Africa
on a shoestring

<><><><><><><><><><><><>

Hugh Finlay
Geoff Crowther
David Else
Mary Fitzpatrick
Paul Greenway
Andrew Humphreys
Ann Jousiffe
Frances Linzee Gordon
Jon Murray
Miles Roddis
Sarina Singh
Deanna Swaney
Dorinda Talbot
David Willett
Jeff Williams

<><><><><><><><><><><><>

Africa

8th edition

Published by

Lonely Planet Publications
Head Office: PO Box 617, Hawthorn, Vic 3122, Australia
Branches: 150 Linden St, Oakland, CA 94607, USA
10a Spring Place, London NW5 3BH, UK
71 bis rue du Cardinal Lemoine, 75005 Paris, France

Printed by
Colorcraft Ltd, Hong Kong

Photographs by

| David Else | Hugh Finlay | Frances Linzee Gordon |
| Mike Reed | David Wall | |

Front cover: Tuareg man, Algeria (Frans Lemmens, The Image Bank). Dune skiing is a developing
sport, but can cause environmental damage, particularly if the dunes are vegetated.

First Published
November 1977 (Africa on the Cheap)

This Edition
January 1998

**Although the authors and publisher have tried to make the information as
accurate as possible, they accept no responsibility for any loss, injury or
inconvenience sustained by any person using this book.**

National Library of Australia Cataloguing in Publication Data

Africa.

8th ed.
Includes index.
ISBN 0 86442 481 7.

1. Africa – Guidebooks. I. Finlay, Hugh.

916.04329

text & maps © Lonely Planet 1998
photos © photographers as indicated 1998

Hugh Finlay

After deciding there must be more to life than civil engineering, Hugh took off around Australia in the mid-70s, working at everything from spray painting to diamond prospecting, before hitting the overland trail. He joined Lonely Planet in 1985 and has written *Jordan & Syria* and co-authored Nepal and contributed to other LP guides including *Kenya, East Africa, India* and *Australia*. He lives in central Victoria, Australia, with his partner Linda and his daughters Ella and Vera.

Geoff Crowther

Born in Yorkshire, England, Geoff took to his heels early on in search of the miraculous, taking a break from a degree in biochemistry. The lure of the unknown took him to Kabul, Kathmandu and Lamu in the days before the overland companies began digging up the dirt along the tracks of Africa. In 1977, he wrote his first guide for Lonely Planet – *Africa on the Cheap*. He has also written *South America* and *Korea & Taiwan*, and has co-authored guides to *India, Kenya, East Africa* and *Malaysia, Singapore & Brunei*.

David Else

After hitchhiking through Europe for a couple of years, David Else kept heading south and first reached Africa in 1983. Since then, he has travelled all over the continent, from Cairo to Cape Town, and from Sudan to Senegal, via most of the bits in between. He has written several guidebooks for independent travellers including Lonely Planet's *Trekking in East Africa* and *Malawi, Mozambique & Zambia*. He has also co-authored and contributed to several other Lonely Planet guides including *West Africa, East Africa* and *Africa – the South*. When not in Africa, David lives in in the north of England, where he's permanently chained to a word processor, and travel means driving to London and back.

Mary Fitzpatrick

Mary grew up in Washington, DC. She has worked for the past three years on development projects in Mozambique, and is presently based in Liberia. Mary has travelled extensively in Africa, the Indian sub-continent and Europe, much of it on bicycle.

Paul Greenway

Paul got his first tropical disease in 1985, and has had the 'travel bug' ever since. He has been to over 50 countries, and has learnt to say 'one beer, please' in just about every known language. Gratefully plucked from the security and blandness of the Australian Public Service, he is now a full-time traveller, writer, photographer and drifter. Paul has worked on Lonely Planet's *Indonesia, Madagascar & Comoros, Indian Himalaya, Mongolia* and *Iran* guides. He is based in Adelaide, South Australia, where he eats and breathes Australian rules football, relaxes to tuneless heavy rock and will do anything (like going to Mongolia and Iran) to avoid settling down.

Andrew Humphreys

Born in England, Andrew stayed around just long enough to complete his studies in architecture before relocating to Egypt. He spent three years documenting Cairo's decaying Islamic monuments and then worked for the country's biggest English-language periodical, *Egypt Today*. In 1991, an unexpected turn of events deposited Andrew in newly independent Estonia where he began by working for *Tallinn City Paper*, before moving on to co-found a new pan-Baltic newspaper. While living in Estonia, a chance meeting with Lonely Planet led to Andrew updating the Baltic chapters of *Scandinavian & Baltic Europe* which earned him the dubious privilege of being despatched to Siberia to work on *Russia, Ukraine & Belarus*. He also co-authored *Central Asia*. Returning to the Middle East, Andrew updated *Israel & the Palestinian Territories*, co-ordinated *Middle East* and wrote the *Jerusalem city guide*.

Ann Jousiffe

After spending a decade working in advertising, Ann escaped the rat race to work as a freelance writer and photographer specialising in the Middle East and North Africa. Based in London, she has written the Libya section of *North Africa* and the new guide to *Lebanon*. Between spending her time in deserts and ancient ruins and working on documentaries, she leads tours to Libya and collapses in front of the television in her London flat with a glass or two of red wine.

Frances Linzee Gordon

Frances grew up in the Highlands of Scotland but later went to London University, where she read Latin. Overcome by feelings of usefulness and employability, she decided modern languages might be more the thing, and went and worked in Spain, Germany and Belgium for a couple of years. After returning to London, she worked for a travel trade publisher, and read French and European law, politics and economics with the University of Lille at the French Institute. She now works – even more usefully – as a travel writer and continues to live in London. Frances has contributed to Lonely Planet's *Mediterranean Europe* and co-authored *Morocco*.

Jon Murray

Jon Murray spent time alternating between travelling and working with various publishing companies in Melbourne, Australia, before joining Lonely Planet as an editor. He was soon travelling again, this time researching Lonely Planet's guidebooks. He co-authored *South Africa, Lesotho & Swaziland* and *Africa – the South* and has updated books on a variety of destinations, including West Africa, Papua New Guinea, Bangladesh and Australia. He lives near Daylesford, Victoria, on a bush block he shares with quite a few marsupials and far too many rabbits.

Miles Roddis

Always an avid devourer and user of guidebooks, Miles came late to contributing to them. Over 25 years he lived, worked, walked and ran in eight countries, including Laos, Sudan, Spain and Egypt. He celebrated retirement by cycling 12,000 miles around the rim of the USA. Convinced that the bike is humankind's greatest invention, but for velcro, he enjoys agitating for cyclists' rights. Wild about wilderness, he's trekked, among other trails, the Zagros mountains in Iran, Britain's Pennine Way and the Pyrenees from the Atlantic to the Mediterranean. He writes for outdoor and athletic magazines and has contributed to Lonely Planet's *Walking in Britain*.

Sarina Singh

After a felucca sail trek down the Nile and whirlwind trip to Greece and Switzerland, Sarina made a New Year's resolution to really live life. After finishing a business degree in Melbourne, she bought a one way ticket to India. There she did a marketing executive traineeship with Sheraton Hotels, but later drifted into journalism. Writing mainly about India, assignments also took her to the Middle East, Nepal, Kenya, Zanzibar and Pakistan. After 3½ years in India Sarina returned to Australia, did a post-graduate journalism course and wrote two television documentary scripts. Other Lonely Planet books she has worked on are *India, Rajasthan* and *Mauritius, Réunion & Seychelles*.

Deanna Swaney

After completing university studies, Deanna Swaney made a shoestring tour of Europe and has been addicted to travel ever since. Despite an erstwhile career in computer programming, she managed intermittent forays away from encroaching yuppiedom in midtown Anchorage, Alaska, and at first opportunity, made a break for South America where she wrote Lonely Planet's *Bolivia*. Subsequent travels resulted in *Tonga, Samoa* and *Iceland, Greenland & the Faroe Islands*. She has also worked on *Zimbabwe, Botswana & Namibia, Brazil, Mauritius, Réunion & Seychelles, Madagascar & Comoros* and *Africa – the South* and contributed to guides to South America and Scandinavia.

Dorinda Talbot

Born in Melbourne, Victoria, Dorinda began travelling at the age of 18 months – to visit her grandparents in Blighty – and has since taken in a fair slice of the world, including Papua New Guinea, South East Asia, the United States, Britain and Europe. Dorinda studied journalism at Deakin University in Geelong before working as a reporter in Alice Springs and sub-editor in Melbourne and London. Still based in London, she now works as a freelance journalist and travel writer. Dorinda also helped to update *Canada, Mediterranean Europe* and *Morocco*.

David Willett

David is a freelance journalist based on the mid-north coast of New South Wales, Australia. He grew up in Hampshire, England, and wound up in Australia in 1980 after stints working on newspapers in Iran and Bahrain. He spent two years working as a sub-editor on the Melbourne Sun before opting to live somewhere warmer. Between jobs he has travelled extensively in Europe, the Middle East and Asia. He lives with his partner, Rowan, and their seven year old son, Tom. David has worked on Lonely Planet's *Australia, NSW, Greece, Mediterranean Europe, Western Europe, Indonesia* and *South-East Asia*. He is currently working on *Tunisia*.

Jeff Williams

Jeff was born in Greymouth, New Zealand, and currently lives with his wife Alison and son Callum in Brisbane in the Australian state of Queensland. He is variously author, co-author or contributor to Lonely Planet's *Western Australia, South Africa, Lesotho & Swaziland, New Zealand, Tramping in New Zealand, Australia, Outback Australia* and *Washington DC & the Capital Region*. He enjoys skiing, climbing and walking, and was fortunate enough to walk along the Dogon Escarpment in Mali while updating this guide. He would like to return to show Callum the Sahel desert.

From the Authors

Hugh Finlay *Thanks to Pat & Susan Hayward for detailed info on shipping vehicles from Ghana to South Africa. Thanks also to all the other authors for their cooperation and prompt replies to the many problems which arose during the project.*

Geoff Crowther *Thanks to the following people for their help and/or hospitality: Alice Njoki Chege (Nairobi, Kenya), Joe Essien (Lagos, Nigeria), Ado Hassan (Kano, Nigeria), KK Sun (Kano, Nigeria), Chuks Nnadozie (Aba, Nigeria), Jan Boettcher (Yaoundé, Cameroon), Maurice Walé (Bafoussam, Cameroon), the Mobil and Amosco mob in Malabo, Equatorial Guinea, and all the immigration/passport officials and police who hassled and extracted money from me in Nigeria, Cameroon, Equatorial Guinea and elsewhere. May they prosper!*

David Else *Firstly, a big thank-you to my wife Corinne; although I string the words together, most of our research trips in Africa are very much joint projects. Many thanks also to the Higgs and Taylor families of Dargle Dale, South Africa for providing friendship, hospitality, email and fax line, a magical device for saving camp fuel and (most appreciated) a base to come back to at the end of our trip. Thanks also to: Mike Deady, a Kiwi traveller who suddenly found himself roped into Lonely Planet research duties when I was laid up with malaria in Beira; Geoff Perrott of Cape Town, for good company and various tips; Jane Jackson of Makuzi Beach, Malawi, who provided sound advice and Fansidar when it was Corinne's turn for malaria; Tim Truluck of Lusaka, for a comprehensive lowdown on the city; Pam and Chris Badger for a base in Lilongwe; and Ian Colclough, who joined us in northern Mozambique masquarading as a linguist, mechanic and experienced traveller – he was a pretty good cook, and we couldn't have done that bit of the trip without him.*

Mary Fitzpatrick *Thanks and love first of all to my husband, Rick, for all the fun, companionship and support on life's journey. I'd also like to express my gratitude in particular to Lynda Schuster for the encouragement and advice; to Talia Owen-Frigyik for the proofreading assistance in Maputo; and to Lucy Hollands, without whose help I might still be laid up with malaria. In Ghana, a special thank you to Emmet Murphy for the numerous informative tips on Accra. For their very generous time and assistance, many thanks to Andrew Snow in Abidjan;*

Karen Gladding and Jim Freund in Accra; Mary Beth Leonard in Lomé, Brian Paul Reublinger and Robin Stern in Cotonou; John Reddy, Brian Aggeler, Daniel Meijering and Matthias Banzhas in Ouagadougou; and Gorom-Gorom, and Kathleen List, Bob Wong, John Hare and David Gorman in Monrovia. Finally, my appreciation to the many others who helped along the way, including Heather, Victoria, Maureen, Austin and Steve in Côte d'Ivoire, Cory, Rich, Holly, Genevieve and Brie in Togo, Harmony, Rachel, Audrey, Bonnie and Jesse in Burkina Faso, and Harriet, Ann and John in Ghana.

Paul Greenway In Madagascar, plenty of thanks must go to: Paul Saxton from the American embassy, and his family, who invited me to my first Thanksgiving dinner; the many helpful staff at several ANGAP offices throughout the country whose names I never knew (nor could remember); the ever-smiling Samoela Andriankotonirina, the librarian at the WWF office in Tana; the lovely Jacky Andriamalala, from the American Cultural Center; and Clare Wilkinson and Connie Boylan (UK) and Natasha Amor (Australia). In the Comoros, thanks also to: Issouffou Oihabi, a Comoran English teacher on Mohéli, who helped with the Comoran language section, and continues to teach though he and his colleagues have not been paid for over nine months; Zaki Muhieddine from Tropic Tours & Travel in Moroni; and Marie Ali Saïd from the Tourism Office in Moroni. For wonderful letters thanks also to: Heike Alber and Andreas Letto (Germany); Sanne Friedrich (Switzerland); the remarkable John Kupiec (USA); Patrick Lachenmeier (Switzerland); Isabelle Loots and Uwe Hübler (Germany); Yves Périsse (France); and Benjamin Schmidt (Germany) for his comments about cycling around Madagascar.

Ann Jousiffe I would like to thank Abdurazzag Gherwash and Abubakr Karmos of Winzrik for all their help and support, Dr Abdulrahman Yedder of the Ministry of Tourism for his invaluable advice and vast knowledge, Dr Guima Anag from the Department of Antiquities in Tripoli and his colleague Dr Fadl Ali in charge of Antiquities in Cyrenaica. Thanks also to all my friends, old and new, in Libya who have always been so kind and hospitable and helped me on my travels.

Frances Linzee Gordon With thanks to all of the following for making the trip possible: the tourist boards across Morocco, and particularly to Mr Abderrahim Bentbib, the délégué of Marrakesh and to Mr Ali El Kasmi and his efficient team in London. With thanks to all of the following for making the trip memorable: Abdennebi for his fluent-Arabic-in-10-hours, to Claire Oxford, Sara Topping and Sarah Wilson for a night of vengeance in a seedy bar in Fès,

keep up the standards girls; to Mohammed for the midnight tour of the medina and kif dens of Chefchaouen disguised in his grandfather's cape; to Ahmed, the Berber boy and his dog for help digging my car from a sand dune; and finally thanks to all those many, many individuals whose names I never knew, but whose warmth, candour and generosity never failed to astound me, and which I shall not forget.

Jon Murray Thanks to the travellers I met while researching this book, and to the many South Africans who provided information and hospitality. As usual, people running hostels were a mine of information.

Miles Roddis Thanks to Tristan and Damon for helping out their Dad without a moan or groan and Ingrid for her infinite tolerance and for a heart and hearth that are always warm.

In CAR I'd like to thank Tony Boomer, Martin Garber, Damien Jonckers, Ito Kazuto, Tony Mokombo, Dieudonn Ngounaji, Ian Ransom, Corinne Vandenberghe, Janet Varner and Junior Zongavodot. In Chad: Craig Boucher, Randa Chichakli, Chris Dio, Bashar Issa, Johanna and Rene Peter, Nicole Poirier, Tressa Rappold, Samir Zoghbi and Carrie Zwicker. In Djibouti: Mohamed Abdillahi, Mincka Buijs and Markus Gellrich, Jean-Philippe de la Rue, Philippe Lambrecht and Christian Touraine. In Eritrea: Dr Negusse Araya, Simon Bush, Chris Caul, Ato Habtemicael, Rod Hicks, Paul Highfield, Debbie McGrath and the VSO team, especially Kara, Becky and Stuart, Woizero Alam Hagos, Pam and Jim Richards, Tedros Tekeste and Ato Yemani Sayoum. In Ethiopia: Alem Birhan Kiros; Don Barnes, another Yorkshireman with wanderlust; Girma Menbaru; Tony Hickey; Mike and Patsy Sargent for local knowledge, friendship renewed and a home after so many nights on the road; Yohannes Tadese, Ato Zeyede Haile; and for their letters and superbly documented information, a joy to read: Dr Guido Groenen, Luc Lauwers and Micke Denys (HOL), Bruce and Cheryl McLaren (NZ), and Sandra and Richard Roik (CAN). In Sudan: Abdel Ghani Abdalla, Rob and Sue Beckley, Alan 'Bill' Harzia' Fenwick, Gibril Gamar, Adam Gordon, Mohammed Majzoub, Ralph Rouse, and the small kindnesses of so many Sudanese, fleetingly met and still remembered.

Sarina Singh In Mauritius, a warm thanks to Joy and Sheena Joymungul for making me feel like part of the family, Abeydin and Ramesh for their enthusiasm, Sandrine Lincoln, Ricardo Lacour and Mr Bissoondoyal. On Rodrigues, thank you to Jean-Marc Begue for showing me the island in a style all of his own. In Réunion, special thanks to the inimitable Carl Houart for his prolific help, friendship – and for giving me a break from speaking French! Thanks also to Chris Verboven for his assistance (and for introducing me to the local brew), Laure Dupont, Gilles Le Cointre, François Gillet and Richard Stratford. In the Seychelles, a huge thank you to Alain and Ginette St Ange, Pat McGregor, Basil Ferrari, Wix Nibourette, George Julienne and the mighty media mogul – Jean François Ferrari!

Deanna Swaney I'd especially like to thank Annemarie Byrne of Durban for her friendship and boundless hospitality. For their help and expertise, thanks to: Aulden Harlech-Jones, who shared his expertise on the Windhoek area; Ian Robertson Rodger and Petra Bosse of Footprints; and Marie Holstensen and Grant Burton, Pam and Colin, Susan and Ragnar, Cletius, and Victor, all of whom shared with me the magic of Mudumu at Lianshulu Lodge in the Caprivi. Also helpful and hospitable were Marie and Brian Harlech-Jones in Windhoek; Wendy Holland-Quayle in Rundu; Karen, Mike and Sebastian at Shaka's Spear; Jack and Eve Drew, Carol Ann van As and Desmond in Maun; all the friendly folks at Nkwasi Lodge in Rundu; André, Mike, Dave and Lex at Mokolodi in Gaborone; and Iain McIntosh, Richard Sheppard and Paul Quinn in Livingstone. Virginia Luling of Survival International in the UK provided information on the San and the Himba. LP author David Else, UK, provided help with Namibia; and George Monbiot, UK, offered direction on conservation issues.

In Zimbabwe, thanks to Hans, Valerie and Tammy van der Heiden, Val Bell, Marion at Manicaland, and Bruce and Iris Brinson. Thanks also to Charlotte Hindle, UK, for her assistance and eagle-eyed observations. Also, special love and thanks to Mike and Anna Scott in Bulawayo. Travellers who enhanced a typically frantic update experience included Scott McKenzie and Keely Davison, Jouke Andringa and Wil Henson, Catherine McEvoy, Marisa Kelly and of course, Hershel T Bear.

Finally, for their continuing tolerance and support, the best of my love and wishes go to Robert Strauss of Kyre Park, Earl Swaney of Fresno, Jonny Morland of TINSTAR Bug-Free Software, and Dave Dault and Keith and Holly Hawkings back home in Anchorage. My portion of this book is dedicated to the memory of Dr Dale Stevens, who helped set me along the road many years ago.

Dorinda Talbot Many thanks to Ali El Kasmi and Jamal El Jaidi of the Moroccan National Tourist Office in London; Ahmed El Khemlichi of the Agadir Tourist Office; Rick Kramer in Rabat; Abdellah El Moumni in Taroudannt, Brahim Aziam, Brahim Toudaoui and Mohammed Amgif in Imlil; Phillip Masbridge of Exodus; Mike McHugo of Discover; Belghit Tihami in Rissani; and Amar Oussou of the Er-Rachidia Tourist Office. A round of applause also to Dawn Chapman, Brian Lackmaker and John Tuckey in London. I'm particularly grateful for all the information and insights received from fellow travellers and for the truly humbling hospitality shown to me by the people of Morocco.

David Willett My thanks to all the many friends I have made in Tunisia in the course of my travels, particularly to the Grar family (Larbi, Nejia, Kamel, Lamia and Anis) of Sousse; Kamel bin Brahim from the ONTT in Tunis; and to Chokri ben Nassir. Thanks also to Rowan and Tom for holding the fort at home during my repeated absences.

Jeff Williams Thanks to Ali and Callum at home in Brisbane; Sunkule in The Gambia for the trip to Gunjur Beach and the forest walk; friends in Guinea-Conakry and Guinea-Bissau (especially Fallou N'Dime in Bissau for the endless cups of tea); Aldiouma Ongoiba in Bamako, Mali, one of the most honest guides you could ever meet; the staff at the Hôtel Plateau in Dakar, Senegal; and a host of friendly people in several countries who shared laughter and advice, never expected anything in return, but also never gave me their names.

This Edition

For this edition of Africa we had people all over the place! The only countries which weren't visited by Lonely Planet researchers were Algeria, Angola, Burundi, and Somalia (but the chapters were updated with all available information) – simply because it was unsafe to do so.

Hugh Finlay coordinated the project, updating the introductory chapters, wading through the mountain of valuable letters we receive from Africa travellers, and checking and cross-checking the entire book to ensure the entire manuscript was as accurate and up-to-date as possible. He also travelled to East Africa and updated the Kenya and Uganda chapters, and did a desk update of Angola, Liberia (before Mary Fitzpatrick visited there) and Somalia.

In North Africa we had Frances Linzee Gordon and Dorinda Talbot update Morocco and Spanish North Africa, David Willett covered Tunisia and Algeria, Ann Jousiffe went to Libya and Andrew Humphreys did Egypt.

Jeff Williams spent time in West Africa updating the chapters on Cape Verde, The Gambia, Guinea, Guinea-Bissau, Mali,

Mauritania, Niger, Senegal and Sierra Leone. The remaining countries in West Africa (Benin, Burkina Faso, Côte d'Ivoire, Ghana, Liberia and Togo) were covered by Mary Fitzpatrick.

The Central African countries of Cameroon, Congo, Congo (Zaïre), Equatorial Guinea, Gabon, Nigeria, São Tomé and Príncipe were done by Geoff Crowther, who also covered Burundi, Tanzania and Rwanda in East Africa. Miles Roddis travelled to Chad and the Central African Republic, and made a second trip covering Djibouti, Eritrea, Ethiopia and Sudan.

In Southern Africa, David Else updated Malawi, Mozambique and Zambia, and also wrote the Social Etiquette section in the Regional Facts for the Visitor chapter. Deanna Swaney was responsible for Botswana, Namibia and Zimbabwe, while Jon Murray researched the South Africa, Lesotho and Swaziland chapters.

Out in the Indian Ocean, Paul Greenway went to Madagascar, Comoros and Mayotte, and Sarina Singh covered Mauritius, Réunion and the Seychelles.

From the Publisher

The editing and proofing of this edition was coordinated by Cathy Lanigan. Kristin Odijk provided a huge amount of assistance during proofing. The editorial team also included Katrina Browning, Miriam Cannell, Michelle Coxall, Liz Filleul, Justin Flynn, Martin Hughes, Russell Kerr, Andrew McKenna, Mary Neighbour, Suzi Petkovski, Richard Plunkett, Diana Saad, Paul Smitz and Isabelle Young.

Margaret Jung coordinated the mapping and design, with cartographic assistance from Verity Campbell, Chris Klep, Anthony Phelan, Jacqui Saunders, Andrew Smith, Sandra Smythe, Geoff Stringer, Lyndell

Taylor, Andrew Tudor and Glenn van der Knijff.

Simon Bracken designed the cover and Adam McCrow produced the back cover map. Kerrie Williams did the indexing. Leonie Mugavin kept us informed of African news updates in the final days before going to press.

Thanks to LP author, David Else, for checking the trekking sections, and Australia's Ethiopian Consul, Graham Romanes, for updates on Ethiopia.

Thanks

A special thanks to all the people who wrote to us from all over the world with their tips, advice and tales. Their names appear on page 1055.

Warning & Request

Things change – prices go up, schedules change, good places go bad and bad places go bankrupt – nothing stays the same. So, if you find things better or worse, recently opened or long since closed, please tell us and help make the next edition even more accurate and useful.

We value all of the feedback we receive from travellers. Julie Young coordinates a small team who read and acknowledge every letter, postcard and email, and ensure that every morsel of information finds its way to the appropriate authors, editors and publishers.

Everyone who writes to us will find their name in the next edition of the appropriate guide and will also receive a free subscription to our quarterly newsletter, Planet Talk. The very best contributions will be rewarded with a free Lonely Planet guide.

Excerpts from your correspondence may appear in new editions of this guide; in our newsletter, Planet Talk; or in updates on our Web site – so please let us know if you don't want your letter published or your name acknowledged.

Contents

Contents

Map Legend

BOUNDARIES

.... International Boundary
.... Regional Boundary

ROUTES

.... Freeway
.... Highway
.... Major Road
.... Unsealed Road or Track
.... City Road
.... City Street
.... Railway
.... Underground Railway
.... Tram
.... Walking Track
.... Walking Tour
.... Ferry Route
.... Cable Car or Chairlift

AREA FEATURES

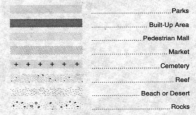

.... Parks
.... Built-Up Area
.... Pedestrian Mall
.... Market
.... Cemetery
.... Reef
.... Beach or Desert
.... Rocks

HYDROGRAPHIC FEATURES

.... Coastline
.... River, Creek
.... Intermittent River or Creek
.... Rapids, Waterfalls
.... Lake, Intermittent Lake
.... Canal
.... Swamp

SYMBOLS

✪ CAPITAL	.... National Capital	☯	☗	.... Embassy, Petrol Station
◉ Capital	.... Regional Capital	✈	✝	.... Airport, Airfield
▧ CITY	.... Major City	⛱	✿	.... Swimming Pool, Gardens
● City	.... City	❖	🐘	.... Shopping Centre, Zoo
● Town	.... Town	⚜	⊼	.... Winery or Vineyard, Picnic Site
● Village	.... Village	←	A25	One Way Street, Route Number
▪	⌂	.... Place to Stay, Hut or Lodge	🏛	⚐	.... Stately Home, Monument
▼	☕	.... Place to Eat, Pub or Bar	🏰	▣	.... Castle, Tomb
✉	☎	.... Post Office, Telephone	⌒	🌴	.... Cave, Oases
❶	❾	.... Tourist Information, Bank	▲	❉	.... Mountain or Hill, Lookout
◗	P	.... Transport, Parking	⛯	⚓	.... Lighthouse, Shipwreck
🏛	✚	.... Museum, Border Crossing	)(	@	.... Pass, Spring
⬚	⛏	Caravan Park, Camping Ground	⚐	⚑	.... Beach, Surf Beach
✚	✚	.... Church, Cathedral		⁂	.... Archaeological Site or Ruins
⌘	☒	.... Egyptian Temple, Pyramid			.... Ancient or City Wall
☪	ॐ	.... Mosque, Hindu Temple			.... Cliff or Escarpment, Tunnel
✚	★	.... Hospital, Police Station			.... Train Station

Note: not all symbols displayed above appear in this book

Introduction

This vast and diverse continent, stretching from the shores of the Mediterranean to the Cape of Good Hope and encompassing the world's largest desert and one of its most extensive rainforests, is the adventurer's last frontier. Africa is a land of contrasts: the stunning oases and barren mountains of the Sahara Desert, the inspiring beauty of snow-capped Kilimanjaro rising sheer from the East African plateau, the lush and mist-covered volcanoes and lakes of the Rift Valley, colourful tribal people and the lure of ancient Egypt. Perhaps nowhere in the world will you find such a variety of cultures, vistas, contrasts and contradictions, cities (ancient and modern) and roaming big game.

Since the Leakey excavations in northern Tanzania, Africa has been regarded as the birthplace of humanity. It was also home to one of the cradles of civilisation. Pharaonic Egypt flourished and declined over a remarkable 5000 years until it was finally eclipsed by the Roman Empire. The monuments that the ancient Egyptians left are among the wonders of the world, and their ideas strongly influenced other civilisations.

Later, Christianity took hold of northern Africa until it was swept aside by the armies of Islam in the 8th century AD. Some of Islam's greatest cultural achievements were produced on African soil. Cairo was, for many centuries, the cultural and political centre of the Islamic world.

Elsewhere on the continent, highly skilled and organised civilisations, empires and kingdoms flourished and foundered, particularly in West Africa and southern Africa. Not even the advent of the European maritime nations and the consequent slave trade to the Americas succeeded in completely destroying the legacy of the past. On the east coast, the Shirazi and Omani coastal trading cities remain.

The 1990s have seen great changes in the political map of Africa and 'multiparty democracy' is now all the rage. In many cases the changes have only been made under pressure from outside – 'reform or lose your foreign aid' has been the message coming from the West. As a result, a number of corrupt and oppressive regimes have been swept aside, while others have simply put on a different face and called themselves multiparty.

It would be irresponsible to suggest that all African countries enjoy political and social stability – some are embroiled in endless rounds of political turmoil – but there's one thing you can be certain of in Africa: there's never a dull moment! You need to keep an eye on the newspapers, your wits together, your eyes and ears open and your mouth in check. Do that, and you're in for the adventure of a lifetime.

Travelling in Africa is certainly no package tour. It requires determination, patience and stamina. Always remember to respect other people's customs and sensibilities, and regardless of their politics, religion or whatever else, you will always have a friend. Hospitality is synonymous with Africa. This continent and its people have a great deal to teach and offer to the other people of the world. Treat it and them with respect.

Africa has the largest game reserves on earth. Considering the pressures of population growth, it is nothing short of miraculous that the governments of the countries concerned have chosen to maintain these sanctuaries and to spend scarce resources to pay for the wardens and rangers to keep poaching to a minimum.

No other continent is even vaguely comparable to Africa. It offers everything you could possibly conceive of. Go and experience it.

Regional Facts for the Visitor

PLANNING
When to Go
One of the main things to bear in mind when planning a trip to Africa is the weather – that red line on the map may be fine in the dry season but may become a sea of mud when it rains (or it may not exist at all!).

The following table gives a general guide to the ideal time to travel in each region, but obviously, this is only a rough guide and there are major variations within each region.

Region	Best Time to Travel
North Africa	mid-March to mid-June
West Africa	November to March
Central Africa	June to September
East Africa	January to April
Southern Africa	May to October

What Kind of Trip?
Independent Travel The classic way to travel through Africa is overland and independently. It can often be unpredictable, uncomfortable, unreliable, unsafe, tiring, unhealthy and even downright scary, but it is never dull and you'll have the time of your life. Travelling this way is the only way to see Africa at ground level, and it opens up the greatest opportunities for meeting and mixing with Africans.

Travelling solo gives you the greatest flexibility, but you'll also need to be fond of your own company, as there will be times when you have no other! It almost goes without saying that you also need a healthy dose of common sense and a strong instinct of self-preservation.

Overland Safari Truck Overland trucks carrying foreign tourists have been raising dust along the roads and tracks of Africa for well over 20 years, and are responsible for opening up many of the routes and attractions available to travellers today. These trips have always been popular, particularly among first-time travellers who want to get out there and do it, but perhaps don't have the confidence to tackle it alone. They are also a good option for solo women as they offer a much greater degree of personal security. Other people join as they just like to party and enjoy the camaraderie.

This mode of travel has big pluses and minuses. The major advantages are that you don't have the worries – how you're going to get from A to B, deal with the difficult border official or decide what to do when the route you planned to take is closed – all these things are the responsibility of someone else and you can relax. This can also be seen as a major disadvantage because it is these very dealings that are part of the challenge of a trip to Africa. Another big drawback is that a group of a dozen or more foreigners is unwieldy and hardly inconspicuous, and the arrival of an overland truck in a small and isolated community can be a bit like the circus coming to town. Interaction on a one-to-one basis is rare.

Maps
Lonely Planet has several excellent quality atlases. Look out for *Zimbabwe, Botswana & Namibia, Egypt, Kenya,* and *South Africa, Lesotho & Swaziland.* Michelin also produce good quality maps to Africa. The Michelin African series consists of the following:

Map	Area Covered
No 953	North & West Africa
No 954	North & East Africa
No 955	Central & South Africa
No 969	Morocco
No 172	Algeria & Tunisia
No 175	Côte d'Ivoire

You won't find Michelin maps in Africa; buy them before you leave home. There are a number of alternatives, but these usually cover regions which are much smaller. The Bartholomews series are also extensive, but older versions do have serious omissions.

What to Bring

Bring the minimum possible. An overweight bag will become a nightmare. A rucksack is preferable to an overnight bag, since it will stand up to rougher treatment.

Choose a pack which will take some rough handling – overland travel destroys packs rapidly. Make sure the straps and buckles are sewn on well and strengthened, if necessary, before you set off.

Some people take a strong plastic bag that will completely enclose the pack. It can be used on dusty journeys when your pack is in the luggage compartment of a bus or strapped onto the roof.

A sleeping bag is more or less essential. It gets very cold in the desert at night and you'll definitely need one if visiting mountainous areas. You'll also be glad of it on long bus or train journeys as a supplement to the wooden seats or sacks of maize. A sheet sleeping bag – similar to the ones used in hostels – is also good when it is too hot to use a normal bag. It's cool and it keeps mosquitoes off your body.

Take clothes for both hot and cold climates, including at least one good sweater for use at night in the mountains and the desert. You needn't go overboard, however, and take everything in your wardrobe. Things like T-shirts, cotton shirts and sandals are very cheap in most places, and it's usually more interesting and economical to buy these things along the way.

In some places (particularly Islamic countries) you should be aware of local dress codes and not wear revealing clothes. This includes brief shorts, short skirts and see-through garments. Africans generally dress very modestly – a fact which many travellers seem to either overlook or ignore. When in Rome ...

Some people take a small tent and a portable stove. These can be very useful and save you a small fortune, but they do add considerably to the weight of your pack. Many local people carry portable stoves around with them. If you take a stove make sure it's leak-proof! Gaz stoves have been highly recommended by many travellers and the gas canisters are available throughout East and West Africa. However, kerosene is the fuel most widely available and the one which local people use.

Don't forget the small essentials: a combination pocket knife or Swiss Army knife; needle and cotton and a small pair of scissors; sunglasses; a towel and toothbrush; contraceptives; tampons; and any specific medicines. Most toiletries – toilet paper, toothpaste, shaving cream, shampoo etc – are available in all the capital cities and large towns.

A water bottle is another essential, especially on long bus or train rides and when walking in the mountains. Anything that holds less than one litre is of limited use. A torch (flashlight) is also very useful, along with a replacement set of batteries. You'll also find a length of nylon cord useful for hanging up your laundry. If you like reading don't forget to take one or two good novels.

SUGGESTED ITINERARIES

The possibilities are endless. The main factors which will determine your route are time, money, political upheavals and specific area of interest. For those with limited time (say a month or less), it's probably best to limit your journey to one region (North, West, East or southern Africa).

With more time you can look at travelling overland between the regions. The most popular route by far is between Kenya and South Africa via Tanzania, Malawi and Zimbabwe, often slotting in Mozambique or Botswana. It's a route which offers great variety and relatively straightforward travel (as far as anything is straightforward in Africa!). Travel between East and West Africa is complicated by Congo (Zaïre), where the travel situation was uncertain at the time of writing.

For those who want to travel overland all the way from north to south (or vice versa), the only option is the trans-Sahara route down through Morocco, Western Sahara and into Mauritania, the problem here being that without a vehicle you will need to hitch, which is difficult but not impossible. The eastern route through Sudan, Eritrea and

Ethiopia is currently closed due to the closure of the Sudan-Eritrea border, which in recent times has been the only option in this area. The Sudan-Ethiopia border is also officially closed. Also see Overland Routes, under Land, in the Getting Around chapter.

From a security aspect, a number of countries are simply no-go areas as far as tourism is concerned: Algeria, Angola, Burundi, Liberia and Somalia are definitely out; and eastern Congo (Zaïre) is also extremely dodgy. While there may be nothing to stop you actually going to some of these places, it would be a seriously dumb thing to do unless you are prepared to come home in a box.

The most important thing to bear in mind when on the road is that this is Africa, and in Africa things change rapidly. Keep abreast of regional developments and seek reliable local advice before heading into places which may not be secure.

VISAS & DOCUMENTS
Passport

The essential document is a passport. If you already have one, make sure it's valid for a reasonably long period of time and has plenty of blank pages on which stamp-happy immigration officials can do their stuff. Getting a new passport overseas not only takes time but can be expensive since it usually involves communication with your home country, for which you will pay.

If you're British, get one of the 94-page 'jumbo' passports; Australians can opt for a 64-page passport; Americans can have extension pages stapled into otherwise full passports at any of their embassies.

Make a photocopy of the first few pages of your passport before you leave and keep it in a separate place. It could well speed up replacement in case of loss or theft.

Visas

Once you have a passport you can start filling it with visas, and there's no quicker place to do this than Africa! Generally it's best to get visas along the way, especially if your travel plans are not fixed, but keep your ear to the ground regarding the best places to get them.

South Africa, for instance, is a handy place to arrange several visas. Also, two different consulates of the same country may have completely different requirements before they will issue visas. For example, the fee may be different from place to place; one consulate might want to see how much money you have, whereas another won't ask; one might demand an onward ticket, while another won't even mention it; and one might issue visas while you wait, while another insists on referring the application back to the capital (which can delay the process by weeks).

Whatever you do, don't turn up at a border without a visa (where one is required) unless you're absolutely sure you can get one at the border. If not, you may well find yourself tramping back to the nearest consulate – and, in some countries, this can be a long way.

Applying for Visas You'll occasionally come across a tedious, petty power freak at an embassy or consulate whose sole pleasure in life is to be as big a nuisance as possible. If you take the bait and display your anger or frustration, the visa will take twice as long to issue or they'll refuse to issue one at all. If you want that visa then keep your cool. Pretend you have all day to waste and that your patience is infinite.

Another important fact to bear in mind about visas is the sheer cost of them. Very few are free and some are outrageously expensive – you won't get a Congo (Zaïrese) visa anywhere, for instance, for less than US$45. Regardless of what passport you carry, you're going to need quite a lot of visas, particularly in West and Central Africa, and if you're on a tight budget they can eat into your funds in an alarming way. It's a good idea to make a rough calculation of what the visa fees will amount to before you set off, and allow for it.

You also need to be aware that certain countries take a long time to issue visas or impose conditions that make it hardly worth the while. Sudan, Libya and Gabon are the main ones, but beware of Nigeria too. Many Nigerian embassies will only issue visas to

FRANCES LINZEE GORDON

DAVID WALL

DAVID WALL

HUGH FINLAY

The many faces of Africa: young women of Morocco (top) and Burkina Faso (middle left); a Dogon man from Mali (middle right); and East African culture captured on batik (bottom).

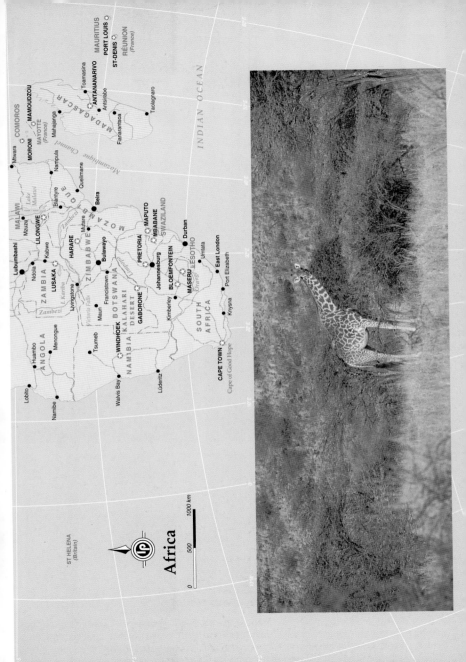

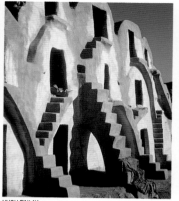
HUGH FINLAY

MIKE REED

DAVID ELSE

DAVID WALL

FRANCES LINZEE GORDON

Africa's diverse architecture and landscapes: the Medenine granary in Tunisia (top left); a striking monument in Johannesburg, South Africa (top right); the windswept sand dunes in the Namib Desert, Namibia (middle left); the amazing rockscape of Ireli in Dogon country, Mali (middle right); and a forest of columns at the landmark Tour Hassan, in Rabat, Morocco (bottom).

citizens or residents of the country where they are located. Avoid this hassle by getting your visa before you leave home. Nigerian embassies also currently slug Brits around US$200 for a tourist visa!

In order to balance what has already been said, it should be mentioned that most visas are easily obtained without fuss. You simply fill in the necessary forms, hand over your photographs and the appropriate fee, and collect your passport the same day or 24 to 48 hours later. It's just that with so many countries, visas assume an importance in Africa which they don't have elsewhere in the world.

Visa Requirements A number of countries demand that you produce a 'letter of recommendation' *(note verbale)* from your own embassy before they will issue a visa. This is generally no problem as your embassy will be aware of this, but you may sometimes have to pay for it. British embassies make you pay through the nose for these letters. For French-speaking countries the letter should read something like this:

Par la présente, nous attestons que Mr...est titulaire de passport No... Il doit se rendre au Congo (Zaïre) pour faire le tourism. Toute assistance que pourrait lui être accordée serait appréciée.
En fait de quoi nous lui délivrons cette lettre pour servir et valoir ce que de droit.

If you plan on going to Libya, you must have the first few pages of your passport translated into Arabic before you apply for a visa. You can have this done either at your embassy in Tunis or before you leave at the passport office in your own country.

Make sure you have plenty of passport-size photographs for visa applications. Twenty-four should give you a good start, although it's easy enough to pick up more en route. Consular officials may refuse to stamp a visa on anything other than a completely blank page, so make sure your passport has plenty of them.

Onward Tickets
Some countries demand that you have a ticket out of the country before they will let you in. So long as you intend to leave from the same place you arrived there is no problem, but if you want to enter at one point and leave from another, this can sometimes be a headache. Fortunately, not too many African countries demand that you have an onward ticket and, of those that do, it's rarely enforced if you are entering overland. It's generally no great problem so long as officials will accept a return bus or rail ticket, since these are usually cheap. If they won't, your options are limited and you're looking at either an airline ticket or what is known as 'sufficient funds'.

Most budget travellers have to rely on buying the cheapest available air ticket out of the country and then refunding it later on. If you do this, make sure you can get a refund without having to wait months for it. Don't forget to ask specifically where you can get the refund (some airlines will only refund tickets at the office where you bought them; some only at their head office), and if you can get the refund in a currency which is useful.

The only other way to avoid this requirement is to have plenty of money (cash or travellers' cheques or both) and/or a major international credit card. It's assumed that if you have US$500 to US$1000 in your possession (or access to it), then you have enough to pay for your return to your own country and the ticket requirement can be waived.

Any or all of the North African countries of Algeria, Libya, Sudan and Tunisia may refuse entry to Israeli nationals and to anyone with Israeli stamps in their passport. In the past, some countries, like Sudan, were extremely strict in enforcing this, even refusing to stamp your passport if it had no actual Israeli stamps in it but had Egyptian stamps issued at the Egyptian side of the Egyptian-Israeli border. The thawing of Arab-Israeli relations has improved this situation, but keep your ear to the ground.

Travel Insurance
A travel insurance policy that covers theft, loss and medical problems is a good idea. The policies handled by STA Travel and

other student travel organisations are usually good value. There is a wide variety of policies available; check the small print:

- Some policies specifically exclude 'dangerous activities', which can include scuba diving, motorcycling and even trekking. A locally acquired motorcycle licence is not valid under some policies.
- You may prefer a policy which pays doctors or hospitals direct rather than you having to pay on the spot and claim later. If you have to claim later make sure you keep all documentation. Some policies ask you to call back (reverse charges) to a centre in your home country where an immediate assessment of your problem is made.
- Check that the policy covers ambulances or an emergency flight home.

International Vaccination Card

An up-to-date vaccination card is almost as important as a passport if you are travelling through a number of countries. They're usually provided by whoever supplies you with your vaccinations. Some countries refuse admission to travellers without current cards, or insist that they have the necessary vaccinations there and then. You cannot be assured of a sterile needle in such circumstances.

International Driving Licence

If you're taking your own transport or thinking of hiring a vehicle to tour certain national parks, get hold of an international driving licence before you set off. Any national motoring organisation will fix you up with this, provided you have a valid driving licence for your own country. The cost of these permits is generally about US$5 and they are valid for one year.

International Student Card

An International Student Card or the graduate equivalent is useful in many places. Some of the concessions available include airline tickets, train and boat fares, and free or reduced entry charges to museums and archaeological sites.

Hostelling International Card

There are a few countries, such as Morocco and South Africa, where a Hostelling International (HI or YHA) card will get you a small discount on hostel accommodation, but its usefulness is pretty limited.

Carnets

If you are taking your own vehicle you will need a *carnet de passage* to enter most African countries. See the section in the Getting There & Away chapter for details.

EMBASSIES

Your home-country embassies can be good places to catch up on news from home. Although this will be in the form of week-old newspapers, most embassies are quite happy for you to come and browse. More important services they provide include replacement of lost passports and getting their citizens home in an emergency – a traveller running out of cash is not considered an emergency.

If you are travelling or living in extremely remote areas for an extended period of time it can be a good idea to register your name and some details of what you are doing with your embassy. If you do this, it is equally important to notify them when you leave the area so that valuable resources are not wasted on looking for you.

For listings of embassies throughout Africa, see the individual country chapters later in this book.

MONEY
Costs

It's very difficult to estimate what a trip to Africa will cost, since so many factors are involved. How fast do you want to travel? What degree of comfort do you consider to be acceptable (where there's a choice)? How much sightseeing do you want to do? Do you intend to hire a vehicle to explore a game park or will you rely on other tourists to give you a lift? Are you travelling alone or in a group? Will you be using the black market or banks? And a host of other things.

Only one thing remains the same in Africa: the pace of change. It's fast, and things like inflation and devaluations can wreak havoc with your travel plans if you're on a very tight budget.

To generalise, you should budget for at least US$10 per day in the cheaper countries (such as Egypt, Malawi and Morocco) and US$25 in the more expensive ones (such as Gabon, Libya and Togo). This should cover the cost of very basic accommodation, food in local cafes or street stalls, and the cheapest possible transport. It won't include the cost of getting to Africa, safaris in game parks, visas or major purchases.

In some countries, particularly in West and Central Africa, you may well find yourself spending considerably more than this upper limit.

Carrying Money

There is no perfectly safe way to keep your money while you're travelling, but the best place is in contact with your skin, where, hopefully, you'll be aware of an alien hand before your money disappears. One method is to wear a leather pouch hung around your neck and kept under cover of a shirt or dress. Another option is to sew an invisible pocket onto the inside of your trousers. Other travellers prefer a money belt. Ideally, your passport should be in the same place, but this isn't always possible.

Wherever you decide to put your money, it's a good idea to enclose it in a plastic bag. Under a hot sun that pouch or pocket will get soaked with sweat – repeatedly – and your cash or cheques will end up looking like they've been through the washing machine.

Which Currency?

However much money you decide on, take a mixture of UK pounds sterling and US dollars, and French francs if you are going to the Francophone countries (mainly West and Central Africa). You'll get a much better rate of exchange for them than you would if you only had pounds sterling or US dollars. Indeed, in the smaller towns (and some of the larger ones too) in these countries you'll have difficulty changing anything *but* French francs.

On the other hand, pounds sterling and US dollars are the preferred currencies in Anglophone and western-oriented countries, such as those on the west coast, East Africa, southern Africa and Congo (Zaïre).

If you take currencies other than these three you'll find it difficult, if not impossible, to find out the exact exchange rate on any particular day except in capital cities, and you may have trouble changing them at all in more remote places.

In some countries, mainly those badly affected by civil war, the local currency is virtually worthless and the US dollar reigns supreme. This applies particularly to Somalia and Congo (Zaïre). In eastern Congo (Zaïre), Ugandan shillings are the preferred currency – you will find it difficult to get rid of New Zaïres at all.

Travellers' Cheques

Take the bulk of your money as travellers' cheques. American Express (Amex), Thomas Cook and First National City Bank cheques are the most widely used and they offer, in most cases, instant replacement in the event of loss or theft. Keep a record of the cheque numbers and the original bill of sale for the cheques in a safe place in case you lose them. Replacement is a lot quicker if you can produce this proof.

You should avoid buying cheques from small banks which only have a few overseas branches, as you'll find them very difficult (if not impossible) to change in many places.

Make sure you buy a good range of denominations when you get the cheques – US$10s, US$20s and US$50s (or the equivalent in pounds sterling or French francs). The reason for this is that if you have too many large bills you may find yourself having to change, say, US$50 in a country that you're only going to stay in for a day or two. You'll end up with a wad of excess local currency which you can only reconvert at a relatively poor rate or not at all. Also, if you are leaving a country by air, most departure taxes (usually US$10 or US$20) have to be paid in foreign currency and change may well be given in local currency.

Travellers' cheques can be difficult to exchange, especially in small places or when the banks are closed. They can often be changed outside of bank hours at large hotels, but the commission charged at such places is often extortionate. It can also be extortionate at certain banks in some countries. There's also the time consumed changing travellers' cheques to be taken into account. In some places it can take hours. These are two reasons why you should bring some cash with you (see below).

Cash

It is vital to carry some cash with you; say up to the equivalent of US$500. Once again, the best currencies are US dollars in East and southern Africa, French francs in West and Central Africa.

While you may not feel comfortable about carrying a few hundred dollars in cash, a contingency fund is necessary in case you really get stuck somewhere – there's not much use having plenty of money if it's in a form no-one can readily use.

Due to the existence of counterfeit bills, it is hard to change US$100 bills anywhere in southern Africa, even at banks, so stick to US$50s.

Credit Cards

A credit card is another way of having secure funds at hand as you can withdraw cash and travellers' cheques from any branch of the credit-card company. This way you can avoid having to carry large wads of travellers' cheques.

All the different credit-card companies have weekly limits on cash and cheque withdrawals which they can execute without reference to your home country. Find out what the limits are before leaving home. If you want more than the limit, this will involve a fax which will take time (sometimes days) and for which you may have to pay.

Amex, Diners Club, Visa and MasterCard are all widely recognised credit cards – you *must*, however, check that you will be able to get cash advances or travellers' cheques against the particular credit card you have in the countries you are visiting, and plan accordingly.

Credit cards also have their uses where 'sufficient funds' are demanded by immigration officials before they allow you to enter a country. It's generally accepted that you have 'sufficient funds' if you have a credit card.

International Transfers

If you run out of money while you're abroad and don't have a credit card, you can ask your bank back home to send you funds by Telegraphic Transfer (TT), assuming you have money in an account there, of course. Make sure you specify the city and the bank branch. If this is done by fax, the money should reach you within a few days. If you correspond by mail the process will take at least two weeks, often longer.

Remember that some countries will only give you your money in local currency, while others will let you have it in US dollars or UK pounds. Francophone countries will usually let you have it in French francs. Find out what is possible before you request a transfer, otherwise you could end up with a lot of unconvertible (and therefore useless) currency, which you may not even be allowed to take out of the country.

Avoid sending bank notes through the post. They'll often be stolen by post-office employees, no matter how cleverly you disguise the contents. There are all sorts of ways of finding out whether a letter is worth opening.

Currency Declaration Forms

A few African countries (such as Algeria, Angola, Cape Verde and Mauritania) still issue currency declaration forms on arrival, although it's a practice which has virtually ceased. You must write down how much money (cash and travellers' cheques) you are bringing into the country. Occasionally these forms may be checked when you leave, and if there are any discrepancies you're in trouble; mostly they're tossed out with barely a glance.

Whatever the case, if you intend using the black market inside the country, you must declare less than you are bringing in and hide the excess.

More details about the forms can be found in the appropriate country chapters.

CFA Franc

Currency in Africa is less complicated than all the various political entities might suggest. Most of the Francophone countries belong to the Communauté Financière Africaine and use the same unit of currency – the CFA franc.

In theory, the CFA francs of one country have the same value as those of another and should be freely interchangeable, but the Communauté consists of two blocks. The West African CFA block (BCEAO) comprises Benin, Burkina Faso, Côte d'Ivoire, Mali, Niger, Senegal and Togo, whose bank notes bear the words 'Banque Centrale des Etats de l'Afrique de l'Ouest'. The Central African CFA block (BEAC), which is composed of Cameroon, the Central African Republic, Chad, Congo, Equatorial Guinea and Gabon, uses bank notes inscribed with the words 'Banque des Etats de l'Afrique Centrale'.

When you go from one zone to another you'll have to change your CFA into those of the other block. It's usually possible to do this on a one-to-one basis, but in some cases there will be a commission to pay.

Both types of CFA are pegged to the French franc at the rate of CFA 100 = FFr 1. The CFAs are, therefore, hard currency and there should be no commission charged for converting French bank notes into CFA bank notes. Normal commission rates apply, however, if you're changing other hard currencies into CFA francs.

Black Market

The major reason for bringing cash with you is that it allows you to take advantage of any difference between the street rate of exchange (otherwise known by the racially suspect term 'black market') and that offered by the banks. Sometimes you can change travellers' cheques on the black market too, but this isn't always the case.

There are some countries in Africa where you can get considerably more for your 'hard' currency on the streets or in shops and hotels than you can in the banks, such as Congo (Zaïre), Eritrea, Libya, Nigeria and Sudan. If you don't take advantage of this, you are going to find many countries very expensive. Conversely, if you do, they'll be relatively cheap.

Some people regard the black market as morally reprehensible. It's certainly predatory and it contributes to the corruption which plagues many African countries. It is, however, a fact of life and its bases are many – greed, unrealistic economic and/or political policies, insupportable external debt and civil war, to name a few. Whether you take advantage of the black market or not is your decision, but there is no point in pretending that it doesn't exist and the fact is that most travellers do take advantage of it.

On the other hand, high black-market rates are becoming less common, especially where a country has secured a loan from either the International Monetary Fund (IMF) or World Bank, or has had its debts 'rescheduled' since these are generally pegged to a demand that their currency be floated against the US dollar. This naturally takes its toll in price hikes (and frequently social unrest), but it does essentially kill the black market.

In some countries the black market is wide open and there appear to be few official constraints on it. In most countries, however, caution and discretion are the name of the game. Being caught unofficially changing money in many African countries can be a serious matter, as can lack of proof that you changed your money anywhere other than a bank (in the event of being searched).

Wherever a black market exists, there are always plenty of touts offering to change money on the street. The conspiratorial half-whisper, 'Change money?', will be one of your most enduring memories of a visit to Africa. The honesty or good intentions of these touts covers a minefield of opinion, and everyone has a story to tell.

It's usually preferable to change money in the relative privacy of a shop or office, and this is in fact where most touts will end up taking you – they are simply 'runners' for the real moneychangers. If you decide to change money on the street, make sure you have the exact amount you want to change available. Don't pull out large wads of notes. Be very wary about sleight of hand and envelope tricks.

Bargaining

In many countries, bargaining is a way of life and includes hotel charges, transport, food, cigarettes etc. Commodities are looked on as being worth what their owners can get for them. The concept of a fixed price would invoke laughter. If you go ahead and pay the first price asked, you'll not only be considered a half-wit but you'll be doing your fellow travellers a disservice, since this will create the impression that all travellers are willing to pay outrageous prices (and that all are equally stupid). You are expected to bargain. It's part of the fun of going to Africa.

All the same, no matter how good you are at it, you'll never get things as cheaply as local people do. To traders and owners of transport, hotels and cafes, you represent wealth – whatever your appearance – and it's of little consequence that you consider yourself to be a 'traveller' rather than a 'tourist'. In the eyes of most, you're the latter.

Bargaining is conducted in a friendly and, sometimes, spirited manner, though there are occasions when it degenerates into a bleak exchange of numbers and leaden head shakes. Some sellers will actually start off at a price four times higher than what they are prepared to accept, though it's usually lower than this. Decide what you want to pay or what others have told you they've paid, and start off at about half of this. The vendor will often laugh heartily or even feign outrage, but the price will quickly drop to a more realistic level. When it does, you start making somewhat better offers. Eventually you should arrive at a mutually acceptable price.

For larger purchases in souks, bazaars and markets, especially in Muslim countries, you may well be served tea as part of the bargaining ritual. Accepting it places you under no obligation to buy. It's just social lubrication.

There will be times when you simply cannot get a shopkeeper to lower the price to anywhere near what you know the product should be selling for. This probably means that a lot of tourists are passing through and if you don't pay those outrageous prices, some mug on a package tour will.

There's no call for losing your temper when bargaining. If you get fed up or it seems a waste of time, politely take your leave. You can always try again the next day.

POST & COMMUNICATIONS

Post

Have letters sent to you c/o Poste Restante, Post Office (PTT in Francophone countries), in whatever city or town you will be passing through. Alternatively, use the mail-holding service operated by Amex offices and their agents if you're a client (that is, if you have their cheques or one of their credit cards). Most embassies don't hold mail and will simply forward it to the nearest poste restante. Plan ahead. It can take up to two weeks for a letter to arrive even in capital cities, and it sometimes takes much longer in smaller places.

The majority of poste restante offices are pretty reliable, though there are a few exceptions. Mail is generally held for four weeks – sometimes more, sometimes less – after which it is returned to the sender. The service is free in most places, but in others, particularly Francophone countries, there is a charge for each letter collected (about US$1 or slightly less). As a rule, you need your passport as proof of identity.

If you're not receiving expected letters, ask staff to check under every conceivable combination of your name – surname, any initials and even under 'M' (for Mr or Ms etc). This sort of confusion isn't as widespread as many people believe, though most travellers have an improbable story to tell about it. If there is confusion, it's generally because of bad handwriting on the envelope or because the sorter's first language is not English, French or another European language.

If you want to make absolutely sure that the fault won't be yours, have your friends address letters as follows:

BLOGGS, Joe
Poste Restante
GPO
Nairobi
Kenya

Make sure the surname is in bold block letters and underlined.

There's little point in having any letter sent by 'express delivery', as it won't get there any quicker on average than an airmail letter.

Telephone

Making international phone calls is generally not too difficult – it's just the cost that hurts! In some places, such as Tanzania, it's outrageously expensive (around US$30 for three minutes), while in other places, such as Uganda, it can be quite cheap (US$7.50). On average you'll pay around US$10 to US$15 for a three-minute call to Europe, the UK, USA or Australia.

Some capital cities have 24-hour phone offices, but there are also plenty where it's only possible to make calls during normal business hours.

BOOKS

Most books are published in different editions by different publishers in different countries. As a result, a book might be a hardcover rarity in one country and readily available in paperback in another. Fortunately, bookshops and libraries search by title or author, so your local bookshop or library is best placed to advise you on the availability of the following recommendations.

Lonely Planet

The following Lonely Planet books are worth getting hold of if you need more detailed information about specific areas of Africa.

Egypt, in its fourth edition, is highly recommended for any traveller who is thinking of spending a lot of time in Egypt. It's packed full of detailed information and peppered with excellent maps.

East Africa, also in its fourth edition, is the book you need if you're going to be spending a lot of time in East Africa and require greater detail than that contained in this book. It covers Kenya, Uganda, Burundi, Rwanda, Tanzania and a thin sliver of eastern Congo (Zaïre). *Kenya* is wholly contained in the East Africa guide, but is the one to get if that's the only country you are going to.

North Africa is the book you need if you're planning to spend a lot of time in the Maghreb; alternatively there are separate guides to both *Morocco* and in 1998, *Tunisia*.

For southern Africa you can't go past the new *Africa – The South* covering all countries south of (but not including) Tanzania, Congo (Zaïre) and Angola. If you require more detail, this area is covered in greater depth by the following Lonely Planet guides: *Malawi, Mozambique & Zambia*; *Zimbabwe, Botswana & Namibia*; and *South Africa, Lesotho & Swaziland*.

Other Lonely Planet guides relevant to the area include *West Africa*; *Central Africa*; *Madagascar & Comoros*; and *Mauritius, Réunion & Seychelles*.

Lonely Planet's *Trekking in East Africa* is an indispensable guide for anyone keen on trekking in this part of the continent.

Lonely Planet's series of travel atlases includes *Zimbabwe, Botswana & Namibia*; *South Africa, Lesotho & Swaziland, Egypt* and *Kenya*.

If want to get a grip on the more common languages on the continent, Lonely Planet can keep you supplied here as well, with phrasebooks for *Egyptian Arabic, Moroccan Arabic, Ethiopian Amharic, French* and *Swahili*.

And to top it off, two titles in Lonely Planet's Journeys travel literature series are based in Africa. *Songs to an African Sunset* by Sekai Nzenza Shand is set in Zimbabwe. It's packed with cultural information and gives an insight into the lives of middle-class, urban Zimbabweans. *The Rainbird* by Jan Brokken interweaves the author's experiences in Gabon with those of famous European travellers such as Stanley, Schweitzer and Mary Kingsley.

Guidebooks

The *Sahara Handbook* by Simon & Jan Glen is the most comprehensive guide you can get for this part of Africa. It's certainly pitched at those taking their own vehicles – almost half the book is taken up by very detailed descriptions of all the possible current routes through the Sahara. There are plenty of maps, illustrations and sketches. It's an excellent book but, because it assumes you'll be sleeping and eating in your own metal box most of the time, it has little to suggest in the way of where to stay and eat, or the cost of transport on trucks and buses.

Durch Afrika by K&E Darr is in German and covers many routes through Africa. It concentrates on information for those taking their own vehicles. There's also a French translation available.

The *Camping Guide to Kenya* by David Else is the best book of its kind for the camping fraternity, with details of every camp site in Kenya whether in towns, mountain areas, the coast, national parks or way out in the bush. The maps are excellent. Those interested in mountain trekking should also buy his book *Mountain Walking in Africa 1 – Kenya*, which is equally excellent.

Travel

Dian Fossey's research on the mountain gorillas of Rwanda is recounted in her book *Gorillas in the Mist*. Alan Moorehead's book *The White Nile* is a superbly evocative account of the exploration of the upper Nile and the rivalry between the European powers.

Journey to the Jade Sea by John Hillaby recounts this prolific travel writer's epic trek to Lake Turkana in northern Kenya in the days before the safari trucks began pounding up the dirt. Other books to look for include *Initiation* by JS Fontaine, *A Bend in the River* by VS Naipaul and *Travels in the Congo* by André Gide.

Two women's accounts of life in East Africa earlier this century have been recent best sellers: *Out of Africa* by Karen Blixen (Isak Dinesen), which was made into a hugely popular movie, and *West with the Night* by Beryl Markham.

Inveterate traveller Dervla Murphy recounts her bicycle trip from Kenya to Zimbabwe in *The Ukimwi Road*, but it is equally revealing about the impact of HIV/AIDS and the people of Africa.

General

For a fairly balanced view of African trends and developments, read Ali Mazrui's *The Africans – A Triple Heritage*. This was the book published in conjunction with the BBC television series of the same name.

The doyen of English-language African authors is Basil Davidson, who has many books to his credit. Try *Africa – History of a Continent* or *The Story of Africa*. Or there's *The Making of Contemporary Africa* by Bill Freund and *A Year in the Death of Africa* by Peter Gill.

Also worth checking out, though written in a somewhat self-righteous high moral tone, is *The Africans* by David Lamb and *Squandering Eden* by Mort Rosenblum & Doug Williamson. Both disaster-style accounts of events and developments in Africa, they are sad and amusing but offer little in the way of analysis.

Africa – Dispatches from a Fragile Continent by Blaine Harden was described by the London *Observer* as 'authoritative, entertaining and mercifully free of giraffes and safari suits'. Harden, a seasoned journalist, offers some remarkable insights into the way things work – or fail to – in contemporary Africa. It's banned in a number of countries, such as Kenya, and you'll be lucky to find it anywhere in Africa; get hold of a copy before you go.

Not exclusively about Africa, but very relevant to bilateral and multilateral aid issues, is *Lords of Poverty* by Graham Hancock, an exposé of the bungling and waste perpetrated by the UN, IMF, World Bank and others.

For novels, current trends in Africa, and cultural and political developments on a more regional basis, write to Heinemann, 22 Bedford Square, London, UK, WC1B 3HH, and ask for a list of their African Writers Series. They are the major publishers of all current literature emanating from Africa in the English language. Try Chinua Achebe (Nigeria), Ngugi wa Thiong'o (Kenya), Elechi Amadi (Nigeria) and Meja Mwangi (Kenya) as starters.

Many of the books published in this series are available in good bookshops in all Anglophone African countries and English-language bookshops in Francophone countries.

MAGAZINES

New African is a monthly publication which covers mostly political and economic issues in Africa, and is probably the best of its kind in the English language. It's available in virtually all Anglophone African countries as well as the UK and USA.

Focus on Africa is a quarterly magazine published by the BBC which also deals with political and economic issues but covers a much wider area of interest, including such topics as sport and music. It doesn't attempt to cover the whole continent in a single issue but concentrates on in-depth feature articles.

Jeune Afrique, arguably the best magazine of the lot, offers investigative journalism *par excellence*. The writers who work for this magazine are obviously very dedicated and informed people. It's published weekly in French and available in all Francophone African countries as well as France.

RADIO

With the dearth of good local news services and the proliferation of propaganda, short-wave radio services such as the BBC World Service or other similar services, like Voice of America (VOA) or Deutsche Welle, are one of the best ways to keep in touch with what's happening across the continent. A small short-wave radio no bigger than a pack of cards is all that's needed to tune in.

Although frequencies change according to region and the time of day, some common BBC frequencies include 17830kHz in West and Central Africa, 6190kHz in southern Africa and 17885kHz in East Africa. For VOA try 6035, 11975 and 15410kHz.

PHOTOGRAPHY

Many African countries have restrictions on what you can photograph. The main reasons for this are fear of espionage and mercenary-backed coups – all very real threats. Other reasons are more personal – religion, tribal myths, press image etc.

In general, if you stay clear of taking pictures of anything connected with the armed forces, bridges, railway stations, post offices, radio/TV stations, prisons and port facilities, you will be OK. If in doubt, ask.

It's a good idea to take most of your film requirements with you, especially if you use slide film, and a set of replacement batteries

for your camera. Film (both colour negative and slide) is readily available in ASA 64, 100, 200 and even 400 in many capital cities, but you will not find ASA 800 or 1600 (essential for photography in jungle conditions) and in many places slide film is not stocked at all. Camera batteries can be hard to find if they are an irregular size.

If you buy film in Africa, check the expiry date carefully and remember that most film will not have been kept in ideal conditions.

Wrap unexposed and exposed film in heavy-duty aluminium foil. It will help to prevent spoilage.

When leaving a country by air, think about those so-called 'film-safe' X-ray machines which you'll have to put your hand baggage through. They probably won't affect 100 or 200 ASA film, but 400 and 800 ASA might be a different matter. Most security personnel are aware of this and will consent to personally examining your camera equipment without you having to put it through the X-ray machine.

TIME

Africa is covered by four time zones (GMT/UTC to GMT/UTC + 3), which you need to be aware of when crossing borders,

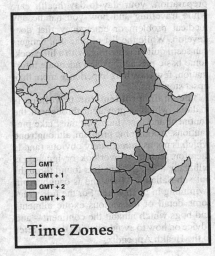

GMT
GMT + 1
GMT + 2
GMT + 3

Time Zones

as the border post on one side may close an hour earlier or later than you anticipate.

Some of the countries in North Africa also have summer time.

ELECTRICITY

Most countries use 220/240V current, some countries have a mixture of 110 and 240V (such as Libya, Madagascar, Mauritania, Morocco and Senegal), while Eritrea is the only country we're aware of which uses solely 110V.

When it comes to sockets, you'll come across virtually every type ever invented – and a few others! Generally where a country has been a European colony, the sockets will be the same as in that European country. In places like Ethiopia, where aid agencies have set up much of the infrastructure, the donors have used whatever was available. The only country with totally non-standard sockets is South Africa, where they have three large round pins (but unlike the British system).

Power surges and total power failures are a part of life in many African countries.

HEALTH

Travel health depends on your predeparture preparation, your day-to-day health care while travelling and how you handle any medical problem or emergency that does develop. While the list of potential dangers can seem quite frightening, with a little luck, some basic precautions and adequate information, few travellers experience more than upset stomachs.

The main problem for travellers is malaria, which is prevalent throughout the continent and for which you must take precautions. Another big problem, although one which is not as immediately obvious (and is therefore easier to overlook or ignore), is bilharzia, a disease which is found throughout sub-Saharan Africa and is caught from swimming in fresh water. For the full, gruesome detail of the various exotic ailments and bugs which inhabit the continent – and advice on how to avoid catching them – refer to the Health Appendix.

WOMEN TRAVELLERS

As if travelling in Africa isn't arduous enough, women, and especially women unaccompanied by a man, face the additional problem of sexual harassment. You may have an 'admirer' who won't go away, or a border official may abuse you verbally. Rape, on the other hand, is in most countries statistically insignificant, perhaps in part because black African societies are not repressive sexually. Generally African men, both black and white, are polite and respectful – when sober.

One reason that women receive this sort of harassment is that they are frequently viewed as 'loose', and clothing can be a major factor in this. Even in major cities where African women dress in modern western gear, most still dress conservatively. It's inadvisable for women to wear anything short or tight, especially in Muslim countries.

If you receive unwarranted attention, act prudish and remote. Or invent an imaginary husband who will be arriving shortly. If you are travelling with a male companion, introduce him as your husband.

It is advisable to avoid dark and lonely places at night, especially when you are unaccompanied.

GAY & LESBIAN TRAVELLERS

Homosexuality is not a major issue in most places, although sex between men is illegal in a number of countries. There are two major exceptions, however, although they are notable for different reasons. The Zimbabwean government is rabidly anti-gay; in March 1997 President Mugabe said: '... gays can never, ever stand as something we approve in Zimbabwe'. At the other end of the spectrum is South Africa, where the new constitution officially bans discrimination based on sexual orientation.

DISABLED TRAVELLERS

Think seriously about coming to Africa if you fit into this category. With the possible exception of South Africa, there are no facilities whatsoever and you'll find it particularly difficult – if not impossible – to get onto public transport, let alone into your room at a hotel with no lifts. Likewise, there are no toilet facilities for disabled people.

SENIOR TRAVELLERS

Providing you are fit and in good health, there is no reason why a trip to Africa should present any unusual problems for senior travellers. Indeed, there are a quite a number backpacking around the continent at any time. What you can't expect, however, is any special provision being made for older people, such as discounts or other preferential treatment.

TRAVEL WITH CHILDREN

This presents few problems other than those you would encounter anywhere else in the world. Africans in general are very friendly, helpful and protective towards children (and their mothers). On the other hand, if you want reasonable toilet and bathroom facilities, you'd be advised to stay in a mid-range hotel. You'd also be well advised to avoid feeding your children street food. Canned baby foods and powdered milk formula are available in most major towns and cities but not elsewhere. Your major concern is good medical facilities in case of sickness. These are few and far between. Your fall-back here is a pharmacy. Most of these stock the usual range of medicines and you will not need a doctor's prescription to buy them.

Most hotels will not charge for a child under two years of age, and for those between two and 12 years old sharing the same room as their parents usually costs 50% of the adult rate. In

better places you may also get a cot thrown in for this price. Likewise, most reasonable restaurants will cater for children – smaller portions at a comparable price. See Lonely Planet's *Travel with Children* for additional advice and ideas.

PUBLIC HOLIDAYS

Public holidays obviously vary from country to country, but some are observed in virtually all countries. These include New Year's Day and Christmas Day. Often, days slated as official public holidays pass and you'd never know; other times, everything shuts down in a place. In each chapter we have listed the official holidays for each country.

In Muslim countries, or countries with a significant Muslim population, Muslim holidays are observed. These fall on a different day each year, as the Muslim calendar differs from the Gregorian calendar. See the Islamic Holidays table in this section for exact dates.

Ramadan is a month when devout Muslims fast (food *and* drink) during daylight hours. Although there are no public holidays during this month, it can be a difficult time as many restaurants don't open until after dark and the locals often get a bit testy by late afternoon if they've had nothing to eat or drink all day. Office hours are generally shorter too. Although you won't be expected to follow suit, it is polite not to eat, drink or smoke in public during Ramadan.

WORK

It's difficult, though by no means impossible, for foreigners to find jobs. The most

Islamic Holidays

Hejira Year	New Year	Prophet's Birthday	Ramadan Begins	Eid al-Fitr	Eid al-Adha
1418	09.05.97	18.07.97	31.12.97	31.01.98	08.04.98
1419	28.04.98	07.07.98	20.12.98	20.01.99	28.03.99
1420	17.04.99	26.06.99	09.12.99	09.01.00	17.03.00
1421	06.04.00	15.06.00	29.11.00	30.12.00	06.03.01

likely employment areas are the safari business, teaching, advertising and journalism but, except for teaching, it's unlikely you'll see them advertised and the only way you'll find out about them is to spend a lot of time getting to know resident expatriates. You will also need to be able to prove that you have the relevant qualifications and/or experience in the field. Basically the rule of thumb is that if an African can do the job there's no need to hire a foreigner.

The most fruitful area in which to look for work, assuming that you have some experience and the relevant skills, is the 'disaster industry'. A number of cities are awash with UN and other aid agencies servicing famines and other humanitarian disasters throughout the continent. But remember that the work is tough, often dangerous, and the pay low. To find such work you would, again, have to spend a lot of time getting to know the expatriates involved in the field.

Freelance work in the fields of journalism, literature and the film industry is also possible. However, work permits and resident visas are usually not the easiest of things to arrange.

ACCOMMODATION

There are many different types of places where you can stay cheaply in Africa. They range from hostels in countries such as Egypt, Kenya, Morocco, South Africa, Tunisia and Zimbabwe, to religious missions in the Francophone countries, to government rest houses in Malawi and Namibia.

Religious missions can be good places to stay. The missions in larger centres often have purpose-built guesthouses. These are usually very clean and well maintained, and cost about the same as an equivalent decent hotel (ie they're not rock-bottom cheap). In the more remote places, the story is very different. Some missions are happy to accept travellers; many don't, often because travellers have abused hospitality in the past. If you are offered accommodation, leave a donation equivalent to what a night in a hotel would cost, and if you've been fed take this into account too.

Where there are no hostels there are often youth centres which offer floor space or a bed in a dormitory. Most of these places shouldn't cost more than a few dollars a night but, if you're put up for free, please leave a reasonable donation.

The next option is a cheap hotel. What you get depends largely on what you pay. If you're paying less than US$5 a single then, as likely as not, the hotel will double as a brothel. Even US$10 a single won't guarantee that the hotel isn't used for the same purposes in some places. Things like a fan, private bathroom or a mosquito net will all bump up the price of a room.

In cities and towns where there are distinct 'African' and so-called 'European' quarters (the latter are generally the parts of a city constructed initially by the colonial authorities), the cheapest hotels will be in the African quarter. Hotels in the European quarter will generally offer similar facilities to those you find in most western countries.

Some cities are very expensive, even for budget accommodation. Top of the list is anywhere in Libya or Gabon, and Dakar (Senegal) and Abidjan (Côte d'Ivoire). Avoid these places if you're on a very tight budget.

The problem with many African hotels under US$25 a night is that maintenance is negligible. This is especially true of plumbing and electrical fittings. Not only are they installed initially in an inexpert manner, but their owners expect them to outlive the life of the building itself. They obviously don't, but no-one is going to fix them.

Ali Mazrui (The Africans – A Triple Heritage) endearingly described this common phenomenon as 'squelching'. So, when you find something squelched, welcome to Africa! Don't waste your time and energy complaining. Someone may have a look at 'the problem' – but nothing will ever be done to rectify it. Lateral thinking works wonders. On the other hand, most hotels, even in the budget range, do provide clean linen.

More and more African countries are setting up purpose-built camp sites, but where there are no such places you can usually find a place to pitch a tent. In some countries you will be obliged to first seek permission from the village elder or chief (and it's common courtesy to do so). Never assume, however, that your gear is safe, even at a camp site which is supposedly guarded 24 hours a day. Don't camp (or sleep out) on beaches except where there's a camp site. There's a good chance your gear will be stolen and/or you'll be mugged.

Many camp sites not only offer facilities for camping, but also have huts (*paillottes*, *bandas*, *rondavels* etc) for those without tents. They're usually very good value and most are constructed in local style and materials.

In the past, the US Peace Corps, British VSO, Canadian CUSO and other volunteer organisations used to welcome travellers to their rest houses, but most now refuse to allow travellers to stay. The reasons are various, but it basically comes down to the fact that many travellers abused their hospitality, didn't contribute to their keep, overstayed their welcome or simply became too numerous. It's still possible to stay with these people here and there, but you should largely assume you're not welcome.

ECOLOGY & ENVIRONMENT
Environmental Problems
Sub-Saharan Africa faces many environmental challenges, both immediate and in the coming years. With a predominantly rural population which depends heavily on agriculture and other natural resources, severe environmental degradation in the form of soil erosion, declining soil fertility, deforestation, desertification, water pollution and loss of biodiversity are all cause for huge concern.

Considering the average population growth rate of around 3%, it has been estimated that the region will be home to in excess of one billion people within the next 30 years. It is also predicted that by the year 2000 something like 300 million Africans will not have access to adequate water. Already two-thirds of the rural population and one quarter of the continent's urban dwellers have insufficient water. Deforestation continues apace, and threatens the sustainability of major ecosystems such as the primary forest of the Congo Basin, which accounts for more than 90% of Africa's remaining primary forest. According to conservative estimates, Nigeria has lost about 30% of its total area to desertification, which still continues at the rate of 500m a year.

Travellers should be aware of their impact on the environment. For example, activities such as sand dune skiing can cause environmental damage. In coastal areas, vegetation can be damaged and even when there is no vegetation, there are still life forms making a home in the sand which can be affected.

While the figures paint an alarming picture, the outlook is certainly not all bleak. Across the continent governments and aid bodies are instituting projects, many of them community based, aimed at tackling the problems on a local level.

Wildlife Management
The management of wildlife is another major issue in Africa, and one which sparks heated debate. It is easy for western environmentalists to put pressure on African countries, insisting that more land be set aside solely for wildlife. While this is a laudable aim in theory, it fails to take into account the situation on the ground: local people often depend utterly on the land for their survival, and if they are completely excluded, as is often the case, their livelihood is threatened. Many Africans still equate protected wildlife areas with exclusive reserves and hunting grounds which were very much a part of the colonial scene in many countries. To an African villager trying to grow crops and herd animals in order to feed his family, wild animals can only be seen as a threat; it's hard to appreciate a wildlife reserve when elephants regularly trample your crops. Unless some tangible benefit can reach these people as a result of proclaiming protected areas, this attitude will be hard to change.

While there is an obvious need for wildlife to be protected, the problem must be approached with the consultation and cooperation of the people most affected by national parks. Many, although far from all, governments are committed to responsible wildlife management, and there is currently close to half a million sq km of Africa given over entirely to designated national parks and game reserves. Given the pressures for land in Africa, this is an extraordinarily high figure.

SOCIETY & CONDUCT
Social Etiquette
Basics As in any part of the world, the best way to learn about a society's conduct is to watch or listen to the locals. The first thing to remember is not to worry: Africans are generally very easy-going towards foreigners, and any social errors that you might make are unlikely to cause offence (although they may cause confusion or merriment). Having said that, there are a few things that are frowned upon wherever you go. These include: public nudity, open displays of anger, open displays of affection (between people of same or opposite sex) and vocal criticism of the government or country.

Common Courtesies A few straightforward courtesies may greatly improve your chances of acceptance by the local community, especially in rural areas. Pleasantries are taken quite seriously, and it's *essential* to greet someone before going any further, even if you're just shopping in the local market or asking directions. Learn the local words for hello, goodbye and how are you, and use them unsparingly.

Great emphasis is also placed on handshakes. There are various local variations, involving linked thumbs or fingers, or the left hand touching the right elbow, which you'll pick up by observation, but these are reserved for informal occasions (not greeting officials). A 'normal' western handshake will do fine in most situations. Sometimes, people who know each other continue to hold hands right through their conversation, or at least for a few minutes.

Dealing with Officials & Elders As in most traditional societies, older people are treated with deference. Teachers, doctors and other professionals (usually men) often receive similar treatment. Likewise, people holding positions of authority – immigration officers, government officials, police, village chiefs and so on (also usually men) – should be dealt with politely.

In many African countries officials are normally courteous and fairly efficient, although there are always exceptions, and in some countries inefficiency, corruption and unpleasantness are the rule. On your side, manners, patience and cooperation will get you through most situations. Even if you meet somebody awkward or unpleasant, the same rules apply. It is one thing to stand up for your rights, but undermining an official's authority or insulting an ego may only serve to waste time, tie you up in red tape and inspire closer scrutiny of future travellers.

Women & Children At the other end of the spectrum, children rate very low on the social scale. They are expected to do as they're told without complaint and defer to adults in all situations. Unfortunately for half the region's population, the status of women is only slightly higher than that of children. For example, an African man on a bus might give his seat to an older man, but not normally to a woman, never mind that she is carrying a baby and luggage and minding two toddlers. In traditional rural areas, women are expected to dress and behave modestly, especially in the presence of chiefs or other esteemed persons. Visitors should act in the same way.

Visiting Villages When visiting rural settlements, especially away from areas normally reached by tourists, it is a good idea to request to see the chief to announce your presence and request permission before setting up a tent or wandering through a village. You will rarely be refused permission. Visitors should also ask permission before drawing water from a community well. Avoid letting water spill on the ground, especially in dry areas. If you want to wash your body or your clothing, fill a container with water and carry it elsewhere, and try to minimise your water use.

Meals Most travellers will have the opportunity to share an African meal sometime during their stay and will normally be given royal treatment and a seat of honour. Although concessions are sometimes made for foreigners, table manners are probably different from what you're accustomed to.

Before eating, a member of the family may pass around a bowl of water, or jug and bowl, for washing hands. If it comes to you first as honoured guest and you're not sure of the routine, indicate that the bowl should be taken to the head of the family, then do what they do when it comes to you.

The African staple – maize or sorghum meal – is the centre of nearly every meal. It is normally taken with the right hand from a communal pot, rolled into balls, dipped in some sort of sauce (meat gravy or vegetables) and eaten. As in most societies, it is considered impolite to scoff food; if you do, your hosts may feel that they haven't provided enough. For the same reason, it may be polite *not* to be the one who takes the last handful from the communal bowl. If your food is served on separate plates and you can't finish your food, don't worry; again this shows your hosts that you have been satisfied. Often containers of water or home-brew beer may be passed around from person to person; however, it is not customary to share coffee, tea or bottled soft drinks.

Giving & Receiving Gifts If you do visit a remote community, tread lightly and leave as little lasting evidence of your visit as possible. In some African societies it isn't considered impolite for people to ask others for items they may desire; but likewise it isn't rude to refuse. So if a local asks for your watch or camera, say 'no' politely, explaining it's the only one you've got, and all will be fine. If you start feeling guilty about your relative wealth and hand out all your belongings, you may be regarded as strange. Reciprocation of kindness is OK, but indiscriminate distribution of gifts from outside, however well intentioned, tends to create a taste for items not locally available, erodes well-established values, robs people of their pride and, in extreme cases, creates villages of dependent beggars.

On the other hand, if you're offered a gift, don't feel guilty about accepting it; to refuse it would bring shame on the giver. To politely receive a gift, local people may accept it with both hands and perhaps bow slightly, or they may receive it with the right hand while touching the left hand to their right elbow; this is the equivalent of saying 'thanks'. You can try this if you think it's appropriate. Spoken thanks aren't common and local people tend to think westerners say 'thank you' too often and too casually, so don't be upset if you aren't verbally thanked for a gift.

Photographing People Ask permission before taking shots of people. Respect their right to privacy. Respect them as individuals. Many of these people have customs which are totally at odds with your own.

Most Muslim women strongly resent having their photographs taken by strangers, and you could get yourself into a lot of trouble by doing so without permission. The same goes for many tribal people, especially the Maasai of Kenya and Tanzania. Where people have been exposed to tourism for a long time, however, it's generally a question of negotiating a price.

This might strike you as nonsense or as an example of a people spoiled by tourism. Yet who is exploiting whom? You come through briefly with your expensive camera gear and an (apparently) endless supply of leisure time in search of local colour, and then you're gone, having contributed nothing to the local economy and, sometimes, not even having spoken to anyone. They go back to their humble lifestyle; you jump on a 747 and go back to the land of plenty. How would you feel if you were an extra on a film project and didn't get paid?

Dress Despite their often exuberant and casual approach to life, Africans are generally quite conservative, and foremost here is modesty in dress. Many travellers get around in T-shirts and shorts which is acceptable (only just) in most areas, but you should be much more circumspect in isolated areas and in Muslim countries. Here women should wear tops that keep the shoulders covered and skirts or pants which reach at least to the knees. Shorts on men are likewise not particularly appreciated.

When doing official business with people such as civil servants, embassy staff and border officials, your position will be much enhanced if you're smartly dressed and don't look like you've just spent five weeks on a truck without a wash (even if you have!).

Child Prostitution

Child prostitution is prevalent in parts of Africa, particularly in areas where so-called 'sex tourism' is big business. Even though all countries have laws which protect the rights of minors, governments generally have been less than vigorous in tackling the problem of child abuse.

Apart from the damage to the child, there is also the health risk to consider (street children and others involved in child prostitution often have high rates of HIV infection) and the fact that people caught using child prostitutes may be subject to criminal proceedings in their own country.

Getting There & Away

AIR

Buying an ordinary economy-class ticket is not the most economical way to go, but it does give you maximum flexibility and the ticket is valid for 12 months.

Students and those under 26 (under 29 in the USA) can often get discounted tickets so it's worth checking first with a student travel bureau (such as STA Travel) to see if there is anything on offer. Another option is an advance-purchase ticket (Apex) which is usually between 30 and 40% cheaper than the full economy fare but has restrictions. You must purchase your ticket at least 21 days in advance (sometimes more) and you must stay away for a minimum period (usually 14 days) and return within 180 days (sometimes less). The main disadvantage is that stopovers are not allowed and changing your dates of travel or destination then incurs extra charges. Standby fares are another possibility. Some airlines will let you travel at the last minute if there are seats available just before departure. These tickets cost less than the economy fare but are usually not as cheap as the Apex fares.

Of all the options, however, the cheapest way to go is via the so-called 'bucket shops'. These are travel agencies which sell discounted tickets. Airlines only sell a certain percentage of their tickets through bucket shops so the availability of seats can vary widely, particularly in the high season. You have to be flexible with these tickets, although if the agents are sold out for one flight they can generally offer you something similar on another.

Most bucket shops are reputable organisations, but there is always the occasional fly-by-night operator who sets up shop, takes your money for a bargain-basement ticket and then either disappears or issues you with an invalid or unusable ticket. Check carefully what you are buying before you hand over money.

Bucket shops generally advertise in newspapers and magazines; many different routes are available and there's a lot of competition, so it's best to telephone first and then rush round if they have what you want.

The UK

You can find bucket shops by the dozen in London, and there are also several magazines with lots of bucket-shop ads which will give you a good idea of current fares.

Trailfinder is a magazine put out three times a year by Trailfinders (☎ (0171) 938 3366), 194, Kensington High Street, London W8 7RG. Trailfinders can fix you up with all your ticketing requirements for anywhere in the world, as well as insurance, immunisation and books. They have been in business for years and are highly recommended. All the staff are experienced travellers. Trailfinders is open Monday to Saturday from 9 am to 6 pm (until 7 pm on Thursday).

The Africa Travel Centre (☎ (0171) 387 1211), 21 Leigh St, London WC1H 9QX, specialises in travel to and around Africa. It has discounted flight prices to most major cities in Africa, as well as information on what safaris are available, along with costs. You can book your safaris in advance here, as well as your airline ticket. Office hours are Monday to Friday from 9.30 am to 5.30 pm and Saturday from 10 am to 2 pm. As with Trailfinders, they're highly recommended.

From these sources, you'll find discounted fares to Cairo (Egypt), Nairobi (Kenya), Dar es Salaam (Tanzania), Kilimanjaro (Tanzania), Harare (Zimbabwe), Johannesburg (South Africa), Lagos (Nigeria), Accra (Ghana), Banjul (The Gambia) and a number of Moroccan cities, but usually not to the Francophone countries. Most of them tend to use eastern European and Middle Eastern airlines.

Typical one-way/return fares from London to Africa include the following: Cairo UK£160/210; Cape Town UK£269/510; Dar es Salaam UK£320/640; Johannesburg UK£270/450; Lilongwe (Malawi) UK£399/

799; Nairobi UK£230/359; and the Seychelles UK£385/770.

There are no direct flights from the UK to Kilimanjaro, but you can fly via Dar es Salaam. The fare from Dar es Salaam to Kilimanjaro is UK£75/150.

Fares to Moroccan destinations can be incredibly cheap if you're lucky enough to track down an agent who has spare seats on a charter flight. Charter flights to The Gambia can be equally cheap depending on the season.

Also well worth checking out are these travel agencies:

Campus Travel
    52 Grosvenor Gardens, London SW1W 0AG (☎ (0171) 730 8111). Open from 8.30 am to 6.30 pm weekdays and from 9 am to 5 pm on Saturday.
CTS
    220 High St, Kensington W14 4NL (☎ (0171) 937 3366). Open from 9.30 am to 6 pm weekdays and from 10 am to 1 pm on Saturday.
STA Travel
    86 Old Brompton Rd, London SW7 3LQ (☎ (0171) 581 4132). Open from 9.30 am to 7 pm weekdays and from 10 am to 4 pm on Saturday.

If you are thinking of flying to Cairo, it may be cheaper to take one of the budget buses from London or one of the other northern European cities to Athens (see the Bus section below) and to buy a ticket to Cairo from there. These buses are advertised in various newspapers and magazines.

Europe

A charter-flight company popular with travellers in Europe is Nouvelles Frontières. They charter flights from Paris to various African destinations and they have offices in several European countries. Their main contact addresses are:

France
    87 Rue de Grenelle, 75015 Paris (☎ 08 03 33 33 33)
    11 Rue d'Maxo, 13001 Marseilles (☎ 91 54 18 48)
Belgium
    2 Blvd March, Lemonnier, 1000 Brussels (☎ (02) 547 44 44)

Switzerland
    10 Rue Chantepoulet, 1201 Geneva (☎ (022) 732 04 03)

Air France is also worth checking out for flights from Paris to West African destinations, since it offers student discounts for those under the age of 26.

North America

In the USA, the best way to find cheap flights is by checking the Sunday travel sections in major newspapers such as the *Los Angeles Times* or the *San Francisco Examiner* on the west coast and the *New York Times* on the east coast. STA Travel or Council Travel are also worth trying.

North America is a relative newcomer to the bucket-shop traditions of Europe and Asia, so ticket availability and the restrictions attached to them need to be weighed against Apex or full economy-price tickets.

It may well be cheaper in the long run to fly first to London from the east coast of the USA using Virgin Atlantic (from around US$500 one way), or standby on other airlines for a little more, and then to buy a bucket-shop ticket from there to Africa, or to go overland. But you must do your homework to be sure of this.

South America

Just about the only convenient flights between South America and Africa are those operated by Varig and South African Airways (SAA). There are no direct flights between Rio de Janeiro and Cape Town, but Varig flies between Rio de Janeiro and Johannesburg twice a week via São Paulo on Tuesday and Friday from US$1079/1096 one way/return. You can then fly from Johannesburg to Cape Town for US$130 return.

Asia

There are bucket shops (of a sort) in New Delhi, Bombay and Calcutta. In New Delhi, Tripsout Travel, 72/7 Tolstoy Lane (behind the Government of India tourist office on Janpath), can be recommended. It's popular with travellers and has been in business for many years. The usual airlines are Pakistan International Airlines (PIA) and Air India which fly from Karachi to Nairobi and from Delhi and Bombay to Nairobi, respectively. From Karachi, the standard economy fare is around US$296/430 one way/return. From Delhi costs around US$535/775 one way/return.

Australasia

For Australians and New Zealanders there are a number of route options to Africa. There are direct connections with Qantas from Perth to Harare and Johannesburg twice a week, and with South African Airways direct to Jo'burg, also twice a week. A return ticket from Sydney or Melbourne to Harare costs around A$1700 to A$2000, depending on the season.

Another option between Australia and Africa is the weekly Air Mauritius flight from Perth to Mauritius, from where there are flights to Nairobi (twice weekly) and other points in southern Africa. The fare to Nairobi is A$2000 from Sydney or Melbourne, and you can have a stopover in Mauritius.

The newest route from the east coast of Australia is with EgyptAir, which flies to Cairo from Sydney twice a week. Return fares from Sydney or Melbourne to Cairo are A$2000 to A$2100, depending on the season.

Other cheap options include going via Bombay with Air India, via Karachi with PIA, via Bangkok with Ethiopian Airlines or via Kuala Lumpur with Malaysia Airlines. The price of any of these routes from Sydney or Melbourne is around A$2000.

It obviously makes sense for Australasians to think in terms of a round the world ticket or an Australia/New Zealand to Europe round-trip ticket with stopovers in Asia and Africa. It shouldn't be too much trouble for a travel agency to put together a ticket which includes various Asian stopovers plus an African stopover. Having this added to a ticket bumps up the price and you may have to go through several travel agencies before

you get the ticket you want as many of them know very little about deals via Africa.

It's probably best to start your search for a ticket by looking in the travel section of the Saturday issue of either the *Sydney Morning Herald* or the *Age* or by visiting a travel bureau such as STA Travel.

LAND
Europe

Most travellers heading for North Africa arrive via one of the ferries across the Mediterranean Sea to Morocco. Details of these services are given in the Sea section below.

Bus There's a wide choice of buses available from places like London and Amsterdam, as well as from other northern European cities. The cost of these has, however, crept up to the point where, for not much extra (or even less), you can fly.

The Moroccan national bus line, CTM, in conjunction with Eurolines, runs buses from London several times a week. The cost to Tangier or Marrakesh is around UK£128 one way. Contact Eurolines (☎ (0171) 730 8235) in London for details.

From Paris the fares vary according to destination and season. Telephone Eurolines (☎ 01 43 54 11 99) in Paris for information. One-way tickets to Tangier, Rabat and Casablanca cost US$124 (US$150 in high season). To Marrakesh and Agadir the fare is US$150 (US$176), while to Meknès, Fès and Ouarzazate it's US$158 (US$184).

Train Buses are fine if you can handle them over long distances, but with a train you have the option of a couchette (a bed converted from seats) and therefore hope of a good night's sleep. The cheapest fare from London to Morocco is UK£137/225 one way/return, which compares very favourably with the CTM bus fares.

Middle East

It's also possible to travel from Europe overland to Africa via the Middle East. There are land crossings between Israel and Sinai (Egypt), or you can catch a ferry from Aqaba in Jordan (see the Sea section below) to Sinai.

There are two crossing points from Israel, one at Taba on the Gulf of Aqaba and the other at Rafah on the north Sinai coast.

There are direct daily buses from Tel Aviv to Cairo (except on Saturday). The one-way fare is about US$30. Using local transport works out cheaper. From Eilat, catch a local bus to the border (US$1) at Taba, walk over the border and catch a bus to the Abbassiya terminal in Cairo (US$20).

TAKING YOUR OWN VEHICLE

Not so long ago travelling the length of Africa in your own vehicle was one of the great overland adventures. Unfortunately these days, due to civil wars and closed borders, the complete trans-Africa trip is no longer a viable option. If you arrive in Morocco it is possible to get into West and Central Africa, which is fine if you only want to go that far and don't mind returning the same way (or shipping your vehicle south from Ghana to Cape Town, which is a costly exercise), but at the time of writing it was uncertain how safe it was to travel through Congo (Zaïre). Similarly, there is no reliable overland route south from Sudan. Southern Sudan is closed, as are the Sudanese borders with Eritrea and Ethiopia, which effectively cuts off any southern route on the eastern side of the continent.

The other option is to ship your vehicle direct to a port, such as Mombasa or Cape Town, and bypass the problem areas. Given the expense that this entails, it hardly seems worth it; you would be better off getting yourself to one of these cities and buying something locally, and this is what most people seem to do these days.

For information on shipping a vehicle between African countries, see the Getting Around chapter.

Carnets

A *carnet de passage* (sometimes known as a *triptyque*) is required for many countries in Africa, with the exception of Morocco, Algeria and Tunisia. You also don't need to prearrange it for most West African countries, South Africa, Namibia, Lesotho, Malawi, Zambia or Zimbabwe. These countries issue a free Temporary Import Permit (TIP) at the border on entry.

The purpose of a carnet is to allow an individual to take a vehicle into a country where duties would normally be payable, without the necessity of having to pay those duties. It's a document which guarantees that if a vehicle is taken into a country but not exported, then the organisation which issued it will accept responsibility for payment of import duties. Carnets can only be issued by national motoring organisations and before they will issue the document they have to be absolutely sure that if the need to pay duties ever arose they would be reimbursed by the individual to whom the document is issued.

Before getting a carnet you should consider the following:

- Insurance companies designate certain countries as 'war zones' and no insurance company will insure against the risks of war. And you must have insurance to get a carnet.
- If you intend to sell the vehicle at some point, arrangements have to be made with the customs people for the carnet entry to be cancelled.
- Though you don't need a carnet to take a foreign-registered vehicle into Algeria, if you have to abandon it in the desert, you'll be up for import duties which are twice the new value of the car.

Car Insurance

Legislation covering compulsory third-party insurance varies considerably from one country to another. In some places it isn't even compulsory. Where it is, you generally have to buy the insurance at the border but the liability limits on these policies are often absurdly low by western standards and if you have any bad accidents you could be in deep shit. Also, you can only guess whether or not the premium is simply pocketed by the person collecting it or is actually passed on to the company. If you want more realistic cover then you will have to arrange it before you leave.

If you're starting from the UK, the company that everyone recommends for insurance policies and for detailed information on carnets is Campbell Irvine Ltd (☎ (0171) 937 6981), 48 Earls Court Rd, London, W8 6EJ.

Guidebooks

Taking a vehicle around Africa requires thorough preparation and is really outside the scope of this book. An excellent guide which discusses all aspects of this is *Sahara Handbook* by Simon & Jan Glen, although it is now 10 years old. Another, which doesn't confine itself to the Sahara, is *Overland & Beyond* by Jon & Theresa Hewatt. In German, a very good book is *Durch Afrika* by K&E Darr – a French translation is also available.

Selling Cars in West Africa

For many years, large numbers of European travellers and other entrepreneurs bought second-hand cars in northern Europe, drove them across the Sahara Desert and sold them in West Africa. The practice has largely died out in recent years, mostly due to the reduced scope for big profits and the problems involved in getting to West Africa these days. With the current troubles in Algeria, the only viable route across the Sahara is through Morocco and the Western Sahara region into Mauritania.

SEA

The following list of ferry routes starts from Spain and moves east to finish with Saudi Arabia. It's not an exhaustive list but includes most of the ferries you are likely to use.

Which ferry to take depends largely on where you want to travel and how much you want to pay. Obviously the shorter the route, the cheaper the fare, which makes the Spain to Morocco ferries the cheapest at around US$20 per person and US$60 for a car. Next are those from southern Italy to Tunis, the cheapest being from Trapani in Sicily, but then your onward travel options in Tunisia are severely limited.

Whichever route you want to take, all are heavily subscribed in the summer months and if you plan to take a vehicle across, it is imperative that you book well in advance, especially for the Tunisian crossings. You don't need to do this between Spain and Morocco as there are many more sailings.

Spain to Morocco

There's a variety of car ferries operated by Compañía Trasmediterranea, Islena de Navigación SA, Comarit, Limadet and Transtour. Jetfoils also make the crossing from Algeciras to Tangier and Ceuta (Spanish Morocco). The most popular service is the Algeciras to Tangier route, although for carowners the service to Ceuta might be more worthwhile because of the availability of tax-free petrol in the enclave. Other routes are Tarifa to Tangier, Almería to Melilla (Spanish Morocco) and Málaga to Melilla. The majority are car ferries of the drive-on/drive-off type.

On most of the routes, more boats are put on in high season, from June 15 until September 15.

If you want the latest information on Trasmediterranea's services, contact Southern Ferries (☎ (0171) 491 4968) at 179 Piccadilly, London W1V 9DB, UK, or the Trasmediterranea offices either in Madrid (☎ (01) 431 0700) at Calle Pedro Muñoz Seca 2 or in Barcelona (☎ (03) 412 2524) at the Estación Marítima, Muelle Barcelona 1.

There are various reductions available on some of the services. Pensioners of EU nations and people under 26 should enquire about them before buying tickets.

Algeciras to Tangier Trasmediterranea, the Spanish government-run company, runs at least nine daily car ferries between Algeciras and Tangier in tandem with Islena de Navigación, Limadet and Comarit. Depending on demand, the number of boats can be as high as about 20.

Whichever boat you end up on, the fares remain the same, although there are a few variations: on Comarit's boats children up to the age of four travel for free, whereas the age limit is two on Trasmediterranea's boats (in both cases children aged up to 12 years pay half fare). In addition to each line's official outlet at the Estación Marítima in

Algeciras, there is a plethora of other ticket offices at the port and along the waterfront.

The one-way adult fare is US$21. The fee for cars is between US$67 and US$110, depending on the dimensions of the car. Motorcycles and bicycles cost US$19 to take across. The crossing takes 2½ hours. Eurail and Inter-Rail pass holders are entitled to a 20% discount on ferry tickets between Algeciras and Tangier and should make a point of asking for it.

If you don't have a vehicle to take across, Trasmediterranea's jetfoil service is quicker (some would say more nauseating) than the ferry. It leaves Algeciras daily at 9.30 am and Tangier at 3.30 pm. In the high season there is usually an afternoon service too. The run takes an hour and costs the same as the ferry.

It costs more travelling from Tangier than it does to Tangier. The fare per person from Tangier by ferry or jetfoil is US$23. Cars up to 6m long cost US$72; over this length the charge is US$34 for every extra metre. The charge for bikes and motorcycles is US$20.

Tangier is swamped with agencies where you can buy tickets but, as a rule, it's probably best to go to the port early and get a ticket on the spot.

Algeciras to Ceuta (Spanish Morocco)
There are at least six ferry and six jetfoil crossings on this route in either direction, except on Sundays, when there are only four. Around Easter and Christmas the number of services can rise to 10 a day each way.

The ferry trip takes 1½ hours and the fare is US$13 (slightly more in high season; children aged between two and 11 years pay half). Vehicles cost from US$60 depending on dimensions. Motorcycles cost from US$14 to US$20 depending on engine size.

The jetfoil costs adults US$21 each way, and the trip takes about 30 minutes.

Tarifa to Tangier
There is a daily ferry from Tarifa to Tangier (one hour, US$21 per person) at 10 am (9 am on Friday). Costs for cars are identical to those for the Algeciras-Tangier ferries. In Tarifa, you can buy your tickets in the morning at the dock or from

Viajes Marruecotur (☎ (956) 68 1821), Calle Batalla del Salado 57.

Almeria to Melilla (Spanish Morocco)
The timetable for services between Almeria and the Spanish enclave of Melilla is not quite so straightforward. In low season there is generally a ferry from Almeria at 1 pm every day except Sunday and Monday, and at 11.30 pm on Sunday. There is no boat on Monday. Going the other way, there is a departure every day except Sunday at 11.30 pm.

In high season (from mid-June to mid-September), the timetable operates on a system of alternating weeks, under which there are two ferries four days of the week (Monday, Wednesday, Friday and Sunday) at 2 am and 6 pm, and one at 10 am on the other days of the week, with the reverse every other week.

The trip takes 6½ to eight hours. The cheapest fare (butaca turista or deck) is US$25 each way. You can also get beds in cabins of four or two, some with toilets. Prices range from US$40 a head for four people to US$67 for single occupation of a twin-berth cabin. Fares are a little higher in high season. A car can cost from US$60 to US$180 in low season, depending on its dimensions. You also pay to take motorbikes across. Buy tickets at the Estación Marítima (about a 10 to 15 minute walk from the train and bus stations) or at travel agents in the centre of town. They accept credit cards.

Málaga to Melilla (Spanish Morocco)
Also operated by Trasmediterranea, ferries leave Málaga daily except Sunday in low season at 1 pm and Melilla at 11 pm (occasionally a Sunday service is put on). In high season there is a regular Sunday service. The journey time is 7½ to 10 hours and fares are the same as for the Almeria-Melilla ferry. As in Almeria, you can buy tickets most easily at the Estación Marítima, more or less directly south from the town centre.

Gibraltar to Morocco
Gibraltar to Tangier Twice a week, the Idriss I ferry links Gibraltar with Tangier.

The voyage costs US$27 one way (US$45 return). The ferry can carry up to 30 cars (the charge for a car is US$50) and runs all year round, leaving Gibraltar at 8.30 am on Monday and 6.30 pm on Friday. From Tangier, it leaves at 9 am on Friday and 5 pm on Sunday. The trip takes about two hours.

The Gibraltar agents are Tourafrica Int Ltd (☎ 79 140), 2a Main St. Several Tangier travel agents sell tickets for the Gibraltar ferry. Tickets to Gibraltar cost US$26 per person and US$56 for a car up to 4.5m long.

Gibraltar to Tetouan Jasmine Lines sometimes runs a catamaran to Restinga Smir (north of Tetouan), usually in the summer, but inclement weather often leads to cancellations. When the going is good (in summer), it runs four or five times a week and costs US$28 one way, US$46 return. The agents are Parodytur (☎ 76 070), in the Cazes Arcade, 143 Main St, Gibraltar.

France to Morocco
Sète to Tangier This car-ferry service is operated by the Compagnie Marocaine de Navigation (Comanav). It is considerably more luxurious (and commensurately more expensive) than the ferries linking Spain and Morocco – it has a swimming pool and a nightclub of sorts on board. The crossing is made between six and seven times per month, usually once every four to five days. As a rule the *Marrakesh*, which can carry 634 passengers, leaves Sète at 7 pm and Tangier at 6 pm.

The trip takes 36 to 38 hours and the fare, depending on class, is between US$250 and US$420 in shared cabins of two to four people. There are sometimes supplements to be paid on top of the fare. Cars under 4m long cost US$308.

There are special reduced fares for students and people under 26; a berth in a cabin of four costs US$180.

You can book tickets for this service at Southern Ferries (☎ (0171) 491 4968), 179 Piccadilly, London W1V 9DB, UK, or in France at the SNCM Ferryterranée office (☎ 01 49 24 24 24), 12 Rue Godot de

Mauroy, Paris 75009. The Sète office (☎ 04 67 74 96 96) is at 4 Quai d'Alger, Sète 34202, France. The port agency in Sète is the Compagnie Charles Leborgne (☎ 6746 6170), at 3 Quai de la République.

In Morocco, Comanav's main office (☎ (02) 30 2412) is in Casablanca, at 7 Blvd de la Résistance. In Tangier, Comanav's office (☎ (09) 93 2649) is at 43 Ave Abou al-Alaa al-Maari.

Sète to Nador The same company runs a similar service at much the same rates between Sète and Nador in the high season (mid-June to mid-September).

France to Algeria
There are a number of options here, operated by the Algerian government-owned Compagnie Nationale Algérienne de Navigation (CNAN), which runs regular services from Marseilles to Algiers, Annaba, Bejaia, Oran and Skikda. These services are fairly pricey, with the cheapest (Marseilles to Algiers) at around US$180.

Given that Algeria is currently not a safe place for travellers (see the Warning in the Algeria chapter), there's not much interest in these services.

France to Tunisia
CTN (Compagnie Tunisienne de Navigation) operates ferries between Marseilles and Tunis. The journey time is 22 hours and the minimum fare is US$130. It's heavily booked in the summer months, so if you have a car you need to book well in advance. For details of sailing times or to book tickets, contact SNCM, 61 Blvd des Dames, Marseilles 13002, France (☎ 04 91 56 63 10), or Southern Ferries in the UK (see the France to Morocco section above).

Italy to Tunisia
Tirrenia Lines offers a year-round weekly service between Trapani (Sicily) and Tunis. The trip takes six hours and the cheapest ticket costs about US$40. There are connections with Cagliari (Sardinia), Genoa and Naples. CTN also operates regular services

between Genoa (all year round) and Naples (from June to September) and Tunis.

The ferries are heavily subscribed; if you are taking a vehicle it is essential that you book well in advance. If you are not taking a car you won't need to book. In Italy, tickets can be booked at Tirrenia (☎ 25 80 41), Ponte Colombo Stazione Maritima, Genoa 16100 or Tirrenia (☎ 31 21 81), Stazione Maritima, Molo Angiono, Naples 80100.

Malta to Libya

There are ferries a few times a week between Malta and Tripoli. The timetables are subject to frequent changes and cancellations due to season, weather and general chaos. The fares are extremely high – a one-way trip costs about US$170.

Greece, Turkey & the Middle East to Egypt

In summer, Misr Shipping Company runs weekly ferries between Alexandria and Rhodes (Greece), Limassol (Cyprus), Antalya (Turkey), Beirut (Lebanon) and Lattakia (Syria). In winter there is no service to Greece or Cyprus.

The Egyptian representative is Menatours (☎ (03) 80 8407) at Midan Saad Zaghloul in Alexandria. The cheapest possible ticket from Lattakia to Alexandria is an airline-style seat on the deck for US$140.

Jordan to Egypt

There is at least one daily car ferry and one speedboat between Aqaba and Nuweiba on the Sinai peninsula. These services offer an alternative to the Israel-Egypt land crossing.

From Aqaba, the car ferries are supposed to leave at noon and 6.30 pm on Sunday and 4 pm on other days – the fare is US$20 and US$100 for a car. This service is invariably late and packed to the brim. Speedboat tickets cost US$27. Tickets can be bought on the day of departure from one of the travel agents in Aqaba, or from Arab Bridge Maritime Co (☎ (03) 31 3235) in central Aqaba.

At the JETT bus office in Aqaba, you can book a ferry and bus right through to Cairo for US$45, although it is cheaper to pay for each leg as you go.

Saudi Arabia to Egypt

Direct ferries take about 36 hours between Jeddah and Suez. There are about two services per week, but getting a berth during the *hajj*, the pilgrimage to Mecca, is impossible. The minimum fare is US$42 for deck class. Check with Al-Aquel Travel (☎ (02) 647 4208), just off Ba'najah and Al-Dahab Sts, Jeddah.

There are also ferries to Port Safaga on Egypt's Red Sea coast from Jeddah (twice weekly, 30 hours, US$60 deck class) and Duba (daily, seven hours, US$30 deck class).

ORGANISED TOURS

A dozen or so European companies offer trips through various parts of Africa, usually using converted 4WD trucks. These are a popular way to travel but certainly won't suit everybody. See the Overland Safari Truck

---

Warning
The information in this chapter is particularly vulnerable to change: prices for international travel are volatile, routes are introduced and cancelled, schedules change, special deals come and go, and rules and visa requirements are amended. Airlines and governments seem to take a perverse pleasure in making price structures and regulations as complicated as possible. You should check directly with the airline or a travel agent to make sure you understand how a fare (and ticket you may buy) works. In addition, the travel industry is highly competitive and there are many lurks and perks.

The upshot of this is that you should get opinions, quotes and advice from as many airlines and travel agents as possible before you part with your hard-earned cash. The details given in this chapter should be regarded as pointers and are not a substitute for your own careful, up-to-date research. ■

section under Planning in the introductory Facts for the Visitor chapter for details on the pros and cons of travelling this way.

The following is a list of some of the companies offering overland Africa trips:

Dragoman, 96 Camp Green, Kenton Rd, Debenham, Suffolk IP14 6LA (☎ (01728) 86 1133; fax 86 1127)

Encounter Overland, 267 Old Brompton Rd, London SW5 9JA (☎ (0171) 370 6951; fax 244 9737)

Exodus Expeditions, 9 Weir Rd, London SW12 0LT (☎ (0181) 673 0859; fax 673 0779)

Explore Worldwide, 1 Fredrick St, Aldershot, Hampshire GU11 1LQ (☎ (01252) 319 448; fax 343 170)

Guerba Expeditions, Wessex House, 40 Station Rd, Westbury, Wiltshire BA13 3JJ (☎ (01373) 826 611; fax 858 351)

Getting Around

Most African countries offer a choice of air travel, train, bus, taxi (shared or private), truck and, in some cases, riverboat and lake ferry.

AIR

Most countries have their own national airline which services a number of domestic routes. They're worth considering if your time is limited, if the distances are large or if the trains are booked out. Fares are often relatively cheap but you shouldn't depend on the scheduling. Delays and cancellations are frequent and, in most cases, the airlines will accept no responsibility for any inconvenience in the event of cancellation.

Unless you are fanatical about only travelling overland, there will be occasions when taking a short international flight is the most practical way of getting from one country to another. This is the case between Morocco and West Africa (land route uncertain), between Cameroon or Gabon and São Tomé (very unreliable boat connections), between Egypt or Sudan and Kenya (civil war in southern Sudan), and between West and East Africa (problems with getting into, and across, Congo (Zaïre).

ROAD
Overland Routes

Due to security problems in Algeria, and the closure of the Eritrea/Sudan border, there is basically only one true overland route south from Europe through northern Africa these days, and that is via Morocco and Western Sahara to Mauritania, and even that's not easily done independently.

The other option, and the most popular one these days if you don't have a vehicle, is to land in Egypt and then fly over Sudan, usually to Kenya or Uganda, although you could also fly to Ethiopia and then proceed south from there.

An alternative route is from Khartoum (Sudan), via the arduous overland route west to the Central African Republic (CAR) and into Congo (Zaïre), but the viability of this route was uncertain at the time of writing following the recent civil war there (crossing into Congo (Zaïre) from Bangui in the CAR is still likely to be difficult), not to mention the poor security situation in western Sudan. Flights from Khartoum to Nairobi or to Kampala (Uganda) are only slightly less than those from Cairo.

Road Conditions

The state of a country's roads reflects both its climate and its political stability. If there's been a long period of instability or rampant corruption, the roads are likely to be in poor shape. In that case, breakdowns and getting stuck are a regular feature of the journey. Don't look too closely at the tyres or the springs of your vehicle: when you see the state of many of the roads you'll know why nothing lasts very long.

In some countries, like the Central African Republic, Congo (Zaïre), Guinea, Mozambique, Sierra Leone and Sudan, the roads have to be seen to be believed – potholes that would swallow a truck, bridges washed away etc. Even the roads in the very centre of some capital cities are not much better!

Desert roads in places like Sudan, Chad, Mali, Niger and Mauritania may be just tyre tracks in the sand or the dust from trucks. Don't pay any attention to red lines drawn on maps in places like this. Many roads are impassable in the wet season.

In the more developed countries – such as Morocco, Tunisia, Egypt, Kenya, Nigeria and all of southern Africa except the former Portuguese colonies – the situation is far better.

Bus

Bus travel is usually quicker than going by rail or truck, but more expensive. Where there is a good network of sealed roads, you may have the choice of going by 'luxury' air-conditioned bus or by ordinary bus. The former naturally costs more but is not always quicker than an ordinary bus. Where there are very few or no sealed roads, the ordinary buses tend to be very crowded and stop frequently to pick up or put down passengers. Book in advance if possible.

Share-taxi

Many countries have shared and private taxis. Share-taxis should definitely be considered. They can cost up to twice the price of the corresponding bus fare but in some places they're only slightly more expensive and they are certainly quicker and more comfortable.

The word 'taxi' doesn't necessarily denote quite the same thing as it does in developed countries. In Africa taxis come in all shapes and sizes, ranging from Toyota minibuses to pick-ups (utilities) and Peugeot 504s. They are also known by many different names – bush taxi (taxi-brousse in Francophone countries), dalla-dalla (Tanzania), matatu (Kenya), taxi in Uganda and taxi-be (Madagascar), to name a few.

They're all basically 'the people's' transport and they leave when full, but 'full' can mean many different things depending on which country you are in. In some, it means that the bus resembles a sardine tin. In others, it means that all the seats are taken. Standards of driving also vary considerably. In Nigeria and Kenya, for instance, they're pretty poor and pile-ups are a regular feature in local newspapers.

You should expect to pay a fee for your baggage in addition to the fare on most buses and taxis in West Africa but usually not elsewhere. Also, in countries where the roads quickly turn into mud baths during the rainy season, the fares on buses and taxis can double and even triple.

Truck

In many out-of-the-way places, trucks are the only reliable form of transport, and although they primarily carry goods, they also supplement this with income from paying passengers. For this reason, most of the time you will be on top of the load, though you can sometimes travel in the cab for about twice what it costs on top.

Lifts on trucks are usually arranged the night before departure at the 'truck park' – a compound or dust patch that you'll find in almost every African town of any size. Just go there and ask around for a truck that's going the way you want to go.

For the most regular runs there will be a 'fare' which is more or less fixed. You'll be paying what the locals pay – but check this out before you agree to a price. If the journey is going to take more than one night or one day, ask whether the price includes food and/or water. Trucks are generally cheaper than buses over the same distance.

Hitching

Hitching is never entirely safe in any country but in much of Africa it's a recognised form of transport, as there is often simply no other option. Travellers who decide to hitch should understand that they are taking a small but potentially serious risk. Trucks are the usual vehicle, although free lifts are the exception (see the Truck section above).

In the more developed countries, where there are plenty of private cars on the road, it's not only possible to hitch for free but, in some cases, very easy indeed, and you may well be offered somewhere to stay the night. Countries where this applies are Ghana, Kenya, Morocco, South Africa, Tunisia and Zimbabwe.

On the other hand, don't expect much in the way of lifts from expatriate workers. They often have a tendency to regard travellers as a lesser form of humanity. Much the same seems to apply to the volunteers who work for agencies such as the American Peace Corps and the British Voluntary Service Overseas (VSO). Perhaps this is because the help given in the past has been abused, so if you are offered help by one of these people, please make sure that you pay your way.

Remember that sticking out your thumb in many African countries is the equivalent of an obscene gesture, although allowances are

---

Warning

Just a word of warning about lifts in private vehicles. Smuggling across borders does go on, and, if whatever is being smuggled is found, you may be arrested even though you knew nothing about it. Most travellers manage to convince police that they were merely hitching a ride and otherwise had nothing to do with the smuggler (passport stamps are a good indication of this), but convincing them can take days. It's unlikely they'll let you ring your embassy during this time, and even if they do you shouldn't count on the embassy's ability to help you.

If you're worried about this, get out before the border and walk through. ■

---

generally made for foreigners. Wave your hand vertically up and down instead.

TRAIN

Travelling by train is generally slow – sometimes very slow – but safer and usually more comfortable than travelling by road. Second-class fares are usually about the same as the corresponding bus fare. For overnight journeys, it's usually possible to take a sleeper in 1st class and sometimes in 2nd class too.

Some train journeys are 'classics' and are used by most travellers to get from one country to another. They include the journeys from Dakar (Senegal) to Bamako (Mali), from Cairo to Aswan (Egypt), from Nairobi to Mombasa (Kenya) and Kampala (Uganda), from Dar es Salaam (Tanzania) to Kapiri Mposhi (Zambia), from Harare (Zimbabwe) to Gaborone (Botswana) and on to Johannesburg (South Africa), and from Johannesburg to Maputo (Mozambique).

BOAT

There are many riverboats and lake ferries in Africa. The main ferry of interest to travellers is the venerable MV *Liemba*, which plies Lake Tanganyika, connecting Kigoma (Tanzania) with Mpulungu (Zambia). This is a classic trip on one of Africa's enduring vessels – well worth taking. The *Mtendere* on Lake Malawi is another which has been running for decades. All the other main lakes – Victoria, Volta and Nasser – have regular ferries.

Travelling by boat can be hazardous, however, as safety regulations (if they exist at all) are often flouted and rarely enforced. Overloading is the most common cause of problems, and this is compounded by poor safety equipment – often there is none at all, and what little there is may be unmaintained and unserviceable. A tragic example of what can happen occurred in 1996 when the MV *Bukoba*, which had a carrying capacity of 430, sank in Lake Victoria with the loss of an estimated 600 lives.

Sea ferries of interest to travellers are those connecting Suez with Suakin in Sudan and Massawa in Eritrea, and those connecting Mombasa (Kenya) with Dar es Salaam and Zanzibar (Tanzania).

On a smaller scale there are many river crossings made by local craft, usually canoes (*pirogues*), which ferry people across, either on a share basis or on demand. Once again, there will be a set fare for such service, and it pays to try to establish the price with local people before paying.

Shipping Vehicles

Look under Sea in the Getting There & Away section of the Ghana chapter for information on shipping vehicles from Ghana to South Africa.

ORGANISED TOURS

See the What Kind of Trip? section under Planning in the Regional Facts for the Visitor chapter. For a list of companies offering overland tours of Africa, see Organised Tours in the preceding Getting There & Away chapter.

Algeria

ALGERIA

Warning
Due to its continuing problems, Algeria was one African nation we were unable to visit. We have updated the information in this chapter as much as possible, but as we were unable to carry out first-hand research much of the detail (including prices) has not been recently verified. Check the current situation before travelling to Algeria. ■

DEMOCRATIC & POPULAR REPUBLIC OF ALGERIA
Area: 2,381,745 sq km
Population: 28 million
Population Growth Rate: 2.5%
Capital: Algiers
Head of State: President General Liamine Zéroual
Official Language: Arabic
Currency: Algerian dinar
Exchange Rate: AD 56 = US$1
Per Capita GNP: US$1640
Inflation: 25% (approximately)
Time: GMT/UTC + 1

Highlights
- Moonlight on the sand dunes at Timimoun
- Well preserved Roman ruins at Timgad and Cuical
- Fascinating architecture of Tlemcen, the old capital of the Maghreb region
- Beautiful oasis towns of Timimoun, Beni Abbès and El Goléa

Algeria has been in the grip of a steadily worsening civil war since the military seized power in early 1992 to prevent an Islamic party from winning the country's first multi-party elections. So far, at least 50,000 people have died, including more than 100 foreigners. Islamic militants have issued repeated threats to kill any foreigners who remain in Algeria. The list of those killed for failing to take the hint ranges from tourists to elderly Trappist monks. Not surprisingly, most foreigners have taken the hint.

While the fighting has been concentrated in the north, the south has problems of its own. A US State Department travel advisory warns that 'bandits have robbed, assaulted, kidnapped and killed travellers in Algeria south of Tamanrasset', effectively closing the overland route to Niger.

At the time of writing there was no reason to hope that the situation might improve and the place looks to be off the travel list for a while to come.

Facts about the Country

HISTORY
The modern state of Algeria is a relatively recent creation. The name itself did not exist until it was coined by the Turks in the 16th century to describe the territory controlled by the regency of Algiers. The present boundaries were set during the French conquest of Algeria in the 19th century.

Before the arrival of the French, Algeria was known to Europeans as the Barbary (a corruption of Berber) Coast, notorious for the pirates who had preyed on Christian shipping since the Moors lost their final foothold in Spain in 1492. Piracy remained a serious

45

ALGERIA

problem until a Barbary fleet was defeated by the US Navy off Algiers in 1815, and it was not eradicated entirely until the French attacked Algiers in 1830 and forced the ruling *dey* to capitulate. It took another 41 years for French domination of the country to become complete.

The main opposition came from the charismatic figure of Abdelkader, the great hero of Algeria's nationalist movement. Abdelkader was a *sherif* (descendant of the Prophet) who ruled a large slice of western and central inland Algeria. The French began their drive against Abdelkader in 1839. The struggle

dragged on for almost six years before his forces were trounced by the French near Oujda in 1844. Abdelkader finally surrendered to the French in 1846. He spent the rest of his life in exile, dying in Damascus in 1883.

The colonial authorities set about changing the face of Algeria. Local culture was actively eliminated, mosques were converted into churches and the old medinas (Arab cities) were pulled down and replaced with streets laid out in neat grids. Symbolic of the change was the conversion of the Great Mosque of Algiers to the Cathedral of Saint Philippe, complete with a cross atop its minaret.

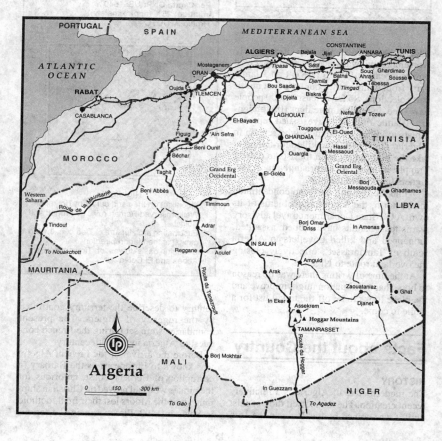

French rule also saw large-scale appropriation of prime farming land for distribution among European settlers – Italian, Maltese and Spanish as well as French.

The fighting that was to become the Algerian war of independence began on 31 October 1954 in Batna, east of Algiers, led by the newly formed National Liberation Front (FLN). The fight was to continue for seven years and cost at least a million Algerian lives. The fighting grew increasingly bitter in the final years. In 1961, militant settlers – fearing that de Gaulle was about to grant independence – formed the underground Organisation de l'Armée Secrète (OAS) and went on a bloody campaign of reprisal against the nationalists.

De Gaulle was unmoved and, on 18 March 1962, agreement was reached for a referendum on independence. The vote was six million in favour and only 16,000 against. The trickle of French settlers returning to France became a flood, with only some 40,000 staying on after independence.

Ahmed ben Bella was the first elected premier of Algeria. He pledged to create a 'revolutionary Arab-Islamic state based on the principles of socialism and collective leadership at home and anti-imperialism abroad'. He was overthrown in 1965 by the defence minister Colonel Houari Boumedienne. His government's emphasis on industrial development at the expense of the agricultural sector – which once employed more than 70% of the workforce – was to have a major impact in later years, with the country becoming heavily dependent on food imports.

Boumedienne died in December 1978 and the FLN elected Colonel Chadli Benjedid to replace him. He was re-elected in 1984 and 1989. There was very little political change in Algeria under Boumedienne and Chadli. The FLN was the sole political party, pursuing basically secular, socialist policies. There was little evidence of opposition until October 1988, when thousands of people took to the streets in protest against government austerity measures and food shortages. The army was called in to restore order and between 160 and 600 people were killed.

The government reacted by pledging to relax the FLN monopoly on political power and work towards a full multiparty system. The extent of the opposition became clear at local government elections held in early 1990, which produced landslide victories for a previously outlawed Islamic opposition party, the Front Islamique du Salut (FIS).

The initial round of Algeria's first free multiparty elections, held in December 1991, produced another landslide for the FIS. The FLN was left looking like a political irrelevance, taking only 15 of the 231 seats up for grabs. To make matters worse for the old guard, Chadli seemed set on seeing the democratic process through regardless of the consequences. The army stepped in to ensure this didn't happen, replacing Chadli with a five person Haut Conseil d'Etat (HCE) led by President Mohammed Boudiaf. The second round of elections was cancelled, FIS leaders Abbas Madani and Ali Belhadj were arrested and others fled into exile.

Boudiaf lasted barely six months before he was assassinated, reportedly by an Islamic militant, amid signs of a growing guerrilla offensive mounted by the newly formed Armed Islamic Group (GIA). Boudiaf was replaced by a hardliner, former FLN stalwart Ali Kafi, who was in turn replaced by a former general, Liamine Zéroual, in January 1994. By now the country had descended into virtual civil war, and the GIA had begun to target foreigners in a bid to sabotage the economy by scaring off western investment.

Charged with defusing the situation, Zéroual announced a one year transitional period leading to fresh elections and set about portraying himself as a man capable of negotiating an end to the violence. Islamic parties were barred from the poll, but the size of Zéroual's victory (66% of the vote) and an impressive voter turn-out raised hopes of a peaceful solution to the country's traumas.

Those hopes were short-lived. Amnesty International puts the death toll at more than 50,000, including more than 100 foreigners, and accuses both sides of atrocities in a war that has become ever more brutal. The GIA, angered by French aid to the government, has extended the war to French soil with a series of bombings and hijackings.

In June 1997 Algeria held its first parliamentary elections since the cancelled elections of 1992. As was expected, the President's newly formed National Democratic rally won comfortably, with the moderate Islamic party, the Movement for a Society of Peace, coming in second. Opposition parties immediately accused the government of fraud but international observers have given the elections guarded approval.

GEOGRAPHY & CLIMATE

Algeria is Africa's second-largest country. About 85% of the country is taken up by the Sahara, while the mountainous Tell region in the north makes up the balance.

The Tell is made up of two main mountain ranges: the Tell Atlas, which run right along the north coast into Tunisia, and the Saharan Atlas, about 100km to the south. The area between the two is known as the High Plateaus. The Sahara covers a great range of landscapes, from the classic dunes of the great *ergs* (sand seas) to the barren peaks of the Hoggar Mountains in the far south.

Summer in the north is hot and humid, and the winters are mild and wet. Summer in the Sahara is ferociously hot, and daytime temperatures seldom fall below 25°C in winter, but nights can be very cold, particularly in the Hoggar. Rainfall ranges from over 1000mm per year in the northern mountains to zero in the Sahara. Some places go decades without a drop.

POPULATION & PEOPLE

Most of the population of around 28 million lives in the north. An estimated 99% are Sunni Muslims.

The majority of people are a mixture of Arab and Berber. Berber traditions are best preserved in the Kabylie region south-east of Algiers, where people speak the local Berber dialect as their first language, French second and Arabic third.

The Tuareg people of the Sahara are also Berbers. Their way of life, cohesiveness and culture have been severely affected by the droughts in the Sahel region (immediately south of the desert proper), and many thousands are now destitute, scratching a bare living on the outskirts of Saharan towns and villages.

LANGUAGE

The main languages are Arabic, French and Berber. Very little English is spoken. See the Arabic and French sections in the Language Appendix for useful phrases.

Facts for the Visitor

VISAS

Unless you've got a Moroccan or Tunisian passport, you need a visa to enter the country. Surprisingly perhaps, it is still possible to get a tourist visa. You should apply to the Algerian embassy or consulate in your home country, or London for Australians and New Zealanders. You'll need to fill in a form, supply three passport photos and produce a hotel booking or proof of an invitation to visit the country.

Charges for a 30 day visa range from free for Australians to UK£26 for Brits. Nationals of Israel, Malawi and Taiwan are not allowed into the country, and if you have a stamp in your passport from any of these countries your visa application will be rejected.

Other Visas

Those wanting visas for Mali and Niger are better off trying the consulates in Tamanrasset than the embassies in Algiers.

EMBASSIES
Algerian Embassies

Representatives in Africa include embassies or consulates in The Gambia, Guinea, Guinea-Bissau, Libya, Mauritania, Morocco (Rabat and Oujda), Niger, Nigeria and Tunisia.

Algeria also has embassies in France,

Germany, the UK and the USA, among others.

Foreign Embassies in Algeria
Countries with diplomatic representation in Algeria include the following, all in Algiers:

France
6 Ave Larbi Alik, Hydra (☎ 69 4488)
UK
Bâtiment B, 7 Chemin Capt Hocine Sliman (☎ 69 2411)
USA
4 Chemin Cheikh Bachir el Ibrahimi, El Biar (☎ 69 1186)

MONEY
US$1 = AD 56

The unit of currency is the Algerian dinar which equals 100 centimes.

Every nonresident must buy AD 1000 (US$18) on entry to the country. Currency declaration forms are issued on arrival and must be kept in good order.

There is no black market to speak of, so you should change at banks where you should get exchange receipts, which are needed on departure.

PUBLIC HOLIDAYS
The following public holidays are observed: 1 January, 1 May, 19 June, 5 July (Independence Day), 1 November and various Islamic holidays (see Public Holidays in the Regional Facts for the Visitor chapter at the beginning of this book).

Getting There & Away

AIR
You can fly from Algeria to Europe, the Middle East and West Africa. There are no direct flights to the Americas, Asia or Oceania. There are daily flights to Tunis and Casablanca.

LAND
Morocco
There are only two crossing points between Algeria and Morocco: Tlemcen-Oujda and Beni Ounif-Figuig.

Tunisia
There are half a dozen crossing points. At the time of writing, the trains had been cancelled, but buses and share-taxis were still running.

Niger, Mali & Mauritania
Algeria's southern borders are frequently closed. For details of the routes (should any or all re-open at any time) see Trans-Saharan Routes in the Getting Around section below.

SEA
France
There is a ferry service across the Mediterranean from Algiers and Oran to Marseilles. See the Getting There & Away section under Algiers for more details.

Getting Around

AIR
Algeria has an extensive domestic air network.

BUS
Long-distance buses are run by the national bus company. They are generally comfortable, reliable and fast where the roads allow. Tickets can be in great demand on less well-serviced routes such as In Salah to Tamanrasset.

TRAIN
The northern train line connects Oran, Algiers, Constantine and Annaba, with additional lines running south from Oran to Béchar and from Constantine to Touggourt.

CAR
If you're taking your own vehicle across the Sahara, or planning to spend time in the

desert, get the *Sahara Handbook* by Simon & Jan Glen.

There are three main routes across the Sahara.

Route du Hoggar The most reliable route as far as transport and facilities are concerned is the Route du Hoggar, running from El Goléa to Agadez (Niger) via In Salah and Tamanrasset.

Route du Tanezrouft Another route runs south from Adrar to Gao (Mali) via Reggane and Tessalit (Mali). This is known as the Route du Tanezrouft. It's more rugged than the Route du Hoggar, takes considerably longer, and there's far less transport along the way.

Route de la Mauritanie The most westerly route is the Route de la Mauritanie, from Béchar to Nouakchott (Mauritania), via Tindouf (in Algeria), Bir Mogrein, F'Derik and Atar (all in Mauritania). This route has not been open for many years.

Algiers

The capital city of Algiers has never been known as a wildly exciting place.

Information
Tourist Information The bookshops along Rue Larbi ben M'Hidi are good places to look for a map of the city. There are good maps posted on boards around the streets of Algiers.

Post & Communications The main post office is at Place Grande Poste, at the southern end of the main street, Rue Larbi ben M'Hidi. It is open Saturday to Wednesday from 8 am to 7 pm and Thursday from 8 am to 1 pm; it is closed on Friday.

The telephone office is on the corner of Rue Asselah Hocine, a block away from the post office towards the harbour.

Things to See
Most of the buildings in the medina are of French origin, but there are some magnificent Turkish palaces around. The main concentration of them is near the **Ketchaoua Mosque** on Rue Hadj Omar. One of the finest houses the **Museum of Popular Arts and Traditions** at 9 Rue Mohammed Akli Malek, which is reached via a stairway to the left about 100m along Rue Hadj Omar.

The concrete monstrosity south of the centre that dominates the city skyline is the **Martyrs' Monument**, opened in 1982 on the 20th anniversary of Algeria's independence. The views from the edge of this area out over the city are the best you'll get.

Places to Stay & Eat
The centre for cheap accommodation is around Place Port Said on the edge of the medina. The best known of the cheap hotels is the enormous *Hôtel el-Badr*, at 31 Rue Amar el-Kamar. More upmarket is the two star *Hôtel Grand Palais*, at 18 Rue Abane Ramdane, not far from Place Port Said.

For local Algerian food, there is a stack of places in the web of the streets between Rue Larbi ben M'Hidi and Rue Abane Ramdane, which run between Place Emir Abdelkader and Place Port Said. More upmarket restaurants are at the Martyr's Monument in the Bois des Arcades.

Getting There & Away
Air The Air Algérie head office (☎ 64 5788) is at the Place Audin. There is a branch office (☎ 63 3847) on the corniche at 29 Blvd Zighout Youssef.

Bus & Train The bus and train stations are on the lower level of the split-level waterfront.

Ferry Tickets to Marseilles (France) are sold at the CNAN office (☎ 63 8932), 7 Blvd Colonel Amirouche. The ferry terminal is near the main train station.

Getting Around
Blue-and-white buses to the airport leave

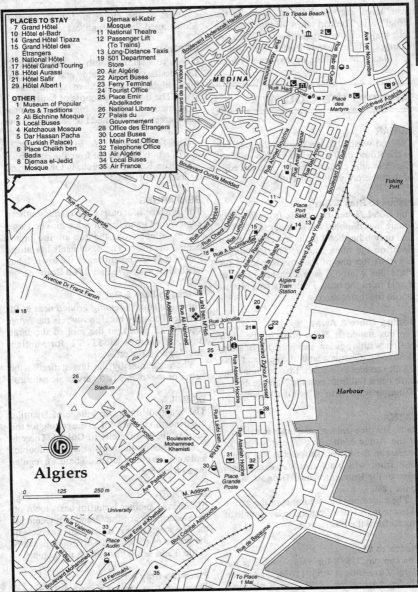

Algiers

from Blvd Zighout Youssef, opposite the Hôtel Safir. The trip takes 40 minutes. The four major city bus stations are at Place des Martyrs, Place Grande Poste, Place Audin and Place 1 Mai. There are taxis everywhere.

Around the Country

ADRAR

This red-washed desert town is the gateway to the Route du Tanezrouft to Gao in Mali. Check in with customs on the southern edge of town before you head south.

Places to Stay & Eat

The *Hôtel Timmi*, one block from the main square, has doubles with shower for US$10. The only other hotel is the expensive *Hôtel Touat* on the main square. The *Restaurant des Amis*, on one of the streets leading off Place des Martyrs, is a pleasant place to retreat from the heat. There is also a restaurant in the bus station.

Getting There & Away

The bus station is 500m north of the town centre with regular services to Béchar, Timimoun, Ghardaïa and Aoulef, and less regular services to In Salah. Taxis to Timimoun leave when full from near the Naftal station, a 10 minute walk north of the main square.

BATNA

Batna is a pleasant regional town in the heart of the Aurès Mountains. There is little of interest in the town itself, but it is a useful base from which to visit the exceptional ruins of the Roman town of **Timgad**, 40km to the east.

The enormous bus station is in the centre of town; taxis leave from an area a couple of blocks from the bus station.

Places to Stay

You can pay US$8 for a tiny double at the *Hôtel Laverdure* (☎ 55 1163), 3 Ave de l'Indépendance, or US$14 for a bit more

comfort at the *Hôtel el Hayat*, on Rue Mohammed Salah Benabbes.

BÉCHAR

If you're heading south to the Route du Tanezrouft, you'll probably end up stopping for a night in this modern administrative town. The town has a couple of banks and a large market next to the big mosque on the main street. The bus and taxi station is close by.

The *Grand Hôtel de la Saoura* (☎ 23 8007), around the corner from the post office at 24 Rue Kada Belahrech, is OK. Singles/doubles cost US$8/12.

BENI ABBÈS

This is a beautiful oasis town on the southern edge of the Grand Erg Occidental. The views are excellent from the top of the dunes behind the town. The oasis itself lies at the foot of the escarpment below the town. It has a beautiful spring-fed pool (**La Source**).

Places to Stay & Eat

There is a small *camping ground* next to La Source. The only hotel in town is the *Hôtel Rym* (☎ 23 3203), at the foot of the large dune. It charges US$17/21 for singles/doubles with breakfast.

The restaurant by the bus station is the better of the town's two very basic eateries.

DJEMILA

The beautiful mountain village of Djemila, 40km north-east of Sétif, is the setting for the ruins of the Roman city of **Cuicul**. There is a hotel right by the ruins (US$10 a double) and a couple of restaurants. There are regular buses from Sétif.

EL-GOLÉA

El-Goléa is another beautiful oasis town on the eastern edge of the Grand Erg Occidental. The water here is some of the sweetest in the whole of the Sahara – so good that they bottle it and sell it throughout the country.

Places to Stay & Eat

There are two camping grounds. The privately owned *Le Palmier* (☎ 83 3319) is the better of the two. It is 200m north of the town centre and charges US$2 per person for shady sites.

The only reasonably priced hotel is the *Hôtel Vieux Ksar*, about 25 minutes walk south of the town centre. The *Restaurant des Amis* in the centre of town stays open late to cater for buses on the Ghardaïa to Adrar run.

EL-OUED

Tagged the 'Town of a Thousand Domes', El-Oued is the major town of the Souf region in the Grand Erg Oriental. As the tag suggests, most of the buildings have domes, built to alleviate the summer heat.

The town is also famous for its carpets, which often bear the traditional cross of the Souf. The prices are better here than in Ghardaïa. The daily **market** in the old part of town is a colourful affair and is at its most animated on Friday.

Places to Stay & Eat

The modern *Hôtel Si Moussa* (☎ 72 8381), near the bus station, has singles/doubles for US$7/9. The *Restaurant El Hoggar*, halfway along the main street, is the pick of a meagre bunch. There is a *hostel* at Nakhla, 16km south of town, where you can stay or camp.

GHARDAÏA

Ghardaïa is actually a cluster of five towns in the river valley of the Oued M'Zab: Ghardaïa, Melika, Beni Isguen, Bou Noura and El-Ateuf. It's inhabited by a conservative Muslim sect, known as the Mozabites, which broke from mainstream Islam some 900 years ago. The area is famous for its rugs. The market in the centre of the old part of Ghardaïa is the place to look for them.

The bus station is just across the riverbed, a few minutes walk from the centre of Ghardaïa.

Things to See

Three kilometres from Ghardaïa's centre, **Beni Isguen** is the religious centre of the M'Zab valley. Foreigners are not allowed to enter without a guide, and not at all on

Friday. It's forbidden to wear shorts, take photos or smoke inside the town.

Melika provides the best overall views of the Oued M'Zab and of Ghardaïa itself. The town is high above the river about 1km to the south-east of Ghardaïa.

Places to Stay & Eat

Camping Bouleila is near the river, 2km south of the town centre on the main road. It has excellent facilities and costs US$2 per person.

The *hostel* (☎ 89 4403) is on the corner that leads up to the Hôtel Rostimedes. A dorm bed costs US$1. The cheap hotels are all on or around Rue Ahmed Talbi, the road that crosses the river to the bus station. The *Hôtel Napht* (☎ 89 0009), just off Rue Ahmed Talbi, compensates for its tiny rooms with an air-con lounge on the 1st floor.

The *Restaurant Oasis* and *Restaurant des Voyageurs*, near the entrance to the old city, are both worth a try, as is the restaurant in the *Hôtel Napht*.

IN SALAH

In Salah is the main town between El Goléa and Tamanrasset. It's built in the red Sudanese style and has a reputation as a laid-back place. The only problem is the one that gives the town its name: salty water. You can't escape the stuff – even the local soft drinks are made from it. Bottled water is not always available.

The bus station is on the main Tamanrasset to El Goléa road, which passes about 1km to the east of In Salah.

Things to See

The most interesting feature of the town is the **creeping sand dune** on the western edge by the Aoulef road. From behind the mosque you can see how the dune is gradually encroaching on the town, and from the top of the dune it becomes apparent that it has actually cut the town in two.

Places to Stay & Eat

Camping Tidikelt is in the centre of town with good, shady sites for US$3 per person.

The only hotel is the upmarket *Hôtel Tidikelt* (☎ 73 0393), near the bus station, charging US$23 for a double with breakfast. It has the only decent food in town.

TAMANRASSET

Tamanrasset, set at the foot of the Hoggar Mountains, is the last major town on the route south to Niger. It has quite a good range of shops and so is a good place to stock up with supplies.

It is also the place to find a lift or rent a vehicle to get to **Assekrem**, a place not to be missed.

If you are heading for Niger (assuming the border is open), be sure to report to the police to get permission to travel south. Passport control is at the border.

Information

There are both Mali and Niger consulates in Tamanrasset. They are on the main street, towards the camping ground. The bus station is on the road to the north of town.

Places to Stay

The camping ground, where most travellers stay, is *Camping Zerib*, 3km south of town near the village of Adriane, which charges US$3 a person.

The *Hôtel Ahaggar* is the cheapest hotel in town at US$7 per person. Another option is the *Hôtel Tinhinane* at US$12/16 for singles/doubles with breakfast.

AROUND TAMANRASSET
Assekrem

Sunrise in the mountains at Assekrem, 75km north-east of Tamanrasset, is an unforgettable experience. It's hard to get there without your own vehicle, but worth the effort.

The travel agents around Tamanrasset will rent a 4WD and driver for about US$150 a day. The vehicles carry up to six people, so if you can get a group together the cost starts to become reasonable.

TIMIMOUN

Timimoun is a beautiful oasis town on the fringe of the Grand Erg Occidental. If you are only able to stop at one oasis, this has to be it. It's an enchanting place, built mostly in the red Sudanese style on the edge of an escarpment. There are fantastic views out over an ancient salt lake to the sand dunes in the distance – magic on a moonlit night.

Places to Stay

Camping le Palmeraie is on the edge of the escarpment, to the left as you enter town. It costs US$3 per person, and there's plenty of shade as well as hot showers.

The *Hôtel Ighzer*, on the main street past the mosque, has spartan doubles for US$8. The *Hôtel Rouge de l'Oasis* (☎ 23 4417) is a fantastic old place. Expect to pay US$25 for a double.

TLEMCEN

Tlemcen is a beautiful old city. It was founded by the Almoravid dynasty, and was the capital of the central Maghreb during its heyday in the 13th century. It thrived on the trans-Saharan trade between black Africa and Europe.

Information

The local tourist office, on Ave Commandant Farradj, just opposite the entrance to the Mechouar, has a good free map of the city.

The bus station is on the basement level of the building on the corner of Rue 1er Novembre and Blvd Gaouer Hocine, about 10 minutes walk from the town centre. The train station is a grand white building about five minutes walk from the bus station.

Things to See

The **Great Mosque** backs onto the main square, Place Emir Abdelkader. The dome above the *mihrab* (prayer niche) has some excellent stalactite decoration and the mihrab itself is covered with delicate stucco work. The **Sidi Bel Hassan Mosque**, at the eastern end of the main square, has been converted into a good little museum.

About 1km to the west of town are the ruins of ancient **Mansourah**. The 4km of walls date from the end of the 13th century.

Two kilometres east of the town centre is the mosque and tomb of **Sidi Bou Mediène**. It is an important example of Merenid architecture and one of the finest monuments in the Maghreb.

Places to Stay & Eat

Camping Municipale is among the olive groves inside the walls of Mansourah, a solid 20 minute walk from the town centre. Facilities are extremely basic.

The pick of the very small bunch of cheap hotels is the *Hôtel Majestic* (☎ 26 0766) on the shady Place Cheikh Bahir Ibrahimi, one block south-east of Place Emir Abdelkader. Singles/doubles are US$7/11. The two star *Hôtel Agadir* at 19 Blvd Khedim Ali, close to the town centre, has good rooms for US$11/15 with shower and breakfast.

The *Restaurant du Coupole*, on Rue 1er Novembre, and the nearby *Restaurant Moderne*, attached to the hotel of that name, both have reasonable set menus for around US$6.

Angola

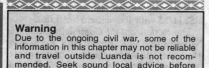

Warning
Due to the ongoing civil war, some of the information in this chapter may not be reliable and travel outside Luanda is not recommended. Seek sound local advice before travelling to Angola. ∎

ANGOLA
Area: 1,246,700 sq km
Population: 11.1 million
Population Growth Rate: 3.2%
Capital: Luanda
Head of State: President José Eduardo dos Santos
Official Language: Portuguese
Currency: New kwanza
Exchange Rate: Kw 5635 = US$1
Per Capita GNP: US$430
Inflation: 3700%
Time: GMT/UTC + 1

Highlights
* Spectacular, palm-tree fringed beaches on Ilha do Mussolo
* The Cidade Alta, the old Portuguese part of Luanda

With security and stability such elusive commodities in Angola, it's hardly surprising that the government has discouraged tourism. Its priorities have been much more basic.

Facts about the Country

HISTORY
Angola endured one of the most backward forms of colonialism. Portugal itself was – in European terms – a relatively undeveloped country. It lacked a substantial industrial base and had neither the inclination nor the resources to develop its African colonies.

While a Portuguese settlement was established at coastal Luanda as early as 1575, it functioned more as a slave-trading port than a colony. Until the end of the 19th century, Portugal was content to milk the area for slaves for its far more lucrative colony in Brazil and to capitalise on the occasional discovery of precious metals and gemstones. It was only when pressure to abandon the slave trade grew that the Portuguese began to settle inland, and even then it was done with convict labour from the prisons of the mother country.

In 1900 there were fewer than 10,000 whites in the colony. By 1950, their numbers had grown to around 80,000, largely because of the coffee boom after WWII. The last 25 years of colonial rule saw immigration from

Portugal increase on a large scale but, even then, about half of the new immigrants were illiterate peasants from the more impoverished parts of Portugal. Not only were the vast majority of them destined to spend only a very short time in the colony, but it seems that few were cut out for life in the Angolan bush. Only 1% of the European population was established in the rural settlements prior to independence.

Popular resistance to colonial rule had its roots in the system of forced labour. After WWII, spontaneous clashes between the various African communities and the colonial administration became increasingly common. The first really serious confrontations took place in 1961 and were directed at European and *mestiço* (mixed race) plantation owners, as well as at the jails in Luanda where political prisoners were held.

The protests were organised by supporters of the Popular Movement for the Liberation of Angola (MPLA) and by the Union of the Populations of Northern Angola (UPNA), soon to become part of the National Front for the Liberation of Angola (FNLA). Some three years after the formation of the FNLA,

a group of southerners broke away to form the National Union for the Total Independence of Angola (UNITA) in protest at what they perceived to be an attempt by tribes of the north to monopolise the movement.

All three groups took to guerrilla warfare shortly after the 1961 uprisings as a consequence of the vicious military and political campaign launched by the colonial authorities. There were few major differences between the three groups as far as objectives were concerned, but there were great differences in the sources from which they drew their support.

The FNLA appealed to tribal allegiances in the country's north and was supported by Congo (Zaïre) and a number of western countries opposed to a Communist takeover of Angola. For this group, the destruction of the MPLA was as important as ousting the Portuguese.

The MPLA emphasised the importance of transcending tribalism and appealed to a broad sense of nationalism. It was linked to the liberation movements in the other Portuguese colonies and was supported by the former USSR and its allies. Its popular base of support was concentrated in the south and centre of the country.

UNITA also drew the bulk of its support from the south, and there was fierce rivalry between it and the MPLA. UNITA certainly had the confidence of the Ovimbundu people in the early stages, but its leaders soon revealed themselves as opportunists. Not only were they prepared to accommodate the right-wing Portuguese forces and exploit superpower rivalry prior to independence, but, once it was granted, they formed an open alliance with South Africa.

Following the overthrow of the fascist regime in Portugal in 1974 by the armed forces, negotiations began on a programme for Angolan independence. A transitional government, representing the three nationalist groups and Portugal, was set up. It broke down, however, and the country was plunged into civil war. It was invaded by regular troops from Congo (Zaïre) in support of the FNLA, and by regular South African forces in support of UNITA. A massive airlift was organised to evacuate the bulk of the white population.

The invasions failed and the MPLA, backed by combat troops from Cuba, Guinea and Guinea-Bissau and with equipment from Mozambique, Nigeria and Algeria, seized control of the bulk of the country by early 1976.

Many years passed, however, before the FNLA and FLEC (Front for the Liberation of Cabinda) were crushed. UNITA continued to wreak havoc in the south and south-east, though its fortunes waxed and waned

according to the extent of South African and US involvement at any particular time. Britain's *Guardian* newspaper reported that UNITA was receiving up to US$50 million a year in covert aid from the USA.

A high-level meeting was held in Luanda in early 1988 between US, Cuban and Angolan officials in an attempt to hammer out a settlement – the withdrawal of Cuban troops in return for peace in Angola and the independence of Namibia. It was certainly a step in the right direction but, in practice, did not result in serious disengagement until 1990, following Namibia's independence and the demise of Communism in Eastern Europe and the USSR.

Despite relying heavily on assistance from its socialist allies, Angola re-established ties with the USA and other western countries. Ironically, the internal conflict didn't prevent the USA from doing business with Angola or exploiting its oil reserves even though, diplomatically, it never recognised the MPLA government in Luanda. The American Chevron and Gulf oil companies operated in the Cabinda enclave for many years. Apart from a South African-inspired attempt to destroy their installations in 1985, which was thwarted by the Angolan armed forces, they were more or less unaffected by the turmoil in the rest of the country.

It looked as if peace was finally in sight for Angola following a cease-fire agreement in Lisbon in June 1991 between the Angolan president, José Eduardo dos Santos, and Jonas Savimbi, the leader of UNITA. All went well until October 1992 when multiparty elections were held and the MPLA won a majority of the vote. UNITA couldn't cope with this and the country was once again at war, despite attempts at mediation by the UN, the OAU, the USA, Russia, Portugal and South Africa. At least 100,000 people have died since hostilities resumed.

Another cease-fire agreement, known as the Lusaka Protocol, was signed between the two parties in November 1994, after UNITA had sustained a string of losses to government forces. A UN force was sent to Angola in 1995 to oversee the demobilisation process of both the army and UNITA, and the formation of the New Angola Armed Forces by June 1996 and a new Government of National Unity & Reconciliation in January 1997. This has not been entirely successful: the UN withdrew in March 1997 and the deadlines have long passed. Even as the demobilisation was supposedly taking place, both UNITA and the army were being trained by foreign mercenaries. Meanwhile Jonas Savimbi has gone bush, declaring that he is 'waiting for the country to implode, then I will take it'.

For the people of Angola the situation looks very bleak – the government simply does not have the funds to maintain even basic services such as water, electricity and garbage disposal; inflation is out of control; an estimated 25% of the population is dependent on foreign aid; and the security situation is far from stable.

GEOGRAPHY & CLIMATE
Around 60% of the country is covered by the plateau which occupies the south and east-central parts of the country. Other regions include a highland plateau in the north and a western coastal desert. The Cabinda enclave is a 7270 sq km province of Angola. It is on the west coast of Africa at the mouth of the Congo (Zaïre) River, and is sandwiched between Congo (Zaïre) to the south and Congo to the north.

There is not a great variation in temperature throughout the year – the climate is generally hot and the daily maximum varies from around 23°C in July and August to 30°C in March. The climate is cooler and wetter in the southern regions. The wet season lasts from November to April, although it is longer in the south.

POPULATION & PEOPLE
The population of around 11.1 million is made up of a number of different ethnic groups, the main ones being the Ovimbundu, Kimbundu and Bakongo. There's also a small number of Angolans of Portuguese descent.

LANGUAGE
Portuguese is the official language and the first language of much of the population, especially in Luanda. In the villages various Bantu languages, such as Kimbundu and Kikongo, predominate. You must speak some Portuguese to survive in Angola; see the Portuguese section in the Language Appendix.

Facts for the Visitor

VISAS
Visas are required by all. If you want to transit by air and stay less than a week, you only need a confirmed hotel reservation and an onward ticket for your visa.

All tourist visa applications made at embassies have to be referred to Direçao de Emigraçao e Fronteiras (DEFA) in Luanda, and take about two weeks to come through. Visas cost around US$50.

EMBASSIES
Angolan Embassies
In Africa, there are embassies in Botswana, Congo, Congo (Zaïre), Namibia, South Africa, Tanzania, Zambia and Zimbabwe. Elsewhere they are in Belgium, France, Italy, Portugal, Spain, Sweden and the UK.

Foreign Embassies in Angola
Congo (Zaïre)
    Rua Cesário Verde 23 (☎ 36 1953)
France
    Rua Reverendo Pedro 31-33, Agostinho Neto (☎ 33 4841)
Gabon
    Avenida 4 de Fevereiro 95 (☎ 37 2614)
Germany
    Avenida 4 de Fevereiro 120 (☎ 33 4516)
Portugal
    Rua Karl Marx 50 (☎ 33 3027)
South Africa
    Calçada do Municipio 3-1 (☎ 33 9126)
UK
    Rua 17 de Setembro (☎ 334582)
Zambia
    Rua rei Cativala 106 (☎ 33 0162)
Zimbabwe
    Avenida 4 de Fevereiro 42 (☎ 33 2338)

MONEY

US$1 = Kw 5635

The unit of currency is the new kwanza (Kw) which equals 100 lweis. Export of local currency is prohibited, and there are thorough checks at the airport.

There are only two official currency exchange points in Luanda: at the Hotel Presidente Meridien and the Banco Nacional de Angola at Avenida 4 de Fevereiro 151. You can only exchange currency from 8 am to noon and from 2.30 to 3.30 pm. Any hard currency is accepted.

There is a flourishing black market (known as the *mercado paralelo* or the *cundonga*), but a government crackdown has made it dangerous to use. The best black-market rates are given by women who change money, known as *kinguilas*. They can be found almost anywhere in Luanda but especially at Avenida 4 de Fevereiro, Rua da Missão and Avenida dos Combatentes.

Inflation is rampant and with the collapse of the currency prices are very unpredictable.

Hotel accommodation (and anything else you buy at a hotel) must be paid for in foreign currency.

PHOTOGRAPHY

Officially a permit is necessary to take photographs, but it's basically a waste of time. You must get a letter of introduction from the tourist office and take it to the Ministry of Information & Culture where the permit will be issued. You'll need two photos and the whole process takes about a day.

Avoid taking photos in Luanda or you'll lose your camera and be fined. Outside Luanda it's generally OK, but be discreet and expect problems with the police.

DANGERS & ANNOYANCES

Never approach the police for assistance, especially the Rapid Reaction Force police (known among local expats as Ninjas because of their black clothes and helmets) as they are usually dangerous and have been known to shoot on sight when drunk.

PUBLIC HOLIDAYS

Public holidays observed include: 1 January, 4 February, 1 May, 25 May (Africa Day), 17 September, 11 November (Independence) and 25 December.

Getting There & Away

You can only enter Angola by air. In Africa this is possible from Addis Ababa (Ethiopia), Brazzaville (Congo), Bujumbura (Burundi), Harare (Zimbabwe), Johannesburg (South Africa), Kinshasa (Congo [Zaïre]), Lusaka (Zambia) and Windhoek (Namibia).

TAAG, the national airline, also flies to Lisbon, Rome, Rio de Janeiro and Moscow.

Getting Around

AIR

Most internal travel in Angola is by air. Almost all flights are heavily booked, especially those to Cabinda. The flights are operated by TAAG, the national airline. Its office in Luanda is on the 5th floor, Rua da Missão 123.

The airport is 4km south of Luanda's centre. Domestic flights leave from a building next to the airport. Taxis to the airport are expensive.

LAND

Bus & Truck

Public transport is virtually nonexistent although trucks (*particulars*) travel all the main routes and take passengers. The roads are horrific. Don't travel at night as the local police often place anti-tank mines on the roads as a security measure!

Bus travel to Lobito, Benguela and Huambo can be arranged through Direçao Nacional dos Transportes Rodoviários (☎ 33 9390), Rua Rainha Ginga 74, 1 Andar, Luanda.

Otherwise, TOURANG can arrange a

number of excursions outside the capital, but they're expensive.

Train

Despite UNITA and South African military activities in the past, the railway system still functions, though only just. The only feasible routes to travel are from Lobito to Benguela and Luanda to N'Dalantando.

For permission to travel, go to the offices of the Empresa dos Caminhos de Ferro de Luanda (☎ 37 0061), Avenida 4 de Fevereiro 42, Luanda, or the Companhia do Caminho de Ferro de Benguela (☎ 2645) at Rua Praça 11 de Novembro 3, Lobito.

Luanda

Luanda is a typical Portuguese colonial city. These days, however, it is very crowded because of the civil war which has resulted in some 1.5 million people (many of them refugees) living in a city designed for around 30,000. It's advisable to stay clear of the *musseques* (shanties) as they are not safe.

Information

For tourist information contact the Agência Nacional do Turismo (☎ 37 2750) at the Palácio de Vidro, or the Ministério do Comércio e Turismo (☎ 34 4525) at Largo do Kinaxixi 14.

Lojas Francas (☎ 37 2832), Ave 4 de Fevereiro 35/36, is the state duty-free shop. Only hard currency is accepted. Livraria Lello on Largo Rainha Ginga is the best bookshop in the city.

There are a number of well-stocked pharmacies in the city centre, but for medical treatment head for the Clinica Sagrada Esperanca on the Ilha.

Things to See

Cidade Alta is the old Portuguese part of the city and has some interesting colonial buildings. The Ministry of Foreign Affairs building is excellent, as is the **Igreja da**

Nossa Senhora da Nazzare on the *marginal* (waterfront).

The **Museu Nacional de Antropologia** on Rue Frederico Engels 59 has good displays of Angolan crafts and information on the history of Luanda. The **Museu da Escravatura**, 20km from the centre at Luanda Sul, is dedicated to the thousands of Angolan slaves who were taken to America.

On **Ilha de Luanda** there are some very attractive beaches, but they have cold, polluted water and a dangerous undertow. This is, however, the place to meet expats as there are a number of decent hotels and restaurants here.

There are spectacular beaches lined with coconut palms, and also lots of bars and restaurants, on **Ilha do Mussulo**. Regular ferries run to Mussulo from the marina at the end of Estrada da Samba.

Places to Stay

Most of the cheaper hotels (around US$20 per double) are in the city centre around the Banco Popular skyscraper. Some are run-down and they are often fully booked, but at least it isn't far to walk between them. They include the *Grande Hotel* (☎ 33 3193), Rua Vereador Castelbranco, the recently renovated *Hotel Continental* (☎ 33 4241), Rua Duarte Lopes 2, and the *Hotel Globo*. The *Logitécnica* (☎ 34 4844), with hot water and air-con, has also been recommended.

Expensive hotels include the *Hotel Presidente Meridien* (☎ 33 0037), Ave 4 de Fevereiro, Caixa Postal 5791.

The *Panorama Hotel* (☎ 33 7843; fax 33 7846), Ilha de Luanda, has a beautiful location and is relatively cheap at US$125!

Places to Eat

The possibilities of eating outside your hotel are fairly limited except on Ilha de Luanda. In town, try the *Restaurante Caixote*, Rua dos Coqueiros 7; the *Pastelaria Primor*, Rua dos Enganos 26; or the *Restaurante a Naue*, Rua da Missão 55.

On Ilha de Luanda you can buy meals of

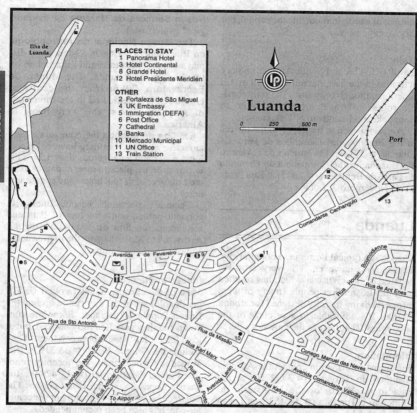

PLACES TO STAY
1 Panorama Hotel
3 Hotel Continental
8 Grande Hotel
12 Hotel Presidente Meridien

OTHER
2 Fortaleza de São Miguel
4 UK Embassy
5 Immigration (DEFA)
6 Post Office
7 Cathedral
9 Banks
10 Mercado Municipal
11 UN Office
13 Train Station

Luanda

fish and rice or goat and maize from the food stalls. You can also eat at *O Surf Restaurant*, and the *Restaurant Barracuda* at the outer end of the island.

Entertainment

There is some interesting nightlife but you need to make friends with local people to find out where it is. The *boîtes* tend to be rather dull and overpriced western-style discos with American or Brazilian music. *Kizombas*, on the other hand, are African-style nightclubs with local music and traditional food; they are great fun.

Things to Buy

The largest and best of the cundongas (black markets) is the Roque Santeiro. It's the place to get fruit, cheap food and interesting souvenirs including masks and fabrics. The masks can be difficult to buy if they're used for *kimbanda* (the cult on which Brazilian *umbanda* was based). Before attempting to buy one, go to the Museu Nacional de Antropologia to get an idea of the range available.

Getting Around

The city buses are crowded and packed to

capacity. A better bet are the *processos* (share-taxis). Ordinary taxis are very expensive.

Around the Country

LUBANGO

Lubango is a nice town untouched by war. It has good access to the coastal town of **Namibe**, where there are excellent beaches. On the route to Namibe you pass the **Tunda-Vala** volcanic fissure, and the **Leba Hill** with its amazing spiral asphalt road.

Places to Stay & Eat

The town has plenty of cheap hotels and restaurants. Try the *Grande Hotel da Huila* (☎ 20 512) on Rua Deolinda Rodrigues.

MALANGE

Malange is Angola's second-largest city and is a pleasant place, despite being surrounded by UNITA troops. Shoot-outs in the streets are common at night, so avoid walking around at that time. To change money head for the municipal market.

Things to see in the area include **Calandula Falls** (1½ hours drive north), **Black Rocks** (110km east) and the **Rio Kwanza waterfalls** (one hour's drive south).

Places to Stay & Eat

The *Malange Hotel* costs US$5 and is good value, although there is no running water.

The *Triangle* in the main street is a favourite among expats, although it is nothing more than an old shipping container with tables inside. The food is surprisingly good.

ANGOLA

Benin

Benin, birthplace of voodoo and seat of one of West Africa's most powerful kingdoms, once had a historical renown which extended far beyond the country's tiny borders. Intrigue abounded about Dahomey, as the country was known until 1975, fuelled by tales of occult religious practices and an elite female fighting force recruited from the wives of the king. Although things are calmer these days, Benin is once again making a name for itself as it embraces democracy with characteristic fervour and is catapulted onto the African stage as a model of reform.

For travellers, Benin still possesses much of the mystique which captivated earlier European imaginations. Colourful voodoo ceremonies, vibrant markets, lagoon villages on stilts and people with a distinct naturalness and vitality make it one of West Africa's most fascinating destinations.

Facts about the Country

HISTORY

Benin and the surrounding area was settled as early as the 13th century by Ewe-speaking people in the south and Voltaic-speaking people to the north. By the 16th century, a number of highly organised, independent kingdoms had been established, the most prominent of which were the Fon states of Allada, Dahomey and Porto Novo in the south, and (somewhat later) the small but powerful Bariba kingdom of Nikki in the north. By the 19th century, following a series of power struggles, the kingdom of Dahomey (based in Abomey) had gained ascendancy over neighbouring states, its power fuelled by the slave trade and a strong military.

With the abolition of the slave trade and tightening of colonial controls, Dahomey's influence began to wane. Despite fierce

REPUBLIC OF BENIN
Area: 112,622 sq km
Population: 5.5 million
Population Growth Rate: 2.9%
Capital: Porto Novo
Head of State: President Mathieu Kérékou
Official Language: French
Currency: West African CFA Franc
Exchange Rate: CFA 500 = US$1
Per Capita GNP: US$370
Inflation: 15%
Time: GMT/UTC + 1

Highlights
- The fascinating palaces of Abomey and voodoo musems of Ouidah
- Natitingou and the superb surrounding countryside

resistance to colonisation, the kingdom finally succumbed in 1894 and by the turn of the century the entire region, including the Bariba kingdom of Nikki, had been incorporated into French West Africa. Opposition to colonial rule was vociferous, fuelled by a small core of the educated elite. As early as 1923 there were anticolonial newspapers in circulation, set up by French-educated Dahomians and former slaves who had returned from Brazil.

Education and trade unionism were major formative influences in the making of the nation between WWII and independence. In addition, many Dahomians were employed by the French in the administrations of other West African colonies. When independence came to most French colonies in 1960, members of this elite cadre were forced to return to Benin, where they became a distinct group of unemployed and disenchanted intellectuals. Their discontent, along with traditional factionalism between the ancient kingdoms, spawned 12 years of coups and power struggles following independence.

In 1972, a group of army officers led by Major Mathieu Kérékou seized power in a coup which initiated almost two decades of military dictatorship. The country took a sharp turn to the left as it embraced Marxism-Leninism in an attempt to break ties with the colonial era and to distance itself from more 'moderate' West African states. Tensions with neighbouring countries flared, resulting in frequent border closures and disruption of trade.

While Kérékou's regime carried out major reforms, particularly in the areas of agriculture and education, Benin was in an economic stranglehold and by 1988 the country was virtually bankrupt. Public servants couldn't be paid, the banking system collapsed and thousands of people lost their savings. With ferment in Eastern Europe and the consequent reduction of support and aid from Eastern bloc countries, Kérékou was forced into accepting multiparty democracy. In March 1990, in a bloodless change of power, a provisional government was set up. It included none of the members of the previous administration except Kérékou, who remained nominal head of state.

Multiparty elections held in March 1991 were won by Nicéphore Soglo, a former World Bank official. However, in the wake of popular discontent over economic austerity measures and increasing autocracy by the Soglo government, Kérékou was voted back into power in March 1996 in balloting which has been viewed as a strong endorsement of Benin's new democratic system.

Although the jury is still out on the extent to which Kérékou has distanced himself

from his previous dictatorial ways, Benin is now being touted as a model of successful democratisation in Africa and the picture for the country is looking brighter than ever before.

GEOGRAPHY & CLIMATE

Benin has a coastline of 121km and a north-south length of almost 700km. Its varied terrain includes the Atakora mountains in the north-west, the Niger plains in the north-east, a fertile central plateau and coastal lowlands.

Southern Benin has a tropical climate with

average temperatures of 28°C. The dry seasons are from December to April and during August. Northern Benin, abutting the Sahel, is less humid, but very hot during March and April. Its dry season lasts from November to May.

ECOLOGY & ENVIRONMENT
Although much of southern Benin was originally covered by rainforests, only small patches now remain. Deforestation and desertification are major environmental problems. In the north, recent droughts have severely affected marginal agriculture, while poaching is threatening the remaining wildlife populations.

POPULATION & PEOPLE
Benin's population of 5.5 million is composed of over 40 ethnic groups, the largest of which are the Fon, the Yoruba, the Bariba and the Somba. Much effort has been devoted to promoting integration and national unity; although underlying north-south tensions persist, Benin's various population groups live in relative harmony. The majority of Beninese follow traditional religions; only 17% are Christian and about 15% are Muslim.

SOCIETY & CONDUCT
Voodoo, the practice of worshipping fetishes believed to have supernatural powers, originated in Benin and eastern Togo. In the 19th century, it was exported to Haiti along with slaves. Both there and in Benin the practice remains strong. Voodoo ceremonies can be colourful events, involving feverish drumming and highly charged dancing by costumed fetish priests.

LANGUAGE
French is the official language. Major African languages are Fon, Yoruba, Bariba and Dendi. For a listing of useful French phrases, see the Language Appendix.

Facts for the Visitor

VISAS
Visas are required for all except nationals of Economic Community of West African States (ECOWAS) countries. Entry visas, valid for 48 hours and extendible in Cotonou, are issued at the Togo-Benin border on the coastal road for US$8 plus two photos.

An international vaccination certificate is required for entry, although it's often not checked at land crossings.

Visa Extensions
Visas can be extended at the Ministry of the Interior in Cotonou. A one month extension will cost you US$12, you need to supply two photos and the visas is issued within three days. Applications are accepted on weekdays between 9 and 11 am.

Other Visas
Burkina Faso, Côte d'Ivoire & Togo
Three-month visas for these countries are issued within 24 hours by the French consulate for US$40 plus two photos. Transit visas cost US$12.
Ghana
One-month visas are issued within 48 hours and cost US$24 plus four photos.
Niger
Visas valid for up to three months cost US$35 plus two photos and are ready the same day if you apply before 10 am.
Nigeria
Visas are issued for residents of Benin only, although your case may be considered if you have a letter of reference from your own embassy or from the Nigerian embassy in your homeland.

EMBASSIES
Benin Embassies
In Africa, there are Beninese embassies in Algeria, Congo (Zaïre), Côte d'Ivoire, Gabon, Ghana, Libya, Niger and Nigeria. Other countries include Belgium, Canada, France, Germany and the USA.

Foreign Embassies in Benin

Foreign embassies and consulates in Cotonou include:

France (consulate)
      just south of Ave Clozel, near the main post office
      (☎ 312638)
Germany
      Pattie d'Oie, near the US Embassy (☎ 312967)
Ghana
      Route de l'Aéroport (☎ 300746)
Niger
      one block behind the post office (☎ 315665)
Nigeria
      Blvd de la Marina, east of Hôtel Sheraton
      (☎ 301142)
UK (honorary consulate)
      (☎ 301120)
USA
      Rue Caporal Anani Bernard, Pattie de'Oie
      (☎ 300650)

The nearest Australian high commission is in Lagos, Nigeria.

MONEY

US$1 = CFA 500

The unit of currency is the West African CFA franc. Foreign currency, other than French francs, can only be changed in Cotonou. The most efficient bank for changing travellers' cheques is the Financial Bank, which also gives cash withdrawals against Visa card (only).

If you are coming from Nigeria, change excess naira into CFA at the border as banks in Benin won't accept them. Going to Nigeria, you can buy naira from some discreet dealers at Gare Jonquet in Cotonou.

POST & COMMUNICATIONS

Cotonou's poste restante is open Monday to Friday from 7 am to 7 pm, Saturday from 8 to 11.30 am. Collected letters cost US$0.50 each.

International calls can be made from the modern telecommunications (OPT) building opposite the post office in Cotonou (open Monday to Saturday from 7.30 am to midnight, Sunday from 9 am to 1 pm). Rates are US$4/6/7 a minute to USA/UK/Australia. You can also send and receive faxes here (US$1 to receive up to four pages on fax

(229) 313837). The country code for Benin is 229; there are no area codes.

By the time this book hits the shelves, Benin may be on-line. Check at the OPT building for information.

DANGERS & ANNOYANCES

Muggings have become increasingly frequent on Cotonou's shoreline. The beach near the Sheraton Hotel is particularly bad, even during the day.

Currents along much of Benin's coastline are dangerous. Seek local advice before taking a swim.

BUSINESS HOURS

Businesses are open weekdays from 8.30 am to 12.30 pm and 3.30 to 7 pm, Saturday from 9 am to 1 pm. Government offices generally close at 6.30 pm, while banks are open weekdays from 8 to 11.30 am and 3 to 5 pm.

PUBLIC HOLIDAYS

Public holidays are: 1 January, 1 May, 1 August (National Day), 15 August, 1 November, 25 December, Good Friday, Easter Monday, Ascension Day, Whit Monday and variable Muslim holidays.

ACCOMMODATION

Options abound, ranging from camping to luxurious hotels. Basic rooms with fan and shared facilities average US$7/9 single/double, while comfortable air-con rooms with attached bathroom start at US$20/24.

Getting There & Away

AIR

Airlines servicing Cotonou include:

Aeroflot	☎ 301574
Air Afrique	☎ 311010
Air France	☎ 301815
Air Gabon	☎ 312067
Cameroon Airlines	☎ 315217
Ghana Airways	☎ 314283
Nigeria Airways	☎ 315824
Sabena	☎ 300355

BENIN

For discounted tickets in Cotonou, try Sitrexci Voyages (☎ 310917). Air Afrique offers student discounts on international flights.

Cotonou's airport is 5km west of the centre. The departure tax is US$5 (payable in CFA).

LAND
Burkina Faso

There's at least one taxi a day from Natitingou to Tanguiéta (45km, US$3). Transport is scarce from Tanguiéta to the border (65km, US$5) except on market day (Monday). From the border the road is sealed. Expect baggage searches and long delays when crossing by bus. It's about 20km from the border to the customs post at Tindangou; from Tindangou, you can catch onward transport to Fada N'Gourma (US$6) and from there to Ouagadougou (three times weekly on Faso Tours, US$4). Time in Burkina Faso is one hour behind Benin.

Niger

Transport between Malanville and Gaya, just over the Niger border, costs US$3. From Gaya, there are minibuses to Dosso (165km, US$4) and Niamey (305km, US$4). The entire journey takes four to six hours depending on police checkpoints and baggage searches.

Nigeria

There is frequent transport between Cotonou and Lagos (120km, three hours, US$6), although it's cheaper to switch taxis at the border. Avoid arriving in Lagos during afternoon rush hour (though traffic in Lagos is a nightmare at any time), and be prepared for hassles with the Nigerian border officials.

Togo

Bush taxis from Cotonou to Lomé (155km, three hours) cost US$5 plus US$1 (negotiable) for luggage, although it's cheaper to take a taxi to the border (US$3), and another from there to Lomé (US$1). Togo's time is one hour behind Benin.

Getting Around

MINIBUS & BUSH TAXI

Minibuses and Peugeot bush taxis are the main means of travel in Benin. On long journeys, minibuses are slightly cheaper than bush taxis; nine-seater bush taxis are cheaper than five-seaters. There is a surcharge for luggage. Be prepared for hard bargaining; for a rucksack the fee should not exceed US$0.60 for most journeys, although drivers may demand over twice that amount.

Some routes and fares are as follows:

Routes & Fares				
From	To	Distance	Duration	Fares (US$)
Cotonou				
	Abomey	135km	3 hours	$3
	Grand Popo	85km	2 hours	$3
	Malanville	730km	15 hours	$16 to $20
	Ouidah	40km	1 hour	$1
	Parakou	415km	8 hours	$12 to $14
	Porto Novo	30km	45 minutes	$1
Parakou				
	Abomey	280km	6 hours	$7
	Malanville	315km	6 hours	$6
	Natitingou	210km	6 hours	$6

TRAIN

Benin's one operational railway line links Cotonou with Bohicon (for Abomey) and Parakou. The train leaves Cotonou daily at 9.56 am, arriving in Bohicon around 1 pm and in Parakou by 7 pm, although construction on the line near Dassa often makes this a 12 hour journey. From Parakou, the train departs daily at 8 am. Tickets are US$10/6 for 1st/2nd class to Parakou (US$3/2 from Cotonou to Bohicon).

In addition, there's an overnight train (US$13) departing Cotonou on Tuesday, Thursday and Saturday at 7.15 pm, and returning from Parakou on Wednesday, Friday and Sunday at 7 pm.

Food is available at stations along the way.

CAR & MOTORCYCLE

There are several car-rental agencies in Cotonou, but all are expensive. It's also difficult to find a taxi willing to negotiate a reasonable all-day rate. For budget travel, it's best to stick to minibuses and bush taxis.

The main north-south road through Parakou and Malanville is sealed and in reasonable condition, although very narrow in parts. The coastal road is also sealed. The road from Parakou to Natitingou is presently under construction.

BICYCLE

Once outside Cotonou, Benin is an excellent country to explore by bicycle, particularly in the north. You can transport your bike in the luggage car of the train (US$1 to Parakou) or on the roof of a bush taxi (up to US$2).

Cotonou

Although Porto Novo is the official capital, most government functions take place in Cotonou. It's a bustling place, with friendly people and an abundance of good eateries. A few streets have been paved in recent years, but many remain sand.

Information

The Direction du Tourisme et de l'Hôtellerie (☎ 314905) sells English and French versions of the booklet *Passeport pour le Benin* for US$1. Good maps are available from the Institut Geographique for US$7.

Pharmacie Jonquet (☎ 312080) is well stocked and open 24 hours daily.

Things to See

The lively **Grand Marché de Dantokpa** sells everything from jeans to pottery. Don't miss the fetish section with its assortment of potions, dried animal organs and other items used in traditional medicine and religion.

The **Centre de Promotion de l'Artisanat** has several small showrooms with everything that's produced in Benin. Craftspeople will make anything to order; bargaining is a must.

Cotonou's **beaches** are plagued by pollution, dangerous currents and muggings. The best is the guarded beach at the Eldorado Beach Club, 3km east of the centre, which is protected by a breakwater. The US$2 fee includes use of the club's popular pool.

Places to Stay

Camping Ma Campagne (☎ 350148), 15km west of Cotonou on the Lomé road, is friendly and secure, although the beach is still 5km away. Camping costs US$3 per person, while ventilated rooms are US$8/12 single/double. A share-taxi from Gare de Dantokpa costs US$0.50.

Near the centre, *Pension de l'Amitié* has decent ventilated rooms from US$8/10 (US$10/12 with attached bathroom and US$20/24 for air-con), while the pink *Hôtel des Familles* (☎ 315125) around the corner has similar ventilated rooms for US$7/8. A few blocks away, the six storey *Hôtel Babo* (☎ 314607) has rundown rooms with fan from US$7/8 (or US$10/12 with attached bathroom).

The clean and central *Hôtel Bodega* (☎ 312974) has singles/doubles with air-con and attached bathroom for US$22/26, although some have only tiny windows.

For a treat, try *Hôtel du Lac* (☎ 331919). Comfortable air-con rooms start at US$50, but you can pile at least three people in. There's a 25m pool and a breezy terrace restaurant with good views of the port.

Places to Eat

The long-standing *Maman Benin* (closed Sunday) has a large selection of West African dishes scooped from steaming pots for US$3 or less. Upstairs is a renovated air-con section serving similar meals for twice the price.

Maquis Le Pili Pili offers some excellent African cuisine in a pleasant setting for US$6.

For cheaper fare, try the street food stalls outside Le Pili Pili, or *Challa Ogot* (evenings only).

BENIN

BENIN

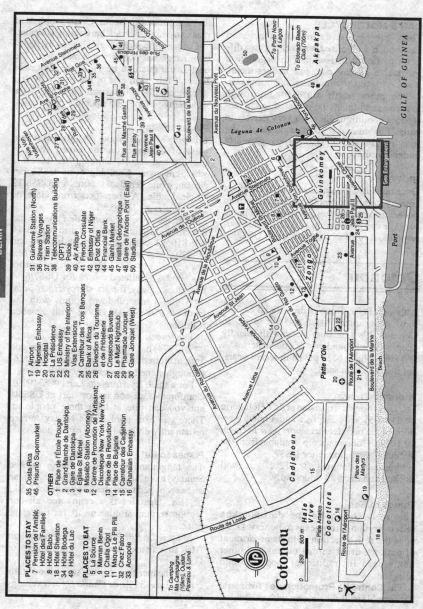

PLACES TO STAY
7 Pension de l'Amitié;
    Hôtel des Familles
8 Hôtel Babo
18 Hôtel Sheraton
34 Hôtel Bodega
49 Hôtel du Lac

PLACES TO EAT
5 La Source
9 Maman Benin
10 Challa Ogot
11 Maquis Le Pili Pili
32 Chez Fatou
33 Acropole

35 Costa Rica
46 Prisunic Supermarket

OTHER
1 Place de l'Étoile Rouge
2 Grand Marché de Dantokpa
3 Gare de Dantokpa
4 Église St Michel
6 Missébo Station (Abomey)
12 Centre de Promotion de l'Artisanat;
    Discotèque New York New York
13 Place de la Revolution
14 Place de Bulgarie
15 Carrefour des Cadjehoun
16 Ghanaian Embassy

17 Airport
19 Nigerian Embassy
20 Hospital
21 La Présidence
22 US Embassy
23 Ministry of the Interior/
    Visa Extensions
24 Carrefour des Trois Banques
25 Bank of Africa
26 Direction du Tourisme
    et de l'Hôtellerie
27 Crossroads Buvette
28 Le Must Nightclub
29 Pharmacie Jonquet
30 Gare Jonquet (West)

31 Guinkomé Station (North)
36 Sirexci Voyages
37 Train Station
38 Telecommunications Building
    (OPT)
39 Police
40 Air Afrique
41 French Consulate
42 Embassy of Niger
43 Post Office
44 Financial Bank
45 Ganhi Market
47 Institut Géographique
48 Gare de l'Ancien Pont (East)
50 Stadium

In the city centre, the popular *Chez Fatou* serves good yassa poulet for US$3, while *La Source* has large portions of chicken for the same price.

Cotonou's best pizzas (from US$7) can be found at *Hôtel Bodega*. Across the street, *Costa Rica* also serves pizza, as well as French cuisine for US$6.

For fast food at all hours, try the slick and efficient *Acropole*, which has hamburgers and other continental food from US$5, and a good patisserie. It's open 24 hours on weekends and weekdays until 1 am.

Entertainment
Crossroads buvette has a pleasant atmosphere, cheap drinks and international cable TV. *Acropole* often has music on weekend evenings.

For nightclubs, try the popular but pricey *New York New York* in the arts centre. It opens at midnight and has a US$10 cover. *Le Must* is much cheaper, but is not recommended for women alone.

Getting There & Away
For minibuses and bush taxis, Gare Jonquet serves the west (Ouidah, Lomé etc), Guinkomé station is for the north (Parakou, Malanville), and Gare de l'Ancien Pont is for eastern destinations (Porto Novo, Lagos). Taxis to Porto Novo and Abomey-Calavi (for Ganvié) leave from Gare de Dantokpa, near the market. Transport for Abomey departs from Missébo station.

Getting Around
Taxi Share-taxis around town cost US$0.50, but are relatively scarce. A private taxi to the airport costs US$4. Coming from the airport, you will probably be quoted double this price.

Motorcycle-Taxi The ample supply of motorcycle-taxis – easily identified by their yellow-clad drivers – means you can whiz around town for US$0.25 a ride, though it's best to use caution as spills are frequent. If your driver gets out of hand, just pay him what he's owed and hop on another one.

A motorcycle-taxi to the airport costs US$0.60; they can usually juggle a backpack.

Around the Country

ABOMEY
Abomey was once the capital of the Fon kingdom, Dahomey, which became the country's name for a while after independence. Its palaces were neglected for many years but restoration is slowly being undertaken. It's one of the most interesting places to visit in Benin. Share-taxis between Abomey and Bohicon cost US$0.50.

Things to See
Abomey's main attraction is **The Royal Palace & Museum**, which in its heyday was

---

Abomey's Royal Palace
Before the arrival of the French, Abomey's royal palace was one of the most impressive structures in West Africa. The first building was constructed in 1645 by the third king of Dahomey. Each successive king built his own palace, so that by the 19th century the compound was enormous, with a 4km perimeter enclosing an area of 40 hectares and a court of 10,000 people. The inner complex consisted of a maze of courtyards, ceremonial rooms, burial chambers and a harem accommodating some 800 wives. Following defeat at the hands of the French in the late 19th century, Béhanzin, the 10th king, ordered it burned as he fled advancing French forces.

Today's museum, which dates from 1818, consists only of the palaces of Ghézo and Glélé, which survived the fire. It covers the history of the Dahomey kingdom and includes royal thrones and tapestries, human skulls that were once used as musical instruments, fetish items and the living quarters of the last king. ■

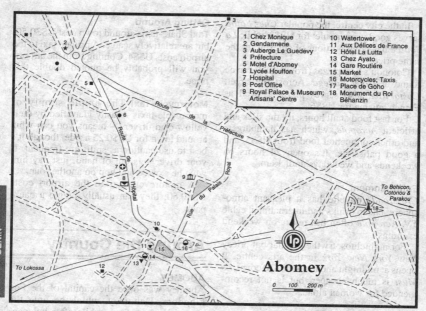

1 Chez Monique
2 Gendarmerie
3 Auberge Le Guedevy
4 Préfecture
5 Motel d'Abomey
6 Lycée Houffon
7 Hospital
8 Post Office
9 Royal Palace & Museum;
   Artisans' Centre
10 Watertower
11 Aux Délices de France
12 Hôtel La Lutta
13 Chez Ayato
14 Gare Routiére
15 Market
16 Motorcycles; Taxis
17 Place de Goho
18 Monument du Roi
    Béhanzin

Abomey

0   100   200 m

To Lokossa
To Bohicon,
Cotonou &
Parakou

one of the largest palaces in West Africa. It's open daily from 9 am to 5.30 pm. The US$3 entry fee includes a guided tour; photography is not permitted.

Next door is an **artisans' centre** (open 9 am to 5.30 pm daily) where you are able to watch craftspeople weaving tablecloths and making sculptures and wall hangings. Prices are reasonable if you bargain.

There are many **fetish shrines** scattered around the countryside, each dedicated to a different spirit. Be respectful when visiting as *juju* (an African fetish) is alive and well here.

Places to Stay & Eat
Near the centre, *Hôtel La Lutta* has a few doubles for US$5 (US$7 with attached bathroom), and an inexpensive restaurant.

The busy but sterile *Motel d'Abomey* (☎ 500075) has overpriced singles/doubles with air-con for US$17/20, as well as nicer bungalows for US$20. If they're not hosting

a conference, you may be permitted to camp on the grounds (US$3 per person).

Chez Monique (☎ 500168), with its shady garden and straw-roofed restaurant, has a much better atmosphere. Rooms cost US$8 (US$14 with fan and private bath). Meals start at US$4.

The modern-style *Auberge Le Guedevy* (☎ 500304) has two good-value rooms with fan and private bath for US$12, and a number of air-con doubles with attached bathroom for US$16. The only drawback is its location 2km north of the market.

The best street food is at *Chez Ayato*, near the gare routière. For reasonably priced cuisine indoors, try *Aux Délices de France* across from the market.

GANVIÉ
Ganvié is one of Benin's premier tourist attractions – a village built on stilts in the middle of a lagoon (Lac Nokoué) and accessible only by *pirogue* (dugout canoe).

BENIN

Residents earn their living from fishing and, increasingly, tourism.

Places to Stay & Eat

Auberge Chez M (☎ 360344) and the more rundown *Expotel Ganvié* (☎ 360034) both have basic singles/doubles for US$4/8, although you may be able to negotiate lower. Anything you drop on the floor at the Expotel will wind up in the lagoon! *Villa Tomoin* is Ganvié's luxury accommodation. Clean singles/doubles with flush toilets and other amenities are US$12/17. All three hotels will prepare meals for around US$4 with advance notice.

On the mainland in Abomey-Calavi, *Auberge du Lac* has basic rooms with mosquito nets, attached bathroom and fan for US$8. It's on the right as you head towards the water. You can pitch a tent in the parking lot outside the deserted *La Pirogue* restaurant at the canoe moorings, but there is no security and no water.

La Source, also by the moorings, serves a variety of dishes for US$4. For cheaper fare, go to the nearby *Bar La Fraicheur* , where two women cook up big pots of food all day for US$0.50 a plate.

Getting There & Away

Tourist pirogues cost US$10/7/5 per person for one/two/five people (US$2 extra per person for a motorised boat). Locals pay US$0.60 to cross the lagoon. To get there, take a share-taxi (US$0.50) or large bus (US$0.25) from Cotonou's Gare de Dantokpa to Abomey-Calavi (not to be confused with Abomey) and walk downhill to the pirogue moorings.

Alternatively, you can try to hire a pirogue independently for less if you continue about 5km past Abomey-Calavi to Akassato and then walk 3km to the village of Sô-Ava. From there, you may be able to negotiate the price down slightly, but the extra hassles with the tourist-wise villagers and several incidents involving capsized pirogues make the savings almost not worth the effort.

GRAND POPO

Grand Popo was once Benin's largest port but is now almost a ghost town. It's set on a beautiful beach, although swimming is restricted due to strong currents.

Places to Stay & Eat

The only accommodation is *L'Auberge de Grand Popo* (☎ 430047), beautifully sited on the waterfront, 3.5km off the main road. From the turn-off you can walk or take a motorcycle-taxi (US$0.40). Comfortable rooms with attached bathroom in a colonial-style villa start at US$27, while less attractive singles/doubles cost US$13/16. All have mosquito nets. Camping is US$2 per person (US$5 to rent a tent), including use of showers. The terrace restaurant offers meals from US$6.

One kilometre back towards the main road is *Les Paillottes Bleues*, which has good meals for US$4. Alternatively, locals will cook seafood for you if you make arrangements beforehand.

MALANVILLE

If you get stuck in this border town, *La Rose des Sables*, 2km south of town near the police checkpoint, has ventilated rooms for US$10.

NATITINGOU

Natitingou is an excellent base for excursions to Pendjari Park and the surrounding Somba country. There's a good **market** every fourth day with a fascinating mix of traders. The area around Natitingou is superb for cycling. Ask around at the market for rentals.

Places to Stay & Eat

Auberge Tanekas (☎ 821352), 2km south of the centre, has ventilated singles/doubles with attached bathroom from US$9/11.

Hôtel Kanta Borifa (☎ 821166), 500m north of Auberge Tanekas, has similar rooms for the same price, as does the friendly *Auberge Le Vieux Cavalier* (☎ 821324), 1.5km east of town.

Hôtel Tata-Somba (☎ 821124), 1km west

of the centre, has luxurious rooms with all the amenities for US$40/48; discounts are available during the low season (June through August). You can arrange visits to Pendjari Park from here, including booking accommodation (see later in this chapter).

OUIDAH

In precolonial days, Ouidah was the most important port in Benin. It was from here that slaves were shipped to the Americas; their path has been memorialised by the 4km *Route des Esclaves*.

Ouidah is also the centre of the voodoo cult in Benin, and its three museums devoted to voodoo history and culture are well worth a visit. The **Musée d'Histoire**, housed in an old Portuguese fort, is dedicated to the links between voodoo practitioners and the slaves transported to Brazil and Haiti. It's open daily (US$2 admission). The tiny **Musée des Tapisseries et des Tentures** and the neighbouring **Musée des Arts et Cultures Vodun** have fascinating collections of voodoo masks, artwork and photos. Both are open daily until 6.30 pm; there is no entry fee.

The **Temple des Serpents** is interesting if you're keen to see sleepy snakes. Entry costs US$2.

Places to Stay & Eat

L'Ermitage has a few basic but clean doubles for US$8; they'll prepare meals on request. It's north of the centre, one block east of the Maison du Peuple.

The more upmarket, central *Oasis Hôtel* (☎ 341091) has air-con doubles with attached bathroom for US$21 (US$27 for a triple) including breakfast; meals are US$6. Across the street, *Well Chic* has inexpensive African fare.

In the south-west corner of town near the art museums, the busy *Oriki Maquis Motel* (☎ 341004) has ventilated singles/doubles with attached bathroom for US$12/13 (US$22 for an air-con double) and meals for US$5.

PARAKOU

Parakou is Benin's central trading town and has a strong Muslim presence. There's not much to see but, being the terminus of the railway line, it's a popular overnight stop.

Places to Stay & Eat

The best value is *Hôtel Les Canaris* (☎ 611169), 800m east of the train station. Good singles/doubles with attached bathroom are US$9/13, while more basic ventilated rooms start at US$4/5. There's also a reasonably priced restaurant.

Hôtel OCBN, one block east of the train station, has dingy but clean air-con rooms with attached bathroom for US$14/20, while the nearby *Motel Terminus* (☎ 610519) has clean rooms which have mosquito nets for US$12/16 with fan/air-con.

Le Souvenir, on the same road as Hôtel OCBN, has inexpensive meals. In the centre, *Restaurant Estomac* serves amiyo poulet and other dishes for under US$4; the adjoining *Bar 1,2,3* is also popular.

PARC DE LA PENDJARI

Pendjari is one of West Africa's better game reserves. It's open from 15 December to 15 May, with the best viewing time near the end of the dry season. Although you may have to search a bit, sightings of baboon, elephant, hippo and warthog are fairly common. Plans are underway to fully merge Pendjari with neighbouring parks in Benin and Burkina Faso.

There are three *campements*. The two main ones, both near the Porga entrance, are expensive (from US$28) and open only in the high season. Reservations can be made c/o Hôtel Tata-Somba in Natitingou (see earlier). The third, at Tanougou, is more basic but is open all year. Singles/doubles are US$12/16, (US$8/12 from June to August). You can also camp on the grounds of the Porga campements for US$4 per person. Entry to the park is US$6, plus a camera fee of US$1 and a surcharge of US$1 per night.

PORTO NOVO

Porto Novo looks more like an overgrown village than the official capital of Benin. It was named by the Portuguese after a town to which it bore a resemblance. Porto Novo has a number of delightful old colonial buildings, which are in various stages of decay, as well as two excellent museums.

The **Ethnography Museum** (☎ 212554), open daily from 9 am to 12.30 pm and 3 to 6 pm, houses a collection of masks, weapons and musical instruments, and a display on the town's history.

The **Palais du Roi Toffa** (☎ 213566), also known as Musée Honmé, was once the residence of King Toffa, who signed the first treaty with the French. It's open daily from 9 am to noon and 3.30 to 6 pm. Admission to each is US$2.

Places to Stay & Eat

Hôtel La Détente has basic ventilated doubles for US$5. Better value is the nearby *Hôtel Malabo* (☎ 213404) where large, ventilated singles/doubles with private facilities start at US$7/8 (US$12/14 with air-con). Both hotels serve simple fare for under US$4.

Hôtel Beaurivage (☎ 212399) has views of the lagoon and comfortable doubles from US$20.

For inexpensive African food try *Festival Ambiance*. *Casa Danza* has three-course meals for US$6.

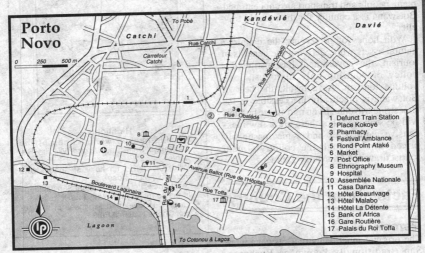

1 Defunct Train Station
2 Place Kokoyé
3 Pharmacy
4 Festival Ambiance
5 Rond Point Ataké
6 Market
7 Post Office
8 Ethnography Museum
9 Hospital
10 Assemblée Nationale
11 Casa Danza
12 Hôtel Beaurivage
13 Hôtel Malabo
14 Hôtel La Détente
15 Bank of Africa
16 Gare Routière
17 Palais du Roi Toffa

Botswana

Botswana, formerly Bechuanaland, is an African success story. A long-neglected British protectorate, Botswana achieved its independence in 1966, and then discovered three of the richest diamond-bearing formations in the world. Politically and ideologically it affiliates itself with its fellow black majority-governed states and enjoys enlightened nonracial policies and health, educational and economic standards which, with the exception of South Africa, are unequalled in black Africa.

Beyond the narrow eastern corridor where the capital, Gaborone, and most development, people and transport are concentrated, Botswana is a country for the intrepid traveller.

With hopes of preserving the country's natural assets while deriving the benefits of tourism, the government has instituted a policy of courting only high-cost, low-volume tourism. As a result, the best of Botswana is practically inaccessible to the shoestring traveller. Even mid-range budgets will be stretched, but there are a few inexpensive camp sites and some reasonably priced trips through the country's main tourist draw, the Okavango Delta.

Facts about the Country

HISTORY

The original inhabitants of Botswana were San (traditionally known as Bushmen, though this name is now considered derogatory), who have inhabited the Kalahari for at least 30,000 years. They were followed by the Khoi-Khoi (formerly called Hottentots, which is also now considered derogatory), who probably originated from a San group cut off from the mainstream.

In the 1st or 2nd century AD, the agricultural and pastoral Bantu migrated from the north. Relations between the San, Khoi-Khoi

REPUBLIC OF BOTSWANA
Area: 582,000 sq km
Population: 1.5 million
Population Growth Rate: 1.6%
Capital: Gaborone
Head of State: President Quett KJ Masire
Official Languages: English, Satswana
Currency: Pula
Exchange Rate: P3.63 = US$1
Per Capita GNP: US$3130
Inflation: 11%
Time: GMT/UTC + 2

Highlights
- Wildlife-packed wonderlands of the Okavango Delta and Moremi Wildlife Reserve
- Wild Kalahari, with its vast spaces and incredible night skies
- 'Wilderness Louvre' of ancient San paintings in the beautifully haunting Tsodilo Hills
- Largely undeveloped expanses of wildlife-rich Chobe National Park

and Bantu societies appear to have been amicable; they traded, intermarried and mixed freely. The Tswana people, a Bantu group which colonised the country's south-eastern strip sometime during the 14th century, today represent Botswana's largest population group.

Aggression after the 1818 amalgamation of the Zulu tribes in South Africa scattered Tswana villages and pushed some into the heart of the Kalahari. In response they regrouped and the society became highly structured. In each of the Tswana nations, the king's subjects lived in centralised towns and satellite villages, one allocated to each clan under the control of village leaders. By the second half of the 19th century, some of these towns had grown to a considerable size.

The orderliness and structure of the town-based society impressed the early Christian missionaries who arrived in 1817. None of them managed to convert great numbers of Tswana people but they advised the locals,

sometimes wrongly, in their dealings with the Europeans that followed – explorers, naturalists, traders, miners and general rabble.

Meanwhile, the Boers, feeling pressure from the British in the Cape, began their Great Trek across the Vaal River. Confident that they had heaven-sanctioned rights to any land they might choose to occupy in southern Africa, 20,000 Boers crossed into Tswana and Zulu territory and established themselves as though the lands were unclaimed and uninhabited (indeed many were, having been cleaned out earlier by Zulu factions).

Prominent Tswana leaders Sechele I and

Mosielele refused to accept white rule and incurred the violent wrath of the Boers. By 1877 the worsening situation provoked the British annexation of the Transvaal and launched the first Boer War.

Violence continued until the Pretoria Convention of 1881 when the British withdrew from the Transvaal in exchange for Boer allegiance to the crown. In 1882 Boers again moved into Tswana lands and subdued Mafeking (Mafikeng), threatening the British route between the Cape and suspected mineral wealth in the area now known as Zimbabwe.

Again, the Tswana lobbied for British protection. In 1885, after petitions from John Mackenzie, a friend of the Christian Khama III of Shoshong, Britain resigned itself to the inevitable. Lands south of the Molopo River became the British crown colony of Bechuanaland and were attached to the Cape Colony (now part of South Africa), while the area north became the British protectorate of Bechuanaland (which is now Botswana).

A new threat to the chiefs' power base came from Cecil Rhodes' British South Africa Company (BSAC). By 1894 the British had all but agreed to hand over control of the country to Rhodes. A delegation of unhappy Tswana chiefs sailed to England to appeal directly for continued government control, but their pleas were ignored. As a last resort, they turned to the London Missionary Society (LMS), which supported their cause out of fear the BSAC would allow alcohol in Bechuanaland. Public pressure mounted and the government was forced to concede.

At this stage the chiefs grudgingly accepted that their rites and traditions would be affected by Christianity and western technology. The cash economy was, by then, firmly in place and the Batswana (people of Bechuanaland) actively participated.

Each chief was granted a tribal 'reserve' in which he was given jurisdiction over all black residents and the authority to collect taxes. He would retain a 10% commission on all monies collected, and the sale of cattle, draught oxen and grain to the Europeans streaming north in search of farmland and minerals provided a good economy for the protectorate.

It was short-lived, however. The construction of the railway through Bechuanaland to Rhodesia and an outbreak of foot-and-mouth disease in the 1890s destroyed the transit trade. By 1920 maize farmers in South Africa and Rhodesia were producing so much grain that Bechuanaland no longer had a market. In 1924 South Africa began pressing for Bechuanaland's amalgamation into the Union of South Africa. When the Tswana chiefs refused to amalgamate, economic sanctions destroyed what remained of their beef market.

Resident Commissioner Sir Charles Rey determined that no progress would be forthcoming as long as the people were governed by Tswana chiefs, and he proclaimed them all to be local government officials answerable to colonial magistrates. So great was the popular opposition to the decision – people feared that it would lead to their incorporation into South Africa – that Rey was ousted from his job and his proclamation was annulled.

During WWII, 10,000 Batswana volunteered for the African Pioneer Corps to defend the British Empire. After the war the heir to the Ngwato throne, Seretse Khama, went to study in England, where he met and married Ruth Williams, an Englishwoman.

The regent, Seretse's uncle, Tshekedi Khama, was furious at this breach of tribal custom (some accused him of exploiting the incident as a means to gain power in his nephew's place) and the South African authorities, still hoping to absorb Bechuanaland into the Union, were none too happy either. Seretse's chieftaincy was blocked by the British government and he was exiled from the protectorate to England. Bitterness continued until 1956, when Seretse Khama renounced his right to power, reconciled with his uncle and returned to Bechuanaland with his wife to serve as a minor official.

The first signs of nationalist thinking among the Batswana occurred as early as the late 1940s, but during the 1950s and early

1960s all of Africa was experiencing political change as many former colonies gained their independence. As early as 1955 it had become apparent that Britain was preparing to release its grip on Bechuanaland. University graduates returned from South Africa with political ideas, and although the country had no real economic base, the first Batswana political parties surfaced and began thinking about independence.

Following the Sharpeville Massacre in 1960, South African refugees Motsamai Mpho of the African National Congress (ANC), Philip Matante, a Johannesburg preacher affiliated with the Pan-African Congress, and KT Motsete, a teacher from Malawi, formed the Bechuanaland People's Party. Its immediate goal was independence for the protectorate.

In 1962 Seretse Khama and the Kanye farmer Quett Masire formed the more moderate Bechuanaland Democratic Party (BDP). They were soon joined by Chief Bathoen II of Ngwaketse.

The BDP formulated a schedule for independence. They promoted the transfer of the capital city into the country (from Mafikeng to Gaborone) and drafted a new nonracial constitution to allow a peaceful transfer of power. General elections were held in 1965 and Seretse Khama was elected president. On 30 September 1966 the Republic of Botswana gained independence.

Sir Seretse Khama (he was knighted shortly after independence), who was no revolutionary, mainly adopted a neutral stance towards South Africa and Rhodesia.

Botswana was economically transformed by the discovery of diamonds near Orapa in 1967. The mining concession was given to De Beers, with Botswana taking 75% of the profits from the mines.

Although Sir Seretse Khama died in 1980, his Botswana Democratic Party still commands a substantial majority within the Botswana parliament. Dr Quett Masire, who has served as president since then, continues on his predecessor's path, while the government in general cautiously follows similar pragmatic and pro-western policies. There is, however, growing urban support for the BDP's rival party, the Botswana National Front.

Since 1994, Botswana's military outlay has increased dramatically; that only some of this build-up can be explained by the country's peacekeeping efforts on the continent has neighbours and observers concerned.

Currently, Botswana's biggest problems are unemployment, urban drift and a rocketing birth rate (currently the third-highest in the world).

GEOGRAPHY & CLIMATE

With an area of 582,000 sq km, landlocked Botswana extends over 1100km from north to south and 960km from east to west. With an average elevation of 1000m, most of Botswana is a vast sand-filled basin characterised by scrub or savannah. The Kalahari (Kgalagadi) covers 85% of the country in the central and south-western areas.

Botswana's rainy season runs from November to March. Wildlife viewing is best during the dry winter months (late May to August), when animals stick to water sources. Winter days are normally clear, warm and sunny, while nights are quite cold.

POPULATION & PEOPLE

Botswana's population is around 1.5 million, with 60% claiming Tswana heritage. The small European and Asian populations live mainly around Maun and other larger towns; the Herero, Mbukushu, Yei, Kalanga, Kgalagadi and San people are distributed through remote areas of western Botswana.

LANGUAGE

English is the official language and the medium of instruction in secondary schools. The most common language, however, is Setswana, which is understood by over 90% of the people and is the medium of instruction in the primary schools.

It's polite to greet people you encounter; for men, say *Dumêla rra*; for women, use *Dumêla mma*. The useful book *First Steps in Spoken Setswana* is available in Gaborone, Maun and Francistown.

BOTSWANA

Facts for the Visitor

VISAS

Visas aren't required for nationals of most Commonwealth countries, Western Europe (except for Spain and Portugal), Israel, Namibia, South Africa or the USA.

Entry permits for 30 days are issued at the border; for extensions, apply to Immigration & Passport Control at the Department of Immigration (☎ 374545), off Khama Crescent, PO Box 942, Gaborone.

EMBASSIES
Botswana Embassies

In Africa, Botswana has embassies or high commissions in Harare (Zimbabwe), Lusaka (Zambia) and Windhoek (Namibia). Elsewhere, apply for visas at British embassies and high commissions.

Foreign Embassies in Botswana

The following countries have diplomatic representation in Gaborone:

France
    761 Robinson Rd, PO Box 1424 (☎ 353683)
Namibia
    BCC building, 1278 Lobatse Rd, PO Box 1586 (☎ 314227)
UK (high commission)
    Queens Rd, The Mall, Private Bag 0023 (☎ 352841)
USA
    Badiredi House, off Khama Crescent, PO Box 90, Gaborone (☎ 353982)
Zimbabwe
    Orapa Close, PO Box 1232 (☎ 314495)

MONEY

US$1 = P3.63

Botswana's unit of currency is the pula (P), which is divided into 100 thebe. 'Pula' means 'rain', which is as precious as money in this largely desert country. There is no black market.

Full banking services are available only in major towns, where banking hours are from 9 am to 2.30 pm on Monday, Tuesday, Thurs-day and Friday; from 8.15 am to noon on Wednesday; and from 8.15 to 10.45 am on Saturday. On Saturday, Barclays Bank at the Gaborone Sun Hotel is open from 8.30 am to 2 pm. In remote villages, travelling banks are available at regular intervals – in some places for just an hour or two per month.

Most credit cards are accepted at hotels and restaurants in larger towns. Credit card cash advances are available through Barclays or Standard Chartered banks in Gaborone, Lobatse, Maun and Francistown. Elsewhere, you must wait for authorisation.

Costs

Supermarket, fast-food and restaurant prices are comparable to those in Europe, North America and Australasia. Budget travel is not impossible as long as hitching is permitted. However, if you can't afford a flight into the Okavango, a day or two at Moremi Reserve or Chobe National Park, or a 4WD trip through the Kalahari, think twice before visiting this country.

Buses and trains aren't too expensive but they won't take you to the most interesting sites. The cheapest vehicle hire is extremely expensive and 4WD hire is out of reach for most travellers. The independent traveller's biggest thorn in the side is national park entry fees (see National Parks & Reserves later in this chapter).

POST & COMMUNICATIONS

In major towns, post offices are open from 8.15 am to 4 pm. The best poste restante address is the post office on The Mall in Gaborone, but it's not 100% efficient.

Botswana's country code is 267; there are no regional area codes. Gaborone and Francistown have telephone offices for international calls. Telephone boxes are found near post offices in major towns, but for international calls you'll need pockets full of coins.

HEALTH

Compared with most of Africa, Botswana's health services are competent and well supplied with equipment and medicines.

Malaria is a risk in the northern part of the country from November to June. Tap water in most towns and villages is generally safe to drink. There are clinics in large villages and hospitals in the major centres.

DANGERS & ANNOYANCES

The Botswana Defence Force (BDF) takes its duties seriously and is best not crossed. Avoid State House in Gaborone at all times, and don't even walk past it after dark.

ACCOMMODATION

Many lodges have camp sites charging around US$6 per person, but few are readily accessible to towns. National park camps are rudimentary, and foreigners, who pay US$18.50 per day just to *be* in the park, must shell out another US$7.50 to set up a tent and use whatever facilities that may exist. With the exception of camp sites, accommodation is subject to a 10% government bed tax.

Unofficial camping is possible if you can get out of sight, but you must be self-sufficient in food, water, transport, petrol and so on. Around villages, ask the local chief or the police for permission to camp and directions to a suitable site.

More upmarket options range from inexpensive tented camps to luxury lodges. Some lie along the road system; others are in remote wilderness areas. In the Okavango, prices range from US$7.50 at Oddball's to over 100 times that at Abu's Camp, which features circus elephant rides. Hotels in Botswana are like hotels anywhere but are generally more expensive. Basic rooms start at US$20 to US$30.

Getting There & Away

AIR

Botswana is served by Air Malawi, Air Tanzania, Air Zimbabwe, British Airways, South African Airways, UTA, Zambia Airways and Air Botswana, but you'll normally find long-haul fares are cheaper to Harare, Windhoek or Johannesburg than to Gaborone.

LAND

Overland entry into Botswana is normally straightforward, although vehicle tyres and passengers shoes must be passed through a cattle-dip solution on entry! Border crossings open between 6 and 8 am and close sometime between 4 and 10 pm.

Namibia

There are three major land crossings between Botswana and Namibia: Ngoma Bridge, Mohembo-Shakawe, and Mamuno-Buitepos. The 54km transit route through Chobe National Park to Ngoma Bridge is relatively well travelled, and if you avoid the riverfront tourist drives you'll also avoid park fees. Most motorists refuel in Kasane, so it's better to look for lifts at the petrol station than along the transit route turn-off near Kazungula.

Public transport between Botswana and Namibia includes the bus and minibus services between Livingstone (Zambia), Victoria Falls (Zimbabwe) and Windhoek, which cross into Namibia at Ngoma Bridge. See Getting There & Away in the Zimbabwe chapter.

There's also a Trans-Namib bus between Ghanzi and Gobabis (Namibia). From Ghanzi, it leaves at 8 am Friday, passes the Buitepos border around noon and arrives in Gobabis at 4 pm. To hitch this route, wait at the petrol station in Ghanzi. Hitching and bus services should improve in the next few years with the completion of the Trans-Kalahari highway between Gaborone and Windhoek.

South Africa

Most traffic between Botswana and South Africa passes through the road and rail crossing at Ramatlabama-Mmabatho; the Tlokweng Gate, 20km from Gaborone; or the Lobatse-Zeerust post. Other posts, most of which lie along backroads across the Limpopo River in the Tuli Block or on the Molopo River in southern Botswana, are open only from 8 am to 4 pm. Travellers rarely encounter much fuss.

An easy way to reach Johannesburg is by minibus (US$15); they leave when full from the Gaborone bus terminal. To be assured of a seat, arrive as early as possible. Minibus services leave Lobatse for Mafikeng in the morning (US$4).

Greyhound (☎ 372224) runs buses from Gaborone to Johannesburg (US$22) four times a week from the Kudu Service Station Shell Garage on Queen's Rd.

Zambia

Travel between Botswana and Zambia is via the Kazungula ferry over the Zambezi, which runs between 6 am and 6 pm. It's free for vehicles registered in Botswana, and for pedestrians, but otherwise it's US$10 for cars and US$20 for pick-ups. On the Zambian side, you can catch trucks to Livingstone, Lusaka and points beyond.

Zimbabwe

Bus Express Motorways (☎ 304470) in Gaborone runs to Francistown, Bulawayo and Harare twice weekly. Between Kasane and Victoria Falls, United Touring Company operates a transfer service for US$20.

The no-frills Zimbabwe Omnibus Company has daily (except Sunday) service between Francistown and Bulawayo. Chitanda & Sons runs twice-weekly express buses from Gaborone to Harare via Francistown and Bulawayo.

The bus and minibus lines between Livingstone (Zambia), Victoria Falls (Zimbabwe), and Windhoek (Namibia) pass through Kasane. See Getting There & Away in the Zimbabwe chapter for details.

Train There are overnight trains daily from Gaborone to Bulawayo. You can choose between 1st and 2nd class sleepers or economy-class seats. Security may be dodgy, especially in crowded economy class. These trains normally have a buffet car, but don't leave your luggage unattended, even to go for a meal. Fares are US$33/27/9 in 1st/2nd/economy class.

Sexes are separated in 1st and 2nd class sleepers unless you book a whole compartment or a two person coupé. When there's a buffet car, you must pay in pula or South African rand; Zimbabwe dollars aren't accepted in Botswana. Customs and immigration formalities are handled on the train.

Hitching

Hitching between Bulawayo and Francistown via Plumtree is fairly easy. It's best to hitch into Botswana in the morning. For lifts between Victoria Falls and Kazungula-Kasane, wait at the Kazungula Rd turnoff about 1km south-east of Victoria Falls town.

Getting Around

AIR

The national carrier, Air Botswana, operates scheduled domestic flights between major towns. Fares are high, but you'll get some relief with 14 day advance purchase. There are four flights weekly between Gaborone and Francistown (US$123), three between Gaborone and Kasane (US$193), and daily flights between Gaborone and Maun (US$173).

BUS & MINIBUS

Along the Lobatse to Francistown highway corridor, bus and minibus services depart when full. Other services operate between Serule and Selebi-Phikwe; Palapye, Serowe and Orapa; Francistown, Nata and Kasane; Francistown, Nata and Maun; Maun, Ghanzi and Mamuno; and Maun and Shakawe. The route through Chobe National Park between Kasane and Maun is served only by safari companies.

TRAIN

Rail travel is a relaxing and effortless way to pass through the dusty Botswana scrub, and the line running through Francistown, Gaborone and Lobatse is a reliable and inexpensive way to travel. In 1st/2nd/economy, the fare between Gaborone and Francistown is US$31/25/8. Bedding costs an additional US$2 per night.

BICYCLE

Botswana's only concession to cyclists is that its terrain is mostly flat. Even on major roads, villages are widely spaced and the 110km/h speed limit is largely ignored; when a semitrailer passes at 150km/h or more, cyclists can literally be blown off the road. On unsealed routes, cyclists may encounter deep sand.

HITCHING

Given Botswana's erratic public transport, many locals and travellers rely on hitching. The standard rate on main routes is about US$0.05 per 10km; drivers normally bring this up before prospective passengers climb aboard. Remember there is always some risk associated with hitching.

Hitching the backroads is another issue. Between Lobatse and Ghanzi, through the Tuli Block, or between Maun and Chobe, Moremi, Ghanzi or Namibia, hitchers need camping gear and sufficient food and water for several days of waiting. For trips further afield – to the Makgadikgadi Pans, the Tsodilo Hills or Gcwihaba Caverns – lifts must be arranged in advance; the best places to look are the lodges at Maun, Nata, Shakawe or Ghanzi.

For the Lobatse to Ghanzi trip, try the Botswana Meat Corporation in Lobatse. From Kasane, the direct route to Maun across Chobe National Park is a trying and expensive hitch (due to park fees), and the laboriously roundabout Kasane-Nata-Maun route is actually quicker and more practical.

Gaborone

Gaborone is a sprawling village suffering from the growing pains, drabness and lack of definition that accompany an abrupt transition from rural settlement to modern city. Although it has a few interesting sights, it is one of the continent's most expensive cities and is certainly nothing to go out of your way for.

Gaborone lacks any definite central business district, and urban action focuses on the dispersed shopping malls. The main one, The Mall, is between the town hall and the government complex of ministries and offices on Khama Crescent.

Information

The tourist office on The Mall is Botswana's only helpful office. The quickest place to exchange cash or travellers' cheques is the Gaborone Sun Hotel branch of Barclays Bank.

The post office is on The Mall. There are phones outside the post office and the National Museum. For overseas calls, go to Botswana Telecom on Khama Crescent. Fax services are available at the Copy Shop (fax 35 9922), in Hardware House on The Mall.

For visa extensions go to the Department of Immigration (☎ 374545), near the corner of State Drive and Khama Crescent. For reading material, try the Botswana Book Centre on The Mall, or Botsalo Books in the Kagiso Centre, Broadhurst. For book exchange, see J&B Books upstairs at Broadhurst North Mall.

Things to See

The **National Museum** complex on Independence Ave, north-east of The Mall, is a good place for perusing Botswana's past and artistic present. The **National Gallery** in the same building is a repository for traditional and modern African and European art.

To climb **Mt Kgale**, which overlooks Gaborone, take any Lobatse bus to the Kgale lookout or hitch along the new Lobatse road to the satellite dish, 8km from town. About 200m towards town (opposite the dish), cross a concrete stile over a fence, turn left, and follow the fence until it enters a shallow gully, where a set of whitewashed stones lead up the hillside to the summit.

The **Gaborone Game Reserve** has a selection of wildlife (including rhinos in a guarded enclosure) and is just 1km east of

BOTSWANA

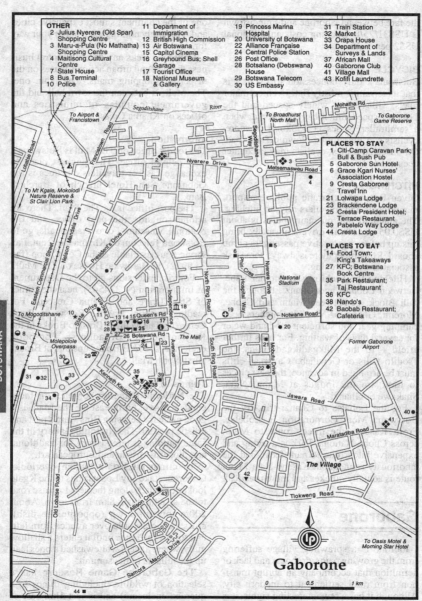

OTHER
2 Julius Nyerere (Old Spar) Shopping Centre
3 Maru-a-Pula (No Mathata) Shopping Centre
4 Maitisong Cultural Centre
7 State House
8 Bus Terminal
10 Police
11 Department of Immigration
12 British High Commission
13 Air Botswana
15 Capitol Cinema
16 Greyhound Bus; Shell Garage
17 Tourist Office
18 National Museum & Gallery
19 Princess Marina Hospital
20 University of Botswana
22 Alliance Française
24 Central Police Station
26 Post Office
28 Botsalano (Debswana) House
29 Botswana Telecom
30 US Embassy
31 Train Station
32 Market
33 Orapa House
34 Department of Surveys & Lands
37 African Mall
40 Gaborone Club
41 Village Mall
43 Kofifi Laundrette

PLACES TO STAY
1 Citi-Camp Caravan Park; Bull & Bush Pub
5 Gaborone Sun Hotel
6 Grace Kgari Nurses' Association Hostel
9 Cresta Gaborone Travel Inn
21 Lolwapa Lodge
23 Brackendene Lodge
25 Cresta President Hotel; Terrace Restaurant
39 Pabelelo Way Lodge
44 Cresta Lodge

PLACES TO EAT
14 Food Town; King's Takeaways
27 KFC; Botswana Book Centre
35 Park Restaurant; Taj Restaurant
36 KFC
38 Nando's
42 Baobab Restaurant; Cafeteria

BOTSWANA

Gaborone

0   0.5   1 km

To Oasis Motel & Morning Star Hotel

Broadhurst. Access is from Limpopo Drive by vehicle only; it costs US$3.70 per person and US$2 per vehicle.

Places to Stay

The cheapest place to camp is the *St Clair Lion Park*, 17km south of town, where sites cost US$7.50 per person. By the time you read this, there'll also be the new *Citi-Camp Caravan Park*, beside the Bull & Bush Pub, with 50 camp sites, just 15 minutes walk from the city centre.

At the *Mogotel Hotel* (☎ 372228), in Mogoditshane, single/double rooms cost US$19/28. It's clean and accessible by minibus from the centre, but lone women may be uncomfortable.

A great choice is the *Mokolodi Nature Reserve* (☎ 353959), 12km south of town. Self-catering chalets beside a dam cost US$35/52 (three/six beds) on weekdays and US$44/66 at weekends, while beds at the Environmental Education Centre cost US$9 (for transport details, see Around Gaborone which follows).

Lolwapa Lodge (☎ 301200), Lot 2873 Mobutu Drive, has single/double rooms with bath and use of cooking facilities starting at US$24/39, including breakfast. *Pabelelo Way Lodge* (☎ 351682), at Plot 838 Pabelelo Way, is less formally organised and charges US$28/45.

The cosy *Brackendene Lodge* (☎ 312886; fax 306246), three minutes walk from The Mall, has single/double rooms with shared bath starting at US$24/29, including breakfast. Rooms with bath are US$27/32.

The *Cresta Gaborone Travel Inn* (☎ 322777; fax 322727), north of the railway station, has single or double rooms with bath and TV for US$45. There's also a great bar, a takeaway and live (loud) music at weekends.

Places to Eat

At *Food Town* dining hall on The Mall, a filling dose of stew or mealies costs US$1.50. Burgers, chips and snacks are found at the office workers favourite lunch spot, *King's Takeaways*, on The Mall.

For something livelier, check out *Nando's*, in the African Mall, which does delicious Portuguese-style peri-peri chicken. For such off-beat specialities as pickled spinach, goat, mopane worms and chibuku (sorghum beer), try the market near the train station.

The African Mall also has other good places. Most popular is the folksy *Park Restaurant*, which does great pub meals and full dinners, including pizzas, steak, chicken, crêpes, ribs, salads and other delights. It's open daily for lunch and dinner. Next door is the *Taj*, which dishes up Indian and Mauritian cuisine; the US$8 buffet lunch is served daily. *Da Alfredo* at Broadhurst North Mall specialises in seafood and Italian cuisine. For lunch the *Terrace Restaurant*, on the terrace of the Cresta President Hotel, serves the likes of spinach quiche, cream of asparagus soup, vegetable curries, sweets and coffee specialities. For a wide choice of sweets and vegetarian dishes, try the *Kgotla* in the Broadhurst Mall Shopping Centre.

A good choice all day long is the *Baobab Restaurant & Cafeteria*, which does traditional Tswana meals for a set price. The restaurant serves salads, grills, pasta and game dishes. It's open daily from 6.30 am until late.

At the *Bull & Bush Pub*, meals cost US$7 to US$10; on Thursday nights it has all-you-can-eat pizza. From Nelson Mandela Drive, look for the west-pointing sign reading 'Police Housing Bull & Bush'.

A real treat is the wonderful outdoor restaurant and bar at the *Mokolodi Nature Reserve*. Game meat is sometimes available.

Entertainment

The 450 seat theatre in the *Maitisong Cultural Centre* (☎ 371809) is used for cultural events. The *Capitol Cinema* on The Mall runs mainly Hollywood films; the *Gaborone Film Society* and *Alliance Française* screen classic films.

A hit with affluent Gaborone youth is *Night Shift* in the Broadhurst North Mall. For African disco go to the *Platform* in the Gaborone Sun Hotel. The *Blue Note* in

Mogoditshane specialises in Congo (Zaïrese) kwasa-kwasa music.

In town, a favourite is *Sinatra's* in the Maru-a-Pula (No Mathatha) Shopping Centre. The disco operates from Thursday to Sunday nights.

Anglophiles may like the *Bull & Bush Pub. Harley's* bar at the Park Restaurant imitates a rebel watering hole in the USA, complete with Budweiser and Harley-Davidson décor. There's live music on Friday and Saturday nights.

Getting There & Away

Intercity buses, and minibuses to outlying villages, arrive and depart from the bus terminal over the Molepolole flyover from the town centre. Most buses leave when full, so make sure you arrive in the morning, especially if you are travelling to Francistown or Johannesburg.

Gaborone also has daily rail connections to and from Bulawayo, Francistown and Lobatse.

Getting Around

Small white minibuses, known as taxis, are recognisable by their blue number-plates, circulate on set routes and cost US$0.25. The standard circuit takes in all the major shopping centres. Conventional taxis (called 'special taxis') are normally ordered by phone and don't circulate on the streets.

AROUND GABORONE
Mochudi

Mochudi, 40km north of Gaborone, was settled by the Kwena in the 15th century and in 1871 by the Kgatla, who were forced from their lands by north-trekking Boers. Today Mochudi has some interesting mud-walled architecture and a prominent *kgotla* (council house and village court). There's also a royal kraal, where two Kgatla chiefs are buried, and a museum. On weekdays a screenprinting workshop operates in the courtyard.

Mochudi buses depart from Gaborone when full, at least six or seven times daily.

Mokolodi Nature Reserve

The 3000 hectare Mokolodi Nature Reserve, 12km south of Gaborone, concentrates on wildlife education for schoolchildren, but also helps protect Botswana's wildlife; even white rhino have been reintroduced from South Africa. Guided two-hour game walks or drives cost US$5.50.

Admission to the reserve is US$1.75 per vehicle, plus US$1.75 per adult and US$0.90 per child. There are also comfortable chalets, dormitories and a super restaurant.

Mokolodi offers transfer services from town for US$9 for up to three people plus US$3 for each extra person. Otherwise take a Lobatse minibus 12km south of Gaborone and get off at the turning 2km south of the turn-off for Mokolodi village. From there, it's 1.5km west to the reserve entrance.

Around the Country

FRANCISTOWN

Francistown was originally conceived as a gold-mining centre, but industry and commerce have now taken over the economy and the town has become an expanding retail and wholesale shopping mecca.

Francistown isn't Africa's most exciting city, but there is a new cultural and historical museum, the **Supa-Ngwao**, just off the new Nata road.

Places to Stay

The best deal is the friendly *Marang Hotel* (☎ 213991; fax 213991), 5km from the centre on the old Gaborone road. You can camp on the secluded, grassy lawn on the bank of the Tati River for US$4.50. Comfortable single or double rooms or rondavels on stilts cost US$66. Single caravans with bath and toilet cost US$25. If you're walking or hitching from the town centre, turn left toward 'Matsiloje' at the Thapama Lodge roundabout.

In the Satellite township is the quirky *Satellite Guest House* (☎ 214665; fax 202115). Air-con single/double rooms cost US$33/44

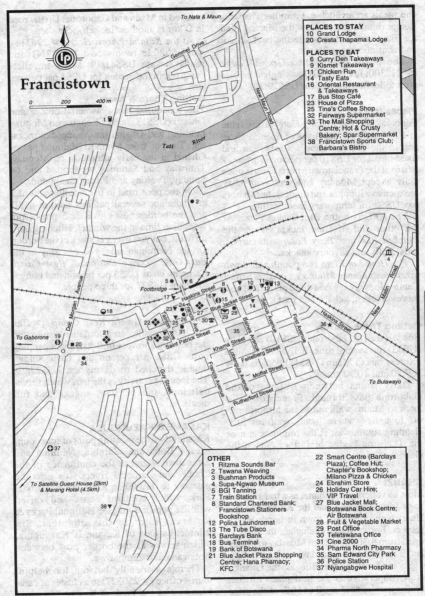

Francistown

0   200   400 m

To Nata & Maun

Gemmel Drive

New Maun Road

Tati   River

Footbridge

Haskins Street

Doc Morgan Avenue

To Gaborone

Blue Jacket Street

Tainton Ave

Francis Ave

Selous Avenue

First Avenue

Haskins Street

New Main Road

Saint Patrick Street

Blames Avenue

Feitelberg Street

Lobengula Avenue

Khama Street

Moffat Street

Francis Avenue

Rutherford Street

Guy Street

To Bulawayo

To Satellite Guest House (2km) & Marang Hotel (4.5km)

BOTSWANA

PLACES TO STAY
10 Grand Lodge
20 Cresta Thapama Lodge

PLACES TO EAT
6 Curry Den Takeaways
9 Kismet Takeaways
11 Chicken Run
14 Tasty Eats
16 Oriental Restaurant
    & Takeaways
17 Bus Stop Café
23 House of Pizza
25 Tina's Coffee Shop
32 Fairways Supermarket
33 The Mall Shopping
    Centre; Hot & Crusty
    Bakery; Spar Supermarket
38 Francistown Sports Club;
    Barbara's Bistro

OTHER
1 Ritzma Sounds Bar
2 Tswana Weaving
3 Bushman Products
4 Supa-Ngwao Museum
5 BGI Tanning
7 Train Station
8 Standard Chartered Bank;
   Francistown Stationers
   Bookshop
12 Polina Laundromat
13 The Tube Disco
15 Barclays Bank
18 Bus Terminal
19 Bank of Botswana
21 Blue Jacket Plaza Shopping
    Centre; Hana Phamacy;
    KFC
22 Smart Centre (Barclays
    Plaza); Coffee Hut;
    Chapter's Bookshop;
    Milano Pizza & Chicken
24 Ebrahim Store
26 Holiday Car Hire;
    VIP Travel
27 Blue Jacket Mall;
    Botswana Book Centre;
    Air Botswana
28 Fruit & Vegetable Market
29 Post Office
30 Teletswana Office
31 Cine 2000
34 Pharma North Pharmacy
35 Sam Edward City Park
36 Police Station
37 Nyangabgwe Hospital

and meals are available. From the Thapama Lodge roundabout, follow the Marang road for 3km; turn left opposite the deaf school and continue about 250m.

The newly refurbished *Grand Lodge* (☎ 212300; fax 212309) has singles/doubles with toilet and shower for US$29/39.

Places to Eat

For breakfast, the *Marang Hotel* offers value at US$6/2.50 for English/continental style, and in the evening there's a salad bar and fixed menu for US$10 per person. *Barbara's Bistro* at the Francistown Sports Club is open daily except Monday and serves up tasty inexpensive lunches and dinners, but visitors pay US$2 for temporary membership.

The *KFC* is in the Blue Jacket Plaza. At the other end of Blue Jacket St are the *Chicken Run* and *Tasty Eats*, with curries, rotis, grills and savoury snacks.

The *House of Pizza* is a popular sit-down pizza restaurant. *Milano's*, in the Smart Centre, does great wood-fired pizza, and also serves chicken, kebabs and pasta.

Getting There & Away

Bus services to Gaborone (US$10) and Nata (US$3) run several times daily. The Mahube Express bus to Maun (US$11) departs daily at 9.30 and 10.30 am.

Daily trains between Bulawayo and Gaborone pass through Francistown. To hitch to Maun, walk out to the airport turn-off to a tree where locals wait for lifts. Heading south, wait at the roundabout near the Thapama Lodge or further out on the Gaborone road.

GHANZI

Most travellers visit Ghanzi as a transit point to or from Namibia, and the Kalahari Arms Hotel is the centre of town in nearly every respect. For currency exchange, the bank is open from 8.30 am to 1 pm Monday to Friday and 9 to 11 am on Saturday.

Short of visiting the villages, the Ghanzi-craft cooperative is the best place for San crafts; they're sold at 30 to 50% of the price charged in Maun and Gaborone. Up the road in **D'kar** is another fine self-help shop.

At the *Kalahari Arms Hotel* (☎ 296311), single/double rooms cost US$37/41 and rondavels are US$41/49. Many travellers camp out in the garden for US$4 per person.

Getting There & Away

The scheduled bus between Lobatse and Ghanzi (US$17) leaves Lobatse on Monday morning and Ghanzi on Wednesday morning. The bus from Maun to Mamuno passes Ghanzi in the early afternoon on Monday, Thursday and Saturday westbound and on Sunday, Tuesday and Friday eastbound.

On the poor road to the Namibian border at Mamuno, several patches require 4WD and the border post closes at 5 pm (4 pm Namibian time in the winter). Hitching isn't difficult, but you may get stuck at the border. On the Namibian side, you can stay at the *East Gate Service Station & Rest Camp*. Camping costs US$3 per person and bungalows are US$27 for three people.

GWETA

The popular *Gweta Rest Camp* (☎ /fax 612220) provides an affordable respite and the best hot showers in Botswana. Camping costs US$6 per person and basic single/double thatched rondavels are US$27/29. The focus of activity is the bar, which serves delicious, inexpensive, snacks and full meals.

KASANE & KAZUNGULA

Kasane sits at the meeting point of four countries – Botswana, Zambia, Namibia and Zimbabwe – and at the confluence of the Chobe and Zambezi rivers. It's also the gateway to 11,000 sq km Chobe National Park, which contains dense and varied wildlife populations (see National Parks & Reserves later in this chapter). Six kilometres east of Kasane is Kazungula, which serves as the border post between Botswana and Zimbabwe.

There's a friendly but not too helpful tourist office (☎ 250327) in a cluster of caravans east of the bank in Kasane. To avoid queuing to change money at the main Barclays Bank, try the branch at the Cresta Mowana Lodge.

Places to Stay & Eat

The best choice is the *Chobe Safari Lodge* (☎ 250336), right on the river. Camping costs US$6 and includes an excellent amenities block with hot showers. The main lodge has basic single/double rondavels for US$37/43; it also has chalets with en suite facilities for US$50/56 and suites with river views for US$55/61.

For a splash-out, try the beautiful *Cresta Mowana Lodge* (☎ 312222; fax 374321). It was designed by a Polish architect and may well be Botswana's loveliest building. Single/double rooms, all with river views, cost US$97/163.

If you're not eating at the lodges, you're limited to fast food at *Tuskers Restaurant & Takeaway* or *Savas Superette*, diagonally opposite the petrol station.

Getting There & Away

From the Lucky-7 Lo-Price Store (also called the Gumba Shop) in Kazungula, a daily minibus leaves at 6 am for Francistown. To be picked up elsewhere, book at the Chobe Safari Lodge. Between Kasane and Victoria Falls, UTC runs daily transfers for US$20 per person. They pick up at Kasane hotels between 9.30 and 10 am.

MAUN

Maun is firmly entrenched as the service centre of western Botswana, and for tourists it's a staging point for trips into the Okavango Delta (see National Parks & Reserves later in this chapter).

The 2.5 sq km **Maun Environmental Education Centre**, east of the Thamalakane River, offers four hiking trails and game hides where you can observe wildlife. When it's complete, foreigners will pay US$3.70 admission. Pick up a map at the entrance.

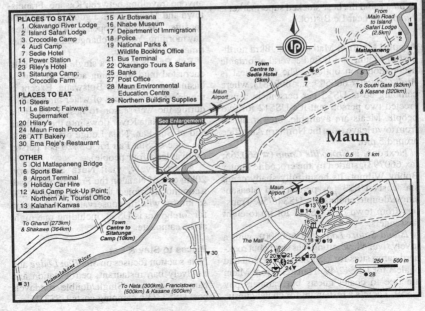

PLACES TO STAY
1 Okavango River Lodge
2 Island Safari Lodge
3 Crocodile Camp
4 Audi Camp
7 Sedie Hotel
9 Power Station
23 Riley's Hotel
31 Sitatunga Camp;
   Crocodile Farm

PLACES TO EAT
10 Steers
11 Le Bistrot; Fairways
   Supermarket
20 Hilary's
24 Maun Fresh Produce
26 ATT Bakery
30 Ema Reje's Restaurant

OTHER
5 Old Matlapaneng Bridge
6 Sports Bar
8 Airport Terminal
9 Holiday Car Hire
12 Audi Camp Pick-Up Point;
   Northern Air; Tourist Office
13 Kalahari Kanvas

15 Air Botswana
16 Nhabe Museum
17 Department of Immigration
18 Police
19 National Parks &
   Wildlife Booking Office
21 Bus Terminal
22 Okavango Tours & Safaris
25 Banks
27 Post Office
28 Maun Environmental
   Education Centre
29 Northern Building Supplies

Maun

BOTSWANA

The new **Nhabe Museum** outlines the natural history and culture of the area.

Some camping gear is sold at Northern Building Supplies on the corner of the main Maun and Nata roads, or you can hire equipment from Kalahari Canvas.

Places to Stay & Eat
The cheapest in-town place is the new *Power Station*, which should be open by the time you read this. Camping costs US$5 per person.

The *Sedie Motel* (☎ 660177; fax 660374) 5km north of town, charges US$47/59 for singles/doubles with breakfast and transfers from the centre. Camping costs US$3.50 per person.

When the legendary Duck Inn flew south, the local hangout shifted to *Le Bistrot*, which serves excellent meals, including a mean satay.

In The Mall, a good place is *Hilary's*, which does earthy meals, including vegetarian fare. The best greengrocer is *Maun Fresh Produce* and the best-stocked supermarket is *Fairways*, near Le Bistrot.

Around Maun In Matlapaneng, 8km northeast of Maun, you'll find several affordable accommodation options. The friendliest is *Audi Camp* (☎ 660599; fax 660581), where camping costs US$3 per person; in a pre-erected two person tent it's US$12 for two people. Meals are available. Free transfers from town leave from the Northern Air office around 5 pm.

Next door is *Crocodile Camp* (☎ 660265; fax 660793), started by the crocodile hunter Bobby Wilmot. Its beautifully shady camp site costs US$3 per person and pleasant single/double chalets are US$46/50. Transfers from town cost US$11 for up to eight passengers.

Island Safari Lodge (☎ 660300), with a lovely river-view setting, has shady but rock-hard camp sites for US$3.50 per person and chalets for US$42/49. Transfers from Maun are free to chalet guests but campers pay US$9. There's a restaurant for chalet guests;

campers and others must book well in advance or just eat at the bar.

Getting There & Away
The bus terminal is at the north-eastern corner of The Mall. There are three daily Mahube Express buses to Nata (US$5.50, four hours) and Francistown (US$8.50, 6½ hours). To Shakawe, there's a reliable daily bus at 8.30 am.

There's also a Sesennye bus which goes three times weekly to Mamuno (on the Namibian border) via Ghanzi.

For hitching east toward Nata, a good spot is Ema Reje's Restaurant on the Nata road. If you're hitching to or from Kasane, the cheapest and easiest option is to take the long route via Nata. If you manage to catch a lift north through Moremi and Chobe, remember that you must pay park fees for each day you spend in either park.

NATA
Nata is an obligatory refuelling stop for anyone travelling between Kasane, Francistown and Maun, so it's a good place to look for lifts. The bank is open only on Wednesday morning. You can change money at other times at Nata Lodge.

Sua Pan is mostly a single sheet of salt-encrusted mud stretching across the lowest basin in north-eastern Botswana. Except in the driest years, flocks of water birds gather during the wet season to nest at the delta where the Nata River flows into the northern end of Sua Pan. Nata Lodge offers trips to the edge of Sua Pan for US$20 per person (with at least four people).

Alternatively, visit **Nata Sanctuary**, 20km east of Nata on the Francistown road, a community project which has set aside 230 sq km for wildlife conservation. Admission for foreigners is US$3, including one night at the camp site.

Places to Stay & Eat
Nata's action focuses on *Sua Pan Lodge* and its lively bar, restaurant, petrol station and camping ground. Single/double rondavels cost US$33/39; camping costs US$3.25.

At friendly *Nata Lodge* (☎ /fax 611210), 10km east of Nata, three-bed chalets cost US$50, four-bed tents are US$37 and camp sites are US$3.50. Accommodation in its self-catering bush camp beside the Nata River costs US$30 per person, including transfers.

SEROWE

With a population of 90,000, sprawling Serowe, the Ngwato capital, is Botswana's largest village and is known for its uniquely intricate **woodcarvings**. The **Khama III Memorial Museum** (closed Sunday) shows the history of the Khama family.

Atop **Thathaganyana Hill** are the ruins of an 11th century village and the **royal cemetery**, with the grave of Khama III marked by a bronze duiker, which is the Ngwato totem. However, police consider this a sensitive spot, and visitors need a police escort.

The new 12,000 hectare **Khama Rhino Sanctuary**, 20km north-west of town, is a safe house for seven of Botswana's 16 rhinos. For information, contact Raymond & Norma Watson at the Dennis Service Station on (☎ 430232; fax 430992), PO Box 60, Serowe.

Places to Stay & Eat

The *Serowe Hotel* (☎ 430234), which is on the Palapye side of town, has bright single/double rooms starting at US$45/52.

The run-down *Tshwaragano Hotel* (☎ 430377), on the hillside above The Mall, has grimy single/double rooms which cost US$37/45.

The best option for meals is either the Serowe Hotel or *Tshukudu (Rhino) Takeaways* at the Engen petrol station. You'll find Indian and Chinese takeaways at the *Central Supermarket Restaurant* in The Mall.

SHAKAWE

For travellers, Shakawe serves as a border crossing to and from Namibia or a staging point for trips to the Tsodilo Hills, 40km away. Activity focuses on Wright's Trading Store, the self-service supermarket and the bottle store.

Places to Stay & Eat

For accommodation, try the lovely and charming *Drotsky's Cabins* 5km south of town. Chalets cost around US$33 per person and camp sites, when they are available, are US$4.50. At the *Shakawe Fishing Lodge*, 8km south of town, camping costs US$6 per person. Meals are also available.

In the compound opposite Wright's is *Mma Haidongo's Nice Bread Bakery* selling home-baked bread. There are also two basic African restaurants.

Getting There & Away

The daily bus to Maun leaves at 9 am and takes eight hours. Drivers should note that although Shakawe has been granted a petrol station permit, as yet petrol is available only from The Brigades. It's sold from drums in a military compound, north along the river beyond the secondary school.

TSODILO HILLS

The four Tsodilo Hills – Male, Female, Child and North hill – rise abruptly from a rippled, ocean-like expanse of desert and they are threaded with myth, legend and spiritual significance for the San people. More than 2750 **ancient rock paintings** have been discovered at over 200 sites. As in most of southern Africa, the majority of these are attributed to ancestors of the modern San.

West of the Male Hill is a decrepit San village whose tragically dispossessed inhabitants are sadly preoccupied with flogging trinkets to tourists and awaiting hand-outs. Further south sits the Mbukushu village, which has flooded the surrounding country with its cattle (to the dismay of the original San inhabitants, who hold the area sacred).

San guides to the major rock paintings are available for around US$4 per group. As yet there are no facilities in the Tsodilo Hills, but suitable *camp sites* are found around the bases of the hills and water is available from the borehole for cattle, several hundred metres from the airstrip.

Getting There & Away

There are two main access routes: one is

BOTSWANA

signposted 7km south of Sepupa and the other turns off opposite the entrance to Shakawe Fishing Lodge. However, both roads are horrid and the latter is a contender for the Planet's Worst Drive. Shakawe Fishing Lodge hires out 4WD vehicles for the trip to the hills for US$150 per day plus US$1 per kilometre, including fuel; drivers should gear up for a challenge.

Travellers have attempted to walk or hitch the 40km from the main road, but the Kalahari is not to be taken lightly. Let someone know you're going and be sure the majority of the weight you're carrying is water. You'll need a *minimum* of 6L per person for two days.

Upon arrival, check in with the Mbukushu chief and sign his guest book. Incidentally, no-one in the village is authorised to charge for visits to the hills (unless you're hiring a guide).

TULI BLOCK

The Tuli Block is a 10 to 20km wide swathe of freehold farmland extending 350km along the northern bank of the Limpopo from Buffels Drift to Pont Drift. The main attraction is the 90,000 hectare **Tuli Game Reserve**, which takes in both the Mashatu and Tuli game reserves. They offer lots of wildlife and some of Botswana's best landscapes: savannah, rock kopjes, river bluffs, riverine forests and tidy villages.

Mashatu Game Reserve is Africa's largest private game reserve. No wild camping is permitted and the only public access is via the corridor road to the cableway and border crossing at Pont Drift, which closes at 6 pm.

Places to Stay

The beautifully situated *Tuli Safari Lodge* (☎ 482 2634) is attached to the privately owned Tuli Game Reserve. The lodge is quite expensive, but does run a self-catering rondavel camp which costs US$240 for up to six people including use of a vehicle and driver.

Limpopo Safaris Camp (☎ Johannesburg (011) 780 3374), has basic huts for US$30 per night, including wildlife-viewing activities. Bring your own food.

Budget access to Mashatu Game Reserve is out of the question (except for the short road corridor between the Motloutse River and Pont Drift); the least expensive single/double plans cost US$186/297.

Getting There & Away

There's an occasional bus from Selebi-Phikwe to Bobonong, Molalatau, or (rarely) to Mathathane, just over 20km from Platjanbridge. Hitching is possible but slow; the easiest route from the Francistown to Gaborone road is from Serule, via Selebi-Phikwe, to Zanzibar. Alternatively, hitch from Gaborone through South Africa to Pont Drift, where you can ride the cableway across the river for US$5.50.

National Parks & Reserves

For foreigners, admission to Botswana's national parks and reserves is US$18.50 per person per day, plus US$7.50 per person for camping. Those on organised tours get a bit of a break and pay only US$11 per person per day plus US$4 for camping.

Advance bookings for entry and camp sites are required for Chobe, Moremi and Makgadikgadi & Nxai Pans; otherwise, you'll be denied entry to the parks. Bookings by fax or in person are available 12 months in advance through the Parks & Reserves Reservations Office (☎ 661265; fax 661264), PO Box 20364, Boseja, Maun. For Chobe, you could also contact the Kasane Wildlife Office (☎ 650235) which is at the Chobe Gate, near Kasane. In Gaborone, you should book through the national parks offices (☎ 371405) in Tsholetsa House, opposite Debswana House on The Mall. Be sure to include the name of the park and requested camping ground, the dates, the number of campers and whether they are foreigners or Botswana citizens or residents.

Payment (in Botswana pula) must be received within one month or you forfeit the booking.

Organised Tours

All of the following tour companies are in Maun. Audi Camp runs economical overland trips through Moremi, Chobe, Makgadikgadi & Nxai Pans, the Okavango Panhandle and even to the Tsodilo Hills and Gcwihaba Caverns, for US$45 per person per day, including transport, food and driver/guide, but excluding camping gear and park fees.

Island Safaris does custom mobile safaris to anywhere you want to go, including transport and a driver/guide, for US$186 per day for up to six people, plus US$0.50 per kilometre over 100km.

Bush Camp Safaris runs customised mobile safaris for US$112 per day for the vehicle only. Guides start at US$26 for up to five people, and more for larger groups. All-inclusive safaris are US$130 per person per day.

You may also want to check out the big overland trucks, most of which stay at Island Safari Lodge. Some go north and you may be able to join in for minimal cost plus food and park fees.

CHOBE NATIONAL PARK

Chobe is best known for its wildlife-packed riverfront, and the main draw is the elephant population, which numbers over 73,000. A good way to enjoy the riverfront is on the river trips offered by Kasane-area lodges, but you must pay the park fees in addition to the cruise prices. Chobe Safari Lodge, Kubu Lodge, Cresta Mowana Lodge and Chobe Game Lodge run three hour afternoon 'booze cruises' for around US$17 (Safari Lodge guests are entitled to discounts), plus park fees. Kubu Lodge also does a catamaran tour to the four-way frontier for US$9 per person.

Kubu Lodge and Chobe Safari Lodge run 2½-hour game drives along the riverfront routes at 6.15 am and 4 pm. Game drives average around US$15 per person, plus park fees.

Places to Stay & Eat

Serondela Camp, 10km west of the park gate, is Chobe's most accessible camp site, with toilets, cold showers and lots of wildlife. However, it will soon be replaced by Ihaha Camp, further west, at which time Serondela will become a picnic site.

Outside the western entrance to the Chobe transit route, near the Namibian border, is the new *Buffalo Ridge Campsite*. This high-ground spot with hot and cold showers, flush toilets and clean borehole water charges US$3 for camping. A lodge and restaurant are being constructed across the valley.

Savuti Camp, in the wild and hard-to-access heart of Chobe (4WD only), is what park rangers call a 'rough camp', meaning

BOTSWANA

Chobe's Elephants

An estimated 73,000 elephants inhabit Chobe National Park, and herds of up to 500 elephants wreak havoc along the riverfront, as evidenced by the trampled bush and the numbers of rammed, flattened, uprooted, toppled and dismembered trees that litter the landscape.

Until recently, the Botswana government maintained that the best course was to let nature handle the problem. Indeed, hunting bans were imposed in the hope that the pressure on the riverfront vegetation would decrease once elephants felt safe to migrate elsewhere. Unfortunately, the pachyderms have continued to multiply and refugees have even migrated from neighbouring countries to this safe haven.

In 1990 the Botswana government decided culling would begin the following year and, as in Zimbabwe, entire herds (rather than individual elephants) were to be shot. These plans didn't go ahead and the elephant population continued to boom. In 1996, however, the government sanctioned a hunt of 80 elephants. ■

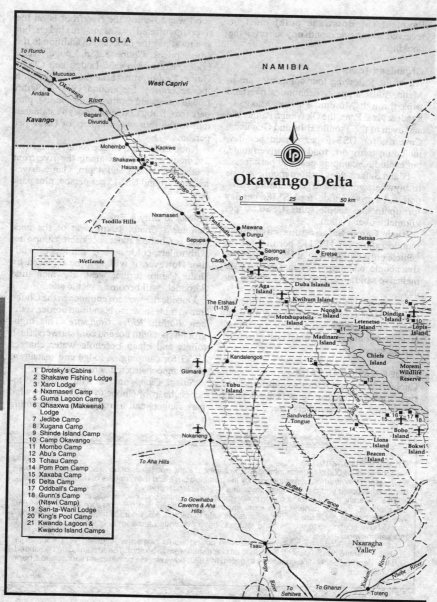

Okavango Delta

ANGOLA

NAMIBIA

To Rundu

Mucusso

West Caprivi

Andara

Okavango

River

Kavango

Bagani
Divundu

Mohembo

Kaokwe

Shakawe
Hauxa

Okavango

Nxamaseri

Tsodilo Hills

Panhandle

Mawana
Dungu

Sepupa

Seronga
Gqoro

Cada

Eretse

Betsaa

Aga
Island

Duba Islands

Kwihum Island

The Etshas
(1-13)

Motshupatsila
Island

Ngoqha
Island

Letenetso
Island

Dindiga
Island

Lopis
Island

Madinare
Island

Kandalengoti

Chiefs
Island

Moremi
Wildlife
Reserve

Gumare

Tubu
Island

Bobo
Island

Sandveldt
Tongue

Lions
Island

Bokwi
Island

Nokaneng

Pom Pom Camp

Beacon
Island

To Aha Hills

Buffalo

Fence

To Gcwihaba
Caverns & Aha
Hills

Nxaragha
Valley

To Aha Hills

Tsau

Thaoge

River

To
Sehitwa

To Ghanzi

Toteng

Nhabe River

0   25   50 km

Wetlands

1 Drotsky's Cabins
2 Shakawe Fishing Lodge
3 Xaro Lodge
4 Nxamaseri Camp
5 Guma Lagoon Camp
6 Qhaaxwa (Makwena)
   Lodge
7 Jedibe Camp
8 Xugana Camp
9 Shinde Island Camp
10 Camp Okavango
11 Mombo Camp
12 Abu's Camp
13 Tchau Camp
14 Pom Pom Camp
15 Xaxaba Camp
16 Delta Camp
17 Oddball's Camp
18 Gunn's Camp
   (Ntswi Camp)
19 San-ta-Wani Lodge
20 King's Pool Camp
21 Kwando Lagoon &
   Kwando Island Camps

BOTSWANA

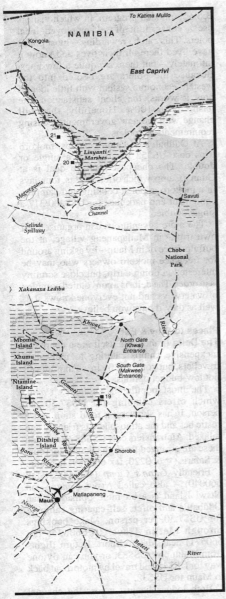

it's prone to invasion by wildlife. Due to high water, Savuti is closed from January to March.

For other options, see Kasane earlier in this chapter.

Getting There & Away

Chobe's northern entrance lies 8km west of Kasane and is accessible to conventional vehicles; however, to proceed beyond the riverfront area requires a 4WD with high clearance. Hitching isn't permitted in the park, so look for lifts in Kasane (at the petrol station) or just outside the park gate.

OKAVANGO DELTA & MOREMI WILDLIFE RESERVE

Described as 'the river which never finds the sea', the Okavango disappears into a 15,000 sq km maze of lagoons, channels and islands. It's the largest inland delta in the world and abounds with birdlife and other wildlife including elephant, zebra, buffalo, wildebeest, giraffe, hippo and kudu.

While it's challenging to visit the delta on a shoestring, mid-range budgets are accommodated and most independent visitors manage a trip by *mokoro*, a dugout canoe well suited to the shallow waters of the delta. The best months to visit are July to September, when water levels are high and the weather is dry.

Moremi Reserve is the area of the Okavango Delta officially cordoned off for the preservation of wildlife, encompassing over 3000 sq km where large chunks of dry land rise between the wetlands: Chief's Island, deep in the Inner Delta, and the Moremi Tongue, to the north-east. Hitching from Maun is slow, and everyone must book and pay for Moremi camp sites in advance.

Mokoro Trips

Most visitors want to do at least a short mokoro trip through the Okavango Delta. Generally, the further you travel from Maun, the better your chances of seeing wildlife, and the best protected wildlife habitat lies inside Moremi Reserve.

Next best for wildlife is the Inner Delta,

the area west and north of Chief's Island, where you will find the classic delta scenery. Accommodation is available in nearly every price range, but access is normally by plane.

The cheapest area to visit, which is accessible by a combination of 4WD vehicle, motorboat and mokoro, is the Eastern Delta. There aren't yet any controls on operations and polers (mokoro pilots and guides) are normally unlicensed freelancers hoping for enough experience to move up to bigger delta camps.

Mokoro trips are normally arranged through the camps, each of which has its own pool of licensed guides/polers. Enquire in advance as to whether you're expected to provide food for your poler. The poler will normally provide a sack of mealies or rice and a cooking pot, while travellers will have to come up with other cooking implements and provisions.

Note that if you enter Moremi on your mokoro trip, you'll be charged national park fees of US$11 per person per day plus US$4 per person to camp (these fees are reduced because mokoro trips qualify as organised tours). Outside the reserve, you won't see as much wildlife – no elephants or lions – but the natural element is just as lovely and you'll see fewer tourists.

Most polers assume visitors want to enter Moremi and will do so as a matter of course, so if park fees are a problem, inform your poler at the outset. Also advise the poler if you'd like to break the trip with bushwalks around some of the palm islands.

The cheapest organised trips are arranged by Audi Camp and Island Safari Lodge, both in Maun. These range from US$15 per day with Audi Camp to US$20 per day with Island Safari Lodge for two people, plus a tip for the poler (say P5 to P10 per day) and a one-off transfer fee to the departure points above the buffalo fence on the Boro or Santadadibe rivers. These start at US$22 per person with Audi Camp and US$40 with Island Safari Lodge.

There's also the Community Development Company (☎ 661225), PO Box 20402, Maun, which has set up a culture and ecology-minded program, in which visitors use a consortium of self-employed local polers. This can be rewarding – most polers have lived there all their lives and know it intimately – but there are quite a few bugs. Because the polers are booted into the western economic system with little idea of how it works, the client satisfaction rate hasn't been 100%. Hopefully, that will change with the new government licensing requirements for polers.

At Oddball's or Gunn's camps, mokoro trips cost US$58 per day for a single or double. The cheapest package deal is at Gunn's Camp, which offers flights, four days in a mokoro, a poler, cooking and camping equipment and park fees for US$200/317 a single/double.

The more adventurous can organise their own trip – in Matlapaneng village, at the buffalo fence or in Maun – by asking around for freelance mokoro owners who may be interested in doing a trip, but close scrutiny is in order. The delta is a convoluted complex of waterways and not everyone knows it as well as they'd have you believe.

Places to Stay & Eat

The Delta In the delta itself are a couple of inexpensive camps catering to mid-range travellers, but you must fly in, so they're still not low-budget options.

The most popular is *Oddball's Camp*, which offers camping for US$7.50 per person. It has showers, a food shop and a rustic bar and the atmosphere is friendly and relaxed. Air transfers cost US$88 return, and these are arranged through Okavango Tours & Safaris (☎ 660220; fax 660589) in Maun.

Friendly *Gunn's Camp* (☎ 660023; fax 660040) – also called *Ntswi Camp* – on Ntswi Island is a bit more upmarket than Oddball's and offers self-catering camping for US$7.50 per person. Make bookings through Merlin Travel (☎ 660635; fax 660571) near Maun airport. Return flights from Maun cost US$83, or you can fly one way for US$45 and travel by motorboat back to Maun for US$38.

Both lodges lie just across the channel

from Chief's Island and Moremi Reserve, about 70km from Maun. In theory, campers should carry food and other supplies from outside but you're limited to 10kg of baggage. Most people rely on camp meals and hire equipment from the camp shops.

Moremi Reserve There's a developed camp site at *South Gate* but more interesting is the undeveloped site at *Third Bridge*, literally the third log bridge from South Gate, 48km away. However, it's becoming popular with overland groups and is no

longer pristine. Only swim at Third Bridge in broad daylight, and watch for crocodiles. Don't camp on the bridge itself or sleep in the open, since there are lots of lions in the area.

The third Moremi camp site is at *Xakanaxa Lediba*, 25km from Third Bridge on a narrow strip of land surrounded by marsh and lagoon. With one of the largest heronries in Africa, the area offers excellent birdwatching. *North Gate*, at the northern entrance to the reserve, has a less-than-appealing camp site.

Burkina Faso

Burkina Faso is a land of contrasts. It's the place where ancient Sahelian empires and coastal kingdoms met, where northern desertscapes yield to southern waterfalls and greenery, where bleak savannah is transformed by vivid textiles and picturesque villages. In the markets, turbaned traders on camels mix with farmers on donkey-drawn carts in a colourful swirl of diverse ethnic groups. Burkina Faso is one of the world's poorest countries, yet the Burkinabè are exceptionally friendly and enterprising. While discovering Burkina Faso takes time, most travellers who come to the country will be captivated by its surprises.

Facts about the Country

HISTORY
The earliest known inhabitants of present-day Burkina Faso were the Bobo, Lobi and Gurunsi, who were in the area by the 13th century. By the 14th century, Mossi peoples had begun to move westward from settlements near the Niger River. From the 15th century, centralised Mossi kingdoms developed, the most important ones being at Ouagadougou and Ouahigouya.

The powerful Mossi states were still in existence as late as 1896, when Ouagadougou was taken by the French. Over the next decade, the French annexed additional territory, including the lands of the Bobo and the Lobi, and by the early 20th century had established a protectorate over the entire region. However, tribal chiefs were permitted to retain their traditional seats and Mossi kings continued to influence the course of politics until independence in 1960. The French redrew the borders between their adjacent territories repeatedly, and it wasn't until 1947 that the borders of Upper Volta (as Burkina Faso was known until 1984) were finally defined.

BURKINA FASO
Area: 274,122 sq km
Population: 10.4 million
Population Growth Rate: 2.9%
Capital: Ouagadougou
Head of State: President Captain Blaise Compaoré
Official Language: French
Currency: West African CFA franc
Exchange Rate: CFA 500 = US$1
Per Capita GNP: US$230
Inflation: 8%
Time: GMT/UTC

Highlights
- Peaceful Banfora and the beautiful surrounding countryside
- Relaxing Bobo-Dioulasso and its biennial cultural festival
- Gorom-Gorom's windswept vistas and fascinating desert market

---

Between the two World Wars, the French authorities forced the Mossi to supply labour for European-owned plantations in Côte d'Ivoire. The system was abolished in principle by the late 1940s but continued in practice until independence. To escape forced recruitment many Mossi went to Ghana, only to be exploited there by British plantation owners. Labour emigration is still a problem, with substantial numbers of young Burkinabè working in Ghana and Côte d'Ivoire.

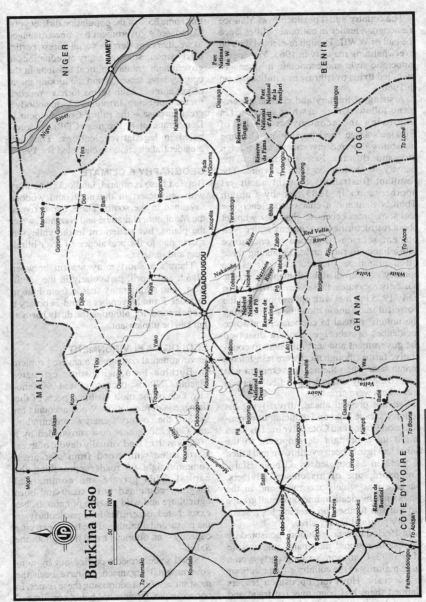

Burkina Faso

NIGER

NIAMEY

Niger River

MALI

Mopti

Koutiala

Skasso

Kokoko

Sindou

Bantora

Niangoloko

Réserve de
Bontioli

CÔTE D'IVOIRE

Ferkessédougou

To Abidjan

To Bamako

Koro

Bankass

Tiou

Ouahigouya

Tougan

Dédougou

Nouna

Boromo

Pâ

Safiri

Bobo-Dioulasso

Koudougou

Parc
National des
Deux Bales

Diébougou

Gaoua

Kampti

Loropéni

To Bouna

Ouessa

Haméle

Léo

Sabou

Wa

GHANA

Balé

Makoyé

Gorom-Gorom

Doti

Bani

Bogandé

Fada
N'Gourma

Kaya

Kongoussi

Djibo

Yako

Kantchari

Koupéla

Tenkodogo

Bittou

Zabré

Tébéle

P.O

Bolgatanga

Diapaga

Pama

Tindangou

Dapaong

Natitingou

Parc
National
du W

Parc
National
de la
Pendjari

Parc
National
d'Arli

Réserve du
Singou

Réserve
de Pama

BENIN

TOGO

To Lomé

To Accra

OUAGADOUGOU

Nakambe

Tolessé

Nobéré

Nazinon River

Parc
Nobéré
de P.O

Réserve de
Nazinga

White Volta

Red Volta
River

Volta Noire

Mouhoun River

Téra

0   50   100 km

BURKINA FASO

The country's first president was Maurice Yaméogo, a leader in national politics since the end of WWII. Though re-elected with an overwhelming majority in 1965, Yaméogo's autocratic style and economic mismanagement led to his overthrow in a military coup in 1966.

A string of military and civilian governments followed, none of which succeeded in improving the economy or the lot of Burkina's large rural population. Ongoing instability deterred investment and foreign aid, and Burkina Faso continued to be heavily dependent on Côte d'Ivoire. The resultant frustrations brought about yet another coup in 1983, led by Captain Thomas Sankara, a charismatic, energetic and sometimes eccentric character who set about restructuring the economy with development schemes designed to encourage self-reliance in rural areas. Financing these often grandiose projects as well as the country's external debt demanded drastic austerity measures; these were introduced in early 1985 but met with opposition from the powerful trade union movement. Following the unions' refusal to cooperate, and some incidences of sabotage, Sankara dissolved the government and sent ministers to cooperative farms (though most were reinstated a month later when the new government was formed). Many union leaders fled overseas and others were arrested.

Sankara pressed ahead, diversifying his country's trade links and reducing its dependence on France and Côte d'Ivoire. His ideas might have brought development to the Sahel had he not been overthrown and killed in 1987 in a coup led by Captain Blaise Compaoré, one of his closest advisers. Sankara was widely mourned, and in the years since his death, numerous small groups have arisen focused on keeping his revolutionary political legacy alive.

In 1991, a new constitution sponsored by Compaoré restored multiparty rule and, in May 1992, Compaoré's ruling party won a large majority in the country's first elections in 14 years. However, opposition leaders claimed there had been massive fraud and that some 65% of the population did not vote. Compaoré's government has since managed to weather considerable social unrest, particularly among students angry at reductions in government grants. Political tensions in the country have lessened and the lurking threat of yet another coup seems to have receded for the time being. In mid-1997 – to nobody's great surprise – the ruling Congrès pour la Démocratie et le Progrès (CDP) predominated in legislative elections. The next presidential election is scheduled for 1998.

GEOGRAPHY & CLIMATE

Burkina Faso is an arid, landlocked country with semidesert in the north and wooded savannah in the south. Three major rivers, the Mouhoun, Nakambé and Nazinon, water the plains, but settlement in the valleys is sparse due to the prevalence of river blindness and malaria.

There's a short rainy season between March and April, particularly in the southwest, with a long rainy season from June to October. From November to mid-February it is cooler and dry, although the dusty harmattan can be unpleasant.

ECOLOGY & ENVIRONMENT

Environmental damage is a severe problem in Burkina Faso, with some estimates placing GNP loss because of it at 9% annually. One of the most visible aspects of this damage is deforestation. Wood accounts for 94% of the country's energy consumption, and Ouagadougou is now surrounded by a 70km swath of land virtually devoid of trees. Carts laden with wood from afar are a common sight on roads approaching the capital. This private and commercial logging, combined with slash-and-burn agriculture and wild grazing of animals, has exacerbated desertification, particularly in the north, and diminished the land's carrying capacity – an ominous trend throughout the Sahel.

Small-scale projects carried out by nongovernmental organisations have been the most successful at addressing these issues. In one example, farmers are being encouraged to return to the traditional practice of building *diguettes*, stone lines laid along field contours which slow water run-off, thereby maximising water penetration, reducing erosion and conserving soil. The diguettes have had an amazingly beneficial impact, in some instances increasing soil levels by 15cm in one year.

POPULATION & PEOPLE
Burkina Faso is one of the most densely populated of the Sahel countries, with 10.4 million people. Important ethnic groups include the Mossi, Bobo, Gourma and Fulani. About 45% of the population still follow traditional beliefs, around 40% are Muslim and 10% are Christian.

LANGUAGE
French is the official language. Major African languages are Moré, Dioula, Gourmantche and Peul. For a listing of useful French phrases, see the Language Appendix.

Facts for the Visitor

VISAS & DOCUMENTS
Visas are required for all except nationals of Economic Community of West African States (ECOWAS) countries.

Cholera and yellow-fever vaccination certificates are usually checked on arrival at the airport and at most land borders.

Visa Extensions
Visas can be extended at the Sûreté (room 22) in Ouagadougou (open weekdays from 7.30 am to 12.30 pm and 3 to 5.30 pm). A one month extension costs US$20 plus two photos and is usually ready the same day if you go early.

Other Visas
Benin & Niger
The French consulate will not issue visas for these countries, so plan ahead.

Central African Republic & Togo
The French consulate issues three-month visas to these countries within 24 hours for US$20 plus two photos. Three-day transit visas cost US$6.

Côte d'Ivoire
One-month visas cost US$40 for most nationalities plus three photos and are issued within 24 hours.

Ghana
One-month visas cost US$24 plus four photos and are issued within two to three days.

Mali
One-month visas cost US$16 plus two photos and are issued within 24 hours.

Nigeria
Visas are issued for residents of Burkina Faso only, although your case may be considered if you have a letter of reference from your own embassy or from the Nigerian embassy in your homeland.

EMBASSIES
Burkina Faso Embassies
In Africa, Burkina Faso has embassies in Algeria, Côte d'Ivoire, Egypt, Ghana, Libya, Mali, Morocco and Nigeria. Its embassies in other countries include Belgium, Canada, France, Germany, Italy, and the USA. There is an honorary consul in the UK. Elsewhere, visas can usually be obtained from French embassies or consulates.

Foreign Embassies in Burkina Faso
Foreign embassies and consulates in Ouagadougou include:

Algeria
near Place des Nations Unies (☎ 306401)
Canada
Rue Agostino Neto (☎ 311894)
Côte d'Ivoire
near Place des Nations Unies (☎ 318228)
Denmark
Rue Agostino Neto (☎ 313192)
France
Blvd de la Révolution (☎ 306774)
Germany
Rue Joseph Badoua (☎ 306731)
Ghana
Ave d'Oubritenga (☎ 307635)
Mali
2569 Ave Bassawarga (☎ 381922)
Netherlands
south of Place des Nations Unies (☎ 306134)
Nigeria
Ave d'Oubritenga (☎ 306667)

BURKINA FASO

Senegal
a few blocks west of the southern end of Ave Yennenga
UK (consulate)
Tobacco Marketing Consultants Ltd, 306 Rue 13.04 (☎ 311137)
USA
Ave Raoul Follereau (☎ 306723)

The Canadian embassy handles Australian affairs. The nearest British embassy is in Abidjan, Côte d'Ivoire.

MONEY

US$1 = CFA 500

The unit of currency is the West African CFA franc.

Banque Internationale du Burkina (BIB) in Ouagadougou charges no commission on travellers' cheques. Outside Ouagadougou, banks generally require proof of purchase to change travellers' cheques. At present, no bank in Burkina Faso gives cash advances on a credit card.

POST & COMMUNICATIONS

Ouagadougou's poste restante (open weekdays from 7.30 am to 12.30 pm and 3 to 5 pm) charges US$1 per collected letter and will hold mail for one month. There is also a poste restante in Bobo-Dioulasso.

International phone calls can be made easily from the telecommunications centre (ONATEL) next to the main post office in Ouagadougou from 7 am to 10 pm daily. Rates are US$4 per minute to Europe and US$5 to the USA and Australia. You can also send and receive faxes here Monday to Saturday from 7.30 am to noon and 3 to 5.30 pm (US$1.50 per received page; fax (226) 338130). The country code is 226; there are no area codes.

DANGERS & ANNOYANCES

Police roadblocks and baggage searches add hours to journeys; on some stretches near the borders, checkpoints are less than 10km apart.

A photo permit is required, although this is rarely enforced. Permits are free and issued on the spot by the hard-to-find sec-retariat of the Ministry of Tourism (open weekdays 7 am to 12.30 pm and 3 to 5.30 pm) located in an unmarked yellow building on Ave Ouedraogo, north of the train station. Even with this permit, don't photograph anything associated with the military or the police.

In Ouagadougou, watch your valuables. Ave Yennenga and the area around the marketplace are notorious for pickpockets.

BUSINESS HOURS

Businesses are open weekdays from 7.30 am to 12.30 pm and 3 to 5.30 pm and on Saturday from 9 am until 1 pm. Banking hours are weekdays from 7.30 to 11 am and 3.30 to 5 pm.

PUBLIC HOLIDAYS

Public holidays are: 1 January, 3 January, 8 March, 1 May, Ascension Day, 4 August (Revolution Day), 5 August (Independence Day), 15 August, 15 October, 1 November, 11 December, 25 December, Easter Monday and variable Islamic holidays (see Public Holidays in Regional Facts for the Visitor for details of Islamic holidays).

ACCOMMODATION

Finding a place to stay is rarely a problem, although vacancies are rare in the capital during FESPACO (see the Ouagadougou section) and in Bobo-Dioulasso during the national culture festival in April. Single/double rooms with fan and shared facilities average US$7/9, while air-con rooms with attached bathroom start at US$20.

FOOD

Tô is the millet or sorghum-based pâté eaten as a staple in Burkina Faso. In larger towns, many people start the day with bread and *yaourt* (yoghurt) at streetside coffee stalls.

Getting There & Away

AIR

Airlines servicing Ouagadougou include Air France (☎ 306065), Air Ivoire (☎ 306207), Air Algérie (☎ 312301), Aeroflot (☎ 307129),

Sabena (☎ 305880), Air Afrique (☎ 306020) and Air Burkina (☎ 315325). Both Air Burkina and Air Afrique offer student discounts on international routes.

Ouagadougou's airport is 8km from the centre; the international departure tax is US$7, payable in CFA. Bobo-Dioulasso's airport services intra-African routes only.

LAND
Benin
The road to Benin via Fada N'Gourma is sealed to the border. There are regular connections between Ouagadougou and Fada via bus (three times weekly on Faso Tours, US$4) and bush taxi or minibus (daily, US$6). Minibuses and taxis from Fada to the border (US$6) are infrequent and fill up slowly. Time in Benin is one hour ahead of Burkina Faso.

Transport is scarce from the border along the dirt road to Tanguiéta (65km, US$5), except on market day (Monday). There's at least one taxi a day from Tanguiéta to Natitingou.

Côte d'Ivoire
Bus BFCI/Sans Frontières has daily buses (10 am and 3 pm) from Ouagadougou to Ferkessédougou (585km, 12 hours, US$24), Yamoussoukro (925km, 18 hours, US$27) and Abidjan (1175km, 24 hours, US$29). UTB has daily departures from Ouagadougou to Abidjan (US$32).

Train Alternatively, there's a train between Burkina Faso and Côte d'Ivoire, departing Ouagadougou on Tuesday, Thursday and Saturday at 8 am and arriving in Abidjan 27 hours later (US$48/32 for 1st/2nd class). There are no sleeping berths and no student discounts; food is available at stations along the way. Unfortunately, the train has been allowed to deteriorate, so it's no longer as pleasant a trip as it used to be.

Ghana
Ghana's state bus company, which is STC (☎ 308751), has a bus every Monday and Friday from the main gare routière in Ouagadougou to Accra (US$20) via Tamale (US$12) and Kumasi (US$16). Tickets should be booked in advance at STC's office on Ave Kwame Nkrumah in Ouagadougou.

There's also an X9 bus to Pô (15km from the Ghanaian border) leaving Ouagadougou Monday, Tuesday and Saturday at 8 am (3 hrs, US$4). From Pô there are one or two taxis a day to the border (US$2) and on to Bolgatanga in Ghana (45km, one hour, US$2).

You can also travel from Bobo-Dioulasso via Hamale to Wa (320km) though traffic is scarce and you must travel in stages.

Mali
Faso Tours has a bus to Bamako via Bobo-Dioulasso, departing Ouagadougou on Thursday at 8 am (542km, 12 hours, US$25); book well ahead. There's also an X9 bus on Monday, Wednesday and Saturday mornings from Ouaga to Djibasso on the Mali border (US$10). Many travellers break the journey at Sikasso (US$10 from Bobo). You can also go from Bobo to Ségou (twice weekly bus, US$10).

BFCI/Sans Frontières has a bus from Bobo-Dioulasso to Bamako for US$16 (daily except Saturday). Bush taxis run from Mopti to Bobo-Dioulasso most days for around US$10. These taxis can take all day to fill, and an overnight stop at the border is likely. (The nearby campement has rooms for about US$6.) Again, many travellers do this trip in stages: a bush taxi from Ouahigouya to Koro is US$6; from Koro to Bankass it's US$5; and from Bankass to Mopti it's US$6.

Niger
Express buses to Niamey (500km, 12 hours, US$14) leave Faso Tours in Ouagadougou on Monday at 7 am; book in advance. An X9 bus does the journey on Tuesday mornings for the same price.

Minibuses to the Niger border leave from Ouagadougou's main gare routière (US$10). For Niamey, you must change vehicles at the border. It's US$4 from the border to Niamey. Neither minibuses nor taxis are plentiful and you must try to leave Ouaga early or you won't make it to the border before it closes

BURKINA FASO

at 5.30 pm. Niger is one hour ahead of Burkina Faso.

Togo

The road is sealed from Ouagadougou to Lomé. The only direct bus to Lomé leaves from Faso Tours on Wednesday at 7 am (965km, 24 hours, US$20); frequent police checkpoints on both sides make this journey agonisingly long.

A direct taxi to Lomé (US$25) is more expensive than travelling in stages, as taxis in Togo are cheaper. Take a minibus first to Bitou (40km from the border, US$8), then from there to Dapaong (US$1). Expect heavy searches at the border, which closes at 6.30 pm.

Getting Around

AIR

In addition to its international flights, Air Burkina has flights several times a week between Ouagadougou and Bobo-Dioulasso.

BUS

Fares have remained static over the past few years, but they are still too high for many locals and all forms of transport except express buses take a long time to fill.

Examples of transport costs (buses) and travel times are shown below, together with some of the main bus companies servicing the routes. Buses are almost always cheaper than taxis.

TRAIN

You can travel between Ouagadougou and Bobo-Dioulasso on the Abidjan-bound express, which departs Ouagadougou on Tuesday, Thursday and Saturday at 8 am and arriving in Bobo around 3 pm (US$14/10 for 1st/2nd class). In the opposite direction, the train departs Bobo at 12.55 am on Tuesday, Thursday and Saturday mornings, arriving in Ouaga around 8 am. Service on the *Étalon*, which used to connect Bobo and Ouaga, has been discontinued.

There's also a train on Saturday between Ouagadougou and Kaya, leaving Ouaga at 8.20 am, arriving in Kaya about 9.45 am, and returning to Ouaga at 2.10 pm the same day (US$4/3 for 1st/2nd class).

CAR & MOTORCYCLE

All main roads to neighbouring countries are sealed and in good shape. Most secondary routes are dirt or mud. The road from Ouagadougou to Gorom-Gorom is paved as far as Kaya, unsealed but in decent condition to Dori, and rough from there onwards.

Cars can be rented at several hotels in Ouagadougou, including the RAN Hôtel and Hôtel de l'Indépendance. Rates are expensive, and many agencies require a driver for excursions outside the capital.

HITCHING

Hitching is not common in Burkina Faso, and you will probably have a long wait. Virtually all drivers expect payment. Also see Hitching in the Getting Around chapter.

Bus Routes & Fares				
From	*To*	*Distance*	*Duration*	*Fares (US$)*
Bobo-Dioulasso				
	Banfora	85km	1 hour	$2 (STMB)
Ouagadougou				
	Bobo-Dioulasso	355km	6 hours	$8 (STBF)
	Djibo	205km	5 hours	$7 (STMB, X9)
	Fada N'Gourma	220km	4 hours	$6 (X9)
	Gorom-Gorom	265km	8 hours	$8 (STMB, X9)
	Kaya	100km	2 hours	$3 (STMB, STGF)
	Ouahigouya	180km	3 hours	$4 (STBF, STGF, STMB)
	Pô	140km	3 hours	$4 (X9)

The Mossi & the Moro-Naba
The Mossi are famous for having the longest continuous royal dynasty in West Africa, dating back about 500 years to the founding of their empire at Ouagadougou. There were four Mossi kingdoms, each with its own king or *naba*. Strongly individualistic, they were one of the few peoples in the Sahel to successfully resist the Muslims, even sacking Timbuktu, a Muslim stronghold, at the height of its power in 1333.

The Moro-Naba of Ouagadougou is the emperor of the Mossi and the most powerful traditional chief in Burkina Faso. No order of his is ever disobeyed, and he's very well in with the government, which always consults him before adopting any major new policy or programme. Most Moro-Nabas have been imposing-looking persons, in part due to their ritual drinking of millet beer, and the present one, the 37th, is no exception. ■

Ouagadougou

Ouagadougou became the capital of the Mossi empire in 1441 and, 250 years later, was chosen as the permanent residence of the Moro-Naba, the Mossi king. The town grew up around the imperial palace and was extended during colonisation, with its more recent expansion largely fuelled by the country's rural exodus.

With its wide avenues and bicycle lanes, Ouagadougou has a relaxed atmosphere. Although there is not much by way of sights, it's a pleasant place to spend some time.

Information
The tourist office (☎ 306060) next to Hôtel de l'Indépendance, on the east side of Ave de la Résistance du 17 Mai, sometimes has maps of Ouagadougou for sale. A better bet is the Institut Géographique on the north side of Blvd de la Révolution near the Sûreté, which sells Ouaga maps (US$7) and country maps. The main post office is just west of Place des Nations Unies.

Things to See & Do
The **Musée National**, housed in the Maison du Peuple, has an interesting collection of masks. It's open Tuesday to Saturday from 9 am to 12.30 pm and 3 to 6 pm. Entry is US$1.

The **Grand Marché** is in the centre of town and there are some good craft stalls

upstairs. Another place for crafts is the **Centre Artisanal**, on Ave Dimdolobsom, where you can watch artists working with bronze, wood and pottery. Prices here are fixed and high; it's open Tuesday to Saturday from 8 am to noon and 3 to 6 pm, and Monday from 3 to 6 pm.

Special Events
Ouagadougou's Pan-African Film Festival, FESPACO, held in late February in odd-numbered years, is the major African film event and attracts international attention. Other cultural events take place simultaneously, including a craft market with products from all over the continent for sale.

Places to Stay
The dreary *Camping Ouaga* near the gare routière charges US$3 a person for camping or US$6 for a stuffy bungalow. To get there, catch bus No 3 from town to the gare routière, then follow the signs for 1km.

In town, *Fondation Charles Dufour* (☎ 303889) has a 15-bed dormitory and a few small rooms; all beds are US$4. The rooms are a bit grubby, but most beds have mosquito nets, and there's a kitchenette and secure parking. If it's full, you can sleep on a mattress on the floor or camp in the tiny garden (US$4).

Solo females may want to try the *mission catholique* (☎ 306490) which has spotless rooms with shared facilities for US$8. Men will have to make do with the more spartan

BURKINA FASO

PLACES TO STAY
3 Hôtel Le Pavillon Vert
9 RAN Hôtel
22 Hôtel de l'Independance
31 Hôtel Delwendé
42 Hôtel Idéal
46 Fondation Charles Dufour
49 Fraternité
49 Mission Catholique
50 Pension Guigsème
55 Hôtel de la Paix

PLACES TO EAT
15 La Fontaine Bleue
16 Le Verdoyant
27 L'Eau Vive
37 Sindabad's; Ciné Burkina
38 Marina Supermarket

43 Chez Awa; Restaurant Riale
44 Café Salif
51 Nabonswende

OTHER
1 Ghanaian Embassy
2 Nigerian Embassy
4 STMB Buses
5 Ministry of Tourism Secretariat/ Photography Permits
6 Train Station
7 X9 Buses
8 Camp Militaire
10 Air France
11 Musée National; Maison du Peuple
12 ONATEL Telecom
13 Post Office

14 Centre Artisanal
17 Sûreté
18 Institut Géographique
19 Palais Présidentiel; Ministries
20 French Embassy & Consulate
21 Tourist Office
23 FESPACO
24 Place des Nations Unies
25 Gare Routière; Total Station
26 Wassa Club
28 Place du 2 Octobre
29 BCEAO Bank
30 Faso Tours
32 BIB Bank
33 Grand Marché

34 Canadian Embassy; Danish Embassy
35 US Embassy
36 BICIA Bank
39 Grande Mosquée
40 Palladium Nightclub
41 STC Booking Office
45 Cemetery
48 Cathedral
52 Jimmy's Discoteque; Maquis Pili Pili
53 Taxi-Brousse Bar
54 Mosque
56 Moro-Naba Palace
57 BFCI/Sans Frontières Buses
58 Sahel's Nightclub
59 Airport

accommodation at the nearby *Fraternité*, where rooms start at US$8.

On Ave Yennenga are several seedy but cheap hotels. *Hôtel de la Paix* (☎ 335283) has acceptable singles/doubles for US$8/10 (US$13/14 for air-con with attached bathroom). Just up the street is *Pension Guigséme* with basic rooms for US$6; this place is not for lone women. *Hôtel Idéal* (☎ 306502) has ventilated singles/doubles for US$11/13, plus a restaurant and a nice porch.

The best lower-range hotel in the centre is *Hôtel Delwendé* (☎ 308757) which has clean singles/doubles for US$13/16 (US$16/19 with air-con). There's a pleasant terrace overlooking the street and a restaurant with meals for under US$4.

On the outskirts of town, the mellow *Hôtel Le Pavillon Vert* (☎ 310611) attracts a lot of travellers. Large, airy singles/doubles with fan and shared facilities cost from US$8/10 (US$26/27 for air-con and attached bathroom), and the outdoor restaurant serves a variety of dishes from US$3.

Places to Eat

There are many inexpensive street stalls near Ave Yennenga and Ave Loudun. *Riale* serves chicken & chips for US$2. The friendly *Chez Awa* is even cheaper. Nearby is the tidy *Café Salif* with fwa and other dishes for US$1. *Nabonswende* sells yoghurt and spiced meat sandwiches.

In the city centre behind the Ciné Burkina building, *Sindabad's* has Lebanese dishes for under US$2.

For more upmarket dining, try the pleasant *Le Verdoyant* (closed Wednesday) on the east side of Ave Dimdolobsom, which has good pizza and other dishes from US$7, though service is slow. Nearby, *La Fontaine Bleue* has an attractive outdoor setting and serves delectable but pricey continental and African cuisine.

For something out of the ordinary, try *L'Eau Vive* on the north side of Rue du Marché (closed Sunday). It's run by an order of nuns and has very good continental cuisine from US$7.

Entertainment

Ouagadougou has a plethora of nightclubs. One of the liveliest places is *Sahel's* which has drumming and live reggae music every night (no cover charge). It's best to go in a group, as the surrounding area is not well lit.

The strip near *Jimmy's Discoteque* is better lit and hopping on most evenings. Jimmy's is expensive (US$5 cover). However, *Maquis Pili-Pili* next door has cheap food and live blues music on weekends. Across the street, *Taxi-Brousse* has outdoor tables where you can watch the scene on the street for free.

Closer to the centre, *Palladium* features live music and has a large dance floor as well as good brochettes and street food (US$1 cover). *Wassa Club*, also central, is open until 1 am and sometimes has live music (US$1 cover on weekends).

Non-guests can use the swimming pools at the RAN Hôtel and Hôtel de l'Indépendance for US$2.

Getting There & Away

The main gare routière for bush taxis and minibuses to destinations throughout Burkina Faso is 4km south of the centre, near the airport. Take a share-taxi (US$0.50) or bus No 3 (US$0.35) which runs along Ave Bassawarga. Minibuses to the borders of Togo, Benin and Côte d'Ivoire also leave in the morning from the gare routière at the Total station near the Wassa Club.

The X9 bus depot is on Ave Yatenga; there are frequent services to Bobo-Dioulasso, fewer to the rest of the country. STMB, STBF and BFCI/Sans Frontières also have buses to Bobo and other destinations. Buses to Kaya and on to Dori, and buses to Ouahigouya depart from the south-east corner of the railway station. Faso Tours buses leave from the Faso Tours office west of the Grand Marché on the north side of Rue Patrice Lumumba.

For information on train services to and from Ouagadougou, see the information under Côte d'Ivoire in the main Getting There & Away section of this chapter, and see Train in the main Getting Around section.

Getting Around

Share-taxis around town cost US$0.40 for a short ride. Private taxis charge at least US$1. To the airport, the fare is US$3; metered taxis (orange) are more expensive.

There are several bus lines running through the city. Destinations and stops are clearly marked; most routes cross Ave Nelson Mandela at some point. The base fare is US$0.20.

Around the Country

BANFORA

Banfora is a quiet town in a beautiful area, excellent for exploring on bicycle. The pretty **Cascades de Karfiguéla**, 12km north-west of town, are worth a look at any time, but are best in the rainy season. The **Dômes de Fabedougou**, an escarpment-type formation not far from the cascades, is good for rock climbing. Ask at your hotel or local repair shops for bicycle and motorcycle rental.

Ten kilometres west of Banfora is **Lake Tengrela** which has hippo and interesting birdlife. A trip in a *pirogue* (dugout canoe) costs US$2.

About 40km from Lake Tengrela is the town of **Douna** which is close to the interesting **Peaks of Sindou** and villages reminiscent of those in Mali's Dogon region. To get there, you'll need to hire a motorcycle or private car.

Places to Stay & Eat

The best value hotel is *Hôtel Le Comoé* (☎ 880151) at the southern edge of town. It has a shady courtyard, a restaurant with meals from US$3 and ventilated rooms from US$9 (US$13 with attached bathroom and US$21 for air-con).

Hôtel Fara (☎ 880117) isn't as good but is much more central, just behind the gare routière. Singles/doubles cost from US$14/15 (US$18/21 with attached bathroom). The luxurious *La Canne à Sucre* (☎ 880107) has air-conditioned singles/doubles for US$28/32 and an expensive garden bar and restau-

rant. Jean, the French owner, has maps and lots of information about the surrounding countryside.

Café Djana serves good meals under a large *paillotte* (thatched awning) from US$3.

Getting There & Away

STMB has daily connections to Bobo (US$2) and Ouagadougou (US$9) and goes at least three times a week to Gorom-Gorom (US$18), Ouahigouya (US$13) and Djibo (US$16). Sotocof and Rakieta also have frequent connections to Bobo. All three companies have stations near the market. Minibuses and taxis leave from the gare routière north of the centre.

BOBO-DIOULASSO

Bobo, as it is more commonly known, is Burkina Faso's second largest city. It's a pleasant, relaxing place and many travellers spend time here. During the last week of April in even-numbered years, Bobo hosts a national culture festival with many music, dance and theatre performances.

A word of warning: you stand a good chance of being mugged if you walk by the river. Don't trust 'guides' who offer to take you.

Information

BIB bank changes US$ and French franc travellers' cheques, but charges commission and requires proof of purchase. Poste restante in Bobo charges US$1 per collected letter. Librairie Socifa (bookshop) sometimes has maps of Burkina Faso in stock.

Things to See

Bobo's **Grande Mosquée** is a beautiful example of Sahelian architecture and the No 1 sight in town. The **Grand Marché** has some good bargains including beads and carvings.

Bobo's small but interesting **Musée Provincial** has a display of regional artwork and full-scale examples of traditional buildings. It's open Tuesday to Sunday from 8.30 am to noon and 3.30 to 6 pm. Entry costs US$1.

The **old city quarter** (*vieux quartier* or Kibidwé district), a fascinating maze of alleyways, adobe houses and artisans' shops, is a great place to wander. Crafts are also cheaper in this section. If you're lucky, you may see the **Fête des Masques**, which takes place here seven times a year and involves spirited dancing late into the night by men covered in colourful feathers and wearing wooden masks.

Places to Stay

The best value is the clean and friendly *Le Pacha* (☎ 980954), 3km west of the centre near the gare routière. Spotless rooms with mosquito net are US$7 (from US$8 with fan and US$20 for attached bathroom and aircon). Camping in the enclosed compound is US$2 per person including use of shared facilities. The pleasant but pricey garden restaurant (closed Tuesday) has meals from US$5.

Another good place for camping is *Casafrica* (☎ 980157) which charges US$3 per person. It has decent ventilated singles/doubles with mosquito net for US$8/10 and a restaurant with brochettes and other meals from US$3. A taxi from the centre costs US$0.40.

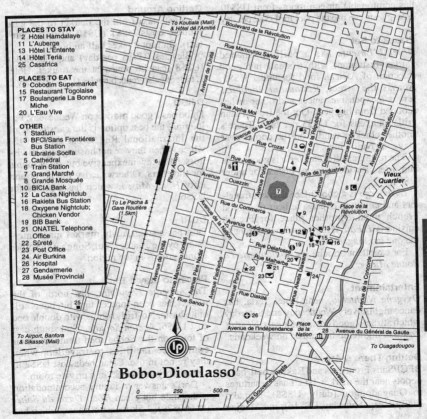

PLACES TO STAY
2 Hôtel Hamdalaye
11 L'Auberge
13 Hôtel L'Entente
14 Hôtel Teria
25 Casafrica

PLACES TO EAT
9 Cobodim Supermarket
15 Restaurant Togolaise
17 Boulangerie La Bonne Miche
20 L'Eau Vive

OTHER
1 Stadium
3 BFCI/Sans Frontières Bus Station
4 Librairie Socifa
5 Cathedral
6 Train Station
7 Grand Marché
8 Grande Mosquée
10 BICIA Bank
12 La Casa Nightclub
16 Rakieta Bus Station
18 Oxygene Nightclub; Chicken Vendor
19 BIB Bank
21 ONATEL Telephone Office
22 Sûreté
23 Post Office
24 Air Burkina
26 Hospital
27 Gendarmerie
28 Musée Provincial

Bobo-Dioulasso

0   250   500 m

To Koutiala (Mali) & Hôtel de l'Amitié
Boulevard de la Révolution
Rue Mamourou Sanou
Avenue de l'Unité
Rue Alpha Moi
Avenue de la Liberté
Rue Crozat
Rue Joffre
Avenue Ponty
Avenue Ouezzin
Rue du Commerce
Avenue de la Nation
Avenue Ouédraogo
Rue Delafosse
Rue Malherbe
Rue Diakité
Avenue de l'Indépendance
Rue Sanou
Avenue Mamourou Konaté
Avenue Père Nadal
Avenue Faidherbe
Avenue de l'Unité
Rue de l'Industrie
Coulibaly
Place de la Révolution
Vieux Quartier
Avenue Birger
Avenue de la République
Avenue Diawara
Avenue de la Révolution
Avenue Awata Diawara
Avenue de la Concorde
Place de la Nation
Avenue du Général de Gaulle
To Ouagadougou
Place Amoro
To Le Pacha & Gare Routière (1.5km)
To Airport, Banfora & Sikasso (Mali)
Ave Gouverneur Résta
Ave Louveau

BURKINA FASO

In the heart of town, the popular *Hôtel L'Entente* (☎ 971205) has large ventilated singles/doubles for US$9/11 (US$20/21 for attached bathroom and air-con), while *Hôtel Teria* (☎ 971972) charges US$10/11 for singles/doubles with attached bathroom and mosquito net (US$17/19 with air-con).

Hôtel Hamdalaye (☎ 982287) is in a busy area, but its ventilated rooms with attached bathroom are excellent value at US$9/11 (US$7/9 for shared bath, and US$16 for air-con). Hamdalaye's restaurant has meals from US$5.

For luxury, head to *L'Auberge* (☎ 971767) on the north side of Ave Ouédraogo, which has comfortable air-con rooms from US$40. Non-guests can use the pool for US$2 per day.

Places to Eat

Hôtel L'Entente has a paillotte-shaded garden restaurant with a small but good selection of African food for under US$5. Across the street, *Restaurant Togolaise* serves inexpensive sauces and other dishes scooped from big pots. Out the front a man grills chickens for US$3 per bird. There's another chicken vendor on the corner near Oxygene Nightclub.

The restaurant at *Hôtel Teria* is good value and offers a wide range of dishes for under US$4.

L'Auberge is a good place to meet travellers and enjoy an expensive beer or a good French meal. Another place for French cuisine is *L'Eau Vive*, a sister restaurant to the one in Ouagadougou.

For excellent brioche try *Boulangerie La Bonne Miche*.

Entertainment

Oxygene Nightclub, near Hôtel Teria, has dance nights every Wednesday and Saturday which attract a good crowd of locals. Nearby, *La Casa* nightclub has music on weekends.

Getting There & Away

BFCI/Sans Frontières and Rakieta both have depots near the market. BFCI has departures to Ouagadougou (daily, US$8), Bamako (daily except Saturday, US$16), and Abidjan (daily, US$24). Buy tickets well in advance. Rakieta has several departures daily for Banfora (US$2) and Ouagadougou (US$8).

Minibuses and bush taxis congregate at the gare routière west of town, although it seems that very few of these actually leave. With luck, there are daily departures for Ouagadougou (US$8), Bamako (US$16), Ferkessédougou (US$12), Yamoussoukro (US$20) and Abidjan (US$24).

For information on train services between Bobo-Dioulasso and Ouagadougou, see Train in the main Getting Around section of this chapter.

Getting Around

A private taxi from the market to the gare routière costs US$1 (US$0.40 in a share-taxi). On foot it takes half an hour.

Bicycles (US$5 per day) and mobylettes (US$8) can be rented at the market. Hôtel L'Entente also rents bicycles (US$5 per day).

DJIBO

Djibo has a good **market** on Wednesday. For lodging, the best option is the *guesthouse* of the International Red Cross (☎ 551013) which, when they're not hosting official visitors, has a few inexpensive but clean rooms for travellers. Otherwise, try the noisy and dirty *Hôtel Massa*, which has doubles for US$6.

DORI

Dori has a small, daily **market** made interesting by the Tuareg, Peul, Songhaï and other ethnic groups in the region.

Places to Stay & Eat

The *Auberge Populaire*, just north of the market, has been spruced up a bit, but is still quite basic. No-frills rooms with double bed cost US$6. *Accion Sociale*, 2km south-east of town on the Sebba road, rents out their conference facilities to travellers when they're not in use. Clean beds cost US$2 in a dormitory and US$3 in a private room.

Dori's answer to luxury accommodation is the stale but clean *Hôtel Oasis du Sahel* (☎ 660329), 1.5km east of town, which has ventilated singles/doubles in converted trailers for US$15/19 (US$19/29 with air-con which cuts off at midnight), and an acceptable restaurant.

FADA N'GOURMA

Fada is a convenient overnight stop for those travelling to/from Niger or Benin. Taxis in all directions take a long time to fill up; for Benin, you may have to wait several days. For more details on getting to Fada, see Benin in this chapter's Getting There & Away section and Bus in this chapter's Getting Around section.

Places to Stay & Eat

The best place to stay is the *Auberge* opposite the market. Basic singles/doubles with fan are US$10/11 (US$12/14 with air-con). The outdoor bar/restaurant is the most popular eatery in town, with meals from US$3.

Auberge Liberté, opposite the gare routière, is much worse. Filthy singles/doubles with revolting communal toilets are US$7/14.

Just up from the Auberge at the intersection with the main road, there's a *coffee stand* with yoghurt and minced-meat sandwiches. *Restaurant de la Paix*, next to the Auberge, has standard fare for US$3.

GOROM-GOROM

Gorom-Gorom has one of the best **markets** in Burkina Faso on Thursday. About 40km north-west are the shifting **sand dunes** of Oursi. Transport is scarce in these parts, and the road from Kaya is often washed out for several weeks during the rainy season.

Places to Stay & Eat

The grubby *Auberge Populaire* has rooms for US$6. There is neither electricity nor running water. The only other option is the declining but comparatively luxurious *Le Campement Hôtelier* (☎ 660144), which has singles/doubles for US$12/13 (US$4 per person for camping). There's water, but no electricity, and mediocre, overpriced meals.

Getting There & Away

The best connections from Ouagadougou are with STMB (Monday, Wednesday and Friday at 7.30 am, US$8); X9 also departs three times a week from Ouagadougou. From Banfora, there is a direct STMB bus at least three times a week (US$18). A minibus from Dori costs US$3. Service to Gorom-Gorom is frequently interrupted during the rainy season.

KOUDOUGOU

Koudougou, the country's third largest city, has no real attractions. However, the surrounding region is worth exploring for its friendly people and many picturesque villages, such as **Goundi**, 8km away. At **Sabou**, the junction with the main road to Bobo-Dioulasso, is a lake inhabited by supposedly 'sacred' crocodiles – on the shores lurk touts and guides.

Places to Stay & Eat

In the heart of town across from the Total station, *Hôtel Yeleba II* has grungy rooms for US$8. *Hôtel Relais de la Gare* (☎ 440138), just up from the train station, has basic ventilated rooms for US$9. The upmarket *Hôtel Photo Luxe* (☎ 440087) at the eastern end of town has spotless rooms with fan and private bath from US$12 (US$19 for an air-con double), and a restaurant with meals for US$4.

For cheap eats, try *Chez Tanti* near the train station, or the *brochette stand* next to Hôtel Relais de la Gare.

OUAHIGOUYA

If you're heading for Dogon country in Mali, the most direct route from Ouagadougou is through Ouahigouya, Burkina Faso's fourth largest city. North-west of town, on the Mali road, *L'Amitié* (☎ 550521) has clean, ventilated doubles from US$9/18 fan/air-con (same-sex couples pay a US$4 surcharge), and meals for US$6. The bar next door can be noisy. Another option is *Hôtel Dunia* (☎ 550595), near the hospital, which has rooms for US$12/30, including fan/air-con and attached bathroom.

National Parks & Reserves

Burkina Faso has several national parks and reserves, most of which are accessible only with your own vehicle.

A permit costs US$20 (US$10 for residents of Burkina Faso) and is valid for unlimited entries to any of the parks for one tourist season (which is 15 December to 31 May).

Without private transport, your best bet is to head to **Parc National des Deux Bales**, halfway between Ouaga and Bobo near Boromo. Although the main section of the park is 120km from Boromo, there are several areas within 10km of Boromo where elephant sightings are common.

The only place to stay in Boromo is the *Relais Touristique* (☎ 440684) which charges US$7/9 for singles/doubles. The staff are very helpful and will assist in arranging a park permit, hiring a guide, and renting a motorcycle to visit the areas nearby.

Burundi

Burundi is a small and beautiful mountainous country. Sandwiched between Tanzania, Rwanda and Congo (Zaïre), it has magnificent views over Lake Tanganyika.

Burundi has had a stormy history of tribal wars and factional struggles between the ruling families. This has been further complicated in recent times by colonisation, first by the Germans and later by the Belgians. Intertribal tensions have been a problem in recent times, but never more so than the present – the situation looks very bleak indeed and the country is not safe to visit.

Burundi is one of the most densely populated countries in the world, with 230 people per sq km. Despite this, there are very few urban centres. The only towns of any size are the capital, Bujumbura, and Gitega.

Facts about the Country

HISTORY
The original inhabitants of the area were the Twa Pygmies, who now comprise only 1% of the population. They were gradually displaced from about 1000 AD onwards by Hutu, mostly farmers of Bantu stock, who now make up 85% of the population.

In the 16th and 17th centuries, the country experienced another wave of migration. This time it was the tall, pastoral Tutsi from Ethiopia and Uganda, who now make up 14% of

REPUBLIC OF BURUNDI
Area: 27,835 sq km
Population: 6.4 million
Population Growth Rate: 3%
Capital: Bujumbura
Head of State: President Pierre Buyoya
Official Languages: Kirundi, French
Currency: Burundi franc
Exchange Rate: BFr 316 = US$1
Per Capita GNP: US$190
Inflation: 20%
Time: GMT/UTC + 2

Highlights
- Cultural exhibits in Bujumbura
- Chutes de la Kagera, spectacular in the wet season
- Kibabi Hot Springs near Kilemba

the population. The Tutsi gradually subjugated the Hutu in a type of feudal system, similar to that of medieval Europe. The Tutsi became a loosely organised aristocracy with a *mwami* (king) at the top of each social pyramid. Under this system the Hutu relinquished their land and mortgaged their services to the nobility in return for cattle – the symbol of wealth and status in Burundi.

At the end of the 19th century, Burundi and Rwanda were colonised by Germany. However, they were so thinly garrisoned that the Belgians were easily able to oust the German forces during WWI. After the war,

BURUNDI

the League of Nations mandated Burundi (then known as Urundi) and Rwanda to Belgium.

Taking advantage of the feudal structure, the Belgians ruled indirectly through the Tutsi chiefs and princes, granting them wide-ranging powers to recruit labour and raise taxes. The Tutsi were not averse to abusing these powers whenever it suited them.

The establishment of coffee plantations and the resulting concentration of wealth in the hands of the Tutsi urban elite further exacerbated tensions between the two tribal groups.

In the 1950s, a nationalist organisation based on unity between the tribes was founded under the leadership of the mwami's eldest son, Prince Rwagasore. But in the run-up to independence he was assassinated with the connivance of the colonial authorities, who feared their commercial interests would be threatened if he came to power.

Despite this setback, challenges were raised to the concentration of power in Tutsi hands when independence was granted in 1962. It appeared that the country was headed for a majority government. This had already happened in neighbouring Rwanda, where a similar tribal imbalance existed.

Yet in the 1964 elections, even though Hutu candidates attracted a majority of votes, Mwami Mwambutsa refused to appoint a Hutu prime minister. Hutu frustration boiled over a year later in an attempted coup staged by Hutu military officers and political figures. Though the attempt failed, it led to the flight of the mwami into exile in Switzerland. He was replaced by a Tutsi military junta. A wholesale purge of Hutu from the army and the bureaucracy followed, but in 1972 another large-scale revolt saw more than 1000 Tutsi killed.

The military junta responded to this challenge with what amounted to selective genocide. Any Hutu with wealth, a formal education or a government job was rooted

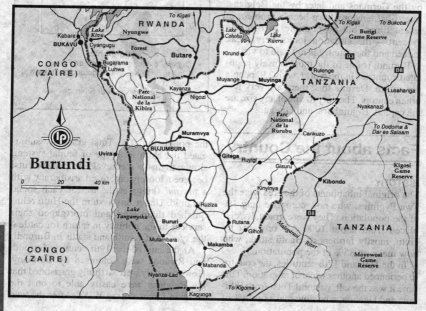

out and murdered, often in the most horrifying way. After three months, 200,000 Hutu had been killed and 100,000 had fled to Tanzania, Rwanda and Congo (Zaïre). Neither the Christian missions inside the country nor the international community raised any protest against this carnage.

In 1976 Jean-Baptiste Bagaza came to power in a bloodless coup, and in 1979 he formed the Union pour le Progrès National (UPRONA), ruling with a central committee and small politburo. As part of a so-called democratisation programme, elections in 1982 saw candidates (mostly Tutsi and all approved by UPRONA) voted into the National Assembly. The elections gave the Hutu a modicum of power in the National Assembly, but it was limited.

During the Bagaza years, there were some half-hearted attempts by the government to remove some of the main causes of intertribal conflict, but these were mostly cosmetic.

In 1985 the government tried to lessen the influence of the Catholic Church, which it believed was sympathetic to the Hutu majority. Its fears of a church-organised Hutu revolt were heightened by the fact that Hutus were in power in neighbouring Rwanda. Priests were put on trial and some missionaries were expelled from the country.

Bagaza was toppled in September 1987 in a coup led by his cousin, Major Pierre Buyoya. This regime improved relations between the government, on one side, and the Catholic Church and international aid agencies on the other. It also attempted to address the causes of intertribal tensions yet again by gradually bringing Hutu representatives back into positions of power in the government. However, there was a renewed outbreak of intertribal violence in the north of the country in August 1988. Between 4000 and 24,000 people were massacred and thousands more fled into neighbouring Rwanda.

Then, in 1992, Buyoya finally bowed to international pressure and announced that multiparty elections would be held the following year. For a time, it seemed that sense and reason might prevail over the endless cycle of bloodletting which had scarred the country's history. However, it was not to be.

Elections held in June 1993 brought a Hutu-dominated government to power, headed by Melchior Ndadaye (also a Hutu). However, a dissident army faction, led by Colonel Sylvestre Ningaba, staged a bloody coup in late October the same year, and assassinated the president. The coup failed when army generals disowned the plotters, but, in the chaos which followed the assassination, thousands of people were massacred in intertribal fighting and an estimated 400,000 refugees fled across the border into neighbouring Rwanda. Surviving members of the government, who had holed up in the French embassy in Bujumbura, were able to reassert some degree of control several days later with the help of loyal troops.

In April 1994 President Ntaryamira was killed in the same plane crash that killed Rwanda's President Habyarimana, sparking the diabolical massacres there. Sylvestre Ntibantunganya was immediately appointed as the interim president. Nevertheless, both Hutu militias and the Tutsi-dominated army passed up no opportunity to go on the offensive. No war was actually declared but at least 100,000 people were killed in these clashes between mid-1994 and mid-1996, most of them in counter-reprisals.

In July 1996, Buyoya, the former president, carried out a successful coup and took over as the country's president with the support of the army. It's too early to say what will happen but it doesn't look good.

GEOGRAPHY & CLIMATE

Burundi occupies a mountainous 27,835 sq km. The capital, Bujumbura, is on the northern tip of Lake Tanganyika.

Burundi has a variable climate. The lower land around Lake Tanganyika is hot and humid, with temperatures around 30°C. In the more mountainous north, the average temperature is around 20°C. The rainy season lasts from October to May, with a brief dry spell in December and January.

POPULATION & PEOPLE

The population of 6.4 million is about 14% Tutsi, 85% Hutu, and 1% Twa Pygmies.

LANGUAGE

The official languages are Kirundi and French; Swahili is also useful. Hardly anyone speaks English. See the Language Appendix for useful French and Swahili phrases.

Facts for the Visitor

VISAS

Visas are required by all visitors to Burundi. Transit visas cost US$10 and a one month tourist visa costs US$20. You will need two photos and can generally get your visa the day you apply, if you apply early enough.

There's no extra charge for requesting a multiple-entry visa, so if there's any chance you will need this, get it now rather than later.

Tourist visas can be extended at the immigration office in Bujumbura. Extensions cost US$5 per month and take 24 hours to issue. Apply early in the morning, as it's very busy in the afternoon.

For some reason, certain Burundi embassies (including Nairobi in Kenya) will not issue visas, telling you to get them at the border. The Burundi embassies in Kampala and Kigali will only issue visas to residents.

Other Visas

Visas for the following neighbouring countries can be obtained in Burundi:

Congo (Zaïre)
  Visa costs are the same as in other countries (see the Congo (Zaïre) chapter for details), three photos are required and the visa is issued in 24 hours.
Rwanda
  A one month multiple-entry visa costs US$30, requires two photos and is issued in 24 hours.
Tanzania
  Visas require two photographs and are issued in 24 hours. Costs vary according to your nationality (see the Tanzania Facts for the Visitor section for details).

EMBASSIES

Burundi Embassies

There are Burundi embassies in Algeria, Egypt, Ethiopia, Kenya, Libya, Tanzania (Dar es Salaam and Kigoma), Uganda and Congo (Zaïre) (Kinshasa and Bukavu).

Outside Africa, there are Burundi embassies in Belgium, Canada, France, Germany, Russia, Switzerland and the USA.

Foreign Embassies in Burundi

Foreign embassies in Bujumbura include:

Rwanda
    24 Ave du Zaïre (☎ 26 865)
Tanzania
    Ave de l'ONU
Congo (Zaïre)
    Ave du Zaïre
USA
    BP 34, 1720 Bujumbura (☎ 223 454)

MONEY

US$1 = BFr 316

The unit of currency, the Burundi franc (BFr), is divided into 100 centimes, though you're unlikely to come across these.

The exchange value of the Burundi franc fluctuates according to the international currency market, particularly the value of the US dollar and the French franc, and devaluations are not uncommon.

Commission rates for changing travellers' cheques are bad news at most banks – some charge up to 7%! The Banque de la République du Burundi is the best place to exchange. Banking hours are Monday to Friday from 8 to 11.30 am. Outside these hours, you can change travellers' cheques at one of the large hotels in Bujumbura (eg Novotel, on Chaussée du Peuple Burundi).

There's a relatively open black market in Bujumbura. For currencies other than the US dollar, stick with the bank.

Tanzanian shillings can also be bought here, which is handy if you're heading for Kigoma, but the rate is not that good. The nearest Tanzanian banks are in Kigoma.

POST & COMMUNICATIONS

The postal service is reasonably efficient, but poste restante at the main post office (PTT) in Bujumbura is poorly organised.

Rates for international telephone calls are extremely high; however, connections from the main post office in Bujumbura take no more than a few minutes.

The country code for Burundi is 257. There are no telephone area codes within Burundi.

HEALTH

You should take precautions against malaria in Burundi. You should also avoid bathing in Lake Tanganyika, where there is reedy vegetation, due to the risk of bilharzia. See the Health Appendix for other health information.

PUBLIC HOLIDAYS

Public holidays include: 1 January, 5 February, 1 May, 1 July, 15 August, 3 September, 13 October, 1 November, 25 December and Easter Monday.

Getting There & Away

AIR

International airlines servicing Burundi include Aeroflot, Air Burundi, Air France, Air Tanzania, Air Zaïre, Cameroon Airlines, Ethiopian Airlines, Kenya Airways and Sabena.

LAND
Rwanda

There is a choice of two routes. Which one you take will depend on whether you want to go from Bujumbura to Butare and Kigali direct, or via Cyangugu (Lake Kivu).

The Bujumbura to Butare route is the more direct, but you are seriously warned not to take it as the northern section of Burundi is out of control of the central government and it's a dangerous area.

From Bujumbura to Cyangugu, take a taxi to the Congo (Zaïre)/Burundi border, cross to Uvira, take a minibus to Bukavu and cross into Rwanda to arrive at Cyangugu. The road between Uvira and Bukavu goes back into Rwanda part of the way (but not through Cyangugu) before re-entering Congo (Zaïre) so you'll need a multiple-entry Rwandan visa and a multiple-entry Zaïrese visa. Rwandan transit visas are available at the border if you don't have a multiple-entry visa. The security situation in Eastern Congo (Zaïre) means that this route is also highly doubtful.

Congo (Zaïre)

From Bujumbura to Bukavu, the route is identical to the route described above for getting to Cyangugu via Uvira.

LAKE
Tanzania & Zambia

The two routes available both use Lake Tanganyika at different points. A direct route is to Kigoma on the venerable MV *Liemba*. However, a more interesting route, using lake taxi and minibus, is via Nyanza-Lac and Gombe Stream National Park (the chimpanzee sanctuary across the border in Tanzania).

Ferry The MV *Liemba* connects Burundi with Tanzania and Zambia, although services to/from Burundi may be cancelled due to the disturbances there.

The schedule for the MV *Liemba* is more or less regular but the ferry can be delayed for up to 24 hours at either end, depending on how much cargo there is to load or unload.

Officially, the MV *Liemba* departs once a week from Bujumbura, on Monday at about 6 pm, and arrives in Kigoma (Tanzania) on Tuesday at 8 am. See the Tanzania Getting There & Away section for details of life on board this fine old vessel.

The fares on the MV *Liemba* from Bujumbura to Tanzania and Zambia (in US dollars) are:

Port	1st class	2nd class	3rd class
Kigoma	$19	$15	$12
Mpulungu	$78	$62	$48

In addition, port fees of US$2 are payable upon boarding in Bujumbura. Tickets for the ferry can be bought from SONACO, Rue des Usines (off Blvd du 1er Novembre), Bujumbura, on Monday morning from 8 am. Tickets must be paid for in US dollars; local currency is not acceptable.

To save money when going all the way from Bujumbura to Mpulungu, buy a ticket to Kigoma, then once the boat docks, get off, immediately make a reservation for a 1st or 2nd class cabin and change money into Tanzanian shillings. Pay for your ticket the following morning at 8 am using the shillings you changed. This will save you approximately US$35/26 on 1st/2nd class tickets.

Lake Taxi & Minibus The alternative to the MV *Liemba* is to travel partly by minibus and partly by lake taxi between Bujumbura and Kigoma, via the Tanzanian border village of Kagunga and the Gombe Stream National Park.

From Bujumbura, minibuses go daily to Nyanza-Lac (US$4). You must go through immigration here; the office is about 1km from the town centre towards the lake. After that you take a minibus (US$1) to the Burundi border post. From this post to the Tanzanian border post at Kagunga, it's a 2km walk along a narrow track. From Kagunga, there are lake taxis to Kigoma (actually to Kalalangabo, about 3km north of Kigoma), which cost US$2, leave some time before dawn and take most of the day. The taxis call at Gombe Stream (about halfway), where you can get off if you like. The fare to Gombe Stream is US$1, as is the fare from there to Kigoma.

Getting Around

MINIBUS
To get around, there are modern, Japanese-made minibuses, not overcrowded and cheaper than share-taxis. They are not that frequent, however, since the troubles started in 1994 because some three-quarters of the owners, who were Rwandans, have decamped and gone back to Kigali. You can usually find one heading in your direction any day between early morning and early afternoon at the *gare routière* (bus station) in any town or city.

Bujumbura

Sprawling up the mountainside on the north-eastern tip of Lake Tanganyika, Bujumbura overlooks the vast wall of mountains on the other side of the lake in Congo (Zaïre). The Burundi capital is a mixture of grandiose colonial town planning (wide boulevards and imposing public buildings) and dusty crowded suburbs like those which surround many African cities.

More English is spoken here than in most parts of Rwanda or Eastern Congo (Zaïre). Also noteworthy is the height of many of the people – they are Tutsi and they're huge!

Bujumbura has a slightly sleazy atmosphere and is certainly not the friendliest place in the world. You are advised not to walk along Ave de la Plage between the Cercle Nautique and the port, even during the day, as there have been reports of muggings. Rue des Swahilis, in the same area, should also be avoided. You're also advised to avoid the Buyenzi and Mbwiza areas of town as there's a constant vendetta between the army and Hutu militias in those areas.

Information
The tourist office is on Blvd de l'UPRONA, but the information available is limited.

The main post office is in the city centre, on the corner of Blvd Lumumba and Ave du Commerce. The international telephone service is housed in the same building.

Things to See
The **Musée Vivant** is a reconstructed traditional Burundian village with basketware, pottery, drum and photographic displays. Occasionally there are traditional drum shows. Entry costs US$0.50.

PLACES TO STAY
1 Hôtel Albatross
6 Novotel
8 Hôtel Burundi Palace;
  Acapulco
16 Hôtel Résidence
23 New Tourist Hôtel

PLACES TO EAT
9 Aux Délices Restaurant
11 Boulangerie-Pâtisserie
  Trianon; Alliance
  Française
13 Restaurant Pizza Oasis
26 Cercle Nautique

OTHER
2 BP & FINA Stations
3 SONACO
4 Stadium

5 Tourist Office
7 Air Tanzania
10 American Cultural Center
12 Ethiopian Airlines
14 Tanzanian Embassy
15 Congo (Zaïre) & Rwandan
  Embassies
17 Banque Commerciale du
  Burundi; US Embassy
18 Market; Minibuses
19 Post Office
20 Banque du Crédit de
  Bujumbura; Sabena
21 Banque de la République
  du Burundi
22 Aeroflot
24 Islamic Cultural Centre;
  Mosque
25 Musée Vivant;
  Parc des Reptiles

To Butare
& Kigali

Ave de la Jeunesse

Buyenzi

Mbwiza

Avenue de l'Hôpital

Avenue de l'Université

To Airport, Uvira & Bukavu

Rue du Marais

Boulevard du Port

Rue des Usines

Boulevard du 1er Novembre

Avenue du Stade

Chaussée du Peuple Burundi

Boulevard de l'UPRONA

Avenue Victoire

Mission

Rue de l'Amitié

Avenue du Zaïre

Avenue France

Chaussée Prince Rwagasore

Avenue du Marché

Avenue des Pêcheurs

Place de
l'Indépendance

Rue de Tanganyika

Rue de l'Imbo

Rue des Swahills

Avenue de la Plage

Lake Tanganyika

Avenue du Commerce

Rue
Industrie

Avenue des Paysans

Ntahangwa

Rue
Science

Avenue de Révolution

Boulevard Lumumba

Avenue du Marché

Avenue de l'Enseignement

Avenue du 18 Septembre

Avenue du 13 Octobre

Rue Gouvernement

Rue Eucalypt

Boulevard de la Liberté

Avenue Pierre Ngendandumwe

Boulevard de Yaranda

Boulevard du 28 Novembre

Bujumbura

0   100   200 m

BURUNDI

Adjacent to the Musée Vivant is the **Parc des Reptiles**, which exhibits just what you might expect. Entry costs US$2.

Opposite the reptile park, the **Musée de Géologie du Burundi** is dusty and run-down but has a good collection of fossils. Entry is free.

The **Islamic Cultural Centre** and mosque is a beautiful building near the main square. Paid for by the Libyan government, it is well worth visiting.

Places to Stay

It can be difficult to find a reasonably priced place to stay in Bujumbura. The main reason for this is the continual clashes between the army and those opposed to the government or, on a more basic level, intertribal clashes between the Tutsi and Hutu. It's a dangerous place to be. Gunfire and violent house searches are common occurrences especially at night. As a result, most of the budget hotels have been closed for several years now. This is particularly true of the suburb of Mbwiza, about 10 minutes walk north-east of the city centre, where many of them used to be found. One that is still operating is the *Hôtel Albatross*, on the corner of Chaussé du Peuple Burundi and Ave de la Jeunesse. It's very reasonably priced.

The *Hôtel Résidence* (☎ 23 886) is close to the city centre and has a variety of rooms, ranging from US$10.

The cheapest place to stay in the city centre is the *Hôtel Burundi Palace*, which has singles/doubles for US$10/15.

Places to Eat

One of the best places in town for breakfast is *Kappa*, Rue Science, which is extremely popular with local office workers between 8 and 9 am. It also has the best strawberry cakes 'on earth', according to a long-time resident.

A good place for excellent coffee and home-made ice cream is the *Café Polar* on Chaussée Prince Rwagasore, one block back from Ave du Zaïre.

The *Cotton Club*, in the Asian part of town, has cheap food and good rock or folk

music all the time. Don't be late, as food runs out early.

Super-Snack-Sympa, behind the market, has good pizzas, lasagne and a special 'hamburger', all with vegetables, cream and tortilla bread, for US$1.50.

Very popular not only with travellers but with local people is the *Acapulco*, on the corner of Blvd de l'UPRONA and Chaussée du Peuple Burundi, next door to the Hôtel Burundi Palace. It's very good, quite cheap and serves western-style food.

Entertainment

Most nightclubs are by the lake shore in the vicinity of the upmarket Hôtel Club des Vacances. The best ones are the *Black & White* and the *Bamboo*. A taxi from the city centre costs about US$3; it's not safe to walk.

Getting There & Away

Air The Air Tanzania office is in the city centre on Place de l'Indépendance. Kenya Airways is represented by the travel agent on Ave du Commerce. The international airport is 11km from the city.

Around the Country

GITEGA

Gitega is the second-largest town in Burundi and it is home to the **National Museum**. Although small, the museum is well worth a visit and is very educational. Entry is free.

A good day trip from Gitega is to the **Chutes de la Kagera** near Rutana. These waterfalls are spectacular in the wet season (October to January) but there is no public transport there, so you will have to hitch. There's a Catholic mission at the Chutes where you can stay.

Places to Stay & Eat

The *mission catholique* in Gitega has a huge guesthouse and is probably the best place to enquire about budget accommodation.

A good place to eat here is the *Foyer Culturel*, which does good, cheap food but has slow service. For a small splurge, the *Pakistani restaurant* in the town centre offers excellent value for money.

KAYANZA

Kayanza is on the road north to Kigali, near the Rwandan border. It has a good market on Monday, Wednesday and Saturday.

The missions won't take guests, so stay at the *Auberge de Kayanza*, which costs US$8 a double.

Minibuses from Bujumbura cost US$3 and take about two hours.

KILEMBA

The principal attraction here is the **Kibabi Hot Springs**, 16km from town. There are several pools of differing temperature, the main one hovering around 100°C. A little further uphill is a waterfall, and another deep pool where it's safe to swim.

Most people stay at the *Swedish Pentecostal Mission*, which has a very good guesthouse. A bed in the dormitory costs US$2, while rooms with shower and toilet and the use of a kitchen cost US$4 per person.

SOURCE DU NIL

This is supposedly the southernmost source of the Nile, though Ugandans dispute this. It is no more than a trickle – not exactly a riveting sight. You can stay at the *mission catholique* in Rutana, 7km away.

Cameroon

Travellers to this country are in luck. In the north, there are hobbit-like villages perched on rocky cliffs and Waza National Park, one of the best game reserves in Central Africa.

In the south-west, you could climb Mt Cameroon, in Foumban you can see the unusual royal palace of the Bamoun tribe, and follow this with a trip to Bandjoun where you can see the most impressive chief's compound in Central Africa. Finally, there is the beautiful coastal region around Kribi where there are long, isolated beaches of squeaky white sand.

Facts about the Country

HISTORY

If Zambia is Africa's most geographically artificial country, then Cameroon is its most socially artificial. Never at any time were its diverse tribal and linguistic groups united, and the history of Cameroon since independence has been dominated by the intense and, at times, brutal drive towards the goal of unification.

Before the area was colonised, the south and east of the country were inhabited by Bantu peoples. On the central Bamiléké Plateau there were a number of well-organised and independent chiefdoms. The northern part of the country was settled by a complex mix of Negroid, Hamitic and Arab-related peoples who formed the empires of Bornu, Mandara and finally, Sokoto. By the late 19th century, the whole of the north was ruled by the Emir of Yola, who was himself a vassal of Sokoto.

These different areas developed more or less independently due to their different trade links with places further afield. The coastal peoples, for instance, were strongly influenced by the slave trade until well into the 19th century. Though the Portuguese first made contact at the end of the 15th century,

REPUBLIC OF CAMEROON
Area: 475,500 sq km
Population: 13.2 million
Population Growth Rate: 2.8%
Capital: Yaoundé
Head of State: President Paul Biya
Official Languages: French, English
Currency: Central African CFA franc
Exchange Rate: CFA 575 = US$1
Per Capita GNP: US$790
Inflation: 7%
Time: GMT/UTC + 1

Highlights
- Attending the open-air mass in Yaoundé
- Climbing Mt Cameroon, West Africa's highest mountain
- The elaborate end-of-Ramadan celebrations in Foumban
- Exploring the villages and markets around Maroua

no attempt was made to colonise the area until the 19th century.

A commercial treaty was signed between one of the chiefs of Douala and the British in 1856. When the British later showed no interest in a request by local chiefs to declare a protectorate over the area, they turned to the Germans, who obliged in 1884. By WWI, most of the country had been 'pacified' and the Muslim chiefs of the north brought into subjection. After WWI the area was divided between the

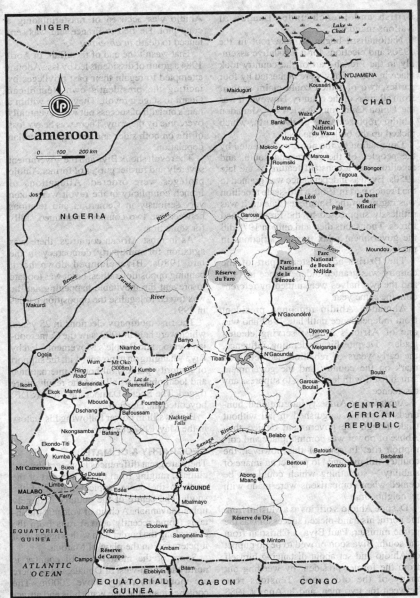

British and French under League of Nations mandates.

Nationalism began to take root in the 1950s and elections for a legislative assembly in the French part of the country took place in 1956. They were contested by four parties, two of which could claim support from all areas of the country. However it was the Union Camerounaise led by Ahmadou Ahidjo, representative of the north, which picked up the bulk of the seats.

Domination by the north was resented by the peoples of the centre and south, and rebellion was a constant feature of the late 1950s. Even as independence was granted to the French part in 1960, a full-scale rebellion was raging on the Bamiléké Plateau. It was ruthlessly suppressed by the French armed forces. Thousands died and only in 1975 did the government relax travel restrictions in the area.

The British-administered part of the country was granted independence in 1961 and the two halves were united by referendum the same year.

Ahmadou Ahidjo remained president from independence until late 1982 and was one of Africa's longest serving elected leaders. Despite his moderating influence, the early years of rebellion had left their mark on the country and the government armed itself with legislation to suppress any dissidence.

According to Amnesty International, hundreds of people languished in jail without trial, though the government denied this. Abuse of power was commonplace and corruption rife. In spite of this however, the country still managed to project an image of stability – something which could not be denied when comparisons were made with its neighbours.

Despite Ahidjo's origins as a Muslim from the north, his hand-picked successor was the prime minister, Paul Biya, a Christian from the south. Biya soon proved to be no puppet of Ahidjo and set about distancing himself from the former president by weeding out many of the old guard. Tensions rose between the two men, and in August 1983

Ahidjo was accused of masterminding a coup plot. He fled to France and was sentenced to death *in absentia*.

That wasn't the end of the affair. In April 1984 a group of dissidents led by Issa Adoum attempted to regain their past privileges by inciting the president's own Republican Guard to stage a revolt. They came within a hair's breadth of success but were eventually overcome by the army. There was heavy loss of life on both sides and among the civilian population.

The revolt shook Biya and the government severely and further purges of former Ahidjo protégés were ordered. Allegations of French complicity in the revolt were taken very seriously in Cameroon and relations between the two countries remained chilly for some time.

As in most African countries, there was agitation for multiparty democracy in the late 1980s. Biya clamped down hard, banning opposition rallies, but it was too late to prevent the inevitable happening and he was forced to legalise the opposition parties in 1991.

The first multiparty elections in 25 years, which were held in 1992, saw the Cameroonian Democratic People's Movement – led by Biya – hanging on to power (with the support of minority parties), although international and local observers all said the results were rigged. The Social Democratic Front (SDF) boycotted the election.

Biya is still in power following his victory in the May 1997 elections.

GEOGRAPHY & CLIMATE

There are great differences in geography and climate, ranging from the near desert of the north to the dense tropical forests of the south. The centre of the country is largely upland savannah. A chain of volcanic mountains (some recently active) runs from the coast along the border area with Nigeria until it peters out on the plain of Maroua.

Some of the most beautiful country is north and north-west of Douala, where there are mountains rising above 2000m. The cooler climate, the fine waterfalls and attractive villages make it one of the most popular areas of the country to visit.

POPULATION & PEOPLE

The population is around 13.2 million. Islam is the predominant religion of the north whereas in the centre and south of the country it is a mixture of Christianity and Islam. The western part is predominantly Christian and is also the centre of Bamoun culture, with its many festivals and feast days which are celebrated with music and dancing. Many of the tribes living in the mountains of the north and the rainforests of the south are animist.

LANGUAGE

French and English are the official languages, but English is rarely heard, except in larger towns in the far west of the country. There is also a wide diversity of African languages. See the Language Appendix for useful French phrases.

Facts for the Visitor

VISAS

Visas are required by all except nationals of Germany and are not available at any border. They are available at Douala airport only if you reside in a country without a Cameroon embassy, or can prove that you have been away from your home country for more than three months.

You can get visas to Cameroon fairly easily in all neighbouring countries, but in Libreville (Gabon) and Lagos (Nigeria) the Cameroon embassies insist that applicants have an onward airline ticket. A 90-day, multiple entry visa costs up to US$60 plus one or two photos and is issued in 24 hours.

You must carry your passport with you at all times (or a photocopy of the relevant pages including the Cameroon visa page) otherwise the police or army will give you a hard time (which translates into a bribe) or possibly arrest you (which costs even more).

Visa Extensions

Visa extensions can be obtained in Yaoundé as well as in any of the regional capitals, usually without any problems. Bring along a photo and expect to pay about US$20.

Other Visas

Central African Republic (CAR)
The CAR embassy, open weekdays from 7.30 am to 3.30 pm, issues visas which are valid for three months from the date of issue and allow visits of up to one month's duration; bring US$60 and two photos. Visas are issued in 24 hours.

Chad
The embassy, which is open weekdays from 7.30 am to noon and from 2.30 to 3.30 pm, issues visas within 24 hours. You'll need two photos and US$30 for a one month visa. Visas are not available at the Kousséri border.

Congo
Visas to the Congo cost US$70. You will need one photo and the visa is valid for up to two months, depending on what you request. The application form asks for the date of your arrival but it's irrelevant – it doesn't appear on the visa. The embassy is open weekdays from 8 am to 3 pm and issues visas within 24 hours.

Congo (Zaïre)
Visas to Congo (Zaïre) are very expensive and cost the same in Yaoundé as elsewhere in Central Africa. The Congo (Zaïrese) embassy also requires two photos and gives same-day service.

Equatorial Guinea
The embassy in Yaoundé is open weekdays from 8 am to 2 pm and gives same-day service for visas if you come fairly early in the morning with one photo and US$60. Make sure you request a multiple-entry visa (same price) in case of ferry or airline cancellations, which are frequent.

Gabon
The Gabonese embassy is open weekdays from 8 am to 3 pm. One-month visas to Gabon cost US$80 plus US$10 for a telex, and take about one week to issue.

Nigeria
Nigerian visas can be obtained from the embassy in Yaoundé or the consulates in Douala or Buea. The embassy's visa section gives 48-hour service. Visas are valid for one-month stays and you must bring three photos and an onward airline ticket (or a photocopy of the same). Visa fees vary greatly but range from free up to US$36 (but a staggering US$214 for UK passport holders). They may also demand a letter stating why you want to visit Nigeria, unless you have a written invitation from a citizen.

Other Countries

The British embassy in Yaoundé and the consulate in Douala issue visas to Botswana. The Gambia, Ghana, Kenya, Malawi, Sierra Leone, Uganda, Zambia and Zimbabwe. The French embassy in Yaoundé and the French consulate in Douala are open for visa service Monday to Saturday from 8 am to noon and issue visas to Côte d'Ivoire, Togo and Burkina Faso, but not to Niger. Bring two photos and US$25. Visas are collected in 24 hours.

EMBASSIES
Cameroon Embassies

In Africa there are Cameroon embassies in Algeria, Angola, the Central African Republic, Chad, the Congo, Congo (Zaïre), Egypt, Equatorial Guinea, Ethiopia, Gabon, Liberia and Nigeria (Lagos and Calabar).

Foreign Embassies in Cameroon

Belgium
 Rue 1851, Bastos (☎ 20 0519)
Benin
 BP 1083 (☎ 22 3495)
Canada
 Immeuble Stamatiades, Ave de l'Indépendance, Centre Ville (☎ 23 2311)
Central African Republic (CAR)
 Rue 1810, Bastos (☎ 20 2155)
Chad
 Rue Mballa Eloumden, Bastos (☎ 21 1624)
Congo
 Rue 1816, off Rue 1810, Bastos (☎ 21 2455)
Congo (Zaïre)
 Blvd de l'URSS, Bastos (☎ 22 5103)
Equatorial Guinea
 Rue 1872, Bastos (☎ 20 4149)
France
 Rue Joseph Atemengué near the Place de la Réunification (☎ 23 4013)
Gabon
 Rue 1793, off Rue 1810, Bastos (☎ 20 2966)
Germany
 Ave de Gaulle, Centre Ville (☎ 21 0056)
Niger
 (☎ 21 3260)
Nigeria
 off Ave Monseigneur Vogt, near Marché du Mfoundi, Centre Ville (☎ 22 3455)
Senegal
 Blvd de l'URSS, Bastos (☎ 22 0308)
UK
 Ave Churchill, near the Hôtel Indépendance, Centre Ville (☎ 22 0796)

USA
 Rue de Nachtigal, near Place de l'Indépendance, Centre Ville (☎ 23 0512)

MONEY

US$1 = CFA 575

The unit of currency is the CFA Central African franc.

Currencies other than French francs attract various commissions depending on what you are capable of negotiating and where you are changing but it's unlikely you'll get more than CFA 500 for US$1.

No bank will accept or change Nigerian naira. West African CFA are also a problem: Some banks will change one for one; others will only do it less a commission.

All banks charge commission for changing travellers' cheques. Rates vary, but if you are changing less than US$500 the commissions are punitive. Once commissions are deducted assume you'll be getting around CFA 485 to the US dollar.

There is no black market for either cash or travellers' cheques.

There are no banks in Banyo or Tibati. The nearest bank to these places is in N'Gaoundéré. There is no bank at Garoua-Boulaï (on the Cameroon-CAR border) but you can change cash with the police or at the petrol station.

Except at travel agents and airline offices, credit cards are totally useless in Cameroon. No bank will advance you cash or sell you travellers' cheques against a card regardless of your credentials.

POST & COMMUNICATIONS

Both Yaoundé and Douala have reliable poste restantes. There's a charge of CFA 200 for each letter collected.

The Intelcam offices in Yaoundé, Douala and elsewhere are very efficient and you are virtually guaranteed instant connection. The charges for international calls depend on distance, and phonecards are available. Reverse-charge calls are not accepted but you can make arrangements to receive incoming calls.

In addition to Intelcam, there are literally thousands of privately owned *cabines téléphoniques* in the main cities and towns which offer phone and fax facilities but they charge up to 50% on top of the Intelcam rates. As with Intelcam, reverse-charge calls are not accepted but they will take incoming calls for a small fee.

The country code for Cameroon is 237. There are no area codes.

PHOTOGRAPHY

You do not need a photo permit but many officials will tell you that you do. They're just fishing for a bribe. If you encounter problems, go to the Ministry of Information & Culture in a regional capital and ask for an official letter stating that you do not need one. There will be a fee to pay for this but it will get you off the hook should you run into any more hassles.

Don't take photographs of anything vaguely connected with the military, train stations, post offices, bridges or government buildings.

DANGERS & ANNOYANCES

The security situation in Cameroon has deteriorated significantly in recent years. In Douala and Yaoundé travellers get robbed every day, especially outside the banks and at the markets and *gares routières* (bus stands), where conditions are usually very crowded and perfect for robberies. Walking around at night anywhere in Douala or Yaoundé is extremely risky and unwise – take taxis.

The police in Cameroon are some of the worst in Central Africa and you'll constantly be stopped for passport and vehicle document checks. If you don't have these (or a photocopy of the relevant pages) then you're in trouble and that means a substantial bribe. Don't get caught. Explanations or excuses will not be entertained.

PUBLIC HOLIDAYS

Public holidays observed in Cameroon include: 1 January, 11 February, Good Friday, Easter Monday, 1 May, 20 May (National Day), 15 August, 25 December, and Muslim holidays (see Public Holidays in the Regional Facts for the Visitor chapter).

ACCOMMODATION

There are no purpose-built camp sites. Camping, except in the mountains of the north, is unwise due to the very real possibility of theft.

Most budget travellers stay at Christian mission hostels, *campements* and small hotels which are priced between US$4 and US$10 in the small towns and up to US$15 in the cities.

FOOD

Cameroon has some of the best food in Central Africa, and consequently you'll also find it in other countries, such as Gabon. One of the main ingredients, manioc leaves, usually translates as *feuille* on menus.

As in all African cooking, sauces in Cameroon are accompanied by rice *(riz)* or a thick mashed potato-like substance which comes in at least three, slightly different forms – *couscous*, *pâte* (pronounced 'paht') or *fufu* – any of which can be made from rice, corn, manioc, plantains or bananas.

Street food is also excellent, consisting mainly of spiced *brochettes* grilled over charcoal and stuffed into a French bread roll along with salad and a dressing. You'll be eating a lot of these if you're on a budget, and why not at around US$1.50 a serve.

Getting There & Away

AIR

Cameroon Airlines is the national carrier, connecting Yaoundé and Douala with the capital cities of all the neighbouring countries.

Other airlines represented in Cameroon include Air Afrique, Air France, Air Gabon, Sabena and Swissair. Most of these airlines use Douala airport rather than Yaoundé but some have connections to Yaoundé.

Another airline of interest to travellers,

which has a fleet of much smaller aircraft, is Air Affaires Afrique. This connects Douala with Malabo and Bata (Equatorial Guinea) and São Tomé and Principe (São Tomé e Principe).

The departure tax on domestic flights is US$1 and on international flights it's US$20.

LAND

Central African Republic

The standard route is via the border town of Garoua-Boulaï and on to Bouar from there. Coming from the north, there are minibuses from N'Gaoundéré to Garoua-Boulaï (US$8, 10 hours) along bad dirt roads. Coming from the south, take the train from Yaoundé to N'Gaoundal and a minibus from there to Garoua-Boulaï via Meidougou (seven hours on the train and 4½ on bad roads – a total cost of US$12).

Direct buses run two or three times weekly from Garoua-Boulaï to Bangui (US$20) and stop overnight in Bouar. Trucks cost the same and also overnight there.

An alternative more southerly route is the train to Belabo and from there by road to Bertoua, Batouri and Berbérati. The roads on all of these routes are dirt and in bad condition. Those in the CAR are generally better and connections are reasonably good.

Chad

The standard route along good, sealed roads is from N'Gaoundéré to N'Djamena via Garoua and Maroua by minibus. This takes two days with an overnight stop in Maroua and costs about US$20. Star Voyages have the best minibuses between N'Gaoundéré and Maroua. From Maroua there are bush taxis to the border at Kousséri (US$8, four hours), where there's a bridge across the river to N'Djamena. On the Chadian side, the border closes at 5.30 pm sharp. Try to get across the border into N'Djamena before the border closes as accommodation in Kousséri is expensive.

Gabon & Equatorial Guinea

There are lots of bush taxis and minibuses headed south from Yaoundé to Ebolowa

(US$4, 2½ hours). From Ebolowa south to Ambam takes another five hours.

In Ambam the road splits, the easterly route heading for Bitam, Oyem and Libreville (Gabon) and the westerly route heading for Ebebiyin and Bata (Equatorial Guinea). On both routes you'll find a ferry to take you across the Ntem River. The ferries cross back and forth every hour, and if they're not operating you can always take a *pirogue* (canoe). From either river crossing it's another half-hour or so to the border where you should have no problem finding vehicles headed for Ebebiyin (just 2km across the border in Equatorial Guinea) or Bitam (30km into Gabon).

You can also cross into Equatorial Guinea from Ipono, a short distance south of Campo on the coast, by pirogue to Lendé or Yenguë (US$8) from where there are pick-ups to Bongoro and Bata – but, on entry, you'll be hit for up to US$2 for the port authority, US$4 for the police and US$32 for customs (the latter is negotiable). There is no accommodation in Lendé or Bongoro.

Warning When heading into Gabon, you absolutely must get an entry stamp in Bitam from immigration. The standard fine for infractions is US$95!

Heading into Equatorial Guinea along the coast, Cameroon immigration is in the centre of Campo – you can't miss it and the officers are polite.

Nigeria

The most popular crossing is in the south via Mamfé and Ekok. Unless you have through-transport, it's a 1km walk from Ekok to Mfum (the Nigerian border village). From Mfum take a taxi to Ikom (US$1) from where there are share-taxis to Calabar (US$3, 2½ hours). The border closes at 7 pm. If you're stranded, there are cheap places to stay. The road between Mamfé and the border is so bad in the rainy season that drivers sometimes demand more money than usual.

In the extreme north, the standard route is from Maroua to Maiduguri via Banki (the border). Minibuses from Maroua to Banki cost US$3 and take about one hour. From the Nigerian side there are share-taxis to Maiduguri (US$2, 1½ hours). Be prepared for multiple immigration and customs checkpoints on the Nigerian side.

Another feasible crossing point is from Garoua to Yola. This is mainly of interest to those intent on visiting the Yankari Game Reserve near Bauchi.

SEA
Equatorial Guinea
It's very unlikely you will find a ship between Douala and Malabo on the island of Bioko, although there are small, open-topped, wooden boats which depart virtually every day loaded to the gunwales with beer bound for Malabo. There's very little room on board, no shelter and no food but they shouldn't cost more than around US$40.

Gabon
There are occasional freight boats which ply between Douala and Libreville which *may* take passengers. Fares are negotiable, but don't expect any comforts. Bring your own food and drink.

Nigeria
Various boats ply back and forth every day between Idenao (in Cameroon 50km north-west of Limbe) and Oron (in Nigeria south of Calabar). There are two classes of boats. One is a small speedboat which is fairly reliable (although there are no life-jackets or safety equipment) and takes about four hours and costs up to US$35. The other is a large cargo boat, often loaded down with smuggled goods. These boats are cheaper (typically around US$10) and for this reason are preferred by the locals. However, they are much more unreliable, usually take longer, and you cannot be certain where they'll drop you as this often depends on where the cargo is headed.

From Oron, there are speedboats to Calabar which go when full (12 people), cost US$1.50 and take half an hour. There's also a regular daily ferry which costs less than US$0.60 but takes 1½ hours.

Warning Cameroon and Nigeria have been fighting an undeclared war over possession of the Bakassi peninsula between Oron and Idenau for several years. As a result, foreigners are not welcome in this area and you can expect major hassles from immigration officials (ie bribes) if you do decide to take the above route.

São Tomé
There are infrequent passenger-carrying freighters between Douala and São Tomé. In Douala, enquire at the shipping offices on the waterfront below the Hôtel Méridien.

Getting Around

AIR
Air Cameroon and Air Affaires Afrique connect the capital, Yaoundé, and the port city of Douala with all the main regional capitals including Bertoua, Bafoussam, Bamenda, N'Gaoundéré, Garoua and Maroua. Air Cameroon is the cheaper carrier but schedules constantly change so you must make enquiries. Both companies accept credit cards.

BUS
There are large modern buses on two of the most heavily travelled routes: Yaoundé to Douala and Yaoundé or Douala to western Cameroon (Bafoussam and Bamenda). These buses are much more comfortable than minibuses or share-taxis and just as fast. They run to relatively set schedules and, unlike minibuses and taxis, are generally not stopped along the way by police.

From Yaoundé they take about three hours to Douala (US$6), 4¼ hours to Bafoussam (US$6) and six hours to Bamenda (US$8). From Douala to Bafoussam and Bamenda the journey times and prices are about the same. These buses depart when full (which can take up to two hours beyond the official departure time) and there's no advance booking. Simply turn up on the day you want to travel.

Other than the above, there's a choice of minibuses and share-taxis which depart from various gares routières. Costs are minimal and in line with bus prices.

Many of the major arterial roads in Cameroon are sealed and in good condition. However, some major routes are still unsealed, including Bertoua to N'Gaoundéré (via Garoua-Boulaï), Foumban to N'Gaoundéré (via Tibati) and the Nigerian border through Mamfé to Bamenda. Driving on these roads, especially during the rainy season, can be tortuous.

TRAIN

The rail system in Cameroon is excellent and much preferable to going by road, where available. The main line runs from Douala to N'Gaoundéré via Yaoundé and Belabo. There are other lines from Douala to Kumba and Nkongsamba but you can forget about those as they are just about moribund.

There are three departures daily between Yaoundé and Douala (4½ hours, US$8/5 in 1st/2nd class). You cannot book seats in advance – just turn up about half an hour before departure.

Between Yaoundé and N'Gaoundéré there are two departures daily (12 hours, US$31/16 in 1st/2nd class). To Belabo (for those heading for Garoua-Boulaï and the CAR), the fares are US$17/8. First class can be booked in advance but 2nd class tickets can only be bought on the day of travel.

All the above trains have a restaurant car where you can buy meals, soft drinks and beer.

Yaoundé

The capital of Cameroon, Yaoundé is hilly, green and picturesque. The climate is relatively cool, although it still gets sticky and sudden downpours are common. It has a huge market (the Marché Central), two museums, many cinemas, several bookshops and well-stocked supermarkets, as well as many lively discos and bars. The population is around one million.

Information

The main post office is in the heart of town at Place Ahmadou Ahidjo. To make telephone calls and send faxes, go to Intelcam across the street.

Bag snatching in broad daylight is on the increase. The areas around the Intelcam building, Score supermarket and the main city market are the worst spots, but you should be careful everywhere. The train station isn't too bad but never leave your pack unattended. Walking around at night is an invitation to robbery – always take a taxi.

Things to See

Built in 1967, the Benedictine monastery has the excellent **Musée d'Art Cameroonais** which definitely should not be missed; it's a five minute walk from the Hôtel Mont-Fébé. Even the monastery's **chapel** is decorated with a beautiful array of Cameroonian textiles and crafts. Take a share-taxi to get there.

The building housing the new **Musée National** is in the administrative district off Ave Marchand (better known as Ave des Ministères) several hundred metres south of the Hilton Hotel.

If you're in Yaoundé on a Sunday morning, don't miss the **open-air mass** outside the Paroisse de N'Djong Melen in Melen, several kilometres west of the city centre and just north of the university. The mass, which takes place from 9.30 am to noon, is a fantastic blend of African and western culture, with African music, drums, dancing and a women's chorus – highly recommended. Take a share-taxi to get there.

Places to Stay

Most travellers stay at the *Foyer International de l'Eglise Presbytérienne* (also known as the Presbyterian mission or called the *mission protestante*), Rue 1115, off Rue Joseph Essono Balla, which is very close to Carrefour Nlongkak (a main roundabout) at the border of Bastos and Etoa-Meki. Look for four huge, concrete water towers – it's at

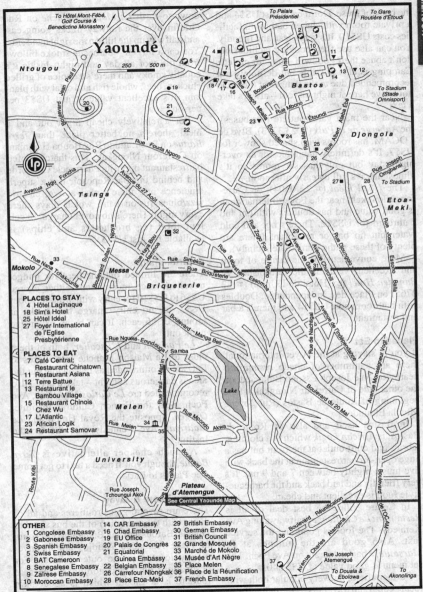

Yaoundé

To Hôtel Mont-Fébé,
Golf Course &
Benedictine Monastery

To Palais
Présidentiel

To Gare
Routière d'Étoudi

Ntougou

0   250   500 m

Bastos

To Stadium
(Stade
Omnisport)

Djongola

Rue Fouda Ngono

Tsinga

Avenue du 27 Août

Etoa-
Meki

Avenue Ngu Foncha

To Stadium

Mokolo

Messa

Briqueterie

University

Lake

Melen

Plateau
d'Atemengue

See Central Yaoundé Map

To Douala &
Ebolowa

To
Akonolinga

PLACES TO STAY
4 Hôtel Laginaque
18 Sim's Hotel
25 Hôtel Idéal
27 Foyer International
    de l'Eglise
    Presbytérienne

PLACES TO EAT
7 Café Central;
   Restaurant Chinatown
11 Restaurant Asiana
12 Terre Battue
13 Restaurant le
    Bambou Village
15 Restaurant Chinois
    Chez Wu
17 L'Atlantic
23 African Logik
24 Restaurant Samovar

OTHER
1 Congolese Embassy
2 Gabonese Embassy
3 Spanish Embassy
5 Swiss Embassy
6 BAT Cameroon
8 Senegalese Embassy
9 Zaïrese Embassy
10 Moroccan Embassy

14 CAR Embassy
16 Chad Embassy
19 EU Office
20 Palais de Congrès
21 Equatorial
    Guinea Embassy
22 Belgian Embassy
26 Carrefour Nlongkak
28 Place Etoa-Meki

29 British Embassy
30 German Embassy
31 British Council
32 Grande Mosquée
33 Marché de Mokolo
34 Musée d'Art Nègre
35 Place Melen
36 Place de la Réunification
37 French Embassy

the back of these. Dorm beds cost US$4 and a private room with shared bathroom facilities costs US$10. It's very clean and friendly. You can also use their cooking facilities but don't abuse their goodwill – pay for gas etc. Camping is also possible but definitely not recommended due to the danger of theft. Do not arrive here at night on foot – always take a taxi.

Near the main gare routière (for buses), the *Auberge de la Paix* (☎ 23 3273), Blvd de l'OCAM, has rooms with shared shower for US$7. It's definitely habitable for an overnight stay but only has six rooms so it's almost always full by early afternoon.

The *Hôtel Idéal* (☎ 22 0304), on Carrefour Nlongkak, near the Foyer International, is good value and has doubles with fan and bathroom for US$12. There's hot and cold water but no bar or restaurant (there are plenty of these in the immediate vicinity).

More convenient for the centre of town and excellent value is the refurbished *El Panaden Hotel* (ex-Hôtel de l'Unité) (☎ 22 2765) on Place de l'Indépendance. Doubles with bathroom cost US$14 and there's a bar and restaurant.

Places to Eat

If you're staying at the Foyer International, there are a number of cheap *restaurants* nearby on Rue Joseph Essono Balla and, on the other side of Carrefour Nlongkak, at the beginning of Route de Bastos (Rue Joseph Mballa Elounden).

In Bastos itself and also on Route de Bastos, is *African Logik* which is a clothing, fabrics and craft outlet at the front but has a huge open-air bar/restaurant at the back with live music nightly between 7 and 9 pm. It's very friendly and laid back and the barbecue-style food is excellent and cheap.

In Centre Ville, the best deal of all is *Restaurant Le Challenge*, halfway along Ave Kennedy. The food is good and the service fast. Also good are the lunches at *Le Marsaille*, a bar/restaurant on Ave Foch. The set menu is good value at US$4.40.

Further afield, but very popular both with local people and travellers, is the delightfully down-to-earth *La Maison Blanche* on Rue Graffin over the railway tracks going east and halfway up the hill on the right hand side. You can't miss it – barbecue smoke billows from the roof all day and night. Inside it's equally smoky and there's a choice of grilled chicken, beef, whole fish and offal with plantain. It's excellent value at just US$3 per person.

For a relatively cheap night out and a meal, there's no better place than *Terre Battue* on Rue Lamido Rey Bouba Hamman, off Carrefour Nlongkak. This thatch-roofed bar/restaurant opposite Pharmacie Concorde and behind the Bar Reposoir has a superb ambience and there's also a live, electric jazz/blues fusion band which plays there every night. There's no cover charge. Excellent food (eg brochettes and chips) is available for just US$3.

Entertainment

There are limited options here for budget travellers since most discos either charge US$6 to US$10 for entry with drinks at about US$2, or, no entry charge but drinks at around US$6 each. It can be an expensive night out.

Le Parisien and *L'Escalier,* both of them close to La Maison Blanche (see Places to Eat) are recommended as reasonable but the area is dangerous at night – take a taxi. Also recommended are *Le Catios Nightclub*, Ave Foch, near the French Cultural Institute, *Oxygen*, opposite the Royal Hotel, and *Le Madrigal*, Ave Kennedy near the Goethe Institut.

A much cheaper alternative is *Terre Battue*, though you'll need a taxi to get home (see Places to Eat).

Getting There & Away

There are several gares routières and all of them, with the exception of the bus stand to Douala, Bafoussam and Bamenda (just south of Place Ahmadou Ahidjo) are inconveniently located in the outer suburbs. For destinations north and north-east, the gare routière is at Étoudi which is about 5km north of the city centre.

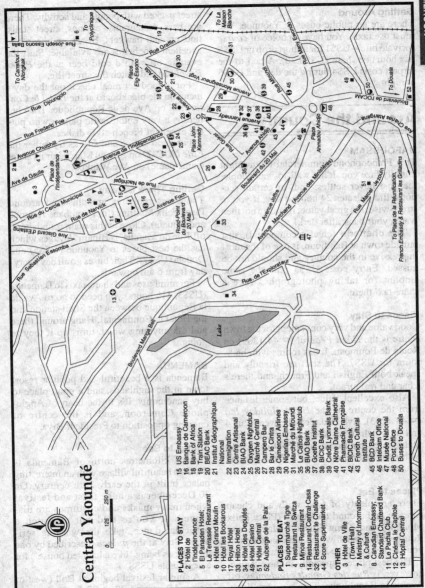

Central Yaoundé

0   125   250 m

PLACES TO STAY
2   Hôtel de
     Indépendence
5   El Panaden Hotel
6   Le Terrasse Restaurant
10   Hôtel Grand Moulin
17   Hôtel les Bookarous
33   Royal Hotel
34   Hilton Hotel
49   Hôtel des Députés
51   Hôtel Casino
52   Auberge de la Paix

PLACES TO EAT
1   Supermarché Tigre
4   Restaurant la Switza
9   Minoa Restaurant
14   Restaurant Central Casa
32   Restaurant le Challenge
44   Score Supermarket

OTHER
3   Hôtel de Ville (Town Hall)
7   Ministry of Information
     & Culture
8   Canadian Embassy;
     Standard Chartered Bank
11   Le Pacha Club
12   Cinéma le Capitole
13   Hôpital Central
15   US Embassy
16   Banque de Cameroon
18   Bank of Africa
19   Train Station
20   BEAC Bank
21   Institut Géographique
     National
22   Immigration
23   Centre Artisanal
24   BIAO Bank
25   Oxygen Nightclub
26   Marché Central
27   Cameron Bar
28   Bar le Cintra
29   Cameroon Embassy
30   Nigerian Embassy
31   Marché du Mfoundi
35   Le Califos Nightclub
36   BIAO Bank
37   Goethe Institut
38   BICIC Bank
39   Crédit Lyonnais Bank
40   Notre Dame Cathedral
41   Pharmacie Française
43   French Cultural
     Institute
45   BCD Bank
46   Intelcam Office
47   Musée National
48   Post Office
50   Buses to Douala

Getting Around

There are no public buses in Yaoundé. You must use taxis. You have a choice of *course* (private hire – US$1 for a short drop or US$5 per hour) or share (US$0.30). A taxi to the airport costs US$4 during the day and US$6 at night.

Around the Country

BAFOUSSAM

This Francophone commercial town might initially faze you. It has wall-to-wall people, the dust never settles, and, in certain sections, life pulsates 24 hours a day. If you're street-wise, it's great value; if you're not then watch your back after dark!

The **chefferie** (chief's compound), just outside town at Bandjoun, is one of the most impressive in the country and should not be missed. Entry costs US$3 plus the same amount for taking photographs. Take a share-taxi there.

Places to Stay

Good value and very convenient for the town centre is the *Hôtel Fédéral* (☎ 44 1309) on Route de Foumban. It has rooms with bathroom for US$7. The staff are friendly and speak both English and French, and there's a bar and restaurant.

Also excellent value, but some distance from the centre, is the *Hôtel Holiday Inn* (☎ 44 1263), Ave Dada Jean between Rue 4 and 5, which offers spotlessly clean rooms with shared bathroom for US$9 or US$10 with own bathroom. There's also a bar and restaurant.

Places to Eat

There are plenty of *food stalls* and cheap *cafes* in and around the centre (Place Felix Moumie) and along Rue du Marché and Route de Foumban which are convenient if you're staying at the Hôtel Fédéral.

The best place, especially in the evening, however, is *Rue des Grandes Endemies*, off Ave de la République. This is a very lively street packed with people and activity. There are bars, restaurants, casinos, street stalls, hookers and hawkers. Beers are cheap and excellent brochettes are available. Start the evening off with a cold beer at the *Poker Royal* bar and watch the street life.

For a good set meal check out the day's menu on the blackboard at the *Hôtel le Continental* on Ave de la République. The chef here is a very enthusiastic person who puts out excellent French-style dishes.

For good coffee and snacks try either the *Café UCCAO* on Rue du Marché or its sister (same name) on Ave Wanko.

Getting There & Away

The gares routières are clustered around Place Felix Moumie (for Foumban, Yaoundé and Douala). Close to this main roundabout, off Rue du Marché, is Binam Voyages which has the best buses to Yaoundé (US$5) and Douala (US$7). Their buses go all day every-day from 6 am onwards.

For minibuses and share-taxis to Bamenda (US$3, 1½ hours) you need to go to Ave de la République between the Shell station and the Hôtel le Continental. Hang around there and ask anything which turns up if they're going.

BAMENDA

Bamenda is a beautiful and popular resort town in the highlands, and a good place to buy handicrafts. It's in the heart of Anglophone Cameroon, and is the centre of ongoing opposition to President Biya.

Things to See

Twenty kilometres north of Bamenda is **Bafut**, a beautiful village with an interesting palace built in the early 20th century. On 20 December is a huge feast and festival when many masks and costumes are displayed. If you're told not to watch a particular dance, take the warning seriously. Stay at the *palace* (described by one traveller as being 'like a haunted house') for a negotiable US$8.

A similar festival begins at **Bali** (west of Bamenda) around 20 to 22 December and

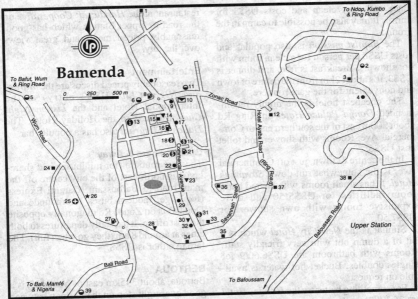

Bamenda

To Ndop, Kumbo & Ring Road

To Bafut, Wum & Ring Road

To Bafut, Wum & Ring Road

To Bali, Mamfé & Nigeria

To Bafoussam

Upper Station

PLACES TO STAY
1	Presbyterian Church Centre
3	Baptist Mission
12	Mondial Hotel
15	International Hotel
24	Unity Hotel
33	Savannah Hotel
34	Holiday Hotel
35	Donga Palace Hotel
36	New City Hotel
37	Ayaba Hotel
38	Skyline Hotel

PLACES TO EAT
14	Snack Concorde
23	Bread Shop
28	Dallas Restaurant
30	New Life Supermarket

OTHER
2	Nkwem Motor Park (Minbuses & Taxis to Bafoussam, Yaoune & Douala)
4	Handicraft Cooperative
5	Ntarkison Motor Park (Vehicles to Bafut & Wum)
6	Amumba Express (Buses)
7	Linkup Project (Handicrafts)
8	Mobil Station
9	Cameroon Airlines
10	Post Office
11	Garanti Express (Buses to Douala & Yaoundé)
13	Tourist Office
16	Texaco Station
17	Photo Victory
18	BIAO Bank
19	Crédit Lyonnais Bank
20	BICIC Bank
21	Total Station
22	Prescraft (Craft Shop)
25	Hospital
26	Police
27	BP Station
29	Market
31	SGBC Bank
32	Mezan Pharmacy
39	Bali Motor Park (Vehicles to Bali & Mamfé)

goes on for several days. At this time the nobles, princes, princesses and palace staff dress in traditional costume and honour the Fon. Market day here is Thursday. Buses from Bamenda cost US$1.60.

Places to Stay
The best place to stay is the *Presbyterian Church Centre*. It is in large, well-kept grounds on top of a hill about a 10 minute walk from the town centre. It's a well-run

place and very clean and costs US$3 for dorms. It may also be possible to camp in the grounds.

The *Baptist mission* is also popular and costs US$8 per person for a clean room with hot showers. Breakfast is free, and dinner is US$3. It's about 2km from the centre of town and convenient for the gare routière.

The cheapest hotel is the highly recommended *Donga Palace Hotel* on Ring Rd about 200m east of the southern end of Commercial Ave. Rooms with shower and toilet cost US$6.

In the centre of town, just off Commercial Ave, is the somewhat run-down *Savannah Hotel*. It has small rooms with shared bathroom facilities for US$5.50 and more expensive rooms with own shower for US$7.50.

Similar is the *New City Hotel* which is a bit of a dump but with very friendly staff. Rooms with bathroom are US$6.60/9 for singles/doubles. Bucket hot water is available on request.

For something better try the *Holiday Hotel* (☎ 36 1382) on the southern end of Ring Rd. Small rooms with bathroom and a balcony cost US$10.

Far better and only slightly more expensive is the *International Hotel* (☎ 36 2527), Commercial Ave, which offers spacious rooms with own balcony and bathroom from US$12.

Places to Eat

The *New City Hotel* offers excellent cheap meals (US$2) and will cook you anything you want given sufficient notice. *Snack Concorde*, in the same block as the International Hotel, off Commercial Ave, also does reasonable food but the service is slow. It's popular in the evenings, especially at weekends when there's music.

One of the most popular upmarket places is *Dallas Restaurant* on the southern end of Ring Rd, west of Commercial Ave. You can sit on the front verandah or inside and eat roasted fish, chicken or steak with chips for US$10.

Another place worth checking out is the restaurant at the *Handicraft Cooperative* on the road to Upper Station which has good, reasonably priced meals and great views over the city.

Entertainment

Two reasonably priced discos are the *Maracana Night Club* (US$2 entry) at the International Hotel and the *Lisbon Night Club* just next to the Holiday Hotel. The *Dallas Restaurant* also has a popular bar.

Getting There & Away

The gare routière (for minibuses and share-taxis) is north-east of the city centre off the main road to Bafoussam. Garanti Express (for large, modern buses to Yaoundé and Douala) is on Zonac Rd diagonally opposite the post office. It has daily departures to both cities at around 8 am (they go when full). The fare to either is US$8.

BERTOUA

Bertoua, about 345km east of Yaoundé, is a good overnight stop on the journey between Yaoundé and Garoua-Boulaï (the CAR border).

Places to Stay & Eat

One of the cheapest places to stay and convenient for the gare routière is the *Hôtel Jenyf* which has rooms with shared bathroom facilities for US$7 and others with own bathroom from US$9.

More comfortable and with better facilities is the *Hôtel de l'Est* (☎ 24 2342), about 200m east of the gare routière opposite the post office on the main road through town. It offers singles/doubles with fan and shared bathroom facilities for US$9/12 or US$14/21 with own bathroom, air-con and TV. There's a bar and restaurant. There's also a nightclub (entry US$3).

BUEA

Buea (pronounced 'bwaya'), on the lower slopes of Mt Cameroon (4095m), is the base for climbing the mountain. Even if you don't climb, Buea is cooler and less humid than the coast which is half an hour away.

Climbing Mt Cameroon

Mt Cameroon is the highest mountain in West Africa. You don't need any special equipment to climb and there is a series of huts where you can stay en route. The season for climbing is between mid-November and mid-May. It's too wet the rest of the year.

It takes about three to 3½ days to do the trip up and back, and even at that pace it's hard work. Bring a change of warm clothes, a sleeping bag, food and water. Warm clothes are essential because it is extremely cold at the top, and waterproof gear is a good idea. Water cannot be guaranteed at the huts and it needs to be boiled or sterilised. There is no firewood beyond the second hut.

You must have a permit and guide, obtainable from the tourist centre on the main drag in town. The official rates are US$16 per person per day (one to four people), US$14 per person per day (five to nine people) and US$12 per person per day (10 or more people). Foreign students pay US$10 per person per day. The price includes the guide and one porter per two people. Extra porters cost US$4 per day.

Places to Stay & Eat

The cheapest place to stay is the friendly *Presbyterian mission* which is clean and has beds with shared bathroom facilities for US$5 and others with attached bathroom for US$6. Meals are available on request.

Excellent value and very friendly is the *Mountain Village* set in well-tended gardens off the main top road going south-west – turn right just after the Nigerian Consulate. Clean doubles with bathroom cost US$10 and bucket hot water is available on request. There's a bar and Francis or Gloria will cook good meals of fish or chicken with chips for US$3. It's a very mellow place.

More expensive and on the same top road, but closer to the main roundabout, is the *Parliamentarian Flats Hotel* (☎ 32 2459) which has doubles with bathroom for US$13. It's clean, quiet and comfortable and has a bar and restaurant. Breakfast costs US$2.

There are hardly any restaurants along the top road so you should eat at your hotel.

Getting There & Away

The bus stand for minibuses to/from Limbe, Douala and Kumba is at Mile 17, way down the hill from the centre of Buea. Leaving Buea, you'll need to take a taxi there (US$1). Coming into Buea, it's much easier as there are always plenty of people wanting to share a taxi (US$0.25). Minibus fares from Mile 17 are US$1.80 (Douala), US$0.60 (Limbe) and US$2 (Kumba).

DOUALA

Douala is the largest city and the industrial centre of Cameroon. It has a delightful, tropical ambience not unlike Singapore before the high-rise boom – leafy, colonial decay rubs shoulders with the modern, marble-façades of banks, five-star hotels and business houses. It's a very lively and cosmopolitan city which you could very well grow to like a lot.

Many people will tell you it has a bad reputation for muggings and you will almost certainly meet someone to whom this has happened. You do need to be street-wise, especially at night, but it's not as bad as some people make out.

Information

The main post office and Intelcam (telephone and fax services) is on the western side of Place du Gouvernement in Bonanjo.

Nigerian visas are available from the Nigerian consulate on Blvd de la Liberté, Akwa. The French consulate in Bonanjo issues visas for Togo and there's also an Equatorial Guinea consulate on Blvd de la République.

Several western countries, including Belgium, France, Italy, Norway, Sweden, the UK (above Standard Chartered Bank, Blvd de la Liberté) and the USA, have diplomatic representation in Douala.

Thomas Cook (☎ 42 9291) is at Transcap Voyages on Rue de Trieste.

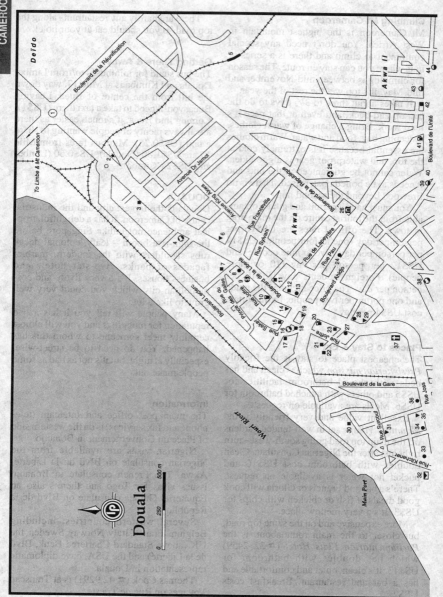

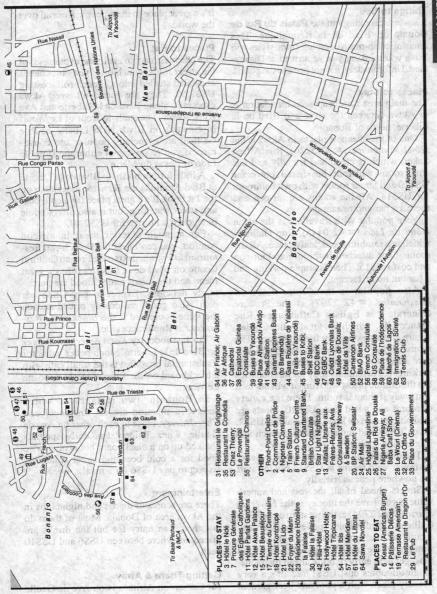

PLACES TO STAY
3 Hôtel le Ndé
7 Procure Générale
    des Églises Catholiques
11 Hôtel Parfait Gardens
12 Hôtel Akwa Palace
15 Hôtel Beauséjour
17 Temple du Centenaire
18 Hôtel Kontchupé
21 Hôtel le Lido
22 Foyer du Marin
23 Résidence Hôtelière
    la Falaise
30 Hôtel la Falaise
42 Ritz-Hôtel
51 Hollywood Hôtel;
    Hôtel Tropicana
54 Hôtel Ibis
57 Hôtel Méridien
61 Hôtel du Littoral
64 Sawa Novotel

PLACES TO EAT
6 Keissi (American Burger)
8 Pâtisserie Délices
19 Terrasse Americain;
    Le Wouri (Cinema)
29 Le Pub

31 Restaurant le Grignotage
35 Restaurant la Comédia
53 Chez Thierry;
    Le Provençal
55 Restaurant Chinois

OTHER
1 Rond-Point Deïdo
2 Commissariat de Police
4 Nigerian Consulate
5 Train Station
8 French Cultural Centre
9 Standard Chartered Bank;
    British Consulate
10 Star Light Nightclub
13 Alitalia; Librairie aux
    Frères-Réunis; Avis
16 Consulates of Norway
    & Sweden
20 BP Station; Swissair
24 Air Mali
25 Hôpital Laquintinie
26 Palais du Roi de Douala
27 Nigeria Airways; Ali
    Baba Craft Shop
28 Le Wouri (Cinema)
32 Post Office
33 Place du Gouvernement

34 Air France; Air Gabon
36 Air Afrique
37 Cathedral
38 Equatorial Guinea
    Consulate
39 Buses to Yaoundé
40 Place Ahmadou Ahidjo
41 Shell Station
43 Garanti Express Buses
    (to Bamenda)
44 Gare Routière de Yabassi
    (Taxis to Yaoundé)
45 Buses to Kribi;
    Shell Station
46 BCC Bank
47 SGBC Bank
48 Crédit Lyonnais Bank
49 Musée de Douala;
    Hôtel de Ville
50 Cameroon Airlines
52 BIAO Bank
56 French Consulate
58 US Consulate
59 Place de l'Indépendence
60 Marché de Lagos
62 Immigration; Sûreté
63 Tennis Club

CAMEROON

Things to See

It's worth checking out the **Palais du Roi de Douala** on Blvd de la République. This amazing mish-mash of architectural styles will leave you thinking you've arrived at Disneyland. Unfortunately, it's not open to the public.

Places to Stay

The main area for cheap accommodation is in Akwa between the river and Blvd de la Liberté, north of Bonanjo.

One of the cheapest places in Akwa is the *Hôtel Kontchupé* (☎ 42 5226), Rue Alfred Saker, which is clean and friendly and has small rooms with toilet but shared shower for US$10 and larger rooms with own bathroom for US$14. All the rooms are air-con and there's a bar and restaurant.

Very popular with travellers is the clean *Hôtel de Lido* (☎ 42 0445), Rue Gallieni, which is a rambling, old, leafy place. All the rooms have attached bathroom and air-con and cost US$15. There's ample parking and a bar but no restaurant.

Also popular is the *Centre d'Accueil Missionaire* (☎ 42 2797) at the Procure Générale des Eglises Catholiques, Rue Franceville, which is great value, quiet, secure and an extremely friendly place. The rooms all have attatched bathroom and air-con, there's a swimming pool and ample parking. It's essentially only for missionaries but the affable priest who runs it will not turn you away if there is room. There is a variety of rooms and a bed costs US$10. Meals are available except on Sunday (breakfast US$2, lunch US$8 and dinner US$6). French and English are spoken.

The *Temple du Centenaire* on Rue Saker is similar with rooms at US$14 but the staff are nowhere near as friendly.

Streets ahead of all the rest and superb value if you have the money is the *Foyer du Marin* (☎ 42 2794) at the western end of Rue Gallieni. Comfortable, spotlessly clean and secure, all the rooms have air-con and hot water but there are only eight of them so you must get here early or book ahead by phone. Singles/doubles cost US$17/22. It's a very friendly place with a pool and beer garden.

It's a great place to meet people from all over the world.

Places to Eat

The cheapest way to eat in the evenings is at the *street stalls*, which offer tasty brochettes and salad stuffed into a French roll, costing US$1.60. They are found all over Akwa especially along Blvd de la Liberté and Ave King Akwa. The stalls in front of Le Wouri (a cinema) on Blvd de la Liberté at Rue Gallieni are especially popular and convenient if you're staying at either the Hôtel le Lido or Foyer du Marin.

A little further north on Blvd de la Liberté at Blvd Ahidjo is the *Terrasse Americain* on the 1st floor. It's a great place for a cold beer and street watching, but it also offers ndolé or chicken with rice for US$2.40.

For a much classier meal in air-con comfort, you can't beat the French-run *Restaurant la Fofani*, next to the French Cultural Centre on Blvd de la Liberté. It has a great menu and the salads and seafood are particularly delicious. Expect to pay US$5 per dish. Also good, reasonably priced and on the same boulevard is the *Black Taste Restaurant* at Rue Franceville.

For fast-food, try *Kesst American Burger* on Blvd de la Liberté. Much better value for a substantial breakfast is the small cafe with a blackboard on the street directly opposite Le Wouri.

In Bonanjo, two restaurants which deserve a mention are *Le Provençal* and *Chez Thierry*, close to each other on Ave de Gaulle. Chez Thierry has daily specials chalked up on a blackboard but is otherwise good for a cold beer and street watching. Expect to pay US$6 for a meal.

Entertainment

There are scores of discos and nightclubs in the Akwa area of Douala. Most of them do not charge an entry fee but the drinks are priced anywhere between US$6 and US$10 each.

Getting There & Away

Air Cameroon Airlines is on Ave de Gaulle

one block south of Rue Joss. Air Affaires Afrique has an office at the airport but its main office is across the other side of the highway from the airport terminal (about 2km).

Bus The main gare routière, where you'll find express buses for Yaoundé, Limbe and Bamenda, is around Place Ahmadou Ahidjo and along Blvd de l'Unité (the area known locally as 'Douche').

The gare routière for minibuses and share-taxis to Yaoundé and Kribi are nearby at the eastern end of Blvd de l'Unité at the junction with Rue Nassif (known as Yabassi).

For minibuses to Limbe, Buea, Bafoussam, Bamenda and other points north and north-west the gare routière is inconveniently located in Bonaberi across the Wouri River bridge about 6km west of the city centre next to the large concrete water tower and a Mobil station. It's well organised but you'll need a taxi (US$2).

Getting Around
A taxi between Akwa or Bonanjo and the airport costs US$4 during the day and US$6 at night.

A share-taxi anywhere in the city costs US$0.30 but you must know the name of a landmark to shout out when the driver slows down. Private hire costs US$2 for a drop or US$6 per hour.

FOUMBAN
Foumban is on the north-eastern edge of the mountains near Bafoussam. It's an interesting place with many old, traditional houses in the surrounding countryside and the German-inspired **Fon's Palace** (or Palais Royal) with its excellent museum. The palace is open daily from 8 am to 5.30 pm and entry costs US$4 including a guide (they speak English and French).

There's also another interesting museum, the **Musée des Arts**, not far from the palace which is free of charge. Excellent woodwork can be picked up from the artisan shops outside both the palace and the other

museum. You can expect high-pressure salesmanship.

The best time to be in Foumban is at the end of Ramadan – the celebration here is one of the most elaborate anywhere in Africa.

Places to Stay & Eat
Most travellers return to Bafoussam where the accommodation is generally better.

The cheapest place to stay is the *mission catholique*, which is in pleasant surroundings on the main drag on the eastern side of town, a five minute walk east of the gare routière. The accommodation is excellent and the people very friendly. A donation of US$3 is expected.

Diagonally opposite the mission, the *Hôtel Beau Regard* (☎ 48 2182) has rooms with shared bathroom for US$8 and others with own bathroom for US$10. There's a bar and restaurant but cheaper food is available from the shack next door.

Getting There & Away
Minibuses from Bafoussam cost US$2 and take about two hours. Going back to Bafoussam, many minibuses only go as far as Foumbot (about halfway) where you will have to change.

GAROUA
This is the commercial hub of the north and there's a lively market on Saturday. Many foreigners live here. However, it's a sprawling place with little of real interest.

Places to Stay & Eat
On the main drag facing the *stationnement Mobil* (parking area), the *Auberge le Salam* (☎ 27 2216) is reasonable value at US$4 a single with shared bathroom and US$5/7 a single/double with own bathroom. There is a good restaurant here and another next door.

Further afield along Rue de Petit Marché are two other places which are popular with budget travellers. The first is *Auberge de la Cité* which is clean and friendly and has doubles with bathroom and air-con for US$13. Close by is *Hôtel le Saré* which is quiet, clean and friendly and has doubles with fan for US$10 or US$12 with air-con.

If you're staying at either of the above two hotels, the street they're on is lined with lively bars and cheap restaurants.

Getting There & Away

The gare routière is out on the highway quite a long way north of town. There are minibuses to Maroua and N'Gaoundéré.

GAROUA-BOULAÏ

Garoua-Boulaï is the small town on the Cameroon/Central African Republic) border through which virtually all travellers pass between the two countries. It's basically a one horse town with a couple of petrol stations and bars.

Places to Stay & Eat

The only serious place you can consider staying, unless you're camping with a group, is the Polish *mission catholique* which is a very friendly place where you might get a dorm bed for a donation, or there are rooms for US$10. It's near the military checkpoint before the turn-off to the actual border coming from the north.

Other than this, there are one or two very basic *auberges* at the two gares routières and along the only main street where you can find a bed for US$3 but don't expect any facilities. Ask at the main bar in the centre of town for directions.

For cooked food, take anything you can find and don't be late.

Getting There & Away

Getting to, or away from, Garoua-Boulaï, even in the dry season, involves a major effort along narrow, pot-holed, rutted dirt-tracks hemmed in on either side by two-metre high elephant grass plus there are overturned trucks to negotiate around. If it rains, you have major problems. A 4WD is almost obligatory. Count on 10 hours from either Bertoua or N'Gaoundéré. There are minibuses but, seriously, you'd be better off arranging a lift in a 4WD vehicle beforehand.

KRIBI

The beaches at Kribi, south of Douala, are better than those north of Limbe and are a popular place for overlanders to spend Christmas. All along the coast, small places to stay (usually in people's homes) have sprung up and you'll find that fresh seafood is readily available.

The **Chutes de la Lobé** (waterfalls), which cascade into the sea at Grand Batanga, about 8km south of Kribi, are picturesque but have become very commercialised so food and souvenirs are very expensive.

Going north, there are good beaches at **Costa Blanca** (12km), **Cocotier Plage** (15km) and **Londje** (24km).

Unfortunately, Kribi's popularity has also attracted thieves and they're pretty gung-ho. *Never* walk along the beach alone even in daylight and don't even think about it after dark – even if you're part of a group.

Places to Stay & Eat

Most of the hotels in Kribi itself are quite expensive; for cheaper accommodation and more privacy most people head off to one of the nearby beaches.

In Kribi itself, try the *Hôtel de la Paix*, with rooms from US$9, or you can often camp on or near the beach in people's front yards – just ask them.

The best value hotel on the beach is the *Auberge Annette II* (☎ 46 1057) with rooms from US$19. For something cheaper, try the *Manapani*, about 1km behind Annette II, which offers large rooms with bathroom, sleeping four people for US$14. There's a good restaurant and disco across the road.

Camping on any of the beaches is unwise unless you're a sizeable group and are prepared to mount a 24-hour guard.

For food in Kribi, *La Balise*, next door to Annette II, is recommended. It isn't cheap but the food is good.

Going south over the river towards the Hôtel les Polygones d'Alice, there is a *circuit* (informal restaurant) on the left hand side run by a local fisher and his wife where you can get excellent cheap seafood if you order in advance. If there's a group of you, ask them to put a table and light on the beach so you can dine there.

LIMBE

Limbe, west of Douala, is a complete contrast to the flat swamplands of the country's major port city. Rainforests tumble down from the slopes of Mt Cameroon into a bay dotted with islands. It's a popular weekend playground for those from Douala with some cash to spend but, most of the week, you wouldn't know it.

Limbe (previously called Victoria) was once the capital of the British part of Cameroon and the well-maintained **Botanical**

Gardens are part of its colonial legacy, though originally laid out by the German colonial regime.

Beaches

The best beaches are north of town and designated by their distance from Limbe. Beach resorts have been built on the best spots. The nearest decent beach, Mile 6 Beach, is a popular spot but has an oil refinery next to it. Mile 11 Beach is better. There's a US$1 'gate fee' for either.

There's no budget accommodation available and camping on the beach is dangerous

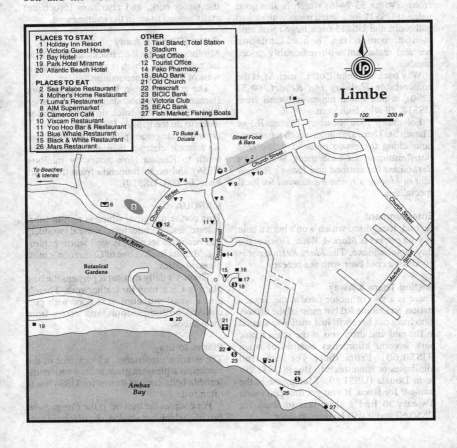

PLACES TO STAY
1 Holiday Inn Resort
16 Victoria Guest House
17 Bay Hotel
19 Park Hotel Miramar
20 Atlantic Beach Hotel

PLACES TO EAT
2 Sea Palace Restaurant
4 Mother's Home Restaurant
7 Luma's Restaurant
8 AIM Supermarket
9 Cameroon Café
10 Vixcam Restaurant
11 Yoo Hoo Bar & Restaurant
13 Blue Whale Restaurant
15 Black & White Restaurant
26 Mars Restaurant

OTHER
3 Taxi Stand; Total Station
5 Stadium
6 Post Office
12 Tourist Office
14 Fako Pharmacy
18 BIAO Bank
21 Old Church
22 Prescraft
23 BICIC Bank
24 Victoria Club
25 BEAC Bank
27 Fish Market; Fishing Boats

Limbe

on account of muggers and thieves so you're looking at day trips from Limbe.

Places to Stay & Eat

Forget about camping in Limbe – it's too dangerous.

The best choice in town – and one with sea breezes and views – is the *Bay Hotel* (☎ 33 2332), on a rise close to the seafront. It offers a variety of rooms from US$12, all of which have air-con and bathroom. You can order meals at the nearby *Black & White Bar/Disco*.

Almost next door is the *Victoria Guest House* (☎/fax 33 2446) which is also good value at US$11 for a small room with shared bathroom and US$13 for a large room with own bathroom and fan. The hotel has its own bar and restaurant with reasonably priced meals.

Way back up the hill, off Church St, is the comfortable *Holiday Inn Resort* (☎ 33 2290), which has a range of rooms from US$12, all with bathroom.

For cheap food, head up Douala Rd or Church St. There are numerous cheap restaurants along these two roads. Try *Yoo Hoo Bar/Restaurant* for bush meat, *Sea Palace Restaurant* for seafood and *Luma's Restaurant* or *Mother's Home Restaurant* for local specialities.

Entertainment

A good, local disco which won't burn a hole in your pocket is *Black & White Disco* at the Bay Hotel annexe. The *Mars Restaurant* is good for a cold beer with sea breezes.

Getting There & Away

There is a sort of motor park at the Texaco station on Douala Rd but most of the drivers who hang out here will just stuff you around in the end and drop you at the main motor park several kilometres outside of town (US$0.60). From there you can find minibuses or share-taxis to Buea (US$1.20) or to Douala (US$1.80). Mutengane is the turn-off for Buea. If you get dropped there, it's easy to find a share-taxi to Buea for US$0.60 and it will be door-to-door.

MAMFÉ

Mamfé, the closest major town to the Nigerian border at Ekok, is a friendly town where English is spoken. There's no bank at the border, so look around for Nigerian naira here.

Places to Stay & Eat

The *Great Aim Hotel* and the *African City Hotel*, both near the motor park, have clean double rooms at US$8 with bathroom. More expensive is the *Little Paradise Hotel*, which has very good rooms for US$15.

There are several good places to eat near the motor park, and also *suya* (brochette) stalls around town in the evenings.

Getting There & Away

Minibuses and pick-up trucks all leave from the motor park, which is about 500m south-west of the main intersection.

The road to Ekok, between Mamfé and Bamenda, is the most dangerous in Cameroon, which is why truck drivers demand so much to do the trip. At US$16 for a seat in a crowded, dangerous pick-up truck this route isn't much cheaper than the longer route south to Kumba (five hours by minibus, US$9) and on to Bamenda from there (six hours by taxi, US$10).

MAROUA

This northern region, which is rich in tribal culture and architecture, natural wonders and beautiful scenery, is well worth exploring. Maroua itself is one of Cameroon's most pleasant cities.

The city's daily **market** is perhaps the best place in Cameroon for leatherwork. There's also a small **museum** next door with pre-colonial costumes, tools and crafts from local tribes.

Places to Stay

The *mission protestante*, a block east of the market, is a pleasant place to stay with comfortable beds in clean dorms for US$4 but is often full.

For couples the best bet is the *Campement Bossou*, which has shaded, circular mud huts

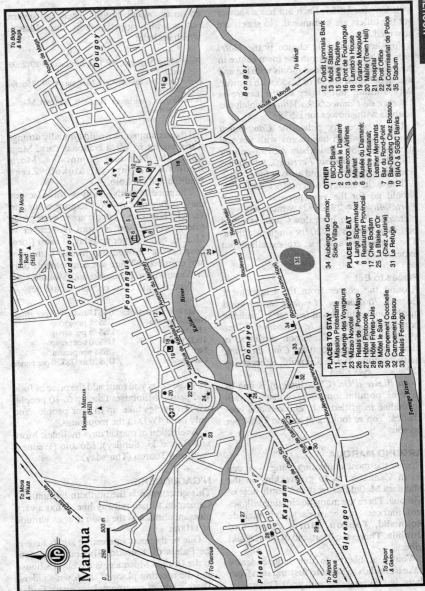

Maroua

0   250   500 m

To Bogo & Maga

To Mindif

Dougoy

Bongor

Route de Maga

Route de Mindif

To Mora

Hosère Red (Hill)

Djoudandou

Founangué

Kaliao River

Boulevard de Renouveau

Avenue du Marché

Avenue du Kakataré

Domayo

Boulevard Lamino-Kora

To Mora & Waza

Route — Plaasa

Rue de Camp SIC

Boulevard Diarengol

Hosère (Hill)

Rue 96 Camp SIC

Pitoaré

Kaygama

Gjarengol

Ferngo River

To Garoua

To Airport & Garoua

To Airport & Garoua

PLACES TO STAY
11 Mission Protestante
14 Auberge des Voyageurs
23 Mizao Novotel
26 Relais de Porte-Mayo
27 Hôtel Protocole
28 Hôtel Frères-Unis
29 Môtel le Saré
30 Campement Coccinelle
32 Campement Bossou
33 Relais Ferringo

PLACES TO EAT
4   Large Supermarket
17 Restaurant Provincial
18 Chez Bodjam
25 La Blaise d'Or
31 Le Refuge

34 Auberge de Camice;
    Soko Village

OTHER
1   BICIC Bank
2   Cinéma le Diamaré
3   Market
6   Musée du Diamaré;
    Centre Artisanal;
    Leather Merchants
7   Bar du Rond-Point
9   Bar-Dancing Chez Bossou
10 BIAO & SGBC Banks
12 Crédit Lyonnais Bank
13 Mobil Station
15 Gare Routière
16 Pont de Founangué
18 Lamido's House
19 Grande Mosquée
20 Mairie (Town Hall)
21 Hospital
24 Commissariat de Police
35 Stadium

with fans for US$5. Each hut has a shower but the toilets are communal. No sheets are provided.

Another reasonable choice is the *Hôtel Frères-Unis*, 3.5km from the town centre in the Pitoaré quarter. Clean rooms with fan and shared bath cost US$4, or US$5 with shower. Very similar, but closer to the centre is *Auberge de Camice/Soko Village* which has doubles with shower for US$5.

Up in price, try either the *Campement Coccinelle*, which has rooms with fan and shower for US$7 and others with air-con for US$11, or the *Relais Ferringo*, which has doubles with shower and air-con for US$12.

Those in search of comfort and style should go for the very popular *Relais de Porte-Mayo* (☎ 29 2692) which has very pleasant, air-con bungalows with attached bathroom for US$16/20 for singles/doubles. The restaurant and bar are excellent but expensive.

Places to Eat

Around the corner from the Campement Bossou, *Restaurant Mandela* serves good meals (including breakfast) at reasonable prices. The *Caféteria le Kassaryel* (Chez Moussa), next to Cameroon Airlines, is clean, cheap and popular. *Chez Bodjam*, halfway along Ave de Kakataré, offers cheap Lebanese-style food.

La Blaise d'Or (Chez Justine) is one of several popular outdoor eateries which specialise in grilled fish, chicken and brochettes. You're looking at around US$4 per person.

AROUND MAROUA

One of the most interesting things you can do in Cameroon is to go trekking in the Mandara Mountains west and north-west of Maroua. There are many fascinating villages and markets in the area which include **Roumsiki, Tourou, Mora, Ziver** and **Oudjilla**. This is the heartland of the Kapsiki tribe.

You're at liberty to trek independently (take a minibus to Mokolo first and start from there, but take a guide with you). Otherwise,

go on an organised tour. There are several outfits which organise these from Maroua which include:

Porte Mayo Voyages, BP 112, Maroua (☎ 29 2692; fax 29 2985)

Jean-Remy Zra Teki, BP 507, Maroua (☎ 29 3356; fax 29 2100)

Jean-Jacques Andrianne, Suntours, BP 680, Maroua (no ☎/fax)

All these companies would typically arrange a trip taking in Waza National Park, Maga Lake, the Mandara Mountains, Mora, Roumsiki, Djingliya, Mokob, Ziver, Oudjilla and Mokolo.

The price depends mainly on three factors: the number of days you require a support vehicle; how many people are in your group (the tourist season is from November to March), and whether you stay in *sarés* (local hospices) or campements (hotels with creature comforts). There are campements only in Waza, Maga, Roumsiki and Mokolo.

Typical daily costs per day would be:

Guide fees for trekking	US$11 to US$15 per group
Normal vehicle	US$58 per group
Minibus	US$76 per group
4WD vehicle	US$90 per group
Saré	US$5 per person
Campement	US$20 to US$30 per person

To these costs you must add the price of food and petrol. Minibuses take up to 10 people; 4WD vehicles take up to four people. You only need 4WD in the mountains.

A selection of market days includes: Mora and Roumsiki (Sunday); Mokolo (Wednesday), and Tourou (Thursday).

N'GAOUNDÉRÉ

This quiet town is the northern terminus of Cameroon's main railway line. It has a very pleasant climate as the town is at an altitude of 1100m.

One of the most interesting sights here is the **Palais du Lamido**. This building, next to the Grande Mosquée, is the chief's house and the meeting place of the town's elders. There's a brief ceremony here every Friday and Sunday morning, which is well worth seeing for the interesting costumes. Entry costs US$5 and photography is positively encouraged.

Places to Stay & Eat

The *Collège Catholique Mazenod* has cheap, attractive rooms for only US$4. If it's full, try the *mission presbytériéne* not far from the train station.

For a cheap hotel, try the *Auberge Centrale* (☎ 25 1936), close to the train station (signposted), where many travellers stay. It has rooms with one/two beds and private bath for US$10/13. The restaurant serves good, cheap food.

The *Hôtel le Relais* (☎ 25 1138) at the back of Cinéma du Nord, is a popular hotel. It's very clean, all the rooms have a bathroom and cost from US$13. There's also a bar and restaurant.

Cheap food is available from street stalls in the train station forecourt. For a cheap breakfast, the *Restaurant le Letahi* and the *Santana Express Restaurant*, opposite the gare routière, are great value.

On the street parallel to the main drag (Ave de la Grande Mosquée), opposite the BICIC bank, are several, cheap restaurants which can be recommended. They include *Le Cristal* and *Le Meilleur*.

On the main drag itself, the *Restaurant Pizzaria le Plaza* is popular with Peace Corps volunteers. Almost opposite, is the old-established *Restaurant La Girafe*, a sort of landmark, which does lunches and dinners.

Yoghurt and ice cream are best at the *Bar Laitier* (known locally as the Kanti Kossam).

For entertainment, the best place is the nightclub *Le Marhaba*.

Getting There & Away

If you're heading south to Yaoundé, take the train! Otherwise, there are daily mini-buses (sardine cans) and also ordinary buses

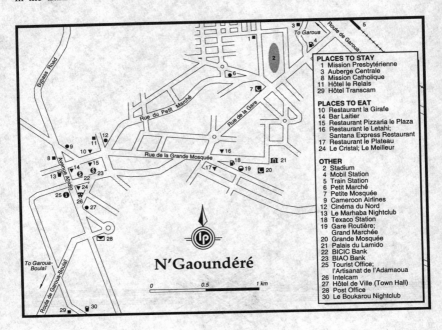

PLACES TO STAY
1 Mission Presbytérienne
3 Auberge Centrale
8 Mission Catholique
11 Hôtel le Relais
29 Hôtel Transcam

PLACES TO EAT
10 Restaurant la Girafe
14 Bar Laitier
15 Restaurant Pizzaria le Plaza
16 Restaurant le Letahi;
   Santana Express Restaurant
17 Restaurant le Plateau
24 Le Cristal; Le Meilleur

OTHER
2 Stadium
4 Mobil Station
5 Train Station
6 Petit Marché
7 Petite Mosquée
9 Cameroon Airlines
12 Cinéma du Nord
13 Le Marhaba Nightclub
18 Texaco Station
19 Gare Routière;
   Grand Marchée
20 Grande Mosquée
21 Palais du Lamido
22 BICIC Bank
23 BIAO Bank
25 Tourist Office;
   l'Artisanat de l'Adamaoua
26 Intelcam
27 Hôtel de Ville (Town Hall)
28 Post Office
30 Le Boukarou Nightclub

N'Gaoundéré

(preferable) to Garoua-Boulaï, Garoua and Maroua from the gare routière at the petrol stations on Rue de la Grande Mosquée.

WAZA NATIONAL PARK

This is the best known of Cameroon's national parks. Here you can see elephant, giraffe, hippo, ostrich, antelope, gazelle, lion and many different varieties of birdlife. April is the best time to see lions but there are sightings at other times.

Entry to the park (open 15 November to 15 June) costs US$6 but this allows you to visit as many times as you like in one year. A guide is compulsory in each vehicle, and they cost US$5.

Places to Stay

There's no accommodation in the park, but you can camp at the entrance, or stay at *Chez Suzanne*, a bar-restaurant in the tiny village of Waza, just north of the park entrance. Basic rooms cost US$8.

The *Campement de Waza* (☎ 29 1007) is the place to head for if money is no object. It has stone cottages on a beautifully landscaped hill and costs more than US$37 for the cheapest room. Non-guests can use the facilities, which include a bar and swimming pool.

Getting There & Away

If you're not part of a group, getting to Waza is going to be expensive since a vehicle alone will cost around US$65 per day including a driver. Check out the safari companies mentioned in the Around Maroua section – they may have a group which is about to go.

Cape Verde

The islands of Cape Verde lie some 645km off the coast of Senegal and are one of the smallest and poorest of the African nations. Despite considerable foreign investment to service package tourists from Europe, the islands are far from being an exotic tropical paradise and few independent travellers visit them. Cape Verde makes its impression subtly through its cultural independence, pleasant atmosphere and people.

Facts about the Country

HISTORY
Previously uninhabited, the islands were colonised by the Portuguese in 1462, the labour and most of the population being slaves taken from the West African coast.

The importance of the islands for the Portuguese lay not so much in any inherent wealth they may have possessed, but in their strategic placement between Africa, America and Europe. Cape Verde was long one of the most important slaving stations of the region. Even when the Portuguese were forced to drastically curtail their slaving activities, as a result of British navy intervention in the 19th century, the islands continued to flourish as the centre of the slave trade between West Africa and the Spanish Antilles.

The Portuguese, despite being unable and unwilling to care much for the welfare of the Cape Verdeans, clung stubbornly to their control of the islands. And while Portugal continued to neglect the economic and political development of its mainland African colonies, Cape Verde, with its light-skinned population, was regarded as a special case, and efforts were made to keep it bound more closely to Portugal and separate from Africa.

In the first Portuguese colony to have a school for higher education, the growth of a rich indigenous literature was fostered.

REPUBLIC OF CAPE VERDE
Area: 4035 sq km
Population: 407,000
Population Growth Rate: 2.3%
Capital: Praia
Head of State: President António Mascarenhas Monteiro
Official Languages: Portuguese, Kriolu (Creole)
Currency: Escudo
Exchange Rate: CV$90 = US$1
Per Capita GNP: US$915
Inflation: 5%
Time: GMT/UTC -1

Highlights
- A carnival in the lively city of Mindelo
- Hiking on volcanic Fogo
- Listening to Cape Verdean music in a Praia nightclub
- Relaxing at Tarrafal beach

This found expression in the magazines *Claridade*, *Certeza* and *Suplemento Cultural*, among others. The ideas expressed in these magazines revealed Cape Verde's growing sense of identity as an African nation. This was accelerated after WWII and led to the formation of the African Party for the Independence of Guinea-Bissau & Cape Verde (PAIGC).

Under the leadership of Amílcar Cabral, the PAIGC began to pressure the colonial

Cape Verde

☐ Uninhabited Islands   0   50   100 km

(MPD) won 70% of the vote and formed a new government under the leadership of Dr Carlos Veiga, prime minister, and António Monteiro, president.

There were major setbacks in the 1990s – an extreme and lengthy drought necessitated emergency food aid from abroad. The slow economic progress in the wake of the drought led to a splintering of the MPD and one defector established the Partido da Convergência Democrática (PCD). In the December 1995 parliamentary elections, the MPD won 50 of the 72 seats and the PCD only one seat. In the presidential election of February 1992, Monteiro was returned easily – there was no opposition candidate.

GEOGRAPHY & CLIMATE

Cape Verde's islands cover 4035 sq km, are of volcanic origin and consist of 10 islands, nine of which have been settled in the course of time, and eight smaller islets. The islands fall into two groups, depending on their relation to the wind: Barlaventos (the windward islands), comprising Santo Antão, São Vicente, Santa Luzia, São Nicolau, Sal and Boa Vista; and Sotaventos (the leeward islands), comprising Maio, Santiago, Fogo and Brava. The island of Fogo was rocked by a volcanic eruption in April 1995 and the inhabitants living in the caldera had to be evacuated. Since 1760 there have been seven eruptions.

Daily temperatures range from 20°C to a maximum of around 29°C from August to October (the best time to visit), when there can also be rainstorms; rainfall the rest of the year is minimal. The islands are also known for their strong winds.

ECOLOGY & ENVIRONMENT

The Cape Verde islands are plagued by soil erosion. Winds, steep run-offs and torrential rain all combine to cause extensive erosion. The problem was highlighted in 1984, on Santiago, when flash floods, exacerbated by cultivation in steep areas and the reduction

authorities to grant independence. The fascist regime in Lisbon was in no mood to come to terms with these demands and reacted with increasing violence and repression, forcing PAIGC to adopt guerrilla tactics from 1961 onwards.

In Guinea-Bissau the party was relatively successful, so that by 1973 it was possible to make a unilateral declaration of independence. However, guerrilla warfare in the jungle is one thing, but on barren islands in the middle of the Atlantic, it is quite another. Cape Verde had to wait until the fascists were toppled in Portugal before independence was granted in 1975.

One of the aims of the PAIGC was the union of Cape Verde and Guinea-Bissau. Between independence and 1980, efforts were made to achieve this, but hopes were dashed in 1980 when the president of Guinea-Bissau, Luiz Cabral, was overthrown in a coup by the prime minister, João Vieira. Cape Verde then went its own way under the African Independence Party of Cape Verde (PAICV).

In 1991 the first-ever multiparty elections were held, and the newly formed party Movimento para a Democracia in vegetation (for firewood), swept millions of tonnes of valuable topsoil into the sea. And when the rains stop, the country is plagued by drought.

There have been concerted attempts to redress the problem. Since 1976 there has been a programme to construct check-dams to control streams, to dig contour ditches to control run-off and an ambitious (and now proving successful) attempt at reafforestation. A type of acacia, well suited to local conditions, has been widely planted and the islands are now achieving self-sufficiency in the production of wood fuel – perhaps for the first time in their history.

POPULATION & PEOPLE

The population is around 407,000. The racial mixture consists mainly of mestizo (mixed race) people, with some Africans and a few whites. Nearly 98% of the population is Roman Catholic.

The intermixing of Portuguese settlers and their African slaves has resulted in a distinct and highly individual 'Creole' culture.

LANGUAGE

Portuguese is the official language, but Cape Verde Kriolu (or Creole, the result of an intermingling of Portuguese and various West African languages) is the everyday language of virtually everyone. Those familiar with Spanish and Italian will soon be greeting, farewelling and counting with a degree of competence.

Facts for the Visitor

CAPE VERDE

VISAS

Visas are required for all visitors except nationals of West African countries, but, if you are coming from a country which has no Cape Verdean embassy, they can be issued on arrival by air at a cost of US$5.

Portuguese speakers can apply direct to the Ministerio de Negocias Estrangeiros, Direcção de Imigração, Cape Verde. If you can't speak Portuguese, most Portuguese embassies will assist you in filling out the necessary forms and will process your application if there is no Cape Verdean embassy in the country where you apply. You need two photos, an onward ticket, and an International Vaccination Card for cholera and yellow fever.

At the Cape Verdean embassy in Lisbon, visas cost the equivalent of US$6 and are issued within 24 hours; you'll need one photo. No onward ticket is required.

Other Visas

The Senegalese embassy in Praia issues visas within a day or two. The French embassy in Praia issues visas within 24 hours to Francophone countries, such as Togo, Burkina Faso and Côte d'Ivoire.

EMBASSIES
Cape Verde Embassies

Cape Verde has embassies in Algeria, Angola, Argentina, Germany, Guinea, Italy,

---

A Rich Literary Tradition

Cape Verde, tiny in size, produces a wealth of literature. The works written prior to independence focused on liberation, were mainly in Kriolu (Creole) and the dominant organ was the journal *Claridade*. Post-independence, the themes expanded to include the mass emigration from the islands by the 'Americanos' and racial discrimination; a new journal, *Raizes*, replaced *Claridade*.

For more information on books and the many authors try: the Instituado Caboverdiano do Livro e do Disco, Praia (☎(238) 61 2068); the James P Adams Library, Rhode Island College, USA (many Cape Verdeans migrated to Rhode Island); Norman Araujo, *A Study of Cape Verdean Literature*; and Duncan T Bentley, *The Atlantic Islands*. For photographs of the islands and people (and books and magazines), the best source is the collection of Ronald Barboza, Barika Photography, 176 Court St, New Bedford, Massachusetts, USA 02740. ■

the Netherlands, Portugal, São Tomé & Príncipe, Russia and the USA. In West Africa, the only consulate is in Senegal, but visas are relatively easy to obtain here (three passport photos are required). Note that there is no representative in the UK.

Foreign Embassies in Cape Verde
Brazil, China, Cuba, France, Germany, Norway, Portugal, Russia, Senegal and the USA have embassies or consulates in Cape Verde (in Praia or Mindelo). There is an honorary British consulate in Mindelo.

MONEY
US$1 = CV$90

The unit of currency is the Cape Verde escudo (CV$), which equals 100 centavos. You will see it written as 100$00 for 100 Es; although the last two zeros are for centavos, you are unlikely to deal with anything smaller than a 50 centavo piece. Currency declaration forms are sometimes issued on arrival; they are checked on an equally voluntary basis on leaving.

There is no bank at Praia airport, making excess escudos hard to get rid of at the last minute (they are worthless outside the country). There are branches of the Banco Comercio do Atlântico in the major towns; they change travellers' cheques.

POST & COMMUNICATIONS
The CTT postal service, including poste restante (Lista da Correios), is very reliable. Telephones are also the domain of the CTT. Quite cheap international calls can be made from CTT offices on the main islands. The offices are generally open from 8 am to noon and around 2.30 to 5.30 pm.

To dial abroad prefix the country code with 0; phone cards of CV$1000 and CV$2000 are available from outlets positioned close to suitable booths. Cape Verde's country code is 238; there are no area codes.

PUBLIC HOLIDAYS & SPECIAL EVENTS
Public holidays observed in Cape Verde are: 1 January, 20 January (National Heroes' Day), 1 May, 1 June (Youth Day), 5 July (Independence Day), 15 August, 1 November and 25 December. Each island seems to celebrate its own festival, with the party going on for about a week; there are February *carnarvals* (carnivals) in Praia and Mindelo.

Getting There & Away

AIR
This is really the only viable option for getting to the islands; there are infrequent sea services, but they will probably end up costing as much as the plane ticket. There are regular flights from Lisbon (from US$1150 return, excursion fare) and less frequent flights from other European centres, South America and South Africa.

Probably the most useful flight for travellers is the three times weekly direct Dakar-Praia flight with the Cape Verde airline (TACV) or Air Senegal for about US$460 for the round trip. Air Bissau (TAGB) also has a flight every Wednesday from Praia to Bissau, and there are a couple of flights a week from Banjul to Praia with Gambia Airways.

A new international airport is expected to open in Praia in 1998; it will take Airbus 310 flights (and similar aircraft) from Europe. All other international flights land at the international airport on the island of Sal; TACV provides the internal connection from here to Praia and Mindelo.

The only travel agent is Cabetur, with offices in Praia and Mindelo and on Sal (☎ 41 1545; fax 41 1098).

Getting Around

AIR
There is a network of expensive internal flights between the islands with TACV. Between Praia, Mindelo and Sal there are flights at least once daily.

ROAD

Travel on the islands is by bus or truck. Taxis are generally very expensive and there are not many of them. If you hitch successfully, ask about the expected cost of the ride to avoid later misunderstandings.

You can rent cars on Santiago, Fogo, São Vicente and Sal; about US$50 per day for 100km.

BOAT

There are two boats, the *Sotavento* and the *Barlavento*, which sail in a circle around the islands, one of them clockwise, the other counterclockwise. They're not good for touring the islands.

There are other, smaller boats which connect the various islands on more or less regular schedules. The São Vicente-Santo Antão trip is a *rough* 50 minutes, with no shortage of seasick passengers!

Around the Islands

Every island has something of interest, but by and large, the pace of life is slow. Santiago, for instance, is very African and is where the majority of Africans live. The markets are very colourful, and it's worth making enquiries about the dates of local festivals in honour of various deities. Music is an integral part of these festivities.

Because of the rocky coastline, there are only a few beaches – the most beautiful is at Tarrafal (Santiago). Another is the black volcanic-sand beach on the west coast of Fogo, south of São Felipe, the main town on the island. Fogo is very popular now and accommodation is scarce. The volcano on this island also offers spectacular views. The beaches are anything but overrun, and the water is warm year-round (between 20°C and 27°C).

SAL

This flat, desert island, home to the international airport, is a package-tour destination for Europeans with large wallets and a yen for the tropics without local involvement. The village of **Santa Maria** caters for them (it is 18km from Espargos). Independent travellers should head for the main village of **Espargos**, where you'll have no difficulty finding a pensão (pension) or a restaurant.

Places to Stay & Eat

The best place to stay in Espargos is *Pensão Doña Angela* (☎ 41 1327), which has singles/doubles for US$17/21; the food is good. There's also the *Residencial Central* (☎ 41 1366) on the main square, which has pleasant rooms for US$17/24; it serves meals (US$6) and good coffee.

Similar is the *Hotel Atlántico* (☎ 41 1210), which offers bed and breakfast (B&B) for US$28/36.

Across the road from the Atlántico is the new bar-restaurant *Arcada*, with a pleasant terrace. The friendly and pleasant *Caravellas* has dishes for about US$6.

SANTIAGO

This is the main island and location of the capital, **Praia**. It's not the more beautiful of the archipelago's two cities (this distinction belongs to Mindelo), but it is a pleasant place with its centre perched on a rocky plateau known as **Plató**. This central area is surrounded by urban sprawl in three directions. The city's two beaches, **Praia Mar** and **Quebra-Canela**, are west of the centre.

About 10km west of Praia is **Cidade Velha** (the Old City), the first town built by the Portuguese on the islands. There are great views of the village on the climb up to **Fort Real de São Felipe**.

Some 20km inland from Praia, the village of **São Domingos** is the closest green agricultural valley to the capital. There are one or two shops selling handcrafts.

São Jorge dos Orgãos, in a beautiful valley not far from São Domingos, is dominated by the nearby 1394m peak of Santo António, the highest point on the island.

Near Assomada, the second largest town on Santiago, you can look for the gigantic **silk cotton tree**, which is 50m in circumference at the base. Ask for the village of Boa

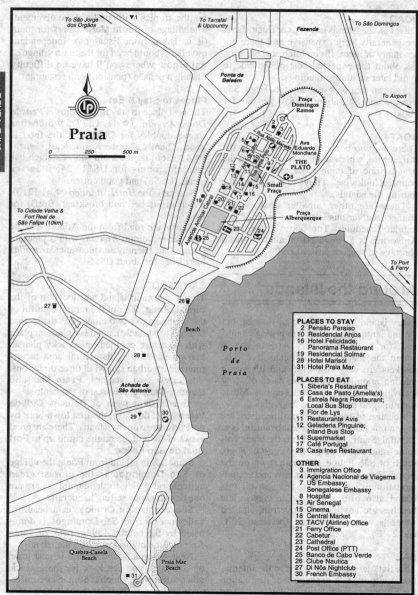

To São Jorge
dos Orgãos

To Tarrafal
& Upcountry

To São Domingos

Fazenda

To Airport

Ponta de
Beleém

Praça
Domingos
Ramos

Ave
Eduardo
Mondlane

THE PLATÔ

Small
Praça

Praça
Alberquerque

To Port
& Ferry

LP

Praia

0   250   500 m

To Cidade Velha &
Fort Real de
São Felipe (10km)

Rua Abílio Macedo

Avenida Amílcar Cabral

Beach

26

27

28

29   30

Achada de
São Antonio

Porto
de
Praia

Quebra-Canela
Beach

Praia Mar
Beach

31

PLACES TO STAY
2   Pensão Paraiso
10 Residencial Anjos
16 Hotel Felicidade;
    Panorama Restaurant
17 Residencial Solmar
28 Hotel Marisol
31 Hotel Praia Mar

PLACES TO EAT
1   Siberia's Restaurant
5   Casa de Pasto (Amelia's)
6   Estrela Negra Restaurant;
    Local Bus Stop
9   Flor de Lys
11 Restaurante Avis
12 Geladaria Pinguine;
    Inland Bus Stop
14 Supermarket
17 Café Portugal
29 Casa Ines Restaurant

OTHER
3   Immigration Office
4   Agencia Nacional de Viagems
7   US Embassy;
    Senegalese Embassy
8   Hospital
13 Air Senegal
15 Cinema
18 Central Market
20 TACV (Airline) Office
21 Ferry Office
22 Cabetur
23 Cathedral
24 Post Office (PTT)
25 Banco de Cabo Verde
26 Clube Nautica
27 Di Nôs Nightclub
30 French Embassy

CAPE VERDE

Entrada – once there, you would have to be blind to miss the tree.

At the northern end of Santiago is the island's second largest settlement, **Tarrafal**, which is famous for its beaches. It can be reached by bus from Praia.

Places to Stay & Eat

It's on the Platô in Praia that you'll find the best selection of cheap hotels and restaurants. One of the cheapest is *Pensão Paraiso* (☎ 61 3539), near the *liceu* (secondary school) on Rua Serpa Pinto, which has singles/doubles for US$12/15.

More expensive is the *Hotel Felicidade* (☎ 61 5585) on Rua Serpa Pinto, which has rooms from US$15/32. The Sunday buffet lunch at the *Panorama*, on top of the Felicidade, is highly recommended. The *Residencial Solmar* on Avenida Amílcar Cabral, a block south of the central market, has rooms for around US$29/41.

For generous serves of authentic Cape Verdean food, try *Casa de Pasto (Amelia's)* on Avenida Amílcar Cabral. It's open daily and a three-course meal costs US$6.

For a bit of a rage with the younger set, head to *Di Nôs*, 1km south-west of the Platô, reputedly the best nightclub in town. It hots up from 10.30 pm Friday to Sunday, and entry is US$5. Other venues are *Clube Nautica*, by the beach just south of the Platô and the popular *Flor de Lys* on Ave Eduardo Mondlane.

In São Jorge dos Orgãos, the *Pensão Sossego* (☎ 61 3637), situated in beautiful surroundings with great views, has rooms from US$14.

In Tarrafal, there are bungalows to rent at the *Bungalows do Tarrafal* (☎ 61 3232) for US$18 per night, payable in advance, or you can stay at *Pensão Ta-Ta* for US$20 per night, including breakfast. There are a couple of bars near the *praça* (main plaza).

SANTO ANTÃO

This is the greenest of the islands, particularly on its northern side, though the south is quite dry and resembles a moonscape. The mountainous centre is covered with Africa's highest pine forests, planted in the 1950s, and dotted with houses. Because of the more viable environment on this island, which has allowed a higher percentage of local people to stay, it is the most unspoiled of them all. It's recommended that you take a trip from Porto Novo to Ribeira Grande for the experience of driving over the top of the **Delgadinho**, a backbone of rock about as wide as the HiAce minibus you'll be sitting in. From either side of the road, you can look down almost sheer 1000m slopes.

The most important town on the island is **Ribeira Grande**, which has a few pleasant pensões where you can stay. *Residencial Aliança* (☎ 21 1246) has clean rooms, some for as little as US$22. For food try the *Cantinho* by the Aliança, and for entertainment there is bound to be an improvised disco in full swing somewhere.

The village of **Paúl** is one of the highlights of the island. Here you'll find perfectly preserved Portuguese architecture, yet no-one can even remember any Portuguese living here. There is a nearby canyon which leads up to the mountainous centre. A comfortable place to stay is the modern *Pensão Vila do Paúl*, where you can rent a good room with balcony from US$14. The attached *restaurant* has delicious food.

SÃO VICENTE

The town of **Mindelo** is very reminiscent of a deserted Portuguese provincial town, though it also displays British influences – brass bands play in the bandstand in the city park on Sunday! If possible, try to visit Mindelo at the end of February, when the local people pride themselves on their mini version of Rio's carnival.

Places to Stay & Eat

In Mindelo, the best place to stay is the *Pensão Chave d'Ouro* (☎ 31 1050), which has a lot of different rooms, some for as little as US$9 (top floor). The new *Hotel Rialto* on Rua N'Krumah comes recommended and is a little more expensive than the Chave d'Ouro. Also recommended (by readers) is the clean, friendly *Pensão Chez Loutcha*

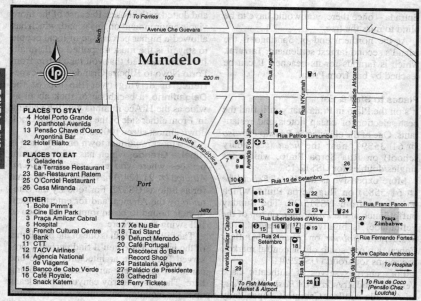

Mindelo

0   100   200 m

PLACES TO STAY
4 Hotel Porto Grande
9 Aparthotel Avenida
13 Pensão Chave d'Ouro;
   Argentina Bar
22 Hotel Rialto

PLACES TO EAT
6 Geladeria
7 La Terrasse Restaurant
23 Bar-Restaurant Ratem
25 O Cordel Restaurant
26 Casa Miranda

OTHER
1 Boite Pimm's
2 Cine Edin Park
3 Praça Amilcar Cabral
5 Hospital
8 French Cultural Centre
10 Bank
11 CTT
12 TACV Airlines
14 Agencia National
   de Viagems
15 Banco de Cabo Verde
16 Café Royale;
   Snack Katem
17 Xe Nu Bar
18 Taxi Stand
19 Defunct Mercado
20 Café Portugal
21 Discoteca do Bana
   Record Shop
24 Pastalaria Algarve
27 Palácio de Presidente
28 Cathedral
29 Ferry Tickets

(☎ 31 1636) on Rua de Coco, with rooms from US$22. More expensive is the *Hotel Porto Grande* (☎ 31 3838) on the praça – avoid the noisy front rooms.

The small bars in and around the harbour have their own special atmosphere and are worth visiting. Try the *Café Royale*, *Snack Katem*, *Café Portugal* or the *Pastalaria Algarve* on Rua Libertadores d'Africa. For traditional Cape Verdean food, go to the Chave d'Ouro (about US$5). The *Argentina Bar*, next door, is a good drinking hole.

Central African Republic

This area of Africa has been plundered for centuries. As a result, the Central African Republic (CAR) is an underdeveloped, fragmented and poverty-stricken country yet one which, with an enlightened government, could be prosperous. The CAR stagnates, however, because of the rapaciousness of its rulers and the negative influence of foreign interests.

Although the country has important mineral deposits and could export significant amounts of produce, little of the wealth generated seeps down to the population at large. Most of it is frittered away by a tiny elite on luxury items and, in some cases, on extreme self-aggrandisement.

To travellers, Central Africans, particularly outside the capital, are usually open, friendly and generous. If it's the 'real' Africa you're looking for, rural CAR may be it.

Facts about the Country

HISTORY

Archaeological remains indicate extensive settlement in the region long before the rise of ancient Egypt and, later, an advanced culture whose artisans were coveted from far afield. However, organised society was decimated by the slave trade – from two directions. Tens of thousands of slaves were dragged off westward for transportation to the Americas while Arab conquerors from the north completed the devastation. As recently as the 19th century, some 20,000 slaves from Central Africa were sold every year on the Egyptian market.

Into this shattered society, the French erupted in the 1880s. They parcelled the land into 17 concessions, ceded to European companies in exchange for around 15% of profits and a fixed annual payment. In need of labour, these companies forcibly, often brutally, conscripted the local population.

CENTRAL AFRICAN REPUBLIC
Area: 624,975 sq km
Population: 3.3 million
Population Growth Rate: 2.6%
Capital: Bangui
Head of State: President Ange-Félix Patassé
Official Language: French
Currency: Central African CFA franc
Exchange Rate: CFA 575 = US$1
Per Capita GNP: US$310
Inflation: 20%
Time: GMT/UTC + 1

Highlights
- The Chutes de Boali - dramatic waterfalls in the rainy season
- Butterfly-wing art at the Centre Artisanal in Bangui

Resistance continued to the French until the late 1920s when it was finally broken as a result of the combined factors of French military action, famine and severe epidemics of smallpox.

The first signs of nationalism sprang up after WWII in the form of Barthelemy Boganda's Mouvement d'Evolution Sociale de l'Afrique Noire. Boganda's party was instrumental in forcing the French to grant independence in 1960, the year after Boganda was killed in a mysterious plane crash. The leadership was taken over by David Dacko, the country's first president.

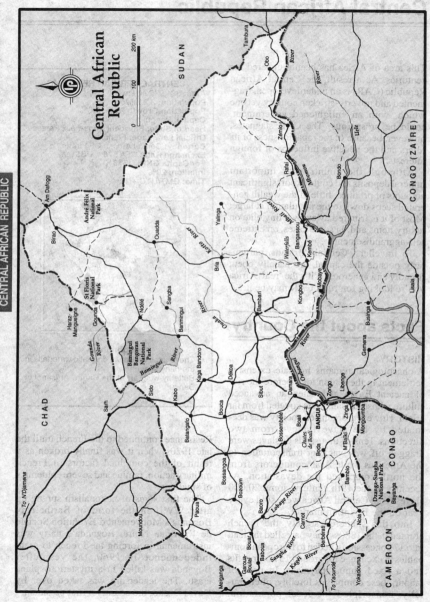

Central African
Republic

Dacko's rule quickly became highly repressive and dictatorial and in 1966 he was overthrown by army commander and close relative, Jean-Bédel Bokassa.

So began 13 years of one of the most sordid and brutal regimes Africa has ever experienced as Bokassa progressively took over the most important government portfolios and snuffed out all opposition. Offenders would be publicly clubbed to death – often with Bokassa's personal involvement.

France, coveting the uranium deposits at Bakouma and the exclusive big-game hunting grounds near the Sudanese border (patronised by former French president Giscard d'Estaing), nevertheless continued to indulge Bokassa and bail out his economy.

Using the country's mineral resources as the carrot, Bokassa negotiated loans from South Africa and private US banks and squandered virtually all this money on prestigious projects, many of which were never completed. He then embarked on his final and most asinine fantasy – to have himself crowned 'emperor' of a renamed Central African Empire. Despite the worldwide derision which the 1977 coronation provoked, the French picked up most of the tab of more than US$20 million, equivalent to the CAR's annual GNP.

Such excess, together with news of a massacre of school children in Bangui, made Bokassa even more of an embarrassment to his backers. Shortly afterwards, France, with David Dacko as its protégé, began to plot his downfall.

In 1979, France abruptly cut off aid to the 'empire'. While Bokassa was in Libya seeking funds, they flew in former president Dacko, supported by 700 French paratroopers, to stage a coup.

Bokassa initially found refuge in Côte d'Ivoire and then later in a chateau outside Paris. Meanwhile, Dacko's takeover proved unpopular and he came to rely increasingly on the presence of French paratroopers.

He in turn was overthrown in 1981 and replaced by André Kolingba, who created a one party state in late 1986. All opposition groups were banned and their supporters were jailed, harassed or forced to flee the country.

Believing that Kolingba wouldn't dare impeach him, Bokassa flew back to the CAR, only to be convicted of treason, murder and cannibalism. He was sentenced to death, but this was commuted to life imprisonment. He was confined to the folly at Berengo which he had constructed when in power, and his death in 1996 passed almost without comment in the local media.

In 1993 Kolingba's 12 years of absolute rule ended when he was defeated in presidential elections and Ange-Félix Patassé became the country's new leader. As Patassé stacked the government with his fellow-tribesmen, political power was snatched for the first time away from the riverine clans of the south.

In 1996, the army, still dominated by southern officers, came out of their barracks shooting on four occasions. Despite French intervention, there is every sign that traditional rivalries will continue to disrupt the country.

GEOGRAPHY & CLIMATE

The country is one immense plateau varying in height between 600 and 700m, with distinct climatic zones. In the south there are dense tropical rainforests with high humidity. The north of the country is dry scrub and forms part of the Sahel. The rainy season lasts from May to October in the south, and from June to September in the north.

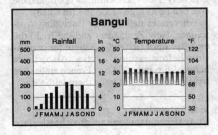

POPULATION & PEOPLE

The population stands at around 3.3 million. Most lived a traditional lifestyle in villages in the bush until Bokassa forcibly relocated them near the main roads. About 85% of the people are engaged in agriculture.

The equatorial forest of the south-west is home to some 15,000 Pygmies. Preserving their nomadic hunter-gatherer lifestyle, they harvest and hunt for their own consumption and to barter at the nearest village.

LANGUAGE

French is the official language, though Sango, known as the national language, is the lingua franca of most people. Very little English is spoken. See the section on French in the Language Appendix.

Sango

Sango, originally a trading language spoken along the Oubangui River, is the mother tongue of no more than 7% of Centrafricains. But everybody understands it. And because it favours no-one, it's the accepted language of communication between speakers of different languages – of which there are over 100 in the CAR. So, while French is the *official* language, Sango is formally recognised as the *national* language. ∎

Facts for the Visitor

VISAS

CAR embassies in neighbouring countries generally issue visas within 24 hours, and the cost can be as high as US$63 (in Chad).

For certain nationalities (including Australians, New Zealanders and the Irish) the embassy must first radio Bangui for permission before issuing a visa. Also, these nationalities may find that French embassies have no authority to issue them with visas.

Visa Extensions

Visa extensions are an expensive hassle since you pay the full price of a new one (US$42, for example, to extend a 12 day transit visa for a further month).

Other Visas

Burkina Faso, Côte d'Ivoire, Gabon, Mauritania, Senegal & Togo
Visas are available from the French consulate. They cost US$42 and are good for stays of up to 90 days. Ask for the visa section (not the consulate), which is only open from Monday to Friday, 8 to 10 am.

Cameroon
Visas cost US$63 for a stay of up to three months. You'll require one photo, and visas take 48 hours to issue. The embassy is open from Monday to Friday, 8 am to 3 pm.

Chad
Single-entry visas cost US$15 and are good for three-month stays. The embassy gives same-day service if you arrive early in the morning. It's open Monday to Thursday from 8 am to 3.30 pm and until noon on Friday.

Congo
The Congolese embassy requires two photos and US$63 to issue visas (usually the same day) valid for up to two months. It is open weekdays from 7 am to 2 pm and Saturday from 9 to 11 am.

Congo (Zaïre)
You'll need two photos, and visas are issued the same day, but first check that the border is open. Prices vary from US$42 for a one month single-entry visa to US$126 for a three month multiple-entry visa. The Congolese (Zaïrese) embassy is open from Monday to Friday from 8.30 am to 3.30 pm.

Nigeria
A one month visa varies in cost (free for Americans, US$23 if you're French and a swingeing US$214 for Britons). For a two month visa, double these costs. The embassy is open weekdays from 8 am to 3 pm and issues visas within 24 hours. Bring two photos.

Sudan
If you're going overland, your request must be sent to Khartoum, a process that can take up to two months. Not even an air ticket to Khartoum and beyond will necessarily exempt you from this process. Moreover, overland visas are issued only during the period from 15 October to 15 April. Two photos and US$40 are required. The embassy is open Monday to Saturday from 7.45 am to 2 pm (until noon on Fridays).

EMBASSIES
CAR Embassies

In Africa there are CAR embassies in Cameroon, Chad, Congo, Congo (Zaïre), Côte d'Ivoire, Egypt, Morocco and Nigeria. Where there is no CAR embassy, visas can generally be obtained from the French embassy.

Elsewhere there are embassies in Belgium, Canada, France, Germany and the USA.

Foreign Embassies in the CAR

Countries with embassies in Bangui include:

Cameroon
  Rue du Languedoc (☎ 61 1687)
Chad
  Ave Valéry Giscard d'Estaing, near Place de la République (☎ 61 4677)
Congo
  Ave Boganda (☎ 61 1877)
Congo (Zaïre)
  Rue Gamal Abdel Nasser (☎ 61 8240)
France
  Blvd Général de Gaulle (☎ 61 3000)
Germany
  Rue Gamal Abdel Nasser (☎ 61 0746)
Nigeria
  Km 3, Ave Boganda (☎ 61 0744)
Sudan
  Ave de la France (☎ 61 3821)
USA
  Ave David Dacko (☎ 61 0200)

If you're British and in trouble, contact the British honorary consul (☎ 61 3602).

MONEY

US$1 = CFA 480

The unit of currency is the Central African CFA franc, made up of 100 centimes. There are no restrictions on the import or export of local currency.

No banks outside Bangui change money, except in Berbérati.

Check commission rates, which can be outrageous, before changing travellers' cheques. Exchange rates are generally low: up to 25% lower than the prevailing internationally accepted rate! Banking hours are Monday to Friday from 7 am to noon.

POST & COMMUNICATIONS

The mail service is very slow. The poste restante in Bangui is efficient and charges US$0.50 per letter but only keeps them for a limited period.

You can send faxes and telexes from the post office and phone from the nearby Socatel office. Rates for three-minute calls are US$10 to Europe and US$20 elsewhere.

The country code for CAR is 236.

HEALTH

A yellow fever vaccination is required, as is a cholera shot if you've visited an infected area within the previous six days. Chloroquine-resistant malaria is a major problem. Swimming is not safe anywhere because of bilharzia (schistosomiasis). AIDS is also a very serious problem. See the Health Appendix for details.

DANGERS & ANNOYANCES
Crime & Petty Theft

If you're travelling overland through the CAR, expect the worst from provincial police, particularly if you're driving. Armed highway robbery in northern and central areas is on the increase.

Also see the Warning in the Bangui section.

Photography

Be very careful of what you photograph, as the police are always suspicious and people may resent your intrusion. See the Photography section in the Regional Facts for the Visitor chapter.

PUBLIC HOLIDAYS

The CAR's public holidays include: 1 January, 29 March (Boganda's Remembrance Day), 1 May, 30 June (National Prayer Day), 13 August (Independence), 15 August, 1 November, 1 December (National Day), 25 December and Easter Monday.

Getting There & Away

AIR

The CAR is served by Air Afrique (☎ 61 4700), Air France (☎ 61 4900), Air Gabon and Cameroon Airlines.

The airport departure tax is US$8 for all destinations.

LAND
Cameroon
The most popular crossing point is Garoua-Boulaï. Direct buses (US$20) run two or three times weekly from Bangui and stop overnight in Bouar. Trucks cost the same and also stop overnight in Bouar.

From Garoua-Boulaï, take a minibus to N'Goundal via Meidougou (4½ hours) and the train from there to Yaoundé (seven hours). For northern Cameroon, take a minibus from Garoua-Boulaï to N'Gaoundéré (US$8, 10 hours).

An alternative more southerly route is via Berbérati, Batouri and Bertoua. The roads on the CAR side are reasonably good; those in Cameroon are dirt and in poor condition.

Chad
There's only one minibus a week (US$19) between Bangui and Sido, the border town on the route to Sarh. There are, however, daily trucks from Bangui to Kaga Bandoro (US$9). From there a daily truck (US$8) leaves early for Sido, the border town. If you miss this, you'll have a long wait and probably a second overnight in Kabo, where the barrier and police post close at 5.30 pm. The police station is also the frontier post so be sure to have your passport stamped there – and don't take any nonsense from the underling at the border in Sido who'll try to extract a fee for letting you through. Once you're over the border, a pick-up for Sarh costs US$5 and takes around five hours. Allow a minimum of two long days for the trip from Bangui to Sarh.

The alternative route via Paoua and Cameroon is not recommended since beyond Bossangoa there are few vehicles and almost as many bandits.

Congo
Between late May and early December a riverboat of the French-managed Société Centrafricaine de Transports Fluviaux (SOCATRAF; ☎ 61 4315 for news of depar-tures) leaves Bangui about every two to three weeks for Brazzaville. Cabins are basic, the downriver journey takes about seven days and the cost per person is US$25. For tickets, ask for Madame Kezza at SOCATRAF.

Congo (Zaïre)
Both of the once-popular Oubangui River crossings from the CAR to Congo (Zaïre), Zongo to Bangui and Mobayi-Mbongo to Mobaye, are currently closed to foreigners.

At the time of writing only the Bangassou border crossing is likely to be open. For a vehicle, the cost of the ferry – which is often out of order – is 'negotiable'. You'll have to bargain hard to pay anything less than 10 litres of diesel fuel. Without a vehicle you have the additional option of taking a pirogue. Congolese (Zaïrese) officials may demand outrageous sums for allowing in your camera, binoculars or video and invent fees such as a fictitious road tax. There are several minibuses daily between Bangui and Bambari (US$10) and between Bambari and Bangassou (US$13).

Sudan
Your only option – and it's a tough one – is from Bangui to El Obeid via Birao in the north-eastern corner of the CAR. The trip can easily take a month, much longer in the rainy season when roads become a quagmire. There's very little traffic and travellers have reported waiting two weeks in Birao for a truck. Before you set out check the fluctuating security situation in western Sudan – and whether the border's open.

The potential route to Sudan from Bangui to Juba via Bangassou is out until the civil war in southern Sudan is resolved.

Getting Around

ROAD
Road conditions are poor throughout the country. The only sealed roads lead from Bangui to M'Baïki (107km south-west), to midway between Bossembélé and Baoro

(some 275km north-west) and to Sibut (188km north-east). Expect frequent potholes on all but the Bangui to M'Baïki stretch.

During the dry season, dirt roads to major towns, the Cameroon border and the Chad border as far as Kaga Bandoro and Bossangoa are mostly in good condition. But when the rains begin, the laterite becomes very muddy and slippery. During and after heavy rainstorms, portions of the Bangui to Cameroon border road can be closed for days so that the large trucks don't tear up the road.

Overcrowded 24-seater minibuses connect Bangui with all major towns. Trucks and pick-ups are called *occasions* in the CAR and are a popular way to travel. Their prices are much the same as minibus fares.

Bangui

Bangui, the capital of the CAR, lies beside the Oubangui River. All major avenues radiate from the Place de la République, the hub of the capital. It's a desolate urban space as many of the buildings were shelled or torched during the 1996 army mutinies.

The heart of the African quarter is the unmarked Km 5 intersection west of town (known variously and confusingly as K-Cinq, Kam Cinq or even PK – pronounced payka – Cinq). It has the largest market, lots of bars and various dancing places. K-Cinq and Ave du Lieutenant Koudoukou, which leads off from it, are the city's liveliest areas but also the most dangerous. Muggers, sometimes drunk, are on the streets here day and night and you should never venture here alone.

Warning

Bangui is one of the most dangerous cities in Central Africa for petty thievery, pickpocketing and, increasingly, violence. Avoid groups of young men and, if you go out at night, always take a taxi.

Information

The post office is open Monday to Friday from 6.30 am to 1.30 pm.

The immigration office is about 1km up the hill to the north of the Presidential Palace. Ask for directions at the army post behind the palace.

Avoid the BIAO bank where staff are surly and commission rates vicious. At the UBAC bank service is friendly and there's no commission for sums under CFA 500,000.

The Martin Luther King Center next to the US embassy has an air-con library with magazines, newspapers and rolling CNN. Open weekdays from 8.30 am to 1.30 pm, it shows free movies every Friday at 7.30 pm.

The Maison de la Presse carries a good stock of French books and magazines and it also has a small range from the international press.

Things to See

The **Musée de Boganda** (US$1) on Rue de l'Industrie is well organised and has helpful guides. There's an interesting collection of local musical instruments which you can try out and there are also good displays on the Pygmies and their culture.

For artisan goods, head for the **Centre Artisanal**, open daily until 6 pm. You'll find ebony carvings, porcupine-quill bracelets, leather goods, batiks, appliqué, African costumes, malachite, grass dolls, woodcarvings and masks. Many of the artefacts are common to the whole Congo basin but don't miss the butterfly-wing collages, which are special to the CAR.

For your eyes only since his prices are sky-high, visit the **Perroni gallery** beside the port. Cyr Perroni came to the CAR from Martinique over 40 years ago and has trained many of the artisans whose products are sold at the Centre Artisanal.

The **Marché Central** in the centre of town, normally bustling and open mornings only, was being extensively renovated at the time of writing. Avoid the market at Km 5. There are more thieves than things for sale here and there's a good chance you'll be mugged.

PLACES TO STAY
2 Centre Protestant Pour la Jeunesse
9 Iroko Hotel
13 Centre d'Accueil Touristique Dalango
21 National Hotel
86 Sofitel Bangui

PLACES TO EAT
1 Restaurant Mirandela
14 Food Stands
28 Restaurant le Relais de Sica
29 Restaurant le Perroquet
30 Snack Bar Les Sept Epis
36 Restaurant le Bistro de l'Enflure
38 Restaurant Le Relais des Chasses
42 Snack Bar Dakota
48 Dias Frères Supermarket
49 Restaurant Chez Malée
51 Salon de Thé de la Terrasse
52 Restaurant New Montana; Manovo Safaris
53 Pâtisserie la Marquise
79 Restaurant Ewaton
80 Cheap Food Stalls
82 Restaurant le Petit Piment
83 Restaurant l'Arbre du Voyageur

OTHER
3 Assemblée Nationale
4 Commissariat Central
5 Gare Routière ONAF
6 University
7 Mosque
8 Bar ABC Nightclub
10 Gare Routière Km 5
11 Le Punch Coco Night Club; Restaurant de l'Amitié
12 Marché Mamadou M'Baïki
15 Nigerian Embassy
16 World Wide Fund for Nature Office
17 Mission St-Charles
18 Bar les Trois Palmiers
19 Lycée
20 Stadium
22 Air France
23 Congo (Zaïre) Embassy
24 Institut Pasteur
25 Hospital
26 Sudan Embassy
27 Cathedral
31 Centre Artisanal
32 European Development Fund Office
33 Mission Evangélique
34 Petroca Station; Bamag Supermarket

35 Rond-Point Boganda
37 Public Gardens
39 Musée de Boganda
40 Cameroon Embassy
41 Le Meringue Nightclub
43 Cinéma Club
44 Apic Photo Service
45 US Embassy; Martin Luther King Library
46 Le Phénix Night Club
47 Tsiros Auto Rental
50 Congo Embassy
54 Maison de la Presse
55 Camico
56 Renault Dealer/Garage
57 Le Songo Nightclub
58 Air Gabon Office
59 German Embassy
60 BEAC Bank
61 Post Office
62 Socatel

63 UNICEF Office
64 Presidential Palace
65 UBAC Bank
66 Police
67 Air Afrique Office
68 Place de la République
69 BIAO Bank
70 Marché Central
71 Perroni Art Gallery
72 Pharmacie Henguibe
73 SOCATRAF Building; Taxi Stand for Ouango
74 Petrol Station
75 CFAO General Store
76 SCKN Department Store
77 Chad Embassy
78 Radio Station
81 Immigration Office
84 French Embassy
85 Ferry for Zongo, Commissariat du Port; Pirogues

To Km 12, Sibut, Bossembélé & Bouar

To Airport

Avenue du Lt Koudoukou

Avenue des Martyrs

Avenue Ben Zid

Malikama

Avenue Yakité

Mustapha

Meskine

Avenue Yakité

Avenue du Lt Koudoukou

Avenue Castors

Avenue Boganda

Mamadou M'Baïki

Km 5

Bacongo

Bangui

0   250   500 m

To M'Baïki

To M'Baïki

Avenue de l'UDEAC

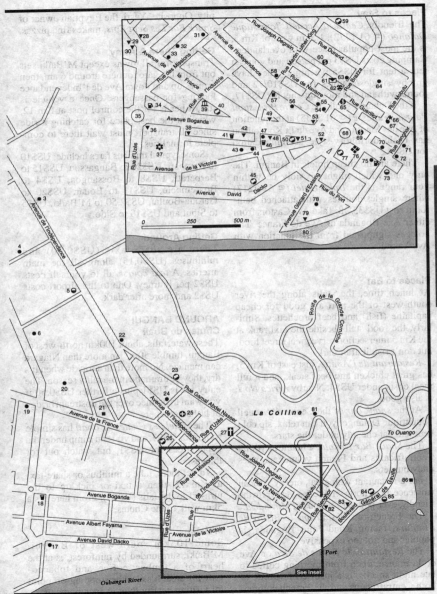

CENTRAL AFRICAN REPUBLIC

Places to Stay

The friendly *Centre d'Accueil Touristique Dalango* (☎ 61 1772), 1.5km west of Km 5, is the most popular place with overlanders. Camping costs US$3 per person and you can rent a tent for US$5 per night. They have grubby singles/doubles for US$10/12 and rooms with fan and mosquito net for US$17.

If the Dalango's full, the *Centre Protestant Pour la Jeunesse* (☎ 61 3935) at the junction of Ave des Martyrs and Ave du Lt Koudoukou has basic dormitory-style accommodation for US$4.

There are no cheap hotels in Bangui. The only one which might possibly be within your range is the *Iroko Hotel* (☎ 61 2217) where singles/doubles with attached bathroom cost US$33/38. Take Ave Castors from either Ave Boganda or Ave de France. The hotel is signposted from the junction with Ave Yakité.

Places to Eat

At lunch time, the stalls along the river south-west of the port are good for cheap capitaine (fish) and beef brochettes. Similarly, the food stalls beside the taxi rank at the Km 5 intersection serve great street food, but don't risk it after dark.

Restaurant de l'Amitié, just east of Km 5, has great chicken and beef steak, and a full meal costs under US$4. Nearby *Africa No 1* is also good.

At the *snack bar* of the Centre d'Accueil Touristique Dalango, you can relax, sip cold beer and eat cheaply under the stars.

The *Snack Bar Dakota*, a haunt of young Centrafricains and French volunteers, does juicy burgers.

For a restaurant with great, breezy African ambience, head north on Ave des Martyrs to the friendly, ever-popular *Restaurant Mirandela*.

The French-run *Restaurant le Bistro de l'Enflure*, facing Rond-Point Boganda, is popular and not too expensive.

The *Restaurant le Relais de Sica* on Ave de la France, open from morning coffee to late night snacks, is a justified favourite of both Centrafricains and the French community. Opposite, Yusri, the Egyptian owner of *Snack Bar Les Sept Epis*, makes fine pizzas.

Getting There & Away

Transport for all towns except M'Baïki sets out from the gare routière around 6 am, then cruises up and down Ave de l'Indépendance looking for passengers. Once a vehicle is full, it heads for the control post at Km 12, which is the best place for catching a ride since all transport must wait there to complete formalities.

Some typical minibus fares include: US$10 to Bambari, US$20 to Bangassou, US$15 to Berbérati, US$8 to Bossangoa, US$4 to Bossembélé, US$11 to Bouar, US$20 to Garoua-Boulaï, US$2.50 to M'Baïki, US$5 to Sibut and US$19 to Sido.

Getting Around

There are share-taxis (US$0.20) and minibuses (US$0.15) along all the main arteries. A *taxi course* all to yourself costs US$2 per journey. One to the airport costs US$2 and more after dark.

AROUND BANGUI
Chutes de Boali

These waterfalls, about 100km north-west of Bangui, tumble 50m, 1m more than Niagara can manage. No more than a trickle when it's dry, they're dramatic in the rainy season. The entry fee is US$1 plus a further US$0.50 if you want to bounce over the upstream bridge of lashed creepers.

The *Hôtel des Chutes de Boali* has simple rooms for US$7, and you can camp under the kapok trees for US$1, but watch out for thieves.

To get there, take a minibus or share-taxi to Km 12, then a taxi or pick-up to the turn-off to the falls (US$3). From here it's a 5km walk to the Chutes.

M'Baïki

Some 105km south-west of Bangui, M'Baïki, surrounded by rainforest, is at the heart of a timber, coffee and tobacco-growing area. It's also the stopping-off point for visiting nearby Pygmy encampments.

One bus (US$2.50) and several pick-ups each day leave Bangui from the lane beside Le Punch Coco nightclub at Km 5. At Berengo, you'll pass a folly which Bokassa built on his tribal lands. Satisfyingly, it now functions as a rural development centre and chicken farm. Also, some 10km north-east of M'Baïki, is the village of Sabe, famous for its ebony sculptures.

The only hotel, the *New Deal Motel*, 200m from the bus station, may not be as cosmopolitan as its name but it offers clean singles/doubles you can lock at US$3/4.

Around the Country

BOSSEMBÉLÉ

This is the second-largest town on the route between Cameroon and Bangui.

If you need a room, try the unmarked *auberge* (guesthouse) on the main drag 150m west of the market. Rooms cost US$3. Otherwise there's the nearby *Auberge de 7 Jours* or the spartan *Auberge Yolowana* (US$2).

BOUAR

Bouar is a frequent stopping place on the road between Bangui and the Cameroon border. The area is dotted with megalithic stone monuments. It's also the site of a large French military base and theft can be a problem.

A room at the *Auberge Chez Pauline* next to the bus station is US$4 after haggling. Pauline and other family members are always around, so your gear is safe. You can park safely and eat well at the *Auberge le Maigaro* (US$4/7 a single/double).

KAGA BANDORO

If you find yourself overnighting here, *Le Samaritain* has singles/doubles for US$3/4, each with an edifying biblical text painted in large red letters. Or else try the *Auberge Koui Na Lo* 100m west of the market square. Avoid the particularly grubby auberge in the square itself.

SIBUT

Sibut, which marks the end of the blacktop road from Bangui, straggles around the junction where roads lead north to the Chad border and east to Bambari and Bangassou.

You can eat and sleep at the *Bar-Dancing la Paillotte du Carrefour* (US$3) on the main street or at the *Restaurant-Auberge le Distingué* just south of the junction.

Chad

A short trip taking in N'Djamena, southern Chad and the Lake Chad area, particularly in conjunction with a side trip to Waza Game Park in northern Cameroon, is well worth the effort. Travel to the far north is not recommended because of the long-standing border dispute with Libya and the fields of uncharted land mines, relics of Chad's long civil war.

Facts about the Country

HISTORY

For three decades after independence from the French in 1960, Chad was torn apart by violent conflicts in which thousands lost their lives.

Its recent bloody history of factionalism was largely the result of the reversal of traditional power relationships brought about by French colonialism. Before the French, the Muslim kingdoms of Ouadaï and Baguirmi dominated the area. Basing their economies on the slave trade, they raided the black peoples of the south who could offer little resistance. The French, likewise, conquered the south easily but the northern kingdoms weren't fully subdued until 1916, nearly 20 years later.

The French introduced cotton into the south and encouraged the development of a market economy which led to the breakdown of the old social order. The cultivation of cotton brought modest investments and the building of schools, though the north was neglected until the 1950s. As a result, educated southerners were much better placed to lead the nationalist movement after WWII.

The first nationalist movement, the Parti Progressiste Tchadien (PPT), was set up in 1947 with the resounding slogan 'No more cotton, no more chiefs, no more taxes'. Since this struck at the heart of the colonial system,

REPUBLIC OF CHAD
Area: 1,284,000 sq km
Population: 6.2 million
Population Growth Rate: 2.4%
Capital: N'Djamena
Head of State: President Colonel Idriss Deby
Official Languages: French, Arabic
Currency: Central African CFA franc
Exchange Rate: CFA 575 = US$1
Per Capita GNP: US$130
Inflation: 40%
Time: GMT/UTC + 1

Highlights
- Abéché, a desert-locked Muslim town, one-time capital of the powerful Ouadaï sultanate
- The small Sao-Kotoko museum, created by the villagers of Gaoui, near N'Djamena
- N'Djamena's bustling central market, the Grand Marché

France at first supported the feudal Muslim forces of the north.

After the PPT abandoned its radical stance in 1950 and integrated itself into the colonial structure, the French were able to install a compliant territorial assembly, known as the Loi Cadre. This body assumed responsibility for the country's internal autonomy, granted in 1956.

The Loi Cadre had limited support and in 1958 the Union Nationale Tchadienne (UNT) was formed by trade unionists, students and intellectuals. It demanded full

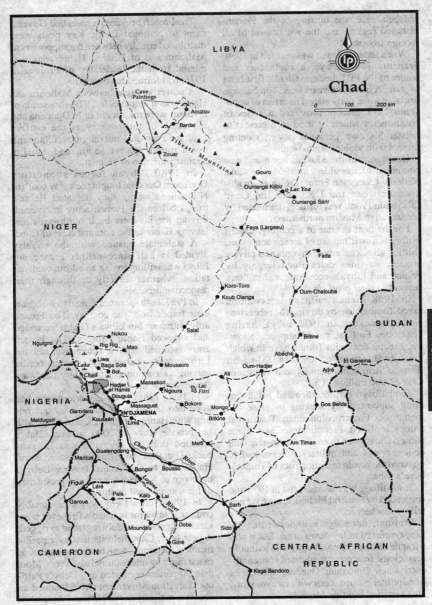

independence, the ousting of the French-installed regime and the withdrawal of all foreign troops.

When independence was granted in 1960, François Tombalbaye, a southerner and leader of the PPT, became Chad's first head of state. A mere two years later, Tombalbaye declared a one party state. His arrest of opposition UNT leaders provoked a series of conspiracies which he used as a pretext to bolster his own personal power, meeting dissent with violent repression.

Resistance in the Muslim north and east continued to smoulder. In 1966, the Chad National Liberation Front (Frolinat), an alliance between the UNT and the Chad Liberation Front, was formed, dominated by conservative Muslim northerners.

For the next quarter of a century, Chad's history is a swirling sea of arcane acronyms, shifting alliances, ethnic myopia and private armies, its tides determined largely by France and Libya's economic and military support to their protégés.

In 1968 French military intervention saved Tombalbaye by driving the rebels into isolated pockets. In 1972 Libya, having bankrolled Frolinat, cut off support following a secret deal with Tombalbaye in which the Libyans occupied the 114,000-sq-km Aouzou Strip in northern Chad in return for CFA 23,000 million of aid.

Tombalbaye further alienated his dwindling supporters by seeking to erase the memory of French colonialism. Traditional names replaced French street and place names. Christian names were banned and all civil servants and military officers had to undergo the *yondo* initiation rites of Tombalbaye's tribe.

Tombalbaye was assassinated in 1975 and succeeded by General Malloum, his rival and fellow southerner.

Frolinat, once again underwritten by Libya, refused to lay down arms. But it was a fragile alliance of conflicting and mutually suspicious interests, temporarily strengthened when Goukouni Oueddei spliced its five splinter groups, each with its own army, into a unified fighting force.

The French brokered a so-called Government of National Unity. Key posts were distributed equally between the supporters of Malloum and of Hissène Habré who, dismissed from the leadership of Frolinat in 1976, had formed his own army.

A power struggle between Malloum and Habré was inevitable. In 1979, thousands of civilians were massacred in N'Djamena and the south of the country as the conflict assumed a regional and religious colour with north pitted against south, and Muslim against Christian or animist.

In 1980 Libyan forces supporting Goukouni Oueddei fought their way south to N'Djamena where they defeated Habré's troops before the French army intervened, driving the invaders back northwards and leaving Habré as the nominal ruler of Chad.

A stalemate ensued with the country divided in half since neither France nor Libya was willing to risk an all-out confrontation, whether directly or through their respective protégés.

In 1987, both sponsors agreed to withdraw their forces from the country. The French duly withdrew but Libya's Gaddafi reneged and attacked Habré's forces. The French army returned with a vengeance and the Libyans were pushed back over the border leaving vast amounts of military hardware strewn across the desert.

In 1990, Idriss Deby, a warlord who had gone into self-exile in Sudan after quarrelling with Habré, swept back into Chad with his private army of 2000 soldiers. Habré claimed that the invasion was Libyan-backed but the French this time stayed aloof. Habré fled to Cameroon, leaving Deby a clear run to N'Djamena and the presidency of his war-ravaged country.

In 1996, Idriss Deby was a predictably comfortable victor in Chad's first ever presidential elections, widely regarded as rigged. A year later, Chad held its first ever parliamentary elections, which were regarded as much fairer by international observers. More than 50 parties competed and Deby's Patriotic Salvation Movement (MPS) gained an absolute majority in the National Assembly.

GEOGRAPHY & CLIMATE

Landlocked Chad is one of the world's poorest countries, and its development is hampered by insufficient and primitive communications as well as by political turmoil.

Chad has potential wealth with important deposits of uranium, wolfram and cassiterite in the Tibesti; gold in Mayo Kebbi; gold, uranium, iron and bauxite in the east; and oil reserves in the Lake Chad and south-west regions. Chad is also Africa's second largest producer of both cotton and gum arabic.

The country has three distinct climatic zones. The south is tropical, with as much as 1000mm of rain per year. There, the dry season runs from November to May and, while temperatures usually range from 20 to 25°C, they can rise to 40°C just before the rains. The centre, where N'Djamena and Lake Chad are located, blends scrub and desert and pre-rains temperatures can rise to over 45°C. The north forms part of the Sahara Desert and includes the Tibesti Mountains which rise to nearly 3500m, some of the highest in North Africa.

ECOLOGY & ENVIRONMENT

The Chadian countryside has suffered badly from the twin ravages of nature and people. The Sahel drought of the 1970s and early 1980s destroyed centuries-old patterns of existence and cultivation. And poachers, taking advantage of the anarchy of nearly two decades of civil war, shot to oblivion much of its wildlife. Now, new drought-resistant cereals are being introduced and, with affluent tourism in mind, the wildlife parks are being restocked and monitored.

POPULATION & PEOPLE

Chad has a population of around 6.2 million. The country stands at an ethnic crossroads where Arab Africa meets black Africa. Black Africans of the south are in the majority and have traditionally dominated the government and civil service. The north is populated by people of Arab descent as well as nomadic Tuareg, Peul-Fulani and Toubou.

The difference between these two broad groups is profound. Southerners are mostly peasant farmers tilling fertile land, people of the monsoon, who are animist or Christian. Those of the north are desert-dwelling pastoralists, people who live with the hot, rasping harmattan, who are Muslim. And – most important of all in the collective memory – north and south also means historical enslavers and ex-slaves.

LANGUAGE

French and (since 1996) Arabic are joint official languages but there are more than 50 local languages, the main ones being Sara, spoken primarily in the south, and, in the north, Turku, often referred to as Chadian Arabic. See the Language Appendix for useful French and Arabic words and phrases.

Facts for the Visitor

VISAS

Only German and French citizens do not need visas. Visas are usually valid for three months and can be renewed without difficulty. The cost is generally around US$15, but can be as high as US$30. You can obtain a Chadian visa in every country in West and Central Africa (except The Gambia and São Tomé). French embassies no longer issue Chadian visas in countries where Chad has no diplomatic representation. Note that Chadian visas are now available in Niger.

You must register at the sûreté, on Ave Félix Éboué, within 72 hours of arriving in N'Djamena. The immigration office (open 7.30 am to 3.30 pm from Monday to Friday) is on the right side of the compound. Registration is free and you'll need patience and two photos.

Visa Extensions

Visa extensions are issued at the sûreté office in N'Djamena.

Other Visas

Burkina Faso, Côte d'Ivoire, Gabon, Mauritania, Senegal & Togo

Visas are issued within 24 hours by the French consulate (open weekdays, 9 am to noon for visa enquiries). A five day transit visa costs US$6. One valid for up to three months costs US$63. For either, you'll need three photos.

Cameroon

A single-entry visa costs US$42 for a stay of up to a month. The embassy is open from 7.30 am to 3 pm, Monday to Thursday and until 12.30 pm on Friday. One photo is required and it takes 48 hours to issue visas. At the time of writing, the embassy was not issuing cheaper transit visas to people who just want to pass through Cameroon en route to Nigeria.

Central African Republic

The CAR embassy, open weekdays from 7.30 am to 1.30 pm, requires two photos and takes 24 hours to issue visas which cost US$63 for a single-entry visit of up to one month. As at all CAR embassies, in the case of citizens from Australia, New Zealand and Ireland, the embassy must first radio Bangui (US$10 fee) for approval, which normally arrives within 24 hours.

Congo (Zaïre)

The Congo (Zaïrese) embassy is open from 8 am to 2 pm Monday to Thursday and until noon on Friday and Saturday. requires two photos. A single-entry one-month visa costs US$52 and you'll need two photos.

Niger

If possible, get your Niger visa before leaving home since you can't get one in N'Djamena – or anywhere else in Central Africa. But you can easily obtain one in Kano or Lagos (Nigeria), Cotonou (Benin) or Addis Ababa (Ethiopia).

Nigeria

The Nigerian embassy, open weekdays from 8 am to 3.30 pm, requires two photos and 48 hours to process visas. They're reluctant to issue visas for longer than a month and the cost varies: free for Americans, US$23 for the French and a massive US$214 for Britons.

Sudan

Single-entry visas, valid for one month from the date of issue, cost US$61 and require two photos. In principle, all applications are referred to Khartoum, a process which normally takes two to three weeks. The embassy is open from 8 am to 12.30 pm, Monday to Friday.

EMBASSIES
Chadian Embassies

Chad has embassies in the neighbouring Central African Republic (CAR), Cameroon, Libya, Niger, Nigeria and Sudan.

Chad also has embassies in, among other places, Algeria, Belgium, Congo (Zaïre), France, Germany, Italy and the USA.

Foreign Embassies in Chad

Countries with diplomatic representation in N'Djamena include:

Cameroon

Rue des Poids Lourds, 500m north of Camp Koufra (☎ 52 2894)

Central African Republic

Rue 1036, near Rond-Point de la Garde (☎ 52 3206)

Congo (Zaïre)

Ave 26 Août, near Rond-Point de la Garde (☎ 52 5935)

France

Off Ave Félix Éboué, near Place de l'Étoile (☎ 52 2575)

Nigeria

Ave Charles de Gaulle, near Cinéma Vog (☎ 52 2498)

Sudan

Left then first right off Rue de la Gendarmerie (☎ 52 5010)

USA

Ave Félix Éboué, near Hôpital Central (☎ 51 6211)

If you're British and in trouble, contact the British honorary consul on ☎ 52 3645.

MONEY

US$1 = CFA 575

The unit of currency is the Central African CFA franc, made up of 100 centimes although shopkeepers and market traders normally quote prices in rials (one rial = CFA 5). Banks that exchange money include the Banque Internationale pour l'Afrique Occidentale (BIAO; which exacts a fat commission) and the Banque de Développement du Tchad (BDT). Banking hours are 7.15 am to 12.15 pm, Monday to Thursday, and to 11 am on Friday and Saturday.

Bottom-end and middle-range hotels in Chad are significantly more expensive than in neighbouring Cameroon, Nigeria and Niger but are roughly comparable to those in the CAR. Food prices are correspondingly high as well.

POST & COMMUNICATIONS

The postal service is reliable and international telephone connections, which are made by satellite, are usually good. To make a call, go to Telecommunications at the post office in N'Djamena or next to the museum in Sarh. Costs are high: expect to pay US$19 for a three minute call to the USA.

The country code is 235.

The King Meets The President

Don't believe those rumours that Elvis is rocking on the moon. You'll find him and his guitar in N'Djamena post office beside a sax-wielding Bill Clinton or paired with Richard Nixon. Each appears on Chadian postage stamps, together with Marilyn Monroe, John Lennon, Tina Turner, Jackie Kennedy (in a set of nine different poses), Bob Marley and – most bizarre of all – Madonna, who's not everyone's idea of Islamic womanhood. ■

PHOTOGRAPHY

Theoretically you need a photo permit from the Ministry of Information but since it costs US$25 and can take up to a week to be issued, few people bother. See also the Photography section in the Regional Facts for the Visitor chapter.

HEALTH

A yellow fever vaccination is mandatory, as is a cholera shot if you're within six days of having visited an infected area. Chloroquine-resistant malaria is on the increase. See the Health Appendix for further information.

DANGERS & ANNOYANCES

In N'Djamena, avoid the riverside area between the French embassy and the Novotel la Tchadienne. And don't walk on the footpath outside the President's Palace. Soldiers in both these areas are excessively trigger-happy.

N'Djamena, once one of the safest cities in Africa, has experienced an increase in pickpocketing and petty street crime, but rarely violence. You're at particular risk around the Grand Marché and on Ave Charles de Gaulle.

PUBLIC HOLIDAYS

Chad's public holidays include: 1 January, 1 May, 25 May, 11 August (Independence), 1 November, 28 November, 1 December, 25 December, Easter Monday, and variable Islamic holidays (see Public Holidays in the Regional Facts for the Visitor chapter).

Getting There & Away

AIR

Airlines servicing Chad include Air Afrique (☎ 52 4020), Air Chad, Air France (☎ 52 4981), Cameroon Airlines, Ethiopian Airlines and Sudan Airways.

The airport departure tax is US$17 for international flights and US$3 for domestic flights.

LAND

Cameroon & Nigeria

The usual overland point of exit is by bridge across the Chari River to Kousséri in Cameroon. Minibuses run from N'Djamena to the border and on to Kousséri (US$0.40). From Kousséri there are bush taxis to Maroua in Cameroon (US$8, four hours) and minibuses from there to N'Gaoundéré (Star Voyages is best). There are also bush taxis from Kousséri to Maiduguri in Nigeria. The border into Cameroon closes at 5.30 pm sharp.

Central African Republic

The usual route from southern Chad into the CAR is via Sarh and the border town of Sido. There are several bush taxis and an unreliable minibus each day from Sarh to Sido (US$5; five hours). Across the border, you'll probably have to overnight and change vehicles in Kaga Bandoro unless you're lucky enough to coincide with the one minibus per week heading straight through to Bangui

CHAD

(US$19); there's also a daily truck from Sido to Kaga Bandoro (US$8). Count on at least two long days from Sarh to Bangui.

The alternative route via Cameroon and Paoua (CAR) is not recommended since between the border and Bossangoa in CAR there are few vehicles and almost as many bandits.

Niger

N'Djamena to Niamey via the top of Lake Chad and Zinder is a hard slog of a week or more. Officials en route, particularly at the Nguigmi border post, are brutish and you can't rely on finding food or water between Mao and Zinder.

N'Djamena to Mao by bush taxi, probably changing vehicles in Massakori, costs US$10. Just outside Mao, you can stay at either the *mission catholique* or the *mission protestante* for a reasonable donation. In town, the *Centre de Culture de la Jeunesse* has double rooms at US$15.

There are infrequent pick-ups from Mao to Nokou (US$6) and from Nokou to Nguigmi in Niger (US$20, 1½ to three days). Equally infrequent pick-ups take the shorter route to Nguigmi via Rig Rig (US$20 to US$25). Both options are very sandy.

Between Nguigmi and Zinder there's one bus a week, leaving Nguigmi every Friday. Otherwise, look for a ride to Diffa (150km, US$4) as there are pick-ups (US$12) and at least one minibus a day (US$10) between Diffa and Zinder.

Get your passport stamped in Mao and Diffa and remember that Niger uses West African CFA francs, so buy some in advance.

Getting Around

AIR

Air Chad's sporadic internal flights connecting N'Djamena with Moundou, Sarh and Abéché are unreliable outside the rainy season.

ROAD

During the rainy season, travelling is, at best, slow and difficult. Southbound travel will become easier once the blacktop road, under construction between Bongor and Moundou, is completed.

The only bus services are those from N'Djamena to Sarh and Moundou in the south. Trucks and pick-ups are the main form of public transport.

N'Djamena

During Chad's civil war N'Djamena suffered badly. A lot of reconstruction has taken place although there are still many bomb sites and bullet-marked facades. The commercial and Muslim districts are bustling by day, especially in and around the lively market (the Grand Marché). They lose their vitality at sunset so, for nightlife, head for the African quarter which stays vibrant until late.

You're advised to dress respectably in N'Djamena to avoid offending local people.

Information

The post office is open from 7 to 11.30 am and 3.30 to 5.30 pm, Monday to Friday and Saturday mornings.

Librairie Al Akhbaar, opposite Air Afrique, has a good selection of books and journals in French and also has a few English-language newspapers and magazines.

Things to See

The small **National Museum**, on Ave Félix Éboué, looted during various invasions of the city, is being renovated and is worth a look. It's open from 8 am to noon every day except Sunday. The **Grand Marché** has a great atmosphere.

Places to Stay

There is little cheap accommodation in N'Djamena and neither the Peace Corps nor the Catholic mission normally welcome travellers.

If you're a sound sleeper, *Ma Carrière* restaurant/nightclub has rooms with fan and external shower/toilet for US$8. The surly owner of the *Auberge Dunia* will start at something ridiculous but will accept US$16 for his rooms with en suite bathroom and air-con (when his generator's working).

The *Hôtel l'Hirondelle* (☎ 52 5470), just east of the Grande Marché, has a selection of unattractive singles/doubles for US$12/21.

The low-life *Auberge le Boukarou* (☎ 52 2329) on Rue de Bordeaux is primarily a brothel. Its intensively occupied rooms (US$15) have fans, showers and basins. The bar is active but the ambience is subdued, so noise isn't a major problem. *Auberge la Plantation*, about 1km south of the bridge and on a regular minibus route, has clean rooms with ceiling fan and en suite toilet/shower for US$16.

If you fancy pampering yourself a little, try the *Auberge la Métropole* (☎ 51 6292). Its air-con rooms with en suite toilet/shower at US$26/31 and its restaurant are good value for money.

The upmarket *Novotel la Chadienne* (☎ 52 4312) lets you camp in its grounds.

Places to Eat
In the Grand Marché area, you'll find street meat sellers and restaurants serving a main dish (un plat) for US$1.25. The *N'Djamena City* and *Oasis* restaurants are recommended and you can also get reasonable meals at the restaurant of the *Hôtel l'Hirondelle*.

For good, reasonably priced food in a relaxed, rooftop setting, visit *Restaurant Etoile du Chad* on Ave Charles de Gaulle.

There's also a range of cheap restaurants to the north and south of the junction of Rue du Canal St Martin and Ave Charles de Gaulle. On the north side, *Al Ikhlasse* is clean, cheap and friendly. For African food, don't miss the *Senegalese restaurant*, just opposite, tucked away behind an unsigned green door and only open at lunch times. About 1 pm, the *patronne* begins ladling out delicious platefuls (US$1.25) of tiéboudienne (fish with mixed vegetables and rice) and by 2 pm she's scraping the bottom of the pot.

Also good for street meat and snacks is the area around the junction of Ave Mobutu and Blvd des Sao. Nearby is *Restaurant Tantine Zam Zam*, open only for dinner (US$3) and famous for its grilled fish. Or you can dine well and drink beer under a *boukarou* (a straw hut) in the garden of *Restaurant Le Pélican* (around US$4).

And all over town at any time of day you can cool off and rehydrate with a half-litre mug of fresh fruit juice, squeezed while you wait.

Getting There & Away
Buses and trucks for Sarh and Moundou leave from the Station de Chagoua at the intersection of Ave Charles de Gaulle and the Voie de Contournement.

If you're heading for Cameroon, the Rond-Point du Pont is the terminus for minibuses which go across the bridge and on to the border station (US$0.40).

Getting Around
You can walk to the airport by day (after dark you're inviting trouble) or take a taxi (US$4). Coming from the airport, you'll pay double unless you bargain hard.

Around town, a share-taxi costs US$0.30 per seat and a minibus is US$0.20. Alternatively it's US$2 for a *taxi course*, all to yourself.

Alternatively, you can easily hire a bike (around US$1.50 a day) and enjoy the independence.

AROUND N'DJAMENA
Gaoui
About 12km due east of the Palais du 15 Janvier and accessible by bike is the pottery village of Gaoui. Today's inhabitants, the riverine Kotoko, regard themselves as descendants of the ancient Sao who used to people the region. They've constructed their own museum, the **Sao-Kotoko Museum**, which displays, in addition to contemporary fishing, household and agricultural implements, finds from the 6th century BC Sao kingdom whose capital lies under today's village.

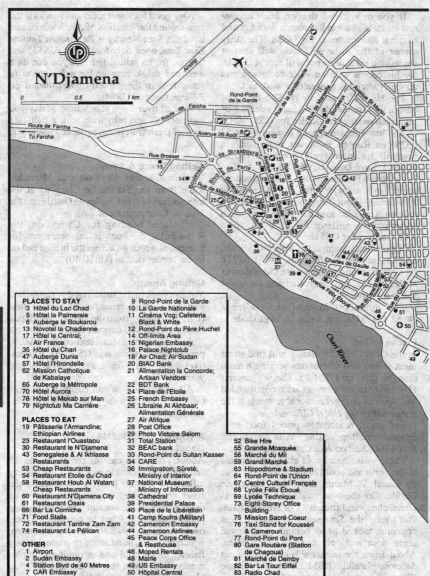

N'Djamena

0   0.5   1 km

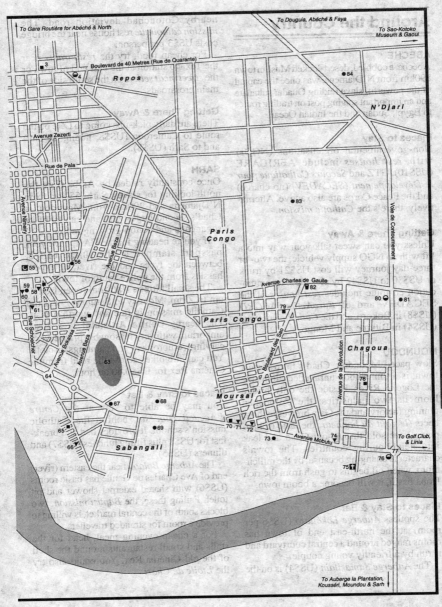

To Gare Routière for Abéché & North

To Douguia, Abéché & Faya

To Sao-Kotoko Museum & Gaoui

Boulevard de 40 Metres (Rue de Quarante)

Repos

■ 3

● 4

N'Djari

Avenue Zezerti

Rue de Pala

Avenue Nimeiry

Avenue Bokassa

Paris Congo

● 83

Voie de Contournement

Avenue Charles de Gaulle

⊞ 82

80 ◐ ● 81

55

56

Avenue Baza

59

58

57

60

61

62

79

Paris Congo

Rue Schoelcher

Avenue Baza

63

64

Chagoua

Boulevard des Sao

Avenue de la Révolution

78

● 67

● 68

Moursal

70 71 72

73

74

Avenue Mobutu

To Golf Club, & Linia

65

● 69

Sabangali

76

77

75

CHAD

To Auberge la Plantation, Kousséri, Moundou & Sarh

Around the Country

ABÉCHÉ

Abéché, a cobbled, desert-locked Muslim town 890km from N'Djamena, was once the capital of the powerful slave raiding Ouadaï sultanate and an important staging post on trading routes to Egypt, Sudan and the Indian Ocean.

Places to Stay

Non-governmental organisations (NGOs) with *rest houses* include AFRICARE (US$10), GTZ and *Secours Catholique pour le Développement (SECADEV)* (no charge) and the Peace Corps are also active. Alternatively, there's the *Catholic mission*.

Getting There & Away

Unless you can sweet-talk your way into a lift with an NGO supply vehicle, the two- or three-day journey will cost US$21 by truck or US$30 to US$42 by pick-up. Accommodation en route includes *rest houses* of the SECADEV and of *EuroAction ACORD* (US$8) in Bokoro, and the *Catholic missions* (US$4) in Bitkine and Mongo.

MOUNDOU

Slow-paced Moundou, Chad's third largest town, is a thin ribbon unravelled alongside the Logone River. Beside the only bridge loom its two industries: the Cotonchad ginning factory and the Gala brewery whose beers (*le goût du bonheur*, the taste of happiness) are sold throughout Chad and leak into neighbouring countries. The town's character is changing because, by the millennium, when oil begins to gush from the rich Doba basin, it will become a boom town.

Places to Stay & Eat

The spotless *Auberge Lokouaro* (US$6 per room) at the north-east end of town has rooms ranged around a central courtyard and is run by a friendly young couple.

The *Auberge Samaritain* (US$4) is on the nearby Cotonchad deviation road. The *mission catholique* rest house near the bridge costs US$3 per person.

For cheap food, try the *restaurants* near the Texaco station at the east end of town or the *street meat sellers* on the south side of the main crossroads.

Getting There & Away

There are daily pick-ups going to Léré on the route to Cameroon (US$8, taking all day) and to Sarh (US$8).

SARH

Once constantly raided by Arabs from the north looking for slaves, Sarh, 550km from N'Djamena and 290km from Moundou, is Chad's second largest city and capital of its sugar cane and cotton-growing region.

If you're heading for the CAR, have your passport stamped at the sûreté office, between the lycée and the river, or expect hassles from the police south of town.

The small **Musée National** (open from 7 am to 2 pm, Monday to Saturday) near the Catholic mission is free and worth a visit. The nearby **Centre Artisanal** is a dusty emporium with very reasonably priced wood carvings, embroidery and paintings on cloth. You can hire bikes across the road from the Cinéma Rex for US$0.40 an hour.

Places to Stay & Eat

You may be able to stay at the *Centre d'Accueil Diocésin*, behind the Catholic mission's school. It provides bed and breakfast for US$8 plus filling lunches (US$7) and dinners (US$5).

The *Auberge Bolaou* near the eastern (river) end of Ave Charles de Gaulle has basic rooms (US$6) with shared external shower and pit toilet. Failing these, the *Baptist mission*, two blocks south of the central market, is willing to provide a room for stranded travellers.

For a cheap evening meal, head for the stalls and small restaurants around the shell of the old Cinéma Rex. You could also try the *Étoile de Chari*.

Comoros & Mayotte

The four islands of the Comoros archipelago – three of which form an independent Islamic republic and one, Mayotte, which has opted to stick with France – lie between the northern tip of Madagascar and the African mainland.

The Comoros is one of Africa's big surprises. Most Comorians are polite, friendly and honest, and their colourful culture is still uncorrupted by tourism. The islands themselves are some of the world's most beautiful with scores of empty, spectacular beaches and a mysterious ambience reminiscent of Zanzibar. You'll also find picturesque old Arab towns, unique wildlife, luxuriant vegetation, an active volcano and lots of great hiking opportunities. Best of all, there's hardly a tourist in sight.

Facts about the Country

HISTORY

Like Madagascar, the Comoros islands were originally settled by people of Malay and Polynesian origin around the 6th century AD. Since then the population has become more mixed as a result of successive waves of immigration by Africans, Arabs and Shirazians. The Shirazians arrived from the Persian Gulf area between the 10th and 15th centuries, during the heyday of Swahili coastal trade, and set up a number of rival sultanates on the islands. Their wealth was based upon the slave and spice trades.

During the European scramble for African colonies in the late 19th century, the French scooped up the islands one by one. Their conquest was made considerably easier by the rivalry between the sultans, and the Sultan of Mayotte sold out to the French for annual payments.

In the early days of the colonial period the islands were administered from Madagascar,

---

FEDERAL ISLAMIC REPUBLIC OF THE COMOROS & MAYOTTE

Area: 1660 sq km (Comoros); 375 sq km (Mayotte)
Population: 550,000 (Comoros); 88,000 (Mayotte)
Population Growth Rate: 3.6% (Comoros); 3.8% (Mayotte)
Capital: Moroni (Comoros); Mamoudzou (Mayotte)
Head of State: President Mohamed Taki Abdul Karim (Comoros)
Official Languages: Arabic, French (Comoros); French (Mayotte)
Currency: Franc Comorien (Comoros); French franc (Mayotte)
Exchange Rate: CFr 372 = US$1 (Comoros); FFr 5.2 = US$1 (Mayotte)
Per Capita GNP: US$510 (Comoros); US$600 (Mayotte)
Inflation: 15%
Time: GMT/UTC + 3

Highlights
- Laze on the Grande Comore beaches of Itsandra, Galawa and Bouni
- See the turtle reserve off the southern coast of Mohéli
- Hike up Mt Karthala on Grande Comore
- Visit the quirky village of Moya on Anjouan
- Stay at the quaint Moya Plage Hotel on Anjouan

---

but they became a separate territory in 1947 and a form of internal autonomy was granted in 1961. Seven years later, however, a strike by local students led to mass demonstrations

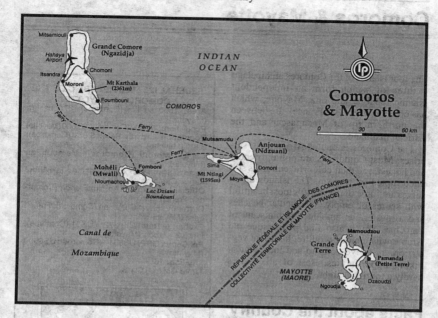

and the French were forced to allow the formation of political parties.

Tensions between the parties grew steadily over the next few years, and, in late 1974, the French held a referendum in which 94% of the population voted in favour of independence, while in Mayotte 64% were against it. Less than a year later, the president, Ahmed Abdallah, announced a unilateral declaration of independence while Mayotte's deputies cabled France requesting French intervention. Two weeks later, the Federal Islamic Republic of the Comoros (minus Mayotte) was admitted to membership of the UN and the Organisation of African Unity (OAU).

One month later Abdallah was overthrown in a coup by Ali Soilih, who imposed a form of Maoist-Marxist socialism and set about obliterating the past. Further change came with the arrival of 29 mercenaries led by Bob Denard. The mercenaries struck at dawn on 13 May 1978 while most of the 2000-strong army were on Anjouan. Abdallah returned two weeks later to a rousing welcome and Ali Soilih was shot to death by the mercenaries. The economy was denationalised, relations with France re-established and children sent back to school. The country quickly returned to relative stability.

Abdallah declared a one-party state which remained in force until 1989 when he was assassinated by his presidential guard. The following year, multiparty elections were held in which Said Mohammed Djohar won. There was another abortive coup in 1992, and, in September 1995, Denard and his merry men attempted another takeover of the islands but were thwarted by French commandos. In the most recent elections held in December 1996, Mohammed Taki Abdul Karim was elected president. He chose an 11 member cabinet under Prime Minister Ahmed Abdou, the 60 year-old former finance minister.

The future of the Comoros in the 1990s is

not good. The economy is totally dependent on agricultural produce (vanilla, cloves, fish) for export income, but output is declining due to soil degradation and commodity prices are in a slump. One hope is to develop the islands' tourism potential, but currently this remains largely unrealised.

GEOGRAPHY & CLIMATE

The four islands of the Comoros archipelago are the tips of the volcanic mountain range rising from the Canal de Mozambique (Mozambique Channel). The archipelago stretches for about 300km from north to south and covers a land area of 2236 sq km.

The hot, wet and humid period is between November and April, when the monsoon winds or *kashkazi* bring moisture from the north-west. The rest of the year is cool (*fraîche*), and is dominated by the south-east trade winds (*koussi*). This is the best time to visit the Comoros and Mayotte.

ECOLOGY & ENVIRONMENT

While deforestation through slash-and-burn farming does take place, a small population and limited development ensures that a lot of the hills and forests of Mohéli and Anjouan remain relatively untouched. On Grande Comore, more often the force of nature – primarily the mighty Karthala volcano – has made the greatest impact on the local ecology. On Mayotte, tourism and development have resulted in pollution, deforestation and urban sprawl.

There have been some attempts to protect the environment: a national park has been set up around the islands to the south of Mohéli to protect turtle and other marine life; and several regions around Grande Comore are also part of a marine reserve.

POPULATION & PEOPLE

The population is around 638,000, and the vast majority is Muslim. Most Comorians are descended from slaves from the African mainland who mixed with traders and settlers of Malagasy, Arab and Persian origin. On Mayotte, there is a minority of permanent French residents.

Comorians love to dance, especially on Mayotte. Dances such as the *mougodro*, a circular dance where everyone joins in, and the prenuptial dance, *wadaha*, are important parts of many religious and cultural events. A lot of the architecture and planning of Comorian towns are reminiscent of the influential Zanzibar, while in the countryside, you will see many half-built homes – started when a daughter is born and often not finished until she is married. In Mayotte, *banga* homes built by unmarried men are fascinating.

LANGUAGE

Arabic and French are both official languages, but the most commonly spoken language is Shimasiwa (Comorian), a language similar to Swahili. If you speak some French, you will be able to get by easily; otherwise see the Language Appendix for useful French phrases. There are currently no Comorian-English dictionaries or phrase books, and almost no-one speaks English. French speakers can get a Comorian-French dictionary in Mayotte or Moroni.

Comorian

There are local dialects on each of the islands, but the following phrases will be understood everywhere.

Greetings & Civilities

Welcome.	*Karibu.*
Hello.	*Salama.*
Good day.	*Bariza.* (Grande Comore)
Good day. (in response)	*M'bona.*
How's it going?	*Ndje?/ Njeje?* (Anjouan)/ *Habare sa?* (Mohéli & Mayotte)
Fine. (in response)	*Ndjema/Sijouha.*
Please.	*Tafatvali.*
Thankyou.	*Marahaba.*
Goodbye.	*Kwaheri.*
Good night.	*Lala ha unono.*

Useful Words & Phrases

I don't understand.	*Ntsu elewa.*

COMOROS & MAYOTTE

I don't speak Comorian.	*Mimi tsidji ourogowa shimasiwa.*
Yes.	*Aiwa.*
No.	*Uh uh.*
My name is ...	*Mi opara ...*
European/ foreigner	*mzungu*
It is beautiful.	*Udjisa.*
How much is this?	*Ryali nga?/ Beyi hindri?*
very expensive/ inexpensive	*ngohouzo anli/ rahisi*
I would like to go to ...	*Ngamwandzo nende ...*
I'm hungry/thirsty.	*Ngamina ndzaya/ nyora.*
I'm looking for a place to eat/ sleep.	*Tamtsaho pvahanou nililye/nilale.*

Facts for the Visitor

TOURIST OFFICES

The tourist office (☎ 74 42 42) in Moroni, just north of town, is worth visiting if you have any specific enquiries; otherwise, they are more involved in implementing policy. The tourist office (☎ 61 09 09) in Mayotte, just up from the ferry terminal in Mamoudzou (look for the signs) is definitely worth visiting as soon as you arrive. It hands out maps, and lists of hotels, diving centres and so on.

VISAS

All visitors to the Republic of Comoros can obtain a visa on arrival – at the international airport at Moroni, on Grande Comore; or, if you arrive by boat, a local immigration official will look after you. The cost for visas are: 24 hours (free); 2-5 days (40 FFr); 6-15 days (80 FFr); 16-45 days (133 FFr). You *must* have enough French francs to pay for the visa when you arrive (there are no banks at the airport or ports).

Mayotte has the same entry regulations as metropolitan France. Citizens of Canada, most European countries and the US may enter for up to three months without a visa.

Australians and New Zealanders must have French visas which are valid for stays of up to three months. They should be obtained from home, but you can get them at French consulates in Madagascar (200 FFr), and in Réunion, the Seychelles and Mauritius.

EMBASSIES

Comorian Embassies

There are Comorian embassies in Paris, New York, and Antananarivo in Madagascar; and consulates in Cologne, Nairobi and Brussels, but as you get visas on arrival, you are unlikely to need to contact them.

Foreign Embassies in Comoros

France
next to Hôtel Karthala, Moroni (☎ 73 06 15); also consulate on Anjouan
Madagascar (consulate)
opposite Volovolo market, Moroni (☎ 73 22 90)

MONEY

| US$1 | = | CFr 372 |
| US$1 | = | FFr 5.2 |

The currency of the Republic of Comoros, called the 'Franc Comorien' locally, is tied to the French franc – 1FFr equals CFr 75. Mayotte uses French francs exclusively, and you can use French francs in the Comoros for hotels, meals and air transport. Travel is not cheap. Expect to spend at least US$35 per day per person; a lot more if you are spending any time in Mayotte.

It is important to note that there are no banks at the international airports at Moroni and Mayotte, so you must have enough French francs for a visa, taxi and so on until you get to a bank.

In the Comoros, major currencies in cash and travellers' cheques can be exchanged at the Banque d'Industrie et Commerce, with branches in Moroni and Mutsamudu. There is no bank on Mohéli; instead there is a mobile bank which arrives by plane every fortnight. On Mayotte, you can change major currencies in cash and travellers' cheques at the Banque Française Commerciale (BIC) in Mamoudzou or Dzaoudzi. Both branches also have automatic teller machines (ATMs) for after-hour withdrawals with major credit cards – but don't rely on them.

POST & COMMUNICATIONS

All capitals of the four islands have post offices and telephone exchanges, but you are advised to use Mamoudzou and Moroni post offices for sending and receiving mail. Telephone cards, or *telecartes*, are available in the Comoros and Mayotte, making long-distance calls from anywhere fairly easy. From Mayotte and Moroni, you can even send and receive faxes from private operators near the post offices. The country code for the Comoros and Mayotte is 269.

DANGERS & ANNOYANCES

The only place where you are likely to have any trouble is the Hahaya airport on Grande Comore: you may be latched on to by 'official' tourist guides who are actually hotel touts, and the taxi drivers at the airport are unscrupulous, so be wary.

Women travellers can rest easy. Other than dressing with some modesty away from the resorts, there is no cause for concern.

PUBLIC HOLIDAYS

Most holidays in the Comoros are religious and based on the lunar calendar, so the dates change each year. During Ramadan, many places will close, transport will be limited and tempers may be short. *Id-ul-Fitr*, the end of Ramadan, is celebrated in grand style. The only standard public holidays are: New Year's Day (1 January), OAU Celebration Day (25 May) and Independence Day (6 July). Mayotte celebrates major Islamic holidays, as well as Bastille Day (14 July) and Christmas. See Public Holidays in the Regional Facts for the Visitor chapter for detail of Islamic holidays.

ACTIVITIES

The Comoros and Mayotte are promoting diving as a tourist attraction, but it is not as spectacular, for example, as the Seychelles. On Grande Comore, the Le Galawa Beach Hotel (see under Places to Stay in the Moroni section) has an excellent diving centre; on Mayotte, contact Le Lambis (☎ 60 06 31).

Hiking is superb among the hills of Mohéli, and the two-day climb of the Mt Karthala volcano, on Grande Comore, is popular. For information about local tours or activities, contact Tropic Tours & Travel (☎ 73 02 02) in Moroni; or Mayotte Aventures Tropicales (☎ 61 19 68) on Mayotte.

FOOD & DRINK

Comorian cuisine is a blend of Indian, Arabic, French and African cooking. Most of the standard meals include some combination of rice and meat, or fish, flavoured with locally grown spices such as vanilla, cardamom, coriander, black pepper, cloves, nutmeg and cinnamon.

Islamic law prohibits the drinking of alcohol. However, you can buy South African beer and other alcohol in upmarket hotels, and locals often imbibe *trembo*, a home brew of coconut milk and fruit juice. If you drink tea, try a cup of strong *thé artisan* at one of the cafes along the tiny streets of the old town in Moroni.

Getting There & Away

AIR

Currently, the only link between the islands and Europe is the weekly Paris-Moroni charter service by Corsair (part of Nouvelles Frontières airlines) – otherwise you can fly to/from Paris via Réunion. Air Mauritius and Air Austral connect Moroni with Mayotte, Réunion and Mauritius; Air Austral links Mayotte with Mahajanga and Nosy Be (both in Madagascar), Kenya and the Seychelles; and Amicale Comores Air and Air Madagascar link Moroni with Madagascar every week; Air Mad often also flies to Kenya. The Malagasy consulate handles tickets for Air Madagascar.

To/from mainland Africa, Emirates airlines flies to Moroni from Dubai or Johannesburg twice a week; and Interair flies between Johannesburg and Moroni.

COMOROS & MAYOTTE

If you are travelling around the islands in the Indian Ocean, enquire about Air Austral's Indian Ocean Pass.

The Comoros and Mayotte do not have separate departure taxes; they are included in the price of your ticket.

SEA

The main connections by sea to the Comoros and Mayotte are with Mahajanga, on the west coast of Madagascar, and with the island of Zanzibar, in Tanzania. If you hang around the relevant ports, you will find something going your way at least once a week – but conditions on the boat, and on the seas, may be rough.

Getting Around

AIR

Following the demise of Air Comores, four quirky airlines – Aeromarine, Air Archipel, Comores Sans Frontières and Amicale – now link the three islands of the Comoros (but not Mayotte) on most days. Flights are fairly cheap, and a worthy alternative to the long, and sometimes rough, inter-island boats. At the time of writing, the only air link between Mayotte and the Comoros is the Air Austral Moroni-Mayotte flight.

BOAT

Every day, one or two different boats travel between Mayotte and Anjouan, and between Anjouan and Grande Comore; fewer boats go via sparsely-populated Mohéli. Between Mayotte and Anjouan there are no flights, so a boat (a hefty US$80) is the only option. Some of the better inter-island boats are the *Villa de Sima* and *Tratinga*.

LOCAL TRANSPORT

Public road transport in the Comoros and Mayotte is by *taxi-brousse*, mainly covered Peugeot 504 pick-ups. Routes extend to most of the accessible towns and villages on the islands. There is no set timetable and they depart when full. Taxis are quite cheap. Ridic-

ulously expensive car and motorcycle hire is available on Grande Comore and Mayotte.

Grande Comore (Ngazidja)

Grande Comore, known as Ngazidja by the Comorians, is the largest, and geologically the youngest, of the Comoros islands. It is 60km from north to south and 20km east to west, with a population of 220,000, of which 22,000 live in the capital, Moroni.

The island's most prominent geographical feature is Mt Karthala (2361m), the active volcano which bubbles at the roof of the island. The coast is mostly raw, black lava with semi-submerged coral on the outer edge.

MORONI

The capital of the Comoros, Moroni, which has one of the best harbours in the country, had its beginning as the seat of an ancient sultanate which traded within the region, primarily with Zanzibar. In Comorian, 'Moroni' means 'in the heart of the fire', probably in reference to Mt Karthala. It is the most developed island, and the only one with resorts, or any decent transport or organised tours.

Things to See

The **Arab quarter**, which takes in Badjanani, Mtsangani and the port, is a convoluted maze of narrow streets lined with buildings dating to Swahili times. It's exotic and intriguing. There are several busy markets, but the new one at Volovolo is less interesting.

The Centre Nationale de Documentation et de Recherche Scientifique (CNDRS) **museum**, which houses numerous scientific, historical and cultural displays about the Comoros and Mayotte, is certainly worth a look.

Places to Stay

Most places include breakfast, but you may get a discount if you don't want it. The *Pension Karibu* (☎ 73 01 17), lost in the

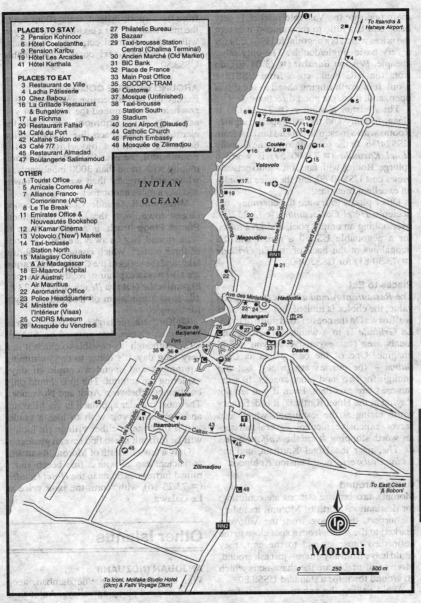

PLACES TO STAY
2 Pension Kohinoor
6 Hôtel Coelacanthe
9 Pension Karibu
19 Hôtel Les Arcades
41 Hôtel Karthala

PLACES TO EAT
3 Restaurant de Ville
4 Ladha Pâtisserie
10 Chez Babou
16 La Grillade Restaurant
   & Bungalows
17 Le Richma
20 Restaurant Falfad
34 Café du Port
42 Kalfane Salon de Thé
43 Café 7/7
45 Restaurant Almadad
47 Boulangerie Salimamoud

OTHER
1 Tourist Office
5 Amicale Comores Air
7 Alliance Franco-
   Comorienne (AFC)
8 Le Tie Break
11 Emirates Office &
   Nouveautés Bookshop
12 Al Kamar Cinema
13 Volovolo ('New') Market
14 Taxi-brousse
   Station North
15 Malagasy Consulate
   & Air Madagascar
18 El-Maarouf Hôpital
21 Air Austral;
   Air Mauritius
22 Aeromarine Office
23 Police Headquarters
24 Ministère de
   l'Intérieur (Visas)
25 CNDRS Museum
26 Mosquée du Vendredi

27 Philatelic Bureau
28 Bazaar
29 Taxi-brousse Station
   Central (Chalima Terminal)
30 Ancien Marché (Old Market)
31 BIC Bank
32 Place de France
33 Main Post Office
36 SOCOPO-TRAM
37 Customs
38 Taxi-brousse
   Station South
39 Stadium
40 Iconi Airport (Disused)
44 Catholic Church
46 French Embassy
48 Mosquée de Zilimadjou

INDIAN OCEAN

To Itsandra &
Hahaya Airport

Sans Fils

Coulée
de Lave

Volovolo

Boulevard de la Corniche

Magoudjou

Route Magoudjou

Boulevard Karthala

RN1

Hadjudia

Ave des Ministères

Mtsangani

Place de
Badjanani
Port

Dashe

Basha

Rue
Itsambuni

Caltex

Zilimadjou

Ave de République Populaire de Chine

To East Coast
& Boboni

RN2

Moroni

0   250   500 m

To Iconi, Moifaka Studio Hotel
(2km) & Falhi Voyage (3km)

COMOROS & MAYOTTE

maze opposite the Volovolo market, is very basic and has little to recommend it except the price, which is a negotiable US$12/24 for a very basic single/double. The only other cheapie, *Pension Barakat* (☎ 73 04 40), up from the BIC bank, costs from US$18 a room. It is worth ringing ahead to see if it is open, and, if so, get good directions.

The *Pension Kohinoor* (☎ 73 28 08) is clean, friendly and the staff speak English. Rooms with a mosquito net and fan cost from US$24/36. In the south of town, the friendly *Hôtel Karthala* (☎ 73 00 57) is worth a splurge. Rooms with fans, mosquito nets and views cost US$40/60, and the price includes an excellent breakfast.

Other places to try are the charming, but decrepit, *Hôtel Coelacanthe* (☎ 73 25 75), overlooking an empty pool, and lava rocks, for a negotiable US$50 a room; and the bungalows at the back of the *La Grillade* (☎ 73 30 81) for US$50/60.

Places to Eat

The *Restaurant Almadad* is clean and good value; the choice is limited, but the manager is effusive. On the coastal road north of town, *La Grillade* is in a wonderful setting and meals aren't as expensive as you would imagine. One of the best places is *Chez Babou* – the curries are pricey, but big enough for two, and other snacks, like the samosas, are excellent. Even if you are not staying at the Hôtel Karthala, it is definitely worth eating at the restaurant, which also serves (expensive) alcohol. Several patisseries worth stopping at are the *Kalfane Salon de Thé*, near the Hôtel Karthala, and the *Ladha Pâtisserie*, near Pension Kohinoor.

Getting Around

Moroni's taxi-brousse stations are confusing: for destinations north of Moroni, including the airport, they leave from the Volovolo market; to the south, from a spot close to the unfinished mosque; and to the east, they could leave from anywhere – just ask around. More comfortable are the share-taxis which go around town for a standard US$0.80.

Avoid paying the extortionate taxi fares from the airport; instead, walk 100m out to the main road and get a taxi-brousse (but you will need some local currency). To Hahaya airport, a share-taxi costs a reasonable US$2.50.

AROUND GRANDE COMORE

Except for two expensive resorts, there is nowhere to stay around the island, but you can easily camp. **Chomoni** is probably the nicest east-coast beach due to its position beside a sheltered bay. Little-visited **Foumbouni**, the island's third largest community with more than 3000 inhabitants, is whiter and brighter than west-coast towns and has a more exotic feel.

Mitsamiouli, Grande Comore's second largest town, with the sandy palm-lined, **Planet Plage** beach, is a pretty village to walk around. Not far away are **Lac Sale**, one of three craters, which contains a beautiful lake, and the rocks of the **Chaine du Dragon** are also worth exploring. Nearby, the super-expensive *Le Galawa Beach Hotel* (☎ 73 81 18) costs a minimum of US$100 per night for a single.

Mt Karthala, the largest volcanic crater in the Indian Ocean, last erupted on 5 April 1977. Although it's possible to climb it in a very long day, it's better to carry camping equipment and spend a couple of days exploring the summit. The trek should only be attempted between April and November. The most popular approach is via M'vouni and Boboni. If you wish to hire a guide, you'll find one in either village (in fact, it will be difficult *not* to find several guides).

Only a few km north of Moroni, **Itsandra**, an ancient capital with a fine beach and a ruined fortress, is home to the *Hotel Isandra* (☎ 73 23 16), with rooms the same price as Le Galawa.

Other Islands

ANJOUAN (NDZUANI)

With its dramatic Cirque de Bambao, steep coastlines and plunging valleys, Anjouan is the most topographically varied of the islands. Its highest peak, Mt Ntingui, rises to 1595m. With more than 180,000 people, it is also the most heavily populated of the islands and has suffered the most environmental devastation of the Comoros.

Mutsamudu

Mutsamudu is one of the Comoros' most picturesque, yet grimy, towns. Sites of interest include the crumbling old **citadel** and the **Sultan's palace**, near the **Mosquée du Vendredi**. There's also an easy walk up the river gorge to the **Dziancoundré waterfall**.

The cheapest accommodation, *Hôtel du Port*, near the harbour, is noisy but cheap for US$13 per room. The restaurant there is always closed. The dilapidated *Hôtel Al-Amal* (☎ 71 15 30) is the upmarket place (there is a pool) but is overpriced at a negotiable US$40/53 for a single/double. The best choice, for accommodation and food, is *La Papilotte* which costs US$24/32 for singles/doubles.

Moya

The village of Moya nestles on the southwest coast beside the island's best beach – a great place to spend a few days. Tiny bungalows at the *Moya Plage Hotel* (☎ 71 14 33) cost a reasonable US$13 per night; excellent, pre-ordered meals cost US$10.

MOHÉLI (MWALI)

Mohéli, with a population of 23,000, is the smallest, wildest, least populated and least developed island of the Comoros. The capital, Fomboni, with 5600 people, is little more than a village. The island measures 30km from east to west and 15km from north to south at its widest point, covering a total of 290 sq km.

The island's wild centre is ideal for hikers and some of the nicest areas may be reached on day walks from Fomboni. Perhaps the most interesting destination is the sulphurous crater lake, **Dziani Boundouni**, near the island's south-eastern tip.

Off the south coast is an island-studded **marine reserve** where the beautiful beaches serve as sea turtle nesting sites. You can catch a lift across from Nioumachoua with local fisherfolk in motorised *pirogues* (dugout canoes).

Places to Stay & Eat

There are only two places to stay on the island. The *Hotel Mledjélé* is dreadful and should be avoided: it is dirty and noisy and it costs a ridiculous US$20 per room. The *Relais de Singani* (☎ 72 02 49), west of town, is far better, but still not good value at US$30/36 for a single/double. The hotel has the only real restaurant on the island, but pre-order all meals if you are not staying there.

The Green Turtle

A local taste for turtle meat has ensured that two species of turtle have all but vanished, so the green turtle (*Chelonia mydas*), which used to live on all three islands, now only survives on several small islands off Mohéli. However, recent conservation efforts have successfully educated locals, particularly in Nioumachoua, about the need to protect the turtles; there are beach patrols during the egg-laying season, and poaching eggs is now illegal.

The green turtle is more than 1m long, and weighs around 130kg to 180kg. The female will wade to a remote area of the beach, and bury her first lot of eggs in the sand. The same female will somehow return to the exact spot about two or three times at intervals of about two weeks and bury more eggs. She can lay up to 200 eggs during one season.

The best place to start organising a trip to the islands, and if the right time (ask locally) to watch them lay their eggs, is at Nioumachoua, an easy taxi-brousse trip from Fomboni. You can hire a pirogue to Chissioua Ouénéfou island, and camp at the beach at the southern end of the island. Bring your own food and water, and please be very careful of the turtles and the local environment. ■

Mayotte (Maore)

Shaped like an exuberant sea horse standing on its head, Mayotte (population 88,000) is the southernmost and geologically the oldest of the Comoros islands, with low, rounded hills and an encircling reef. Politically, it is not part of the République Fédérale et Islamique des Comores, but a Collectivité Territoriale of France, and its people are EU citizens.

The 'island' is actually three main islands: Grande Terre, the large central island, with the largest town, Mamoudzou; Pamandzi, or Petite Terre, where the airport is located; and the four-hectare rock of Dzaoudzi, the former capital, which is the headquarters of the Foreign Legion.

Things to See & Do

A good day walk, beginning along Rue de la Convalescence in Mamoudzou, leads to the summit of **Mt Mtsapéré** (572m). Alternatively, you can climb **Mt Choungui** in the south. The route runs between the villages of **Kani-Kéli** and **Chirongui**.

On the south-western tip of the island is **Ngoudja**, Mayotte's finest beach. Other great beaches include **Plage Moya**, and the chocolate-coloured beach at **Soulou**, where the 8m-high waterfall, **Cascade de Soulou**, plunges directly into the sea.

On Pamandzi island, the crater lake **Dziani Dzaha** and the ruins of **Bagamayo**, a 10th-century Shirazian settlement, are worth a look.

Places to Stay & Eat

There is nothing remotely cheap on Mayotte. The cheapest options are *Le Lagon Sud* (☎ 60 06 20), and the *Hôtel Royal* (☎ 60 12 45), both next door to each other on the road to the airport, which cost from US$40 per room; and the *Villa Raha* (☎ 62 03 64) in Pamandzi village from US$30 per room. The only central option is the *Hôtel Caribou* (☎ 61 14 18), opposite the ferry terminal in Mamoudzou, which costs a steep US$70/80 for a single/double.

In Mamoudzou, a popular place to eat is the *Mimosa* snack bar in the market square. The *Bar 5/5*, right at the ferry terminal, does excellent sandwiches and reasonably priced beer. For a splurge, try *L'Estanco* for pizzas; or *Les Terrasses* for the views.

The only way to eat cheaply is to visit the sprawling *market* in Mamoudzou or the *SNIE* supermarkets in Mamoudzou and Dzaoudzi. Otherwise, there are several small food stands beside the ferry terminals in Mamoudzou and Dzaoudzi which sell brochettes and other fried titbits.

Getting Around

From the airport, take a taxi (US$1.50) to Dzaoudzi from where a ferry leaves every 30 minutes to the main town of Mamoudzou, which is small enough to walk around. The fare for the shortest ride in a share-taxi around either island is US$0.80. Taxis-brousse, which hang around the ferry terminal at Mamoudzou, go to every corner of the main island (Grande Terre).

Congo

REPUBLIC OF THE CONGO
Area: 342,000 sq km
Population: 2.6 million
Population Growth Rate: 3%
Capital: Brazzaville
Head of State: President Pascal Lissouba
Official Language: French
Currency: Central African CFA franc
Exchange Rate: CFA 575 = US$1
Per Capita GNP: US$720
Inflation: 5%
Time: GMT/UTC + 1

Highlights
* Friendliness of the locals, particularly in the countryside
* Markets and food stalls of Brazzaville
* Beautiful beach and relaxed atmosphere of Pointe-Noire

Everybody usually finds something to like about the Congo – there are clean beaches and you can go dancing to the music of some of Africa's most popular recording stars. Getting around is half the adventure.

Facts about the Country

HISTORY

The slave trade resulted in the establishment of a number of small independent kingdoms along the coast of Congo, the capital of each being a trading post; milking the interior for a regular supply of slaves. This exploitation started the radicalisation of Congo's people.

When the slave trade was finally abolished, the coastal kingdoms gradually collapsed. In the 1880s the French explorer Savorgnan de Brazza floated a plan to divide up the whole of the Congo territory (which then included Gabon and the Central African Republic) between concessionary companies. The most accessible areas taken over by the French were bled dry and the population was devastated by famines.

The remaining population was then subjected to yet another form of exploitation with the construction of the railway to Pointe-Noire between 1924 and 1930. In order to secure sufficient labour for the project, the French authorities unleashed what were virtually press gangs.

Because of such conditions, anti-colonialism quickly took root. In the early years it manifested itself in the form of Matswanism, a quasi-religious movement named after Matswa, one of the first resistance leaders. By the end of WWII, Congolese youth, student and trade union movements had become closely connected with developments in the wider communist world, and resistance to the French took on a more stridently political colour.

189

CONGO

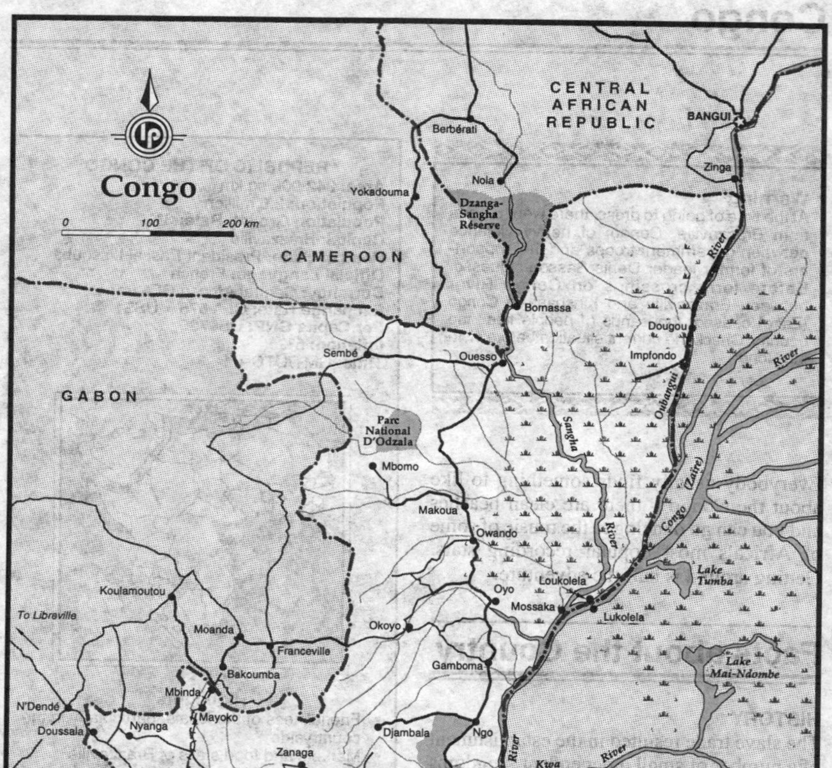

Congo
0
100
200 km
CENTRAL
AFRICAN
REPUBLIC
BANGUI
Berbérati
Zinga
Nola
Yokadouma
Dzanga-
Sangha
Réserve
CAMEROON
Bomassa
Dougou
Impfondo
Sembé
Ouesso
GABON
Parc
National
D'Odzala
Mbomo
Makoua
Owando
Oyo
Loukolela
Mossaka
Lukolela
Lake
Tumba
Koulamoutou
To Libreville
Moanda
Franceville
Okoyo
Gamboma
Lake
Mai-Ndombe
Bakoumba
Mbinda
N'Dendé
Mayoko
Doussala
Nyanga
Djambala
Ngo
Zanaga
Léfini
Réserve
Mah
Lac
Bleu
Makabana
Kibangou
Sibiti
Mont
Bélo
Madingo
BRAZZAVILLE
Loubomo
Kouilou
Madingo-Kayes
Kinkala
Boko
KINSHASA
Pointe-Noire
Chicamba
Chutes de Béla
(Béla Falls)
Chutes de
Loufoulakari
(Loufoulakari Falls)
ANGOLA
Cabinda
Bandundu
Kikwit
Kwango
Kwilu
River
Kasai
River
Kwa
River
Congo
River
Congo
(Zaïre)
Sangha
River
Oubangui
River
CONGO
(ZAÏRE)
ATLANTIC
OCEAN
ANGOLA

CONGO

By the time independence was granted in 1960, the mass movement had become a strong, well-organised political force. Such a movement naturally represented a threat to continued French interests and control, and so the colonial authorities attempted to groom moderate politicians to lead the country after independence.

Youlou was one such politician, and he became president after independence in 1960. Some three years later, however, when Youlou attempted to break the power of the unions by arresting their leaders, he was deposed by Massembat-Debat.

Youlou's overthrow, however, was only the beginning of the struggle, since the forces of repression inherited from the colonial era – the army, police and gendarmerie – remained unpurged. By 1968, the army and the civil defence had reached a stalemate and a coup was staged in which Massembat-Debat was replaced by Captain Marien Ngouabi, a left-wing army officer from the north.

In the mid-70s, Ngouabi came under pressure from French and other European interests to organise the partition of oil-rich Cabinda, the Angolan enclave sandwiched between Congo and Congo (Zaïre), with Congo (Zaïre). His failure to bring this about cost him the support of the French. In 1977 he was assassinated.

The running of the country was taken over by a military commission headed by the army chief of staff, Yhombi. The Congolese Workers' Party (PCT) was eclipsed and the government took a decided turn to the right, though it still used the language of the left. In early 1979, after a series of street demonstrations organised by the trade unions' federation, the PCT met to reassert itself.

Yhombi was ousted, the military commission dissolved and its powers handed over to the central committee of the PCT. Colonel Sassou-Nguesso was named the new head of state and Yhombi was arrested for the embezzlement of several billion Central African CFA francs.

As with many other countries in Africa in the 1990s, the Congo has seen multiparty democracy sweep aside the old order. Elections were held in 1992 and the public gave the thumbs down to the PCT. Pascal Lissouba, head of the Union Panafricaine pour la Démocratie Sociale, was sworn in as the new president.

Though the Congo now has an elected government, those in power have yet to make the hard decisions needed if the country is to avoid Congo (Zaïre)-style chaos. Foreign aid donors are still jittery about the state of the economy. The one bright spot is the country's oil reserves, which are gradually being developed.

GEOGRAPHY & CLIMATE

The narrow coastal plain is low-lying and dry with grassland vegetation. Further inland the Mayombe and Chaïlou highlands and plateaus are forested and deeply dissected by gorges and valleys. The northern part of the country has equatorial rainforests with an average annual rainfall of 1100mm.

The rainy season lasts from October to May, with a brief dry spell around the end of December. Temperatures average between 21 and 27°C.

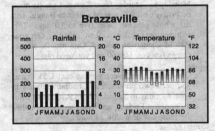

POPULATION & PEOPLE

The population is around 2.6 million. The main tribal groups are the Vili, Kongo, Teke, M'Bochi and Sanga.

LANGUAGE

French is the official language. The main African languages are Lingala and Munukutuba. See the Language Appendix.

CONGO

Facts for the Visitor

VISAS

Visas are required by all except nationals of France. Two-week visas valid from the date of entry cost US$60 to US$70 and you need one or two photos. Onward tickets are not required and visas are issued in 24 hours. The visa form asks for your expected date of entry but you don't need to answer the question.

Other Visas

Burkina Faso, Côte d'Ivoire & Togo

Visas for these countries are issued by the French embassy. The visa section is open on weekdays from 8 to 10.30 am, and visas are issued in 24 hours. You'll need US$25 and two photos.

Cameroon

Three-month, multiple-entry visas cost US$60 and you need one photo and an onward airline ticket; however, if you're travelling overland, the airline ticket requirement may be waived. The embassy is open weekdays from 7 am to 2 pm and issues visas within 24 hours.

Central African Republic

Brazzaville is not a good place to get a visa to the CAR because the embassy, which is open Monday to Saturday from 8 am to 1 pm (to noon on Friday), must first send a telex to Bangui, and the whole process takes five to 10 days. This requirement applies to all nationalities. Get your visa in Cameroon instead. One month, single-entry visas cost US$60 and you need two photos.

Chad

One-month, single-entry visas cost US$30 and you need two photos. The Chadian embassy is open Monday to Saturday from 9.30 am to 2 pm (to noon on Friday), and visas are issued either the same day or within 24 hours.

Congo (Zaïre)

The Congolese (Zaïrese) embassy in Brazzaville has been difficult in the past regarding the issue of visas to nonresidents of the Congo but this phase seems to have passed. However, it's probably best to obtain your visa elsewhere. The cost of visas varies depending on how long you want to stay and whether you want multiple entry (see the Congo (Zaïre) chapter for details). You will also need two photos and a letter of introduction from your own embassy. Visas are issued in 24 hours. The embassy is open weekdays from 8.30 to 11 am.

Gabon

Visas cost US$80 plus US$10 for a telex to Libreville and you need two photos. Because of the telex requirement you can wait a week or more for a reply. Visas are valid for three months from the date of issue. The embassy is open weekdays from 8 am to 2 pm.

Nigeria

The cost of Nigerian visas varies according to your nationality (see the Nigerian chapter for details). You also need two photos, an onward airline ticket (or photocopy of it) and either a letter of invitation from a resident/company in Nigeria or a letter explaining why you want to visit Nigeria. Visas can take up to two weeks to be issued but it's usually less than that. Visas are valid for a stay of one month. The embassy is open Monday to Friday from 7.30 am to 3.30 pm.

EMBASSIES

Congolese Embassies

In Africa, there are Congolese embassies or consulates in Angola, Cameroon, the CAR, Chad, Congo (Zaïre), Egypt, Gabon, Guinea, Mozambique and Senegal.

Elsewhere, there are Congolese embassies in Belgium, France, Germany, Italy, the UK and the USA.

Foreign Embassies in the Congo

Many countries use their embassies in Kinshasa, Congo (Zaïre), just across the river from Brazzaville, to handle their affairs in the Congo.

Embassies in Brazzaville include:

Belgium
    Ave Lumumba, west of Place de la Poste (☎ 83 2963)
Cameroon
    Rue Général Bayardelle (☎ 83 3404)
Central African Republic
    Rue Fourneau (☎ 83 4014)
Chad
    22 Rue des Écoles (☎ 83 2222)
Congo (Zaïre)
    130 Ave de l'Indépendance (☎ 83 2938)
France
    Ave Alfassa (☎ 83 1086)
Gabon
    Ave Monseigneur Augouard (☎ 83 0590)
Germany
    Place de la Mairie (☎ 83 2990)
Nigeria
    11 Blvd du Maréchal Lyautey (☎ 83 1316)

UK (consulate)
   Côte de l'Hôtel Méridien, 26 Rue Lyantey (☎ 83 8527)
USA
   Ave Amilcar Cabral (☎ 83 2070)

MONEY

US$1 = CFA 575

The unit of currency is the Central African CFA franc.

The rates at the UCB bank seem to be the most favourable, especially for large transactions.

The representatives for American Express are Delmas Voyages (☎ 83 3957), BP 2345, Ave Fexlix Éboué, Brazzaville, and Manucongo Voyages (☎ 94 2629), BP 616, Ave de Loango, Pointe-Noire.

Warning

There are no restrictions on the importation of cash but some travellers report that the export of more than CFA 25,000 in cash is prohibited. Since customs searches are thorough both on entry and departure, make enquiries before leaving the country.

POST & COMMUNICATIONS

The post is fairly reliable, and international calls can be made either from the post office or from Congo Phone next to Aeroflot on Rue de Reims, Brazzaville. You can send a fax or telex from the post office on Place de la Poste or, at much more expensive rates, from the Méridien and M'Bamou Palace hotels in Brazzaville.

The country code for the Congo is 242. There are no area codes within the country.

PHOTOGRAPHY

Exercise extreme caution when taking photographs. Photos of the airport, government buildings, the harbour, ferries, dams, radio stations etc are strictly forbidden.

DANGERS & ANNOYANCES

Security is a major problem in Brazzaville. Do not walk around at night. Also avoid travelling at night outside the major cities.

PUBLIC HOLIDAYS

Public holidays observed in the Congo are: 1 January, 8 February, 6 March (Tree Day), 8 March, 1 May, 15 August (National Day), 25 December, 31 December, Good Friday and Easter Monday.

Getting There & Away

AIR

The only flight connections with East Africa are provided by Ethiopian Airlines. Cameroon Airlines, Air Gabon and Air Afrique provide flight connections with various West African cities. Connections to Europe are by Air France, Sabena and Swissair.

LAND & RIVER

Central African Republic

Between approximately May and early December there is one Congolese riverboat about every two to three weeks from Brazzaville to Bangui, stopping at some 13 Congolese villages and at Zinga en route. Prices to Bangui are: US$25 deck class, US$33 intermediate, US$70 tourist class, and US$300 1st class with meals. The trip takes about 14 days upstream.

If the steamers aren't operating you could take a barge, such as the *M'Bamou* which operates between the two capitals, pulled by a tug. The barges take at least twice as long but they are often far less crowded and there are departures about every week. The fare is also low at around US$25.

Congo (Zaïre)

Apart from flying, the only way to get to Congo (Zaïre) is by ferry between Brazzaville and Kinshasa (US$23). It departs hourly in both directions between 8 am and noon and then at 2 and 3 pm. The journey itself only takes about 20 minutes but the bureaucracy at either end makes the whole thing a three hour affair. The first ferries in the morning are the most crowded and should be avoided if possible because of the increased risk of being robbed.

CONGO

Gabon

The major route connecting Brazzaville and Libreville is by rail and road via Loubomo, N'Dendé and Lambaréné; the stretch between Brazzaville and Loubomo is normally done by train. There are daily trucks going north from Loubomo to Kibangou (US$4, three hours). Between Kibangou and N'Dendé in Gabon (185km), you'll find only occasional trucks. The N'Dendé to Libreville trip usually takes two days by a series of trucks and/or minibuses and costs about US$50. Altogether, the Brazzaville to Libreville trip takes a minimum of six days.

The alternative Brazzaville to Libreville route takes about four days and is mostly by train. From Brazzaville take a Pointe-Noire train to Loubomo and another train from there to the border at Mbinda (see also the Train entry in the following Getting Around section). In Gabon, take a series of minibuses or trucks to Moanda (about US$9), and from there the *Transgabonais* train to Libreville (US$52/42 in 1st/2nd class, nine hours).

Getting Around

AIR

Domestic flights by the national carrier, Lina Congo, are totally unreliable and dependent on chartered Air Gabon planes. There are, however, two private and fairly reliable companies: Aéro Service (☎ 94 2221) and Trans Air Congo (☎ 94 3567), which fly between Brazzaville and Pointe-Noire three to four times daily. The fare on Aéro Service is US$113; on Trans Air Congo it is US$90. There are also flights between Brazzaville and Loubomo (Dolisie) for US$60.

ROAD

Road conditions are pretty poor. There are no sealed roads outside Brazzaville, the capital. Roads are frequently closed during the rainy season to protect their surfaces.

There are minibuses and taxi pick-ups linking Brazzaville with Loubomo (Dolisie), Owando (nine hours) and Djambala (nine

hours), but not with Pointe-Noire. On other routes, you'll have to catch a truck. Between Brazzaville and Loubomo, the road is bad – take a train.

TRAIN

The main line runs between Brazzaville and Pointe-Noire via Loubomo, plus there's a branch line north from Loubomo to Mbinda, close to the Gabonese frontier.

There are three trains daily in either direction along the main line and the trip takes about 12 hours, although delays are common. Fares vary according to the train – from US$15 to US$22 in 2nd class. Students with international student identity cards can get discounts of 50% on the cheaper train, but you must get a permit from an office at the university in Brazzaville, near the French cultural centre. There are also daily trains on the branch line from Loubomo to Mbinda (US$22/12 in 1st/2nd class, 12 hours).

Brazzaville

This is an interesting place, very green and sprawling with a **basilica**, **markets** and the **National Museum**, all of which are worth visiting. The city was, for a time, the capital of Free France (a movement opposing the German occupation) during WWII. The most interesting part of Brazzaville is the suburb of **Poto-Poto**.

About 10km from Brazzaville are the **Congo river rapids** – they're a worthwhile excursion.

Places to Stay

Brazzaville is an expensive city for accommodation. The best value places are the Catholic missions. One is at the *Église Sacré Coeur*, better known as the Cathedral, behind the Méridien Hôtel. The rooms (mostly single) are very clean and go for US$8 per person. Another is the *Église Kimbanguiste* in the Plateau des 15 Ans, near the Hôtel Majoca. It charges US$10 for a clean room with two single beds. The people

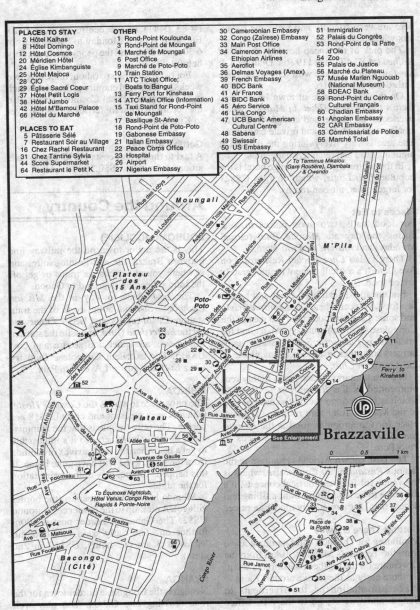

Brazzaville

CONGO

here are very friendly and welcome travellers wholeheartedly.

The pick of the cheap hotels is the *Hôtel Kalhas* (☎ 83 4742) at 119 Rue Djambala. It has fairly clean rooms with fans and private bathrooms for US$16.

On the opposite side of town in Bacongo there's the popular *Hôtel du Marché*, which overlooks the market and charges US$16 for small rooms with fans and private bathrooms. The area is very lively during the day but at night it's dead and relatively dangerous.

In the centre, a good mid-range hotel is the popular *Petit Logis*, which charges US$21 for large, quiet, air-con rooms.

Places to Eat

For food stalls, two good places to look during the day are *Marché Total* (closed Monday) and *Marché de Poto-Poto*.

There's also *Chez Rachel Restaurant* on Ave Orsi. It's a small place with moderately priced food.

For cheap African bush meat and breakfast food, you can't beat *Chez Tantine Sylvia* and some 15 other food stalls just east of the Congolese (Zaïrese) embassy. Also good for breakfast is *Pâtisserie Sélé*. Passable hamburgers and other fast foods are available in the *American Club*.

A more upmarket place that's highly recommended is the *Restaurant le Petit K*, which is in Bacongo facing the eastern side of the Marché Total gare routière. The best place for Cameroonian food is the *Restaurant Soir au Village* at 14 Rue Mbetis in Poto-Poto.

The best known African restaurant is the famous *Restaurant la Congolaise*, which is the venue for frequent musical concerts. It's the place to head to if you want a filling and decent meal for a relatively moderate price.

Getting There & Away

Minibuses for Owando and Djambala leave from the Terminus Mikalou, 10km from the city centre on the northern outskirts of town. Be there early as they leave around 7 am.

For information on the riverboats to Bangui and Ouesso, go to the ATC office (☎ 83 0441) in the centre on Ave Félix Éboué. It is open Monday to Saturday from 6.30 am to 1 pm and the people there are very helpful.

For barges to Ouesso (about one every two weeks) and Bangui enquire at the port, which is just below the Hôtel Cosmos. This is also the departure point for ferries across the river to Kinshasa.

Getting Around

A taxi to the airport costs US$6. Share-taxis around town cost US$0.35.

Around the Country

LOUBOMO (DOLISIE)

This is the major town on the railway line between Brazzaville and Pointe-Noire, and is where you either change trains or get off the train if heading overland to Gabon.

The best place to stay is the *Mission Catholique St-Paul*, 500m north of the train station. Clean rooms cost US$9. Otherwise try the *Buffet de la Gare*, opposite the station. The rooms are quiet and secure and cost US$15. For excellent Congolese food try *Chez Évélaine*, just off Ave de la Paix.

MBINDA

The only place to stay is the *Comilog Hostel* which is very pleasant and costs US$18 per person. The only trouble is that the administrator doesn't sleep there, so it's impossible to get a bed when the train arrives in Mbinda from the south as he will have gone home. If this happens to you, stay at the train station for the night.

Mbinda is 7km from Lekoko (the border village). A pick-up to the border costs around US$2. The Gabonese border post is 100m further on. The daily train to Loubomo leaves at 5 am (12 hours, US$12 in 2nd class).

NYANGA

Nyanga is the Congolese border town for the road crossing into Gabon. You may well have to overnight here. There's no electricity or running water, but there are simple rooms next to the market (US$3) or there's one hotel with rooms for US$5.

PARC NATIONAL DE ODZALA

Opened to tourism in June 1996, Odzala is *the* place to view gorillas in Central Africa – if not the whole of Africa – but it takes a little effort to get there. To arrange a visit you must first contact ECOFAC in Brazzaville. The office is behind the hardware store Structor (known to all taxi drivers) and the friendly manager is called Jean Marc Froment. The two-week trip costs US$600 including the return flight from Brazzaville, food and tented accommodation. Recent travellers have reported seeing up to 100 gorillas in the time they spent there.

POINTE-NOIRE

The only real attraction of this fairly relaxed city is the beautiful beach just a short walk from the main drag.

Places to Stay

All of the cheap places are in the Cité area, except the *mission catholique* (☎ 94 1636), better known as La Procure or Le Vichy. It is in the modern commercial centre, a block south of the well-known Hôtel Migitel, and

has clean rooms ranging in price from US$8 to US$13.

In the Cité, the *Motel Kingoy* (☎ 94 1846), roughly 2km north-east of the Rond-Point Lumumba on Ave Jeudi, used to be popular but these days is very dirty. Rooms cost US$14/26 with fans/air-con and private showers. The *Motel Mapila* (☎ 94 4009) is similar in quality and has rooms from US$13 with air-con and private bathroom.

If you'd like to be within walking distance of a beach, try the *Hôtel le Ndey (No 1)* (☎ 94 0517), about 300m from Pointe-Noire Bay, off Ave de Loango. Rooms cost from US$13.

Places to Eat

Chez Gaspard is perhaps the city's best African restaurant and a popular place to eat. It has dishes from US$3. *Chez Roro* is similar in standard and price, as is the *Restaurant Bibaka*, where grilled meats are the speciality. Late at night the Bibaka turns into a nightclub.

The *Restaurant Mikado* on Ave de Gaulle is a tiny cafe offering braised chicken and fish and other grilled dishes, mostly for US$4, and large beers for US$2.

The most popular meeting place for expatriates, day and night, is the *Vegas Pub & Restaurant* on Ave du Port near the Cercle Naval.

Congo (Zaïre)

The Amazonia of Africa, this vast country is the archetypal explorer's dream. In the heart of the tropics, Congo (Zaïre) is covered with endless rainforests, mountains, volcanoes, enormous rivers and abundant wildlife. It also has one of the most diabolical transport systems in the world. In short, it has everything that adds up to genuine adventure.

Any traveller who has been to Congo (Zaïre) will entertain you for hours with the most improbable stories you're ever likely to come across. There's certainly no rushing through this place – even if you want to – and whichever route you choose, it'll take a long time to reach the other side.

Facts about the Country

HISTORY
The earliest inhabitants of Congo (Zaïre) were groups of hunters and gatherers who lived communally in the densely forested areas without a structured kinship system, much as the Pygmies still do. Settled communities sprang up along the rivers and at the edges of the forest as progressive waves of migrating Bantu and Nilotic tribes moved into the area from the north.

By the 14th century, the first great king-

DEMOCRATIC REPUBLIC OF CONGO
Area: 2,345,410 sq km
Population: 46.5 million
Population Growth Rate: 1.7%
Capital: Kinshasa
Head of State: President Laurent Kabila
Official Language: French
Currency: Nouveau Zaïre
Exchange Rate: NZ 158,000 = US$1
Per Capita GNP: US$400
Inflation: 150%
Time: GMT/UTC +1 (West), GMT/UTC +2 (East)

Highlights
- The mountain gorilla groups and chimpanzees of the Parc National des Virunga and the lowland gorillas of the Parc National de Kahuzi-Biéga
- The volcanoes of the Parc National des Virunga
- The Great Lakes of Tanganyika, Kivu, Edward and Albert
- Travelling on the Congo (Zaïre) riverboat, *Le Grand Pousseur*
- The live music of Kinshasa

---

doms had come into being. Foremost among these was the kingdom of Kongo which controlled a large part of the coastal area around the mouth of the Congo (Zaïre) River. Further south, the most important kingdoms were the Luba, Kuba and Lunda.

By the 17th century, the Portuguese demand for slaves for their Brazilian plantations had far outstripped the numbers that could be supplied by the Kongo. In their efforts to procure sufficient numbers, Portuguese raiding parties began to undermine the economy of the Kongo, and war erupted in 1660. The Kongo were resoundingly beaten by the superior fire power of the Portuguese, who called the country Zaïre and the kingdom went into rapid decline.

The kingdoms of the interior, however, continued to grow by trading slaves and ivory for firearms, cloth and luxuries with the Portuguese.

Despite the centuries of trade with European powers, there was no direct penetration of the interior until the 19th century. It was the British journalist Henry Morton Stanley who, after going in search of David Livingstone (whom he found at Lake Tanganyika), turned his attention to exploring the area and paved the way for colonising this part of Africa. King Leopold II of Belgium laid claim to a vast region of central Africa and was successful in getting the other European powers to ratify his claim at the Berlin Conference in 1884-85.

While King Leopold II remained the sole owner of this vast territory, its inhabitants

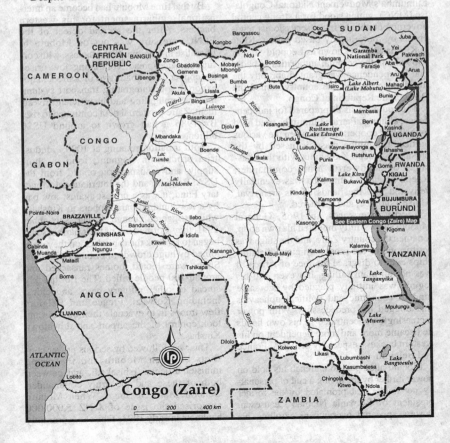

Congo (Zaïre)

were subjected to one of the most preposterous forms of foreign domination ever to disgrace the face of Africa. When news of the worst atrocities leaked out King Leopold II was forced to hand over the territory to the Belgian government. Colonial administration by the Belgian government, however, resulted in little real change.

Only in the 1950s, with independence movements sweeping over other African colonies, did the Belgian authorities relax their paternalistic rule and allow a number of African political parties to emerge.

The main force to emerge was Patrice Lumumba's Mouvement National Congolaise (MNC), which stood for a strong central government able to resist secessionist tendencies by more locally based parties. Riots at Kinshasa (then known as Leopoldville) in 1959 shook the colonial authorities so badly that independence was granted abruptly the following year and the country named the Democratic Republic of Congo.

The country was ill-prepared for independence, although Patrice Lumumba tried hard to maintain cooperation between the various parties. Lumumba was dismissed by the president, Joseph Kasavubu, with the assistance of a powerful army commander, Joseph Mobutu. Lumumba was eventually delivered into the hands of his arch-rival, Moise Tshombe, and murdered.

Shortly afterwards, in 1965, General Mobutu successfully mounted his own coup, renamed the country Zaïre, and the stage was set for one of the most pernicious dictatorships ever to disgrace the face of Africa. It was not all plain sailing, however, and his regime was initially plagued by the same kind of economic and political upheavals that dogged his predecessors. With power increasingly concentrated in his own hands he became more and more dependent on his western backers, especially the USA, France and Belgium.

Mobutu attempted to entrench his hold on power further by instituting a cult of personality not unlike that promoted by the former president of Romania Nicolae Ceausescu. Posters appeared everywhere extolling his virtues as the perfect African leader and anyone with any caution kept their mouth firmly shut.

It couldn't last forever, of course, but his regime did eventually survive for a remarkable 32 years. One of the strongest challenges to his position came in 1977 when some 5000 guerrillas of the Front de Libération Nationale du Congo (FLNC) invaded Shaba province from Angola and got as far as the important mining town of Kolwezi. They were only expelled with foreign assistance. A year later the same thing happened.

By that time Mobutu had become an international embarrassment for his western backers. After the second defeat of the FLNC, pressure was put on Mobutu to liberalise his regime. Nevertheless, with corruption widespread, continuing low prices for copper and cobalt (two of Zaïre's major exports), a disintegrating transport system, massive smuggling and insufficient investment, Zaïre's external debt continued to rise. By 1986 it had grown to around US$6 billion.

With inflation running at 1000%, industrial production stagnant, food in short supply, and a suspension of aid from the USA, Belgium and the International Monetary Fund, it was a protest against low pay by a few hundred paratroopers in Kinshasa which triggered change. In late September 1991, they stormed out of their barracks and began to ransack the capital. Soon they were joined by huge crowds of ordinary civilians. Shops were looted, homes ransacked and around 100 people killed. The riot quickly spread to other military bases and cities, including Kolwezi. France and Belgium flew troops in to evacuate their citizens and took control of the airport and downtown Kinshasa.

This was followed by serious power conflicts between Mobutu and the prime minister, Etienne Tshisekedi, and between both of these and the army commander, General Marc Bokungu. When Mobutu authorised the issue of a NZ 5,000,000 banknote in early 1993, Tshisekedi promptly declared it illegal tender. Traders, therefore, refused to accept it. Unfortunately, it was in these NZ 5,000,000 notes that the troops were paid. Faced with fistfuls of worthless paper, they rioted and, in the process, trashed and looted many cities, including Bukavu, Kinshasa and Goma. Large areas of these cities were reduced to ruin and economic activity ground to a halt.

In mid-1994 agreement was reached on a plan for multiparty elections and a new democratic constitution but it was all window-dressing. Meanwhile, Mobutu withdrew to the opulence of his remote palace at Gdabolite in northern Zaïre yet, remarkably, managed to cling onto power. Then, in mid-1996, he virtually deserted the country for three months to undergo prostate cancer therapy in Switzerland followed by a long convalescence in his villa in France.

By the time Mobutu returned in late December, a guerrilla army known as the Alliance of Democratic Forces for the Liberation of Congo-Zaïre (ADFL), led by Laurent Kabila, had emerged, seemingly from nowhere, and taken over the whole of eastern Zaïre stretching from Uvira to Bunia. In the process, the incompetent and indisciplined Zaïrese army were sent packing west towards Kisangani with the ADFL in hot pursuit. Perhaps the most significant event of this campaign, however, was that the ADFL broke the grip of the Interahamwe (Hutu militants responsible for the genocide in Rwanda two years earlier) on the refugee camps around Goma and Bukavu. Even the UN had failed to do this. Within weeks, hundreds of thousands of Rwandan refugees were streaming back to their homeland. However, tens of thousands of refugees fled deep into central Zaïre ahead of the ADFL advance – relatively few made it back alive.

Mobutu attempted to reverse the gains made by the ADFL but his commanders and their troops were, by then, thoroughly demoralised. Kisangani, Lubumbashi and Mbuji-Mayi, as well as many other important centres fell to Kabila's rebel forces virtually without a fight but not before Mobutu's unpaid troops had gone on their usual rampage or rape and pillage. The final crunch came in May 1997 when Kabila's forces entered Kinshasa, again, virtually without a fight. Mobutu had fled to Morocco several days earlier and his cronies to Brazzaville and elsewhere. Kabila was installed as the new president several days later to the apparent delight of the people of Zaïre and the reserved acceptance of his victory by the western powers, South Africa and a number of Anglophone African countries, notably Uganda. Mobutu died of prostate cancer in Morocco in September 1997.

It remains to be seen whether Kabila can win the confidence of his people, keep the alliance together and get the country back on its feet. So far, he has shown little enthusiasm for democratisation despite this having been made a condition of renewed aid from western donors. In addition, the majority of his ministers are of ethnic Tutsi (Banyamulenge) origin and considered outsiders by many in what has been renamed the Democratic Republic of Congo. A new constitution has been promised along with elections in 1999 but the signs are not promising that his regime will be substantially better than that of Mobutu's. Press censorship remains in force, all political activity is banned except that of his own party, the ADFL, and many prominent politicians who had the courage to oppose Mobutu have been ignored entirely.

It's been suggested by some observers that Kabila is seriously lacking in statescraft having spent some 30 years away from the centre of power and that his victory has created unrealisable expectations amongst the population. These need to be addressed urgently if Congo (Zaïre) is not to dissolve, once again, into warring regional factions.

GEOGRAPHY & CLIMATE
The greater part of the country consists of a huge, flat basin through which the rivers Zaïre, Kasai and Oubangui flow to the Atlantic Ocean. Most of the region is covered by lush, tropical rainforest.

Further south in Shaba province, the forest

gives way to savannah. The country's eastern borders run the length of the Rift Valley, taking in Lakes Albert, Edward, Kivu, Tanganyika and Mweru. Here the land rises into a string of mountains, some of which, such as the Ruwenzoris, approach the 5000m mark.

Temperatures vary between 20 and 30°C in the central forest area and between 15 and 25°C on the high plateau. The best time to visit is from June to September in areas south of the equator and from November to March in areas north of the equator. These periods correspond to what might be called the 'dry' season.

ECOLOGY & ENVIRONMENT

Much of Congo (Zaïre) is dense rainforest but indiscriminate and uncontrolled hunting of wild animals, particularly primates (such as the gorilla and chimpanzee) and ungulates (such as the okapi), have put these species on the endangered list. For a while, during the 1970s and 1980s, they were, to a degree, protected from further poaching because of the large influx of tourist dollars which encouraged local people living adjacent to their habitats to protect them. However due to the civil war many safari companies switched their operations to Rwanda and Uganda resulting in a considerable reduction in tourist receipts. When this happened in Rwanda two years before, a number of gorillas disappeared as army personnel sought to supplement their incomes with trophy hunting. It remains to be seen whether the same thing has happened to the gorilla groups in eastern Congo (Zaïre) but the news will probably not be encouraging. The same applies for the okapi.

The Pygmy communities of the north-east have long been exposed to tourism, particularly long-haul overland safari trucks, and as a result, most are thoroughly commercialised with a consequent degradation of their traditional culture and lifestyle. There's not a great deal that can be done about this except to minimise your impact and don't throw money around. The only way you will get to know these people is to spend some time in the area and avoid brief encounters which are based around commercial transactions.

Other threats to the environment are the logging and mining industries. Quite a number of deals were signed with Laurent Kabila even before he'd won the civil war. What the contents of those deals were is anyone's guess but the motivation was clearly to secure money to continue the civil war and to procure arms. It's unlikely that concern for the environment featured strongly.

POPULATION & PEOPLE

The population is approximately 46.5 million and consists of up to 200 different ethnic groupings, several of which straddle the borders with neighbouring countries. The most prominent of these groups are the Kongo, who live in the Kinshasa area; the people of Kwangu-Kwilu; the Mongo, who live in the forest areas; the Luba in the south; the Bwaka; and the Zande in the north and east. The Banyamulenge of eastern Congo (Zaïre) are related to the Tutsi of Rwanda and Burundi and formed an important part of Laurent Kabila's rebel forces.

LANGUAGE

French is the official government language. However, Lingala, which is spoken in Kinshasa and along the rivers, is the official language of the armed forces. Other major languages spoken in particular areas are Swahili, Tshiluba and Kikongo. Very little English is spoken.

Facts for the Visitor

VISAS & DOCUMENTS
Visas

The cost of visas varies depending on what you want but you will also need two to four photos and a letter of introduction from your own embassy. An onward airline ticket and health certificates are rarely asked for but have at least the latter handy.

Depending on where you get them, single-entry, one-month visas cost from US$42 to

US$75 and three-month multiple-entry visas up to US$126 to US$225. The exception is Zambia where you can pick up a one month visa for US$20. Visas are generally issued within 24 hours.

You can get a visa in all nine neighbouring countries, except Sudan. The Congolese (Zaïrese) embassy in Brazzaville (Congo) sometimes refuses to issue visas to travellers who are not residents of the Congo.

Warning You must carry your passport with you at all times.

Visa Extensions Avoid having to get a visa extension – it's time-consuming and all officials are on the make so it will cost you a lot of money. Get a visa valid for as long as you think you'll need in the first place. Otherwise, visa extensions are available in Kinshasa and all provincial capitals.

Travel Permits

There are special requirements for travel to the middle of Congo (Zaïre) in the mining regions of Kasaï Oriental and Kasaï Occidental (particularly the cities of Mbuji-Mayi, Kabinda and Kananga). For either area you must first obtain a *permit de circulation* as otherwise the police will assume you are a smuggler. The only exception is for those travelling by train to/from Lubumbashi.

In Kinshasa, these permits are issued by the Département de l'Administration du Territoire (☎ 32 098) at 41 Ave des Trois Z in Gombe. Because getting such a permit often takes a week or two, most travellers to these areas simply bribe their way through, but this can get quite expensive. The permits, likewise, are not cheap.

A special exit permit from the Congo (Zaïre) immigration department is necessary before you can cross the river from Kinshasa to Brazzaville (Congo).

Other Visas

Burundi
    The embassy is open every day, except Sunday, from 7.30 am to 2.30 pm (to 12.30 pm on Saturday). One-month visas are issued in 24 to 48 hours and you need US$20 (US dollars only) and two photos. You can also get visas to Burundi at the Burundian consulate in Bukavu.

Cameroon
    The embassy is open for applications weekdays only from 11 am to 1 pm. Three-month, multiple-entry visas cost US$60 and you need two photos and an onward airline ticket (unless you're travelling overland). They are valid for three months from the date of issue and take 24 hours.

Central African Republic (CAR)
    The CAR embassy, which is open weekdays from 8 am to 2 pm, issues visas within 24 hours *if* it's not necessary to telex Bangui first. If a telex is necessary, the visas can take up to a week to issue. They cost US$60, you need two photos and they're valid for a stay of one month.

Congo
    The Congo embassy, which is open weekdays from 8.30 am to 1 pm, takes 48 hours to issue one-month visas. They cost US$70 and you need two photos. On occasion, you may also need a letter of introduction from your own embassy.

Gabon
    The Gabonese embassy is open weekdays from 9 am to 3 pm. Visas cost US$80 plus US$10 for a telex to Libreville and you need two photos. You may also need a letter of introduction from your own embassy. Visas take a week or more to come through because of the telex requirement. They are valid for a stay of one month.

Rwanda
    The embassy is open weekdays between 8 am and 3 pm and issues visas in 24 to 48 hours. They cost US$10 and you need two photos plus you may also need a letter of introduction from your own embassy (this requirement varies). Visas are valid for a stay of one month. There are no Rwandan consulates anywhere else in Congo (Zaïre).

Tanzania
    The embassy takes 48 hours to issue visas and requires two photos and a letter of introduction from your own embassy (not required if your country doesn't have a Congolese (Zaïrese) embassy). Fees vary according to your nationality (see the Tanzanian chapter for details). The embassy is open weekdays from 8 am to 2.30 pm and visas are valid for stays of up to three months. Visas are also available on arrival by air.

Uganda
    The Ugandan embassy is open weekdays from 9 am to 2 pm and issues visas in 24 hours. The cost varies according to your nationality but is usually US$25 and you need two photos (see the Uganda chapter for details).

Zambia
    The Zambian embassy issues visas in 48 hours and requires two photos, a letter of introduction

from your own embassy and your International Health Certificate. The charges vary according to your nationality (see the Zambia chapter for details). The embassy in Kinshasa is open weekdays from 8 am to 3 pm but only receives visa applications on Monday, Wednesday and Friday. There is also a consulate in Lubumbashi which gives same-day service.

EMBASSIES
Congolese (Zaïrese) Embassies
In Africa there are Congolese (Zaïrese) embassies in most West and Central African countries (except Equatorial Guinea and São Tomé & Príncipe), as well as Angola, Burundi, Egypt, Ethiopia, Kenya, Morocco, Mozambique, Rwanda, South Africa, Sudan, Tanzania, Tunisia, Uganda, Zambia and Zimbabwe.

Elsewhere they are found in France, Germany, the UK and the USA, among other places.

Foreign Embassies in (Congo) Zaïre
Foreign embassies in Kinshasa include:

Benin
    3990 Ave de Cliniques (☎ 30 492)
Burundi
    4687 Ave de la Gombe (☎ 33 353)
Cameroun
    Blvd du 30 Juin (☎ 34 787)
Canada
    17 Ave de la Justice (☎ 21 801)
Central African Republic
    11 Ave Pumbu, near Rond-Point Batétéla (☎ 33 571)
Congo
    Blvd du 30 Juin, east of Rond-Point Batétéla (☎ 34 028)
France
    3 Ave République du Tchad (☎ 22 669)
Gabon
    Blvd du 30 Juin (☎ 50 206)
Germany
    Ave des Trois Z (☎ 27 720)
Kenya
    5002 Ave de l'Ouganda, near Rond-Point Petit Pont (☎ 33 205)
Nigeria
    Blvd du 30 Juin, west of Place de Nelson Mandela (☎ 33 343)
Rwanda
    50 Ave de la Justice (☎ 33 080)

Uganda
    Ave des Travailleurs
UK
    Ave des Trois Z (☎ 34 775)
USA
    310 Ave des Aviateurs (☎ 25 881)
Zambia
    54 Ave de l'École (☎ 21 802)

MONEY
US$1 =   NZ 158,000

The unit of currency is the Nouveau Zaïre (NZ), which is probably going to change name under the new regime.

The currency is extremely unstable and inflation is out of control. What the exchange rate will be by the time you read this is anyone's guess. You can safely assume it will be 15 to 50% better than the official rate. As a rule of thumb, assume that the price of a litre bottle of Primus beer equals US$2 and work from there.

If you enter Congo (Zaïre) from the CAR at Bangassou, customs officials will hand you a currency declaration form. If you fill it in incorrectly they'll confiscate any excess they find as well as fine you. Currency forms are not issued anywhere else in Congo (Zaïre).

Changing travellers' cheques at banks in Congo (Zaïre) is for mugs only. Not only is it a hassle and time-consuming with commissions varying from 2% to 10%, but most banks won't do it anyway, especially outside Kinshasa. You must bring cash to this country if you want to get around and pay reasonable prices for commodities. And you must change money on the black market, where necessary. This is illegal, of course, so be discreet or you face losing the lot. On the other hand, many traders demand to be paid in hard currency rather than Nouveau Zaïres so you won't have to change money too often if you bring plenty of small denominations with you. You'll find that US dollars are the preferred currency.

An important consideration with local currency is that the largest note (NZ 1 million) is only worth around US$5. Notes of this size, however, are the exception rather than the rule: NZ 100,000 or less is more common. This means that if you change US$100 you'll be handed a stack of notes which will fill your pockets.

Credit cards are useless in Congo (Zaïre).

POST & COMMUNICATIONS

Forget about the postal service in Congo (Zaïre). It's a joke.

International telephone connections are fairly good in the major cities but elsewhere they're hopeless. The country code for Congo (Zaïre) is 243. There are no area codes.

PHOTOGRAPHY

Photography permits are required and are valid only in the region of issue, so a permit issued in Kinshasa is not valid for Kisangani. In Kinshasa, permits are issued weekday mornings at the headquarters of the Office National du Tourisme (ONT) at 11 Ave du 24 Novembre. In Kisangani permits are issued by the Voix de Zaïre (which also probably going to change name) while in the south they are issued by the Division de la Culture, Arts et Tourisme in Lubumbashi. The cost of these permits depends on the official you deal with but is not normally excessive.

Warning

Even with a permit you must be extremely cautious; if you photograph anything in the cities police are likely to ask questions and to fabricate some rule you've violated. Moreover, taking photos of dams, government buildings, airports, bridges, ports and army personnel (ie anything of military importance) is forbidden.

HEALTH

Take precautions against malaria, it's even more important if you stay in Congo (Zaïre) a long time. We've met very few American Peace Corps volunteers in Congo (Zaïre) who haven't had at least one bout of malaria, despite the fact they were taking antimalarial drugs.

Vaccination against yellow fever is required for Congo (Zaïre).

Tap water is not safe to drink, so purify it first.

Another condition you might pick up, especially if you only wear thongs, is jiggers (tropical fleas which burrow under your skin). Get them pulled out at a clinic. They're easy to remove if you know what you're doing.

If you are trekking the Ruwenzoris you may suffer altitude sickness. For information on this and other medical problems, see the Health Appendix.

DANGERS & ANNOYANCES

Mobutu's regime was characterised by corrupt and frequently drunk officials, police and army personnel many of whom had not been paid for months. They were notorious for hassling everyone and anyone, but particularly travellers, and bribes were *de rigeur* if you wanted to avoid trouble or arrest.

It remains to be seen whether Kabila and his ministers can reverse this ingrained habit. Many of his troops in the civil war were raw recruits with little or no education and large numbers of them were only in their teens. It's perhaps early days to comment but it will probably be a long time before anything can be done to stamp out corruption. That being the case, don't expect things to change too quickly. If you are confronted with this situation it's essential to keep your composure. Never get angry or start shouting. Calm negotiation and whatever humour you can muster is the name of the game. And always carry your passport with you to keep hassles to a manageable level.

Uniformed personnel apart, street crime is a major problem in the cities. Kinshasa has the worst reputation and when the euphoria of Mobutu's overthrow has worn off then street crime is likely to return to previous levels. Even walking around Kinshasa during the day poses a serious risk. *Never* walk around at night – always take a taxi.

PUBLIC HOLIDAYS

The following public holidays are observed in Congo (Zaïre): 1 January, 4 January, 1 May, 24 June, 30 June, 1 August, 14 October, 27 October, 17 November, 24 November and 25 December.

Getting There & Away

AIR

Many African airlines fly to Kinshasa, especially from West Africa, including Cameroun Airlines and Nigeria Airways. Ethiopian Airways and Cameroun Airlines connect Kinshasa with East Africa. Sabena, Air France and Swissair provide connections between Europe and Congo (Zaïre).

LAND

Burundi

The overland routes between Congo (Zaïre) and Burundi are dangerous because of the civil war in northern Burundi. You're seriously advised not to travel in this area.

Rwanda

The two main crossing points from Congo (Zaïre) to Rwanda are between Goma and Gisenyi (at the northern end of Lake Kivu) and between Bukavu and Cyangugu (at the southern end of Lake Kivu).

Between Goma and Gisenyi there are two crossing points: one on the Poid Lourds (a rough road) north of the ritzy part of Gisenyi, and one on a sealed road along the lake shore. It's only 2 to 3km either way and there are taxis or motorcycles on both routes.

It's a 3km walk or taxi ride from Bukavu to the border at Ruzizi where you can walk between the two posts. From the Rwandan border post of Cyangugu it's a short minibus ride to Kamembe (the commercial and transport hub of Cyangugu).

Uganda

Rutshuru to Kisoro Before the recent problems, this was the most reliable crossing with a distance of about 30km between the two towns. There are a few morning pick-ups from Rutshuru to the border. The border posts are next to each other and crossing into Uganda is very straightforward. From the Ugandan side there are very crowded pickups to Kisoro and Kabale.

There's no reasonable accommodation on the Congolese (Zaïrese) side of the border but there are several hotels in Kisoro.

Rutshuru to Kasese This route follows the road from Rutshuru to Katunguru on the Kasese to Mbarara road through the Ishasha border post, Kihihi and Rukungiri. On the Ugandan side there is a steady trickle of traffic along this route, so hitching to Ishasha shouldn't be too much of a problem, and there's even the occasional taxi (pick-up).

Beni to Kasese The route from Beni to Kasese via Kasindi, Mpondwe and Katwe involves hitching unless you can find a minibus. The road from Beni to Mpondwe (in Uganda) is very bad if wet. It's 3km from Kasindi to the border post at Bwero and you'll probably have to walk. Friday is market day so there are a number of trucks in both directions. There's basic accommodation at Bwero and Kasindi.

Other Crossings There are less-used border posts further north, between Mahagi and Pakwach and between Aru and Arua but they're dangerous because of the activities of the lunatic rebels of the Lord's Resistance Army, who are opposed to the Ugandan government. Kidnap or a bullet in the head are real possibilities.

Sudan

You can forget about going to Sudan from north-east Congo (Zaïre) at present because of the civil war between the Sudanese government and the Sudan People's Liberation Movement. It's a very dangerous area.

Zambia

The railway line south from Lubumbashi is connected to the Zambian system but there are no through passenger services. For road transport, go to the Route de Kibushi on the south side of Lubumbashi. There you'll find pick-ups, minibuses or shared taxis to the border (Kasumbalesa) that take about five hours (it's a bad road).

The border crossing is a breeze and the Congolese (Zaïrese) officials are cordial and speak English. From here, you can walk to the Zambian border and take a shared taxi to Chililabombwe. From Chililabombwe take a bus to Lusaka or a shared taxi to Kitwe from where there are trains south to Lusaka.

LAKE & RIVER
Central African Republic
Both of the once popular Oubangui River crossings from Congo (Zaïre) to the CAR, Zongo to Bangui and Mobayi-Mbongo to Mobaye, are currently closed to foreigners. The only crossing likely to be open is Ndu to Bangassou. Even so, you are not guaranteed entry into the CAR as this depends on the political situation. Expect to pay 'fees' (for cameras etc) and bribes on both sides of the river.

For a vehicle, the cost of the ferry is 'negotiable'. Note, this ferry often doesn't run at all. You'll have to bargain hard to pay anything less than 10L of diesel fuel. Without a vehicle you have the additional option of taking a pirogue.

Once into the CAR, there are several minibuses each day between Bangassou and Bambari (US$13) and between Bambari and Bangui (US$10). They depart very early in the morning and take about nine hours for each segment during the dry season.

The customs post at Bondo is a hive of official rip-off merchants. Unless you have declared cash and cameras on entry into the CAR, they may well be confiscated. Very thorough searches are made here.

Congo
Apart from flying, the only way to get to the Congo is by ferry between Kinshasa and Brazzaville (US$23). It goes hourly in either direction between 8 am and noon and then at 2 and 3 pm. The journey itself takes about 20 minutes but the bureaucracy at either end extends it into a three hour affair. The first ones in the morning are the most crowded and should be avoided if possible because of the increased risk of being robbed.

As with leaving by air from Kinshasa airport, you will be forced to accept the services of a team of 'protectors' to guide

you through the numerous checkpoints to the boat. These services do not come cheaply but you won't get on unless you pay.

Tanzania
SNCZ used to operate boats from Kalemie to both Uvira and Kigoma on Lake Tanganyika. They may still operate but would be very unreliable.

Getting Around

Getting around Congo (Zaïre) is an exercise in initiative, patience and endurance. It also promises some of the most memorable adventures you're ever likely to have. To enjoy it to the full, you need to forget anxieties about how long it takes to get from A to B, the sort of food you will be eating and the standard of accommodation you're likely to find. Nothing can be guaranteed, nothing runs on time and in the wet season you could be stranded waiting for a lift for weeks.

Apart from the riverboats on the Congo (Zaïre) and Kasai rivers and the railways in the east and south-east of the country, the only way of getting around the country is to hitch lifts on trucks. There are few public buses.

In general the roads are diabolical so you'll probably end up at your destination covered in mud, bruised, battered and thoroughly exhausted. You'll find that free lifts are the exception rather than the rule. The price of lifts often reflects the difficulty of getting there rather than the distance.

AIR
Air Zaïre, the national carrier, is moribund. As a result, small, private airlines operating small planes have mushroomed. Some of these are regional; others operate country-wide. The only trouble is that they tend to come and go and are dependent on the political situations. They are also relatively expensive but they may be the only practicable way of getting from one point to another.

The best way to find out what is available

is to ask around in the bar of the best hotel in town, wherever you are. Drinking the night before flying might be taboo in the West but it certainly isn't in Congo (Zaïre).

LAND

The most well travelled route through Congo (Zaïre) used to be from Bangassou in the CAR across the Oubangui River to Ndu and on from there to Buta. From there you had the choice of heading south to Kisangani or east to Isiro and Beni (and from there into East Africa).

Kisangani to Bukavu

The most reliable route is the partially completed German/Chinese-built road which connects Kisangani and Bukavu. Between Kisangani and Walikale the road is fine, but between there and the Parc National de Kahuzi-Biéga it's still as rough as guts. The normal route goes north from Goma to Komanda via Butembo and then west to Kisangani via Mambasa and Bafwasende.

Kisangani to Goma

This route goes east to Epulu and Komanda, then south through Beni and the Parc National des Virunga to Goma. The worst stretch is between Epulu and Komanda; allow three days for the Kisangani to Komanda stretch in the dry season and six in the wet.

Goma to Bukavu

Most travellers go by boats (see the Lake & River entry later in this section), but there may also be the occasional bus which takes six hours in the dry season.

Bukavu to Uvira

The quickest and most comfortable route loops through Rwanda for part of the way. There are several buses daily in both directions that leave when full (usually between 7.30 and 8 am).

In theory, since you have to cross two borders on this route, you will need a Rwandan transit visa and a multiple entry visa for Congo (Zaïre). In practice, this is not always enforced but don't take that for granted. Rwandan transit visas are available at the border though the charge seems to vary from US$10 to US$20. There's no Rwandan consulate in Bukavu. Re-entering Congo (Zaïre) is usually no problem; officially, you never left.

Kisangani to Kalemie & Lubumbashi

The first part of this journey involves getting from Kisangani to Kindu, from where there is a railway all the way to Lubumbashi. At Kabalo there is a branch line to Kalemie on Lake Tanganyika.

Kisangani to Kindu The train from Kisangani to Ubundu is supposed to run twice a week but it's often cancelled because of fuel shortages and derailments. You may have to wait for days. The journey generally takes 16 to 20 hours but has been known to take 30. Take food and water, although supplies such as groundnuts, corn, corn, elephant meat, caterpillars and beer can be bought at stops on the way.

When you get to Ubundu you may be lucky and connect with the riverboat down to Kindu. This only runs intermittently so, again, you'll probably be waiting around. The journey takes four to five days.

If something goes wrong with either the Ubundu train or the boats and you get sick of hanging around, you can attempt to get to Kindu by road. However, it's very difficult as there's almost no traffic and the Lubutu to Punia stretch of 'road' was aptly described by one traveller as 'the most desperate piece of road I've ever experienced'. The whole trip from Kisangani can easily take two weeks.

Kindu to Kalemie & Lubumbashi The Kindu-Lubumbashi train departs once a week in each direction, usually on Friday or Saturday from Kindu and on Wednesday from Lubumbashi, but delays are frequent. The journey can take as little as 2½ days but usually takes longer, up to five days. In theory, student concessions of 50% are available if you have a student card and authorisation. In practice, you can forget about it.

Try not to travel on this train alone, especially if you are a single woman. It's not unknown for gangs of thieves to terrorise passengers with the connivance of the railway staff. There are also many drunks on it who can get violent. The fares are around US$170/50 in 1st/3rd class.

Those heading for Kalemie (and Tanzania) must change trains at Kabalo. From Lubumbashi to Kalemie the fare is the same as for Kindu to Lubumbashi.

On all these trains, food can be bought along the way or from the dining car.

Kinshasa to Lubumbashi

The first part of this trip involves getting to Ilebo (930km) where the railway to Lubumbashi begins. The most direct way is by ONATRA river steamer down the Kasai River from Kinshasa to Ilebo. It goes in each direction once every two weeks (sometimes only once a month) and takes about four days.

If you don't want to take the steamer there are plenty of cargo barges, either in Kinshasa or Kwamouth, which go to Mangai, about one day's ride by truck from Ilebo.

Another possibility is to go by road. SOTRAZ, Ave Kianza, Kinshasa (about 6km from the centre), runs daily buses from Kinshasa to Kikwit (about 12 hours). From Kikwit there are trucks to Ilebo on a daily basis.

The railway line connects Ilebo with Lubumbashi via Kananga and Kamina. There are both ordinary and *rapide* trains on this line between Kananga and Lubumbashi, but only ordinary trains between Ilebo and Kananga. The ordinary train takes six days and the rapide four.

In theory, both trains run in both directions once a week; in practice they go at any time, so keep going to the station and making enquiries.

You should bring food and water, although limited supplies are available en route and there's a buffet car in 1st class. The fare from

Ilebo to Lubumbashi is US$65/45 for 1st/3rd class.

If you're coming up from Lubumbashi on the train, buying a ticket there can be a major hassle. They're only sold when the train has actually arrived. Then, of course, all hell breaks loose with people pushing, screaming and shouting.

This is a pretty rugged train trip. It's a combination of Noah's Ark and a Calcutta slum: millions of screaming kids, pots and pans, vast amounts of luggage, dried fish, bush meat and anything else you can imagine. Nothing works and everything is broken; there's no water available; the toilets are horrendous; and large cockroaches will be your constant companions. The train stops frequently in the middle of nowhere so that ticket inspectors can eject ticketless passengers (there are always plenty of them) and you can expect the usual litany of dumb and tedious questions from officialdom.

LAKE & RIVER
Kinshasa to Kisangani

Riverboat The Congo (Zaïre) riverboat (*Le Grand Pousseur*) is the only semi-reliable means of transport between Kinshasa and Kisangani via Lisala and Bumba. Unfortunately, departures are becoming less and less frequent and can be up to two months or more apart. This means you must contact ONATRA, the boat's operator, to try and ascertain when it will turn up at any of the river ports (there's radio contact with the boat).

The boat consists of a variable number of barges lashed together and pulled by a tug. Each barge has a dining room and at least one bar. First class is up at the front in the tug and consists of two-bunk cabins with showers and toilets. Each of the barges has an upper-deck 2nd class consisting of four-berth cabins with communal showers and toilets, and a lower-deck 3rd class where you make do with deck space.

Second class is quite acceptable but 3rd class is always crowded and strictly for those with an iron constitution. If your group occupies a whole 2nd class cabin you can lock it

Le Grand Pousseur

The Congo (Zaïre) riverboat between Kinshasa and Kisangani is one of Africa's classic journeys. It's essentially a floating village. It consists of a tug up front with a variable number of barges strung out behind it. Regardless of the discomforts and hassles you may experience it should not be missed. Each barge rages 24 hours a day to loud music with people drinking (the Congolese (Zaïrese) love their Primus beer!), smoking and dancing. There can be up to 2000 people on board.

There are market stalls, smoked fish, all manner of wildlife (both dead and alive) destined for the chopping block in Kisangani or Kinshasa (including monkeys, tortoises and crocodiles with their jaws wired shut), pots and pans and other paraphernalia both profane and sacred. Pigs and goats are slaughtered on board, prostitutes ply their trade and all manner of deals are struck round the clock for various commodities. You certainly won't ever forget it! ∎

for the duration of the voyage, which isn't a bad idea as there are always thieves on board.

The fares between Kinshasa and Kisangani are US$325 (1st class), US$115 (2nd class) and US$100 (3rd class). Going downriver from Kisangani to Kinshasa, the fares are about half of the above. All fares include meals.

Student reductions of 30% are available on the fares (minus the cost of meals) but you need a *lettre d'attestation* from a local educational institute. In Kinshasa a letter of confirmation from your embassy suffices.

The journey upriver from Kinshasa to Kisangani takes 12 days on average. The trip downriver is naturally somewhat faster. From January to May when the river is at its lowest journey times are often much longer as the boats seem to get stuck on the sandy bottom at least every other day.

When buying 1st or 2nd class tickets it's important to make sure the barge number is written on the ticket, otherwise it will be almost impossible to find an empty cabin. When the boat arrives, get on the appropriate barge and find the person who allocates cabins. If for any reason you end up in 3rd class with a 2nd class ticket, kick up a polite but determined fuss. Even then, there's no absolute guarantee you'll get a cabin straight away or that you won't end up in a cabin with more than four people. Organisation on these boats is chaotic and military personnel are allowed to occupy cabins without a ticket, so no-one knows just how much space will be available at each stop.

In 1st class you get three substantial meals a day, which are basic but edible and are mainly western-style meat and vegetables. In 2nd and 3rd class, breakfast is *mandazi* (a kind of steamed bread) and tea, and lunch/dinner is rice, beans and offal. It's not exactly cordon bleu but you won't starve. If you don't like the food, the boat calls at plenty of places where food is available or where you can buy fresh fish, meat and fruit. Local people come alongside the boat in their dugouts selling food. It's also possible to buy meals in the 1st class dining room for US$5. Water is taken from the river and not filtered.

Be very careful about taking photographs on this boat and ask the captain's permission first. If you do it without permission, you'll be arrested by soldiers and have to pay bribes. They may also confiscate your camera and film.

Cargo Barge If the riverboat isn't due for weeks or months, it may be possible to persuade the captain of a cargo barge to take you up or down the river.

These cargo boats are similar to the riverboat. They're much slower than the normal boat but they are also cheaper and infinitely more spacious than 3rd class on the boat. There are no canteens on board, however, so you'll have to buy your food from dugouts which come out to the barges or, occasionally, on shore. Expect to spend a lot of time stranded on sandbanks when the river is low.

Goma to Bukavu

In theory, there are three boats which ply between Goma and Bukavu on Lake Kivu, but much of the time at least two of them will be out of service. If they're running, it's a pleasant trip with incomparable views of the Virunga volcanoes across the lake. None of the boats call at Rwandan ports, nor do the Rwandan ferries call at Congolese (Zaïrese) ports.

The boats are the *Karisimbi*, the *Vedette* and the *Mulamba*. The first two are government owned and operated. The *Vedette* is purely a passenger boat, while the *Karisimbi* takes freight, including motorcycles. Both are crowded and not overly comfortable.

The *Mulamba* is a privately owned vessel which carries beer from the Primus factory in Bukavu to Goma once a week. It is a far more comfortable boat to travel on (if you go 1st class) and is only slightly more expensive than the *Vedette*. The fares on the *Mulamba* are US$15/8 in 1st/2nd class.

All three boats take from seven to eight hours to make the crossing. Tickets should be bought a day in advance, so you need to make enquiries in Bukavu or Goma regarding the schedules, which are variable. In Bukavu, tickets for the *Mulamba* can be bought at the ACT office on Ave du Président Mobutu.

Kinshasa

The rest of Congo (Zaïre) may be pretty wild and untamed but Kinshasa, the capital, sprang from the jungle into the fast lane a long time ago. On the one hand, it's huge (4.5 million people), muggy and very dangerous, particularly since the riots of 1991 and 1993. On the other hand, it's somewhat cheaper than its twin city, Brazzaville, and the once-legendary nightlife may regain its vibrancy with the new government. Moreover, despite the widespread destruction during the riots, it still has a few modern shops and restaurants of some repute.

Kinshasa is still one of the focal points of modern African music but, since 1991, the music scene has lost much of its vibrancy as even the locals are afraid to go out at night.

Information

Tourist Office The Office National du Tourisme, or ONT (☎ 33 945), is at 11 Ave du 24 Novembre and is open weekdays from 8 am to 1 pm. The people here are responsible for issuing photography permits.

Money Among the best banks for changing money are Barclays at 191 Ave de l'Équateur and Citibank at the corner of Aves Col Lukusa and Longole.

Travel Agencies The best travel agency by far is AMIZA at 600 Ave des Aviateurs, two blocks west of the US embassy, at the corner of Ave de l'Équateur.

Bookshop & Maps

Kinshasa's best bookshop is the Librairie du Kioske at the Hôtel InterContinental. For (old) city maps and maps of Congo (Zaïre), try the Institut Géographique (IGZA) on Blvd du 30 Juin just east of Place de Nelson Mandela.

Dangers & Annoyances

Kinshasa is a dangerous city at any time of day but particularly at night. Thieves and muggers abound and violent crime is common. Not only that, but police and army personnel seeking bribes constantly target travellers. You must carry your passport with you at all times to minimise the hassles and keep bribes to a minimum. If you don't have your passport when stopped, you'll be arrested, taken for questioning and that will cost you even more.

Another delightful experience awaits you if you arrive in Kinshasa by air. Here you'll be surrounded by gangs of military personnel in civilian clothes who will hold you, your luggage and your passport hostage until you give them money. None of these gangs will let you go until you've parted with at least US$100 per person. Then you'll be faced with the problem of finding a taxi into

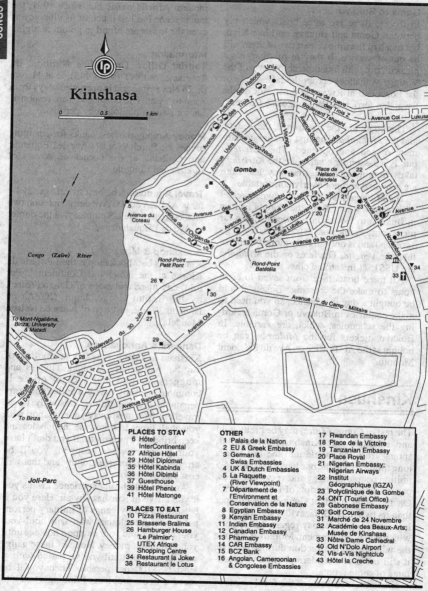

Kinshasa

0   0.5   1 km

PLACES TO STAY
6 Hôtel InterContinental
27 Afrique Hôtel
29 Hôtel Diplomat
35 Hôtel Kabinda
36 Hôtel Dibimbi
37 Guesthouse
39 Hôtel Phenix
41 Hôtel Matonge

PLACES TO EAT
10 Pizza Restaurant
25 Brasserie Bralima
26 Hamburger House 'Le Palmier'; UTEX Afrique Shopping Centre
34 Restaurant la Joker
38 Restaurant le Lotus

OTHER
1 Palais de la Nation
2 EU & Greek Embassy
3 German & Swiss Embassies
4 UK & Dutch Embassies
5 La Raquette (River Viewpoint)
7 Département de l'Environment et Conservation de la Nature
8 Egyptian Embassy
9 Kenyan Embassy
11 Indian Embassy
12 Canadian Embassy
13 Pharmacy
14 CAR Embassy
15 BCZ Bank
16 Angolan, Cameroonian & Congolese Embassies

17 Rwandan Embassy
18 Place de la Victoire
19 Tanzanian Embassy
20 Place Royal
21 Nigerian Embassy; Nigerian Airways
22 Institut Géographique (IGZA)
23 Polyclinique de la Gombe
24 ONT (Tourist Office)
28 Gabonese Embassy
30 Golf Course
31 Marché de 24 Novembre
32 Académie des Beaux-Arts; Musée de Kinshasa
33 Nôtre Dame Cathedral
40 Old N'Dolo Airport
42 Vis-á-Vis Nightclub
43 Hôtel la Creche

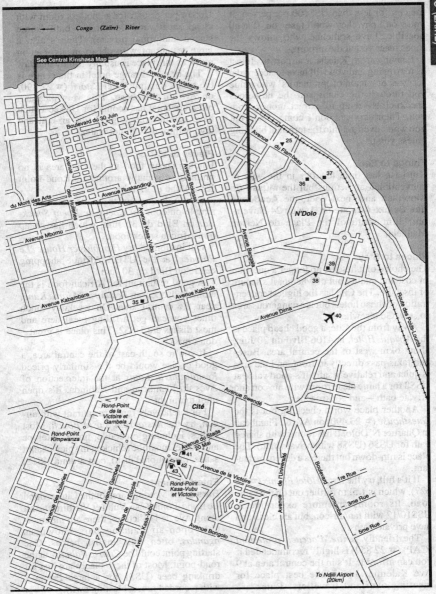

the city for less than US$100 per person. If you won't pay, they won't take you. If at all possible, have someone who knows the ropes meet you at the airport.

Leaving from Kinshasa airport is almost as harrowing and you will have to accept the services of a team of 'protectors' who guide you through the chaos and the numerous checkpoints set up to extract money from you. Their services don't come cheap but you won't even get into the terminal building unless you pay.

Things to See

Kinshasa has little to offer in the way of conventional attractions but the **Musée de Kinshasa** and, next door, the **Académie des Beaux-Arts** are on Ave du 24 Novembre, 1km south of the Place de Nelson Mandela.

Places to Stay

The choice of a hotel is no longer a question of cost and quality but of whether it's secure or insecure. The Cité has the highest concentration of cheap hotels but is a dangerous area to stay. Go elsewhere.

Away from the Cité, a good cheap place is the *Afrique Hôtel*, at 4106 Blvd du 30 Juin, about 6km west of the central area. Buses and taxis pass directly in front, and the area is quiet and relatively safe. It's good value at US$8 for a large clean room with air-con and private bath – and cockroaches.

Another place worth checking out is the *Guesthouse* (☎ 23 490) on Ave du Flambeau in Quartier N'Dolo. It has rooms with shared bath for US$6 (US$8 with private bath). The place is run-down but there's a decent restaurant.

If it's full, try the large *Hôtel Phenix* (☎ 26 627), which is 1.5km further out on the same road. Its rooms are more expensive at US$10/12 with fan/air-con, but are clean and have private baths.

The friendly *centre d'accueil protestant* (CAP) (☎ 22 852) is highly recommended if you can afford it. It's in the central area at 9 Ave Kalemie, and is the best place for meeting overland travellers. Rates are US$14 per person for a spotless room with clean sheets and decent hot bath (some shared and some private). There's also a large restaurant with cheap meals. Get in quick as this place is usually full by midday.

The best mid-range hotel in the centre is the small, tranquil *Hôtel Estoril* (☎ 27 790) on Ave du Flambeau. This very pleasant, old-style hotel has rooms for US$26 which have comfortable single beds, air-con and own bathroom with hot water.

Places to Eat

Finding cheap food in the Cité area is no problem, especially around Le Rond-Point Kasa-Vubu et Victoire.

Just to the west of the central area is the simple outdoor *Au Coeur de Boeuf Snack-Bar* on Blvd du 30 Juin, which has cheap non-African snack food.

Out in Gombe, try *Hamburger House 'Le Palmier'* at the UTEX Afrique shopping centre on Blvd du 30 Juin.

A good restaurant for African food is the unmarked, open-air *Restaurant Mama Kane*, near the central area. On weekday lunch times you can get a filling meal here and most dishes are US$2. This place is great – don't miss it.

If you're south-east of the central area, a good choice would be the similarly priced *Restaurant le Lotus* at the intersection of Aves du Flambeau and Kabinda. It's open until midnight.

For a relatively fancy restaurant with air-con, try the *Restaurant Sur le Pouch*. Most dishes, including crocodile, turtle, antelope and poulet moambé (chicken in spicy peanut sauce, the national dish), cost around US$8.

Entertainment

Bars In the Matonge area of the Cité, around Le Rond-Point Kasa-Vubu et Victoire and all along Ave de la Victoire, there are innumerable open-air dancing bars known as *ngandas*, often with English names. One starting point could be *Club le Palmare* at the rond-point. Most of these places are just for drinking beer (US$1 for a large Primus), with recorded music blasting away.

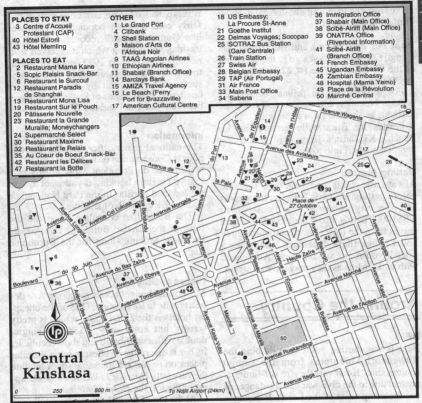

PLACES TO STAY
3 Centre d'Accueil Protestant (CAP)
40 Hôtel Estoril
43 Hôtel Memling

PLACES TO EAT
2 Restaurant Mama Kane
5 Sopic Plaisirs Snack-Bar
6 Restaurant le Surcouf
12 Restaurant Paradis de Shanghai
13 Restaurant Mona Lisa
19 Restaurant Sur le Pouch
20 Pâtisserie Nouvelle
23 Restaurant la Grande Muraille; Moneychangers
24 Supermarché Select
30 Restaurant Maxime
32 Restaurant le Relais
35 Au Coeur de Boeuf Snack-Bar
42 Restaurant les Délices
47 Restaurant la Botte

OTHER
1 Le Grand Port
4 Citibank
7 Shell Station
8 Maison d'Arts de l'Afrique Noir
9 TAAG Angolan Airlines
10 Ethiopian Airlines
11 Shabair (Branch Office)
14 Barclays Bank
15 AMIZA Travel Agency
16 Le Beach (Ferry Port for Brazzaville)
17 American Cultural Centre

18 US Embassy; La Procure St-Anne
21 Goethe Institut
22 Delmas Voyages; Socopao
25 SOTRAZ Bus Station (Gare Centrale)
26 Train Station
27 Swiss Air
28 Belgian Embassy
29 TAP (Air Portugal)
31 Air France
33 Main Post Office
34 Sabena

36 Immigration Office
37 Shabair (Main Office)
38 Scibé-Airlift (Main Office)
39 ONATRA Office (Riverboat Information)
41 Scibé-Airlift (Branch Office)
44 French Embassy
45 Ugandan Embassy
46 Zambian Embassy
48 Hospital (Mama Yemo)
49 Place de la Révolution
50 Marché Central

Central Kinshasa

0   250   500 m

To Ndjili Airport (24km)

Nightclubs Nightspots with musicians are all in the Cité, mostly in the Matonge area. On weekdays, because of security problems, people tend to come here after work and leave by 9 pm.

Going to the Cité definitely involves a serious risk, especially at night, so if you decide to take the plunge, remove all valuables, go with friends if possible and don't stay out late.

A good place to start on weekends is the *Hôtel la Creche*. It has a band playing on its rooftop terrace. One of the most well known places is the open-air *Vis-à-Vis* next door to

the Hôtel la Creche, where well known bands play Fridays to Sundays from around midnight.

Things to Buy
One of the best places to buy art is the Maison d'Arts de l'Afrique Noir, which is a very small shop at the intersection of Aves Col Lukusa and Bandundu, in the city centre.

Getting There & Away
Bus SOTRAZ has buses to Kikwit and Boma. They leave from the Gare Centrale, near the railway station. Minibuses to Kikwit

leave from the gare routière in Ngaba, about 7km from the centre.

Boat For reservations and information on Congo (Zaïre) riverboats go to the 2nd floor of the ONATRA office (☎ 22 109) on Blvd du 30 Juin.

For information on private barges, try AVC or Nocafex, adjacent companies at the harbour, behind the railway station.

Ferries for Brazzaville leave from 'Le Beach', Kinshasa's ferry port. If arriving here, take a taxi into town.

Getting Around
Always use taxis and negotiate the fare before getting in. Taxis between the airport and the city centre (25km) cost up to US$100. There's also a courtesy bus which leaves from the Hôtel InterContinental three hours before flight departures – negotiate a price if you're not staying there. Also check with your airline as they may have transport.

Around the Country

BENI
Beni is the starting point for climbing the Ruwenzori Mountains from the Congo (Zaïre) side. However, they're off-limits at present due to the civil war and the danger of encountering units of the Lord's Resistance Army which use the foothills of the mountains to launch raids into Uganda.

Places to Stay & Eat
Three reasonable places to stay are the *Hôtel Sina Makosa*, *Hôtel Jumbo* and the *Hôtel Beni*. They all cost US$6 for a room.

The restaurant at the *Hôtel Walaba* is good. Their bread is baked on the premises. Good breakfasts are available from the *Restaurant du Rond-Point* on the roundabout.

BUKAVU
Built over several lush tongues of land jutting out into Lake Kivu and sprawling back up the steep mountainside behind,

Bukavu was once an attractive city with a fairly cosmopolitan population. However, like Goma, it is still recovering from the trashing and looting which it received from rioting troops in early 1993 and again during the civil war of late 1996. It was also stretched to the limit by the presence of hundreds of thousands of Rwandan refugees between mid-1994 and late 1996.

Information
The national parks office, Institut Zaïroise pour la Conservation de la Nature (IZCN), is at 185 Ave du Président Mobutu. It's here that you make a booking if you want to visit the lowland gorillas in the Parc National de Kahuzi-Biéga north of Bukavu.

The Burundian consulate is on the top floor of the Sinelac Building, 184 Ave du Président Mobutu (look for the Burundian flag).

Places to Stay
Most of the budget hotels are along Ave des Martyrs de la Révolution. One of the cheapest hotels is the *Hôtel Taifa*, which is pretty scruffy but costs only US$4/5 a single/double with a washbasin and shower cubicle. Its bar is one of the liveliest in town. Similar places on or just off the same street include the very tatty *Hôtel de la Victoire* and, cheapest of the lot, the *Hôtel Moderne*.

At the top of the hill, where the minibuses for Uvira leave, is the *Hôtel Nambo*. It's really too far from the city centre for convenience but is a good place to stay if you're going to take an early morning bus to Uvira.

Mid-range hotels are generally along Ave du Président Mobutu. One exception is the *Hôtel Joli Logis*, on Ave des Martyrs de la Révolution. Set in a garden, it's popular and has large rooms with hot bath for US$7/10 a single/double. Also recommended is the *Tchikoma Hôtel*, close to Place du 24 Novembre. There's a bar and restaurant with reasonable food.

On Ave du Président Mobutu, the best bet is the *Hôtel Canadien* (☎ 2021), almost opposite the Burundian consulate. It's a

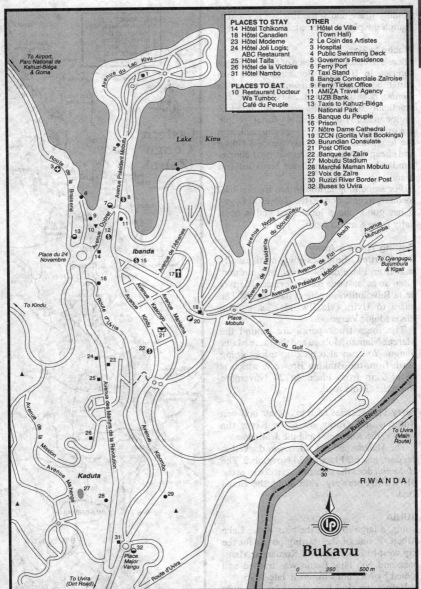

PLACES TO STAY
14 Hôtel Tchikoma
18 Hôtel Canadien
23 Hôtel Moderne
24 Hôtel Joli Logis;
   ABC Restaurant
25 Hôtel Taifa
26 Hôtel de la Victoire
31 Hôtel Nambo

PLACES TO EAT
10 Restaurant Docteur
   Wa Tumbo;
   Café du Peuple

OTHER
1 Hôtel de Ville
  (Town Hall)
2 Le Coin des Artistes
3 Hospital
4 Public Swimming Deck
5 Governor's Residence
6 Ferry Port
7 Taxi Stand
8 Banque Comerciale Zaïroise
9 Ferry Ticket Office
11 AMIZA Travel Agency
12 UZB Bank
13 Taxis to Kahuzi-Biéga
   National Park
15 Banque du Peuple
16 Prison
17 Nôtre Dame Cathedral
19 IZCN (Gorilla Visit Bookings)
20 Burundian Consulate
21 Post Office
22 Banque de Zaïre
27 Mobutu Stadium
28 Marché Maman Mobutu
29 Voix de Zaïre
30 Ruzizi River Border Post
32 Buses to Uvira

Bukavu

0   250   500 m

friendly place and some English is spoken, though the plumbing needs attention.

Places to Eat

There's a reasonable choice of cheap African eateries in Bukavu. For atmosphere you can't beat the *Restaurant Docteur Wa Tumbo*, near the Place du 24 Novembre. It's practically a hole in the wall, with no electricity and only bench seating for 10 people at a squeeze. The owner is very amenable and the food, though extremely basic, is filling and cheap. The *Café du Peuple*, next door, is similar but is only open for breakfast and lunch.

For something a little better, try the *ABC Restaurant* next door to the Hôtel Joli Logis. It has good, cheap local food and is open daily from 8 am to 4 pm.

Getting There & Away

Bus & Truck Minibuses going north usually start from Place du 24 Novembre, but they often do at least one run up Ave des Martyrs de la Révolution to collect passengers. The buses to Uvira (via Rwanda) leave from Place Major Vangu.

The main truck parks are around the Marché Maman Mobutu and the Place Major Vangu. You can also pick up trucks going north from the Bralima Brewery, which is about 2km from Place du 24 Novembre along the Goma road.

Ferry Three ferries used to operate between Bukavu and Goma on Lake Kivu: the *Vedette*, the *Karisimbi* and the *Mulamba*.

The *Vedette* and the *Karisimbi* docked at the port, just off Place du 24 Novembre. The *Mulamba* does the beer run, so it docks at the BRALIMA brewery, 2km along the Goma road.

BUNIA

Bunia, a large town in the hills above Lake Albert, is one of the starting points for the trip west to Kisangani via Komanda, Mambasa and Nia Nia. Bunia was trashed and looted by Mobutu's troops in late 1996.

Before the civil war, Bunia had the only

international airport in this part of Congo (Zaïre), other than Goma. There were TMK flights to Entebbe (Uganda) for US$165 and domestic flights to Beni for US$75, plus departure taxes (US$7 for domestic and US$35 to US$55 for international).

Places to Stay & Eat
The *Hôtel Semliki* is a good place to stay but is expensive at US$20 for a room. Nearby, and similar in price, is the *Hôtel Ituri*.

Going up in price, the *Hôtel Rubi* on the main street is one of the best.

BUTA
Buta is about halfway between Bangassou (CAR border) and Kisangani. You should avoid this town if at all possible and never stay here overnight. It's crawling with corrupt and rapacious officials who will go to any lengths to 'fine' you or extract bribes. Having currency in excess of that declared on your currency form is their favourite ruse – you'll have it confiscated *and* you'll have to pay a 'fine'.

BUTEMBO
With a population of some 100,000, Butembo is a large town about halfway between Goma and Bunia. There's a good market and excellent views of the surrounding countryside. It was trashed and looted by Mobutu's troops in late 1996.

Trucks leave from the 'Concorde' at the Goma end of town.

Places to Stay & Eat
Most of the cheapies are near the market. The *Logement Apollo II* has electricity in the evenings and bucket showers. The *Semliki Hôtel* at the north end of town on the main road has doubles without shower or toilet but does have a good restaurant.

Somewhat more expensive is the *Hôtel Ambiance*. It has electricity, running water, showers and washing facilities.

The *Oasis Hôtel* has excellent meals and there's a bar and disco. Similar in price is the *Hôtel Kyavagnendi* at 55 Ave Bukavu.

GOMA
Goma is a dusty, somewhat run-down town at the foot of the brooding Nyiragongo volcano at the northern end of Lake Kivu. It's not far from the chain of volcanoes that make up the Parc National des Virunga on the border between Congo (Zaïre) and Rwanda. The town became a household word in mid-1994 when it was swamped with as many as a million Rwandan refugees fleeing the fighting in their country. They have since returned home but the environmental scars remain.

Like Bukavu, it is an important business, government and resort town with a fairly cosmopolitan population. There's quite a contrast between the ritzy landscaped villas down by the lake shore and the Cité behind it.

Goma, like other towns in eastern Congo (Zaïre), was trashed and looted by rioting troops in early 1993 and again in late 1996 at the start of the civil war. As a result, many places are closed or lie in partial ruin.

Places to Stay
Do not camp anywhere in Goma. Your security cannot be guaranteed.

The best value for money places are the mission hostels. The *mission catholique*, about 300m from the post office along Ave du Rond-Point, is exceptionally clean and quiet and is totally secure. The rooms are very small, cost US$3/6 a single/double and have a washbasin.

Next door is the *centre d'accueil protestant* (☎ 549), which is a good deal less austere than its Catholic neighbour. The hostel is often full but the restaurant is worth a visit.

A much better bet than these places is the *Hôtel Lumumba*, not far from the post office at the main traffic roundabout.

One of the cheapest mid-range places is the *Hôtel Jambo*, behind the Banque du Peuple.

Places to Eat
The *Kairuza Rendez Vous Restaurant* (formerly La Famille) serves cheap and tasty food. The owner speaks some English and is

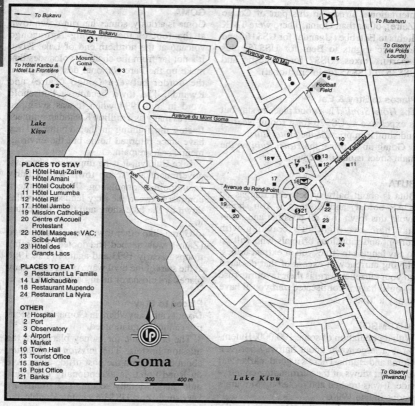

PLACES TO STAY
5 Hôtel Haut-Zaïre
6 Hôtel Amani
7 Hôtel Couboki
11 Hôtel Lumumba
12 Hôtel Rif
17 Hôtel Jambo
19 Mission Catholique
20 Centre d'Accueil
   Protestant
22 Hôtel Masques; VAC;
   Scibé-Airlift
23 Hôtel des
   Grands Lacs

PLACES TO EAT
9 Restaurant La Famille
14 La Michaudière
18 Restaurant Mupendo
24 Restaurant La Nyira

OTHER
1 Hospital
2 Port
3 Observatory
4 Airport
8 Market
10 Town Hall
13 Tourist Office
15 Banks
16 Post Office
21 Banks

Goma

0   200   400 m

Lake Kivu

To Gisenyi
(Rwanda)

a good source of information. The market in Goma has a good selection of food if you are doing your own cooking.

Try the *Cafe Tora*, on the southern side of the main roundabout opposite the post office. It used to be well known for its French cuisine but was trashed in 1993. It may have reopened. The *Restaurant Yeneka* at the centre d'accueil protestant is also worth a try – the food is unexciting but even the heartiest eaters should be satisfied with the portions.

Getting There & Away
The Rwandan town of Gisenyi is only some

3km east of Goma along the lakeshore road. Visas are available at the border.

See the Land and Lake & River entries of the Getting Around section earlier in this chapter for more details on how to get to Goma.

ILEBO
On arrival in this town you'll be escorted to the immigration office where you have to register. The railway line to Lubumbashi starts here.

Places to Stay
The best of the cheap places is the *mission*

catholique about 3km out of town and a long walk uphill.

For a cheap hotel try the *Hôtel Frefima* or the *Hôtel Machacador*. Desperadoes can doss at the *Hôtel Ngongo Ngomda* which has cheap rooms but no running water and what appears to be the entire cockroach population of the Congo basin.

The *Hôtel des Palmes* is a pleasant old colonial-style place and offers rooms from US$12.

Getting There & Away
Occasionally trucks run to Idiofa (about 24 hours away) and there are two ferries across the Kasai River daily.

KALEMIE
Kalemie is Congo (Zaïre)'s main port on Lake Tanganyika. It's a pleasant, relaxed place, though there is a lot of smuggling activity on the lake.

Places to Stay
The best deal in town for accommodation is the *Hôtel du Midi*. More expensive but good value is the *Hôtel de la Gare*, which has large beds and cold showers. The best hotel in Kalemie is the *Hôtel du Lac*.

KANANGA
With a population of well over half a million, this is one of Congo (Zaïre)'s largest cities. Some 20km outside town, however, is a large army camp so, as in Kamina, expect aggressive police, army patrols and lots of prostitutes. You also need a permit to visit.

Kananga has a good **museum** if you are interested in local crafts.

Places to Stay
The cheapest hotel is the *Hôtel Kamina*. Others include the *Hôtel Palace* in the town centre and the *Hôtel Musube* (☎ 2438) on Ave du Commerce.

KAYNA-BAYONGA
This town is a truck-stop on the road between Goma and Butembo, especially for drivers going south as they are not allowed to go through the national park (Virunga) at night. As far as views are concerned, this is to your advantage because otherwise you would miss seeing the Kabasha escarpment.

Trucks leave around 5.30 am, either from the Hôtel Italie or from the market. After that you'll have to rely on transport passing through from elsewhere.

Places to Stay & Eat
Although there are a few small *logements* in the town centre, most truck drivers (and therefore travellers looking for a lift) stay at the *Hôtel Italie* about 3km north of the town. It's clean and bucket showers are available. There's no electricity so it's down to kerosene lamps.

If you stay at the Italie you'll probably have to eat there too – there's a choice of western or local food.

KISANGANI
Kisangani is the main city on the middle reaches of the Zaïre River, and is a major hub for travellers. It was once a fairly pleasant city, but it is in serious decline following riots and looting in 1993. It fell to Laurent Kabila's forces without a fight in March 1997.

Things to See
For something to do, visit the **Wagenia Fisheries** at Boyoma Falls (also known as Stanley Falls). It's somewhat touristy but still OK. You'll see the fishers dropping conical baskets into the falls to catch fish. Touts check the hotels and will find you. The cost is around US$5 per person plus US$20 per group.

Places to Stay
Most travellers used to stay at the Greek-run *Hôtel Olympia* but there are very few travellers coming through these days. Camping is possible but ill-advised and costs US$1. Rooms with (almost nonfunctional) communal facilities cost from US$3 to US$8. Food tends to be on the expensive side but it's good.

Also reasonable is the *Hôtel Kisangani*

CONGO (ZAÏRE)

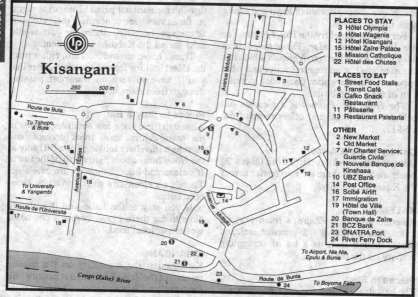

Kisangani

0   250   500 m

Route de Buta

To Tshopo,
& Buta

To University
& Yangambi

Route de l'Université

Avenue de l'Église

Avenue Mobutu

Avenue Mobutu

Congo (Zaïre) River

To Airport, Nia Nia,
Epulu & Bunia

Route de Bunia

To Boyoma Falls

PLACES TO STAY
3 Hôtel Olympia
5 Hôtel Wagenia
12 Hôtel Kisangani
15 Hôtel Zaïre Palace
18 Mission Catholique
22 Hôtel des Chutes

PLACES TO EAT
1 Street Food Stalls
6 Transit Café
8 Cafko Snack
   Restaurant
11 Pâtisserie
13 Restaurant Psistaria

OTHER
2 New Market
4 Old Market
7 Air Charter Service;
   Guarde Civile
9 Nouvelle Banque de
   Kinshasa
10 UBZ Bank
14 Post Office
16 Scibé Airlift
17 Immigration
19 Hôtel de Ville
   (Town Hall)
20 Banque de Zaïre
21 BCZ Bank
23 ONATRA Port
24 River Ferry Dock

which has a pleasant garden, bar and terrace. Rooms with shower and toilet cost US$7. The *Hôtel Wagenia*, on the main road about a kilometre from the post office, is similar.

More expensive is the large *Zaïre Palace Hôtel* (☎ 2664), a kilometre west of the post office. Clean, carpeted rooms with bath cost US$20, while air-con apartments are US$35.

Places to Eat
Many of the restaurants were victims of the 1993 riots and the resulting lack of visitors.

The *PO Cafeteria*, beneath the post office, is good value. For cheap beans and rice head for the stalls on the north side of the market. The *Pâtisserie* near the Hôtel Kisangani is good for pastries.

Most of the restaurants are Greek-owned and the food is generally expensive. The air-con *Cafko Snack Restaurant*, on the main drag, charges around US$5 for steak or fish. The Olympia and Wagenia both have decent, though not cheap, restaurants.

Getting There & Away
Good places to try for lifts are the beer depots and warehouses. Otherwise, take a taxi to Kibibi, about 6km from the centre, and try from there.

The train/ferry trip to Kindu is likely to take two weeks.

LUBUMBASHI
The capital of Shaba province, Lubumbashi is in the heart of the copper belt. It's a pleasant city but, like many other cities in eastern and southern Congo (Zaïre), it was not spared the effects of rioting troops in 1991 and 1993. Many hotels and restaurants closed and may never reopen.

Information
The Division de la Culture, Arts et Tourisme, near the centre of town at 1206 Ave Ndjamena 1206, is responsible for issuing photography permits. There's a French cultural centre on Ave Président Mobutu.

Places to Stay & Eat

One of the cheapest places is the *Hôtel de la Paix* near the hospital but it's a real dive and only for the desperate. The *Hôtel du Globe* (☎ 22 3612) at 247 Ave Mwepu near the railway station has OK rooms with bath for US$10, and there's a restaurant and bar.

The *Hôtel du Shaba* (☎ 22 3617) at 487 Ave Mama-Yemo, a reasonable mid-range place, has rooms with cold baths for US$20.

The best spot for eating and meeting people (locals and the occasional traveller) is the *Café Mokador* on Ave Président Mobutu. The *Snack Bar* next door is a good place for breakfast but it's expensive.

Getting There & Away

Trucks and minibuses for the Zambia border at Kasumbalesa (US$3, five hours) leave from the south side of town on Route de Kipushi.

MT HOYO

Mt Hoyo is about 13km off the Beni-Bunia road close to Komanda. Mt Hoyo's attractions are the **Chutes de Venus** (waterfalls) and the **Grottoes** (caverns).

The waterfalls and grottoes are managed as an extension of Parc National des Virunga so you have to pay US$20 (in hard currency) for a seven day visiting permit. This includes the services of a compulsory guide; pay at the Auberge du Mont Hoyo. A photography permit costs extra.

Places to Stay & Eat

The *Auberge du Mont Hoyo* charges US$30 for a three bed chalet, or there are basic rooms for US$6. If you have a tent you can camp for US$2 per person including the use of toilet and showers. Meals are expensive.

RUTSHURU

Rutshuru is the town closest to the gorilla groups which are found on the slopes of the Muside and Sabinyo volcanoes (which Congo (Zaïre) shares with Rwanda and Uganda) in the Parc National des Virunga.

Places to Stay & Eat

Probably the best place is the *catholic mission guest house*, about 4km outside town. It's a friendly place and costs around US$3 per night per person. Showers and meals are available and you may be able to camp in the mission grounds free of charge.

A cheaper option is the unnamed *lodging house* about 50m north of the police station on the opposite side of the road. It has basic rooms, bucket showers and an earth toilet. The owner is very friendly and may help you find transport.

The *Hôtel Gremafu*, close to the truck park, is very clean but has no electricity or running water.

UVIRA

Uvira, on the north-west tip of Lake Tanganyika facing Bujumbura across the lake, is not a particularly attractive or interesting place.

The actual port, Kalundu, is some 4km south of Uvira.

Places to Stay & Eat

One of the cheapest places is the *Hôtel Babyo La Patience*, Ave Bas-Zaïre near the mosque. If it's full, the *Pole Pole* is clean and reasonably priced. There's no running water but there's a bar and good brochettes (grilled kebabs) for sale. Another good place which is clean and quiet is the *Hôtel Rafiki*.

National Parks

PARC NATIONAL DE KAHUZI-BIÉGA

Lying between Bukavu and Goma, this park was first created in 1970 with an area of 600 sq km, but was expanded to 6000 sq km in 1975. Its main purpose is to preserve the habitat of the lowland gorilla (*Gorilla gorilla graueri*), which was once found all the way from the right bank of the Congo (Zaïre) River to the mountains on the borders with Uganda and Rwanda. These days, like the mountain gorillas living on the slopes of the volcanoes on the borders between Congo (Zaïre), Rwanda and Uganda, they are an endangered species.

Visiting the Gorillas

There are 20 families of gorillas in this park but only four of them are habituated to human contact. Adults can visit any day of the year including public holidays, but children under 15 years of age are not allowed.

Visits should be booked in advance in Bukavu at the Institut Zaïroise pour la Conservation de la Nature (IZCN), 185 Ave du Président Mobutu.

The entry fee is US$125 payable in hard currency (cash or travellers' cheques). This includes a compulsory guide and trackers (who chop through the vegetation) though they all expect a tip at the end. Camera fees are additional to the park entry fee. You need fast film, ASA 800 to ASA 1600, for taking photographs of the gorillas.

You must have appropriate footwear and clothing, preferably a pair of stout boots and waterproof clothes. The guides can generally locate a group of gorillas within two hours though it can take as long as five hours.

Places to Stay

It's possible to stay at the park gate at Tshivanga. If you don't have camping gear, the only shelter you'll get is a roof over your head – there are no beds or other facilities. Only tea and beer are available at the gate, so bring other supplies with you, either from Miti (which has a good market and basic stores) or, preferably, Bukavu. The charge for staying at the gate is US$3.

Getting There & Away

To get to the gate at Station Tshivanga you have the choice of catching a bus and walking the last few kilometres, or of taking a taxi from Bukavu. The taxi is really only feasible if there's a group of you. It does mean though that you can probably set off from Bukavu in time to reach Tshivanga by 8 am, see the gorillas and be back in Bukavu by mid-afternoon if you're lucky.

If you have to use public transport you'll need a minimum of two days. The first day you take one of the buses which run frequently from Place du 24 Novembre in Bukavu to Miti along a surfaced road. From

Miti it's 7km to Tshivanga and lifts are difficult to find. You may have to walk so it's best to plan on staying at Tshivanga for the night and seeing the gorillas the next day. If you do this, bring your own food and drink with you.

PARC NATIONAL DES VIRUNGA

This park covers a sizeable area of the Congo (Zaïre)-Uganda and Congo (Zaïre)-Rwanda borders, stretching all the way from Goma almost to Lake Albert via Lake Edward. Much of it is contiguous with national parks in Uganda and Rwanda.

Created in 1925, the Virunga was Congo's (Zaïre's) first national park and covers an area of 8000 sq km. For administrative purposes the park has been divided into four sections. From the south these are: Nyiragongo, Nyamulagira and Karisimbi; Rwindi and Vitshumbi; Ishango; and the Ruwenzoris.

Entry to any part of the Parc National des Virunga (except if you're passing straight through on transport between Rutshuru and Kayna-Bayonga) costs US$45 for a seven day permit, except for visits to the Djomba or Bukima gorillas which cost US$125 and to the chimpanzees at Tongo which cost US$65. The higher fees cover you for a seven day permit. You can go from one part of the park to another without paying twice, so long as your permit is still valid.

All these fees are payable in hard currency (cash or travellers' cheques) at the respective park headquarters.

At the time of writing this whole area was very unstable and travel in the area was definitely not advised. Check locally to see if things have improved before attempting to visit the park.

Djomba

Djomba is on the slopes of Muside and Sabinyo volcanoes along the border with Rwanda. To see the gorillas, you must be at the departure point by 8 am to pay the fee and be allocated to a group. The fee includes a compulsory guide and an armed ranger, both of whom will expect a tip from each person at the end (US$2 is about average).

Note that as well as gorilla-viewing fees, which must be paid in hard currency, everything at Djomba has to be paid for in hard currency or in Ugandan shillings. No-one accepts Nouveau Zaïres.

Places to Stay & Eat There's an excellent hut at the park headquarters, which has two dormitories with four beds in each (good value at US$5 per bed). Clean sheets are provided and there's an earth toilet outside. There's also ample camping space (US$5 per tent) with a tap and earth toilet.

You can buy meals at the park headquarters for US$1.

Getting There & Away To get to Djomba from Goma, first go to Rutshuru. The turn-off for Djomba is about 2km before Rutshuru and is clearly signposted. From the turn-off it's about 26km to the Congolese (Zaïrese) border village of Bunagana over a very rough road. Transport is sporadic and there are no regular minibuses, so you'll have to hitch or walk.

At Bunagana, you'll be met by local children and youths who will offer to guide you up to the park headquarters (7km, 2½ hours) at Djomba and/or carry your bags. Don't pass up their services or you'll get lost in the maze of farms and paths along the way.

Coming from Uganda, you need a Congolese (Zaïrese) visa to enter *unless* you are only going to visit the Djomba gorillas and then return to Uganda afterwards. If you intend to return to Uganda after seeing the gorillas, Congolese (Zaïrese) immigration will charge you US$50, retain your passport and allow you to go to Djomba. When you return, you get your passport back. This is cheaper than buying a tourist visa. Re-entry into Uganda costs US$20 or US$25, depending on nationality, unless you already have a multiple-entry visa.

Bukima

After booking in Goma, get to the Station de Rumangabo on the Rutshuru road, 45km

from Goma (a two hour drive). A guide will take you up the mountain (a four hour walk), where you stay overnight. The next morning there's a two hour walk to find one or other of the three families of habituated mountain gorillas *(Gorilla gorilla beringei)*, after which you return to Rumangabo the same day.

Places to Stay There's a hut with cooking facilities and firewood at the station where you pay entrance fees and there's also a cleared camp site here, though it has no facilities. Otherwise, get a room with one of the locals. There's also a very basic mountain hut *(gîte)*, which you can use, but it has no beds or water.

Tongo Chimpanzee Sanctuary

Tongo is Congo's (Zaïre's) first chimpanzee sanctuary, and it's a pity there are not more, as poachers are decimating the numbers of these primates elsewhere in the country.

Viewing starts at 6 am, but as it can often take four or five hours before the group is located, expect a strenuous walk. There are also colobus monkeys and baboons as well as a wide variety of birdlife. Butterflies are everywhere.

Places to Stay & Eat Besides a camp site with toilets, shower and kitchen (US$1 per person per night), there's also the *Sokomutu Lodge*, with electricity and hot water for US$20 a double (hard currency). The lodge is on a beautiful site above the village of Tongo, looking out towards the Virunga Mountains.

Getting There & Away Take transport from Goma to Rutshuru but get off at Kalangera village, about 10km south of Rutshuru. From there, a 17km dirt track leads you to Tongo. Market day in Tongo is Friday, so this is the best day to get a lift along this road. Otherwise, it's a pleasant four hour walk.

Porters congregate at the turn-off for Tongo and will carry your pack to Tongo for about US$2.

Nyiragongo

This volcano (3470m), which broods over Goma, used to be a spectacular sight when it was erupting but it is now merely smoking. Since it only takes five hours up and three hours down, the climb can be done in one day if you set off very early. However, a one day trip isn't recommended because the summit is only clear of mist or cloud in the early morning and again, briefly, in the late afternoon; it's better to make it a two day event.

The starting point is at Kibati, about 15km north of Goma on the Rutshuru road. Here you find the Camp des Guides: a long, white, unmarked building set back above the road at the foot of the volcano. Either hitch or walk to this place.

The US$45 entry fee is paid at the camp and includes the services of a guide (who will expect a tip at the end). Porters can also be hired at Kibati. Bring all your food and drink from Goma, as there's nothing for sale at Kibati. Firewood is also in short supply.

Places to Stay It's possible to stay at the *Camp des Guides* the day before you go up the mountain but there's no regular accommodation. You can camp at the free camp site about 2km south of the Camp des Guides.

Nyamulgira

You will need at least three days to climb Nyamulgira volcano (3056m). As at Nyiragongo, you'll have to tip the guides extra. Bring all your food requirements and a tent,

as there's nowhere to stay at the Nyamulgira base camp. The trip starts at Kibati (see the section on Nyiragongo).

Rwindi & Vitshumbi

The main attraction in this part of the park is the game: lion, hyena, hippo, giraffe, antelope, elephant, buffalo and many others. The Queen Elizabeth National Park in neighbouring Uganda (which is contiguous with the Parc National des Virunga) used to be much the same but was sadly depleted of wildlife during that country's civil wars. You cannot hire vehicles to tour this part of the Virunga, so you'll be reliant on other tourists.

The lodge at Rwindi is somewhat expensive. If you can't afford it enquire about cheap rooms in the drivers' quarters. There's also a small guesthouse in the nearby village.

Ruwenzori Mountains

This is the most northerly part of the Parc National des Virunga, and its major appeal for travellers is climbing the mountains. However, we've not heard of anyone doing this for several years and, in any case, it may still be dangerous as the foothills were used as a base for launching raids into Uganda by the Lord's Resistance Army. That danger has substantially passed due to cooperation between Laurent Kabila's forces and the Ugandan army but there may be surviving rag-tag units of rebels still operating. Climb from the Ugandan side until the situation becomes clearer.

Côte d'Ivoire

For many years, Côte d'Ivoire was the jewel of West Africa. Its strong economy attracted thousands of workers from neighbouring countries, and sizeable French and Lebanese communities established themselves in the commercial capital, Abidjan.

Although a heavy debt and an autocratic government have cast shadows on Côte d'Ivoire's role as regional showpiece in recent years, the country still gleams, with an excellent road network, comfortable long-distance buses and some impressive skyscrapers in Abidjan. It also continues to enjoy an enviable degree of political and economic stability in comparison with some of its neighbours.

For travellers, Côte d'Ivoire offers a culture rich with festivals and some of the most outstanding art work in West Africa. Other attractions include great beaches, forested mountains in the western region around Man, the faded but charming colonial capital of Grand-Bassam and a plethora of colourful open-air restaurants.

Facts about the Country

HISTORY

Although Côte d'Ivoire has been populated since early times, its original inhabitants were displaced or assimilated by waves of southward migration resulting from the collapse of the kingdoms of Mali and Songhaï in the 15th and 16th centuries. Important states which arose from the 16th century onwards included the Krou, who migrated eastward from Liberia; the Senoufo and Lubi, who moved southward from Burkina Faso and Mali; the Malinké who came from Guinea into the north-west; and the Akan peoples, including the Baoulé, who migrated from Ghana eastwards. Until the 19th century, these states remained largely insulated from European influence due to Côte d'Ivoire's inhospitable coastline and densely forested interior.

In the 1840s, however, the French embarked on a systematic plan to give their traders a commercial monopoly in the region. Treaties were signed with local chiefs, and by the turn of the century, the French had assumed control of the entire area. French colonial policy in Côte d'Ivoire was based on stimulating the production of cash crops – cocoa, palm oil, timber and bananas – and ensuring that there would be a sufficient supply of labour on plantations established by French expats. To implement

REPUBLIC OF CÔTE D'IVOIRE
Area: 322,465 sq km
Population: 14.2 million
Population Growth Rate: 3.4%
Capital: Yamoussoukro
Head of State: President Henri Konan Bédié
Official Language: French
Currency: West African CFA Franc
Exchange Rate: CFA 500 = US$1
Per Capita GNP: US$610
Inflation: 4%
Time: GMT/UTC

Highlights
* Man area, with its waterfalls, hills and hiking
* Fishing villages and beaches near Sassandra
* Grand-Bassam, the relaxing colonial capital

this, a 'head tax' was imposed on the indigenous population in 1903. This measure, together with large-scale forced labour used for the construction of roads, railways and public buildings, led not only to considerable suffering and social dislocation, but also to a mass exodus from the eastern Agni region to Ghana.

In 1944 Félix Houphouët-Boigny, the son of a wealthy Baoulé chief, founded the Syndicat Agricole Africain to protest the colonial authorities' preferential treatment of French planters in the recruitment of farm labour. The pressure group soon acquired a broad appeal, leading to mass demonstrations in Abidjan during 1948-49 in favour of greater African participation in the colony's administration. Fifty-two people were killed and over 3000 arrested during those years, but in the face of continued repression by the French authorities, and having gained the commodity price increase his group had campaigned for, Houphouët-Boigny then adopted a more conciliatory approach. The French reciprocated by making Houphouët-Boigny the first African to become a minister in a European government. At independence in 1960 he became the country's

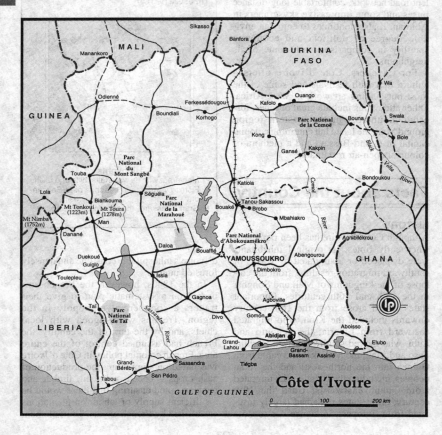

first president, and for the next three decades guided the country on an unwavering neo-colonialist course of almost total reliance on France.

While Houphouët-Boigny ruled with an iron hand politically and tolerated no dissent, he liberalised the agricultural sector, promoting the phenomenal expansion fuelling the 'Ivoirian miracle.' For almost two decades, the economy maintained an annual growth rate of nearly 10% – the highest of Africa's non oil-exporting nations.

During the 1970s, Côte d'Ivoire remained one of Africa's most politically stable and outwardly wealthy countries. Yet, by the mid-1980s, the rumblings of discontent could be heard. A downturn in the economy, due largely to the world recession and a severe drought in 1983-84, was exacerbated by Houphouët-Boigny's penchant for spending millions of dollars on flashy projects, such as the basilica where his funeral was held. The country's external debt tripled and real GNP began to stagnate.

In 1990, faced with rising unemployment and crime, a continued decline in living standards and a lack of educational facilities, Ivoirian students and civil servants took to the streets in unprecedented and violent anti-government protests. The crisis forced Houphouët-Boigny to act, and within months he announced the transition to multiparty democracy. Opposition parties hastily formed to contest the presidential election in October 1990, but the main challenger, Laurent Gbagbo of the Front Populaire Ivoirienne, was trounced by Houphouët-Boigny.

Despite the election victory, the ageing president's last few years in office were anything but peaceful. Mass demonstrations against corruption and repression continued, climaxing in calls for the president's resignation. In reply, security forces arrested students and opposition leaders, including Gbagbo. In mid-1993 civil servants and students went on strike over nonpayment of salaries and allowances.

Houphouët-Boigny's death in December 1993 marked the end of an era for Côte d'Ivoire as he was one of the few African leaders to have ruled since independence. In true form, he died without naming a successor, leaving Henri Konan Bédié, his godson and the speaker of parliament, to claim the 'constitutional' right to take over the presidency. Bédié was sworn in, despite challenges by Prime Minister Alassane Ouattara (whom many expected would assume the role) and despite a call by the opposition for a transitional government to be installed until scheduled elections were held in 1995.

In October 1995 Bédié overwhelmingly won re-election against a fragmented and disorganised opposition. Since then, he has tightened his hold over political life, sending several hundred opposition supporters to jail, including over 20 journalists. In contrast, the economic outlook has improved, at least superficially, with decreasing inflation, steady growth rates and agreements reached in principle to reschedule or relieve significant portions of the country's massive foreign-debt burden. In early 1996, the government enacted a new economic strategy focused on diversifying agricultural earnings and developing nonagricultural sectors, including tourism. Yet, serious social problems shadow the picture, with over two-thirds of Côte d'Ivoire's urban population living in slums and the highest incidence of HIV in West Africa (12% of the population).

What the future holds for Côte d'Ivoire is uncertain. However, despite the tarnishing of its image in recent years, it is unlikely that the 'elephant of Africa', as the country promotes itself, is ready to relinquish its leading regional role soon.

GEOGRAPHY & CLIMATE

The topography of Côte d'Ivoire is an unexciting mix of plains and low hills, with a small mountainous area around Man to the west. The south's equatorial rainforest (much of which has been logged) becomes woodland savannah in the north.

Average temperatures fluctuate between 27 and 30°C. From May to October the south

CÔTE D'IVOIRE

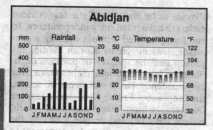

has its heaviest rainfall. In the north the driest months are from December to February.

ECOLOGY & ENVIRONMENT

Deforestation is one of Côte d'Ivoire's most serious environmental problems. Rainforests are being cut down at a shocking rate, with barely three million hectares of forestland now remaining from 16 million at independence. Between 1977 and 1987 alone, Côte d'Ivoire lost over 40% of its woodland. Meanwhile, agricultural lands have expanded from 3.1 million hectares in 1965 to nearly eight million in the mid-1990s. The timber industry is one of the major culprits; although it is illegal to cut trees north of the 8th parallel, logging continues unchecked in many areas, and timber is an important export. As a result, the only remaining virgin forest in the country is the 3600 sq km Parc National de Taï in the far south-west of the country.

POPULATION & PEOPLE

Côte d'Ivoire's population of 14.2 million is comprised of over 60 different tribes, the major ones being the Baoulé, Agni, Bété, Malinké, Dan and Senoufo. In addition to the indigenous population there are large numbers of expatriate workers from Burkina Faso, Mali, Guinea, Benin, Togo and Senegal, as well as many French and Lebanese nationals.

About 60% of the population embrace traditional beliefs, with Muslims and Christians equally making up the balance.

LANGUAGE

French is the official language. Major African languages include Baoulé and Agni in the south, Mandé and Senoufo in the north, and Dioula, the universal language of commerce. For a listing of useful French phrases, see the Language Appendix.

Facts for the Visitor

VISAS

Visas are required for all foreigners except nationals of Economic Community of West African States (ECOWAS) countries. US passport holders do not need visas for stays of less than 90 days.

Yellow-fever vaccination certificates are obligatory.

Visa Extensions

Visas can be extended at police headquarters near the main post office in Abidjan. An extension, valid for up to three months, costs US$24 plus two photos and is ready the same day if you apply early. The visa section is open weekdays from 8 am to noon and 3 to 5 pm.

Other Visas

Benin

    A one month visa costs US$40 plus one photo and is issued the same day.

Burkina Faso

    A three month multiple-entry visa costs US$26 plus three photos and is issued within 48 hours. The embassy is open weekdays from 8 am to 12.30 pm and 1.30 to 4.30 pm. The consulate in Bouaké also issues visas.

Ghana

    A one month visa costs US$24 plus four photos and is issued within 48 hours. The embassy is open Monday, Wednesday and Friday from 8.30 am to 1 pm.

Guinea

    A one month visa requires three photos and is issued within 24 hours. The cost varies from US$40 for Australians to US$64 for Americans. The consulate is open weekdays from 8.30 am to 4 pm.

Liberia

A three month visa costs US$40 plus two photos and is issued the same day. The embassy is open weekdays from 9 am to 12.30 pm and then 1.30 to 4 pm.

Mali

A one month visa costs US$20 plus two photos and is issued the same day. The embassy is open weekdays from 8 am to noon and then 12.30 to 4.30 pm.

Senegal

A one month visa costs US$6 plus two photos and is issued within 36 hours.

Sierra Leone & Kenya

Visas are issued within 24 hours by the UK embassy for US$36 plus one photo and a copy of your airline ticket. Applications can be picked up weekdays between 8.30 and 10.30 am.

Togo

The French embassy issues one month visas for Togo (one year for US passport holders) for US$20 plus two photos.

EMBASSIES
Côte d'Ivoire Embassies

In Africa, Côte d'Ivoire has representations in Algeria, Angola, Burkina Faso, Congo (Zaïre), Egypt, Ethiopia, Gabon, Ghana, Morocco, Nigeria, Senegal, South Africa and Tunisia. Other countries with Côte d'Ivoire embassies include Belgium, Brazil, Canada, Denmark, France, Germany, Italy, the UK and the USA. Where there is no Côte d'Ivoire embassy, visas are generally issued by French embassies or consulates.

Foreign Embassies in Côte d'Ivoire

Foreign embassies and consulates in Abidjan include:

Algeria

53 Blvd Clozel, Plateau (☎ 212340)

Benin

Rue des Jardins, Deux Plateau (☎ 414413)

Burkina Faso

Ave Terrasson de Fougères, Plateau (☎ 211313); consulate in Bouaké (☎ 634431)

Canada

Immeuble Trade Centre, Ave Nogues, Plateau (☎ 212009)

France

Rue Lecour, Plateau (☎ 200505)

Germany

Immeuble Le Mans, Ave Boutreau-Roussel, Plateau (☎ 214727)

Ghana

Immeuble Corniche, Blvd du Général de Gaulle, Plateau (☎ 331124)

Guinea

Immeuble Crosson Duplessis, Ave Crosson Duplessis, Plateau (☎ 222520)

Liberia

20 Ave Delafosse, Plateau (☎ 331228)

Mali

Maison du Mali, Rue du Commerce, Plateau (☎ 323147)

Niger

Blvd Achalme, Marcory (☎ 262814)

Nigeria

Blvd de la République, Plateau (☎ 211982)

Senegal

Immeuble Nabil, Ave Général de Gaulle, Plateau (☎ 332876)

UK

Immeuble Les Harmonies, Blvd Carde, Plateau (☎ 226850)

USA

Rue Jesse Owens, Plateau (☎ 210979)

The Canadian embassy handles Australian affairs.

MONEY
US$1 = CFA 500

The unit of currency is the West African CFA franc.

SGBCI is the only bank which gives cash advances against credit cards (Visa), and the only place which changes both American Express (Amex) and Thomas Cook travellers' cheques. Citibank and BICICI will exchange Amex travellers' cheques, while BIAO exchanges Thomas Cook cheques. Many banks require proof of purchase before exchanging travellers' cheques.

POST & COMMUNICATIONS

Poste restante in Abidjan's main post office (Plateau) is open weekdays from 7 am to noon and 2.30 to 5.30 pm. Identification is required to collect letters, which cost US$1.20 each and are held for one month.

International telephone calls and faxes can be made easily from Monday to Saturday from 7 am to 6.30 pm and Sunday from 8 am to noon on the 1st floor of the nearby EECI building. A three minute (minimum) call to

Australia/USA/UK costs US$10/8/7 (US$6/5 for evening calls to the USA/UK). You can also make international calls using phone cards, although denominations above US$5 are frequently sold out. The country code for Côte d'Ivoire is 225; there are no local area codes.

DANGERS & ANNOYANCES

Although tougher enforcement measures have decreased crime rates somewhat in recent years, the incidence of mugging and theft in Abidjan remains high. The two bridges connecting Treichville with Plateau should be avoided by pedestrians at all hours. Caution should also be exercised in Treichville, Adjamé and Plateau; it's best to take a taxi in the evenings.

Much of the coastline is plagued by riptides and other dangerous currents and many swimmers drown every year. Seek local advice before going in.

BUSINESS HOURS

Business hours are weekdays from 8 am to noon and 2.30 to 6 pm, and Saturday until noon. Government offices are open weekdays from 7.30 am to noon and 2.30 to 5.30 pm, while banks are open weekdays from 8 to 11.15 am and 2.45 to 4.30 pm.

PUBLIC HOLIDAYS & SPECIAL EVENTS

Public holidays are: 1 January, 1 May, 7 August (Independence Day), 15 August, 1 November, 15 November, 7 December, 25 December, Easter Monday, Ascension Day, Whit Monday and variable Islamic holidays. See also Public Holidays in the Regional Facts for the Visitor chapter.

Some of the more interesting of Côte d'Ivoire's many colourful festivals include the Fêtes des Masques (see the boxed story in the Around Man section later in this chapter); Fête de l'Abissa, in late October or early November in Grand-Bassam; Fête du Dipri, in Gomon (100km north-west of Abidjan) in March or April; and Carnival, in Bouaké in March.

ACCOMMODATION

Finding somewhere to sleep in Côte d'Ivoire is rarely a problem. Most towns have a selection of budget hotels, where a basic ventilated room with communal shower and toilet costs from US$5. Rooms with private facilities and air-con start at US$12. There are always plenty of mid-range hotels.

FOOD

If there's one thing not to miss in Côte d'Ivoire, it's having a meal in a *maquis*, small open-air restaurants with low, wooden tables, sandy floors and good music. The menu is nearly always identical – *poisson* or *poulet braisé* (fish or chicken cooked over the embers of a low fire) topped with tomato and onion, and accompanied by *attiéké* (grated manioc, not unlike couscous).

Other Ivoirian specialities include *foutou*, boiled and pounded yams or plantains eaten as a staple food with sauce; and *kedjenou*, a chicken and vegetable stew served with rice or foutou.

Getting There & Away

AIR

As one of West Africa's major commercial and banking centres, Abidjan is serviced by most European airlines and many African airlines.

Air Ivoire, the national airline, has flights to Monrovia (Liberia) for US$254, Ouagadougou (Burkina Faso) for US$132, Accra (Ghana) for US$84, Bamako (Mali) for US$142 and Conakry (Guinea) for US$205.

Abidjan airport is at Port Bouët, 15km south-east of the city centre. There's a US$10 departure tax (payable in CFA).

LAND
Burkina Faso
Bus There are daily CTM and UTRAFER buses from Abidjan to Ferkessédougou (nine hours, US$8). From Ferkessédougou you can get a bush taxi to Bobo-Dioulasso

(230km, five hours, US$8) or on to Ouagadougou (US$16).

BFCI/Sans Frontières has direct buses daily to Ouagadougou from Abidjan (1175km, 24 hours, US$29), Yamoussoukro (925km, 18 hours, US$27) and Ferkessédougou (585km, 12 hours, US$24). UTB also has daily departures from Abidjan to Ouagadougou.

Train The Abidjan-Ouagadougou 'express' train leaves Treichville station on Tuesday, Thursday and Saturday at 7.30 am, and is scheduled to arrive in Bouaké at 1.45 pm, Ferkessédougou at 6.45 pm, Bobo-Dioulasso at 1 am the following day and Ouagadougou around 7.30 am, although the trip invariably takes several hours longer. Fares to Ouagadougou are US$48/32 for 1st/ 2nd class (US$32/22 to Bobo-Dioulasso). There are no sleeping cars and no student discounts; food is available at stations along the way. Unfortunately, the train has been allowed to deteriorate, so it's no longer as pleasant a trip as it used to be.

Ghana

The most popular route to Ghana is from Abidjan to Accra (550km, 12 hours) along the sealed road via Aboisso and Takoradi. There is a daily (except Sunday) Ghanaian STC bus, which departs from the STC bus station south of Treichville at 8.30 am and costs US$17 plus a *dash*, or bribe, for the border guards, plus US$1 for luggage. However, as these buses are often held up for several hours at the border, it's generally quicker and cheaper to take a taxi-brousse from Abidjan to Aboisso and then another to Elubo at the border, from where cheaper Ghanaian vehicles head to Takoradi and destinations further east.

You can also cross into Ghana from Abidjan to Kumasi (555km) going via Agnibilékrou. There are no direct buses, but you can do the journey in stages from Abidjan to Abengourou, then from there to the border. Don't forget to call in for an exit stamp from the police/immigration at Agnibilékrou. From the Ghanaian border there are taxis heading to Kumasi.

On the northernmost route from Ferkessédougou to Bole (370km), taxis go from Ferkessédougou to Bouna (eight to 12 hours, US$15) and then from there to the Ghanaian border (US$2). From the border, there's a canoe across the river and transport to Bole on the other side.

Guinea

A taxi or minibus from Danané will drop you at the border (50km, 1½ hours, US$5), which is open 24 hours, from where you can catch transport to Lola (35km) and on to Nzérékoré (45km). Be sure to get your passport stamped at the police commissariat in Danané.

An alternative route goes via Odienné and Kankan, but this is in poor condition and infrequently travelled. You will probably have to hitch a ride with a truck. Allow two days.

Liberia

The main route into Liberia is from Danané to Sanniquellie (90km) via Kahnple. Since the situation in Liberia is unstable, you'll need to check with the police commissariat in Danané to find out if the border is open. If so, you should be able to get a minibus from Danané to the border (1½ hours, US$2) and a taxi on the other side. You should take an armed escort and plenty of presents to give away.

Mali

From Ferkessédougou, minibuses go to the border, where you can transfer to a taxi for Sikasso. There are also some 'through' minibuses to Bamako, although these sometimes transfer passengers to taxis at the border, where the new driver then demands more money; try to delay payment until you're well into Mali.

From Odienné to Bougouni, there is very little traffic and only one bus a week from Odienné to Bamako (US$20). The bridge at Manankoro (on the Mali side of the border) is usually underwater throughout August.

There are direct buses at least three times per week from Abidjan all the way to Bamako (40 hours minimum, US$30), but most travellers don't take them as the trip is very gruelling and there's not much of interest along the way.

Getting Around

AIR
Air Ivoire flies from Abidjan to Korhogo (US$48) and Man (US$48).

BUS & BUSH TAXI
There is a good network of buses and bush taxis between major towns. Buses are preferable to taxis since they have a fairly definite departure time, are less expensive, do not charge extra for luggage and (usually) respect the one-seat-per-person principle.

Some examples of fares and journey times are listed below.

TRAIN
The only train is the Abidjan-Ouagadougou express. For details, see Burkina Faso in the earlier Getting There & Away section.

CAR
Renting a car in Côte d'Ivoire is expensive. Given the excellent bus network, it's generally not worth the extra hassles.

Most of Côte d'Ivoire's main roads are sealed and in excellent condition. One exception is the road from Korhogo to Odienné, which is paved only as far as Boundiali.

Road travel at night is not recommended due to frequent accidents and sporadic incidents of ambushing and banditry.

Abidjan

The gleaming high-rise commercial centre of Côte d'Ivoire is undoubtedly the New York of West Africa, and it's just as vibrant

Routes & Fares

From	To	Distance	Duration	Fares (US$)	Departs From
Abidjan					
	Aboisso	120km	2 hours	$2	STA from Adjamé or Gare de Bassam
	Bouaké	355km	5 hours	$6	STIF or UTB from Adjamé
	Ferkessédougou	590km	9 hours	$8	CTM or UTRAFER from Adjamé
	Grand-Bassam	45km	45 minutes	$1	UTAB from Adjamé via Gare de Bassam, from where minibuses and taxi-brousse also leave
	Korhogo	640km	10 hours	$8	UTRACO from Adjamé
	Man	580km	9 hours	$8	Fandasso, BAN, Tramoci or CTM from Adjamé
	Sassandra	260km	5 hours	$5	AMT from Adjamé
	Yamoussoukro	200km	3 hours	$4	UTB or YT buses from Adjamé
Korhogo					
	Bouaké	285km	5 hours	$5	CK or UTRACO from across the Grand Marché
	Ferkessédougou	55km	1 hour	$2	UTRACO or minibus from Agip station
	Odienné	290km	6 hours	$7	postal van from post office daily (except Sunday) at 8 am (get there early)
Odienné					
	Man	275km	5 hours	$6	one minibus/taxi-brousse daily or the 7 am daily (except Sunday) postal van from behind the post office
Yamoussoukro					
	Man	330km	6 hours	$9	CTM from the CTM depot near the Agip station

once you get out of the central business district of Plateau, which virtually shuts down after business hours.

Indeed, Abidjan (population 3.5 million) causes culture shock if you've become accustomed to the more dilapidated capitals of neighbouring states. There are stark contrasts between affluence and poverty, ankle-deep mud and six-lane highways, straw-roofed huts and 30-storey buildings, Paris fashions and rags. Some like it; others hate it.

Orientation
Abidjan, built on the banks of an enormous lagoon, is divided roughly into six parts. Plateau, with its wide streets, supermarkets and offices, is the business and government centre. Connected to it by two bridges is Treichville, a vibrant quarter (although unsafe at night) where the main train station is located. To the east of Treichville is Marcory, a more intimate area, with cheap hotels and excellent street food.

North of Plateau is Adjamé, with the main *gare routière* (bus station), while to the east, across a spur of the lagoon, is Cocody, a somewhat exclusive residential suburb which spreads northwards into the upscale residential and restaurant area of Deux Plateaux. The international airport and main marine port are at Port Bouët, to the south-east alongside the Atlantic Ocean.

Information
Tourist Office There is a tourist information office (☎ 206500) in the large building opposite the post office in Plateau, but visiting it is essentially a waste of time.

Travel Agencies SDV Voyages (☎ 202198) in Treichville is the Amex representative and staff will assist in booking flights. Saga Voyages (☎ 329870), opposite Air Afrique in Plateau, can assist with finding discounted fares.

Medical Services The Polyclinique St Anne-Marie (PISAN) in Cocody is frequented by foreigners residing in Abidjan.

Musée National
The recently renovated museum has an interesting collection of masks, pottery and other art work, and is worth checking out. Most buses from Treichville or Plateau to Adjamé pass by here (eg bus Nos 2 and 86).

Cathédrale St-Paul
This striking, modern cathedral doesn't rival the basilica at Yamoussoukro, but it's worth a visit. For good views over Plateau, go to the 2nd floor.

Île Boulay & Abobo-Doumé
For a break from the city, SOTRA Tourisme (☎ 321737) offers a 1½ hour boat trip across the lagoon to Île Boulay, south-west of Plateau. The boats leave from the Gare Lagunaire (Ferry Terminal) in Plateau at 3 pm on Wednesday, 9 am and 3 pm on Thursday, and 9.30 am and 3 pm on Saturday, and cost US$4 per person.

Alternatively, take one of the frequent boats from Plateau or Treichville to Abobo-Doumé. On Sunday the bars here often have live music as well as Abidjan's cheapest beers.

Places to Stay
Camping Abidjan's two closest camping grounds are tiny, beachfront places surrounded by cement walls. Both charge US$2 a person for camping and US$3 for a very basic room.

Camping Vridi, in the Vridi Canal area south of Abidjan, is usually deserted these days as the water supply is down and there's no electricity. Up the road are a few street food stalls. From Plateau, take bus No 18 or 53 (or bus No 24 from Treichville) to the Coco Beach sign, then walk back 500m.

Better is the friendly *Camping Coppa-Cabana*, which is 17km east on the road to Grand-Bassam. To get here, take a share-taxi (US$1) from Gare de Bassam in Treichville.

Treichville This area, colourful by day, is not safe to wander in at night. If you want to stay here, *Hôtel Le Prince* (☎ 241738), near the corner of Ave 20 and Rue 19, is relatively

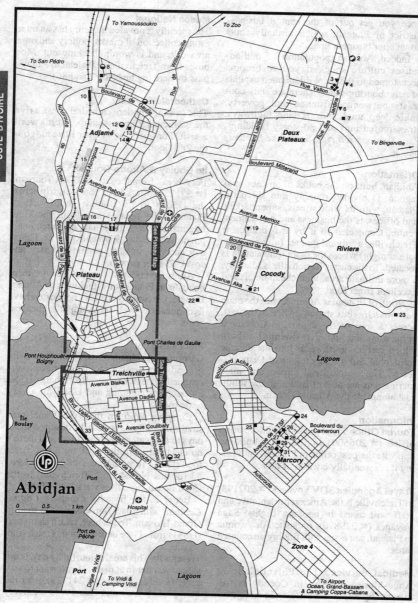

Abidjan

0   0.5   1 km

To Yamoussoukro
To Zoo
To San Pédro
To Bingerville
To Vridi &
Camping Vridi
To Airport,
Ocean, Grand-Bassam
& Camping Coppa-Cabana

Lagoon
Adjamé
Deux
Plateaux
Plateau
Riviera
Cocody
Treichville
Île
Boulay
Marcory
Port
Port de
Pêche
Port
Zone 4
Lagoon
Lagoon

Boulevard de Gaulle
Rue Vallon
Rue des Jardins
Boulevard Latrille
Boulevard Mitterand
Avenue Mermoz
Boulevard de France
Rue Washington
Avenue Aka
Boulevard Achalme
Boulevard du Cameroun
Avenue de la Sté
Autoroute de l'Ouest
Boulevard Abobaqua
Avenue Reboul
Boulevard de la Corniche
Blvd du Général de Gaulle
Boulevard de la Paix
Pont Charles de Gaulle
Pont Houphouët Boigny
Avenue Blaka
Avenue Dadié
Rue 12
Avenue Coulibaly
Blvd Valéry Giscard d'Estaing (Autoroute)
Blvd Nanan Yamoussou
Boulevard de Marseille
Boulevard du Port
Digue de Vridi
Rue Williamsville

See Plateau Map
See Treichville Map

Hospital

Rue Vallon

To Vridi &
Camping Vridi

PLACES TO STAY

7	Le Provençal
9	Hôtel Patience
13	Hôtel de la Gare; L'Escale
14	Hôtel Banfora
22	Hôtel Ivoire
23	Hôtel Forum Golf
25	Hôtel Hamanieh
26	Hôtel Konankro
28	Hôtel Pousada
29	Hôtel Copacabana

PLACES TO EAT

3	Score Supermarket
4	L'Automatic
6	Le Phenecien; Hyatt Supermarket
19	Allocodrome
27	Pâtisserie La Genoise
31	Maquis Le Vatican; Maquis du Petit Marché

OTHER

1	Commissariat de Deux Plateaux
2	Benin Embassy
5	Centre Commercial du Vallon; BICICI Bank
8	Gare Nord (SOTRA)
10	Adjamé Train Station
11	Share-Taxis for Grand-Bassam
12	Gare Routière de Adjamé
15	Marché d'Adjamé
16	Musée National
17	Cathédrale St-Paul
18	Polyclinique St Anne-Marie
20	Marché de Cocody
21	Institut Géographique
24	Gare de Marcory (SOTRA)
30	Petit Marché de Marcory
32	Share-Taxis for Adjamé
33	Treichville Train Station
34	Gare de Bassam
35	STC Bus Station

secure and a good deal, with clean air-con doubles from US$12.

A step down is *Hôtel Le Succès*, with basic rooms for US$6 (US$7/9 for fan/air-con).

The only hotel in this area approaching mid-range is the run-down *Treichôtel* (☎ 240559), which has decent doubles with attached bathroom from US$20.

The cheapest acceptable place near the train station is the desolate *Hôtel L'Ariegeois* (☎ 249968), with basic rooms for US$14.

Marcory The best option is *Hôtel Konankro* (☎ 261328), which has good value singles/doubles with attached bathroom and fan for US$12/15 (US$17/20 with air-con).

Nearby, *Hôtel Pousada* has decent rooms for US$8/12 with fan/air-con, if you don't mind sleeping in a very active brothel. Nevertheless, it's better than *Hôtel Copacabana*, where the only redeeming aspect is that it's cheap, with basic rooms for US$8.

For luxury in this area, head to *Hôtel Hamanieh* (☎ 269155), a modern multi-storey place with singles/doubles for US$36/50.

All buses heading to Gare de Marcory (such as Nos 2, 3 and 74) pass close to these hotels; get off at the intersection of Ave de la TSF and Blvd du Cameroun.

Plateau Budget lodging is scarce in Plateau. The *Hôtel des Sports* (☎ 331958) on Rue du Commerce has singles/doubles with attached bathroom for US$12/14 (US$22/24 for air-con).

Overlooking the lagoon, the *Grand Hôtel* (☎ 321200), with its shuttered windows, is like something out of the Left Bank in Paris. Comfortable rooms with all the amenities are US$42/56. The entrance is at the end of a dark and dangerous alleyway.

Adjamé The chaotic *Hôtel de la Gare*, just south of the gare routière, is the cheapest option, with bad rooms for US$6 (US$8 with fan).

Better is the nearby *Hôtel Banfora* (☎ 370252), which has air-con rooms with attached bathroom from US$16. Further north, *Hôtel Patience* (☎ 372241) is not quite as nice as the Banfora. Rooms are US$13/15 with fan/air-con (US$17 with attached bathroom).

Deux Plateaux Apart from private guest-houses, the cheapest place is *Le Provençal* (☎ 411567), with comfortable air-con rooms from US$20.

Places to Eat

Treichville The exterior of *Chez Babouya* is unimposing, but inside the décor resembles a scene from *The Arabian Nights*. A meal of

CÔTE D'IVOIRE

PLACES TO STAY
34 Hôtel des Sports; Bar
39 Grand Hôtel

PLACES TO EAT
5 Maquis du Stade;
 Maquis Sanh-Bé-La
7 Maquis Le Diplomat
9 La Casablancaise
11 Hamburger House
14 Charlie Express
20 Score Supermarket

OTHER
1 UK Embassy
2 Cathédrale St-Paul
3 Nigerian Embassy
4 Burkina Faso Embassy
6 US Embassy
8 French Embassy
10 Sabena
12 Marché
13 BICICI Bank
15 Citibank
16 Liberian Embassy
17 Air France
18 Air Afrique

19 SGBCI Bank
21 BIAO Bank;
 Saga Voyages
22 Police Headquarters
23 Post Office
24 Presidential Palace
25 Train Station
26 Tourist Office
27 EECI Building;
 Telecom Office
28 Air Burkina
29 Air Ivoire
30 Immeuble Trade Centre
 (Canadian Embassy)
31 Guinean Consulate
32 Air Guinée;
 Ghana Airways;
 Cameroon Embassy
33 Immeuble Nabil
 (Senegalese Embassy)
35 Gare Sud (SOTRA)

36 SOTRA Tourisme
37 Ghanaian Embassy
38 Nigerian Airways
40 Malian Embassy
41 Gare Lagunaire
 (Ferry Terminal)

Plateau

To Adjamé
To Cocody & Deux Plateaux

Boulevard Carde
Avenue Jamot
Ave Jean Paul II
Boulevard Roume
Avenue Crozet
Avenue Marchand
Avenue Terrasson de Fougères
Boulevard Angoulvant
Avenue Franchet d'Esperey
Rue Gourgas
Rue Jesse Owens
Rue Lecoeur
Boulevard du Général de Gaulle
Avenue Chardy
Avenue Delafosse
Avenue Anoma
Avenue Lamblin
Rue Botreau-Roussel
Boulevard Clozel
Boulevard de la République
Place de la République
Avenue Houdaille
Avenue Crosson Duplessis
Avenue Nogues
Rue du Commerce
Boulevard du Général de Gaulle
Pont Houphouët-Boigny
Pont Charles de Gaulle

Stadium
Lagoon
Lagoon

0 150 300 m

To Treichville
To Treichville

excellent Moroccan or Senegalese cuisine plus wine comes to about US$12.

Much cheaper is the friendly *Le Pot Noir* near Hôtel Le Prince, with all sorts of sauces and other specialities for under US$3.

Marcory Dining tends to be more relaxed in Marcory than in Treichville. The *Petit Marché area* is known for its barbecued fish (from US$2 to US$4 depending on the size), broiled nightly at streetside stalls.

Nearby is *Maquis Le Vatican*, a terrace restaurant with a noteworthy reputation among expatriates. It offers first-rate food at reasonable prices and the service is excellent.

Pâtisserie La Genoise is a friendly place, with coffee, pastries and simple dishes for around US$3.

Plateau Cheap restaurants in the Plateau area are few and far between. One of the least expensive is the *Maquis Sanh-Bé-La*, a quiet place off the street with poulet kedjenou and other delicacies for under US$3. Around the corner, the bustling *Maquis du Stade* is also good, with a variety of dishes for under US$4. It's open weekdays until 6 pm.

On Rue Jesse Owens, *Maquis Le Diplomat* serves a simple plat du jour (dish of the day) for US$2.

La Casablancaise is a pleasant cafe, with a variety of selections for under US$5.

Inexpensive fast food is sold from the *Charlie Express* kiosk at the Pyramid building. For burgers and fries, there's *Hamburger House* on Ave Chardy.

Adjamé In Adjamé, *L'Escale* next to Hôtel de la Gare has a good selection of inexpensive dishes.

Cocody *Allocodrome*, a large open-air compound where some 30 vendors grill fish, chicken and beef while patrons eat on the benches, is very popular in the evenings. Prices are cheap – there's plenty here for under US$2.

Deux Plateaux Near the intersection of Rue Vallon and Rue des Jardins are many morning *coffee stalls* serving baguettes and other cheap snacks. *L'Automatic* on Rue des Jardins has inexpensive poulet and chawarmas. *Le Phenecien* near the Hyatt Supermarket has excellent Lebanese food at reasonable prices.

Entertainment
Treichville There are several popular bars and nightclubs near the train station. *Midnight Express* has music and dancing daily from 10 pm. The US$8 cover is often waived if you get there early. Nearby, *Hit Parade* has good music and attracts a mix of locals and expatriates; there's an expensive (US$10) cover. Further up, *La Canne à Sucre* on Blvd Delafosse is an energetic nightclub.

Marcory Around the Petit Marché are a number of easy-going terrace bars. They're perfect for a drink in the late afternoon (particularly on weekends), when crowds gather to watch local soccer teams competing on the small dirt square at the centre of the open-air market area.

Plateau The *Hôtel des Sports* has plenty of interesting characters, but beers are expensive. On the same street, *Le Cinoche* is an old theatre with a DJ and dance music. It's formal and pricey at US$10, but still attracts a good crowd.

Getting There & Away
Air Airlines serving Côte d'Ivoire include: Air Afrique (☎ 220500), Air Burkina (☎ 328919), Air France (☎ 219093), Air Guinée (☎ 326064), Air Ivoire (☎ 213434), Ghana Airways (☎ 322783), Nigerian Airways (☎ 322601), Sabena (☎ 212936) and South African Airways (☎ 215839). All have their offices in Plateau.

Bus Gare Routière d'Adjamé, Abidjan's main bus station, is a nightmare. You'll have fewer hassles if you decide in advance which bus company you want to travel with and head straight for its depot.

To avoid the chaos of Adjamé on arrival

COTE D'IVOIRE

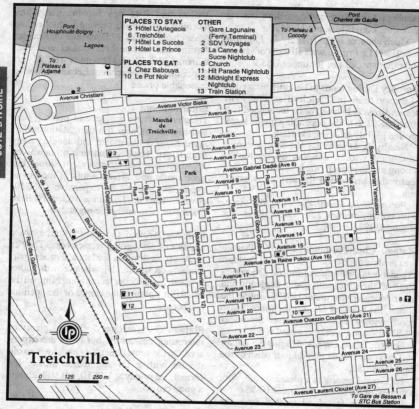

PLACES TO STAY
5 Hôtel L'Ariegeois
6 Treichôtel
7 Hôtel Le Succès
9 Hôtel Le Prince

PLACES TO EAT
4 Chez Babouya
10 Le Pot Noir

OTHER
1 Gare Lagunaire
 (Ferry Terminal)
2 SDV Voyages
3 La Canne à
 Sucre Nightclub
8 Church
11 Hit Parade Nightclub
12 Midnight Express
 Nightclub
13 Train Station

Treichville

0   125   250 m

in Abidjan, disembark at Yopougon station on the outskirts of the city, one stop before Adjamé; almost all buses stop at Yopougon. A taxi to the city centre costs slightly more, but it's well worth the extra money. This doesn't work as well on departure, as buses are often full when they leave Adjamé, with no seats left by the time they get to Yopougon. Whatever you do, avoid arriving at Adjamé at night as robberies and muggings are common.

Gare de Bassam in Treichville serves destinations east as far as Aboisso. Nearby is the depot for Ghana's STC buses.

Train For information on train services between Abidjan and Bouaké, see the main Getting Around section of this chapter.

Getting Around

Bus Abidjan's SOTRA buses are well organised, but overcrowded during rush hours. Stops are signposted and the buses generally run from 6 am to 9 or 10 pm. You can buy tickets (US$0.35 base fare, US$0.50 for additional zones) either from ticket counters at the main depots or as you board. The principal bus stations are Gare Sud in Plateau and Gare Nord (north of the main gare routière) in Adjamé. A few bus routes of interest include:

No 2 – Gare Nord, Marché de Adjamé, Plateau post office, Marché de Treichville, Treichville train station, Gare de Marcory

No 3 – Adjamé train station, Cathédrale St-Paul, Plateau, Marché de Treichville, Gare de Bassam, Gare de Marcory

No 6 – Gare Sud to the airport via Treichville

No 21 – Cocody to Plateau and Treichville

No 24 – Treichville to Vridi Beach

No 82 – Gare Sud to Deux Plateaux

Taxi Taxis are plentiful and have meters, which they generally use. The trip from the train station in Treichville to the gare routière in Adjamé costs US$2; to the airport costs US$6. Double tariffs apply between midnight and 6 am. It's best to put on the seat belt unless you want to risk a fine from the police.

Ferry The daily lagoon ferry service con-nects the Gare Lagunaire in Plateau (below the Gare Sud) to Treichville and Abobo-Doumé (US$2) every eight minutes or so from 6 am to 8.30 pm.

Around the Country

BONDOUKOU
Bondoukou, a renowned centre for Islamic studies, is known for its many mosques and for the decoratively sculpted **Abron Tombs**. There are several hotels in town, and street food is available.

BOUAKÉ
Bouaké is one of Côte d'Ivoire's largest towns, and an important commercial and trading centre. There's not a lot to see except for the **Grand Marché**, the **Grande Mosquée** and lively nightlife in the Koko district.

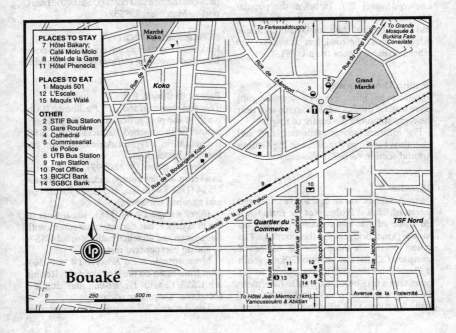

PLACES TO STAY
7 Hôtel Bakary;
    Café Molo Molo
8 Hôtel de la Gare
11 Hôtel Phenecia

PLACES TO EAT
1 Maquis 501
12 L'Escale
15 Maquis Walé

OTHER
2 STIF Bus Station
3 Gare Routière
4 Cathedral
5 Commissariat de Police
6 UTB Bus Station
9 Train Station
10 Post Office
13 BICICI Bank
14 SGBCI Bank

To Ferkessédougou

To Grande Mosquée & Burkina Faso Consulate

Grand Marché

Marché Koko

Koko

Rue de l'Avenir

Rue de l'Aéroport

Rue du Camp Militaire

Rue de la Boulangerie Koko

Avenue de la Reine Pokou

Quartier du Commerce

Avenue Gabriel Dadié

La Route de Carnival

Avenue Houphouët-Boigny

Rue Jacque Aka

TSF Nord

Avenue de la Fraternité

Bouaké

0   250   500 m

To Hôtel Jean Mermoz (1km),
Yamoussoukro & Abidjan

There's a Burkina Faso consulate opposite the mosque, which issues visas within 24 hours or less for US$26 plus three photos.

Places to Stay & Eat
In town, the dreary *Hôtel Bakary* has basic, dirty rooms for US$4 (US$6 with fan). The nearby *Hôtel de la Gare*, in an unmarked pink building, is the same price and almost as bad.

The *Hôtel Phenecia* (☎ 634834) is more expensive, but a big step up, with good rooms, including attached bathroom, from US$15, and a restaurant with French fare for US$7.

South of the town centre, *Hôtel Jean Mermoz* (☎ 638027) has good value rooms for US$8/12 with fan/air-con. Full breakfast costs US$2, and there's a *maquis* nearby for lunch or dinner.

For inexpensive African food, head to the Koko district and ask around for the well-known *Maquis 501*. In town, the popular *Maquis Walé* has pleasant veranda seating and good Ivoirian fare for US$4. *L'Escale*, directly across the road, has chawarma and other Lebanese dishes from US$1.

Getting There & Away
Minibuses to Odienné (via Ferkessédougou) leave several times a week from the area near the Agip station in the centre of town.

For information on other bus, taxi and train travel to/from Bouaké, see the Getting Around section earlier in this chapter.

DANANÉ
Danané stands in an attractive, forested region of Côte d'Ivoire. Not far from town are some of the last remaining **ponts de lianes** (vine bridges) in the country. The easiest to visit are those near the villages of **Lieupleu** (22km) and **Vatouo** (30km), south of Danané on the road to Toulépleu. To get there, take a taxi-brousse towards Toulépleu; the bridges are a 4km walk east off the main road. A private taxi will cost US$9 return.

There's a negotiable entry fee to Lieupleu bridge of US$2.

Places to Stay & Eat
Hôtel Tia Étienne (☎ 700388) has clean rooms for US$7/12 with fan/air-con and attached bathroom, and a restaurant with decent meals from US$4. It's 500m west of the gare routière for Man.

Hôtel de la Frontière (☎ 700210), 100m down the road, has small, dim rooms from US$6 and serves meals for US$5. There's a lot of stagnant water around this place and many mosquitoes.

The more luxurious *Hôtel Les Lianes*, opposite the gare routière for Man, has one basic room for US$5 and numerous air-con doubles with attached bathroom for US$14.

Getting There & Away
The gares routière for Man and the gare routière for Liberia and Guinea are at opposite ends of the town. It's a long walk between them; a taxi costs (US$0.40). Transport to Man costs US$3.

FERKESSÉDOUGOU
Ferkessédougou is a convenient transit point for those travelling to/from Mali or Burkina Faso.

Places to Stay & Eat
The run-down *Hôtel La Paillotte*, 100m north of the post office, has ventilated bungalows with attached bathroom for US$5. It's set out as a typical African village, but has seen better days.

Hôtel Koffikro (☎ 880197), west of the market in a quiet compound, has rooms for US$4 (US$5 with fan, and US$8 for air-con and attached bathroom).

Hôtel Refuge (☎ 880288), south-west of the post office, has decent-value rooms with fan/air-con and attached bathroom for US$7/8, and an inexpensive restaurant.

More upscale is *La Réserve* (☎ 880050), 2km from town on the Bouaké road. Rooms are US$8/12 with fan/air-con and attached bathroom. There's no restaurant.

The *Arc en Ciel* maquis near the market

has good, cheap food, as do *La Savane* and *La Primature*, near the gare routière.

Getting There & Away
The main gare routière (for Abidjan, Mali and Burkina Faso) is at the northern end of town near the post office. CTM and UTRAFER buses have their depots nearby. Transport to Korhogo leaves from a small car park to the west of the market.

GRAND-BASSAM
About 45km south-east of Abidjan and set among coconut palms is Grand-Bassam, the capital of Côte d'Ivoire from 1893 to 1900. A yellow-fever epidemic forced the French to abandon the place and move the capital to Bingerville, yet the port struggled on and remained important until the Vridi Canal (which opened up Abidjan's Port Bouët to the ocean) was cut in 1950. From that point on it declined rapidly.

These days it's a place for dreamers, full of dilapidated colonial buildings and old churches which give it the air of a ghost town. Grand-Bassam is also the nearest place to Abidjan for beaches, although currents are dangerous. They're virtually deserted during the day, but don't sleep on them as chances are you'll be robbed.

Lodging in Grand-Bassam tends to fill up quickly on weekends, so get there early.

Things to See & Do
The old **Governor's Palace** is now a museum containing exhibits of African art and culture, as well as old photographs of the colonial days. Entry is free (though a tip is appreciated), and it's open from 9 am to noon and 3 to 5 pm (closed on Monday and on Tuesday morning).

At the entrance to town, coming from Abidjan, there's a long row of **artisan stalls** selling caneware, wooden furniture and other crafts. You'll find more crafts at the **Centre Céramique** and the interesting

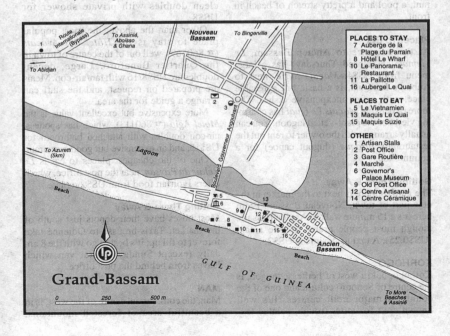

PLACES TO STAY
7 Auberge de la Plage du Parrain
8 Hôtel Le Wharf
10 Le Panorama; Restaurant
11 La Paillotte
16 Auberge Le Quai

PLACES TO EAT
5 Le Vietnamien
13 Maquis Le Quai
15 Maquis Suzie

OTHER
1 Artisan Stalls
2 Post Office
3 Gare Routière
4 Marché
6 Governor's Palace Museum
9 Old Post Office
12 Centre Artisanal
14 Centre Céramique

Grand-Bassam

0   250   500 m

GULF OF GUINEA

Centre Artisanal in the old town, Ancien Bassam. All are open daily.

Places to Stay
Set back on the sand between hotels Le Wharf and La Paillotte is the informal *Le Panorama*. It has three spartan doubles with shared facilities for US$6, and a simple restaurant serving one or two dishes for US$5.

The small and friendly *Auberge Le Quai* (☎ 301075) has decent rooms for US$13/19 with fan/air-con.

The only other moderately priced option is the well located but atmosphereless *Auberge de La Plage du Parrain* (☎ 301541), which has ventilated doubles with attached bathroom from US$13.

For more upscale lodging, try the relaxed *Hôtel Le Wharf* (☎ 301533). It's tucked away from the seafront, but has airy singles/doubles with air-con and attached bathroom for US$36/50 (US$34/46 in the low season). There's an expensive restaurant, a pool and a pretty stretch of beach in front.

Places to Eat
At the entrance to Ancien Bassam, *Le Vietnamien* (closed Thursday) has a large menu from US$4. *Maquis Suzie*, next to Auberge Le Quai, is a basic but agreeable place, with a few inexpensive dishes. The more expensive *Maquis Le Quai* has charming views of the plant-veiled lagoon. You can usually arrange with the owner to rent out the restaurant's *pirogue* (dugout canoe) for a nominal fee.

Getting There & Away
The gare routière is next to the market in the new part of town, Nouveau Bassam. From here it's a 15 minute walk to Ancien Bassam, though most people prefer to take a taxi (US$0.25). A taxi to Assinié is US$2.

KORHOGO
Korhogo, 55km west of Ferkessédougou, is the centre of Senoufo culture and one of the country's major craft centres. It's well known craft for *toiles* (rough, painted textiles) which you'll see hung up around Côte d'Ivoire.

Things to See & Do
The best place to see toiles is at the superb **Centre Artisanal**. It's run as a cooperative and the prices are fixed but reasonable.

The **museum** on Ave Coulibaly has an interesting selection of masks. It's closed Sunday and Monday; admission is free.

Within walking distance of Korhogo are a number of traditional **Senoufo villages** which specialise in crafts, including making *waraniéné* (woven shirts and trousers), *torgokaha* (baskets and hats) and *foro* (musical instruments). You'll have no trouble finding a guide in Korhogo.

Places to Stay & Eat
The cheapest place is the *Centre Artisanal*, which has a couple of cheap, basic rooms for US$4. The *mission catholique*, near the cathedral, is also inexpensive, with large, clean doubles with private shower for US$8.

Other than the above, the most popular place to stay is the *Hôtel des Avocats* (☎ 860569), well out of the centre of town in the Quartier Banaforo. Large, decent doubles are US$8/16 with fan/air-con. Meals are prepared on request, and the staff can arrange a guide for the area.

More expensive but excellent value is the *Motel Agip* (☎ 860113), which has spotless, air-con doubles with attached bathroom for US$15, and an expensive but good restaurant.

One of the cheapest places to eat is *Le Relais du Paysan*, near the post office, which offers Ivoirian food from US$2 a plate.

Getting There & Away
Most buses have their depots just south of the market. Taxis-brousse to Odienné take forever to fill up; it's best to go with the 8 am daily (except Sunday) postal van which leaves from behind the post office.

MAN
Man, the commercial centre of the west, is in a beautiful area of forested mountains,

though the town itself is not particularly attractive.

The area's drawcard is the culture of the Dan people, who settled this area in the 14th century after migrating from further west. They had little contact with the other peoples of Côte d'Ivoire or with Europeans until very late in the 19th century. Their masks, which are used in initiation ceremonies, are full of character, and their incredible stilt dances are famous throughout the area.

Information

The new Bourse de Tourisme (☎ 791213)

hasn't much to offer except a list of approved guides to take you exploring further afield.

Although there are branches of all major banks here, it's often difficult to change travellers' cheques in denominations other than French francs.

Places to Stay

Centre Béthanie (☎ 790092), run by a Swiss nun, is a very popular place that offers excellent value. Spotless singles/doubles/triples cost US$8/9/10 with attached bathroom (US$12/13 for air-con doubles/triples), and breakfast is US$3. It's on a peaceful hill

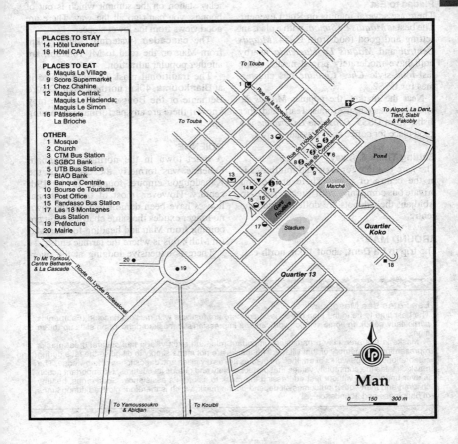

PLACES TO STAY
14 Hôtel Leveneur
18 Hôtel CAA

PLACES TO EAT
6 Maquis Le Village
9 Score Supermarket
11 Chez Chahine
12 Maquis Central;
Maquis Le Hacienda;
Maquis Le Simon
16 Pâtisserie
La Brioche

OTHER
1 Mosque
2 Church
3 CTM Bus Station
4 SGBCI Bank
5 UTB Bus Station
7 BIAO Bank
8 Banque Centrale
10 Bourse de Tourisme
13 Post Office
15 Fandasso Bus Station
17 Les 18 Montagnes
Bus Station
19 Préfecture
20 Mairie

Man

about 3km from the town centre (US$1 by taxi). From Centre Béthanie, it's 3km to the waterfalls and a disintegrating vine bridge.

In town, the new (and unfinished) *Hôtel CAA* is good value, though you need to walk through a construction site to get to the rooms. Clean doubles are US$7/12 with fan/air-con and attached bathroom.

The centrally located *Hôtel Leveneur* (☎ 791481) has air-con doubles with attached bathroom from US$14, and a good restaurant.

Places to Eat

There are several maquis on Rue Leveneur. The best is *Maquis Le Simon*, with a pleasant setting and good food from US$4. *Maquis Central* and *Maquis Le Hacienda* nearby both have moderately priced meals, while fast-food-style *Chez Chahine* has chawarmas for US$2.

Near the market, the popular *Maquis Le Village* has carpe braisé (braised carp) and other dishes from US$5. *Pâtisserie La Brioche* is a good place for coffee and croissants.

Getting There & Away

The gare routière for taxis and minibuses is in the centre of town. There are several private bus companies with direct services to Abidjan; their depots are dotted around the centre.

AROUND MAN

The trip to **La Dent**, about 12km north-east of Man, is a popular excursion. Aptly named, it's a bald, tooth-like rock formation which rises out of the surrounding forest and is visible from Man on clear days. The views from the top make the somewhat arduous climb well worth it (provided the harmattan isn't blowing). To get here, take a taxi to the village of Glongouin and negotiate a price for a guide (you'll need one). Expect to pay about US$12. The climb to the top takes about two hours.

Another hiking possibility is to **Mt Tonkoui** (1223m), also visible from Man. It's about 32km to the top from Man, but as there's a TV relay station on the summit which is out of bounds, you can't go all the way. There are good views from the lower slopes.

The **cascades** (waterfalls), about 5km from Man on the road to Mt Tonkoui, are another popular attraction.

The traditional mask-dancing centre is at **Biankouma**, 40km north of Man. Centre Béthanie or the Bourse de Tourisme may know if there are any performances coming up.

ODIENNÉ

A quiet town in the northern savannah, Odienné was formerly the capital of the Kabadougou empire, founded in the 19th century. However, most of the traditional houses have been demolished, so the town no longer exudes the same charm. If you are coming from Man and heading for Bamako (in Mali), this is where the tarmac ends.

There is expensive lodging at the over-

Les Fêtes des Masques

The best time to be in the Man region is when there are festivals with masked dancing (February is particularly good). In some villages you can see impressionistic masked dancers on stilts up to 3m high.

Masks in this area play a particularly important role, and each village has several great masks representing the memory of that village. The masks are not made simply to disguise the face during celebrations or to be works of art; their main roles are as divinities and depositories of knowledge. The mask dictates the community values that protect society and guards its customs. No important action is ever undertaken without first addressing the mask to ask for its assistance. Good crops, healthy children and many other outcomes all depend on the mask, which is therefore glorified during times of happiness and abundance. ■

priced *Hôtel Les Frontières* (☎ 800283) to the west of town, with rooms for US$22, and cheaper rooms at *La Savane*, near the town centre, for US$10.

For inexpensive Ivoirian fare, try *Le Yancadi* or *La Bonne Auberge*, both near the town centre.

SASSANDRA

Sassandra, once an important timber port at the mouth of the river of the same name, is a peaceful fishing and trading village about 260km west of Abidjan. Most travellers come here for the delicious, cheap seafood and the superb beaches, which stretch some 25km west of town; the more remote of them are only feasible if you have your own transport. Plenty of people will offer to take you upriver in a pirogue; be prepared to bargain.

Places to Stay & Eat

The relaxing *Chez Tanti Youyou*, at the eastern end of town on the river bank, has tiny doubles with mosquito nets and fans from US$8, and new bungalows with attached bathroom for US$17. Tanti serves excellent shrimp kedjenou and other meals at reasonable prices.

On the main road into town is the French-run *Hôtel Grau* (☎ 720520), which charges US$10 for rooms with fan or US$20 for spacious rooms with air-con and attached bathroom. *Hôtel Eden* (☎ 720474), on the same road, has good rooms for US$12 per person.

The closest beach accommodation is *Chez Ralph's*, which has camping for US$2 per person and a few simple huts for US$4.

Around 15km west of Sassandra at Latéko Plage, Raymond and his brothers rent out simple *bungalows* on the sand for US$6. There's no electricity or running water at this friendly, relaxing place, but they can arrange clean water for bathing and will cook meals on request. To get here, either make arrangements in Sassandra for taxi drop-off and pick-up, or be prepared to walk.

Back in town, the *Safari Restaurant*, next to the gare routière, offers a mouthwatering array of dishes (including Sassandra's best stuffed crab), while *La Terrace*, on the hill below the lighthouse, has good food and ocean views. There's lots of street food near the gare routière.

YAMOUSSOUKRO

Though this former village – the birthplace and final resting-place of Félix Houphouët-Boigny – has been the official capital of Côte d'Ivoire since 1983, Abidjan remains the commercial and diplomatic centre.

Carved out of the bush with little imagination and totally out of touch with the environment, Yamoussoukro is a treeless expanse of endless lawns and vast boulevards as well as a huge presidential palace and the enormous Basilique de Notre Dame de la Paix, which dominates the city's skyline.

Things to See

The **Presidential Palace** (which is where Houphouët-Boigny is buried) has its own **crocodile lake**. The crocodiles are fed daily at 5 pm.

Despite its incongruity – or because of it – most visitors pay a visit to the **Basilique de Notre Dame de la Paix**, built in the late 1980s under orders from former President Houphouët-Boigny. You must register at the south-western gate, but there's no entry charge. Once you've reached the entrance, guardians will offer their services as guides (for a fee), but they're not compulsory. The lift to the upper gallery costs US$2. The basilica is open Tuesday to Saturday from 9 am to noon and 2 to 5.30 pm, and all day on Sunday. There are no restrictions on photography.

Places to Stay & Eat

In the central market neighbourhood is *Hôtel Las Palmas*, which charges US$6 to US$10 for small rooms with shower and fan. Nearby, *Hôtel Akwaba* (☎ 642594) has rooms for US$8/10 with fan/air-con, and a reasonably priced restaurant.

A good place close to the gare routière is *Hôtel Les Artisans* (☎ 640227), which has spotless rooms for US$8/12 with fan/air-con. It's behind the post office on a small street paralleling the main road. There's a *maquis* nearby for meals.

The cheapest option is *Les Confidences du Ciel*, a small hotel west of the post office with dark rooms (request one with a window) for US$5/7 with fan/air-con. To eat, you'll have to go back towards the city centre.

For comfort, try *Le Bonheur I* (☎ 660061) opposite the gare routière, which has modern air-con doubles with attached bathroom from US$16 to US$22, or *Hôtel Agip* (☎ 643043) across the street, which has good value rooms for US$14 and a restaurant.

A maze of *food stalls* crowds the gare routière and some good *maquis* dot the area south-east of the market. Many of these have pleasant terraces or lake-side seating. Two of the best are *Maquis Les Alizés* and the slightly more expensive *Maquis Le Palmier*. *Maquis Le Jardin* is good but expensive at around US$7 for a meal.

Getting There & Away

UTRAFER, UTRACO, CTM and YT buses all have their depots near the Agip station. UTB departs from the Shell station. BFCI/Sans Frontières buses depart from the Gare du Burkina on Rue de la Mosquée. Taxis-brousse congregate at the Total station near the Score supermarket.

National Parks

Most of Côte d'Ivoire's national parks are either closed or inaccessible unless you have your own vehicle. Proposals to create a new park to protect some of the country's last remaining patches of pristine coastal rainforest were cancelled when the government went ahead with the controversial construction of the coastal road between Sassandra and Grand-Lahou, despite opposition from environmentalists.

PARC NATIONAL D'ABOKOUAMÉKRO

This park is just to the north-east of Yamoussoukro. Transport and guides can be arranged through the Direction du Tourisme in Yamoussoukro, though there's not much to see in the park. It costs US$20 per day for a guide, plus US$4 admission.

PARC NATIONAL DE LA COMOË

Comoë is the best known and the largest (11,500 sq km) of Côte d'Ivoire's parks. Occupying a huge chunk of woodland savannah, it is a haven for birds and a variety of wildlife, including lion, elephant and hippo. The park is open from December to May. Accommodation is available only at the park boundaries – in Kafolo and Ouango in the north, and Gansé and Kakpin in the south.

PARC NATIONAL DE LA MARAHOUÉ

Marahoué occupies 1000 sq km of semi-dense forest between Bouaflé and Daloa. Though less well known than Comoë, it's easier to reach. There are no lion here, so you can walk in the park, but it is difficult to see elephant due to the dense undergrowth; many days it's difficult to find any wildlife at all.

From the park entrance, a path leads 15km to the Marahoué River, home to hippo. The park is open all year and entry costs US$5. The closest lodgings are at Bouaflé and Daloa, on the main Yamoussoukro-Man route.

PARC NATIONAL DU MONT SANGBÉ

North of Man in a mountainous region, this small park is currently inaccessible and does not have lodging facilities, although there are plans to establish these in the near future.

PARC NATIONAL DE TAÏ

This park, near the Liberian border, is in virgin rainforest and is known for its chimpanzee communities. However, access is difficult and you'll have to head to the village of Taï for hotel accommodation. As the park is closed for research, a special visitor's permit must be obtained in advance from the Forestry Ministry in Abidjan.

Djibouti

Djibouti was the last French colony on the African mainland to gain its independence, in 1977. It consists of the port and town of Djibouti and an enclave of semidesert hinterland.

Facts about the Country

HISTORY

The area, now known as Djibouti, was once the grazing land for a number of nomadic tribes, including the Afars (from eastern Ethiopia) and the Issas (from Somalia). Islam was introduced to the region around 825 AD and Arab traders controlled the economy until the 16th century.

The French, seeking to counter the British presence in Aden on the other side of the Bab al-Mandab strait, made agreements in 1862 with the Afar sultans of Obock and Tadjoura, which gave them the right to settle. In 1888 construction of Djibouti began on the southern shore of the Gulf of Tadjoura. This area was settled by Somalis, mainly of the Issa clan, and French Somaliland began to take shape.

France and the emperor of Ethiopia then signed a pact designating Djibouti as the 'official outlet of Ethiopian commerce'. This led to the construction of the Djibouti-Addis Ababa railway, which remains of vital strategic and commercial importance to Ethiopia.

As early as 1949 there were anticolonial demonstrations by the Issas, who were in favour of the reunification of the territories of Italian, British and French Somaliland. Meanwhile, the Afars were in favour of French rule. The French supported the Afars, and in 1958 placed Ali Aref and fellow Afars in control of local government.

This didn't stifle opposition, however. There were serious riots, especially after the 1967 referendum which produced a 60.4% vote in favour of continued rule by France –

Highlights
- A sunset walk along L'Escale causeway
- A boat trip across the Gulf of Tadjoura
- Eating Red Sea fish, baked, barbecued or grilled
- Flamingoes, wilderness and weird natural chimneys belching steam at Lac Abbé

a vote achieved partly by the arrest of opposition leaders and the massive expulsion of ethnic Somalis. After the referendum, the colony's name was changed from French Somaliland to the French Territory of the Afars and Issas. Many of those who were expelled went to join the Somali Coast Liberation Front, which increased its terrorist activities within the colony during the early 1970s.

In 1976 Ali Aref was forced to resign following huge demonstrations in support of

249

DJIBOUTI

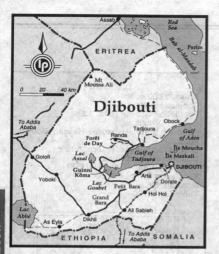

DJIBOUTI

the opposition People's Progress Assembly (RPP), a moderate inter-ethnic party led by Hassan Gouled Aptidon, an Issa, and Ahmed Dini, an Afar.

France reluctantly granted independence in 1977, when Hassan Gouled Aptidon became president, and his party, the RPP, the only legal political party.

Only a few months before Iraq's invasion of Kuwait in 1990, Djibouti signed a military pact with Baghdad, which supplied coastal patrol vessels and other armaments. It also had a long-standing military pact with Paris and had recently secured an annual grant of US$1.7 million from the USA.

Hassan Gouled skilfully gave lip service to opposition to the military build-up in the Gulf while allowing France to considerably increase its military personnel in Djibouti. He also allowed use of Djibouti's naval-base facilities, to which Italian and US warships also had access. He also managed to retain the support of Saudi Arabia and Kuwait for the modernisation of Djibouti port, the country's most important development project.

In November 1991 Afar rebels, united in the Front for the Restoration of Unity and Democracy (FRUD), launched a civil war in the north, their traditional territory. Accusing the Issa-dominated government of favouring its own kind in the labour market, FRUD demanded multiparty elections.

After four months of bloodshed and several hundred casualties, Hassan Gouled, under pressure from France, finally agreed to concessions. A new constitution was approved in the 1992 referendum, with a 70% turn-out. In the elections of December 1992, the RPP got 72% of the votes, the rest going to the new Party of Democratic Renewal, the only other party to compete.

A peace accord was signed in December 1994 between FRUD and the government. However, this agreement is a fragile one and ethnic hostility continues to simmer.

There is still no clear potential successor to Hassan Gouled, in power since independence and reportedly in declining health.

The year 1999 will be decisive for Djibouti: scheduled presidential elections will coincide with a significant reduction in French military personnel which will cause an estimated loss of revenue of some 35% to an already chronically sick economy.

GEOGRAPHY & CLIMATE

Djibouti's 23,000 sq km can be divided into three geographic regions: the coastal plain, the volcanic plateaus in the south and central parts of the country, and the mountain ranges in the north. Essentially the country is a vast wasteland, with practically no arable land.

The climate is generally hot, with a cooler season (including occasional rain) from November to mid-April, when temperatures average 25°C. At the peak of the hot season, the thermometer can peak at 45°C and the humidity is correspondingly high.

POPULATION & PEOPLE

The population, more than 90% of which is Muslim, numbers 430,000, swollen by an additional 150,000 refugees who fled recent conflicts in neighbouring Ethiopia and Somalia. It consists, in broadly equal proportions, of Afars, ethnically linked with Eritrea and Ethiopia, and Issas, whose links are with

A Question of Dress

The French, civil or military, men or women, are the ones in the short shorts. The local men, by contrast, all wear either trousers or a *futa*, Djibouti's version of the sarong. The women wear modestly long dresses or skirts and drape themselves with a *shalma*, a gauze-thin brightly coloured length of fabric. ■

Somalia. There are also sizeable minorities of Somalis of the Gadaboursi and Issaq clans, as well as Yemenis and some 10,000 French, of whom over 4000 are military personnel.

LANGUAGE

French and Arabic are joint official languages. (See the Language Appendix for useful phrases.) Afar and Somali are also spoken. Very few people speak English.

Facts for the Visitor

VISAS

All visitors, except nationals of France, need visas. They cost US$20 to US$22 and are valid for one month.

Other Visas

Ethiopia
A one month visa costs US$63 (US$70 for US nationals). You need one photo and may be asked to produce an onward air ticket. The consulate receives applications only on Sunday, Tuesday and Thursday from 9 to 11 am, and you collect the next day.

France
The consulate issues visas on behalf of African francophone countries, none of which are represented in Djibouti. Visas cost US$29, and are issued within 48 hours. Bring two photos. Opening hours are Sunday to Thursday from 8 am to noon.

Yemen
Visas, which are issued the same day, cost US$33 for Americans, US$53 for French citizens and US$56 if you're British. Everyone pays an additional US$3 for an Arabic translation of the application and you need two photos. Opening hours are Saturday to Thursday from 8.30 am to 1.30 pm.

EMBASSIES

Djibouti Embassies

There are Djibouti diplomatic representation in Belgium, Egypt, Ethiopia, France, Kenya, Somalia, Tunisia, the USA and Yemen. Where there is no Djibouti embassy, visas can be obtained from the French embassy.

Foreign Embassies in Djibouti

Embassies in Djibouti city include:

Ethiopia
Rue Clochette (☎ 350718)
France
Ave Maréchal Foch (☎ 350325)
(consulate) Ave Maréchal Lyautey (☎ 352503)
USA
Ave Maréchal Foch (☎ 353995)
Yemen
Between Ave Maréchal Foch and Plateau du Serpent (☎ 352975)

If you're British and find yourself in trouble, ring the UK honorary consul (☎ 353844).

MONEY

US$1 = DFr 175

The unit of currency is the Djibouti franc (DFr). There are no import or export restrictions.

There's no currency exchange at the airport. Banks in central Djibouti are open Sunday to Thursday from 7.30 am to 1.30 pm. The major banks are on Place Lagarde. Authorised moneychangers, whose shops are on the southeast side of Place Ménélik, are open all day.

Djibouti is a very expensive country to travel in.

POST & COMMUNICATIONS

International postal services work with French efficiency from Djibouti city.

There are several phone booths around town which accept cash or phonecards. You can also call and buy phonecards from designated shops.

International telephone calls are best placed at the post office. Like everything else in town, they're expensive: US$9 for three minutes to Europe, US$12 to Australia and US$15 to the USA. The country code for Djibouti is 253; there are no area codes.

BUSINESS HOURS & PUBLIC HOLIDAYS

Friday is the weekly holiday for offices and government institutions.

Djibouti observes the following holidays: 1 January, 1 May, 27 June (Independence), 25 December and variable Islamic holidays. See also Public Holidays in the Regional Facts for the Visitor chapter.

Getting There & Away

AIR

Djibouti is served by Aeroflot, Air France (☎ 352010), Air Tanzania, Corsair (☎ 350 413), Ethiopian Airlines (☎ 351007), Yemenia and the national carrier, Djibouti Airlines (☎ 351006). Both Yemenia and Air Tanzania are represented by Savon et Ries Travel Agency (☎ 351305).

Yemenia has two flights a week across the Red Sea to Sana'a and one each to Aden (US$134) and Taiz (US$140), while Djibouti Airlines flies once a week to Taiz (US$114).

The charter company, Corsair, has a weekly flight to Paris which, at US$514, is considerably cheaper than Air France's fare.

The airport departure tax for international flights is US$17 for flights to neighbouring countries and US$29 for further-flung destinations.

LAND
Eritrea

Only tracks and dirt roads used by Afar nomads lead to Eritrea. They're a risk – not because of the security situation, but since there's no formal frontier post, you may have trouble leaving Eritrea without an entry stamp in your passport.

Ethiopia

There's an irregular bus service as far as the first village over the border, from where you can catch a connection to Dire Dawa in Ethiopia.

The rail journey is preferable; it's comfortable if you buy a 1st class ticket (US$20) and the scenery's spectacular. Unless you're an obsessive railway buff, it's better to take the train as far as Dire Dawa, rest up overnight and continue to Addis Ababa by bus.

Somalia

Since Somalia is still extremely unsafe for travellers, delete it from your itinerary.

SEA

All boats leaving Djibouti waters sail from the commercial port. It's all but impossible to fix a hitch or paying passage on a cargo boat. Dhows only occasionally head for west coast Red Sea ports. Most are Yemeni owned and ply only between Djibouti and Aden. Travellers have arranged crossings, but it'll take patience and your toughest bargaining skills.

Getting Around

Since the peace agreement of late 1994, it's possible to travel everywhere except in the extreme north-west. North of the Gulf of Tadjoura, stick to the main tracks; there are still many leftover landmines.

The peace is fragile, so check with your consulate if you plan to travel outside the areas included in the section on Around the Country later in this chapter.

BUS

The road network links all major villages in the country with the capital. Buses leave when full, so anticipate a wait. The standard one-way bus fare from the capital to almost any place in Djibouti is US$3.

TRAIN

You can take the Djibouti-Addis Ababa train to Ali Sabieh. It leaves Djibouti at 6 am, and is crowded and slow. A 1st class ticket (US$3) gets you a guaranteed seat.

CAR

Vehicle rental is only worthwhile if you want to go desert bashing. For this, a basic 4WD will set you back around US$125 a day. Try Sarco (☎ 354969) or Frado (☎ 354930).

BOAT

Small ships (US$3) leave daily and unpredictably from L'Escale in Djibouti for both Tadjoura and Obock, on the north coast of the Gulf of Tadjoura.

Djibouti

The city, barely 100 years old, is home to at least two-thirds of the nation's population. It makes its money from the commercial port, the railway to Ethiopia and the French military presence.

Information

The tourist office near Place Ménélik is open Saturday to Wednesday from 7.30 am to 12.30 pm and 4.30 to 6.30 pm (mornings only on Thursday). It sells a good map of Djibouti city for US$1.75.

The Maison de la Presse carries a wide range of French newspapers and magazines, and a small selection of international newspapers.

Things to See & Do

A walk around central Djibouti is a must, as is a stroll past the **presidential palace** and along the causeway to **L'Escale** in the cool of the evening. There, you can see dhows, fishing skiffs and pleasure boats moored in the small marina.

The **Le Marché Central** (Central Market) extends from Place Mahamoud Harbi eastward along and below Blvd de Bender. Have a look in particular at the sprigs of qat, a mild stimulant, kept fresh under wet sacking.

To get a glimpse of the underwater riches of the Red Sea without getting wet, check the **Aquarium Tropical de Djibouti**, open daily from 4 to 6.30 pm, except during Ramadan.

Qat

Qat is a mild stimulant which grows in the highlands and is used extensively in East Africa and southern Arabia. One of the few things that runs to schedule in Djibouti is the daily Ethiopian Airlines cargo plane bearing qat. It arrives punctually at 1 pm every day and fresh supplies are on the street no more than an hour later. ■

The entrance fee is US$2. (At the time of writing it was closed, as one of the tanks had ruptured, releasing a tidal wave of over 3000L of water. It's expected to reopen once the safety of the remaining two tanks has been confirmed).

Places to Stay

The bar/hotels in the quartier Africain (African quarter) are the cheapest. They're about as rough as you can get and invariably double as brothels. Single rooms are not available – you pay per bed.

Between mid-April and late-October, you'll need a room with air-con if you're to be comfortable. The following hotels have air-con in all bedrooms.

The friendly *Hôtel Sheikh Gabood* (☎ 351067), the *Hôtel Restaurant Horseed* (☎ 352316) and its neighbour, the more down-at-heel *Red Sea Hotel* (☎ 352309), each charge US$11 for a bed in a double room with communal bathroom.

The *Hôtel Bienvenue* (☎ 354622) in the heart of town charges US$17 for singles, US$29 for doubles with communal bathroom and US$40 for a double with private bathroom. The surly staff of the *Hôtel de Djibouti* (☎ 356415) offer plain rooms and communal facilities up on the roof for US$17 per person and rooms with TV, fridge and private bathroom for US$29/40. The *Djibouti Palace Hotel* (☎ 350982), which has seen better days, has singles/doubles/triples with the same facilities as the Hôtel de Djibouti for US$26/34/51.

The *Auberge Sable Blanc* (☎ 351161), which is a converted villa, has a friendly

DJIBOUTI

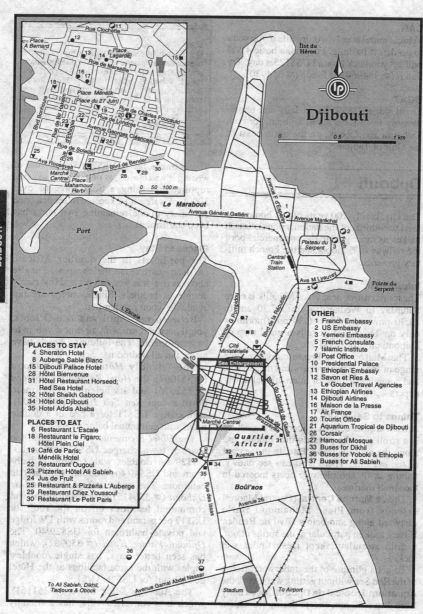

Djibouti

0   0.5   1 km

PLACES TO STAY
4 Sheraton Hotel
8 Auberge Sable Blanc
15 Djibouti Palace Hotel
28 Hôtel Bienvenue
31 Hôtel Restaurant Horseed;
    Red Sea Hotel
32 Hôtel Sheikh Gabood
34 Hôtel de Djibouti
35 Hotel Addis Ababa

PLACES TO EAT
6 Restaurant L'Escale
18 Restaurant le Figaro;
    Hôtel Plein Ciel
19 Café de Paris;
    Ménélik Hotel
22 Restaurant Ougoul
23 Pizzeria; Hôtel Ali Sabieh
24 Jus de Fruit
25 Restaurant & Pizzeria L'Auberge
29 Restaurant Chez Youssouf
30 Restaurant Le Petit Paris

OTHER
1 French Embassy
2 US Embassy
3 Yemeni Embassy
5 French Consulate
7 Islamic Institute
9 Post Office
10 Presidential Palace
11 Ethiopian Embassy
12 Savon et Ries &
    Le Goubet Travel Agencies
13 Ethiopian Airlines
14 Djibouti Airlines
16 Maison de la Presse
17 Air France
20 Tourist Office
21 Aquarium Tropical de Djibouti
26 Corsair
27 Hamoudi Mosque
35 Buses for Dikhil
36 Buses for Yoboki & Ethiopia
37 Buses for Ali Sabieh

Le Marabout

Port

L'Escale

Avenue Général Galliéni

Avenue F d'Esperey

Avenue Maréchal

Foch

Plateau du
Serpent

Central
Train
Station

Ave M Lyautey

Pointe du
Serpent

Îlot du
Héron

Avenue G Pompidou

Blvd de la République

Cité
Ministérielle

See Enlargement

Marché Central

Blvd du Général de Gaulle

Ave de
Brazzaville

*Quartier
Africain*

Avenue 13

Rue des Issas

Boûl'aos

Avenue 26

Stadium

Avenue Gamal Abdel Nassar

To Ali Sabieh, Dikhil,
Tadjoura & Obock

To Airport

Enlargement

Rue Clochette

Place
A Bernard

Place
Lagarde

Rue de Marseille

Place Ménélik
(Place du 27 Juin)

Rue de Charles Foucauld

Rue de Londres

Avenue Georges Clémenceau

Rue de Soleillet

Ave Roosevelt

Blvd de Bender

Marché
Central

Place
Mahamoud
Harbi

Blvd Bonhoura

Rue de Bir Hakeim

Rue d'Ethiopie

0   50 100 m

pension atmosphere. Its double rooms with private bathroom cost US$34.

Places to Eat

First, a question of vocabulary. Joints on the south side of Place Ménélik aren't always what they seem... Among the genuine eating establishments are even more pick-up bars, also innocuously labelled 'Restaurant'.

In the souk (market) area below Blvd de Bender, there are a number of small restaurants where you can eat for US$3 to US$5. Check out the *Restaurant Petit Paris*. For finger-licking, spicy oven-baked fish (US$8), try *Chez Youssouf*. There are also several modest, clean restaurants along Avenue 13.

The fancier *Restaurant Ougoul* serves great barbecued fish (US$7 to US$9) and good French cooking (US$6 to US$11). *Le Figaro* has superb meat or fish dishes for US$10 to US$15. *L'Auberge* is a more homey place for a grill or pizza (US$9 to US$11).

For the most authentic pizza in town (US$6 to US$11), prepared by the Italian proprietor, visit the *Pizzeria* at the Hôtel Ali Sabieh (evening only).

At *Restaurant L'Escale* you can savour the food and the fine views of the harbour.

For the best and widest range of fresh fruit juices in town, visit *Jus de Fruit*.

Getting Around

There are no buses between town and Djibouti-Ambouli international airport, from where a taxi costs US$6 after bargaining. Taxis aren't metered; US$3 is a fair price for a journey within the city.

The central hub for city minibuses (US$0.20) is on Place Mahamoud Harbi.

AROUND DJIBOUTI

The best beaches near Djibouti are at **Doralé**, to which buses run on the tarmac road, and the less accessible **Khor-Ambado**. They're 8km and 15km west of Djibouti, respectively.

The islands of **Maskali** and **Moucha** lie in the Gulf of Tadjoura. You can hire a boat to get there, then camp safely overnight.

Around the Country

The four district capitals, Ali Sabieh, Dikhil, Obock and Tadjoura, are very small towns, and the pleasure lies as much in the trip there and back as in the destination.

Buses (US$3) run to Ali Sabieh and Dikhil, while Obock and Tadjoura are best reached by ferry from L'Escale. For other destinations, such as the lakes, you'll need to hire a 4WD or join a tour organised by one of the three experienced travel agents, ATTA (☎ 354848), La Caravane du Sel (☎ 356618) and Le Goubet (☎ 352350).

ALI SABIEH

You can reach Ali Sabieh by train or bus from the capital. The 95km road from Djibouti city crosses two spectacular desert plains **Petit Bara** and **Grand Bara**. At the eastern end there's a centre where you can windsurf on wheels on the great salty plain.

Around town are several traditional round **Afar huts**.

You can stay at the *Hôtel la Palmeraie* (☎ 426198), where a double room costs US$29.

DIKHIL

Dikhil, a town of some 30,000 inhabitants, 118km west of Djibouti city on the sealed road to Ethiopia, is a starting point for 4WD expeditions west to Lac Abbé (see The Lakes in this section).

You can stay either at the *Hôtel la Palmeraie* (☎ 420164)), where a double room with air-con costs US$29 or US$20 with fan, or at the *Kouta Boya tourist camp* for US$11 per person.

OBOCK

Obock is the place where colonisation of the region began in 1862, when the Afar sultans of Obock sold their land for 10,000 thalers to the French. Its importance declined rapidly after 1888, when the construction of Djibouti port began.

You can reach Obock by ferryboat from

L'Escale in Djibouti. By road, a 4WD is essential for the last stage from Tadjoura (see below).

TADJOURA

Tadjoura gave its name to the gulf separating the Afar and Issa lands. The town itself isn't spectacular, but its setting is attractive, particularly when viewed from the sea. Within 10km of the town there are several peaks rising to more than 1300m.

You can stay at the *Hôtel Restaurant le Golfe* (☎ 424091) for US$29 a double. From here, there are superb coral reefs no more than 10m offshore.

The best way to arrive is by boat from L'Escale in Djibouti. There's also a good tarmac road from Djibouti, the Route de l'Unité, constructed since the peace accord, but there's no bus service.

THE LAKES

You can visit **Lac Assal** in one day by taking the tarmac road from Djibouti. At 150m below sea level, it's an aquatic wilderness surrounded by dormant volcanoes and black lavafields.

On the way you pass **Lac Goubet**, a seawater loch known locally as 'the pit of demons', then cross a stark, apocalyptic volcanic neck separating the two lakes.

Lac Abbé can only be reached by 4WD and requires at least two days and a guide. It's a dawn gathering place for flamingoes where weird natural chimneys formed by the escape of underground steam dot the foreshore.

Egypt

Birthplace of one of the greatest civilisations the world has known, modern Egypt still retains the glory of the Pharaohs in the extraordinary monuments they left behind, particularly the pyramids and the temples around Luxor and Aswan. The centuries following the long era of Pharaonic rule brought Greeks, Romans, Arabs, Turks and Europeans – to mention only the main players – to this seat of power, and all have left their mark.

Modern Cairo, the over-bloated capital and the continent's largest city, is a chaotic collision of the Middle East, Africa and the remnants of 19th century European colonisation. Away from the life-giving Nile lie harsh deserts, occasionally softened by pockets of life in the oases. South-east of the famous Suez Canal stretches Sinai, a region of harsh beauty fringed by the aquatic marvels of the Red Sea reefs, one of the world's best diving locations.

While Egypt has always been a popular country for overland travellers, unfortunately deteriorating relations with its southern neighbour mean that at present it is almost impossible to travel cross country down into Sudan.

Facts about the Country

HISTORY

Egypt was one of the first centres of civilisation in the world. Its recorded history stretches back at least 6000 years, beyond even the time of the Pharaohs.

That history is inextricably linked to the Nile. Ever since the earliest known communities settled the Nile Valley, it has inspired and controlled the religious, economic, social and political life of Egyptians. For many centuries the narrow, elongated layout of the country's fertile lands hampered the fusion of the early settlements, but the Nile

Highlights
- Giza's pyramids, one of the Seven Wonders of the World
- The Tutankhamun treasures at the Egyptian Museum in Cairo
- The great temples of Karnak and Luxor
- Sinai's fantastic marine life, accessible even to snorkellers

broke the barriers by providing an avenue for commercial traffic and communication.

The small kingdoms eventually developed into two important states: the Upper Kingdom, covering the valley as far as the Delta, and the Lower Kingdom, consisting of the Delta itself. The unification of these two states by Menes in about 3000 BC set the scene for the greatest era of ancient Egyptian civilisation. More than 30 dynasties, 50 rulers and 2700 years of indigenous (and occasionally, foreign) rule passed before

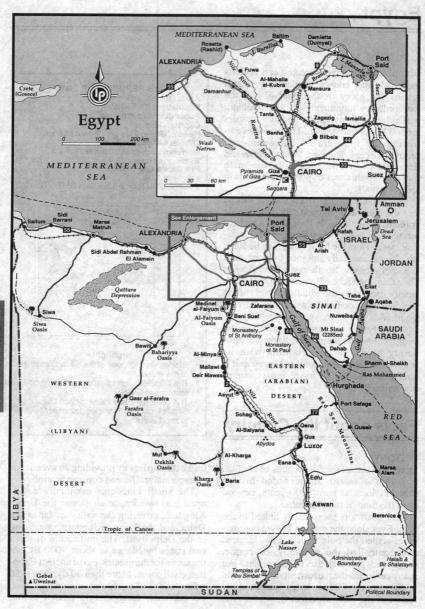

EGYPT

Egypt

0   100   200 km

MEDITERRANEAN SEA

Enlargement map:

MEDITERRANEAN SEA

Baltim — Damietta (Dumyat) — Port Said
Rosetta (Rashid) — L. Burullus — L. Manzala
ALEXANDRIA — Fuwa — Al-Mahalla al-Kubra — Mansura — Ismailia — Suez Canal
Damanhur — Tanta — Zagazig — Ismailia
Benha — Bilbeis
Wadi Natrun — Giza — CAIRO — Suez
Pyramids of Giza — Saqqara

0   30   60 km

Main map labels:

Crete (Greece)

MEDITERRANEAN SEA

Sallum — Sidi Barrani — Marsa Matruh — Sidi Abdel Rahman — El Alamein
Qattara Depression
Siwa — Siwa Oasis
Bawiti — Bahariyya Oasis
Qasr al-Farafra — Farafra Oasis
Mut — Dakhla Oasis
Al-Kharga — Kharga Oasis — Baris

WESTERN

(LIBYAN)

DESERT

LIBYA

Gebel Uweinat

ALEXANDRIA — Port Said — Tel Aviv — Amman
Rafah — Jerusalem — ISRAEL — Dead Sea — JORDAN
Al-Arish
CAIRO — Suez — Taba — Eilat — Aqaba
Medinet al-Faiyum — Zafarana — SINAI — Nuweiba — SAUDI ARABIA
Al-Faiyum Oasis — Beni Suef — Mt Sinai (2285m) — Dahab
Monastery of St Anthony
Monastery of St Paul — Sharm el-Sheikh — Ras Mohammed
Al-Minya — EASTERN — Hurghada
Mallawi — (ARABIAN) — Port Safaga
Deir Mawas — DESERT — Quseir
Asyut — RED SEA
Sohag — Qena — SEA MOUNTAINS
Al-Balyana — Qus — Luxor
Abydos — Esna — Marsa Alam
Esna — Edfu
Aswan — Berenice

Tropic of Cancer

Lake Nasser

Administrative Boundary
To Halaib & Bir Shalatayn

Temples of Abu Simbel

SUDAN

Political Boundary

Alexander the Great ushered in a long, unbroken period of foreign domination.

Many of the kingdoms showed remarkable vitality, and the ruined cities and monuments which they left are testament to their skill and inventiveness. Thanks to the dry desert climate, these remains are well preserved, although many bear the scars of vandalism over the centuries – the Romans were among the worst offenders.

The kingdoms fell apart from time to time as a result of decadence, religious conflicts and invasion – the Assyrians, Persians and Macedonians all conquered Egypt in their time – but it is a measure of the strength of the Egyptian culture that it was able to revitalise and absorb conquerors. Even after conquest by Alexander, who finally eclipsed the Egyptian dynasties, the subsequent rulers (the Ptolemies) were more Egyptian than Greek.

Although Egyptian civilisation has always known influences from the Middle East through trade and conquest, it is now known that the early Egyptian kingdoms had far more contact with Africa than was previously supposed. There is evidence that they sent trading missions and expeditions to West Africa and as far south as the rainforests of the Congo basin, and influenced civilisations that were to emerge there later.

The Ptolemies ruled Egypt for 300 years until the defeat of Mark Antony's navy at the hands of the Romans at the battle of Actium in 31 BC and the subsequent suicide of Antony and Cleopatra VII ushered in a long period of obscurity under Roman rule.

Egypt remained a backwater of the Roman Empire until taken by the armies of Islam in 640 AD. In the following centuries, under a succession of varied Islamic dynasties, Cairo became one of the greatest centres of Islamic culture, and scholars from all over the known world came here to study. It's the legacy of this era that makes Cairo such a fascinating city to explore.

In the early 16th century Egypt became part of the Ottoman Turkish Empire which, at its height, included most of North Africa, Saudi Arabia, the Middle East, Greece and a large part of eastern Europe. However, as the vitality of this empire waned and the sultans became virtual recluses in Constantinople, Egypt became autonomous under the rule of a headstrong local satrap, Mohammed Ali. He and his successors hoped to make Egypt economically independent, and various monumental public works projects were undertaken, the greatest of them being the Suez Canal. Mismanagement sent the country bankrupt, however, and by 1882 British and French comptrollers were in charge of its finances. When war broke out in 1914, Egypt was made a British protectorate presided over by a puppet monarchy.

The founder of the modern nation was Colonel Gamal Abdel Nasser, who overthrew the effete monarchy in a coup in 1952. A fervent nationalist and tough negotiator, Nasser became one of the most prominent politicians of the developing world. Skilfully playing on the rivalry between the Americans and the Soviet Union, he was able to attract the aid he needed for the construction of the Aswan Dam and procure military hardware to fight Israel.

The wars with Israel had a devastating effect on the country's economy, diverting much-needed funds for development into the armed forces. They also resulted in the closure of the Suez Canal for many years and the occupation of Sinai by the Israelis. It was Anwar Sadat, Nasser's successor, who was instrumental in reaching a peace treaty, the Camp David Accord, with Israel in 1979 despite condemnation by every other Arab state. Egypt recovered Sinai and moved closer to the USA.

Sadat's willingness to talk peace with the Israeli state cost him his life. He was assassinated in 1981 during a military parade by members of the Muslim Brotherhood – an uncompromising political organisation that aimed to establish an Islamic state in Egypt.

Leadership of the country since Sadat's assassination has been in the hands of Hosni Mubarak, who has maintained a pragmatic attitude towards regional politics. His years in power have seen the rehabilitation of Egypt in the Arab world, and in 1990-91 his government lined up with the USA in the anti-Iraq alliance, profiting from participation in the Gulf War to the tune of a US$14 billion debt write-off. Maintaining Egypt's role as a peace broker between Israel and the rest of the Arabs, Mubarak has also reduced tensions on his 'western front', normalising relations with Libya. The situation in the south has been less happy, with arguments flaring between Cairo and Sudan over possession of the disputed Halaib region.

Mubarak's greatest worries are at home, where his biggest headache remains how to deal with rising Islamic fundamentalist violence – hundreds of people have been killed in clashes between government forces and members of the Gama'a al-Islamiyya (Islamic League). A number of those fatalities were tourists; the Gama'a has declared tourism, and hence tourists, a legitimate target in its fight with the government over the introduction of *shari'a* (Islamic law) – a fight that hides the more pressing issue of a young population increasingly frustrated by economic woes.

GEOGRAPHY & CLIMATE
For most Egyptians the Nile Valley is Egypt. To the east of the valley is the Eastern (Arabian) Desert, a barren plateau bounded on its eastern edge by a high ridge of mountains. To the west is the Western (Libyan) Desert, a plateau punctuated by huge clumps of bizarre geological formations and luxuriant oases.

Terrain in Sinai extends from the high mountain ridges, which include Mt Sinai (Gebel Musa) and Mt St Catherine (Gebel Katerina – the highest in Egypt at 2642m), in the south to desert coastal plains and lagoons in the north.

Most of the year, except for the winter months of December, January and February, Egypt is hot and dry. Temperatures increase as you travel south from Alexandria, the only city in Egypt to receive any substantial rainfall. Summer temperatures range from a scorching 50°C in Aswan to 31°C on the Mediterranean coast. At night in winter the temperatures sometimes drop as low as 8°C, even in the south.

ECOLOGY & ENVIRONMENT
Despite being a signatory to various international conventions aimed at protecting vulnerable or endangered species and important natural habitats, Egypt has a long way to go where environmental awareness and protection is concerned. Migrating birds are being killed in Egypt in massive numbers while en route from Europe to Africa; waterfowl are hunted in protected wetlands breeding areas; and ivory and other illegal animal products are traded in shops. The coral reefs of the Red Sea are under enormous threat from irresponsible tourism and opportunistic development. Freshwater lakes are being poisoned by industrial and agricultural toxins. Air pollution in Cairo is so bad that it is eating away at the antiquities.

On a more positive note, the government has started to set aside protected zones, such as the Zaranik area on Lake Bardawil, the Elba region on the Red Sea coast and the Naqb, Ras Abu Gallum and Dahab regions in Sinai. However, with the exception of Ras Mohammed National Park in Sinai, where full-time rangers are employed to patrol the park, there is little active enforcement of protection laws within these zones.

POPULATION & PEOPLE
Egypt's population has, in a sense, become its greatest problem. Counted at close to 61.5 million in a 1996 census, it is predicted to reach 65 million by the year 2000.

Anthropologists divide the Egyptian people very roughly into three racial groups.

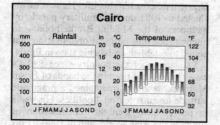

Responsible Tourism

As long as outsiders have been stumbling upon or searching for the wonders of Ancient Egypt, they have also been crawling all over them, chipping bits off them or leaving their own contributions engraved on them. When visiting the monuments, question how important it is for you to climb to the top of a pyramid or take home a bit of stone belonging to a Pharaonic column.

If visiting Ras Mohammed National Park, remember it's illegal to drive off the tracks – doing so spells disaster for the fragile desert environment.

Rubbish: there's lots of it in Egypt, and tidy-town awards do not feature here. Some of the refuse – plastic mineral water bottles for instance – is actually recycled in many ways, so don't be too quick to point an accusing finger at the Egyptians. However, there is no doubt that inadequate waste disposal and little regard for environmental issues produces some ugly sights. More than one traveller has reported being disgusted by the garbage left behind by visitors climbing Mt Sinai – try not to add to it.

When diving or snorkelling, heed the requests of instructors *not* to touch or tread on coral. Also, don't collect or remove anything, don't litter and don't feed the fish. ∎

The largest is descended from the Hamito-Semitic race that has peopled the Nile (as well as many other parts of North Africa and neighbouring Arabia) for millennia. Also included in this race are the Berbers, a minority group who settled around Siwa in the Western Desert.

The second group, the truly Arab element, is made up of the Bedouin Arab nomads who migrated from Arabia. Nearly 500,000 Bedouin survive in the harshest, most desolate parts of the Western and Eastern deserts and Sinai. But, despite being the country's most isolated population group, with the inevitable influx of outsiders into their domains, the Bedouin are gradually becoming more settled and less self-sufficient.

The third group are the Nubians, the original people of Nubia, the region between Aswan in the south of Egypt and Khartoum in Sudan, which was known in ancient times as Cush. Their traditional way of life – based on agriculture, fishing and the transport of goods up and down the Nile – existed virtually unchanged until early this century when the Aswan Dam was built. As the waters gradually rose, the Nubians' homeland was consumed; the final assault came with the building of the High Dam near Aswan in 1971, which entirely devoured their traditional lands. Many of the 60,000 or more displaced people were resettled in Aswan and around Kom Ombo, while others were repatriated to Sudan.

LANGUAGE

Arabic is the official language in Egypt, but English and, to a lesser extent, French are widely understood in the cities. Lonely Planet's *Egyptian Arabic Phrasebook* is a useful tool for getting around. See also the Language Appendix.

Facts for the Visitor

VISAS

All foreigners entering Egypt, except nationals of Malta and Arab countries, must have a visa.

Visas can be obtained in most neighbouring countries with little fuss. In the UK, a single-entry tourist visa costs most western applicants the equivalent of UK£15 (about US$22).

You can also get a visa on arrival in Egypt by air or sea but not by land. At the new terminal of Cairo airport the process is simple, and visas cost US$19 or UK£12 – get them from the Bank Misr desk just before immigration.

The single-entry visa is valid for presentation for three months and entitles the holder to stay in Egypt for one month. Also available are multiple-entry visas (for three visits).

While you can't get an Egyptian visa at the border with Israel, it is possible to visit Sinai between Sharm el-Sheikh and Taba (on the Israeli border) without a visa. You are also permitted to visit St Catherine's Monastery. On arrival, you are issued with an entry stamp, free of charge, allowing you up to 14 days in the area.

You can get a visa, with much fuss, on the boat from Jordan.

Visa Extensions & Re-entry Visas

Extensions of your visa beyond the first month can be obtained for six/12 months and cost US$3.50/11. You need one photograph and a modicum of patience.

If you do not have a multiple-entry visa, it is also possible to get a re-entry visa, valid to the expiry date of your visa and any extensions, at most passport offices including the Mogamma in Cairo. A single/multiple re-entry visa costs US$3/4.

Note that there is a two week grace period beyond the expiry date of your visa.

Other Visas
Algeria
    Visas cost US$34 for one month, US$56 for three. Applications (with four photos) are accepted between 10 am and noon on Sunday and Monday only, and take anywhere between one and four weeks to process.
Eritrea
    Visas valid for a month are issued within 24 hours. You need a letter of introduction from your embassy and two photos. The visa costs US$45.
Ethiopia
    A letter of introduction and two photos are required. The visa costs US$20 and is issued in one or two days. Some people have been refused visas without an air ticket showing an onward flight.
Kenya
    Visas valid for three months and good for travel in Kenya for a month cost US$8 for most western nationals. You need one photo.
Libya
    It is possible to visit Libya, but generally only 10-day visas are issued, and only for some nationalities (see the Visa section in the Libya chapter for details). The process can be long and complicated, so give yourself a few weeks. If you get the thumbs up, the visa will cost around US$30.

Sudan
    Visas take up to a month to issue and cost US$50. Five photos and a letter of recommendation from your embassy are required.
Tunisia
    Visas can be obtained with relatively little sweat. You need two photos. EU citizens pay nothing, others US$7.

EMBASSIES
Egyptian Embassies

In Africa there are Egyptian embassies in Benin, Burundi, Cameroon, the Central African Republic, Congo, Côte d'Ivoire, Ethiopia, Ghana, Guinea, Guinea-Bissau, Kenya, Libya, Mali, Morocco, Senegal, Somalia, Sudan, Tanzania, Uganda and Zimbabwe.

Foreign Embassies in Egypt

Most countries throughout the world are represented through embassies in Cairo. Some of them include:

Algeria
    14 Sharia Brazil, Zamalek (☎ 341 8527)
Australia
    World Trade Centre, 11th floor, 1191 Corniche el-Nil (☎ 575 0444)
Canada
    6 Sharia Mohammed Fahmy al-Sayed, Garden City (☎ 354 3110)
Central African Republic
    13 Sharia Mahmoud Azmi, Mohandiseen (☎ 344 6873)
Chad
    12 Midan al-Rifai, Doqqi (☎ 349 4461)
Congo (Zaïre)
    5 Sharia Al-Mansour Mohammed, Zamalek (☎ 341 1069)
Djibouti
    11 Sharia al-Gezira, Agouza (☎ 345 6546)
Eritrea
    13 Sharia Mohammed Shafik, Mohandiseen (☎ 303 0517)
Ethiopia
    3 Sharia Ibrahim Osman, Mohandiseen (☎ 347 7805)
France
    29 Sharia al-Giza, Giza (☎ 570 3916)
Kenya
    7 Sharia Mohandis Galal, Mohandiseen (☎ 345 3907)
Libya
    7 Sharia As-Saleh Ayoub, Zamalek (☎ 340 1864)

Morocco
    10 Sharia Salah ad-Din, Zamalek (☎ 340 9849)
Somalia
    27 Sharia Somal, Doqqi (☎ 337 4038)
South Africa
    21-23 Sharia al-Giza, Giza (☎ 571 7234)
Sudan
    3 Sharia Ibrahimi, Garden City (☎ 354 5043)
Tunisia
    26 Sharia al-Gezira, Zamalek (☎ 340 4940)
Uganda
    9 Midan al-Missaha, Doqqi (☎ 348 5544)
UK
    7 Sharia Ahmed Ragheb, Garden City (☎ 354 0850)
USA
    5 Sharia Latin America, Garden City (☎ 355 7371)

MONEY

US$1 = E£3.40

The official currency of Egypt is the pound (E£). In Arabic it is called a *guinay*. A pound is equal to 100 piastres (pt) or 1000 millims. The Arabic word for piastre is *irsh* or *girsh*.

Most foreign hard currencies, cash or travellers' cheques can be readily changed in Egypt. Money can be officially changed at American Express and Thomas Cook offices, commercial banks, foreign exchange (forex) bureaus and some hotels.

American Express, Visa, MasterCard, JCB cards and Eurocard are good for purchases in a wide range of stores displaying the appropriate signs.

Visa and MasterCard are good for cash advances from many branches of Banque Misr and the National Bank of Egypt, as well as Thomas Cook. Outside the big cities and tourist hubs, cash advances are more problematic. Excess E£ can be exchanged back into hard currency at the end of your stay, or during if you wish, at some banks, forex bureaus and offices of Thomas Cook and American Express.

Eurocheques can be cashed at some banks, but watch the charges – you need your Eurocheque card and passport.

The black market for hard currency is negligible and few travellers can be bothered hunting it out for the fraction of the difference it makes.

Tipping & Bargaining

Tipping in Egypt is called *baksheesh*. Salaries and wages in Egypt are much lower than in western countries, so baksheesh is regarded as a means of supplementing income. Services such as opening a door or carrying your bags warrant 25 pt (US$0.07) to 50 pt (US$0.15). A guard who shows you something off the beaten track at an ancient site should receive about E£1 (US$0.30). Baksheesh is not necessary when asking for directions.

In hotels and restaurants, a 12% service charge is included at the bottom of the bill, but the money goes into the till rather than into the pocket of the waiter or the woman who cleaned your room. If you want to tip someone, you'll have to do so directly.

Bargaining is part of everyday life in Egypt. Almost everything is open to haggling – from hotel rooms to the fruit juice you buy at a local stand. When buying souvenirs in bazaars, don't start bargaining until you have an idea of the true price, and never quote a price you're not prepared to pay.

POST & COMMUNICATIONS
Post

The Egyptian postal system is slow but eventually most mail gets to its destination. Receiving and sending packages through customs can cause tremendous headaches but there is generally little problem with letters and postcards. They can take anything from four to 10 days to get to Europe and from one to three weeks for the USA or Australia. Postcards and letters up to 10g cost US$0.25.

Mail can be received at American Express offices or at the poste restante in most Egyptian cities. American Express offices are the better option.

Telephone

Local telephone calls cost 10 pt (US$0.03) from pay phones – if you can find one that works. Many kiosks and small shops have

EGYPT

telephones for public use, for 50 pt (US$0.15) per local call. Major hotels usually charge E£1 (US$0.30).

Card phones are on the increase. You'll find these bright orange phones mainly in telephone offices, where you can buy phonecards (135 units for US$4.50). You can call direct anywhere in Egypt or abroad (dial 00 and the country code). Otherwise you'll have to book a call at the exchange, with a three minute minimum. Cheap rate is from 8 pm to 7.59 am. Egypt's country code is 20. Area codes include: Alexandra 03; Cairo 02; Aswan 097; Luxor 095; and Sharm el-Sheikh & Na'ama Bay 062.

Fax, Telegraph & Email

Fax machines are available for sending and receiving documents at the main telephone and telegraph offices in the big cities, at EMS offices, at most three- to five-star hotels and at some of the smaller hotels as well. The average charge is US$2.50 per minute but the machines are slow and a single sheet usually takes two minutes to go through. Telexes and telegrams can also be sent from telephone offices.

Cairo has several email servers. The best place to get current information is to visit one of the city's two cybercafes: the best of the two is on the 6th floor of 2 Midan Simon Bolivar, immediately behind the Semiramis InterContinental Hotel; the other is in the basement of the Nile Hilton shopping mall.

HEALTH

If you need a doctor, your embassy should be able to help find one. There are hospitals throughout Egypt, but facilities are often dubious.

Bilharzia is prevalent in Egypt. The Nile and the Nile Delta are infested with the bilharzia parasite and the microscopic snail which carries it. We strongly recommend that you do not drink, wash, paddle or even stand in the shallows of the Nile.

For more general health information see the Health Appendix.

DANGERS & ANNOYANCES

An entire book could be written from the comments and stories of women travellers about their adventures and misadventures in Egypt. At the very least, pinching bottoms, brushing against breasts or making lewd suggestions seem to be considered by some Egyptian men as perfectly natural means of communication with the unknown foreign woman. Flashing and masturbating in front of the victim occasionally occur, but serious physical harassment and rape are not significant threats in Egypt

Also be on your guard for pickpockets in the main tourist centres.

Terrorism

Apart from the middle region of the country Egypt is generally safe. The concerted campaign against tourism by Islamic extremists in 1993-94 seems to have been brought under control and the authorities have embarked on campaigns to reassure the world how safe Egypt is. However, the danger of being caught in the cross-fire, however statistically slight, should at least be borne in mind.

Middle Egypt Travel Warning
For the moment we strongly advise against independent travel in the region south of Al-Minya and north of Qena. Despite governmental claims to the contrary, violence and random acts of terrorism are still common in this area. Any travellers passing through will most likely pick up a police escort who may well insist that you take the next bus out. ∎

BUSINESS HOURS

As Egypt is a mainly Muslim country, Friday is the principal day off during the week, although most government offices and banks are shut on Saturday too. To confuse the issue, many shops close on Sunday, a hangover from colonial rule. Working hours are roughly 8 am to 3 pm, although shops remain open until 8 or 9 pm. During Ramadan (see Public Holidays in the Regional Facts for the Visitor chapter) the hours are from 10 am to 1 pm.

PUBLIC HOLIDAYS

Public holidays in Egypt are: 1 January, 25 April (Sinai Liberation Day), 1 May, 18 June, 23 July (Revolution Day), 6 October (celebrating the early successes of the 1973 War), Easter among the Coptic Christian community and variable Islamic holidays (see Public Holidays in the Regional Facts for the Visitor chapter).

ACTIVITIES

Many visitors to Egypt choose to pass on the monuments and deserts, instead flying directly into Sinai or Hurghada for a week or two of underwater sightseeing. The waters of the Red Sea are reckoned to offer some of the world's most spectacular diving. There's a plethora of dive operators in Sinai (at Na'ama Bay, Sharm el-Sheikh, Dahab and Nuweiba) and on the Red Sea coast (Hurghada, Port Safaga and Al-Quseir). Most of the clubs offer every possible kind of dive course, from one-day introductions (a single dive is about US$60) to open-water certification courses which stretch over about five days and cost from US$280 to US$400 depending on the operator and location.

By contrast, you can hire a mask, snorkel and fins from most Sinai dive centres for around US$3 per day.

Before leaping into the water, it is an idea to become familiar with dangerous creatures like lionfish, stonefish, barracuda and moray eels. Remember not to touch or stand on the coral – it can be painful and certainly does the coral no good.

ACCOMMODATION

The whole gamut of accommodation possibilities is available in Egypt, and for many travellers emerging from less comfortable parts of Africa, Egypt may seem like heaven. There are few youth hostels as such but the no-star to two-star bracket of hotels can throw up some great treats – and also its fair share of dumps. Prices generally start at around US$5 for a bed in a shared room and go up to about US$15. Some three-star places, which can cost up to US$50, are very good.

FOOD & DRINK

Egypt offers a fairly typical range of Arab-Middle Eastern cuisine. The cheap daily staples include *fuul* (fava beans, with a variety of ingredients such as oil, lemon, salt, meat, eggs and onions added to spice it up) and *ta'amiyya*, the local version of felafel.

An Egyptian speciality that is cheap, filling and nutritious is *kushari*, a combination of noodles, rice, black lentils, fried onions and tomato sauce. Other typical dishes are *chawarma*, *kebab* and *kofta*, all of them variations on the lamb, goat or camel-meat theme. Beef is not common and pork is forbidden. In the big cities and tourist centres, a wide range of western food is available.

Tea (*shay*) and coffee (*ahwa*) are the main drinks, but a pleasant option is *karkaday*, a hibiscus tea that is equally pleasant hot or cold. Also try *sahleb*, a sweet, milky drink made from rice flour, grapes, coconut and various nuts, including hazelnuts and pistachios. Beer is widely available – the local variety is marketed under the name Stella.

Getting There & Away

AIR

Many travellers fly to Egypt from Europe, and some of the better deals can be found in London (where it is possible to get return flights for as little as about UK£240). In addition, it may be worth checking the possibility of charter flights to Cairo, Sinai or Luxor/Aswan.

Going the other way, there are rarely spectacular deals from Cairo. Flights further south into Africa booked from Egypt are also very expensive.

EGYPT

LAND

Israel & the Palestinian Territories

See the introductory Getting There & Away chapter at the beginning of the book for details of crossing into Egypt from the Middle East.

Libya

There are direct buses running between Cairo (or Alexandria) and Benghazi and Tripoli. See the Sallum section for information about getting to/from the border itself.

Sudan

People determined to drive into Sudan, or at least get their vehicles in, can try to negotiate for a boat to transport them from the docks at the High Dam, south of Aswan, to Wadi Halfa. In March 1993, some travellers took two cars and two trail bikes across for US$1500. There are at least 10 cargo vessels operating on the lake, and most of them can carry a motorcycle or 4WD.

SEA

Greece & Cyprus

There are ferries from Alexandria to Greece and Cyprus. See the introductory Getting There & Away chapter at the beginning of the book for details.

The Middle East

There are car ferries between Nuweiba in Sinai and Aqaba (Jordan), and between Suez and Jeddah (Saudi Arabia). Again, see the introductory Getting There & Away chapter for details.

Sudan

The most common way of travelling between Sudan and Egypt used to be by ferry from Wadi Halfa up Lake Nasser to Aswan. However, because of continuing bad relations between the two countries this service has been indefinitely cancelled.

The only option these days is by one of the two Red Sea ferries. The weekly ferry MS *Raneem I* plies between Port Safaga (near Hurghada) and Suakin (Sudan). The ferry leaves Port Safaga on Friday, arriving in

Suakin on Monday. The cost is US$90 for a deck seat (little shade), US$110 for an indoor Pullman seat, and US$130 for a 2nd class cabin. Travel agents in Cairo sell tickets.

The MV *El-Maharousa* connects Suez with Suakin. It leaves Suez at around 4 pm on Sunday, and arrives in Suakin three days later. Second class consists of reasonable two-berth cabins, and the cost is US$103.

A number of travellers have reported being given compulsory injections on arrival at Suakin, despite having a vaccination certificate full of stamps. The needles used are single-dose ones, but no-one has yet been able to establish what the jab is for!

Getting Around

AIR

Domestic air fares are expensive even by international standards. The return fare from Cairo to Aswan is US$336, to Luxor it's US$243, to Hurghada US$264 and to Sharm el-Sheikh US$277. Other destinations include Abu Simbel, Al-Arish, Al-Kharga and Marsa Matruh.

Air Sinai (to all intents and purposes EgyptAir by another name) has flights from Cairo to Sharm el-Sheikh and Taba (Ras an-Naqb; in winter only).

BUS

Buses service just about every city, town and village in Egypt. Intercity buses, especially on shorter runs and in Upper Egypt, tend to become quite crowded, and you'll be lucky to get a seat.

Deluxe buses travel between some of the main towns, especially between Cairo and Alexandria. They are fast and comfortable, with air-con (it doesn't always work), toilet and, unfortunately, non-stop noisy video. A direct bus between Cairo and Alexandria costs from US$4.50 to US$8; to Aswan it is about US$15.

TRAIN

Trains travel along more than 5000km of

track to almost every major city and town in Egypt from Aswan to Alexandria. A timetable for the main destinations, in shoddy English, is updated every year (valid to 30 June) and occasionally actually available for a small fee.

Trains range from the luxury Wagon-Lits sleepers that run between Cairo, Luxor and Aswan to rattling old 3rd class museums, packed to the hilt with people, chickens and just about every imaginable kind of baggage and household item. Student discounts of up to 50% are available for holders of ISIC cards. You can travel from Cairo to Aswan for around US$3 in 3rd class with a student card – cheap but painful.

CAR & MOTORCYCLE

Driving in Cairo is a crazy affair, but in other parts of the country, at least in daylight, it isn't necessarily so bad. You drive on the right in Egypt. For more information on road rules, suggested routes and other advice, it might be worth picking up a copy of *On the Road in Egypt – A Motorist's Guide* by Mary Dungan Megalli.

Petrol is readily available. *Benzin aadi*, or normal petrol, costs US$0.25 a litre. *Mumtaz*, or super, is more expensive at US$0.30 a litre. Lead-free fuel was introduced in 1995 but it's not a big seller yet.

SERVICE TAXI

Travelling by 'servees' taxi (or *bijous*) is the fastest way to go from city to city. They travel on set routes and in most places congregate near bus and train stations. Each driver waits with his Peugeot 504 taxi until it's full. Fares tend to be a little higher than on the buses.

MICROBUS

A slightly bigger version of the service taxi is a van that would normally take about 12 people. More often than not they cram on as many as 22 people. These run on fewer routes than the service taxis, and generally cost the same.

BICYCLE

Bicycles are a practical way of getting around a town and its surrounding sites. In most places, particularly Luxor, you can rent bicycles; prices start at around US$2 per day.

HITCHING

It is easy to hitch in Egypt, but drivers are used to being paid for giving you a ride. You'll probably not save much money by hitching, but it can be a good way to meet people. Obvious cautions apply to women hitching. Also see Hitching in the introductory Getting Around chapter.

BOAT

The felucca, the ancient sailing boats of the Nile, are still the most common means of transport up and down the river. Sunset is one of the best times to take a felucca ride, but you can arrange a few hours of peaceful sailing at any time from just about anywhere on the Nile. The best trip to make is the journey between Aswan and Esna, Edfu or Kom Ombo; this takes from one to three days.

LOCAL TRANSPORT
Bus

Cairo and Alexandria are the only cities in Egypt with their own bus systems. It's a cheap way to get around, but they can get ridiculously crowded at times.

Metro

Cairo is the only city in Egypt (indeed in Africa) with an underground rail system. It's fast, inexpensive and usually not crowded – at least by comparison with the city's overburdened forms of public transport.

Tram

Cairo and Alexandria are the only two cities in Egypt with tram systems. Alexandria's trams are relatively efficient and go all over the city but they also get quite crowded. Cairo's trams are similar but only a few lines remain.

EGYPT

Taxi

There are taxis in most cities in Egypt. A short run in Cairo costs US$0.60; a run of about 20 minutes (from, say, the centre to Mohandiseen) is worth US$1. Even if you bargain you will inevitably pay two or three times what you ought to – the only way to pay the proper fare is to know it before you get into the cab and not to raise the subject of money at all, just hand the driver the proper sum at your destination.

Multiple hire is the rule rather than the exception.

Microbus

Privately owned and usually unmarked microbuses (in the form of a minibus) shuttle around all the larger cities. For the average traveller, they can be difficult to use, as it is quite unclear where most of them go. The exception is the run from Midan Tahrir in Cairo to the pyramids. Most of the smaller cities and towns have similar microbuses doing set runs around town.

Hantour & Careta

Hantours, also known as *caleches*, are horse-drawn carriages which are popular tourist vehicles in Luxor and Aswan.

Caretas are donkey-drawn carts with plastic awnings and wooden seats which are used as local taxis in some towns on the Mediterranean coast. They're also common in Siwa Oasis.

Cairo

Dubbed Al-Qahira ('the victorious') by Fatimid rulers in 969 AD, hence 'Cairo', the former Byzantine Christian city of Babylon was subsumed to become one of the key capitals of the Muslim world. Cairo became the religious and intellectual capital of Islam under Salah ad-Din. In 1250 the Mamelukes, a dynasty of slave-soldiers, took the reins of power. The monuments remaining in what is today called Islamic Cairo are a legacy of the Mamelukes. The city's days as an imperial centre came to an end with the arrival of the Ottoman Turks in 1517.

All these periods have endowed the city with a rich variety of Arab, Coptic, Turkish and European monuments, in addition to the Pyramids, the Sphinx and other reminders of Pharaonic times.

Information

Visa Extensions You can obtain visa extensions at the Mogamma, the great white building on Midan Tahrir. The offices (on the 1st floor) are open Saturday to Wednesday from 8 am to 4 pm and Thursday until 2 pm.

Tourist Office The head office of the Egyptian Tourist Authority (☎ 391 3454) is at 5 Sharia Adly, about three blocks east of Sharia Talaat Harb. It's open every day, usually from 8.30 am to 8 pm.

Money The Banque Misr exchange offices at the Nile Hilton and inside Shepherd's Hotel (next door to the Semiramis InterContinental Hotel on the Corniche) are open 24 hours a day, as are the money-changing booths at the airport. The Nile Hilton, the Semiramis on the Corniche and the Marriott Hotel in Zamalek also have ATMs which dispense cash to Visa card holders.

American Express has several offices in Cairo. Its downtown office (☎ 574 7991), at 15 Sharia Qasr el-Nil, is open Saturday to Thursday from 8.30 am to 4.30 pm, Friday from 9 am to 3 pm. Thomas Cook also has a handful of offices in Cairo; in central Cairo its office (☎ 574 3955) is at 7 Sharia Mohammed Bassiuni and is open daily from 8 am to 5 pm.

Post & Communications Cairo's main post office, in Midan Ataba, is open from 7 am to 7 pm, supposedly seven days a week (be wary on Friday and public holidays). The poste restante is through the last door down the side street to the right of the main entrance, opposite the EMS fast mail office, and is open from 8 am to 6 pm (Friday and holidays from 10 am until noon).

There are telephone offices on the north

side of Midan Tahrir, near the tourist information office on Sharia Adly and on Sharia Mohammed Mahmud in the Telecommunications building.

Cairo has several email servers –for more information, see under Post & Communications in the Facts for the Visitor section earlier in this chapter.

Travel Agencies The area around Midan Tahrir is teeming with travel agents. De Castro Tours (☎ 574 3144) at 12 Sharia Talaat Harb has always seemed to offer the best flight deals. Down the road at No 10, Norma Tours (☎ 76 0007) also touts itself as being a cheap airfare specialist.

Bookshops Among the better bookshops for guides, maps and general literature in English are the Anglo-Egyptian Bookshop at 165 Sharia Mohammed Farid; the American University in Cairo Bookstore inside the university entrance on Sharia Mohammed Mahmud; Lehnert & Landrock at 44 Sharia Sherif; and Shorouk, on Midan Talaat Harb.

For books in French go to Livres de France on Sharia Qasr el-Nil, just south of the junction with Sharia Sherif.

Emergency For the Cairo Ambulance Service call ☎ 123 or ☎ 77 0123, but be prepared for a lengthy wait. For the police, in emergencies call ☎ 122 or ☎ 90 0112. For the tourist police call ☎126.

Pyramids of Giza & the Sphinx

Considered one of the Seven Wonders of the World, the Pyramids of Giza are possibly the most visited monuments in Egypt. The pyramids of Cheops and Chephren, which have stood for 46 centuries, are the largest, while that of Mycerinus is much less impressive. Before them lies the Sphinx. Mystery surrounds the meaning of this feline character, 50m long and 22m high, carved from a single block of stone. Known in Arabic as Abu al-Hol ('father of terror'), the Sphinx is the centrepiece of the nightly sound and light performances (US$9, half for students).

Entrance to the grounds of the pyramids, open from 7 am to 7.30 pm, costs US$6, as does entry to the Pyramid of Cheops (open from 8.30 am to 4 pm) and the Solar Boat Museum (open from 9 am to 4 pm). Students pay half.

A taxi from Midan Tahrir should not cost more than US$3. You can also get minibuses and microbuses from in front of the Nile Hilton.

Egyptian Museum

Full of statuary, artworks, sarcophagi and many other relics, much of the archaeological glory of ancient Egypt resides, in

---

The Pyramids of Giza

It was not an obsession with death, or a fear of it, on the part of the ancient Egyptians that led to the construction of these incredible mausoleums; it was their belief in eternal life and their desire to be at one with the cosmos. A Pharaoh was the son of a god, and the sole receiver of the *ka*, or life force, that emanated from the god. The Pharaoh, in turn, conducted this vital force to his people, so in life and death he was worshipped as a god.

A pyramid was not only an indestructible sanctum for the preservation of a Pharaoh's ka, nor simply an incredible, geometric pile of stones raised over the mummified remains of a Pharaoh and his treasures to ensure his immortality. It was the apex of a much larger funerary complex that provided a place of worship for his subjects, as well as a visible reminder of the absolute and eternal power of the gods and their universe.

The mortuary complexes of Cheops, Chephren and Mycerinus, who were father, son and grandson, included the following: a pyramid, which was the Pharaoh's tomb as well as a repository for all his household goods, clothes and treasure; a funerary temple on the east side of the pyramid; pits for the storage of the Pharaoh's solar boats (known as barques), which were his means of transport in the afterlife; a valley temple on the banks of the Nile; and a causeway from the river to the pyramid. ■

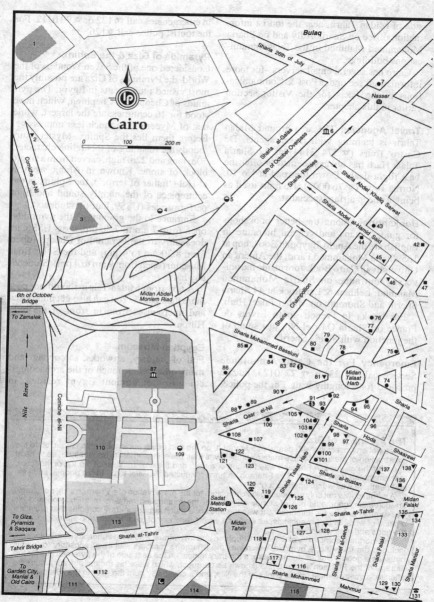

Cairo

0   100   200 m

Bulaq

Sharia 26th of July

Nasser Ⓜ

1

2

Comiche el-Nil

Sharia al-Galaa

6th of October Overpass

🏛 6

7

3

5

4

Sharia Ramses

Sharia Abdel Khaliq Sarwat

Sharia Abdel al-Hamid Said

43

44

42

△5

46

47

Sharia Champollion

76

77

75

Sharia Mohammed Bassiuni

85

80   79

78

86

84 83 82 💲

81

Midan Talaat Harb

74

6th of October
Bridge

To Zamalek

Midan Abdel
Moniem Riad

Nile River

Comiche el-Nil

87 🏛

90

88 89

Sharia Qasr el-Nil

91 93 92

94 95

96

Sharia Hoda

Sharia

106

105

104

103

102

98 97

99

100

101

137 138

136

108

107

121 122

123

110

109

Shaarawi

Sharia al-Bustan

120

119

124

Midan
Falaki

To Giza,
Pyramids
& Saqqara

Sadat
Metro
Station Ⓜ

125

126

Sharia at-Tahrir

133

134

135

113

Midan
Tahrir

118

127 128

Sharia Yusef al-Gendi

Sharia Falaki

Sharia Mansur

Tahrir Bridge

To Garden City,
Manial &
Old Cairo

117

116

Sharia Mohammed
Mahmud

129 130

131

111

112

Ⓒ

114

115

EGYPT

To Ramses Train Station,
Mubarak Metro Station,
Midan Ulali (Intercity Buses) &
Midan Ahmed Hilmi (Intercity Buses)

To Happyton
Hotel

Sharia Zaky

Sharia al-Tawfiqiyya

Sh Orabi

14

Midan
Orabi

Imad ad-Din

Sharia Alfi Bey

Sharia al-Gomhuriya

8

9

10

11

13

12

15 16

17 18

19

20

21

22

25

24

23

Sharia 26th of July

Ezbekiya

Gardens

26

27

28

29

30

31

32

33

34

35

36

37

38

Sharia Adly

41

Sharia Talaat Harb

40

39

49

52

53

54

58

59

60

Midan
Opera

Midan

Midan
Ataba

65

Overpass

Sharia Abdel Khaliq Sarwat

48

50

51

55

56

57

61

Midan
Mustafa
Kamel

Overpass

64

To Khan el-Khalili,
Madrassa of Al-Ghouri
& Islamic Cairo

62

63

Sharia Qasr el-Nil

70

68

69

Sharia Sherif

Sharia Mohammed Farid

Sharia al-Gomhuriya

Sharia Abdel Aziz

66

71

72

73

Sharia Rushdi

67

Mohammed Sabri Abu Alam

Sharia Aref

139

Footbridge

Sharia al-Bustan

140

132

Abdin

Midan
al-Gomhurriya

Abdin
Palace

To Museum of
Islamic Art
& the Citadel

EGYPT

PLACES TO STAY
- 3 Ramses Hilton
- 12 Tawfikia, Safary & Sultan Hotels
- 20 Windsor Hotel
- 23 Hotel Nitocrisse
- 25 Grand Hotel
- 26 Claridge Hotel
- 27 Hotel Minerva
- 29 Scarabee Hotel
- 31 Cairo Khan Hotel
- 33 Pension Roma
- 37 Hotel Tee
- 38 Hotel Select
- 42 Pensione de Famille
- 44 Odeon Palace Hotel
- 47 Hotel Beau Site
- 49 Hotel des Roses
- 54 Panorama Palace Hotel
- 61 Hotel Petit Palais
- 66 New Riche Hotel
- 72 Cosmopolitan Hotel
- 77 Gresham Hotel
- 80 Pensione Suisse
- 84 Hotel Viennoise
- 85 Anglo-Swiss Hotel
- 95 Tulip Hotel
- 99 Golden Hotel
- 103 Lotus Hotel
- 107 Cleopatra Palace Hotel
- 110 Nile Hilton
- 111 Semiramis Inter - Continental Hotel
- 112 Garden City House
- 118 Ismailia House Hotel
- 119 Sun Hotel
- 136 Amin Hotel

PLACES TO EAT
- 2 Paprika Restaurant
- 8 Cafe el-Agatey
- 10 Ash-Shams Teahouse
- 13 Casablanca Restaurant; Nicolakis Liquor Store
- 16 Alfi Bey Restaurant
- 18 International Public Meal Kushari
- 19 Peking Restaurant
- 22 Ali Hassan al-Hatti
- 39 Excelsior Restaurant
- 41 Amira Restaurant
- 45 Coin de Kebab Restaurant
- 46 Fu Shing Chinese Restaurant
- 48 At-Tahrir Kushari Restaurant
- 50 KFC

- 53 GAD Restaurant
- 59 Garden Groppi's Cafe
- 81 Groppi's Cafe
- 83 La Pacha Restaurant
- 88 Arabesque Restaurant
- 90 Caroll Restaurant
- 96 Teahouse
- 97 Felfela Garden Restaurant
- 98 Felfela Takeaway & Cafeteria
- 105 Estoril Restaurant
- 116 McDonalds
- 117 KFC; Pizza Hut
- 125 Crystal Bakery
- 127 Fatatri at-Tahrir
- 128 At-Tahrir Kushari Restaurant
- 129 El-Fornaia Etman Bakery
- 130 24-Hour Sandwich Shop
- 132 Cafeteria el-Shaab; Fiteer Place
- 135 Lux Kushari Restaurant
- 138 Wimpy Bar

OTHER
- 1 Radio & TV Building
- 4 Buses to Upper Egypt
- 5 Trams to Heliopolis
- 6 Entomological Society Museum
- 7 Isaaf Pharmacy
- 9 Souk Tawfiqiyya
- 11 Liquor Store
- 14 Cafeteria Port Tewfik
- 15 Shahrazad Night Club
- 17 Horus Exchange
- 21 Telephone & Fax Office
- 24 Pussy Cat Bar
- 28 Lehnert & Landrock Bookshop
- 30 Palmyra Nightclub
- 32 Honolulu Nightclub
- 34 International Vaccination Centre
- 35 Tourist Authority; Tourist Police
- 36 Telephone & Fax Office
- 40 Cinema Metro
- 43 Hostelling International Office
- 51 Anglo-Eastern Pharmacy
- 52 Kodak Photo Shop
- 55 Cap d'Or Cafeteria
- 56 Turkish Airlines
- 57 Banque Misr

- 58 Anglo-Egyptian Bookshop
- 60 EgyptAir
- 62 EMS Office
- 63 Poste Restante
- 64 Post Office; Post Office Museum
- 65 Hebton Bus Company
- 67 Egypt Free Shop
- 68 Libyan Arab Airlines
- 69 Disco Nightclub
- 70 Livres de France
- 71 Olympic Airways
- 73 Photo Centre
- 74 Bulgarian Airlines
- 75 Swissair & Austrian Airlines
- 76 Radio Cinema
- 78 Madbouly Bookshop
- 79 Atelier du Caire Gallery
- 82 Thomas Cook; Gulf Air
- 86 Mashrabia Art Gallery
- 87 Egyptian Museum
- 89 Royal Jordanian Airlines
- 91 American Express
- 92 Air France
- 93 Tunis Air
- 94 Shorouk Bookshop
- 100 Czech Airlines
- 101 EgyptAir
- 102 Norma Tours
- 104 De Castro Tours; Hungarian Airlines
- 106 KLM
- 108 TWA
- 109 Bus Terminal; Minibus Station
- 113 Arab League Building
- 114 Mogamma
- 115 American University (AUC) Bookstore
- 120 Telephone & Fax Office
- 121 British Airways
- 122 Sudan Airways
- 123 Goethe Institut
- 124 Misr Travel
- 126 Air India
- 131 Telephone Office
- 133 Souk Mansur
- 134 Brazilian & Yemeni Coffee Shop
- 137 Cairo-Berlin Art Gallery
- 139 Cafeteria Horeya
- 140 Post Office

somewhat chaotic fashion, in this museum on Midan Tahrir. The star attractions are the treasures found in Tutankhamun's tomb in Luxor – particularly the gold mask of the boy king. Second in popularity are the mummies of 11 kings and queens who ruled Egypt between 1552 and 1069 BC, on display once more after Islamic disapproval of exhibiting the dead kept them hidden away for 15 years.

The museum is open from 9 am to 5 pm daily; closed Friday between noon and 2 pm in summer and between 11.30 am and 1.30 pm in winter. Entry is US$6; the Royal Mummy Room costs an additional US$18. All fees are halved for students.

Islamic Cairo & Khan al-Khalili

Enter the warren of districts like Al-Muski, Darb al-Ahmar and Gamaliya, and you submerge yourself in a world that, but for cars and radios, has hardly changed in hundreds of years.

Dominating the skyline at the southern end of the area known as Islamic Cairo is the **Citadel**, which Salah ad-Din began building in 1176. Within its imposing crenellated walls various edifices have been added over the centuries, the most impressive of which is the Turkish-style **Mosque of Mohammed Ali**, built by the 19th century ruler of the same name. The Citadel is open from 8 am to 5 pm in winter and until 6 pm in summer; entry is US$6.

Facing the Citadel across the square beneath its western walls are the enormous **Mosque of Sultan Hassan** (1362) and the **Ar-Rifa'i Mosque** (1911), where the Shah of Iran is interred. Entry to the two costs US$3.50; baksheesh is needed to see the Shah's tomb.

One kilometre south-west of Sultan Hassan, along Sharia Saliba, is one of the largest mosques in the world, that of **Ibn Tulun** (879), named for the 9th century commander sent to rule in the name of Baghdad, but who instead established his own dynasty. Entry is US$2. Next door is the fascinating **Gayer-Anderson House**. This museum is actually two houses which were occupied and restored by a British major, John Gayer-

Anderson, between 1935 and 1942, and then bequeathed to Egypt. Entry is an expensive US$5.

Heading north from the Citadel/Sultan Hassan, you pass through a labyrinth of twisting lanes to reach **Bab Zuweila**, the surviving southern gate of Salah ad-Din's city and once a place of execution. There are great views from its twin minarets, accessible through the neighbouring **Mosque of Mu'ayyad**. Entry is US$2.

Walk up the market street, Sharia al-Muizz li-Din Allah, and just before meeting traffic-congested Sharia al-Azhar you pass by the grand **Al-Ghouri** mausoleum and madrassa complex. The building on the right side (east) of the street is the venue for twice-weekly Sufi dancing performances – see Entertainment later in this section.

Some 150m east along Sharia al-Azhar is the mosque and university of **Al-Azhar**, built in 970 and the oldest university in the world. Admission is US$2. Cross the busy road and you find yourself in the maze of **Khan al-Khalili**, Cairo's sprawling bazaar and a souvenir shopper's paradise – bargain hard.

Museum of Islamic Art Established in 1881, this comparatively little-visited museum on Midan Ahmed Mahir houses an extensive collection of Islamic decorative art, and is well worth a look. It is open from 9 am to 4 pm (closed Friday) and admission costs US$5.

Old Cairo

Once known as Babylon, this remains the seat of the Coptic Christian community. There is a **museum** (entry US$5) with mosaics, manuscripts, tapestries and other Christian artwork.

Al-Muallaqa, or the **Hanging Church** (entry US$6), is the centre of Coptic worship. Among the other churches and monasteries here, **St Sergius** is supposed to mark one of the resting places of the Holy Family in its flight from King Herod. The easiest way to get here from Midan Tahrir is by metro. Get out at the Mari Girgis station.

EGYPT

Places to Stay

Camping The *Motel Salma* (☎ 384 9152) is about the only camping possibility. It's next to the Wissa Wassef Art Centre at Harrania, south of Giza. Camping costs US$2 per person with your own tent or campervan, or you can stay in overpriced, claustrophobic cabins.

Hostels The *Manial Youth Hostel* (☎ 364 0729) at 135 Sharia Abdel Aziz as-Saud is near the Manial Palace on Roda Island. It's in reasonable nick with clean toilets, although the beds are nothing great; it costs US$2.50 with a membership card, US$3.60 without.

Hotels The area of central Cairo from Midan Tahrir to Sharia 26th July is full of budget possibilities.

About the cheapest are three places one block north of Sharia 26th July, all in a single building above the Souk at-Tawfiqiyya, a busy little market lane. On the 1st floor is the friendly and popular *Sultan Hotel* (☎ 77 2258); the 5th floor is home to the *Tawfikia* (☎ 75 5514) and *Safary* (☎ 575 0752) hotels. They are all basic and offer beds in simple dorms for about US$2.

The *Pensione de Famille* (☎ 574 5630) in Sharia Abdel Khaliq Sarwat, just off Sharia Talaat Harb, is in a building that should have been condemned years ago. The beds are a little lumpy, but at US$2.40/3.20 for a single/double (excluding breakfast), you can't go too far wrong.

Two of the city's most popular travellers' haunts are down by Midan Tahrir. One is the new *Sun Hotel* (☎ 578 1786) at 2 Sharia Talaat Harb (9th floor) which has decent-sized singles/doubles with big, comfortable beds for US$7/12, or US$4.50 per person in a four bed room. The other is the 8th floor *Ismailia House Hotel* (☎ 356 3122) right on Midan Tahrir (No 1). It is clean and bright and the showers are piping hot. Singles cost US$6, doubles come at US$12, while a bed in a share room (a double with two extra rickety beds crammed in) costs US$4. The same people own the *Hotel Petit Palais* (☎ 391 1863), at 45 Sharia Sarwat. The bathrooms are spotless, and unlike at the Ismailia,

each room has hot water; prices are comparable.

The *Gresham Hotel* (☎ 575 9043) on the 3rd floor at 20 Sharia Talaat Harb, hasn't changed its room rates in years and is now pretty good value. Single rooms cost US$7, or US$10 with private bath and air-con. Doubles without/with bath go for US$12/14 and are all air-con.

The *Pension Roma* (☎ 391 1088) at 169 Sharia Mohammed Farid, near the junction with Sharia Adly, is tucked away in a side alley. All the rooms have shiny hardwood floors and antique furniture. Single/double rooms without bath are US$6/11. A room with four beds can be had for US$19.

The *Happyton Hotel* (☎ 92 8671) at 10 Sharia Aly el-Kassar, in a quiet back street off Sharia Imad ad-Din, is one of the best value mid-range options and is handy for both central Cairo and Ramses station. A relaxed place with a small, open-air roof-top bar and a restaurant, it has singles/doubles with air-con and private bathroom for US$12/15.

The *Lotus Hotel* (☎ 575 0966) at 12 Sharia Talaat Harb (opposite Felfela Cafeteria), is another good middle-priced hotel. You'll pay US$10/19 for a single without/with bath; doubles are US$19/25.

The *Cosmopolitan Hotel* (☎ 392 3663) in Sharia Ibn Taalab, just off Sharia Qasr el-Nil, has beautifully plush old rooms with dark, lacquered furniture, central air-con and tiled bathrooms with tubs. Some rooms have balconies and there's a wonderful, old, open elevator. Singles/doubles cost US$40/50.

Places to Eat

Cairo is full of cafes and snack bars where you can eat staple snacks such as chawarma, kushari, fuul and ta'amiyya for no more than US$0.30. For those with a more timid palate there are also plenty of western fast-food places around.

One of the best places for a cheap meal in Cairo is *El-Tabie El-Domiati* at 31 Sharia Orabi not far from Orabi metro station. The portions are large, the service fast and friendly, the setting clean and the food excellent. It's predominantly vegetarian and has a great salad bar and delicious ta'amiyya. A filling meal for two costs as little as US$2.

For good kushari go to the *At-Tahrir* on Sharia Abdel Khaliq Sarwat, just off Talaat Harb. There's also a second *At-Tahrir* kushari restaurant on Sharia at-Tahrir. A medium *(metawasit)* serving is extremely filling and costs less than US$1. The *International Public Meal Kushari*, on the corner of Sharia Imad ad-Din and Sharia Alfi Bey, is also very popular.

For meat eaters, the *Casablanca*, opposite the Grand Hotel on Sharia Talaat Harb, serves up a whole roast chicken, bread and salad for US$3.50, while *Ali Hassan al-Hatti*, just north of Sharia 26th July, is a good kebab and kofta place with lots of character. Try their speciality called 'moza', which is roast lamb on rice, for US$4.50.

The *Excelsior*, on the corner of Sharia Talaat Harb and Sharia Adly, is popular with the cinema crowds and serves beer but it's overpriced. Directly over the road is the *Amira*, a 24-hour eatery where film extras are sometimes recruited. You can get a delicious lentil soup for US$0.50 or a number of other small dishes for around US$0.60.

The *Felfela Garden* at 15 Sharia Hoda Shaarawi, just off Sharia Talaat Harb, is one of the better all-round restaurants in Cairo, although its enormous popularity with locals and foreigners alike means there are quite a few dishes you could get elsewhere for less. *Felfela Cafeteria*, just around the corner from the main restaurant, has excellent ta'amiyya, chawarma, kofta and fuul sandwiches, from US$0.25.

Midway down Mohammed Bassiuni, a few doors shy of the Thomas Cook office, is *La Pacha* (no sign, just look for the stained wood frontage and push open the door) which serves simple but very good and filling Egyptian fare; recommended are the liver and rice (US$1) and the macaroni bechamel (US$1).

At 166 Sharia at-Tahrir is the 24-hour *Fatatri at-Tahrir*, an excellent place for a sweet or savoury fiteer (Egyptian pancakes) from US$2.

Entertainment

On Wednesday and Saturday nights from 9 pm (9.30 pm in winter) you can treat yourself to a display of *raqs ash-sharqi*, or Sufi dancing in the *Madrassa of Al-Ghouri* in Islamic Cairo. (Sufis are adherents of a Muslim mystical order which emphasises dancing as a direct personal experience of God.) Admission is free and it's advisable to come early, especially in winter, as the small auditorium can get quite crowded.

There are a few cinemas that occasionally show decent movies. Check the daily *Egyptian Gazette* or weekly *Middle East Times* newspapers.

Getting There & Away

Bus There are several bus stations scattered throughout Cairo. From Midan Abdel Moniem Riad, just around the corner from the Ramses Hilton on Sharia al-Galaa, there are frequent services to Alexandria (2½ hours, US$2 to US$8), at least one bus a day to Marsa Matruh (five hours, US$10), nine buses to Port Said (three hours, US$3 to US$5) and one to Sharm el-Sheikh (eight hours, US$15) at 11 pm. There are also daily buses to Luxor (11 hours, US$12), Aswan (12 hours, US$15) and Hurghada (six hours, US$7 to US$9).

There are also cheaper buses to these destinations and to most towns along the Nile leaving from Midan Ahmed Hilmi, behind Ramses train station. From Midan Ulali, also near Ramses station, the East Delta Bus Company has buses to the Suez Canal towns. To Suez costs US$1.50. Buses to Libya also leave from here.

Nearly all the East Delta buses to Sinai leave from the Sinai Terminal at Midan Abbassiya, on the way to the airport. The exception is the 5 pm bus to Sharm el-Sheikh which leaves from Midan Ulali. They are expensive: to Sharm el-Sheikh costs from US$9 to US$15; to St Catherine's costs US$12; and to Nuweiba costs from US$12 to US$16.

Buses to the Western Oases leave from a small lot at 45 Sharia al-Azhar, off the main road to Khan al-Khalili.

Train Trains to all destinations leave from the main station at Midan Ramses. The daily Wagon-Lits train to Luxor and Aswan leaves at 7.45 pm, arriving in Luxor at 5 am and in Aswan at 11 am. For either destination it costs US$133 one way in a 1st class sleeper compartment, or US$86 in 2nd class (US$160 return), which includes all meals. There is no student reduction.

Tickets for 1st and 2nd class seats on the overnight air-con express trains to Luxor (US$14/8) and Aswan (US$18/10) must be bought in advance. They can be found at a window on platform 11.

Getting Around
The Airport Bus No 422 runs hourly between 6 am and midnight from Midan Tahrir to the new Terminal II for US$0.07. Several buses operate from various points in the city to the old terminal – some shuttle to the new terminal too. No 400 goes from Midan Tahrir, as does minibus No 27. Taxis from central Cairo should not cost more than US$6.

Bus & Minibus The main station is in front of the Nile Hilton at Midan Tahrir. Fares for buses are very cheap – usually US$0.07. Minibus fares are slightly more. Bus No 815 goes from Midan Tahrir to Al-Azhar and Khan al-Khalili. Minibus No 83 goes from Midan Tahrir to the Pyramids and No 54 goes to the Citadel. The numbers are sometimes in Arabic numerals only, so it pays to learn them (see the Arabic section in the Language Appendix).

AROUND CAIRO
Memphis & Saqqara
There is not much left of the former Pharaonic capital of Memphis, 24km south of Cairo, but the museum contains a fairly impressive statue of Ramses II. A few kilometres away is Saqqara, a vast site strewn with pyramids, temples and tombs. The star attraction there is the **Step Pyramid** of Zoser, the first decent attempt at pyramid building. Entrance for the whole area is US$6, with an additional charge of US$3 to visit some of the newly opened tombs. The site is open from 7.30 am to 4 pm (5 pm in summer).

Getting There & Away A taxi from central Cairo costs about US$20 shared among a maximum of seven people. This is the best way for those on a tight budget to get to and around Saqqara. Stipulate the sights you want to see and how long you want to be out and bargain hard.

Birqash Camel Market
On the edge of the Western Desert, 35km north-west of Cairo, the Camel Market is an easy half-day trip from Cairo but, like all of Egypt's animal markets, it's not for animal lovers or the faint-hearted. Hundreds of camels are sold here everyday, most having been brought up the 40-Days Road from western Sudan. The market is most lively on Friday and Monday mornings, from about 6 to 9 am; admission is US$0.60.

Getting There & Away The cheapest way to get to the market is to take a taxi (US$1.20) to the site of the old camel market at Imbaba, from where microbuses shuttle back and forth to Birqash. Alternatively, on Fridays only, the Sun Hotel (☎ 578 1786) at 2 Sharia Talaat Harb organises a minibus tour (US$6 per person; minimum five people) from the hotel departing at 7 am. A taxi there and back costs around US$17; make sure to negotiate waiting time.

Around the Country

ABU SIMBEL
That Ramses II's **Great Temple of Abu Simbel** is there to be marvelled at is thanks to a US$40 million UNESCO effort to move it out of the way of the rising waters of Lake Nasser in the 1960s.

The temple was dedicated to the gods Ra-Harakhty, Amun, Ptah and the deified Pharaoh himself. Guarding the entrance, the four famous colossal statues of Ramses II sit majestically, each more than 20m tall, with smaller statues of the king's mother, Queen Tuya, his wife Nefertari and some of their children. The other temple at the Abu Simbel complex is the rock-cut **Temple of Hathor**. The admission fee for both temples is US$9 (US$4.50 for students).

Places to Stay
There are two hotels at Abu Simbel. The *Nefertari Hotel* (☎ 31 6402) is about 400m from the temples. It has singles/doubles for US$60/75, inclusive of breakfast and taxes. They will also let you camp for about US$6 – you get to use the showers and pool. The *Nabalah Ramses Hotel* (☎ 31 1660) is in the town of Abu Simbel, about 1.5km from the temple site. Singles/doubles are US$39/74, although deals are possible. It is more economical to stay in Aswan.

Getting There & Away
Most people visit Abu Simbel from Aswan and many hotels there band together to arrange minibus trips to the temple leaving at about 5 am. The cheapest price is about US$7. Alternatively, a bus departs from Aswan at 8 am and from Abu Simbel at about 2 pm; the trip takes about 3½ to four hours one way and costs US$8.

ABYDOS
See the Middle Egypt Travel Warning earlier in this chapter on page 264.

According to mythology, the head of the god Osiris was buried here after his brother Seth killed him, and so Abydos became the most important site of his worship. The **Cenotaph Temple of Seti I** honours seven gods, including Osiris and the deified Pharaoh himself. To the north-west lies what's left of the **Temple of Ramses II**, built by Seti's son. The site is open from 7 am to 5 pm and admission is US$3.50.

Places to Stay
Right in front of Abydos is the *Osiris Park Restaurant & Camp* (☎ 81 2200), where a bed in a tent costs US$1.60. You can pitch your own tent for US$1 per person. The only other option is the *Abydos Hotel* (☎ 81 2102), 200m before the Osiris. It has simple, overpriced rooms for US$9/15.

Getting There & Away
Trains and buses from Asyut, Sohag, Qena and further afield stop at the township of Al-Balyana, from where service taxis and microbuses go to the temple complex.

ALEXANDRIA
Established in 332 BC by Alexander the Great, the city became a major trade centre and focal point of learning for the whole Mediterranean world. Its ancient library held 500,000 volumes and the Pharos lighthouse was one of the Seven Wonders of the World. In the 7th century, Alexandria was eclipsed and reduced to a backwater when the conquering Muslims made their capital in what was to become Cairo. Napoleon's arrival 11 centuries later and Alexandria's subsequent redevelopment as a major port attracted people from all over the world, but the Revolution of 1952 put an end to much of the city's pluralistic charm.

Orientation & Information
Alexandria, home to five million people, is a true waterfront city, nearly 20km long from east to west and only about 3km wide. The focal point of the city is Midan Saad Zaghloul (the area is generally known as Ramla), a large square running onto the waterfront. The main tourist office (☎ 807 9885) is at the south-west corner of the midan, while in the streets to the south and west are the central shopping area, airline offices, restaurants and cheaper hotels. The main post office is a small office just east of Midan Orabi and there's a telephone office at the tram station (Mahattat ar-Ramla), east of Midan Saad Zaghloul, which is open 24 hours a day.

If you need to extend your visa, go to the passport office at 28 Sharia Talaat Harb.

The tourist police are above the main tourist office, while the main police station is by Misr train station on Sharia Yousef.

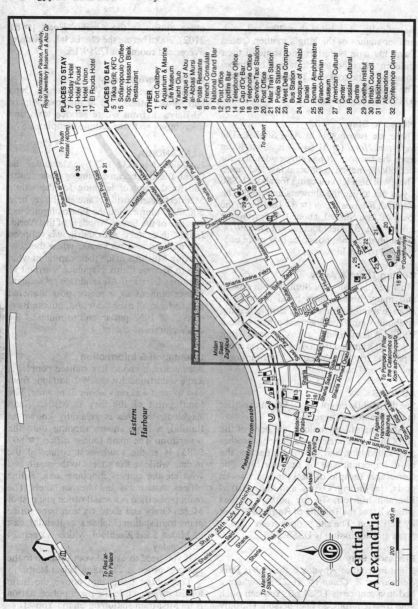

PLACES TO STAY
7 Holiday Hotel
10 Hotel Fouad
11 Hotel Union
17 El Rouda Hotel

PLACES TO EAT
5 Tikka Grill; KFC
15 Sofianopoulo Coffee Shop; Hassan Bleik Restaurant

OTHER
1 Fort Qaitbey
2 Aquarium & Marine Life Museum
3 Yacht Club
4 Mosque of Abu al-Abbas Mursi
6 Poste Restante
8 French Consulate
9 National Grand Bar
12 Post Office
13 Spitfire Bar
14 Telephone Office
16 Cap d'Or Bar
18 Telephone Office
19 Service-Taxi Station
20 Post Office
21 Misr Train Station
22 Police Station
23 West Delta Company Bus Station
24 Mosque of An-Nabi Daniel
25 Roman Amphitheatre
26 Graeco-Roman Museum
27 American Cultural Center
28 Russian Cultural Centre
29 Goethe Institut
30 British Council
31 Bibliotheca Alexandrina
32 Conference Centre

To Mortazah Palace, Rushdy,
Royal Jewellery Museum & Abu Qir

To Youth Hostel (400m)

To Airport

Eastern
Harbour

Pedestrian Promenade

Sharia al-Geish

Sharia Port Said

Sharia Mustafa Kamel

Mustafa

Sharia Iskander al-Akbar

Sharia Rateb Pasha

Yousef

Champollion

Sharia Amine Fekry

Sharia Hussein

Sharia Safia Zaghloul

Sharia Sultan Hussein

Sharia an-Nabi Danial

al-Hurriya

Sharia Talaat Harb

Tariq

See Around Midan Saad Zaghloul Map

Midan Saad Zaghloul

Sharia Zangarli

Sharia Salah Salem

Sharia Ahmed Orabi

Midan
Orabi

Midan
Tahrir

Sharia an-Nasr

al-Nasr

Sharia 26th July (Corniche)

Sadd

Sharia al-Awal

Sharia Ras at-Tin

Tawfiq

Ras at-Tin

To Ras at-Tin Palace

To Maritime Station

To Agami & Hanoville Beaches

Sharia Ibrahim al-Awal

To Pompey's Pillar & the Catacombs of Kom ash-Shuqafa

al-Hurriya

r Gomhurriya

Midan al-

Central
Alexandria

0   200   400 m

Things to See

Despite its long and colourful history, there isn't that much left to see in Alexandria. You can get some idea of the splendours it must have once contained in a visit to the **Graeco-Roman Museum**. It's at 5 Sharia al-Mathaf ar-Romani and is open from 9 am to 4 pm daily, except Friday, when it closes at 11.30 am for two hours. Admission is US$5.

The only example of a Roman theatre found in Egypt is the **Roman Amphitheatre** in Alexandria, not far from the main Misr train station. It is still in quite a good state of repair. It's open from 9 am to 4 pm and entry is US$2.

Dating back to the 2nd century AD, the **Catacombs of Kom ash-Shuqqafa** held about 300 corpses. Open from 8.30 am to 4 pm, they are in the south-west of the city, near tram line No 16. Admission is US$3.50. Not far away is the famed, misnamed and very missable **Pompey's Pillar**. Admission is US$2.

The Mameluke sultan, Qaitbey, built a **fortress** on the foundations of the destroyed Pharos lighthouse in 1480. In the 19th century, Mohammed Ali expanded its defences but it was badly damaged during British bombardments in 1882. Admission is US$3.50 during the day, US$6 in the evening. Take the No 15 tram.

Once the summer residence of the royal family, **Montazah Palace**, at the eastern extremity of the city, is now reserved for the president and his VIPs, but the gardens are still a pleasant place to wander around for the day. Entry to the grounds costs US$1.60. Bus No 260 from Midan Orabi passes the gardens on its way to Abu Qir, as does bus No 250 from Misr station.

The city **beaches** are not overly enticing, although locals flock to them in summer. Maamoura, just east of Montazah Palace, is good, but Agami and Hannoville, about 17km west of central Alexandria, are better. Buses and minibuses go there from Midan Saad Zaghloul.

Places to Stay

Hostels The *Youth Hostel* (☎ 597 4559) at 13 Sharia Port Said costs US$2 for members in dorms (eight beds) or US$3 to US$4.50 in one of the new double rooms. Non-members pay US$1.30 extra.

Hotels The *Hotel Acropole* (☎ 80 5980), 4th floor, 1 Sharia Gamal ad-Din Yassin, is pleasant and centrally located, one block west of Midan Saad Zaghloul. It costs from US$4.50/7 for a single/double, depending on the location of the room. Across the street is the *Hotel Triomphe*. Its rooms have sagging beds but, they are only US$2.30/3.50 for a single/double.

A few doors down from the Triomphe, on Sharia Gamal ad-Din Yassin, is a building with four pensions. The cheapest is the 5th floor *New Hotel Welcome House* (☎ 80 6402). The other three – the *Hotel Gamil* (☎ 81 5458), *Hotel Normandie* (☎ 80 6830) and the *Mekka* (☎ 80 8940) – are all on the 4th floor.

One block west of these pensions is the *Hotel Union* (☎ 80 7312). This hotel, on the 5th floor, is great value. Some rooms have TVs, sparkling tiled bathrooms, balconies and fantastic harbour views. Singles/doubles without bath cost US$8/9, or US$11/14 with bath.

Down on Midan Orabi, the *Holiday Hotel* (☎ 80 3517) is popular with travellers on overland trucks. Singles/doubles with private bathroom cost US$11/16; US$9/12 without.

Also very central is the *Metropole Hotel* (☎ 48 21465) at 52 Sharia Saad Zaghloul, which has a bit of old world class. There is a cosy little bar downstairs. Singles/doubles cost about US$22/31.

The *Cecil Hotel* (☎ 483 7173), overlooking Midan Saad Zaghloul, is something of an institution in Alexandria. Its history is one of romance and intrigue. Guests over the years have included Somerset Maugham, Lawrence Durrell and Winston Churchill, and during WWII it was the headquarters of the British Secret Service. These days, rooms start at US$114/140.

Places to Eat

There are many places to eat along Sharia Safia Zaghloul. At the Mahattat ar-Ramla

EGYPT

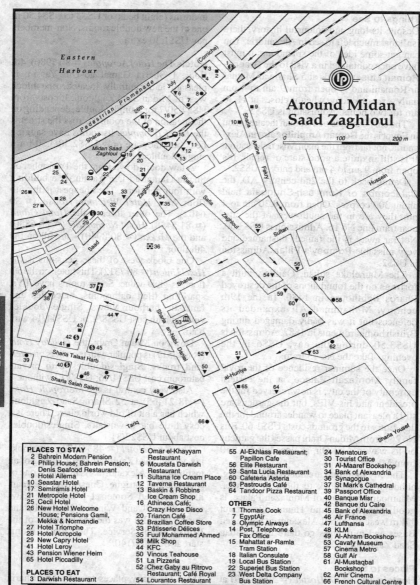

Around Midan Saad Zaghloul

Eastern Harbour

Midan Saad Zaghloul

0   100   200 m

PLACES TO STAY
2 Bahrein Modern Pension
4 Philip House; Bahrein Pension;
    Denis Seafood Restaurant
9 Hotel Ailema
10 Seastar Hotel
17 Semiramis Hotel
21 Metropole Hotel
25 Cecil Hotel
26 New Hotel Welcome
    House; Pensions Gamil,
    Mekka & Normandie
27 Hotel Triomphe
28 Hotel Acropole
29 New Capry Hotel
41 Hotel Leroy
43 Pension Wiener Heim
65 Hotel Piccadilly

PLACES TO EAT
3 Darwish Restaurant

5 Omar el-Khayyam
    Restaurant
6 Moustafa Darwish
    Restaurant
11 Sultana Ice Cream Place
12 Taverna Restaurant
13 Baskin & Robbins
    Ice Cream Shop
16 Athineos Café;
    Crazy Horse Disco
20 Trianon Café
32 Brazilian Coffee Store
33 Pâtisserie Délices
35 Fuul Mohammed Ahmed
38 Milk Shop
44 KFC
50 Vinous Teahouse
51 La Pizzeria
52 Chez Gaby au Ritrovo
    Restaurant; Café Royal
54 Lourantos Restaurant

55 Al-Ekhlass Restaurant;
    Papillon Cafe
56 Elite Restaurant
59 Santa Lucia Restaurant
60 Cafeteria Asteria
63 Pastroudis Café
64 Tandoor Pizza Restaurant

OTHER
1 Thomas Cook
7 EgyptAir
8 Olympic Airways
14 Post, Telephone &
    Fax Office
15 Mahattat ar-Ramla
    Tram Station
18 Italian Consulate
19 Local Bus Station
22 Superjet Bus Station
23 West Delta Company
    Bus Station

24 Menatours
30 Tourist Office
31 Al-Maaref Bookshop
34 Bank of Alexandria
36 Synagogue
37 St Mark's Cathedral
39 Passport Office
40 Banque Misr
45 Banque du Caire
46 Bank of Alexandria
46 Air France
47 Lufthansa
48 KLM
49 Al-Ahram Bookshop
53 Cavafy Museum
57 Cinema Metro
58 Gulf Air
61 Al-Mustaqbal
    Bookshop
62 Amir Cinema
66 French Cultural Centre

end of the street, close to the seafront, there are a number of cafes, juice stands, chawarma stands and bakeries. If you're content with a croissant and a cup of coffee, try the *Brazilian Coffee Store* on Sharia Saad Zaghloul. Established in 1929, it's the oldest coffee shop in the city. The *Trianon Café* in the Metropole Hotel is another of Alexandria's superb cafes.

Fuul Mohammed Ahmed, at 317 Sharia Shakor, is without doubt the best place in town for a cheap, simple meal of fuul or ta'amiyya, plus all the usual accompaniments. There's also a popular takeaway section. *Al-Ekhlass* at 49 Sharia Safia Zaghloul serves very good but pricey Egyptian food. Kebab and kofta cost about US$4.50.

Elite at 43 Sharia Safia Zaghloul, close to the Cinema Metro, has a bit of class and culture at reasonable prices. The walls are decorated with prints by Chagall, Picasso and others. It serves pizza and moussaka (sometimes), or you can just sit down for a beer (US$1.60 including complimentary pastry nibbles).

Down towards Midan Orabi, *Hassan Bleik* at 18 Sharia Saad Zaghloul serves excellent Lebanese food in a small restaurant nestled behind a patisserie. Mezzes go for less than US$1 and sanbousak (puff pastry with meat/cheese/spinach) for US$0.75. It's open from noon to 6 pm.

ASWAN

Over the centuries Aswan, Egypt's southernmost city, has been a garrison town, the gateway to Africa and the now inundated land of Nubia, a prosperous marketplace at the crossroads of the ancient caravan routes and, more recently, a popular winter resort. In and around Aswan – the most attractive of the Nile towns – you can see a variety of Pharaonic monuments, a Coptic Christian monastery, the High Dam and Lake Nasser, the huge artificial lake that backs up behind the dam into Sudan. Aswan is also the best base from which to visit the awesome temple at Abu Simbel.

Things to See

Once the core of what is now Aswan, **Elephantine Island** is characterised by its huge grey (elephant-like?) boulders. Ongoing excavations have revealed a small town, temples, fortifications and a Nilometer at the southern end of the island. There is a small museum; admission is US$3.

Lord Kitchener turned what is now known as **Kitchener's Island** into a flourishing garden, which it remains. Entry is US$3 and you have to hire a boat to get there.

Over on the west bank of the Nile, the elaborate **Mausoleum of the Aga Khan** is modelled on Fatimid tombs in Cairo. It is no longer open to visitors. South of the mausoleum, cut into the high riverside cliffs, the **Tombs of the Nobles** are the tombs of local dignitaries dating from the Old and Middle Kingdom. Admission is US$3.50 (half that for students). Hours are 8 am to 4 pm in winter, to 5 pm in summer.

The well-preserved 6th century Coptic Christian **Monastery of St Simeon** is a half-hour hike or short camel ride from the felucca dock near the Mausoleum of the Aga Khan. To get to the west bank, take the ferry from in front of the tourist office (when the river is low, ferries leave from in front of the Abu Simbel Hotel).

Back on the east bank, **Sharia as-Souk**, is one of Egypt's most colourful markets. South of the town centre, on the road to the Aswan Dam, a **Nubian Museum**, to showcase Nubian art and architecture, is under construction. Ask the tourist office if it has opened.

The **Fatimid Cemetery**, opposite the Nubian Museum, is a collection of low stone buildings with domed roofs topped by crescents. Across the road from the cemetery (a five to 10 minute walk away if you follow the road) is the impressive **Unfinished Obelisk**, a huge discarded obelisk on the edge of the northern granite quarries. Entry to the site costs US$3.

Philae Temple South of Aswan and relocated to escape flooding in the 1960s, the Temple of Philae was dedicated to Isis, who found the heart of her slain brother, Osiris, on the now submerged Philae Island. Most of the temple was built by the Ptolemies and Romans, and early Christians turned the hypostyle hall into a chapel. It is possible to organise taxi trips to the boat landing at Shellal south of the Old Dam, or you can walk if you can get a lift to the dam. The temple complex is open from 8 am to 4 pm in winter and from 7 am to 5 pm in summer; admission is US$6.

High Dam This colossal structure controls the unpredictable annual flooding of the Nile and is a source of hydroelectric power. It is 3600m long and 111m deep. Trips to Abu Simbel (see the Abu Simbel section earlier in this chapter) usually include a stop at the dam or you can take one of the six daily trains to Saad al-Ali station.

Places to Stay

Camping There's a camping ground next to the Unfinished Obelisk. Facilities are basic (cold showers only) but there are grassy spaces and a few trees to provide shade. It costs US$1 per person plus US$1.50/0.60 for a car/motorcycle.

Hostels The *Youth Hostel* (☎ 32 2235) is on Sharia Abtal at-Tahrir, not far from the train station. At US$2 for a bed in a share double or triple, it's not a bad deal. The rooms have fans, the showers and toilets are clean and the place is generally empty.

Hotels North of the train station, the *Rosewan Hotel* (☎ 32 4497) has clean, simple, rather small singles/doubles with shower/toilet combinations for US$5/8, or US$3/7 without shower. All rooms have fans and tiled floors and, according to some disgruntled travellers, bugs. Next door, the *Hotel El-Saffa* (☎ 32 2173) is starting to show its age but is still OK at US$1.50/3 for rooms with sinks and balconies. A few rooms also have showers with hot water.

A few blocks north is the *Mena Hotel* (☎ 32 4388). The cool, carpeted rooms have

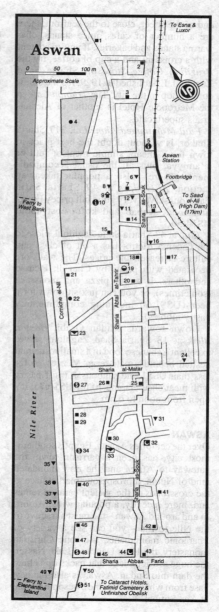

PLACES TO STAY
1 New Abu Simbel Hotel
2 Mena Hotel
3 Rosewan & El-Saffa Hotels
7 Marwa Hotel
9 Youth Hostel
13 Noorhan Hotel
14 El-Amin Hotel
15 Ramses Hotel
17 New Bob Marley Hotel
18 Cleopatra Hotel
20 Nubian Oasis Hotel
21 Abu Simbel Hotel
25 Aswan Palace Hotel
26 Happi Hotel
28 El-Salam Hotel
29 Hathor Hotel
30 Victoria Hotel
40 Horus Hotel
41 Molla Hotel
42 Hotel al-Oraby

43 Abou Shelib Hotel
45 El Amir Hotel
46 Memnon Hotel
47 Philae Hotel

PLACES TO EAT
6 Restaurant Derwash
8 El Dar Restaurant
11 Esraa (Kofta Place)
12 El Nasr (Pizza Place)
16 Medina Restaurant
24 El Masry Restaurant
31 Al-Sayyida Nefisa Restaurant
35 Saladin Restaurant
37 Aswan Moon Restaurant
38 Emy Restaurant
39 Monalisa Restaurant
49 Panorama & El-Shati Restaurants
50 Restaurant el-Nil

OTHER
4 Governorate Building
5 Tourist Office
10 Tourist Office; Nile Valley Navigation Office
19 Bus Station
22 Cultural Centre
23 Post Office
27 Banque Misr
32 Mosque
33 Post Office (Poste Restante)
34 Bank of Alexandria
36 Dr Ragab Papyrus Museum
44 Mosque
48 Banque du Caire
51 Thomas Cook

TVs, phones, showers, toilets and small balconies. Singles/doubles are US$4.50/7.

South of the train station, across the street from the youth hostel, is the *Marwa Hotel*, which at US$1 is about as cheap as you'll find. Another cheapie is the *New Bob Marley Hotel* (☎ 32 3123), one block east of the Medina Restaurant on Sharia as-Souk's. For US$1.50 per person you get a reasonable double room with fan and balcony. The newer air-con rooms cost a bit more.

The relatively new *Nubian Oasis Hotel* (☎ 31 2126), just off Sharia as-Souk, is one of Aswan's most popular travellers' haunts. It has good clean rooms for US$2 per person with private bath, slightly less without. There's a large lounge area and a roof garden where Stellas cost US$1.50.

On a quiet side street towards the southern end of the souk is the relatively new *Hotel Al-Oraby* (☎ 31 7578). The staff are friendly, and the communal bathrooms are clean (though prone to flooding). It charges US$2 per person in a room with fan; air-con is slightly more. It's a 15 to 20 minute walk from the train station.

The *Ramses Hotel* (☎ 32 4000) on Sharia Abtal at-Tahrir is a good deal and, according to some travellers, the best value hotel in

Aswan. Singles/doubles with showers, toilets, air-con, colour TV, mini-refrigerators and Nile views cost about US$10/16.

Further away from the Nile is the *Oscar Hotel* (☎ 32 3851), which has become something of a travellers' favourite. Rooms cost US$7/10. There's a rooftop terrace where beers (US$1.50) are available.

The *Abu Simbel Hotel* (☎ 32 2888) on the Corniche used to be a middle-range place but is so decrepit that it is now a definite bottom ender. Double rooms with shower cost US$8 for one or two people. The views from here are superb.

Continuing south along the Corniche, the new 34-room *Memnon Hotel* (☎ 32 2650) is above the National Bank of Egypt (but can only be entered through the back alley). Air-con doubles with private bath, comfortable beds, and views over the alley/Nile cost US$7/10; singles are slightly cheaper. It's good value.

Places to Eat
The *Restaurant Derwash* on the south side of the Aswan Station Square has been recommended by some travellers. A block from the station is *Samah*, a little ta'amiyya stall. Down a side street, a bit further, is *El-Nasr*

which has pizza (or 'betza' as they prefer to spell it), as well as fried fish and chicken.

Next to the youth hostel is an OK place called the *El-Dar*, which serves nice vegetable soup, although portions are small. Alternatively you could try *Esraa*, a tiny kofta place just down the road. The *Medina Restaurant* on Sharia as-Souk, across from the Cleopatra Hotel, is also recommended for its kofta and kebab. It does a vegetarian meal for US$1.30 which includes a cola.

The *Al-Sayyida Nefisa*, tucked away in a side alley in the heart of the souk, is a good-value little place, serving kofta for US$1.50, soup for US$0.30, and a meal of rice, salad, vegetables and bread for US$0.75.

There are three places on the Corniche where you can sit out on a barge in the river and get decent food and beers. Of the three, the *Aswan Moon Restaurant* remains the most popular among foreigners and Egyptians. Main courses go for about US$3.50 and a beer is US$1.80. Another of the three, the *Emy Restaurant*, does especially nice fruit cocktail drinks. The view from its top deck at sunset is bliss, and the beers are the cheapest in town.

The tiny *Restaurant el-Nil* is on the Corniche a few doors along from Thomas Cook. A full meal with fish (carp from Lake Nasser), chicken or meat with rice, vegetables, salad, tahini (sesame seed paste) and bread should cost about US$3.

Getting There & Away

Bus The bus station is in the middle of town. There are two daily buses to Abu Simbel (US$8 return) but neither of them has air-con. One leaves at 8 am and arrives back at about 5.30 pm; the other is a night service departing at 5 pm. You should book in advance.

There are hourly buses to Kom Ombo (one hour, US$0.50), Edfu (1½ hours, US$0.60), Esna (two hours, US$0.75) and Luxor (four to five hours, US$1.80). A direct bus for Cairo (12 hours) leaves at 3.30 pm and costs US$15. The bus leaving an hour later costs US$3 less.

Train There's a handful of trains running daily between Cairo and Aswan, although only three of them can be used by foreigners. The most expensive is the Wagon-Lits train (No 85) which departs at 3 pm. Express train Nos 981 and 997 to Cairo leave at 5.45 am and 6.30 pm. For details of fares see the Cairo Getting There & Away section.

Tickets for the train to Luxor (four hours) cost US$6/3.50 in 1st/2nd class on the afternoon service, and about a dollar more on the morning train.

Felucca A trip down the Nile would not be complete without at least a short felucca ride. The most popular trip is downstream from Aswan to Edfu – most captains won't go further. The trip takes about two or three days. There's no shortage of captains or touts along the Corniche trying to sell rides. Get a group of people to go together (a comfortable number is six; more than eight is a tight squeeze). Officially, feluccas can carry a minimum of six passengers and a maximum of eight, for the following prices: US$7 to Kom Ombo, US$13 to Edfu and US$15 to Esna. On top of this you must add US$1.50 for police registration and extra for food.

EDFU

The attraction in this town is the Greek-built **Temple of Horus**, the falcon-headed son of Osiris. It took about 200 years to complete and it has helped fill in a lot of gaps in knowledge about the Pharaonic architecture it imitates. It is open from 7 am to 4 pm in winter and from 6 am to 6 pm in summer. Admission is US$6.

There are two cheap *hotels* in Edfu, near the temple, and a couple of small places to eat near the square.

Getting There & Away

There are frequent connections to Edfu from Luxor and Aswan. Service taxis are the best bet. They cost US$1.50 from Luxor and US$1 from Aswan. The buses are slightly cheaper.

HURGHADA (AL-GHARDAKA)

The only attractions of this one-time fishing village are the water, or rather what's in it. The town and the coast for 20km south resemble a kind of permanent building site – every square centimetre of beach will soon be backed by some hotel resort.

The main town area, Ad-Dahar, where virtually all the budget accommodation is located, is at the northern end. South is the port area of Sigala and then the resort strip.

Things to See & Do

There is a small **aquarium** near the Three Corners Hotel, but most people come here to dive or snorkel and view the rich sea life directly. Hurghada is crawling with dive clubs and agents for snorkelling trips. One of the popular snorkelling day trips is to **Giftun Island**, which costs between US$7 and US$12. Some of the reputable dive clubs take snorkellers out to better sites and, by going with one of them, you're almost assured of reef protection practices being put into action.

Diving trips of one day or more are possible. Subex (☎ 54 7593) in Ad-Dahar is highly recommended for shorter trips and Rudi Kneip (☎ 44 2960) in Sigala has years of experience taking diving safaris.

To get a rough idea of prices, see the Activities section of Facts for the Visitor.

Places to Stay

Hostels Hurghada's old *Youth Hostel* (☎ 44 2432) is on the resort strip, opposite the Sonesta Beach Resort. It costs US$2 a night (US$2.60 for non-members). At the time of writing, a big new hostel was due to open about 5km north of Ad-Dahar.

Hotels Hurghada is full of places to bed down. Captain Mohammed's *Happy House* on the main square by the mosque in the centre of Ad-Dahar is a clean basic place to stay for US$2 per person. Near the main Coptic church is the homely *My Place – Raoul's Budget Paradise*. It's not a bad deal at US$1.50 a head.

The *Hotel Sosna* (☎ 44 6647) is a bit over the top with clean rooms for US$6/9 without

bath, or US$7/10 with. Better value is the *Shakespear Hotel* (☎ 44 6256) at the top end of Sharia Abd al-Aziz Mustafa. Its very spacious, comfortable doubles with communal baths cost US$7.

On the slope up behind the Aboudi Bookshop in Ad-Dahar is the comfortable *Alaska* (☎ 54 8413) which charges US$2.50 per person plus US$0.60 for breakfast. Close by is the small *Luxor Palace Hotel* (☎ 54 9260) with singles/doubles for US$3/6, breakfast included.

The *Sea Horse Hotel* (☎ 54 8704), north of the big mosque, is an old but quite OK three-star place. In winter, rooms cost US$29/32 with breakfast, but come down about US$7 in summer. The nearby *Al-Gezira Hotel* (☎ 54 7785) is quite a good deal, if you don't mind taking half board (obligatory), with singles/doubles costing US$20/26.

Places to Eat

The *Al-Baron* is a cheap and cheerful little eatery in Ad-Dahar. A satisfying meal costs about US$1. A block north of the Baron and in a side lane to the right is the cosy *Aladin's Lamp*. It does a small plate of calamari for US$1.60 and chicken for US$2, and can arrange beers.

One of the most popular budget places on Sharia Abd al-Aziz Mustafa is the *Bell Riviera*. It does an excellent lentil soup for US$0.40, calamari for US$2.60, and you can also get breakfast for US$1. There are a few other cheap eating places around the Happy House Hotel, including one called *Zeko*, which is just across the square.

Arlene's, on Sharia Abd al-Aziz Mustafa, is one of the few places in Egypt where you'll find nachos. It also serves beer.

For cheap fare in Sigala you could try the kushari and ta'amiyya places just up from the *Samos* Greek restaurant or, better still, *Baracoda* near Thomas Cook. This tiny place serves passable pizzas for US$1. A couple of kilometres along the road, past the Moon Valley Village, is the best located *Felfela* restaurant in the country. Sitting on a rise and a gentle bend in the coastline, it is a splendid place for a modestly priced meal.

Getting There & Away

Bus Superjet's terminal is near the main mosque in Ad-Dahar. It has buses to Cairo (six hours, US$12) at noon and 2.30 and 5 pm, and a daily bus to Alexandria (seven hours; US$18) at 2.30 pm. The Upper Egypt Bus Co operates from the main bus station at the southern end of Ad-Dahar. It runs buses almost hourly to Cairo (six hours, US$7 to US$12) from between 6 am and midnight.

Boat One vessel plies the waters from Hurghada to Sharm el-Sheikh, departing Sunday, Tuesday and Thursday from Hurghada. Book ahead. You can do this at Al-Shaymaa Sea Trips (☎ 54 6901) on Sharia Abd al-Aziz Mustafa, Ad-Dahar. The trip costs US$29 one way and the boat departs from the port in Sigala some time between 9 and 10 am.

LUXOR

The sheer grandeur of Luxor's monumental architecture, and its excellent state of preservation, have made this village-city one of Egypt's greatest tourist attractions. Built on and around the 4000-year-old site of ancient Thebes, Luxor is an extraordinary mixture of exotic history and modern commercialism.

Information & Orientation

What most visitors today know as Luxor is actually three separate areas: the city of Luxor itself, the village of Karnak a couple of kilometres to the north-east (both on the east bank of the Nile) and the monuments and necropolis of ancient Thebes on the west bank.

The city – actually a small provincial town – of Luxor is the main accommodation centre. It has only three main thoroughfares: Sharia al-Mahatta runs between the train station and the gardens of Luxor Temple; the Corniche runs along the river; and Sharia al-Karnak runs parallel to it and out towards the Karnak temples.

The main tourist office (☎ 37 3294) is next

to the New Winter Palace Hotel. It's open from 8 am to 8 pm and the staff let you leave messages for other travellers. The main banks have branches on or near the Corniche. There is also an exchange booth open long hours on the Corniche in front of the tourist office. American Express (☎ 37 2862) and Thomas Cook (☎ 37 2196) have offices at the old Winter Palace Hotel.

The main post office is on Sharia al-Mahatta and there's a branch office in the Tourist Bazaar. The central telephone office is on Sharia al-Karnak and is open 24 hours; there's another, open from 8 am to 10 pm, below the resplendent entrance of the New Winter Palace Hotel.

The East Bank

The most spectacular of the east bank sites are the **Temples of Karnak**, which are one of the most overwhelming monuments of the Pharaonic legacy. General admission to the temples is between 6 am and 5.30 pm (winter) or 6.30 pm (summer); tickets cost US$6. Local microbuses make the short run to the temples from the centre of Luxor.

The Karnak temples' **sound and light show** easily rivals the one at the Great Pyramids. There are three or four performances a night, in English, French, German, Japanese, Italian, Spanish or Arabic. The show costs US$10 (no student discount).

In the centre of town is **Luxor Temple**, built by the New Kingdom Pharaoh Amenophis III. It was added to over the centuries by Tutankhamun, Ramses II, Alexander the Great and the Arabs, who built a mosque in one of the interior courts. The temple is open daily from 6 am to 9 pm (winter) or 10 pm (summer), and admission is US$6.

Luxor Museum has a small but well-chosen collection of relics from the Theban temples and necropolis, including pottery, jewellery, furniture and stelae. The museum is open daily from 9 am to 1 pm and 4 to 9 pm (winter) or 5 to 10 pm (summer). Entry costs US$5.

The West Bank

The west bank of Luxor was the necropolis

of ancient Thebes. Five ferries cross the Nile – two tourist and three local, at least one of which also carries vehicles. Foreigners pay US$0.70 on all of them.

From the Al-Fadlya Canal junction it is 3km to the Valley of the Queens, 7km to the Valley of the Kings, and 2km straight ahead to the ticket office (where student tickets can be bought), past the Colossi of Memnon. There is another ticket office where the tourist ferries land on the west bank of the Nile but student tickets are not available from here. To see everything would cost about US$100 (without a student card) and take a lot of time. Tickets are only valid for the day of purchase, so choose carefully. You can buy tickets for the Valley of the Kings at the site itself.

The places most worth visiting include the **Valley of the Kings** whose tombs were designed to resemble the underworld, with a long, inclined rock-hewn corridor descending into either an antechamber or a series of sometimes pillared halls and ending in the burial chamber. Entry to groupings of three tombs is US$6 a time. Tutankhamun's tomb, discovered in 1922 by Howard Carter and far from being the most interesting, requires a separate ticket for US$12. Better are the tombs of Ramses VI, Queen Tawsert/ Sethnakt, Tuthmosis III and Saptah.

The most impressive tomb of all is the recently opened **Tomb of Nefertari** whose stunning wall paintings are hailed as the finest in all of Egypt. Visitors must pay a hefty US$30 admission to enter the tomb and are permitted to stay for 10 minutes only. It's in the **Valley of the Queens**, where five more tombs are also open to the public (US$3.50).

Above ground the **Deir al-Bahri (Temple of Hatshepsut)**, which rises out of the desert plain in a series of terraces to meet the cliff faces behind, is also well worth including on any itinerary. Entry is US$3.50.

Places to Stay

The tourist trade is extremely seasonal in Luxor, so visitors in winter will often pay more than in the hotter months.

Camping The *YMCA* camping ground on Sharia al-Karnak costs US$1 per night. It's very basic. The *Rezeiky Camp* (☎ 38 1334), just up the road, charges US$3 per person, for which you get access to the dinky swimming pool and showers.

Hostels The *Youth Hostel* (☎ 37 2139) is in a street just off Sharia al-Karnak. Rooms are clean and have at least three beds. With a membership card it costs US$1.80 (US$2.10 without).

Hotels – East Bank Close to the railway station is the *Anglo Hotel* which charges US$3/4.50 for a single/double with breakfast and shared bathroom. It's clean and the management is friendly.

The area around Sharia Mohammed Farid and Sharia Television teem with little budget pensions and hotels. The *Oasis Hotel* (☎ 38 1699) has pokey singles but decent doubles with bath for US$2/4, slightly more with air-con. All rooms have fans and the shared bathrooms are new and clean.

Two streets past the Oasis, then down a dead-end alley off to the right, is the *Grand Hotel* (☎ 37 4186). Newly renovated and, for the time being at any rate, very clean, it has a small roof-top terrace with great views, and decent shared bathrooms with hot water. Doubles with fans and a bit of furniture go for US$1.50.

On a dusty lane off Sharia Ahmed Orabi the *Atlas Hotel* (☎ 37 3514) isn't bad at US$2 per person (plus US$0.70 if you want breakfast). The nearby *Fontana Hotel* (☎ 38 0663), however, is more popular with travellers, although at US$3/4.50 for a room with shared facilities, or US$6 for a double with air-con and private bathroom, it's a little overpriced.

In a lane opposite the old garage on Sharia Television, the 2nd-floor *Pension Roma*, run by a friendly Egyptian guy and his English wife, is small, homely and OK value at US$1.50 for a pokey double with shared facilities. A few streets away on Sharia el-Kamr, the *Happy Land* (☎ 37 1828) has been highly recommended by several readers as

EGYPT

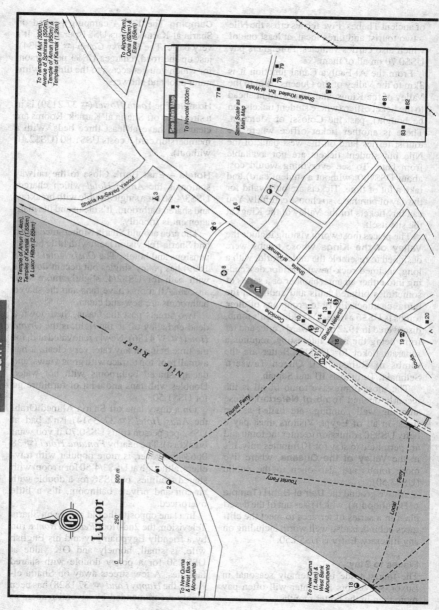

Luxor

To Temple of Mut (300m),
Avenue of Sphinxes (500m),
Temple of Amun (900m) &
Temples of Karnak (1.2m)

To Airport (7km),
Qena (62km) &
Esna (55km)

To Temple of Amun (1.4m),
Temples of Karnak (1.65m) &
Luxor Hilton (2.65m)

Sharia As-Sayed Yaoust

Corniche

Sharia al-Karnak

Nile River

Sharia Nefertiti

Sharia Khaled Ibn el-Walid

See Main Map

Same Scale as
Main Map

To Novotel (300m)

Souq

Tourist Ferry

Tourist Ferry

Local Ferry

To New Qurna
& West Bank
Monuments

To New Qurna
(1.4km) &
West Bank
Monuments

0   250   500 m

EGYPT

PLACES TO STAY

3 Rezeiky Camp
4 Pola Hotel
5 Youth Hostel
6 YMCA Camping Ground
10 Merryland Hotel
11 Windsor Hotel
13 Philippe Hotel
14 Nile Hotel
16 Mercure ETAP Hotel
20 Emilio Hotel
21 Mina Palace Hotel
25 Venus Hotel
26 Pyramids Hotel
27 Nobles Hotel
28 St Catherine Hotel
29 Sphinx Hotel
30 El-Shazly Hotel
31 Nefertiti Hotel
36 Horus Hotel
41 Hotel El Salam
43 Saint Mina Hotel
44 Negem ei-Din Pension
47 New Kamak Hotel
49 Anglo Hotel
50 Akhnation Hotel
51 Arabesque Hotel
52 Luxor Wena Hotel
54 New Winter Palace
55 Old Winter Palace;
    Thomas Cook; EgyptAir;
    Amex; Misr Travel;
    AA Gaddis Bookshop
59 Mubarak Hotel
60 Salah ad-Din Hotel
62 Oasis Hotel
63 Grand Hotel
64 New Nour Hotel
65 Atlas Hotel
66 Princess Pension
67 Everest Hotel
68 Santa Maria Hotel
69 Shady Hotel
70 Pension Roma
71 Fontana Roma
73 Titi Hotel
74 Moon Valley Hotel
75 Happy Land Hotel
76 Novotel
77 Club Med Belladona
    Resort
78 St Joseph Hotel
79 Flobater Hotel
82 Gaddis Hotel
83 Isis Hotel

PLACES TO EAT

24 El Dar Restaurant
32 Amoun & El-Hussein
    Restaurants
37 Abu Negem el-Din
39 Abu Ashraf
40 Mensa Restaurant
46 New Kamak Restaurant;
    Salt & Bread Cafeteria
48 Twinky's Patisserie
57 Fleer Restaurant;
    El Dabaawy Restaurant
56 Sayida Zeinab (Kushari
    Restaurant
61 Restaurant Abu Hager
72 Mish Mish Restaurant
80 Kings Head Pub

OTHER

1 Ticket Office
2 Taxis to West Bank
    Monuments
7 Service-Taxi Station
8 Hospital
9 Luxor Museum
12 Banque Misr
15 Bank of Alexandria
17 Dr Ragab's Papyrus
    Museum
18 Taxis & Donkeys to
    West Bank Monuments
19 Telephone Office
22 Brooke Hospital for
    Animals
23 Police Station
33 Entrance to
    Luxor Temple
34 Luxor Temple
35 Bus Station
38 Post Office
42 Pharmacy La Confiance
45 Train Station;
53 Post/Telephone Offices
    Tourist Bazaar (Tourist
    Office & Tourist Police)
56 National Bank of Egypt
81 Passport Office

one of the cleanest and friendliest places in town. It charges only US$1.50 for its cheapest rooms, including breakfast. A better single with private bath costs US$3.

North of Sharia al-Mahatta, the *Hotel El Salam* (☎ 37 2517) is deservedly popular with the impecunious. At US$1.50/3, the prices are reasonable and include use of a washing machine. The rooms have fans. Doubles with bath cost US$4.50.

For anyone with a bigger budget, the *Saint Mina Hotel* (☎ 38 6568), just north of the train station, is a very good deal – it is relatively new, and although the rooms are small, they are modern and clean with air-con or fans. A single room with bath is US$9, but singles/doubles without bath go for US$6/10.

Hotels – West Bank

Opposite the Medinat Habu temple complex is the *Habou Hotel* (sometimes spelt 'Habu'). It has dark, dingy, overpriced rooms for US$3/6.

The *Mersam Hotel* (☎ 38 2403), also known as the *Ali Abd el-Rasul Hotel* or the *Sheik Ali Hotel*, is opposite the Antiquities Office. Rooms in the main building are somewhat better than the primitive mud-wall rooms in an adjacent building. Singles/doubles cost US$7/9 in summer, though prices double in winter.

The *Abdul Kasem Hotel* (☎ 31 0319) is near the Temple of Seti I on Sharia Wadi al-Melouk. It has rooms for US$6/9 and is one of the best lower-budget places on the west bank. It rents bicycles for US$1.50 a day.

Pharaohs Hotel (☎ 31 0702) is the only middle-range place to stay on the west bank. It's near the Antiquities Office and has 14 rooms, most with air-con or strong overhead fans, wallpaper and tiled floors. There's a small restaurant which is renowned for its sun-baked bread. Single/double rooms with fan cost US$9/12, or US$18/21 with air-con.

Places to Eat

The *New Karnak Restaurant* and next door the *Salt & Bread Cafeteria* serve cheap meals for about US$1.30. The latter offers many entrees, including kebab, pigeon and chicken; the former has rather small portions of chicken or other meat dishes.

The *Mensa Restaurant*, on Sharia al-Mahatta, has basic food that's a bit overpriced. Dishes include chicken, pigeon stuffed with rice, sandwiches, and chicken with French fries and mixed vegetables. A meal costs about US$2.50.

A little more expensive is *El-Hussein*, on Sharia al-Karnak, where most main dishes cost around US$2.50 plus service. They do tasty fish in a tomato and basil sauce and acceptable, if smallish, pizzas for US$2. Next door the *Amoun Restaurant* serves oriental kebab, chicken, fish and various rice and vegetable dishes for similar prices.

Up the road from the El-Hussein is the small and busy local hangout, the *Abu Negem el-Din*, where half a chicken costs US$1.50 and a plate of macaroni US$0.60. Try the tagen, a kind of stew, with or without meat, cooked in a clay casserole pot.

There is a huddle of small eateries and cafes in the lanes around Sharia al-Mahatta between the Amoun Restaurant and the police station, where the food is cheap and the atmosphere busy. One of them, the tiny *El-Dar Restaurant*, is up on the 1st floor of a building in an alley off Sharia al-Karnak. The portions tend to be a bit small, but you can get a beer here for US$1.80.

At the northern end of Sharia Television is another cluster of small diners, a juice stand and a very good, no-name, open-air *fiteer place*. It's sandwiched between a teahouse and the El-Dabaawy Restaurant – just look for the flashing 'Pizza' sign.

A little further along Sharia Television is *Sayyida Zeinab*, one of Luxor's best kushari joints. The prices are written in English, so there's no attempt to rip off tourists and the portions are large.

Further up Sharia Television, near the Titi Hotel, is the *Mish Mish* restaurant. Try their Mish Mish salad – a kind of mixed salad with hummus and cold meats, enough to constitute a light meal for US$1.80. They serve a version of pizza too.

A new and very trendy travellers' hangout

is the 24-hour *Kings Head Pub* on Sharia Khaled ibn el-Walid near the passport office. This place is England through and through – from the dart board and billiard table to the western music and counter meals. The food is very good though the prices are inflated.

Most of the mid-range hotels have their own restaurants, generally rooftop jobs of varying quality.

Getting There & Away

Bus The bus station is behind the Luxor Temple on Sharia al-Karnak (the garage on Sharia Television is not a pick-up point). There are two departures to Cairo: at 4.30 pm (US$10) and 7 pm (US$12). Buses leave for Aswan (four to five hours, US$1.80) about every hour from 6 am to 3.30 pm. The same buses go to Esna and Edfu.

Train The Wagon-Lits train for Cairo leaves at about 8.30 pm, with other services at 11 am and 11 pm. See the Cairo Getting There & Away section for more details. First and 2nd class tickets to Aswan (four hours) cost US$6/3.50 on the 6.30 am train, and slightly more on the 4.30 pm service.

MARSA MATRUH

The large waterfront town of Marsa Matruh, built around a charming bay of clear Mediterranean waters and clean white sandy beaches, is a popular summer destination with Egyptians. There's a tourist office (☎ 93 1841) on the ground floor of the Governorate building one block west of Sharia Iskendariyya on the corner of the Corniche. It is open daily from 8.30 am to 6 pm (until 9 pm in summer).

Things to See & Do

Set in the caves Rommel used as his headquarters during part of the El Alamein campaign, this pretty poor excuse for a **museum** contains a few photos, a bust of the Desert Fox and what is purported to be his greatcoat. It's closed in winter. Nearby is **Rommel's Beach**, where he used to take a break from warring.

The best **beaches** are outside the grotty town. The pick is Agiba, 24km west of Marsa Matruh. A pick-up goes out there.

Places to Stay & Eat

The *Youth Hostel* (☎ 93 2331), a couple of blocks south of the Awam mosque, is OK. Members pay US$1.50 for a comfortable enough bunk bed in a cramped room of six or eight.

A popular travellers' stop is the *Ghazala Hotel* (☎ 93 3519) which is just off Sharia Iskendariyya; the entrance is sandwiched between some shops and is easily overlooked. They charge US$2 a head for a basic but clean bed. *Queen Mary* is a four-storey pension (there's no sign or telephone) one block back from the water, next to the Awam mosque. In winter, it has doubles with private bathroom for US$4.50 (prices are five times higher in summer). The *Dareen Hotel* (☎ 93 5607), near the road to Sallum and Siwa, has reasonably comfortable rooms with own bath and breakfast for US$8/12 (US$3 more in summer).

The *Panayotis Greek Restaurant* on Sharia Iskendariyya does a decent plate of fish for US$5 and calamari for US$4.50. You can also get a beer here. Across the road is the *Alex Tourist Restaurant*, serving kebabs, kofta and the like, and also beer.

For excellent pizza (summer only), head down to the Corniche. Just after the Negresco Hotel you'll find *Pizza Gaby*, where most of the pizzas cost around US$3.

Getting There & Away

Marsa Matruh has two bus stations – one near the tourist office and the other, the main station, up near the railway line. There are numerous buses from both stations to Alexandria (four hours, US$3.30 to US$6.50) and Cairo (five hours, US$5 to US$10) – the cheaper buses are those from the main station which don't have air-con; the expensive ones are the West Delta and Superjet buses departing from near the tourist office.

Buses for Siwa (five hours, US$3) leave daily at 7.30 am and 3.30 pm, and in addition on Saturday, Monday and Wednesday at 5.30 pm.

EGYPT

MONASTERIES OF ST ANTHONY & ST PAUL

These two Coptic Christian monasteries, in the mountains overlooking the Gulf of Suez near Zafarana (about a third of the way from Cairo to Hurghada), can be conveniently visited from Hurghada. You don't need permission to visit, but if you intend to stay overnight you do need permission from the monasteries' Cairo residences.

St Paul's won't take visitors during Lent. It has separate *guesthouses* for men and women, and women must dress 'decently'. If you can't stay in the guesthouse, you can camp in the dry riverbed nearby. Food and lodging are free, but don't abuse the hospitality; bring your own food if you can.

St Anthony's, about 45km from the Red Sea coast, is more modernised. The visiting hours are from 9 am to 5 pm. It's worth climbing the 500m up the mountain behind the monastery to see **St Anthony's Cave**. St Anthony's *guesthouse* is for men only.

Getting There & Away

To get to St Paul's, take a bus along the coastal road north from Hurghada and get off at the turn-off for the monastery, south of the Zafarana lighthouse. From there it's a 13km walk on a dirt track across baking desert with very little traffic – don't rely on getting a lift.

To get to St Anthony's, take the road inland to the Nile Valley from Zafarana and take the monastery turn-off. From there it's a 10km walk. As with St Paul's, you may have to walk this stretch.

SALLUM

Some 214km west of Marsa Matruh, Sallum is the last town before the Libyan border. There's not much to it, but you can visit a Commonwealth **war cemetery** or go for a swim at one of the outlying beaches. There are a couple of small hotels and cafes. Buses for Marsa Matruh depart three times a day, some of which go on to Alexandria.

The Egyptian-Libyan border crossing point of Amsaad, just north of the Halfaya Pass, is 12km on from Sallum. Service taxis run up the mountain between the town and

the Egyptian side of the crossing for US$0.60 to US$0.90. Once you get through passport control and customs on both sides (you can walk through), you can get a taxi on to Al-Burdi. From there you can get buses on to Tobruk and Benghazi.

SINAI

It was on Mt Sinai that Moses received the Ten Commandments, but over the centuries the sixth has been broken here with monotonous regularity. Armies have crossed backwards and forwards, most recently from Israel, which occupied the peninsula from 1967 until 1982 when, under the Camp David Agreement, it agreed to pull out. Wedged between Africa and Asia, its northern coast is bordered by the Mediterranean Sea, and its southern peninsula by the Red Sea gulfs of Aqaba and Suez.

The area is populated mainly by Bedouins, although other Egyptians are settling there, mostly to take advantage of the tourist trade.

The splendours of the underwater world of the Red Sea and the grandeur of the desert mountains are the main attractions. For general information about diving, see Activities in the Facts for the Visitor section.

Warning

Despite what local tour operators may tell you, some areas of Sinai still contain land mines left from the wars with Israel. Be very wary about going off the beaten track.

Ras Mohammed

Declared a national marine park in 1988, the headland of Ras Mohammed is about 30km short of Sharm el-Sheikh, at the southern tip of the peninsula. Camping permits (US$1.50 per person per night) are available from the visitor's centre inside the park but camping is allowed only in designated areas. Take your passport with you, and remember that it is not possible to go to Ras Mohammed if you only have a Sinai permit in your passport.

Sharm el-Sheikh & Na'ama Bay

The south coast of the Gulf of Aqaba, between Tiran Island in the strait and Ras Mohammed, features some of the world's most amazing underwater scenery.

Na'ama Bay is a resort that has grown from virtually nothing since the early 1980s, while Sharm el-Sheikh, initially developed by the Israelis, is a long-standing settlement. They are 6km apart. An open-sided public bus (US$0.30), known as a *tof-tof*, runs every 40 minutes or so until about 11 pm between them. Pick-ups do the same run for the same price.

Diving & Snorkelling Na'ama itself has no reefs, but the stunning Near and Middle gardens and the even more incredible Far Garden can be reached on foot from the bay. Some of the most spectacular diving is off Ras Mohammed and in the Strait of Tiran. There is also good snorkelling at most of the popular coastal dive sites, including Ras um Sid near the lighthouse at Sharm. The deep drop-offs and strong cross currents at Ras Mohammed are not ideal for snorkelling. There are several wrecks including the prized *Thistlegorm*.

Any of the dive clubs and schools can give you a full rundown on the possibilities. Among the better and more established are Aquamarine Diving Centre (☎ 60 0276); Aquanaute (☎ 60 0187); Camel Dive Club (☎ 60 0700); Red Sea Diving Club (☎ 60 0342) and Red Sea Diving College (☎ 60 0313). There's a modern decompression chamber just outside Sharm el-Sheikh.

Places to Stay The *Youth Hostel* (☎ 60 0317), which is up on the hill in Sharm el-Sheikh near the Clifftop Hotel, costs US$3 with breakfast. It's open from 7 to 9 am and 2 to 11 pm.

The *Clifftop Hotel* (☎ 60 0251) has quite pleasant singles/doubles with TV, air-con, fridge, phone and bathroom for US$43/56 including breakfast.

Safety Land (☎ 60 0359), almost opposite the bus station, has dorm beds in a large tent

for US$7 or there are hot cement bungalows with fans at US$11/18 for singles/doubles.

In Na'ama Bay the *Pigeon House* (☎ 60 0996), on the northern edge of town, has comfortable huts with fans and breakfast for US$11/16.

Places to Eat There are a couple of small restaurants/cafes in the shopping bazaar behind the bus station in Sharm el-Sheikh. The *Sinai Star* does some excellent fish meals for about US$4 a person. The nearby *Brilliant Restaurant* does a range of traditional Egyptian food at moderate prices.

Safety Land can arrange meals (fish or calamari for US$7) and snacks (omelettes and salad), and you can dine within metres of the water. Beers are a reasonable US$1.80.

In Na'ama Bay the *Tam Tam Oriental Café*, jutting onto the beach, is a laid-back place serving up cheap Egyptian fare. *Viva* on the promenade is popular with divers and instructors.

Getting There & Away The main bus station is on the main road halfway between Sharm el-Sheikh and Na'ama Bay. To get there catch the tof-tof or flag one of the frequent passing taxis or minibuses. Superjet has a bus to Cairo (US$15) leaving at 11 pm. The East Delta Co's direct services to Cairo (seven hours) cost from US$8 to US$15. They depart at 7, 8 and 10 am and 1, 4 and 11.30 pm and midnight. There are frequent buses in the opposite direction to Dahab (1½ hours, US$2) and on to Nuweiba (US$3) and Taba (US$4.50). The 7.30 am bus goes on to St Catherine's Monastery (US$4.50).

There's a ferry to Hurghada on Monday, Wednesday and Saturday, leaving Sharm el-Sheikh at 9 or 10 am. Tickets (US$30) can be booked through most hotels or at Thomas Cook in Na'ama Bay.

Dahab

The village beach resort of Dahab ('gold') is 85km north of Sharm el-Sheikh on the Gulf of Aqaba. There are two parts to Dahab – in the new part, referred to by the locals as

EGYPT

Dahab City, are the more expensive hotels, bus station, post and phone offices and bank. Assalah, the other part of Dahab, was a Bedouin village and is about 2.5km north of town. It now has more low-budget travellers and Egyptian entrepreneurs than Bedouins in residence. Most travellers come here simply to laze around. Please respect local sensitivities and refrain from sunbathing topless. There's a lot of dope around, but be discreet.

There are seven dive clubs – among the better are Inmo (☎ 64 0370), Nesima (☎ 64 0320) and Fantasea (☎ 64 0043). They offer the full range of diving services as well as combined camel/diving safaris. Snorkellers tend to head for Eel Garden, just north of the village. You can hire snorkelling gear from places along the waterfront.

In the morning, camel drivers and their charges congregate along the waterfront to organise camel trips to the interior of Sinai. Prices for a one day trip including food start at US$15.

Places to Stay & Eat Most, if not all, low-budget travellers head straight for Assalah. There's a plethora of so-called camps, which are basically compounds with simple stone and cement huts with two or three mattresses, generally costing US$1.50 to US$3 per person. Many of the camps are introducing proper rooms with private bathroom, but these are considerably more expensive than the huts. Prices here are always negotiable. The *Auski*, *Star of Dahab* and *Mirage Village* are all good camps.

Heading south from Assalah, the new *Starcosa Hotel* (☎ 64 0366) is a comfortable place offering singles/doubles with fans, private bathroom and hot water for US$15/20 including breakfast.

A string of places along the waterfront in Assalah serve breakfast, lunch and dinner, and most seem to have identical menus hanging up out the front – a meal costs around US$3.

Few people seem to stay at the *Dolphin Camp* but the food here is good, the servings generous and it's one of the few camps where you can drink a beer with your meal. *Tota*, a

ship-shaped place in the heart of Assalah, has the best Italian cuisine on the strip. Next door, the *Italy Pizzeria* arguably does better pizzas.

Getting There & Away The bus station is in Dahab City. The most regular connection is to Sharm el-Sheikh, (1½, US$2), with about six or seven buses running between the two. There are buses to Nuweiba (US$1.80) at 10.30 am and 6.30 and 10.30 pm. The 10.30 am service goes on to Taba (US$3). The 9.30 am bus to St Catherine's (US$3) takes two to three hours. Buses to Cairo (nine hours) leave at 8 am (US$14), 11 am (US$13) and 9.30 pm (US$15).

Nuweiba

The beach and port town of Nuweiba, hardly Sinai's most attractive spot, is 87km north of Dahab. It is divided into three parts. To the south is the port with a major bus station and banks and fairly awful hotels. A few kilometres further north is Nuweiba City, where the tourist resort hotels and one of the area's two dive centres are located, as well as a couple of good places to eat. About 2km north of here, draped along the northern end of Nuweiba's calm bay, is Tarabin, a once tranquil beach-side oasis which, especially during Israeli holidays, is rapidly turning into a party and pick-up place.

Once again, underwater delights are the feature attraction and scuba diving and snorkelling the prime activities. At the Bedouin village of **Mizela**, 1km south of Nuweiba port, you can swim in a bay which has been frequented, for the past few years at any rate, by a dolphin. The village elders charge visitors US$2 to swim and US$1.50 for a mask and snorkel.

Places to Stay & Eat There are three fairly unimpressive hotels you can stay in by the port. The new *Motel Marina* is the best of the trio. Small doubles with shower and air-con are US$9; larger quads cost US$21.

In Nuweiba City, with your own tent you can camp at the *Morgana Restaurant* for US$1, but there's precious little shade. The

Helnan Nuweiba Hotel (US$3) and *City Beach Village* (US$1.50) also take campers.

There are a couple of simple camps with a few huts along the beach south of the Al-Waha Tourism Village, including the overpriced *Sinai Star* and the relaxing *Duna*. The *Helnan Nuweiba Holiday Camp*, next to the hotel, has cabins for US$12/15 a single/double. The nearby *Al-Waha Tourism Village* (☎ 50 0420) has large tents at US$4.50/5 for one/two people or stuffy bungalows (no fan) for US$7/10.

The *City Beach Village*, halfway between Nuweiba City and Tarabin, is one of the best options. You can camp out in one of their reed huts for US$3 per person or go for a clean, comfortable room for US$10/15. In Tarabin you can get a mattress in a bamboo or concrete hut at one of the camps for US$1.50.

Besides the hotels and camps, there's not much to speak of at the port or in Tarabin. In Nuweiba City, *Dr Shishkebab* and *Sendbad* are both excellent budget diners.

Getting There & Away Buses going to or from Taba stop at the Helnan Nuweiba Hotel (11 am and 3 pm to Cairo; 6.30 am and 4 pm to Sharm el-Sheikh) and at Dr Shishkebab in Nuweiba City. They usually also call in at the port but they do not stop at Tarabin.

Nuweiba to Taba

Despite ongoing development in the region, there are still some desolate beaches backed by stunning blue waters and pockets of fringing reefs along this stretch of road. At **Maagana**, there's a row of huts, in honeycomb formation, stretched out along a lovely bay. Another 7km on is **Barracuda Village** which has a series of waterfront stone huts.

At **Basata** (☎ 50 0481), 23km north of Nuweiba, is another simple, clean and carefree travellers' settlement. Its bamboo huts cost US$5 per person. A set dinner costs between US$3.50 and US$5 depending on whether it's vegetarian or with fish. It's advisable to book ahead if you want to stay here.

Taba is the busy crossing point into Israel,

open 24 hours daily. There is a small post and telephone office in the 'town', along with a hospital, bakery and an EgyptAir office (often closed). You can change money at booths of Banque du Caire (unreliable opening hours) and Banque Misr (open 24 hours), both 100m before the border, or at the Taba Hilton Hotel.

St Catherine's Monastery

Twenty-two Greek Orthodox monks live in this ancient monastery at the foot of Mt Sinai. The monastic order was founded in the 4th century AD by the Byzantine empress Helena, who had a small chapel built beside what was believed to be the burning bush from which God spoke to Moses. The chapel is dedicated to St Catherine, the legendary martyr of Alexandria, who was tortured on a spiked wheel and then beheaded for her Christianity.

There is no entry charge to St Catherine's Monastery, but you are only allowed to see the **skull room** (full of the bones of deceased monks), the beautiful **chapel** and some of the icons and jewelled crosses. St Catherine's is open to visitors from 9 am to noon daily except on Friday, Sunday and holidays, when the monastery is closed.

Mt Sinai

At a height of 2285m, Mt Sinai (Gebel Musa is the local name) towers over St Catherine's Monastery. It is revered as the place Moses received the Ten Commandments from God. It is easy to climb – you can take the gentle camel trail or the 3000 Steps of Repentance, carved out by a monk. It takes two to three hours, and most people either stay overnight or climb up in time for sunrise – bring a torch (flashlight). It gets freezing cold in winter.

Places to Stay & Eat St Catherine's Monastery runs a *hostel* which offers a bed in a single-sex dormitory (seven beds) for US$10, and rooms with three beds and private bathroom for US$12 a head. The facilities are basic but clean.

Right by the roundabout, 2km west of the monastery, is the expensive *St Catherine's*

Tourist Village, where singles/doubles cost US$114/135 including breakfast and dinner. Next door is the somewhat grubby *Al-Fairoz Hotel*, where a dormitory bed costs US$4.50 and a mattress in a big tent or in the open air is US$2.30.

In the village of Al-Milga, about 3½km from the monastery, there's a bakery opposite the mosque and a couple of well-stocked supermarkets in the shopping arcade. Just behind the bakery are a few small restaurants, the most reasonable of which is *Look Here*.

The new *Panorama Restaurant*, on the main road near the post office, has pizzas for US$2 to US$5 and sandwiches, pancakes, burgers and soups.

Getting There & Away Buses leave from the square in Al-Milga to Sharm el-Sheikh (US$4.50) via Dahab (US$3) between noon and 1 pm; to Suez (US$5) at 6 am; to Cairo (US$12 – from Taba via Nuweiba) at 10 am; and to Taba (US$6) via Nuweiba (US$3) at 3.30 pm.

SIWA OASIS

The lush and productive Western Desert oasis of Siwa, famous throughout the country for its dates and olives, is 300km south-west of Marsa Matruh and 550km west of Cairo, near the Libyan border. There are no banks or international phones here.

Apart from date palms, there are a couple of **springs** where you can swim, the remains of a **temple** to Amun, some Graeco-Roman **tombs** and a small **museum** of local traditions. The town centre is marked by the remnants of a medieval mud brick **fortress** and **minaret**. Several shops around town sell local crafts such as basketware and jewellery.

Places to Stay & Eat

There are about half a dozen places to stay of which the *Yousef Hotel* remains the cleanest and friendliest. Beds are US$1.50 a night in a share room or US$2.50 in a private room with bathroom. Second choices include the newish *Palm Trees Hotel*, just off the main

square, which charges US$2 a night, and the slightly cheaper but grottier *El Medina*.

The town's top hotel is the 20-room *Arous el-Waha* (☎ 6100). Recently renovated, all the rooms have bathrooms with constant hot water and fans. Singles/doubles will cost US$11/17.

Of the town's handful of eating places the most popular is the *Abdu Restaurant*, across the road from the Yousef Hotel. At the nearby *Alexander Restaurant* you can get excellent lentil soup, vegetarian shakshooka and couscous.

Getting There & Away

The West Delta Bus Co station is on the main square in Siwa. There's a daily bus at 6.30 am to Alexandria (10 hours, US$4), stopping at Marsa Matruh (five hours, US$2) on the way. On Sunday, Tuesday and Thursday, there's a second bus to Alexandria, once again via Marsa Matruh. It departs at 10 am, has air-con and costs US$6 to Alexandria and US$3 to Marsa Matruh. You should book ahead for these services. An additional daily service to Marsa Matruh leaves at 1 pm and costs US$2; no bookings are taken.

SUEZ CANAL

The Suez Canal, one of the greatest feats of modern engineering, links the Mediterranean with the northern end of the Red Sea. Opened in 1869, the canal is now an important source of revenue for Egypt; each ship that passes through the canal is charged a fee based on its size and weight.

The three principal cities along the canal are not top of the list of tourist attractions. Suez suffered badly in the 1967 and 1973 wars and is above all a transit point for tankers, pilgrims to Mecca and people travelling between Sinai and the rest of the country. However, Port Said and, to a lesser extent, Ismailia are full of some attractive examples of late 19th and early 20th century colonial-style architecture.

Port Said

A city of 400,000 people, Port Said was founded in 1859. It is effectively built on an island, connected to the mainland by a bridge to the south and a causeway to the west. Because Port Said is a duty-free zone, there are customs controls on the way in and out of Port Said, and at the train and bus stations. If you are shopping, check before you buy whether the items will be subject to duties.

One of the most pleasant things to do in Port Said is simply to walk the canal-side streets and marvel at the four-storey buildings with wooden balconies and verandahs. You can't miss **Suez Canal House**, the Moorish-style building right on the canal, which you can't enter. The **National Museum** has a good collection of artefacts from all stages of Egyptian history and merits more visitors than it gets. Admission is US$3.50.

Places to Stay & Eat The *Youth Hostel* (☎ 22 8702), near the stadium, costs US$1 with membership card and slightly more without. It has basic bunks in rooms of about 20 beds.

The area around the canal is crawling with little dives. The very basic *Pension Rivoli*, in a lane off Sharia al-Gomhurriya, charges US$1.50 a night for a bed but a much better deal is the *Akri Hotel* (☎ 22 1013), at 24 Sharia al-Gomhurriya. It has clean singles and doubles without bath for about US$4.50/6. The rooms have a bit of charm and are nicely furnished.

Round the corner from the Akri Hotel is the very cheap and very good *Restaurant Soufer*, where arguably the best hummus in Egypt is prepared. Across the road from Akri Hotel is *Reana*, a Chinese-Korean restaurant, and *Cecil*, a spit-and-sawdust bar, which is open until quite late.

Getting There & Away There are three bus terminals but the most useful is in front of the railway station from where Superjet buses leave for Cairo (three hours, US$4.50) 11 times a day. There's also a bus from here to Alexandria (four hours, US$8) at 3.30 pm. Book ahead. There are also four buses daily to Alexandria from the East Delta Bus Co terminal near the Farial Gardens.

There is one slow train to Cairo each day; the 2nd class ordinary/air-con fare is US$1.60/3, while 2nd-class ordinary fare is.

WESTERN DESERT OASES
The five main oases of the Western Desert are attracting a growing number of travellers, but still remain off the main tourist trail. The government has dubbed the string of oases the New Valley Frontier District and hopes to develop the area and so create new possibilities for an exploding population.

Getting There & Away
EgyptAir has two services a week from Cairo to Al-Kharga with one-way fares from US$117.

Asphalt roads link all the oases, four of them in a long loop from Asyut round to Cairo. Siwa (see earlier this chapter), out near the Libyan frontier, is linked by road to Bahariyya but as yet no public transport uses this route.

From Cairo, there are daily buses to: Al-Kharga (nine hours, US$6 to US$9), Dakhla (12 to 14 hours, US$8 to US$11), Farafra (10 to 11 hours, US$7) and Bahariyya (six hours, US$3 to US$4). There are also buses, service taxis and microbuses which link all the oases.

Kharga
About 240km south of Asyut is the largest of the oases, Kharga. The town, Al-Kharga, is the administrative centre of the New Valley Governorate, which also includes Dakhla and Farafra oases. The town is of little interest, but to the north you'll find the **Temple of Hibis**, built for the god Amun by the Persian emperor Darius I.

You can camp in the grounds of the *Kharga Oasis Hotel* for US$2 per person. The four storey *Waha Hotel* (☎ 90 0393) is a reasonable cheapie. If you're coming in from Dakhla, the bus can drop you off at the entrance. Singles/doubles cost US$1.60/3 without bath, or US$3/5 with bath.

Dakhla
Located 190km west of Kharga is the oasis of Dakhla, containing two small towns, Mut

and Al-Qasr. The former is the bigger and has most of the hotels and public utilities. There are government-run **hot springs** 3km to its north. Another 30km brings you to the remarkable medieval mud-brick town of **Al-Qasr**. Watch out for the 12th century minaret.

It's possible to camp near the dunes west of Mut, in Al-Qasr or at the Mut Talata springs for US$1 per person. The only other option in Al-Qasr is the friendly *Al-Qasr Hotel* (☎ 94 0750) on the main road near the entry to the old town. It has four big rooms for US$2 per person. On the ground-floor is a tea house and restaurant which serves good basic fare such as chicken, rice, fuul and salad.

The best deal in Mut is the *Gardens Hotel* (☎ 94 1577), where singles/doubles without bath or fan cost US$3/3.50; with bath US$3.50/4.50. It also has a restaurant and you can rent bikes for US$1.50.

Farafra
Some 300km north-west of Dakhla, Farafra is the smallest and most untouched of the oases. There is really nothing much to see here, except for the palms and fruit trees bearing everything from dates to apricots. About 45km north of town is the stunning **White Desert**, to which you can organise excursions from the town.

There is a *camp site* on a hillock above Bir 6, a hot spring 6km west of town, but the site has no trees, so it's relentlessly hot during the day. The only other place to stay is the *Tourist Rest House* about 1km out along the road to Bahariyya. It costs US$3 per person in comparatively comfortable triple rooms with fans.

Bahariyya
About 185km from Farafra is the oasis of Bahariyya (from where it is another 330km to Cairo). Buses will bring you to Bawiti, the main village. The attractions are limited here to various **springs**. One of the best, Bir Ghaba, is accessible only by 4WD. Ask at the Alpenblick Hotel. You can also go walking to **Black Mountain**.

The *Paradise Hotel* is a pretty dingy place in the centre of Bawiti which charges US$1 a bed. *Ahmed's Safari Camp*, about 4km out of Bawiti has become a bit of a favourite among travellers and trans-Africa groups. It has cool, pleasant, domed double rooms with private bathroom for US$3, rooms with shared facilities for US$1.50, basic reed huts at US$1, and a roof where you can sleep under the stars for US$0.60.

More expensive is the *Alpenblick Hotel* in Bawiti. Large double rooms without/with private bath (and hot water) go for US$10/13 including breakfast. It also has a camp site.

Equatorial Guinea

Away from the mainland town of Bata and the island capital of Malabo, Equatorial Guinea is a land of tropical forests, with cloud-covered volcanoes providing a backdrop to almost every view on Bioko Island.

Facts about the Country

HISTORY

The original inhabitants of mainland Equatorial Guinea were Pygmies and the Ndowe people were the first wave of Bantu migration into the area in the 12th and 13th centuries. The final wave of Bantu migration came in the 13th century with the warlike Fang who quickly became the dominant and most numerous of the tribal groups, as a result of war and intermarriage with the Ndowe. They made foreign occupation attempts a dangerous venture, but they were forced to retreat from the coastal region during the centuries of slave trading by the British, Dutch and French. With the abolition of slavery they once again reoccupied the coast. The island of Bioko was first settled by the Bubi between the 13th and 15th centuries.

The first part of the country to have contact with Europeans was the island of Pagalu, which was visited by the Portuguese in 1470. Portugal subsequently settled Pagalu and the other islands in the Gulf of Guinea – Bioko, São Tomé and Príncipe – until, in the 18th century, it exchanged Bioko and Pagalu as well as parts of the mainland with Spain for certain regions in Latin America.

Bioko itself became an important slave-trading base for several European nations, including Britain, during the early 19th century.

Britain's interest in the island waned as naval bases were set up on the mainland, and control passed back to Spain. Cocoa plantations were started on the island in the late

REPUBLIC OF EQUATORIAL GUINEA
Area: 28,050 sq km
Population: 492,000
Population Growth Rate: 2.6%
Capital: Malabo
Head of State: President Brig Gen (Ret) Teodoro Obiang Nguema Mbasogo
Official Language: Spanish
Currency: Central African CFA franc
Exchange Rate: CFA 575 = US$1
Per Capita GNP: US$430
Inflation: 35%
Time: GMT/UTC + 1

Highlights
- The Spanish colonial architecture of Malabo
- Luba's lively bar life and good beaches
- The rainforests of Bioko and Rio Muni

19th century, making Malabo Spain's most important possession in equatorial Africa. The mainland enclave of Rio Muni was largely ignored, and the interior wasn't even explored by the Spanish until the 1920s.

Equatorial Guinea attained independence in October 1968 under the presidency of Macias Nguema. Several months after independence, however, relations with Spain deteriorated rapidly when it was discovered that the country had almost no foreign currency reserves.

Following a stormy meeting with Nguema, the Spanish ambassador was ordered to leave and a state of emergency was declared. The stage was set for a 10-year dictatorship where the brutality was on a par with that perpetrated by Amin in Uganda and Bokassa in the Central African Republic (CAR). Many thousands of people were tortured and executed in the jails of Malabo and Bata, or beaten to death in the forced-labour camps of the mainland. By the time Nguema's regime was toppled in 1979 only one-third of the 300,000 Guineans who lived there at independence remained.

It wasn't just political figures, intellectuals and expatriates who were persecuted. The Catholic Church, too, was dragged into the net. Priests were arrested and expelled for plots real or imaginary, and in 1975 all mission-run schools were closed, effectively putting an end to formal education in the country. This was followed in 1978 by the forced closure of all churches.

With the country in shambles, bankrupt and all economic activity at a standstill, even Nguema's closest colleagues began to suspect that he was insane, and he was toppled in a coup in August 1979. He was executed a month later.

The new government was headed by the

present leader, Obiang Nguema Mbasogo (Macias Nguema's nephew), and it seemed for a while that order and some degree of political freedom might be restored. To a degree it was, but the situation was still far from ideal.

On the other hand, the government did make at least one major constructive move, which was to join the CFA franc zone. This enabled the country to trade more extensively with its neighbours Gabon and Cameroon. It also prompted the International Monetary Fund (IMF) and the World Bank to come up with loans and have the country's foreign debt rescheduled.

Equatorial Guinea has since embarked on the path to multiparty democracy, despite a further hiatus in relations with Spain in the late 1980s. Progress had been slow but multiparty elections were held in 1993 and again in 1996. However, power still firmly rests with Obiang Nguema and his kinsmen.

Oil, however, has changed the picture – at least for some. Mobil has two rigs offshore of Bioko Island and they came on line in early 1997. If the income from this is spent wisely, it will transform the lives of the country's inhabitants.

GEOGRAPHY & CLIMATE

The most economically important part of Equatorial Guinea, Bioko, is formed from three extinct volcanoes. It's a rugged, jungle-covered island and its main products are cocoa, coffee, bananas and palm oil. The nation's capital, Malabo, is also here.

The mainland, Rio Muni, has been largely bypassed in the 20th century. Though there are a number of coffee plantations, it's mostly gently rising, thickly forested country with an abundance of wildlife and interesting villages where traditional beliefs survive.

The rainy season runs from April to January, and humidity is high at this time.

POPULATION & PEOPLE

The population of Equatorial Guinea is around 500,000. The largest tribal group is the Fang, who make up about 80% of the population of Rio Muni (320,000). Minor tribal groups include the Kombe, Balengue and Bujeba. On Bioko the most numerous group was formerly the Bubi, but for economic reasons many Fang were forced to migrate to the island, where they now outnumber the others.

LANGUAGE

Spanish is the official language, but isn't as widely spoken as its status suggests. Some French is spoken. The main local language is Fang; Bubi is common on Bioko. See the Language Appendix.

Facts for the Visitor

VISAS

Visas are required by everyone. The Equatorial Guinea embassy in Yaoundé and the consulate in Douala (Cameroon) both give same-day service without problems. Single-entry visas valid for a stay of one month cost US$60 (US$72 in Douala) and you need one photo (three in Douala). Multiple-entry visas may cost more.

Visa Extensions

Visa extensions for an extra 15 days are obtainable in Malabo and Bata for US$20 plus a photo. They are issued in 24 hours.

Other Visas

Cameroon

> Multiple-entry visas, valid for a stay of three months, are obtainable at the embassy in Malabo or the consulate in Bata. They cost US$60 plus one photo, and are issued the same day in the afternoon.

Gabon

> The Gabonese embassy in Malabo and the consulate in Bata both issue visas to Gabon, usually quickly and without any major hassles. They cost US$80 plus US$10 for a telex to Libreville and require two photos. Visas can take about one week to issue, but are usually issued in a few hours.

EQUATORIAL GUINEA

Nigeria

The embassy in Malabo and the consulate in Bata issue visas without hassle but the price varies according to your nationality. Expect US$30 (but a staggering US$214 for UK passport holders!) plus you also need three photos and an onward airline ticket. The visa allows for a stay of one month (renewable).

São Tomé & Príncipe

The embassy in Malabo is on Calle de Acacio Muñe. It's a little hard to find as there's no plaque and the flag is half-hidden by trees and shrubs – it's just a family house. Visas valid for a stay of seven days (renewable) cost US$30 and you need one photo. You collect your passport within three hours.

Other Countries

For visas to Burkina Faso, the Central African Republic, Chad, Côte d'Ivoire and Togo, enquire at the French embassy in Malabo.

EMBASSIES
Equatorial Guinean Embassies

In Africa there are embassies or consulates in Cameroon (Yaoundé and Douala), Ethiopia, Gabon, Morocco, Nigeria (Lagos and Calabar) and São Tomé & Príncipe. Other countries with embassies or consulates include France, Germany, Spain and the USA.

Foreign Embassies in Equatorial Guinea

Countries with diplomatic representation in Malabo include:

Cameroon
    Calle de Rey Boncoro (☎ 2263)
France
    Carretera del Aeropuerto (☎ 2005)
Gabon
    Calle de Argelia (☎ 2420)
Nigeria
    Paseo de los Cocoteros (☎ 2386)
Spain
    Parque de las Avdas de África (☎ 2020)

The US embassy and British high commission in Yaoundé, Cameroon handles US and UK relations with Equatorial Guinea. The British consulate recommends the French embassy in Malabo for help.

MONEY

US$1 = CFA 575

The unit of currency is the Central African CFA franc.

Currency exchange is straightforward but there's little choice of banks. The best in Malabo is the BIAO on Calle de Argelia. Cash can also be changed with expatriates in the bar at the Hotel Ureca, the Pizza Place and at Le Bantu disco.

In Bata, go to the BEAC bank where the commission is much lower. Cheques and cash can also be changed at the Pizzaria Central.

Warning

Officially, travellers carrying cash in excess of CFA 50,000 must declare it on entry, otherwise the difference may be confiscated on exit.

POST & COMMUNICATIONS

Both of these are reliable, including poste restante (lista de correos in Spanish), in Malabo and Bata. Don't count on it elsewhere.

Both Malabo and Bata (but nowhere else) have satellite communications with the rest of the world and connections are virtually guaranteed. Telephone/fax charges per minute are US$4 to the USA, US$6.50 to the European Union (EU) or Australia. Phone cards are available.

The country code for Equatorial Guinea is 240. The area code for Malabo is 09, and for Bata it's 08.

PHOTOGRAPHY

A photo permit is essential if you want to keep your film and camera and avoid major hassles with the police. This takes 24 hours but costs a whopping US$50. A request must be typed (preferably in Spanish, but French or English are grudgingly accepted) on official stationery (US$3), obtainable from the Ministry of Culture, Tourism & Francophone Relations on Calle de Kenia. (The Ministry will let you use their typewriters.) This permit is almost as important as your passport. Get one!

Don't take photographs of anything vaguely connected with the government, the military, communications facilities, the airports or the presidential palace.

PUBLIC HOLIDAYS

Holidays observed in Equatorial Guinea include: 1 January, 1 May, 25 May, 12 October (Independence), 10 December, Good Friday and Easter Monday.

ACCOMMODATION

Those on a budget will find themselves staying mainly at guesthouses (known in Spanish as *hostales* or *residencias*). These can be either private houses with a few guest rooms or small hotels. Costs vary between US$4 and US$10. Meals are sometimes available.

Hotels, as such, tend to be expensive and scarce even in Malabo and Bata. You're looking at a minimum of US$30 a night with private bathroom but without air-con.

Getting There & Away

AIR

Two airlines connect Malabo and Bata with Douala (Cameroon) twice weekly. They are Ecuato Guineana de Aviacion (EGA; ☎ 94 497), which costs US$124 return Malabo to Douala or US$90 weekend special, and Air Affaires Afrique (☎ 93 179 and 8 254), which charges US$240 return to/from Malabo. Cameroon Airlines also flies between Douala and Malabo (US$125 return) at least once a week.

EGA also connects Malabo and Bata with Libreville (Gabon) weekly (US$286 return).

The only direct connection with Europe is with Iberia which flies Malabo to Madrid.

The airport departure tax for international flights is US$10.

LAND
Cameroon

The usual route is via Ebebiyin and Ambam (Cameroon). From the Cameroon border

town of Kye Ossi it's pretty easy to get a truck or minibus to Ambam and on to Ebolowa.

You can also enter Cameroon via the coast by pick-up or minibus from Bata and Bongoro to either Yengué or Lendé on the Rio Ntem. From either of these villages (where you go through immigration and customs) there are daily motorised *pirogues* (dugout canoes) across the river to Ipono (Cameroon) for US$8 which leave when full. From Ipono, there are pick-ups to Campo and others from there to Kribi.

Gabon

From Bata there are pick-ups to Mbini, and from there to Acayalong. Pirogues take you to Cogo (the police station handles Equatorial Guinean customs and immigration) and across the Estuario del Muni to Cocobeach (Gabonese customs and immigration). The pirogue journey takes about four hours including the stop at Cogo and costs US$8. From Cocobeach it's another 2½ hours to Libreville by pick-up.

Going from Bata to Libreville via Acurenam is not an option as you cannot cross the border at that point.

SEA
Cameroon

You can forget about boats between Malabo and Douala unless you want to sit it out on one of the nightly beer runs in a small, open-topped boat with no facilities whatsoever. They dock in Malabo at the new port, and shouldn't cost more than US$40.

Getting Around

AIR

EGA operates flights between Malabo and Bata in either direction daily except Monday (US$56).

MINIBUS

On the mainland, there are minibuses from Bata to Mbini (US$3; one hour, including a ferry from Bolondo to Mbini) and others from there to Acalayong (US$10; six hours).

Going inland, there are minibuses between Bata and Ebebiyin which take eight to 10 hours during the dry season. There are also bush taxis and minibuses along the Bata to Mongomo and Bata to Evinayong routes which take about five or six hours.

BUSH TAXI

On Bioko, there are good bush taxi connections between Malabo and the island's two other major towns, Luba (US$3; one hour) and Riaba (US$4; 1½ hours).

BOAT

The *Acacio Mañe*, a large passenger boat, sails from Malabo to Bata every night and back again the following day. The journey takes 12 hours and costs US$24 in deck class and US$40 in cabin class. There's a bar on board and food is available.

Bioko Island

MALABO

The capital of Equatorial Guinea, Malabo, is a relatively small but beautiful town. It's full of Spanish colonial buildings and open plazas with cloud-capped Pico Malabo (3106m) as a backdrop which, incidentally, is a military area and out of bounds.

Though allowed to deteriorate for many years, the town is now looking quite smart after the president ordered a face-lift and everyone got down to it with brush and paint! Malabo is where Frederick Forsyth wrote his novel *The Dogs of War*.

Places to Stay

The cheapest budget hotel is *Residencia Ana José/Hostal Residencia*, in the centre of town on Ave de la Independencia. Owned by an old Spanish lady, it's clean and pleasant with rooms for US$8.

Also good value are the *Hostal Nely* and the *Hostal Chana*, opposite each other on Avenida de las Naciónes Unidas. Both of them

offer clean double rooms with fan and shared bathroom facilities for US$10. The Nely has a bar and the manager speaks English.

Considerably more expensive is the *Bar Restaurant Hotel Candy* (☎ 2093), at the junction of Calle Hipolita Eworo and Calle de Paulio Pun, which has doubles with bathroom and fan for US$30.

Places to Eat

Cheap places to eat include *El Guiso*, on Calle de Mongomo between Calle de Rey Boncoro and Calle de Nigeria; *La Toya*, on Calle de Nigeria near the junction with Avenida de Bata; and *Café-Bar Elvis*, on Calle de Acacio Muñe between Calle de Nigeria and Calle del Alcalde Balboa.

For an excellent, tasty lunch at around US$4, give *Restaurant Gué-Gué* on Avenida de la Independencia a try.

Up in price, *El Barín*, diagonally opposite the Gué-Gué, is a popular place for lunch and dinner. Known as the Spanish Bar, it's run by Spanish people and the food is excellent. Light seafood meals with chips cost around US$3. The pavement bar is equally popular.

For Chinese cuisine, try either the *Bar Restaurant Chino* or the *Restaurante Cantong*. Prices are similar to those at El Barín.

Very popular with expatriates is *Pizza Place*, Avenida de la Independencia, which is Lebanese-run. The food is superb and the salads are a meal in themselves but it can be expensive (up to US$8).

The new *Mesa Verde* on Calle de Argelia is similarly priced, offers European-style food and also has a terrace overlooking the bay.

Entertainment

Popular bars include *La Cubana* (known locally as Delphine's), a pavement bar with cheap, cold beers which is open afternoons and evenings; the *American Bar/Restaurant* on the corner of Avenida 3 de Agosto and Calle de Acacio Muñe; and *El Barín*.

The most popular disco/nightclub is *Le Bantu* at the junction of Calle del Alcalde Balboa and Calle de Acacio Muñe. Entry is free, beers cost US$2 and it gets going

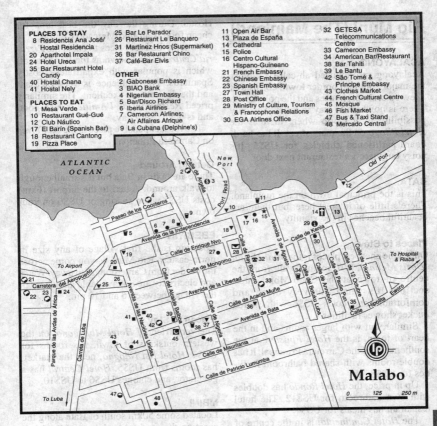

PLACES TO STAY
8 Residencia Ana José/
Hostal Residencia
20 Aparthotel Impala
24 Hotel Ureca
35 Bar Restaurant Hotel
Candy
40 Hostal Chana
41 Hostal Nely

PLACES TO EAT
1 Mesa Verde
10 Restaurant Gué-Gué
12 Club Náutico
17 El Barín (Spanish Bar)
18 Restaurant Cantong
19 Pizza Place

25 Bar Le Parador
26 Restaurant Le Banquero
31 Martínez Hnos (Supermarket)
36 Bar Restaurant Chino
37 Café-Bar Elvis

OTHER
2 Gabonese Embassy
3 BIAO Bank
4 Nigerian Embassy
5 Bar/Disco Richard
6 Iberia Airlines
7 Cameroon Airlines;
Air Affaires Afrique
9 La Cubana (Delphine's)

11 Open Air Bar
13 Plaza de España
14 Cathedral
15 Police
16 Centro Cultural
Hispano-Guineano
21 French Embassy
22 Chinese Embassy
23 Spanish Embassy
27 Town Hall
28 Post Office
29 Ministry of Culture, Tourism
& Francophone Relations
30 EGA Airlines Office

32 GETESA
Telecommunications
Centre
33 Cameroon Embassy
34 American Bar/Restaurant
38 Bar Tahiti
39 Le Bantu
42 São Tomé &
Príncipe Embassy
43 Clothes Market
44 French Cultural Centre
45 Mosque
46 Fish Market
47 Bus & Taxi Stand
48 Mercado Central

Malabo

around 11 pm. Much more down-to-earth is the *Bar/Disco Richard*.

The *Centro Cultural Hispano-Guineano* is a lively spot and hosts many cultural events as well as the occasional dance.

Getting Around
There are taxis in Malabo but it's small enough to walk around. To the airport (about 7km) costs US$6.

AROUND BIOKO
Luba
For the best beaches on the island of Bioko,

head towards Luba, 50km (an hour's taxi ride) south-west of Malabo. It's a pleasant, relaxing place to spend a weekend. Luba is the island's second-largest town with about 1000 inhabitants.

Places to Stay & Eat On the waterfront at the western edge of town is the popular *Hotel Jemaro*, which has recently renovated rooms on the 2nd floor with balconies and a view across the beach for US$10. It's run by an old man who speaks Spanish and French. The seafood here is excellent (US$4 per dish).

EQUATORIAL GUINEA

Rio Muni (The Mainland)

ACALAYONG

Acalayong (pronounced ah-cah-LYE-ong), the major southern border town, consists of a few bars, shops, houses and the police post. There is nowhere to stay in town. The only possibility is at **Cogo** where there is the *Hotel Bilogo* on the main street. It has hardboard-partitioned cubicles for US$5. It's noisy but there's a restaurant next door.

BATA

This is the principal town on the mainland. There's little of interest here, but there are beautiful beaches in the vicinity.

Places to Stay

One of the cheapest places is the *Mini-Hostal 'Doris Melina'*, a 10 minute walk from the centre of town at the Cogo-Mbini intersection. It's small but very clean and comfortable and costs US$6 with shared bucket shower facilities.

Similar, but with larger rooms and in the heart of town, is the *Hotel Finistère* at the southern end of the Carretera Principal. It has double rooms with shared bathroom facilities for US$8.

Up in price, the *Hotel Rondo* has doubles with own bathroom for US$12. The hotel restaurant has meals for US$4.

The *Hotel Continental* is in the centre of town on the 2nd storey of a building on Calle del Mercado, about 200m north of Mercado Central. It's not the cleanest of places but has rooms for US$12.

The best place to stay is the *Apartamentos Nnang Afang* which costs US$16 (after negotiation) for a room with own bathroom.

Places to Eat

For street food at night, try the intersection just west of the hospital or near the Mini-Hostal. During the day the best area for cheap food is around Mercado Central.

Among the best places to eat is the *Pizzaria Central* (also known as the Bar Central) which is popular with expatriates, mostly Spaniards. The ambience is very pleasant and the desserts are excellent. The similarly priced *Restaurant de l'Amitié* is also good and is open every day.

The most expensive place is the *La Ferme* on Carretera Principal.

Getting Around

There are taxis in Bata but it's small enough to walk around. A taxi to the airport (6km) costs US$1 when sharing or US$6 on your own.

EBEBIYIN

Ebebiyin is the first village of any size in north-eastern Rio Muni as you come across the border from Cameroon, 2km away. Water and electricity are not available anywhere in the village between 6 and 10 pm.

Places to Stay

The very friendly *Hotel Mbengono*, on the western outskirts of town, has rooms for US$4. *Hotel Nsi Ndogno*, near the market, has rooms from US$5. *Hotel Central* has a generator, and charges US$6 to US$10.

MBINI

Located some 50km south of Bata along the coast on the road to Acalayong, Mbini is a pleasant, small town at the mouth of the Rio Benito. It's a good destination if you're looking for deserted beaches.

There are two places to stay in town. Immediately on your left as you disembark from the ferry is the *Hostal Restaurant Pantala* ... (the rest of the sign is missing), which has reasonable rooms for US$5. Kerosene lamps and mosquito coils are provided and meals are available. The *Hotel Parador*, further towards the plaza, is similar.

Eritrea

Eritrea is Africa's newest country, formed in 1993 when its people voted in a referendum to secede from Ethiopia. This was the final chapter in a war which had lasted for more than 30 years, during which Eritreans learned to fend for themselves. This same spirit of self-reliance has been the force behind massive highway construction and rural regeneration programmes, including the planting of over a million tree seedlings. Eritrea is a buoyant, vigorous, though impoverished nation, keen not to become anybody's client. Its people have a dignity, self-respect and disinterested friendliness that is a particular tonic if you've just arrived from the hustling and hassles of Ethiopia or Egypt. Get there before things change.

Facts about the Country

HISTORY

During the 1st millennium BC, tribes from present-day Yemen migrated to the southern highlands of Eritrea, settling on both sides of today's Eritrean-Ethiopian border. The descendant of their language, Ge'ez, is still used in church liturgy, and the contemporary Tigrinya and Amharic languages are still written in its script.

The celebrated Axumite kingdom flourished in Eritrea from the 1st to the 9th century AD. While Axum itself was in today's Ethiopia, important Axumite towns – in particular the sea port of Adulis – were built in Eritrea.

After Islam's rise in the 7th century AD, Axum's decline began. Adulis was destroyed in 710, and for centuries the dividing line between the Muslim coast of the Red Sea and the Christian Ethiopian highlands moved back and forth over what is now Eritrea.

From the early 16th century to the late 19th century, the Egyptians and the Ottoman

---

ERITREA
Area: 124,000 sq km
Population: 3.6 million
Population Growth Rate: 3.3%
Capital: Asmara
Head of State: President Isaias Afwerke
Official Languages: Arabic, Tigrinya
Currency: Ethiopian birr
Exchange Rate: Birr 7.2 = US$1
Per Capita GNP: US$120
Inflation: 11%
Time: GMT/UTC + 3

Highlights
- The spectacular winding descent from the central highlands to Massawa on the Red Sea coast
- Asmara's National Museum – once it reopens
- Local cuisine, washed down with a glass of mead, in the Milano Restaurant, Asmara
- The dusty alleys of Massawa
- Keren's seething Monday livestock market

Turks fought each other for control of the Eritrean coast and its ports.

In 1869 the Italian Rubattino Shipping Company bought some land in the Bay of Assab. In 1885 the Italians extended their rule to Massawa. They then marched upon the highlands despite severe military setbacks in Dogali in 1887 and Adwa in 1896. What had started as the acquisition of a couple of ports soon developed into large-scale

ERITREA

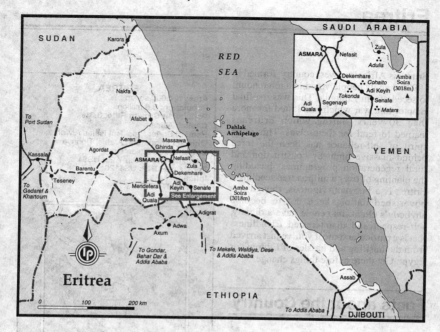

Eritrea

agricultural colonialism, and thousands of Italian peasants settled in the region in the last quarter of the 19th century.

A series of border treaties were signed: with the French over the southern border of present-day Djibouti; with the British over the northern border of Sudan; and with Ethiopia over the greatest length of the border. Eritrea's present-day frontiers and the foundations of an Eritrean identity had been laid.

The Italians invested heavily in Eritrea, building roads, railways, ports and factories, and establishing plantations. Indeed, it's questionable whether Italy was a net beneficiary from its investments in Eritrea.

In 1936 Mussolini invaded Ethiopia from Eritrea. When the Allied forces defeated the Italian army in 1941, Italy was forced to give up its three African possessions: Eritrea, Libya and southern Somalia. Eritrea was administered by the British until 1952, when a contentious United Nations (UN) resolu-

tion granted Eritrea self-government within a federal union with Ethiopia.

Gradually more and more Eritreans turned against the Ethiopians who, they felt, were colonising their country. In 1961 a few Eritreans attacked an Ethiopian police station with two stolen pistols – an incident regarded today as the starting point of Africa's longest war this century. In 1962 Ethiopia's Emperor Haile Selassie unilaterally, and in defiance of the UN, annexed Eritrea as Ethiopia's 14th province.

The Eritrean Liberation Front (ELF), founded the previous year, was by no means homogeneous. Separate Muslim and Christian guerrilla groups attacked Ethiopians here and there, gradually winning support from the people but building internal tensions too. Between 1965 and 1969, hundreds of ELF fighters were killed, not only by Ethiopians but also by their co-fighters.

In 1970 the Eritrean People's Liberation

The Railway

The Italian-built railway which curled its way up from Massawa on the coast to 2128m before dropping to Asmara was, with its 30 tunnels and 65 bridges, a masterpiece of civil engineering. Neglected, its rails ripped up for trench reinforcement, it was one of the many casualties of war. Come peace, the Eritreans asked for international help in its rehabilitation. Too costly, said the Italian consultants. Other donors shied away or imposed crippling conditions. So the Eritreans are going it alone, pulling old railway workers and blacksmiths out of retirement, calling upon volunteers, thumbing their noses at international donors and making *their* railway one more symbol of self-reliance. ■

Forces (EPLF, later Front) was founded. With its ideological roots in Marxism, the EPLF fought a bitter civil war from 1972 to 1974 against the more conservative, Arab-supported ELF. The ELF lost ground steadily, and in 1987 the remaining ELF leadership merged with the EPLF. The EPLF has since abandoned hardline Marxism while carrying out land reform and other significant changes.

In 1974 Mengistu Haile Mariam, a Communist dictator, rose to power in Ethiopia, and in 1977 the Soviet Union began its massive support of the Ethiopian army. As a result, in 1978 the EPLF, which was on the point of overrunning the whole country, was forced to withdraw from the towns it controlled in the face of aerial raids, heavy artillery and tanks. This event is commemorated as the 'Strategic Withdrawal', crucial to the survival of the resistance.

From 1978 to 1986, the Ethiopian army carried out eight major offensives against the EPLF, all of which were repulsed. The fighting grew from hit-and-run guerrilla attacks to a war between two permanent armies, with frontlines and trenches in the style of WWI.

In 1988 the EPLF inflicted major losses on the Ethiopian army, capturing its northern headquarters in Afabet and taking Keren, the second-largest town in Eritrea. In 1990 the Ethiopians lost the port of Massawa and then blanket-bombed it. Finally, in 1991 the EPLF entered Asmara unopposed.

A Provisional Government of Eritrea (PGE) was established under the leadership of Isaias Afwerke, a senior EPLF military commander, who is now president of the country.

Less than a decade after the bitter, protracted civil war, there's a unique harmony between Eritrea and Ethiopia. This is primarily because, as Eritrea was gaining its independence, Ethiopia itself was engaged in its own revolutionary struggle against Mengistu's regime in Addis Ababa. And because Isaias Afwerke and Meles Zenawi, the Ethiopian head of state, are both friends and battle-seasoned commanders who fought against a common enemy. The two leaders immediately resolved the major issue that was blocking Eritrea's independence: Eritrea guaranteed landlocked Ethiopia vital sea access through the port of Assab.

In April 1993 the PGE held a referendum, regarded as clean and free by international monitors, in which Eritreans voted for independence by the resounding figure of 99.8%.

The country is now run by the People's Front for Democracy and Justice (PFDJ), a political offshoot of the EPLF. A constitutional commission has finalised a draft constitution which will be submitted for approval to a Constituent Assembly, for which elections were held in 1997.

GEOGRAPHY & CLIMATE

Eritrea is bordered to the west by Sudan, to the south by Ethiopia and to the south-east by Djibouti. It has three climatic zones: the densely populated central highlands, the Red Sea coastal plain to the east and the western lowlands.

Several mountains exceed 2500m, with the highest peak, Amba Soira, reaching 3018m. The country is generally arid or semi-arid, with no permanent rivers or sizeable lakes. Offshore lies the Dahlak Archipelago, the largest in the Red Sea.

The highland climate is moderate, with an

ERITREA

average annual temperature of 16°C and afternoon temperatures which never exceed 30°C. The main rainy season is from late June to early September, with lighter rains in March and April.

On the coastal plain, daily temperatures range between 18°C and 32°C from December to February, when there are light rains. Between June and August, afternoon temperatures frequently exceed 40°C and the humidity is high. The driest and hottest part of the country is the low-lying south-eastern Danakil Province, which very rarely receives rain.

In the western lowlands, temperatures can also reach 40°C during the hottest months of April to June.

The average annual rainfall along the coastal belt is less than 200mm. However, at around 1500m, in a tiny pocket on the long descent from Asmara and the plateau to Massawa and the coast, there's a tropical, intensively cultivated area which receives more than 1000mm of rain annually.

POPULATION & PEOPLE

Eritrea's population is 3.6 million. The country is ethnically diverse, with nine major tribes or clans: Afar, Bilen, Hadareb, Kunama, Nara, Rashaida, Saho, Tigre and Tigrinya.

Around 80% of the population live in rural areas, some 35% of them nomadic or semi-nomadic.

The population is about half Muslim and half Christian. The predominantly agricultural Christians (of the Eritrean Orthodox church) live mainly in the highlands, while the majority of Muslims are concentrated in the coastal areas and towards the Sudanese border.

The New Eritrean Woman
Over one third of freedom fighters were women. In liberated, secular Eritrea, they now enjoy equal property rights, the right to divorce and to custody of children in any settlement, the entitlement to vote and the ability to acquire land. All of this is guaranteed by law. ∎

LANGUAGE

Arabic, common in the coastal areas, and Tigrinya, used widely in the highlands, are recognised as joint official languages. Each of the nine ethnic groups speaks its own language: Afar, Bilen, To Bedawi, Kunama, Nara, Arabic, Saho, Tigre and Tigrinya. Amharic, a legacy of Ethiopian rule, is also still widely spoken.

Until independence, only Arabic, Tigre and Tigrinya had a written form. Nowadays, Eritrea is developing a script, using the Latin alphabet, for the remaining six languages as a way of reinforcing regional culture and identity.

You'll find English surprisingly useful, not least because during the war most families had at least one member abroad, and most returnees from Western Europe or North America speak it fluently.

Facts for the Visitor

VISAS

Visa requirements vary arbitrarily from one Eritrean consulate to another. In principle, you're supposed to get your visa from the embassy in your home country, or the one deemed to serve your country. This isn't always observed, particularly if you can show that you've visited other countries between leaving home and applying. If you're applying en route, you may be asked to produce a letter of recommendation from your embassy, or an onward ticket, or neither.

A one month visa issued by the embassy in Addis Ababa states that it's valid from the date of issue. However, the Department of Immigration in Asmara confirms the more liberal interpretation of 'from the date of arrival in Eritrea'.

Visa Extensions

The Department of Immigration in Asmara will extend your visa for a further month in return for US$35 and one photo.

Other Visas
Djibouti
French Nationals are exempt. A one month visa, issued the same day, costs US$20. Bring two photos. The embassy is open from 7 am to 3 pm on weekdays.

Egypt
A one month visa costs US$15 and is issued the same day. You need one photo. The consulate is open from 10 am to 1 pm on weekdays.

Ethiopia
A one month visa costs US$63, payable in cash (travellers' cheques are not accepted). Bring one photo and reserves of patience; the obstacle course from office to office *can* be completed in one visit. The embassy is open Monday to Thursday from 8 am to noon and until 11.30 on Friday.

Saudi Arabia
If you're travelling by boat to Egypt via Jeddah (see under Sea in the following Getting There & Away section), you can get a 72 hour transit visa, valid for one month from the date of issue (the authorities in Jeddah will extend this if there's no connecting ferry within three days). It costs US$15, and you need one photo and an Egyptian visa already stamped in your passport. The visa section is open from 10.30 am to 2.30 pm on weekdays.

Sudan
There's currently no Sudanese embassy in Asmara. It was closed by the Eritreans who, as a calculated slight, allow the premises to be used as the headquarters of the National Democratic Alliance, a consortium of Sudanese opposition groups in exile. Now there's style!

EMBASSIES
Eritrean Embassies
Eritrea has embassies or consulates abroad in Australia, Belgium, Canada, Djibouti, Egypt, Ethiopia, Germany, Kenya, UK, USA and Yemen, among other countries.

Foreign Embassies in Eritrea
Countries with diplomatic representation in Asmara include:

Djibouti
Andinnet St (☎ 181010)
Egypt
5 Degiat Afwerk St (☎ 124935)
Ethiopia
Franklin D Roosevelt St (☎ 120736)
France
Victory St (☎ 126599)

Saudi Arabia
20-24 Workers' St (☎ 121071)
UK (consulate)
Emperor Yohannes Ave (☎ 120145)
USA
Franklin D Roosevelt St (☎ 120342)
Yemen (consulate)
Tesfalidet St (☎ 114434)

MONEY
US$1 = Birr 7.2
US$1 = Nakfa 7.2

After independence, Eritrea used the Ethiopian birr, which equals 100 cents, pending the introduction of its own currency, the nakfa. Eritrea allows the export and import of birr to and from Ethiopia, without having to complete a currency declaration form (however, the Ethiopians have their own regulations; see the Money section in the Ethiopia chapter for details). Currency import and export arrangements for the nakfa were still being discussed at the time of writing.

Eritrea is refreshingly free of street moneychangers. If you do indulge, you're taking a big risk for a trivial gain.

Credit cards are very rarely accepted outside Ethiopian Airlines offices and a few of the top hotels in Asmara.

POST & COMMUNICATIONS
International mail can be slow, but it almost invariably reaches its destination.

For international phone calls, the Telecommunications Office in Asmara is swift and efficient; less so in the provinces. A three minute call costs US$8 to the USA, US$8.50 to the UK and US$11.60 to Australia. The country code for Eritrea is 291. The area code for Asmara is 01.

TFanus Enterprise (☎ 124050; email tfanus@gemel.com.er) offers Internet access, charging US$0.70/0.25 per outgoing/incoming messages.

BOOKS
Eritrea at a Glance, edited by Mary Houdek & Leonardo Oriolo, is an excellent, locally produced guide, written primarily for expat residents.

HEALTH

Malaria is endemic in the western lowlands, Keren and on the coastal plain, where dengue fever is also prevalent.

In the highlands, the sun's rays are fiercer than they feel. It would be wise to plaster on the sunblock especially in the early days of your stay.

If you arrive by air, the sudden change to living at over 2000m may induce mild altitude sickness. Symptoms, which usually disappear after a couple of days, are headaches, lightheadedness and shortage of breath. Also see the Health Appendix.

DANGERS & ANNOYANCES

There are still thousands of uncharted mines around the countryside. Never stray off the road or a well-trodden track.

Eritrea is one of the safest countries in Africa to travel around. All the same, follow the example of the locals and make sure you're off out-of-town roads by dusk.

BUSINESS HOURS & PUBLIC HOLIDAYS

In 1997 the government decreed working hours for public sector bodies of 7 am to noon and 2 to 6 pm. Time will tell whether such a punishing schedule can be made to stick.

Shop hours are variable, the majority closing between 2 and 4 pm. Muslim shopkeepers close for Friday prayers; Christians close on Sunday afternoon.

National and Eritrean Orthodox public holidays fall on 1 January, 7 January, 19 January, 8 March, 1 May, 24 May, 20 June, 1 September, 11 September and 27 September. Easter and Islamic holidays are variable (see Public Holidays in the Regional Facts for the Visitor chapter).

FOOD & DRINK

In true Italian style, Asmara's innumerable bars serve espresso, macchiato (with just a splash of milk) and cappuccino, while restaurants offer *primi piatti* (entrées) and *secondi piatti* (main courses).

For typical local dishes, see the section on Food & Drink in the Ethiopia chapter. The terms are the same except for *wat*, the fiery sauce, which is known as *zigne* in Tigrinya, and *t'ej*, or mead, which is called *meis* here, while home-brew beer, *t'ella*, enjoys the splendid – and unfairly deprecating – name, *sewa*. If you prefer vegetarian food, ask for *nai tsom*, a selection of vegetable dishes traditionally served during times of fasting. As in Ethiopia, everything is served on *injera*, the carbohydrate staple with the texture of those hot towels that the better airlines pass round after takeoff.

Melotti beer and the local Asmara ouzo or gin with tonic are refreshing, but Asmara wine is no cause for celebration.

Coffee is normally served ultra sweet unless you specify otherwise when you order.

Getting There & Away

AIR

Eritrea is served by EgyptAir (☎ 127492), Ethiopian Airlines (☎ 125436, 127512), Lufthansa (☎ 182707) and Saudia (☎ 120 166). Eritrean Airlines doesn't actually fly yet, but acts as a ticketing agency for Lufthansa. Airport departure tax is US$10.

LAND
Djibouti

Travel overland to Djibouti is for the seriously adventurous only. There are only tracks and dirt roads used by Afar nomads.

Ethiopia

There are two tarmac routes from Asmara to Ethiopia. The first goes via Mendefera and Adi Quala to Axum in Ethiopia. This is the choice if you want to travel Ethiopia's Historic Route (see Around the Country in the Ethiopia chapter). There are three buses a week (US$3), which take about six hours to Axum, excluding time at the border. You need to book a day in advance.

The Ethiopian leg of the second route, which goes via Dekemhare and Senafe then over the frontier to Adigrat, is less gruelling than the Historic Route – but infinitely less interesting. There are three buses a week (US$12.50) between Asmara and Addis Ababa. The journey takes three days, with the first overnight stop at Mekele in Ethiopia.

There's also a good road from Assab in southern Eritrea to Addis Ababa – but getting from Asmara to Assab is an altogether different experience (see the Assab entry in Around the Country later in this chapter).

Sudan

For the moment, don't even try travelling overland to Sudan. The Eritrean side is quite safe, but the border is officially closed to foreigners and there's sporadic, but fierce, fighting on the Sudanese side.

When diplomatic relations are restored and the security situation improves, it will again be possible to take a bus directly from Asmara to Kassala in Sudan. The previous journey time of up to three days will be reduced by the extension of the sealed road from Asmara, ultimately as far as Teseney.

SEA

The Saudi Baabour Line's car/passenger service sails about once a week between Massawa and Jeddah, sometimes calling in Suakin in Sudan. In Asmara, you can get advance information from the Red Sea Shipping & Tourist Agency (☎ 120143) or Saik Trading & Services (☎ 119168). In Massawa, tickets (US$82) for the 32 hour journey can be booked at Saik Trading & Services/Nakfa Travel Agency (☎ 552642) opposite the open-air cinema, or at the minute office of Shumdehan (☎ 552715) behind the Banco d'Italia. You can only book the onward trip to Suez (US$66 deck class) once you arrive in Jeddah – try Wadi Alneel Company or ETC Shipping. See also Saudi Arabia under Other Visas in the earlier Facts for the Visitor section.

Getting Around

AIR

Eritrean Airlines, whose future pilots and ground staff are currently undergoing training abroad, runs only two domestic flights a week. They are between Asmara and Assab and cost US$38 one way. As first priority it intends to introduce flights from Asmara to Massawa, Teseney and the Dahlak Archipelago.

BUS

Reconstructing Eritrea's war-shattered road network has been one of the government's prime objectives; twice as much funding goes into it as into developing all other communications. As you travel, you'll see young people undertaking their national service or gangs of volunteers at work.

The road between Asmara and Massawa and both routes to the Ethiopian border are tarmac, as well as the stretch between the capital and Agordat via Keren. There are plans to extend the sealed road to Teseney, then as far as the Sudanese frontier. A new tarmac road between Dekemhare and Barentu is also under construction.

There's no road through the Danakil depression to Assab, only a dirt track, traversable in a 4WD vehicle with local guidance.

The long-distance bus services are pretty reliable. You have to be at the bus station by 6 am to be guaranteed a seat. You can't usually buy tickets the day before.

ORGANISED TOURS

Eritrean Tour Service (ETS; ☎ 124999) in Asmara arranges half-day tours of the capital for US$5 to US$8, depending upon numbers subscribed. It also offers weekend return travel to Massawa and transport to the beach at Gurgusum, all for US$8. Its rental vehicles are reliable; a saloon car costs US$25 to US$27 per day and a 4WD is US$90 to US$97.

Two other agencies with a reputation for putting together tailor-made tours are Explore Eritrea Travel Agency (☎ 121242) and Travel House International (☎ 120208), the latter being one of the very rare places in Eritrea to accept credit cards.

For bicycle touring, Robel Mocconen (c/o Berhanu Brothers Travel agency ☎ 116414) runs very reasonably priced one day tours from Asmara and trips to Keren or Massawa, which include an overnight camp.

ERITREA

Asmara

Asmara has an average annual temperature of 17°C. It's one of the most European cities in Africa, with its palm boulevards and elegant villas. From October to March, gardens are a riot of jacaranda, hibiscus and bougainvillea. Mostly built by the Italians, it seems scarcely to have changed since they left. It's a city where traffic lights both work and are observed, streets have name plaques and platoons of sweepers are out in force early every morning. It's also safe, even after dark, despite a few recent and atypical incidents.

With a population of around 400,000 Asmara remains uncrowded, as a result of positive government discrimination in favour of the countryside. It's thus been spared – unlike Khartoum or Addis Ababa – an influx of the rural dispossessed, driven by drought and war, both of which Eritrea has suffered just as grievously as its neighbours.

Information
Banks are open Monday to Friday from 8 am to noon and 2 to 5 pm; also on Saturday morning. You can change money at the Commercial Bank of Eritrea on Liberation Ave. The exchange office on the ground floor of the First of September Stadium has longer opening hours (including Sunday morning from 8.30 to 11.30 am), and service is rapid and efficient.

Awghet, the government bookshop, on Liberation Ave, has a wide range of books on Eritrea's recent history.

Things to See
Asmara is essentially a city for strolling around. To get your bearings, take the short walk north of the long-distance bus station and up the hill to the **Cherhi Recreation Centre & Viewpoint**.

In both architecture and atmosphere, Asmara is two towns, bisected by Liberation Ave. Take a walk on the south side, the old colonial quarter, an area of elegant villas and wide, shaded streets. Other relics of this era are the icing sugar confection of the old **Governor's Palace**, still awaiting a new role, and the splendid **post office**, all marble and Ionic pillars.

On the north side of Liberation Ave, you'll find more bustle and animation, particularly in and around the **market**.

The dominant red-brick **Catholic Cathedral**, constructed in 1922, could have been lifted straight from Lombardy. White-robed worshippers mingle outside the Eritrean Orthodox **Kiddisti Mariam (St Mary's) Cathedral**, built at the same time. Nearby is the main mosque, **Al Khulafa al Rashidin**.

The excellent **National Museum** has three separate sections: archaeological, ethnographic and military. Previously housed in the splendid Governor's Palace, it will, alas, remain closed until it finds a new location.

Out towards the airport, **Den Den military camp** is popularly known as the tank graveyard. Tanks, armoured cars and other detritus of war have been brought here and dumped as rusting reminders of Eritrea's recent past.

Places to Stay
There are so many *albergos* (inns) and pensions within easy reach of Liberation Ave that you'll have no trouble finding bottom-end accommodation. Rates are US$2 to US$5 for singles, slightly more for doubles.

Both the *Eritrea* (☎ 120058) and *Luam* pensions have singles/doubles with communal bathroom for US$3/4. The *Mitslal Hotel* (☎ 118670) has doubles for US$6. The spacious doubles (US$6) at the *Africa Pension* (☎ 121436), a converted villa, are particularly good value. The *Legese Hotel* (☎ 125 054) also has rooms for US$6/9. The more modest *Diana Hotel* (☎ 121529) has rooms for US$7/10. In much the same category, rooms at the *Central* (☎ 121656) and *Victoria* (☎ 121648) pensions cost US$5/6.

If you prefer a private bathroom, the *Keren Hotel* (☎ 120740), a delightful if run-down colonial relic built in 1899, has rooms for US$14/19. The *Shagay Hotel* (☎ 126562), with rooms at US$12/15, is clean and friendly. The *Ambassador Hotel* (☎ 126 544), also

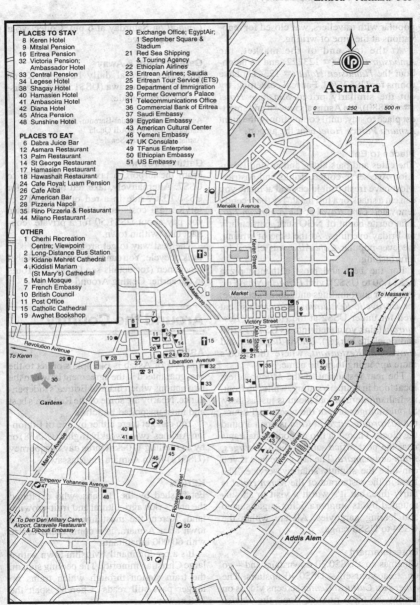

Asmara

PLACES TO STAY
- 8 Keren Hotel
- 9 Mitsial Pension
- 16 Eritrea Pension
- 32 Victoria Pension; Ambassador Hotel
- 33 Central Pension
- 34 Legese Hotel
- 38 Shagay Hotel
- 40 Hamasien Hotel
- 41 Ambasoira Hotel
- 42 Diana Hotel
- 45 Africa Pension
- 48 Sunshine Hotel

PLACES TO EAT
- 6 Dabra Juice Bar
- 12 Asmara Restaurant
- 13 Palm Restaurant
- 14 St George Restaurant
- 17 Hamasien Restaurant
- 18 Hawashait Restaurant
- 24 Cafe Royal; Luam Pension
- 26 Cafe Alba
- 27 American Bar
- 28 Pizzeria Napoli
- 35 Rino Pizzeria & Restaurant
- 44 Milano Restaurant

OTHER
- 1 Cherhi Recreation Centre; Viewpoint
- 2 Long-Distance Bus Station
- 3 Kidane Mehret Cathedral
- 4 Kiddisti Mariam (St Mary's) Cathedral
- 5 Main Mosque
- 7 French Embassy
- 10 British Council
- 11 Post Office
- 15 Catholic Cathedral
- 19 Awghet Bookshop
- 20 Exchange Office; EgyptAir; 1 September Square & Stadium
- 21 Red Sea Shipping & Touring Agency
- 22 Ethiopian Airlines
- 23 Eritrean Airlines; Saudia
- 25 Eritrean Tour Service (ETS)
- 29 Department of Immigration
- 30 Former Governor's Palace
- 31 Telecommunications Office
- 36 Commercial Bank of Eritrea
- 37 Saudi Embassy
- 39 Egyptian Embassy
- 43 American Cultural Center
- 46 Yemeni Embassy
- 47 UK Consulate
- 49 TFanus Enterprise
- 50 Ethiopian Embassy
- 51 US Embassy

ERITREA

popular with travellers, was closed for renovations at the time of writing.

At the top end of the market, the *Ambasoira Hotel* (☎ 123222) and its neighbour the *Hamasien Hotel* (☎ 123411) have rooms for US$35/42. For real cossetting, try out the similarly priced *Sunshine Hotel* (☎ 127880). It's Asmara's newest and smartest place to stay, until completion of the giant *Asmara Palace Hotel* near the airport.

Places to Eat
The cafes and bars along and around Liberation Ave serve coffee, drinks and pastries. Most have fresh fruit juices and at many you can eat a snack or a full meal. Try the recently renovated *Cafe Royal* or the *American Bar*, a favourite haunt of NGO staff, particularly on Friday evenings. At the time of writing, the ever-popular *Cafe Alba* was closed for refurbishing.

For the best and most authentic pizza (US$1.50 to US$2), visit *Pizzeria Napoli* or, in fancier surroundings and more expensive, the *Caravelle Restaurant*. You can also eat well for under US$2 at the *Hamasien Restaurant* (sink your teeth into its US$0.75 fish and omelette burger), *Dabra Juice Bar* and *Hawashait Restaurant*, where the food's more appealing than the name.

The rear restaurant of the *Milano* offers local food in a superb setting, while, up front, its Italian/international menu is just as tasty. Should hunger bite in the wee small hours, the *Ristorante Pizzeria Rino* is open around the clock. There's a trio of good restaurants near the post office square: the *St Georges*, *Palm* and *Asmara*. The last is the best if you can take the slightly smarmy service. The food in the restaurant of the *Keren Hotel* is fairly dire, but it's worth a visit to sit surrounded by its amphora, icing-sugar stucco and leering gargoyles. All are within the US$4 to US$6 range.

Entertainment
Cinemas cost US$0.30 downstairs and – go on, treat yourself – US$0.40 upstairs. The *American Cultural Center* screens videos on Friday at 6.30 pm, as does the *British*

Council on Saturday at 6 pm. Collect your ticket in advance.

Getting There & Away
There are several daily buses to Keren (US$1) and Massawa (US$1.25). Long distance routes include:

Asmara-Keren-Agordat-Barentu-Teseney
Asmara-Mendefera-Adi Quala
Asmara-Dekemhare-Senafe

Getting Around
From the airport, a taxi costs US$5.50 to US$7. Alternatively, take red bus No 1 for US$0.10. A ride in a red or white bus or service taxi costs under US$0.15. In town you pay about US$1.50 for a private 'contract taxi' within town.

The best way to get around Asmara is to walk or cycle. You can hire a bike from Robel Mocconen (for details see Organised Tours in the earlier Getting Around section).

Around the Country

ASSAB
The port of Assab is Ethiopia's outlet to the sea, guaranteed in the agreement between the two nations which marked Eritrea's independence. Nearby are some of the Red Sea's best and most unspoiled **beaches**.

You can get there either by one of Ethiopian Airlines' twice weekly flights (US$38) or by a gruelling 1100km three day bus journey (US$14) from Asmara via Massawa.

KEREN
Established by the Italians, who exploited the area's rich agricultural and fruit-growing land, Keren, the most important highland town after Asmara, is a commercial centre with 60,000 inhabitants.

It's a predominantly Muslim town with a large Christian minority. The peeling sign on the train station through which trains no longer pass still reads 'Cheren', spelt the Italian way.

There's a small, helpful tourist office 200m from the bus station.

The heart of town is the small **Gira Fiori**, or floral roundabout, bordered by hotels, restaurants and cafes. These and the remaining run-down **villas**, the resplendent **Ministry of Local Government building** and the **San Antonio cathedral**, a diminutive cousin of the one in Asmara, still impart a distinct Mediterranean feel. For an overview, sip a beer at sunset on the rooftop terrace of the Keren Hotel.

Keren has a colourful daily **market**, which is frequented by people of various tribes from the surrounding area and is particularly renowned for its silversmiths' street. Each Monday, there's a bustling livestock market just to the south of town.

The Italian and British **war cemeteries** are sombre and moving reminders of one of the major battles between the Allies and Mussolini's forces in 1941.

The **shrine of St Mariam Darit**, a half-hour walk to the east of the Italian cemetery, nestles inside the trunk of a giant baobab tree.

Places to Stay & Eat

The *Eritrea Hotel* (☎ 401298) and the *Sicilia* (☎ 401059), its neighbour and Keren's oldest hotel, both offer singles/doubles with communal bathroom for US$3.50/4. A room with vast private bathroom at the Sicilia costs US$7. Both have pleasant, shaded courtyards.

On the Gira Fiori, prices are similar at the *Red Sea Hotel* (☎ 401628), while the nearby *Keren Hotel* (☎ 401639) charges US$11/14.50 with private bathroom and US$8/11 without.

You can eat well at the Keren Hotel and at the *Peace and Love Restaurant*, also on the Gira. The restaurant at the Senhit Hotel, known to one and all as *Areggai's*, after its extrovert owner, is great for local food.

Getting There & Away

Between Keren and Asmara, there are at least 10 buses daily travelling the 91km journey. Tickets cost US$1 and the trip takes 2½ to three hours.

MASSAWA

Massawa (also spelt Mitsiwa and often called Batsi) is 115km by road from Asmara. Successor to the ancient port of Adulis, it was once known for its pearl-diving and salt-panning industries. During the Fascist build-up in the early 1930s, it was the busiest port on the east African coast. However, the city was almost levelled by bombing raids in 1990, an act of gratuitous vengeance by the Ethiopians after they lost the port to the EPLF.

Almost every pre-1990 building bears its battle scars, and the remaining ruins, empty lots and hillocks of rubble are a constant visual reminder of Massawa's blitz. But this predominantly Muslim city is being faithfully reconstructed and becoming once again a thriving Red Sea port whose dusty alleys are fascinating to roam.

What is collectively called Massawa is really three entities. The mainland, with its new blocks of popular housing, is of little interest. Across the first causeway is **Taulud Island**, symbolically guarded by three gutted tanks, the first to battle their way across the causeway during Massawa's liberation. This was the old Italian quarter. Among the trim villas, note the **palace of Signor Melotti**, who made his fortune from the Asmara Brewery.

The port and old town, a blend of Egyptian, Turkish and Italo-Moorish architecture, are over a second, much shorter causeway leading to **Massawa (Batsi) Island**.

Places to Stay

The cheapest hotels are on Massawa Island, including the *Hotel Lido* and the *Asmara*, *Ghenet*, *Yossuf*, *Modern* and *Massawa* hotels. Each charges US$4 to US$6 for a double with communal bathroom.

The *Torino Hotel* (☎ 552855) is the only hotel on Massawa Island with air-con. The price of US$21 for a double room includes free entry to the rooftop nightclub. Bear that fact in mind if you're a light sleeper. The noise carries to its neighbour, the *Savoya*, where doubles with/without private bathroom cost US$8/6.

The better hotels are all on Taulud Island. Once over the causeway from the mainland, turn left at the church and within 500m you'll pass four of the main five hotels. The first, the *Hotel Corallo* (☎ 552406), costs US$8/5.50 for doubles with/without private bathroom and US$17 for a double with aircon. The *Hotel Luna* (☎ 552272) is in the same price range.

Between these two is the clean *Central Hotel* (☎ 552002), where all rooms have aircon and cost US$17/14 with/without private bathroom. The *Dahlak Hotel* (☎ 552818) is beside the causeway to Massawa Island. Rooms cost US$30/45 – to be paid in dollars – and all have air-con and private bathroom.

At the south end of Taulud Island is the *Red Sea Hotel*, Massawa's ritziest and most expensive. Severely damaged during the war, it was preparing to reopen at the time of writing.

Places to Eat

On Massawa Island there are plenty of small, cheap restaurants, such as the *Denkalia* on the main street or the *Seghen* beside the port.

There are also two superb fish restaurants: the *Adulis* on the square beside the main mosque, which offers grilled or baked fish for US$3.50 plus a national and international menu; and, just around the corner, Abu Bakr's long-established *Sallam Restaurant*, serving only fish – but such fish – for US$2.50.

At the *Eritrea Restaurant* you can get two main courses for US$4 or an excellent fish zigne for US$2.

The hotels on Taulud Island all have reasonable but unexciting restaurants. If you fancy a blow-out with great views of the port, indulge in the *Dahlak Hotel's* Saturday-only evening buffet.

Getting There & Away

Buses leave from the quayside on Massawa Island. Several travel daily between Asmara and Massawa (US$1.25), taking around four hours.

The road is spectacular, winding down from 2300m to sea level and passing briefly through Eritrea's most fertile area. The track of the former railway runs alongside or within view of the road for much of the journey.

For a weekend travel option from Asmara, see the Organised Tours section in the introductory Getting Around section. For boats to Jeddah, refer to Sea in the introductory Getting There & Away section.

AROUND MASSAWA

The best and most accessible beach near Massawa is at **Gurgusum**, 8km north of town. Taxis charge US$7 from Massawa. Minibuses at a tenth of the price leave from the bus stand in Massawa and run fairly frequently, especially at weekends. You can overnight at the *Gurgusum Beach Hotel* (☎ 552911), where doubles cost US$25/33 according to season, or at the nearby *Hamasien Beach Hotel* (☎ 552725), where doubles, mostly with communal bathroom, are US$17. For both, it's essential to reserve at weekends.

The beaches and waters around the 210 islands of the undeveloped **Dahlak Archipelago** offer spectacular, unspoilt diving and snorkelling. However, it doesn't come cheap – you pay a fee of US$30 for a three day permit. Dahlak Sea Touring (☎ 552489) rents diving, camping and fishing gear. A boat with capacity for six costs US$208 per day and US$275 for up to eight people. More modestly, you can take a boat for four (US$28) and spend the day lazing and snorkelling on **Green Island**, half an hour off the coast.

Ethiopia

Throughout the 1970s and 1980s, the world knew Ethiopia as its most persistently famine-prone country. But since the change of government in 1991, agricultural production is increasing, heavyweight state corporations are slowly being privatised and tourism, from a zero base, is already the country's second biggest foreign-exchange earner after coffee.

Now's the time to go there before it becomes yet another stopping point on the international package-tour itinerary. Travelling can be tough and Ethiopians on the street, still adjusting to the presence of foreigners after so many years of isolation, can be mind-numbingly irritating. But you'll meet many more who are innately kind and dignified, and who will go out of their way to help you. The scenery is spectacular, the culture rich, unique and infinitely diverse – and you'll have the satisfaction of knowing that you got there among the first.

Facts about the Country

HISTORY

Ethiopia is unique among African countries for having never been colonised, only occupied by the Italians for five years before and during part of WWII. It's also a founding member and the continental headquarters of the Organisation of African Unity (OAU).

Ethiopia is also special because, geographically so close to the Prophet Mohammed's homeland, it has an indigenous Christian church. Dating back to the 4th century AD, the church has successfully resisted Islam. And it resisted equally successfully the more recent onslaught of Marxist-Leninist doctrine during Mengistu Haile Mariam's dictatorship in the 1970s and 1980s.

Unlike most African nation states, its roots are deep. The Ethiopians have kept a record of their rulers for almost 5000 years, but much of their history is not confirmed by other

ETHIOPIA	
Area:	1,127,000 sq km
Population:	55 million
Population Growth Rate:	3.1%
Capital:	Addis Ababa
Head of State:	Prime Minister Meles Zenawi
Official Language:	Amharic
Other Languages:	Tigrinya, Orominya
Currency:	Birr
Exchange Rate:	Birr 6.6 = US$1
Per Capita GNP:	US$380
Inflation:	10%
Time:	GMT/UTC + 3

Highlights

- The rock churches of Lalibela
- A boat trip on Lake Tana
- The Blue Nile Falls near Bahar Dar
- The castles of Gondar
- Ethiopia's birdlife – over 850 recorded species
- Looking down over Addis Ababa from the heights of Entoto Natural Park

sources. Ethiopia's first entry into world history, the Queen of Sheba's visit to King Solomon around 1000 BC, is documented in the Bible and Yemeni folklore. Her son, Menelik I, is regarded as the first emperor of Ethiopia, ruling from 982 to 957 BC. The 237th and last emperor of the dynasty was Haile Selassie, who ruled from 1930 to 1974.

The first evidence about the kingdom of Axum comes from the 3rd century BC. It

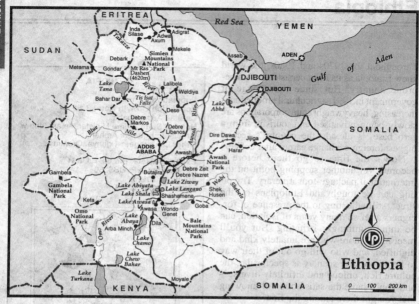

Ethiopia

gradually grew in power, conquering not only the powerful state of Meroe in Sudan but also the kingdoms of southern Arabia.

According to local tradition, ancient Ethiopians were Jews and, indeed, a community of Ethiopian Jews, known as Falashas, lived near Gondar until the late 1980s, when the last few were airlifted to Israel. Christianity was brought to Axum by the Syrian youth Frumentius, who converted Emperor Ezana and was later consecrated as the first bishop at Axum in 330 AD.

After the Prophet Mohammed's death in 632 AD, the armies of Islam spread out from Mecca but, even though Axum lost parts of the Red Sea coast to the Arabs, large scale hostilities didn't occur.

The first major challenge to the Axum empire came from pagan tribes further south. The Ethiopian emperors were forced, as a result, to adopt the life of nomadic military commanders living in temporary tented cities. Ethiopian Christian priests became

monks and hermits in order to keep the religion alive. Eventually the tribes were pacified, the kingdom revived and its capital was moved south to Amhara Province.

Muslims gradually expanded into eastern Ethiopia between the 12th and 14th centuries, establishing short-lived kingdoms. In the 16th century, the Ottoman Turks began to support the various Muslim kingdoms, most notably that of Ahmed Gragn the 'Left-Handed', by providing firearms and artillery. Only the intervention of the Portuguese in 1542 saved the Christian empire from collapse.

After a remarkable life span, the Axum empire broke down into its constituent provinces in the 18th century, and 100 years of constant warfare between numerous warlords followed. The shattered empire was eventually reunified by Ras Kassa, who had himself crowned emperor at Axum under the name of Tewodros in 1855.

Tewodros, an abrupt character, was as much disliked by British envoys as by his own vassals. A military expedition led by General Napier was mounted by the British in 1867. After a long siege of his fortress in Magdala, Tewodros shot himself.

His successor, Yohannes IV, fought his way to the throne using British arms acquired in exchange for help at Magdala. After him, Menelik II continued building up stocks of European arms, which he used in 1896 at Adwa to stop Italy's expansion from Eritrea, which it had occupied in 1889. He increased the size of his empire at the expense of the Afars, the Somalis of the Ogaden and Harar, and the Oromos of the south-west.

In 1936 the country was overrun by Mussolini's Italian troops, who remained until 1941 when they surrendered to Allied forces during WWII, after which Ethiopia resumed its independence.

Eritrea remained under British administration until 1952, when a United Nation's (UN) resolution granted it self-government within a federal union with Ethiopia. However, in 1962 Haile Selassie unilaterally annexed Eritrea as a province of Ethiopia. This led to the outbreak of guerrilla warfare, since the Eritreans regarded the annexation as colonisation by another African nation.

Although Haile Selassie had established himself as a national hero during the campaigns against the Italians and had become a respected African statesman through his role in the creation of the OAU, his country remained feudal. The constant accumulation of wealth by the nobility and the church, the hardship of millions of landless peasants, the famines and the war in Eritrea all produced widespread resentment of his rule.

In 1974, against a background of strikes, student demonstrations, army mutinies and peasant uprisings, Haile Selassie was deposed and held under armed guard in his palace until his death several months later.

Overnight, Ethiopia was plunged into drastic social revolution as a clique of junior army officers imposed a military dictatorship on the country. Mengistu Haile Mariam emerged as leader of the Derg, the new governing party. He threw out the Americans, instituted a number of radical reforms, jailed trade union leaders, banned church activities and appealed to the USSR for economic aid.

Months of chaos and excess followed. As the country slipped even further into disorder, the Eritreans stepped up their guerilla campaign and the Somalis pressed their longstanding claims over the Ogaden desert, invading in force and occupying most of the lands of the ethnic Somalis.

The regime, on the point of collapse, retained power only with the massive intervention of Soviet and Cuban troops, who helped to throw the Somalis back across the border and reverse some of the losses sustained in Eritrea. Yet even the Soviets were unable to break the back of the Eritrean liberation fighters.

Mengistu dictated radical rulings to change the country, both politically and economically. *Kebeles*, or people's committees, controlled the lives of everyone in every town and village, nightly curfews were enforced, vast population transfers were carried out to fight famines (a move that backfired devastatingly), and conscription was enforced for all 18 to 30-year-old males (later increased to include those up to 70 years old!).

However, despite these Draconian social controls and the massive military support of its communist allies, in the 1980s Mengistu faced not only the Eritreans but several other regional guerilla armies, notably the Tigray People's Liberation Front. Finally, with the Soviets withdrawing from all their Cold War fronts, the fall of Massawa (Ethiopia's principal port) to the Eritreans in 1990 and yet another major famine ravaging the country, the Derg collapsed. In May 1991, Mengistu fled the country and the government was taken over by a coalition of rebel groups, headed by the 36-year-old Tigrayan rebel commander, Meles Zenawi.

The new government inherited six million people facing famine, a shattered economy, an empty treasury, and moribund industrial and agriculture sectors. Despite these overwhelming problems and occasional clashes with the separatist guerillas of the Oromo Liberation Front and the Ogaden National Liberation Front, the transitional government moved the country towards democracy.

The new constitution, ratified in 1994, is unique in that it allows each of the nine regions to secede – even to the point of full independence, by analogy with Eritrea.

In May 1995, in Ethiopia's first ever parliamentary elections, regarded as free and fair, the Ethiopian People's Revolutionary Democratic Front (EPRDF) won a resounding 98% of the votes – scarcely surprisingly since the poll was boycotted by all the main opposition parties.

Meles Zenawi was confirmed as Prime Minister by the new parliament. Although his council of ministers has representatives from a range of ethnic groups, key positions rest with Tigrayans, to the pique of the Amhara, the traditional holders of political power. Among the government's priorities are food security and expanding the role of the private sector, although the disbanding of monolithic state enterprises proceeds very slowly. Even so, and even though the country started from a low base, it achieved an impressive 10.2% economic growth rate in 1996.

GEOGRAPHY & CLIMATE
The high central plateau varies from 2000 to 3000m, with several mountains of over 4000m. It's dissected by numerous river valleys, the most important being the Blue Nile (the Abbay) flowing from Lake Tana, and split diagonally by the Rift Valley which crosses East Africa.

Although Ethiopia is relatively close to the equator, the central plateau enjoys a temperate climate, with an average annual temperature of 16°C. Only in the east, towards the Red Sea, and west, near Sudan, does it get very hot.

The *kremt*, or main rainy season, occurs between mid-June and mid-September. Light rain also falls during March and April.

ECOLOGY & ENVIRONMENT
Ethiopia's forests are declining alarmingly. Because of the demands for fuel, construction and fencing, at least 77% have been destroyed in the last 25 years. King Menelik II's response in the 1880s to a similar crisis, once he had denuded the hills around Addis Ababa for his new capital, was to import the eucalyptus from Australia.

But the eucalyptus, fast-growing and aggressive, now dominates native species, just as the introduction of the rabbit from Europe threatened indigenous Australian mammals. What's more, it's shunned by wildlife, inhibits plant life around its base and consequently contributes to soil erosion.

PLANT, a group of volunteers within the Ethiopian Wildlife & Natural History Society, encourages a return to native species by growing seedlings in its nurseries. More than 150,000 have been planted by schools, farmers and local Non-Governmental Organisations (NGOs). Through its education programmes and support for schools wishing to start nurseries, it makes people aware of the importance of biodiversity.

POPULATION & PEOPLE
Ethiopia has a population of around 55 million people. Almost 90% of Ethiopians work on the land. There are more than 80 ethnic groups. The largest of these (some 40% of the population) are the Oromo. They live in the centre and south of the country, having migrated from further south in the 15th century. The Amhara and Tigrayans, who live in the north and west, together constitute some 32% of the population.

Muslim and Christian, Christian and Muslim, nobody knows the exact balance, which varies according to who's talking. Roughly 40% of the population are Christian, another 40% are Muslim and the rest follow traditional faiths. In the main, the highland people are Christian, while Muslims predominate in the east and towards the Sudanese border.

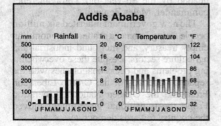

Addis Ababa

	Rainfall				Temperature	
mm		in	°C			°F
500		20	50			122
400		16	40			104
300		12	30			86
200		8	20			68
100		4	10			50
0	J F M A M J J A S O N D	0	0	J F M A M J J A S O N D		32

LANGUAGE

There are almost as many languages – from a variety of families: Semitic, Hamitic, Nilotic and Omotic – as there are peoples in Ethiopia. Amharic, or Amarinya/Amarigna, was the sole official language until 1991, but Tigrinya (also spelt Tigrigna), spoken in the northern areas, and Orominya, spoken in the south, have now achieved semi-official status.

Amharic and Tigrinya use the script of Ge'ez, the language of church liturgy with its daunting syllabary of 231 letters. Orominya uses Roman script.

English is the language of education from junior high school onwards and many people manage more than a smattering. Arabic is spoken in the east and west.

Amharic

Some Amharic words and phrases that you may find useful include:

Greetings & Civilities

Hello.	*tenaystelegn*
How are you?	
(to men)	*denaneh?*
(to women)	*denanesh?*
response (to men or women)	*dena*
OK.	*ishi*
Please.	*ibakih*
Thank you.	*amesegunalhu*

Useful Words & Phrases

Yes.	*ow (very breathy)*
No.	*yelem/aydelem*
I want ...	*afellegallo ...*
I don't want ...	*alfellegem ...*
How much does it cost?	*sint no wagaw?*
expensive	*wud*
cheap	*rekash*
One tea please.	
(to men)	*ante shai ebakah*
(to women)	*ante shai ebakish*
tomorrow	*nega*
tomorrow morning	*nega twat*
What is it?	*minduno?*

Food & Drink

banana	*mooz*
bread	*dabo*
sour bread	*injera*
coffee	*buna*
egg	*encual*
milk	*wa'tat*
raw minced meat and onion	*kitfo*
sauce	*wat*
tea	*shai*
water	*wuha*
soda water	*ambo*

Getting Around

left	*graa/carmachina*
right	*kagn*
road	*mengad*
Where are you going?	*wadyet te-hedaleh?*
Where is ...	*... yetno?*
Which is the road to ...?	*ye ... mengad yet no?*

Numbers

1	*and*
2	*hulet*
3	*sost*
4	*arat*
5	*amist*
6	*sidist*
7	*sabat*
8	*simint*
9	*zetegn*
10	*assr*
20	*haya*
25	*haya amist*
30	*salassa*
40	*arba*
50	*hamsa*
60	*silsa*
70	*saba*
80	*samagna*
90	*zetana*
100	*moto*
1000	*shi*

Note that 'gn' is always pronounced 'ny' as in *canyon* or the Spanish *señor*.

Facts for the Visitor

VISAS & DOCUMENTS

Everyone except Kenyan nationals needs a visa. You may be asked to produce an onward air ticket or visa for the next country on your itinerary plus proof that you have sufficient funds. Visas are single entry only and cost US$63 each – particularly expensive if you plan a round trip to Eritrea or Djibouti.

Yellow fever and cholera inoculations are mandatory if you arrive from an infected area.

Visa Extensions

Visa extensions (US$20) aren't always readily granted to travellers. They are available from the Immigration Office just off Churchill Ave in Addis Ababa. Exit visas are only required for stays of over 30 days.

Other Visas

Djibouti
One-month visas cost US$22, require one photo and are issued after 24 hours. French nationals are exempt. The consular section is open daily between 9 am and noon.

Eritrea
Visas are issued the following day in return for one photo and US$25 – in cash; travellers' cheques aren't accepted. The visa section is open from 9 to 11 am.

Kenya
Open from 9 am to noon, the embassy offers same-day service. Visas, valid for three months, cost US$29 for US nationals, and US$38 for French and Australians. You need one photo. For a list of countries, such as Germany, Ireland and the UK, whose nationals don't require visas, see the Visas section in the Kenya chapter. Visas can also be bought at the border.

Sudan
All visa applications are referred to Khartoum, from where a decision, not always favourable, routinely takes a month or more. In return for four photos and US$60, the visa, if granted, is valid for one month. Consular hours are from 9 am to noon (to 11 am on Friday).

EMBASSIES
Ethiopian Embassies

Ethiopia has embassies in the following countries: Djibouti, Egypt, Eritrea, France, Germany, Italy, Kenya, the UK and the USA. There is a consulate in Australia.

Foreign Embassies in Ethiopia

Countries with embassies in Addis Ababa include:

Djibouti
off Bole Rd (☎ 613006)
Egypt
Entoto Ave, near Sidist Kilo Square (☎ 550021)
Eritrea
Ras Makonnen Ave (☎ 512844)
France
Omedia St (☎ 550066)
Germany
Afewerk St (☎ 550433)
Kenya
Fikre Maryam Aba Techan St (☎ 610033)
Sudan
off Roosevelt St (☎ 516477)
UK
Fikre Maryam Aba Techan St (☎ 612354)
USA
Entoto Ave (☎ 550666)

MONEY
US$1 = Birr 6.6

The unit of currency is the birr, which equals 100 cents. You can't import or export any local currency from Ethiopia – not even to Eritrea, which has also been using birr.

There's a black market but it gives you less than a 10% advantage. If you indulge, change money in shops and never, ever in the Mercato or Piazza areas of Addis Ababa, where there's a fair chance of being robbed or swindled. Outside the capital, you'll have difficulty exchanging anything but dollar bills. Only Ethiopian Airlines and the Hilton, Sheraton, Ghion and Ethiopia hotels take credit cards, and there's a reluctance everywhere to accept travellers' cheques; even Ethiopian Airlines turns its nose up at them.

Currency declaration forms are issued on arrival. Officially, excess birr can be reconverted on leaving, less US$30 per day of your stay (as you're supposed to spend at least that much daily). It's better to spend up since the amount you can convert seems to be at the whim of the official on duty and the process is deliberately tortuous.

POST & COMMUNICATIONS

The postal service is slow but usually reliable and best in Addis Ababa. The officials in the post office run a flourishing private business selling old stamps to foreigners.

You can make international telephone calls and send faxes from the Telecommunications Centre in Addis Ababa. A three minute call to the UK costs US$6.25, to the USA US$8 and to Australia US$9.75.

The country code for Ethiopia is 251. The area code for Addis Ababa is 01, for Axum it's 03, and for Gondar it's 08.

HEALTH

There's bilharzia in *all* of Ethiopia's rivers and lakes, except Lake Langano which is believed to be bilharzia free. Outside Addis Ababa, make sure you boil or add purifying tablets to all drinking water: 'I've never been in a more faecally contaminated environment', says an NGO doctor with over two decades of third world experience.

Many of the bar girls and their clients are HIV positive.

Malaria, although no problem in the highlands, is prevalent at lower altitudes.

Be wary of salads as there's a good chance of picking up liver fluke, and pesticide usage is far from controlled. Eating raw *kitfo* (minced meat) is a national custom best avoided as tapeworms are common.

In spite of this litany, with only a little care you can have a sickness-free time in Ethiopia. Also see the Health Appendix.

DANGERS & ANNOYANCES

In bigger towns, especially Addis Ababa, beware of thieves and pick-pockets. They often work in gangs, and you may have difficulty telling a beggar from a thief.

Armed robbery is mainly confined to the countryside and occurs mostly at dusk, which is why buses tend to drive from 6 am to 5 pm only.

In addition to theft, there are the small-scale swindlers. Shouts of 'You, you!' invariably mean someone wants money from you, no matter how they open the conversation, and self-proclaimed guides find you anywhere, anytime.

Gay Lib hasn't reached Ethiopia yet. There's a real risk of violence – and up to 10 years imprisonment – if you're caught with your trousers down.

Water supply is often limited to a few hours a day, particularly in the provinces, so turn on the tap before you strip for a shower.

BUSINESS HOURS & PUBLIC HOLIDAYS

Government offices are open Monday to Thursday from 8.30 am to 5.30 pm with a lunch break between 12.30 and 1.30 pm. On Friday and Saturday, hours are 8.30 to 11.30 am. Offices and shops are closed on Sunday.

Ethiopia uses the Julian solar calendar, made up of 12 months of 30 days and a 13th month of five or six days – hence the tourism slogan '13 months of sunshine'. The year begins on 11 September in the Western Gregorian calendar, and the Julian calendar is some seven and a half years behind our own.

Time also follows a different system, using 12-hour cycles which start at 6 am and 6 pm western time. Eccentric this may be, but interpreting time from dawn to dusk is just as logical as our own way, based upon noon and midnight. All the same, be careful: if you're told your bus leaves at 11 *kelayleetu* (the equivalent of our 'in the morning'), you're in for an early wake-up; they mean it will depart at 5 am. Conversion's no big deal; just subtract six hours from western time or add six to local time. And many Ethiopians are familiar with western usage for both times and dates, so in practice there's rarely ambiguity.

Public holidays include: 7 January (Ethiopian Orthodox Christmas), 19 January, 2 March, 6 April, 1 May, 5 May, 28 May, 11 September (Julian New Year) and 27 September, plus Orthodox Easter and Islamic holidays. For more information on Islamic holidays, refer to Public Holidays in the Regional Facts for the Visitor chapter.

FOOD

Everywhere, *injera* and *wat* (called *zigne* in Tigrinya) are the staple food. Injera is the national foam-rubber bread, guaranteed to produce earth-shattering flatulence. Flour from *teff*, a cereal peculiar to Ethiopia, is mixed with yeast, left to go sour and then baked on a clay platter over a wood fire. Wat, the sauce in which meat or vegetables are simmered, comes in two varieties: red, fiery *kay wat* and yellowish, milder *alicha wat*.

Common protein dishes are *doro* (chicken), *bug* (lamb), *assar* (fish), *tibs* (fried meat), and *kitfo* (minced or ground meat).

Tasty vegetarian dishes include *shuro* (a lentil and chickpea mush), *kuk* (chick peas) and *misur* (black lentils). Or ask for *ye sim magib*, a selection of vegetable dishes traditionally served during times of fasting.

Fasting

Ethiopian Orthodox Christians take fasting seriously. Like Muslims, they eschew pork. Every Wednesday and Friday they abstain from meat and dairy products (and many from fish, too). On these days and during their 40 day Lent, you won't find such dishes on restaurant menus, except in fancy places catering for foreigners. ∎

DRINKS

Sparkling mineral water, *Ambo*, is safe and refreshing. Traditional alcoholic drinks are *t'ella* (beer), *t'ej* (mead) and *arakie* (grain spirit). T'ella, the local home brew, is made from barley in the highlands and maize in the

---

Coffee

The southern region of Kefa has a strong claim to be the original home of coffee. Used in Ethiopia as early as 1000 AD, the coffee bean was taken to Yemen in the 14th century, spreading from there to the rest of the world. ∎

---

lowlands. T'ej is, of course, made from honey, served in the smarter restaurants from a *birille*, a delicate fluted bottle. Go easy; it can glue you to your seat. And treat arakie with even greater respect.

You can get good espresso, macchiato (with just a splash of milk) and cappuccino, all normally served ultrasweet unless you specify otherwise.

Getting There & Away

AIR

Airlines serving Ethiopia include the national carrier, Ethiopian Airlines (☎ 512222), Air Djibouti (represented by Sun Travel Agency; ☎ 614312), Egypt Air (☎ 122565), Kenya Airways (☎ 513018), Lufthansa (☎ 515666) and Saudia (☎ 512637).

Ethiopian Airlines is one of Africa's largest and best airlines. The fleet consists of modern jets, and international schedules are generally reliable. The network of flights to African capital cities is extensive, and Ethiopian Airlines is one of the very few which connects West and East African countries.

Ethiopian Airlines flies daily to Asmara, Eritrea for US$119/237 one way/return. Ethiopian Airlines and Air Djibouti each have two flights a week to Djibouti for US$137/274. Ethiopian Airlines also offers an attractive excursion return ticket for US$296, valid for two months, to Sana'a in Yemen, including a stopover in Djibouti.

The departure tax for international flights is US$10.

LAND

Djibouti

The journey by road is possible but wearying. Most travellers prefer to travel by bus from Addis Ababa to Dire Dawa then by train the following day to Djibouti (this leg of the trip costs US$20 for a 1st class guaranteed seat, which is well worth paying the extra, and takes 12 hours). Alternatively, you can do the whole journey by train in two days, overnighting in Dire Dawa.

Eritrea

Three buses a week run from Addis Ababa to Asmara (US$12.50), taking three days via Dese, Mekele and Adigrat. The alternative, following the Historic Route via Bahar Dar, Gondar and Axum, is infinitely more interesting but more gruelling. For details, see the Getting There & Away section for each town in Around the Country later in this chapter. Another option is to fly from Addis Ababa to Axum (US$65), then travel by bus to Asmara (US$3; about six hours, excluding time at the frontier).

There's a good tarmac road from Addis Ababa to the Eritrean port of Assab. From Assab, however, it's a tough, broiling journey along desert tracks to Massawa – or indeed to anywhere.

Kenya

Buses from Addis Ababa to the border at Moyale take a couple of days with an overnight in Dila. Trucks over the border travel in convoys because of the risk of banditry and you'll have to wait some time until one assembles. They take two to three days from Moyale to Nairobi.

Somalia

Somalia remains anarchic and the Ethiopian side of the frontier is also unsafe. Stay well away.

Sudan

The whole length of the frontier, along which there's sporadic fighting, is closed to travellers.

The usual overland route to Sudan – via Eritrea – is also currently blocked since the border between the two countries is closed and just as dangerous. For more information, see Sudan under Land in the Getting There & Away section of the Eritrea chapter.

Getting Around

AIR

Ethiopian Airlines (☎ 512222) has a strong internal network and its prices are reasonable. Addis Ababa to Axum via Bahar Dar, Gondar and Lalibela, for example, costs US$107 one way and US$174 return, while a one way ticket to Dire Dawa is US$49.

It's essential to reconfirm all onward flights and to verify your departure time the day before. And don't set out on a round trip with one leg open-ended or you risk being stranded.

BUS

There's a good network of dirt-cheap, dead-slow buses along all major roads. In the bigger towns, buy your ticket the day before to avoid paying double or more to the touts who've snapped up the last remaining seats. In the wet season, you may be temporarily delayed, but all major towns remain accessible.

TRAIN

The trip between Addis Ababa and Dire Dawa costs US$11/7/3.50 in 1st/2nd/3rd class, and takes about 14 hours. Unless you're a railway buff, you'll prefer the bus option, which is swifter and scenically more varied.

ORGANISED TOURS

Experience Ethiopia Travel (☎ 152336), is friendly, informed and environmentally and socially aware. National Tour Operations (NTO; ☎ 159274), once a state monopoly, remains the biggest. Other companies in Addis Ababa with a proven track record are Caravan Tours (☎ 516501), Travel Ethiopia (☎ 510168) and the upmarket Yumo International (☎ 518878).

Addis Ababa

Addis Ababa means 'new flower' in Amharic. So to call it only Addis makes as much sense as an Ethiopian calling the Big Apple 'New'.

Addis Ababa is 2400m above sea level. It's one of Africa's largest inland cities with a population of around three million, of whom one million have arrived since the 1991 revolution, putting an immense strain on all resources. Founded in 1887 by

Menelik II, it supplanted Entoto (see Around Addis Ababa later in this section) as the capital of Ethiopia.

The city has grown rapidly since the establishment of the United Nations Economic Commission for Africa (UNECA) in 1958 and particularly since the foundation in 1963 of the OAU, which also has its headquarters in Addis Ababa.

Warning
Violence is uncommon but pick-pockets and con artists prey particularly around the bus station, in the Mercato (Market) and on the triangle of streets around the stadium. You're at risk walking the streets of the city centre after dark.

Information
The Ethiopian Tourism Commission near Maskal Square can provide information and a brochure or two. The friendly counter staff of Experience Ethiopia Travel also readily dispense information on all aspects of travel.

Changing money at the main branch of the Commercial Bank of Ethiopia on Churchill Ave is relatively painless. The foreign section is upstairs. Opening hours are Monday to Friday from 8 am to 3 pm and Saturday from 9 to 11 am.

The British Council (☎ 550022), on Adwa Ave, has a good library and an active cultural programme.

Things to See
The **Ethnographic Museum** at the Institute of Ethiopian Studies in the grounds of Addis Ababa University is well worth its US$3 entry fee. Its two main sections on local crafts and on regions and peoples make it an ideal place to start learning about Ethiopia's rich ethnic diversity. It also has an impressive array of religious crosses, triptychs and murals – plus, incongruously enough, Haile Selassie's bedroom and bathroom. It's open Tuesday to Friday from 8 am to 5 pm and on weekends from 10 am to 5 pm.

The **National Museum** is open daily from 8.30 am to 5.30 pm; entry costs US$1.50. The **Addis Ababa Museum** is in a beautiful

wooden house, once a nobleman's palace. It's open daily from 8.30 am to 6 pm, and entry is US$0.30. The guides, who expect a tip, are well informed.

Within the UNECA headquarters in **Africa Hall** are huge, richly coloured stained-glass windows by internationally renowned Ethiopian artist Afewerk Tekle, which portray the history and diversity of Africa's people.

Giorgis Cathedral (St George's Cathedral) was built in 1896 to commemorate the victory over the Italians at the Battle of Adwa. Beside it is a small museum; entry is US$1.50.

Addis Ababa has one of the largest open-air markets in Africa, known as the **Mercato**, where you can buy everything from vegetables to gold and silver jewellery.

Lucy & Her Ancestors
The star of the National Museum is Lucy. When her 3.5 million-year-old skull and incomplete skeleton were found in 1974, she caused a radical rethink of the timescale for humankind's development.

But beside Homo Ramidus Afarensis, 4.4 million years old and discovered recently in the same area, she's a mere teenager. ■

Places to Stay
Many cheap hotels in Addis Ababa are a combination of noisy street bar, brothel and a few double rooms, though some are surprisingly well kept and suitable for travellers. Foreigners are routinely charged two to four times local rates.

There's a profusion of budget hotels in the US$2 to US$3 range around the Piazza. Nearby, there's the *Alternative National Hotel* (☎ 551678) – not to be confused with its downtown upmarket namesake – has singles/doubles for US$3.75/US$4.50. However, its ground floor restaurant and bar can be noisy. Just down the hill, the *Baro Hotel* (☎ 551447), a travellers' favourite

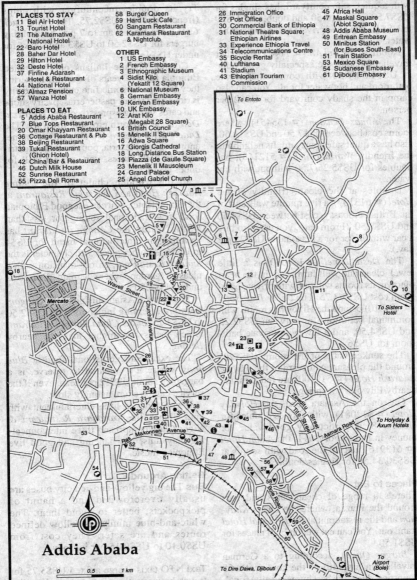

PLACES TO STAY
11 Bel Air Hotel
13 Tourist Hotel
21 The Alternative
   National Hotel
22 Baro Hotel
28 Baher Dar Hotel
29 Hilton Hotel
32 Deste Hotel
37 Finfine Adarash
   Hotel & Restaurant
44 National Hotel
56 Almaz Pension
57 Wanza Hotel

PLACES TO EAT
5 Addis Ababa Restaurant
7 Blue Tops Restaurant
20 Omar Khayyam Restaurant
36 Cottage Restaurant & Pub
39 Tukal Restaurant
   (Ghion Hotel)
42 China Bar & Restaurant
46 Dutch Milk House
52 Sunrise Restaurant
55 Pizza Deli Roma

58 Burger Queen
59 Hard Luck Cafe
60 Sangam Restaurant
62 Karamara Restaurant
   & Nightclub

OTHER
1 US Embassy
2 French Embassy
3 Ethnographic Museum
4 Sidist Kilo
   (Yekatit 12 Square)
6 National Museum
8 German Embassy
9 Kenyan Embassy
10 UK Embassy
12 Arat Kilo
   (Megabit 28 Square)
14 British Council
15 Menelik II Square
16 Adwa Square
17 Giorgis Cathedral
18 Long Distance Bus Station
19 Piazza (de Gaulle Square)
23 Menelik II Mausoleum
24 Grand Palace
25 Angel Gabriel Church

26 Immigration Office
27 Post Office
30 Commercial Bank of Ethiopia
31 National Theatre Square;
   Ethiopian Airlines
33 Experience Ethiopia Travel
34 Telecommunications Centre
35 Bicycle Rental
40 Lufthansa
41 Stadium
43 Ethiopian Tourism
   Commission

45 Africa Hall
47 Maskal Square
   (Abiot Square)
48 Addis Ababa Museum
49 Eritrean Embassy
50 Minibus Station
   (for Buses South-East)
51 Train Station
53 Mexico Square
54 Sudanese Embassy
61 Djibouti Embassy

Addis Ababa

0   0.5   1 km

To Entoto

To Sisters
Hotel

To Holyday &
Axum Hotels

To Dire Dawa, Djibouti

To
Airport
(Bole)

Mercato

Wavell Street

Churchill Avenue

Ras Makonnen Avenue

Asmara Road

Bole Road

with a quiet, safe courtyard, has singles for US$7.50 to US$10.50 and doubles at US$9 to US$12. All have private bathroom and hot water.

Rooms at the *Bel Air* (☎ 114655), another travellers' haunt, are especially good value at US$4.50/7.50 with communal/private bathroom and hot water for all. You can also camp in the shady courtyard for US$2 per person.

The *Almaz Pension* (☎ 155451), where rooms cost between US$7.50 and US$13.50, also has a quiet safe courtyard. Its neighbour, the friendly *Wanza Hotel* (☎ 512168), has doubles for US$5.25/7.50 without/with hot water.

Doubles at the clean, friendly *Sisters Hotel* (☎ 613137), a five minute walk east of the British embassy, cost between US$4.50 and US$7.50. (From here, you can also hire a car with driver for a reasonable US$23 per day.)

The *Deste Hotel* (☎ 151030) is a little jewel, clean and well furnished, in the heart of town. Its rooms without/with private bathroom cost US$3/3.75. The *Baher Dar Hotel* (☎ 154310) behind the Hilton has rooms with communal bathroom for between US$2.25 and US$4.50, and a few with private bathroom for US$6.

The sunken baths of the rooms (US$20) around the pleasant courtyard of the *Finfine Adarash Hotel* (☎ 519100) are fed from the nearby Filwoha hot springs.

Out on the Asmara road, the *Holyday Hotel* (☎ 612081), with singles/doubles for US$16/18, is particularly good value for money in its category, as is the *Axum Hotel* (☎ 613916) just up the road with rooms at US$30/34.50 for singles/doubles.

Places to Eat

There's a range of cheap cafes and bars around the Piazza, where the *Omar Khayyam* and the restaurant at the *National Hotel* stand out. You can eat well at both places for US$1.50.

Burger Queen, according to a German traveller, in his 54th of the continent's 55 countries, does 'the best burger in all Africa'.

Try its double queenburger with chips (french fries) for US$2.75. The *Hard Luck Cafe*, open from 9 am to 7 pm, has bulging burgers for US$2.50 to US$3 and steaks for under US$4.

Considering the Italians only occupied Ethiopia for five years of wartime austerity, they left behind some fine cuisine. The city is rich in pizzerias, pasticcerias, pastry shops and cafes serving espresso coffee. The *Pizza Deli Roma* is worth crossing town for. The *Dutch Milk House* is, despite its name, another good pizzeria, popular with expatriates. At both places, you can eat well for under US$4.

In the wooden chalet of the *Finfine Adarash Hotel* and the *Tukul Restaurant* at the Ghion Hotel, you can eat good Ethiopian food in a traditional setting for less than US$4. Nearby, the *Cottage Restaurant* has an impressive international menu for US$4 to US$6. Another place with character is the *Sunrise Restaurant*, an old mansion with a pleasant garden, where a main dish costs under US$3.50.

You can eat Asian cuisine at the *Sangam Restaurant* serving Indian food for US$2.50 to US$4.25, or the *China Bar & Restaurant*, which locals rate higher than the nearby *Beijing*.

The excellent international food at *Blue Tops*, where it's essential to reserve, is a bargain at about US$12 per head, even if the service can be excruciatingly slow.

If you fancy a little entertainment with your dinner, the *Karamara Restaurant & Night Club*, comprising three interconnecting clay huts, has dancing and good live Ethiopian music.

Getting Around

Bus The big yellow-and-red city buses are usually overcrowded and a haunt of pickpockets; better to avoid them. The white-and-blue minibuses follow defined routes and are safer. They cost from US$0.10 to US$0.15 per journey.

Taxi NTO taxis charge a fixed US$5.75 for travel between the airport and all major hotels. Ordinary taxis are cheaper (around US$4), although you'll initially be quoted something outrageous. In town, always agree on the fare before starting out. A reasonable rate is US$1.50 to US$2. You can also hire a taxi by the hour for US$3 to US$4 or per day for under US$25.

Bicycle You can hire bikes by the hour or day from the empty lot just north of the stadium.

AROUND ADDIS ABABA
Slip the Ethiopia Heritage Trust's excellent book *Twenty One-Day Trips from Addis Ababa* into your pocket. For a copy, ring the Ethiopia Heritage Trust (☎ 158802) enquire at the British Council (☎ 550022) or ask at major bookshops.

Entoto
Entoto is the horseshoe shaped ridge to the north and east of Addis Ababa. You can ramble undisturbed – a rare privilege in Ethiopia – around the recently established **Entoto Natural Park** and enjoy superb views of the city and surrounding country-side.

Menelik II briefly established his capital here in 1881, constructing the Entoto Maryam Church, which today has a small adjacent museum (entry US$1.50) and St Raguel's Church, before descending to the valley a mere six years later. To get there, hire a taxi or take a No 17 bus to its terminus, then hike on and up for some 3km.

Debre Zeit
The small town of Debre Zeit, which can be very crowded at weekends, is 45km and an hour's drive from Addis Ababa. You can also visit it en route to the Rift Valley Lakes (see Around the Country). At 1900m, it's warmer than Addis Ababa and the base for visiting the nearby crater lakes, all rich in birdlife. **Lake Bishoftu**, just outside Addis Ababa, is the most accessible and **Lake Hora**, a 2km walk away, the most attractive. Buses run frequently from Addis Ababa.

Around the Country

The towns of Axum, Bahar Dar, Gondar and Lalibela constitute what is known as Ethiopia's Historic Route.

AXUM
Axum is the country's holiest city. Here, every Ethiopian Orthodox Christian believes, resides the original Ark of the Covenant. And it was here that King Ezana in the 4th century decreed Christianity to be the state religion. At this time, it was the capital of the powerful Zagwa empire, which was linked by caravan routes to southern Arabia through its port of Adulis (now buried 60km south of Massawa in Eritrea), and which maintained regular contacts with Nubia, Egypt, Greece and Rome.

Things to See
The huge granite monoliths, or steles, of the **Stele Field**, just beyond the museum, are symbols of this ancient grandeur. One, sadly broken, measures 30m, making it the largest monolith in the world.

You buy a ticket (US$7.50) for the Stele Field and other archaeological sites from the **museum**, which is open daily from 8 am to noon and 2 to 6 pm. It has a dusty clutter of interesting but appallingly documented finds from local sites.

Beside the museum is the **St Mary of Zion** church, Ethiopia's holiest shrine, built in the 17th century on the site of a 4th century Axumite church. According to local tradition, the original Ark of the Covenant lies in a building in the grounds, having been smuggled from Jerusalem by Menelik I, but neither you nor anyone are allowed to set eyes upon it. The church is dwarfed by a modern one, built by Haile Selassie in 1965. The church **museum** has a small but impressive collection of bibles, crosses and crowns. Entry to the compound is a hefty US$9.

Just to the north-east of the Stele Field is a modern reservoir, known as **Queen**

ETHIOPIA

Sheba's Pool. From there, a pleasant half-hour walk takes you to **King Kaleb's Palace**. On the way, a nondescript corrugated iron hut houses a half-buried stele with inscriptions in Ge'ez, Sabean (forerunner of Ge'ez) and Greek. The **Pentaleon Monastery**, with superb views of Axum and the distant mountains of Eritrea, is a further half-hour walk beyond the palace. Entry is US$1.50.

The underground **Tomb of King Basen**, in town, and the remains of the so-called **Palace of Queen Sheba**, just beyond the airport, are also worth a visit.

The Stolen Stele of Axum
In 1937 Mussolini's troops looted Axum's finest stele, all 24m of it. It stands in front of Rome's UN Food and Agricultural Organisation headquarters, exposed to the city's traffic pollution, slowly and irrevocably deteriorating. But in 1997, the 50th anniversary of its theft, the Italian government finally agreed to return the obelisk to its rightful place. ■

Places to Stay & Eat
Axum's cheap hotels are on the main street. The *Gorgira Hotel*, the *Abraha We Atsbaha* and the *Queen of Sheba* are all in the US$2.50 to US$3 range. The *Ghenet* has overpriced singles/doubles with communal bathroom for between US$3.75 and US$9, and better value singles with private bathroom for US$7.50.

The *Africa* (☎ 751701) has rooms for US$7.50/10.50, while rooms at the *Atse Kaleb* (☎ 750222) cost US$6/9. Both are friendly, with good restaurants and rooms with private bathroom plus hot water, ranged around courtyards of mature greenery.

Of the two government hotels, the *Axum* (☎ 750205) is central and has character, with rooms for US$24/36. You can camp in the grounds for US$2.25 per person. The *Yeha*, with rooms for US$36/48, is on a hillock north-east of the Stele Field. Both offer a reasonable three course dinner for US$4.25.

Getting There & Away
The airfare between Addis Ababa and Axum is US$65 one way. Axum to Gondar by bus (See the Gondar entry later in this section) takes a day and a half. There are regular minibuses to Adwa, 25km east, and a daily bus service to Adigrat and Mekele, on the main transport route between Addis Ababa and Asmara in Eritrea.

BAHAR DAR
Bahar Dar sits on the southern shore of the 3600 sq km Lake Tana. For a great view of the town and Lake Tana, cycle 5km downstream from the bridge on the Blue Nile's east bank to a commanding hillock, topped by a former palace of Haile Selassie.

The tourist office is on the airport road. You can hire bicycles outside the Ghion and Blue Nile Spring hotels. Bahar Dar has a bustling Saturday **market**.

Lake Tana's Monasteries
The lake has 37 islands, many with monasteries (admission usually US$1.50) dating from the 11th to 16th centuries. Women are not allowed on some of the islands.

Getting to the islands is expensive. The 'official' boats of the Marine Transport Authority charge US$25 per hour – not so outlandish if you team up with other travellers since the boats can take 25 passengers. For a small group, a private boat at US$12 to US$15 is considerably cheaper.

The return boat trip to the most popular monastery, **Kidene Mehret** on the Zege peninsula, takes about three hours. On the way back, you can visit a couple of the small island monasteries, **Kebran Gabriel** (men only) and **Debre Maryam**, plus the inlet where the Blue Nile flows from Lake Tana.

Blue Nile Falls
Known locally as Tis Isat, the Blue Nile Falls are some 400m wide and 50m deep, are impressive at any time and at their best from October to December, after the rainy season.

The falls used to be the haunt of some of the most disagreeable and aggressive hangers-on in all of Africa, however that has changed now. At the Tourist Information Centre in the nearby village of Tis Abbay, a 40 minute walk from the falls, collect its brochure with its easily followed map in return for US$2.25 admission (students US$0.75). You can either come back by the same path or make a circular route, crossing the Blue Nile by papyrus boat (don't pay more than US$1 per person).

Several buses make the 32km, 45 minute journey daily from Bahar Dar to Tis Abbay for US$0.50; the first leaving about 6 am and the last returning at about 3 pm. Unfortunately, under pressure from local tour operators, taxis have been banned from this route so, unless you cycle, the only other option is an expensive trip with one of these tour operators.

Places to Stay & Eat

The US$1 to US$1.50 hotels are between the bus station and the market. The *Mulu Hotel*, *Blue Nile Hotel* and *Daga Pension* (☎ 200070) all have showers and charge US$3.

The rooms at the *Guna Terara Hotel* (☎ 200976) are set around a quiet courtyard, and cost US$6. The *Tekie Hotel* (☎ 200808) has rooms for US$4.50/9 for singles/doubles and the communal showers have hot water.

The *Blue Nile Spring Hotel* (☎ 200038), a 3km minibus ride on the Gondar road, has rooms with private bathroom for US$7.50/13.50 beside a sprawling garden, where you can camp.

The *Ghion* (☎ 200111) has rooms for US$24/36 – more than a third cheaper than its fellow government hotel, the *Tana* (☎ 200626). Both have pleasant lakeside lawns and terraces, and good US$3.75 set menus.

Food and comfort are superior at the new *Dib Anbessa Hotel* (☎ 201436), with rooms at US$27/40. You can also eat well for around US$1 at the friendly, unpretentious *Enkutash Restaurant*, 100m from Bahar Dar's only cinema.

Getting There & Away

A one-way flight from Addis Ababa costs US$38. A taxi from the airport costs US$3. The bus (US$5.50) takes two days to cover the 565km, passing through the spectacular Blue Nile Gorge and stopping overnight in Debre Markos, where a room at the Tourist Hotel costs US$4.50. The 180km bus journey (US$2) to Gondar takes six hours.

DIRE DAWA & HARAR

Dire Dawa was established by the French in 1902 as they pushed the Djibouti to Addis Ababa railway westward. The walled town of Harar, essentially Muslim, was founded in 1520 and, with its 99 mosques, is the fourth most holy in Islam.

You can fly (US$49 one way) from Addis Ababa or take the bus, which follows a scenic route, or the train (US$8, about 20 hours).

Places to Stay

In Dire Dawa, the noisy *Makonnen Hotel* near the train station charges US$5, while the *National* and *Continental* charge US$3. The clean, new *Sai Hotel* has doubles with private bathroom for US$12.

In Harar, cheap hotels include the *Dessic* and *Tourist* (US$2), the *Wantimu* (US$3) and the *Tewodros*, where a double with private bathroom costs US$4. The *Belayneh Hotel* is also good value for money at US$6.

The *Ras Hotel* chain has a branch in both towns, with overpriced doubles at US$33.

GONDAR

About 750km north of Addis Ababa, Gondar was the capital of Ethiopia from its foundation by Emperor Fasilidas in 1632 until 1886.

The piazza – a grandiose name for an unremarkable small square – is the heart of the modern town, where you'll find the Post & Telecommunications and Ethiopian Airlines offices and, up the stairs on the east side, the tourist office.

Things to See

The **Royal Enclosure** occupies an area of 76,000 sq metres. The first and most impressive castle within its surrounding walls was built by Emperor Fasilidas around 1640 and the remainder by his descendants over the next hundred years.

Entry to the compound, which is open from 8.30 am to 12.30 pm and 1.30 to 5.30 pm, costs US$7.50. In principle, the guides are free but they're well informed; it's their livelihood and they merit a tip.

Your ticket also admits you to the **Bath of Fasilidas**, the Emperor's bathing pool and pavilion, which is by the stadium, about 2km out of town on the Bahar Dar road. Continuing for about 1km, take a steep track to the right beyond the hospital to reach the ruined **Palace of Kusquam**; entry costs US$2.25. There's also the splendid **Debre Birhan Selassie Church**, with fine murals and painted ceiling, an easy walk north-east of town. Entry costs US$2.25.

Don't be persuaded to visit the 'Falasha village', about 7km out of town; there's only one Falasha left after the mass emigration to Israel – and even her credentials are dubious.

Places to Stay & Eat

Take a long shower before coming to Gondar since there's a chronic shortage of water. There are some US$1 to US$1.50 hotels near the bus station. Walking north along the main street, the *Ethiopia Hotel* (☎ 110203) costs US$1.25 per person and rooms at the *Kassegn Alemayehu* (☎ 110060) go for US$3.75. Both have popular bars and restaurants. At the *Tourist Hotel* (☎ 110436), you pay US$3.75/6 for singles/doubles, while rooms at the *Yimam* (☎ 110470) cost US$7.50.

The *Misrak Pension* (☎ 110069) has singles/doubles with private bathroom (rarely with water, however) for US$7.50 to US$10.50. Its neighbour, the *Fogera Hotel*, once the residence of General Grazzi, commander of the Fascist forces, has huge rooms with bathroom for US$10/13.75 after mild bargaining. Its restaurant is grim.

For round-the-clock water, choose the new *Nile Gondar Hotel* (☎ 111610), which has its own well. Rooms cost US$15/20. The attractive *Goha Hotel* (☎ 110634), with rooms for US$36/48, has superb views and does a good set menu for US$3.

You can camp in the grounds of the run-down *Terara Hotel* (☎ 110153), with a fine overview of the Royal Enclosure, for US$3.50 per person.

Getting There & Away

One-way flights from Addis Ababa cost US$50. The bus to Bahar Dar (US$2) takes six hours. You can travel to Axum (355km) in one long day by taking the early bus (US$3.25) to Inda Silase (also called Shire), then a connection to Axum (65km, US$1). A bus also runs to Mekele (US$6.50) via Axum and Adigrat, overnighting in Inda Silase.

LALIBELA

What makes Lalibela's 11 **rock churches** unique is that most are hewn straight from the bedrock, so their roofs are at ground level. Originally called Roha, the town takes its present name from the 12th century King Lalibela who, says the legend, established his capital there according to divine instructions revealed in a dream.

All 11 churches were built within a century; some, says another legend, with the help of angels – who must have been working overtime to have completed the massive Bet Abba Libanos church overnight. The churches have been kept alive by generations of priests who guard their treasures of ornamented crosses, illuminated bibles and illustrated manuscripts.

Tickets, valid for all 11 churches for the duration of your stay, cost an extortionate

---

The Lalibela Cross

In 1997 a priest, entering the church of Medhane Alem for his morning vigil, discovered that its 800-year-old holy cross had been stolen. The cross, believed to have belonged to King Lalibela himself, is more important to Ethiopian Christians than any relic of Rome or Jerusalem and its theft was treated as a national disaster. It's the most spectacular example among hundreds of stolen Ethiopian historical treasures, most of which find their way onto the European art market. ■

US$15. Your visit will be a misery unless you hire a guide. You'll be assailed as soon as you enter town. To engage a reputable guide at a fair price, go to the tourist office or the Seven Olives hotel.

For exhilarating views and a temporary reprieve from the constant pestering, make the four hour round trip trek to the **Asheton Maryam monastery**; entry costs US$3.

The tourist office is on the west side of town, beside the high school. The Ethiopian Airlines office is in room 26 of the Seven Olives Hotel, at which you can change money, including travellers' cheques.

Places to Stay & Eat
Of the budget hotels, the friendly and central *Fikresalem* has rooms for US$3 and good local food for US$1. The *Lasta*, as basic as you can get, has singles/doubles for US$1.50/ 2.25, while rooms at the *Kadent*, less of a blockhouse, cost US$3/3.75.

The *Serkie's Hotel*, on the west side of town, is good value at US$2.25 per person, while the 'alternative' *Roha Hotel*, popular with travellers, charges US$4.50 a head. All the above have communal bathrooms. Prices at the *Asheton*, another travellers' favourite, are the same as the Roha's but its doubles have private bathrooms.

At the western extremity of town, the new private *Lal Hotel*, with rooms for US$21/48 and a good restaurant, is much better value than the two government hotels: its neighbour, the *Roha*, and the glum, run-down *Seven Olives*, both charge US$36/48 and you can camp at the latter for US$6 per tent. The set meal at each costs US$4.25.

For cheap, local food, try the *Manharia* or *Tiszeta* restaurants on the north side of the main drag. Both are signed in Amharic only.

Getting There & Away
One-way flights from Addis Ababa cost US$50 and from Gondar a bargain US$14. Once the new road connecting Lalibela with the capital is completed, it will be possible to make the bus journey in one long day. At the time of writing, the journey took two days with a change of bus in Weldiya.

RIFT VALLEY LAKES
The wide valley through which the highway to Kenya slices is generally fertile and lush.

Distances from Addis Ababa to the seven lakes are:

Ziway	160km
Langano, Abiyata and Shala	205km
Awasa	273km
Abaya and Chamo	505km

Lake Ziway
Lake Ziway is great for bird-watching. From the jetty, you can take a boat to Tullo Guddo island. You can stay and eat well at the *Bekelle Molla* (US$4.50) or the new *Ziway Tourist* (US$5.25) hotels. Both, at the southern end of town, have doubles with private bathroom.

Lakes Langano, Abiyata & Shala
These lakes, one brown, one silver and one blue, respectively, form a trio. The latter two are designated a national park, though very much in name only. Lake Abiyata is shallow and rich in birdlife, with up to 200,000 flamingo in season. Lake Shala nestles in a crater over 250m deep. There's a fine view from the hill above the narrow neck separating the two.

Only Lake Langano has accommodation. It's also the only lake that's bilharzia-free and safe for swimming. You can stay at the *Wabe Shebelle Hotel*, US$29.50 for up to four people, or the *Bekele Molla*, where doubles cost US$9 and US$22.75, and you can camp for US$1.50 per tent. Prices rise at weekends. Both have restaurants, the latter outstandingly mediocre.

You can swim in the hot springs (entry US$0.50) at **Wondo Genet**, in the hills 17km east of Sheshamene, from where buses run. Its *Wabe Shebelle Hotel* (☎ (06) 201576) has doubles for US$21; more at weekends.

Lake Awasa
There's plenty of budget accommodation in Awasa town. Of the two lakeside *Wabe Shebelle* hotels, No 1 has doubles for US$19,

while No 2 is both cheaper and friendlier. There's a pleasant 1km walk along the flood embankment between them.

Lakes Abaya & Chamo

From Arba Minch, where there's a range of accommodation, these lakes lie 3km north-east and 8km south-east, respectively, within Nechi Sar National Park. The scenery's wild and the wildlife, including crocodile, plentiful.

Tourism & Development

The NGO Farm Africa has established a luxury camp beside Lake Langano. At US$85 for a double tent and full board, it's beyond the budget of most travellers but you have the satisfaction of knowing that your money goes to the local people. They run the camp – 42 of them working as guides, cooks, gardeners and so on. Profits in only two years have funded a clinic, a new school, piped drinking water – and a tree nursery to compensate the villagers for giving up their traditional wooding rights. ∎

National Parks

For Abiyata-Shala and Nechi Sar national parks, see the previous Rift Valley Lakes section.

BALE MOUNTAINS NATIONAL PARK

This 2400 sq km park, rich in endemic animals and birds, is some 400km south of Addis Ababa. Within it are the Sanetti Plateau, Africa's highest moorland, and Tullu Demtu, at 4377m Ethiopia's second highest mountain. You can arrange one to five-day treks, on foot or by mule, at the park headquarters in Dinsho, from where there's an interesting 1km nature trail. There's self-catering accommodation at the lodge for US$8 for a double or US$2 in a dormitory, or you can camp. It's advisable to book (☎ Addis Ababa (01) 516938).

SIMIEN MOUNTAINS NATIONAL PARK

This park is excellent for trekking, with spectacular views and a large variety of wildlife: baboon, ibex, Simien fox and predatory birds, including the rare lammergeyer. You can make round trips of between three and 10 days either on foot or by mule, building in an ascent of Africa's fourth highest peak, the 4620m Ras Dashen.

The starting point is at **Debark**, 101km and about four hours by bus (US$1.25) from Gondar. Daily fees, payable at the national park office, are: US$10 per person per 48 hours, US$3.50 for a camp site per day and US$3 for an armed 'scout'. You pay US$7.50 per day for an English-speaking guide (including their own park fees), plus US$1.50 for a mule and muleteer. You can hire a tent for US$3 per night.

In Debark, you can stay at the *Simien Hotel*, where a double costs US$3.75.

Lonely Planet's *Trekking in East Africa* guide covers trekking in the Simien Mountains in detail.

Gabon

Few travellers get to Gabon. The hassles associated with getting a visa and the expense put most people off. Nevertheless, the contrasts are spectral. From the virgin rainforests of the interior to the glitzy modernity of the capital, Libreville, Gabon has the lot, but travelling is not easy once you leave the main roads and the railway. Traditional African culture has all but disappeared under the onslaught of oil money and French influence, though it's still worth passing through if you're taking the western coastal route north or south.

Facts about the Country

HISTORY

Gabon appears to have been populated originally by Pygmies who lived in small family units along riverbanks, but they survive today only in the more remote parts of the country. They were displaced by migrating peoples from the north between the 16th and 18th centuries, principally the Fang who came from what are now Cameroon and Equatorial Guinea.

Contact with Europeans, starting with the arrival of the Portuguese in 1472, set a train of events in motion which had a profound effect on tribal social structures. The Portuguese largely ignored the area, preferring to base their activities on the nearby islands of Bioko and São Tomé. However, British, Dutch and French ships called in along the coast regularly to trade for slaves, ivory and precious tropical woods.

The capital, Libreville, was established as a settlement for freed slaves in 1849 on the site of a French fort constructed in 1843. The capital of the region was transferred to Brazzaville (Congo) in 1904, and six years later Gabon became a French colony in French Equatorial Africa. The country became independent in 1960 under the pres-

GABONESE REPUBLIC (RÉPUBLIQUE GABONAISE)
Area: 267,665 sq km
Population: 1.3 million
Population Growth Rate: 1.8%
Capital: Libreville
Head of State: President El Hadj Omar Bongo
Official Language: French
Currency: Central African CFA franc
Exchange Rate: CFA 575 = US$1
Per Capita GNP: US$3500
Inflation: 30%
Time: GMT/UTC +1

Highlights

- Visiting the Musée des Arts et Traditions in Libreville
- Lazing on a beach at Cap Estérias
- Experiencing the abundant wildlife in Gabon's reserves
- Taking a pirogue trip into the lake region near Lambaréné

idency of M'Ba, who died in a French hospital in 1967.

Gabon was once regarded as the economic miracle of equatorial Africa. The newly independent nation got off to an extravagant start. With the money rolling in from the sale of oil, manganese ore, iron ore, chrome, gold and diamonds, the country sported a per capita income higher than that of South Africa and only slightly lower than that of Libya.

That was before the oil glut, the recession of

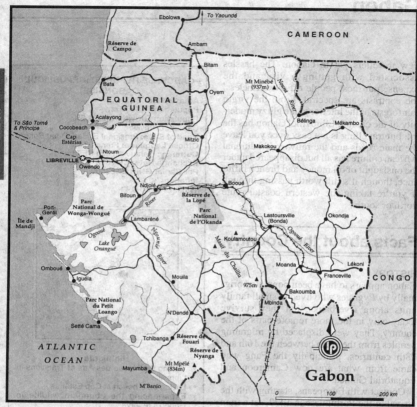

Gabon

the early 1980s and the downturn in the steel industry (the major consumer of manganese). All these wreaked havoc with the Gabonese economy, but external factors were not the only reasons for the change of fortunes.

In 1976 an ambitious four-year plan, with a budget of US$32 billion, was announced, with the intention to create a modern transport system, encourage local industry and develop mineral deposits. Most of the money was squandered on misguided projects.

The downturn in the country's earnings, however, did not prevent the completion of the US$140 million presidential palace, or the staging of one of the most extravagant Organisation of African Unity (OAU) summits ever held or ever likely to be held again.

Gabon has been ruled since 1967 by President El Hadj Omar Bongo (who adopted Islam in 1974). With a personal bodyguard composed of European mercenaries and Moroccan troops, the presence of 400 French airborne crack troops as well as numerous French political and military advisers, Bongo has been able to project a remarkable image of stability for the country.

From 1968 the country was a one party state, with lucrative ministerial posts frequently shuffled between a small number of political faithfuls.

In mid-1978, with the oil industry on the downturn, 10,000 Beninois workers were expelled after Benin's then President Kérékou renewed his allegations that Gabon had been used as a staging post for the 1977 attempt by airborne mercenaries to invade Benin. Again, in 1979, an atmosphere of xenophobia was created towards refugees from Equatorial Guinea.

In 1990 Bongo ended more than two decades of one party rule by legalising opposition parties. Multiparty elections were held in December 1993. Although Bongo won, he only gained a little over 50% of the vote. Wrangles continued over the role of opposition until negotiations held in France resulted in the Paris Agreement in September 1994. The timing of elections and the role of the parliament remains the subject of debate.

GEOGRAPHY & CLIMATE
Gabon consists of a narrow, low-lying coastal strip which rises to a series of plateaus with peaks over 1500m. Tropical rainforests cover three-quarters of the country and deep river valleys dissect the country into small, relatively isolated units. The climate is hot (the average temperature is 27°C) and humid. The dry season extends from May to September, with a short dry spell in mid-December.

POPULATION & PEOPLE
The population numbers about 1.3 million, most of whom are of Bantu origin. The Fang makes up about a third of the population.

LANGUAGE
French is the official language, but in the interior there are many local languages spoken, including Fang, Bapunu and Bandgabi. See the Language Appendix for useful French phrases.

Facts for the Visitor

VISAS
The Gabonese authorities seem to regard virtually all foreigners with suspicion. As a result, everyone needs a visa, and they take up to a week or more to come through since applications have to be referred to Libreville by telex.

Visas cost US$80 plus US$10 for the telex and require two photos. In theory, you also need an invitation from a resident or citizen of Gabon and an onward airline ticket, but these requirements may be waived at embassies in adjoining countries, especially Equatorial Guinea (at the embassy in Malaba and the consulate in Bata) where visas can be issued in a few hours.

The only exception to the above rules concerns São Tomé & Príncipe, where there is no embassy. If you fly into Libreville from São Tomé, you can buy a visa on arrival for US$50, but it will most likely be just a four day transit visa (possibly renewable).

A fee of US$12 will be charged to enter overland into Gabon at Cocobeach.

Visa Extensions
These are available from SEDOC in the Zone Industrielle and cost US$100.

Other Visas
Benin
> Visas are good for stays of two weeks, require two photos and cost US$7.50. The consulate is open from Monday to Wednesday from 9 am to noon and 3.30 to 5.30 pm, and issues visas within 24 hours.

Burkina Faso, Chad & Togo
> You can get visas for these countries from the French consulate, which is open weekdays from 7 to 11 am, and issues visas within 24 hours.

Cameroon
> Multiple-entry, 90-day visas for Cameroon cost US$60 and you need two photos and an onward airline ticket. The airline ticket may be subject to negotiation. The embassy issues visas in 24 hours if you make your application in the morning. The embassy is open weekdays from 8 am to 1 pm.

GABON

Central African Republic
Visas cost US$60, require two photos and are good for a one month stay. They are issued in 24 hours. The embassy is open weekdays from 8 am to 1.30 pm. However, for Australians, New Zealanders, Irish and a few other nationalities, the embassy must first telex Bangui, a process that can take a week or more.

Congo
Visas to the Congo cost US$70 and require one photo. They are issued in 24 hours and are valid for a stay of two weeks from the date of entry. The embassy is open on weekdays from 8 am to 2 pm.

Congo (Zaïre)
The cost of visas varies, but you will need two photos and a letter of introduction from your own embassy. Single-entry, one-month visas cost US$75 (US$120 for multiple entry), single-entry, two-month visas cost US$135 (US$180 for multiple entry) and single-entry, three-month visas cost US$200 (US$225 for multiple entry). The embassy is open weekdays from 9 am to 3 pm and Saturday until noon, and issues visas within 24 hours.

Equatorial Guinea
Visas cost US$60, require one photo and are issued in two to three days. The visas are valid for a stay of one month. The embassy is open weekdays from 8 am to 3 pm.

Nigeria
The cost of visas varies depending on your nationality (see the Nigerian chapter). One-month visas require two photos, an onward airline ticket, and a letter of invitation from a resident or citizen of Nigeria or a letter explaining why you want to visit Nigeria. Visas are generally issued within 48 hours, but they can take up to one week. The embassy is open from 8 am to 3 pm.

São Tomé & Príncipe
Visas cost US$30 and you need two photos. Applications are only accepted on Monday and Wednesday between 8 and 11 am. You then collect your passport the following day between 3 and 5 pm.

EMBASSIES
Gabonese Embassies

In Africa, Gabon has embassies in Cameroon, the Congo, Congo (Zaïre) Côte d'Ivoire, Egypt, Equatorial Guinea (Malabo and Bata), Mauritania, Morocco, Nigeria, Senegal and Togo.

Outside Africa, there are embassies in Belgium, Canada, France, Germany, Italy, Japan, Spain, Switzerland, the UK and the USA.

Foreign Embassies in Gabon
Countries with diplomatic representation in Libreville include:

Benin
Blvd Léon Mba, Quartier Derrière Prison (☎ 73 7692)

Cameroon
Blvd Léon Mba, Quartier Derrière Prison (☎ 73 2800)

Central African Republic
North of Voie Express, near the airport (☎ 73 7761)

Congo
Gué-Gué, just off Blvd Ouaban near Citibank (☎ 67 7078)

Congo (Zaïre)
Gué-Gué, just off Blvd Ouaban near Citibank (☎ 73 8141)

Côte d'Ivoire
Immeuble Diamont, Blvd de l'Indépendance (☎ 72 0596)

Equatorial Guinea
Blvd Yves-Digo, before L'Église d'Akébé, Akébéville (☎ 76 3015)

France
Rue Ange Mba (☎ 74 3420)

Germany
Immeuble des Frangipaniers, Blvd de l'Indépendance (☎ 76 0188)

Nigeria
Blvd Léon Mba, Quartier Derrière Prison (☎ 73 2201)

São Tomé & Príncipe
Blvd de l'Indépendance (☎ 72 0994)

UK
BP 476 (☎ 72 2985)

USA
Blvd de l'Indépendance, near the Novotel Rapontchombo (☎ 76 2003)

MONEY
US$1 = CFA 575

The unit of currency is the Central African CFA franc, made up of 100 centimes.

The conditions for changing travellers' cheques at the banks are very similar to those in Cameroon and other Central CFA franc countries, except that the commissions charged can be punitive – make enquiries before you change. As elsewhere, cash has the edge.

There are banks in the largest towns (eg Franceville, Lambaréné, Moanda etc), but many of them refuse to change money or travellers' cheques other than those denominated in French francs or CFA francs.

The American Express (Amex) representative is Eurafrique Voyages (☎ 76 2787), BP 4026, Rue de la Grande Poste, Libreville. Amex travellers' cheques can be arranged here against a credit card and personal cheque for 3% commission.

It's almost impossible to change CFA francs to French francs at banks – staff will tell you they don't have any.

POST & COMMUNICATIONS

Poste restante is available, but it is expensive at US$1 per letter.

International telephone connections are good. Telephone rates are high – about US$7 per minute to Europe or the USA. Almost all the public telephones in Libreville are card phones. You can buy these cards in various denominations at the communications centre in the centre of Libreville, east of the Air Afrique office.

Gabon's country code is 241; there are no area codes.

PHOTOGRAPHY

Photography is a touchy subject in Gabon. Never take a photograph of the airport, any government buildings or military installations, vehicles or personnel. If you do, your film and camera will be subject to confiscation.

PUBLIC HOLIDAYS

Public holidays observed in Gabon include: 1 January, 12 March, 1 May, 17 August (Independence Day), 25 December, Easter Monday and variable Islamic holidays. Also see Public Holidays in the Regional Facts for the Visitor chapter for dates of Islamic holidays.

Getting There & Away

AIR

Air Gabon (the national airline), Ecuato Guineana de Aviacion (the Equatorial Guinea airline), Air São Tomé e Príincipe (the São Tomé airline) and Sabena, among others, service Gabon through Libreville. You'll find that there are good connections with other countries in East and Central Africa.

Flights to São Tomé are best booked through Mistral Voyages (☎ 76 0421), Immeuble Diamant, Blvd de l'Indépendance. Return tickets cost US$360 (US$280 weekend special) and the flight takes about 80 minutes.

LAND

Cameroon

Travelling by *taxis-brousse* (bush taxis) and minibuses from Libreville to Yaoundé takes about three days.

From Bitam there are plenty of vehicles to the border, from where it's half an hour to the Ntem River. Ferries operate regularly, or you can take a *pirogue* (dugout canoe). From the river you head for Ambam, from where it's five hours to Ebolowa and another 2½ hours to Yaoundé (US$4).

Congo

The major route connecting Libreville and Brazzaville is by road and rail via Lambaréné, N'Dendé and Loubomo; the total trip should take a minimum of six days.

The Libreville to N'Dendé section usually takes two days by a series of trucks and/or minibuses, and costs about US$50. Between N'Dendé and Kibangou (185km) in the Congo, you'll find only occasional trucks. There are daily trucks going south from Kibangou to Loubomo (US$4, three hours). The stretch between Loubomo and Brazzaville is normally done by train.

Be sure to get an exit stamp at N'Dendé, 40km before the border.

The alternative Libreville to Brazzaville

route takes about four days and is mostly by train. From Libreville, take the daily *Transgabonais* train to Franceville but get off at Moanda (US$52/42 in 1st/2nd class, nine hours), and from there a series of minibuses or trucks to the border at Mbinda (about US$9). From Mbinda take a train to Loubomo and then take another from there to Brazzaville.

Equatorial Guinea

The Libreville to Bata (Equatorial Guinea) route is via the border town of Cocobeach (Gabonese customs and immigration), where you should spend the night as accommodation is a problem until you get to Mbini or Bata.

From Libreville it's 2½ hours to Cocobeach by pick-up. From Cocobeach there are daily motorised pirogues across the Estuaire du Muni to Cogo (Equatorial Guinean customs and immigration) and then on to Acalayong. The pirogues leave when full, cost US$8 and take about four hours (including the stop at Cogo). You'll be charged an 'exit fee' of US$10 at Cocobeach and a similar 'entry fee' at Cogo, but the fee is negotiable. From Acalayong there are pick-ups to Mbini and there are others from there to Bata.

Going from Libreville to Bata via Acurenam is not an option as you cannot cross the border at that point.

SEA
Cameroon

There are occasional freight boats that ply between Libreville and Douala which *may* take passengers. Fares are negotiable, but don't expect any comforts and bring your own food and drink. Enquire at Port Môle (the old port) in Libreville about the possiblility.

São Tomé

The *Solmar II* sails from Libreville to São Tomé on a fairly regular schedule, and the one-way fare is US$72.

Getting Around

AIR

Air Gabon has flights from Libreville to Lambaréné, Port-Gentil and Franceville. Student discounts of 30% are available.

ROAD

Most of the roads are dirt and, although generally well maintained, can become treacherous in the rainy season. Local driving standards are poor and truck drivers are invariably drunk. Most truck drivers stop at a bar on average every hour, so it takes a long time to get anywhere using this form of transport and it's far from safe.

Minibuses go in all directions, but the number of people travelling is relatively small, so don't expect much choice of vehicles, even from Libreville. From Libreville to Franceville, Moanda or Lastoursville, it is just as cheap to travel 2nd class on the train as on a minibus and it's a lot faster.

For other destinations, you can sometimes cut costs slightly by taking trucks; the place to catch them in Libreville is on the outskirts of town at Km 5.

TRAIN

The *Transgabonais* runs four times a week between Owendo (a few kilometres south of Libreville) and Franceville via Booué and Lastoursville, and is very efficient and punctual. First class is excellent and 2nd class very comfortable, though there's no guarantee of a seat in 2nd class. Both classes are pretty crowded. Every train has a buffet car selling sandwiches, soft drinks and beer. First/2nd class fares from Libreville to Franceville cost US$55/44.

BOAT
Libreville to Port-Gentil

There are several boats which do the run between Libreville and Port-Gentil almost every day, and they all cost between US$34 and US$39. The fastest is the *Elsa-Dorothie* (*'la vedette'*) which takes four hours, with five departures a week in either direction. Uro-Gabon also has two small boats, which leave every morning in each direction and take five hours. Finally, there is the slower *La Léombi* (the *grand bateau*, or large boat), which is better for those with considerable luggage. It takes eight hours, with one round trip every two days.

Port-Gentil to Lambaréné

There are also boats along the Ogooué River between Port-Gentil and Lambaréné (some go on to Ndjolé). The smaller boats leave Port-Gentil on Monday and Friday, tickets cost US$27 and the trip takes about 10 hours. The larger *Azingo* makes only one round trip a week, leaving Port-Gentil on Monday and Lambaréné on Thursday. The *Azingo* is more like a floating village and potentially more fun if you don't mind sleeping overnight on board. First/2nd class fares are US$31/20, and it takes 1½ days upriver and 24 hours downriver, with stops at lots of villages en route.

Ndjolé to Lambaréné & Port-Gentil

In addition to the scheduled ferries, it's possible to get rides on oil barges along the Ogooué River. At Ndjolé there is a Mobil oil depot, from where barges run to Lambaréné (US$8, seven hours) and Port-Gentil on a semi-regular basis. Enquire at the depot in Quartier Bingoma about getting on board, though it's generally best to speak directly with the captains.

Take your own food and drink with you. There are two stores near the dock in Ndjolé where you can buy bread, cheese and groceries of all kinds. Also, take a mat to sit on as the barges are somewhat dirty and there are no cabins.

Libreville

Libreville can be an interesting city if you take the time to get to know it. Each *quartier* (quarter) has its own character and is peppered with bars and boutiques. It might look a far cry from towns in the interior with its wide boulevards and sealed roads, but it doesn't take too long to get out of this area. The main drawback to Libreville is cost – it's one of the most expensive cities on the continent.

Information

Gabontour (☎ 74 6788), the government's travel advisory service, has a small office at the airport.

The bank at the airport operates strange hours, but is generally open Monday to Friday from 8 to 10.30 am and 6 to 8 pm.

The main post office, Centre Ville, is on Blvd de l'Indépendance. To make any long-distance calls, go to the communications centre on Ave Félix Éboué, east of Air Afrique.

One of the best travel agents is Mistral Voyages (☎ 76 0421), Immeuble Diamant, Blvd de l'Indépendance.

Things to See

Don't miss **L'Église St-Michel** (St-Michel Church) in N'Kembo, 1km east (further inland) from Mt Bouët. It's a beautiful building, the entire facade of which is covered with mosaics and local wood, carved to depict stories from the Bible.

The **Musée des Arts et Traditions**, on the ocean road next to the modern Elf Gabon building two blocks north of the Novotel Rapontchombo, has numerous examples of indigenous art, musical instruments and masks. Good tours are conducted in French.

Le Village des Artisans, near the US embassy on Blvd de l'Indépendance, is worth a visit for masks, wooden statues, carved bowls, plates and soapstone, although most of the items are imported from the Congo, Ghana and Congo (Zaïre).

Places to Stay

The most popular place to stay is the *Maison Libermann* (☎ 76 1955) near the gare routière. It's friendly, clean, quiet and comfortable, and has hot showers. Singles/doubles cost US$16/18. Directly opposite is the *Maison Emilie de Villeneuve Soeurs*

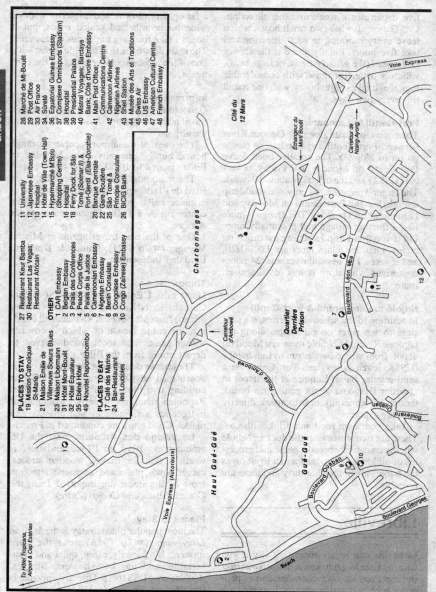

PLACES TO STAY
19 Mission Catholique
   St-Marie
21 Maison Emilie de
   Villeneuve Soeurs Blues
23 Hôtel Mont-Bouët
31 Hôtel Mont-Bouët
32 Hôtel Equateur
35 Edéné Hôtel
49 Novotel Rapontchombo

PLACES TO EAT
17 Café des Marins
24 Bar-Restaurant
   les Loucioles

27 Restaurant Keur Bamba
30 Restaurant Las Vegas;
   Restaurant Africain

OTHER
1 CAR Embassy
2 Belgian Embassy
3 Maison Libermann
4 Peace Corps Office
5 Palais de la Justice
6 Cameroonian Embassy
8 Benin Consulate
9 Congolese Embassy
10 Congo (Zairese) Embassy

11 University
12 Japanese Embassy
13 Hospital
14 Hôtel de Ville (Town Hall)
15 Hypermarché M'Bolo
   (Shopping Centre)
16 Hospital
18 Ferry Dock for São
   Tomé (Solmar II) &
   Port-Gentil (Elisa-Dorothie)
20 Banque Centrale
22 São Tomé &
   Principe Consulate
26 BICIG Bank

28 Marché de Mt-Bouët
29 Post Office
33 Air France
34 Sûreté
36 Equatorial Guinea Embassy
37 Complexe Omnisports (Stadium)
38 Hospital
39 Presidential Palace
40 Mistral Voyages; Barclays
   Bank; Côte d'Ivoire Embassy
41 Main Post Office;
   Communications Centre
42 Cameroon Airlines;
   Nigerian Airlines
43 Shell Station
44 Musée des Arts et Traditions
45 Swiss Air
46 US Embassy
47 American Cultural Centre
48 French Embassy

GABON

Libreville

0   250   500 m

To Kango,
Lambaréné,
Cocobeach
& Oyem

Route de Kango

To Train
Station &
Owendo

(Autoroute)

Échangeur
de Kango

Akébé Plaine

Glass

Likouala-
Moussaka

To Owendo, Port, Train
Station, Brazzaville,
Loubomo & Kibangou

Akébéville

Petit
Paris

Mt-Bouët

Montagne Sainte

N'Kembo

Quartier
Louis

Batavia

Nombakélé

Estuaire
du Gabon

Port Môle

Pompidou

Boulevard Joseph Deemin

Rue Pierre Barro

Boulevard de l'Indépendance (Boulevard de la Mer)

Boulevard Omar Bongo

Ave Jean Paul II

Boulevard Bessieux

Rue Montagne

Montée Lorraine

Rue Alsace
Lorraine

Cours Pasteur

Cours Oureau

Rue Laford

Rue Angé Mba

Rue Parant

Rue Pecqueur

Ave Col

Avenue Félix Éboué

Rue Noémbé

Rue M. Bouët

Avenue Nkoutan

Rue Albert Bivoull

Bivd

Rue des Frères

Boulevard Léon Mba

Rue Marc N'Doumi

Boulevard Léon Mba

Rue Vincent Loubenri

Rue Batavia

Boulevard Yves Digo (Route de Akébaville)

Carrefour
Léon Mba

13

29

36

35

28

30

31

34

32

33

27

26

25

20

24

23

21

14

15

16

17

18

19

37

38

39

40

41

42

43

44

45

46

47

48

49

Blues (a catholic mission), which has rooms for US$14.

Similar is the *Mission Catholique St-Marie*, which charges about the same. The two storey dormitory lodging is next to the church.

Among the hotels, the best is the well-managed *Hôtel Mont-Bouët* (☎ 76 5846). Relative to other hotels in town, it's an outstanding deal at US$20 for a spotless room. It's secure, offers luggage storage and is centrally located – only a seven minute walk from the gare routière down Rue Mt-Bouët towards the city centre.

Next in line price wise is the *Ebéné Hôtel* (☎ 74 4093) on Rue Ndona, near the Complexe Omnisports in Akébéville. The rooms, which cost from US$22 to US$27, are fairly large and have fans, but the hotel is fairly run-down compared to the Mont-Bouët.

Places to Eat

Across from the gare routière you'll find several Senegalese restaurants, including the *Restaurant Rio Nunez*, where you can get breakfast for US$1. The *Restaurant de la Gare Routière* on the south-east side of the gare is another reliable place for a meal, but it closes early (7 pm).

Rue Ndona is lined with cheap restaurants and street-food places. One is the *Restaurant Las Vegas*, which has standard Senegalese food and is very crowded at lunch time with single men. The *Restaurant Africain* next door is similar.

If you're staying at Maison Libermann, try the *Bar-Restaurant les Loucioles*, which is slightly upmarket compared to the food places at the gare routière.

In the city centre, the cheapest place to eat is probably the *Pam-Ly* food stall on Rue Pecqueur, a few metres inland from the Blvd de l'Indépendance.

For the best American fast food in Central Africa, head for the ultra-modern *American Burger* (marked 'American Food') at the Hypermarché M'Bolo shopping centre.

For more upmarket West African cooking, there's the *Restaurant Keur Bamba*, a very modest place on Rue d'Alsace Lorraine.

The cheapest French restaurant in town is probably *Restaurant Chez Nous* on Ave Col Parant. Main dishes cost around US$6, and you have the choice of eating inside or out on the front terrace.

Getting There & Away

Taxi-Brousse & Minibus Most minibuses leave from the gare routière just north of the Marché de Mt-Bouët, but you can also find them further east at the gare routière on Blvd Léon Kalfa near the Voie Express.

Train The gare routière for the *Transgabonais* is just before Owendo, about 10km south of town. A share-taxi to the train station costs US$1 compared to up to US$10 for a private taxi.

Getting Around

The cheapest way to get to/from the airport is on one of the taxi-buses which pass in front of the airport. They're all headed to the gare routière in Mt-Bouët and charge US$0.50. A private taxi to the airport or the train station will cost you up to US$10 (negotiable).

Fares for a share-taxi are US$0.30 for short trips and around US$1 for longer ones. Fares for a privately hired taxi are US$2 for a short drop and US$3 for a longer drop.

AROUND LIBREVILLE

The beaches north of the city toward the airport are very pleasant. **Cap Estérias**, which you can get to by taxi for US$1, is popular, as is Pointe-Dénis, across the estuary from Libreville.

At **Pointe-Dénis** there is a small hotel and an excellent but expensive restaurant. Day trips and overnight camping are both possible. There are a few local bars in the fishing villages nearby where you can also find food, entertainment and possibly accommodation.

The only way across the estuary is by outboard canoe, which runs on an erratic schedule from Port Môle.

Around the Country

COCOBEACH

Local people here are very friendly, and it's quite likely you'll be offered a place to stay. If not, there's the *Hôtel Chez Tante Mado*, which charges US$10 for a basic double and offers reasonably priced bush meat for dinner.

FRANCEVILLE

Franceville is the terminus of the railway line from Libreville and is the largest town in south-eastern Gabon. It derives its importance from the nearby manganese and uranium mines, and also from the fact that the president was born close by at Bongoville – hence the impressive range of facilities in the town.

It's a sprawling city with little of interest to the traveller.

Places to Stay & Eat

The best value for money is the friendly *Paroisse St-Hilaire* (☎ 67 7183), 1.5km east of the Grand Marché on the Route de Bongoville, where rooms start at US$11. If it's full, try the *Motel Joumas* (☎ 67 7616), 1km to the south on Rue Principal. It is way overpriced at US$28 for an air-con room. The French-run *Hôtel Poubara* (☎ 67 7370) is similarly priced but much better value.

There are plenty of cheap restaurants at both the Marché Poto-Poto and the Petit Marché. For a splurge, you'll have to go to one of the big hotels and pay around US$13 for a meal.

LAMBARÉNÉ

Gabon's third largest city is built on an island in the middle of the Ogooué River.

Things to See

Lambaréné's big attraction is the **Schweitzer Hospital** about 8km from town. The hospital is still fully functioning and a new, large annexe was built in 1981. It's one of Gabon's finest hospitals. Albert Schweit-

zer's office, home, library, laboratory and treatment centre are still there, although deteriorating.

Part of the hospital is a museum, and guided tours are available. The guide is sometimes Albert Frey, an old Alsatian Protestant preacher and godson of the famous doctor. His English is shaky, but his enthusiasm makes up for it. There's no entrance fee, although a donation is expected.

From Lambaréné you can take a pirogue trip into the **lake region**, where hippos and other wildlife can be seen (especially during the dry season). This is expensive, since it takes most of the day to go far enough to see much. You're looking at around US$75 for a half-day trip shared by up to five people, but getting a group together is difficult as there are so few travellers around.

Places to Stay

The largest and best known cheapie is the *Hôtel Lépopa*, next to the Bar-Dancing le Capitole. Prices range from US$7 to US$13 per room.

La Petite Auberge, two blocks south-east, is run by a friendly English-speaking man from Benin. The slightly grubby rooms have mosquito nets and fans, and cost US$5.

On the island itself there are two cheap places worth checking: the *Hôtel Angleterre* and an unmarked pink-coloured *case de passage*, both with rooms for US$7. The beds are clean enough, but the bucket showers are filthy.

The best mid-range places are the two Catholic missions on the northern side of the island. There's the *Mission de l'Immaculée Conception*, which charges US$12 for a very clean, comfortable room; and the *Mission Catholique St-François-Xavier*, which has a charge of US$9 for a dorm bed or US$12 for a double room.

At Lac Evaro, about 1½ hours upriver from Lambaréné and on a very picturesque island, is the *Hôtel du Lac Evaro* (☎ 78 1075), run by Mr Legrand, his nephew and the nephew's Mauritian wife (a great cook!). It offers simple but very decent accommodation in cottages for US$27, a swimming pool and bar. Mr Legrand will pick you up from Lambaréné if you call ahead.

Places to Eat
The nuns at one of the missions recommend the Senegalese-run *Touba* restaurant down by the river (near the bridge). *Chez Tante Marie*, south of the river by the soap factory, is recommended for its excellent selection of bush meat (monkey, wild boar, gazelle, crocodile etc). Marie herself is a friendly woman and good for a chat.

Also good for a splurge is *Chai TT*, owned and operated by a friendly French woman called Tété. The place has air-con, and serves French and Gabonese food in a simple style – much like a restaurant in the French provinces.

MOANDA
Moanda is one of Gabon's manganese mining centres and, as a result, it has one of the largest French expatriate communities in the country. The area of town in which they live has all the amenities you would expect to find in France, though the African miners' quarters resemble a small version of Soweto.

Places to Stay & Eat
The excellent value *Mission Catholique St-Dominique*, which is on the same road as the post office, offers spotlessly clean rooms with air-con and shared clean showers and toilets for US$12. Otherwise try the friendly *Hôtel Ampassi*, also on the main drag, with rooms for US$13. There's a good African restaurant next door.

MOUILA
This is the major town between Lambaréné and the Congo border.

For a cheap room try the *mission catholique*, the *mission protestante* or the *Mess Militaire*.

N'DENDÉ
This is the last village of any size before the Congo border. If you are heading for the Congo, remember that you must get an exit stamp before going on to the border.

The *mission catholique* charges US$8 for a double, or there's a *case de passage* west of the main intersection for the same price.

Expect to pay US$7 to get to the Congo border or Mouila by local transport.

NDJOLÉ
There's nothing particularly interesting to recommend this town which has grown up around the port. There's no cheap accommodation, but you may be stuck here for the night. The best value accommodation is the *Hôtel la Vallée* near the central market, where rooms cost US$11. The train station is 11km out of town.

OYEM
Oyem is the largest city in the north. It is in the heart of a cocoa-growing area, and is home to a large number of Muslim Hausa traders from Nigeria.

There's a *mission catholique* and a *mission protestante*, both of which may have cheap accommodation. Otherwise there's the *Hôtel la Cabosse* (☎ 98 6088), near the gare routière, which charges US$15/18 for singles/doubles.

National Parks

Because Gabon has so few people, wildlife is still quite abundant in many areas. Gorilla, chimpanzee, leopard, mandrill, monkey, antelope and elephant are fairly common. Along the coast and in the lagoons there are still quite a few crocodile, hippo, manatee and, offshore in season, humpback whales.

RÉSERVE DE LA LOPÉ
The easiest wildlife reserve to get to is Réserve de la Lopé, which borders both the railway and the road. Get off at the village of Lopé, two stops before Booué. This is the best place in the country to see wildlife, but you need your own vehicle to explore the park – you're not allowed in on foot and budget travellers are not well catered for

(camping is not allowed inside the park, for instance).

Established in 1982, the park consists of open savannah and small but dense forests beside the riverbeds. Except during the rainy season, the animals tend to favour the dense forest and you won't see much other than buffalo. For car rentals, try Gustave at the Au Nid des Routiers in Lopé or the game wardens, who have a vehicle at their disposal. The park entry fee is US$12.

Places to Stay & Eat

At the park entrance, *Le Campement* is a mid-range place with chalets for US$21 but no restaurant.

Cheaper is *Au Nid des Routiers*, a small hotel at the eastern end of Lopé run by Gustave. It has basic but clean rooms for US$8 a night. Gustave is friendly and helpful, and also runs a small restaurant with meals at reasonable prices (order in advance as supply is very limited).

The Gambia

The Gambia is a small narrow country, 500km long and only 25km to 50km wide, almost completely surrounded by Senegal. It's one of Africa's most pleasant and interesting countries, and would still be worth visiting even if it hadn't been made famous by Alex Haley, author of *Roots*, tracing his ancestors back to the village of Juffure.

The Gambia offers unspoilt traditional villages, superb beaches, a friendly English-speaking population, a now stable political environment and an endless variety of birdlife (some 400 species in and around Banjul). And its small size is surely one of its appealing characteristics – you can traverse the country from the beach resorts to the unhurried upcountry/upriver centres such as Basse Santa Su in a day.

A downside to this otherwise pleasant country are the hordes of package tourists, isolated in their fortified hotels, who seldom venture away from their protected strip of beach and hotel charge cards – they seldom speak to a Gambian who doesn't work in the hotel. The locals ironically refer to these hotels as 'South Africa' but, as they are of great importance to the local economy, the apparent air of 'apartheid' is tolerated.

REPUBLIC OF THE GAMBIA

Area: 10,690 sq km
Population: 1.2 million
Population Growth Rate: 4.1%
Capital: Banjul
Head of State: Chairman of the Armed Forces Provisional Ruling Council President Yahya Jammeh
Official Language: English
Currency: Dalasi
Exchange Rate: D 9.35 = US$1
Per Capita GNP: US$380
Inflation: 5%
Time: GMT/UTC

Highlights
- A trip up the Gambia River by boat
- The mysterious Wassu Stone Circles
- Market day at Basse Santa Su
- Lazing at one of the Atlantic Coast resorts

Facts about the Country

HISTORY

The Gambia's first contact with Europeans was in 1456, when Portuguese navigators landed on James Island about 30km upriver from the sea. Although they did not establish a settlement they continued to monopolise trade along the West African coast throughout the 16th century. In those days salt, iron, pots and pans, firearms and gunpowder were exchanged for ivory, ebony, beeswax, gold and slaves.

The first settlement was made by Baltic Germans, who built a fort on James Island in 1651. They were displaced in 1661 by the British, who themselves were constantly under threat from French ships, pirates and the mainland African kings, who would cut off supplies from time to time. Fort James finally lost its strategic importance when new forts were built at Barra and Bathurst (now Banjul) at the mouth of the Gambia River. These were better placed to control the movement of ships, but Fort James continued to be an important collection point for slaves bound for the Americas until the trade was abolished in 1807.

THE GAMBIA

During the early 19th century the British continued to extend their influence further upstream. In the 1820s the territory was declared a British protectorate. It was ruled for many years from Sierra Leone, but in 1888 The Gambia became a crown colony in its own right. Meanwhile, the surrounding territory of Senegal had become a French colony. The following year the British and French signed a treaty establishing a border between The Gambia and Senegal.

The colony became self-governing in 1963, but the British considered independence to be impractical both economically and politically, and a possible merger with Senegal was debated. Although a Treaty of Association was signed, the country became independent in 1965. At this time its official name became *The* Gambia. Dawda Jawara, leader of the People's Progressive Party, became president.

Despite the less-than-perfect conditions for most Gambians, President Jawara remained generally popular. So it came as something of a surprise when, in July 1994, he was overthrown in a reportedly bloodless coup led by Lieutenant Yahya Jammeh and a group of young military officers. The takeover process was relatively smooth and many Gambians felt that the young Jammeh had their interests at heart. A constitutional referendum was held in August to determine the shape future elections would take.

In the September 1996 presidential election, which seemed to all intents and purposes democratic (given also that opposition parties were only allowed to come into the open a few weeks before the polls), the now-retired Colonel Jammeh was swept into power with 56% of the vote; his main opposition, rival Ousainou Darboe, polled 36%.

Darboe went into hiding for a short time immediately after the election result became clear, declaring that something was wrong. Many expats and a number of prominent locals came out in support of The Gambia, seeing it as an opportunity for The Gambia to achieve legitimacy on the world stage.

GEOGRAPHY & CLIMATE

The main geographical feature is the Gambia River, and there are few significant variations in altitude or vegetation, which consists largely of savannah and saline marshes. Baobab trees are a significant feature of the savannah.

The dry season stretches from November to April (the best time to visit) with the main rains between July and October.

POPULATION & PEOPLE

Latest estimates put the population at about 1.2 million, making The Gambia one of Africa's most densely populated countries. Most are rural dwellers, although 20% of the country's total population live in Banjul, Serekunda and Brikama. About 90% are Muslims. Ethnic groups include the Mandinka (Mandingo), Wolof, Fulani, Jola and Serahuli.

The population continues to expand, while deforestation and drought have combined to create their own serious problems. Many young Gambians have been forced to search for jobs elsewhere – mainly in Britain and France. Those who cannot leave have become beach boys (known locally as bumsters or bumsas) and hang around the tourist resorts selling handcrafts or drugs, acting as guides, trying to arrange marriages with European women, or simply thieving.

LANGUAGE
English is the official language. African languages include Wolof (the main trading language), Mandinka and Fulani.

Facts for the Visitor

VISAS
Visas are required by all except nationals of the Commonwealth countries, Belgium, Canada, Denmark, Finland, Germany, Iceland, Ireland, Italy, Luxembourg, the Netherlands, Norway, Spain and Sweden. The cost varies but is about US$15 for Americans.

Those who don't need visas are given a stay permit at the border or airport. This can be extended free of charge at the immigration office in Banjul. For all visitors it is important that you have a passport valid for six months beyond your period of stay.

Other Visas
Banjul is a good place to get visas for West African countries, as the city centre is small and easy to walk around. Applying for any of the visas below, you'll need one or two photos.

Guinea
  Visas are issued for US$40 in 24 hours.
Guinea-Bissau
  One-month visas are issued for US$11 and the process takes a few hours. (Guinea-Bissau visas are also available on the spot at the consulate in Ziguinchor, Senegal, for US$20.)
Mali
  Seven-day visas are issued, although travellers have reported that getting visas for longer stays (up to one month) is not too difficult. The cost is US$25, and the process takes half a day.

Mauritania
  One-month visas are issued immediately for about US$5.
Senegal
  One-month, multiple-entry visas take 24 hours to issue and cost US$25. New Zealanders, for some unknown reason, wait a long period for Senegalese visas.
Sierra Leone
  Visas are issued in 48 hours. Costs vary: US$32 for Britons; around US$25 for most other western countries; free for Americans.

EMBASSIES
Gambian Embassies
In Africa, The Gambia has embassies in Côte d'Ivoire, Ghana, Guinea-Bissau, Nigeria, Senegal and Sierra Leone.

Foreign Embassies in The Gambia
Countries with embassies in Banjul include:

Belgium & France (honorary consulates)
  14 Wellington St (CFAO Supermarket), Banjul (☎ 22 7473); also an honorary Belgian consulate at the Kairaba Hotel
Côte d'Ivoire (consulate)
  1A Hill St, Banjul (☎ 22 7168)
Guinea
  Above Marché Juboo (a shop), next to Gambia Airways, Wellington St (look for the flag) (☎ 22 6862)
Guinea-Bissau
  1st floor of building next to African Heritage Restaurant, Wellington St, (☎ 22 8134)
Mali (consulate)
  VM Company Ltd, about 50m from bus station on Cotton St (☎ 22 6947)
Mauritania
  Off Kairaba Ave (formerly Pipeline Rd), on a minor road near Weezo's Nightclub, Fajara (☎ 49 6518, 49 4098)
Senegal
  Corner of Nelson Mandela (formerly Cameron St) and Buckle Sts (☎ 22 7469)
Sierra Leone
  Hagan St, between Hill and Anglesea Sts (☎ 22 8206)
UK
  48 Atlantic Rd, Fajara, opposite the Medical Research Council (☎ 49 5133; fax 49 6134)
USA
  Kairaba Ave (formerly Pipeline Rd) (☎ 49 2856; fax 49 2475)

MONEY

US$1 = D 9.35

The unit of currency is the dalasi (D) which equals 100 bututs. There are no restrictions on its import or export. Exchange rates have been stable for the last few years, and you get only 5% more on the black market. In some banks, travellers' cheques sometimes have a higher exchange rate than cash. There's a bank at the airport, but if it's closed the police will help you find a moneychanger.

There are banks in Banjul, Bakau, Serekunda and large upcountry towns. In Banjul, black-market moneychangers can be found around the main post office and MacCarthy Square. You'll also find them at Bakau (at the stalls near the CFAO supermarket), Serekunda (although there is a chance of being ripped off here if you don't know what you're doing), at the borders and at the towns on the Trans-Gambia Highway.

If you've come in from Senegal and have no dalasi, CFA are accepted for many items (including bush taxis) although, since the 1994 CFA devaluation, rates are bad.

POST & COMMUNICATIONS

The main post office is in Banjul, near the Albert Market. The telephone system is handled by Gamtel, with offices and kiosks in Banjul, Bakau, Serekunda and most upcountry towns, where you can dial direct overseas 24 hours a day. The lines are excellent and calls to Europe cost about US$5 for three minutes. The country code for The Gambia is 220; there are no area codes.

DANGERS & ANNOYANCES

Petty thefts and more serious muggings have increased in Banjul city centre, Serekunda and on the beaches around Bakau and Fajara. With common sense (ie keeping your wealth out of sight), you'll be OK here during the day. The major problem is walking in these areas at night. Don't do it.

Many visitors also complain about the beach boys (known as bumsters or bumsas) who wait outside hotels and offer tourists anything from souvenirs to sex. It's best to ignore these guys completely (presuming you don't want any of their services): don't even shake hands or try to explain that you want to be on your own. Verbal abuse is the usual response, but it's all hot air.

A combination of tourism and urban deprivation around Banjul also means grass and harder drugs are available. If this is your scene, go carefully: the police will be severe if you have even a small amount, as there's a chance of a backhander from you to avoid arrest. Tourists have been busted recently at the airport and on the beach.

PUBLIC HOLIDAYS

The following public holidays are observed: 1 January, 18 February (Independence), 1 May, 15 August, 25 December, Good Friday, Easter Monday and other variable Islamic holidays (see Public Holidays in Regional Facts for the Visitor for dates).

ACCOMMODATION

In Banjul and the nearby Atlantic Coast resorts of Bakau, Fajara, Kotu Strand and Kololi there's a very wide choice of places to stay, ranging from simple hostels to international-standard hotels. Upcountry there are a few smart tourist lodges, but your choice is normally limited to basic local-style rest houses.

FOOD & DRINK

In every town there's at least one cheap restaurant (chophouse) with prices around US$1 for *domodah* (peanut stew with rice). Around Banjul there are many restaurants catering for the tourist trade, providing meals like grilled chicken & chips for US$3.

Tea and coffee (usually with bread) is available at street stalls in every town, usually around the market or bus station. The Gambia's national beer is JulBrew, consistently decent and available in small bottles, or on draught in the more upmarket establishments. Local palm wine and various 'fire-waters' (made from distilled sugarcane or rice) are also available, especially in upcountry areas.

THE GAMBIA

Getting There & Away

AIR

Airlines flying between The Gambia and Europe include Sabena, SwissAir, Gambia Airways and Air Gambia. There are also numerous cheap charter flights, as The Gambia is popular with European package tourists between November and April.

Gambia Airways, the national airline, flies to Freetown, Bissau, Conakry, Dakar, and Nouakchott. Other regional airlines include Air Gambia, Ghana Airways, Nigeria Airways, Air Bissau, Air Guinée and Air Senegal. Wherever you fly in West Africa, shop around the airlines, as prices vary considerably – you can get a Dakar-Banjul return fare for as low as US$90. Most airlines have their offices in central Banjul.

The departure tax is US$15 (150 dalasi), payable in hard currency. Some charter flights include the tax in the ticket price.

LAND
Senegal

The Gambia is completely surrounded by Senegal (except at the coast), and all journeys involve changing transport at the border. Only vehicles travelling between north and south Senegal on the Trans-Gambia Highway are allowed to cross the border, but passengers on public transport cannot end their journey in The Gambia.

Banjul to Dakar From Banjul take the ferry (US$0.30) across the river to Barra. There you'll find numerous taxis and pick-ups (US$0.50) to the border at Karang, from where bush taxis go to Dakar for about US$10 (payable in CFA), or minibuses for US$5. The journey takes six to eight hours depending on your luck with connections and the ferry. Small boats can take you across the river here; the fare should be no more than the ferry fare.

Serekunda to Ziguinchor Minibuses and bush taxis go from Serekunda 'garage' (bus and taxi station). A Peugeot 504 from Serekunda to the border costs US$3 (payable in dalasi or CFA), and from there to Ziguinchor is about US$4.

Basse Santa Su to Tambacounda Pick-ups run from Basse Santa Su to Velingara for US$1, and from there bush taxis go to Tambacounda for US$4. Travelling either way on this route you must get a stamp in your passport from the immigration official at the police station in Basse.

SEA
Senegal

Some intrepid travellers get rides on ocean-going *pirogues* (open wooden boats) from Banjul to Dakar and Ziguinchor in Senegal. There are no set schedules or prices, and you should note that these boats are notoriously unsafe.

Getting Around

ROAD

Frequent government (GPTC) buses run between Banjul and Basse, as do bush taxis and minibuses. Upcountry services often require a change of vehicle at Soma. Fares are reasonable: for example, to travel the length of the country from Banjul to Basse by bus costs US$6, or US$8.50 on the 'super-express'. Wherever you go by bush taxi or minibus, there's usually a baggage charge of around US$0.50.

Hitching is quite feasible on the south bank road, but not on the north bank road because traffic is light.

BOAT

Gambia River Excursion Ltd, also known as Samba River Venture (☎ 49 5526), runs a weekly service between Lamin Lodge (near Lamin village, between Serekunda and Abuko) and Jangjang-bureh Camp, near Georgetown. It stops at several places along the river and overnight at Tendaba Camp and Sofin Yama Camp. The boat has a bar and toilet, but no cabins. Meals are available. You can sleep in bungalows at each camp or on the sundeck (mattresses, mosquito nets and blankets are provided), which costs an extra US$5.

The one-way trip between Lamin Lodge and Georgetown costs US$80 per person. You can leave the boat at any of the 10 or so intermediate stops: Lamin to Tendaba Camp is US$27, to Farafenni is US$37, and to Kuntaur (near the Wassu Stone Circles) is US$70. Downstream prices are the same. The upstream boat leaves Lamin Lodge every Wednesday at 8 am and arrives at Jangjang-bureh on Friday afternoon. The downstream boat leaves Jangjang-bureh every Saturday at 7 am and arrives at Lamin Lodge on Sunday evening.

Banjul

Banjul is an island separated from the mainland by mangrove creeks. It has an air of neglect and decaying colonial elegance, and from some of its features – particularly its terribly potholed streets – you'd never pick it as a capital city. The impressive new arch at the entrance to the city lulls you into thinking that the city will be magnificent – it's not.

Indeed, most people who work in Banjul desert it at night for Serekunda, a lively town on the outskirts now bigger than Banjul itself, or for the nearby Atlantic coast resorts of Bakau, Fajara, Kotu Strand and Kololi. Nevertheless, Banjul does have a life of its own that is distinctly different from the tourist-oriented resorts, and it's full of activity during the day.

Serekunda, south of Banjul and a few kilometres inland from the resort strip, is by far the nation's largest concentration of population and the true reflection of real Gambian life.

Information
Only a trickle of independent tourists make it to the Ministry of Information & Tourism

(☎ 22 7181), in The Quadrangle, just before the presidential palace and adjacent to MacCarthy Square. Unfortunately the level of help is abysmal and the pamphlets horribly out of date.

The immigration office is on the ground floor of the building near the corner of Dobson and Anglesea Sts.

Banks in Banjul include Standard Chartered (☎ 22 1681) and Meridien BIAO (☎ 22 5777), both on Buckle St, and BICIS (☎ 22 8145) at 11A Wellington St.

The Banjul Travel Agency (☎ 22 8473) on Buckle St handles flights on most airlines and is quite efficient.

Name Changes
In Banjul, Cameron St is now Nelson Mandela St, Leman St is now OAU Blvd, and Independence Drive is now July 22 Drive; although the old names are still used by locals. In Bakau/Fajara/Serekunda, Pipeline Rd is now Kairaba Ave, New Town Rd is Garba Jahumpa Rd, and Cape Rd is Saitmatty Rd.

Things to See & Do
In Banjul, the **National Museum** on Independence Drive is well worth a visit for its history and ethnology exhibits, which are all well labelled and explained in detail. Entry costs US$1 and it's open Monday to Thursday from 8.30 am to 4 pm, and Friday and Saturday from 8 am to 12.30 pm.

Taking a **boat trip** through the creeks and mangrove swamps around Banjul is a popular activity. You can team up with some other people and have one of the tour companies arrange your trip, or find a local boat operator and arrange it yourself. Alternatively take a shorter, cheaper trip with a hand-paddled canoe. You can ask at the river bank along Wellington St between Albert Market and the ferry pier, or at Denton Bridge where the highway between Banjul and Bakau/Serekunda crosses the creek.

Places to Stay
Banjul The cheapest place (for the desperate only) is the *Teranga Hotel* (☎ 22 8387) at 13

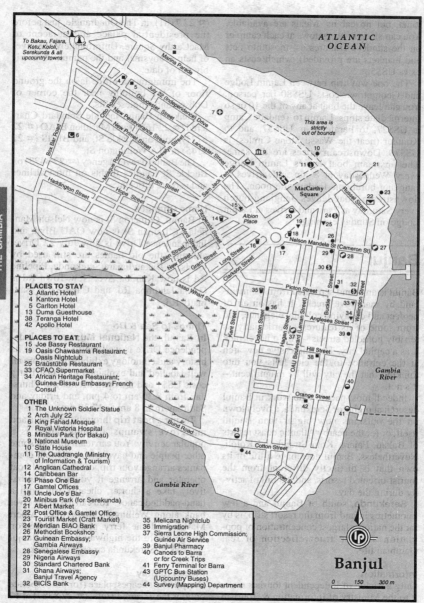

ATLANTIC OCEAN

To Bakau, Fajara,
Kotu, Kololi,
Serekunda & all
upcountry towns

Marina Parade

July 22 (Independence) Drive

Gloucester Street

Otu Road

New Perseverance Street

New Primet Street

Box Bar Road

Mosque Road

Llewelyn Street

Lancaster Street

This area is
strictly
out of bounds

Haddington Street

Hope Street

Ingram Street

Sam Jack Terrace

MacCarthy
Square

Russel Street

Albion
Place

Fitzgerald Street

Oxford Street

Allen Street

New Street

Grant Street

Long Street

Clarkson Street

Nelson Mandela St (Cameron St)

Lasso Wharf Street

Picton Street

Kent Street

Dobson Street

Hagan Street

Buckle Street

Anglesea Street

Wellington Street

OAU Boulevard (Leman Street)

Hill Street

Gambia
River

Orange Street

Bund Road

Cotton Street

Gambia River

Broom St

PLACES TO STAY
3 Atlantic Hotel
4 Kantora Hotel
5 Carlton Hotel
13 Duma Guesthouse
38 Teranga Hotel
42 Apollo Hotel

PLACES TO EAT
15 Joe Bassy Restaurant
19 Oasis Chawaarma Restaurant;
Oasis Nightclub
25 Braustüble Restaurant
33 CFAO Supermarket
34 African Heritage Restaurant;
Guinea-Bissau Embassy; French
Consul

OTHER
1 The Unknown Soldier Statue
2 Arch July 22
6 King Fahad Mosque
7 Royal Victoria Hospital
8 Minibus Park (for Bakau)
9 National Museum
10 State House
11 The Quadrangle (Ministry
of Information & Tourism)
12 Anglican Cathedral
14 Caribbean Bar
16 Phase One Bar
17 Gamtel Offices
18 Uncle Joe's Bar
20 Minibus Park (for Serekunda)
21 Albert Market
22 Post Office & Gamtel Office
23 Tourist Market (Craft Market)
24 Meridian BIAO Bank
26 Methodist Bookshop
27 Guinean Embassy;
Gambia Airways
29 Senegalese Embassy
29 Nigeria Airways
30 Standard Chartered Bank
31 Ghana Airways;
Banjul Travel Agency
32 BICIS Bank

35 Melicana Nightclub
36 Immigration
37 Sierra Leone High Commission;
Guinée Air Service
39 Banjul Pharmacy
40 Canoes to Barra
or for Creek Trips
41 Ferry Terminal for Barra
42 GPTC Bus Station
(Upcountry Buses)
44 Survey (Mapping) Department

Banjul

0   150   300 m

Hill St, which has dirty rooms for US$9. Much better is the friendly *Duma Guesthouse* (☎ 22 8381) on the corner of Oxford St and Sam Jack Terrace, where you pay US$12.50 for clean doubles with fans or US$15 with attached bathroom.

The best value is the *Kantora Hotel* (☎ 22 8715) on Independence Drive, which has clean singles/doubles for US$16/20 including breakfast (with air-con it's US$21/25).

The *Apollo Hotel* (☎ 22 8184) on Orange St near Buckle St has singles/doubles with attached bathrooms at US$25/35 with air-con. Couples can share a single.

The only mid-range choice in town is the *Atlantic Hotel* (☎ 22 8601; fax 22 7861), with air-con singles/doubles for US$85/110, and all the tourist facilities; it costs considerably less in the off season.

Across the river from Banjul in Barra, and about 300m from the ferry, is the *Black Cow Cross Cultural Arts Centre*. This is a hippyish alternative where you can learn drumming and dance. The price of US$10 includes full board in traditional grass tents and compound rooms; food is traditional chop served in a communal bowl.

Bakau A long-time travellers' favourite is the friendly *Atlantic Guest House* (☎ 49 6237) on Atlantic Rd in Bakau. It's the only budget hotel right on the coast, with a nice garden and clean doubles for US$15 to US$20 (shared bathroom) and US$25 (private bathroom). During the low season, rates drop to around half-price. Breakfast is available, and nearby are some bar-restaurants, a bakery and a small food shop. Boat trips on the nearby creeks can be arranged.

Near the CFAO supermarket, the *Ramona Hotel* (☎ 49 5127) has singles/doubles at US$15/20, with fans and decent bathrooms. The modern and slightly sterile *Friendship Hotel* (☎ 49 5829), next to Independence Stadium, has spotless rooms with attached bathroom, fans, air-con, mosquito nets and reliable hot water. The price is a steal at US$20 a double.

A good option for discerning independent travellers are the excellent double rooms in

Yvonne Class (☎ 49 6222, ask for Sunkule), the country's best restaurant which is on the same street as Amies Beach Hotel and about 200m further on – expect to pay about US$20 and a surcharge of US$5 for air-con.

For cheaper accommodation, some travellers find families to stay with. Expect to pay about US$10 per night for a double, although with bargaining you may get a reduction. For longer stays you can rent a local compound with bedroom, bathroom and kitchen for around US$75 to US$100 per month. Some travellers recommend the pleasant, friendly *Overlanders Rast* (☎ 99 1953; ask for Monika or Heinz) in Sukuta, a village near Serekunda; rooms cost from US$10.

Mid-range hotels include the good-value *African Village Hotel* (☎ 49 5034), on Atlantic Rd near the CFAO supermarket, with views of the ocean, rooms with attached bathroom at US$35/45, a pool and private beach; and the excellent *Cape Point Hotel* (☎ 49 5005), near the top-end Sunwing Hotel, where comfortable rooms are US$20/30 with a continental breakfast. *Amies Beach Hotel* (☎ 49 5035), a little further on from the Cape Point, has rooms for US$38 (US$45 with air-con). Renovation should by now be complete, so prices will probably have gone up.

Fajara The peaceful *Malawi Guesthouse* (☎ 39 3012) is popular, with double rooms at US$10 to US$18. Not far away, the *Fajara Guest House* (☎ /fax 49 6122) has doubles at US$20 to US$30. The owner often meets flights at the airport. If you're flying in, you can even phone from abroad to arrange a free pick-up (remembering a taxi fare is US$15). *Francisco's Hotel & Restaurant* (☎ 49 5332) has very nice air-con rooms at US$35/45 with a full breakfast.

A cheap place to stay (and recommended by readers) is the *Blue Moon Café* (☎ 37 2758) which is on 16th St, parallel to Kairaba Ave (two blocks behind the US embassy); singles/doubles are US$8/10.

In Kotu Strand (beyond Fajara), the *Bakotu Hotel* (☎ 49 5555), near the beach, has rooms with breakfast for US$37/47. A few kilometres south, in Kololi village, is the friendly *Kololi Inn & Tavern* (☎ 46 3410), with rooms for US$15/20 in pleasant thatched bungalows. The *Mango Tree*, a block to the west, has been recommended by travellers; doubles are US$16 (about US$11 out of season).

Between Fajara and Serekunda, off Kairaba Ave, the *Kenifeng YMCA Hostel* (☎ 39 2647) has clean basic rooms with shared bath for US$8/13 with breakfast.

Serekunda The dreary *Jalakunda Hotel* has rooms at US$13, but you'll get a better deal at the *Green Line Hotel* (☎ 39 4245), about 200m from the market, with clean air-con rooms with attached bathroom for US$15/23, including breakfast.

Places to Eat & Drink

Banjul In the centre, the *Joe Bassy Restaurant* off Albion Place serves basic sandwiches for around US$1.50. There are a few cheap chop houses in the area around Clarkson St. The *Oasis*, on Clarkson St between Dobson and Hagan Sts, serves good Lebanese chawarma for US$2.

A popular place for tourists is the *African*

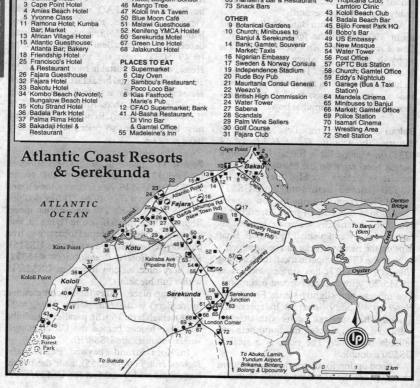

PLACES TO STAY		
1	Sunwing Hotel	
3	Cape Point Hotel	
4	Amies Beach Hotel	
5	Yvonne Class	
11	Ramona Hotel; Kumba Bar; Market	
13	African Village Hotel	
15	Atlantic Guesthouse; Atlanta Bar; Bakery	
18	Friendship Hotel	
25	Francisco's Hotel & Restaurant	
26	Fajara Guesthouse	
32	Fajara Hotel	
33	Bakotu Hotel	
34	Kombo Beach (Novotel); Bungalow Beach Hotel	
35	Kotu Strand Hotel	
36	Badala Park Hotel	
37	Palma Rima Hotel	
38	Bakadaji Hotel & Restaurant	

42	Kairaba Hotel; Senegambia Hotel; Belgium Consul
46	Mango Tree
47	Kololi Inn & Tavern
50	Blue Moon Café
51	Malawi Guesthouse
52	Kenifeng YMCA Hostel
60	Serekunda Motel
67	Green Line Hotel
68	Jalakunda Hotel

PLACES TO EAT	
2	Supermarket
6	Clay Oven
7	Sambou's Restaurant; Poco Loco Bar
8	Klas Fastfood; Marie's Pub
12	CFAO Supermarket; Bank
41	Al-Basha Restaurant, Di Vino Bar & Gamtel Office
55	Madeleine's Inn

62	Samburger Fastfood
63	Hansen's Bar & Restaurant
73	Snack Bars

OTHER	
9	Botanical Gardens
10	Church; Minibuses to Banjul & Serekunda
14	Bank; Gamtel; Souvenir Market; Taxis
16	Nigerian Embassy
17	Sweden & Norway Consuls
19	Independence Stadium
20	Rude Boy Pub
21	Mauritania Consul General
22	Weezo's
23	British High Commission
24	Water Tower
27	Sabena
28	Scandals
29	Palm Wine Sellers
30	Golf Course
31	Fajara Club

39	Bantaba Hotel
40	Tropicana Club; Lamtoro Clinic
43	Kololi Beach Club
44	Badala Beach Bar
45	Bijilo Forest Park HQ
48	Bobo's Bar
49	US Embassy
53	New Mosque
54	Water Tower
56	Post Office
57	GPTC Bus Station
58	Church; Gamtel Office
61	Garage (Bus & Taxi Station)
64	Mandela Cinema
65	Minibuses to Banjul
66	Market; Gamtel Office
69	Police Station
70	Isamari Cinema
71	Wrestling Area
72	Shell Station

Atlantic Coast Resorts & Serekunda

Heritage Restaurant (☎ 22 6906) at 16 Wellington St, just south of Picton St, where snacks are around US$3, meals US$5 to US$9 and a small beer US$1.50. It has an upstairs terrace overlooking the street.

The Austrian-style *Braüstüble* at 77 OAU Boulevard, half a block south of MacCarthy Square, has draught beer (US$1.50 for a small glass) and sandwiches, plus meals in the US$4 to US$8 range.

For a cheap drink during the day, try *Uncle Joe's* on the roundabout at the corner of Nelson Mandela (formerly Cameron) and Clarkson Sts. More upmarket is *Melicana Nightclub* on the corner of Dobson and Picton Sts. If you're searching for low-life after dark, try the *Phase One Bar* on Long St, or the *Caribbean Bar* on the corner of Allen and Ingram Sts, but it's best to go with a street-wise Gambian friend.

Bakau & Fajara Finding cheap food here is difficult. *Chez Awa* in the market on Atlantic Rd is popular with the local traders, and for cheap beer *Marie's Pub* on Old Cape Rd is a basic place with Gambian clientele and reggae music. Other than these, most places cater mainly for tourists, including *Klas Fastfood* on Old Cape Rd (with cheap meals at US$3) and the *Kumba Bar*, next to the Ramona Hotel, with meals such as burgers or chicken & chips for around US$4 and small beers around US$1.

Also good is the *Atlanta*, next to the Atlantic Guest House, doing meals such as grilled chicken & chips for US$4, or the *Malawi Guest House* (see Places to Stay) which serves good home-cooked food in the same price range.

In Bakau, *Sambou's* has a varied menu with most dishes in the US$5 to US$7 range, and small beers for US$1.20. The *Cape Point Restaurant*, next to the Sunwing Hotel, is similar. For Indian food try the deservedly popular *Clay Oven* (☎ 49 6600) close to the actual Cape Point at the corner of Old Cape Point Rd.

Between Kotu and Kololi, the *Bakadaji* (☎ 46 2307), near the Palma Rima Hotel, is reckoned to be the best African restaurant in town. The Thursday and Saturday evening buffets for US$8 are good value.

In the resort areas there are many specialist restaurants, although none are cheap, and most of the upmarket hotels have all-you-can-eat buffets in the US$10 to US$15 range. Some travellers make the most of this deal by forgoing breakfast and lunch and then stuffing themselves silly at the evening buffet.

The best restaurant in The Gambia and well worth a splurge is *Yvonne Class* (☎ 49 6222) at 24 Cape Point Rd. For what you get it is good value – a shrimp cocktail is US$4.50, medallions of succulent butterfish US$6.50 and desserts cost from US$3.

Serekunda The best place for cheap food is around the market and bus station, where there are several streets of bars, cafes doing drinks and bread, and Senegalese-style *gargotes* (cheap restaurant) doing basic rice dishes.

Entertainment

Nightclubs In Banjul, the raunchy *Oasis Nightclub* on Clarkson St is lively, particularly at weekends or when a band is playing, although visitors can get hassled here and it's worth going with a Gambian friend to avoid this. It's open from 10.30 pm to 6 am and entry costs US$1. Serekunda is livelier at night than Banjul and has several clubs catering for locals.

The beach area and Serekunda have by far the best selection of clubs serving up a wide range of hypnotic music. *Eddy's* on Finding Dailey St in Serekunda buzzes on Friday and Saturday nights playing *mbalax* (Senegalese style) and reggae. *Scandals*, near the US embassy in Kairaba Ave North, is worth the US$2.50 entrance fee.

For Mexican music and food, a little incongruous in The Gambia, *Weezo's*, also in Kairaba Ave North (formerly Pipeline), gets going after 11 pm, with a sophisticated local crowd and a good African-style restaurant (with Mexican snacks). There is always something happening at the *Bantaba Hotel* in Kololi.

THE GAMBIA

Tourists and expats seem to prefer discos catering to them, such as *Bellingo* at the Kombo Beach Novotel, where the cover alone is US$3. They don't know what they are missing.

Wrestling In Serekunda, traditional wrestling matches are popular events with tourists and locals. The preliminaries involve decorated wrestlers strutting around the ring, accompanied by groups of supporters with drums and whistles. For the fight itself, anything goes, including biting, kicking and punching. No fancy hand-locks or technical throws – just get him down!

The 'arena' is about 1km west of the market, and matches take place from 5 to 7 pm on most Saturdays and Sundays (except during Ramadan). The entrance fee is US$1 (considerably less than the US$15 that the big hotels charge to bring you here). Occasionally matches are at the big stadium in Bakau, but the atmosphere is not so good there.

Getting There & Away
Bus Government (GPTC) buses from Banjul to Georgetown and Basse Santa Su leave from the bus station on Cotton St in Banjul and another terminus in Serekunda. There are several each day: regular buses cost US$6; express buses cost US$7; and the super-express bus costs US$8.50. It's best to go to the bus station the day before to check times. Reservations are not possible but the buses are rarely full.

Bush Taxi Bush taxis and minibuses to upcountry destinations south of the river, and to the southern border with Senegal, leave from the 'garage' (bus and taxi station) in Serekunda. Bush taxis to the northern border with Senegal (from where you get transport to Dakar) and along the north side of the river leave from Barra.

Car Rental There are various car rental agencies based at the tourist hotels, but for cheaper deals Village Tours, at the African Village Hotel in Bakau (☎ 49 5384), has small saloon cars for US$45 per day (a driver is available at no extra charge). Madeleine's Inn in Fajara (☎ 39 1464) has tatty runarounds for US$36 per day. Prices do not include fuel (around US$1 per litre).

Getting Around
The Airport The airport at Yundum is about 20km from Banjul city centre. A taxi from the airport is US$10 to Serekunda, and US$12 to Bakau, Fajara or Banjul. Drivers keep to the official fares (listed on the wall at the taxi rank), so bargaining is not required. Going to the airport you should get at least 30% off this price.

There are no buses to/from the airport itself, but minibuses running along the main road between Serekunda and Brikama pass the turn-off, 3km from the airport.

Minibus & Share-Taxi For getting around Banjul and the coast resorts, minibuses and share-taxis are cheap and frequent. In Banjul vehicles to Bakau leave from opposite the

---

The Bump & Grind

If you like to witness absolute mayhem from behind the safety of a fence, you can't miss the weekend wrestling matches in Serekunda, 2km east of the market. Just ask for *boreh* (the Wolof word for these proceedings), or for *les luttes*, the term used for such bouts in Senegal.

It is a definite highlight of a trip to The Gambia, a real chance to mix with locals and a great chance for photographs (if you have a telephoto lens). Anything goes out in the arena and the shouting, drumming and whistling of the crowd is positively deafening. The winning wrestlers, covered in grease and charms (to ward off attackers), definitely deserve a few of your dalasi after their moments in the dust. The best time for the action is from 5 to 7 pm; entry is about 10 dalasi (US$1). ∎

Shell station on July 22 Drive, and to Serekunda from any of the roads off MacCarthy Square. From Bakau, vehicles to Banjul (US$0.30) and Serekunda (US$0.30) go from opposite the market.

Taxi Having a taxi to yourself (known as a 'town trip') is expensive. From Banjul they cost about US$4 to Bakau, US$6 to Fajara, and US$8 to Kotu Strand. Around town, a short trip costs from US$1 to US$2. Bargaining is definitely required.

Bicycle & Moped Rental Many of the major beach hotels rent bikes and mopeds, and there are also several private outfits with bikes to rent. Prices start at around US$8 per day for a bike and US$20 for a moped, but with some fairly easy negotiation you can normally pay half this, and even better deals are possible if you hire a bike for a few days. Cycling is a great way to see the country, particularly along the north bank of the river. You can always put your bike on top of a bush taxi if you get tired.

Around the Country

ABUKO NATURE RESERVE

Abuko is rare among African wildlife reserves in that it's easy to reach – only 20km south of Banjul. It is also well managed, with an amazing diversity of vegetation and animals, including sitatunga, duiker, green vervet and red colobus monkey.

More than 200 species of bird have been recorded here, particularly in the winter when numerous species migrate from Europe. Stars of the show include the Senegal parrot, lily trotter, pelican, pied kingfisher and glossy starling, plus several types of colourful turacos, flycatchers and sunbirds. The reserve is open every day from 8 am to 6 pm, and entrance is US$1.50. Take some food and plenty to drink, and sit in one of the cosy hides and watch the birds pass.

To get there, take a private taxi (expensive at US$30) or a minibus headed for Brikama

from Banjul or Serekunda (cheap at US$0.75). The reserve is signposted.

BASSE SANTA SU

Basse Santa Su, more commonly called Basse, is The Gambia's most easterly town of any size, at the end of the tar road. It's quite a lively place, with an interesting riverside market and waterfront with many old shops.

There have been recent outbreaks of meningitis here – make sure your innoculations are up to date.

Places to Stay & Eat

The tatty but friendly *Plaza Hotel*, overlooking the main square, has doubles for US$5 and the basic but clean *Apollo 2 Hotel* on the main street has singles/doubles priced from US$3/6. The *Government Rest House*, about 2km from town, also has rooms for US$5 a person. In a different league is the *Linguere Motel* on the town's edge, where clean doubles with attached bathrooms cost US$15.

There are several tea shacks opposite the taxi park and there's street food in the market. Cheap restaurants include *No 1* and *Ebrima's* with meals from US$1 and the optimistically titled *No Flie Restaurant* near the police station which has meat and rice for US$2. The coldest beers in town are at the almost legendary *Uncle Peacock's Faladu Bar* and the music is hot at the *London Club* at the Jem Hotel.

Getting There & Away

Buses between Banjul and Basse leave throughout the day, and bush taxis run between Basse and Georgetown or Soma. If you are coming into Basse from Senegal don't forget to report to the immigration official at the police station.

BIJILO FOREST PARK

This small reserve is on the coast at Kololi, near the Senegambia Hotel, and is easy to reach by taxi, minibus from Serekunda or hired bike. You follow a 4.5km footpath to see various monkeys and numerous birds. On weekdays a guide is available. Entrance is US$1.50, and the reserve should be supported as it helps prevent more hotel development down this part of the coast.

GEORGETOWN

Georgetown, on the north of MacCarthy Island in the Gambia River, is about 300km upstream from Banjul. The island is 10km long and 2.5km wide, and much of it is covered with fields of rice and groundnuts. The town was important during colonial times, but it now has a tranquil ambience.

A few kilometres south of Kuntaur (west of Georgetown) is the **River Gambia National Park**. There is a primate research project here but casual visitors are not allowed to visit – you can cruise past the islands in a boat (which can be hired in Kuntaur – prices start at about US$20 for a five hour trip).

Places to Stay & Eat

The *Government Rest House* has good clean rooms and hot water showers for US$5 per person – you may be required to 'book'. Better value is the friendly *Alakabung Lodge* at the other end of the main street, where a double thatched hut with its own shower and clean shared toilets costs US$5 per person.

On the east side of town is the large *Baobolong Camp*, where self-contained double chalets cost about US$15 per person. On the north side of the river at Lamin Koto is *Jangjang-bureh Camp*, with good self-contained bungalows for US$20 per person; canoes can be hired for US$8 per hour.

There's a cheap *chop house* near the market, otherwise eating is limited to what the lodges provide; they all have reasonable meals for US$2 to US$6. If you are after a cold beer you can't go wrong at *Tida's Bar*.

Getting There & Away

MacCarthy Island is reached by ferry from either the south or north bank of the river. The southern ferry is reached by turning off the main Banjul to Basse road. Some buses go there, but on the express bus you have to get off at Bansang and take a bush taxi back to the ferry (US$1). The southern ferry is free

for passengers, then pick-ups take you across the island to Georgetown (US$0.20). Georgetown can also be reached from Lamin Lodge near Banjul for about US$80 per person (see the main Getting Around section earlier).

GUNJUR

This magical, small fishing village, about 15km south of Brikama, is the antithesis of the beach resorts around Banjul. Trouble is it takes about two hours and a taxi and three bush taxi rides to get there – taxi to Serekunda, bush taxis to Brikama, Gunjur village and then to the beach (say US$5).

The great *restaurant* at the beach, which specialises in locally caught seafood, should be open by the time you read this – just ask the villagers the way to Sunkule Beach. There is safe swimming about 100m away, a nearby lagoon which is home to a wide variety of migratory birds, and a patch of original forest behind. Just go!

The *Gunjur Beach Motel* (☎ 48 6026) has single/double bungalows (with toilets and showers) for US$20/30.

JUFFURE, ALBREDA & JAMES ISLAND

When Alex Haley, the American author of *Roots*, traced his origins to **Juffure**, a village some 25km from Barra, the place quickly became a major tourist attraction (an Afro-American Disneyland). The legend lives on, but Juffure is definitely overrated and actually no different from countless other riverside villages (although more full of tourists and touts). Nearby are **Albreda Fort** and **James Island**, reached by boat for US$10 return, although all you see are some walls, arches and an old cannon.

To get to Juffure, take an early ferry to Barra, dodge the touts, and find a bush taxi (US$1) – or take an organised tour for around US$50. A third option: don't bother going.

WASSU STONE CIRCLES

About 25km north-west of Georgetown near the town of Kuntaur are the **Wassu Stone Circles**, which archaeologists believe are burial sites constructed about 1200 years ago. Each stone weighs several tonnes and is between one and 2.5m in height. (The museum in Banjul has more information.) There's a bus most days between Kuntaur and the northern Georgetown ferry which will drop you near Wassu.

WEST KIANG NATIONAL PARK

Also called Kiang West, this area of bush and riverine forest on the south bank of the river, some 150km by road from Banjul, is a refuge for several species of monkey and antelope plus, of course, many types of bird.

The park's actual status is unclear: you may be allowed to visit independently, but most people stay at nearby Tendaba Camp and reach the park by a 4WD or organised boat trip.

The tired looking *Tendaba Camp* has bungalows for US$14 per person plus US$4 for breakfast and about US$5 for lunch and US$9 for dinner. It was the country's first inland tourist hotel. The camp is about 5km north of the main highway and is easy to reach by car.

Ghana

For much of its history, Ghana has played a pivotal role in West Africa. From the height of Ashanti power to the more recent era of Kwame Nkrumah's fiery speeches and impassioned pan-Africanism, developments in Ghana have influenced the course of regional politics and economics. After suffering almost two decades of severe decline, Ghana again appears to be on the upswing, with a slowly but steadily growing economy and a government cautiously joining the ranks of emerging African democracies.

For travellers, the country is one of the friendliest and easiest to get around in West Africa. Clamouring, colourful markets, richly-hued textiles, old coastal forts steeped in the history of their slave-trading past, secluded, palm-fringed beaches, Mole National Park, and towns like Kumasi – capital of the Ashanti kingdom – are only some of the highlights.

Facts about the Country

HISTORY

Present-day Ghana has been inhabited since at least 4000 BC, although little evidence remains of its early societies. Successive waves of migration from the north and east resulted in Ghana's present ethnographic composition. By the 13th century a number of kingdoms had arisen that were strongly influenced by the Sahelian trading empires such as those of ancient Ghana (which incorporated western Mali and present-day Senegal). Among these early kingdoms were the Akan states of Bono and Banda in the northern orchard bush, which gradually expanded south along the course of the Volta River to the coastal grasslands.

By the 18th century, the powerful Ashanti kingdom of the Akan had conquered most of the other states and taken control of trade

---

REPUBLIC OF GHANA
Area: 238,537 sq km
Population: 17.1 million
Population Growth Rate: 2.8%
Capital: Accra
Head of State: Flight Lt Jerry Rawlings (President)
Official Language: English
Currency: Cedi
Exchange Rate: C 1700 = US$1
Per Capita GNP: US$390
Inflation: 55%
Time: GMT/UTC

Highlights
- Laid-back beaches and fishing villages, and ancient forts along the coast between Accra and Dixcove
- The vibrant streets and markets of Accra
- Cultural Kumasi, ancient Ashanti capital

---

routes to the coast. Its capital, Kumasi, was highly organised, with facilities and services the equal of those in most European cities of the time. The ruler, known as the Asantehene, employed literate Muslim secretaries from the north to manage trade with the Sahelian kingdoms and govern distant provinces.

Europeans began to arrive in the late 15th century, lured initially by trade in gold and ivory. However, with the establishment of European plantations in the Americas during the 16th century, slaves rapidly replaced gold

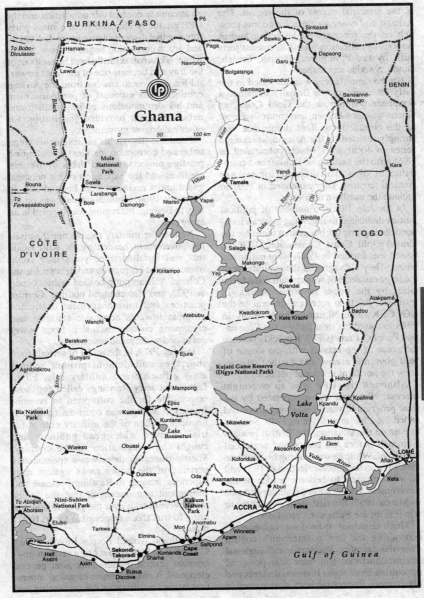

BURKINA / FASO

To Bobo-
Dioulasso

Hamale

Tumu

Paga

Pô

Navrongo

Bawku

Sinkassé

Lawra

Bolgatanga

Garu

Dapaong

Nakpanduri

Gambaga

Sansanné-
Mango

BENIN

Wa

Ghana

0   50   100 km

Mole
National
Park

Sawla

Larabanga

Bole

Damongo

Nterso

Yapei

Buipe

White

Volta

River

River

Oti

Tamale

Yendi

Kara

Bimbilla

TOGO

Bouna

To
Ferkessédougou

River

Black

Volta

CÔTE
D'IVOIRE

Kintampo

Yeji

Makongo

Salaga

Daka

River

Kpandai

Kete Krachi

Atakpamé

Badou

Wenchi

Atebubu

Kwadiokrom

Berekum

Ejura

Kujani Game Reserve
(Digya National Park)

Hohoe

Sunyani

Mampong

Lake
Volta

Kpandu

Kpalimé

Agnibilékrou

River

Bia

Ejisu

Kumasi

Kuntansi

Nkawkaw

Akosombo

Ho

Bia National
Park

Wiawso

Lake
Bosumtwi

Obuasi

Akosombo
Dam

Volta

River

LOMÉ

Aflao

To Abidjan

Aboiso

Nini-Suihen
National Park

Dunkwa

Koforidua

Aburi

Keta

Ada

Elubo

Oda

Asamankese

Kakum
Nature
Park

ACCRA

Tema

Tarkwa

Mori

Anomabu

Winneba

Half
Assini

Axim

Elmina

Komenda

Shama

Cape
Coast

Saltpond

Apam

Sekondi-
Takoradi

Busua
Dixcove

Gulf of Guinea

GHANA

as the principal export of the region. The Ashanti and other southern kingdoms grew rich on the proceeds of delivering human cargoes to collection points in coastal forts built by the Portuguese, British, French, Dutch, Swedes and Danes.

By the time slavery was abolished in the early 19th century, the British had gained a dominant position in the Gold Coast, as Ghana was then known, and controlled most of the coastal forts. This dominance was strongly resisted by the Ashanti, sparking a series of local wars which culminated in 1874 with the sacking of Kumasi and establishment of a British protectorate over Ashanti territory, later expanded in 1901 to include the northern territories.

In the late 1920s, a number of political parties dedicated to regaining African independence sprang up, but neither these nor the United Gold Coast Convention (UGCC), which was formed in 1947, were nationally based. They also ignored the aspirations of the large numbers of workers attracted to the cities by the boom in public works. In response, the then secretary-general of the UGCC, Kwame Nkrumah, broke away in 1948 to found his own party – the Convention People's Party (CPP). It quickly became the voice of the masses with the slogan of 'self-government now' and, for the first time, drew the north into national politics.

Although the CPP was an overnight success, Nkrumah was exasperated by the slow progress towards self-government and called for a national strike in 1949. Seeking to contain the situation, the British brought Nkrumah before the courts and sentenced him to jail. While he was serving his sentence the CPP won the general election of 1951 and he was released to become leader of the government. Ghana gained its independence in March 1957, the first African country to win it from the European colonisers.

Much remained to be done, however, to consolidate the new government's control over the country. Factional and regional interests surfaced and there was powerful opposition from some traditional chiefs and big farmers. Repressive laws were passed in an attempt to contain this opposition and the CPP gradually changed from a mass party into one that dispensed patronage. Individual and group corruption began to grow. Meanwhile, Nkrumah skilfully kept himself out of the fray and became one of the most powerful leaders ever to emerge from the African continent. His espousal of pan-Africanism and his denunciations of imperialism and neocolonialism provided inspiration for other nationalist movements.

Laudable though his achievements were, unbridled corruption, reckless spending on prestige projects, unpaid debts to Western creditors and the expansion of his personal guard into a regiment were his undoing. In February 1966, while Nkrumah was on his way to Beijing, his regime was toppled in an army coup.

Neither the military regime nor the civilian government headed by Dr Kofi Busia that was installed three years later could overcome the corruption and debt problems. Colonel Acheampong headed the next coup in 1972, and also changed nothing. Corrupt practices and mismanagement obstructed progress towards economic stability, and continuing civilian exclusion from power generated widespread resentment.

In May 1979, in the midst of serious food shortages and demonstrations against army affluence and military rule, Flight Lieutenant Jerry Rawlings called for those responsible for the corruption to be confronted. Rawlings was court-martialled but his denunciation of the military elite at his trial received widespread publicity and caught the imagination of the country. Shortly thereafter there was a spontaneous uprising of the junior ranks against their superiors, leading to Rawlings' release and subsequent announcement that the junior ranks were to take over the government and bring to trial those responsible for its bankruptcy.

Rawlings' Armed Forces Revolutionary Council was handed over to a civilian government several months later after general elections. A major 'house-cleaning' operation began, resulting in the sentencing and execution of some senior officers, including Acheampong. But the new president, Hilla Limann, was uneasy with Rawlings' continued popularity and eventually accused him of attempting to subvert constitutional rule. This provoked a second takeover by the Armed Forces Revolutionary Council in December 1981. Rawlings has been the head of state ever since.

Many of the policies adopted by the Revolutionary Council – particularly the strict austerity measures suggested by the IMF and the World Bank – aggrieved radicals both within and outside the government. These measures, however, drew support from the traditional Ashanti chiefs who had been suspicious of the radical speeches made in the early days of the revolution. Priority was given to rehabilitating the cocoa, mining and timber industries (to the detriment of Ghana's few remaining forests, which are estimated to be logged at 2% a year).

In 1992, under pressure from influential supporters and changes in neighbouring countries, Rawlings announced a hastily organised referendum on a new constitution and lifted the 10-year ban on political parties. Opposition groups formed along traditional lines – the Danquahists (following in the footsteps of Dr Danquah, the father of Ghana's Right) and the Nkrumahists (whose leftist ideology was based on the ideals of the nation's first president). But divisions in both camps were strong and, without a united opposition front, Rawlings triumphed at the November 1992 presidential election, winning 60% of the vote. The opposition claimed the ballot had been rigged although independent monitors concluded that it was 'free and fair'. Humiliated, the main opposition parties then withdrew from the following month's parliamentary election, leaving the way clear for Rawlings' National Democratic Congress (NDC) to sweep the board and for Rawlings to be sworn in as president.

In December 1996, Rawlings was reelected with 57% of the vote – this time in elections popularly acknowledged as free and fair and considered by many observers

to signal solidification of Ghana's commitment to democracy. Other areas are looking up as well. Despite high rates of inflation and unemployment, the economy is stabilising, with an average 4% real GDP growth for the past several years. The recent appointment of Ghanaian Kofi Annan as UN Secretary General has boosted morale. Hopes are high that Ghana, a country with a wealth of human and natural resources, will again take on a leading role in Africa.

GEOGRAPHY & CLIMATE

Most of Ghana consists of wooded hill ranges and wide valleys with a low-lying coastal plain. The damming of the Volta River in the mid-1960s has created one of the largest lakes in Africa.

Along the humid coastal region, the rainy seasons are from April to June and September to November. In the hotter and drier north, the rainy season lasts from May to September. Average temperatures vary between 25 and 29°C.

ECOLOGY & ENVIRONMENT

Commercial logging, wood fuels extraction and agricultural deforestation have decimated Ghana's forests from over eight million sq km at the early part of the century to less than two million sq km now. Marine and coastal resources are also threatened by high coastal population concentrations and erosion.

The most effective efforts in combating these problems are being carried out by non-governmental organisations. World Wide Fund for Nature, for example, is spearheading a project in collaboration with local groups which encourages the government and timber companies to adhere to estabished stewardship principles for sustainable forest management. Another bright note is an amazingly successful World Health Organisation project which has facilitated resettlement of deserted riverbank communities in the country's north by controlling the humpback fly which causes river blindness.

The Stool

Stools have unique significance in Akan society. As a symbol of the unity between the spirits of the ancestors and the living members of the lineage, the stool is often the first gift given by a father to his son and by a man to his future bride. In the case of royalty, the stool represents power and symbolises the unity of the state with its people. When a ruler dies, the Ashanti often say that 'the stool has fallen'.

Historically, certain designs, such as those where the seat is supported upon the image of a leopard or elephant, were restricted to particular ranks within Ashanti society, with the larger and most elaborate stools belonging to the higher echelons. The most famous is the Golden Stool or *Sika Gwa Kofi*, which is said to have been captured from heaven by Okomfo Anokye, the chief priest of the first *asantehene* (Ashanti king), and which represented the union of the various Ashanti states. Not even the supreme Ashanti king may sit on this stool, which is brought out only on rare occasions. ■

POPULATION & PEOPLE

Major ethnic groups include the Akan, Ewe, Mole-Dagbane, Guan and Ga-Adangme. Over half of the country's 17.1 million people are Christians and about 15% are Muslim, though a high proportion of both persuasions also follow traditional religions.

LANGUAGE

English is the official language. At least 75 African languages and dialects exist. The main ones are Akan and related languages such as Fante-Twi and Nzima, Ga, Ewe, Mole-Dagbane, Grusi and Gurma.

Facts for the Visitor

VISAS & DOCUMENTS

Visas are required for all except nationals of Economic Community of West African States (ECOWAS) countries, and should be arranged in advance. Proof of yellow fever vaccination is checked at the airport and at most land borders.

A permit is necessary to export any traditional craftwork (including kente cloth, woodcarvings etc) which is deemed to be either very old or very large. Permits cost around US$1 per piece and are issued from the small office to the right after entering the main building at the Arts Centre in Accra.

Visa Extensions

Visas can be extended at Immigration Head-quarters in Accra. Applications are accepted on weekdays between 8.30 am and noon and require two photos, a letter stating why you want to stay longer, proof of onward transport and US$6 for each additional month. Immigration retains your passport during processing, which takes at least two weeks – and often much longer. The experience is guaranteed to be frustrating.

Other Visas

Benin
A one month visa costs US$20 (payable in US$, West African CFA francs or FF) plus two photos and is issued within 48 hours, often faster.

Burkina Faso
A three month visa costs US$40 (payable in US$, West African CFA francs or FF) plus three photos and is issued within 24 hours.

Côte d'Ivoire
A one month visa requires US$17 and a two week visa US$11 (payable in cedis only) plus two photos and is issued within 48 hours.

Togo
A one month visa costs US$20 (payable in US$, West African CFA francs or FF) plus three photos and is issued within 48 hours.

EMBASSIES
Ghanaian Embassies

In Africa, there are Ghanaian embassies in Algeria, Angola, Benin, Burkina Faso, Côte d'Ivoire, Egypt, Ethiopia, Guinea (Conakry), Namibia, Nigeria, Sierra Leone, Tunisia, Togo and Zimbabwe. Other countries with Ghanaian embassies include Canada, France, Germany, the UK and USA.

Foreign Embassies in Ghana

Foreign embassies and consulates in Accra include:

Benin
19 Volta St, Airport residential area (☎ 774860)
Burkina Faso
off 2nd Mango Tree Ave, Asylum Down (☎ 221988)
Canada
46 Independence Ave, near Sankara Circle (☎ 228555)
Côte d'Ivoire
18th Lane, south of Danquah Circle (☎ 774611)
Denmark
67 Dr Isert Rd, North Ridge (☎ 226972)
France
12th Rd, off Liberation Ave north of Sankara Circle (☎ 774480)
Germany
7th Ave Extension, North Ridge (☎ 221311)
Japan
8 Tito Ave (☎ 775616)
Netherlands
89 Liberation Ave, Sankara Circle (☎ 773644)
Togo
Cantonments Rd (☎ 777950)
UK
Abdul Nasser Ave, south of Ring Rd (☎ 221665)
USA
Ring Rd East (☎ 775347)

The nearest Australian high commission is in Lagos; the Canadian high commission in Accra can assist Australians with passport and consular services.

MONEY

US$1 = C 1700

The unit of currency is the cedi (C) which equals 100 pesewas.

There are foreign exchange bureaus (forex) in all major towns and cities, although many of those outside Accra will not handle travellers' cheques. It's best to shop around as rates can differ significantly. For cash transactions, many forex bureaus give a better rate for US$50 or US$100 bills than for smaller denominations. In general, bank rates are slightly lower than those of forex bureaus, and rates for travellers' cheques are lower than those for cash.

Currency declaration forms are often issued on arrival, but only rarely collected on departure.

Barclays Bank (in Accra and Kumasi) gives cash withdrawals against Visa and MasterCard. There's a commission plus a US$3 fee for the approval telex; it's often a long wait.

Be sure to exchange any remaining cedis before departing Ghana, as it's often difficult to do so in neighboring countries.

POST & COMMUNICATIONS

Poste restante at the main post office in James Town, Accra, is open weekdays from 8 am to 5 pm and on Saturdays from 9 am to 2 pm. There's no fee for collected letters.

International telephone calls can be made from Ghana Telecom's office on High St in Accra. It's open daily from 7 am to 8 pm; there are additional phone booths requiring a phonecard which stay open round-the-clock. Phonecards can be purchased at the Telecom office weekdays until 7 pm and weekends until 4 pm. A three minute (minimum) call to Australia costs US$6; to the USA and UK it's US$5. There are also direct-dial telephones for the USA and UK in the main lobby of the Telecom office.

You can send and receive faxes here between 8 am and 6 pm on weekdays and on Saturdays from 8 am to 2 pm (US$0.40 per received page, fax (233-21) 665960 or 662680). Incoming faxes are registered and held indefinitely.

In Kumasi, there's an efficient 24 hour telecommunications office at the main post office, and a poste restante window (open weekdays from 8 am to 4.30 pm). In both Accra and Kumasi, you will need a minimum value of US$8 on a phonecard to make an international call.

All major towns have private telecommunications services, although they are invariably more expensive than Ghana Telecom.

The country code for Ghana is 233. The telephone area code for Accra is 21, and for Kumasi it's 51.

Email

Ghana is on line. At the Internet Cafe in Accra you can log on, Web surf and send

GHANA

emails for US$5 per hour. It's near White Bells on Kojo Thompson Rd.

BOOKS

No Worries! (US$12), published by the North American Women's Association, has practical information about Accra targeted at long-term visitors. *Ghana – A Travellers' Guide* (US$18) by Jojo Cobbinah contains some interesting cultural titbits. Both are on sale at the Labadi Beach and Novotel hotels.

DANGERS & ANNOYANCES

Photo permits are not required, but you should be discreet with cameras. It's prohibited to photograph anything associated with the government or military, including airports, ports, dams and Christiansborg castle in Accra.

Much of Ghana's coastline is plagued with dangerous currents. Seek local advice before taking a swim.

BUSINESS HOURS

Businesses are open weekdays from 8 am to 12.30 pm and from 1.30 to 5.30 pm, Saturdays from 8.30 am to 1 pm. Banking hours are weekdays from 8.30 am to 2 pm (3 pm on Fridays).

PUBLIC HOLIDAYS & SPECIAL EVENTS

Public holidays are: 1 January, 7 January, 6 March (Independence), 1 May, 1 July, 25-26 December, Good Friday and Easter Monday.

Ghana's rich cultural tapestry has given rise to many colourful festivals. Some of the more interesting ones are Akwasidee (see the upcoming Kumasi section) and Aboakyer (Deer Hunt Festival), held annually in Winneba on the first weekend in May.

ACCOMMODATION

Lodging is rarely a problem in Ghana, although it's not as cheap as it once was. Basic rooms with fan and shared bath average US$5/7 per single/double, while more comfortable rooms with attached bathroom and air-con start at US$15.

FOOD & DRINK

'Chop bars' are the place to go for inexpensive and tasty Ghanaian food (usually around US$1). *Fufu* (fermented cassava) is a staple, often accompanied by sauces made from groundnuts (peanuts) or okra.

Pito, a home-made millet beer, is drunk from calabash bowls in villages in the northeast.

Getting There & Away

AIR

Ghana Airways (☎ 221150 or 773321) connects Accra with all capitals of the coastal states except Bissau (Guinea-Bissau) and Monrovia (Liberia). Service is friendly, although cancellations and delays are frequent. Ghana Airways also has non-stop flights to Accra twice weekly fom New York and London.

Other airlines servicing Ghana include KLM (☎ 226925), Swiss Air (☎ 231921), Alitalia (☎ 301973), Lufthansa (☎ 221086), British Airways (☎ 667900), Air Afrique (☎ 663986), Aeroflot (☎ 225604) and South African Airways (☎ 230722). For cheap flights to Europe and elsewhere, try M&J Travel (☎ 773153) in Accra.

Kotoka airport is 10km from the city centre. There is a US$20 departure tax (payable in US$).

LAND
Burkina Faso

The usual route is to Ouagadougou via Bolgatanga, Navrongo and Pô. There's a direct STC bus to Ouagadougou from Accra (1000km, 24 hours, US$27) every Saturday at 8 am and from Kumasi (720km, 20 hours, US$21) on Wednesdays at 10 am. However, it's cheaper to do the trip in stages.

From Bolgatanga there are one or two taxis a day to the border (45km, one hour, US$2) and on to Pô (US$2), 15km from the Ghanaian border. There's an X9 bus from Pô to Ouagadougou three times a week (three hours, US$4). You can also enter Burkina Faso between

Wa and Bobo-Dioulasso going via Hamale (320km); traffic is scarce and there's no direct transport.

Côte d'Ivoire

The most convenient route is via Elubo and Aboisso on the coastal road. STC buses from Accra to Abidjan (550km, 12 hours, US$23) leave daily at 8 am, although it's generally quicker and cheaper to take a bush taxi from Takoradi to Elubo and catch onward transport from there to Aboisso and Abidjan.

Another crossing is from Kumasi via Agnibilékrou; there are no direct buses on this route.

On the northernmost route from Bole to Ferkessédougou (370km), there's transport from Bole to the river (the border), which you cross by canoe. A taxi from there to Bouna costs US$2; transport from Bouna to Ferkessédougou costs US$15 and takes eight to 12 hours.

Togo

Frequent minibuses and taxis ply the coastal road between Accra and Aflao/Lomé (200km, three hours, US$9). There are few hassles on the Ghanaian side, but Togolese officials will do everything possible to extract some money from you. Once out of customs and immigration, you're actually in Lomé and only 1km from some of the popular hotels.

From Kpandu to Kpalimé (40km) there are direct share-taxis, but it's faster to take one to the border and then walk 1.5km via a well-trodden footpath to the Togolese border post; it's the first track on the right after leaving Ghanaian customs. North of Kpandu on the Hohoe-Yendi road, there's an obscure though easy crossing to Badou.

In the north, you can cross from Tamale via Yendi to Sansanné-Mango (220km) or Kara (260km) and from Bawku via Sinkassé to Dapaong (70km); transport is scarce on these routes.

SEA

Ships connect Tema with ports in numerous countries, including Nigeria, Côte d'Ivoire, Cameroon and South Africa. Enquire at the harbour authority in Tema for details; the Black Star Line's office in Tema (☎ (022) 202888) will also have information.

Shipping Vehicles

If you need to ship a vehicle between Ghana and South Africa, the following information, supplied by Pat and Susan Hayward, may be of help.

The first step is to find a reliable agent in Tema, the new port for Accra. Liner Agencies (☎ (0221) 2987), PO Box 214, Tema, are recommended, but it depends a bit on who has a boat going, and when. Liner also have a tie-up with Ellerman & Bucknall, who have offices in major cities in South Africa, and it is they who take care of things at the South African end.

Establishing a firm price is difficult as it depends on the US dollar price of oil at the time. Expect to pay around US$135 to the agent in Ghana for hire of a shipping container and handling charges. The actual freight cost, payable in South Africa, is about US$900, and added to this are the port and handling charges of about US$120 at the South African end.

You need to get your vehicle containerised a day or two in advance, and get the all-important document, the 'Bill of Lading', which you need to retrieve your cargo at the other end. The boats take about a week to travel from Tema to Cape Town.

On top of all this, there is the cost of getting yourself to South Africa to pick up your vehicle! Ghana Airways to Johannesburg costs around US$720.

So, the all-up cost of getting yourselves and your vehicle to South Africa is around US$2700 (assuming two people).

Getting Around

AIR

From Accra, there are domestic flights several times a week to both Kumasi (US$30) and Tamale (US$50) on Airlink. Bookings can be made at M&J Travel in either Accra (☎ 773153) or Kumasi (☎ 24132). Golden Airways (☎ 760627) and Fan Air (☎ 762120) in Accra also have flights between these cities.

BUS
Ghana's government-run STC buses connect most major towns and some smaller ones on more or less fixed schedules. Service has deteriorated in recent years and it's frequently quicker and cheaper to travel with one of the numerous private bus companies. On most routes, City Express is the cheapest, while GPRTU buses generally fill up most quickly. Vehicle conditions vary widely, although buses on major routes are usually in decent shape.

Sample routes, fares and journey times follow, with STC and City Express schedules given as a point of reference.

TRAIN
Ghana's railway system links Accra, Kumasi and Takoradi in a single-track triangle. The trains are comfortable but slow and food is available at stops along the way. Tickets are sold on the day of departure, although sleepers should be booked in advance.

Between Kumasi and Takoradi, trains

depart Kumasi at 6 and 11 am and depart Takoradi at 6 am and noon. They take about nine hours (less for the 6 am express which costs an additional US$0.20 per ticket) and cost US$4/3 for 1st/2nd class. Additionally, there's an overnight sleeper at 8 pm in each direction arriving the following day by 7 am (US$5/4).

Between Accra and Kumasi there are overnight trains only, departing daily in either direction at 8.30 pm, arriving around 9 am the following day (US$4/3 for 1st-class sleeper/2nd-class seating).

Between Accra and Takoradi, there's an overnight train departing in each direction at 7.15 pm, arriving the next day by 8 am (US$5/4 for 1st/2nd-class seats, US$7/4 for a sleeper).

ROAD
Most main roads are in decent condition, with the exception of some badly potholed stretches between Kumasi and Tamale. The road from Tamale to Bolgatanga is being resurfaced, but is in poor condition at present. Almost all secondary routes are unsealed. Car rental is expensive.

There are occasional police checkpoints on the roads; usually they're angling for a 'dash',

Routes & Fares					
From	To	Distance	Duration	Fares (US$)	Departs From
Accra					
	Cape Coast	165km	3 hours	$3	two STC buses daily
	Kpandu	250km	5 hours	$4	STC bus daily except Sunday
	Kumasi	255km	5 hours	$5	hourly STC buses
	Paga	830km	18 hours	$13	STC three times weekly
	Takoradi	240km	4 hours	$4	hourly STC buses
	Tamale	640km	12 to 14 hours	$11	daily STC bus
	Wa	710km	15 to 18 hours	$13	weekly (Saturday) STC bus
Bolgatanga					
	Tamale	160km	4 hours	$3	City Express three times daily
Cape Coast					
	Kumasi	200km	4 hours	$3	daily City Express
Kete Krachi					
	Tamale	285km	11 long hours	$9	daily City Express bus
Kumasi					
	Tamale	380km	6 to 8 hours	$7	twice daily STC and City Express buses
Tamale					
	Wa	300km	7 hours	$8	daily City Express bus

but are not very insistent. Taxis generally get through more quickly than buses, which are sometimes held up for baggage checks.

The eastern route between Accra and Tamale (570km) via Ho and Yendi necessitates several transfers plus a ferry crossing and can't be done in one day. Most of the route is unsealed.

HITCHING

Hitching is relatively easy, but if it's a free lift you want, confirm this before getting in.

BOAT

The *Yapei Queen* makes regularly scheduled passenger runs up the Volta River from Akosombo to Yeji, stopping at many villages along the way. The boat departs Akosombo on Monday at 4 pm, arriving in Yeji the next day around 3 pm, and returning to Akosombo on Wednesday at 2 am. Tickets may be purchased in advance or on the day and cost US$20 for 1st-class cabins (attached bathroom, air-con doubles) and US$9/8 for 2nd/3rd-class seating; first class often fills up quickly as there are just two cabins. The ride winds past beautiful coastal hills and is a great alternative to road travel. The *Yapei Queen* also has occasional unscheduled cargo runs to Buipe (US$24/13/9 for 1st/ 2nd/ 3rd class). In addition, there are unscheduled cargo runs (3rd-class only) to Yeji and Buipe on the *Buipe Queen* and the *Volta Queen*.

Onward transport from Buipe to Tamale is US$2. From Yeji, there are two ferries daily to Makongo (US$4), from where you can get onward transport to Tamale.

Make bookings at the dock, or through the Volta Lake Transport Co at Akosombo port (☎ (0251) 686) or in Accra (☎ 665300).

TRO-TRO, MAMMY WAGON & BUSH TAXI

Minibuses (tro-tros) and bush taxis (usually Peugeot 504s) operate on all major and secondary routes. Mammy wagons (generally some sort of converted pick-up truck) are common on local routes and in rural areas. Both tro-tros and mammy wagons are cheaper than taxis and buses.

Accra

Accra is a sprawling, vibrant, friendly city, bustling 24 hours a day. There's no central high-rise district. Instead, the business and government offices are scattered all over town – perhaps a legacy of when Accra was villages controlled by seven branches of the Ga tribe, each with its own chief.

Information

Scantravel Ltd (☎ 664456), just off High Street, is the American Express representative and can also assist with domestic and international travel arrangements.

Mobil publishes a useful map of Accra, for sale at its petrol stations (US$5).

Things to See

For an intense and colourful introduction to Ghanaian life, customs and humour, walk around the area between High St and Tudu Rd in the James Town area, especially the **Makola Market** on Kojo Thompson Rd.

The **National Museum** (☎ 221633) has fascinating displays on various aspects of Ghanaian history and culture. It's open daily from 8.30 am to 5.30 pm; entry costs US$1 plus an optional US$0.50 photography fee.

The **Arts Centre** (Centre for National Culture) has a wide selection of crafts, including kente cloth, wooden and brass sculptures, beads and drums, however it's very touristy and haggling is essential.

Accra's three **forts** – James Fort, Ussher Fort and Christiansborg Castle (the Castle), built in the 17th century by the British, the Dutch and the Danes respectively, are off-limits. James Fort is a prison and Christiansborg Castle is where the president works. Stay clear of the Castle, as security here is tight.

Places to Stay

For details on beach accommodation, see the Around Accra section.

Kojo Thompson Rd Area There are many budget hotels on or near Kojo Thompson Rd.

GHANA

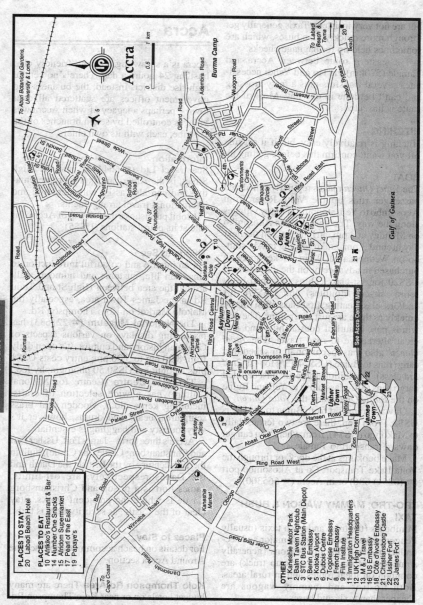

Accra

To Aburi Botanical Gardens,
University & Lomé

To Kumasi

To Cape Coast

Gulf of Guinea

To Labadi
Beach &
Tema

Burma Camp

Osu
Area

Asylum
Down

Kaneshie

Usher
Town

James
Town

See Accra Centre Map

0   0.5   1 km

PLACES TO STAY
20 Labadi Beach Hotel

PLACES TO EAT
10 Afrikiko's Restaurant & Bar
14 Number One Snacks
15 Afridom Supermarket
17 Pearl of the East
19 Papaye's

OTHER
1   Kaneshie Motor Park
2   Balm Tavern Nightclub
3   STC Bus Station (Main Depot)
4   Benin Embassy
5   Kotoka Airport
6   Dubois Centre
7   Togolese Embassy
8   French Embassy
9   Film Institute
11 Immigration Headquarters
12 UK High Commission
13 M & J Travel
16 US Embassy
18 Côte d'Ivoire Embassy
21 Christiansborg Castle
22 Ussher Fort
23 James Fort

The cheapest is the *YMCA* (☎ 224700 – men only) on Castle Rd, which has a canteen and four or six-bed dorms for US$2 per person. The *YWCA* (☎ 220567 – women only) down the road is much more rundown and has rooms only during school holidays (US$2 per person in a four-bed dorm or US$3 per person in a double).

Other cheap options are the seedy *Hotel de California* (☎ 226199), with stuffy rooms for US$5/6 per single/double, or the *Nkrumah Memorial Hotel* (☎ 228451), which has basic singles/doubles with shared bathroom for US$6/8.

Much better is the *Cavalry Methodist Church* (☎ 234507), east of Kojo Thompson Rd, which has seven good rooms for US$6/9 per single/double (US$8/11 with air-con).

The *Bellview Hotel* (☎ 667030) has friendly staff and clean, ventilated rooms for US$9/15 per single/double; its good restaurant serves Ghanaian dishes from US$2.

The comfortable *St George's Hotel* (☎ 224699) has air-con singles/doubles with attached bathroom for US$20/24.

Ring Rd Central Area Asylum Down, a quiet residential area south of Ring Rd Central, has several good options. *Asylum Down Lodge* (☎ 233104) has doubles for US$5 and a pleasant outdoor bar and restaurant, while the nearby *Lemon Lodge* (☎ 227857) has ventilated doubles for US$6. *Korkdam Hotel* (☎ 223221) next door is a step up, with ventilated rooms from US$12 (US$15 with air-con) and a bar and restaurant.

Just north of Ring Rd, the *New Haven Hotel* (☎ 222053) charges US$5/7 for clean singles/doubles.

For those seeking luxury, the quiet *Gye Nyame Hotel* (☎ 223321) in Asylum Down has comfortable air-con rooms with TV and refrigerator for US$35/42 per single/double.

Places to Eat

Street stalls and chophouses are dotted all the way from the post office in James Town to Nkrumah Circle. One of the best is the popular *Variety Chop Bar* which has a good atmosphere and many dishes for US$1 to US$3. Further north, *White Bells* has cheap sandwiches, hamburgers and various Ghanaian dishes from US$1.

In Asylum Down, *Spicy Chicken* serves chicken and snacks for under US$3, while the nearby *Bus Stop* has fast food for US$2.

In James Town, *Casan Casan* offers a good variety of Chinese and Ghanaian dishes from US$2; seating is on a terrace overlooking the street.

Number One Snacks on Danquah Circle is a cheap, open-air, 24-hour Lebanese restaurant/bar. *Papaye's* in Osu Area has hamburgers and fast food from US$2.

On Liberation Ave is *Afrikiko's*, an open-air restaurant/bar/disco which has good food – Ghanaian for around US$3 and continental from US$5.

Accra has many Chinese restaurants. One of the least expensive is *Pearl of the East* in Osu Area; its varied menu starts at US$2.

Entertainment

Accra is a lively place into the early hours. Most nightclubs have a US$3 cover charge.

Glen's on Farrar Ave, one block west of White Bells, is a small New York-style bar with music and dancing. The nearby *Miracle Mirage* has outdoor tables and a disco with a good DJ.

Afrikiko's (see Places to Eat above) often has live music on the weekends and is a popular place in the evenings.

In north Kaneshie, the *Balm Tavern* has live jazz music on weekends in an open courtyard; get a local to show you the way.

Ryan's Irish Pub in Osu Area is not cheap, but is perhaps the only place in West Africa where you can get a Guinness on tap.

The *theatre* at the Arts Centre just off High Street puts on many interesting performances by West African playwrights, some of which are reasonably priced (around US$2). The *National Theatre* has inexpensive matinee performances of local plays (some in Fante-Twi).

Accra is a good place to get acquainted with Ghana's growing film industry. The *Film Institute* behind Afrikiko's has frequent evening showings of local and foreign

GHANA

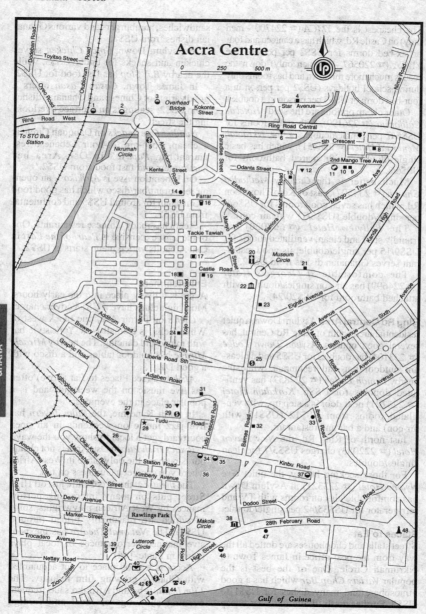

Accra Centre

0   250   500 m

Dodeban Road
Toyitso Street
Otublohum Road
Oyoo Road

Ring Road West

To STC Bus Station

Overhead Bridge
Kokonte Street
Star Avenue
Ninja Road

Ring Road Central

Nkrumah Circle
Akasanoma Street
Paradise Street
5th Crescent
2nd Mango Tree Ave
Kente Street
Odanta Street
Eseefo Road
Mango Tree Ave
Kenda High Road
Machiel Street
Semora Avenue
Manjo Avenue

Farrar Avenue
Tackie Tawiah
Prange Street
Museum Circle
Castle Road
Eighth Avenue
Kojo Thompson Road
Nkrumah Avenue
Adutrom Road
Brewery Road
Graphic Road
Seventh Avenue
Morocco Road
Sixth Avenue
Independence Avenue
Sixth Avenue

Liberia Road Nth
Liberia Road Sth
Adjaben Road
Agbogbloshi Road
Tudu Crescent Road
Barnes Road
Liberia Road
Nasser Avenue

Tudu Road

Amponakwa Road
Okai-Kwei Road
Mamleshie Road
Hansen Road
Station Road
Kimberly Avenue
Kinbu Road
Oval Road

Commercial Street
Derby Avenue
Market Street
Kojoo Lane
Rawlings Park
Trocadero Avenue
Nettey Road
Zion Street
Lis Street
Lutterodt Circle
Pagan Road
Thorpe Road
High Street
Makola Circle
Dodoo Street
28th February Road

Gulf of Guinea

movies (US$2), as does the *Rex Cinema* on Barnes Rd near Dodoo Street.

Non-guests can use the Novotel's *swimming pool* for US$4.

Getting There & Away

The main STC depot is on the western side of town near Lamptey Circle. All STC buses depart from here, except for those to Ho, Kpandu, Hohoe and Aflao, which leave from the smaller STC depot next to Tudu station.

Most other buses (including GPRTU), tro-tros and share-taxis for points north depart from the Neoplan station west of Nkrumah Circle. Transport to points west, including Cape Coast, Takoradi and Abidjan leaves from Kaneshie motor park, while transport for Tema, Ho and Aburi leaves from Tema station. Bush taxis and tro-tros for Aflao/Lomé and Akosombo leave from Tudu station.

Getting Around

Most city tro-tros leave from Tema station, although some also go from the motor park just west of Nkrumah Circle. Tro-tros to Labadi and Osu leave from the Labadi lorry park on High St near Thorpe Rd. Tro-tros are cheaper than taxis but also more crowded.

Taxis have no meters but are cheap if you hail them when they already have passengers;

it's US$0.30 between each major intersection or roundabout (US$0.20 in a tro-tro). A private ('dropping') taxi costs around US$1 per trip, depending on the distance. Taxi drivers will assume that tourists want 'a drop', so make your intentions clear if that's not the case.

A private taxi from the airport to the city centre should not cost more than US$7 (half that going to the airport). Alternatively, share-taxis (US$0.30) and tro-tros (US$0.20) to No 37 Roundabout pass along the main road, 200m from the airport. A share-taxi from the airport into Nkrumah Circle will cost US$0.80.

AROUND ACCRA

Beaches

Labadi Beach, about 8km east of central Accra, is the private strip of coastline of the five star *Labadi Beach Hotel* (☎ 772501); the beach is open to non-guests for US$2.

About 7km further east is **Coco Beach** and an overpriced resort (☎ 712887). The beach has deteriorated in recent years, although you can still camp for US$2.

Some 30km west of Accra is **Kokrobite Beach** and the renowned Academy of African Music & Arts Ltd (AAMAL), which attracts well known musicians from all around West Africa and has live music and drumming every weekend from 2.30 to 6 pm. It's *the* place to come for drumming lessons.

There's lodging at the pleasant but declining *Kokrobite Beach Resort* (☎ (027) 555042 – a mobile phone) which is owned and run by AAMAL. Basic singles/doubles with shared facilities cost US$7/8, while ventilated doubles with attached bathroom cost US$12. Water supplies are erratic, and the bar and restaurant expensive.

Better is the laid-back *Big Milly's Backyard*, on the beach, where you can camp for US$2 per person. There are also rooms from US$4/6 per single/double, and good, inexpensive meals for US$2. Follow signs for AAMAL to the last village, then continue straight down towards the water.

To get to Kokrobite, take a tro-tro from Kaneshie motor park in Accra (US$0.70), or take a Winneba-bound tro-tro to the sign posted turnoff for AAMAL. It's 8km from here on a badly potholed road – easily hitched on weekends but difficult on weekdays.

Aburi Botanical Gardens

The peaceful Aburi gardens on Akwapim Ridge, 35km north of Accra, were laid out by the British over 100 years ago. There's an old colonial-style *resthouse* (☎ (0876) 22022) which charges US$9 for basic triples and from US$11 for chalets with attached bathroom (often fully booked on weekends). Its restaurant, *Rose Plot*, serves basic fare from US$2 but it has difficulty competing with the food and the view at the *Royal Restaurant*, about 200m away. Just outside the gardens coming from Accra is the *Restaurant May & Lodge* which has a good view and four rooms for US$8.

Admission to the gardens costs US$0.50. To get there, take a minibus from Tema station (US$0.80).

Around the Country

ADA

Halfway between Accra and Lomé, Ada is near the Volta River estuary and some sublime beaches. There's a basic *camp site* on the estuary and a *chop bar*. Alternatively, the *Paradise Beach Hotel* (☎ (0968) 277) has rooms from US$50.

AKOSOMBO

Most people come to Akosombo to view the dam holding back the immense Lake Volta. From Akosombo port, you can take a boat north to Yeji (for details see Boat in the Getting Around section of this chapter). The dam is 2km after Akosombo village and the port is another 4km beyond. A permit (which includes a guide) is necessary to visit the dam; they're issued by the Volta River Authority in Akosombo free of charge.

On Sunday at 10.30 am, the *Dodi Princess* makes a popular six-hour excursion on the lake, including a two-hour stop on Dodi Island. Tickets (US$5) can be arranged through the Volta Hotel. Bring a picnic lunch or buy a plate of chicken on the boat for US$4.

Places to Stay & Eat

The ritzy *Volta Hotel* (☎ (021) 662639) has exclusive views of the dam and rooms from US$80. In Atimpoku, the *Benkum Motel* has basic singles/doubles for US$5/6. The much nicer *Zito Guest House* (☎ 474), north-west of the Mobil Station between Akosombo and Atimpoku, has four clean rooms with fan, bath and enormous bed for US$11. There are several *chop bars* in Atimpoku, none of them distinguished.

In Akosombo, the *Maritime Club* (closed Wednesday), 300m after the port, is a lively weekend spot, with views of the lake and meals for US$3.

Getting There & Away

A tro-tro from Accra's Tudu station costs US$3. Alternatively, buses and tro-tros from Tema station heading to Ho will drop you in Atimpoku, from where it's 8km to Akosombo village and taxis to the dam and port.

APAM

Apam is a dirty, dusty town with an old Dutch fort overlooking a picturesque harbour.

You can generally arrange to sleep in the

fort for US$1 per person, although the interior is filthy. There's no water and you'll need to bring a torch. Just off the main road, *King Pobee Hotel* has ventilated doubles for US$7. There are *chop bars* in town.

BOLGATANGA

Bolgatanga is a fast growing town and the regional capital of the Upper East Province. It's also the northern craft centre, particularly for basketware and leather goods.

The **Paga Crocodile Ponds** near the Burkina Faso border are only worth visiting in the dry season (December to April) when the crocs are voracious enough to come out of the water for food.

Places to Stay & Eat

The best value is the *Catholic Social Centre*, north of the centre. Clean singles/doubles with fan and shared bath are US$4/5; dormitory beds are US$2.

Hotel Bolco, in the centre behind the police station, has ventilated doubles with bucket baths for US$4. *Sandgardens* (☎ 3464) is also cheap with singles/doubles from US$4/5, although it's inconveniently located at the eastern edge of town.

Black Star Hotel (☎ 2346) gets the tour groups. Doubles are US$4/10 for communal facilities/attached bathroom.

The clean and friendly *All People's Canteen* next to the post office has cheap chop from US$1. Alternatively, you can eat cheaply at *Comme-çi, Comme-ça* near Sandgardens, although the food is inferior. For coffee or snacks, try the *Travellers' Inn* near the market.

Getting There & Away

The STC depot is at the southern end of town. Taxis and minibuses leave from the centre, while OSA buses for Tamale leave from the depot next to Sandgardens.

CAPE COAST

Cape Coast, known as *Oguaa* in the local Fante language, is a bustling town. Its 17th-century **castle**, constructed by the Swedes, became headquarters for the British colonial administration until the capital was moved to Accra in 1876. The castle is open daily from 9 am to 5 pm. Entry is US$2.50 (US$5 with guide) including a non-negotiable photo fee.

There are good batiks and other crafts at the **Cape Coast Women's Coop** near the centre.

Places to Stay & Eat

The only budget option near the centre is the dumpy *Palace Hotel* (☎ 33556) on Aboom Rd, which has singles/doubles for US$5/7 (US$8 for a double with attached bathroom); its restaurant serves Ghanaian dishes from US$2.

The *Savoy Hotel* (☎ 32805), to the east on Ashanti Rd, has doubles with attached bathroom for US$12, US$17 for fan/air-con.

The cosy, new *Amkred Guest House* (☎ 32868) off Jukwa road north of the motor park, has comfortable rooms with attached bathroom for US$18, US$20 for fan/air-con. The friendly caretaker will prepare good, reasonably priced meals with advance notice.

The *University of Cape Coast* sometimes has rooms to rent out. Enquire at the residence hall.

There are street *food stalls* at the intersection of Commercial St and Ashanti Rd, south of Kotokuraba market. For snacks, try the Kingsway store.

DIXCOVE & BUSUA

Dixcove is a tiny village with a dirty beach and a picturesque **fort**. A 20 minute walk over the hill lies the village of Busua and a beautiful stretch of coastline (although the section near town is dirty).

Each morning and evening, Busua is a hive of activity as colourful fishing boats come and go. At dusk, the town's main street is lit with kerosene lanterns and, in this cosy ambience, locals sit, chat and trade.

Places to Stay & Eat

In Dixcove, the only option is the *Quiet Storm Hotel* which charges US$7/9 for a large but grubby room. Meals are available upon request.

In Busua, the only hotel is the *Busua Beach Resort* (☎ 774582 in Accra) which has a restaurant, generator and pricey accom-

GHANA

modation in fully equipped chalets from US$40. Alternatively, you can stay in village guesthouses – all the locals know where these are. The best is *Mary's* place, near the beach, with three very basic rooms for US$5 and a bucket shower. *Elizabeth's* is similar but is at the back of the village and the rooms (US$2/4 per single/double) are not as cool. *Sabina's*, near the resort, has a couple of small rooms for a negotiable US$3/5. All will prepare meals on request.

There's no shortage of locals who'll offer to cook some of the day's catch for you. *Frank's* and the nearby *Daniel's* are in stiff competition for the market on banana pancakes.

Getting There & Away

There are several tro-tros daily from Takoradi's Tema station to Dixcove. Tro-tros from Takoradi to Busua are infrequent; it's best to walk the 3km from Dixcove. Alternatively, you can take any transport along the coastal road to Agona Junction, 20km west of Takoradi, from where you can walk or take a tro-tro 12km south to either Dixcove or Busua.

ELMINA

Elmina is the site of Ghana's oldest fort, Fort St George, constructed by the Portuguese in the 15th century, and Fort St Jago (Sao Iago), built by the Dutch 150 years later. It was from here that the Portuguese controlled their trading interests in West Africa before being displaced by the Dutch in 1637. Both forts were later ceded to the British.

Fort St George (Elmina castle) is open daily from 9 am to 5 pm. Admission costs US$2.50 (US$5 with guide), including a non-negotiable photo fee. The hilltop **Fort St Jago** is under renovation, but it's worth the hike up for good views of the harbour.

During Elmina's colourful **Bakatue festival** on the first Tuesday of July, local chiefs parade through town in their full regalia, followed by singers, dancers and men on stilts.

Places to Stay & Eat

The only budget option is the *Nyansapow Hotel* (☎ 33955), also known as Hotel Hol-

lywood. Ventilated doubles start at US$6; meals can be arranged with advance notice.

East of town are two hotels catering to the well-heeled. The drab *Oyster Bay Hotel* (☎ 33605) has no atmosphere and lots of cement. Acceptable bungalows start at US$30.

The *Elmina Motel* is under renovation, but once it's completed will be a multi-star resort with amenities and prices to match.

There is very little street food in Elmina; the only relatively cheap place to eat is the open-air *Gramsdel J*, on the beach at the eastern edge of town.

KETE KRACHI

The original town of Kete Krachi, once an important stop on slave trading routes, was flooded when Lake Volta was created. The new town is one of the lake's main ports.

If it's still open, the *Education Guesthouse* is the best place to stay. Otherwise, the *Simon Hotel*, 2km from the lake, has rooms for US$4. There's street food in town.

KPANDU

Kpandu (pronounced 'pandu') is close to the eastern shore of Lake Volta on one of the main Ghana to Togo routes.

The *Revco Hotel* has been recommended; it has ventilated doubles for US$5.

KUMASI

Kumasi, ancient capital of the Ashanti kingdom, is a major cultural and economic centre with a population of around one million. Almost nothing remains of the original city, which was razed by the British in 1874 during the Fourth Ashanti War and burned in 1901. However, with its many colourful festivals and rich cultural heritage, Kumasi is a fascinating place to explore.

Things to See

National Cultural Centre At the Cultural Centre (open daily), you can watch brassworkers, woodcarvers, weavers and drum and sandal-makers work, as well as buy their products. It also has a library and the tiny but intriguing **Prempeh II Museum**, which illustrates Ashanti history and culture with photographs, traditional stools, cloths and ritual objects. The museum is open Monday from 2 to 5 pm and Tuesday to Sunday from 8 am to 5 pm; admission costs US$0.50. There's also a helpful tourist office (☎ 26243) on the grounds, open weekdays from 9 am to 5 pm and Saturday until noon.

Military Museum This museum, in old Fort St George, is open Tuesday to Saturday from 10 am to 5 pm. The US$0.50 entry fee gets you a guided tour of the 1896 fort, with its collection of weapons, uniforms and photographs of Ghanaian colonial military history.

Asantehene's Palace It is possible to visit the Ashanti king's palace (Manhyia palace) and adjoining museum, but don't expect too much pageantry or historical romance. The present palace was built in 1995 in honour of the current Asantehene's 25th jubilee. It's open daily from 9 am to 5 pm. Admission is US$3 (US$1 for students); no photography is permitted. As the Asantehene's health isn't very good these days, his previously regular appearances have become more sporadic. However, you can occasionally arrange to meet the queen mother by advance appointment at the Secretariat on the eastern side of the palace grounds. If you're lucky enough to get an audience, etiquette demands presentation of a bottle or two of schnapps when meeting the royals.

Central Market Kumasi's market sprawls, crowded and confusing, across the railway line, selling everything from foodstuffs to

---

Ghanaian Textiles
Kente cloth is one of West Africa's most famous – and most expensive – textiles. Its designs, composed of woven geometrical figures, all have meaning. Kente cloth is traditionally worn on joyous events, and exclusively by men. In contrast, *adinkra* cloth – a cotton material with dark geometric designs or stylised figures stamped on it – is worn primarily on solemn occasions (adinkra means farewell), and by both men and women. ■

---

kente cloth, northern Muslim smocks, beads, Ashanti sandals, batik and bracelets. Other curiosities include smoked bush meat (monkey, bat etc) and fetish items (vulture heads, parrot wings and dried chameleons).

Festivals
The 42-day cycle of the Ashanti religious calendar culminates in **Akwasidee**, a public ceremony involving the Asantehene, other chiefs and fetish priests at the palace. The tourist office at the Cultural Centre can advise you of the exact dates.

Places to Stay
Best value by far is the *Presbyterian Guesthouse* (☎ 23879), a beautiful place with shady, flowering trees close to the city centre. It's also the only place in central Kumasi where you can camp. Basic but spacious doubles cost US$2 per person, and there's a small kitchen. The only bad point is that there's no running water, although the large drum is usually kept full.

In the city centre, the *Montana Hotel* charges US$4/5 for dark singles/doubles. Better is the *Nurom Inn – Annex 2*, also central, with clean ventilated singles/doubles for US$3/4.

Mensah Memorial Hotel (☎ 26432) has ventilated singles/doubles for US$4/5, but no restaurant.

Hotel de Kingsway (☎ 26228) is an old British hotel with good, air-con rooms with attached bathroom from US$14 and a restaurant with meals for US$3.

For comfort, try *Noks Hotel* (☎ 24162) on a quiet side street. Doubles with amenities start at US$35, although they are sometimes willing to discount this rate.

Places to Eat
There are many street *food stalls* next to the railway line close to Kejetia Circle and alongside the eastern wall of the stadium.

The popular *Abotare Ye Chop Bar* near the STC bus station has inexpensive Ghanaian dishes. *Sister's Inn*, closer to the centre, has similar fare.

For more upmarket African food try the *Kentish Kitchen* at the Cultural Centre (open

GHANA

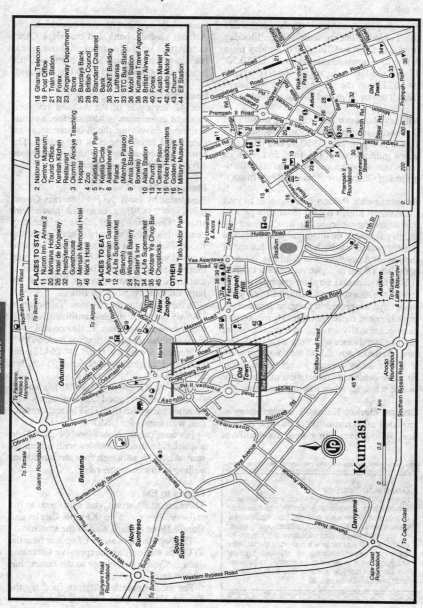

PLACES TO STAY
11 Nurom Inn - Annex 2
20 Montana Hotel
26 Hotel de Kingsway
32 Presbyterian
     Guesthouse
37 Mensah Memorial Hotel
46 Nok's Hotel

PLACES TO EAT
12 Adehyeman Gardens
     A-Life Supermarket
     (Branch)
24 Windmill Bakery
27 Sister's Inn
34 A-Life Supermarket
35 Abotare Ye Chop Bar
45 Chopsticks

OTHER
1 New Tafo Motor Park
2 National Cultural
    Centre; Museum;
    Tourist Office;
    Kentish Kitchen
    Restaurant
3 Okomfo Anokye Teaching
    Hospital
4 Zoo
5 Kejetia Motor Park
6 Kejetia Circle
7 Asantehene's
    Palace
    (Manhyia Palace)
9 Anoca Station (for
    Bonwire)
13 Alaba Station
14 Central Prison
15 Police Headquarters
16 Golden Airways
17 Military Museum
18 Ghana Telecom
19 Post Office
21 Train Station
22 Forex
23 Kingsway Department
    Store
25 Barclays Bank
28 British Council
29 Standard Chartered
    Bank
30 SSNIT Building
31 Lufthansa
33 STC Bus Station
36 Mobil Station
38 Kumasi Travel Agency
39 British Airways
40 Forex
41 Asafo Market
42 Asafo Motor Park
43 Church
44 Elf Station

daily until 7.30 pm). It has a variety of dishes including a few vegetarian platters from US$2. *Adehyeman Gardens* (ah-DESH-eh-mans) also has good Ghanaian cuisine for US$3, as well as an outdoor dance floor (watch out for pickpockets).

For good-value European fare, try the *Windmill Bakery*, down an alley behind the Kingsway store. It's open all day and has generous servings from US$2.

Chopsticks (evenings only) is one of Kumasi's top restaurants. It has a large selection of Chinese dishes averaging US$4.

Getting There & Away

All OSA/City Express buses as well as buses, minibuses and taxis for Accra and other points south depart from Kejetia motor park. Buses to Bolgatanga, Bawku and Ouagadougou depart from New Tafo (Kurofuforum) motor park. Minibuses to Tamale and destinations in the Upper West depart from Alaba station off Zongo Rd, while all local/regional transport as well as some minibuses to Accra depart from Asafo market. The STC has its own depot on Prempeh Rd.

For information on train travel see the Getting Around section at the start of this chapter.

AROUND KUMASI
Lake Bosumtwi

This 100m-deep crater lake some 30km from Kumasi is a popular weekend picnic spot. It's a sacred lake dedicated to the god Twi, and is said to be safe to swim in. To get there, take a tro-tro (US$0.70) from Asafo station to Abono, the lakeside village.

On the lakeshore, the rundown *Sabon du Lac* has basic doubles with filthy shared facilities for US$9. There's no running water, and drinking water can be hard to find. Alternatively, you can stay at the *Government Resthouse*, high on a hill about 30 minutes walk from the lake; it's US$30 for a chalet with two double beds. There's water and a kitchenette, but you'll have to bring your own food.

Craft Villages

There are a number of these within 30 minutes drive of Kumasi. The families who live and work here have, for generations, produced regalia for Ashanti chiefs as well as, more recently, tourists.

The craft villages include **Ahwiaa** (known for its carving), **Ntonso** (adinkra cloth), **Bonwire** (weaving), and **Kurofuforum** (brass casting). The easiest way to visit the villages is to hire a taxi for the day.

LARABANGA

If you're en route to Mole National Park, it's worth stopping at Larabanga to see its famous **mosque**. It's Malian in appearance (mud and pole construction) and is Ghana's oldest, supposedly dating to 1421. Tradition has it that it was built by a certain Ibrahim, who also founded the town. There's a negotiable US$0.50 entry fee. A new **tourist information centre** should be up and running by now, with tips about the area and bicycle rentals. The Salia brothers are also a wealth of information.

If you're travelling by public transport, take the daily 6 am City Express bus from Tamale to Bole, disembarking at Larabanga. You can then continue on to Mole on the evening bus from Tamale, which stops at Larabanga about 5 pm.

MOLE NATIONAL PARK

Mole park was established in 1971 and now covers 5100 sq km. It is home to elephant, antelope, buffalo, the occasional lion and many bird species. The best time to visit is towards the end of the dry season (March to June). Vehicle rental is relatively inexpensive, but the park's 4WD is frequently under repair. Alternatively, you can hire a guide for a walking tour (US$2 an hour, plus tip). Entry to the park costs US$3.

Places to Stay

The park's *hotel* (☎ (071) 22563) overlooks a reservoir and the river plain, and is the best place to observe wildlife. From here you can often see antelope, waterbuck, kob, green monkey, wart hog, baboon, crocodile and sometimes a herd of elephant. Doubles start at US$11 (US$14 for a triple) and camping is allowed on the grounds for US$2 per person. There's electricity from 7 to 10 pm, running water, and a restaurant; order meals well in advance. In the dry season it's advisable to book ahead, especially for weekends.

There are a few other places to camp in the park, however you'll need a vehicle to reach them.

Getting There & Away

To get to Mole, there's a daily OSA bus from Tamale which leaves at 2.30 pm and arrives at the park's hotel about 7 pm (US$3). The bus returns to Tamale the next day at 5.30 am. Otherwise, from Tamale take a bus heading to Bole and get off at Larabanga just after Damongo (2½ hours). From there it's a 5km walk; hitching is virtually impossible.

NAKPANDURI

This sleepy unspoilt village, 65km south of Bawku, is perched on top of the Gambaga escarpment. There are paths along the edge with superb views (except during the harmattan).

The *Government Resthouse*, serenely situated on the rim of the escarpment, offers a couple of basic rooms for US$2; if it's full you can camp. There's street food at the junction in the village, 1.5km from the resthouse.

Public transport from Bawku (US$2) is scarce, except on that town's market day (every three days, the same as Bolgatanga's).

NAVRONGO

If you want to overnight here en route to or from Burkina Faso, the *Catholic Mission* on the south-east side of town has clean rooms for US$3.

TAKORADI

Takoradi, Ghana's second-largest port along with the naval base of Sekondi 10km to the east, is of little interest to travellers. You may find yourself spending a night here, however, en route to or from Côte d'Ivoire or Ghana's coastal towns.

Places to Stay & Eat

The *Zenith Hotel* on Califf Ave has nothing to recommend it other than its price. Ventilated

singles/doubles with shared bath are US$3/5. There's a restaurant and loud music at night.

The *Embassy Hotel* (☎ 2212) on Liberation Rd has similar rooms and even louder music for US$6/8, while the *Amenlah Hotel* (☎ 2543) near the market has cheaper ventilated singles/doubles for US$3/4. The well-maintained *Ahenfie Hotel* (☎ 4272) has clean, ventilated rooms with semi-detached bathroom for US$14/18.

The best option is the relaxing *Beachway Hotel* (☎ 4734) at the southern end of town. Good value singles/doubles with fan and shared bath are US$7/9. The friendly staff will prepare meals for around US$3.

There's plenty of street food near the market. *Furama Restaurant* at the Harbour View Hotel has moderately priced Chinese and Ghanaian food.

TAMALE

Tamale is a commercial town and capital of the Northern Province. Though of little interest in itself, it's the jumping-off point for Mole National Park and Larabanga.

Places to Stay & Eat

Most travellers stay at the *Al Hassan Hotel* (☎ 23683) as it's near the truck park. Basic ventilated singles/doubles are US$3/4 (US$5 for a double with attached bathroom).

A few kilometres out of town on the Bolgatanga road, the *Christian Services Guest House* has ventilated rooms from US$4 (US$7 for attached bathroom). Across the street is the *Catholic Mission* (☎ 22265) which has good singles/doubles with attached bathroom for US$8/9. A taxi from the centre costs US$0.40.

For moderate luxury, head for the *Las Hotel* (☎ 22158) on the Salaga Rd. Decent rooms with fan and private bath are US$15/18 per single/double, and there's a restaurant serving Chinese food for around US$4.

The best place for a meal is *Crest Restaurant's* rooftop terrace near Barclays Bank; good Ghanaian food starts at US$2. Nearby, *Sparkles Restaurant* (closed Sunday) has Chinese and Ghanaian meals from US$1.

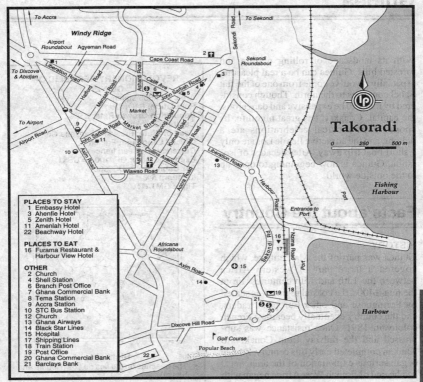

PLACES TO STAY
1 Embassy Hotel
3 Ahenfie Hotel
5 Zenith Hotel
11 Amenlah Hotel
22 Beachway Hotel

PLACES TO EAT
16 Furama Restaurant &
     Harbour View Hotel

OTHER
2 Church
4 Shell Station
6 Branch Post Office
7 Ghana Commercial Bank
8 Tema Station
9 Accra Station
10 STC Bus Station
12 Church
13 Ghana Airways
14 Black Star Lines
15 Hospital
17 Shipping Lines
18 Train Station
19 Post Office
20 Ghana Commercial Bank
21 Barclays Bank

Takoradi

0   250   500 m

GHANA

WINNEBA

Winneba is a pleasant town with a good
beach. A tro-tro from the main (Swedru)
junction into town costs US$0.30.

On the first weekend in May, Winneba is
home to the renowned Deer Hunt Festival
(*Aboakyer*), in which two teams compete to
capture an antelope for sacrifice to the tribal
god Penkye Otu. The first to capture the
animal alive and bring it back to the village
chief wins. The next day the sacrificial offering is made to Penkye Otu.

Places to Stay & Eat

About 1.5km west of the town centre, right
on the beach, is the *Sir Charles Tourist*

Centre (☎ 189). The atmosphere is drab but
the facilities it offers – restaurant and bar and
a quiet, clean beach – are tempting. Basic
rooms cost from US$4 (US$7 with fan),
while attractive chalets are US$15.

The *Army Resthouse* (☎ 208) is set well
back from the shore on the south campus of
the Advanced Teacher Training College. It's
nowhere near as nice as the Sir Charles;
rundown doubles are US$6 and you must
bring your own food or eat in town.

If you don't mind being almost 4km from
the centre on the Swedru road, the *Yeenuah
Hotel* (☎ 161) has a breezy balcony, a restaurant and ventilated singles/doubles for
US$5/12.

Guinea

With its landscape of rolling pasture and forested hills, Guinea can be a real pleasure, especially if you've come from one of the flat Sahel countries to the north. Though considered by many to be expensive and dangerous, the capital, Conakry, has great nightlife. Its spontaneous musical celebrations are a delight, and the attractive Îles de Los are only a short boat trip away. After decades of isolation, Guinea is now beginning to open up to the outside world.

Facts about the Country

HISTORY

Guinea was part of the Mali empire, which covered a large part of western Africa between the 13th and 15th centuries. From the mid-1400s, the coastal region was settled by Portuguese and other European traders, and the country eventually became a French colony in 1891. Once resistance was suppressed and the railway from Conakry to Kankan completed early this century, France began serious exploitation of the area.

The end of French West Africa began with Guinea. It was granted independence in 1958 under the leadership of Sekou Touré. Guinea's isolation resulted from Touré's rejection of a French offer of membership in a commonwealth as an alternative to total independence, declaring: 'We prefer poverty in liberty to riches in slavery'. French reaction was swift: financial and technical aid was cut off, and massive amounts of capital were withdrawn from the country. Guinea withdrew from the Central Africa CFA franc zone and introduced its own currency, the syli.

In the mid-1960s Sekou Touré decided to model Guinea on the revolutionary Chinese pattern, introducing state-run farms and industries which were to prove disastrous. As the decade rolled on, he became increasingly

REVOLUTIONARY REPUBLIC OF GUINEA
Area: 245,855 sq km
Population: 6.6 million
Population Growth Rate: 2.9%
Capital: Conakry
Head of State: President Lansana Conté
Official Language: French
Currency: Guinean franc
Exchange Rate: GFr 1000 = US$1
Per Capita GNP: US$530
Inflation: 5%
Time: GMT/UTC

Highlights
- The beaches on the Îles de Los (Roume and Kassa)
- A spontaneous musical performance in a Conakry side street
- The Fouta Djalon plateau

obsessed with opposition to his rule. 'Conspiracies' were detected in one group after another, show trials were held, and dissidents were imprisoned or executed. By the end of the 1960s there were some 250,000 Guineans living in exile.

Towards the end of his presidency, Touré changed many of his policies. A major influence was the Market Women's Revolt of 1977, in which several police stations were destroyed and some local governors were killed, as part of the fight against state plans to discourage private trade.

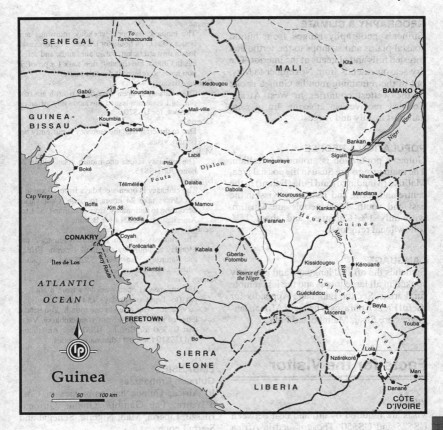

SENEGAL

To
Tambacounda

MALI

Kita

BAMAKO

Gabú

Koundara

Kedougou

GUINEA-
BISSAU

Koumbia

Mali-ville

Gaoual

Bankan

Boké

Labé

Pita

Fouta

Djalon

Dinguiraye

Siguiri

Niani

Télimélé

Dalaba

Mandiana

Cap Verga

Dabola

Niani

Boffa

Km 36

Mamou

Kouroussa

Kankan

Kindia

Faranah

Haute

Guinée

Milo River

CONAKRY

Coyah

Forécariah

Kabala

Gberia-
Fotombu

Kissidougou

Kérouané

Îles de Los

Ferry Route

Kambia

Source of
the Niger

Guinée

ATLANTIC
OCEAN

Guéckédou

Forestière

FREETOWN

Macenta

Beyla

Touba

Bo

Lola

Guinea

SIERRA
LEONE

Nzérékoré

Man

0   50   100 km

LIBERIA

Danané

CÔTE
D'IVOIRE

Niger River

Cap Verga

GUINEA

Touré died in March 1984. Just one month later a military coup was staged by a group of colonels, including Lansana Conté, who became president. He introduced austerity measures to secure an IMF loan, and a new currency, the Guinean franc, replaced the syli. In 1991, Conté bowed to pressure to introduce a multiparty political system.

Presidential elections were held in late 1993. In mid-December the land borders were closed while voting and counting took place. The borders remained closed into early 1994 – weeks after the election, which Conté won with 51% of the vote. General elections are planned for 1998 or 1999, but it remains to be seen if the Guinean people can wait that long. In February 1996, there was a mutiny by troops in Conakry and about 50 people were killed. Conté sacked his defence minister.

Today, Guinea is relying on its mineral reserves (which include bauxite, copper, iron, diamonds and possibly uranium) to pull it out of its position as one of the world's poorest countries. The quality of life and standard of living has improved for most Guineans; many exiles have returned, free enterprise is encouraged and people can talk openly without fear of repression.

GEOGRAPHY & CLIMATE

Guinea's geography ranges from humid coastal plains and swamps to the fertile and forested hills and plateaus of the interior. The dry season extends from November to May, but in the remaining months Guinea is one of the wettest countries in West Africa: Conakry receives an amazing 4m of rain, half of it in July and August.

POPULATION & PEOPLE

Guinea's population is around 6.6 million. The main groups are Susu in the coastal area, Malinké (Mandingo) and Fula (Fulani) in the centre and north, and Tenda and Kissi in the east and south. Most people are Muslim, with only 1% Christian, and about 15% follow local religions.

LANGUAGE

French is the official language and is widely spoken in all large towns and the less remote rural areas. See the Language Appendix for useful French phrases. The main African languages are Susu, Malinké and Fula.

Facts for the Visitor

VISAS

Visas are required by all, and cost between US$25 and US$50. Those issued in Africa may only be good for stays of two weeks, but you can sometimes get longer. For an extension go to the immigration office (☎ 44 1439) in Conakry, corner of 1st Blvd and Ave Tubman (8th Ave).

Other Visas

In Conakry you can get visas to many African countries. You'll need between one and four photos for each visa application.

The French embassy issues visas to Burkina Faso, the Central African Republic, Chad and Togo within 24 hours. The cost of each is about US$10 (FFr50).

Ghana
    The embassy is open weekday mornings and issues visas in 24 hours for US$50. The form asks for an onward ticket, sufficient funds, and referees in Ghana, but the staff don't ask for proof; if you have no referee it doesn't matter.
Guinea-Bissau
    The embassy is open weekdays from 8 am to 1 pm, and visas are issued the same day, often on the spot, for US$20.
Liberia
    Due to the civil war, the embassy is currently not issuing visas.
Mali
    The embassy issues one-month visas within 24 hours for US$15.
Nigeria
    The embassy is open weekdays from 10 am to 2 pm. Visas take 24 hours to issue. Cost varies according to nationality, from less than US$1 for Americans to US$214 for Britons.
Senegal
    The embassy is open from 8.30 am to 2 pm Monday to Thursday and until 1 pm on Friday and Saturday. Visas cost US$20 and are issued within 24 hours.
Sierra Leone
    The embassy is open weekdays from 8 am to 3 pm (to 1 pm on Friday) and gives same-day service, for visas of up to one month. You need a letter of introduction from your embassy. Visas cost US$30 for Britons, US$15 for Americans and US$10 for most other nationalities.

EMBASSIES
Guinean Embassies

In Africa, Guinea has embassies in Côte d'Ivoire, The Gambia, Ghana, Guinea-Bissau, Liberia, Mali, Nigeria, Senegal and Sierra Leone.

Foreign Embassies in Guinea

Countries with a diplomatic mission in Conakry include:

Canada
    Near Cité Douanes, Corniche Sud, Matam (☎ 41 2395; fax 41 4236)
Cape Verde (consulate)
    Quartier Minière (☎ 42 1137)
France
    Corner of Blvd du Commerce and 8th Ave (☎ 41 1605; fax 41 2708)
Germany
    Corner of 2nd Blvd and 9th Ave (☎ 44 1506)

Ghana
Place des Martyrs, Imm Kaloum, Ave de la République, behind Sabena (☎ 44 1510)
Guinea-Bissau
Quartier Bellvue, Commune de Dixinn (☎ 44 4398)
Mali
La Minière, Commune de Dixinn (☎ 41 1539)
Nigeria
Corniche Sud, 750m beyond Place du 8 Novembre (☎ 41 4375, 46 1341)
Senegal
Corniche Sud, 1.5km beyond the Nigerian embassy (☎ 46 2834)
Sierra Leone
Route Donka, just south of Carrefour Bellvue, Commune de Dixinn (☎ 44 5099)
UK (honorary consul)
Mrs Val Treitlein, opposite the Coléah Lycéem, Quartier Mafanco (☎ 46 1734; fax 44 4215)
USA
Corner of 2nd Blvd and 9th Ave (☎ 44 1521)

MONEY

US$1 = GFr 1000

The unit of currency is the Guinean franc (GFr). The exchange rate offered by black-market dealers is at best 10% higher than the bank rate, but only for cash; in Conakry these dealers operate at the airport and in the city centre next to the post office on 4th Blvd.

There's a bank at Conakry airport but the rates are low for travellers' cheques. Neither this bank nor any other will change back Guinean francs into hard currency when you leave. However, the moneychangers will help you out – everything seems fairly open, but it's worth being as discreet as possible.

POST & COMMUNICATIONS

The postal service is quite reliable between Conakry and Europe or the USA, although it's terrible to/from towns outside the capital.

For international phone calls in Conakry go to the Novotel. If you have little money to spare and plenty of time to waste, go to the post office. The country code is 224; there are no area codes.

DANGERS & ANNOYANCES

Outside the capital, Guinea is a safe country, but Conakry itself is a bad place for street crime. Be particularly careful in markets and bus stations where thieves and pick-pockets abound. It's more likely, however, that the only time you will be 'robbed' is by the police or soldiers – they set up roadblocks at night, delight in holding your papers until you pay a bribe, then allow you to proceed down the 'closed' street. Unless you have a lot of time on your hands, offer them about GFr2000 (US$2).

PUBLIC HOLIDAYS

Public holidays include: 1 January, 1 April, 1 May, 27 August (Market Women's Revolt), 1 October (Independence Day), 1 November (Armed Forces Day), 25 December, Easter Monday and variable Islamic holidays (see the Regional Facts for the Visitor chapter for details of Islamic holidays).

ACCOMMODATION & FOOD

There aren't many budget hotels in Conakry. Outside of Conakry, most towns have at least

Outdoor Guinea

Guinea is one of the best places in West Africa for the outdoor enthusiast. Apart from the Casamance in Senegal (when the political situation permits) there are few places in West Africa where you can walk or mountain-bike so freely.

The Fouta Djalon is the main focus for hikers and bikers. A command of simple French and adequate supplies (water, purification tablets and packaged food) ensure you can wander/cycle freely. Things to look for are La Voile de la Mariée (Bridal Veil) Falls and Mont Gangan near Kindia; the picturesque towns of Dalaba and Pita (and nearby attractions such as Les Chutes de Kinkon); and the great hiking/mountain-biking route from Pita to Télimélée (part of the Paris-Dakar Rally in 1995).

The really adventurous could consider canoeing down the Niger River from Faranah to Kouroussa (two weeks, 350km); the trip is best done at Christmas time. ■

one place to stay, often with quite basic, but cheap, facilities.

In most towns, street food – grilled fish or meat (with onions and crumbled Maggi cube), peanuts and cakes – is available, and there are usually one or two basic eating houses doing cheap meals of rice and sauce. Only the larger towns have anything like a restaurant, where you might also find meat, chicken or chips.

Getting There & Away

AIR
European airlines serving Guinea include Air France, KLM, Sabena and Aeroflot. Ghana Airways and Air Afrique also have flights to/from Europe.

Within Africa, Conakry is connected to Bamako, Niamey and all the capital cities along the West African coast. For example, to Freetown (Sierra Leone) on Gambia Airways and Ghana Airways costs US$60/80 one way/return, and to Banjul (The Gambia) and Dakar (Senegal) the one-way/return fares are both around US$165/180. Most of the airlines have their offices on or near Ave de la République, in the centre of Conakry.

For international flights, there's no airport departure tax. For domestic flights, the tax is around US$5.

LAND
Côte d'Ivoire
The usual route to Côte d'Ivoire is via Macenta, Nzérékoré, Danané and Man. Getting to Nzérékoré from Conakry is straightforward. It is easy to get from Conakry to Macenta by bus, and on to Nzérékoré by bush taxi. From Nzérékoré bush taxis run to Lola (45km), and from there to the border (35km), which is open 24 hours. From the border a taxi or minibus takes you to Danané (50km, 1½ hours, US$5), near Man.

An alternative route goes via Kankan and Odienné, passing through Mandiana and Tindila, but this is in poor condition and

infrequently travelled. Bush taxis run between Kankan and Mandiana; for the rest of the route you will probably have to hitch a ride with a truck. Allow two days.

Guinea-Bissau
The usual route to Guinea-Bissau goes via Labé and Koundara to Gabú. Getting from Conakry to Koundara is straightforward. Catching rides between Koundara and Gabú, however, is difficult. With luck you may find a truck or pick-up going direct for around US$10. Expect it to take a day to cover this 100km stretch.

Alternatively, from Koundara there are irregular bush taxis to Seréboïdo, the last village in Guinea, but from there you may have to walk to the border and hope for a pick-up to Gabú. Your best chance of getting connections is at Seréboïdo's weekly market on Sunday: vehicles go from Koundara on Saturday and return to Gabú on Sunday or Monday.

Mali
The usual route from Conakry to Bamako goes via Kankan and Siguiri. From Kankan, there's a bus most days to the border at Kourémalé, via Siguiri, for US$10. Bush taxis also go this way for about the same price (although many drivers who say they are going to Bamako are actually only going towards Bamako and stop at the border). You cross the Niger River twice on decrepit ferries which break down frequently. When this happens, you have to take a pirogue and find a vehicle on the other side.

Once you cross the border (at Kourémalé) into Mali, there's a bus three times a week to Bamako (US$4.50), and bush taxis (which sometimes start at Siguiri) on most other days. Bush taxis travel on this route when there is no bus. If you get stuck at the border, there is a campement with rooms for US$3.

Senegal
The usual route to Senegal goes via Labé and Koundara, from where vehicles head for Tambacounda or Velingara most days. Some

may go all the way to Dakar (US$55) or Ziguinchor. Between Koundara and Kaliforou (the border town), the scenery is beautiful but the road is pitiful. The whole trip between Labé and Dakar takes between 25 and 35 hours. Trucks trundle from Koundara or Labé to Tambacounda and cost around US$20.

During the wet season the stretch between Labé and Koundara is very slow or impassable as the trucks tear up the road, causing other vehicles to get stuck.

Sierra Leone

There are plenty of private buses and bush taxis running directly between Conakry and Freetown via Pamelap, costing about US$15. You can do it in a day if you leave Conakry early (see the Conakry Getting There & Away section).

You can also enter Sierra Leone from Faranah: a good dirt road (with little traffic) goes south-west to the Guinea border town of Gberia-Fotombu. From there to the Sierra Leone checkpoint is 12km, and from there you may find a truck heading for Kabala.

There are other possible routes. From Guéckédou, go 30km west to the border town of Nongoa, then take a canoe across the river to reach Koindu (from where buses and bush taxis go to Kenema and Freetown). Alternatively, from Kindia, take a pick-up truck to Kamakwie, then a bush taxi on to Makeni.

BOAT

Mali

A barge carrying passengers goes once weekly from Kankan to Jikuroni (upstream from Bamako) between July and November, or when the river is high enough. The trip costs US$10 and takes four days.

Sierra Leone

A fast luxurious hydrofoil once operated between Conakry and Freetown; the fare was US$40/70 one way/return. It may resume, so inquire in Conakry.

Getting Around

AIR

Air Guinée, Guinée Air Service and Guinea Inter Air have domestic flights from Conakry to Boké, Kissidougou, Kankan, Siguiri, Labé and Koundara. There's usually one or two flights per week to each destination, but schedules change constantly.

BUS

SOGETRAG, the government bus company, runs between Conakry and all the main upcountry towns (except Nzérékoré, although they may start when the road from Macenta is tarred), with services from once to three times a week. Its large 'Transguinée' buses are comfortable and good value. Some sample prices are: Conakry to Kankan US$23, Conakry to Labé US$12, and Conakry to Macenta US$17. There are also private buses running on some of these routes, for around the same price, although they're not so reliable.

BUSH TAXI

Bush taxis in Guinea are usually Peugeot 504s, made to carry six people but usually carrying up to 12 people, plus children, goats, bananas, live poultry and often a few more people on the roof (we have even seen two passengers on the bonnet!). Because the long-distance buses are cheap and reliable, bush taxis do the relatively shorter runs between major towns.

Some sample fares are Mamou to Labé US$6, Mamou to Faranah US$7, Faranah to Kissidougou US$5, Kissidougou to Kankan US$8, Kissidougou to Guéckédou US$3, Guéckédou to Macenta US$2.50 and Macenta to Nzérékoré US$8.

Minibuses cover the same routes as bush taxis. They are cheaper, more crowded, significantly more dangerous and worth avoiding unless there's no alternative.

In Guinea the term *gare voiture* is used, rather than gare routière, for the bus and bush-taxi park.

GUINEA

Conakry

After being run down by Sekou Touré for a quarter of a century, Conakry is once again an open and vibrant place. The main avenues have been repaved (although side streets are still dirty), and glitzy new shops, restaurants and nightclubs are constantly popping up.

On the down side, street crime in Conakry has increased considerably, particularly around the central Marché du Niger and at the Gare Voiture de Madina, so always be on your guard. The police love a bribe, so factor such eventualities into your daily expenses.

For budget travellers there's little in the way of cheap accommodation, and for many visitors there's not much of interest to see or do in the city. Other visitors love the place for the very reason that it is very much an 'African' capital with all the attendant dangers, heaps of unexpected surprises, good music venues and idyllic islands offshore (for a weekend blast).

The rest of Guinea has beautiful landscapes, friendly people and is a great place to visit, so, if you wish to avoid a 'walk on the wild side', plan your escape from Conakry quickly.

Orientation & Information
Conakry is a long, narrow city, built on the Kaloum peninsula. In the city centre are the banks, airline offices, several restaurants and some hotels. Two km out of the centre the peninsula narrows, and at Place du 8 Novembre the road divides: Route Donka to the west, Corniche Sud to the east, and the Autoroute up the middle. If you take a left on Route Donka you reach the buzzing Camayenne quarter. Ten km north of the centre are the lively Rogbane and Taouyah quarters.

Conakry has no tourist office, but local events are advertised in *Dyeli*, a listings magazine available free at large hotels, airline offices and some restaurants.

Banks for changing money include the BICIGUI on Ave de la République, or the BIAG, around the corner on Blvd de Commerce. Rates and commissions vary for cash and travellers' cheques, and for the number (and even the type) of cheques changed.

Things to See & Do
The **Palais de la Présidence** near the Novotel was going to be the venue for the Organisation of African Unity conference in 1984, which was cancelled when Sekou Touré died. It now serves as the office of the president. It is forbidden to come here at night.

The **Musée National**, by the Corniche Sud on 7th Blvd, has a modest collection of masks, statues and musical instruments. It should be open in the mornings from Monday to Saturday, but often isn't; entry is free.

The beaches on the **Îles de Los**, 5 to 10km south-west of Conakry, are popular at weekends. Expatriates prefer the **Île de Roume**, reached by hiring a motorised pirogue from the beach near the Novotel for about US$25. Guineans prefer Soro Beach on **Île de Kassa**, reached by public boat (US$1 return) leaving every Sunday at 9 am from the port and returning at 5.30 pm. Mr Coza (contact Karou Voyages) also runs day trips to the Îles de Los (about US$20) or to Kindia, Bridal Falls and Le Chien Qui Fume Mountain (US$50).

Places to Stay
City Centre The homey and reliable *Pension Doherty* (☎ 44 1764) on 5th Ave between 8th and 9th Blvds (in a residential area), has clean singles/doubles with attached bathroom from US$23/28 (US$6 extra for air-con), a good-quality restaurant and attractive garden area.

The *Hôtel du Niger*, near the Marché du Niger, has rooms with fans, attached bathroom and hot water for US$25/35 (US$10 extra for air-con) including a good breakfast. *Samaya Accommodation*, near the corner of 9th Ave and Route du Niger, is close to Lips nightclub – its proximity is reflected in the price for a room (US$25 per night or US$5 per hour!)

The *Hôtel Kaloum* (☎ 44 3311) on Ave de la République near Blvd du Commerce, is currently closed for renovations – expect the price to go up considerably when it reopens (perhaps US$60/80 for singles/doubles).

Outside the City Centre In the Kipé area,

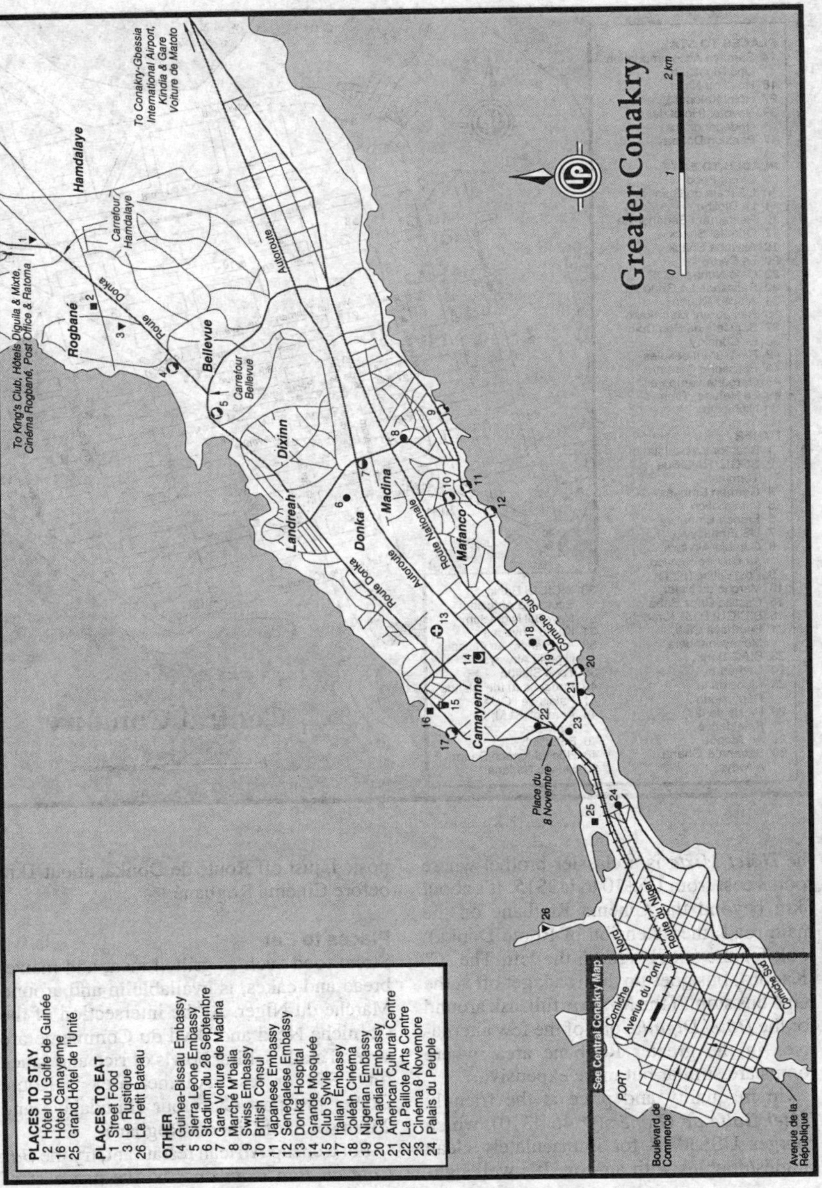

Greater Conakry
0 1 2 km
PLACES TO STAY
2 Hôtel du Golfe de Guinée
16 Hôtel Camayenne
25 Grand Hôtel de l'Unité
PLACES TO EAT
1 Street Food
3 Le Rustique
26 Le Petit Bateau
OTHER
4 Guinea-Bissau Embassy
5 Sierra Leone Embassy
6 Stadium du 28 Septembre
7 Gare Voiture de Madina
8 Marché M'balia
9 Swiss Embassy
10 British Consul
11 Japanese Embassy
12 Senegalese Embassy
13 Donka Hospital
14 Grande Mosquée
15 Club Sylvie
17 Italian Embassy
18 Coléah Cinéma
19 Nigerian Embassy
20 Canadian Embassy
21 American Cultural Centre
22 La Paillote Arts Centre
23 Cinéma 8 Novembre
24 Palais du Peuple
To King's Club, Hôtels Diguila & Mixte, Cinéma Rogbané, Post Office & Ratoma
To Conakry-Gbessia International Airport, Kindia & Gare Voiture de Matoto
Hamdalaye
Carrefour Hamdalaye
Rogbané
Route Donka
Bellevue
Carrefour Bellevue
Autoroute
Dixinn
Landreah
Donka
Madina
Route Nationale
Mafanco
Corniche Sud
Camayenne
Place du 8 Novembre
See Central Conakry Map
PORT
Corniche Nord
Avenue du Pont
Route du Niger
Boulevard de Commerce
Avenue de la République

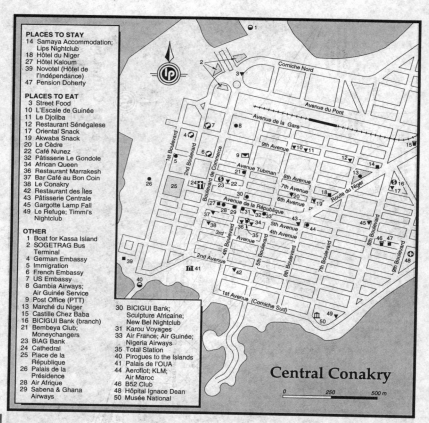

PLACES TO STAY
14 Samaya Accommodation;
   Lips Nightclub
18 Hôtel du Niger
27 Hôtel Kaloum
39 Novotel (Hôtel de
   l'Indépendance)
47 Pension Doherty

PLACES TO EAT
3 Street Food
10 L'Escale de Guinée
11 Le Djoliba
12 Restaurant Sénégalese
17 Oriental Snack
19 Akwaba Snack
20 Le Cèdre
22 Café Nunez
32 Pâtisserie Le Gondole
34 African Queen
36 Restaurant Marrakesh
37 Bar Café au Bon Coin
38 Le Conakry
42 Restaurant des Îles
43 Pâtisserie Centrale
45 Gargotte Lamp Fall
49 Le Refuge; Timmi's
   Nightclub

OTHER
1 Boat for Kassa Island
2 SOGETRAG Bus
  Terminal
4 German Embassy
5 Immigration
6 French Embassy
7 US Embassy
8 Gambia Airways;
  Air Guinée Service
9 Post Office (PTT)
13 Marché du Niger
15 Castille Chez Baba
16 BICIGUI Bank (branch)
21 Bembeya Club;
   Moneychangers
23 BIAG Bank
24 Cathedral
25 Place de la
   République
26 Palais de la
   Présidence
28 Air Afrique
29 Sabena & Ghana
   Airways
30 BICIGUI Bank;
   Sculpture Africaine;
   New Bel Nightclub
31 Karou Voyages
33 Air France; Air Guinée;
   Nigeria Airways
35 Total Station
40 Pirogues to the Islands
41 Palais de l'OUA
44 Aeroflot; KLM;
   Air Maroc
46 B52 Club
48 Hôpital Ignace Dean
50 Musée National

Central Conakry

0   250   500 m

GUINEA

the *Hôtel Mixte* is a classier brothel where
rooms cost from US$10 to US$15. It's about
3km beyond the Cinéma Rogbané on the
main road (the extension of Route Donka);
look for the small sign on the left. The 'C'
(Kaporo) bus goes up this road; get off at the
Kipé bus stop. If the Mixte is full, ask around
for the *Hôtel Diguila*, one of the few alternatives in the greater Rogbané area, where
rooms are similar but more expensive.

Up in quality and price is the friendly
Hôtel Golfe de Guinée (☎ 46 4310), which
charges US$30/38 for immaculately clean
singles/doubles with air-con. It's well sign-

posted, just off Route de Donka, about 1km
before Cinéma Rogbané.

Places to Eat
Street food such as grilled meat and maize,
bread and cakes, is available in and around
Marché du Niger. At the intersection of the
Corniche Nord and Blvd du Commerce are
several stalls selling bowls of rice and sauce
for US$1 or less. Another area is Route
Donka just past Carrefour Hamdalaye and
250m south of Cinéma Rogbané.

For a cheap African restaurant, try the *Bar
Café au Bon Coin* on 4th Ave just east of

Blvd du Commerce, where rice and sauce is around US$1.50, or the friendly Senegalese-run *Lamp Fall*, on 8th Blvd two blocks south of Route du Niger, a gargotte where good filling meals are around US$3.

Some of the cheapest (US$1.50 a dish) and best food (delicious poisson and poulet yassa) is found at the *Restaurant Sénégalese*, on the corner of 9th Ave and 7th Blvd. Another fairly cheap place is *Le Djoliba* on 9th Ave, between 5th and 6th Blvds (where tourism students hone their skills).

For inexpensive Lebanese chawarmas, kafta sandwiches and hamburgers for around US$1.50, and meals like grilled chicken and chips for US$2.50, go to *Oriental Snack* on 8th Blvd near the junction with Route du Niger, and *Akwaba Snack*, near the Hotel du Niger. More expensive is the *Pâtisserie Centrale*, on Ave de la République, where burgers and pizzas start at US$3. Upmarket Lebanese food can be found at *Le Cèdre*, between 5th and 6th Blvds.

More expensive but good-value restaurants in the centre include *Restaurant Marrakesh*, near the corner of 5th Ave and 4th Blvd, which has lunch platters for about US$6 and a full dinner for about US$12; and *Le Refuge*, on Corniche Sud near the museum, which serves French food (it has Timmi's Nightclub attached).

Entertainment

Conakry has several nightclubs. In the centre is the seedy, crowded and always lively *Bembeya Club*, on the corner of Ave Tubman and 4th Blvd, a block south of the post office. This club is not for the faint-hearted, and the surrounding area is known for thugs and thieves. Slightly better clubs: *B52*, on 5th Ave just down from the Pension Doherty; the buzzing *Le Djoliba* on 9th Ave; *Lips*, across from the BICIGUI Bank on Route du Niger, a great place to dance (see Places to Stay earlier); and *Castille Chez Baba*, a happening place with a wide range of music, which is near the corner of Route du Niger and Avenue du Pont.

The smarter places, with cover charges, are in the suburbs and these include *King's Club* (US$3 cover), just past Cinéma Rog-

bané, and the expensive *Eden Park* (US$8 cover), 1km or two beyond. *Le Palace* on Ave de la République used to be a flashy, favourite pick-up joint – it reopens as *New Bel* and promises to be upmarket.

The best night haunt in the whole of Conakry is the unpretentious *Club Sylvie* in Camayenne, a stone's throw away from the glitzy Hôtel Camayenne. It is always packed and fairly hums from 8 pm until the wee small hours – the beer is cold, there are plenty of street stalls outside to satisfy that early-morning hunger and lots of taxis on hand.

Getting There & Away

Bus & Bush Taxi All SOGETRAG long-distance buses leave from Gare Voiture de Madina on the Autoroute, 6km from Conakry centre, reached by taxi (US$3) or a city bus on route 'A' from the Ave de la République.

There are buses to Macenta (via Mamou, Faranah, Kissidougou and Guéckédou, US$17), Pita (via Kindia and Mamou, US$11), Kissidougou (via Mamou and Faranah, US$15), Kankan (via Faranah and Kissidougou, US$23) and Labé (US$12). Big bags cost US$3 regardless of where you get off.

All long-distance buses depart at 8 am. For most buses reservations are not possible; you have to go early (around 6 am) to the ticket office at the gare voiture on the day of departure. At this time, get a taxi to drop you right by the ticket office (US$0.50 extra to go into the gare voiture), as it's still dark and this is a favourite haunt for thieves. Tickets can be bought the day before for the Kankan bus only (at the Gare Voiture de Matoto, several kilometres beyond the airport).

Private buses and bush taxis direct to Freetown (Sierra Leone) leave from the Gare Voiture de Matoto. They take all day and are supposed to leave around 8 am, but it's often later.

Bush taxis and minibuses for destinations such as Kindia and Mamou leave from Gare Voiture de Madina. Long-distance bush taxis from Conakry to places beyond Mamou are less common as the buses are so popular. Bush taxis (and also some buses) running

GUINEA

overnight stop outside Conakry until dawn before finishing their trip. Any local trip involves passing through the onerous roadblock 'Km 36', where the police do anything to extract bribes from drivers and passengers before dropping the chain which blocks the road.

Getting Around

The Airport Taxis from the city centre to the airport (13km) cost from US$3 to US$5 depending on your bargaining powers. From the airport the drivers start with outlandish figures like US$50, then show you the 'official tariff sheet' which says fares are US$10. After you've walked away a few times you should get your ride for US$5. Alternatively, it's easy to catch a bus or share-taxi from the airport to the centre; just walk across the road and hail a share-taxi or take the 'A' bus (marked 'Port' or 'Ville') for US$0.20.

Bus SOGETRAG has two main city bus lines: both start at the roundabout next to the port and go along Ave de la République and Route du Niger to Place du 8 Novembre, where the 'C' bus takes Route Donka to Kaporo, out beyond Rogbané, and the 'A' bus either continues on the Autoroute or takes the parallel Route Nationale east to Matoto, out beyond the airport.

Taxi For a seat in a share-taxi around town just stand at the side of the road appropriate to the direction you want to go in and shout your destination as the taxi passes. It costs US$0.20 for a ride of up to about 3km, double for longer rides. A taxi for an hour should cost about US$2.50 if you bargain well.

Around the Country

COYAH

Coyah is a small town about 50km from the centre of Conakry on the main road which leads to all the large towns in the country. It is where Guinea's bottled mineral water comes from.

The *Hôtel Mariani* has reasonable rooms with attached bathroom for US$12, and there are some basic eating houses around the bus-park area. *Chez Claude* is a decent French restaurant which is open daily except Friday; one of the six or so selections on the menu will cost from US$7 to US$10.

Buses and bush taxis go regularly to Kindia or Mamou.

THE FOUTA DJALON

Most of West Africa is flat and a welcome exception is the Fouta Djalon. This plateau, a beautiful area of green rolling hills, where the temperature is cooler than the lowlands, is a must for any visitor to Guinea (and well worth the effort it takes to get there). At the heart of the plateau are the towns of Dalaba, Pita and Labé. There are many options for **hiking**, and it is undoubtedly one of the best places in the region for this activity. The best time to visit is from November to January.

The towns below are listed in order of distance from Conakry.

Mamou

Mamou is a grimy junction town, where the road into the Fouta Djalon branches off the main road from Conakry. It is said that the thieves here are smarter than those in Conakry – and that is *smart*!

The cheapest place to stay is the *Hôtel Luna*, on the north side of the town centre, with rooms for US$5, and slightly better ones for US$8.

For cheap food, there's a couple of basic eating houses near the gare voiture in the market. A popular cheapie is the *Restaurant de l'Unité*, on the Labé road, where filling meals are US$1. Other reliable places are *Café de Guinée le Relais* and *Clos St-Catherine*.

Dalaba

During the colonial period Dalaba was a therapeutic centre, perhaps due to its 1200m altitude and scenic position. Today it's a good base for day hikes in the surrounding area. For an idea of routes, go either to the Centre d'Acceuil or to the large boulders on the edge of the escarpment to the west of the Hôtel Tangama, where you get good views and from where paths lead down into the valley. You can also follow the dirt road that leads along the edge of the escarpment from the Centre d'Acceuil.

Places to Stay & Eat All the places to stay are on the south-western edge of town. Cheapest is the *Étoile de Fouta*, a dingy bar/restaurant/nightclub with a few rooms of varying quality for US$4. Nearby, the new *Hôtel Tangama* (☎ 61 0400) has clean doubles from US$7 (about US$20 with private bath).

Further down the road is the *Centre d'Acceuil*, also called Villa Présidential. (The president used to holiday here, but the chandeliers and embroidered curtains are now faded and covered in dust.) For reasonable rooms with attached bathroom, the caretaker charges the same as the Hôtel Tangama.

The meals at the Tangama are the best in Dalaba but they are not cheap (main meals are around US$10). In the centre of town the *Restaurant Tinka* and the *Renaissance Bar* do cheap meals, and near the gare voiture are several simple cafes. For a drink try *Bar Le Relais 55*.

Getting There & Away The gare voiture is next to the market. Buses to/from Labé and Pita pass through six times per week in each direction. Daily bush taxis also go to/from Mamou and Labé, both for US$2 (to Conakry it is about US$10 by bush taxi).

Pita

Roughly halfway between Dalaba and Labé is the small but interesting town of Pita – as good as an escape as you will get in West Africa. Stop off and enjoy!

Nearby are **Les Chutes du Kinkon**, reached by going north on the main road for 1km, then left down a dirt road for 10km. There are waterfalls above and below the hydroelectric power station, and both falls make for nice walks through villages and hills – you can easily walk to them (and back) in a day. Permission to visit the falls is needed from the police (as the strategic

power station is nearby). Camping is definitely prohibited.

The road from Pita to Télimélé (and on to Kindia), to the west, has some beautiful sections and would be extremely challenging to a mountain biker.

Places to Stay & Eat The definitely rustic *Hôtel Kinkon*, on the north side of town behind the public gardens, charges US$4 a room; there are attached washing cubicles for which you can order hot water. The much-vaunted *Centre d'Accueil* was not open when we visited (US$5 when it is).

You can eat at one of the cheap *stalls* on the main street (grilled meat with onions and Maggi) where the buses and bush taxis stop. Nearby are coffee shops such as the *Buenos Aires* and *Café Restaurant Montréal*. The slightly adventurous can wander off the main street to find a fabulous *Mauritanian restaurant* to the west side of the road (opposite the video club Le Sapin), where excellent chawarma, kafta and couscous can be had for a song.

Two good bars are tucked away in the middle of no-persons land to the west of the main road. The *Hilton Bar* is the more exciting, due to the total absence of lighting.

Labé

Labé, 400km from Conakry, is at the end of the tarred road through the Fouta Djalon. It's Guinea's third-largest town and not particularly attractive, but it is a major hub for traffic to/from Senegal and Guinea-Bissau.

Changing money in the bank takes ages; one of the shops near the Hôtel de l'Indépendance may be able to help. Find the charismatic Belgian, Pascal Diez.

Places to Stay & Eat For US$2 you can get a bed at the dingy *chambre de passage* in the gare voiture. If you want luxuries like sheets and windows try the *Hôtel du Tourisme* on the southern side of town, where rooms with double beds are US$5 (US$8 for two single beds). The shared toilets are dirty, but the restaurant is OK, with meals around US$2.

The *Grand Hôtel de l'Indépendance* near

the gare voiture has rooms for US$15 and meals for US$2.50 (it also has a much cheaper version across the road). Other choices are the *Hôtel Saala*, just out of town on the Pita road (US$10 for clean rooms) and the *Hôtel Tata*, close to the centre (rooms are US$20).

There are several inexpensive restaurants around the gare voiture. The *Restaurant Tata* is good for Italian; *Mamadou Oury Ly* is a good cafe; for a drink, try *Le Makoumba*, which is a lively place near the Hôtel de l'Indépendance.

Getting There & Away Air Guinée has scheduled flights to Conakry (US$40). Vehicles for Koundara (US$7) and Senegal go from Gare Voiture Dakar on the western outskirts of town. From the gare voiture in the centre, the bus goes to Conakry three times per week (US$12). Bush taxis leave daily for Mamou (US$6), Pita (US$1.50) and, if there's no bus that day, for Conakry (US$12).

GUÉCKÉDOU

Guéckédou is near the borders of Sierra Leone and Liberia (both of which can be reached from here) and is a major smuggling centre. The town itself is quite unattractive, but the weekly market (Wednesday) is huge. Traders from all over Guinea, plus many more from Sierra Leone, Liberia, Mali and Côte d'Ivoire, come to do business.

A place to stay is the *Hôtel Mafissa*, on the south-western edge of town, 1km along the road between the hospital and the gendarmerie, heading towards Sierra Leone. It has singles/doubles for US$3/6, although it is often full on market day. There is a good *restaurant* at the Hibiscus Hôtel and *coffee shops* near the truck park.

KANKAN

Kankan, on the banks of the Milo River, is Guinea's second city but it's a quiet place. The principal sights are the open market (with its large arched entrances), the covered market, the Grand Mosquée, and the old presidential palace overlooking the river.

Many Malinké (Mandinka) people regard this as their spiritual home.

Places to Stay & Eat

The *Hôtel Buffet de la Gare* next to the defunct railway station has half-decent rooms upstairs for US$10, and some more out the back, which are worse, for US$6. Another option, at about the same price, is at *Chez Madame Marie* (sometimes called *Le Refuge*), which is 1km from the centre of town on the Kissi road. More upmarket is the *Hôtel Bate*, where small but good rooms with attached bathroom are US$22, and US$29 with air-con (meals are US$5, snacks US$2).

At *Le Caleo* restaurant, down a side street near the open market, you can get meals from US$3.50 and snacks from US$1.50. For cheaper fare, there's a row of coffee and bread *stalls* near the open market.

Getting There & Away

Kankan's main gare voiture, for all southbound traffic, is by the bridge over the river. A bus from Conakry to Kankan costs US$23, and from Kankan to Kissidougou by bush taxi is US$8.

KINDIA

Kindia, nestled beneath Mount Gangan, is 135km from Conakry. The **Bridal Falls (Le Voile de la Mariée)** are 12km beyond town, 2km off the road to your right, but they're only worth visiting during or just after the rainy season. There's a small *restaurant* at the falls where meals cost US$5, and a bungalow can be rented for US$20. Any bush taxi for Mamou will drop you at the junction.

The *Hôtel Buffet de la Gare*, north of the town centre on the road to Mamou, has rooms for US$10. The new *Le Bungalow* (☎ 61 0143), just outside town on the Kindia bypass, is run by Madame Watty and her two sons; B&B in rooms with nets and fans is US$30, dinner is about US$10.

Another possibility is the *Hôtel/Bar Phare de Guinée*, 2km south on the Conakry road, with rooms with electricity for US$8 (but no fans or running water).

For street food, look around the market

and the gare voiture. For coffee and snacks, visit *Café King Kindy* two blocks south-east of the market. Drinking? Stagger to the *Bar Guinéen* or the buzzing *Le Bananier*.

KISSIDOUGOU

Kissidougou (often called Kissi) is a junction town where the main road from Conakry divides north to Kankan and south to Guéckédou and Nzérékoré. It lies next to the greatest area of remnant forest in this part of Africa.

The *Kissi Hôtel* has decent doubles with electricity and bucket baths for US$7. More expensive are the rooms, with attached bathroom, at the *Hôtel de la Paix*, reached by taking the road which runs north from the market. A number of readers recommend the *Hotel Nelson Mandela*, south of the main roundabout, which has clean rooms with air-con for US$15.

For onward travel, bush taxis go from the gare voiture to Faranah for US$5, to Kankan for US$8, to Mamou for US$14 and to Guéckédou for US$2.50.

MACENTA

Macenta is in south-east Guinea, at the end of the tar road from Conakry. It is inhabited by the Toma people, known for their interesting ceremonies and dancing. Beyond Macenta, the road south to Nzérékoré is in bad condition.

Near the gare voiture the *Hôtel Magnetic* has rooms for US$5. For cheap food, go to the unnamed *restaurant* up the hill from the Hôtel Palm, where bowls of rice and sauce are US$1.

Four km from town, on the Liberia road, is the smart *Hôtel Balaki* with simple rooms from US$10 and doubles with attached bathroom from US$25; meals are US$4.

Bush taxis to Nzérékoré (US$8) go from the gare voiture on the east side of town; all other traffic goes from the gare voiture on the west side. Bush taxis from Macenta to Guéckédou are US$2.50 and to Kissidougou US$3.

NZÉRÉKORÉ

In the far south-eastern corner of the country, Nzérékoré is the major city in Guinea's forest country (Guinée forestière). It's a lively place – a smuggling centre, a vital transport hub and a refugee centre for those fleeing the civil wars in Liberia and Sierra Leone.

The cheapest places in town seem to be the *Hôtel Orly*, *Bakuli Annexe* and *Bar Hanoi*, all with basic rooms for about US$3. Better is the friendly *Hôtel de l'Unité*, where very clean doubles (with bathroom, running water and towels) cost US$5. A reader suggests the *mission catholique* on a main street in the centre. These places sometimes have rooms, sometimes not.

Nzérékoré has four gares voitures: on the south-western side of town for vehicles toward Liberia, on the north-western side for big trucks, on the north-eastern side for vehicles going north to Kankan and east to Lola and the Côte d'Ivoire border, and on the northern outskirts of town for Macenta.

SOURCE OF THE NIGER

The Source of the Niger (Les Sources) is just north of the Sierra Leone border, near the remote settlement of Forokonia (72km from the main road). It looks like any other muddy stream, but romantics may want to visit anyway.

Before you set out, be aware that this is a border region and potentially sensitive. It is also a sacred area for the local people. Make enquiries about the current situation at the Hôtel de Ville in Faranah. Once in Forokonia, you will need a guide to show you to Les Sources; local youths charge about US$2. You can also find somewhere to sleep in the village – expect to pay US$5 for a bed in a hut and a meal.

The Source of the Niger is south of Faranah, about 170km by road. The best way to get there is on a truck from the Faranah market. About halfway along the main road between Faranah and Kissidougou, a dirt road branches off south, through the villages of Bambaya and Kobikoro, to reach Forokonia. From here it's only 7km to Les Sources – a three to four hour walk.

GUINEA

Guinea-Bissau

Guinea-Bissau is a gem – with a pleasant capital, sleepy towns, quiet beaches and beautiful offshore islands. Don't fall into the trap of believing it's all paradise though. While travelling here, you should remember that the country is still very poor and that for most people life is a continual struggle to make ends meet.

Facts about the Country

HISTORY

Guinea-Bissau was part of the Mali empire when Portuguese traders (the first Europeans to reach this region) made contact in the 1440s. Control of the interior was not established until 1915 and, unlike other colonies, Portuguese Guinea (as it was then called) was not developed. However, while other African nations were gaining independence in the late 1950s and early 1960s, in Guinea-Bissau Portugal refused to relinquish power. The result was the longest war of liberation in the history of Africa, fought by the African Party for the Independence of Guinea and Cape Verde (PAIGC) from 1961 until the early 1970s.

When independence was unilaterally declared in 1973 nearly all the preparations had been made for national administration. Although the new government was recognised around the world, it wasn't until Portugal's fascist regime was overthrown in 1974 that the Portuguese finally withdrew.

The leader of the PAIGC was Amílcar Cabral, although he was murdered about six months before independence by Portuguese agents, and was succeeded by his half-brother, Luiz Cabral, who became president of the country. Many of the PAIGC's leaders came from the Cape Verde islands and the party was committed not only to the liberation of Guinea-Bissau and Cape Verde but to the unification of the two. This idea was stalled in 1980 when Luiz Cabral was over-

---

REPUBLIC OF GUINEA-BISSAU
Area: 36,125 sq km
Population: 1.1 million
Population Growth Rate: 2.1%
Capital: Bissau
Head of State: President João Bernardo Vieira
Official Language: Portuguese
Currency: West African CFA Franc
Exchange Rate: CFA 575 = US$1
Per Capita GNP: US$220
Inflation: 5%
Time: GMT/UTC

Highlights
- Wandering through the colonial jumble of Bissau
- Boat trips to the Bijagos Archipelago
- Exploring the ruined fort at Cacheu

---

thrown by prime minister, João Bernardo Vieira. Although the countries are allies, the unity idea has been dropped.

Since the coup, Guinea-Bissau has been ruled by Vieira. He has turned out to be remarkably independent and determined, willing to tackle the country's enormous problems with a high degree of intelligence and sensitivity. Gone are the expensive and largely prestigious projects favoured by his predecessor. The emphasis is now on implementing small schemes appropriate to the country's needs.

At the end of 1991, after many years of one-party rule, several opposition parties were registered. In March 1993, the leader of one of these new parties, João da Costa, led an abortive coup attempt against Vieira's government. Presidential elections were held in July 1994 and Vieira won with 52% of the vote.

Although many countries have helped out with loans it seems that Guinea-Bissau is destined to remain one of the world's poorest nations. The country still cannot produce enough food for its people, all manufactured goods have to be imported and electricity will remain a scarce commodity since the country is too flat for production of hydro-electricity (blackouts are commonplace).

GEOGRAPHY & CLIMATE

Much of the country is low-lying with numerous rivers, mangrove swamps and

Memories of the Revolution

If you want to see how colonialism has effectively ruined a country then Guinea-Bissau is the place. The war of liberation was Africa's longest – from 1961 until the African Party for Independence in Guinea and Cape Verde (PAIGC) held elections (in liberated areas only) in 1973. Rampant inflation, a huge national debt and a run-down city (Bissau) were the consequences of the rapid and greedy departure of the Portuguese.

In Bissau, look at the decaying, neglected colonial buildings (some still with fading slogans from the revolutionary war); the old fort and the mausoleum of revolutionary hero Amílcar Cabral; the fist-shaped Pidjiguiti monument and the pier where many dock workers were gunned down in the 1959 strike. Then marvel at the polite and friendly manner in which the inhabitants of the city now greet you – on the basis of their hard-won equality. ■

forest giving way to savannah inland, and to hills on the border with Guinea. The rest of the country consists of offshore islands.

Rainfall is heavy, especially on the coast, and it's generally hot and humid. The coolest months are December and January; the hottest are April and May.

POPULATION & PEOPLE
The population stands at just over one million. There are numerous groups including the Balante, Fulani, Manjak and Mandinka. There are also quite a few mestizos of mixed European and African descent.

About 55% follow tribal religions, 40% are Muslim and the rest are Christian. Nearly all the Portuguese and Lebanese traders left after independence although many have returned in the last few years and have taken up the reins of business.

LANGUAGE
Portuguese is the official language but Kriolu is the common tongue. Many other regional African languages are spoken, mainly Wolof, and quite a few people understand French. See the Language Appendix.

Facts for the Visitor

VISAS
Visas are required by all, except citizens of Cape Verde and Nigeria. Typically, visas are valid for a month and extensions are easy to obtain at the central police station in Bissau. If you stay for more than a month, you may need an exit visa.

Note that the French embassy issues visas to Burkina Faso, Côte d'Ivoire, Togo, Chad, the Central African Republic and possibly Mauritania (you'll need to check). Most of these cost between US$10 and US$20.

Other Visas
The Gambia
    The embassy is open weekday mornings. Visas cost around US$5 and are issued the same day if you arrive early. Two photos are required.

Guinea
    Visas cost about US$40 (payable in hard currency). You need two to four photos and endless patience. A letter of introduction from your embassy may speed things up and it's important to dress neatly. The embassy's hours are from 8.30 am to 3 pm Monday to Thursday and to 1 pm on Friday. The embassy is sometimes open on Saturday morning until noon.
Senegal
    Visas cost from US$10 to US$20, depending on your nationality, and are issued in 48 hours. You need four photos.

EMBASSIES
Guinea-Bissau Embassies
In Africa, Guinea-Bissau has embassies in The Gambia, Guinea and Senegal. There's also a consulate in Ziguinchor (Senegal).

Foreign Embassies in Guinea-Bissau
Countries with a diplomatic mission in Bissau include:

France
    Bairro de Penha, Avenida de 14 Novembro, near the Hotel Hotti Bissau (☎ 25 1031)
The Gambia
    Avenida de 14 Novembro, about 1km from Mercado de Bandim
Guinea
    Corner of Rua 12 and Rua Osvaldo Vieira (☎ 21 2681)
Mauritania
    Avenida de 14 Novembro, opposite the Gambian High Commission
Senegal
    Off Praça dos Heróis Nacionais, facing TAP Air Portugal (☎ 21 2636)
UK & Netherlands (honorary consul)
    Jan van Maanen, Mavegro, Estrada de Santa Luzía
USA
    On the airport road, an extension of Avenida de 14 Novembro (☎ 25 2273/4; fax 25 2282)

MONEY
US$1 =   CFA 575

The unit of currency is now the West African CFA franc. When this book was being researched, Guinea-Bissau's currency was the peso, a notoriously weak currency, and one responsible for a rampant inflation rate in the country. However, in mid-1997, as a means of improving the economic conditions in the country, Guinea-Bissau joined the ever expanding CFA Franc zone. By the end of 1997, the peso had been completely withdrawn.

Banks will change cash and travellers' cheques, with a preference for French francs over US dollars. In Bissau, moneychangers hang out at the Mercado Central and near the post office – treat them with a degree of suspicion. The money-changing bureaus in the area near the central market are a better bet.

Hotels accept payment in West African CFA francs, French francs or US dollars. The Hotti Bissau (formerly the Sheraton) and Hotel du 24 de Setembro accept most credit cards (but not MasterCard).

POST & COMMUNICATIONS

The postal service out of the country and international phone connections are quite good, but the poste restante is unreliable.

You can buy phonecards from the post office and then use the phone booths directly outside on the street. A card with 100 *impresos* (pulses) costs about US$10 and gives you a three minute call to Europe.

The country code for Guinea-Bissau is 245. Area codes include 021 for Bissau and 041 for Bafará.

PUBLIC HOLIDAYS

Public holidays include: 1 January, 20 January (death of Amílcar Cabral), 8 March (International Women's Day), 1 May, 3 August (Pidjiguiti Day), 24 September (Independence), 14 November, 25 December and variable Islamic holidays (see the Public Holidays in the Regional Facts for the Visitor chapter).

ACCOMMODATION

The choice of budget hotels in the capital has shrunk recently as most of the cheapies have shut their doors. For this reason, most travellers head upcountry or to the islands where accommodation is more reasonably priced and usually good value.

FOOD & DRINK

In Bissau, there are few street stalls selling food such as brochettes or roasted corn. Even coffee stalls, common in neighbouring countries, are difficult to track down. However, in the last few years, the city's choice of patisseries, ice cream shops and smart restaurants has grown considerably. Beer, usually the Portuguese Sagres or Superbock, is plentiful and relatively cheap. The adventurous can sample palm wine, caña rum, or *caña de cajeu* (made from cashews).

Getting There & Away

AIR

European airlines serving Bissau include Portugal's TAP (via Lisbon), Aeroflot and the French company EAS. Most visitors arriving by air fly to Dakar (Senegal) and then change to a regional airline.

Within West Africa, Air Senegal and Air Bissau (TAGB) fly to Dakar (US$145 one way); Air Senegal stops in Ziguinchor. TAGB flies to Conakry in Guinea (US$135) and to Banjul in The Gambia (US$110). Departure tax is US$15.

LAND
Guinea

Most travellers heading overland to Guinea take the northern route via Gabú, Koundara and Labé. Vehicles between Gabú and Koundara are irregular although you may find a truck going all the way (for around US$10 in Guinean francs or West African CFA francs). Your best bet is on Saturdays, when trucks and pick-ups go from Gabú to the border town of Sereboïdo, which has a big market on Sundays. On Sunday and Monday you can get transport to Koundara and Labé. From Gabú to Labé may take three days, on a scenic route through the Fouta Djalon foothills (impassable in the wet).

Public transport is best found at the bus/truck park on the eastern side of Avenida 14 de Novembro in Bissau.

Senegal

The main route from Bissau to Ziguinchor is via Bula, Ingore and São Domingos. It's sealed all the way, but there are two ferry crossings which can cause delays and make the journey anything from three to six hours. Bush taxis leave the main garage (bus park) in Bissau for Ziguinchor (US$8), mostly before 9 am (if you leave later it is likely that you will miss a ferry connection and be forced to stop overnight). Passengers have to pay for the ferry crossings (US$0.20).

The coast route between Ziguinchor and Bissau via Canchungo is not viable as there is no longer a ferry between Cacheu and São Domingos (the *Cacheu* is currently beached).

Getting Around

BOAT

From Bissau port ferries, operated by Rodo-fluvial (it provides a timetable of sorts), leave once a week for Bubaque Island (leaves Friday, returns Sunday); once a week for Bolama Island and Catió near the Guinean border (leaves Tuesday, returns Friday); and every weekday morning for Enxudé just across the bay from Bissau.

LOCAL TRANSPORT

Public transport around the country consists of minibuses and bush taxis on the main routes, and pick-ups called *kandongas* on rural routes. Fares are cheap: for example, across the country from Bissau to Gabú is US$3. On any trip, baggage is 10% extra.

Bissau

Bissau is a small city which used to be quiet and empty, but since the mid-1980s it has become increasingly like other African cities or, as some say, more 'Senegalised'. The central part of town has an air of decay, with abandoned buildings overgrown with creepers. However, it's still a very laid-back place

– you won't be hassled by youths in the street and, as long as you steer clear of the port at night, there's very little chance of being robbed.

Information

The Centro do Informacão e Turismo, on Avenida do 3 de Zgosto, Bissau, offers lots of smiles and goodwill, but has little information. Some of the carvings sellers, on Avenida Amílcar Cabral (near Pensão Centrale), seem to know all the possibilities and willingly offer information (ask for Fallou N'Dime, in particular).

The banks, the moneychangers and the post office are all on Avenida Amílcar Cabral, opposite the cathedral.

The French Cultural Centre on the Praça Ché Guevara has magazines, a library and a small snack bar. The American Cultural Center, in the embassy, also has a selection of English-language newspapers.

Things to See

The **Museu Nacional**, at the Complex Escolar on Avenida 14 de Novembro, out towards the Hotel Hotti Bissau, has a small collection of traditional artefacts and is open daily from 9 am to 2 pm. More interesting is the **Centro Artístico Juvenil**, a training centre for young local artists, on Avenida de 14 Novembro (closed Sundays).

The **presidential palace** at the northern end of Avenida Amílcar Cabral, overlooking Praça dos Heróis Nacionais, is worth a glance. No photos are allowed here, and don't walk up the streets on each side.

At the port end of Avenida Amílcar Cabral is the imposing **Pidjiguiti monument** – in the shape of a fist? – dedicated to the 50 or so Bissau dockworkers who were killed during a strike on 3 August 1959. This bloody massacre firmed the resolve of Guinea-Bissauans to win their independence from the Portuguese colonists.

The **port** at the southern end of Avenida Amílcar Cabral is interesting, as are the nearby narrow streets full of old Portuguese-style buildings. The **fort**, Fortaleza d'Amura, is used by the military and is not generally

PLACES TO STAY
1 Hotel do 24 de Setembro
14 Hotel Caracol
42 Hotel Apartmentos Jordani
44 Grande Hotel
47 Pensão Sergio Centeio
(Pensão Lunar)
48 Pensão Centrale
53 Pensão Proquil
54 Hotel Tamar

PLACES TO EAT
2 Restaurant-Bar Djumbai
3 Restaurant Casa Santos
15 Restaurant Le Cedre
18 Restaurant Delas Africana
20 Restaurant Atentadora
27 Lebanese Takeaway
30 La Bodeguita;
Bar Noë

31 Café Universal;
Gelataria Baiana
35 Asa Branca
36 Gelataria Italiana
38 Restaurant Trópicana;
TAGB Air Bissau
40 Supermarket
45 Confeitaria Dias & Dias
62 Brisa do Mar

OTHER
4 Tropicana Nightclub
5 Mosque
6 Coquiero Nightclub
7 Mosque
8 Bus Park (for Senegal)
9 Mauritanian Embassy
10 Museo Nacional
11 Gambian High Commission
12 Cabana Nightclub

13 Caracol Market
16 Mercado de Bandim
17 Bus Park
19 Bus Park
21 Presidential Palace
22 Praça dos Heróis
Nacionais
23 TAP Air Portugal
24 Senegalese Embassy;
Confeitaria Imperio
25 UDIB Cinema
26 Swedish Embassy
28 Capitol Nightclub
29 Guinean Embassy
32 Praça Ché Guevara
33 French Cultural Centre
34 Bar Galleon
37 Dutch Co-operation Service

39 Mercado Centrale
41 Correio (Post Office)
43 Hospital Simão
Mendes
46 Fortaleza d'Amura
49 Cathedral
50 BIGB Bank &
Change Bureau
51 BCGB Bank
52 Pharmacy
55 Aeroflot
56 Petrol Station
57 Club Malila
59 Pidjiguiti Monument
59 Rodofluvial Office
60 Guinémar Shipping Co
61 Tourist Office
63 Pirogues to Enxudé

Bissau

0   150   300 m

GUINEA-BISSAU

open to visitors. The **mausoleum** of Amílcar Cabral is here and with the utmost politeness and persistence you may be allowed to pay your respects to this quintessential African hero. However, keep your camera out of sight anywhere near the fort.

The **Mercado Centrale** (central market), just west of Avenida Amílcar Cabral, is a lively place to wander around in the morning. For more practical items go to the **Mercado de Bandim**, at the start of Avenida de 14 Novembro; it's the apotheosis of a lively African market.

For a glimpse of rural village life, take a short trip to **Enxudé** (pronounced en-SHOU-day), just across the river from Bissau. The ferry runs every weekday, remains an hour on the other side then returns. The one-way cost is US$2. For information on the departure times, enquire at the Rodofluvial office.

Places to Stay

Your cheapest option is to ask around at the garage (bus park) on Avenida de 14 Novembro. Some travellers have found locals to stay with who charge about US$8 for a room and a meal – it will be appreciated if you pay for the ingredients of the meal.

The very tired *Grande Hotel* (☎ 21 3437) on Avenida Pansau Na Isna has rooms with air-con and showers for US$15. The state of the toilets reflects the general malaise in accommodation standards in this part of the world. Its only saving grace is the nice terrace.

The better *Pensão Centrale* (☎ 20 1232) on Avenida Amílcar Cabral has been a favourite for many years with clean rooms for US$15 or so. This price is negotiable if you stay for three nights or more (say US$13.50). Some travellers have reportedly been overcharged, so confirm the rates when you check in. There is a restaurant which serves huge Portuguese-style meals of the day.

The *Pensão Proquil* (☎ 21 2629) on Rua 2 is a Portuguese-style apartment block with air-con rooms with attached bathroom; expect to pay from US$15 for a clean room. Also in this price range is the friendly *Hotel Caracol* (☎ 21 3227), on Avenida Caetano

Semedo (also known as Estrada de Bor), about 1km west of Mercado de Bandim. Singles/doubles are US$15/25 and filling meals in the restaurant cost US$2.50.

Up in price and quality is the recently renovated *Hotel Apartmentos Jordani* (☎ 20 1719), on Avenida Pansau Na Isna opposite the Grande Hotel, where good singles/doubles with air-con and attached bathroom cost US$50/70. Just watch out for the pet monkey – he'll scare the living daylights out of you.

The *Hotel Tamar* (☎ 21 4876), on the corner of Avenida 12 de Setembro and Rua 2 (in a fascinating old quarter of town), has also undergone an improvement in facilities. Tidy rooms with attached bathroom cost from US$40 a double and there is an attached restaurant.

Places to Eat

Street food in Bissau is limited to peanuts, deep-fried dough-balls (doughnuts) and chawarma sandwiches around the Mercado Centrale and the Mercado de Bandim, where there are also a few coffee and bread stalls. At the bus park, out of town on Avenida de 14 Novembro, you'll find some basic eating houses selling coffee, bread and cheap bowls of sauce (occasionally chunks of meat). For imported delights, try the *supermarket* in Rua Justino Lopes, near the central market.

The cheapest place in the centre is the nameless hole-in-the-wall around the back of the Grande Hotel but you may need to order a few hours in advance here. Nearby is *Confeitaria Dias & Dias* where you can buy fresh bread and pastries to take away.

The *Café Universal* on Praça Ché Guevara is an old restaurant with meals for US$2 and beers for US$1. The *Pensão Centrale* (see Places to Stay) offers a three course Portuguese evening meal (with a banana) for US$3. It's one of the best deals in town, although the quality is varied and the meals are sometimes cold. The meals at *Hotel Apartmentos Jordani* (see Places to Stay) are prepared with a greater degree of culinary excellence.

Other options include the *Restaurante-Bar Atentadora*, under the water tower at the junction of Avenida do Brazil and Avenida Francisco Mendes, where meals such as grilled fish cost an expensive US$6.

The upmarket *Gelataria Baiana*, a sidewalk cafe on Praça Ché Guevara, serves ice cream, sandwiches, pastries and coffee (and in this buzzing part of town is a great place to watch the passing parade). Around the corner, and a couple of blocks up Avenida Domingos Ramos, is a hole-in-the-wall *Lebanese takeaway* which serves hamburgers, pizza and chawarma. There are tables set out on the footpath.

For full-scale meals try *Restaurante-Bar Trópicana* in a pleasant garden setting on Rua Osvaldo Vieira, which has main dishes from US$4. If you crave a Guinness flick to the *Restaurante-Bar Djumbai* near the Hotel do 24 de Setembro – you won't be disappointed. The *Restaurant Le Cedre* on Avenida Caetano Semedo, near the Hotel Caracol, has Lebanese meals from US$5. At the *restaurant* in the courtyard of the Hotel Apartmentos Jordani (see Places to Stay), you can get an excellent chicken, rice and salad lunch for US$5.

Right on the port, with its kitchen in an old shipping container and a sheltered garden bar arrayed before it, is a great restaurant, *Brisa do Mar*; good meals of chicken and rice are about US$4.

Entertainment
The best laid-back place in town by far (and with the vote of all who go there) is the recently expanded *Bar Galleon* on Praça Ché Guevara. Expect a sophisticated crowd, good music, prompt service and pleasant banter from its two French owners. Other nightclubs include the *Capitol*, near the corner of Rua 14 and Rua Osvaldo Vieira, currently about the most happening place in town; and the *Coquiero* on 2nd Avenida de Cintura, described by knowledgeable locals as 'not too good'.

Getting There & Away
Bus & Bush Taxi The main *garage* (bus park) is on Avenida de 14 Novembro, about 2km from Mercado de Bandim. In the morning, there's a minibus every hour or so to Bafatá (US$2) and Gabú (US$3), and two or more bush taxis to São Domingos and Ziguinchor (Senegal). There are fewer vehicles in the afternoon.

Boat Ferries to the islands of Bubaque and Bolama, and to Enxudé and Catió, are operated by Rodofluvial. Sailing days and times are posted in its office on Avenida do 3 de Agosto. For details, see the text on Bolama and Bubaque islands in the Bijagos Archipelago section later in this chapter.

Getting Around
The Airport Taxis are plentiful at the airport, but they charge an extortionate US$10 to US$20 for the trip into the city centre (10km). A seat in a share-taxi between the city centre and the airport is about US$1, or alternatively the bus costs US$0.20. To find a share-taxi or bus into the city centre, walk 700m from the airport to the roundabout at the start of Avenida de 14 Novembro, the highway into the city.

Bus The modern Bissau city buses (called Paragem) travel along Avenida de 14 Novembro between the airport and city centre, passing the bus park and Mercado de Bandim. These are the most useful for visitors; all rides cost US$0.20.

Taxi Share-taxis are cheap and easy to use in Bissau. Stand by the side of the road in the direction you want to go and shout your destination as the taxi passes. Fares vary according to the distance but expect to pay about US$0.20 for every 1 or 2km.

Around the Country

BAFATÁ
This is a quiet little town (about 10,000 people) on a hill by a river, with old Portuguese-style houses and shops built on narrow streets. About 12km to the west of Bafatá are

the ruins of **Gêba**, once an important Portuguese trading post.

There are a couple of places to stay. *Apartmentos Gloria*, a few streets behind the main road on the right side as you come in from Bissau, has basic rooms for US$4. Nearby is *Pensão Fa*, which costs about the same.

For food there's the *Piscina Café*, by the empty swimming pool near the market, or *Restaurant-Bar Cassumae Kep* next to the church.

THE BIJAGOS ARCHIPELAGO

The Bijagos Archipelago is the group of islands off the coast of Guinea-Bissau. Several are uninhabited, while others are home to small fishing communities that are rarely, if ever, visited by foreigners. The following islands are the easiest ones to reach.

Bolama Island

Bolama Island is closest to the mainland and to Bissau. The main town, also called Bolama, was the capital during colonial days but it has been slowly crumbling away since 1941 when the capital was transferred to Bissau. About 4km south of the town is a good beach, although the ones at the south-western end of the island, about 25km from Bolama, are reckoned to be better.

There are no hotels but if you're friendly towards the local people someone will probably invite you to stay. If you are given food and lodgings you should pay the going rate.

Getting There & Away The ferry for Bolama leaves Bissau every Friday or Saturday and returns Sunday. For departure times, check at the Rodofluvial office near the port in Bissau. The fare is US$3 each way.

Bubaque Island

Bubaque Island is at the centre of the archipelago and is one of the easiest islands to reach. It's a delightful place on which to pass a few days or weeks and there is a choice of places to stay in the island's town, which has a market, a bakery, small cafes and a post office.

Things to See & Do Taking boat rides to nearby islands or walks through the forest,

palm groves and fields around the town are pleasant ways to pass the time.

Most visitors come for the **beaches** and there's a little one near the hotel that's fairly quiet but a bit dirty. Much better is **Praia Bruce** (Bruce Beach) at the southern end of the island, about 18km from Bubaque town. The Hotel Bijagos runs a shuttle bus to this beach which costs US$2 per person (minimum four people). Some travellers have managed to hire bikes to get there.

Before you go to any beach, check the tides. When the tide is low the sea is a long way out and you'll have to wade through thigh-deep mud before you can swim.

Places to Stay Cheap places to stay in Bubaque town include *Pensão Pauline Cruzponte* (☎ 82 1135), where the rooms are clean but strangely damp. Singles/doubles cost US$10/12 with breakfast, and meals start at US$3 with beers for US$1. To get there follow the main street from the port up the hill for 400m or so. It's on your left behind a large hut. Another similar budget place, the *Campini*, also known as *Chez Nattie la Cubanne*, has been recommended by readers.

A little further along the same dusty or muddy track is the friendly *Pensão Cadjoco* (☎ 82 1185) or *Chez Patricia*, where clean single/doubles with mosquito net and separate bucket showers cost US$9/13. It also serves breakfast (US$2), other meals (US$4) and beers (US$1). This place is set in a lush garden with its own well so lack of water is never a problem. Patricia is Italian and her home-made seafood pizzas are the best! Boat trips to neighbouring islands can be arranged for the day, or longer if you have camping gear. There's also a tide table so you know when it's worth going to the beach.

Moving up the price scale, the *Hotel Bijagos* (☎ 82 1144), about 2km from the town, has single/double rooms in bungalows with fans for US$15/18 (an extra US$5 for air-con). A good breakfast is included. Meals cost US$4 and beers are US$1. The hotel will arrange to pick you up from the airport if you give advance warning.

Places to Eat Apart from the places above, try the *Restaurant Saia*, a French-Senegalese place on the street between the port and the police station; meals are around US$5. *L'Escale*, another French place by the port, has a reputation for good seafood dishes. There's also fresh food and bread at the market.

Getting There & Away Air Bissau (TAGB) flies at least twice a week between Bissau and Bubaque for US$48 one way, US$88 return. The service is fairly reliable. In Bubaque the TAGB representative lives next to Casa Adelio, a pensão near the church, and can sell you a ticket on the spot. If he's not there, check in Denis' Bar opposite.

The ferry leaves Bissau every Friday/Saturday for Bubaque and returns on Sunday. The trip takes four to six hours and the departure time depends upon the tide – check at the Rodofluvial office near the Bissau port. The cost is US$4 (one way) on the lower deck, slightly more on the upper deck. Tickets are sold from a small booth at the port gates. It's worth getting there at least an hour in advance to get a good place. You can buy beer and canned drinks on the boat.

Galinhas Island

Galinhas is a small island between the islands of Rubane and Bolama, about 60km south of Bissau. The *Aldeia Touristica de Ambancana* has ordinary rooms at US$5 per person, or rooms with attached bathroom for US$7 per person. Until this hotel was built in 1993 the island was very rarely visited by tourists. It's a friendly and interesting place and we've heard from people who intended to visit for a only few days but stayed for 10. In Bissau, you can get details from the Electrodata photocopy shop near the Shell station, 100m from the port.

CACHEU

Cacheu (pronounced CASH-ay-you) is a small coastal town about 100km north-west of Bissau. Its sleepy ambience makes it worth a visit. Don't miss the **fort** where Sir Francis Drake and Sir John Hawkins did battle with the Portuguese in 1567. The

cannons are still in place, and there are also some large bronze figures.

The modern, and rarely used, *Hotel Baluarte* (☎ 92 1102) has decent doubles with attached bathroom for US$10. There's a small eating house next to the port office. The good-value meals have to be ordered in advance.

To get to Cacheu from Bissau take a minibus to Canchungo (US$3) and then a pick-up to Cacheu (US$0.50). Pick-ups leave very early from Cacheu for Canchungo (to connect with the first minibus to Bissau).

GABÚ

In the east, 200km from Bissau, Gabú is a lively town and the country's major transport hub outside Bissau, with connections to Guinea and The Gambia.

The *Pensão Miriama Sadje Djalo's*, near the market, has basic rooms for US$6 and with a few hours notice meals can be served. Nearby and better is the French-run *Hotel Suitte* (☎ 51 1255), a hunting lodge of sorts. Small clean rooms cost US$15. A reader recommends the *Oasis*, a new place with rooms from US$7.

The pleasant *Hotel Madina Boé* (☎ 51 1236), on the edge of town, has double tin-roofed bungalows from US$10; less noisy in the rain are the thatch-roofed bungalows at US$15. Meals are about US$4 and beers less than US$1. For other meals try the *chophouses* or the *Bar-Restaurant-Disco Esplanada* near the market.

Minibuses to/from Bissau cost US$3. If you're heading for Guinea, look around the market for trucks on their way to Koundara, Koumbia and Boké.

SÃO DOMINGOS

Most travellers pass through the border town of São Domingos without stopping.

If you are caught here for the night, the *Hotel Yal*, diagonally across from the police post, has basic rooms for US$5. It also serves cheap meals, or you can buy bread and fruit from the market. Travellers have told us about the *Campamento Zulu* which has bungalows for about US$15; meals such as chicken are also provided with notice.

Kenya

Not only has Kenya been recognised as the 'cradle of humanity' (as a result of the Leakeys' famous Rift Valley digs), but it has one of the most diverse and colourful collections of tribal people anywhere on the continent. It also has some of the largest, best stocked and most accessible game parks in Africa, coral reefs and palm-fringed white-sand beaches along the Indian Ocean littoral, Mt Kenya, ancient Swahili cities which rival Zanzibar and endless possibilities for adventure in the arid north.

The Swahili word 'safari' is almost synonymous with Kenya, which is why the country attracts so many foreign visitors each year. Despite the fact that there is stiff competition for the tourist dollar from neighbouring Tanzania and, increasingly, Uganda, Kenya is unlikely to lose its rating as East Africa's top destination in the near future.

Facts about the Country

HISTORY

Kenya has been a major migratory pathway for millennia. The first wave of immigrants was the tall, nomadic Cushitic-speaking people from Ethiopia, who began to move south around 2000 BC. They were to reach as far as central Tanzania. A second group of pastoralists, the Eastern Cushitics, followed them around 1000 BC and occupied much of central Kenya.

The rest of the ancestors of the country's medley of tribes arrived from all over Africa between 500 BC and 500 AD. The Bantu-speaking people (such as the Gusii, Kikuyu, Akamba and Meru) arrived from West Africa, while the Nilotic speakers (such as the Maasai, Luo, Samburu and Turkana) came from the Nile Valley in southern Sudan.

While migrations were going on in the interior, Muslims from the Arabian Peninsula and Shirazis from Persia (now Iran)

REPUBLIC OF KENYA
Area: 582,645 sq km
Population: 28.2 million
Population Growth Rate: 2.9%
Capital: Nairobi
Head of State: President Daniel arap Moi
Official Languages: Swahili, English
Currency: Kenyan shilling
Exchange Rate: KSh 56 = US$1
Per Capita GNP: US$230
Inflation: 5%
Time: GMT/UTC + 3

Highlights
- Visiting Lake Turkana, Kenya's largest lake and a famous archaeological site
- Trekking Mt Kenya, Africa's second highest mountain
- The spectacular annual wildebeest migration at Masai Mara National Reserve, Kenya's most popular safari park
- Amboseli National Park, home to the endangered black rhino; stunning Mt Kilimanjaro backdrop

began to visit the East African coast from the 8th century onwards. As a result, a string of relatively affluent and Islamic-influenced coastal towns sprang up along the East African coast from Somalia to Mozambique.

In the 16th century, most of the Swahili trading towns, including Mombasa, were either sacked or occupied by the Portuguese, and this marked the end of the Arab monopoly of Indian Ocean trade. Two centuries of

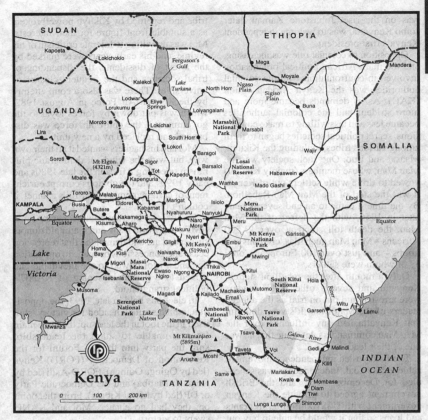

Kenya

harsh colonial rule followed, but by 1720 control of the coast reverted to the Arabs.

By the mid-19th century, the British were interested in the suppression of the slave trade and set up a consulate in Zanzibar. Later an agreement was reached between the British and the Germans as to their spheres of interest in East Africa.

By the late 19th century, the interior of the country had been opened up by the British, and the Mombasa-Uganda railway was built.

White settlement in the early 20th century was initially disastrous, but the British settlers finally succeeded in putting the colony on a more realistic economic footing by establishing mixed agricultural farms. Other European settlers established coffee plantations about the same time.

During this period, more and more Kikuyu were migrating to Nairobi or being drawn into the colonial economy in one way or another. They weren't at all happy about the alienation of their land, and this led to demands for the return of land.

An early leader of the Kikuyu political association, Harry Thuku, was jailed by the British in 1922. While Thuku's star was on the wane, that of another member of the tribe was on the rise. Johnstone Kamau, later Jomo Kenyatta, was to become independent Kenya's first president.

Opposition to colonial rule was increasing, and the main African political organisation involved in confrontation with the colonial authorities was the Kenya African Union (KAU). As its demands became more and more strident and the colonial authorities became less and less willing to make concessions, secret political societies began to form among various tribes, including the Kikuyu, Maasai and Luo. One such society was the Mau Mau, whose members (mainly Kikuyu) vowed to drive white settlers out of Kenya. It was the start of the Mau Mau Rebellion. By the time it came to an end several years later in 1956, with the defeat of the Mau Mau, the death toll stood at over 13,500 Africans – Mau Mau guerrillas, civilians and troops – and just over 100 Europeans, only 37 of whom were settlers.

Only a month after the rebellion started, Kenyatta and several other KAU leaders were arrested and put on trial as the alleged leaders of the Mau Mau. It's very doubtful that Kenyatta had any influence over the Mau Mau commanders, let alone that he was one of their leaders.

The Kikuyu-led independence movement achieved its goal. Independence was scheduled for December 1963, and the British government agreed to provide the Kenyan government with US$100 million in grants and loans so that it would be able to buy out European farmers in the highlands and restore tribal lands.

Kenyatta was released from house arrest in mid-1961 and assumed the presidency of the Kenya African National Union (KANU). Independence came on 12 December 1963, with Kenyatta as the first president and KANU as the ruling party. Under Kenyatta's presidency, Kenya developed into one of Africa's most stable and prosperous nations.

In 1964 Kenya effectively became a one party state following the opposition KADU party's voluntary dissolution.

Kenyatta died in 1978 and was succeeded by Daniel Arap Moi, a member of the Tugen tribe and regarded by Kikuyu powerbrokers as a suitable front figure for their interests. Moi was unwilling to tolerate criticism of his regime, and his early years were marked by the arrest of dissidents, the disbanding of tribal societies and the frequent closure of universities. There was also a coup attempt by the Kenyan Air Force in August 1982, which was put down by forces loyal to the government – the entire air force was disbanded and replaced by a new unit.

Moi and his backers wanted it all their own way, but with the winds of democratic pluralism sweeping Africa in the late 1980s and early 1990s and the obvious corrupt enrichment of certain members of Moi's cabinet, it couldn't last.

In 1990 the International Monetary Fund (IMF), the World Bank and major aid donors suspended aid and demanded that repression cease and concessions be made to opposition demands. Moi bowed to the inevitable and agreed to a partial loosening of KANU's political stranglehold.

In elections held in late 1993, the opposition, which seemed headed for victory, shot itself in the foot in the lead-up: the three main figures, unable to share the leadership, split the party into three – Forum for the Restoration of Democracy (FORD)-Kenya (led by Oginga Odinga), FORD-Asili (led by Kenneth Matiba) and the Democratic Party or DP (led by Mwai Kibaki). From that point on, they had no chance. Moi and KANU swept to victory.

In 1995 a new party was launched with the intention of drawing all of the opposition under one umbrella and agreeing on a single presidential candidate to contest the next election. This was Safina, founded by Richard Leakey (whom Moi had sacked as director of the Kenya Wildlife Service) and other prominent opposition MPs. Despite being refused official registration, Safina has made some headway in bringing the opposition together.

A great deal depends on the outcome of the latest elections, which were due to be held in late 1997. The months leading up to the elections saw serious outbreaks of violence in various places, particularly Mombasa. As was the case in 1992, it seems that Moi was doing everything to ensure his survival, despite the cost to Kenya as the economy took a hammering from jittery aid doners and the IMF suspending payments. As long as Moi fails to undertake serious reform, true multiparty democracy in Kenya will remain elusive and the likelihood of serious civil unrest remains high.

It's not just political survival the government has to worry about. Kenya still has one of the highest population growth rates of any country in the world (around 3%). The strain on health and educational facilities is showing, and the situation seems unlikely to improve. Add to this hundreds of thousands of people of working age who can't find work, and you have a recipe for increased social turmoil and political instability. Not a promising prospect.

GEOGRAPHY

Kenya straddles the equator and covers an area of 582,645 sq km, which includes around 13,600 sq km of inland lakes.

The country can be roughly divided into four main zones: the coastal belt, which features hot, humid weather all year; the Rift Valley and central highlands, the most scenic area, with its lakes and mountains and agreeable climate; western Kenya, with the northern tea plantations fading away to semi-desert in the south and the popular game reserve of Masai Mara on the Tanzanian border; and the north and east of the country, which consists of vast semiarid bushland where rainfall is sparse and cattle-grazing is the main activity.

CLIMATE

Kenya's geographical diversity means its climate is varied. However, the rainy seasons are March to May (the 'long rains') and October to November (the 'short rains'). During these times downpours occur mostly in the late afternoons; the days start out warm and sunny. Travelling in Kenya at this time is not generally a problem as the roads are good and the bursts of rain are short.

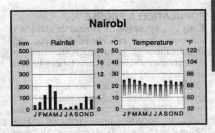

ECOLOGY & ENVIRONMENT
Pressure for Land

The pressure for land in Kenya is enormous due to the high population growth. This particularly applies to people who live in the immediate vicinity of national parks and reserves, where they face a dual problem: not only is the land reserved for animals, but these same animals wander outside the parks, and they can often do tremendous damage in the process.

Finding a solution to the conflict between people and animals will not be easy. Compensating local people out of the tourist receipts from national parks and reserves is one approach which has gained favour recently.

Environmental Problems

Again, the tourist industry is the cause of some of Kenya's major environmental problems. Parks such as Amboseli and Masai Mara are criss-crossed with tracks and crawling with tourist minibuses. The problem is particularly bad in the Mara where minibuses seem to go pretty much where they please, as regulations are not policed by the local Narok council, which administers the reserve.

Another environmental problem is poaching. A few years ago, the Kenya Wildlife Service (which controls the national parks but not the reserves) managed to get this under control. Unfortunately, Richard Leakey, the man in charge of KWS, fell foul of the government. He was sacked, his position filled by another white Kenyan with less enthusiastic (some would say less 'aggressive') designs and the anti-poaching force was relieved of its heavy weaponry.

POPULATION & PEOPLE

Kenya's population of around 28 million is made up almost entirely of Africans, with small (although influential) minorities of Asians (about 80,000), Arabs (about 40,000) and Europeans (about 40,000).

There are more than 70 tribal groups among the Africans. Distinctions between many of them are blurred – western cultural values are becoming more ingrained and traditional values are disintegrating. Yet, even though the average African may have outwardly drifted away from tribal traditions, tribe is still the most important part of a person's identity.

It's probably true to say that most Kenyans outside the coastal and eastern provinces are Christians of one sort or another, while most of those on the coast and in the eastern part of the country are Muslim. The Asian population is Muslim, Hindu and Sikh. Christian missionary activity is intense.

LANGUAGE

English and Swahili are the official languages and are taught in schools throughout Kenya, but there are many other major tribal languages, including Kikuyu, Luhia, Luo and Kikamba, as well as a plethora of minor tribal languages.

It's extremely useful to have a working knowledge of Swahili, especially outside urban areas and in remote parts of the country, since this will open doors and enable you to communicate with people who don't speak English.

See the Language Appendix for some useful Swahili words and phrases. For more detailed help with the language, see Lonely Planet's *Swahili phrasebook*.

Facts for the Visitor

VISAS

Visas are required by all visitors except nationals of Commonwealth countries (but not Australians, New Zealanders, Sri Lankans and United Kingdom passport holders), Denmark, Ethiopia, Germany, Ireland, Italy, Norway, Spain, Sweden, Turkey and Uruguay. Those who don't need visas are issued a Visitor's Pass on entry which is valid for a stay of up to six months.

The cost of a three month visa is roughly the local equivalent of US$30, though this does vary. Two photos (sometimes three) are required, but you normally do not have to show an onward ticket or a letter from a travel agent confirming that you have booked one. Visas are valid for a period of three months from the date of issue. Kenyan visa applications in Tanzania and Uganda are simple and straightforward, and payment is accepted in local currency.

Visas are also available on arrival at Jomo Kenyatta international airport in Nairobi for US$20. Transit visas issued at the airport are valid for three days only and are definitely not extendable.

So long as your visa remains valid you can visit either Tanzania or Uganda and return without having to apply for another visa. This does not apply if you are visiting any other countries.

Visa Extensions

Visas can be renewed in Nairobi at the immigration office (☎ (02) 332110), Nyayo House (ground floor), on the corner of Kenyatta Ave and Uhuru Highway; the office in Mombasa (☎ (011) 311745); or at immigration on the 1st floor of Reinsurance Plaza, on the corner of Jomo Kenyatta Highway and Oginga Odinga Rd, Kisumu, during normal office hours.

A three month extension costs US$30. Remember that you don't need a visa for re-entry into Kenya if you're only going to Tanzania or Uganda *as long as your visa remains valid*.

Other Visas

Since Nairobi is a common gateway to East Africa and the city centre is easy to get around in, many travellers spend some time here picking up visas for other countries they intend to visit.

Congo (Zaïre)
Visa fees are the same for all nationalities. Single-entry/multiple-entry visas cost US$45/70 for a month; US$80/100 for two months and US$115/135 for three months. Two photos are required and visas are delivered the same day if you apply before 11 am.

Ethiopia
One-month visas cost US$63, require one photo and take 48 hours to issue. Applications must be submitted before noon.

Rwanda
Double-entry, seven-day transit visas cost US$27; one-month visas cost US$36, require two photos and are delivered the same day if you apply before noon. If you are travelling overland, it's much cheaper (US$20) to get a visa on arrival at the border.

Somalia
At the time of writing, the embassy was not functioning and anyone could get into Somalia without a visa. See the Somalia chapter for the advisability of travelling to the country.

Sudan
Visas are difficult to get because of the civil war and all applications have to be referred to Khartoum. An onward ticket is necessary, so get one before you apply.

Tanzania
The cost of a visa depends on your nationality and ranges from US$55 for British nationals, US$45 for Americans, US$26 for Japanese, US$16 for Germans and US$10 for others. One photo is required and visas take half an hour to issue. Visas are also available on arrival at Namanga, Kilimanjaro airport (Arusha), Dar es Salaam airport and Zanzibar

Uganda
Most nationalities don't require visas. For those that do they cost up to US$25, require two photos and are delivered the same day if you apply before noon.

EMBASSIES
Kenyan Embassies
In Africa, there are Kenyan embassies or high commissions in Burundi, Congo (Zaïre), Egypt, Ethiopia, Nigeria, Rwanda, Somalia, Sudan, Tanzania, Uganda, Zambia and Zimbabwe.

Outside Africa, there are Kenyan embassies and high commissions in virtually all western and Commonwealth countries. Where there is no Kenyan embassy or high commission, visas can be obtained from the British equivalent.

Foreign Embassies in Kenya
Countries which maintain diplomatic missions in Kenya (Nairobi unless otherwise stated) include:

Australia
Riverside Drive (☎ 445034; fax 444617)

Belgium
Limuru Rd, Muthaiga (☎ 741564; fax 741568)
Mitchell Cotts building, Mombasa (☎ 220231; fax 312617)

Burundi
Development House, Moi Ave (☎ 218458; fax 219005)

Canada
Comcraft House, Haile Selassie Ave (☎ 214804; fax 226987)

Congo (Zaïre)
Electricity House, Harambee Ave (☎ 229771)

Djibouti
Comcraft House, Haile Selassie Ave (☎ 339633; fax 339168)

Egypt
Harambee Plaza, Haile Selassie Ave (☎ 225991; fax 21560)

Eritrea
Rehema House, Westlands (☎ 443163; fax 443165)

Ethiopia
State House Ave (☎ 723027; fax 723401)

France
Barclays Plaza, Loita St (☎ 339783; fax 220435)

Germany
Williamson House, 4th Ngong Ave (☎ 712527; fax 714886)
Palli House, Nyerere Ave, Mombasa (☎ 314732; fax 314504)

Israel
Bishops Rd (☎ 722182; fax 715966)

Italy
International House, Mama Ngina St (☎ 337356; fax 337056)
Jubilee bldg, Moi Ave, Mombasa (☎ 314705; fax 316654)

Japan
ICEA bldg, Kenyatta Ave (☎ 332955; fax 216530)

Madagascar
Hilton Hotel, Mama Ngina St (☎ 226494; fax 218393)

Malawi
Waiyaki Way, Westlands (☎ 440569; fax 440568)

Mauritius
Union Towers, Moi Ave; this is also the Air Mauritius office (☎ 330215)

Mozambique
159 Kyuna Rd, Kyuna (☎ 581857; fax 582478)

Netherlands
    Uchumi House, Nkrumah Ave (☎ 227111; fax 339155)
    ABN Bank building, Nkrumah Rd, Mombasa (☎ 311043)
New Zealand
    Minet-ICDC House, off Nyerere Rd (☎ 722467; fax 722549)
Rwanda
    International House, Mama Ngina St (☎ 334341; fax 336365)
Seychelles
    Agip House, Waiyaki Way, Westlands (☎ 445599; fax 441150)
Somalia
    There is currently no functioning Somali embassy.
South Africa
    Lonrho House, Standard St (☎ 228469; fax 223687)
Sudan
    Minet-ICDC House, Mamlaka Rd (☎ 720853)
Tanzania
    Continental House, corner of Uhuru Highway and Harambee Ave (☎ 331056; fax 218269)
    Palli House, Nyerere Ave, Mombasa (☎ 229595; fax 227077)
Uganda
    Uganda House, Baring Arcade, Kenyatta Ave (☎ 330801; fax 330970)
UK
    Visa & Immigration Section, Bruce House, Standard St (☎ 335944; fax 333196)
    The actual embassy is on Upper Hill Rd, west of the city centre.
USA
    Moi Ave (☎ 334141; fax 340838)
Zambia
    Nyerere Rd (☎ 724796; fax 718494)
Zimbabwe
    Minet-ICDC bldg, Mamlaka Rd (☎ 721045; fax 726503)

MONEY
US$1 = KSh 56

The unit of currency is the Kenyan shilling (KSh), which equals 100 cents. Import/export of local currency is allowed up to the amount of KSh 100.

The currency is fairly stable and there is no black market to speak of. If you are offered a high rate on the street you are being set up for a scam.

You can get US dollars cash if you make a withdrawal against your home account using a Visa card at Barclays Bank.

Travellers' cheques attract a 1% commission at some banks but none at all at others. Foreign exchange (forex) bureaus are common, open long hours and don't charge commission. Banking hours are Monday to Friday from 8 or 9 am to 2 pm and on the first and last Saturday of the month from 9 to 11 am. The branch of Barclays Bank at Nairobi airport is open 24 hours.

Kenya is a good place to have funds transferred to. It generally takes only a few days. You can collect your money entirely in US dollars travellers' cheques, but the money is transferred first into Kenyan shillings then back into dollars.

POST & COMMUNICATIONS
The Kenyan postal system is generally very reliable. An alternative mail drop is American Express Clients Mail. Postal addresses are: Express Kenya Ltd, PO Box 40433, Nairobi; and Express Mombasa, PO Box 90631, Mombasa.

International phone calls are easy to make from post offices. To Europe or the USA it's US$3 per minute, to Australia and New Zealand it's US$4 per minute. Calls are marginally cheaper from a private phone.

The country code for Kenya is 254. The area code for Nairobi is 02 and for Mombasa 011.

PHOTOGRAPHY
Film is widely available in Nairobi and the price is fairly competitive compared to what you'd pay at home in the west. You'll easily find 64, 100, 200 and 400 ASA slide film in Nairobi and Mombasa, but 800 ASA is hard to find and 1600 ASA almost impossible to get.

DANGERS & ANNOYANCES
Travelling in Kenya is basically trouble-free but you definitely need to keep your wits about you, especially in Nairobi. The city has gained a reputation as one of the worst in Africa for petty crime, and it gets worse by the day. Nairobi attracts a lot of tourists – of both the budget and the well-heeled variety

Police: Friend or Foe?

For visitors from western countries, it comes as something of a surprise to find the local police force are not seen by the local people as protectors and upholders of law and order. Any encounter between police and civilians is likely to end up with money changing hands, regardless of the situation. Basically they are a major cause of hassle to be avoided at all cost; you keep your head down and hope they don't notice you.

A recent example of police excess occurred on the busy Thika road just outside Nairobi late in 1996. Traffic police caused severe chaos when, for two hours, they stopped motorists and demanded a 'Christmas present' of KSh 500 (US$10)! ■

– and this, in turn, attracts thieves. If you flaunt your wealth, act visibly disorientated or simply don't pay attention to what is happening around you, a thief will notice and you'll be followed.

It's particularly bad on city minibuses (*matatus*). Here thieves use the 'instant crowd' technique. Trickster scams include the penniless refugee who, when you try to help, lands you in trouble with bogus plain-clothes police, complete with fake ID cards. If you find yourself in this situation, insist on going to the police station – but along the main roads. Refuse to go down back alleys. Better still, don't patronise the 'refugee' in the first place.

Beware also of friendly strangers offering you food and drinks – these may be laced with drugs to knock you out so that you can be easily robbed.

Apart from scams, outright mugging can also happen, but it's mainly confined to Nairobi and tourist spots on the coast. Don't walk down dark alleys or across parks at night, and don't get visibly drunk in a nightclub or bar and then walk back to your hotel. Use taxis at night. Even when walking around in daylight you need to be aware of your surroundings.

Lastly, always have enough small change handy for everyday transactions and keep the rest concealed.

PUBLIC HOLIDAYS

Public holidays observed in Kenya are: 1 January, 1 May, 1 June, 10 October (Moi Day), 20 October (Kenyatta Day), 12 December (Independence), 25 and 26 December, Good Friday, Easter Monday and variable Islamic holidays. For more information on Islamic holidays, see Public Holidays in the Regional Facts for the Visitor chapter.

Getting There & Away

AIR

As the main gateway into East Africa, Nairobi is serviced by airlines from all over the world but particularly from Europe, Asia and the rest of Africa.

To West Africa, Ethiopian Airways is best – it has a large fleet and is one of the few African airlines servicing virtually all the capital cities on the east-west axis.

From the north, the main options into Nairobi are from Athens, Cairo and Khartoum, but it's expensive.

Most of the cheapest tickets to Europe sold by agents in Nairobi are for Aeroflot, Air India, Pakistan International Airlines and Sudan Airways flights.

The cheapest tickets available for flights to Asia are with Ethiopian Airways and Air India (to Bombay direct).

The airport departure tax for international flights out of Nairobi or Mombasa is US$20 or the equivalent in another hard currency or Kenyan shillings.

Tanzania

The cheapest options between Kenya and Tanzania are the flights between Nairobi and

Dar es Salaam (US$136) and Mombasa and Zanzibar (US$55), though you must add the US$20 departure tax to these prices. The Mombasa-Zanzibar flight with Kenya Airways is very popular – you need to book at least two weeks ahead.

LAND
Ethiopia
The border crossing at Moyale is frequently used by travellers and overland trucks, and presents few problems.

The only transport between Marsabit and Moyale are trucks. The trip takes two to four days and costs US$9 from Marsabit and US$11 to US$18 from Isiolo.

There are buses going north from the Ethiopian side of Moyale but they start early at around the break of dawn. A few kilometres out of town, you'll encounter the first of many police check points. At the border, ensure your passport is stamped both by immigration (at the checkpost) and customs (100m further on), otherwise you will be sent back to the border.

Somalia
There's no way you can get overland from Kenya to Somalia at present (unless you're part of a refugee-aid convoy). Even if you attempted it, the Kenyan police or the army would turn you back. Moreover, the entire border area is infested with well-armed Somali *shifta* (bandits), making any attempt to cross it a dangerous and foolhardy venture.

Sudan
As with Somalia, there's no way you can get overland between Kenya and Sudan at present. The furthest north you're going to get is Lokichokio, and you'll be lucky to get that far unless you're with a refugee-aid convoy.

Tanzania
Bus There are several land connections by bus between Kenya and Tanzania.

Mombasa to Dar es Salaam Hood Bus/Cat Bus has three weekly departures from Mombasa via Tanga (12½ hours, US$7). In Mombasa, the office is on Kenyatta Ave.

You can also do the trip in stages, but you may have to walk the 6km between the border and Horohoro.

Nairobi to Arusha & Moshi Between Nairobi and Arusha there's a choice of normal buses and minibus shuttles.

The minibus shuttles take about four hours and cost US$18. Riverside Shuttle departs Nairobi daily at 8.30 am from opposite the Norfolk Hotel on Harry Thuku Rd. Davanu Shuttle (☎ (02) 222002), which has its office at Windsor House, 4th floor, University Way, Nairobi, departs Nairobi for Arusha daily at 8.30 am and 2 pm.

Much cheaper is Arusha Express, which operates full-sized buses and has its office among the cluster of bus companies on Accra Rd in Nairobi. It operates a daily service leaving Nairobi at 8.30 am (US$7, four hours).

It's also easy, but less convenient, to do this journey in stages, and since the Kenyan and Tanzanian border posts are next to each other at Namanga, there's no long walk involved.

Nairobi to Dar es Salaam Direct buses from Nairobi to Dar operate roughly every second day. The buses park outside the Arusha Express office on Accra Rd, and have a sign on the bus door giving the departure time (some travel by day, others at night); tickets can be booked with the bus crew who hang out on the bus. The journey takes 10 to 12 hours and costs US$18.

Voi to Moshi The crossing between Voi and Moshi via Taveta is also reliable as far as transport goes (buses, matatus and share-taxis), as long as you go on a Wednesday or Saturday, which are the market days in Taveta.

Kisii to Musoma/Mwanza There are no direct buses between Kenya and Tanzania through the Isebania border post, and doing it in stages is a pain. There's very little traffic on the road between the border at Isebania and Musoma, so give yourself plenty of time.

Train Through service to Tanzania has recently recommenced, with a weekly connection between Voi and Moshi. From Voi the departure is on Saturday at 5 am, arriving at Moshi at 11.30 am. The fare from Voi to Moshi is US$9/5 in 1st/2nd class.

Uganda

The main border post which most overland travellers use is Malaba, with Busia being an alternative if you are coming from Kisumu.

Bus Akamba operates three direct buses between Kampala and Nairobi daily; the regular services cost US$16, depart at 7 am and 7 pm, and the journey takes around 12 to 14 hours. The Royal service is significantly more expensive (US$42), but very comfortable and includes lunch. Its office in Nairobi is on Lagos Rd.

Mawingo also operates daily buses at 3 pm. These are marginally cheaper than Akamba.

If you are doing the journey in stages, there are frequent matatus until the late afternoon between Malaba and Tororo (Uganda), and from there to Kampala (US$5).

The Ugandan and Kenyan border posts are about 1km from each other at Malaba, and you can walk or take a *boda-boda* (bicycle taxi).

The other entry point into Uganda from Kenya is via Busia further south. There are frequent matatus between Kisumu and Busia and between Busia and Jinja. Akamba has direct buses on this route connecting Kisumu and Kampala. The buses leave Kisumu daily at noon and cost US$11.

Train The weekly train from Nairobi to Kampala is an excellent way to travel between the two capitals, and the border crossing is a breeze as the immigration officials come through the train and you don't even have to leave your compartment.

Departure from Nairobi is at noon on Tuesday, arriving in Kampala on Wednesday at 9.30 am. The fare is US$78/63 (but much

cheaper in the opposite direction), and the train is often subject to delays of anything up to six hours.

SEA & LAKE
Tanzania

Sea It's possible to go by dhow between Mombasa, Pemba and Zanzibar, but sailings are very infrequent these days. More reliable is the ferry MS *Sepideh*, operated by Zanzibar Sea Ferries Ltd (☎ (011) 311486), which connects Mombasa with Tanga, Pemba, Zanzibar and Dar es Salaam. The schedule varies according to the season but it's usually twice a week in either direction. From Mombasa the fares are US$65 to Dar, US$50 to Zanzibar, and US$40 to Tanga or Pemba.

Lake Victoria After a ferry disaster in 1996 which cost 600 lives, services were suspended, although it's likely that the ferries between Kisumu and Mwanza will once again be running. Make enquiries at the port office. Even when the two ports were connected, cancellations were frequent.

Originally the boat left Mwanza at 6 pm on Thursday and arrived in Kisumu at 10 am the following day. The fare from Kisumu was US$21/17/11 in 1st/2nd/3rd class.

Getting Around

AIR

Kenya Airways, the national carrier, connects the main cities of Nairobi, Mombasa, Kisumu and Malindi. One of the most popular flights is the Nairobi-Malindi-Mombasa route, which operates daily in either direction (US$65 one way). Book well ahead.

A number of private airlines operate light aircraft which connects the main cities with smaller towns and certain national parks. The airlines are Prestige Air Services (☎ (02) 501211), Eagle Aviation (☎ (02) 60615) and Skyways (☎ (011) 221964); they all operate out of Nairobi's Wilson airport and/or Mombasa's Moi airport.

KENYA

BUS

Buses are generally cheaper than trains and journey times are quicker. Unlike the trains, which usually travel at night, many buses travel during the day, so you may prefer to take a bus if you want to see the countryside. Akamba is one of the best companies and has the most comprehensive network. KBS Stagecoach is also good.

MATATU (MINIBUS)

Matatus are notorious for their involvement in horror road-smashes. Still, many travellers use them, and in some cases there is no alternative. If there is (such as a bus or train), take that instead. The Mombasa-Nairobi road is particularly notorious for smashes.

As in most East African countries, you can always find a matatu which is going to the next town or further afield, so long as it's not too late in the day. Simply ask around the drivers at the matatu park. Matatus leave when full and the fares are fixed.

TRAIN

Kenyan trains are a very popular mode of travel – they generally run on time and are considerably safer than travelling by bus or matatu. First class consists of two-berth compartments with washbasin, drinking water, wardrobe and drinks service. Second class consists of four-berth compartments with washbasin; 3rd class is seats only. Sexes are separated in 1st and 2nd class unless you book the whole compartment. Third class can become a little wearing on the nerves during long journeys, especially overnight journeys (which most are).

There is a dining car on most trains, offering expensive meals of only average quality, and the service is not great either. All meals and bedding are included in the 1st and 2nd-class fares.

Nairobi to Kisumu

The train departs daily from Nairobi at 6 pm, arriving in Kisumu at 7.10 am the next day. In the opposite direction it departs daily at 6.30 pm, arriving in Nairobi at 7.35 am the next day. The fares are US$35/24 in 1st/2nd class.

Nairobi to Malaba

There are trains to the Ugandan border at Malaba on Friday and Saturday at 3 pm from Nairobi, arriving at 8.45 am the next day. In the opposite direction they depart Malaba on Saturday and Sunday at 4 pm and arrive at 9 am the next day. The fares are US$47/32 for 1st/2nd class.

Nairobi to Mombasa

There's one train daily in either direction at 7 pm, arriving at 8.30 am the next day. The fares are US$49/35 for 1st/2nd class, including meals and bedding whether you want them or not. Book in advance.

CAR

Taking Your Own Vehicle

If you are bringing your own vehicle to Kenya, you should get a free three month permit at the border on entry, so long as you have a valid *carnet de passage* for it (see Taking Your Own Vehicle in the main Getting There & Away chapter). If you don't have a carnet you should be able to get a free one week permit at the border, and after a week you must get an 'authorisation permit for a foreign private vehicle' from Nyayo House in Nairobi. This costs a few dollars and soaks up time.

Large foreign-registered vehicles are not permitted into Kenyan game parks and reserves.

Rental

Renting a vehicle to tour Kenya (or at least the national parks) is a relatively expensive way of seeing the country, but it does give you freedom of movement and is sometimes the only way of getting to the more remote parts of the country.

The major consideration when hiring a vehicle is whether to take a 2WD or 4WD. Outside the rainy season, a 2WD vehicle may be perfectly adequate in some parts of the country, including Amboseli, Masai Mara and Tsavo national parks. Most companies have a policy of insisting that you take a 4WD vehicle if you're going upcountry and to off-the-beaten-track parks.

To give you some idea of average costs, the base rates for a 2WD saloon car are between US$17 and US$27 per day plus US$0.15 to US$0.30 per kilometre (usually with a daily minimum of either 50 or 100km), plus Collision Damage Insurance (CDW) of between US$11 and US$16 per day and Theft Protection Insurance (TPW) of around US$11 per day. Daily unlimited kilometres rates vary between US$70 (one day) and US$57 (eight to 30 days) plus the two insurance rates quoted above.

Unless you're paying by credit card, you'll also have to leave a returnable deposit – at least enough to cover the total rental.

Pay attention to the amount of the excess you may be liable for when taking out CDW and TPW insurance, as it can be as high as US$700!

An International Driving Permit or your own national driving licence is required. Some companies stipulate a minimum age of 23 for drivers, but with others it is 25.

BOAT
Lake Victoria Ferry
On Lake Victoria, there are very limited services connecting Kisumu with other Kenyan ports on the lake.

Dhow
Sailing on a dhow along the East African coast is one of Kenya's most worthwhile and memorable experiences. There's nothing quite like drifting along the ocean in the middle of the night with the moon up high and the only sounds being the lapping of the waves against the side of the boat and subdued conversation. It's enjoyable at any time of day, however, even when the breeze drops and the boat virtually comes to a standstill.

There are no creature comforts aboard these dhows, so when night comes you simply bed down wherever there is space. Take drinking water and food with you, although fish is often caught on the way and cooked on deck over charcoal. Dhows can be picked up in Mombasa, Malindi and Lamu.

ORGANISED SAFARIS
There are essentially two types of organised safari available – those where you camp at night and those where you stay in game lodges or luxury tented camps at night. Whichever you choose, they typically start and end in either Nairobi or Mombasa, though there are a number of exceptions.

Game drives typically last two to 2½ hours. The best (in terms of sighting animals) are those in the early morning and late afternoon when the animals are at their most active.

Camping Safaris
Camping safaris cater for budget travellers and for those who are prepared to put up with discomfort. They are no-frills safaris. There are none of life's little luxuries, such as flushing toilets, running water or iced drinks, so they can be quite demanding, depending on where you go, and you'll be expected to lend a hand. You'll end up sweaty and dusty, and there may well be no showers available – even cold ones. On the other hand, you're in for an authentic adventure in the African bush with nothing between you and the animals at night except a sheet of canvas and the embers of a dying fire.

Another plus for these safaris is that you'll probably find yourself with travellers from the four corners of the earth.

The price of your safari should include three meals a day cooked by the camp's cook(s), though on some safaris you'll be expected to help with the preparation and clean up. Food is of the 'plain but plentiful' variety.

The price will also include all the necessary camping gear (except a sleeping bag, which you must provide or hire locally).

The amount of baggage you're allowed to bring is limited. Excess gear can usually be stored at the safari company's offices.

There are also a number of somewhat more expensive camping safaris which utilise permanent camp sites with showers and pre-erected tents fitted with mosquito nets, beds and sheets.

Remember that at the end of one of these safaris your driver/guide and the cooks will expect a reasonable tip. This is only fair, since wages are low and these people will have made a lot of effort to make your trip a memorable one. Be generous.

Safari Options

If possible, it's best to go on a safari which lasts at least five days (preferably longer), since otherwise a good deal of your time will be taken up driving to and from the national parks and Nairobi. You'll also see a great deal more on a longer safari and have a much better chance of catching sight of all the major animals.

A three day safari typically takes you to Amboseli or Masai Mara. A four day safari would take you to Amboseli and Tsavo, or to Masai Mara, or to Samburu and Buffalo Springs. A five day safari would take you to Amboseli and Tsavo, or to Masai Mara and Lake Nakuru. A six day safari would take you to lakes Nakuru, Bogoria and Baringo plus Masai Mara, or to Lake Nakuru, Masai Mara and Amboseli.

Safari Costs

There's a lot of competition for the tourist dollar among the safari companies, and prices for the same tour are very similar. Generally, the longer the tour, the less it costs per day.

For camping safaris you are looking at around US$75 to US$80 per day for a short safari, less (per day) for a longer one (five or more days).

Choosing a Safari Company

There is no doubt that some safari companies are better than others. The major factor to take into consideration before you decide to go with any particular company is whether it operates its own safaris with its own vehicles or whether it is just an agent for other safari companies. If the company is actually an agent then obviously part of what you pay is their commission, but, most importantly, if anything goes wrong or the itinerary is changed without your agreement, you have very little comeback and you'll be pushing shit uphill to get a refund. We get letters about this *all* the time from travellers to

whom it has happened. Unfortunately, the situation isn't so easy to avoid.

Another aspect of the safari business in Kenya is that there's a good deal of swapping of clients when one company's vehicle(s) are full for any particular safari and another's are not. This may mean you end up travelling with a different company from the one you booked with. Reputable companies won't do this without informing you, but agents certainly will.

Despite the pitfalls, a number of reliable companies offer camping safaris with their own vehicles and with excellent track records. They include:

Best Camping Tours
2nd floor, Nanak House, corner of Kimathi and Banda Sts, PO Box 40223, Nairobi (☎ (02) 229667)
Bushbuck Adventures
Barclays Bank bldg, Kenyatta Ave, PO Box 67449, Nairobi (☎ (02) 212975)
Come to Africa Safaris Ltd
3rd floor, Rehema House, between Kaunda and Standard Sts, PO Box 69513, Nairobi (☎ (02) 213186; fax 213254)
Exotic Safaris
1st floor, South Wing, Uniafric House, Koinange St, PO Box 54483, Nairobi (☎ (02) 338811)
Gametrackers Camping Safaris
Kenya Cinema Plaza, Moi Ave, PO Box 62042, Nairobi (☎ (02) 338927)
Safari-Camp Services
Barclays Plaza, PO Box 44801, Nairobi (☎ (02) 330130)
Safari Seekers
5th floor, Jubilee Insurance Exchange bldg, Kaunda St, PO Box 9165, Nairobi (☎ (02) 226206)
Savuka Tours & Safaris
3rd floor, Pan Africa House, Kenyatta Ave, PO Box 20433, Nairobi (☎ (02) 725907)

This is by no means an exhaustive list, nor is there any implication that companies not included here are unreliable.

Other Safaris

Camel Safaris Four main companies offer camel safaris at present. Contact Camel Trek Ltd (☎ (02) 891079), Nairobi; Desert Rose Camels (☎ (02) 228936), PO Box 44801, Nairobi; Yare Safaris (☎ (02) 214099),

Nairobi; or Gametrackers Camping Safaris (address above), also in Nairobi.

Walking Safaris For those who want to get around but don't want to spend the entire time in a safari bus, there are a number of companies offering walking safaris. Contact Bushbuck Adventures, Gametrackers (see addresses above) or Hiking & Cycling Kenya, PO Box 39439, Nairobi (☎ (02) 218336).

Do-it-Yourself Safaris This is a viable proposition in Kenya if you can get a group together to share the costs, since you will have to rent a vehicle and camping equipment.

Doing it yourself has several advantages over organised safaris. The main one is flexibility – you can go where you want, stop whenever you like and stay as long as you like. You don't have to follow the standard tourist routes. Another advantage is that you can choose your travelling companions.

The main disadvantage is the extra effort you have to put in to organise the safari. It can also be a worry if you don't have mechanical skills and/or tools and the vehicle breaks down. There's also the security of the vehicle and its contents to think about if you want to leave it somewhere and go off walking. Good maps are difficult to find, so navigation in remote areas can also be a problem.

As far as costs go, it's probably true to say that organising your own safari will cost at least as much and usually more than a company-organised safari.

Nairobi

The capital of Kenya, with a population of around one million, Nairobi is very cosmopolitan. It's lively, interesting, pleasantly landscaped, and a good place to get essential business and bureaucratic matters sewn up.

You'll meet travellers from all over the world here, plus there are all the things that you won't have seen for months if you've been hacking your way across from West Africa. It's a great place to stay and to tune in to modern urban African life. However, security is a definite concern and many travellers hate the place because of it.

Information
Money The branch of Barclays Bank at the international airport is open 24 hours a day, seven days a week. There are plenty of forex bureaus around town.

Post & Communications The main post office is on Haile Selassie Ave. The poste restante is well organised. This is also the best place to post parcels from.

The Extelcoms office is also on Haile Selassie Ave, almost opposite the post office. It is open from 8 am to midnight. It also has telex and fax facilities.

Nairobi's telephone area code is 02.

Travel Agencies The best places to try for discounted air tickets are Flight Centres (☎ 210024; fax 334207), Lakhamshi House, Biashara St, and Let's Go Travel (☎ 340331; fax 336890) on Standard St, opposite Bruce House and close to the Koinange St intersection.

Bookshops The Nation Bookshop, which is next door to the New Stanley Hotel, and the Westland Sundries shop beside it on Kenyatta Ave are both excellent.

Medical Services If you need medical treatment, try Dr Sheth on the 3rd floor of Bruce House on Standard St. There is also a dentist on the same floor.

Otherwise, go to Nairobi Hospital. The Aga Khan Hospital in Parklands opposite Mrs Roche's guesthouse is also good. Avoid Kenyatta Hospital.

You can get vaccinations at City Hall Clinic, Mama Ngina St. It is open for jabs from 8.30 am to noon Monday to Friday. If you want a gamma globulin shot (for hepatitis A) go to Dr Sheth.

Camping Equipment Hire If you want to hire anything from a sleeping bag to a

KENYA

folding toilet-seat, tent or mosquito net, the
best place to go to is Atul's (☎ 225935) on
Biashara St. It has the lot at reasonable
prices.

Things to See

The **National Museum** has a good exhibi-
tion on prehistoric people, an incredible
collection of native birds, mammals and
tribal crafts, and a good section on the
culture, history and crafts of the coastal
Swahili people. Opening hours are from 9.30
am to 6 pm daily, and admission is US$4.

Opposite the museum, the **Snake Park**
has living examples of most of the snake
species found in East Africa – some of them
in glass cages, others in open pits. Hours and
entry charges are as for the museum.

The **Railway Museum** on Station Rd is
slowly rotting away and is hardly worth a
visit these days. It's open daily from 8 am to
4.45 pm; entry is US$4.

The **Kenyatta Conference Centre** is
Nairobi's most prominent landmark. There
is a viewing level on the 28th floor, which
costs US$2. Photographs from the top level
are permitted.

Places to Stay

Camping The best place to camp in Nairobi
is *Upper Hill Campsite* (☎ 720290),
Menengai Rd, off Hospital Rd, which is itself
off Ngong Rd. It offers camping for US$3
per person in green, shady surroundings. If
you don't have camping equipment there's
dormitory accommodation for US$4, as well
as a few private double rooms. Facilities
include hot showers, a mellow bar, restaurant
(open for breakfast, lunch and dinner), a
fireplace with comfortable chairs, a library,
a collection of games and a covered workshop for vehicle maintenance. It's a great
place to stay, close to the city (15 minutes
walk) and people are very friendly.

You could once say the same of *Mrs
Roche's* on Third Parklands Ave opposite the
Aga Khan Hospital, a place which has been
making travellers welcome for over 25 years.
However, security is not well attended to,
and many travellers have had their tents

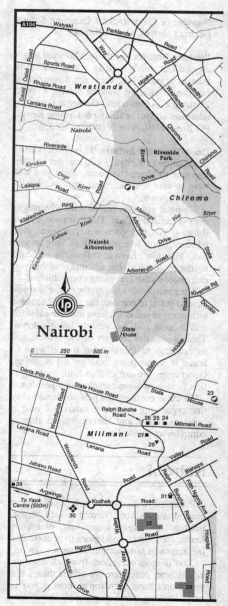

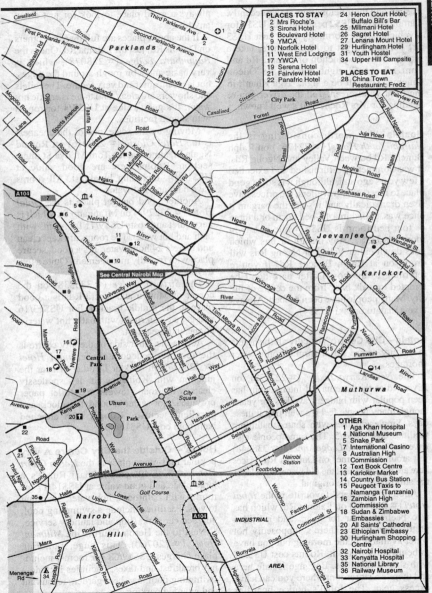

slashed and their belongings stolen recently. Camping costs US$2 per night plus US$1 for a vehicle, while dormitory beds cost US$3 per person. To get to Mrs Roche's, take a matatu from the junction of Latema Rd and Tom Mboya St right outside the Odeon Cinema. There'll be a sign, 'Aga Khan', in the front windscreen. Tell the driver you're heading for Mrs Roche's. It's well known.

Hostels Also worth considering is the *Nairobi Youth Hostel* (☎ 721765) on Ralph Bunche Rd between Valley and Ngong Rds. It was completely refurbished and extended a few years ago and, although it is still a good place to meet other travellers, the prices have risen dramatically and it's not the bargain it once was. A bed in a 16-bed dorm or a three or four-bed room is US$6, while in a twin room it's US$7. Any matatu or bus which goes down either Valley or Ngong Rds will drop you at Ralph Bunche Rd. If you're returning to the hostel after dark don't be tempted to walk back from the centre of the city. Many people have been robbed. Always take a matatu or taxi (US$4).

Hotels – City Centre Virtually all the hotels in the city centre suffer from chronic water shortages.

The *New Kenya Lodge* (☎ 222022), on River Rd at the Latema Rd intersection, has been popular with budget travellers for years, though many people feel it's well past it these days. Singles/doubles with shared bathroom facilities cost US$3/5. The same people also have the *New Kenya Lodge Annexe* (☎ 338348) just around the corner on Duruma Rd. Prices here are the same as at the old place, but it lacks the atmosphere of the original.

Another travellers' favourite is the *Iqbal Hotel* (☎ 220914) on Latema Rd, which has also been popular for years and is still a pretty good place. There's supposedly hot water available in the morning but you have to be up early to get it. Rooms cost US$3/7 with shared facilities. Baggage is safe here and there's a storeroom where you can leave excess gear. The Iqbal's notice board is

always a good place to look for just about anything.

If the above places are full there are others on Dubois Rd, just off Latema Rd. One is the *Bujumbura Lodge* (☎ 228078), which is very basic and a bit rough around the edges, but is clean, quiet and very secure. The toilets and showers are clean, and there is erratic hot water. It's good value at US$3/4 for rooms with shared facilities.

Moving up the scale, one of the cheapest is the *Hotel Gloria* (☎ 228916) on Ronald Ngala St, almost at the Tom Mboya St intersection. Rooms here are good value at US$11/14, including breakfast. All rooms have bath and hot water.

Another good budget place is the *Dolat Hotel* (☎ 222797) on Mfangano St, which is very quiet and costs US$9/11 for rooms with bath and hot water. The rooms are kept clean and there's 24 hour water. It's a good, secure place with friendly management. Quite a few travellers stay here.

The *Sirikwa Lodge* (☎ 333838) on the corner of Munyu and Accra Rds is a good place in the middle bracket. For US$13/16 you get a clean room with bath, hot water, a phone and breakfast.

Across the other side of the city centre is the recently redecorated *Terminal Hotel* (☎ 228817) on Moktar Daddah St near the junction with Koinange St. It's spotlessly clean, with soap, towels and toilet paper provided, hot water around the clock and excellent security. Rooms with attached bathroom cost US$16/20.

Hotels – Outside the City Centre A very popular mid-range place is the *Heron Court Hotel* (☎ 720740) on Milimani Rd. It's a large place and good value at US$14/17 for rooms with bathroom, hot water, soap and towels. Facilities include a swimming pool, guarded car park, shop and laundry service.

Next to the Heron Court is the *Milimani Hotel* (☎ 720760). This huge, rambling place charges US$49/68 for rooms, including breakfast and taxes. Facilities include a swimming pool, bar, beer garden, restaurant and guarded parking.

Places to Eat

There are a lot of very cheap cafes and restaurants in the Latema/River Rds area and at the top end of Tom Mboya St, where you can pick up a very cheap, traditional African breakfast of mandazi (a semi-sweet doughnut) and tea or coffee.

The *Malindi Dishes* restaurant on Gaberone Rd is well worth trying at least once. As the name suggests, the food here has the Swahili influence of the coast, and so coconut and spices are used to good effect.

For a good solid meal (mixing western and local cuisine) such as steak and matoke (mashed plantains and maize) or maharagwe (kidney beans), try *Cafe Helena* on Mama Ngina St opposite City Hall. At around US$2 the meals are excellent value.

An excellent place for submarine sandwiches, cakes and decent coffee is the *Pasara* cafe on Standard St. It does a good breakfast here for US$5.

If you're staying at Mrs Roche's in Parklands, the *Stop'n'Eat* tin shed up the road offers ugali (maize meal) and ngombe (beef) at very modest prices.

Kenya is the home of all-you-can-eat lunches at a set price and Nairobi has a wide choice of them, most offering Indian food. One of the best is the *Supreme Restaurant* on River Rd, which offers excellent Indian vegetarian food for US$4. It also has superb fruit juices.

The *Minar* chain of upmarket Indian restaurants are great places for Sunday lunch, as they do a good-value US$8 all-you-can-eat buffet. There is a branch on Banda St.

At the *Calypso* in the basement of Bruce House on Standard St you can get a good English-style breakfast for US$2.

For a breakfast splurge, try one of the buffets at a major hotel. The *Illiki Cafe* on the ground floor of the Ambassadeur Hotel on Moi Ave is excellent value, and you can make a pig of yourself for US$7.

The *West African Paradise Restaurant* in Rank Xerox House, Westlands, offers a wide range of food from a number of West African countries.

One of the best Chinese restaurants is the *Rickshaw Chinese Restaurant* in Fedha Towers, Standard St.

For Italian food, there is the long-running and very popular *Trattoria* on the corner of Wabera and Kaunda Sts. However, a cheaper place is *La Scala* on Standard St near Muindi Mbingu St. This place also has western dishes such as steaks and burgers.

For steak eaters who haven't seen a decent doorstep since they left Argentina, Australia, Uruguay or the USA and are looking for a gut-busting extravaganza, there's no better place than the *Carnivore* (☎ 501709), out at Langata just past Wilson airport. Whether it's lunch or dinner, there's always beef, pork, lamb, ham, chicken, sausages and at least three game meats. Meals are not cheap here, but it is open slather. It costs US$17 for lunch from Monday to Saturday and US$19 on Sunday; dinner is US$19 daily. To get there take bus No 14, 24 or 124 from Moi Ave, opposite the US embassy, and tell the conductor where you are going; the restaurant is a 1km signposted walk from where you are dropped off; hitch or take a taxi home.

Much more modest, and worth it for the atmosphere, are the 20 or more wooden shacks of the *NSSF Market* on the corner of Loita St and Kenyatta Ave. Here you can eat good choma for around US$2, and also sample many other Kenyan dishes such as matoke and kenyege. This is a very popular place among the city's office workers, and although foreigners are a rare sight, you'll be warmly welcomed.

Entertainment

Cinemas Nairobi is a good place to take in a few films, and at a price substantially lower than what you'd pay back home. If you don't want scratched films you should go to one of the better cinemas such as the *Kenya* on Moi Ave, or the *Nairobi* or *20th Century* on Mama Ngina St.

Discos Perhaps the most popular disco is the *Florida 2000* on Moi Ave near City Hall Way. Entry costs US$2 for men (US$3 on Saturday) and half that for women, and it's open until 6 am. Also very popular is the *New*

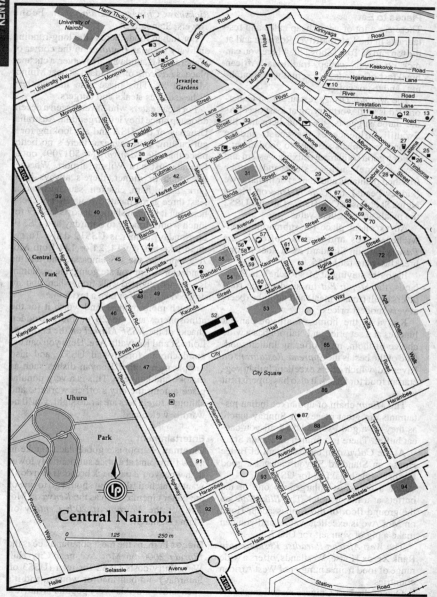

Central Nairobi

0   125   250 m

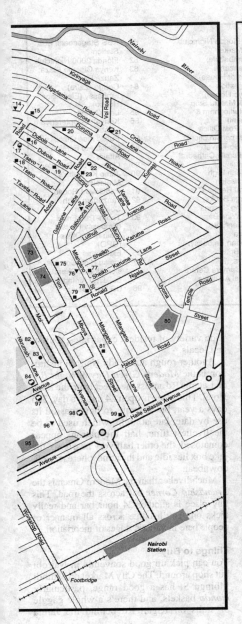

Continued from previous page

PLACES TO STAY
- 2 Nairobi Safari Club
- 3 Suncourt Hotel
- 4 Parkside Hotel
- 7 Meridien Court Hotel
- 11 Marble Arch Hotel
- 15 New Kenya Lodge
- 16 New Safe Life Lodging
- 18 Hotel Greton
- 19 Bujumbura Lodge
- 20 New Kenya Lodge Annexe
- 23 Sirikwa Lodge
- 25 Oriental Palace Hotel
- 26 Iqbal Hotel
- 37 Terminal Hotel; Dove Cage Restaurant
- 38 Embassy Hotel
- 39 Grand Regency Hotel
- 47 Inter-Continental Hotel
- 55 Sixeighty Hotel
- 66 New Stanley Hotel; Thorn Tree Cafe; Nation Bookshop
- 68 Oakwood Hotel
- 72 Hilton Hotel
- 74 Ambassadeur Hotel
- 75 Solace Hotel
- 77 Dolat Hotel
- 78 Terrace Hotel
- 79 Hotel Gloria
- 81 Princess Hotel
- 99 Hotel Hermes

PLACES TO EAT
- 9 Dhaba Restaurant; Nyama Choma Terrace & Bar
- 10 Supreme; Mayur & Zam Zam Restaurants
- 14 Bull Cafe
- 24 Malindi Dishes
- 28 Nairobi Burgers
- 29 Nakumatt Supermarket
- 30 Minar Restaurant
- 33 Slush Happy Eater
- 36 Kenchic Inn; Hoggers Eating Place; Afro Unity Bar
- 40 Hard Rock Cafe; Kenya Airways (Barclays Plaza)
- 44 Harvest Cafe
- 45 NSSF Market (Nyama Choma Stalls)
- 51 Beneve Coffee House
- 54 Calypso & Dragon Pearl Restaurants (Bruce House)
- 56 Great Chung Wah Chinese Restaurant
- 58 La Scala
- 60 Cafe Helena; Coffee Bar
- 61 Trattoria Restaurant
- 62 Pasara Cafe; Rickshaw Chinese Restaurant
- 67 Supermac
- 69 Caprice
- 70 Jax Restaurant

Continued on next page

Continued from page 429			41	New Florida Nightclub	80	KBS Stagecoach Bus
71	I'ora Blu		42	City Market		Station
76	New Bedona Cafe		43	Air Zimbabwe;	82	Florida 2000 Nightclub
96	Tamarind Restaurant;			Air Tanzania	83	Kenya Cinema Plaza;
	American			(Chester House)		Zanze Bar
	Cultural Center		46	Immigration	84	Congo (Zaïre)
				(Nyayo House)		Embassy (Electricity
OTHER			48	Bus & Matatu Stop		House)
1	Police			(for Hurlingham &	85	Law Courts
5	Bus Stop			Milimani)	86	Kenyatta Conference
	(for Westlands)		49	New Post Office		Centre
6	Maasai Market			(under construction)	87	Public Map Office
8	Moi Ave Post Office		50	Let's Go Travel	88	Ministry of Foreign
12	Akamba Bus Office		52	Holy Family Cathedral		Affairs
13	Bancko Tours & Travel		53	City Hall	89	Office of the President
17	DPS Peugeots		57	Ugandan High	90	Jomo Kenyatta's
	(Shared Taxis)			Commission		Mausoleum
21	Coast Bus, Mawingo,		59	Central Rent-a-Car	91	Parliament House
	Goldline, Arusha		63	Prestige Books;	92	Tanzanian High
	Express Bus Lines			Dancing Spoons		Commission
22	Matatus for Embu,			Cafe; Wine Bar;	93	Thorn-Tree Email
	Isiolo & Nanyuki			20th Century		(Embassy House)
27	Modern Green Day &			Cinema	94	Main Post Office
	Night Bar		64	Rwandan Embassy;		(GPO)
31	McMillan Memorial			DHL ; British	95	Extelcoms
	Library			Airways	97	Indian High Commis-
32	Jamia Mosque		65	Expo Camera Centre		sion (Jeeva Bharat
34	Flight Centres		73	National Archives		Building) Air India
35	Atul's (Camping Gear)				98	US Embassy

Florida, on the corner of Koinange and Market Sts, which is a most unusually shaped building above a petrol station!

There's a live band/disco every Wednesday night at *Simba Saloon* at the Carnivore restaurant in Langata. Entry costs US$2 per person (free if you eat dinner at the restaurant).

Live Music The *Zanze Bar* on the top floor of the Kenya Cinema Plaza on Moi Ave has live music most nights.

Zingara Percussion is a local group which performs every Saturday afternoon at the *Hoggers Eating Place* on Muindi Mbingu St opposite Jeevanjee Gardens.

Bars The *Thorn Tree Cafe* in the New Stanley Hotel on the corner of Kimathi St and Kenyatta Ave is a bit passé these days, but is still something of a meeting place for travellers.

One of the liveliest bars in Nairobi is *Buffalo Bill's* at the Heron Court Hotel, Milimani Rd. It's extremely popular with a wide variety of resident expatriates, tourists and locals.

Another rough and ready Nairobi institution is the *Modern Green Day & Night Bar* on Latema Rd across the street from the Iqbal Hotel. This place is open 24 hours a day, 365 days a year, but it seems to have passed its use-by date; late at night, which used to be the liveliest time, half the patrons appear comatosed, the other half very nearly so, the juke box lies idle and the atmosphere is, well, downbeat.

Much livelier than the Modern Green is the *Friendship Corner* bar across the road. This tiny place is another 24 hour bar and really kicks on. You'll come across all manner of people here in various stages of inebriation.

Things to Buy

You can pick up good souvenirs in Nairobi but shop around. The City Market on Muindi Mbingu St has a good range, particularly *kiondo* baskets, and there's a whole gaggle of stalls on Kigali Rd behind the Jamia

Mosque – bargain fiercely. The Maasai market is held on Tuesday at the northern end of Moi Ave. The tribespeople come to town with their goods (carved gourds, beads etc); it's a great atmosphere.

Even though they originated in Tanzania (where they're much cheaper), *makonde* wood carvings have caught on in a big way in Nairobi. You can buy some really fine examples at bargain-basement prices from hawkers. Expect to pay around half to two-thirds of the price first asked.

The Spinners Web describes itself as a 'consignment handcraft shop' and sells goods made in workshops and by self-help groups around the country. Its shop is on Waiyaki Way in Westlands, near Viking House.

Getting There & Away
Air All the major European, Asian and African airlines fly into Nairobi and have offices in the city. Most travellers find that it's cheaper to buy an air ticket from a travel agent.

Bus Most long-distance bus offices are along Accra Rd near the junction with River Rd. For Mombasa there are numerous companies (such as Coast, Akamba, Mawingo, Goldline and Malaika) doing the run, both by day and night. They all cost around US$7 and the trip takes around eight hours with a meal break on the way. Akamba, perhaps the most reliable, has daily services to many parts of the country and to Kampala. Its office is on Lagos Rd, just off Latema Rd. Also good is KBS Stagecoach on Ronald Ngala St.

The main country bus station is just off Landhies Rd, about a 15 minute walk from the budget hotel area. There is at least one departure daily, and often more, to virtually every main town in the country.

Share-taxi Most of the companies have their offices around the Accra and River Rds area. DPS has daily Peugeots to Kisumu (US$9, four hours), Busia (US$13), Nakuru (US$4, two hours) and Malaba (US$9). Departures are only in the morning so you need to be at the office by around 7 am.

For the Tanzanian border at Namanga, taxis leave from the top side of the service station on the corner of Ronald Ngala St and River Rd. They run throughout the day, take about two hours and cost US$7. A better bet is the buses direct to Arusha. Davanu Shuttle (US$18), from the Norfolk Hotel, and Arusha Express (US$7), on Accra Rd, depart daily at 8.30 am.

Getting Around
The Airport Wilson international airport is 15km out of town off the road to Mombasa. The cheapest way of getting into town is on the No 34 city bus, but don't even think about it as a great number of people have been ripped off on this bus.

The only other way to/from the airport is by taxi – the only option if you have a dawn or late-night flight. The standard fare is US$17.

To Wilson airport (for small aircraft to Malindi, Lamu etc) take bus No 15, 31 or 125 from Moi Ave opposite the US Embassy.

Bus Useful buses include the No 46 from outside the new post office on Kenyatta Ave for the Yaya Centre in Hurlingham, or No 23 from Moi Ave at Jeevanjee Gardens for Westlands.

Taxi Taxis operate from ranks at the train station, the museum and outside most main hotels. The taxis are not metered but the fares are remarkably standard and few cabbies try to overcharge. Around US$4 gets you just about anywhere in the city centre. Outside the centre, the fare generally rises to US$6.

AROUND NAIROBI
Nairobi National Park
Nairobi National Park is the most accessible of all Kenya's game parks, being only a few kilometres from the city centre. Virtually all of Kenya's big game, except elephant, are represented here. Entry to the park costs US$27 per person plus US$4 for a vehicle.

If you want to hitch a ride through the park from the main gate, the No 24 city bus from Moi Ave goes right by it. Many safari com-

KENYA

panies offer tours of Nairobi National Park. They usually depart twice a day from Nairobi and cost US$50.

Bomas of Kenya

You can see traditional dances and hear songs from the country's 16 ethnic groups at this cultural centre in Langata. There is a daily performance at 2.30 pm (3.30 pm on weekends) and entry costs US$5. Bus No 15, 125 or 126 from outside Development House, Moi Ave, will get you there in about half an hour.

Around the Country

DIANI BEACH

Diani Beach, on the coast south of Mombasa, is a typical 'tropical paradise' beach, but is also the most developed of the beaches in this area. Most of the beachfront is taken up with resorts ranging from expensive upwards. Do not walk between the highway at Ukunda and the beach road, as it's notorious for muggings. Take a matatu or a KBS bus.

Places to Stay

The only cheap accommodation is *Dan Trench's*, behind the Trade Winds Hotel. It has good camping for US$3 and cheap rooms for US$5. One of the few mid-range places to stay is *Diani Beachalets* (☎ (0127) 2180) at the southern end of the beach. There is a range of bandas (huts) available from US$14 to US$23.

Getting There & Away

From the Likoni ferry (Mombasa) there are KBS buses (No 32) every 20 minutes or so from early morning until around 7 pm. There are also plenty of matatus.

ELDORET

There is little to see or do in Eldoret but it's a convenient place to stop for the night.

Places to Stay

One option for campers is the *Naiberi River*

Campsite, some 22km south-east of town on the C54 road to Kaptagat. As well as camping (US$3), there is a dormitory (beds for US$5) and a few very comfortable double cabins with attached bathroom for US$22. The owner works in Eldoret during the day, so if you ring before 5 pm on weekdays he can give you a lift out to the site. The contact number is ☎ (0321) 32644.

The *Mahindi Hotel* (☎ (0321) 31520), on Uganda Rd close to the bus and matatu station, is good value at US$5/7 for singles/ doubles with private bath. The hotel has a restaurant, and the noise from the Silent Night Bar (!) downstairs can sometimes be distracting.

Also in this area is the *Sosani View Hotel*, with single/double rooms with hot bath for US$5/7.

A popular mid-range place is the *New Lincoln Hotel* (☎ (0321) 22093) on Oloo Rd, which is quiet and has guarded car parking. Rooms with attached bathroom are good value at US$6/8, including breakfast.

Places to Eat

A popular lunch-time spot is *Otto Cafe* on Uganda Rd.

For a more upmarket meal or snack try the flash new *Sizzlers Cafe* on Kenyatta St. Also good is the*Elcove Restaurant* on Oloo Rd opposite the New Lincoln Hotel.

Getting There & Away

There are bus, minibus, share-taxi and matatu departures throughout the day for Kisumu (US$3), Nakuru (US$3), Nairobi (US$5), Kericho (US$3) and Kitale (US$2).

ISIOLO

Isiolo, where the tarmac ends, is the frontier town for north-eastern Kenya – a vast area of forested and barren mountains, deserts, scrub and Lake Turkana, and home to the wild and colourful Samburu, Rendille, Boran and Turkana peoples.

Isiolo is the last place going north which has a bank, fuel or food supplies until you get to either Maralal or Marsabit.

Places to Stay & Eat
The best budget place is the *Jamhuri Guest House*, across the road from Barclays Bank, which is excellent value at US$4/5 for a single/double.

The modern *Desert Trails Lodge*, clearly visible behind the BP station on the main street, is good value at US$5/8 with a bathroom shared between two rooms.

Getting There & Away
Akamba operates three buses daily to Nairobi (US$5, seven hours).

Mwingi Buses operates irregular buses to Marsabit (US$6), supposedly a couple of times a week, but this is very flexible. The same company also operates less frequent buses to Moyale on the Ethiopian border (US$6 from Marsabit).

KILIFI
Kilifi, a coastal town north of Mombasa, consists of the small village of Mnarani (or Manarani) on the southern bank of the creek and Kilifi itself on the northern bank. It's a small town which you can walk around within minutes.

The **Mnarani Ruins**, on the southern bank of Kilifi Creek overlooking the ferry landing, are the remains of one of a string of Swahili city-states which dotted the East African coast.

Places to Stay
The best place is *Tushaurine Boarding & Lodging* (☎ (0125) 22486), one of a number of cheapies near the bus station. Simple rooms with mosquito net and shared bathroom facilities cost US$3/5 a single/double.

Up the price scale is the *Dhows Inn* (☎ (0125) 22028) on the main road south of Kilifi Creek. It's a fairly small place, with a number of double rooms surrounding a well-kept garden. A room here with mosquito net and bath costs US$10.

Places to Eat
A cheap and very popular place to eat, for both lunch and dinner, is the *Kilifi Hotel* at the bus station.

For a splurge, go for a meal at the very agreeable *Sahani Tamu Restaurant* on the northern side of the creek, opposite the Mnarani Club. The food here is mainly Italian and seafood, and is very well prepared and presented. Main dishes are in the US$4 to US$6 range.

KISUMU
Kisumu, on Lake Victoria, is Kenya's third largest town. It has a very easy-going, almost decaying, atmosphere, but with the recent increase in cooperation between the former partners in the community, Kisumu's fortunes may once again be on the rise. International ferries run to Mwanza in Tanzania and the town is a busy transhipment point.

Things to See
The **Kisumu Museum** is well worth a visit. It's on Nairobi Rd within easy walking distance of the town centre, and is open daily from 9.30 am to 6 pm; entry is US$4.

Places to Stay
Campers should head for *Dunga Refreshments* (☎ (035) 42529) at Hippo Point, right on the shores of Lake Victoria, 3km south of town. Camping costs US$2 per person. There's also a dormitory block which costs US$5 per bed. The complex includes a very pleasant restaurant with reasonably priced meals. It's a mellow place to stay and highly recommended.

The cheapest option in town is the *YWCA* (☎ (035) 43192) on the corner of Omolo Agar and Nairobi Rds. It has dorm beds (three people per room) with shared facilities for US$3.

A good budget option is the *Razbi Guest House* (☎ (035) 44771), upstairs on the corner of Oginga Odinga Rd and Kendu Lane. It's very secure, the rooms are clean, and a towel and soap are provided. The rates are US$3/4 for singles/doubles with shared cold-water bath.

On Oginga Odinga Rd, there's the *Mona Lisa Guest House* (behind the restaurant of the same name), which has rooms with

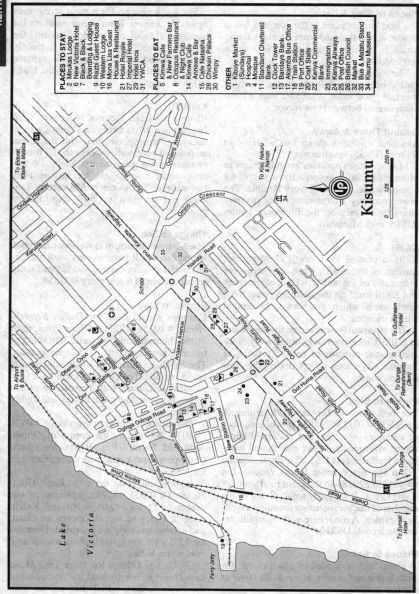

PLACES TO STAY
2 Mirukas Lodge
6 New Victoria Hotel
7 Black & Black
   Boarding & Lodging
9 Razbi Guest House
10 Western Lodge
16 Mona Lisa Guest
   House & Restaurant
21 Hotel Royale
27 Imperial Hotel
29 Hotel Inca
31 YWCA

PLACES TO EAT
5 Kimwa Cafe
   & New Farmers Bar
8 Octopus Restaurant
   & Night Club
12 Kimwa Cafe
14 Annex & Bar
15 Cafe Natasha
28 Chicken Palace
30 Wimpy

OTHER
1 Kibuye Market
   (Sundays)
3 Hospital
4 Mosque
11 Standard Chartered
   Bank
12 Clock Tower
13 Barclays Bank
17 Akamba Bus Office
18 Port Office
19 Train Station
22 Craft Stalls
   Kenya Commercial
   Bank
23 Immigration
24 Kenya Airways
25 Post Office
26 British Council
32 Market
33 Bus & Matatu Stand
34 Kisumu Museum

Kisumu

To Eldoret,
Kitale & Malaba

Ondek Highway

Karume Road

Ochieng Avenue

Obunga Road

Jomo Kenyatta Highway

Crescent

Omino

To Kisii, Nakuru
& Nairobi

Nairobi Road

Nairobi Road

N2se Road

Uhuru Road

Oginga Ager Road

To Gulfstream
Hotel

Anaawa Avenue

School

To Airport
& Busia

Ondiri Road

Oyoo Street

Otiena Road

Gor Street

Accra Street

Mosque Road

Angawa Avenue

Jevanjee Road

Nairobi Road

Oginga Odinga Road

Kendu Lane

Marine Drive

Kenyatta Street

New Station Road

Angawa Avenue

Got Huma Road

N2se Road

Ombili Road

Achieng Road

Oneka Road

Odera Row

To Dunga
Refreshments (3km)

To Dunga

To Sunset
Hotel

Lake
Victoria

Ferry Jetty

0   125   250 m

To Gulfstream
Hotel

attached bathroom for US$4/6 – excellent value.

The mid-range *New Victoria Hotel* (☎ (035) 21067) on the corner of Kendu Lane and Gor Mahia Rd is good value, especially if you get one of the front rooms with a balcony and views of Lake Victoria. Doubles cost US$14, including breakfast.

Places to Eat

One of the most popular restaurants is the *Mona Lisa* on Oginga Odinga Rd. It's a friendly place where you can meet lots of people.

For a splurge, go for lunch or dinner (about US$11) at the *Hotel Royale* and soak up the atmosphere. The service and food are excellent.

Out at Hippo Point, *Dunga Refreshments* has good food at budget prices, plus you can eat outside right on the water's edge.

Entertainment

Everyone in search of action goes to the excellent disco/bar/restaurant complex called *Octopus Night Club* on Ogada St.

Getting There & Away

From Kisumu there are matatus to, among other places, Nairobi (US$6), Busia (US$2), Kakamega (US$2) and Eldoret (US$3). There are also trains to Nairobi; fares are US$35/24 for 1st/2nd class.

KITALE

Kitale is another in the string of agricultural service towns which dot the western highlands.

The **Kitale Museum** has a variety of indoor exhibits, including good ethnographic displays about the Turkana people.

Places to Stay

If you want to camp, the only place in the area is *Sirikwa Safaris*, about 23km north of Kitale on the Kapenguria road. It's run by Jane and Julia Barnley at their farmhouse and is a beautiful place to stay. Camping with your own tent costs US$5, or there are 'permanent' furnished tents for US$17/22.

To find Sirikwa Safaris, look for the sign on the right-hand side 1km after the small village of Kesagen. Kapenguria matatus from Kitale go right by Sirikwa (US$1), and the drivers all know it.

Best of the usual bunch of cheapies/brothels is the *New Kitale House* on Moi Ave, which offers singles with clean sheets and shared bath for just US$3. Next door is the *Hotel Mamboleo* (☎ (0325) 20172), where singles/doubles with attached bathroom cost US$4/6 and there's hot water in the showers.

The most popular mid-range place in Kitale is the *Bongo Hotel* (☎ (0325) 20593) on Moi Ave, which has rooms for US$10/13 with private bath, including breakfast.

Places to Eat

The *Executive Restaurant*, at the lodge of the same name on Kenyatta St, is a very popular lunch-time spot. The menu is extensive, and the food is good and reasonably priced.

The *Bongo Hotel* on the corner of Moi Ave and Bank St has a slightly more upmarket restaurant which is a good place for an evening meal.

Getting There & Away

For Lodwar and Kalekol in the Turkana district, there is usually one minibus per day for US$6; you'll just have to ask around. The Nissan matatus are more reliable and leave about five times daily (five hours, US$7).

LAKE NAIVASHA

Lake Naivasha, near the town of Naivasha, is one of the Rift Valley's fresh-water lakes and its ecology is quite different from that of the soda lakes. It's home to an incredible variety of bird species and one of the main focuses of conservation efforts in Kenya.

Almost opposite Hippo Point, a couple of kilometres past Fisherman's Camp, is **Elsamere**, the former home of the late Joy Adamson of *Born Free* fame. It is now a small conservation centre.

Places to Stay

There are a couple of budget options on the lake shore. The most popular place is

Fisherman's Camp (☎ (0311) 30088) on the southern shore. You can camp here for US$3 per person, plus there are tents for hire at US$4. There is also a range of bandas from US$6. It's a very pleasant site with grass, shady acacia trees and a bar.

Another possibility is *Burch's Campsite* (☎ (0311) 21010) about 1km beyond the Yelogreen Bar & Restaurant towards Fisherman's Camp. Pitching your tent in this shady camp site costs US$3 per person, or there are basic but adequate twin-bed rondavels for US$8, or bigger, self-contained four-bed rondavels with attached bathroom for US$17 a double plus US$5 for each extra person. This includes bedding, cooking equipment and use of a gas stove.

Getting There & Away
There are fairly frequent matatus between Naivasha town and Kongoni on the western side of the lake. It's 17km to Fisherman's Camp from the turn-off on the old Naivasha-Nairobi road.

LAKE TURKANA
Heading north from Maralal, the lushness of the Horr Valley gradually peters out until, finally, you reach the totally barren, shattered lava beds at the southern end of Lake Turkana. Top the ridge here, and there it is in front of you – the Jade Sea. It's a breathtaking sight – vast, yet totally barren. You'll see nothing living here except a few brave, stunted thorn trees. When you reach the lake shore, you'll know why – it's a soda lake and, at this end, highly saline. If you decide to take a dip, watch out for crocodiles.

A little further up the lake shore is **Loyangalani**, with an airstrip, post office, fishing station, luxury lodge, two camp sites and a Catholic mission (which may reluctantly sell petrol), all of it surrounded by the yurt-like, stick and doum-palm dwellings of the Turkana tribespeople. Taking photographs of people or their houses here will attract 'fees'.

On the west side of the lake, most travellers head on from Lodwar to **Kalekol**, a fairly dismal little town a few kilometres from the lake shore. To get out to **Ferguson's Gulf** on the lake it's a hot 1½ hour walk.

Places to Stay & Eat
Loyangalani The first camp site is the *El-Molo Camp*, which has excellent facilities, including good showers and toilets, a swimming pool, large dining-hall and bar (with cold beers!) and electricity until 9.30 pm (kerosene lanterns after that). Camping costs US$2 per person per night or there are bandas with attached bathroom for US$35.

The other camp site, adjacent to El-Molo, is *Sunset Strip Camp,* which is similar.

Kalekol The only option is the basic *Safari Hotel,* which has a reasonable restaurant.

Getting There & Away
On the western side of Lake Turkana there are daily matatus and buses between Kitale and Lodwar and Kalekol. On the eastern side, you're on your own.

LAMU
On the Indian Ocean coast and with an almost exclusively Muslim population, Lamu's Kenya's oldest inhabited town. It has changed little in appearance or character over the centuries. Access is still exclusively by diesel-powered launch from the mainland (though there's an airstrip on nearby Manda Island) and the only vehicle on the island is that owned by the District Commissioner. The streets are far too narrow and winding to accommodate anything other than pedestrians and donkeys.

Men still wear the full-length white robes known as *khanzus*, and the *kofia* caps, and women cover themselves with the black wraparound *bui bui* as they do in other Islamic cultures, although here it's a liberalised version.

There are probably more dhows to be seen here than anywhere else along the East African coast, and local festivals still take place with complete disregard for camera-toting tourists. The beach at Shela remains magnificent and uncluttered, and nothing happens in a hurry. It's one of the most

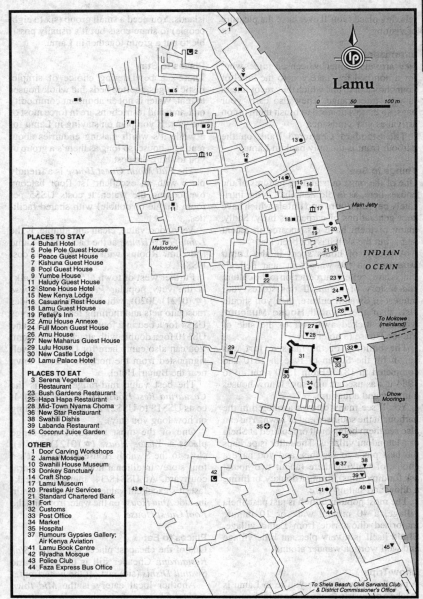

Lamu

0   50   100 m

To Matondoni

Main Jetty

To Mokowe (mainland)

INDIAN OCEAN

Dhow Moorings

To Shela Beach, Civil Servants Club & District Commissioner's Office

PLACES TO STAY
4   Buhari Hotel
5   Pole Pole Guest House
6   Peace Guest House
7   Kishuna Guest House
8   Pool Guest House
9   Yumbe House
11 Haludy Guest House
12 Stone House Hotel
15 New Kenya Lodge
16 Casuarina Rest House
18 Lamu Guest House
19 Petley's Inn
22 Amu House Annexe
24 Full Moon Guest House
26 Amu House
27 New Maharus Guest House
29 Lulu House
30 New Castle Lodge
40 Lamu Palace Hotel

PLACES TO EAT
3   Serena Vegetarian Restaurant
23 Bush Gardens Restaurant
25 Hapa Hapa Restaurant
28 Mid-Town Nyama Choma
36 New Star Restaurant
38 Swahili Dishis
39 Labanda Restaurant
45 Coconut Juice Garden

OTHER
1   Door Carving Workshops
2   Jamaa Mosque
10 Swahili House Museum
13 Donkey Sanctuary
14 Craft Shop
17 Lamu Museum
20 Prestige Air Services
21 Standard Chartered Bank
31 Fort
32 Customs
33 Post Office
34 Market
35 Hospital
37 Rumours Gypsies Gallery; Air Kenya Aviation
41 Lamu Book Centre
42 Riyadha Mosque
43 Police Club
44 Faza Express Bus Office

relaxing places you'll ever have the pleasure of visiting.

Information

New arrivals are met by licensed guides who, for a nominal fee, take you to the hotel of your choice or to one which they recommend in your price range. They also carry your bags, so there's no need to brush them off on arrival as just a nuisance.

The Standard Chartered Bank on the harbour front is the only bank in Lamu.

Things to See

One of the most outstanding features of the houses here, as in old Zanzibar, is the intricately **carved doors and lintels** which have kept generations of carpenters busy. Sadly, many of them have disappeared in recent years, but the skill has not been lost.

A couple of hours spent in the **Lamu Museum**, on the waterfront near Petley's Inn, is an excellent introduction to the culture and history of Lamu. If this stokes your interest in Swahili culture, then you should also visit the **Swahili House Museum**, which is tucked away off to the side of Yumbe House (a hotel).

The building of the massive **fort** was begun by the Sultan of Paté in 1810 and completed in 1823. From 1910 right up to 1984 it was used as a prison. It now houses a library and aquarium.

You'll see many **dhows** anchored in the harbour at the southern end of town. You can also see them being built or repaired at Shela or Matondoni villages. The latter is perhaps the best place to see this, and you have a choice of walking there (about two hours, ask for directions), hiring a donkey, or hiring a dhow and sailing there.

The most popular **beach** is just past Shela village, a 40 minute walk or 10 minute motorised dhow ride from Lamu village. **Shela** itself is a very pleasant little village and well worth a wander around.

Dhow Trips

A popular activity while you're in Lamu is to take a dhow trip to one of the neighbouring islands. You need a small group (six to eight people) to share costs but it's usually possible to put a group together in Lamu.

Places to Stay

There's a bewildering choice of simple, rustic lodges, rooftop beds and whole houses to rent. Water is not an abundant commodity on Lamu and restrictions are in force most of the year. If you plan on staying in Lamu for a while it's worth making enquiries about renting a house, so long as there's a group of you to share the cost.

The *Full Moon Guest House* is a friendly place with an excellent 1st floor balcony overlooking the water. It costs US$5 per room (single or double) with shared facilities.

Very good value, clean and simple, is the *Lamu Guest House* at the back of the Lamu Museum. Rooms with fan and bath cost US$11.

Further west of town (15 minutes walk) is the very popular *Peace Guest House* (☎ (0121) 3020), which is clean, provides mosquito nets and morning tea, and charges US$4 for a bed in a four-bed dormitory and US$10 for a double with attached bathroom. You can also camp here for US$2. It's well signposted from the northern part of town near the Buhari Hotel.

The best value mid-range place is the *Casuarina Rest House* (☎ (0121) 3123). It costs US$18 to US$27 a double (depending on how long you stay).

One of the most beautiful mid-range places is *Yumbe House* (☎ (0121) 33101), close to the Swahili House Museum. It's a four storey traditional house with a central courtyard. At US$18/34, including breakfast, it's excellent value. Others in this vein include *Amu House* on the waterfront and the *Pool Guest House*.

Places to Eat

One of the cheapest places is the *New Star Restaurant*. Cheaper still is the very basic *Swahili Dishis* (sic) just off the waterfront.

Another local eatery is the *Mid-Town Nyama Choma* cafe on the main square by the fort. There are no prizes here for culinary excellence, but for a cheap meat meal it's the place to go.

The very popular *Bush Gardens* is on the waterfront. Service can be slow, but the food is very good and the atmosphere pleasant. The *Hapa Hapa Restaurant* close by is also good.

The rooftop terrace at *Petley's Inn* serves surprisingly inexpensive food and is open to non-guests of the hotel. This is also one of the very few places where you can have a beer (US$1) or other alcoholic drinks with your meal.

Getting There & Away
There are daily flights to Lamu from Nairobi and Malindi.

Buses leave for Malindi at 7 am. The fare is US$9 and the journey takes about five hours. Book in advance. When coming to Lamu, the buses terminate at the ferry jetty on the mainland not far from Mokowe. From here you take a motorised ferry to Lamu for US$1.

If you do decide to go to Lamu by bus, you should be aware that there is a possibility your bus may be held up by shifta toting AK47s, in which case you'll be robbed or, at worst, robbed and shot. Make enquiries locally as to the current situation before setting off on this route.

LODWAR
The hot and dusty administrative town of Lodwar is the only town of any significance in Kenya's north-west. The town has a post office and a branch of the Kenya Commercial Bank.

Places to Stay
Best of the cheapies is the *Mombasa Hotel*. The friendly Muslim owners charge US$4/6 for singles/doubles. If you have a mosquito net you can sleep in the courtyard. The *Africana Silent Lodge* is also recommended.

Another good option, and the only one for campers, is the *Nawoitorong Guest House* (☎ (0393) 21208). The turn-off is signposted 1km south of Lodwar on the main road, and

from there it's a further 2km. This place, built entirely of local materials, is run by a local women's group. Camping costs US$2 and meals are available. There's also one banda which costs US$5/7, including breakfast.

The *Turkwel Hotel* (☎ (0393) 21201) is the town's social focus and also has the best accommodation. Rooms with fan and bath cost US$6/8.

Getting There & Away
There are daily buses and matatus to Kitale. The trip costs US$7 and takes around seven hours.

Matatus also run from Lodwar to Kalekol near Lake Turkana if demand warrants, but you can't count on them.

MALINDI
Malindi was an important Swahili settlement as far back as the 14th century, and often rivalled Mombasa and Paté for control of this part of the East African coast.

These days, on account of its excellent beaches, it has experienced a tourist boom similar to that north and south of Mombasa, and resort hotels are strung out all the way along the coast. It's a popular port of call for travellers heading north from Mombasa or south from Lamu.

Information
There is a tourist office next door to Kenya Airways, opposite the shopping centre on Harambee Rd. The immigration office is next to the Juma Mosque and pillar tombs on the waterfront.

Warning
Don't walk back along the beach to your hotel at night. Many people have been mugged at knife-point, although these days the beach appears to be safer. Go back along the main road (which has lighting) or take a taxi.

Things to See & Do
The most popular place to visit is the **Malindi Marine National Park**, south of town, where you can rent a glass-bottomed boat to take

KENYA

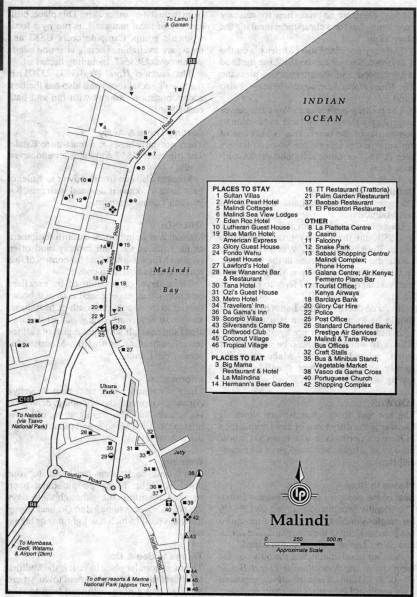

To Lamu & Garsen

B8

To Lamu & Garsen

INDIAN

OCEAN

Lamu Road

Harambee Road

Malindi Bay

Uhuru Park

C103

To Nairobi (via Tsavo National Park)

B8

Tourist Road

Jetty

To Mombasa, Gedi, Watamu & Airport (2km)

Tourist Road

To other resorts & Marine National Park (approx 1km)

PLACES TO STAY
1 Sultan Villas
2 African Pearl Hotel
5 Malindi Cottages
6 Malindi Sea View Lodges
7 Eden Roc Hotel
10 Lutheran Guest House
19 Blue Marlin Hotel;
    American Express
23 Glory Guest House
24 Fondo Wehu
    Guest House
27 Lawford's Hotel
28 New Wananchi Bar
    & Restaurant
30 Tana Hotel
31 Ozi's Guest House
33 Metro Hotel
34 Travellers' Inn
36 Da Gama's Inn
39 Scorpio Villas
43 Silversands Camp Site
44 Driftwood Club
45 Coconut Village
46 Tropical Village

PLACES TO EAT
3 Big Mama
   Restaurant & Hotel
4 La Malindina
14 Hermann's Beer Garden

16 TT Restaurant (Trattoria)
21 Palm Garden Restaurant
37 Baobab Restaurant
41 El Pescatori Restaurant

OTHER
8 La Piattetta Centre
9 Casino
11 Falconry
12 Snake Park
13 Sabaki Shopping Centre/
    Malindi Complex;
    Phone Home
15 Galana Centre; Air Kenya;
    Fermento Piano Bar
17 Tourist Office;
    Kenya Airways
18 Barclays Bank
20 Glory Car Hire
22 Police
25 Post Office
26 Standard Chartered Bank;
    Prestige Air Services
29 Malindi & Tana River
    Bus Offices
32 Craft Stalls
35 Bus & Minibus Stand;
    Vegetable Market
38 Vasco da Gama Cross
40 Portuguese Church
42 Shopping Complex

Malindi

0   250   500 m

Approximate Scale

you out to the coral reef. The variety and colours of coral and fish are simply amazing. Snorkelling gear is provided. People come around the hotels to ask if you are interested in going. The usual price is US$11 per person, which includes a taxi to/from your hotel, hire of the boat and the park entry fee (US$5).

Places to Stay
By far the best place is the *Fondo Wehu Guest House* (☎ (0123) 30017), about 15 minutes walk from the bus station. You may need to ask directions, as it can be a little hard to find. Beds in the airy upstairs dorm cost US$4, and comfortable singles/doubles cost US$6/9. The price includes an excellent breakfast and free laundry service. Tasty snacks are also available.

Next best is probably *Ozi's Guest House* (☎ (0123) 20318) close to the foreshore. Rooms, each with fan and mosquito net, cost US$6/11, including breakfast.

Another popular place is the *Silversands Camp Site* (☎ (0123) 20412), 2km south of the town centre along the coast road. It costs US$2 per person to camp here, but there is very little shade. The Silversands also has bandas for rent from US$5 to US$8 per double.

For mid-range accommodation try the *Malindi Cottages* (☎ (0123) 20304) out on Lamu Rd, close to the Eden Roc Hotel. There are several fully furnished cottages with attached bathroom surrounding a swimming pool. Each cottage sleeps up to five adults and costs US$27 per night.

You can get hot showers and also use the swimming pool, bar and restaurant at the *Driftwood Club* (near the Silversands Camp Site on the coast road) by paying US$2 for temporary membership.

Places to Eat
Excellent value is the *Palm Garden* on Harambee Rd, opposite the petrol station. Also worth visiting for its excellent milk shakes and fruit juices is the *Malindi Fruit Juice Garden* on the Lamu road near the casino.

It's possible to get fish & chips for around US$4 and the cheapest cold beer in town at US$1 from the *Baobab Restaurant* on Vasco da Gama Rd.

Not far from the Baobab is *El Pescatori Pizzeria & Grill Bar*, which is worth checking out for lunch and dinner if you like pizza or spaghetti.

Entertainment
The most famous bar/disco is the *Stardust Club*, which generally doesn't get started until late (10 or 11 pm) and costs US$4 entry (more on Saturday night).

The liveliest tourist bar is the makuti-roofed *Hermann's Beer Garden*. Also fairly popular is the *Fermento Piano Bar* on the top floor of the shopping centre diagonally opposite the Sabaki Centre.

Getting There & Away
There are several buses daily in either direction between Mombasa and Malindi. The trip costs US$1 and takes about 2½ hours. Matatus also do this run.

There are two Faza Express buses to Lamu daily from Malindi (KSh 300). They leave from outside the New Safari Hotel in the centre of town at 8.30 am. There's no booking office so just turn up. These buses originate in Mombasa so they're usually pretty full on arrival and a writhing mass of humanity on departure. It's a lousy eight hour journey if you're lucky; 11 hours if you're unlucky.

MARALAL
Maralal is high up in the hills above the Lerochi Plateau (essentially a continuation of the central highlands), north of Nyahururu and Nanyuki, north-west of Isiolo, and connected to all these towns by gravel roads.

It's an attractive area of grassy undulating plains and coniferous forests. The town itself, while a regional centre, retains a decidedly frontier atmosphere. The main attraction is the **Camel Derby** which takes place here in October.

Places to Stay
The best place is the popular *Yare Club & Campsite* (☎ (0368) 2295), 3km south of

town on the Isiolo to Nyahururu road. You have a choice of camping for US$4 or renting a banda with attached bathroom for US$15/20 a single/double.

In Maralal itself, the most popular place is the *Buffalo Lodge* (☎ (0368) 2228), a fairly modern structure offering rooms with clean sheets, towels and hot water (in the mornings) for US$7 a single or double.

Cheaper and excellent value is the *Kimaniki Boarding & Lodging*, a two storey wooden place offering good rooms for US$2/3.

Getting There & Away

Nissan minibuses travel between Maralal and Nyahururu via Rumuruti on a daily basis, usually in the morning. The trip costs US$4 and takes four to five hours.

Between Maralal and Isiolo there are no direct buses or matatus. To get between the two towns you must first take a bus or matatu to Wamba and change there. Between Wamba and Isiolo there are many matatus and regular buses every day. The cost is US$2 and the journey takes about one hour.

MARSABIT

East of Lake Turkana and north of Isiolo, Marsabit is set in a spectacularly beautiful area at the base of Mt Marsabit (1702m), among thickly forested hills which stand in stark contrast to the desert on all sides.

One of the most memorable sights in Marsabit is the colourful mix of tribespeople you'll see thronging the roads into town. They are the major non-Muslim people in what is otherwise a largely Muslim area.

The **Marsabit National Park & Reserve**, the main focus of interest here, is home to a wide variety of larger mammals. National park fees apply.

Places to Stay

Few camp sites in Kenya would rival the one at Lake Paradise, although there are no facilities (except lake water and firewood). A ranger must be present when you camp here. It costs US$10 per person and only one group can camp at a time, but you can arrange all this at the park entrance gate.

There's also the expensive *Marsabit Lodge* (☎ (0183) 2044).

If you have no camping equipment there's a good choice of lodges in the town of Marsabit. One of the best is the *Marsabit Highway Hotel*. It's very clean and pleasant, and rooms cost US$5 a double.

Getting There & Away

Mwingi buses run irregularly from Marsabit south to Isiolo (US$6). All vehicles, including buses travelling between Marsabit and Isiolo or Marsabit and Moyale, must travel in convoy.

MOMBASA

Mombasa is the largest port on the coast of East Africa. It has a population of nearly half a million, of which about 70% are African, the rest being mainly Asian with a small minority of Europeans. Mombasa's docks serve not only Kenya but also Uganda, Rwanda and Burundi. The bulk of the town sprawls over Mombasa Island, which is connected to the mainland by a causeway which carries the rail and road links.

To a large extent the city has retained its traditional character; there are few high-rise buildings. The old town, between the massive, Portuguese-built Fort Jesus and the old dhow dock, remains much the same as it was in the mid-19th century.

Information

The tourist office (☎ (011) 311231) is just past the giant tusks which arch over Moi Ave. It has a good map of Mombasa for sale, but otherwise is of little help to budget travellers.

Things to See

The old town's biggest attraction is **Fort Jesus**, which dominates the harbour entrance. Begun in 1593 by the Portuguese, it changed hands nine times between 1631 and 1875. These days it's a museum, and is open daily from 8.30 am to 6 pm. Entry to the fort costs US$4 and includes admission to the museum.

Though its history goes back centuries, most of the houses in the **old town** are no

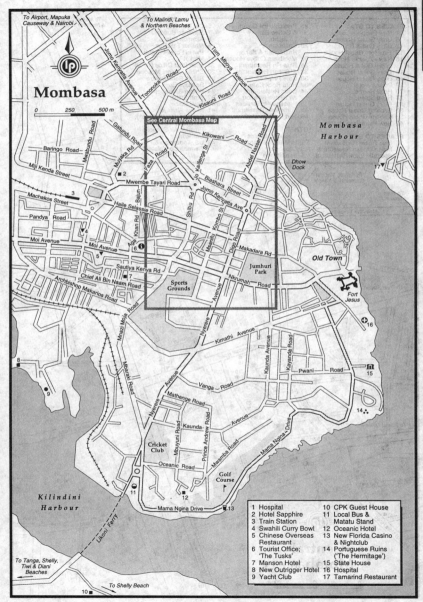

Mombasa

0   250   500 m

To Airport, Mapuka
Causeway & Nairobi

To Malindi, Lamu
& Northern Beaches

*Mombasa
Harbour*

Dhow
Dock

Old Town

Jumhuri
Park

Sports
Grounds

Fort
Jesus

*Kilindini
Harbour*

Cricket
Club

Golf
Course

To Tanga, Shelly,
Tiwi & Diani
Beaches

To Shelly Beach

1 Hospital
2 Hotel Sapphire
3 Train Station
4 Swahili Curry Bowl
5 Chinese Overseas
   Restaurant
6 Tourist Office;
   'The Tusks'
7 Manson Hotel
8 New Outrigger Hotel
9 Yacht Club
10 CPK Guest House
11 Local Bus &
   Matatu Stand
12 Oceanic Hotel
13 New Florida Casino
   & Nightclub
14 Portuguese Ruins
   ('The Hermitage')
15 State House
16 Hospital
17 Tamarind Restaurant

KENYA

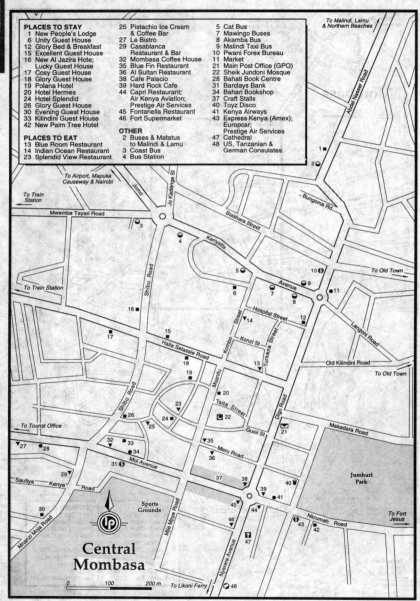

PLACES TO STAY
1 New People's Lodge
6 Unity Guest House
12 Glory Bed & Breakfast
15 Excellent Guest House
16 New Al Jazira Hote;
     Lucky Guest House
17 Cosy Guest House
18 Glory Guest House
19 Polana Hotel
20 Hotel Hermes
24 Hotel Splendid
26 Glory Guest House
30 Evening Guest House
33 Kilindini Guest House
42 New Palm Tree Hotel

PLACES TO EAT
13 Blue Room Restaurant
14 Indian Ocean Restaurant
23 Splendid View Restaurant

25 Pistachio Ice Cream
     & Coffee Bar
27 Le Bistro
29 Casablanca
     Restaurant & Bar
32 Mombasa Coffee House
35 Blue Fin Restaurant
36 Al Sultan Restaurant
38 Cafe Palacio
39 Hard Rock Cafe
44 Capri Restaurant;
     Air Kenya Aviation;
     Prestige Air Services
45 Fontanella Restaurant
46 Fort Supermarket

OTHER
2 Buses & Matatus
    to Malindi & Lamu
3 Coast Bus
4 Bus Station

5 Cat Bus
7 Mawingo Buses
8 Akamba Bus
9 Malindi Taxi Bus
10 Pwani Forex Bureau
11 Market
21 Main Post Office (GPO)
22 Sheik Jundoni Mosque
28 Bahati Book Centre
31 Barclays Bank
34 Bahari Bookshop
37 Craft Stalls
40 Toyz Disco
41 Kenya Airways
43 Express Kenya (Amex);
     Europcar;
     Prestige Air Services
47 Cathedral
48 US, Tanzanian &
     German Consulates

To Malindi, Lamu
& Northern Beaches

Abdel Nasser Road

To Train Station

Mwembe Tayari Road

Jomo Jo Kadenge St

To Airport, Mapuka Causeway & Nairobi

Bungoma Rd

Blashara Street

Kenyatta

To Old Town

Avenue

To Train Station

Shibu Road

Hospital Street

Langoni Road

Street

Konzi St

Kombo

Turkana Street

Old Kilindini Road

To Old Town

Haile Selassie Road

Msanliu

Digo Road

To Tourist Office

Shibu Road

Taita Street

Gusii St

Makadara Road

Moi Avenue

Meru Road

Jumhuri Park

Sautiya

Kenya Road

Mji Moye Road

Sports Grounds

Mnarzi Moja Road

Nyerere Avenue

Nkrumah Road

To Fort Jesus

Central Mombasa

0   100   200 m

To Likoni Ferry

To Fort Jesus

more than 100 years old. However, you'll come across the occasional one which dates back to the first half of the 19th century. The combination of styles and traditions includes the long-established coastal Swahili architecture commonly found in Lamu, various late-19th century Indian styles and British colonial style. There are many examples of the massive, intricately carved doors and door frames characteristic of Swahili houses in Lamu and Zanzibar, as well as fine balconies with beautiful fret and lattice work.

Places to Stay

Mombasa has chronic water problems, so there's no guarantee of getting a daily shower at any of the cheaper places.

A reasonable bet and popular with travellers is the *Cosy Guest House* (☎ (011) 313064) on Haile Selassie Rd, though we have had reports that the owner hassles women. It costs US$5/7 for singles/doubles with shared facilities. The guesthouse will most likely be full if you arrive late in the day.

Just around the corner on Shibu Rd is the *New Al Jazira Hotel*, which has doubles with balcony and shared bath (no fan) for US$5.

Another budget hotel in the town centre, and one which has been popular for years, is the *New People's Lodge* (☎ (011) 312831) on Abdel Nasser Rd, right next to where the buses leave for Malindi and Lamu. Rooms cost US$3/5 with shared showers and toilets, and US$4/7 with private facilities. There's a good, cheap restaurant downstairs.

An excellent value mid-range place is the *Excellent Guest House* (☎ (011) 311744) on Haile Selassie Rd. It offers bed and breakfast in rooms with attached bathroom, towel, soap, toilet paper, mosquito net and fan for US$13/17.

Places to Eat

If you are just looking for fish or chicken with chips try the *Blue Room Restaurant* on Haile Selassie Rd. The *Mombasa Coffee House* on Moi Ave is a good place for fresh coffee and snacks, and you can also buy coffee beans here.

Since many of the restaurants in Mombasa are Indian-owned, you can find excellent curries and thalis, and at lunch time many places offer a cheap, substantial set meal.

One such place is the popular *New Chetna Restaurant* on Haile Selassie Rd, directly under the Cosy Guest House. The food here is south Indian vegetarian (with dishes such as masala dosa and idli) and sweets. An all-you-can-eat set vegetarian lunch costs US$3.

Excellent tandoori specialities can be had at the very popular *Splendid View Restaurant* on Maungano Rd.

For coastal Swahili dishes, the *Recoda Restaurant* on Nyeri St in the old town is recommended. It's a hugely popular place with locals and the tables are set up along the footpath.

Those keen to dine in an atmosphere far removed from Kenya should try the *Hard Rock Cafe*, Nkrumah Rd, next door to Kenya Airways.

Entertainment

The most popular and lively rendezvous is the *Casablanca Restaurant & Bar* on Mnazi Moja Rd just off Moi Ave. This open-air, two storey, makuti-roofed venue is always thronged with an interesting and garrulous collection of westerners, Asians and Africans from early morning until very late.

The best nightclub/disco is the *New Florida Casino & Nightclub* on Mama Ngina Drive.

Things to Buy

There are a lot of craft stalls along Msanifu Kombo St near the junction with Moi Ave, along Moi Ave itself from the Castle Hotel down to the roundabout with Nyerere Ave, and along Jomo Kenyatta Ave close to the junction with Digo Road. Bargain hard.

Biashara St, west of Digo Rd, is the centre for fabrics and *kangas*, those colourful, beautifully patterned wraparound skirts.

Getting There & Away

The bus offices are mainly along Jomo Kenyatta Ave. For Nairobi, there are many buses departing daily in either direction (mostly in the early morning and late evening). The fare is US$5 and the trip takes seven to eight hours.

There are also many departures daily to Malindi. Buses take up to three hours, matatus about two hours. They all depart from outside the New People's Hotel, Abdel Nasser Rd.

There are regular ferries to Zanzibar. See the earlier Kenya Getting There & Away section for details.

Getting Around

A regular public bus runs the 13km to the airport, leaving from the Kenya Airways office on Nkrumah Rd. Any 'Port Reitz' matatu will take you past the airport turn-off (ask to be dropped off), from where it's about a 10 minute walk. The standard taxi fare is US$13.

To get to the beaches south of Mombasa, you must first take the Likoni Ferry from Mombasa Island to the southern mainland. The ferry runs at frequent intervals throughout the night and day. To get to the ferry from the centre of town take a Likoni matatu from outside the post office on Digo Rd.

NAIVASHA

There's very little of interest in the town of Naivasha itself. A small service centre for the surrounding agricultural district, it's a good place to stock up with supplies if you're planning a sojourn by Lake Naivasha (see the earlier Lake Naivasha section).

Places to Stay & Eat

The *Naivasha Super Lodge* has no doubles but the single beds are large enough for a couple; at US$3 these are not bad value.

For more salubrious lodgings, head for the *Naivasha Silver Hotel* on Kenyatta Ave, which has rooms with attached bathroom and hot water for US$5/7 a single/double. There's an upstairs bar and restaurant.

If you appreciate good food, there's essentially only one place to eat in Naivasha, *La Belle Inn*. While not dirt cheap, it's not too expensive, and the food is excellent.

NAKURU

Kenya's fourth largest town is the centre of a rich farming area about halfway between Nairobi and Kisumu on the main road and railway line to Uganda. The big draw for travellers is the nearby **Lake Nakuru National Park** with its prolific birdlife. The **Menengai Crater** and the **Hyrax Hill Prehistoric Site** in the immediate area are both worth a visit.

Places to Stay

The *Amigos Guest House* on Gusil Rd is a very friendly place. Singles/doubles with shared facilities cost US$4/5.

Right in the centre of town is the *Shik Parkview Hotel* (☎ (037) 212345) on the corner of Kenyatta Ave and Bondoni Rd. Rooms cost US$4/7 with breakfast. The rooms overlooking Kenyatta Ave are noisy. Its main attraction is its proximity to the bus and train stations.

Going up in price, an excellent choice is the *Mukoh Hotel* (☎ (037) 213516) on the corner of Mosque and Gusil Rds. Clean and comfortable rooms with private bath cost US$5/8.

Places to Eat

The best place to eat is the *Tipsy Restaurant* on Gusil Rd. Dishes include Indian curries, western food and lake fish.

Getting There & Away

Frequent matatus and buses run to Nairobi (US$3), Naivasha (US$2) and other places to the west.

NARO MORU

The village of Naro Moru on the western side of the mountain is the most popular starting-point for treks on Mt Kenya. There's a post office here but no banks (the nearest are at Nanyuki and Nyeri).

Places to Stay

There are a couple of basic lodges in the village, the *Naro Moru 82 Bar & Restaurant* and the *Mountain View Lodge*, but hardly anyone stays at them.

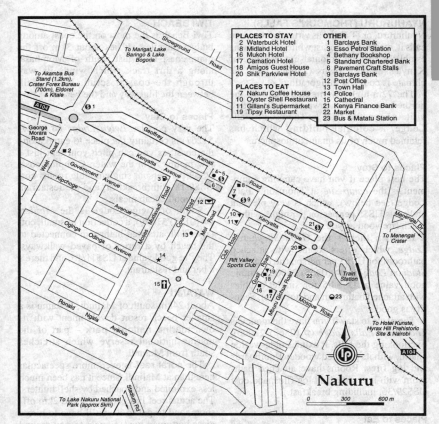

PLACES TO STAY
2 Waterbuck Hotel
8 Midland Hotel
16 Mukoh Hotel
17 Carnation Hotel
18 Amigos Guest House
20 Shik Parkview Hotel

PLACES TO EAT
7 Nakuru Coffee House
10 Oyster Shell Restaurant
11 Gillani's Supermarket
19 Tipsy Restaurant

OTHER
1 Barclays Bank
3 Esso Petrol Station
4 Bethany Bookshop
5 Standard Chartered Bank
6 Pavement Craft Stalls
9 Barclays Bank
12 Post Office
13 Town Hall
14 Police
15 Cathedral
21 Kenya Finance Bank
22 Market
23 Bus & Matatu Station

Nakuru

0   300   600 m

If you're an independent traveller and intent on scaling the summit, think seriously about walking 12km and staying at the *Mt Kenya Hostel & Campsite* on the way to the start of the Naro Moru trail. You can camp here for US$3 or take a bed for US$4.

Just outside the entrance to the hostel is the *Mountain Stop Motel*, which has camping for US$3 and 10 bandas (doubles) for US$5 per banda.

Most people staying in Naro Moru head off to the *Naro Moru River Lodge* (☎ (0176) 62622), which is about 1.5km off to the left down a gravel track from the main Nairobi

to Nanyuki road. It's essentially a top-end place, but it does have a well-equipped camp for US$4 per person per night. There are also dormitory bunkhouses where a bed costs US$6. The main reason for coming to this lodge is to book and pay for any of the mountain huts you might want to stay in along the Naro Moru trail.

Getting There & Away
The plentiful buses and matatus that travel from Nairobi and Nyeri to Nanyuki and Isiolo will drop you off in Naro Moru.

NYAHURURU (THOMSON'S FALLS)

Nyahururu, or 'T Falls' as virtually everyone calls it, was one of the last white settler towns established in the colonial era. It's one of Kenya's highest towns (2360m), and the climate is cool and invigorating.

The 72m-high **Thomson's Falls** on the northern outskirts of town are well worth a visit. Above the falls is Thomson's Falls Lodge, a colonial building which has retained much of its quaint atmosphere.

Places to Stay

The best place if you have camping equipment is the *camp site* at Thomson's Falls Lodge (see below), which is very pleasant and costs US$5 per person per night, with as much firewood as you need.

In town there's the *Good Shepherd's Lodge*, which offers rooms with attached bathroom for US$3 per person (no doubles). *Stadium Lodging* (☎ (0365) 22002) is quite good value at US$4/5 for singles/doubles with attached bathroom and hot water. Security is good.

The place to stay if you have the money is *Thomson's Falls Lodge* (☎ (0365) 22006), overlooking the falls. It exudes olde-worlde charm, with its polished wooden floorboards and log fires. Rooms have attached bathroom with hot water and log fires, and cost US$29/36, including breakfast.

Places to Eat

Meals at the *Baron Hotel* are excellent value. For local colour and a barbecued meal, try the *Tropical Bar & Restaurant* around the corner from the Baron Hotel.

For a minor splurge eat at *Thomson's Falls Lodge*, which has an open-air grill at lunch time. The lodge also has the most interesting bar in town (and one of the liveliest).

Getting There & Away

There are buses and matatus throughout the day until late afternoon to/from Nakuru (US$2), Nyeri (US$3), Nairobi (US$4), Nanyuki, Thika, Kericho, Isiolo and Maralal.

TIWI BEACH

Tiwi Beach is the most on the coast among budget travellers. It lies about 3km off the main coast road just south of Mombasa, along a dirt track which winds its way through the coastal scrub. Don't walk between the highway and the beach.

Places to Stay

The very popular *Twiga Lodge* (☎ (0127) 51267) is certainly *the* place to camp along the coast, as you can pitch your tent just a few metres from the water. Camping costs US$2 per person, single/double rooms cost US$9/18 with breakfast, and the restaurant does good cheap meals.

South of Twiga Lodge is the *Minilets* (☎ (0127) 51059), a collection of small, cottages with attached bathroom connected to the beach by a series of paved walkways. They're good value at US$11/15, and there's a bar and restaurant.

WATAMU

About 24km south of Malindi, Watamu is a smaller beach resort development with its own **marine national park** – part of the marine national reserve which stretches south from Malindi.

The **coral reef** is even more spectacular here than at Malindi, since it has been much less exploited and poached by shell hunters. The actual reef lies between 1 and 2km offshore, and to get to it you'll have to hire a glass-bottomed boat. Expect to pay around US$20 per person.

A few kilometres from Watamu are the famous, eerie **Gedi ruins**, one of the principal historical monuments on the coast. Though the ruins are extensive, this Arab-Swahili town is something of a mystery since it's not mentioned in any of the Portuguese or Arab chronicles of the time. Take a matatu to Gedi village; the ruins are about a 1km signposted walk.

Places to Stay

The two cheap lodges in Watamu village are a bit grim. Much better is the family-run *Villa Veronica/Mwikali Lodge* (☎ (0122) 32083).

This very friendly and secure place offers clean rooms with fan, mosquito net, shower and toilet for US$11/15 a single/double, including breakfast.

The *Watamu Cottages* (☎ (0122) 32211), on the main access road to the village and a hot 15 minute walk, are a good deal at US$14 for a double with bath, including breakfast. The rooms are set in a pleasant garden which also has a swimming pool.

Places to Eat

Friend's Corner is a small duka (shop) on the road between the Come Back Club and Villa Veronica. It has about the best cheap food in town, although the variety is limited.

Hotel Dante is probably the best of the non-resort restaurants. The service is slow, but there's warm beer and a jukebox to distract you while you're waiting.

Getting There & Away

Regular buses run between Watamu and Malindi.

National Parks & Reserves

ABERDARE NATIONAL PARK

This relatively little-visited park essentially encloses the moorland and high forest of the Kinangop plateau, and is often closed during the wet season.

Although there are a number of animals in the park – the rare bongo, black leopard, elephant and rhino – they can be difficult to spot because of the dense forest country. On top of this, there is no cheap accommodation (apart from a couple of basic camp sites), no public transport, hitching is virtually impossible and, as elsewhere, walking requires special permission, so the park is essentially out of reach for anyone without their own transport.

If you wish to camp in the park, reservations must be made at the park headquarters

at Mweiga (☎ (0171) 55024). The charges are standard.

AMBOSELI NATIONAL PARK

Amboseli is the next most popular park after Masai Mara, mainly because of the spectacular backdrop of Africa's highest peak, Mt Kilimanjaro.

Probably the best reason for visiting Amboseli is that you stand the greatest chance of spotting a black rhino. Amboseli also has huge herds of elephant, and to see a herd making its way sedately across the grassy plains, with Kilimanjaro in the background, may be a real African cliche but it is an experience which leaves a lasting impression.

Places to Stay

The only budget accommodation is a *camp site* right on the southern boundary of the park. The only facilities are a couple of long-drop toilets and a kiosk which sells warm beer and sodas, and accepts the payment of camping fees (US$8 per person). The water supply is extremely unreliable, so bring some with you.

LAKE BARINGO NATIONAL PARK

Lake Baringo is a deep freshwater lake north of Nakuru. Although the lake supports many different species of land and aquatic birdlife as well as crocodiles and herds of hippos, the main attraction is the birdlife. The lake is the bird-watching centre of Kenya: of Kenya's 1200 different species of birds, more than 450 have been sighted at Lake Baringo.

Places to Stay

At *Robert's Camp* (☎ Kampi-ya-Samaki 3 – through the operator) you can camp for US$4 per person per night, with bundles of firewood for US$1. There are also bandas with use of cooking facilities for US$11 per person plus 15% tax – demand is heavy at times, so book in advance (PO Box 1051, Nakuru).

Alternatively, try the basic *Bahari Lodge* in the nearby village of Kampi-ya-Samaki.

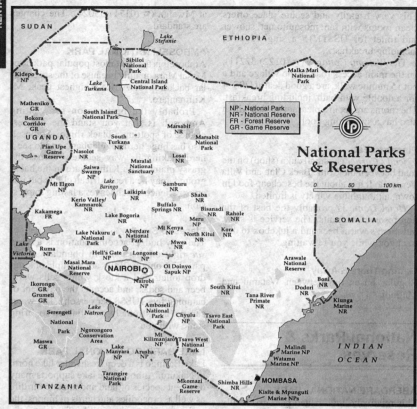

National Parks & Reserves

NP - National Park
NR - National Reserve
FR - Forest Reserve
GR - Game Reserve

0   50   100 km

Getting There & Away

There are three buses per day in either direction between Kampi-ya-Samaki and Nakuru (US$1), as well as a number of matatus (US$2) and Nissan minibuses. The journey takes between 1½ and two hours.

LAKE NAKURU NATIONAL PARK

Like most of the other Rift Valley lakes, Lake Nakuru is a shallow soda lake. Here you will (hopefully) see thousands of flamingo and other birds. Recently, however, the water level has been so low that most of the birds have gone elsewhere.

Nakuru National Park is also home to Rhino Rescue, an organisation set up in 1986 specifically to save the rhino. The park is protected by a 74km electric fence with guard posts every 15km.

The main national park entrance is about 6km from the centre of Nakuru, and the entry fee is US$27 per person per day.

Places to Stay

A good camp site, known as the *Backpackers' Camp Site*, is just inside the park gate. Fresh water is available and there are a couple of pit toilets. Close your tents

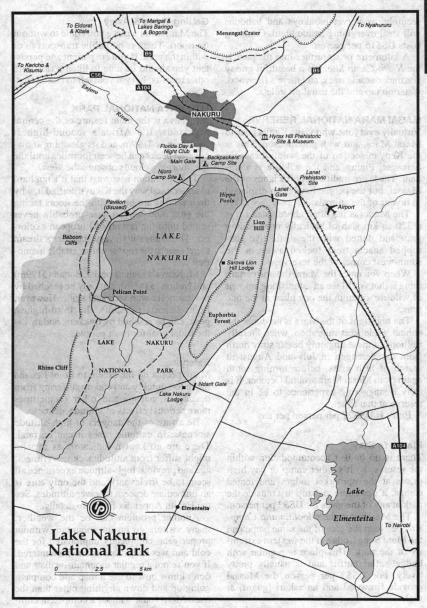

Lake Nakuru National Park

To Eldoret & Kitale

To Marigat & Lakes Baringo & Bogoria

Menengal Crater

To Nyahururu

B5

NAKURU

To Kericho & Kisumu

C56

A104

Njoro River

Hyrax Hill Prehistoric Site & Museum

Florida Day & Night Club

Backpackers' Camp Site

Main Gate

Njoro Camp Site

Lanet Prehistoric Site

Lanet Gate

Airport

Pavilion (disused)

Hippo Pools

Lion Hill

Baboon Cliffs

LAKE NAKURU

Sarova Lion Hill Lodge

Pelican Point

Euphorbia Forest

LAKE NAKURU NATIONAL PARK

Rhino Cliff

Ndarit Gate

Lake Nakuru Lodge

A104

Lake Elmenteita

To Nairobi

Elmenteita

0   2.5   5 km

securely, as vervet monkeys and baboons will steal everything inside them. Camping costs US$15 per person.

A kilometre or so further into the park is the *Njoro Camp Site*. It's a beautiful grassy site under acacia trees, and there's firewood, water on tap and the usual pit toilets.

MASAI MARA NATIONAL RESERVE

Virtually everyone who visits Kenya goes to Masai Mara, and with good reason. This is the Kenyan section of the wildly beautiful Serengeti Plains, and the wildlife is abundant. These are traditionally the lands of the Maasai, but the people have been displaced in favour of the animals.

The Mara (as it's often abbreviated to) is a 320-sq-km slab of basically open rolling grassland dotted with the distinctive flat-topped acacia trees tucked away in the south-west corner of the reserve.

When you enter the Mara, the one certain thing is that you'll see an astonishing amount of wildlife, often in the one place at the one time.

The highlight of the Mara is no doubt the annual wildebeest migration, when literally millions of these ungainly beasts stray north from the Serengeti in July and August in search of lush grass, before turning south again from Masai Mara around October. It is truly a staggering experience to be in the reserve at that time.

Entry is US$27 per person per day.

Places to Stay

There is no budget accommodation within the reserve, so it's either camp or pay high prices at the upmarket lodges and tented camps. It's possible to camp just outside the park at any of the gates for US$3 per person.

The Maasai run the *Oloolaimutia Campsite*, between the gate of the same name and the Mara Sopa Lodge at the western extremity of the park. This place is popular with budget-safari outfits and is usually pretty lively. For US$3 per person the Maasai provide firewood and an askari (guard) at night.

Getting There & Away

The Mara is not a place you come to without transport. There is no public transport to or within the park. If you are patient and persistent you should be able to hitch a ride with other tourists, but get yourself to Narok first.

MT KENYA NATIONAL PARK

Mt Kenya is the main feature of the central highlands. It's Africa's second-highest mountain at 5199m, and its gleaming snow-covered peaks can be seen for miles until the late-morning clouds obscure the view.

This mountain is so vast that it's not hard to understand why the Kikuyu deified it, why their houses are built with the doors facing the peak and why it was probably never scaled until the arrival of European explorers. These days it's every traveller's dream to get near to the top for unforgettable memories.

Mt Kenya's highest peaks, Batian (5199m) and Nelion (5188m), can only be reached by mountaineers with technical skills. However, Point Lenana (4985m), the third-highest peak, can be reached by trekkers, and this is the usual goal for most people.

Safety

Many people do the ascent to Point Lenana much too quickly and end up suffering from headaches, nausea and other (sometimes more serious) effects of altitude sickness.

Be aware of the dangers of high-altitude sickness. In extreme cases it can be fatal. There are no known indicators as to who might suffer from altitude sickness (fitness, age and previous high-altitude experience all seem to be irrelevant), and the only cure is an immediate descent to lower altitudes. See the Health Appendix for more details.

Another problem can be the weather; many visitors go up the mountain without proper gear, completely unprepared for the cold and wet conditions often encountered. If you're not a regular mountain-walker and don't know how to use a map and compass, going up and down anything other than the Naro Moru route without a competent companion or a local guide is simply asking for trouble.

The best times to go, as far as fair weather is concerned, are from mid-January to late February and from late August to September.

Books & Maps

Before you leave Nairobi we strongly recommend that you buy a copy of *Mt Kenya 1:50,000 Map & Guide* by Mark Savage & Andrew Wielochowski. This contains everything most trekkers will need to know.

For keen trekkers looking for more information, or for details on wilder routes and some of the more esoteric variations that are possible on Mt Kenya, get hold of Lonely Planet's *Trekking in East Africa* by David Else.

Clothing & Equipment

You will need a good sleeping bag, a closed-cell foam mat if you are going to sleep on the ground, a good set of warm clothes, headgear and gloves, waterproof clothing, a decent pair of boots or good quality joggers, and a pair of thongs, sandals or spare pair of shoes. If you intend to camp you'll need a tent and associated equipment.

You'll also need a stove, basic cooking equipment and a water container with a capacity of at least one litre per person, as well as water-purifying tablets for use on the lower levels of the mountain. Except in an emergency, using wood gathered from the vicinity of camp sites to light open fires is prohibited within the confines of the national park.

Equipment Hire

Trekking gear can be hired in Nairobi at Atul's (☎ (02) 225935), Biashara St, PO Box 43202; or at Mountain Rock Hotel (☎ (0176) 62625); or Naro Moru River Lodge (☎ (0176) 22018), both at the mouth of the mountain.

Park Fees

Entry fees to the national park are US$10 per day. If you take a guide and/or porters, you'll have to pay their entry fees too (these are US$3 per person per night). Camping fees are an additional US$8 per person per night.

Guides & Porters

Guides, porters and cooks can be engaged at the Naro Moru River Lodge, the Mountain Rock Hotel, the Mt Kenya Hostel or through the Naro Moru Porters & Guides Association (☎ (0176) 6205), PO Naro Moru.

Mt Kenya Route

The three main routes are Naro Moru, Sirimon and Chogoria. The detail we give here is not enough for trekking safely on the mountain – if you're planning to do a trek, get full information from the sources listed above under Guides & Porters.

Naro Moru Route This is the most straightforward and popular of the routes. It's also the least scenic, although it's still a spectacular and very enjoyable trail. You should allow a minimum of four days return, or three days if you have transport between Naro Moru and the Met Station.

Sirimon Route This is the least used of the three main routes, but the driest. It is also the longest approach to Point Lenana, and involves some serious sections of trekking. If you are inexperienced in high mountain conditions, don't attempt this route without a local guide. You should allow a minimum of five days to undertake this trek.

Chogoria Route This route, from the eastern side of the mountain, is undoubtedly the most beautiful of the access routes to the summit and certainly the easiest as far as gradients go. This is a good route if you have a tent and some trekking experience.

Organised Treks

Naro Moru River Lodge (☎ (0176) 22018) does a range of trips, which cost from US$174 per person in a group of eight.

Mountain Rock Hotel (☎ (0176) 62625), between Naro Moru and Nanyuki, also offers a range of organised treks, with some good bargains for travellers.

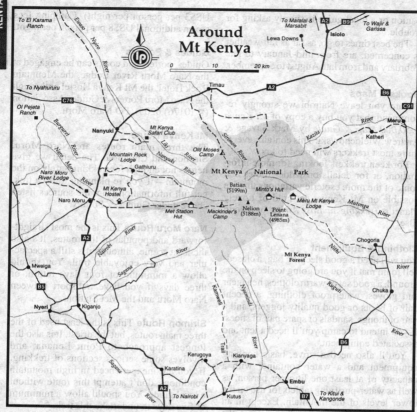

Around Mt Kenya

Places to Stay
There are various huts and bunkhouses on the main routes, so it's possible to stay in them, or you can carry your own equipment and camp. Contact the Naro Moru River Lodge (☎ (0176) 22018) for details of hut fees on the mountain.

NORTHERN GAME RESERVES
Just north of Isiolo there are three national reserves, **Samburu National Reserve**, **Buffalo Springs National Reserve** and **Shaba National Reserve**, each along the banks of the Ewaso Nyiro River and cover-

ing an area of some 300 sq km. The land is mainly scrub desert and open savannah plain, broken here and there by small rugged hills.

The roads inside Buffalo Springs and Samburu are well maintained and it's easy to get around even in a 2WD, though you might need a 4WD on some of the minor tracks.

Entry to each of the three reserves costs US$27 per person per day, plus US$4 for a vehicle per day.

Places to Stay
Buffalo Springs There are four public *camp*

sites close to the Gare Mara entrance gate. However, none of them is particularly safe as far as robberies go. Camping costs US$2.50 per person per night.

For those with adequate finances, there's the *Buffalo Springs Tented Lodge* (☎ (0165) 2234) up at the north-eastern end of the reserve just south of the Ewaso Nyiro River.

Samburu The most convenient places to stay are the public *camp sites* close to the Samburu Lodge and to the wooden bridge which connects the western extremity of Buffalo Springs to Samburu across the Ewaso Nyiro River. Camping costs US$2.50 per person per night.

For those with money, there's four top-range lodges/tented camps, including the *Samburu Lodge*, which has cottages with attached bathroom beside the river. You can also get petrol and organise game drives here.

TSAVO NATIONAL PARK
At just under 20,000 sq km, Tsavo is the largest national park in Kenya. For administrative purposes it has been split into Tsavo West National Park, with an area of 8500 sq km, and Tsavo East National Park, which covers 11,000 sq km. Tsavo West is the more popular and accessible of the two.

Tsavo West National Park
The focus here is the watering holes by the Kilaguni and Ngulia lodges. The **Mzima Springs** are not far from Kilaguni Lodge, and the pools here are favourite haunts of both hippo and crocodile.

Also in the area of the lodges is the spectacular **Shaitani lava flow** and **caves**. The **Chaimu Crater**, south of Kilaguni Lodge, can be climbed.

Places to Stay Tsavo West has a number of *camp sites* at the Tsavo, Mtito Andei and Chyulu gates.

The self-service accommodation at the *Ngulia Safari Camp* and the *Kitani Safari Camp* (☎ (02) 340331 in Nairobi for both) is, by park standards, quite cheap at US$9 per person in fully equipped bandas (minimum charge of US$36).

Getting There & Away The main access is through the Mtito Andei Gate on the Mombasa-Nairobi road at the northern end of the park. A further 48km along the main road away from Nairobi is the Tsavo Gate.

From Voi there is access past the expensive Taita Hills and Salt Lick lodges via the Maktau Gate. This road cuts clear across the park, exiting at the Mbuyuni Gate, to Taveta, from where it's possible to cross into Tanzania and the town of Moshi at the foot of Kilimanjaro.

Tsavo East National Park
Tsavo East consists of vast rolling plains with scrubby vegetation. The entire area north of the Galana River (which constitutes the bulk of the park) is off-limits to the general public. The southern third of the park is open to the public and its rolling scrub-covered hills are home to huge herds of elephant, usually covered in red dust.

The **Kanderi Swamp**, not far into the park from the main Voi Gate and park headquarters, is home to a profusion of wildlife.

It's not advisable to bother with this park unless you have a 4WD vehicle.

Places to Stay There are *camp sites* at the Voi Gate, Kanderi Swamp and the *Mukwaju Camp Site* on the Voi River, 50km in from the main gate.

Lesotho

Lesotho (pronounced le-SOO-too) is a mountainous kingdom, surrounded by South Africa. It's worth a visit, but unless you plan to hike (which is a great way to see some spectacular scenery and experience life in traditional villages) there aren't a lot of options for shoestringers. Organised hiking or pony trekking offer the best short introduction.

Facts about the Country

HISTORY

The first people to occupy Lesotho were the original inhabitants of southern Africa, the hunter-gatherer people known as Khoisan. They have left many examples of their rock art in the river valleys. Lesotho was settled by Sotho peoples comparatively recently, possibly as late as the 16th century.

In the early 19th century European traders arrived and they were soon followed by the Voortrekkers (Boer pioneers). On top of this came the disaster of the *difaqane* (forced migration), caused by the violent expansion of the Zulu state. That the loosely organised southern Sotho society survived this period was largely due to the abilities of King Moshoeshoe (pronounced moshesh). His people formed what became known as Basutoland.

As the difaqane receded a new threat arose. The Boers had crossed the Orange River in the 1830s, and by 1843 Moshoeshoe was sufficiently concerned by their numbers to ally himself with the British Cape government. The resulting treaties did little to stop squabbles with the Boers and in 1868 the British government annexed Basutoland.

In 1910 the advisory Basutoland National Council was formed. In the mid-1950s it requested internal self-government from the British, and in 1960 a new constitution was in place and elections were held for a Legis-

lative Council. The main contenders were the Basutholand Congress Party (BCP), similar to South Africa's African National Congress (ANC), and the conservative Basutholand National Party (BNP).

The BCP won the 1960 elections and demanded full independence from Britain. This was eventually agreed to, with independence to come into effect in 1966. However, at the elections in 1965 the BCP lost power to the BNP and Chief Jonathan became the first prime minister of the new Kingdom of Lesotho.

After losing the 1970 election, Jonathan responded by suspending the constitution, expelling the king and banning opposition parties. Jonathan was deposed by the army in 1986 and the king was restored as head of state. This was a popular move, but agitation for democratic reform rose. In 1990 King Moshoeshoe II was deposed by the army in favour of his son, Prince Mohato Bereng Seeisa (Letsie III). Elections in 1993 resulted in the return of the BCP.

In 1995 Letsie III abdicated in favour of his father, who restored calm to Lesotho after a year of unrest. Tragically, less than a year later he was killed when his 4WD plunged over a cliff in the Maluti Mountains. Letsie III is again the king, and while there have been some rumblings in the army and police, most visitors will not notice anything amiss.

Although the king has practically no constitutional powers he is extremely influential, both as an embodiment of traditional culture and as a major player in the country's labyrinthine politics.

GEOGRAPHY & CLIMATE

Lesotho is surrounded by South Africa. The eastern border is the rugged Drakensberg escarpment. All of Lesotho is over 1000m high, with great ranges reaching 3000m in the centre and east of the country.

Winters are cold and clear. Frosts are common and there are snowfalls in the high country, and sometimes down to lower altitudes. In other seasons snow is not unknown, especially on the high peaks, but rain and mist are more often the bugbears of drivers and hikers. Nearly all of the country's rain falls between October and April, with spectacular thunderstorms in summer. Down in the valleys, summer days can be hot with temperatures ranging from 30 to 40°C.

ECOLOGY & ENVIRONMENT

Erosion is a major problem and the already scarce arable land is becoming degraded. Much of the country's food has to be imported.

The huge Highlands Water Project is creating a series of dams on the Orange River in Lesotho, and sales of water and hydroelectricity to South Africa might make Lesotho more economically independent. As with all large-scale dam projects there is an environmental downside, with valleys being flooded and water-courses diverted.

POPULATION & PEOPLE

Lesotho's 2.1 million citizens are known as the Basotho people. Culturally, most belong to the Southern Sotho grouping.

SOCIETY & CONDUCT
Traditional Culture

Traditional culture consists largely of the customs, rites and beliefs with which ordinary people explain and flavour their lives. There is a supreme being, but more emphasis is placed on ancestors (balimo), who are intermediaries between the people and the forces of nature. Evil is an everpresent danger, caused by boloi (witchcraft; witches can be either male or female) and thkolosi, maliciously playful beings. A ngaka is a learned man, a combination of sorcerer and doctor, who can combat them.

Thanks to the part French missionaries played in the creation of Lesotho, most people are at least nominally Christian and a high percentage are Roman Catholic.

LANGUAGE

The official languages are SeSotho and English. Greetings are an important social ritual in Lesotho, so it's useful to know some.

SeSotho
Greetings & Civilities

Greetings father.	*Lumela ntate.*
Peace father.	*Khotso ntate.*
Greetings mother.	*Lumela 'me.*
Peace mother.	*Khotso 'me.*
Greetings brother.	*Lumela abuti.*
Peace brother.	*Khotso abuti.*
Greetings sister.	*Lumela ausi.*
Peace sister.	*Khotso ausi.*
Thank you.	*Kea leboha.*

If you think the woman/man is older than you then use mother/father; if younger use sister/brother. There are three ways to say 'How are you?':

	Singular/Plural
How do you live?	*O phela joang/*
	Le phela joang?
How did you get up?	*O tsohele joang/*
	Le tsohele joang
How are you?	*O kae?/Le kae?*

The answers to the above questions are:

	Singular/Plural
I live well.	*Ke phela hantle/*
	Re phela hantle.
I got up well.	*Ke tsohile hantle/*
	Re tsohile hantle.
I am here.	*Ke teng/Re teng.*

These questions and answers are interchangeable. When parting, use the following expressions:

	Singular/Plural
Go well.	*Tsamaea hantle/*
	Tsamaeang hantle.
Stay well.	*Sala hantle/*
	Salang hantle.

Useful Words & Phrases

Thankyou.	*Kea leboha.*
How much?	*Ke bokae?*
water	*metsi*
vegetables	*meroho*
meat	*nama*
eggs	*mahe*

Facts for the Visitor

VISAS

Most people need a visa, unless they are citizens of Denmark, Finland, Greece, Iceland, Ireland, Israel, Japan, Norway, San Marino, Sweden or South Africa. Citizens of Commonwealth countries do not need a visa, with the significant exceptions of Australia, Canada, Ghana, New Zealand, Nigeria, India, Pakistan and Namibia.

If you arrive without a visa you *probably* will be given a temporary entry permit which allows you to go into Maseru and apply for a visa at the Immigration Office. A single entry visa costs US$4.50 and a multiple entry visa US$9.

EMBASSIES
Lesotho Embassies

There are Lesotho embassies in Maputo (Mozambique), Nairobi (Kenya) and Pretoria (South Africa). Lesotho is represented in several other countries, including Canada, Germany, the UK and the USA.

Foreign Embassies in Lesotho

Embassies in Maseru include:

France
    37 Qoaling Rd (☎ 32 6050)
Netherlands
    c/o Lancer's Inn (☎ 31 2144)
South Africa
    10th Floor, Lesotho Bank Centre, Kingsway (☎ 31 5758)
UK
    Linare Rd (☎ 31 3961)
USA
    Kingsway (towards Maseru Bridge border post) (☎ 31 2666; fax 31 0116)

MONEY

US$1 = M 4.40

The unit of currency is the maloti (M), which is divided into 100 liesente. The maloti is fixed at a value equal to the South African rand, and rands are accepted everywhere. When changing travellers' cheques you can usually get rand notes and this saves having to convert unused maloti (which aren't easily convertible in South Africa).

The only banks which change money are in Maseru.

POST & COMMUNICATIONS

The telephone system works reasonably well. The country code is 266; there are no area codes. To call from South Africa dial 09-266.

Post offices are open Monday to Friday from 8 am to 4.30 pm, Saturday from 8 am to noon. Delivery is slow and unreliable.

HEALTH

Lesotho has no malaria or bilharzia, although diseases such as hepatitis and dysentery are possible if you don't treat water taken downstream from a village. There is no trouble finding clean water except towards the end of the dry season.

Never venture into the mountains without cold-climate clothing and food for emergencies. Take precautions against sunburn, too. Several lives are lost each year from lightning strikes; keep off high ground during an electrical storm.

See the Health Appendix.

PUBLIC HOLIDAYS

Public holidays include the usual Christmas, Boxing and New Year's days, Good Friday and Easter Monday, plus Independence Day (4 October) and Moshoeshoe Day in early March.

ACTIVITIES
Hiking

Lesotho's high country offers some of the most spectacular hiking country in southern Africa.

The climate is very changeable, so come prepared. Temperatures can plummet to near zero even in summer, and thunderstorms are common. Rain gear and plenty of warm clothes are essential. In summer many rivers flood, and fords become dangerous. Thick fogs can also delay you. By the end of the dry season, especially in the higher areas, good water can be scarce.

There are stores in the towns which sell very basic foodstuffs. In much of the country there are scattered villages but in the southeast the rugged mountains are all but deserted. This makes for great wilderness hiking but don't walk in this area unless you are very experienced, well prepared and in a party of at least three people.

Malealea Lodge (see the following Pony Trekking section) also offers hiking, with a pony to carry your gear if you want.

Pony Trekking

Lesotho's tough little Basutho ponies can take you to some remote and beautiful places. Just keep reminding yourself, as your pony nonchalantly negotiates an apparently sheer cliff, that next to 'tough', the most popular cliché describing these beasts is 'sure-footed'.

On an overnight trek you'll need to take all the necessary gear, plus food and water-purification tablets. Check whether you'll need cooking utensils.

As well as the two places mentioned below, Semonkong Lodge also offers pony trekking. (See Semonkong later in this chapter.)

Malealea Lodge This is probably the best place for pony trekking. Even if you aren't interested in riding or hiking, Malealea is a very pleasant place to stay and it's in beautiful country. There's a range of accommodation: camping costs US$3.50 per person, dorms are US$8 (less if you have your own linen), huts with shared bathrooms are US$11.50, and rooms with attached bathroom are US$16. There are communal kitchens or you can arrange all meals (which are good). There's a village store selling basics, and a bar. The lodge has no phone, but you can book on ☎/fax (051) 447 3200 or (051) 448 3001 in South Africa; email

malealea@pixie.co.za. Allow a couple of days for the booking to go through.

Malealea is 26km from Motsekuoa (52km south of Maseru), which is on the main Maseru to Mafeteng road, just south of Morija. When you get to Motsekuoa, turn off onto the gravel road opposite the Golden Rose restaurant. The lodge can often arrange transfers from Bloemfontein (ask at Taffy's Backpackers) and Maseru. Ubuntu Tours (☎ (011) 648 7066; fax 648 2186 in South Africa) has transfers from Johannesburg.

Self-catering pony treks cost US$16 per person for a day, US$23 per person per day for overnight treks. The price includes a guide and a pack horse on overnight treks (you might have to hire an extra pack horse if you're in a large group).

Malealea can help you organise walking treks, taking along a pack horse to carry the luggage. 4WD tours are also available.

Basotho Pony Project This government-run project aims to preserve the blood-lines of Basutho ponies. The stables are at Molimo Nthuse on the road between Maseru and Thaba-Tseka, on the top of God Help Me Pass.

Treks range from a two hour ride (about US$8) to a week long ride (about US$100). There are minimum numbers on the longer rides, but it's only two or four, so it's easy to get a group together. Contact the tourist office in Maseru for details and bookings. The charges include horses and a guide but not accommodation, food and transport to the centre. Accommodation is in villages along the way, and they charge about US$4 per person a night or US$2.50 if you have a tent. By bus it's about US$2 from Maseru to the stables and the trip takes about two hours. There *should* be four daily buses each way, but there have been problems lately.

ACCOMMODATION

There's very little purpose-built budget accommodation outside Maseru but people are friendly, especially in the mountains. If you ask the village chief for permission to camp he'll often fix you up with a hut. Expect to pay for huts, about US$3 per night.

The missions and Agricultural Training Centres can often provide basic accommodation for about US$3.50.

Getting There & Away

AIR

Lesotho Airways (book through SAA in South Africa) has flights daily between Moshoeshoe airport, 18km from Maseru, and Jo'burg in South Africa for US$72, one way. There's an airport departure tax of US$4.50.

LAND

All the land borders are with South Africa. Most people enter via Maseru Bridge. The major border posts are listed in the table below.

Bus & Minibus Taxi

Minibus taxis run between Johannesburg and Maseru for about US$15. Buses from Maseru for South African destinations leave from the bridge on the South African side of the border.

Car

You can't enter via Sani Pass unless your vehicle is 4WD, but you can leave that way in a conventional vehicle. Most of the other entry points in the south and the east of the country also involve very rough roads. The easiest entry points are on the north and west sides. There's a vehicle departure tax of US$1.20.

Hertz (☎ 31 4460) and Avis (☎ 31 4325) have agents in Maseru, but it's cheaper to hire in South Africa.

Getting Around

AIR

Lesotho Airways flies between Maseru and Qacha's Nek for about US$25. Note that the luggage allowance is only 15kg. The main booking office (☎ 31 7317) is in Kingsway, Maseru.

BUS & MINIBUS TAXI

Slow buses run to many towns. Minibus taxis are quicker but tend not to run long distances. In more remote areas you might have to arrange a ride with a truck, for which you'll have to negotiate a fare. Be prepared for long delays once you're off the main routes.

You'll be quoted long-distance fares on buses but it's better to just buy a ticket to the next major town, as most of the passengers will get off there and you'll be stuck waiting for the bus to fill up again, and other buses might leave before yours.

CAR

Driving in Lesotho is getting easier as new roads are built in conjunction with the Highlands Water Project, but once you get off the tar there are still plenty of places where even a 4WD will be in trouble. Apart from rough

Lesotho Border Posts		
Border Post	*Hours*	*Nearest South African Town*
Caledonspoort	24 hours	Fouriesburg (near Butha-Buthe)
Ficksburg Bridge	24 hours	Ficksburg (near Maputsoe)
Makhaleng	8 am to 4 pm	Zastron (near Mohale's Hoek)
Maseru Bridge	6 am to 10 pm	Ladybrand
Ngoangoana Gate	8 am to 4 pm	Bushman's Nek (near Sehlabathebe)
Qacha's Nek	8 am to 10 pm	north of Matatiele
Ramatseliso's Gate	8 am to 6 pm	north-east of Matatiele
Sani Pass	8 am to 4 pm	Himeville
Sephapho's Gate	8 am to 4 pm	Boesmanskop (south of Mafeteng)
Van Rooyen's Gate	6 am to 10 pm	Wepener (north-west of Mafeteng)

roads, rivers flooding after summer storms present the biggest problems. People and animals on the roads are another hazard.

There are sometimes army roadblocks, usually searching for stolen cars. If you're driving a car hired in South Africa, make sure that you have a letter from the rental agency giving you permission to take it into Lesotho, otherwise there's a small chance that you will be accused of having stolen the car.

You can use any driving licence as long as it's in English or you have a 'certified translation'. There's a fine for not wearing a seat belt.

Maseru

Most of Maseru's 110,000 people have arrived since the 1970s, but for a rapidly expanding Third World city it remains an easy-going place. Maseru is fairly safe but be on your guard at night, especially off the main street.

Information

The Maseru Club is a meeting place for expats and aid workers, who can be good sources of information on out-of-the-way places.

The Department of Lands & Survey sells good topographic maps of Lesotho. The office is on Lerotholi Rd, near the corner of Constitution Rd.

Tourist Office The tourist office (☎ 31 2896; fax 32 3638) is on Kingsway, next to the Hotel Victoria. The staff are friendly but some of their information is out of date.

Money Three banks – Lesotho, Barclays and Standard – are all on Kingsway. These are the only places in the country where you can change money. Banking hours are short: 8.30 am to 3 pm weekdays (1 pm on Thursday) and 8.30 to 11 am Saturday. The last Friday of the month is pay day and there are huge queues.

Post & Communications If you can help it don't use Maseru as a poste restante address.

To make international phone calls go to the public call office, down the lane on the west side of the post office. It's open from Monday to Friday between 8 am and 5 pm, Saturday between 8 am and noon. Calls are very expensive.

Medical Services The Queen Elizabeth II Hospital is on Kingsway, near the Lesotho Sun Hotel.

Places to Stay

Camping & Hostels There's no camping facility in Maseru and free-camping would be risky, but you can camp at the *Khali Hotel*.

The *Anglican Centre* (☎ 32 2046) charges US$6 per person in austere dorms or twin rooms. The centre is about 500m north of Kingsway.

The *Phomolong Youth Hostel* (☎ 33 2900) is a long way from town; it charges US$6 per night. Head out on Main North Rd, go over the bridge and turn right down the Lancers Gap road (not signposted). The hostel is about 2km further on. Minibuses to Lancers Gap run past it.

If you're desperate, you could stay at the *Lesotho Workcamps Association* (☎ 31 4862), 917 Cathedral Rd, behind the impressive Catholic cathedral near the Circle at the end of Kingsway. Head down Main North Rd until you come to a garage; nearby is a dirt road where taxis accumulate. Follow this road until you come to the buildings of the workcamp. The dorms are US$4 per night.

Hotels Add 10% tax to the prices given here. About 5km east of the centre is the *Lakeside Hotel* (☎ 31 3646), off Main North Rd. Singles/doubles are US$25/35 and it's good for the price.

The *Khali Hotel/Motel* (☎ 31 0501) is a large and friendly local place south of Kingsway, beyond the prison. They have rooms from US$20/28 and there's a restaurant. They have an hourly shuttle-bus or you can take a Thetsane minibus on Pioneer Rd,

LESOTHO

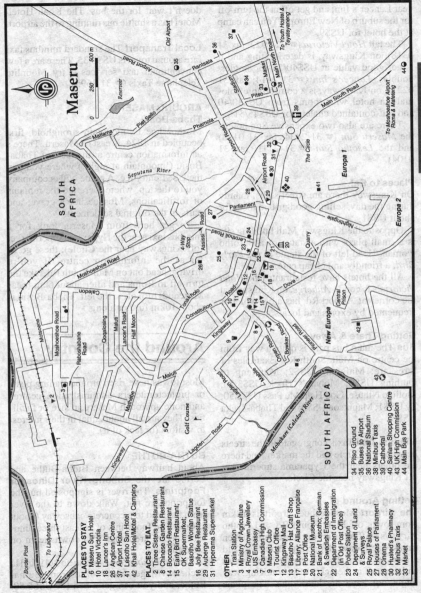

Maseru

0   250   500 m

Reservoir

SOUTH
AFRICA

Seputana River

Old Airport

Airport Road
Rantsala
Stadium
Pitso
Market
Main North Road

Piet Sello
Mattlama
Phamola

Airport Road
4-Way Stop
Assisi Road
Lerotholi Road
Parliament

Main South Road
The Circle
Airport Road

To Youth Hostel &
Toyateyaneng

To Moshoeshoe Airport
Roma & Mafeteng

Europa 1
Europa 2
Nightingale
New Europa
Quarry
Central Prison

Moshoeshoe Road
Caledon
Mohokare (Caledon River)

Raboshabane Road
Mabathoana
Maluti Road
Constitution Road
Kingsway
Lancer's Road
Half Moon
Oopolosing
Forst'holo Road

Kingsway
Motsoene
Mathebe
Maluti Road
Bowker Road
Orpen Road
Mabile
Dove

Golf Course
Lagden Road
Lagden (Caledon) River

SOUTH
AFRICA

To Ladybrand
Border Post
Liqoi

PLACES TO STAY
6   Maseru Sun Hotel
10 Hotel Victoria
18 Lancer's Inn
26 Anglican Centre
37 Airport Hotel
41 Lesotho Sun Hotel
42 Khali Hotel/Motel & Camping

PLACES TO EAT
2   Three Sisters Restaurant
8   Chinese Garden Restaurant
14 Boccacio Restaurant
15 Early Bird Restaurant;
    OK Supermarket;
    Basotho Woman Statue
16 Jolly Bee Restaurant
29 Auberge Restaurant
31 Hyperama Supermarket

OTHER
1   Train Station
3   Ministry of Agriculture
4   Royal Crown Jewellery
5   US Embassy
7   Canadian High Commission
9   Maseru Club
11 Tourist Office
12 Kingsway Mall
13 Basotho Hat Craft Shop
17 Library; Alliance Française
19 Post Office
20 National Museum
21 Bank of Lesotho; German
    & Swedish Embassies
22 Department of Immigration
    (in Old Post Office)
23 Police Station
24 Department of Land
    & Surveys
25 Royal Palace
27 Houses of Parliament
28 Cinema
30 Husted's Pharmacy
32 Minibus Taxis
33 Market
34 Pitso Ground
35 Buses to Airport
36 National Stadium
38 Minibus Taxis
39 Cathedral
40 Sanlam Shopping Centre
43 UK High Commission
44 Main Bus Park

near Lancer's Inn, and get off at the turn-off for the suburb of New Europa. You can camp at the hotel for US$9.

The tall *Hotel Victoria* (☎ 31 2922; fax 31 0318), on Kingsway, is deteriorating and it is not good value at US$40/55 for singles/ doubles. *Lancer's Inn* (☎ 31 2114; fax 31 0223), on Kingsway, is a comfortable colonial-era hotel with rooms from US$30/40 and self-contained chalets for US$45/51.

There are also two expensive Sun hotels: the *Maseru Sun* (☎ 31 2434; fax 31 0158) and the *Lesotho Sun* (☎ 31 3111; fax 31 0104).

Places to Eat

On Kingsway there are street stalls, mainly during the day, selling good grilled meat for about US$1.

Opposite the Kingsway Mall building site is a small plaza with a statue of a Basotho woman. Head left of the statue to the *Early Bird*, a friendly and cheap cafe.

All the hotels have restaurants (the *Hotel Victoria*'s is good). *Auberge*, on Kingsway at the corner of Airport Rd, has a bar which is frequented by expats and locals.

Getting There & Away

Bus The main bus park is quite a way from the centre on Main South Rd. Examples of fares are: Mafeteng US$2; Mafeteng to Quthing US$3; Mohale's Hoek US$3.50; Molimo Nthuse, God Help Me Pass US$2.50; Ty US$1; Maputsoe US$3; and Thaba-Tseka US$6.

Minibus Taxi Taxis congregate in the streets between the Circle and the market, and there are others near the Hyperama supermarket off Kingsway near the Circle.

Getting Around

The Airport Moshoeshoe airport is 18km from town, off Main South Rd. A Lesotho Airways staff bus runs out there half a dozen times each day, departing from the old airport in town. The timetable often varies and the staff at the ticket office on Kingsway might not have the latest one. The plane doesn't wait for the bus. The Khali Hotel/ Motel has a shuttle bus running to the airport.

Local Transport The standard minibus taxi fare around town is US$0.35. There are a few conventional taxi services – try Moonlite Telephone Taxis (☎ 31 2695).

AROUND MASERU
Thaba-Bosiu

Moshoeshoe I's mountain stronghold, first occupied in 1824, is east of Maseru. There's an information centre at the base of Thaba-Bosiu ('mountain at night') where you pay the US$1 entry fee. A guide will accompany you to the top, where there are the remains of fortifications, Moshoeshoe's grave, and parts of the original settlement.

To get here from Maseru, look for a minibus taxi near the Hyperama supermarket (off Kingsway near the Circle); these go as far as the information centre. If you're driving, head out on Main South Rd, take the turn-off to Roma and after about 6km (near Mazenod) turn off to the left. Thaba-Bosiu is about 10km further along.

Around the Country

Most towns have risen around trading posts or protectorate-era administration centres and none approach Maseru in size or facilities. They are all about equal in their interest to visitors (or lack of it).

BUTHA-BUTHE

About halfway between Butha-Buthe and Leribe are the **Subeng River Dinosaur Footprints**. The river is signposted but the footprints are not. Walk down to the river from the road to a concrete causeway (about 250m). The footprints of at least three dinosaur species are about 15m downstream on the right bank.

The *Ha Thabo Ramakatane* hostel is in Ha Sechele village, about 4km from Butha-Buthe, and you can get a bed for US$5.50.

There are basic cooking facilities; bring food.

MORIJA

This village, about 40km south of Maseru on the Main South road, is where you will find the small but interesting **Morija Museum & Archives**. The museum is open Monday to Saturday from 8.30 am to 4.30 pm, Sunday from 2 to 4.30 pm; admission is US$0.50.

Near the museum is the *Mophato Oa Morija* (☎ 36 0219), an ecumenical centre with beds for US$9 and camping for US$4.50 per person. There's also *Ha Matel* (☎ 36 0308; ask for Stephen Gill – he works at the museum), a pleasant self-catering cottage which costs US$14 per person (no minimum number).

ROMA

Roma, 35km from Maseru, is a university town. There are some attractive sandstone buildings and the entry to town by the southern gorge is spectacular.

North of Roma is the important **Ha Baroana rock painting** site. Although suffering from neglect and vandalism it is worth seeing.

To get there from Roma head back to the Maseru road and turn right onto the road heading east to Thaba-Tseka. After about 12km turn off to the left, just after the Ha Ntsi settlement on the Mohlsks-oa-Tuka River.

Places to Stay

Outside Roma, off the Maseru road, is the self-catering *Trading Post Guest House* (☎ 34 0202). The trading post has been here since 1903; so has the Thorn family, who own the store and the guesthouse. The accommodation is good value at US$8 per person in rondavels, US$10 in the main house (a nice old stone building). Camping costs US$2.50 plus US$2.50 per person. Everything is provided except towels.

SANI PASS

This steep pass is the only dependable road between Lesotho and the KwaZulu/Natal Drakensberg. On the South African side the nearest towns are Himeville and Underberg.

From the chalet at the top of the pass there are several day walks, including a long and strenuous one to **Thabana-Ntlenyana** (3482m), the highest peak in southern Africa. There is a path but a guide would come in handy. Horses can do the trip so consider hiring one.

Places to Stay

Sani Top Chalet, at the top of the pass, charges US$16 per person with breakfast, or US$9 for backpackers. There are cooking facilities but bring your own food. In winter the snow is often deep enough to ski (there are a few pieces of antique equipment at the chalet) and horse trekking is available with prior arrangement. Book through Sani Tours (☎ /fax (033) 702 1069 in South Africa). The *Sani Lodge* hostel, in South Africa at the bottom of the pass, arranges trips up the pass.

Getting There & Away

The South African border guards won't let you up the pass unless you have a 4WD, although you can come down from Lesotho without one. The South African border is open between 8 am and 4 pm; the Lesotho border stays open an hour later to let the last vehicles up. Hitching up or down the pass is best on weekends when there is a fair amount of traffic to and from the lodge.

There's no public transport from the pass to other places in Lesotho, although several trucks each day head for Mokhotlong (52km north).

SEHLABATHEBE NATIONAL PARK

Lesotho's only national park is remote and rugged and that is its main attraction. There are relatively few animals other than a rare Maloti minnow (thought to be extinct but rediscovered in the Tsoelikana River), rare birds such as the bearded vulture, and the odd rhebok or baboon. As well as hikes and climbs, the park has horse riding; guided horseback tours are US$12.

For bookings at the park contact the Conservation Division (☎ 32 3600, ext 30), in the Ministry of Agriculture building (the sign says Bosiu Rural Development Project) on Raboshabane Rd, which is off Moshoeshoe Rd in Maseru, near the railway station.

Places to Stay
You can camp in the park but, except at the lodge where camping costs US$2.50 per person, there are no facilities. The lodge has hostel rooms for US$5 and singles/doubles for US$7/12. You can buy firewood and coal here, but for food (very limited) and petrol or diesel you'll have to rely on a small store about 4km west of the park entrance and quite a way from the lodge. You have to book the lodge in Maseru at the Conservation Division of the Ministry of Agriculture.

In Sehlabathebe village is the new, clean *Range Management Education Centre*. It is 1.5km down the road to Sehonghong and it costs US$3.50 in dorms.

Getting There & Away
Sometimes there are charter flights from Maseru to Ha Paulus, a village near the park entrance, and you can arrange to be picked up from there for US$9.

Driving to the park can be a problem as the roads become impassable after heavy rain in spring and summer.

There are several routes, all of which currently require 4WD. The longest is the southern route via Quthing and Qacha's Nek. There's also a route via Thaba-Tseka, then down the Senqu River valley past the hamlet of Sehonghong and over the difficult Matebeng Pass. The park can also be reached from Matatiele in the extreme west of KwaZulu/Natal. This route doesn't have as many difficult sections as the others but it is less well maintained so it is sometimes closed.

A daily bus runs between Qacha's Nek and Sehlabathebe village. The relatively short trip takes 5½ hours and costs US$4.50.

Probably the simplest way in is to hike the 10km up the escarpment from Bushman's Nek in South Africa. From Bushman's Nek to Nkonkoana Gate, the Lesotho border post, takes about six hours. You can also take a horse up or down for US$10.

SEMONKONG
Maletsunyane Falls (also known as Lebihan Falls) are about a 1½ hour walk from Semonkong. The falls are some 200m high and are best in summer.

You can usually find a bed at the *Roman Catholic mission* for a small contribution and there's also *Semonkong Lodge*, which has dorms for US$6, doubles for US$36 and camping for US$4 per person. Book through Peacock Sports (☎ (05192) 2730 in South Africa) in Fontein St, Ficksburg, South Africa. Pony trekking and hiking are offered here.

TEYATEYANENG
Teyateyaneng ('the place of quick sands') is usually known as Ty. The town has been developed as the craft centre of Lesotho and there are several places worth visiting. Some of the best tapestries come from Helang Basali Crafts in the St-Agnes Mission, a couple of kilometres before Ty on the Maseru road.

THABA-TSEKA
This remote town is on the western edge of the central range, over the sometimes tricky Mokhoabong Pass. It was established in 1980 as a centre for the mountain district. You can usually get a bed at the *Farmer Training Centre* for about US$4, and there's apparently also a *guesthouse*.

Liberia

Since the signing of yet another peace accord (the 15th) in August 1996, a tenuous calm has prevailed in Liberia. However, many areas remain factionalised and remote, and the country is not yet a place for independent travellers. If peace solidifies and travel opens up, Liberia has much to offer, including friendly people, lush landscapes and some of the last remaining rainforests in West Africa.

Facts about the Country

HISTORY

Liberia began as a venture by US philanthropists in 1822, the idea being that freed slaves from the plantations would be resettled in Africa. Many of the former slaves refused to go, and the few thousand who did accept had to contend with the hostility of the indigenous people, who resented being alienated from their land and the settlers' attempts to dominate them. By the mid-19th century, more than half of the 5000 black Americans who originally migrated to Liberia had died from tropical diseases or returned to the USA. Some, however, managed to survive, and in 1847 the new country declared itself an independent republic with Joseph Roberts as its first president.

The Americo-Liberians, as the settlers came to be known, saw themselves as part of a mission to bring civilisation and Christianity to Africa. Though constituting only a tiny fraction of the total population, they came to dominate the indigenous peoples and imposed a form of forced labour which anywhere else would have gone under the name of slavery. This continued for almost 100 years, and in 1930 both Britain and the USA cut off diplomatic relations for five years because of the sale of such labour to Spanish colonialists in what was then Fernando Pó (now Bioko in Equatorial Guinea). As late as 1960, Liberia was condemned for its labour

REPUBLIC OF LIBERIA
Area: 111,370 sq km
Population: 2.5 million
Population Growth Rate: 3.2%
Capital: Monrovia
Head of State: President Charles Ghankay Taylor
Official Language: English
Currency: Liberian dollar
Exchange Rate: L$1 = US$1
Per Capita GNP: US$200
Inflation: 10%
Time: GMT/UTC

Highlights
• Mt Nimba and beautiful surrounding hill country
• Remnant rainforest in Sapo National Park

recruitment methods by the International Labour Organisation.

The True Whig Party monopolised power from early in Liberia's history. Despite the country's labour recruitment policies, the party was able to project an image of Liberia as Africa's most stable country. During William Tubman's presidency (1944-71), this image led to massive foreign investment. The huge influx of foreign money, however, soon began to distort the economy and to exacerbate social inequalities, causing hostility to grow between Americo-Liberians and the local population. Tubman viewed

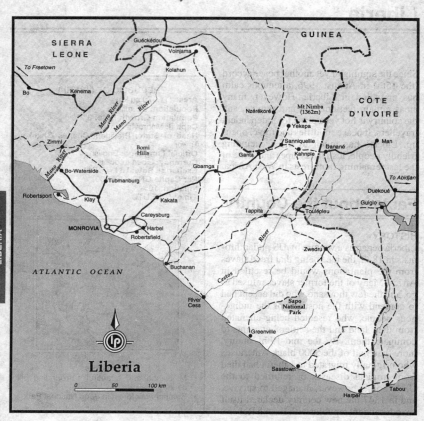

Liberia

0   50   100 km

this development with alarm, and was forced
to concede that the indigenous people would
have to be granted some political and economic involvement in the country; one of his
concessions was to enfranchise them. Until
this point (1963), some 97% of the population had been denied the franchise.

William Tolbert, who succeeded Tubman as
president in 1971, was a strong supporter of
South Africa's efforts to maintain diplomatic
and economic relations with the rest of black
Africa. Tolbert also established diplomatic
relations with Communist countries such as the
People's Republic of China, while at home, he

clamped down on opposition and brought in
harsh laws to deal with anyone considered to
be a threat to his government. Even his
staunchest ally, the USA, began to complain
about violations of human rights.

Resentment of these policies and of
growing government corruption grew. In
1979, several demonstrators were shot in
protests against a proposed increase in rice
prices. Finally, in April 1980, Tolbert was
overthrown in a coup led by Master Sergeant
Samuel Doe. During the accompanying
fighting, Tolbert and many high-ranking
ministers were killed. Of those who sur-

vived, the majority were briefly 'tried', then publicly executed by a firing squad on the beach in Monrovia. Although the coup gave the indigenous population real political power for the first time since the settlers had arrived, it was condemned by most other African countries as well as by Liberia's other allies and trading partners. Over the next few years, relations with neighbouring African states gradually thawed. However, the flight of capital from the country in the wake of the coup, coupled with the financial strains of subsidising a basic annual wage of US$2400, caused Liberia's economy to spiral rapidly downwards.

Samuel Doe (quickly self-promoted to general) survived several coup attempts and maintained his grip on power by any means available, including a sham 'election' held in late 1985 (largely to appease his major creditor, the USA). By the late 1980s, however, it was clear that opposition forces had had enough and were determined to topple him.

During 1990 the main opposition groups, led by Prince Johnson and Charles Taylor, quickly overran most of the country and were poised for the final assault on Monrovia. By mid-year, casualties (both military and civilian) were high, refugees were streaming into neighbouring countries and Liberia lay in ruins. US warships were anchored off the coast and an Economic Community of West African States (ECOWAS) peace-keeping force (known as ECOWAS Monitoring Group or ECOMOG) was dispatched in an attempt to keep the warring factions apart.

It was all to no avail. Refusing to surrender or even step down as president, Doe and many of his supporters were finally wiped out by Johnson's forces. With both Johnson and Taylor claiming the presidency, the ECOMOG forces installed their own candidate, political science professor Amos Sawyer, as head of the Interim Government of National Unity (IGNU). Meanwhile Taylor's National Patriotic Front of Liberia (NPFL) forces continued to occupy about 90% of the country, while the remnants of Doe's former army and Johnson's followers were encamped within Monrovia itself.

In October 1992 Taylor launched a month-long assault on Monrovia. This led to an increase in the ECOMOG force to 15,000 and Taylor started to lose ground. In August 1993 the protagonists finally hammered out a peace accord at a UN-sponsored meeting in Geneva. The accord, known as the Cotonou Agreement, called for the installation of a six month transitional government representing IGNU, NPFL and the third major player, the United Liberation Movement for Democracy (ULIMO), Doe's former soldiers. When its mandate expired in September 1994 a new agreement, the Akosombo Amendment, was signed. It called for the formation of a new five-member Council of State to replace the IGNU. The amendment was rejected by the IGNU, however, which extended its own life span until mid-1995.

In August 1995, yet another peace agreement (known as the Abuja Peace Accord) was signed by the leaders of the main warring factions. This one lasted until 6 April 1996, when fighting erupted in Monrovia between NPFL and ULIMO. During April and May there was widespread looting, major sections of Monrovia were severely damaged and nearly all resident foreigners and United Nations staff were evacuated.

August 1996 saw the negotiation of an amended Abuja Accord which provided for a cease-fire to be implemented by 31 August, disarmament and demobilisation to be completed by the end of January 1997, and elections to be held in late May 1997 (later postponed until 19 July 1997). At the same time, Ruth Perry, a former senator, was appointed to head the Council of State. Despite serious cease-fire violations during the ensuing months and a slow and incomplete disarmament process, the July elections proceeded as scheduled, with Charles Taylor and his National Patriotic Party polling an overwhelming majority (75%) in voting declared by international observers to have been largely free and transparent.

Although there are some signs (such as the partial disarmament and elections) that things are improving, the situation for the people of Liberia remains grim. Hundreds of thousands of Liberians have fled the country and almost half those remaining have been displaced from their home villages. Malnutrition is rife in rural areas, while in Monrovia, infrastructure and utilities have been almost completely destroyed. While hopes persist that a post-election spirit of reconciliation will prevail and provide a foundation for reconstruction of the country, they are tempered by the tragic realities of Liberia's recent past.

GEOGRAPHY & CLIMATE

Liberia's sandy and low coastal plain is intersected by marshes, creeks and tidal lagoons. Further inland is a densely forested plateau and a region of mountains near the Guinea border.

The climate is warm and humid with temperatures ranging from 21 to 33°C. The best time to visit is during the dry season, between November and April.

POPULATION & PEOPLE

The population of 2.5 million consists overwhelmingly of people of indigenous origin, divided into some 16 major tribal groupings, including the Kpelle in the centre, the Bassa around Buchanan, the Krahn in the southeast, the Mandingo in the north and the Kru along the coast. Americo-Liberians account for less than 3% of the total population.

LANGUAGE

English is the official language. Major African languages include Kpelle, Bassa and Kru.

Facts for the Visitor

VISAS & DOCUMENTS

Visas are required for all; there have been several recent incidents of travellers without proper documentation being turned back at the airport. An international health certificate is also obligatory.

After arrival in Monrovia, you must report to the Bureau of Immigration within 48 hours for a visitor's permit (US$25) which will determine the length of your stay. The immigration office also handles visa extensions.

An exit visa is required to leave the country. They're available from the Bureau of Immigration in Monrovia and are valid for one week from the date of issue.

Other Visas

Côte d'Ivoire
> Visas are issued while you wait by the Air Ivoire office (☎ 227436) on the corner of Ashmun and Mechlin streets in Monrovia. A multiple entry visa valid for three months costs US$50 plus one photo.

Guinea
> A single-entry visa valid for three months is available from the Guinean Embassy on Tubman Blvd. It costs US$40 plus two photos and is issued within 24 hours.

Sierra Leone
> Visa service in Monrovia has been suspended since the coup in Sierra Leone. Previously, a single entry visa cost US$50 plus two photos.

EMBASSIES

Liberian Embassies

In Africa there are Liberian embassies in Congo (Zaïre), Côte d'Ivoire, Egypt, Ethiopia, Ghana, Guinea and Sierra Leone.

Foreign Embassies in Liberia

Countries which still have diplomatic representations in Monrovia include:

Belgium
> Bushrod Island Rd (☎ 226209)

Guinea
> 24th St & Tubman Blvd, Sinkor

Nigeria
> Nigeria House, Tubman Blvd, Congo Town (☎ 227345)

People's Republic of China
> 17th St, Sinkor (☎ 226816)

Sierra Leone
> c/o Hotel Africa (☎ 226043, ext 5600)

UK (honorary consul)
> (☎ 226056)

USA
> United Nations Drive, Mamba Point (☎ 226370)

MONEY

US$1 = L$1

The unit of currency is the Liberian dollar (L$, sometimes called the 'liberty'). Officially it's on a par with the US dollar, but on the street it now changes at a rate of approximately L$50 to US$1. Upcountry, you will still find 'JJs' – notes issued by Charles Taylor's people and distinctive because of the picture of Joseph Roberts (the first president of the independent republic) on them. Outside Monrovia, JJs exchange at roughly twice the value of liberties against the US dollar.

Travellers' cheques are virtually useless. If you really get stuck, try the Liberia United Bank (known locally by the acronym LUBI), where you can sometimes change for a 3% commission. Use the Randall St entrance and go upstairs.

POST & COMMUNICATIONS

The main post office on Randall St in Monrovia is open Monday to Friday from 8 am to 4 pm and on Saturday from 9 am to noon. There is no poste restante.

International telephone calls can be made daily between 8 am and 5 pm at the telecommunications building on Lynch St; the lines frequently work. Rates are US$3 per minute to the USA and US$4 to Australia and Europe; a deposit is required. You can also send and receive faxes here (fax 227838). It's US$5 per page to send and US$0.70 per page to receive; incoming faxes will be held indefinitely.

The country code is 231; there are no area codes.

PHOTOGRAPHY

The photography situation under the Taylor government was unclear at the time this book was being researched. However, use caution when taking photos, and definitely don't snap any shots within sight of ECOMOG checkpoints or anything related to the military or the police.

DANGERS & ANNOYANCES

With the increased ECOMOG presence, the crime rate in Monrovia has begun to decrease and travel throughout the country has opened up. However, the present calm is extremely fragile and demobilisation of the warring factions is not complete. Once ECOMOG

pulls out, it is likely that security conditions will deteriorate. If you are going to set off outside Monrovia, get a complete briefing first from people who know the situation.

As there are so few foreigners in the country, expect to be approached frequently – particularly at the Red Light motor park in Monrovia and other unsavoury places – by men in casual clothes carrying official-looking Bureau of Immigration badges and demanding to see your documents. It's more than likely they don't really work for the immigration office, but having your visa in order helps if you're unable to wriggle away from these guys. Try to keep your passport in your own hands.

In Monrovia, there's a midnight to dawn curfew. The city has had no power supply for over seven years, so have a torch handy.

BUSINESS HOURS

Most businesses are open Monday to Friday from 8.30 am to 5 pm and on Saturdays from 9 am until 1 pm. Banks are open from 9.30 am to noon Monday to Thursday and until 12.30 pm on Friday.

PUBLIC HOLIDAYS

Public holidays are: 1 January, 7 January, 11 February, Decoration Day (2nd Wednesday in March), 15 March, 11 April, 14 May (National Unification Day), 26 July (Independence), 24 August, 6 November, 29 November and 25 December.

ACCOMMODATION & FOOD

Hotels in Monrovia are starting to reopen, although anywhere with a generator and water will be expensive. There are few hotels upcountry. Often the only accommodation is with missions or aid organisations, although these frequently do not have sufficient facilities to accommodate independent travellers.

Good chop bars, (cheap streetside restaurants selling local food), are plentiful in Monrovia and there is also a decent selection of more expensive restaurants. Only the most basic provisions are available in many towns outside the capital.

Getting There & Away

AIR

There are direct flights several times a week between Monrovia and Conakry in Guinea (US$165 one way) on Air Guinée and TransAfrica Air, and almost daily between Monrovia and Abidjan in Côte d'Ivoire (US$275) on Weasua and Air Ivoire. Fares are 10% lower if you are affiliated with a tax-exempt organisation. Air Guinée and Air Ivoire are notoriously unreliable.

The main international airport, which is closed, is at Robertsfield, 60km from Monrovia. All flights now use the Spriggs-Payne airfield in Monrovia, about 7km from the centre of town, just beyond Sinkor. There is a US$30 departure tax.

LAND
Côte d'Ivoire

Kingdom Transport Services and Yazu Ltd run a direct bus at least once a week from Monrovia via Sanniquellie to Abidjan and on to Accra in Ghana. It's US$40 to Abidjan (US$60 to Accra), plus approximately US$20 for border fees and other incidental costs. Schedules are irregular, so enquire in advance at the bus companies' office (☎ 226588) near the Bong Mines Bridge.

There are also frequent bush taxis between Monrovia and Ganta, from where you can catch onward transport via Sanniquellie to Danané and Man in Côte d'Ivoire. Monrovia to Man takes 12 to 15 hours.

In the south-east, there's a road connecting Harper with Tabou in Côte d'Ivoire, although you'll have to cross the river that forms the border between the two countries in either a canoe or ferry. Service may be suspended during the rainy season.

Guinea

Daily bush taxis run from Monrovia to Gbarnga and Ganta, from where you can catch onward transport to Nzérékoré in Guinea.

Sierra Leone

Due to recent troubles in Sierra Leone, the border is now closed. If it reopens, bush taxis should again ply the route between Monrovia and Freetown. The road is sealed the whole way except for a nearly impassable section (in the rainy season) between the border and Kenema in Sierra Leone.

SEA

The occasional cargo boats which run between Monrovia and Conakry (Guinea) generally accept a few passengers. Enquire at the port for details.

Getting Around

CAR

Road travel is now possible throughout the country, although until the security situation stabilises further it is unwise to head off without first thoroughly checking things out in Monrovia. Most roads are unsealed and many become nearly impassable during the rainy season. Major exceptions are the sealed routes connecting Monrovia with Bo-Waterside (on the Sierra Leonean border), Tubmanburg and Buchanan, although there are some badly deteriorated stretches on the Buchanan road. The road to Guinea and Côte d'Ivoire is sealed as far as Ganta. The going rate for hiring a car with a driver is US$50 per day within greater Monrovia, more for upcountry or if you want to drive yourself.

MINIBUS & TAXI

There are daily bush taxis from Monrovia to Buchanan, Gbarnga and the Sierra Leonean border, as well as to numerous other destinations. Several taxis per week link the capital with almost everywhere else, although many routes are restricted during the rainy season.

Some examples of journeys and fares from Monrovia are listed in the following table. There is a surcharge for luggage, based on size. For a standard rucksack, the fee should not exceed US$1 for most journeys.

| | | Routes & Fares | | |
From Monrovia	To	Distance	Duration	Cost (US$)
	Bo-Waterside	140km	3 hours	$6
	Buchanan	150km	3 hours	$6
	Greenville	660km	3 days	$60
	Harper	745km	3 days	$80
	Kakata	70km	2 hours	$3
	Sanniquellie	305km	8 hours	$14
	Tubmanburg	70km	2 hours	$3
	Voinjama	395km	11 hours	$30

BOAT

There is a boat which runs several times a week between Monrovia and Harper. The trip takes at least 36 hours and costs US$60. Enquire at the port for details.

Monrovia

Monrovia has suffered badly during the fighting of the last eight years. Infrastructure has been largely destroyed, and many buildings have been gutted. However, despite its initially depressing appearance, the city has some pep. Pick a day when it's not raining, find some Liberian friends, try not to notice all the ECOMOG checkpoints, and soon you'll forget you're walking around in what was only recently a war zone.

Information

Travel Agencies Karou Voyages (☎ 226508) or the nearby Gritaco Travel Agency (☎ 226854) can assist with booking flights out of Monrovia.

Pharmacies The well-stocked Charif Pharmacy on Randall St is open Monday to Saturday from 8 am to 7.30 pm.

Things to See

Ellen's Beach, just beyond Hotel Africa and 10km north of the centre, is popular on weekends, as is **Kendeja Beach**, about 15km out of town towards Robertsfield

Airport, near the stadium. In town, the bustling **Waterside Market** is gradually coming back to life. There are some **artisan stalls** opposite the US Embassy on Mamba Point. Although there's nothing much to see there now, **Providence Island** is of historical interest as the spot where the first expedition of freed American slaves landed. The **Masonic Temple**, gutted after the 1980 coup, was once one of Monrovia's landmarks.

Places to Stay

One of the cheapest places is the *Florida Motel* (☎ 221690), which has basic rooms with small double beds and bucket shower for US$12. Men are not allowed to share a room. If they're full, the imaginatively named *Hotel* on Gurley St across from the Ministry of Transport has similar rooms in a deserted high-rise for the same price. Ask for David, the friendly manager. Both hotels sometimes have power for a few hours in the evening. Women alone would probably not feel comfortable at either of these places.

Nearby, on Carey St, is the long-standing *El Meson* (☎ 227871), with a generator (until 1 am), water supply and rooms for US$25/35/50, depending on size.

The *Ambassador Hotel*, on the beach at Mamba Point, has acceptable rooms, overpriced at US$40 but with nice sea views. There's usually power and water.

Top of the range in Monrovia is the *Mamba Point Hotel* (☎ 226693), where you can sleep in luxury for US$110/165 for singles/doubles, plus 10% tax.

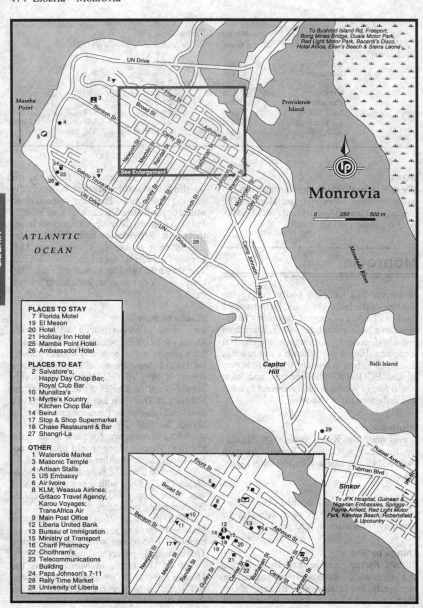

Monrovia

0   250   500 m

PLACES TO STAY
7   Florida Motel
19 El Meson
20 Hotel
21 Holiday Inn Hotel
25 Mamba Point Hotel
26 Ambassador Hotel

PLACES TO EAT
2   Salvatore's;
    Happy Day Chop Bar;
    Royal Club Bar
10 Munaliza's
11 Myrtle's Kountry
    Kitchen Chop Bar
14 Beirut
17 Stop & Shop Supermarket
18 Chase Restaurant & Bar
27 Shangri-La

OTHER
1   Waterside Market
3   Masonic Temple
4   Artisan Stalls
5   US Embassy
6   Air Ivoire
8   KLM; Weasua Airlines;
    Gritaco Travel Agency;
    Karou Voyages;
    TransAfrica Air
9   Main Post Office
12 Liberia United Bank
13 Bureau of Immigration
15 Ministry of Transport
16 Charif Pharmacy
22 Choithram's
23 Telecommunications
    Building
24 Papa Johnson's 7-11
28 Rally Time Market
29 University of Liberia

Places to Eat

Chop bars in Monrovia are good and abundant. A plate of fufu costs under US$1, while dried fish with rice is US$1.50. For self-caterers, Monrovia's supermarkets have a wide selection of reasonably priced products from the USA.

The *Chase Restaurant & Bar* has a good selection of basic dishes for US$6 to US$8. They also serve breakfast from 7 am. *Munaliza's* is less expensive, with palava sauce and fufu from US$2. *Beirut* (Lebanese), *Salvatore's* (Italian/continental) and *Shangri-La* (Indian) have some reasonably priced dishes and are good for more exotic fare.

All the mid-range and top-end hotels have restaurants with mid-range and top-end prices. The downstairs snack bar at the *Holiday Inn Hotel* has pizzas from US$9 and hamburgers and other snacks for under US$4.

For a splurge, try the balcony restaurant at the *Mamba Point Hotel*. Meals average US$20 and up. They also have a pizzeria with a less expensive menu.

Entertainment

Papa Johnson's 7-11 in Mamba Point has good views of the sea and is a popular watering hole for locals and expatriates alike. The *Royal Club*, inside a small house on Broad St, is well frequented at happy hour. *Bacardi's* disco near Hotel Africa attracts a mix of expats and affluent locals. The disco at the *Holiday Inn Hotel* is open daily and draws a good local crowd. The US$4 cover charged by most places is usually negotiable.

Getting There & Away

Taxis for Tubmanburg and the Sierra Leonean border leave from Duala motor park on Bushrod Island Rd. Taxis and minibuses for most other upcountry destinations, including the borders of Guinea and Côte d'Ivoire, leave from Monrovia's main motor park in Red Light about 10km northeast of the centre. Buses to Accra and Abidjan depart from Bong Mines Bridge on Bushrod Island Rd.

Getting Around

Share-taxis operate on a zone system with prices ranging from US$0.10 to US$0.50. It's US$0.20 for a share-taxi from the centre to Duala and US$0.40 to the motor park in Red Light. A share-taxi between the city centre and Spriggs-Payne airfield costs US$0.20 (US$1.50 in a private cab). Good places to catch a taxi include Waterside, Duala and Broad St.

AROUND MONROVIA
Firestone Plantation

The Firestone Plantation – the world's largest rubber plantation – is operating again, although at greatly reduced capacity. There are no regular tours any more, but you're likely to find employees in the grounds who can show you around and explain the tapping process. Stick to the beaten path, as Firestone is one of several areas in Liberia where land mines have been found. The plantation is in Harbel, about 65km east of Monrovia near Robertsfield airport.

Around the Country

BUCHANAN

Buchanan, 150km south-east of Monrovia, is Liberia's second major port. There's not much to see except for the **port** itself and some good **beaches** south of the centre. However, Buchanan makes a pleasant excursion, as the war destruction is not as bad as in most other parts of the country.

For lodgings, try the Ring Rd area. You can sometimes rent a room for a couple of dollars at the old *Lamco compound*.

GANTA

Busy Ganta is a stop on most overland routes through Liberia. The shops aren't quite as well stocked as in Gbarnga, but there are several decent chop houses in town.

GBARNGA

Gbarnga, where Charles Taylor established his headquarters during the war, is Liberia's second city and a bustling place. Cuttington College is on the outskirts of town. Behind the campus, there's a pretty **waterfall**.

Near the Phebe Hospital complex, just before Gbarnga on the road from Monrovia, is *Josephine's*, one of the only hotels in the country outside the capital. It's a flea-ridden place, but Josephine is friendly and her prices are negotiable. She may also be willing to help set you up more cheaply with a family in town.

In addition to the restaurant at Josephine's (which is better than the hotel), there are many chop bars and several other restaurants in Gbarnga.

HARPER

The remote town of Harper, almost on the Côte d'Ivoire border, once had numerous sites of historical and architectural interest, including the residence of the late President William Tubman. Nowadays, it's just a shell of its former self, although the surrounding area is beautiful.

Road access from Monrovia to Harper is via Tappita and Zwedru, then south to the coast along a very bad road. Under good conditions, it's an arduous three day journey in a 4WD; during the rainy season, the road becomes impassable.

ROBERTSPORT

Robertsport, once a relaxing beach town,

was completely destroyed during the war. No infrastructure remains, although the beaches are still beautiful. There's a large lake outside the town which often flows onto the road during the rainy season. Before going, ask around in Monrovia to see if the bridges have been repaired.

SANNIQUELLIE

Sanniquellie, in a pretty, mountainous area, is the last major town before the border with Côte d'Ivoire. The caretaker at the old *Catholic Mission* sometimes has inexpensive rooms to rent.

SAPO NATIONAL PARK

Before the war, Sapo was Liberia's major park, bounded on the west by the Sinoe River and to the north by the Putu mountains. Now, although the vegetation – including significant areas of virgin forest – remains, all park structures have been overgrown. Access to the area that was once Sapo is via the Zwedru-Greenville road.

YEKEPA

Yekepa, about 350m above sea level, has a pleasant climate and good views of the lush surrounding mountains, although the town itself has been destroyed. Given increased stability and infrastructure, the area holds the potential for some good hiking. Nearby is **Mt Nimba**, Liberia's highest peak at 1362m.

Libya

GREAT SOCIALIST PEOPLE'S LIBYAN ARAB JAMAHIRIYA
Area: 1,759,540 sq km
Population: 5.4 million
Population Growth Rate: 3.7%
Capitals: Tripoli and Benghazi
Head of State: Colonel Muammar Gaddafi
Official Language: Arabic
Currency: Libyan dinar
Exchange Rate: US$1 = LD 0.36
Per Capita GNP: US$6500
Inflation: 25%
Time: GMT/UTC 1 (GMT/UTC + 2 April-Sept)

Highlights
- The Roman cities of Leptis Magna and Sabratha, and the Greek cities of Cyrene and Apollonia
- Wonderful desert architecture of Ghadhames
- The stunning scenery and prehistoric cave paintings of the Acacus Mountains area
- The Sahara – not called the greatest desert on earth for nothing

Libya has been conquered and settled at one time or another by Berbers, Phoenicians, Greeks, Romans, Vandals, Byzantines, Arabs, Turks and Italians. The remains of these periods can be seen along the coast and in the desert cities of the Fezzan.

The Roman remains at Leptis Magna, east of Tripoli, are arguably the finest you'll see in the Mediterranean. In the Green Mountains in the east of the country are the Greek cities of the Pentapolis, the best preserved of which is Cyrene.

In the deep south of the country is some of the finest prehistoric rock art in Africa, much of it to be found in the Acacus Mountain area near Ghat.

Also in the Fezzan are the ruins of the Garamantian empire which held sway in the Sahara for 1000 years until the Arab invasion.

Despite Libya's somewhat intimidating reputation, travellers who have visited Libya usually report having a pleasant time. The Libyan people have always had a reputation for their kindness and hospitality to visitors and they will often go out of their way to help.

Facts about the Country

HISTORY
The Romans invaded Tripolitania (the region around Tripoli) in 106 BC and by 64 BC Julius Caesar had completed the occupation. As a Roman province Libya was prosperous,

LIBYA

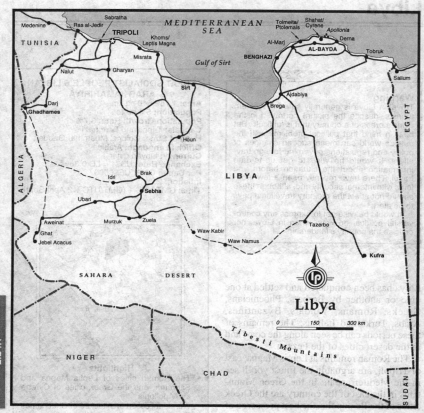

reaching a golden age in the 2nd century AD. The three principal Roman cities of Sabratha, Oea and Leptis Magna provided the empire with grain, oil and a supply of slaves and exotic goods from sub-Saharan Africa.

One of Libya's most celebrated historical figures is Septimius Severus, who was born in Leptis Magna and became emperor of Rome in 193 AD. During his reign he built some of the outstanding public buildings at Leptis as a lasting tribute to his home town.

The decline of the Roman Empire saw the classical cities fall into ruin, and this process was hastened by the Vandals' destructive sweep through northern Africa in the 5th century AD. When the Byzantines took over in the 6th century, efforts were made to refortify and revitalise the ancient cities, but it was only a last flicker of life before they collapsed into disuse. Only Oea, which today is the capital, Tripoli, remains a living city.

The Arab invasion in the 7th century changed the face of Libya forever, as the country quickly became Islamic (it remains so today). Arab rule was culturally fruitful, and there are many examples of early Islamic architecture, especially in the oases of the south.

The Arabs ruled Libya until the Turks conquered the country in the middle of the 16th century. Although nominally ruled by the Sublime Porte (the court of Constantinople), Tripoli was in fact run by a succession of locally appointed rulers who levied a toll on every Christian fleet using the Mediterranean.

Following the Napoleonic wars the European powers began to colonise northern Africa, and the Turks hastened to strengthen their control of Libya, ruling it once more directly from Constantinople. Libya was the last North African possession of the Turks and it was taken from them by the Italians in that country's last-minute bid for colonies in Africa. The Italian period was a devastating one for the Libyan people. The Italians viewed Libya as a 'fourth shore' of Italy and embarked upon a complete 'Italianisation' program. Between 1911 and the end of WWII, half of the indigenous population of one million had been either exiled or exterminated.

Libya suffered the crowning misfortune of being a theatre of war during WWII. The desert campaign left behind huge minefields, some of which remain.

In the post-war years Italy was forced to give up Libya, and the country became an independent kingdom under King Idris, an ageing Senussi leader. His appointment as king was not universally popular, especially outside of his native Cyrenaica, the region around Benghazi.

Fired by growing political discontent and a mood of Pan-Arabism which was sweeping the Arab world, a small group of army officers, led by 27-year-old Captain Muammar Gaddafi, deposed the old king on 1 September 1969 in a coup. Soon after, the British and Americans were ordered to leave the bases they had occupied since WWII, and the 25,000 descendants of the Italian colonists were also forced to pack their bags and leave promptly.

Gaddafi's regime was committed to a more equitable distribution of Libya's enormous oil income, and billions of dollars were spent on roads, schools, housing, hospitals and agriculture.

During the mid-70s Gaddafi wrote the *Green Book*, which he claims is a radical alternative to capitalism and communism. Launching his revolution, he declared Libya to be a *Jamahiriya* (which loosely translates as 'state of the masses'), and set about dismantling the state apparatus and replacing it with People's Committees. In practice however, Libya's government is a military dictatorship.

Almost wholly foreign-owned and controlled at the time of King Idris' overthrow, Libya's oil deposits have been taken over by a government determined to gain control of the country's main natural resource. The foreign oil companies formed a cartel to resist such a development, but by 1973 they had been forced to accept a minimum of 51% Libyan ownership.

Oil money funded the US$27 billion Great Man-Made River Project which pumps water from ancient acquifers the deep desert to the coastal areas. The water is intended to make Libya self-sufficient in food production.

Throughout the 1970s and 1980s Libya adopted a high international profile based on Pan-Arabism, its virulent condemnation of 'western imperialism', its support of liberation movements around the world and military adventurism in neighbouring African countries.

What angered western countries most was Gaddafi's support of real and so-called liberation movements, and particularly his alleged support of international terrorist organisations. While there was probably some truth to the accusations in respect of some of these groups, just as much support (if not more) was being provided by Syria – but Middle Eastern politics demanded that Syria's favour be curried in the search for a peace treaty between Israel and its hostile neighbours.

These activities only served to isolate Libya further from the international community. The most violent reaction came from the USA, culminating in the air strike of April 1986, which killed dozens of people including Gaddafi's adopted baby daughter.

LIBYA

Libya's present isolation from the international community followed the bombing and destruction of a Pan-Am airliner over Lockerbie in Scotland in 1988. Libya was accused of planting the bomb, and two Libyans were named as suspects. The resulting stand-off caused the US to pressure the UN Security Council to impose sanctions on the country. Sanctions still apply today; no aircraft can fly in, out or over Libya, and the trade of military equipment and parts with Libya is forbidden.

Gaddafi's control of the political scene will probably remain for the immediate future, despite occasional outbreaks of civil disobedience and several rumoured military coup attempts. Islamist groups may be his regime's greatest threat in the long term.

GEOGRAPHY & CLIMATE

Libya is the fourth-largest country in Africa with around 1.8 million sq km of mostly desert terrain. The narrow coastal strip receives sufficient rainfall for agriculture and it's here that 95% of the population lives.

Summer is very hot, with temperatures on the coast around 30°C, often accompanied by high humidity, and temperatures in the south often reaching 45°C.

The best times to visit Libya are in the northern spring and autumn, although you may encounter the *ghibli*, a hot, dry, sand-laden wind which can raise the temperature within hours to between 40°C and 50°C.

ECOLOGY & ENVIRONMENT

Due to its small population and large area, Libya has few serious environmental headaches. Far and away the biggest problem is chronic littering; everywhere you look there are piles of rubbish, and they're usually of the non-biodegradable variety. This sometimes spoils beaches and other beauty spots.

Many of Libya's indigenous animals have long been hunted to virtual extinction and their habitats damaged by grazing goats. Attempts to vegetate the encroaching sand dunes have government backing, but it's a slow process. The country's chronic water shortage has been solved by the Great Man-made River Project; although the impact on the Saharan acquifers it drains has not been an issue.

POPULATION & PEOPLE

Libya has a population of 5.4 million, and half of its people are under 15. Libyans consider themselves to be Arab, although ethnically there is quite a mixture of other races including Turkish, Berber and sub-Saharan African.

SOCIETY & CONDUCT

Libya is a conservative Muslim country and foreigners, especially women, should take great care not to infringe the local customs by dressing inappropriately or indulging in loud, flashy behaviour. Alcohol is forbidden and social mixing between the sexes is very limited. Nonetheless, Libyan women are active in public life and often found in business and government jobs.

RELIGION

Libya is almost 100% Sunni Muslim. Religion is important but not too restrictive.

LANGUAGE

Arabic is the official language. All road, shop and other public signs are in Arabic, so that some working knowledge of the language is extremely useful. See the Language Appendix for useful words and phrases. English is often spoken by those in business, and some older Libyans speak Italian.

Facts for the Visitor

VISAS & DOCUMENTS
Visas

Visas are required for all. Nationals of Israel are not admitted; nor are those with Israeli stamps in their passports. Independent tourist visas are not granted to nationals of Australia, New Zealand, UK, USA, Canada or anywhere else without a Libyan People's Bureau. These nationalities need a group tourist visa sponsored by a Libyan tour company (see Organised Tours in the main Getting Around section). Countries without a Libyan People's Bureau (embassy) often have a Libyan Interests Section working out of another embassy. Visas can be processed through these or another nominated Libyan embassy.

Before applying for a visa you *must* have your passport details translated into Arabic. Without this the Libyan embassies will not accept your visa application. You can obtain a stamp in Arabic from most western embassies or passport offices, and the details will then have to be written in by hand.

Visa cost, on average, US$28. Visas are normally valid for a one month stay. Foreigners have to register at a police station within 48 hours of arrival. Usually your hotel will do this for you, but it is important to check. The police station in Tripoli is in Sharia Baladiya. The forms are in Arabic.

Other Visas

Egypt
    Visas are issued by the Egyptian Consulate. They take three days and costs US$50.
Tunisia
    Most EU nationals, citizens of the USA, Canada and Japan do not need a visa to enter Tunisia. Australians and New Zealanders do need a visa and processing can be slow – up to two weeks from the Tunisian embassy in Tripoli. They cost US$7. Double-entry visas are hard to obtain.

EMBASSIES
Libyan People's Bureaus

There are Libyan embassies (People's Bureaus) in most European capitals, and Egypt, Malta and Tunisia. The UK has a Libyan Interests Section which works out of the Saudi Arabian embassy.

Foreign Embassies in Libya

Countries with diplomatic representation in Tripoli include:

Egypt (consulate)
    Sharia Omar al-Mukhtar
France
    Sharia Ahmad Lotfi Said, PO Box 312 (☎ 33 526)

Germany
    Sharia Hasan al-Mashay, PO Box 302 (☎ 30 554)
Tunisia
    Sharia Bin 'Ashur (☎ (021) 607161)
UK
    British Interests Section, c/o Italian Embassy, Sharia Uhari 1, PO Box 912 (☎ 31 191)
USA
    US Interests Section, c/o Belgian Embassy, Tower 4, That Al-Amad Complex (☎ (021) 33 771)

CUSTOMS

All pork and alcohol products are prohibited. Books, magazines and videos may be confiscated.

MONEY

LD 1 = US$0.36

The unit of currency is the Libyan dinar (LD) which equals 1000 dirham. Credit cards are not accepted in Libya, and travellers' cheques are impossible to change. Cash is the only practical option when travelling, and the favoured currency is the US dollar.

A black market exists, but great discretion should be exercised when changing money this way. Hotel staff and shopkeepers are often prepared to change money, but don't ask in front of other people. The current black market rate is six times the bank rate.

All prices quoted in this chapter have been calculated at the *official exchange rate*.

POST & COMMUNICATIONS

Libya's postal system has suffered since the UN embargo as there is now no airmail. There is a high incidence of undelivered mail to and from Libya. A letter to Europe costs US$1. Poste restante services are available in the main cities. The country's international telephone code is 218.

The main post offices also offer public telephone services for both local and international calls. You may be asked for identification, so take your passport or hotel registration card.

PHOTOGRAPHY

Libya is very sensitive about photography

and there are still reports of foreigners being stopped and questioned when taking photographs, especially in Tripoli. The worst thing that may happen is that you will have your film confiscated. There is no problem with taking pictures at tourist sites, but when travelling in the rural areas be careful about photographing people and get their permission first. Do not try to photograph women.

DANGERS & ANNOYANCES

Occasional outbreaks of civil disobedience have happened recently and travellers should be aware of the current situation when they travel to Libya.

BUSINESS HOURS

Libya operates on an Islamic working week, with Friday as the day off. Business hours are from 7 am to 2 pm in summer, and from 8 am to 1 pm and 4 to 6.30 pm in winter. Government offices are open from 8 am to 2pm.

PUBLIC HOLIDAYS

Libya observes all the Islamic holidays (see Public Holidays in the Regional Facts for the Visitor chapter for dates) in addition to the following national holidays: 2 March (Declaration of the Jamahiriya Day); 11 June (Evacuation of foreign military bases Day); 1 September (Anniversary of the Revolution Day); 26 October (Day of Mourning; everything closes, including the borders, and there are no international telephones, telexes, faxes or ferries).

ACCOMMODATION

There is a shortage of cheap hotels in Libya, even in the main cities. Accommodation tends to polarise into overpriced business-class hotels (where you can expect to pay US$120) and cheap but not very cheerful budget-class hotels (about US$30). If you stay in the better hotels you will be expected to pay in hard currency at the official rate (often in advance). In the smaller, cheaper hotels you can often pay in local currency.

There is an abundance of hostels in Libya, mostly well-kept and clean, if somewhat basic. They are a good alternative for those on a budget, and in some far-flung places they may be the only accommodation. They charge around US$7.

FOOD

Libyan cuisine revolves around the North African staple *couscous*, and macaroni-based dishes influenced by the Italians. Lamb and chicken are the most popular meats, followed by camel. Libyan soup, served at almost every meal, is a kind of highly spiced minestrone with lamb and pasta. On the coast the local fish is very good.

If you are travelling to the interior you may come across some Saharan dishes such as *f'taat,* which is made with buckwheat pancakes and layered with sauce and meat.

DRINKS

There is strictly no alcohol on sale in Libya, and unless you have a taste for sweet, fizzy drinks the choice can be frustratingly limited. Tea is always served sweet and the coffee, both Arabic and espresso, is usually very good.

Getting There & Away

AIR

At the time of writing and for the foreseeable future there are no international air services to or from Libya due to the UN air embargo. In normal times Tripoli has good connections with most of the Arab capitals and with Europe and the Far East.

LAND

Chad

Although the border is open and there are reliable connections by truck, only Libyan or Chadian nationals are allowed to cross.

Egypt

There are frequent buses from Benghazi to Alexandria and Cairo, leaving from the bus station in the Funduq Bazaar area. There are also local buses as far as the border, and you can connect with an Egyptian bus on the other side. It is also possible to get a share taxi to and from either side of the border. There are also a few long-distance buses from Tripoli direct to Cairo (US$150) and Alexandria (US$140), which leave from the central bus station off Sharia Omar al-Mukhtar to the west of the medina near the waterfront.

Sudan

The border is open, but only Libyan and Sudanese citizens can cross.

Tunisia

Buses leave from the central bus station and serve Sfax, Gabés, Medenine and Tunis. They usually leave early in the morning and fill up quickly, so it is best to get there early. There are also share-taxis which leave from a stand at the central bus station near the waterfront. The fares are very low but the driving can be erratic.

SEA
Malta

There are connections every other day, but the fare is US$170 one way. See Mediterranean Ferries in the introductory Getting There & Away chapter for details.

Getting Around

AIR

There are only two aircraft left in service offering a dwindling schedule. Tripoli international airport is closed; flights go instead from the military airbase east of Tripoli.

BUS & SHARE-TAXI

The road system in Libya is excellent, smooth and fast. Air-con buses serve all of the main towns and there are services to all but the most out-of-the-way places. Share-taxis taxis also cover most of the country and are as cheap as the buses. In remote areas there may only be one bus a day, so it is important to check the times and to turn up

at least an hour early, as they tend to fill up and leave quickly.

ORGANISED TOURS

Desert safaris and archaeological tours are available from numerous private tour operators. The quality and efficiency of the services offered varies enormously but the costs seem very similar. Desert safaris cost around US$100 per person per day fully inclusive. Archeological tours cost around US$70 per person per day staying the best available hotels. Cheaper options can be negotiated. If you are in a small group, it is possible to arrange a tailor-made itinerary.

Recommended is Winzrik Travel & Tourism Services Company (☎ (021) 361 1123 or 4 or 5; fax 361 1126). Other companies include: Wings Travel & Tours (☎ (021) 333 1855; fax 333 0881); Ghadhames Travel & Tourism (☎ (0484) 2307; fax 2633); and Robban Travel & Tourism (☎ (021) 444 1530; fax 444 8065).

The General Board of Tourism (☎ (021) 50 3041; fax 50 3041 or 46 438) can advise you.

Tripoli

Tripoli is the joint capital of Libya (with Benghazi) and its main port and seat of administration. It has a population of about 1.5 million many of whom are part of the expat workforce. The old part of Tripoli still has considerable charm and an unspoilt air.

Information

The half-dozen main banks are on or near Green Square, on Sharia 1st September, Sharia Al-Magarief and Sharia Omar al-Mukhtar. They are open from 8 am to 2 pm, Saturday to Thursday.

The main post office is on Maidan Al-Jazeer, near the former cathedral (now a mosque) at the end of Sharia Al-Magarief. The public telephone office is in the same building and is open 24 hours a day. There is

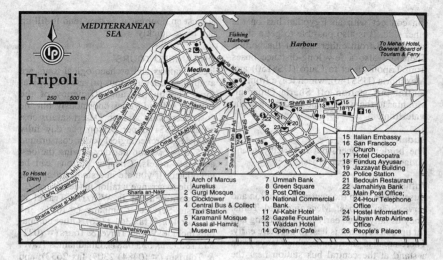

1 Arch of Marcus Aurelius
2 Gurgi Mosque
3 Clocktower
4 Central Bus & Collect Taxi Station
5 Karamanli Mosque
6 Assai al-Hamra; Museum
7 Ummah Bank
8 Green Square
9 Post Office
10 National Commercial Bank
11 Al-Kabir Hotel
12 Gazelle Fountain
13 Waddan Hotel
14 Open-air Cafe
15 Italian Embassy
16 San Francisco Church
17 Hotel Cleopatra
18 Funduq Ayyusar
19 Jazzayat Building
20 Police Station
21 Bedouin Restaurant
22 Jamahiriya Bank
23 Main Post Office; 24-Hour Telephone Office
24 Hostel Information
25 Libyan Arab Airlines Office
26 People's Palace

also a post office on the east side of Green Square.

Things to See

Of all Libyan cities, Tripoli is the most atmospheric and interesting. A lot of its traditional architecture has survived, although much of it is in need of renovation.

The dominant feature of the capital is the **Assai al-Hamra** (the Red Castle), which overlooks the port, Green Square and the old medina. The castle is vast and contains many interconnecting courtyards, mostly dating from the 18th century, and some fine classical statues and fountains from the Ottoman period. There is a good view of the city and the sea from the battlements.

The castle also houses the new **Jamahiriya Museum**, which has an excellent collection of classical antiquities. Opening times are 8.30 am to noon and 2 to 5 pm; entry is US$1.50.

The old walled city, the **medina**, is a labyrinth of narrow streets and covered souks selling traditional jewellery and clothes as well as household goods.

There are several old mosques in the city. Close to the main entrance of the medina off

Green Square is the **Karamanli Mosque**, built by the founder of the Karamanli dynasty, who ruled Tripoli in the 18th century. Many of the family's tombs can be seen in the courtyards of the mosque, surrounded by some fine tilework.

At the northern end of the medina is the **Arch of Marcus Aurelius**, the only Roman monument left in Tripoli. Nearby is one of the finest mosques in the old city, the finely decorated **Gurgi Mosque**, which dates from 1833.

Places to Stay

The *Hostel* (☎ (021) 74755) is at Gargaresh, about 3km from the centre of Tripoli off the main road towards the sea. Charges are US$8 per person per night.

The best of the cheap hotels in town is the *Funduq Ayyussar* (☎ (021) 30 911). It is in a back street in Dahra near the San Francisco Church. Singles/doubles cost US$60 for a room with bath. A couple of doors along is the *Hotel Cleopatra* for the same price.

Places to Eat

The *Bedouin Restaurant* on Sharia Al-Baladiya, almost directly behind the

Al-Kabir Hotel on the corniche, is recommended. The food is Lebanese, and lunch or dinner costs about US$20 for the full works.

There are many cafes serving soft drinks and light snacks around Green Square and along Sharia Al-Fatah. A good one is the new open-air cafe next to the Waddan Hotel, which is a popular gathering place. There are a few traditional cafes near the clocktower in the medina.

Getting Around

Buses serving the city, the suburbs and the airport leave from the main bus station, off Sharia Omar al-Mukhtar near the waterfront.

Long-distance buses and collect taxis also leave from the main bus station to destinations in Libya, Tunisia and Egypt.

Avoid the private black and white taxis, as they are hideously expensive.

Around the Country

BENGHAZI

Benghazi is the second-largest city in Libya, with a population of about 600,000, and is situated on the eastern side of the Gulf of Sirt. Joint capital with Tripoli, it is a major commercial centre and port (the port is built around a large double harbour).

There is little of historical or architectural interest in Benghazi, but it does make a good base for touring the Green Mountain area, and there are bathing beaches nearby.

There is a lively **souk** which is open daily. It is just off Sharia Al-Aguriyah (also known as Sharia Tokrah).

Places to Stay & Eat

There is a *hostel* (☎ (061) 26 201) at the Sports City complex on the south-west side of the inner harbour.

The best cheap hotel is the *Atlas Hotel* (☎ (061) 92 314) on Sharia Gamal Abdel Nasser. Singles/doubles cost US$25/30. Even crumbier is the *Medina Hotel* (☎ (061) 98 046) near the Italian church. Rooms cost US$16.50. There are several cheap restau-

rants in the area, including a good Tunisian one. Snack stalls line the cornice at night.

Getting There & Away

There are buses from Tripoli to Benghazi and Benghazi to Beyda several times a day.

CYRENE

The most splendidly preserved of the five Greek cities of Cyrenaica (the Pentapolis), Cyrene is situated on the crest of a hill next to the modern village of **Shahat**, 220km east of Benghazi. Founded in 600 BC by Greek settlers, the city is a must, not only for its temples but also for the fact that it's essentially a replica of Delphi.

The ruins are 2km from Shahat and are open from 8 am to 5 pm. They are somewhat overgrown and you'll often find yourself walking over mosaics that would be under glass if they were in Europe. The site is closed on Monday.

Twenty kilometres east of Shahat is the ancient port of **Apollonia**, near the village of Susah, whose ruins are now partially submerged (a heaven for divers). You can take a taxi from Shahat. It's a beautiful site with great swimming (technically not allowed). It's closed on Monday.

Places to Stay & Eat

At Cyrene is a *hostel* (☎ (0853) 2102) close to the upper level of the site. At Apollonia is a beach resort *Massif Susah Seahi* (☎ (0853) 2365) which costs US$60 for a room. Dinner can be had for US$20.

In Bayda 12km away there is the *Funduq Gasr al-Bayda* (☎ (084) 23455) where it's US$36/50 for singles/doubles with bath.

Getting There & Away

To get to the ruins from Benghazi take a collect taxi to Al-Bayda (two hours, US$12) and then another to Shahat (US$6). The ruins are 2km from the village. A taxi to Apollonia costs US$10.

GHADHAMES

Ghadhames is a charming oasis town 670km south-west of Tripoli, close to the borders with Algeria and Tunisia. It is worth visiting for the unique desert architecture of the old town, and for the surrounding desert scenery.

The town consists of a maze of cool, covered streets. There is a **museum** in the old Italian fort housing a collection of local artefacts. There is also the Ghadhames **merchant's house**, furnished entirely in the traditional way, which is well worth seeing. It is near the northern entrance to the old town, near the Ain Al-Faras Hotel. The key is at the fort in the museum.

Places to Stay & Eat

There is a *hostel* on the south-eastern outskirts of town. It is clean and modern but lacking in atmosphere.

The somewhat shabby *Ain Al-Faras Hotel* is conveniently located near the entrance to the old town. Rooms with air-con cost US$60. Dinner costs about US$20.

There is a new and comfortable hotel to the south of town called the *Waha Hotel* (☎ 2569/70//71; fax 2568). Singles/doubles cost US$90/105, including breakfast. Meals cost US$45.

Near the fort there is a small *restaurant/cafe* with outside seating serving simple meals for a few dollars.

Getting There & Away

There is a daily air-con bus to and from Tripoli.

GHAT & THE ACACUS

Although not very interesting itself, the town of Ghat, in the far south of the country, is the gateway to the **Acacus Mountain** area where there is a concentration of some of the finest **prehistoric rock art** in Africa, not to mention some of the most dramatic desert scenery in the Sahara.

The town is mostly inhabited by Tuareg people, many of whom eagerly await the arrival of tourists to guide into the desert. There is a deserted old quarter of crumbling mud-brick houses surmounted by an abandoned Italian fort. The old town has a lovely, vernacular-style **mosque** which is well worth seeing.

Organised Tours

There are two main tourism companies in Ghat which can provide advice and facilities for travellers to the area. Acacus Tours (☎ (0724) 2804) and Winzrik Tourism Services Company (☎ (0724) 2600) have offices on the main road which runs through the town, and can provide vehicles, equipment and guides for trips to the Acacus.

A permit is needed for travel to the Acacus, and a guide is compulsory. The above tourism offices can arrange permits (one working day). You need two passport photos and they cost about US$10.

Places to Stay & Eat

There is only one hotel in town, the *Tassili Hotel* (☎ (0274) 2570), run by Winzrik (you can book through its Tripoli office). It is just off the main road, next to the post office. Rooms cost US$30.

Winzrik Tourism Services Company operates a *camp* of palm-frond huts in a wild desert setting near Tadrat, about 10km from Ghat. Contact Winzrik to arrange a stay.

There are no restaurants in Ghat apart from in the hotel. Only a couple of cafes sell snacks.

Getting There & Away

There is a daily bus to/from Sebha via Ubari (five hours). From Sebha there are regular bus services to Tripoli (nine hours).

LEPTIS MAGNA

Leptis Magna is the finest classical site in Libya and should not be missed. The Roman remains cover a large site 120km to the east of Tripoli, next to the modern town of Khoms.

Originally a Carthaginian city, Leptis was to become one of the most important cities in the Roman empire, supplying grain and oil and occupying a key position on the African trade route.

During the reign of the emperor Septimius Severus (193-211 AD) Leptis Magna flourished, and many of the fine buildings seen today date from this period. Among the many buildings are a magnificent carved basilica, a theatre, a gigantic forum and baths which are the largest outside Rome. The site is open daily from 8 am to 5.30 pm except Monday.

The town of Khoms is dull and modern but has a fine stretch of beach running from the town to Leptis Magna.

Places to Stay

The cheapest place is the *Hotel Al-Sherief* (☎ 22816) on Sharia Khoms in the centre of Khoms. Rooms cost US$12/15 for singles/doubles with shared bathroom. Breakfast is an extra US$6.

The *Funduq Seahia* (☎ 22130) is probably a better bet. It is off Sharia Khoms down a side street opposite the bus station. Rooms cost US$15/25 and some have private bathroom.

Getting There & Away

Collect taxis run regularly to Khoms from Tripoli and cost about US$8.

SABRATHA

Sabratha is the sister town of Leptis Magna and is a finely preserved Roman city 68km west of Tripoli. There is a small modern town of the same name, and buses and collect taxis regularly stop there. The ruins are about 1.5km from the town and taxi drivers will take you to the gate for a small fee. The site is open daily from 8 am to 5.30 pm. Keep your ticket for entry to the museum. The highlight of the remains is the stunning rose-coloured, three-tiered **Roman theatre**, somewhat reminiscent of Petra in Jordan.

Places to Stay & Eat

There is a good *hostel* (☎ (024) 2215) right next to the site. The *Funduq Sabratha* near the corner of the main road charges US$22 for a basic room. The *Restaurant Sherazade* is located in an old church on the main road (by the turning to the ruins). Lunch/dinner costs US$8.

Madagascar

Although it has long remained an obscure destination, an increasing number of travellers are discovering Madagascar and its delights – rainforest and desert, high plateaus and tropical islands, some amazing natural features and varied, unique wildlife and flora.

Travelling independently around Madagascar is often not easy, but visitors who have discovered the remote beaches, and explored the forests with endemic lemurs and chameleons, among other delights, say it is all worthwhile. Madagascar has a good range of accommodation and restaurants, and is cheaper than other nearby countries on the African mainland and in the Indian Ocean.

Facts about the Country

HISTORY

Madagascar lies relatively close to the African mainland, but apparently remained uninhabited until around 1500 to 2000 years ago. The majority of the current population has descended from Malay-Polynesian migrants who began to arrive during the 6th century. It isn't clear how these settlers arrived, but they may well have colonised Madagascar after migrating in a single voyage, and then travelling and trading along the coasts of Arabia and eastern Africa.

In 1500, the first Europeans, a Portuguese fleet under the command of Diego Dias, arrived and named the island Sao Lourenço. In the centuries following, there were repeated attempts by the Portuguese, Dutch and British to establish permanent bases. From the end of the 17th century onwards, bands of pirates established bases in Madagascar, especially on Île Sainte Marie (Nosy Boraha).

In the 1790s, the Merina king Andrianampoinimerina unified the Merina tribe of the highlands using European weapons and

REPUBLIC OF MADAGASCAR
Area: 594,180 sq km
Population: 13.9 million
Population Growth Rate: 3.2%
Capital: Antananarivo
Head of State: President Didier Ratsiraka
Official Languages: Malagasy, French
Currency: Franc Malgache (FMg)
Exchange Rate: FMg 4300 = US$1
Per Capita GNP: US$220
Inflation: 20%
Time: GMT/UTC + 3

Highlights
- The endemic wildlife and spectacular rainforest in the Parc National d'Andasibe-Mantadia
- Exhilarating train ride between Fianarantsoa and Manakara
- Luxurious Hôtel Relais de la Reine, near the Parc National de Isalo
- Diving, whale-watching and lazing on glorious beaches on Île Sainte Marie

advisers. The Merina soon became Madagascar's dominant tribe and came to control nearly half the island.

In 1820, Britain signed a treaty recognising Madagascar as an independent state under Merina rule, but once the Suez Canal was built, in 1869, Britain lost interest in Madagascar. In 1890, an Anglo-French treaty ceded control to the French. Four years later, the Merina queen, Ranavalona III, was

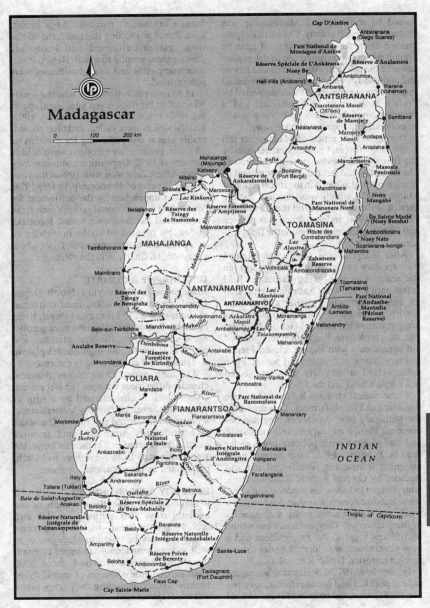

Madagascar

0   100   200 km

Cap D'Ambre
Antsiranana (Diego Suarez)
Parc National de Montagne d'Ambre
Réserve Spéciale de L'Ankàrana
Nosy Be
Réserve d'Analamera
Hell-Ville (Andoany)
Ambilombe
Iharana (Vohémar)
Ambanja
ANTSIRANANA
Tsaratanana Massif (2876m)
Réserve de Marojejy
Béalanana
Sambava
Marojejy Massif
Andapa
Antsohihy
Antalaha
Maroantsetra
Masoala Peninsula
Mahajanga (Majunga)
Sofia River
Boriziny (Port Bergé)
Réserve de Ankarafantsika
Mandritsara
Nosy Mangabe
Katsepy
Mitsinjo
Marovoay
Parc National de Mananara Nord
Soalala
Lac Kinkony
Île Sainte Marie (Nosy Boraha)
Besalampy
Réserve des Tsingy de Namoroka
Réserve Forestière d'Ampijoroa
TOAMASINA
Ambodifotatra
Nosy Nato
Maevatanana
Route des Contrabandiers
Soanierana-Ivongo
Tamborano
MAHAJANGA
Lac Alaotra
Mahambo
Zahamena Reserve
Vohiojala
Ambatondrazaka
Toamasina (Tamatave)
Maintirano
Réserve des Tsingy de Bemaraha
Tsiroanomandidy
ANTANANARIVO
Lac Mantasoa
Parc National d'Andasibe-Mantadia (Périnet Reserve)
Arivonimamo
ANTANANARIVO
Ambila-Lemaitso
Belo-sur-Tsiribihina
Miandrivazo
Ankaratra Massif
Moramanga
Ambatolampy
Lac Tsiazompaniry
Vatomandry
Analabe Reserve
Tsiribihina
Réserve Forestière de Kirindy
Antsirabe
Mahanoro
Morondava
Mania River
TOLIARA
Nosy-Varika
Ambositra
Mandabe
Parc National de Ranomafana
Morombe
Beroroha
Mananjary
Manja
FIANARANTSOA
Fianarantsoa
Zomandao River
Ambalavao
INDIAN OCEAN
Lac Ihotry
Parc National de Isalo
Réserve Naturelle Intégrale d'Andringitra
Manakara
Ankazoabo
Vohipeno
Ranohira
Farafangana
Sakaraha
Ifaty
Andranovory
Betroka
Vangaindrano
Toliara (Tuléar)
Onilahy River
Baie de Saint-Augustin
Anakao
Tropic of Capricorn
Betioky
Réserve Spéciale de Beza-Mahafaly
Réserve Naturelle Intégrale de Tsimanampetsofsa
Bekily
Beraketa
Ampanihy
Réserve Naturelle Intégrale d'Andohalela
Sainte-Luce
Beloha
Réserve Privée de Berenty
Ambovombe
Taolagnaro (Fort Dauphin)
Faux Cap
Cap Sainte-Marie

MADAGASCAR

forced to abdicate and Madagascar was declared a French colony. Colonisation progressed from the expropriation of land by French settlers and companies to the exploitation of the peasantry through forced labour and taxes and development of a coffee-based import-export economy. It was supported by French-built roads and railroads and a French-trained Malagasy elite. As a result, resentment grew against French rule.

During WWII, much of Madagascar fell to the Vichy forces, but they were retaken by the British and handed over to Général de Gaulle in 1943. After the war, resentment of foreign rule culminated in the insurrection of March 1947, which was crushed by the French at the cost of several thousand lives. Finally, in 1960, independence was granted and Philibert Tsiranana became the first president.

After independence, the French retained their military bases and, effectively, still ran the shop. The right-wing Tsiranana held office until 1972, when he brutally repressed an anti-government uprising and popular sentiment demanded that he step down. His army commander, General Gabriel Ramantsoa, then took over. Ramantsoa renegotiated aid agreements with France, closed French military bases and attempted to set up a collectivised society. He also established links with China and the USSR.

These radical changes led to a wholesale departure of French farmers. This reminded the Malagasy how dependent they had become on French capital and technical skill, and the government's policies came under fire. In February 1975, after several coup attempts, Ramantsoa was forced out and replaced by Colonel Richard Ratsimandrava, who pledged to follow his predecessor's policies. Ratsimandrava was shot dead within a week and a rebel army group announced a military takeover. They, in turn, were routed by officers loyal to the ex-president and a new government was formed under former foreign minister, Didier Ratsiraka.

In the late 1970s, Ratsiraka attempted radical political and social reforms, severing ties with France and courting favour and aid from Communist nations. As a result, agricultural production stagnated, the education system collapsed and economic development ground to a halt. Banks, insurance companies and other businesses were nationalised.

In March 1989, Ratsiraka was dubiously 'elected' to his third seven year term, sparking riots. From May 1991 to January 1992, general strikes were called, and after considerable unrest and jockeying for position on all sides, preliminary elections were held in November 1992. Opposition candidate, Professor Albert Zafy, won with 70% of the vote, ending 17 years of dictatorship. In July 1996, Zafy was impeached by the parliament for 'exceeding constitutional powers' and fresh presidential elections were called. Ratsiraka ended 19 months of exile in France to compete, and to the surprise of just about everyone, he finally won the elections.

GEOGRAPHY & CLIMATE

Madagascar is the world's fourth largest island, measuring 1580km from north-east to south-west and 571km east to west. It can be divided geographically into three parallel north-south zones: the low plateaus and plains in the west, the high central plateau and the narrow coastal strip in the east.

The high central spine causes dramatic climatic differences between the wet eastern coast, which is characterised by a strip of coastal rainforest, and the dry western coast, with its savannah and dry forest. The south is considerably more arid and features cactus-like vegetation. On the east coast, the wet season lasts from November to March, punctuated by the occasional cyclone.

ECOLOGY & ENVIRONMENT

Madagascar's unique flora – such as the baobab, travellers' palm (ravinala) and orchid – and the fauna – including the lemur which can only be found in Madagascar, as well as the chameleon – are under constant threat. Since humans arrived about 2000 years ago, countless species of animals have become extinct, including the pygmy hippo and the elephant bird.

Deforestation continues through slash-and-burn farming to grow rice, breed zebu and obtain fuel, and is exacerbated by dramatic urban sprawl. Tragically, over 85% of the country's natural forest has disappeared. Conservationists are desperately trying to save some of the pristine countryside and protect the flora and fauna.

POPULATION & PEOPLE

Madagascar's rapidly growing population of nearly 14 million is composed mainly of the 18 Malagasy tribes as well as Europeans (mainly French), Comorians, Chinese and Indo-Pakistanis. The Merinas represent about 27% of the total while the Betsimisaraka on the east coast account for 15%. Around half the population follow traditional beliefs, and half Christianity.

As in other countries in the region, dance and music are an important part of the Malagasy lifestyle; the *hira gasy* (see the Hira Gasy boxed story), and the *famadihana* 'turning of the bones' funeral ceremony, are probably the most impressive spectacles. Contemporary and traditional music, influenced by mainland African rhythms and instruments from Asia, is becoming increasingly popular in Europe. Another unique aspect of the island is the red-brick houses in the highlands, while homes on the coast are often made from raffia or ravinala palms.

LANGUAGE

The official languages are French and Malagasy. You will have no problems if you speak French. A few people in the tourist industry may speak English, but you will have great difficulty unless you have some grasp of French (or Malagasy). See the Language Appendix for useful French phrases.

Facts for the Visitor

VISAS

All visitors, except citizens of several African countries, must have visas issued by a Malagasy embassy or consulate. Visas are issued for 90 days, and are not generally extendable without special permission. The embassy/consulate will need your passport, four completed forms, four passport photos, a copy of your ticket and a fee of around US$33.

Other Visas

Mayotte & Réunion

The French consulate, at the back of the embassy in Antananarivo, can issue a visa within 24 hours (US$37).

EMBASSIES

Malagasy Embassies

There are diplomatic missions abroad in Australia, Belgium, Canada, France, Germany, Italy, the UK and the USA, and in Africa in the Comoros, Kenya, Mauritius, Réunion and South Africa.

Foreign Embassies in Madagascar

The following countries have diplomatic representation in Antananarivo:

France
  3 Làlana Jean Jaurès, Ambatomena (☎ 23 700)
UK
  Imm NY Havana, 67 Ha (☎ 27 370)
USA
  14-16 Làlana Rainitovo, Ambodirotra (☎ 23 802)

MONEY

US$1 = FMg 4300

The unit of currency is the Malagasy franc or *franc malgache* (FMg). Every major town has at least one branch of the four major banks (BFV, BNI-CL, BMOI and BTM) which will change US and major European currencies in cash and travellers' cheques. Larger branches of the BTM will give cash advances on MasterCard; BFV will do the same with Visa card. Banks are generally open weekdays from 8 am to 4 pm.

The airport at Antananarivo is the only one in the country with moneychanging facilities, so if you arrive at another airport, make sure you have some French francs. If you stay away from resorts, expensive activities and Tana you can live well for about US$15 a day for a single, or US$25 a double.

MADAGASCAR

POST & COMMUNICATIONS

Every major town has a reliable post office and telephone exchange. Sending mail or postcards is cheap, and they invariably reach their destination. International calls can take a while to organise (and be expensive) at post offices, so it's easier to buy a *telecarte* and use a public telephone for all national and international calls. Madagscar's country code is 261 and the area codes for dialling another province are: Antananarivo 02; Toamasina 05; Mahajanga 06; Fianarantsoa 07; Antsiranana 08; and Toliara 09.

DANGERS & ANNOYANCES

Robbery, especially after dark, is a genuine possibility in Antananarivo. Avoid walking too far from your hotel after dark, particularly around Analakely, Araben ny Fahaleovantena, the train station and the numerous stairways. At night, take a taxi, walk in a group, hire a guard from the hotel or restaurant, or stay at a hotel with, or very near to, a restaurant.

PUBLIC HOLIDAYS

Public holidays observed in Madagascar include: 1 January, 29 March (Martyr's Day), 1 May (Labour Day), 24 May (OAU Day), 26 June (Independence Day), 1 November (All Saint's Day), 25 December, 30 December (Republic Day), Good Friday and Easter Monday.

Getting There & Away

AIR

Air France flies to Antananarivo from Paris via Nairobi twice a week. Air Madagascar (affectionately known as Air Mad) connects Tana with Paris via Frankfurt, Zurich or Munich and Nairobi, twice a week. The cheapest option from Europe is the weekly Aeroflot flight from Moscow via Zurich.

Air Mad also flies to the Comoros, Mauritius, Réunion, and the Seychelles. Other regional airlines flying to these islands from Madagascar are Air Mauritius, TAM and Air Austral. Interair and Air Mad fly to/from Johannesburg. If you enter Madagascar with Air Mad, you should receive a 50% discount on domestic flights – a good reason to use Air Mad.

To Mauritius, Réunion, the Seychelles and the Comoros, the departure tax (payable in FFr or FMg) is US$13; to elsewhere, US$20.

SEA

Foreigners do not normally travel to Madagascar by boat, but with some determination, you can do it. However, the trip will be long, possibly rough, and may not be too much cheaper than a flight. The two main ports are Mahajanga, where you can find a ship sailing to Mayotte, and Grande Comore in the Comoros, and probably on to Zanzibar. From Toamasina, cargo boats regularly travel to Mauritius and Réunion.

Getting Around

AIR

Air Madagascar's impressive domestic network reaches most of the country. The main Air Mad office (☎ 22 222) is at 31 Araben ny Fahaleovantena, Antananarivo. The only alternative to Air Mad is the Réunion-based TAM airline (☎ 29 691), which links Tana with major places like Île Sainte Marie, Nosy Be and Mahajanga.

Tickets purchased in Madagascar are not too expensive, but nonresidents must pay in foreign currency (ie, any major currencies in cash, but mainly US$ or FFr in the countryside). The departure tax on domestic flights is US$2 (payable in FMg).

MINI-BUS & TAXI

Most of Madagascar's 35,000km of road (only 4000km of which is tar-sealed) is in an abominable state, and, during the rainy season, even main roads are often impassable. The most popular, inexpensive forms of road transport are the *taxi-brousse* (bush taxi), *car-brousse* (bush mini-bus) and *taxi-be* (Peugeot 404 and 504 estate wagons).

Some runs, such as Antananarivo to Toamasina, are served by larger buses.

These vehicles are usually in a dilapidated state, are always packed well beyond capacity, and regularly break down. Allow plenty of time for all overland trips. On longer trips, the vehicle will often stop for the night, leaving passengers to sleep in the vehicle or out on the ground, or to seek accommodation in a local hotel or private home.

TRAIN

Madagascar's 850km of track connects Antananarivo and Toamasina (the line was closed at the time of research); Tana and Antsirabe (daily); Fianarantsoa and Manakara (twice a week); and Tana and Ambatondrazaka (three times a week). First class is comfortable but not plush; locals normally travel 2nd class, so it's more crowded. One fascinating trip, which is recommended if it is running, is on the Micheline private train between Tana and Toamasina. Enquire at agencies at either station. For all trains, arrive at the station at least an hour before departure to buy your ticket.

BOAT

Between some coastal villages and along rivers, *pirogues* (dugout canoes) are the primary means of transport. For longer trips, with hard bargaining, you'll pay from US$12 to US$18 per day. You can also hire *boutres* (dhows) and *goëlettes* (larger cargo boats), or travel on a cargo vessel which accepts paying passengers.

Daily ferries and regular cargo boats sail from the mainland to the populated islands of Nosy Be and Île Sainte Marie.

Antananarivo

Known locally as Tana, the capital of Madagascar (population around 1.5 million, mostly Merina) is like no other city on earth. The tall, narrow houses with their crumbling red brickwork, terracotta-tiled roofs, wooden balconies and shuttered windows, sprawl up the various levels over the 12 hills

of Tana. Among them rise numerous church spires and crowning the city are the ruins of the former palace of Queen Ranavalona I. Still, Tana is overcrowded and polluted, and there is little reason to linger when there is so much of the country to explore.

Information

At last Madagascar has a Maison du Tourisme (☎ 32 529) in Antananarivo. It is worth visiting if you have any questions, and to pick up a few maps and pamphlets. The office is easy to find on the Place de L'Indépendance. Staff speak French and English.

The main post office is near Hôtel Colbert and has poste restante facilities; the other one is in Analakely, along Araben ny Fahaleovantena. Around these two areas, you'll also find most of the banks, all of which change money. The Librairie de Madagascar bookstore is excellent for guidebooks, maps and novels – all in French.

For medical treatment, head for the Hôpital Joseph Ravoahangy Andrianavalona (☎ 27 979).

Things to See

Tana's massive market, the **Zoma**, extends off Araben ny Fahaleovantena, continues along Araben ny 26 Jona 1960, and climbs the stone steps on either side. Bargains can be found, but avoid carrying bags or cameras and watch for pickpockets and muggers. The **Andravoahangy market** in the northern suburbs is also very busy, interesting, but potentially dangerous.

The **Parc Botanique et Zoologique de Tsimbazaza** is definitely worth a visit. They have lemurs (including an aye-aye), as well as a variety of indigenous birds, reptiles and plants. The **Musée d'Académie Malgache**, also on the zoo grounds, has natural and cultural exhibits, including funerary art. From Analakely, take an ANTAFITA No 15 bus or a taxi. The entrance is opposite the Restaurant Indonesia. You don't have to take any of the very annoying guides who hang around the entrance.

The **Rova** (Palais de la Reine or 'Queen's Palace') recently burnt down, and won't be

MADAGASCAR

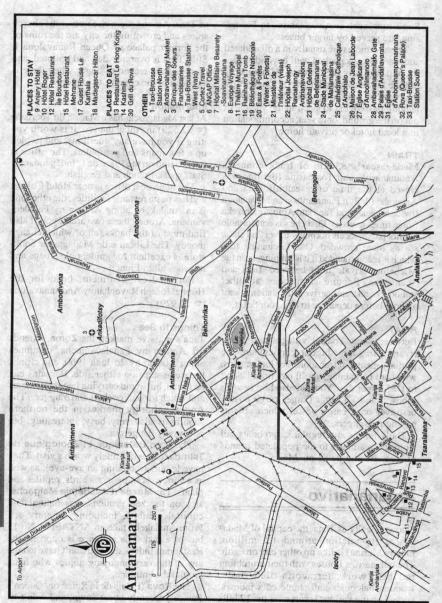

PLACES TO STAY
9 Anjary Hôtel
10 Hôtel Roger
12 Hôtel Restaurant
   Île Bourbon
15 Hôtel Restaurant
   Mehrane
17 Guest House Le
   Karthala
18 Madagascar Hilton

PLACES TO EAT
13 Restaurant Le Hong Kong
14 Kashmir
30 Grill du Rova

OTHER
1 Taxi-Brousse
   Station North
2 Andravoahangy Market
3 Clinique des Soeurs
   Franciscaines
4 Taxi-Brousse Station
   West (Ivato)
5 Cortez Travel
6 ANGAP Office
7 Hôpital Militaire Besarety
   -Soavinandriana
8 Europe Voyage
11 Rainiharo's Tomb
16 Théâtre Municipal
19 Bibliothèque Nationale
21 Eaux & Forêts
   (Water & Forests)
22 Ministère de
   l'Intérieur (visas)
17 Hôpital Joseph
   Ravoahangy
   Andrianavalona
23 Hôpital Général
   de Befelatanana
24 Stade Municipal
   de Mahamasina
25 Cathédrale Catholique
   d'Andohalo
26 Maison de Jean Laborde
27 Église Anglicane
   d'Ambohimanoro
28 Ambavahadimitafo Gate
29 Palais d'Andafiavaratra
31 Église
   d'Amboninampamarinana
32 Rova (Queen's Palace)
33 Taxi-Brousse
   Station South

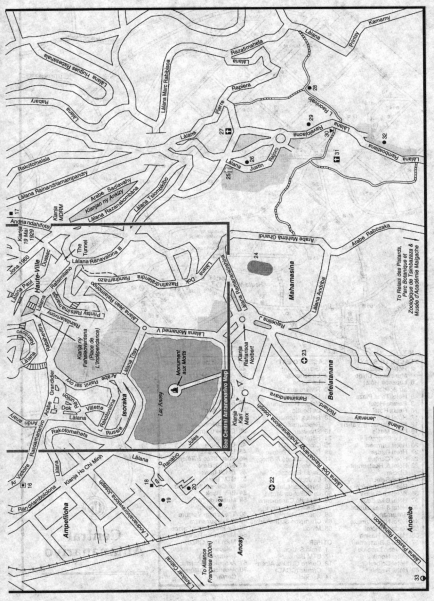

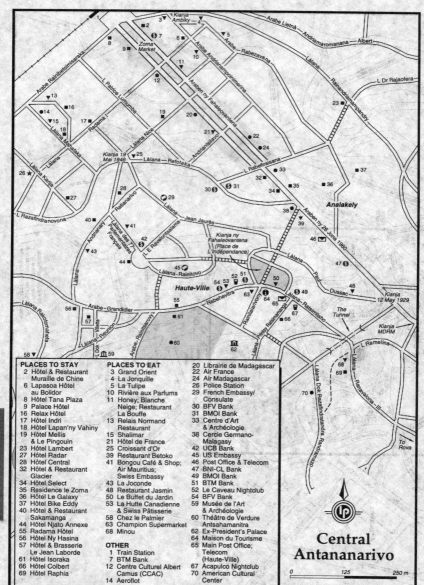

PLACES TO STAY
2 Hôtel & Restaurant
   Muraille de Chine
6 Lapasoa Hôtel
   au Bolidor
8 Hôtel Tana Plaza
9 Palace Hôtel
16 Relax Hôtel
17 Hôtel Indri
18 Hôtel Lapan'ny Vahiny
19 Hôtel Mellis
   & Le Pingouin
23 Hôtel Lambert
27 Hôtel Radar
28 Hôtel Central
32 Hôtel & Restaurant
   Glacier
34 Hôtel Select
35 Residence le Zoma
36 Hôtel Le Galaxy
37 Hôtel Bike Eddy
40 Hôtel & Restaurant
   Sakamanga
44 Hôtel Njato Annexe
55 Radama Hôtel
56 Hôtel Ny Hasina
57 Hôtel & Brasserie
   Le Jean Laborde
61 Hôtel Isoraka
66 Hôtel Colbert
69 Hôtel Raphia

PLACES TO EAT
3 Grand Orient
4 La Jonquille
5 La Tulipe
10 Rivière aux Parfums
11 Honey; Blanche
   Neige; Restaurant
   La Bouffe
13 Relais Normand
   Restaurant
15 Shalimar
21 Hôtel de France
25 Croissant d'Or
39 Restaurant Betoko
41 Bongou Café & Shop;
   Air Mauritius;
   Swiss Embassy
43 La Joconde
48 Restaurant Jasmin
50 Le Buffet du Jardin
53 La Hutte Canadienne
   & Swiss Pâtisserie
58 Chez le Palmier
63 Champion Supermarket
68 Minou

OTHER
1 Train Station
7 BTM Bank
12 Centre Culturel Albert
   Camus (CCAC)
14 Aeroflot

20 Librairie de Madagascar
22 Air France
24 Air Madagascar
26 Police Station
29 French Embassy/
   Consulate
30 BFV Bank
31 BMOI Bank
33 Centre d'Art
   & Archéologie
38 Cercle Germano-
   Malagasy
42 UCB Bank
46 Post Office & Telecom
47 BNI-CL Bank
49 BMOI Bank
51 BTM Bank
52 Le Caveau Nightclub
54 BFV Bank
59 Musée de l'Art
   & Archéologie
60 Théâtre de Verdure
   Antsahamanitra
62 Ex-President's Palace
64 Maison du Tourisme
65 Main Post Office;
   Telecom
   (Haute-Ville)
67 Acapulco Nightclub
70 American Cultural
   Center

Central
Antananarivo

0   125   250 m

opened to the public until it's repaired. For magnificent views of the town, go the **Cathédrale Catholique d'Andohalo** in the nicest part of town.

Places to Stay

The cheapest places sometime double as brothels, and have share bathrooms. The *Hôtel Lapan'ny Vahiny* looks really dingy from the outside, but the rooms aren't too bad for US$2.50; *Hôtel Roger* (☎ 30 969) is noisy but good value at US$7 a room; and the *Relax Hôtel* is very simple but good value at US$5 per room.

Despite its dodgy location, along a stairway, the *Hôtel Lambert* (☎ 22 992) is clean, secure and has a restaurant – rooms range from US$7 to US$12; and the *Hôtel Bike Eddy* (☎ 21 165), in a good, central location, costs US$9 per room.

Better are the new, and very popular, *Hôtel Sakamanga* (☎ 35 809 – advance booking is advised) – with rooms ranging from US$14 to US$20; the friendly and central *Residence le Zoma* (☎ 23 113) for US$19 per room; and *Hôtel Mellis* (☎ 23 425). The Hôtel Mellis is good value (but has no restaurant) if you can get one of the cheap rooms (US$10 to US$12); the other rooms are overpriced.

In the middle range, the tiny, charming *Hôtel Restaurant Île Bourbon* (☎ 27 942) with rooms for US$20 is worth trying to find; and *Hôtel Le Jean Laborde* (☎ 33 045) is in a nicer part of town, with an excellent restaurant and bar, and rooms for about US$24.

The *Guest House Le Karthala* (☎ 24 845) is not great value these days, with rooms from US$20, and is in a dodgy location up a stairway, but it's friendly, and has a good restaurant.

Places to Eat

Tana's *street-stalls* sell everything from yoghurt to sambos (samosas), and around the taxi-brousse stations and along the narrow streets there are plenty of tiny restaurants.

Of the handful of cafes along Araben ny Fahaleovantena, *Blanche Neige* is the best, and serves an excellent cooked breakfast in a quasi-alfresco setting. The *Croissant d'Or*,

near Hôtel Mellis, is also a favourite for breakfast and lunch.

On the Place de L'Indépendance, *Le Buffet du Jardin* is popular. Around the corner, one of our favourites is the *Minou* – though servings are a little small, the price and views are good. The *Restaurant le Hong Kong* is also recommended for Chinese meals, and drinks, while watching people walk by.

At *La Joconde*, just south of the Sakamanga, the friendly manager cooks tasty chicken or steak on an outdoor fire. The *Shalimar* is excellent for curries, but no alcohol is served.

Of the hotels, the *Restaurant Sakamanga* is very good, though prices are a little high. The *Hôtel de France* has a good range of meals, and top-notch service. For a bit of a splurge, try the *Grand Orient* for Chinese and international dishes in a pleasant, sometimes rollicking atmosphere; the *Restaurant Jasmin*; or the *Grill du Rova*, next to what was the Rova, for stupendous views, surprisingly reasonable prices, and, often, live music.

Entertainment

Of the numerous discos around the Hôtel Colbert, the best is arguably the *Acapulco*.

The *Centre Culturel Albert Camus* (☎ 23 647) and *Alliance Française* (☎ 21 107) host many live shows and films for French-speaking locals and visitors. English-speakers

---

Hira Gasy

The *hira gasy* is a unique spectacle of music, dancing and story telling, performed by a number of wildly clad troupes of about 25 performers. The performances begin with a complicated and eloquent *kabary* (discourse by an orator); the message within the kabary is then performed by the troupe in wonderfully exuberant song and acrobatic dances accompanied by tinny trumpet and clarinet music.

The themes are always upbeat, extolling the virtues of honesty and upholding tradition, and encouraging young people to respect their parents. At the end of a large hira gasy, the extent of the audience's response to the performances determines which troupe has won. ■

may want to contact the *American Cultural Center* (☎ 20 238) to find out what they offer.

For a touch of Malagasy culture, a *hira gasy* is often held on Sunday afternoons, near the Alliance Française.

Getting There & Away

Tana has four taxi-brousse stations (*gares routières*). The two main ones are the Taxi-brousse Station North at Ambodivona (take MALAKIA No 4 from Analakely or a taxi) – for Toamasina, Mahajanga and Antsiranana; and the Taxi-brousse Station South (take FIMA bus no 10 or taxi) at Anosibe – for Antsirabe, Fianarantsoa and Toliara.

From the Taxi-brousse Station West, 500m north of the train station, taxis-brousse go to Ivato (for the airport). The Taxi-brousse Station East at Ampasampito serves Manjakandriana, Lac Mantasoa, and Moramanga; take an ANTAFITA bus No 1 or 2 or a taxi.

Getting Around

The Airport Tana's airport is at Ivato, 14km from the city centre. Taxis-brousse go to Ivato, 1km from the airport, every 15 minutes from the Taxi-brousse Station West, but don't even think of using this option after dark. Taxis are better if you have luggage, but drivers will want US$11 for a ride to town – hold out for US$7.50 (check the current rate at the airport information desk).

Bus Most buses within the city begin and end their journeys at Analakely in the centre of town. They are usually so packed, and slow, that taxis or walking are better options.

Taxi Besides walking, the best way to get around is by taxi – especially after dark. The fare around town is about US$2 (more at night), but you'll have to bargain.

AROUND ANTANANARIVO

Easy day trips by regular taxi-brousse from Tana can take you east to **Carion**, from where you can trek to the **Station Forestière d'Angavokely** reserve; and, nearby, to **Lac Mantasoa**, a lovely, peaceful lake, where there are two pricey resorts.

Lac Itasy, about 120km east of Tana, is a dramatic area of volcanic domes. Only 68km south of Tana, **Ambatolampy** is the starting point for the **Station Forestière de Manjakatompo** reserve, and has several excellent restaurants.

About 20km north of Tana is **Ambohimanga**, the original capital of the Merina royal family, and home of the immense **Rova**, the 18th century royal palace, which you can visit.

Around the Country

ANTSIRABE

The delightful town of Antsirabe lies 169km south of Tana. The main attractions are the **thermal baths**, the **Star Brewery** and the two volcanic lakes, **Lac Andraikiba** and **Lac Tritriva**, which are 7km and 18km from town. Both are accessible by horse or bicycle; or you can hike or get a taxi-brousse to Andraikiba. A day trip to the nearby village of **Betafo** is also worthwhile.

Places to Stay & Eat

The cheapest accommodation is the *Hôtel Niavo* (☎ 48 467), just off Rue le Myre de Villers, which charges US$4/6 for a single/double. Better are *Hôtel Rubis*, which is often full, for US$9 a room, and *Hôtel Baobab* (☎ 48 393) for slightly less – both are in the centre of town.

The wonderful *Villa Nirina* (☎ 48 597), just north of town, has spotless rooms for US$14, including breakfast – bookings are recommended. Another good choice is the *Manoro Hôtel* (☎ 48 047), next to the taxi-brousse station, from US$9 per room. The colonial *Hôtel des Thermes* (☎ 48 761) dominates Antsirabe like a royal palace. The rooms aren't great value, but if you want to lap up a bit of luxury, tiny rooms start at US$30/40, and go much higher.

For meals, don't miss the elegant *La Halte* for excellent French food and very low prices. For snacks and drinks head to the *Helena Salon de Thé*. The *Razafimamanjy* may be hard to say, and doesn't look much from the outside, but the meals are great, and they often have live music.

ANTSIRANANA (DIEGO SUAREZ)

Antsiranana, more commonly known as Diego Suarez, sits on a small promontory in a large bay and has one of the finest harbours in the Indian Ocean. It is a pleasant part of the island, and a good place to base yourself while exploring the **Parc National de Montagne d'Ambre** – details from the WWF office (☎ 21 957) in town – but this northern region is remote.

A popular day trip by taxi-brousse, or as an alternative place to stay, is **Plage Ramena** beach, 15km east of town. Another nice break is a small pocket of wilderness known as **Montagne des Français**.

Places to Stay & Eat

Hôtel Diamont, along Rue Bezare, is good value at US$7/9 for a single/double; the *Royal Hôtel* (☎ 22 815), nearby, costs about the same.

Hôtel Maymoune (☎ 21 827), in the centre of town, is quiet and friendly for US$12 per room; more for air-con. Rooms at the *Hôtel Fiantsilaka* (☎ 22 348), on Blvd Étienne, cost US$9, but you can pay too much for a private bathroom and air-con.

The *Nouvel Hôtel* (☎ 22 262), along Rue Colbert, has clean rooms for US$10. The restaurant is great for fish, but is only open in the evenings.

The best places to eat are: the *Hortensia*, which has poor service but good, cheap meals; *Restaurant L'Extrême Orient* for very good Chinese food; and the restaurant at *Hotel L'Orchidée* is good for breakfast.

Several places cater to the expat crowd: the *Valiha* and *L'Amiral* have pizzas; and *La Pirogue*, on Rue Colbert, serves a large range of western meals.

Out at Ramena beach, there are two great places to stay and eat: the *Hôtel L'Oasis* and the *Badamera*, which both cost US$10 per bungalow.

FIANARANTSOA

Fianarantsoa is regarded as the academic and intellectual centre of Madagascar, as well as the heart of its wine-producing region. It is a good place to break up the journey between Tana and Toliara, to wait for the exhilarating **train trip to Manakara**, or to organise a visit to **Parc National de Ranomafana**, or nearby **Ambalavao** village.

Places to Stay & Eat

In a good location in Nouvelle-Ville (the middle part of the town), the basic *Nouvel Hôtel* (☎ 51 055) is good value at around US$4 per room.

Just up from the taxi-brousse station, the *Arinofy Hôtel* (☎ 50 638) is very good, and deservedly popular, from US$6/8 for a single/double.

Worth a short taxi ride from the station is the excellent *Tsara Guest House* (☎ 50 206), where rooms cost US$7/12 without/with bathroom.

Other places to check out are *Hôtel Escale*, near the train station, which may not seem much from the outside, for US$9 per room; and *Hôtel Relais du Betsileo* (☎ 50 823) for the same price.

Long regarded as Madagascar's finest restaurant, *Chez Papillon*, opposite the train station, has slowly been going downhill, but if you want some old-fashioned service and French food, give it a try.

The popular *Panda Restaurant* serves good value Chinese meals, and *Chez Alice* is worth visiting for pizzas and other tasty treats. The food at the *Tsara* and *Arinofy* hotels is also very good. Some expats rate the pastries at the bizarre *Hôtel Sofia* as some of the best in the country.

ÎLE SAINTE MARIE (NOSY BORAHA)

The slender island of Île Sainte Marie (less commonly known as Nosy Boraha) is overtaking Nosy Be as Madagascar's main beach destination. Historically, it served as a haven for Indian Ocean pirates, and near the capital of Ambodifotatra is an appropriately eerie and overgrown **pirate cemetery**. Also worthwhile are **Plage Ankarena** beach in the far south and pools at **Ambodiatafana**, near the island's northern tip.

From July to September, you are virtually guaranteed to see whales; boat trips are expensive but easy to get on, and great fun. South of Île Sainte Marie is the secluded island of **Nosy Nato**, which is easily reached by pirogue from near the airport.

Places to Stay & Eat

Bookings are not generally possible, as there are no telephones on the island. In Ambodifotatra, the *Hôtel-Restaurant Drakkar* is the best choice at US$6 per bungalow, and it serves great meals. The only other hotel in town is *La Zinnia* for US$7 per bungalow.

The island has a growing number of inexpensive beach bungalows (which fit two people), and most also serve meals. The best are: *Hôtel La Baleine*, where a four-person bungalow can cost as little as US$8; *Hôtel Lakana*, where the bungalows above water for US$15 are worth choosing; *Le Mangoustan*, with bungalows from US$3 to US$10, the best value in the bottom range; *Hôtel Atafana*, which is very popular, but now a little overpriced at US$7/15 without/with bathroom; and the remote *Antsara Bungalows*, which cost from US$5 to US$7 per bungalow.

On Nosy Nato, *Hôtel Pandanus* has lovely bungalows for US$6 to US$10. The *Hôtel Orchidées* is magnificent, and very popular – bookings (☎ Tana 35 607) are essential – with rooms for US$20/30 for a double/triple.

For meals, you are usually stuck eating at your hotel, but if you have transport, try the *Il Pirata* for pizza, near Ambodifotatra. The fish at the *Restaurant Au Bon Coin* at Ambodifotatra is excellent.

Getting There & Away

Air Mad flies daily (US$83), and TAM less often for the same price, to Île Sainte Marie from Tana, often through Toamasina. If you are travelling overland to/from Toamasina, the only official ferry (for a ridiculous US$17) leaves daily from Soanierana-Ivongo, though you'll get on a cargo boat

from Maroantsetra, Mananara or Toamasina if you ask around the ports.

Getting Around

To get around the island, hire a mountain bike for US$5/7 for a half-day/one-day; or a tiny motorcycle is great fun for US$20/31. They are available in Ambodifotatra and at major hotels. For the airport you'll have to rely on the island's one taxi-brousse, or a ride on the 'courtesy vehicle' owned by your hotel (for which you will be charged).

MAHAJANGA (MAJUNGA)

Mahajanga is Madagascar's second port (after Toamasina). It's a hot, dusty and lethargic place with long, wide promenades. It is not popular with travellers because it is remote.

For around US$5 to US$7 per room, the best cheapies to stay in are: *Hôtel Kanto* (☎ 22 978) and *Hôtel Tropic* (☎ 23 610). The better places for US$15 per room are *La Ravinala* (☎ 22 968) and *Nouvelle Hôtel* (☎ 22 110).

The *Pakiza* is great for snacks and curries; the *Hôtel Kanto* is good; and the *Sampan d'Or* is excellent for Chinese dishes. For a real treat, take a ferry (it leaves two or three times a day) across the river to **Katsepy**, where you'll find *Chez Mme Chabaud* which has outstanding meals, and bungalows.

NOSY BE

Nosy Be, the largest island off Madagascar, is the main resort island. The main town, **Andoany** (more commonly known as Hell-Ville), has a friendly and colourful market. The most popular beach for budget travellers is **Ambatoloaka**.

A popular day trip by boat is to the islet of **Nosy Tanikely**, which is surrounded by a **marine reserve** and which offers excellent snorkelling. For an overnight trip, visit the volcanic island of **Nosy Komba**, which has a **lemur reserve**, and some excellent beaches. Increasingly popular is a trek up **Mont Passot** or to **Lokobe Reserve**.

Places to Stay & Eat

In Hell-Ville, try the *Hôtel Bienvenue*, but get a room (US$7) at the back with a fan. The quirky *Hôtel de la Mer* (☎ 61 353) is improving, and has a vast range of rooms starting at US$7. Also cheap, but probably doubling as brothels, are the rooms let out by the *Hôtel Venus* and the *Saloon Bar* for US$5.

Good hangouts in Hell-Ville for a drink and a meal are the *Saloon Bar* and, around the corner, the *Nandipo*, full of French expat rugby fans playing pool. Excellent meals are available at the *Restaurant Classic*.

At Ambatoloaka, the cheapest place to stay is the Malagasy-run *Authentique* where bungalows cost US$9. Other (overpriced) places for US$15 to US$18 per bungalow are *Le Robinson* (☎ 61 436) which is quiet, but not on the beach; and *Hôtel Tropical*, which is often full.

There are a dozen great, but pricey, places in Ambatoloaka to eat: for fish, try the *Dauphin Blanc*; *La Ravinala* does good Chinese dishes; and *La Saladerie* serves Italian and Mexican food, among other dishes, right on the beach.

Other recommended bungalows around the island are the cosy *Au Rendezvous de Amis* (about US$10) at Villa Blanche; the nearby *Tsara Loky* (☎ 61 022) (US$35); and *Chez Loulou*, at Andilana, is in a gorgeous location, but very remote, for US$25.

On Nosy Komba, there are a couple of places with bungalows; the best is *Hôtel Les Lemuriens*, which charges US$10 for a simple, but clean, bungalow. Transfers from Andoany costs another US$5/6 one way/ return per person.

Getting There & Away

Air Mad (and, less often, TAM) flies daily (US$150) from Tana to Nosy Be, often via Mahajanga, and usually on to Antsiranana. It is easy to travel 'overland' from Nosy Be to Antsiranana. A ferry from Nosy Be sails to Ankify every one or two hours; best to try in the morning. Then get a taxi-brousse to Ambanja, and on to Antsiranana via Ambilombe.

Getting Around

If you arrive by air, you will have little choice but to pay the high 'tourist prices' charged by taxi drivers. There are very few taxis-brousse around the island. You can hire motorbikes, from the main hotels, and in Andoany, for US$20/35 half-day/one-day; and a taxi with a driver costs US$21/31.

TAOLAGNARO (FORT DAUPHIN)

Taolagnaro, more commonly known as Fort Dauphin, is a small, pleasant town on the far southern coast, which makes it remote and relatively unaffected by tourism. It is a great place to base yourself while exploring the local attractions.

A good day excursion is to **Tranovato**, also known as Îlot des Portugais, an island fort built by shipwrecked Portuguese sailors in 1504. Two-day pirogue and trekking trips are possible around the **Baie de Lokaro** and **Sainte-Luce**. A few hours from Taolagnaro by taxi-brousse are **Ambovombe**, with a great **zebu market** every Monday; and **Berenty Reserve** (see under Réserve Privée de Berenty in the following National Parks & Reserves section) – but avoid the Kaleta Reserve, nearby, which is a poor imitation.

Places to Stay & Eat

The *Hôtel Mahavoky* (☎ 21 332), in a huge, old boarding school, is a charming place with huge rooms for a bargain US$5. The small and friendly *Auberge Maison Age D'Or* is popular and costs from US$5 per room.

Chez Jacqueline, near the taxi-brousse station, costs from US$5 to US$8, but is inconvenient.

In the middle range, the bungalows at *Village Petit Bonheur* (☎ 21 274), on the beach, and the rooms at *Hôtel Kaleta* (☎ 21 287), in town, are good for around US$15.

The best places to eat, the *Mahavoky Annexe* and the *Panorama Restaurant*, both along the main street, are friendly and good value. Also worth trying are the *Sunflower Snack Bar*, for a snack and drink, and *La Detente* for good service, and tasty pasta.

TOAMASINA (TAMATAVE)

Also known as Tamatave, Toamasina, the country's largest port, lies on a scenic stretch of coastline. It's a favoured Malagasy holiday destination and it is worth spending a day pottering around looking at the architecture and tropical vegetation.

The best attraction is the **Jardin d'Essai et Parque Zoologique de l'Ivoloina**, a zoo, with plenty of lemurs, and a botanical garden, created in 1898. It lies along the Ivoloina River, 12km north of town. Charter a taxi, or take a taxi-brousse to Ivoloina, then walk about 7km.

Places to Stay & Eat

Near the train station are several cheap places, but they also serve as brothels. The cheapest is *Hôtel Justin* for as little as US$3 per room; the best is *Hôtel Venance* for US$4, with a decent Malagasy restaurant.

One fun option is the *Hôtel Plage* (☎ 32 090), opposite the stadium, with rooms from US$6; it is worth paying more for a bathroom and views.

Along the main street, Blvd Joffre, the *Generation Hôtel* (☎ 32 105) and *Eden Hôtel* (☎ 33 036) are recommended for rooms at about US$10.

On Blvd Joffre, the popular *Chez Jo* specialises in pizza and grills, and, underneath, the *Croissant d'Or* is the best place for drinks and pastries. *Restaurant Pacifique* is excellent for Chinese food.

Also recommended are *La Recrea*, overlooking the unexciting port; and the *Buffet de la Gare*, at the train station, which is popular with locals.

TOLIARA (TULÉAR)

Dusty Toliara (aka Tuléar) has some fine 'Wild West' architecture, but otherwise the town is of limited interest. There is no beach, only mangroves, so most visitors quickly head north to **Ifaty**, which offers world-class diving and several inexpensive bungalows.

Places to Stay & Eat

The best value place in Toliara is *Chez Micheline* (☎ 41 586), near the northern taxi-brousse station, for US$5 per room. In the centre of town, the appropriately named *Hôtel Central* (☎ 42 880) has huge rooms at US$10. Nearby, the popular *Hôtel Sud* (☎ 41 589) costs from US$11 per room.

The Hôtel Sud does a good continental breakfast; and *Hôtel Plazza*, on the esplanade, has a limited menu, but the setting and food are very good. If you eat at the *Zaza*, nearby, which has great Malagasy food and pizza, you get a free ticket into the disco. The *Maharadjah Restaurant*, near Hôtel Central, does curries in a friendly atmosphere.

In Ifaty, the cheapest beach resort is the *Bamboo Club* (☎ 42 717) for US$18 per bungalow. *Vovo Telo* (☎ 42 684), and *Moramora* (☎ 42 0159), for US$30/40 a double/triple, are also good value. You will have to pay an extra US$13 per person return for a transfer along the very sandy road from Toliara, or rely on rough and irregular public transport.

National Parks & Reserves

For the reserves listed below (except Berenty Reserve), you can get permits, and usually buy an excellent pamphlet with a map and information, at the park entrance, or go to the ANGAP office in Tana: 1 Làlana Naka Rabemanantsoa, Antanimena (☎ 30 518; fax 31 994; email angap@bow.dts.mg). For all other (non-private) parks, get your permit at the ANGAP office in Tana. Permits cost US$12 for a three day visit.

At each park, a guide is compulsory, and the cost is set by ANGAP.

RÉSERVE PRIVÉE DE BERENTY

The 200-hectare Berenty Reserve contains over 115 plant species which provide habitat for a variety of wildlife. Most visitors come for the lemur viewing; most prominent are the ringtail lemur and the acrobatic Verreaux's sifaka, but also abundant is the brown lemur.

Berenty is privately owned, so no permits are required, but the entrance fee is a hefty US$20. The reserve is not near any public transport, so you will have to hire a vehicle from Taolagnaro, or go on an expensive, but very good, tour from *Le Dauphin* hotel for about US$70 per person. There are also bungalows in the reserve. Along the 85km route to the reserve, you can stop to see pitcher plants, three-cornered palms, Antanosy tombs and the other-worldly spiny forest.

PARC NATIONAL DE ISALO

Isalo National Park, established in 1962, takes in 81,540 hectares of haunting and wildly eroded country. Although it has a few lemurs, the main attraction is the landscape.

The most popular hiking destinations are the **Canyon des Singes**, which is filled with lush vegetation, and the **Piscine Naturelle**, a paradisiacal pool fed by a waterfall. Isalo and Ranohira are on the main road and easy to reach.

The village of Ranohira, which is very close to the park, has several places to stay; *L'Orchidée* is the best at US$12 per room (the restaurant is good). For about US$7 per room, *Hôtel Les Joyeux Lemuriens* is popular but becoming overpriced these days; *Hôtel Berny* is better. *Chez R Thomas* is the cheapest.

If you are going to splurge on one hotel during your trip, do it at the spectacular *Hôtel Relais de la Reine* (☎ Tana 35 265), set magnificently in the rocky landscape, a few kilometres south of the park. Rooms cost US$60.

PARC NATIONAL D'ANDASIBE-MANTADIA

More commonly known as Périnet Reserve, this park is the most accessible to Tana and

definitely worth a visit. Most people come to see the indri, the largest of the lemur, and hear its haunting, early morning cry.

For something a little old-fashioned, but not particularly comfortable, the *Hôtel Buffet de la Gare* (☎ 2), at the train station, has singles/doubles for US$7/8 (and more expensive bungalows), and a restaurant and bar. In the village of Andasibe, *Hôtel Les Orchidées* is very cosy for US$5/7 and has a good, if a little pricey, restaurant. Nearer the park is the recommended *Feon'nyala Hôtel* for US$7/9. If you have a tent, you can camp at the park entrance with permission. Alternatively, stay at, and day trip from, Moramanga.

To get to the park, and all the accommodation, catch a taxi-brousse from Toamasina or Tana to the nearby centre of Moramanga, and take another to the village of Andasibe.

PARC NATIONAL DE RANOMAFANA

The 41,600-hectare Ranomafana National Park is home to 29 species of mammal including 12 lemurs; you'll probably see red-bellied lemur, diademed sifaka and red-fronted lemur. It is definitely worth going to the **visitors' centre**, and have a soak in the **thermal baths**; both are in the village of Ranomafana.

The park is a few kilometres from the village (easily reached by taxi-brousse from Fianarantsoa). The run-down *Hôtel Station Thermale de Ranomafana* (☎ 1) charges a hopeful US$7/9 for a single/double. More realistic is *Hôtel Ravinala*, with basic rooms for US$5, and, better is *Hôtel Manja* for US$8 per bungalow. Best of all, camp (you can even hire a two person tent for US$2.50), or stay in the rustic huts (bring your own food), at the ANGAP office at the park entrance.

MADAGASCAR

Malawi

The tourist brochures bill Malawi as 'the warm heart of Africa' and, for once, the hype is true; Malawi's scenery is beautiful and (although we hate to generalise) Malawians really do seem to be among the friendliest people you could meet anywhere.

For most travellers, the country's main attraction is Lake Malawi, stretching some 500km down the eastern border. The high-profile Liwonde National Park is at the southern end of the lake, and there's an ever-increasing number of hotels, lodges and camp sites along the southern and western shores. The diving and snorkelling here are very highly rated.

Facts about the Country

HISTORY

The area now called Malawi was settled by various Bantu tribes who had migrated to the area between the 14th and 18th centuries. The early 19th century brought two more significant migrations. The Yao, armed with guns supplied by Swahili-Arab traders from the east coast of Africa, invaded southern Malawi, killing the inhabitants or capturing them for sale into slavery. At about the same time, groups of Zulus (from present-day South Africa) settled in central and northern Malawi, and became known as the Angoni or Ngoni.

At the height of slaving in the mid-19th century, the Swahili-Arabs (together with dominant tribes) are reckoned to have either killed or sold into slavery 80,000 to 100,000 Africans per year. Those taken from the areas now called Malawi and Zambia were brought to one of the Arab trading centres, such as Nkhotakota, Karonga or Salima, where they were sold to 'wholesalers', and taken across Lake Malawi crammed into dhows. On the other side, they were then marched across Mozambique to the east

REPUBLIC OF MALAWI
Area: 118,484 sq km
Population: 11.1 million
Population Growth Rate: 4.5%
Capital: Lilongwe
Head of State: President Bakili Muluzi
Official Languages: English, Chichewa
Currency: Malawi kwacha (MK)
Exchange Rate: MK 15 = US$1
Per Capita GNP: US$180
Inflation: 80%
Time: GMT/UTC + 2

Highlights
- The relaxing *Ilala* boat trip on Lake Malawi
- Hiking on Mt Mulanje
- The abundant wildlife and beautiful scenery of Liwonde National Park

coast, usually chained or tied to poles of wood to prevent escape. Many also carried elephant tusks, as ivory was another major trade item going from Africa to the outside world. Any slaves too ill to make the journey were simply abandoned. Most died of dehydration or were killed by wild animals.

In the mid-19th century the celebrated explorer David Livingstone reached Lake Malawi (which he called Lake Nyasa) and inspired missionaries to come to Central Africa, aiming to suppress the slave trade by introducing the 'civilised' principles of trade and Christianity.

The area (then known as Nyasaland) was declared a British protectorate in 1891, and settlers, who arrived after the missionaries, began to establish plantations, notably for tea. Nyasaland became a colony in 1907. More and more land was expropriated, a 'hut tax' was introduced and traditional methods of agriculture were discouraged. As a result, increasing numbers of Africans were forced to seek work on the plantations or become migrant workers in Southern Rhodesia (later Zimbabwe) and South Africa.

Opposition to colonial rule didn't become a serious threat until the 1950s. At this time, the Nyasaland African Congress (NAC) was formed, mainly to oppose the federation of Nyasaland with Northern and Southern Rhodesia. Hastings Banda (who had spent the previous 40 years as a doctor in the USA and Britain) was invited to return home and become leader of the NAC. He was so successful in gaining support that the colonial government declared a state of emergency, jailing Banda and other leaders.

Nevertheless, opposition continued and in 1961 the colonial authorities were forced to release Banda and invite him to London for a constitutional conference. In the elections which followed, the NAC (now renamed the Malawi Congress Party or MCP) swept to victory. Shortly afterwards the Federation of Rhodesia and Nyasaland was dissolved and Malawi became independent in July 1964. In July 1966, Malawi became a republic and Banda was made president

Despite his fierce oratory, however, Banda was no radical, and when major political differences began to surface between him and his ministers, Banda demanded they declare their allegiance to him. Rather than do this, many ministers resigned and took to violent opposition. Drawing his support from the peasant majority, Banda was quickly able to smash opposition and drive the leaders into hiding or exile.

With the opposition muzzled, Banda continued to strengthen his dictatorial powers by having himself declared 'president for life', banning the foreign press whenever it suited him, outraging the Organisation of African

Unity (OAU) by refusing to ostracise the South African regime (for which he was handsomely rewarded with aid and trade), and waging pogroms against any group he regarded as a threat.

Banning the Press

It wasn't only newspapers which incurred the wrath of former president Banda. Several books on contemporary history were also banned, including, perhaps not surprisingly, *The Theory and Practice of African Politics* and *Malawi – the Politics of Despair*. Any form of pornography was also prohibited, but this included several medical textbooks because the diagrams were 'indecent'. Even guide-books didn't escape; an early Lonely Planet book called *Africa on the Cheap* (forerunner of *Africa on a shoestring*) was critical of the regime, and was promptly banned. In the early 1980s, travellers with a low-budget look about them often had bags specifically searched for the offending volume. ∎

Although a slight liberalisation was attempted in 1977 with the release of some 2000 detainees (many of whom immediately fled the country), thousands more continued to languish in jail.

In 1978, in the first general election to be held since independence, Banda personally vetted everyone who intended to stand as a candidate, demanded that each pass an English examination (thereby precluding 90% of the population) and even reinstated one of his supporters who had been defeated.

Banda retained his grip on the country through the 1980s. The distinctions between the president, the party, the country and the government became increasingly blurred. Quite simply, Banda *was* Malawi.

The 1990s brought increasing opposition to Banda's totalitarian one-party rule. In 1992 the Catholic bishops of Malawi condemned the regime and called for change. This was a brave action, for even bishops in Malawi could not be guaranteed immunity from Banda's iron grip of control. Demon-strations throughout the country, both peaceful and violent, added their weight to the bishops' move. As a final blow, donor countries cut off all non-humanitarian aid until Banda agreed to relinquish total control.

In 1993 a multiparty political system was introduced. Banda's MCP remained a powerful force, but two other main political parties emerged: the United Democratic Front (UDF), led by Bakili Muluzi, and the Alliance for Democracy (AFORD), led by Chakufwa Chihana. The first full multiparty election held in May 1994 was basically a three horse race. Although there was still a good deal of respect for the octogenarian Dr Banda, the desire for change was greater and the UDF emerged the winner.

The main challenge for President Muluzi's new government was (and still is) to satisfy the heightened expectations of the Malawian people. This at a time when the country's low export earnings have resulted in a devaluation of its currency (the kwacha) and a massive rise in prices, causing considerable hardship and suffering for the Malawian people. There are bright spots, however: peace in neighbouring Mozambique has once again given Malawi access to the port at Nacala; and the end of the Banda era has resulted in the resumption of foreign aid and increased investor confidence.

Despite some shaky periods, Bakili Muluzi remains Malawi's president. He holds this position for a five year term, until the next elections, which are due in 1999.

GEOGRAPHY & CLIMATE

Malawi's total area is just over 118,000 sq km, about 20% of which is taken up by Lake Malawi. Neighbouring Tanzania and Mozambique also have sovereignty over parts of the lake, which they call Lake Nyasa and Lago Niassa, respectively. High plateaus rise up from the shores of the lake and there are some spectacular mountain areas in the north (including Nyika National Park) and the south – notably Mt Mulanje.

In the higher areas, the climate is pleasant, with temperatures averaging around 20°C between November and April, and 27°C from May to October. On the lake shore temperatures are higher. The rainy season lasts from October to April.

ECOLOGY & ENVIRONMENT

For a relatively small country, Malawi has a large number of protected wildlife areas. (More details are given in the National Parks & Game Reserves section towards the end of this chapter.) The national parks are: Nyika, Kasungu, Lake Malawi National Park (around Cape Maclear), Liwonde and Lengwe. The game reserves are: Vwaza Marsh, Nkhotakota, Mwabvi and Majete. Generally speaking, game reserves are less developed than national parks, with fewer accommodation options and a more limited network of roads and tracks.

Despite this impressive number of parks and reserves, poaching was rife through the 1980s and early 1990s. Lip service was paid to wildlife conservation by the Banda government, but there was very little park management. At that time all camp sites and lodges inside parks and reserves were of poor quality, mainly because they were run by the Department of National Parks and Wildlife, and revenue that was raised disappeared into central government coffers (along with about 90% of the national park entrance fees). The new government promised to combat poaching and improve

facilities, but limited resources and a complete lack of commitment meant little changed.

However, since the mid-1990s several parks and reserves have received funds from international donors. For example the German government is assisting at Nyika, the European Union at Kasungu, and South Africa at Liwonde. These have pumped (or will pump) millions of dollars into the parks over the next few years, which should result in improved access roads, management, anti-poaching strategies and staff morale. Part of the deal in most cases is that accommodation should be leased out to private companies instead of being run by the government. Wherever such schemes have been introduced, accommodation and general park standards have improved greatly, although prices have also risen.

POPULATION & PEOPLE

Malawi's population is around 11 million. About 10% inhabit towns and cities while the vast majority live in rural areas, in scattered villages and individual homesteads. Up to a quarter of a million men are generally absent, many working in the mines of Zimbabwe and South Africa.

The main ethnic groups are: the Chewa, dominant in the central and southern parts of the country; the Yao, also in the south; and

---

Traditional Dance in Malawi

The most notable traditional dance in Malawi is the Gule Wamkulu, indigenous to the Chewa people (the largest and most dominant group in the country). The dance reflects traditional religious beliefs in spirits and is connected to the activities of secret societies. Leading dancers are dressed in ragged costumes of cloth and animal skins, usually wearing a mask, and occasionally on stilts.

Other groups have their own music and dance traditions. For example, among the Tumbuka in northern Malawi, the *vimbuza* is a curative dance performed by traditional healers, or witch doctors, to rid patients of sickness. Local anthropologists report that the demand for vimbuza dancers has increased significantly in recent years, and healers from other northern tribes, such as the Ngoni, have adapted the dance into their own curative ceremonies.

More secular in origin are the *beni* dances of the Yao people in southern Malawi. During colonial times many men from the traditionally war-like Yao served as *askaris* (from the Swahili word for guard) in a regiment called the Kings African Rifles. Beni is believed to be a corruption of 'band', and the dance originally satirised what the African soldiers saw as the European military obsession with marching and parades, before developing into a more specific form of its own. Today, dancers still wear a costume inspired by the colonial military uniform (which originated in India), which includes white tunics and red caps – often made from local materials such as sardine tins. ■

MALAWI

the Tumbuka in the north. Other groups include the Angoni (Ngoni) who inhabit parts of the central and northern provinces, the Chipoka in the central area, and the Tonga who live mostly along the lake shore.

LANGUAGE

English and Chichewa are the official languages. Several other African languages are spoken. The following words in Chichewa may be useful:

Greetings & Civilities

Hello.	*moni*
How are you?	*muli bwanji?*
I'm fine.	*ndili bwino*
Good/Fine/OK.	*chabwino*
Thank you/Excuse me.	*zikomo*
Thanks very much.	*zikomo kwambiri*
Goodbye (to person leaving).	*pitani bwino*
Goodbye (to person staying).	*tsalani bwino*
Please.	*Chonde.*

Useful Words & Phrases

Yes.	*inde*
No.	*iyayi*
Where?	*kuti?*
Here.	*pano*
Over there.	*uko*
How much?	*mtengo bwanji?*
I want ...	*ndifuna ...*
I don't want ...	*sindifuna ...*
to eat	*kudya*
to sleep	*kugona*

On toilet doors, *akazi* means women and *akuma* means men.

Food & Drink

chicken	*nkuku*
eggs	*mazira*
fish	*nsomba*
lake perch	*chambo*
meat	*nyama*
milk	*mkaka*
potatoes	*mbatata*
water	*madzi*

Facts for the Visitor

VISAS

Visas are required by all except nationals of Belgium, Commonwealth countries, Denmark, Finland, Germany, Iceland, Ireland, Luxembourg, the Netherlands, Norway, Portugal, Sweden and the USA. Visa extensions are free and available at the immigration offices in Blantyre and Lilongwe, or at regional police stations.

Other Visas

Mozambique
Visas are available in Lilongwe (quick and quiet) and Limbe (busy), near Blantyre. Both offices open Monday to Friday, from 8 am to noon. Transit visas cost US$5 (or US$10 for double transit), require one photo and are issued within 24 hours. One-month, single-entry tourist visas cost US$9, require two photos and take one week to issue, although there is also a four day express service which costs US$15. A three month multiple-entry visa is US$30.

South Africa
Visas are free and take two days to issue. The embassy visa section is open Monday to Friday, 8 am to noon.

Tanzania
Be warned that there is no Tanzanian high commission in Malawi so if you need a visa it must be obtained elsewhere. Lusaka and Harare are the closest places. (If you do need a visa and you're flying into Tanzania, you can get it on arrival at the airport.)

Zambia
Visas cost US$20 and take two days to issue. The visa section is open Monday to Friday, from 9 am to noon.

Zimbabwe
Visas cost US$8 and take a week to issue. The office is open from 8 am to 12.30 pm.

EMBASSIES

Malawian Embassies

In Africa, there are Malawian embassies or high commissions in Ethiopia, Kenya, Mozambique, Namibia, South Africa, Tanzania, Zambia and Zimbabwe. Elsewhere, countries with embassies include France, Germany, the UK and the USA.

Foreign Embassies in Malawi

The following diplomatic missions are in Lilongwe, unless otherwise stated:

Germany
    Convention Drive, Capital City (☎ 782555)
Mozambique
    Commercial Bank Building, African Unity Ave, Capital City (☎ 784100)
    consulate: Kamuzu Highway, Limbe (☎ 643189)
South Africa
    Impco Building (in Capital City Shopping Centre), Capital City (☎ 783722)
UK
    Kenyatta Rd, Capital City (☎ 782400)
USA
    Kenyatta Rd, Capital City (☎ 783166)
Zambia
    Convention Drive, Capital City (☎ 782100/635)
Zimbabwe
    Near Development House, off Independence Drive, Capital City (☎ 784988)

MONEY

US$1   =   MK 15

The unit of currency is the kwacha (MK), which equals 100 tambala. Import or export of local currency is not allowed, but there are few other restrictions (there are no currency declaration forms).

Cities and most towns have banks and foreign exchange bureaus where you can change money. Many small towns have a 'roving' bank, which operates for about an hour on one or two days of the week only. There is also a black market in the major towns: rates are slightly higher than banks and bureaus, but so is the chance of being ripped off. If the banks are closed and you need cash, go to a large hotel (where rates may be low) or try asking at a shop which sells imported items. In restaurants and top-end hotels, prices attract a whopping extra 30% in government taxes.

POST & COMMUNICATIONS

All towns (and many villages) have post offices. Post restante services are available in Blantyre and Lilongwe (see Information in the Lilongwe section for more details).

International calls can be made from public Telecomms phone offices in main towns and cities and cost around US$10 for a three minute minimum. The country code is 265. There are no area codes. Telephone calls within Malawi are inexpensive and the network between the main cities is reliable.

HEALTH

Although the tourist literature (and previous editions of this book!) would have you believe otherwise, there *is* bilharzia in Lake Malawi. However, in some areas (notably around Livingstonia Beach Hotel & Steps Campsite in Senga Bay, and some of the other smart hotels) the weed harbouring the snail which carries the disease has been cleared, and the water is safe. Elsewhere, you can minimise the risk by sticking to places which are free of weed or human habitation. Also see the Health Appendix for further information.

DANGERS & ANNOYANCES

While Malawi has long been regarded as one of the safest countries in Africa to travel in, this is gradually changing, especially in touristy areas, such as Cape Maclear, and in Lilongwe, Blantyre and Zomba at night. Muggings and violence have not yet reached alarming levels, but you do need to keep your wits about you.

ACCOMMODATION

The last few years have seen a dramatic rise in the number of backpackers' hostels. Most are along the lake shore, but there are a few in the cities too. Prices range from US$1 for a dorm bed to about US$5 per person for a room. Camping is about US$2.

Most towns have a council rest house, a government rest house, or both. Prices range from US$1 to US$5, and the conditions are generally spartan. Camping is permitted, although security is sometimes questionable. Definitions of single and double rooms may be determined by the number of beds rather than the number of people. It's not unusual for two people to share a single, paying either the single rate or something just a bit higher.

In the national parks and along the lake

shore, many places offer camping and self-catering chalets. Some camp sites are pretty basic, while others have good facilities. 'Self-catering' in Malawi either means you get the use of a fully equipped kitchen, or the kitchen is staffed by cooks and helpers; you just bring your food – they prepare it (and wash up). The fee you pay (US$10 to US$25) covers this, although tips are of course always appreciated.

THINGS TO BUY

Malawi is famous for its woodcarvings. The best range is at Senga Bay, but there are also pavement stalls in Blantyre and Lilongwe. Note, however, that parcel post is expensive: US$8 plus US$3 per kg. Many travellers carry carvings to Tanzania or Zimbabwe, where rates are cheaper, and post them home from there.

Getting There & Away

AIR

Air Malawi has a pretty good regional network, serving Harare, Nairobi, Lusaka, Johannesburg, Maputo and Beira. Most international flights go through Lilongwe international airport, 27km north of the city, although a few regional flights use Blantyre.

Airport departure tax for international flights is US$20, payable in hard currency.

LAND

Mozambique

Southern & Central Mozambique If you're heading for Mozambique south of the Zambezi, take a local bus from Blantyre to the Malawi border post at Mwanza (US$3), then walk or hitch 6km to Zobué (pronounced Zobway), which is the Mozambique post, from where transport goes to Tete (onward buses to Beira and Maputo). Alternatively take a direct bus between Blantyre and Harare (see Zimbabwe, below), and get off at Tete. There are plenty of moneychangers at both border posts, dealing in kwacha, Zim dollars, US dollars and meticais, but rates are low.

Northern Mozambique If you're heading for northern Mozambique, minibuses run from Mangochi to the last Malawi town of Namwera, or to the Malawi border post at Chiponde, 10km beyond Namwera (the fare to both places is US$2). Then it's 6km to the Mozambique border post at Mandimba; you can try hitching or use a bicycle taxi (US$2). From Mandimba, there's usually a daily *chapa* (bush bus) to Cuamba (US$4), from where you can get a train to Nampula.

You can also reach Cuamba from Malawi by rail. There's a twice-weekly passenger train from Balaka, via Liwonde, to the border at Nayuchi (rail crossing only) which costs US$2. You walk about 1km to the Mozambique border post where you catch a freight train (twice weekly, but not the same two days each week) to Cuamba. The fare is US$1.50, payable in meticais. There are moneychangers at Nayuchi.

From Cuamba there are three passenger trains per week to Nampula (US$3) and freight trains with a wagon for passengers most other days. Three separate train rides, none of which connect, plus a bad line between the border and Cuamba (especially in the rainy season) means this trip can take a day or a week, depending on your luck.

Another road option between Malawi and northern Mozambique involves taking a bus from Blantyre, via Mulanje town, to the border post at Muloza (US$3). From here you walk about 1km to the Mozambique post at Milanje, from where it's another few kilometres into Milanje *vila* (town). From Milanje there's usually a chapa or truck about every other day in the dry season to Mocuba (US$4), where you can find transport on to Quelimane or Nampula.

Tanzania

The only land crossing is at the Songwe River Bridge, in the far north-western tip of Malawi. Between Karonga and the border is a twice-daily bus (US$0.50) and occasional minibuses (US$1). Once across the border, you have to walk or hitch about 7km to the junction with the road between Kyela and

Mbeya. Alternatively, local youths on bicycles will pedal you there for US$1. You can also change money with them. If you're heading north, there's no need to go into Kyela as it's in the wrong direction for Mbeya. From the junction you can find a bus (two or three each day) or a lift to Mbeya.

There are plans for a new bridge upstream from the current border crossing point and to tar the road between Karonga and Mpulungu (Zambia) via Chitipa and Nakonde. From Nakonde, the Tanzania town of Tunduma is just across the border. In the next few years, this may become an easier way of crossing between Malawi and Tanzania.

Zambia

The main border crossing point is about 30km east of Chipata, on the Lusaka to Lilongwe highway. There's a twice-weekly direct service between Lilongwe and Lusaka (book in advance at the Stagecoach depot – not the bus station – on Kamuzu Procession Rd, Lilongwe).

You can also do this journey in stages but it works out little cheaper. Buses go from Lilongwe to the Malawi border post, 2km west of Mchinji, from where it's about 12km to the Zambia border post. Local share-taxis and minibuses cost about US$1.50. From the Zambian side of the border there is a daily bus to Lusaka, otherwise you can find local buses to Chipata, and get a bus to Lusaka from there.

Zimbabwe

There are two international express services between Blantyre and Harare, via Tete (Mozambique). Stagecoach runs a fast and comfortable thrice-weekly service (US$50). There's also a smaller operator called Munorurama with a daily bus from Blantyre's Chileka Rd bus station at 6 am, arriving in Harare some time between late afternoon and midnight (US$15), but one traveller described it as 'the 16-hour trip from hell'. Munorurama's Blantyre office is near Wayfarers backpackers lodge (formerly Doogles).

LAKE
Mozambique

The only option here involves the Malawian ferryboat *Ilala* (see Getting Around) which stops at Likoma Island twice a week. A local boat goes every other day to Cobué (pronounced Kobway) on the Mozambique mainland (US$0.60). From here infrequent trucks go to Lichinga (two days), which is joined by a good road and a terrible railway line to Cuamba.

Getting Around

BUS

Most buses around Malawi are operated by a company called Stagecoach. Top of the range is Coachline, a daily luxury service that runs nonstop between Blantyre and Lilongwe (US$17) and between Lilongwe and Mzuzu (US$19).

Express buses are fast and comfortable with limited stops and no standing passengers. InterCity buses are similar, but with more stops. Express buses charge between US$2 and US$2.50 per 100km, and InterCity buses slightly less. Some sample prices are: Blantyre to Lilongwe US$7; Blantyre to Mulanje US$2; Lilongwe to Monkey Bay US$4; Lilongwe to Mzuzu US$4; and Mzuzu to Nkhata Bay US$1.

For Coachline and Express buses you can buy tickets in advance and have a reserved seat. Note that in Blantyre the luxury Coachline service goes to/from the Mount Soche Hotel; in Lilongwe, it goes to/from the Capital Hotel and the Stagecoach depot near the PTC Hypermarket at the Nico Shopping Centre, *not* the bus station.

A few smaller outfits compete with Stagecoach and include Yanu Yanu and Nyika Express. There are also local minibus services around towns and to outlying villages, or along the roads which the big buses can't manage. Prices are about the same as Stagecoach, or slightly more, depending on the severity of the route.

Once you get off the main routes, the only vehicles you're likely to see are trucks or pick-ups, carrying goods and acting as an unofficial transport service (called *matola*) for local people in rural areas. If you get a lift here, payment is expected (about the same as a bus, ie around US$2 per 100km).

TRAIN

There are daily passenger trains between Blantyre and Balaka (north-west of Zomba) from Monday to Friday (US$2). There's also a twice-weekly service between Limbe and Nsanje (in the far south of Malawi) for US$3. Trains are very slow and crowded, and only slightly cheaper than the bus, so they are rarely used by visitors.

BOAT

A passenger boat called the *Ilala* plies up and down Lake Malawi, once a week in each direction, between Monkey Bay and Chilumba, stopping at about a dozen lakeside villages. (It also sometimes continues north to Itungi in Tanzania, and goes across the lake to Mbamba.) The whole trip, from one end of the line to the other, takes about three days.

Note, however, that this boat is notoriously prone to delays. The official, and infinitely flexible, schedule follows (only main ports shown).

Ilala Schedule

Northbound

Port	Arrival	Departure
Monkey Bay	–	10.00 am or 2.00 pm (Fri)
Chipoka	5 pm or 8 pm	10.00 pm
Nkhotakota	5.00 am (Sat)	6.00 am
Likoma Island	11.00 am	2.00 pm
Nkhata Bay	7.00 pm	5.00 am (Sun)
Chilumba	5.30 pm	–

Southbound

Port	Arrival	Departure
Chilumba	–	3.00 am (Mon)
Nkhata Bay	4.30 pm	2.30 am (Tues)
Likoma Island	8.30 am	11.30 am
Nkhotakota	4.30 pm	5.30 pm
Chipoka	1.00 am (Wed)	3.00 am
Monkey Bay	3.00 pm (Wed)	–

The *Ilala* has three classes: the cabins, which were once luxurious and are still in reasonable condition; the 1st class deck, which is generally quite spacious, with seats, a small shaded area and a bar; and economy, which is the lower deck, is dark and crowded, and also has engine fumes permeating from below.

Some sample routes and fares (US$) follow.

Ilala Routes & Fares

Route	Cabin	1st Class Deck	Economy
	(US$)	(US$)	(US$)
Monkey Bay to Chilumba	$93	$73	$14
Monkey Bay to Nkhata Bay	$66	$50	$10
Nkhata Bay to Nkhotakota	$30	$23	$4.50
Nkhata Bay to Likoma	$18	$11	$2
Nkhata Bay to Mbamba	$16	$10	$2

Reservations are usually required for the cabins. For other classes, tickets for the boat are only sold when it's sighted, so queuing tends to start about a day before the boat is due to arrive. On the other hand, there's no question of anyone being refused – it just keeps filling up!

If you travel economy, you'll probably be allowed on to the 1st class deck to buy a beer, which you can then make last several hours. Food is available, served from the galley on the economy deck; meals of beans, rice and vegetables cost less than US$1.

Another boat called the *Mtendere* was out of service at the time of writing. There are rumours that it is to be refitted, so there's a chance that it may be relaunched, probably running to a schedule that fits in with that of the *Ilala* (which would mean that there would be a boat twice a week going in each direction).

Lilongwe

The capital of Malawi is a pleasantly relaxed but very sprawling city of limited interest to travellers. There are two centres: Capital City (or City Centre), a surprisingly quiet and rather sterile place which has the airline offices and embassies; and the livelier Old Town, with cheap hotels and the bus station. The two centres are at least 3km apart and minibuses run between them.

Information

There are post offices in both Capital City and Old Town. If you want to use the poste restante service, make sure to have your letters addressed specifically c/o Old Town or City Centre post office and *not* to Lilongwe, or else your mail may get lost. The public telephone (Telcomms) office is in Capital City Shopping Centre, in the depths of Centre House Arcade, opposite the entrance to Kandodo supermarket.

The National Parks & Wildlife Office (☎ 723566) on Murray Rd in Old Town handles reservations for government camps and lodges. Next door is the Immigration office (☎ 722995).

Things to See

The large and very animated **market** on Malangalanga Rd in the Old Town is well worth a wander through. You can buy everything here from roasted locusts to wheel bearings.

For something more soothing, a visit to the **Nature Sanctuary** is highly recommended. There's a wildlife information centre and a series of walking trails. Birds are surprisingly varied for such a small area. Mammals include duiker, vervet monkey, porcupine and bushpig. You'll also see hyena, leopard and even tiger – unfortunately in cages. Afterwards, try Annie's au Naturelle, a nice open-air local cafe near the entrance.

Places to Stay

Lilongwe Golf Club is a very popular place to camp; for US$7 per person you get a clean, guarded site with hot showers. Included in the fee is day membership of the club, so you can use the bar and swimming pool. Unfortunately, there have been a few incidents of theft; tents near the perimeter fence have been slashed at night. It's probably safer to camp near the guards' hut.

St Peter's Guest House, near the golf club, has spotless rooms from US$4 per person, and is nearly always full. Remember it's a church place and behave accordingly. Other good cheapies are *Annie's Coffee House* (see Places to Eat), which has a small dorm for US$3 per person and camping for US$2, and *The Gap*, a South African-run backpackers lodge in the suburbs of Old Town, where beds in the dorm are US$3, camping US$1.50, and there are cheap meals – but security is limited.

The *Council Rest House* (opposite the bus station) has very basic rooms for US$4, and slightly better ones for US$6. Three or four people can share a double.

Up the scale a bit is the very pleasant *Golden Peacock Hotel* (☎ 742638), on the corner of Johnstone and Lister Rds, with en suite doubles for US$17, and standard doubles/triples for US$10/12.

Places to Eat

In Old Town, around the market and in the back streets off Kamuzu Procession Rd, are several stalls selling deep-fried cassava or potato chips and roasted meat, at very cheap prices.

At *Annie's Coffee House*, coffee is US$0.50 and chocolate cake just over US$1. Good value snacks, meals (around US$2) and cold drinks are also available. Also in this area is the clean, no frills *Gazebo Restaurant*, which serves good curries for around US$4 and snacks for US$2.

Sunset Restaurant on Kamuzu Procession Rd (behind the insurance building that is opposite the Commercial Bank of Malawi) does standard fry-ups like fish & chips for US$2 and local dishes like nsima and meat for just over US$1. Almost next door, *Byee! Takeaway* has similar food at similar prices. Also nearby is the pleasant *Summer Park*

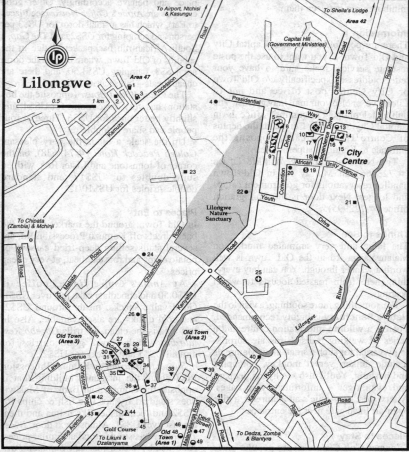

PLACES TO STAY
2 Annie's Lodge
12 Capital Hotel
21 Capital City Motel
23 Lingadzi Inn
30 Lilongwe Hotel
40 The Gap
42 Golden Peacock Hotel;
   Korea Garden Restaurant
43 St Peter's Guest House
44 Lilongwe Golf Club
   (Camping)
46 Council Rest House

PLACES TO EAT
15 Golden Dragon
   Restaurant

17 PTC Hypermarket
27 Modi's
31 Huts
38 Annie's Coffee House
39 Gazebo Restaurant

OTHER
1 Hollywood Nightclub
3 Petrol Station
4 Adventist Health Centre
5 UK High Commission
6 Zambia High Commission
7 French Embassy
8 German Embassy
9 US Embassy
10 City Centre Post Office
11 Capital City Shopping Centre

13 Minibuses to Old Town
14 Zimbabwe High Commission
16 British Council Library
18 ADL House
   (Travel Agents; Clinic)
19 Commercial Bank;
   Mozambique High Commission
20 Reserve Bank Building
22 Entrance to Lilongwe
   Nature Sanctuary
24 Department of Forestry
25 Lilongwe Central
   Hospital
26 Immigration Office;
   National Parks & Wildlife Office
28 Commercial Bank
   of Malawi

29 Minibuses to
   City Centre
32 National Bank
   of Malawi
33 Nico Shopping Centre
34 Stagecoach Bus Depot
35 Old Town Post Office
36 Police
37 Town Hall (Cinema)
41 Petrol Station
45 Map Sales Office
47 Market
48 Local Bus Station
49 Long-Distance
   Bus Station

with ice creams (US$0.60), burgers (US$2) and full meals (US$3).

In City Centre there are a number of cafes. Cheap street food is available at lunch time around the PTC Hypermarket which is where local office workers eat.

Getting Around

The Airport A local bus goes from the bus station near the market to within about 4km of the airport terminal and costs just US$1, but you'll probably have to walk from there as traffic is light. A taxi costs about US$15.

Bus In Old Town, minibuses for the City Centre go from opposite the bus station and from Kenyatta Rd opposite the PTC Hypermarket in the Nico Shopping Centre (US$0.30).

Around the Country

BLANTYRE & LIMBE

Blantyre is the main commercial centre of Malawi, stretching for about 20km, merging into its 'sister city' of Limbe. The city centre is very compact with most of the places of importance to travellers well within easy walking distance. (Unless stated otherwise, every address in this section is in Blantyre, rather than Limbe.)

Information

The tourist office on Victoria Ave has a few leaflets and brochures, and the staff try to be helpful. Blantyre's main post office is on Glyn Jones Rd, and the Telcomms office is on Henderson St, just off Victoria Ave.

Things to See

The **National Museum** is midway between Blantyre and Limbe, just off Kamuzu Highway, the main road that links the two city centres. There's a good display of traditional weapons and artefacts, some donated by an American family whose ancestor had collected them during colonial times. The most impressive thing to see in Blantyre is the **CCAP church**, officially called the Church of St Michael and All Angels, in the mission grounds, just off Chileka Rd.

Places to Stay

Wayfarers Lodge (formerly Doogles) is a backpackers' favourite where camping is US$2 per person and a bed in the dorm US$4. There's a bar, friendly staff and good security. A couple of local budget tour outfits run excursions from here too. Snacks and meals are available, and there are several cheap places to eat just outside the gate.

Cheaper but nowhere near as good is the *District Resthouse* where old, very basic singles/doubles are US$1/2 and new rooms US$2/3. Toilets are filthy and security questionable. If you *really* want to save money, and are travelling to/from Harare on the Munorurama Bus, there's a free *'guesthouse'* (a bare room with mats on the floor) for passengers at their depot next to the main bus station.

Good value, though more expensive, is the Grace Bandawe Conference Centre (☎ 634267), a small church hostel on Chileka

The CCAP Church

The CCAP church was built in Blantyre by missionaries of the Established Church of Scotland who came to Malawi in the 1870s. Their leader was the Rev Clement Scott. With no training in architectural design or construction skills, and with only local handmade bricks and wood available, Scott planned and then oversaw the building of this magnificent church, complete with basilica dome, towers, arches and bay windows. Although extensively renovated in the 1970s, what you see today is pretty much how it looked when it was completed in 1891. After more than a century of service, St Michael's, as it was officially called, is about to be replaced by a new modern church nearby. ■

Blantyre

PLACES TO STAY
- 4 Ryall's Hotel
- 5 Mt Soche Hotel; Map Office
- 19 Hotel & Catering School
- 43 Wayfarers Lodge (ex-Doogles)
- 48 CCAP Mission Resthouse
- 49 District Resthouse

PLACES TO EAT
- 2 Hong Kong Restaurant
- 7 Chick Wings
- 8 Sasha's Bakery
- 12 Modern Fish & Chips
- 13 Maxim's Restaurant
- 14 L'Hostaria
- 16 PTC Supermarket
- 18 Creme Centre
- 20 Kips
- 23 Dafabio Too
- 24 Chimovomwe Restaurant; Central Bookshop
- 27 Lunch Box
- 30 Kandodo Supermarket
- 32 Tai Pan Restaurant
- 35 Downtown Café
- 41 Melting Pot

To Motel Paradise, Chileka Airport, Mwanza, Lilongwe & Tete (Mozambique)

To Grace Bandawe Conference Centre

To Michiru Mountain

To Chikwawa

To National Museum, Mozambique Consulate, Limbe & Zomba

OTHER
- 1 Cathedral of St Paul
- 3 Air Malawi; Seventh Day Adventist Clinic
- 6 National Library
- 9 Petrol Station
- 10 Main Post Office
- 11 Safari Curios; Galaxy Travel
- 15 Commercial Bank of Malawi
- 17 British Airways
- 21 Immigration Office
- 22 Tourist Office
- 25 TBS Bookshop
- 26 Nix Bar
- 28 Manica Travel
- 29 Legends
- 31 Pat's Bar
- 33 Bank of Malawi
- 34 Telcomms Office
- 36 Local Buses & Taxis
- 37 Map Sales Office
- 38 Blantyre Sports Club
- 39 Old Boma
- 40 Municipal Market
- 42 Clock Tower
- 44 Munorurama Bus Station
- 45 Long-Distance Bus Station
- 46 Mwai Private Hospital
- 47 CCAP Church
- 50 Train Station
- 51 Mandala House

0   100   200 m

Rd, about 2km from the city centre, with clean en suite singles/doubles for US$10/14. Breakfast is US$2 and other meals US$3.50. At the nearby *CCAP Mission Resthouse*, a bed in the dormitory costs US$5. This place is spartan, clean and quiet, with big lockers to keep your gear safe, though you need your own padlock.

Places to Eat

For cheap eats, there are stalls around the main bus station selling fried potatoes and fish for around US$0.50, or try the *Downtown Café*, near the local bus station, or the nearby *Kuyesa Restaurant* (open till 7.30 pm).

A good cheap place for takeaway food is Lunch Box on Henderson St, open from 7.30 am to 2 pm only, which offers curry and rice or chicken and chips for US$1.50, and burgers for US$1. Other takeaways (open evenings) include Chick Wings on Glyn Jones Rd and Kips on Hanover Ave.

Places to have a splurge include *L'Hostaria*, where you can enjoy a rustic terrace setting and some large pizzas and pasta dishes from around US$5, and also the *Tai Pan Restaurant* on Victoria Ave, where you can eat a small selection for between about US$5 and US$7, or you can splash out and pay up to US$10 or US$15.

MALAWI

Entertainment

For a wild, late-night bar, try *Pat's* on Victoria Ave. There's a disco, which has a cover charge of US$4 on weekends. Another lively place is *Nix* on Hanover Ave, with live music on weekends.

CAPE MACLEAR

Cape Maclear is the name of a bay and large village on the southern lake shore, about 20km by road from Monkey Bay (the nearest town). It's a travellers' byword for rest and recreation, and just about everyone who comes to Malawi passes through here. You'll meet people here you last saw in Cape Town, Kisangani, Nairobi or wherever.

Information

The nearest bank is at Monkey Bay (open Monday and Thursday mornings).

Much of the lake shore and peninsula around Cape Maclear, the lake itself and several offshore islands are part of Lake Malawi National Park; the park headquarters is at Golden Sands Holiday Resort (see Places to Stay).

Activities

Watersports are big here. Depending on your budget, you can go snorkelling, sailing, kayaking or windsurfing. There are two dive schools: the Scuba Shack at Stevens' Resthouse and Lake Divers at Golden Sands. Their prices are similar: a five day course costs US$130 to US$150. For those already qualified, shore dives are US$15.

Local youths organise day trips to nearby islands for US$10 to US$40 per boat, or around US$4 per person, including snorkelling and lunch (fish cooked on an open fire). Before arranging anything, check with other travellers for recommendations; some of the lads are very good, but others can be sharks.

If you want a day on dry land, there's a good range of hikes in the hills behind the beach. Arrange a guide (recommended for security) either from the village or at the park headquarters; the park rate is US$10 for a full-day trip.

Places to Stay & Eat

The long-running *Stevens' Resthouse* used to be one of *the* places to stay on the backpackers' Cape to Cairo route, but there's stiff competition these days and it's lost some of its once-legendary atmosphere. Clean singles/doubles are US$1/2 (or US$3 for en suite). Breakfast is US$0.50 and other meals are US$1.50 to US$2. The bar on the beach is still a popular place for a drink and to meet other travellers, especially at sunset.

Top Quiet Resthouse (behind Stevens') has simple, clean rooms for around US$1 per person, or US$3 if you want an attached shower. Meals cost US$3. A bit further along the beach is *The Ritz*, with camping for US$0.60, and *The Gap*, where camping is the same price and simple rooms are US$1. Snacks start at US$1, or you can buy burgers and chips or similar for around US$3.

At the southern end of the beach is *Golden Sands Holiday Resort*, with camping and basic chalets for US$3 per person and en suite rondavels for US$5 per person. As this is inside the park you have to pay park fees too (see the National Parks section). The beach here is cleaner and the atmosphere quieter (one traveller said 'more sensible'); suitable for families and people who don't want to party all night. Watch out for the monkeys – they'll run off with anything edible!

At the park Visitor Centre you can arrange lodgings with a local family in Cape Maclear village as part of the *Visitor Stay Experience*, run in cooperation with the American Peace Corps. You stay for about 24 hours and do everything the family does – collect water from the lake, help with cooking traditional food etc. It costs US$6.

In the village, you can get cold drinks, bread, tinned foods and groceries at *Mr Banda's Store*. Nearby is *Chip's Bar* which serves, naturally, deep fried potato pieces plus other takeaway snacks at budget prices.

Getting There & Away

When the dirt road beyond Monkey Bay is in good condition there's a Stagecoach bus to Cape Maclear from Blantyre (US$5) via

Mangochi. The Monkey Bay to Cape Maclear section is US$0.50. Alternatively, the Stevens' truck (see Places to Stay & Eat) runs between Cape Maclear and Monkey Bay a couple of times a day for US$1 per person.

CHINTHECHE

Chintheche (pronounced 'Chin-tejch-ee') is about 40km south of Nkhata Bay with a few shops, a market and a bank that's open twice a week. Nearby is a long stretch of lake shore with several camp sites and lodges.

On the edge of the village, the *Forest Resthouse* has functional but clean wood cabins for US$2.50 per person. On the lake, about 2km south down the main road and another 2km along a dirt track, is *Flame Tree Lodge* run by a friendly English-Malawian couple, where smart self-contained chalets are US$10/14, camping US$2, and meals around US$3. This is a pleasant, quiet place.

About 15km south of Chintheche village (about 55km from Nkhata Bay) is a sign to *Kande Beach Camp*, a basic camp site with long-drop toilets and a long-open bar. Extremely popular with overland trucks, good times and partying is the name of the game here. Individual campers are charged US$1.50.

Another 7km further south is the vastly different *Mwaya Beach Camp*, where the atmosphere is restful and the entrance track is allegedly designed to keep the overland trucks out! Simple chalets cost US$3 per person and camping is US$1.25. There's a bar, snacks and meals for US$1 to US$4, and clean drinking water is free.

CHITIMBA

This small village is where the Livingstonia road turns off the main north-south highway. Places to stay include *Florence Bay Resthouse*, on the junction, where you can sleep for US$0.50 per night. There's cheap food, and you can safely leave your bag here if you want to go to Livingstonia for the day. Next door is the similar *Nyabweka Restaurant & Resthouse*. For a longer stay *Des's Chitimba Beach Campsite* is popular with overlanders, with chalets for US$3, camping for US$1.50, and a lively bar right on the beach.

KARONGA

This is the first/last town of any size in northern Malawi, strung out for about 2km along the main street between a roundabout on the north-south highway and the lake shore. Facilities include the only permanent bank north of Mzuzu.

Places to Stay & Eat

The *Tukumbugwe Hotel* by the roundabout is good value with rooms for US$4. Nearby is the *Chombe Hotel & Restaurant*, charging US$3 per person, with good food. Also nearby are several cheap eating houses (including the recommended *Cross Roads* and *Karonga Restaurant*).

Heading from the roundabout towards the lake, *Safari Lodge* has clean rooms with attached bath for US$8 including breakfast. Another option is *Kankhununu Guest House*, behind the old market, where basic rooms cost US$1.50.

At the end of the road, turn right to reach the friendly *Mufwa Lakeside Centre*, worth the long walk from the roundabout, with clean singles/doubles for US$4/6 and camping for US$1 per person. There is plenty of shade, good food for US$2 and cold beers.

LIKOMA & CHIZUMULU ISLANDS

These two Lake Malawi islands are within the territorial waters of Mozambique but part of Malawi and on the *Ilala* ferry route (see the Getting Around section earlier in this chapter). Likoma Island is dry and sandy, with beaches and good snorkelling. Missionaries settled here in colonial times and their legacy – a huge **Anglican Cathedral** – is a major landmark today and well worth a visit. Visitors seem to fall into two categories: those who love Likoma and stay for weeks, and those who leave as soon as possible. Either way, you'll meet few other tourists. Chizumulu Island particularly can be a perfect hideaway.

Places to Stay & Eat

In Chipyela, Likoma's main settlement, the *Akuziko Resthouse* is clean and good value at US$3 per person. Similar in price is the

Quiet & Cool Resthouse, which also has a restaurant. There are a few other places to eat; try the *women's restaurant* near the jetty. Wherever you go, don't expect a huge menu – the staples here are fish and nsima.

We've been told about a new place called *Chiponde Beach Lodge*, at the south-east end of the island, which charges US$10 per person.

On Chizumulu Island, *Kubira Lodge* is on a good beach with friendly staff. Double rooms cost US$2.50, camping US$0.60, and there's a pleasant bar. Or try the new *Tionge Resthouse & Restaurant*, where prices are the same.

LIVINGSTONIA

This mission station and surrounding small town was founded by Scottish missionaries in 1894 and still exudes a quiet bygone air. It's about 800m above the lake and has some of the most spectacular views in Africa.

Things to See

Exhibits in the fascinating **museum** in the Stone House tell the story of early European exploration and missionary work in Malawi. Nearby is the **church**, built in Scottish style, with a beautiful stained-glass window.

You can walk to **Manchewe Falls**, about 3km from the town. There are several paths, and young boys hanging around the Resthouse (see Places to Stay & Eat below) who will show you the way for a small fee.

Places to Stay & Eat

The *Stone House* has original Victorian furniture and superb views; good value at US$2.50 per night. You can camp on the lawn for US$1.50. You can use the kitchen, or meals can be provided for around US$2 if you order in advance.

If you have just staggered up the escarpment road, the *Resthouse* is about 15 minutes closer than the Stone House and a bit cheaper at US$2, although facilities are a little more basic. Camping, meals and use of the kitchen are also available here – same price as the Stone House.

There are also a couple of camp sites on the road up the escarpment, including *Falls Grocery* opposite the path to Manchewe Falls, where friendly Mr Edwin lets you pitch a tent for US$0.60. There is a dilapidated toilet and water comes from the stream nearby. The shop however is very well stocked with food and drink (including beer).

There are also some shops in Livingstonia town itself selling basic groceries, and a market.

Getting There & Away

From Chitimba on the main north-south highway, a dirt road goes up the escarpment in a series of acute hairpin bands. There is no official public transport but a lift in a pick-up (there's two or three each day) costs about US$1.

The alternative is to walk: it's a 25km steep stretch and takes about five hours. There are shortcuts which can reduce it to three or four hours, but these are even steeper. We heard from a traveller who was mugged on this road. This may have been an isolated incident – probably hundreds of travellers walk up here every year – but it may be worth checking the latest situation before you set off, or taking a local guide.

Livingstonia can also be reached by bus in the dry season from Rumphi.

MONKEY BAY

Monkey Bay, towards the southern end of the lake, is Malawi's main port. There's no beach here, so most travellers head for the nearby delights of Cape Maclear as soon as possible. If you get stuck, the *Council Resthouse* has grotty rooms for US$1 per night. Nicer is *Zawadi Lodge* where rooms are US$3. Camping is allowed in the yard, but no fence means security is very questionable. For eats, try *Gary's Café* opposite. Monkey Bay also has a market, supermarket and excellent bakery, plus a roving bank (but as this is not reliable, you're better off changing elsewhere before you arrive).

About 35km south of Monkey Bay, towards Mangochi, is *Nanchengwa Lodge*, 1.5km west off the main road and reached by a dirt track. This is a friendly hostel for

MALAWI

backpackers and overlanders, in a fishing village on a small bay, with camping on a site that overlooks the beach for US$1.50, a bed in the dorm for US$3 or rooms for US$9. There's a bar and food is available, plus a whole range of activities like snorkelling, diving, hiking and horse riding.

MT MULANJE

Stunning scenery, easy access, clear paths and a series of well-maintained huts make Mt Mulanje a fine hiking and trekking area. If you've got four to six days spare, various traverses of the whole massif are possible.

Mt Mulanje is a forest reserve; you must register for hiking and reserve a bed in the huts at Likabula Forest Station (☎ 465218), about 15km from Mulanje town, at the foot of the main path up the massif. There's no entry charge, but you pay your hut fees (see below) here and can arrange guides and porters, if you want them. The rate is US$4 per day per porter. The Tourist Attendant is a friendly lady called Dorothy; she will make sure the porters you take are reliable.

The Forestry Department produces an information leaflet and map of Mulanje. For more detail, get the *Guide to Mulanje Massif* by Frank Eastwood (available in Blantyre bookshops) or Lonely Planet's *Trekking in East Africa*, which covers several routes on Mulanje.

Mulanje town has a small supermarket (near the Likabula junction) and a market selling fruit and veg.

Warning

The Mulanje massif has notoriously unpredictable weather. Even during dry periods rain, cold winds and thick mists can occur very suddenly. It's easy to get lost. The worst period is between May and August when periods of low cloud and drizzle (called *chiperones*) can last for several days. At this time temperatures can drop below freezing, especially at night. Take warm, waterproof gear and take extra care in conditions of poor visibility. Do not try to cross swollen streams.

Places to Stay

At Likabula, the *Forestry Resthouse* charges US$3 per person per night. You can camp at the forest station for US$0.35 per tent, or outside the rest house for US$1.25, and use the kitchen.

On Mt Mulanje are six *forestry huts*, each with a caretaker and open fires (with firewood). You provide your own food, cooking gear, candles, sleeping bag and stove (although you can cook on the fire). The huts cost US$1 per person per night – an absolute bargain, although this may rise in the future.

The only other place to stay on the massif is the *CCAP Cottage*, on the Lichenya Plateau, run by Likabula CCAP Mission (next to the Forest Station), which costs US$1.25 per night.

Camping is permitted outside the huts (US$0.60 per person) but is not allowed anywhere else on the massif. You can cook and eat in the huts.

MULANJE

The town of Mulanje is the centre of Malawi's tea industry. You may pass through it if you're heading for Mozambique, but most travellers come through on the way to Mt Mulanje, which dominates the town and much of the surrounding area, and is an excellent hiking and trekking area (see above).

Places to Stay & Eat

The *Council Resthouse* and the *Zimbabwe Guest House* both have doubles from US$2. Just downhill from the bus station is the quieter *Mulanje Motel*, with rooms also for US$2. Next door is the smarter *Mulanje View Motel*, with a better choice of rooms from US$3.50 for singles to US$8 for en suite doubles with breakfast. There's also a bar and good-value food in the restaurant.

Camping is possible at the *Mulanje Golf Club*, on the eastern outskirts of town. The US$2.50 cost includes day membership, so you can use the showers, bar and swimming pool, and enjoy the fabulous views of Mt Mulanje from the terrace.

MZUZU

Mzuzu – 'Capital of the North' – has changed in the last decade or so from a sleepy frontier town to a fairly large administrative centre. Most travellers pass through en route to Karonga (US$6 by bus) or Nkhata Bay (US$1).

Places to Stay & Eat

Best value is the *CCAP Resthouse*, about 500m north-east of the bus station. A bed in a clean shared double or triple room costs US$3, and good meals are available. Cheaper is the *Jambo Resthouse* on M'Membelwa Rd, with basic rooms from US$1 per person. Up the scale from here, the *Chenda Hotel*, east of the bus station, has clean en suite singles/doubles at US$10/15 with breakfast. Camping is available at the *Government Tourist Lodge*, on the eastern side of town about 1km from the roundabout, for US$2.

The *Tropicana Restaurant* has very good meals for US$2.50. Another place is the *At'Tayyiba Restaurant* near the bus station, which has meals for around US$2.

NKHATA BAY

The town of Nkhata Bay spreads round a large lake inlet, and is probably the most scenic of Malawi's lake-shore towns. A few travellers have even described it as 'Caribbean'. Despite the influx of foreigners, the town retains its Malawian feel. There's a lively market and a bank where you can change money every weekday morning.

Aqua Africa (☎ 352284) runs diving courses which have been recommended. Prices start at about US$100 for a five day scuba course.

Places to Stay & Eat

At *Backpackers Connection* (☎ 352302), single/double rooms are US$3.50/5 and camping US$1. Almost opposite is the locally run *Africa Bay Backpackers*, with simple chalets on the beach for US$1.50 per person.

At the bottom of the hill is *Safari Restaurant*, a popular travellers' haunt, where you can get omelettes and sandwiches for US$1, pizzas for US$2, and other meals for US$2.50. Nearby is the *Juice Bar*, serving drinks for US$0.30 and huge healthy sandwiches for just over US$1.

On the edge of the centre is the *Heart Hotel*, a friendly no-frills shack and one of the few tourist places in town that is Malawian-run. The owner, Philip, says whatever the other rest houses in town charge, he'll always be the cheapest. Camping costs US$0.35, you can sleep on the floor for US$0.60 or you can take the luxury option of a bed in the new building for US$1 (with breakfast). There have been some incidents of theft here, so don't leave your gear lying around and check the latest situation with other travellers before staying here.

About 20 minutes from the centre (always seems longer with a backpack) is *Njaya*, where reed chalets cost US$5 (for one or two people). Camping or a mat in the dorm is US$1.50. The breezy bar overlooks the lake, and food includes burgers and homemade sausages for US$1.50 and veggie pizzas for US$2.

Next door, the smarter *Chikale Beach Resort* has en suite double chalets for US$8 and triples at US$11. Camping is US$2. In the bar and restaurant right on the fabulous beach, you can get a full breakfast and other meals for about US$3.

A few travellers have been attacked and robbed walking between Njaya or Chikale and town at night. To combat this, the lodges, restaurants and Aqua Africa have got together and will 'lend' their watchman to any travellers. Use this service and you'll have no worries.

NKHOTAKOTA

This is reputedly one of the oldest market towns in Africa and was once the centre of the slave trade in this region. The town is strung out along the main north-south highway, and another road which runs down to the lake. The bus station and a small group of rest houses are about 2km off the main road, from where it's another 2km to the lake.

The best place to stay is the clean and friendly *Pick & Pay Resthouse*, opposite the bus station, which charges US$2/3 for singles/doubles and US$1 for camping. Also good is the *Livingstone Resthouse & Restaurant* with similar prices. The *District Rest House* by the boat jetty has a beautiful terrace overlooking the lake and is good for a beer, but the rooms are terrible.

RUMPHI

Rumphi (pronounced 'Rumpy'), north of Mzuzu, is a good starting point to get to Nyika (see the National Parks section). Places to stay are limited to *Yagontha Hideout Resthouse*, near the bus stand, with simple rooms for US$2 per person, and the friendly and good-value *Simphakawa Inn*, on the edge of town, where clean en suite rooms with hot showers cost US$3.50 (for one or two people).

SALIMA & SENGA BAY

The town of Salima is about 15km from the lake and you may have to stay there for the night before heading down to the beach at Senga Bay. Otherwise it's not worth a stopover. The grotty *Council Resthouse*, opposite the bus station, has dorm beds for US$0.30 and doubles for US$2.50. Better is the *Mai Tsalani Motel*, with double en suite rooms for US$3 and a surprisingly good restaurant.

Minibuses between Salima and Senga Bay cost US$1.

In Senga Bay, *Hippo Hide Resthouse* just off the main street is a backpackers' favourite where no-frills rooms cost US$1.50 per person and camping is US$1. Meals are US$3. The beach is just a few hundred metres away, and the friendly staff arrange boat trips or hikes in the hills. About 2.5km from the main street is *Carolina's Lakeside Chalets* where en suite rooms are US$14 for one or two people and camping is US$1.50. Next door is *Baobab Chalets* where rooms are US$10 and camping is US$1.

At the far end of the main street the topend Livingstonia Beach Hotel runs the *Steps Campsite*, next door. It is reckoned by some travellers to be the best in Malawi. It's clean and safe, with spotless showers and toilets. There's a bar and takeaway serving snacks and fresh bread. The charge is US$4 per person for camping; costly by Malawian standards, but good value compared with some other parts of southern Africa. Beers at the bar are top-end prices, and burger and chips (admittedly fine quality) will set you back US$7. Watersports and activities are available at the hotel.

ZOMBA

Zomba is the old capital of Malawi. It's a good place from which to explore the **Zomba Plateau**, a pleasant hiking area with fantastic views. There's no transport up to the plateau, so you'll have to walk, hitch or take a taxi for US$10.

Places to Stay & Eat

The *Council Resthouse* opposite the bus station is OK; the rooms are clean but the toilet block is disgusting. Dorm beds cost US$0.50, while singles/doubles cost US$2/3. There's a restaurant and noisy bar. For something better try the *Ndindeye Motel* which has large clean rooms at US$3/6 or US$7/13 for en suite with breakfast. The restaurant does meals from US$2.

On the plateau itself, the only budget option is the *Forest Campsite* set among large pine trees. It costs US$1 per person; there are toilets and hot showers. It's one of those places which is beautiful in sunlight and a bit miserable in mist. Bring all groceries from Zomba town as there's no shop.

National Parks & Game Reserves

Malawi has five national parks: Nyika, Kasungu, Lake Malawi (around Cape Maclear), Liwonde and Lengwe. The game reserves are Vwaza Marsh, Nkhotakota, Mwabvi and Majete. All have accommodation, though the reserves have fewer options and a more limited network of tracks (if any). Accommodation ranges from simple camp sites and rest houses to self-catering chalets and comfortable (even luxurious) lodges. These used to be government run, but most have been privatised in the last few years. For more details see the Ecology & Environment section of this chapter.

All national parks and game reserves have an entry fee of US$15 per person per day, plus US$15 per car per day. In parks where walking is permitted, a guide costs US$10 per day. A porter is US$15 per day. (These fees are paid to the park, so it is usual to tip the scouts extra for their services.) All these fees are payable in kwacha.

Reservations for government-run accommodation in the parks and reserves should be made through the Department of National Parks & Wildlife in Lilongwe or Blantyre. Reservations for privately run lodges and camps should be made direct or through an agent. Reservations are recommended but not always essential. You can try your luck and turn up without a booking, but the popular parks may be full at weekends and during holiday times. It is not usually necessary to reserve camp sites, assuming you have your own tent.

Some parks and reserves are difficult to reach without your own vehicle, so only those with easier access are described here. Lake Malawi National Park is described in the Cape Maclear section.

LIWONDE NATIONAL PARK

This is Malawi's best national park: well-managed, with a relatively good stock of wildlife and beautiful scenery. It lies to the south of Lake Malawi, and includes part of the Shire River. Literally thousands of hippo and crocodile live in the river, and there are several hundred elephant in the park, plus plenty of antelope (including impala, bushbuck and kudu).

Places to Stay & Eat

By far the best place to stay is the privately run *Mvuu Camp*. Chalets cost US$34, dome tents US$20, or you can camp for US$10 (all charges per person). There's a fully equipped

kitchen or you can eat at the camp restaurant (breakfast is US$6, dinner US$14), an open-plan thatched affair which overlooks the river and also has a bar (beers US$1). The camp arranges wildlife-viewing trips by boat or vehicle (US$18 for 2½ hours) and walks (US$10). A complete package in a chalet (including all meals, wildlife drives, walks and boat rides) costs US$85. The same deal if you stay in a dome tent is US$70. For more details contact Central African Wilderness Safaris (☎ 781393, 781153; fax 781397) in Lilongwe.

Getting There & Away

The main park gate is 6km east of Liwonde town. There's no public transport beyond here into the park itself, but hitching is not impossible, especially on weekends.

An alternative is the boat transfer service offered by Waterline (☎ /fax 532552), based near Kudya Discovery Lodge in Liwonde town. If you've got the money this is the best way to approach, as you can spot elephant, hippo, crocodile and a host of water birds on the way. They will drop you at Mvuu Camp and wait, returning within 24 hours, for around US$42 per person for groups over two.

MAJETE GAME RESERVE & LENGWE NATIONAL PARK

South and west of Blantyre, the land falls dramatically to form the Lower Shire Valley, probably one of the least visited areas of Malawi. Even when it's cool in the highlands, it can be blisteringly hot down here, quite unlike the rest of the country.

Majete Game Reserve lies about 30km directly to the west of Blantyre, in the area between the River Shire and the border with Mozambique. Lengwe lies to the south of this.

Places to Stay & Eat

These two places are hard to reach without your own wheels, but a fairly accessible and very pleasant place to stay nearby is *Majete Safari Camp* (☎ 423204), just outside the reserve. It's also a useful base for exploring the whole area. Overlooking the river, the camp has en suite chalets at around US$80 per person for full board, simpler chalets and permanent tents from US$20, and camping for US$3. There's a bar, a kitchen for self-catering, or you can buy meals. Trips to Majete, Lengwe and other places in southern Malawi can be arranged here.

Getting There & Away
Majete Safari Camp is 15km north of a small town called Chikwawa, which is on the main road between Blantyre and Nsanje. There are several buses per day to Chikwawa from Blantyre. From here you can try hitching (good at weekends, as the camp is popular with Blantyre residents) or phone the camp for a lift (they take a small charge). If you get stuck as night falls, Chikwawa has a couple of local rest houses, bars and eating houses.

The road between Mwanza (on the Tete road) and Chikwawa, via Mikolongo, was due to be upgraded in 1997. If you're coming from Mozambique, this would be an ideal way to enter Malawi, allowing a visit to Majete and other parts of the Lower Shire area before continuing to Blantyre.

NYIKA NATIONAL PARK
The Nyika Plateau, in the north of Malawi, is a vast upland area and the largest park in the country. It consists mainly of rolling grassy hills, split by forested valleys, and surrounded by steep escarpments.

The range of vegetation attracts a varied selection of wildlife. Most common are the large roan antelope and the smaller reedbuck. You'll also see zebra, wart hog and eland, plus possibly klipspringer, jackal, duiker and hartebeest. You might even catch a glimpse of hyena and leopard. More than 250 species of bird have been recorded.

Nyika is also famous for its wildflowers. The best time to see them is during the rains, but conditions are also good in August and September, when the grassland is covered in colour and small outcrops turn into veritable rock gardens. Over 120 species of orchid alone grow on the plateau.

The national park produces a small infor-

mation booklet, and there are also displays in the information centre at Chelinda Camp. A larger book called *A Visitor's Guide to Nyika National Park* by Sigrid Johnson is available in Blantyre and Lilongwe bookshops, and Lonely Planet's *Trekking in East Africa* covers walking routes on Nyika.

Trekking
Although you are not allowed to *enter* the park on foot, once inside the park walking is allowed. There are several South African style wilderness trails, lasting anything from two days to a week or longer. There's also a popular four-day trek taking in many of Nyika's main attractions including Kaulime Lake, the Zovo-Chipolo Forest, Chisanga Falls, Domwe Peak, the western escarpment and Nganda Peak, the highest point on the plateau.

Another recommended route goes from Chelinda Camp to Livingstonia (three days). Scouts (park rangers) are obligatory and cost US$10 per day. Porters (optional) are US$15 per day. All the scouts speak English and are generally quite knowledgeable about the birds and wildlife; they're good company on a long trek. They receive no extra money from the park for this work, so a tip (of around US$1 or US$2 per day) at the end of your trek is appropriate if the service has been good.

Places To Stay
Chelinda Camp, at the centre of the park, has fully contained chalets for US$10 per double, although improvements (and possibly a price rise) are planned. The camp site charges US$3 per night.

Getting There & Away
In the dry season, there's a daily bus between Mzuzu and Chitipa, going through the park, via Thazima and Kaperekezi gates, with a loop up to Chelinda. (If the bus doesn't go to Chelinda, ask the driver to drop you at the Zambian Resthouse junction, from where you can walk or hitch the 12km to Chelinda.) When the road is tarred to Chelinda (as planned) the bus will run all year.

VWAZA MARSH GAME RESERVE

This pleasant and frequently overlooked reserve, south of the Nyika Plateau, is well worth visiting. Access is pretty straightforward, walking is permitted (with a ranger) and a lot of wildlife can be seen from the main camp, which makes Vwaza an ideal destination for travellers without their own transport.

Mammals include elephant, buffalo, hippo, waterbuck, eland, roan, sable, hartebeest, zebra, impala and puku, all surprisingly easy to see from the area around the lake. The bird life is also excellent.

Places to Stay

The only place to stay is Lake Kazuni Camp, where dilapidated walk-in tents with two beds cost US$5 per person, or you can use your own tent for US$3. The chances are you'll have the camp (plus the scenery and the animals) completely to yourself. A new tented camp is planned at Kazuni, which will probably change mid-range prices. For details contact Central African Wilderness Safaris (☎ 781393, 781153; fax 781397) in Lilongwe.

Getting There & Away

In the dry season, there's a daily bus from Rumphi to Mzimba via Kazuni village, about 15 minutes walk from the entrance gate, from which Lake Kazuni Camp is easily reached. If you miss the bus, ask around in Rumphi about trucks and pick-ups going to Kazuni village; there's usually a couple each day – the ride costs US$2.

Mali

Mali is one of the poorest countries on earth, yet for travellers it is one of the great destinations in West Africa – there's such a variety of places to see and things to do: Bamako, on the banks of the Niger River, has one of the largest markets in the region; Djenné is a well-preserved city dating back to the Middle Ages; Timbuktu has been a magnet for travellers for many years; Dogon Country is one of the world's great trekking areas; and for adventurers, there are Niger River canoe trips.

Facts about the Country

HISTORY

The region that is now the modern state of Mali was part of the empire of Ghana during the 9th century. The empire controlled trade in the Western Sahara until 1076, when it was invaded by Muslim Almoravids from Mauritania. The capital, Kumbi, was built 200km north of the town now known as Bamako.

In the middle of the 13th century, Sundiata Keita, leader of the Mandinka people (also called the Malinké), founded the empire of Mali and converted to Islam as a gesture of friendship to his northern neighbours and trading partners. By the next century the Mali empire stretched from the Atlantic to the borders of present-day Nigeria, and controlled nearly all trans-Saharan trade. Its great commercial cities – like Djenné and Timbuktu – grew rich on the transport of gold, salt and other goods between West Africa and the Mediterranean, and became famous centres of culture and learning, surrounded by a mystique which has endured right up to the present day. When the Mali emperor Mansa Musa passed through Egypt on a pilgrimage to Mecca in the early 1300s he gave away so much gold that the value of Egyptian currency slumped for decades.

On his return from Arabia, Musa brought

REPUBLIC OF MALI
Area: 1,240,140 sq km
Population: 10.8 million
Population Growth Rate: 2.8%
Capital: Bamako
Head of State: President Alpha Oumar Konaré
Official Language: French
Currency: West African CFA franc
Exchange Rate: CFA 575 = US$1
Per Capita GNP: US$300
Inflation: 2%
Time: GMT/UTC

Highlights
- The huge mud-brick Grande Mosquée in the medieval town of Djenné
- Exploring the winding streets and alleyways of legendary Timbuktu
- Trekking along the Bandiagara escarpment in the World Heritage Pays Dogon (Dogon Country)

architects and scholars to Timbuktu and Djenné, establishing mosques, universities and a literate administration. However, in the east of his empire the Songhaï people had established their own city-state around Gao, and by 1400 they were strong enough to raid Mali's capital, Niani. In 1464 they finally eclipsed the empire of Mali and embarked on a systematic conquest of the Sahel.

The Songhaï empire collapsed in 1591 after an invasion from Morocco and an ensuing revolt by its own people. However,

it is unlikely that any empire could have survived for much longer in this region as, by the 17th century, European ships were sailing directly to and from the coast of West Africa, and the trans-Saharan trade routes lost their significance.

Towards the end of the 19th century, Mali became a French colony and the local population was forced to produce cash crops, mainly groundnuts, cotton and gum arabic. Mali became independent in 1960 (though for a few months it was federated with Senegal) and Modibo Keita, the first president, put the country on a socialist road to development. In 1968 Keita was overthrown in a military coup led by Moussa Traoré.

Throughout the 1970s and 1980s, the greatest cause of concern was the continual food shortages. These were conveniently blamed on the droughts suffered by many Sahel countries at this time, but were due largely to government mismanagement. As the food crises worsened, so did relations between the government and the Tuareg people of northern Mali, who had suffered more than most during the droughts.

In 1990, a small number of Tuareg separatists attacked some isolated army posts.

The soldiers' heavy-handed retaliation led to further fighting. Hundreds were killed on both sides and a full-scale civil war seemed imminent. Northern Mali became off-limits to foreigners, and Gao was briefly besieged.

There was also unrest in Bamako. In March 1991 demonstrations in Bamako triggered a government backlash in which more than 150 people were killed. Within days the army, led by Colonel Amadou Touré, took control, arresting President Moussa Traoré.

Touré became leader of the transitional National Reconciliation Council, and commanded considerable respect and support from Malians. In August 1991, the country's constitution was changed to allow for multiparty democracy, and in April 1992 a 'national pact' was signed with the Tuareg. In June 1992, Amadou Touré resigned, allowing elected president Alpha Oumar Konaré to take over.

However, problems continued and in April 1993 there were further serious anti-government riots in Bamako. In November the same year the World Bank suspended aid to Mali and demanded that a series of austerity measures be introduced. Occasional outbreaks of 'banditry' were still occurring in northern Mali in the mid 1990s, and transport around Gao was restricted.

In March 1996, there was a symbolic burning of weapons in Timbuktu to mark the end of the four years of Tuareg insurgency in Mali. The United Nations High Commission for Refugees (UNHCR) began repatriating Tuareg refugees from south-eastern Mauritania and they are slowly returning to their traditional villages near Timbuktu. Unfortunately, because of food shortages they are being forced to give up their nomadic lifestyle.

On 13 April 1997, elections for the Assemblée Nationale were held, however the results were annulled because of several irregularities. It was back to the ballot boxes a month later, and in the two-horse race, the opposition candidate was well and truly left at the barrier – Konaré the incumbent (and candidate for ADEMA – Alliance for Democracy in Mali) managed to snare 96% of the vote and the lone challenger, of the

Party for Unity Development and Progress, bravely gathered the other 4%. Konaré seemed to be back in for five years – but, you guessed it, more irregularities. The race started again in late July with the second round held in early August and ADEMA easily won the election.

GEOGRAPHY & CLIMATE
The northern half of Mali consists of desert, while in the south there is usually enough rainfall to grow crops without irrigation. In between these two areas is the Sahel zone, where cultivation depends largely on the flooding of the Niger River. The rainy season lasts from June to late September although rainfall is rare in the north and light in the Sahel. The coolest part of the dry season is from November to March, although this is when the dusty harmattan winds blow in from the desert. The other months are less dusty but very hot.

POPULATION & PEOPLE
The population is currently estimated at about 10.8 million. The main group is the Bambara (BAM-bah-rah) who live in the region around Bamako and Ségou. Other minority groups include the Songhaï (SONG-guy) and Puel (also known as Fulani). The north, especially around Timbuktu, is populated mainly by nomadic Tuareg (TWA-reg). The Dogon (DOH-ghon), who live on the rocky Bandiagara escarpment 100km east of Mopti, are a fascinating people who have resisted incursion by other groups and have managed to retain many of their traditional beliefs.

LANGUAGE
French is the official language but the most widely spoken (especially in Bamako) is Bambara. Other languages spoken in various areas are Songhaï, Tuareg and Arabic. The Dogon people have some 48 dialects, Sangha being a major one, but even this is not understood by many Dogon. See the Language Appendix for Arabic and French words and phrases.

Dogon Culture

The Bandiagara escarpment *(falaise)*, known as Dogon Country after its inhabitants, is a veritable treasure-trove for the adventurous traveller, with stunning vistas, photogenic architecture and a complex culture.

The Dogon are believed to have arrived at the escarpment around 1500 AD at a time when it was occupied by the Tellem people, who had reached it around 400 years earlier. Push came to shove and the Tellem were forced away by the Dogon, possibly to Burkina Faso. Subsequent incursions were made by African warlords but it was not until 1920 that French soldiers (and a train of 'follow-up' onion-cultivating missionaries) finally 'civilised' the falaise. Fortunately, all the raiders had little impact, and Dogon culture, with its predominantly animist beliefs, survives even to this day.

The real threat to the survival of the culture comes from the latest raider – tourism. The Dogon happily sell parts of their buildings (doors and windows), statuary and authentic masks, in order to get a annual maize supply for their families. The motto for the traveller: Buy only those things which you believe to be easily reproducible by the Dogon. ■

Facts for the Visitor

VISAS

Visas are required for all except French nationals and usually cost around US$15, although they can be as much as US$50 (in Niger); they are not available at the border. Visas are usually valid for one month and can be extended at main police stations for about US$10.

Foreigners must register with the police in Mopti, Gao and Timbuktu. This involves filling in a form, while the police put a stamp and some illegible scrawl in your passport. A US$2 'fee' is usually payable, although some travellers have avoided this by asking for a receipt. In Timbuktu, a traveller refused to pay and spent the night in jail!

Other Visas

In Bamako, the French embassy issues visas to Côte d'Ivoire, Togo, Chad and the CAR, but not to Niger. You can also get visas for the following African countries (note that for each application you'll need from one to four photos):

Algeria
    Visa costs vary according to nationality, and visas are issued in 24 hours.

Burkina Faso
    Visas cost US$20 and are usually issued on the same day if you arrive early.
Guinea
    Visas cost US$30 and are issued within 24 to 48 hours.
Mauritania
    Visas cost US$8 and are issued on the same day.
Nigeria
    Fees vary according to nationality (free for US citizens, US$12 for Australians and US$35 for UK citizens).
Senegal
    Visas cost US$5 and are issued within 24 hours.

EMBASSIES
Mali Embassies

In West Africa, Mali has embassies in Côte d'Ivoire, Egypt, The Gambia, Ghana, Guinea, Sierra Leone, Niger, Nigeria and Senegal. Elsewhere, there are Mali embassies in Belgium, Germany, France and the USA. The Malian embassy in Washington issues one month visas for US$17 in three days (two photos and proof of a return airline ticket are required).

Foreign Embassies in Mali

Countries with embassies in Bamako include:

Algeria
    Badalabougou, Route de Ségou, about 4km south of the river (☎ 22 5176)

Burkina Faso
> off Route de Koulikoro, near the Hippodrome, about 3km east of the city centre (☎ 22 3177)

Canada
> Route de Koulikoro, about 5km from the city centre (☎ 22 2236; telex 2530)

France
> Square Lumumba (☎ 22 6246)

Germany
> on Ave de Farako in Badalabougou, south of the Niger River bridge (☎ 22 3299; fax 22 9650)

Guinea
> west side of the city centre, on a small street off Route de l'Ancien Aéroport (☎ 22 2975)

Mauritania
> Rue Titi Niare, Bagadadji, just off Route de Koulikoro, about 6km from the city centre (☎ 22 4815)

Nigeria
> Route de Ségou in Badalabougou, 1km south of the Pont des Martyrs (☎ 22 5771)

Senegal
> just south of the centre, three blocks west of Square Patrice Lumumba and 50m south of Ave de l'Yser (next to Restaurant du Fleuve)

UK (honorary consul)
> Mr Harvey Smith (BP 2069, ☎ 22 2064)

USA
> corner of Rue Rochester and Rue Mohammed V (☎ 22 5834; fax 22 3712)

MONEY
US$1 = CFA 575

The unit of currency is the West African CFA franc. There are no restrictions on the import or export of local currency.

Commissions vary according to the currency you exchange (and also depend on whether you change cash or travellers' cheques) but they are invariably very high. At all banks the process is slow and the staff dislike anything other than French francs (in all cases you will need your purchase receipts). Some large hotels in Bamako and other main towns will change travellers' cheques, with high commissions. Visa card cash advances are available in Bamako.

Banking hours are generally from 8 to 11 am (sometimes noon) Monday to Saturday. Black-market currency rates are not worth the risk of changing money on the street.

POST & COMMUNICATIONS
Letters posted from Bamako and Mopti to destinations outside Africa generally arrive, but parcel post can be unreliable. The poste restante service in Bamako is reliable.

In Bamako there are many private *télé-centres* where you can make international calls and send faxes. You can also make calls with card phones in the major centres; international calls are expensive.

The country code for Mali is 223. There are no area codes.

DANGERS & ANNOYANCES
Crime in Bamako is on the increase. Several travellers have been robbed at the railway station or near the Maison des Jeunes. If you arrive on the train at night, either stay in the station hotel until dawn or take a taxi to your hotel.

Another danger to watch out for is the men who engage you in conversation about Malian politics, but then turn out to be secret police and threaten to 'arrest' you for subversion. Naturally they settle for a large 'fine'.

The Tuareg rebellion around Gao and Timbuktu officially ended in 1996, and the Malian government's recent peace initiatives seem to have been successful. However, it may be worth checking out the latest situation before you venture beyond these towns.

PUBLIC HOLIDAYS
Public holidays in Mali include: 1 January, 20 January (Army Day), 1 May, 25 May (Africa Day), 22 September (Independence Day), 25 December, Easter Monday and variable Islamic holidays (see Public Holidays in the Regional Facts for the Visitor chapter for details).

ACCOMMODATION
Places to stay in Mali range from backstreet brothels to smart hotels in Bamako and large tourist towns (Ségou, Mopti and Timbuktu). In between these two extremes you'll find *campements* – there's at least one in every town – where accommodation in bungalows or huts is simple but adequate, and sometimes good value.

In Dogon Country, many travellers sleep on the flat roof of village huts, so a blanket or light sleeping bag may be required.

Some upmarket hotels add a tourist tax of US$2 per person per night to the room cost.

FOOD
Food in Mali is very similar to that found in Senegal. For more details see the Food & Drink section in the Senegal chapter. Along the Niger River, restaurants serve grilled or deep-fried *capitaine* (Nile perch).

Getting There & Away

AIR
Airlines flying between Europe and Mali include Sabena, Air France, Aeroflot and Ethiopian Airlines. Air Afrique has regular flights to/from Paris, Marseilles and Rome, and also flies to/from New York via Dakar or Abidjan.

Within Africa, Air Afrique flies from Bamako to Abidjan (Côte d'Ivoire), Niamey (Niger, US$275/300 one way/return), Dakar (Senegal), Ouagadougou (Burkina Faso), Nouakchott (Mauritania) and several other West African capitals. You can get to Conakry (Guinea) on Air Guinée, Guinée Air Service (US$110 one way) and Air France (US$125 one way).

Departure tax at Bamako airport is US$5 for internal flights, and US$18 for other African/international flights.

LAND
Algeria
Check the security situation in Algeria before attempting to enter. At the time of writing it was not safe – foreigners were targets for Islamic agitators (several have been killed). If this is still the case, give it a big miss.

Burkina Faso
Bus Direct buses go from the Sogoniko *gare routière* in Bamako to Bobo-Dioulasso for around US$25, but the trip takes 12 hours so many travellers break it at Sikasso. The Bamako to Sikasso fare is US$6, and from Sikasso to Bobo it's US$10.

You can also get to Bobo from Ségou on the twice weekly bus that leaves from the town's gare routière. The fare is US$10.

Bush Taxi Bush taxis run from Mopti to Bobo-Dioulasso most days for around US$10. These taxis can take all day to fill, and an overnight stop at the border is likely. (The nearby *campement* has rooms for about US$6.) Again, many travellers do this trip in stages: a bush taxi from Mopti to Bankass costs US$6; from Bankass to Koro it's US$5; and from Koro to Ouahigouya it's US$6.

Côte d'Ivoire
The main route to Côte d'Ivoire is via Sikasso and Ferkessédougou. Direct buses go three times per week from the Sogoniko gare routière in Bamako all the way to Abidjan for US$30. It is meant to take 36 hours but can easily be longer; one traveller reported that his bus took 4½ days and that it was 'the most broken-down, overpacked, sweaty, dirty, dusty, smelly, sweltering bus trip' he'd ever had. It's much easier and more pleasant to do this trip in stages: buses from Bamako to Sikasso cost US$6, then from Sikasso to the border by taxi, followed by a minibus to Ferkessédougou it's US$14.

From Bougouni to Odienné there is very little traffic and only one bus a week from Bamako to Odienné (US$20). The bridge at Manakoro (on the Mali side of the border) is usually under water throughout August.

Guinea
The main route to Guinea is from Bamako to Conakry via Kankan. Between Bamako and Kankan there are two choices: via Kourémalé (the border) and Siguiri, or via Bougouni and Mandiana. There's a bus company called Sahel Transport going three times per week from Bamako (leaving the small gare routière – a dusty dead-end street – near the Maison des Jeunes) to Kourémalé (US$4.50). This bus may go on to Siguiri though you're more likely to have to take a

MALI

minibus or bush taxi towards Kankan from the border.

Mauritania

It is possible to travel to Mauritania in your own vehicle. The 1100km route from Néma to Nouakchott is asphalted all the way. The journey from Bamako can be done in three days, but that's pushing it.

Niger

The main route between Mali and Niger is from Gao to Niamey. The national bus line, SNTN, makes one trip per week (US$20, 30 hours). You should buy tickets two days in advance. Other than these buses, there are also occasional slow trucks (two to three days) for about US$15.

Senegal

Travelling by road on public transport between Senegal and Mali involves a lot of short bus and taxi rides. Forget it.

A better bet is the twice-weekly Bamako to Dakar express train. The trip, which takes about 35 hours, departs each city in the morning on Wednesday and Saturday. Large, comfortable, 1st class seats can be reserved in advance; 2nd class is more crowded with less comfortable, though adequate, seating. The 1st/2nd class fares from Bamako to Dakar are US$75/52. The couchettes (sleeping berths) cost from US$110 per person. The trains have dining cars, or you can buy cheap food along the way.

At each border post you have to get your passport stamped. It may be taken by an inspector on the train, but you still have to collect it yourself by going to the office at the border post. Nobody tells you this. So if your passport is taken, ask where and when you have to go to collect it. You may need a stamp at the police station in Kayes too, but this seems fairly arbitrary. Watch out for thieves on the train, especially at night.

BOAT
Guinea

A barge carrying passengers usually departs once a week from Jikuroni (upstream from Bamako) to Kankan between July and November, or when the river is high enough (US$10, four days). For more details ask at the Compagnie Malienne de Navigation (CMN) office in Bamako.

Getting Around

AIR

Internal flights are operated by Air Mali. There are flights three times a week in each direction between Bamako and Timbuktu, stopping at Mopti and Goundam each way. Once per week the flight continues on to Gao.

From Bamako flights to Mopti cost US$90 and to Timbuktu US$120. From Mopti to Timbuktu costs US$65 and to Gao US$90; return fares are double.

BUS & BUSH TAXI

Several private bus companies run safe and comfortable vehicles on the routes between main towns. Fares seem to be fixed and differ very little between the various companies. Major routes include Bamako to Sikasso (US$7), Mopti (US$13) and Gao (US$24 to US$30). The Gao road was often closed during the Tuareg uprising. Buses often had to travel in convoy, protected by troops. Regular, even daily, services may have recommenced by now.

Because buses are better and cheaper, there are very few bush taxis on the main long-distance routes. Bush taxis are either Peugeot 504 seven-seaters (with around 11 people inside) or pick-ups (called *bachés*) carrying about 16 passengers – bachés are slower but about 25% cheaper than 504s. However, on shorter routes, such as Mopti to Djenné (US$4.50) and Mopti to Bandiagara (US$3), bush taxis are the best (or only) way to get around. Luggage usually costs between 5% and 10% of the fare.

You may have to, at some stage, resort to a truck *camion* complete with live poultry, porcine and human cargo (not to mention smelly oil drums and household furniture).

It is not the preferred mode of travel for those with the money, but to many Malians (and you for a brief time) it may be the only means from A to B.

BOAT
Passenger Boat
Large passenger boats, which are operated by the CMN, ply the Niger River between Koulikoro (60km north-east of Bamako) and Gao, via Mopti, Kabara (for Timbuktu) and several other riverside towns. They usually run from August to November, when the river is high. In December and January the service may run between Mopti and Gao.

In theory, one boat heads downstream from Koulikoro every Tuesday and arrives in Gao the following Monday, while another boat heads upstream from Gao every Thursday and arrives at Koulikoro a week later. The journey from Koulikoro to Mopti should take three days and from Mopti to Gao it should take four days, but schedules are very unreliable and the journey along each section can take twice as long as scheduled.

There are three boats, although one always seems to be out of action; the *Kankan Moussa* is the best, and the *Tombouctou* and the *Général Soumare* are more basic. But despite their differences, all the boats have the same fare structure. *Luxe* and 1st class consist of two-berth cabins; 2nd class is a four berth cabin; 3rd class is either an eight berth or 12 berth cabin (although you can also sleep on the upper deck, and hang out there during the day); and 4th class is in the very crowded and basic lower deck (which even the most hardened travellers rate as the pits). You can buy tickets at CMN in Bamako, Mopti, Timbuktu and Gao.

Except in 4th class, meals are included in the fare. The food is bland and boring, and you need your own bowl and fork in 3rd class. Extra food can be bought on board or at stops en route. Beers, soft drinks and bottled mineral water can be bought on the boat, but supplies sometimes run out. Water is drawn from the river and 'purified' by the addition of bleach, but it's best to purify your own or bring some bottled mineral water.

Pirogue & Pinasse
There are also other more traditional boats carrying passengers up and down the river. *Pirogues* are small canoes, either motorised or paddled by hand. *Pinasses* tend to be larger, motorised and have extra features such as a simple cabin. Pinasses are generally faster than pirogues, but not as fast as the large passenger boats.

The most popular routes for travellers are between Mopti and Djenné, and between Mopti and Kabara (for Timbuktu). A ride by pinasse from Mopti to Djenné takes all day and costs US$9. It's also possible to go by non-motorised pirogue which takes two days and costs US$6. Between Mopti and Kabara by large pinasse costs about US$15. The journey varies from three days to two weeks depending on the amount of cargo carried, the size of the boat, and the water level.

Bamako

Bamako is a dusty, low-rise city with a very 'African' feel. Although (or because) it lacks the sophistication of Dakar, many travellers enjoy a short stay here. There are wide boulevards, some lively markets and a central area which is fairly compact and easy to walk around. Not far from the centre is the cosmopolitan Niaréla quartière with good restaurants and pleasant places to stay.

Information
Happily there is a new tourist information office – the Office Malien du Tourisme et L'Hôtellerie (☎ 22 5673) – near the corner of Ave du Fleuve and Rue Mohammed V. OMATHO, as it is known, is open from 7.30 am to 4 pm weekdays. It's early days, but the staff are enthusiastic and this is one of the few places in West Africa where you can get a capital city map and brochures on tourist destinations (Timbuktu, Mopti, Djenné, Ségou, Pays Dogon). The English translation of the French brochures will leave you in stitches, eg '... Markala remains a place

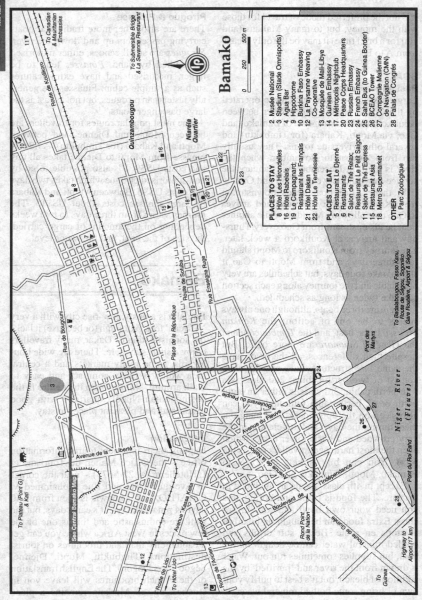

Bamako

PLACES TO STAY
8 Hôtel Les Hirondelles
16 Hôtel Rabelais
19 Le Campagnard;
   Restaurant les Français
21 Hôtel Dakan
22 Hôtel Le Tennessee

PLACES TO EAT
5 Restaurant Le Djenné
6 Restaurants
7 Salon de Thé Relax;
   Restaurant Le Petit Saigon
11 Salon de Thé l'Express
15 Restaurant Asia
18 Metro Supermarket

OTHER
1 Parc Zoologique
2 Musée National
3 Stadium (Stade Omnisports)
4 Agua Bar
9 Hippodrome
10 Burkina Faso Embassy
12 La Paysanne Weaving
   Co-operative
13 Mosquée de Mali-Libye
14 Guinean Embassy
17 Métropolis Nightclub
20 Peace Corps Headquarters
23 Russian Embassy
24 French Embassy
25 Sahel Bus (to Guinea Border)
26 BCEAO Tower
27 Compagnie Malienne
   de Navigation (CMN)
28 Palais de Congrés

0   250   500 m

worth discovering thanks to its morkshops and dom' (eh?).

Banks where you can exchange money in Bamako include the BIAO at Rond Point de la Nation, and BDM and Banque Malienne de Credit et Dépôt (BMCD), which are both on Ave du Fleuve. The BMCD also gives Visa card cash advances. To change travellers' cheques you need purchase slips.

The US Information Center on Rue Baba Diarra (near the train station) has English-language newspapers and magazines in its air-con library. It is open from 8 am to 12.30 pm and from 3 to 6 pm. The Centre Culturel Française on Blvd de l'Indépendance near Rond Point de la Nation screens films.

The best travel agency is ATS Voyages (☎ 22 4435), on Ave du Fleuve just north of Square Lumumba, where the helpful staff speak English; it is also the American Express agency.

Things to See & Do

The **Grand Marché** burnt down in 1993. It's due to be rebuilt but in the meantime all the stalls have moved out to the surrounding streets and the area is as lively as ever. The **Maison des Artisans** on Blvd du Peuple near the Grande Mosquée is also worth a visit, even if you're not buying. There are many gold and silversmiths, plus several stalls selling wood and leather items.

In a complete contrast to that, the **Musée National**, on Ave de la Liberté, north of the city centre, is quiet and well organised with some interesting exhibits including local crafts and Dogon artefacts. The museum is open every day from 9 am to 6 pm, except Monday; entry is US$1.50. The **zoo**, 500m past the museum, is a sorry-looking place, where the animals suffer from neglect.

For a superb **panorama** of the city and the wide Niger River head to Point G, the plateau above Bamako. The road to the top starts near the museum. About halfway up this road, you'll see a sign, 'Point de Vue Touristique' – follow the track for 1km.

Places to Stay

If you arrive late at night at the Sogoniko gare routière, it might be best to stay at one of the nearby *chambres de passage* which offer basic accommodation (a dirty mat on the floor) for around US$1.50.

The clinical *Le Centre d'Accueil Catholique des Soeurs Blanches* on the corner of Rue 133 and Rue 130, west of the city centre, is OK. A bed in the dorm costs US$5.50 and private doubles with nets cost US$14. A friendlier alternative is the nearby *Chez Fanta*, on the corner of Rue 130 and Rue 135, where you can stay for US$6 per night, plus US$1 for breakfast. There's no sign, but locals will point out the house.

Another option in the cheap price range is the *Pension MS No 1* (☎ 22 6377), on Rue Mohammed V, where secure singles/doubles with fans cost about US$15/19. The price includes breakfast (a cup of coffee and enough bread to feed a mouse). Some travellers have slept on the verandah for US$6.

Also worth checking out is the *Mission Libanaise*, an old mission on Rue Poincaré, where clean doubles with nets, fans and hot showers cost around US$18. You can camp in the yard for US$5.

Up the scale a bit there's the *Hôtel-Buffet de la Gare* (☎ 22 5460) which charges US$18/28 for singles/doubles with fans, US$35/50 for rooms with air-con and cold baths. Prices include breakfast and dinner, and drop by US$4 per person if you don't want meals.

The only other option in the city centre is the *Hôtel Lac Debo* (☎ 22 9635), at the junction of Ave du Fleuve and Ave de la Nation, with decent air-con rooms for US$35/40 although, if you insist, they'll give you a slightly older room for US$22/32.

The mid-range *Hôtel Les Colibris* (☎ 22 6637) on Route de Ségou, 3km south of the bridge (a taxi trip), has a relaxed ambience and rooms with bath for US$25/30. Camping is allowed for US$6 per person and US$3 per vehicle.

For a splurge there is the excellent *Hôtel Baobab* (☎ 23 5417) on the south side of the river in the Fasso Kanu district (turn off at Hôtel Les Colibris). This has the best-value rooms in Mali, a great restaurant and a

MALI

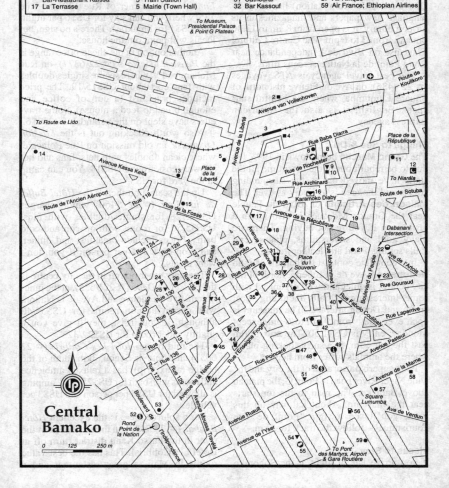

Central Bamako

terrace with superb views; singles/doubles are from US$30/45. It is worth the US$3 taxi fare to stay here.

In the Niaréla district, east of the centre, there are two good mid-range choices. The *Hôtel Dakan* (☎ 22 9196), south of Route de Sotuba, has decent air-con singles/doubles for US$25/32. There is a central courtyard with several *paillottes* (thatched sun shelters). A couple of blocks north, above the Metro supermarket, is the classy, Lebanese-run *Le Campagnard* (☎ 22 96; fax 23 2469), a perennial favourite with aid workers and also Peace Corps volunteers. Comfortable singles/doubles go for US$54/62; each room has air-con, mini-bar, telephone and colour TV. Perhaps it's the little bit of luxury you crave after the privations of the Pays Dogon.

Places to Eat

Cheap street food, mainly beef brochettes and fried plantains, is sold all over town. At the train station there are several *stalls* providing coffee, bread and eggs.

The small *L'Escale de Jumeaux*, opposite the Centre d'Accueil Catholique des Soeurs Blanches, has breakfast and other meals from US$1. To the north is the friendly *Café Mohammed à la Casa*, great for omelettes and coffee; a meal is about US$2.

Near the corner of Rue Bagayoko and Ave Mamadou Konaté in a small *shack*, a friendly Senegalese guy serves meals in the same price range. In the same area, a block south on Ave Mamadou Konaté, is the *Restaurant Joal-Fadiouth*, where a decent meal costs from US$2 to US$3 and large beers are US$1. On the other side of the street the near-legendary '*bean lady*' serves meals for less than US$1. Another cheapie for riz gras is *Gargotte Dunkuta*, behind Cinéma Vox.

Up several large bounds from these places, but still reasonably priced, is the cosy *Ali Baba Café*, on Rue Mohammed V, which has a pleasant atmosphere and snacks such as chawarma for US$1.50, plus pizzas, sandwiches and cakes. Also on Rue Mohammed V is the similar *Salon de Thé la Phoenicia*; sadly, the beers are overpriced.

The *Hôtel-Buffet de la Gare* is worth trying if you want a decent meal for about US$4. At *Bar-Restaurant Kaissa*, near Pension MS No 1, the prices are similar and the food is good. On Ave de la Nation, the slightly disreputable but frequently recommended *Bar Bozo* serves solid meals.

Bamako also has some smarter restaurants serving international cuisines. These include *La Pizzeria* on Rue Mohammed V, where small pizzas cost around US$4 and other meals are in the US$4 to US$7 range; and *Le Bol de Jade*, in the city centre off Ave du Fleuve, a popular place with authentic Vietnamese food. A favourite is *Les Français* in Le Campagnard (see Places to Stay earlier), a haunt of Peace Corps workers and Australian drillers; breakfast is US$5, a lunch platter US$15 and a full dinner (including fabulous wood-fired pizza) from US$17.

Entertainment

The *Buffet de la Gare*, open late for drinks and dancing, sometimes has recorded music, and occasionally the legendary Rail Band performs (US$3 cover charge). Other popular bars are the attractively sleazy *Bar Bozo* (see Places to Eat earlier) and *Disco Colombo*, both along the Ave de la Nation.

Popular nightclubs include *Black and White* near the cathedral; the intriguingly named *37.2* diagonally opposite the US embassy (US$5 cover charge); the heavily advertised *L'Evasion*, off Ave du Fleuve; the African-oriented *Agua Bar* in Rue de Bougouni (US$4 cover charge); and the glitzy *Métropolis* in Niaréla (near the Metro supermarket), where smart Bamakois gyrate beneath a sparkling glitter-ball.

To cool off (and remove the night sweat) after all the gyrating, the pool at the Hôtel de l'Amitié is open to non-guests for US$6 including the use of a towel.

Sunday at the Hippodrome on Route de Koulikoro is a fun day out. In Mali, the lottery is based on horse-racing – picking a trifecta (three horses) to be exact.

Getting There & Away

Bus Nearly all long-distance buses go from the gare routière at Sogoniko (sometimes written Soko Niko), about 6km south of the city centre, and all the bus companies have ticket offices there. It's advisable to go to the gare routière the day before you travel to buy your ticket and to check departure times. Bamabus is particularly reliable.

To get to Sogoniko take a crowded pickup from Square Lumumba along Route de Ségou for US$0.20, or take one of the smart new white-and-blue Taba minibuses along the same route for US$0.30. A taxi from the centre of town costs US$2.

For train services to Dakar (Senegal) see the Getting There & Away section earlier.

Boat For details on the riverboat service from Koulikoro to Gao, via Mopti and Timbuktu, see the main Getting Around section in this chapter. To make bookings in Bamako, go to the office of the Compagnie Malienne de Navigation (CMN, ☎ 22 3802), a small two storey building on the riverbank, west of the Pont des Martyrs. Transport from Bamako to Koulikoro leaves from various points in the city centre. Ask the CMN staff for directions.

Getting Around
The Airport A bus meets most international flights and goes into town for US$3 per person which is good value as taxis between the airport and city centre cost at least US$9 and more usually US$15.

If you're coming from the city centre, you can avoid taxis by taking a Taba city minibus to the major road junction at the southern end of Route de Ségou, from where you can get a taxi the last 5km to the airport for US$2. Alternatively, Taba city minibuses run between town and the airport via Pont du Roi and the highway.

Around the Country

DJENNÉ
Djenné is possibly the oldest and most impressive of Mali's ancient trading cities. Its heyday was during the 15th and 16th centuries, and it seems to have changed little since. It is a mud-brick town through and through, and no modern building detracts from the atmosphere. Market day is Monday.

Its main attraction is the huge **Grande Mosquée** – one of the world's largest mud-brick buildings and a classic example of Sudanese (or Sahelian) architecture. Non-Muslim visitors aren't allowed inside the mosque, but for a fee you can go onto the roof of the Petit Marché building opposite and get a clear view of its exterior.

The **Grand Marché** in front of the mosque is very busy on Monday, but it's quiet during the rest of the week. To tour the town's narrow streets and alleyways, you might consider hiring a guide (US$2 for a few hours), as you'll avoid a lot of hassle, and see much more than you would on your own. Your guide will show you around and also take you onto the roof of a private house, from where you'll get great views.

You may have to register with the police in Djenné (the station is near the post office) – enquire at OMATHO in Bamako.

Places to Stay & Eat
Other than finding a room in someone's house, the only place is *Le Campement* (☎ 42 0009), near the Grande Mosquée, where singles/doubles are US$7/9, or you can sleep on the roof for US$3.50. Meals, such as riz sauce (US$2) and chicken (US$6), are prepared to order.

For better food, search out *Chez Baba* in a courtyard off a back street near the small market, where rice, chicken and dessert costs US$2. You can also stay here for US$3. You can also ask your guide to organise a meal, but agree on a price beforehand.

Getting There & Away
From Bamako, there are direct buses to Djenné on Saturday and Monday from the Sogoniko gare routière (US$14). In Mopti, bush taxis for Djenné leave from the gare routière near the campement (a baché is US$4 and a Peugeot 504 is US$5).

GAO

Like Djenné, Gao was a prosperous Sahelian trading city which flourished during the 15th and 16th centuries. It's been more affected by the 20th century than Djenné, but is still very interesting. Gao was attacked during the Tuareg uprising in 1990, and there are still incidents of banditry in the region. It is still worthwhile checking the current situation before travelling there (or beyond).

It is also important to report to the police here. You may have to pay US$2 (see the section on Visas earlier in this chapter). The police station, opposite the mosque, closes for passport business at noon.

Things to see include the curious **Tomb of Askia**, a 16th-century ruler, and the associated **mosque**; the two good **markets**; and the **waterfront** where you can take a ride in a pirogue which is a relief after all that desert. There's a small ethnological **museum** in the town; entry is US$0.50.

For details on Gao to Bamako transport, see the introductory Getting Around section earlier in this chapter.

Places to Stay

There are a couple of cheap places to stay. *Camping Tizi Mizi* is 4km down the Niamey road. Good double rooms here with fan and shower cost US$12, basic rooms are US$7, or you can sleep on the terrace for US$4. *Camping Yurga* is an older, very basic place near the river about 4km south of town. Hard beds in rooms or on the terrace cost US$3. At either of these places you can put up your own tent for a fee of US$3 per night. (It is illegal to camp within 10km of Gao except at one of these places.)

The only place in Gao itself is the rundown *Hôtel Atlantide*, near the Grand Marché. A single with a shared bath costs from US$9, and a double with bath from US$17 (US$38 with air-con). Prices include breakfast, but this is poor value when you consider that water and electricity are erratic.

Places to Eat

There are several *food stalls* around the market selling grilled meat, spicy sausages and other bargain snacks. Other cheap places are *Le Sénégalaise*, near the Place de l'Indépendance; and the *Blackpool* and *Dikou* for capitaine – these last two places are a couple of blocks from the river.

Other places to eat which have been recommended are the *Bar l'Oasis* and the *Casa Bar* (with brochettes and other snacks). For a drink, go to the *Café Sportif* which has a pleasant garden and decent music, or to *Le Twist Bar*.

HOMBORI

This small village about 250km south-west of Gao is close to some spectacular scenery including, 11km to the south, **Le Main de Fatma**, a giant rock formation bursting out of the ground like an enormous hand and featured on many tourist posters. This offers the best technical rock climbing in West Africa (some say the world) and only those suitably 'wired' can even contemplate its enormity.

For climbers, the small *hôtel* at the base of the rock costs a fraction of what it costs to transport your climbing equipment here. For drinks and food, try *La Belle Sénégalaise*.

MOPTI

Travellers have a love-hate relationship with Mopti, the 'Venice of Africa' – the centre of Mali's tourist industry and fast becoming the Marrakesh of West Africa. It's compact enough to get around easily, big enough to be interesting (a population of 40,000) and it's also a good place to meet people, both other travellers and locals. However, the hordes of touts can drive you crazy, and they are sometimes very hard to get rid of. That said, you can hire great Dogon guides here.

On arrival, you're meant to report to the police near the campement; this costs US$2. Many travellers choose to ignore this rule.

Mopti is 10km to the west of the main Bamako to Gao road, reached by turning off at Sévaré. Most buses from Bamako go all the way to Mopti itself, but your journey may

MALI

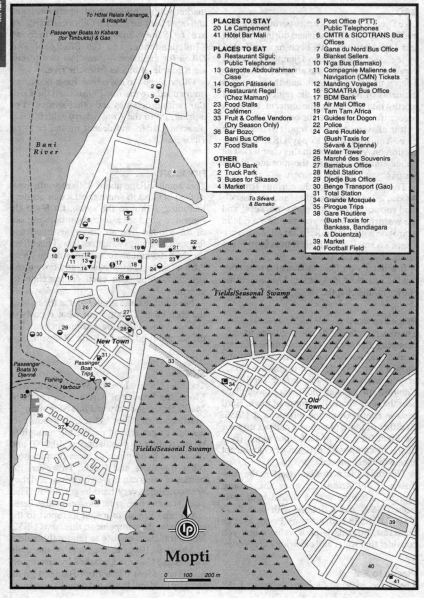

PLACES TO STAY
20 Le Campement
41 Hôtel Bar Mali

PLACES TO EAT
8 Restaurant Sigui;
    Public Telephone
13 Gargotte Abdoulrahman
    Cisse
14 Dogon Pâtisserie
15 Restaurant Regal
    (Chez Maman)
23 Food Stalls
32 Cafémen
33 Fruit & Coffee Vendors
    (Dry Season Only)
36 Bar Bozo;
    Bani Bus Office
37 Food Stalls

OTHER
1 BIAO Bank
2 Truck Park
3 Buses for Sikasso
4 Market

5 Post Office (PTT);
    Public Telephones
6 CMTR & SICOTRANS Bus
    Offices
7 Gana du Nord Bus Office
9 Blanket Sellers
10 N'ga Bus (Bamako)
11 Compagnie Malienne de
    Navigation (CMN) Tickets
12 Manding Voyages
16 SOMATRA Bus Office
17 BDM Bank
18 Air Mali Office
19 Tam Tam Africa
21 Guides for Dogon
22 Police
24 Gare Routière
    (Bush Taxis for
    Sévaré & Djenné)
25 Water Tower
26 Marché des Souvenirs
27 Bamabus Office
28 Mobil Station
29 Djedje Bus Office
30 Benge Transport (Gao)
31 Total Station
34 Grande Mosquée
35 Pirogue Trips
38 Gare Routière
    (Bush Taxis for
    Bankass, Bandiagara
    & Douentza)
39 Market
40 Football Field

To Hôtel Relais Kananga,
& Hospital

Passenger Boats to Kabara
(for Timbuktu) & Gao

*Bani
River*

To Sévaré
& Bamako

Fields/Seasonal Swamp

New Town

Passenger
Boats to Djenné

Passenger
Boat
Trips

Fishing
Harbour

*Old
Town*

Fields/Seasonal Swamp

Mopti

0   100   200 m

end in Sévaré. Regular share-taxis run between Sévaré and Mopti for US$1.

Things to See & Do
The large **Grande Mosquée** was built in 1935; it is best seen from the roof of one of the buildings nearby. The **Marché des Souvenirs**, in the centre of town, is definitely worth visiting for crafts (carpets, beads, silver jewellery etc) and locally made items such as masks and pottery. Mopti is the town in which to buy Fulani wedding blankets – the sellers are outside Restaurant Sigui.

The area around the **port** is also fascinating, and particularly lively in the early morning and at sunset. A **pirogue trip** to nearby fishing villages and Tuareg camps costs around US$2 per hour; ask at Bar Bozo.

Places to Stay
Mopti Many desperate travellers stay at the *Hôtel Bar Mali*, on the southern side of the old town. This is a dirty brothel, which smells of urine, but it has a kind of sleazy charm. Singles/doubles with fans cost US$8/9 but choose carefully as some rooms have no windows and those at the top get hot. The hotel will store baggage for you.

More expensive is *Le Campement* (☎ 43 0032), on your left as you come into Mopti near the gare routière, where basic double rooms with fan and net cost US$18, or US$30 with air-con. The shared bathrooms are also basic. These prices vary according to demand, and rise by at least US$6 in the high season. You can camp in the car park for US$4 per person, and there's a restaurant, serving meals from US$2 to US$4. The bar swarms with local guides in the evening. (If you employ one of them for the Dogon, make it clear that you want none of their salespersons/friends anywhere near!)

Mopti's flashiest choice is the *Relais Kananga Mopti* (☎ 43 0500).

Sévaré To escape Mopti's hustlers, you could think about staying in Sévaré. The *Hôtel Oasis* (☎ 42 0106), in the back streets, has clean doubles with fans for US$15. On the main road, the old, gloomy *Motel de Sévaré* (☎ 42 0111) and the smarter *Hôtel Debo* (☎ 42 0124) both have rooms; the latter has singles/doubles from US$25/32.

The best bet is *Chez Mankan Te* (fax 42 0193) a private home run by a German woman (Jutta). Comfortable doubles with air-con, attached bathroom and breakfast cost from US$15 per person. For directions ask at Mankan Te Restaurant, 1km south of the main crossroads.

Places to Eat & Entertainment
For street food in Mopti, check the *stalls* around the taxi park near the campement or the basic *gargottes* near the harbour's gare routière.

The *Dogon Pâtisserie*, in nice surroundings, is not as expensive as it looks. It has delicious croissants and cakes from US$1 and large cups of good coffee for US$0.50. Close by is *Gargotte Abdoulrahman Cisse* where you can get fried eggs or rice and sauce at very low prices.

Slightly more expensive, but good value, is the *Restaurant Régal* (also called *Chez Maman*), on the waterfront, where the owner is very friendly and meals such as meat and chips cost around US$2 and riz sauce costs US$1.

Nearby, the more expensive *Restaurant Sigui* has African and European meals at around US$3 and large beers at US$2. In the same price range, the *Bar Bozo* at the end of the harbour has views over the river.

The buzzing nightclub/disco is the *Tam Tam Africa*, near the campement. There is an adjoining garden bar and good restaurant (meals from US$5).

Mankan Te Restaurant is the place to eat at in Sévaré, and the adjoining *Bar Americain* is the spot for a drink.

Getting There & Away
Bush taxis (Peugeot 504s and bachés) for Djenné and Sévaré leave from outside the campement. For Bandiagara, Douentza and Bankass go to the gare routière south of the harbour. Buses to all other destinations leave

MALI

from various bus company offices in town (these are indicated on the Mopti map).

SÉGOU

Ségou is a large town (the second biggest in Mali), about halfway between Bamako and Mopti. The Monday **market** is lively and there's an interesting waterfront, several pleasant bars and restaurants. It is far less touristy than Mopti or Djenné.

Places to Stay

The cheapest place to stay in town used to be the *Office du Niger Campement* (☎ 32 0392) – ask if its once-good rooms (US$9 with fans and nets) are still available.

In the town centre, the *Grand Hôtel de France* (☎ 32 0315) has simple rooms for US$11 (or US$22 if you want air-con and bath) set around a pleasant courtyard, which becomes a restaurant and bar at night.

Also in the centre, closer to the river, *L'Auberge* (☎ 32 0145) is very pleasant (luxurious, in fact) with clean singles/doubles with air-con and hot showers and occasionally satellite TV for US$23/33.

Five kilometres from the town centre on the Mopti road is the *Hôtel du 22 Septembre 1960* (☎ 32 0462), with rooms for US$18 (plus US$10 for air-con).

Places to Eat & Entertainment

There's a row of simple *eating houses* on the main street where Bamako to Mopti buses stop. These include *Au Bon Coin* and *Tantie J'ai Faim* where riz sauce is US$1.

In the centre is the landmark *Snack Golfe*, a smart place which offers value meals like steak or chicken and chips, and capitaine, for US$2 to US$4. Nearby are the less stylish, cheaper *Regal* and *Chez Madame Halima*, with meals from US$1.

Travellers recommend *Restaurant Non-Stop*, 3km out on the Mopti road, where good meals cost from US$2 to US$5. The atmosphere is friendly and the tasty pizzas the best in Mali. For dancing, squeeze into the *Beau Rivage*, near L'Auberge.

TIMBUKTU (TOMBOUCTOU)

Few places in the world have a legend as enduring as Timbuktu's. From humble beginnings as a remote Tuareg settlement, it had grown by the 15th century into a major trading city and one of the most famous centres of Islamic scholarship.

Today, it still takes an effort to get here and some travellers are disappointed when they arrive. Like the early European explorers, maybe they expect the streets to be paved with gold (instead they find them clogged with sand). Many are still glad they came – perhaps they haven't seen the Pays Dogon?

Don't forget to register with police at the commissariat; it seems that this is free.

Things to See & Do

Even if this town of 15,000 didn't have a magical name, it would still be a fascinating place to visit. Seemingly lost in the middle of the desert, Timbuktu is a sprawl of low, flat-roofed buildings with dusty, winding streets and alleyways. There are numerous heavy doors decorated with brass studs and surrounded with ornate frames. Some have **plaques** showing where explorers such as René Caillié, Heinrich Barth and Gordon Laing stayed after they reached the city in the early 1800s. Not-so-famous DW Berty's house also gets a plaque – he was leader of the first American trans-Saharan expedition.

The three mud-brick mosques of **Djinguereber**, **Sankoré** and **Sidi Yahya** are interesting (for a small fee you can usually go inside), and the new **museum** near the Sidi Yahya Mosque is definitely worth a visit (entrance US$1).

The **CEDRAB** (Centre des Recherches Historiques Ahmed Baba), to the east of the PTT, has an interesting collection of documents *(tarikh)* chronicling Malian history.

Diré, a small town on the river between Timbuktu and Mopti, is rarely visited by outsiders. If you go by pirogue to Timbuktu you may have to change here. A *café* on the square has rooms for US$3 per night.

Places to Stay & Eat

Officially, there are only two hotels in Tim-

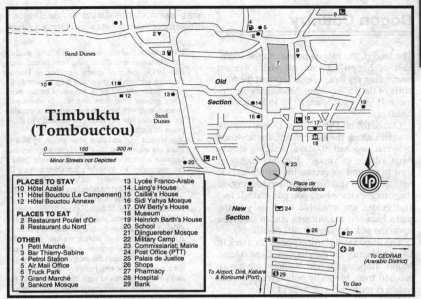

Timbuktu (Tombouctou)

Sand Dunes

Old Section

Sand Dunes

New Section

0   150   300 m

Minor Streets not Depicted

To Airport, Diré, Kabara & Korioumé (Port)

To Gao

To CEDRAB (Ararabio District)

Place de l'Indépendance

PLACES TO STAY
10 Hôtel Azalaï
11 Hôtel Bouctou (Le Campement)
12 Hôtel Bouctou Annexe

PLACES TO EAT
2 Restaurant Poulet d'Or
8 Restaurant du Nord

OTHER
1 Petit Marché
3 Bar Thierry-Sabine
4 Petrol Station
5 Air Mali Office
6 Truck Park
7 Grand Marché
9 Sankoré Mosque
13 Lycée Franco-Arabe
14 Laing's House
15 Caillié's House
16 Sidi Yahya Mosque
17 DW Berty's House
18 Museum
19 Heinrich Barth's House
20 School
21 Djinguereber Mosque
22 Military Camp
23 Commissariat; Mairie
24 Post Office (PTT)
25 Palais de Justice
26 Shops
27 Pharmacy
28 Hospital
29 Bank

buktu. The cheaper is the *Hôtel Bouctou* (☎ 92 1012), usually called *Le Campement*, where singles/doubles are US$15/20 (rooms with attached bathroom are US$10 extra). The older annexe has more character and double rooms on the ground floor with nets and fans cost US$15. Upstairs in the annexe, rooms with a mattress on the floor cost US$6. Supposedly, foreign tourists cannot stay there, although with gentle negotiation you'll probably be allowed.

Up in price and quality, the *Hôtel Azalaï* (☎ 92 1163) has air-con singles/doubles for US$45/55. Travellers also recommend the *Patisserie Asco*.

For good traditional meals starting from US$1. You should go to the *Restaurant Poulet d'Or* near the Petit Marché. Equally good are *Le Sénégalaise* in the main market building and *Restaurant du Nord* near the Grand Marché. All serve tea, bread, eggs, riz sauce and so on.

The *Bar Thierry-Sabine*, on the main street to the west of the centre, has cold beers which are cheaper than the Azalaï's.

Getting There & Away
Timbuktu is served by Air Mali flights (see the main Getting Around section earlier).

During the dry season the Djedje bus company runs a weekly service between Bamako and Timbuktu, via Ségou and Niono. The trip takes three very hard days and costs US$30. If you're coming from Mopti, you can find old Land Rovers going to Timbuktu a few times per week, also for about US$30 per person. This is a long, hot trip through the desert, and breakdowns are common – take plenty of water.

The easiest (and sometimes the only) way to get here is by boat (see the main Getting Around section in this chapter), but note that Timbuktu is not right on the river. You alight at Kabara (11km away), from where a seat in a share-taxi costs between US$1 and US$3 depending on your bargaining powers.

MALI

Dogon Country

The land of the Dogon people, to the south-east of Mopti, is one of Africa's most fascinating regions, centred around the high cliffs of the 150km-long Bandiagara escarpment. If you visit Mali, a trip to Dogon is a must.

One of the best ways to see Dogon country is to trek along the escarpment, for anything between two and 10 days, walking slowly from village to village, allowing plenty of time to see and appreciate the people and the landscape. You can find food and lodgings in the villages (for which you pay a small fee) and guides are available to show you the paths between the villages and to take you up to the old abandoned cliff dwellings.

The three main starting points for a trek in Dogon country are Bandiagara, Bankass and Mopti. Bandiagara and Bankass are easily reached from Mopti by public transport but Sanga is more difficult to get to.

The best times to visit are February, June to mid-July, and mid-September to mid-December. The high tourist season is late July to early September and mid-December to the end of January. From March to May it is too hot for hiking.

TREKKING
Guides

Guides in Dogon Country are not essential, but you'll find things much easier if you take one. They show you the route, help with translation (as few Dogon speak French), find places for you to eat and sleep, and take you to abandoned cliff dwellings. They'll also help you observe such etiquette as the distribution of kola nut and can explain the history and culture of the Dogon people as you go along. In short, a good guide will ensure you actually enjoy your trek.

It is usual to hire your guide at Bandiagara, Sanga or Bankass, but many of the guides from these villages come to Mopti to look for work. (On no account hire a guide in Bamako, as you will be responsible for transport and accommodation to the Dogon.) Remember these points when hiring a guide:

- It is essential that the guide has an official guide's identification card. These have been issued since late 1993, and any guide working in Dogon Country without his own card may be arrested.
- Your guide should be a Dogon. Guides from other groups have less freedom to show you around, and will have to subcontract a genuine local (whom you pay for). The ID card will show place of birth.
- You should like and trust your guide. In Mopti, there are many who may be cheap but they can become unpleasant and unhelpful. Some guides recommended by travellers are (check their ID cards): the trustworthy Aldiouma Ongoiba of Mopti (☎ 43 0439); Abdoulaye Dicko of Bandiagara; Amadou Ouedrago ('L'homme de Dourou') of Mopti; Malick Napo of Sévaré; Oumar Dicko of Timbuktu; Assou Faradj; and Al Haj ('Bouctou'). (Tell us about other reliable guides.)
- All this said, the best advice we can give is for you to prepare a written 'contract' with your guide. Establish both the intended itinerary and the total cost of the trek before you go – both you and your guide should sign the paper. (Add the guide's ID card number and your passport number.) Hidden costs will still creep in, however, and only the most impecunious (or stingy) traveller can avoid these. And a tip for service isn't much to ask – the cost of your tiny sojourn here equates to the average annual salary of a Malian!

Accommodation, Food & Equipment

In the larger villages, a special *case de passage* is reserved for visitors. In smaller villages you'll stay with a family, usually under the stars on the roof. This is a wonderful experience, particularly in the early morning, as the sunlight hits the top of the cliffs and you listen to the sounds of the village stirring around you. Mosquitos can ruin the experience, so plan ahead.

At the place where you sleep, simple food will be provided. Top up the basic meals provided with biscuits, crackers, cheese, tinned meat and fruit. In some of the larger villages, locals sell Coke and beer. More authentic is *konjo* (Dogon millet beer).

Travel light! Essentials include a good hat and a water bottle, as it can get extremely hot on the escarpment and trekkers are at risk of heatstroke and serious dehydration. You should carry at least a litre (or two) of water while walking – two bottles of mineral water for each day is a good rule. Filter and purify well-water before you drink it as there is a serious risk of the dreaded guinea worm.

Also bring a light blanket or sleeping bag for the pre-dawn chill, torch (flashlight) for pitch-black nights, and camera accessories (batteries).

Costs

Visitors to Dogon country must pay for the privilege. Fees are reasonable, and provide the local people with a much-needed source of income. The US$1.50 per person to enter a village allows you to take photos of houses and other buildings (but *not* of people – unless you get their permission) and to visit nearby cliff dwellings. To sleep at a village costs US$1.50 on top of the visit fee. Food costs are usually around US$2 per meal.

Fees for guides are not fixed, and range from US$6 to US$15 per day depending on the size of the group and the length of the trip. The guide fee for two trekkers on a three day trip may be about US$25 but some negotiation is essential. This includes the guide's food and accommodation.

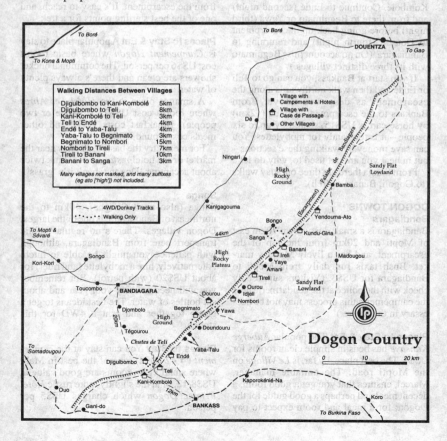

Walking Distances Between Villages

Djiguibombo to Kani-Kombolé	5km
Djiguibombo to Teli	8km
Kani-Kombolé to Teli	3km
Teli to Endé	4km
Endé to Yaba-Talu	4km
Yaba-Talu to Begnimato	3km
Begnimato to Nombori	15km
Nombori to Tireli	7km
Tireli to Banani	10km
Banani to Sanga	3km

Many villages not marked, and many suffixes (eg ato ['high'] not included.

--- 4WD/Donkey Tracks
····· Walking Only

■ Village with Campements & Hotels
▲ Village with Case de Passage
● Other Villages

Dogon Country

0   10   20 km

To Boré
To Kona & Mopti
To Boré
DOUENTZA
To Gao
Dé
Ningari
High Rocky Ground
Sandy Flat Lowland
Bamba
Kanigagouma
Bongo
Yendouma-Ato
Sanga
Kundu-Gina
Banani
Ireli
Yaye
Amani
Madougou
44km
High Rocky Plateau
Tireli
Sandy Flat Lowland
To Mopti & Sévaré
Songo
Kori-Kori
Toucombo
BANDIAGARA
Dourou
Ourou
Idjiel
Nombori
Djombolo
Begnimato
Yawa
Tégourou
High Ground
Doundouru
To Somadougou
Chutes de Teli
Yaba-Talu
Djiguibombo
Endé
Teli
Kani-Kombolé
Kaporokénié-Na
Koro
Ouo
Gani-do
BANKASS
To Burkina Faso

The other cost is transport. In Bandiagara, you can hire a mobylette for US$15 (including petrol) to get to Djiguibombo. A donkey cart is the same price, although slower, and can take four people and their gear. A 4WD may be the best choice for some groups. From Bankass to Endé, you will need a horse/donkey cart; the cost is about US$15.

Routes

From Bandiagara, go to Djiguibombo (20km) where you can stay the first night. From Djiguibombo, drop down the cliffs to Teli, with an optional diversion into Kani-Kombolé. Continue to Endé (second night) and from there to Begnimato or Yawa (third night) before going back up the escarpment to Dourou (fourth night) and returning to Bandiagara. (On no account miss Begnimato with its three distinct villages.)

If you start at Bankass, you can go to Teli or Endé and then walk northwards along the escarpment as described above. From Bankass to the escarpment at Endé (12km) by horse cart is US$15, shared by up to six people – it is too sandy for mobylettes. You can save money by walking these sections – but in heat you are not used to, why do it?

From Sanga there are three one-day walks (to Gogoli, Banani or Ireli).

DOGON TOWNS
Bandiagara

Bandiagara is a small dusty town 70km east of Mopti and 20km from the top of the escarpment, and has a lively Monday market. Bush taxis run daily from Mopti to Bandiagara for US$3. (Visitors supposedly check with the police at the gendarmerie near the campement; this process may not be necessary in the future.)

Places to Stay & Eat The popular *Auberge Kansaye* has beds in simple clean rooms for US$4. The best place, by far, is *Le Village* on the Mopti road. The amiable manager, Marcel, ensures that you get a good room, a decent meal and perhaps a good guide for the Dogon; for a meal and room expect to pay

about US$10 (a chicken meal is about US$2.50).

For food there is a street-side *rotisserie* (selling roast meat), just a block east of the Kansaye. The *Petit Coin*, a few blocks east of the roundabout, serves simple fare, and the *Restaurant Togui* and the *Foyer Dogon*, both west of the centre towards Mopti, are other good places to try. A good place to meet guides, and to get cheap food and beer, is the *Bar Point Raid* near the market.

Bankass

Bankass is 100km from Mopti and 12km from the escarpment. It's easy to reach, and one of the best starting points for a trek.

Places to Stay & Eat A popular place to stay is *Campement Hogon* where basic rooms cost US$6 per person. The communal bucket showers are clean and there's always plenty of water.

A smarter place is the *Hôtel Les Abres* where rooms cost US$22 (for one or two people). Breakfast costs US$2 and other meals cost around US$3.

For meals, try the basic *gargottes* near the market or the hotel *restaurants*. Think twice about accepting 'Dogon tabac'; it's 'grass'!

Sanga

Sanga (also spelt Sangha), 40km to the north-east of Bandiagara, is one of the largest Dogon villages. There's no regular public transport here from Bandiagara, although with patience you might be able to hitch. Alternatively, hire a mobylette (and rider) for about US$20 (with petrol). But remember you will need to carry your gear and about six bottles of water. The best idea is to get a group together and rent a 4WD for this stretch.

Places to Stay You can stay at the *campement* (☎ 42 0092), one of the best in Mali, where smart clean rooms are good value at US$8/12, or at the slightly more rustic *Hôtel Femme Dogon* which charges US$5 per person.

Mauritania

Much of Mauritania forms part of the Sahara Desert – a region of shifting sand dunes, rugged mountain plateaus and rocky outcrops. Only in the oases and along a narrow strip bordering the Senegal River can food crops be grown. Life in this harsh land is affected by overwhelming poverty, lack of resources and ethnic conflicts.

Only a few travellers visit Mauritania these days, mainly because its border with Algeria is closed. If it wasn't for the Parc National du Banc d'Arguin, one of the world's great birdwatching areas, one could almost suggest that Mauritania was *the* place to avoid.

There is a good chance that slavery still exists here, in the east – it was most recently abolished in 1980, for the third time, but many blacks (perhaps 90,000 or so) exist in a relationship with Arab (Moor) masters that could only be described as slavery. To some, this place is the pits – sand and an overwhelming sense of revulsion.

Facts about the Country

HISTORY
Mauritania may be dry and inhospitable these days, but one of the most lucrative of the trans-Saharan trade routes from West Africa to the Maghreb once ran through it. So rich were the pickings in gold, slaves and salt along this route that the Almoravid dynasty in Morocco sought to control the trade. In 1076 they defeated the empire of Ghana, which held sway over what is today Senegal and parts of Guinea and Mali. The Almoravid commanders who had taken part in the campaign quickly asserted their independence from Morocco. Their descendants ruled over this area until defeated by the Arabs in 1674. The conquest resulted in a rigid caste system which has survived largely intact to the present.

MAURITANIA
Area: 1,030,700 sq km
Population: 2.3 million
Population Growth Rate: 2.5%
Capital: Nouakchott
Head of State: President Colonel Maaouya Ould Sid'Ahmed Taya
Official Language: Arabic
Currency: Ouguiya (UM)
Exchange Rate: US$1 = UM 138
Per Capita GNP: US$500
Inflation: 3.5%
Time: GMT/UTC

Highlights
- Birdwatching in the Parc National du Banc d'Arguin
- The Adrâr region of Atâr, Chinguetti and Ouadâne oases

The European nations showed very little interest in Mauritania until the 19th century, when France took over the area. Even then it was little more than an administrative appendage of Senegal. Self-government of a sort was granted in 1957 under the Loi Cadre, and independence was gained in 1960 under the presidency of Mokhtar Ould Daddah. Nevertheless, the French maintained their stranglehold over the economy. In fact, one reason why they granted independence was to prevent the country's absorption by Morocco, which maintained a

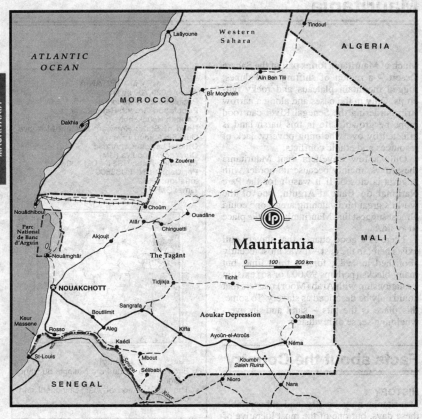

historical claim to the area and refused to recognise Mauritania until 1969.

In the early years of Mokhtar Ould Daddah's regime, opposition first came from the black people of the south who resented his decision to make Arabic, along with French, an official language. The next challenge came from trade unions who objected to the racial inequality in the mining community at Zouérat (the 3000 expatriates there earned two-thirds of the country's entire wage bill). Ould Daddah survived that challenge by nationalising the mines in 1974, withdrawing from the franc zone, substituting the *ouguiya* for the CFA franc.

The signing of an agreement between Spain, Morocco and Mauritania in 1975 resulted in the Spanish Sahara (a Spanish colony) being divided up between Morocco and Mauritania. The Mauritanians took the largely worthless southern third of the colony while the Moroccans took the centre and phosphate-rich north. Both countries immediately found themselves fighting a vicious war with the guerrillas of the Western Sahara's Saharawi Polisario Front, which was supported by Algeria, Libya and Cuba.

Mauritania was incapable, both militarily and economically, of fighting such a war.

Though Ould Daddah reinforced the Mauritanian army of 1800 with a further 17,000 soldiers (at enormous cost), they proved no match for the guerrillas. Even with Moroccan troop reinforcements and French air-power, Ould Daddah was unable to check the guerrillas. In 1978 he was overthrown.

The new regime, headed by Mohamed Khouna Haidallah, dithered for over a year about how to extricate Mauritania from the war. Eventually, however, renewed guerrilla attacks and demonstrations by the black population of the south against the increasing Arab influence forced the regime to renounce all territorial claims to the Western Sahara. In order to curry Arab favour, the new regime threw in its vocal support for Polisario, which quickly led to a break in diplomatic relations with Morocco (restored in early 1985). Support for the guerrilla movement had its benefits, but it didn't prevent the economy from continuing to deteriorate.

With the country slipping further and further into unsustainable debt, Haidallah was overthrown in December 1984 by Colonel Maaouya Ould Taya (who is still in power). Within two months of the coup, the currency was devalued by 16% and food prices rose by 25%. The measures were greeted with satisfaction by Mauritania's creditors and the national debt was rescheduled.

Bloody ethnic riots flared in 1989 between the Moors and black Africans, and many Africans were forced to flee to Senegal. The Islamist (Moor) government was widely denounced for its treatment of black Mauritanians, and the flow of aid from non-Islamic countries dried up.

To counter criticism, Taya introduced a new constitution, under which multiparty elections were held in early 1992. Taya was returned with 63% of the vote, but his government is still largely a military one. Supposed multiparty elections were held for the National Assembly (Majlis al-Watani) in mid-October 1996. There was little opposition to Taya's Democratic and Social Republican Party who, oddly, allowed 'non-partisans' to win eight of the 79 seats.

GEOGRAPHY & CLIMATE

Much of Mauritania's north and central regions form part of the western section of the Sahara, while the south contains a region of savannah and small areas of arable land around the Senegal River. The climate, especially in the desert areas, is hot and dry; much of Mauritania receives little or no rain, although the south does have a rainy season (when crops are cultivated) between July and October. From April to October temperatures can reach 40°C and over, but from December to March the range is 13 to 29°C. The coastal areas are more temperate due to cool sea breezes.

ECOLOGY & ENVIRONMENT

Like most of the Sahel countries, desertification looms as the greatest environmental problem. Nearly 75% of Mauritania's land surface is desert or near-desert. As agriculture expands into marginal lands, augmented livestock herds contribute to overgrazing. Further deforestation results as land is cleared for the livestock and the herders seek out firewood for daily cooking.

The eastern desert is home to the addax antelope, an endangered species. Throughout the rest of the country the animal populations traditionally associated with Africa have long gone – victims of desertification and the hunter's bullet. Perhaps there are a few elephant and leopard left, but you will be lucky to see them.

POPULATION & PEOPLE

The population stands at about 2.3 million, of whom some 26% are urban dwellers. There is ethnic conflict between 'white' Moors, 'black' Moors and black Africans. It's a very traditional and strictly Muslim society with an atmosphere of timelessness.

LANGUAGE

Arabic is the official language, although until recently French was also officialy used.

MAURITANIA

Slavery's Last Stronghold

Slavery was supposedly outlawed in Mauritania in 1980 – yes, as late as 1980! But many people are still enslaved, and may express surprise when they hear of the new law enshrining their emancipation.

The predominantly black African *haratin* – freed slaves or their descendants – make up about 40% of Mauritania's population. Still, it is estimated that 90,000 to 100,000 blacks are still living as 'chattel slaves' to the dominant Moor masters, or *Bidan*.

Most of the blacks living in Mauritania converted to Islam 100 years ago and Islam forbids slavery. Yet the practice continues. This is in spite of attempts to have the issue raised in the US Congress – attempts perhaps thwarted by fears of alienating the Mauritanian government. ■

The Moors speak an Arabic dialect known as Hassaniya, whereas the black Africans of the south speak Pulaar, Soininke and Wolof.

Facts for the Visitor

VISAS

Visas are required for all except nationals of Arab League countries, some African countries, France and Italy. When applying for a visa you will need to produce a yellow fever vaccination certificate and a letter of introduction from your own embassy. Visas are valid for three months and on average cost about US$15, but can be as low as US$5 (The Gambia) and as high as US$40 (the CAR); four photos are required.

Mauritanian embassies can be sticky about issuing visas, in many cases asking for a return air ticket (such as in Morocco).

Other Visas

Visas can be obtained in Nouakchott for the following countries:

Burkina Faso, Chad, Congo (Zaïre), Côte d'Ivoire and Togo
 Three month visas for these countries are available from the French embassy in Nouakchott. You can also get 30 day visas for Congo (Zaïre): US$22 for single entry and more for multiple entries.
Senegal
 The Senegalese embassy issues visas without hassles.

EMBASSIES
Mauritanian Embassies

In Africa there are Mauritanian embassies in Algeria, Côte d'Ivoire, The Gambia, Mali, Morocco, Nigeria and Senegal, and a consulate in Niger. Elsewhere they are found in Belgium, France, Germany, Spain and the USA, and a consulate in Switzerland.

Foreign Embassies in Mauritania

Countries with diplomatic representation in Nouakchott include:

France
 Rue Abdalaye (☎ 51740)
Germany
 Rue Abdalaye (☎ 52304)
Morocco
 South of Rue Abdalaye (☎ 51411; telex 550)
Senegal
 Ave du Général de Gaulle (☎ 52106)
UK
 Unofficial representative (☎ 51756; fax 57192)
USA
 Rue Abdalaye (☎ 52660; fax 52589)

CUSTOMS

As Mauritania is an Islamic republic, importing alcohol is prohibited.

MONEY

US$1 = UM 138

The unit of currency is the ouguiya (UM) which equals five *khoums*. The import or export of local currency is prohibited. Currency declaration forms are issued on arrival and the authorities are sometimes strict about them; at other times they are not even collected when you leave the country.

There is a black market, but few travellers use it, as the rates are not good and if you're caught you will end up in jail.

POST & COMMUNICATIONS

The post office in Nouakchott is open seven days a week and has a poste restante service.

It's fairly easy to make direct-dial phone calls to anywhere in the world (US$5 per minute to the USA, US$3 per minute to Europe. The country code for Mauritania is 222; and 02 is the code for all Mauritanian towns.

Getting There & Away

AIR

There are direct flights from Paris on Air France and Air Afrique; the fare is expensive but specials are available. Flying the other way is about 50% of the cost (if booked and paid for in Mauritania).

Gambia Airways flies between Banjul (The Gambia) and Nouakchott. There are also flights between Las Palmas (Canary Islands) and Nouâdhibou and Nouakchott. There are two flights per week in each direction from Dakar (Senegal) to Nouakchott with Air Afrique (US$240/390 one way/return).

The airport departure tax for flights to other African countries is US$5. Flights to other international destinations attract a tax of US$7.50. Occasionally there are flight delays caused by sandstorms.

LAND
Mali

It is possible to travel to Mali in your own vehicle. The 1100km route from Nouakchott to Néma is asphalted all the way. The journey to Bamako can be done in three days, but that's pushing it.

Morocco

Going across the desert begins at Dakhla,

1703km south of Casablanca. The road is tarred all the way and there are good bus connections. In Dakhla, the army leads a convoy every Tuesday and Friday to the Mauritanian border, where you must wait at least a day or so to pass through customs. From there, vehicles are escorted by Mauritanian police the 60km to Nouâdhibou. All movement is from north to south, ie Europe to Africa.

Senegal

Bush taxis run regularly from Nouakchott to Rosso (the border) for US$10. A *pirogue* (dugout canoe) across the Senegal River is US$2 per person. From Rosso to Dakar costs US$14. The whole journey may be done in a day.

Getting Around

AIR

There are flights between Nouakchott and Nouâdhibou, Atâr, Néma, Tidjikja and Zouérat, among other places. The airport departure tax for domestic flights is US$2.

ROAD

The main roads through Mauritania are: Nouâdhibou to Rosso (Senegal border) via Nouakchott; the Route du Mauritanie from Nouakchott to Tindouf (Algeria) via Atâr, Choûm, F'Dérik and Bîr Moghrein (surfaced only between Nouakchott and Akjoujt); and a highway linking Nouakchott with Néma in the south-east. The road between Nouakchott and Nouâdhibou is diabolical, and most people go via Choûm.

There are both trucks and Land Rovers running between Nouâdhibou and Nouakchott which take between 30 and 48 hours. Take your own food, water, sun protection and warm clothes – and expect a *long* wait while your vehicle collects enough passengers before departing. Land Rovers take at least 18 people!

Nouakchott to Atâr by truck takes about 12 hours. There's usually an overnight stop.

Between Atâr and Chinguetti there are infrequent Land Rovers (US$7) but it's difficult to get from Chinguetti to Ouadâne as transport is limited.

TRAIN

There is one railway line, which runs between Nouâdhibou and Zouérat, where the iron ore mines are located. As you might expect, the trains consist of open-topped ore bogies which make no concessions to comfort and are slow and very dusty. The train has a passenger car attached so, if you don't fancy riding in an ore bogie, take this, but even then don't expect too much: 'everything you've always dreamed of in terms of exotic and romantic discomfort', according to one traveller.

The trains depart Nouâdhibou daily from the new station about halfway between the town centre and Cansado (to the north) at around 1 to 3 pm (☎ 53337 Nouakchott, ☎ 45174 Nouâdhibou). It costs US$8 to Zouérat; the journey typically takes about 20 hours.

Nouakchott

Nouakchott is the capital of Mauritania. There's very little of note to see, but the mosques are worth visiting (though non-Muslims aren't allowed inside). The **Mousquée Saudique**, which was constructed by the Saudi Arabians, is stunning.

The **National Museum** focuses on the life and culture of the country's nomads, but excludes references to the black southerners.

The banks, post office (PTT) and some hotels are along or near Ave Abdel Nasser.

Places to Stay

Campers should head for the *campement* down from the Port des Pêcheurs, although it's not cheap at US$8 per person, and the facilities are dirty.

The cheapest place is the distinctly ordinary *Hôtel Adrar* (☎ 52955), south of the Grand Marché, which costs US$16/24 for an

upstairs double with attached bath (inclusive of breakfast), and US$20/30 for a cheap downstairs room with a window!

More expensive is the noisy *Hôtel Oasis* (☎ 52011), Ave de Gaulle, which costs US$30/40 for singles/doubles. You can get alcohol at the bar (but at US$4.50 a small bottle of beer) – the one plus in this overpriced place.

The *Park Hôtel* (☎ 51444) on Ave Abdel Nasser has good rooms with air-con which cost US$35/45. Better still is the *Hôtel el Amanne* (☎ 52178; fax 53765), around the corner. It charges about US$45/55.

Places to Eat

There are many restaurants along Ave Abdel Nasser where you can buy a simple meal at a reasonable price. The *Phenicia* on Rue Mamadou Konaté does excellent Moroccan and Lebanese food; a meal is from US$3.50. The *El Mouna* across the road is cheaper but has less choice. The *Welcome Burger* on Ave de Gaulle serves burgers, chips and chawarma. On Ave Abdel Nasser, the *Chez Riad* is another good Lebanese standby. For good pita bread head to *El Frisco Snack* on Ave Kennedy.

For Moroccan food go to *Zoubeida* on Rue Ely Ould Mohamed; couscous is about US$2. Chinese/Vietnamese food (and ice cream) can be found at *Le Dragon d'Or*, on a side street facing the Mosquée Saudique. A block behind the Park Hôtel is the *Boulangerie-épicerie Hajjar* for fresh bread and croissants.

The *Lebanese Club* is by invitation only and the *Oasis* and *Novotel* are currently the only hotels serving alcohol. Time to abstain from the dreaded booze, eh?

Things to Buy

Depressed by the lack of entertainment? Then shop away your disappointment. There are interesting wares at Marché Capital, Cinquième Marché and the oft-deserted Artisan Centre on the Rosso road (a taxi will get you there).

MAURITANIA

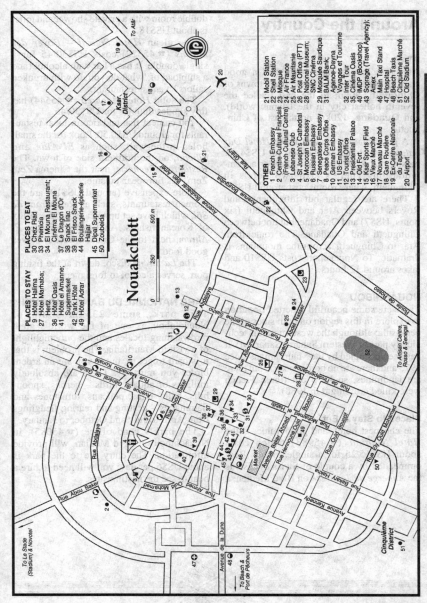

Nouakchott

PLACES TO STAY
9 Hôtel Halima
27 Hôtel Marhaba;
   Hertz
36 Hôtel Oasis
41 Hôtel el Amanne;
   Supermarket
42 Park Hôtel
49 Hôtel Adrar

PLACES TO EAT
30 Chez Riad
33 El Mona
34 El Mouna Restaurant;
   Cinéma El Mouna
37 Le Dragon d'Or
38 Snack Irac
39 El Frisco Snack
44 Boulangerie-épicerie
   Hajjar
45 Dipal Supermarket
50 Zoubeida

OTHER
1 French Embassy
2 Centre Culturel Français
   (French Cultural Centre)
3 Lebanese Embassy
4 St Joseph's Cathedral
5 Moroccan Embassy
6 Russian Embassy
7 Senegalese Embassy
8 Peace Corps Office
10 German Embassy
11 US Embassy
12 Tourist Office
13 Presidential Palace
14 Old Fort
15 Ksar Sports Field
16 Nouveau Marché
17 Vieux Marché
18 Ex-Centre Nationale
   du Tapis
19 Airport
20 Airport
21 Mobil Station
22 Shell Station
23 Mosque
24 Air Mauritanie
25 Poste (PTT)
26 National Museum;
   SNC Cinéma
29 Mosquée Saudique
31 BALM Bank;
   Agence-Dayna
32 Cinéma Oasis
35 Voyages et Tourisme
   Inter Tour
40 IMDP (Bookshop)
43 Soprage (Travel Agency);
   Amex
46 Main Taxi Stand
47 Hospital
48 Beach Taxis
51 Cinquième Marché
52 Old Stadium

0   250   500 m

Around the Country

ATÂR

Atâr is a lovely oasis town and a good starting point for trips to the oasis towns of **Chinguetti**, 80km to the east (called the seventh holiest city in the Islamic world), and **Ouadâne**, 120km north-east of Chinguetti.

A good place to stay at is the *Hôtel Dar Salaam* which has good rooms for US$4 per person. *Le Restaurant* has cheaper accommodation. There's also two hotels in Chinguetti, where rooms cost around US$5.

There are regular but infrequent Land Rovers between Atâr and Chinguetti (six hours, US$7) and Ouadâne, but not between Chinguetti and Ouadâne. The route from Atâr to Chinguetti across the mountains is dramatic. To Nouakchott costs US$10 and takes around 12 hours.

NOUÂDHIBOU

There are some beautiful deserted **beaches** to explore in this region on both sides of the peninsula; although the western part is technically part of Western Sahara (Saharawi), it has been occupied by the Mauritanians since 1975 and there are no border posts – but there are landmines, so keep out (three French were killed crossing it in 1988).

Places to Stay & Eat

The cheapest hotel, and good value, is the *Hôtel Niabina* (☎ 45983) which costs about US$15/25 for a single/double. Recommended by a couple of Swiss cyclists is the *Auberge de Jeunesse* on Blvd Médien; a double room with a private shower and toilet is about US$18.

The clean *Hôtel Sharaf – Foyer des Marins* (☎ 45522) costs US$30/45 for a single/double. It has a bar with alcohol (and a shipload of 'what do you do with drunken sailors?') and a restaurant.

The solid *Hôtel Maghreb* (☎ 45544) has tiny singles/doubles for US$30/45.

You can eat fish and rice in local restaurants for around US$0.50. Look for the small holes-in-the-wall, such as *El Aide* and *Sihgatt*, on the northern side of town. The *Restaurant Recherie*, near the Cinema Zem Zem, has European cuisine.

More expensive (around US$10) are the Korean restaurants, such as *Restaurant de Sôl*, which have set up to cater for the influx of Korean fishers. An Egyptian place, *El Ahrem*, next to the Grand Marché, serves good food.

The *La Siréne* disco, down at the fishing port, serves alcohol to foreigners.

PARC NATIONAL DU BANC D'ARGUIN

This park, some 235km south of Nouâdhibou, is one of the world's great birdwatching locales and the *only* highlight of a visit to Mauritania. The problem is that it is hard to get to, but if you are an ardent birder you must try. There are absolutely millions of aquatic birds – herons, spoonbills, gulls, terns, pelicans, turnstones and flamingoes – nesting and rearing fledglings from April to July and October to January.

The park's head office (☎ 45085), in Nouâdhibou on Blvd Médian, will provide information. The entry fee to the park is about US$6 per day; you will need to hire a boat to see the nesting sites.

Mauritius

Mauritius isn't really on the way to anywhere, but it's well worth visiting on its own merits. It's a beautiful island with an interesting cultural mix, endless sugar cane plantations, striking mountains and some of the finest beaches and aquamarine lagoons in the Indian Ocean.

Facts about the Country

HISTORY

Though visited by Malay and Arab mariners before the arrival of the Europeans, Mauritius remained uninhabited until the end of the 16th century. The first Europeans to call in were the Portuguese under the command of Pedro Mascarenhas. The Portuguese laid no claim to the island and it wasn't settled until the Dutch landed a party in 1598. The island subsequently became an important port of call for Dutch, French and English trading ships, and it was from here that Abel Tasman embarked on the voyage which would lead to the arrival of Europeans in Australia.

The Dutch colonial period saw the introduction of sugar cane and the importation of slaves to harvest it, the decimation of the ebony forests, and the extermination of the dodo and other indigenous birds. The Dutch settlement lasted until 1710, when it was abandoned.

Eleven years later the island was claimed by France and its name was changed to Île de France. The French imported large numbers of slaves from the African mainland and from Madagascar, and set up extensive plantations for the cultivation of sugar, cotton, indigo, cloves, nutmeg and other spices. They also used Mauritius as a base from which to harass British merchant ships on their way to and from India, and from which to mount attacks on Britain's Indian colonies.

It remained a thorn in Britain's side until 1810, when the French forces were defeated by a British naval squadron which launched its attack from the island of Rodrigues. At the end of the Napoleonic Wars the island was ceded to Britain, though under the terms of the treaty the French way of life – its religion, customs, language and laws – was safeguarded.

Under British rule little changed until

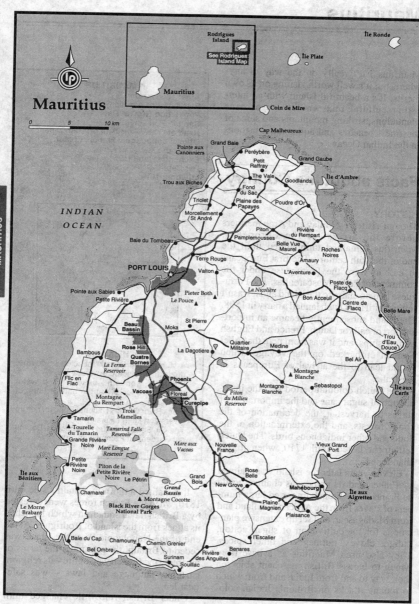

MAURITIUS

Mauritius

0   5   10 km

Rodrigues Island

See Rodrigues Island Map

Mauritius

Île Ronde

Île Plate

Coin de Mire

Cap Malheureux

INDIAN OCEAN

Grand Baie
Pointe aux Canonniers
Peréybère
Petit Raffray
The Vale
Grand Gaube
Île d'Ambre
Trou aux Biches
Fond du Sac
Goodlands
Triolet
Plaine des Papayes
Poudre d'Or
Morcellement St André
Piton
Rivière du Rempart
Baie du Tombeau
Pamplemousses
Belle Vue Maurel
Roches Noires
Terre Rouge
Amaury
PORT LOUIS
Valton
L'Aventure
Poste de Flacq
Pointe aux Sables
Pieter Both
La Nicolière
Bon Acceuil
Centre de Flacq
Petite Rivière
Le Pouce
Belle Mare
Beau Bassin
St Pierre
Moka
Rose Hill
Quartier Militaire
Medine
Trou d'Eau Douce
Bambous
La Dagotiere
Quatre Bornes
La Ferme Reservoir
Bel Air
Flic en Flac
Phoenix
Montagne Blanche
Sebastopol
Vacoas
Floreal
Montagne Blanche
Montagne du Rempart
Curepipe
Piton du Milieu Reservoir
Trois Mamelles
Tamarin
Tourelle du Tamarin
Tamarind Falls Reservoir
Mare aux Vacoas
Grande Rivière Noire
Mare Longue Reservoir
Nouvelle France
Vieux Grand Port
Petite Rivière Noire
Piton de la Petite Rivière Noire
Le Pétrin
Grand Bois
Rose Belle
New Grove
Mahébourg
Île aux Bénitiers
Chamarel
Grand Bassin
Île aux Cerfs
Le Morne Brabant
Montagne Cocotte
Black River Gorges National Park
Plaine Magnien
Île aux Aigrettes
Plaisance
Baie du Cap
Chamouny
Chemin Grenier
Benares
l'Escalier
Bel Ombre
Surinam
Rivière des Anguilles
Souillac

1835 when, despite opposition from French *colons* (colonists), slavery was abolished. Most freed slaves left the plantations and settled in the coastal towns, creating a labour crisis which was solved by importing indentured labourers from India, mostly from Bihar and the southern provinces. When their contracts finished, most of them opted to remain on the islands and by 1860, two-thirds of the island's 300,000 people were of Indian descent.

Politics in the 19th century centred mainly on the struggle of the Franco-Mauritian plantation owners for more representation in the colonial government, but it wasn't until 1936 that the Labour Party was formed. Strikes and demonstrations instigated by the Labour Party from 1937 to the end of WWII were brutally repressed.

Meanwhile, a group of Indo-Mauritian intellectuals, traders and planters combined under the leadership of Seewoosagur Ramgoolam and succeeded in procuring a number of nominations to the Legislative Council. In 1948, under the banner of 'defenders of Hindu interests', they garnered most of the rural vote.

By the time the next elections came around in 1953, the Indo-Mauritians had succeeded in usurping the leadership of the Labour Party, which won a comfortable majority. The working class, however, remained divided and most of the Créoles were frightened into joining the conservative Parti Mauricien Social Démocrate (PMSD).

At the time of independence in 1968, Ramgoolam's Labour Party-CAM (Muslim) alliance won by a narrow majority but in 1969, his mandate was strengthened when he formed a coalition with the PMSD. As a result, pro-South African and pro-French conservatives gained a share of government. In response, the far left-wing Mouvement Militant Mauricien (MMM) was formed.

Initially, the government attempted to suppress it by harassing its members, by postponing general elections for four years and by passing a number of harsh laws curtailing political activity. In 1982 an alliance between the MMM and the Parti Socialist Mauricien gained power under Prime Minister Anerood Jugnauth. In 1983 the MMM split and Jugnauth formed a new party, the Mouvement Socialist Mauricien (MSM), which in alliance with the Mauritius Labour Party governed the country until 1995, when Jugnauth lost the election to Navin Ramgoolam, son of former Prime Minister, Seewoosagur Ramgoolam. Mauritius officially became a republic in 1992.

GEOGRAPHY & CLIMATE

Mauritius is a volcanic island lying about 800km off Madagascar's east coast. The country includes the island of Rodrigues, and other scattered coral atolls such as Cargados Carajos and Agalega. All the islands are surrounded by coral reefs and have a tropical summer (average temperatures 25°C to 30°C) from November to April and a slightly cooler winter between May and October.

ECOLOGY & ENVIRONMENT

Tourism is one of Mauritius' major economic pillars. The expansion of tourist facilities, however, has strained the island's infrastructure and has caused all sorts of problems, including environmental degradation and excessive demand on electric, water, telephone and transport services.

Conservationists are campaigning to protect the fragile marine environment, which has suffered widespread damage in the last few decades. Some of the causes include disturbance from motorboats, fishermen and divers, as well as rising pollution.

Collection of shells and coral for commercial purposes has also been detrimental to the marine environment. We strongly urge you not to buy anything made out of turtle shell nor to buy or take any shells from the beach. Governments are trying to do something about it; please don't contribute to the problems by providing market incentives for the collectors.

POPULATION & PEOPLE

Mauritius has an estimated population of 1.1 million. With around 600 people per sq km,

---

Festivals of Mauritius

Mauritius' vibrant cultural mix is reflected in its numerous festivals. In February/March, the Hindu community celebrates **Maha Shivaratri**. Thousands of Hindus make the pilgrimage to the holy volcanic lake Grand Bassin in honour of Lord Shiva.

In January/February during **Cavadee**, Tamil penitents skewer themselves through cheeks, tongue, arms and back, walk on nail shoes, drag carts on hooks fastened in their flesh and carry heavy wooden frames festooned with images of deities.

Apart from a host of Hindu events, Mauritius also has a number of Chinese, Muslim and Christian festivals. ■

---

it has one of the highest population densities in the world.

Mauritians are a heterogeneous mixture of Indian (around 70% of the total), African, Chinese, French and British elements. Mauritius is often cited as an example of racial harmony – and compared to most other countries it is – but there is still little inter-marriage or social mixing between the various communities.

LANGUAGE

English and French are the official languages of Mauritius, but French is more widely used. The everyday language is Créole, a blend of French and assorted African languages. Most Indo-Mauritians speak Bhojpuri, derived from a Bihari dialect of Hindi. See the Language Section for French phrases.

Facts for the Visitor

VISAS

You don't need a visa for Mauritius if you are a national of a Commonwealth country, the EU, Japan, the USA and just a few other countries. Immigration authorities require that all visitors have onward tickets and can supply the name of their intended accommodation. They may even ask for proof of sufficient funds. Initial entry is granted for a maximum of three months. Extensions for a further three months' stay are available; contact the Passport & Immigration Office (☎ 208 1212) in Port Louis.

EMBASSIES
Mauritian Embassies

Mauritius has diplomatic representation in Australia, Belgium, China, Egypt, Ethiopia, France, India, Italy, Madagascar, Malaysia, Pakistan, South Africa, the UK and the USA.

Foreign Embassies in Mauritius

Countries with diplomatic representation in Port Louis include:

Australia
   Rogers House, 5 President John Kennedy St (☎ 2081700)
France
   14 St George St (☎ 2084103)
UK
   Les Cascades Building, Edith Cavell St (☎ 2111361)
USA
   Rogers House, 5 President John Kennedy St (☎ 2082347)

Other countries with foreign representation in Mauritius include Canada, India and Madagascar.

MONEY
US$1 = Rs 20

The unit of currency is the Mauritian rupee (Rs) which equals 100 cents. All exchange rates are set by the government and there are no differences from bank to bank. There is no black market. Travellers' cheques bring a better rate of exchange than cash. You can import Rs 700 and export up to Rs 350 in local currency, but duty-free items must be bought with foreign currency.

Most credit cards are widely accepted and most banks will issue cash advances on major cards, such as Visa and MasterCard.

Only airport porters expect a small tip.

ACCOMMODATION

You can camp along most public beaches, but there may be security problems.

The main accommodation categories are *pensions de famille* (boarding houses), bungalows or apartments, guesthouses, small Indian or Chinese-run hotels, and luxury beach hotels. At the budget end, remember that the more of you there are and the longer your stay, the lower the rates. December, January, July and August are usually the busiest months, and some hotels hike their rates up at this time.

The best deals are found at guesthouses, apartments and bungalows near the beaches. The cheapest hotels are in the towns, while most of the beach hotels are extremely expensive. If you want this sort of luxury, take advantage of package rates by booking from overseas.

FOOD

Mauritian food largely consists of curry with rice or with *roti* (Indian-style bread). Most restaurants offer Chinese, Indian, Créole or European fare; seafood is often the speciality.

Getting There & Away

AIR

Mauritius is served by a number of European, African and Asian airlines, as well as by the national carrier, Air Mauritius. Air Mauritius has weekly flights to many European destinations including Paris, Munich, Frankfurt, Vienna, Rome, Geneva, Brussels and London.

Air Mauritius also flies weekly to Nairobi, Antananarivo, Harare, Durban, Johannesburg, Cape Town, Mumbai (Bombay),

Delhi, Hong Kong, Singapore, Kuala Lumpur, Jakarta, Perth and Melbourne.

There are several daily flights to Réunion; the return fare (valid for one month) costs US\$132.

Airport tax on international departures is US\$15, payable in local currency.

SEA
Réunion

The MV *Mauritius Pride* operates several times monthly between Mauritius and Réunion. Contact Mauritius Shipping Corporation Ltd (☎ 2412550; fax 2425245), Nova Building, 1 Military Rd, Port Louis.

Getting Around

AIR

Air Mauritius flies daily to Rodrigues Island. The 1½ hour trip costs US\$275 return (for stays of five to 30 days).

Buses from the airport to Mahébourg and Port Louis stop at the shelter outside the gates hourly between 6.30 am and 6.30 pm. After leaving the terminal, continue across the car park about 500m to the bus stop.

ROAD

Bus services are generally good – if a bit slow – and can take you just about anywhere. No service covers the entire island; rather, there are regional services with routes covering the three main regions (north, centre and south).

As a rule, buses stop running at about 6.30 pm, although around Port Louis and Curepipe they often keep going until 11 pm. On standard services, the longest trips cost about US\$1. Express services cost slightly more, but are quicker.

Taxis are quite expensive and usually charge more after dark. Make sure you agree on a price before setting off. To get an idea of how much you should be paying, ask the locals.

MAURITIUS

BOAT

The MV *Mauritius Pride* sails several times monthly to and from Rodrigues Island. Tickets for the 27-hour trip start at US$68 one way.

Contact Mauritius Shipping Corporation Ltd (☎ 2412550; fax 2425245), Nova Building, 1 Military Rd, Port Louis. On Rodrigues, contact Islands' Service Ltd (☎ 8311555; fax 8312089), Port Mathurin.

Port Louis

Port Louis, the burgeoning Mauritian capital, is a wildly busy centre during the day, but virtually dead at night.

There is a distinct Muslim area around Muammar El Khadafi Square and a Chinatown around Royal St.

Information

The tourist office, Mauritius Tourism Promotion Authority (☎ 2011703), is on the ground floor of the Emmanuel Anquetil Building on Sir Seewoosagur Ramgoolam St, however it may be shifting to the Air Mauritius Centre. It's open Monday to Friday from 9 am to 4 pm and until noon on Saturday.

Air Mauritius (☎ 2087700) is at the Air Mauritius Centre, President John Kennedy St.

Things to See & Do

If you wish to see a stuffed replica of a dodo, visit the **Mauritius Institute**. The dodo was a native Mauritian bird which became extinct between 1681 and 1693. The Institute is open from 9 am to 4 pm weekdays except Wednesday, and on weekends until noon. Admission is free.

Père Laval's Shrine, the Lourdes of the Indian Ocean, at Ste Croix, is open daily from 6 am to 6 pm. Other interesting buildings are the **Chinese Pagoda** on Volcy Pougnet St and the **Jummah Mosque** (naturally, it's in the middle of Chinatown!), which is open to visitors from 10 am to noon

daily except Thursday and Friday. For a sensational view over Port Louis, go to the hilltop **Fort Adelaide**.

Worth a visit is the lively **market**, between Farquhar and Queen Sts, which sells everything from medicinal herbs to Malagasy handicrafts. Be sure to bargain hard and beware of pick-pockets. The market is open Monday to Friday from around 6 am to 5.30 pm and on Saturday from 6 am to noon.

Places to Stay

Budget accommodation in Port Louis is limited and lacklustre. Possibly the best option is the *Hotel Le Grand Carnot* (☎ 2403054) at 17 Dr Edouard Laurent St. Doubles cost US$18, including breakfast. Similarly priced but not nearly as good is the *Rossignol Hotel* (☎ 2121983) on Sir John Pope Hennessy St.

Near Victoria Square, the *Tandoori Tourist Hotel & Restaurant* (☎ 2122131) has doubles for US$15. The *Bourbon Tourist Hotel* (☎ 2404407), at 36 Jummah Mosque St, charges US$28 for an air-con double, including breakfast.

Places to Eat

For cheap curries and biryanis, try *Namaste* just off Farquhar St. The locally popular *Snow White* on the corner of Sir William Newton and Queen Sts, serves good lunches. Not far away, the *First Restaurant* offers cheap Chinese food; stir-fried seasonal vegetables cost US$2. On Geoffroy St, the *DSL (Deva Saraswatee Laxmi) Coffee House* specialises in Indian cuisine, including a good choice of vegetarian dishes.

Most of the eating places at the swanky new *Le Caudan Waterfront* (near the harbour) are open until around midnight.

Entertainment

Port Louis is somewhat of a ghost town after dusk, however the *Le Caudan Waterfront* (☎ 2116560) has injected life into the capital. Apart from a swish casino, there's also an impressive three screen cinema complex; the last session is at 9 pm.

Alternatively, night owls can gamble at

MAURITIUS

Port Louis

0   100   200 m

MAURITIUS

PLACES TO STAY
7   Hotel Le Grand Carnot
9   Bourbon Tourist Hotel
28 Rossignol Hotel
33 Tandoori Tourist Hotel & Restaurant

PLACES TO EAT
5   Merchant Navy Club
8   Foong Shing
10 First Restaurant
11 Namaste
16 Cari Poulé
18 Snow White
24 La Flore Mauricienne
27 DSL (Deva Saraswatee Laxmi) Coffee House

OTHER
1   Police Station
2   Muammar El Khadafi Square
3   L'Amicale Chinese Gaming House
4   Immigration Square Bus Station
6   Jummah Mosque
12 Main Post Office
13 Market
14 Le Caudan Waterfront
15 Labourdonnais Square Bus Station
17 Barclays Bank
19 Mauritius Commercial Bank
20 MTTB Travel (Amex)
21 Rogers House; OTS; US Embassy; Australian High Commission; Rogers Aviation; Air Madagascar; Air France
22 Air Mauritius
23 Natural History Museum; Mauritius Institute
25 Tourist Office
26 Central Post Office
29 Police Station
30 Company Gardens
31 Taxi Stand
32 Victoria Square Bus Station
34 Police Station
35 French Embassy
36 Jeetoo (Civil) Hospital

the *L'Amicale Chinese Gaming House* near the corner of Anquetil and Royal Sts. It's open daily until 2 am.

Getting There & Away
Port Louis has two major bus stations, the Immigration Square station for destinations in the north and east and the Victoria Square station for buses to the west and south.

Around the Country

BLACK RIVER GORGES NATIONAL PARK
In the south-west of the island, the forestry station at Le Pétrin is the jumping-off point for hikes into Black River Gorges National Park, the most scenic corner of Mauritius and home to several rare animal species, including the threatened echo parakeet. A day walk will take you from Le Pétrin right down to the coast at Grande Rivière Noire.

The main route from Le Pétrin leads to perpetually rainy Plaine Champagne, which is the largest undeveloped area on the island. The highest point on the Curepipe to Chamarel road is marked by a radio tower at 744m. About 3km beyond is the Rivière Noire lookout, affording a spectacular view over the Black River Gorge, the Rivière Noire Falls and Piton de la Petite Rivière Noire, which, at 828m, is the highest point in Mauritius.

CHAMAREL
The 100m **Chamarel Falls** lie near Chamarel village which is inland from Baie du Cap on the south coast. Further along the same road are the **Coloured Earths**, an intriguing but not mind-blowing area of seven differently coloured layers of earths. Admission to both sites costs US$0.80. There are infrequent buses from Baie du Cap to Chamarel. Most major tour operators run excursions to Chamarel.

CUREPIPE
Curepipe and the other towns nearby owe their size and prominence to the malaria epidemic of 1867 which caused thousands of people to flee infested Port Louis for the healthier hill country. There's not a great deal to do here, but the town offers good shopping and is the centre of the model-ship building industry.

If you're in Curepipe, it's worth climbing up to the rim of the ancient crater, **Trou aux Cerfs**, which affords brilliant views over the island.

Places to Stay & Eat
A good budget choice is the *Welcome Hotel* (☎ 6747292) on Royal Rd, which has doubles for US$20, including breakfast. Also recommended is the similarly priced *L'Auberge de la Madelon* (☎ 6761520; fax 6762550) at 10 Sir John Pope Hennessy St.

You can pick up the usual groceries at *Prisunic* supermarket on Elizabeth Ave. The nearby *Le Pot de Terre* is a terrific little place for cheap snacks; more substantial meals are also available for around US$4.

Nobby's Restaurant on Royal Rd serves great European and Créole cuisine; spaghetti bolognese costs US$6.

GRAND BAIE & PERÉYBÈRE
Some of the island's best beaches are at its northern end. For nightlife, trendy Grand Baie is your best option, while the quieter, lower-budget area of Peréybère lies several km north.

Places to Stay
For shoestringers, self-catering apartments and bungalows are the best bet in Grand Baie. On Royal Road *Ebrahim Flats* (☎ 2637845; fax 2638564) and *Libellule Travel Agent Tours Ltd* (☎ 2636156; fax 2635352), both rent flats from around US$14.

The popular *Les Palmiers* (☎ 2638464; fax 2428711), just off Royal Road, has studios for US$18 and larger flats for US$25.

For something more upmarket, there's the *Colonial Coconut Hotel* (☎ 2638720; fax 2637116) near Pointe aux Canonniers. Doubles, including breakfast and dinner, cost around US$80 in the low season (about 15% more in the high season).

In Peréybère, the easy-going *Jolicoeur Guest House* (☎/fax 2638202) has doubles for US$19, including breakfast.

Casa Florida (☎ 2637371; fax 2636209), Mt Oreb Lane, has double rooms for US$23 and studios for US$34, including breakfast. North towards Cap Malheureux is the basic but cheap *Allamanda* (☎ 2638110), with self-catering flats for just US$10 a double.

Places to Eat
The big Chinese restaurants in Grand Baie, *Palais de Chine*, *La Pagode* and *La Jonque*, are all reasonably cheap and are located near each other on the main road. For standard European fare, try *Café de Paris*. Créole and French cuisine is offered at *La Mediterranée*; seafood curry costs US$10.

Phil's Pub serves drinks from 11 am to 1 pm and from 7 to 11 pm. The attached *L'Assiette du Pêcheur* specialises in seafood; main dishes start from around US$9.

In Peréybère, self-caterers can go to *Stephan Boutique*, but the Grand Baie supermarkets have a much wider choice.

For scrumptious Indian cuisine try *Nirvana*; chicken biryani costs US$7. *Restaurant Café Peréybère* and *Caféteria Peréybère* serve mainly Chinese-oriented meals; main dishes start at around US$4. The beach stalls cook up cheap eats; noodles cost US$1.

Getting There & Around
From Port Louis, take a Cap Malheureux or Grande Gaube bus, which leave frequently from Immigration Square and cost US$0.60.

For moped hire, try Coastal Tour (☎ 2638050) or Ebrahim Travel and Tours (☎ 2637845), both in Grand Baie, which charge around US$10 per day. Bicycles cost at least US$5 per day. For longer rentals, ask for a discount.

MAHÉBOURG
Mahébourg, the nearest town to Sir Seewoosagur Ramgoolam international airport, is a relaxed commercial centre with a small fishing fleet and attractive bay.

Things to See & Do
There's a variety of nautical displays at the **Naval Museum**, located on the outskirts of Mahébourg. It's open from 9 am to 5 pm daily except Tuesday. Admission is free.

The 25-hectare nature reserve, **Île aux Aigrettes**, off the coast near Mahébourg, is perhaps the last remnant of Mauritius' original coastal forest, thanks to Mauritius Wildlife Appeal Fund (MWAF) volunteers.

For a break from beach life, visit the beautiful 900-hectare forest, called **Domaine du Chasseur**. It's at Anse Jonchée, close to the village of Vieux Grand Port. Visitors have a choice of activities, including birdwatching, accompanied mini-safaris and hiking.

Places to Stay & Eat
The down-to-earth *Aquarelle* (☎ 6319479), near the Blue Bay road, offers doubles with common bath for US$19, including breakfast. They also have bungalows for US$21. Not far away is the more upmarket *Hôtel Les Aigrettes* (☎/fax 6319094), which has airy self-catering apartments from US$33 a double.

The *Pension Nôtre Dame* (☎ 6319582), Rue du Souffleur, is run by helpful nuns who charge US$18 for a double room.

A cut above the Mahébourg accommodation is *Chante au Vent* (☎/fax 6319614), which is on the shore about 4km out on the Blue Bay road. Doubles cost US$39, including breakfast.

For wonderful Créole and French cuisine the restaurant at the Aquarelle (see above) is recommended. *Restaurant Monte Carlo* on Rue de la Passe, serves Indian, Chinese and European dishes. Cheap snacks are available at the *Recréation Café* on Rue de Labourdonnais.

MOKA
Moka is an academic centre, with the University of Mauritius and the Mahatma Gandhi Institute. The town's environs have picturesque bubbling brooks, waterfalls,

valleys and towering peaks. **Eureka House** is an 1830s Créole home which has been turned into a museum. It's open from 9.30 am to 5 pm daily except Sunday; entry is US$5.

For energetic climbers, the **Moka Range** contains several moderate challenges – namely Le Pouce, Junction Peak, Pic des Guibies and Snail Rock.

PAMPLEMOUSSES
The **Sir Seewoosagur Ramgoolam Botanical Gardens** at Pamplemousses were started by Governor Mahé de La Bourdonnais in 1735, as a vegetable garden for his Mon Plaisir Château. In 1768, they were transformed by the French horticulturist Pierre Poivre. The main features today are the giant Victoria Regina water lilies, native to the Amazon region.

It's open daily from 8.30 am to 5.30 pm; entry is free. To get there, take the Grand Gaube, Rivière du Rempart, Roches Noires or Centre de Flacq bus from Immigration Square in Port Louis.

TAMARIN
Tamarin, a popular surfing area, has a good public beach with views across the river estuary to Montagne du Rempart. Nearby is the **Casela Bird Park**, which has exotic and endangered birds, including the rare Mauritius pink pigeon. The park is open daily from 9 am to 5 pm; admission is US$5/US$3.80 on weekdays/weekends.

Places to Stay
Chez Jacques (☎ 6836445), on the main road down to the beach, is fading at the edges but is cheap with self-catering apartments from around US$12. They rent out surfboards and bicycles for US$5 (each) per day. Another cheapie is the *Saraja Guest House* (☎ 6836168) on Anthurium Ave, which has basic apartments for US$13.

TROU AUX BICHES
Trou aux Biches is an upmarket beach resort area on the north-west corner of the island.

Some of the best public beaches are at **Mon Choisy**.

Places to Stay & Eat
The *Rocksheen Villa* (☎/fax 2655043), 161 Morcellement Jhuboo (not far from the police station), is homely and has three comfortable rooms for US$20/25 for a single/double, including breakfast. There's also an attractive self-catering studio for US$25.

La Sirène (☎ 2656026), run by Mr Bakaoolah, offers singles/doubles for US$18/25, including breakfast.

For a really cheap feed go to the little *Souvenir Snack*, near the police station. Nearby is the more stylish *Café Créole*; grilled fish costs about US$4.

L'Exotique serves Créole, European and Indian fare; main dishes are around US$6. *Lagon Bleu* specialises in seafood.

RODRIGUES ISLAND
The volcanic island of Rodrigues (population 37,000) lies about 560km east of Mauritius and is 18km long and 8km wide.

Rodrigues is much more mellow than Mauritius, and has far less tourist hype. Port Mathurin is the island's hub, and the best base for visitors.

Things to See & Do
The **Caverne Patate** caves in the south-west corner of the island are worth visiting, but you must first obtain a permit (US$2.50) from the Administration Office (☎ 8311504), Jenner St, Port Mathurin. There are daily guided tours of the caves and you should arrive at the cave entrance at the time specified on your permit. Wear strong shoes. From Port Mathurin, take the La Fouche bus and ask the driver to let you off at the right spot.

Pointe Coton, which has a luxury hotel, is the best beach on the island. There are other fine beaches at **St François, Trou d'Argent** and **Petit Gravier**.

The low-lying sandy islands of **Île Cocos** and **Île aux Sables** are nature reserves. Pick up visitors' permits at the Administration Office in Port Mathurin (see the information earlier in this section). Permits are valid for

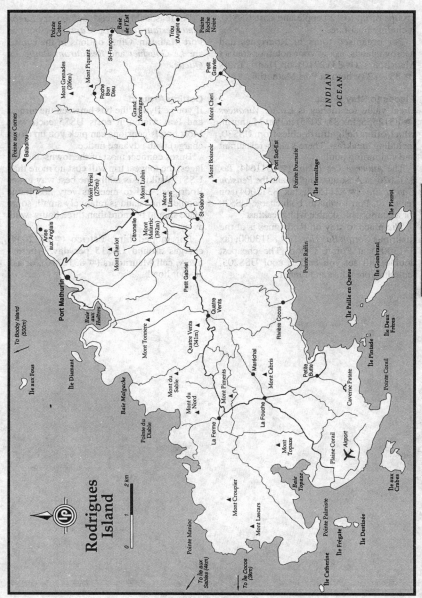

Rodrigues Island

MAURITIUS

groups of up to 12 people and cost US$10, including boat fare.

For organised tours of Rodrigues and nearby islands, ask at your hotel, or contact Mauritours (☎ 8312710) or Henri Tours (☎ 8311823), both in Port Mathurin.

Places to Stay & Eat
Great value for money is *Escale Vacances* (☎ 8312555; fax 8312075) in Port Mathurin, which offers delightful doubles from US$30, including breakfast. There's also a restaurant and swimming pool.

The *Auberge Les Filaos* (☎ 8311644; fax 8312026) at Anse aux Anglais and the *Pension Ciel d'Eté* (☎ 8311587; fax 8312004) on Jenner St, Port Mathurin, both charge US$30 for a comfortable double with breakfast.

The place to stay on Rodrigues is at the luxurious *Cotton Bay Hotel* (☎ 8313000; fax 8313003) at Pointe Coton. The cheapest double will set you back a cool US$205, including breakfast and dinner.

For reasonably priced seafood, try *Lagon Bleu Restaurant* or *Le Capitaine*, both in Port Mathurin. Other options in the capital are *Le Gourmet* and *Restaurant Paille En Queue*.

Getting Around
If you're flying, the bus between the airport and Port Mathurin costs US$5 each way. Most hotels/pensions can pick you up (for a charge) with advance notice.

Buses connect most of the towns and villages; the longest trip will cost no more than US$1. Walking is really the best way to see Rodrigues and to meet its very hospitable people. The island is relatively small, so no place should be more than three hours' walk away.

For moped hire, Patrico (☎ 8312044) charges around US$15 per day. Alternatively, call Mauritours (☎ 8312710), or ask at your hotel.

Morocco

Known by the Arabs as *al-Maghreb al-Aqsa*, 'the furthest land of the setting sun', Morocco has long held a romantic allure for the westerner.

A colourful mix of African, Islamic, Arab, Berber and European influences, the country boasts a rich culture. Its Roman ruins, medieval cities, Berber fortresses and beautiful Islamic monuments are among the best examples of their kind in the world.

Equally varied is the landscape, which includes beaches along the Atlantic and Mediterranean coasts, skiing pistes in the Atlas mountains and vast sand dunes in the Saharan desert.

For those still in search of the exotic and unfamiliar, Morocco won't disappoint. The sights and smells of the *souks* (outdoor markets), the mesmerising geometric designs of the carpets and the taste of newly brewed mint tea all make for a memorable visit.

Morocco is easily accessible from Europe, and for many travellers is their first taste of Africa.

Facts about the Country

HISTORY

The Berbers were the first settlers in Morocco but little is known of their origins. They were first recorded in history as powerful merchants who controlled a large part of the trans-Saharan trade routes.

Among those who traded with the Berbers were the Phoenicians. By the 8th century, they had established colonies all along the North African coast and were the first in a long line of foreign powers to attempt to gain a foothold in this part of Africa.

With the demise of Carthage in 146 BC, the Romans were the next on the scene, but

KINGDOM OF MOROCCO
Area: 710,000 sq km
Population: 27.7 million
Population Growth Rate: 2.2%
Capital: Rabat
Head of State: King Hassan II
Official Language: Arabic
Currency: Dirham
Exchange Rate: Dr 8.88 = US$1
Per Capita GNP: US$1100
Inflation: 6%
Time: GMT/UTC

Highlights

- The imperial cities of Fès, Marrakesh & Meknès, among the best preserved medieval cities in the world
- Trekking through the beautiful scenery and remote Berber villages of the High Atlas Mountains
- The immense ochre-coloured cliffs of the Dadés Gorge, and the red-earthen kasbahs of the Drâa Valley
- Chefchaouen, one of the prettiest villages in Morocco, with its blue-washed houses standing amid the wild and dramatic Rif Mountains

their hold on the area was equally tenuous; the Berbers were never known for their tolerance of foreign domination.

Christianity arrived in the 3rd century AD followed by Islam, which burst onto the world in the 7th century when the Arab armies swept out of Arabia. By the beginning

MOROCCO

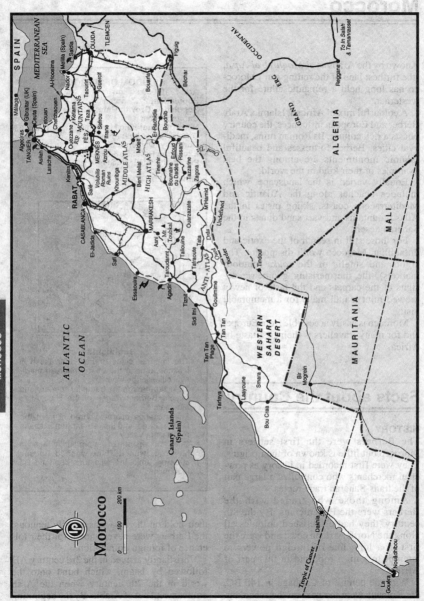

Morocco

MOROCCO

of the 8th century, all of North Africa and most of Spain were under Arab control.

It was not long before the Berbers were in revolt again, and by the 9th century rebellious Kharijite communities had managed to expel non-Berber Muslims from most of North Africa. The Idrissid kingdom sprang up, with Fès as its capital, and for the first time something like a united Morocco existed.

It was short lived. By the 11th century the kingdom and much of North Africa had fragmented. Out of the chaos emerged a fundamentalist Berber movement, the Almoravids, who overran Morocco and Muslim Andalusia in Spain and made Marrakesh their capital.

They in turn were supplanted in the 12th century by the Almohads, who brought Fès, Marrakesh and Rabat to the peak of their cultural development. They too then crumbled as the Christian armies in the north regained Spain and Bedouin tribes in the east took over Algeria and Tunisia.

Next on the scene were the Merenids under whom Morocco again flourished, but increased encroachment by the Portuguese and the fall of Granada in Spain to the Christians in 1492 eventually swept the new dynasty away.

Several short-lived dynasties followed, including the Saadians, and in the 1630s the Alawites, the descendants of whom still rule today. During the rule of sultan Moulay Ismail (1672-1727), the Imperial City of Meknès was constructed. It was a last gasp. As trans-Saharan trade disintegrated and Europe became industrialised, Morocco increasingly became a backwater.

By the end of the 19th century the rule of the sultan, Abd al-Aziz, was paralysed by corruption and the European powers saw growing opportunities to be able to meddle in Morocco's affairs. An uprising led by the sultan's brother, Abd al-Hafid, in 1907 gave the French their chance to move in and a protectorate was established in 1912, with provision for Spanish control of the north.

Under the first French resident-general, Marshal Lyautey, Rabat was made the new capital, the port of Casablanca was developed and French-style *villes nouvelles* (new towns) were built alongside the old towns.

Marshal Lyautey's less enlightened successor, together with some heavy-handed Spanish control of the northern protectorate, prompted an uprising of the Riffian Berbers. Under Abd el-Krim, their leader, they managed to inflict several humiliating defeats on the Spanish and even proclaim a Republic of the Rif. It took a combined Spanish-French force of over 250,000 to defeat them in 1926.

In 1943 the nationalist movement, embodied by the Istiqlal (Independence) Party, put forward proposals demanding independence. These were ignored by the French, who detained the party leaders and sent their sultan, Mohammed V, into exile. Two years later, in 1955, he was allowed to return, now a national hero, and independence was granted the following year.

With the French gone, Sultan Mohammed V became king, and on his death in 1961 was succeeded by his son Moulay Hassan (Hassan II).

Although Morocco is officially a constitutional monarchy, Hassan II, the Commander of the Faithful (amir al-mu'mineen), remains effectively an absolute ruler. In 1970 and 1972, some constitutional reforms were introduced, and in September 1996 a referendum finally approved the creation of a new bicameral parliamentary system in which the lower house is directly elected. This is expected to give greater representation to the opposition parties, although the effects will not properly be known until after elections in the second half of 1997.

The king continues to dictate all economic strategy, however, and this has led to mounting political and social tensions. In May and October 1996, graduates, protesting against high unemployment, staged sit-ins and hunger strikes in Rabat. Tight security continues to prevent serious social unrest.

Despite the imbalance of power, Hassan II remains a respected figure among the majority of his subjects. His popularity soared in 1975 with the Green March, when 350,000

MOROCCO

unarmed Moroccans marched into the phosphate-rich Spanish colony of Western Sahara. Upon the departure of the Spanish troops however, the Polisario Front, which had been struggling for years against Spanish rule, turned to fight its new overlords.

The United Nations (UN) brokered a cease-fire in 1991, and a referendum was promised. As of mid-1997 this had still not taken place. However, relations between both sides seem to be improving. On 6 November 1996, the 21st anniversary of the Green March, King Hassan II confirmed that for the first time in years, direct talks had taken place with Polisario. Prisoners have also been exchanged, while in May 1996 the UN peacekeeping force was reduced by half.

Early in 1997, former US secretary of state James Baker was appointed by the UN as a special envoy to deal with the issue. Baker's immediate mandate was to find a compromise between the two sides which will allow a referendum to proceed. In May 1997 the first of the meetings took place, with representatives from Morocco, Algeria, Mauritania and Polisario.

A population growing by more than 2% a year, economic hardship induced by an International Monetary Fund (IMF) austerity programme, and questions about the threat of fundamentalism to the monarchy and state have all put pressure on Hassan II, but the story is not all bleak. After a tough decade, Morocco is showing signs of pulling out of its economic morass. King Hassan II pins great hopes upon anchoring Morocco as firmly as possible to the European Union's (EU) orbit (including eventual membership). Conversely, Morocco is seen by Europe as a useful ally among Arab states and a bulwark against the diffusion of Islamic fundamentalism. To this end the free trade zone agreement signed between the EU and the kingdom in 1996 should consolidate ties on a long-term basis. A new link between Europe and the Maghreb was created in November 1996, when the 1430km gas pipeline came on stream, carrying Algerian gas to Spain via Morocco.

Tourism, hit hard by the effects of the Gulf War in 1991, recovered strongly in 1996 after a three year recession. It remains the country's second largest hard-currency earner, providing jobs, both formal and 'informal' (ie black market), for half the working population of cities like Marrakesh.

GEOGRAPHY & CLIMATE

Morocco is traversed by four distinct mountain ranges. From north to south, they are the Rif, the Middle Atlas, the High Atlas and the Anti-Atlas. Certain peaks of the High Atlas remain snow-capped throughout the whole year and are among the highest in Africa.

In between the mountain ranges and stretching up toward the Atlantic coast are fertile and well watered plateaus and plains. In the extreme south, at the edge of the Anti-Atlas, the country is characterised by vast, eroded gorges which, like the rivers that flow at their bases, gradually peter out into the endless sand and stony expanses of the Sahara Desert.

The geological variety in Morocco also gives it a wide range of climatic conditions. Weather in the coastal regions is generally mild. In winter, temperatures in the lowlands can reach 30°C during the day to a cool 15°C at night. In summer, day-time temperatures are as high as 45°C. Winter in the higher regions demands clothing suitable for Arctic conditions.

The main rainy season is between November and April. The most pleasant seasons to explore Morocco are spring (April to May) and autumn (September to October).

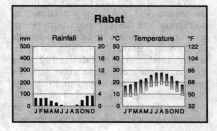

ECOLOGY & ENVIRONMENT

Morocco is said to have the greatest biodiversity in the Mediterranean area, its rich landscape providing a diverse habitat for vegetation, animals and birds.

The country serves as a point of passage, for example, for thousands of migratory birds passing from Europe to Africa. It has the only species of parrot in North Africa, the only forest of Argan trees in the region, as well as colonies of panther and leopard (rarely seen) which have disappeared elsewhere.

For some species, help has inevitably come too late. The famous Barbary lion, found in Morocco at the turn of the century, has been hunted to extinction. A further 34 bird and animal species are said to be in acute danger.

As in many African countries, the greatest cause for concern is the destruction of the natural habitat, particularly the loss of forest to agriculture and urban settlement. This has led to erosion, impoverishment of the land and, in recent years, serious flooding.

Morocco's programme of dam construction and irrigation pumps has not helped either. This has led to the lowering of the water table, and a further decrease in animal and plant species.

On a brighter note, concern for this decline has led to some positive action. On the Atlantic coast several wetland sites have been awarded protected status, and in the Atlas mountains three national parks have been established, with plans to set up another seven. Plantation schemes and educational centres have also been established.

Above all, there has been a move to win the support of the local communities who inhabit these regions. Without their assistance, the problems of deforestation, overgrazing and hunting are likely to continue.

POPULATION & PEOPLE

Morocco has a population of nearly 28 million but at present growth levels it is expected to double by early next century.

Contrary to popular belief, the Berbers are not exotic outsiders but make up the bulk of the population. With the shift towards the industrial cites, however, the distinction between Berbers and Arabs is becoming less and less clear.

In general, the Berbers inhabit the mountainous regions and parts of the desert, and are roughly divided into three groups identified by dialect: those speaking Amazigh from the Middle Atlas, Chleuh from the High Atlas, and Riffian from the mountains of the same name.

Besides the Arabs and Berbers, Morocco once hosted a significant population of Jews who fled Andalusian Spain in the face of the Reconquista. With the creation of Israel in 1948, the Jewish population has dropped to about 30,000.

Growing commercial links with the interior of Africa over the centuries also attracted a population of sub-Saharan Africans, particularly in the south of the country. Many originally came as slaves.

All but a tiny minority of the population is Muslim (Sunni), but in Morocco Islam is far from strictly orthodox. The strict segregation of sexes in public life that is characteristic of Muslim societies is far from uniform in Morocco, and predictably it is in the big

Remedies & Cures

Pre-Islamic folklore is still widespread in Morocco. A trip to a good spice market in any souk will bear that out. In cages, stuffed or dried, you'll find an extraordinary collection of amphibians, reptiles, birds and mammals. What to do with them?

For syphilis of the throat and mouth: 'swallow the ashes of a crow which has been knocked down and stunned, then cremated in a new cooking pot'.

Syphilis used to be so widespread in Morocco that there is a saying: 'He who doesn't have it in this world will have it in the next'. ■

cities, notably Casablanca, where this is least evident. Nevertheless, males generally take the leading public role and, consequently, most travellers' contacts with Moroccans are with men.

SOCIETY & CONDUCT

As a rule, a high degree of modesty is demanded of both sexes, in dress and behaviour. For the tourist too, it pays to respect this convention. Women are strongly advised to cover their shoulders and arms and to opt for long trousers or skirts. Not doing so runs the risk of arousing the ire of the genuinely offended, and attracting constant and unwanted attention from others.

LANGUAGE

Arabic is the official language but French and, to a lesser degree, Spanish are also spoken in the cities. English is spoken in some places. Spoken Moroccan Arabic – *Drama* – is considerably different from the Arabic spoken in the Middle East. Various Berber dialects are widely spoken in the countryside and particularly in the mountains. See the Arabic section in the Language Appendix for useful words and phrases. Or for a more comprehensive travellers' guide to the Arabic language, see Lonely Planet's *Moroccan Arabic Phrasebook*.

Facts for the Visitor

VISAS

Most visitors to Morocco do not require visas and are granted leave to remain in Morocco for 90 days on entry. Exceptions to this rule include nationals of Israel, South Africa and Zimbabwe, who can apply for a one month single-entry visa (US$22) or a three month double-entry visa (US$31). An initial visa can take up to four weeks to be issued.

Visa Extensions

Should the standard 90 day stay be insufficient, it is possible to apply for an extension or even for residence (but the latter is difficult to get).

It is probably easier to simply leave the country and try to re-enter after a few days. Your chances improve if you enter by a different route the second time.

People on visas may prefer to try for the extension. Go to the nearest police station with your passport, three photos and, preferably, a letter from your embassy requesting a visa extension on your behalf. If you are in Rabat go to the Sûreté Nationale office, off Ave Mohammed V in the centre of town. It should take a maximum of four days to process.

Other Visas

Algeria

The diplomatic missions in Rabat, Casablanca and Oujda (see Foreign Embassies in Morocco) issue one-month, single-entry visas which vary in price according to nationality. Australians don't pay anything, US citizens pay about US$30 and Britons about US$40. You need three photos and confirmation of a hotel booking in Algeria. Visas can take up to two weeks to be issued. It is not possible to cross the Moroccan-Algerian land border due to internal conflict in Algeria.

Burkina Faso, Djibouti & Togo

The French embassy in Rabat issues visas for these countries.

Mali

Visas are issued in 24 hours at the embassy in Rabat.

Mauritania

Visas valid for a one month stay are issued in Rabat on the same day at a cost of US$25. You need two photos and a return airline ticket with Air Mauritanie or Royal Air Maroc. A letter of recommendation from your embassy is advisable. If you want to enter overland, buy a return ticket in Rabat (see Information in that section), get the visa and then refund the ticket. You will lose something on the refund but it is the only way to get a visa in Morocco. The only alternative is to get one before leaving Europe. Visas issued in Rabat may be stamped 'Entry at Nouakchott Airport' but land border officials don't seem to worry.

Senegal

The embassy in Rabat issues visas for a stay of either one month (US$14) or three months (US$20). You need two photos and a return airline ticket. Visas are generally issued on the same day.

EMBASSIES
Moroccan Embassies
Morocco has embassies and consulates in the following countries: Algeria, Australia, Canada, Egypt, France, Germany, Israel, Japan, Libya, Mauritania, the Netherlands, Portugal, Spain, Tunisia, the UK and the USA.

Foreign Embassies in Morocco
Most of the developed nations maintain embassies in the capital, Rabat, and there are consulates scattered about in various other cities. They include the following:

Algeria
    46 Blvd Tariq ibn Zayid, Rabat (☎ 76 5092)
    159 Blvd Moulay Idriss I, Casablanca (☎ 80 4175)
    11 Blvd de Taza, Oujda (☎ 68 3740)
Canada
    13 bis Zankat Rue Jaafar as-Sadiq, Agdal, Rabat (☎ 67 2880)
France
    3 Rue Fahnoun, Agdal, Rabat (☎ 77 7822)
    Consulates: Service de Visas, Rue Ibn al-Khattib, off Blvd Hassan II, Rabat (☎ 70 2404); Rue Prince Moulay Abdallah, Casablanca (☎ 26 5355)
Germany
    7 Zankat Madnine, Rabat (☎ 70 9662)
Italy
    2 Zankat Idris al-Azhar, Rabat (☎ 70 6597)
Japan
    39 Ave Ahmed, Balafrej, Rabat (☎ 63 1782)
Mauritania
    Souissi II Villa, No 266, OLM, Rabat (☎ 65 6678)
Netherlands
    40 Rue de Tunis, Rabat (☎ 73 3512)
Senegal
    17 Rue Qadi Amadi, Rabat (☎ 75 4138)
Spain
    3-5 Rue Madnine, Rabat (☎ 70 7600)
    Consulates: 57 Ave du Chellah, Rabat (☎ 70 4147); 31 Rue d'Alger, Casablanca (☎ 22 0752)
Tunisia
    6 Ave de Fès, Rabat (☎ 73 0576)
UK
    17 Blvd de la Tour Hassan, Rabat (☎ 73 1403)
    43 Blvd d'Anfa, Casablanca (☎ 20 3316)
USA
    2 Ave de Marrakech, Rabat (☎ 76 2265)
    8 Blvd Moulay Youssef, Casablanca (☎ 26 4550)

MONEY
US$1 = Dr 8.88

The unit of currency is the dirham (Dr), which is equal to 100 centimes. The import or export of local currency is prohibited. There's no black market as such, but you will occasionally be made an offer. For a few cents more than the bank rate, it's hardly worth the effort.

Banks are generally open from 8.30 to 11.30 am and 2.30 to 4.30 pm Monday to Friday, with the midday break on Friday being slightly longer.

The Banque Populaire seems to be the most efficient of the Moroccan banks. It doesn't charge a commission on travellers' cheques and some branches have exchange facilities open on weekends. Australian and New Zealand dollars are not recognised in Morocco.

ATMs are becoming increasingly widespread throughout the country, though many have a Dr 1000 limit. Many banks accept Visa and MasterCard for cash advances.

Major credit cards are widely accepted for purchases, although the use of them can incur a 5% surcharge. American Express (Amex) is represented by the travel agency Voyages Schwartz in Casablanca, Marrakesh and Tangier.

Some travellers have run into hassles changing money at airports, where in some cases only cash is accepted. Travellers' cheques are not accepted at land borders.

PUBLIC HOLIDAYS
Public holidays observed are: 3 March, 1 May, 23 May (National Day), 9 July (Youth Day), 14 August, 6 November, 18 November (Independence Day) and variable Islamic holidays. See Public Holidays in the Regional Facts for the Visitor chapter for more information on Islamic holidays.

POST & COMMUNICATIONS
Post
The Moroccan post is reasonably reliable, but poste-restante counters sometimes hold items for only a couple of weeks before

MOROCCO

returning them to the sender. There's a small charge for collecting letters and you need your passport.

Parcels have to be inspected by Customs (at the post office) before you seal them and pay for the postage, so don't turn up at a post office with a sealed parcel.

Telephone & Fax

The telephone service has been substantially upgraded, and in all major cities and most towns dozens of *téléboutiques* have sprung up where you can make calls using either coins or phonecards. Téléboutiques also offer fax services.

The country area for Morocco is 212; area codes include Casablanca 02; Marrakesh 04 and Rabat 07.

ACCOMMODATION

You can camp anywhere in Morocco provided you have the site owner's permission. There are many official camping grounds, which vary in price depending on the facilities provided. They are sometimes pretty bare and poor value.

There are youth hostels (*auberges de jeunesse*) at Asni, Azrou, Casablanca, Chefchaouen, Fès, Marrakesh, Meknès, Rabat and Tangier. If you're travelling alone, they are among the cheapest places to stay – around US$3 per night if you have a HI card, slightly more without.

Apart from unclassified hotels (usually the most basic, and costing around US$4 per person), Moroccan hotels are classified according to a set of government guidelines, and there is a fixed maximum price that they're allowed to charge. Rates at the lower end of the scale range from US$8/10 for a single/double with common facilities in a '1-star B' hotel up to US$24/29 for a room with attached bath in a '3-star A' place.

FOOD & DRINKS

Moroccan cuisine is varied and very often delicious. *Harira*, a thick lentil-based broth with meat stock and vegetables, is good and cheap. The main national dishes are *tajine*, a tasty meat and vegetable stew cooked slowly in a round, earthenware dish with a cone-shaped lid, and *couscous*, a steaming mountain of semolina topped with meat, vegetables and a spicy sauce. Grilled lamb *brochettes* (skewered piece of meat cooked over hot coals) are common as is roast chicken served with crispy *frites* (chips; French fries).

Coastal areas offer a range of seafood straight from the ocean, and fresh fruit is plentiful along with dates, figs, almonds and olives.

The national drink is mint tea – Moroccan whiskey, as the locals like to call it – which is made with great ceremony and a great deal of sugar.

Getting There & Away

AIR

Morocco is well linked to Europe, Africa and the Middle East by air. Among the airlines serving Morocco are Air Algérie, Air France, Alitalia, British Airways, GB Airways, Iberia, KLM, Lufthansa, Royal Air Maroc (RAM), Royal Jordanian, Sabena, Saudia, Swissair, EgyptAir and Tunis Air.

There are international airports at Casablanca, Tangier and Agadir. There are also direct flights from Paris to Fès, Ouarzazate, Oujda and Marrakesh. There are no cheap flights from Morocco to Europe.

Algeria

RAM has weekly flights from Casablanca to Algiers for around US$160 one way.

LAND
Algeria

There are two border crossings between Morocco and Algeria: Oujda-Tlemcen and Figuig-Beni Ounif. However, due to worsening internal strife in Algeria, the borders are closed and visas are not issued at all for land crossings. Travel to Algeria is not advisable.

Mauritania

The border between Morocco and Mauritania was open at the time of writing. Cars must cross the border in army-escorted convoys. Check the latest political situation before planning to travel this route.

Convoys leave Dakhla twice weekly, and all travellers must be in a vehicle and supply two passport photos. The Moroccan escort army leaves the convoy 42km from the Mauritanian border.

Spanish North Africa

Ceuta From Tetouan there are plenty of *grands taxis* (share-taxis) to the border at Fnideq (US$2, 20 minutes). Transport dries up from 7 pm to 5 am, although the crossing is open 24 hours. At the border there are informal moneychangers on the Spanish side and national banks on the Moroccan side.

Special buses run every 15 minutes from the border to the Plaza de la Constitución in Ceuta (US$0.50, 20 minutes).

The whole trip from Tetouan to Ceuta should take no more than two hours; often it takes a good deal less. To keep delays to a minimum, it's worth crossing the border either early in the morning or late at night, particularly if you're going by car.

Melilla There are frequent buses and grands taxis from Nador to the border until about 8 pm. It's about 200m to the Spanish border post, and another 150m to the bus stop for local buses to the Plaza de España. Buses run from about 7.30 am until late in the evening.

SEA
Europe
The various ways of getting to Europe are covered in the introductory Getting There & Away chapter.

Getting Around

AIR
If your time is limited and you want to see as much of Morocco as possible, it's worth considering the occasional flight with RAM. If you're 22 years of age or under, or a student under 31, you pay 25% less.

The standard one-way fare from Casablanca to Fès is about US$48. Fès to Agadir is US$120 one way. Casablanca to Marrakesh is US$40 one way.

BUS
There is a good network of buses, and in most Moroccan cities companies gather in a central bus station. The national carrier, Compagnie de Transports Marocains (CTM), sometimes has its own terminal.

CTM is the largest company and has both 1st-class and 2nd-class buses. On longer runs the 1st-class buses are usually comfortable, with video (a dubious asset) and (sometimes in winter) heating. In the south, the local company SATAS is just as good. See the table below listing a range of CTM's 1st-class fares.

CTM 1st-Class Bus Fares			
From	To	Fares (US$)	Duration
Casablanca	Agadir	$14	8 hours
	Chefchaouen	$8	5½ hours
	Fès	$8	5 hours
	Marrakesh	$6	4 hours
	Rabat	$3	1½ hours
	Safi	$6	4 hours
	Tangier	$11	6 hours
Fès	Oujda	$7.50	6 hours
	Tangier	$8	6 hours
Marrakesh	Agadir	$5	3½ hours
	Fès	$12	9 hours
	Ouarzazate	$5	4 hours
	Tangier	$16	10 hours
Tangier	Agadir	$22	15 hours

There is an official charge for baggage storage on CTM buses. On private lines it's usual to give baggage handlers a small tip.

Smaller local companies generally operate only regionally. Some of them are two-bit operations with a broken-down old bus or two, while others match CTM for comfort. They're generally a bit cheaper than CTM.

Don't expect anything other than a CTM long-haul bus to have heating, even on the journeys over the Atlas Mountains in winter. Warm clothing is, essential, particularly if

MOROCCO

there's any chance of being stranded on the passes because of snowdrifts. The Marrakesh to Ouarzazate road is prone to this.

TRAIN

Morocco's Office National des Chemins de Fer (ONCF) is one of the most modern rail systems in Africa. It links most of the main centres, and the trains are generally comfortable and fast. Lines go as far south as Marrakesh, but with Supratours bus link-ups the ONCF can get you as far south as Dakhla.

There are two types of train and two classes on each. The main difference between the normal trains and the *rapides* is not speed (there is rarely any difference), but comfort and air-con with the latter. Second class is more than adequate on any journey, and on normal trains 2nd-class fares are commensurate with bus fares. See the table below listing a range of 2nd-class fares for normal and rapide trains.

2nd-Class Fares for Normal & Rapide Trains			
From	*To*	*Normal/ Rapide Fares (US$)*	*Duration*
Tangier	Casablanca	$8/11	6 hours
	Fès	$7/9	6 hours
	Marrakesh	$14/18	10 hours
Casablanca	Marrakesh	$5/7	4 hours
	Oujda	$15/19	11 hours
Rabat	Fès	$5/9	3½ hours
	Marrakesh	$8/10	4½ hours
	Tangier	$7/8	5 hours

Buy tickets at the station, as a supplement is charged if you buy them on the train. You can get couchettes on the overnight trains from Marrakesh to Tangier and from Casablanca to Oujda. They are worth the extra US$6/5 in 1st/2nd class.

Timetables for the whole rail system are posted in French at most stations.

In addition to the normal and rapide trains, express shuttles (TNR) run frequently between Kenitra, Rabat, Casablanca and Mohammed V airport. From Rabat to Casablanca it's US$2 in 2nd class.

TAXI & CAMIONETTE
Taxi

Shared Mercedes taxis (*grands taxis* or, in Arabic, *taxiat kebira*) link towns to their nearest neighbours in a kind of leap-frogging system. They are generally faster on short routes, but with six passengers (they leave only when full) they can be uncomfortable on longer journeys. If you are a group of five or six, it is worth considering hiring one on scenic routes, at a prearranged price that covers photo stops. Note that not all grands taxis run on set intercity routes for fixed fares. Many of the ranks you will see are for local runs only, but all drivers are willing to take you anywhere – for a price that suits them. As a rule of thumb, fares are approximately US$0.15 per 3km, a little more expensive than buses.

City taxis (*petits taxis*) are useful for cheap trips around towns.

Camionette

In some of the remoter parts of the country, especially in the Atlas Mountains, the only way you can get from village to village is by local Berber *camionette* (pick-up). This is a bumpy, adventurous way to get to know the country and people, but it can mean waiting days at a time for the next lift.

CAR

Many out-of-the-way places in Morocco are difficult to get to without your own transport. Car rental is not cheap, but with four people it's affordable. Charges do vary even among the major international companies (Hertz, Budget, Avis and Europcar/InterRent) and there are any number of local companies that will rent you the same cars for much less, so check things out thoroughly before deciding.

Always haggle for a discount, especially when renting for an extended period. Most companies offer excellent discounts for rentals over one month.

A Renault 4 costs from US$32 to US$50

a day, or US$225 to US$375 for seven days with unlimited kilometres. This includes tax and insurance. A motorcycle will cost around US$25 a day.

Premium petrol (super) costs under US$1 per litre (more in country areas).

HITCHING

Hitching is possible but you'll need a thick skin and considerable diplomatic expertise in the north to guard against aggressive hustlers who may pick you up. They won't take 'no' for an answer and feign outrage if you express lack of interest in whatever they're trying to sell you – usually drugs. It's particularly bad on the road between Tetouan and Tangier. Giving lifts to locals in these areas is, for similar reasons, a bad idea. See also the warning on hitching in the main Getting Around chapter.

Rabat

Morocco's capital is a modern city with enough to keep the sightseer occupied for at least a couple of days.

Rabat's history goes back 2500 years to the time of Phoenician exploration. With the arrival of the Romans, a significant settlement known as Sala Colonia was established. In the 12th century, Rabat's fortunes rose when the Almohad sultan Yacoub al-Mansour used the *kasbah* (the citadel) as a base for campaigns in Spain and built the magnificent Oudaia Gate (Bab Ouadia) and the Tour Hassan, the incomplete minaret of the great mosque. However, after his death in 1199, the city rapidly declined.

Muslim exiles from Spain resettled in Rabat and neighbouring Salé in the early 17th century, and the stage was set for the colourful era of the Sallee Rovers.

During the 17th, 18th and 19th centuries, these notorious pirates plundered thousands of merchant vessels returning to Europe from Asia, West Africa and the Americas.

Information

The Office National Marocain du Tourisme (ONMT; ☎ 68 1531) is on Rue al-Abtal in the west of the city. The syndicat d'initiative (a branch of the main tourist office), more conveniently located on Rue Lumumba, is due to reopen in 1998. The banks are concentrated along Ave Mohammed V.

Things to See

The walled **medina** (old quarter) dates from the 17th century. It is only of mild interest, but there are some good carpet shops inside.

The **Kasbah des Oudaias** is built out on the bluff overlooking the Atlantic Ocean and houses a palace built by Moulay Ismail, now containing a **museum** of traditional art. It's open every day, except Tuesday, from 9 am to noon and 3 to 5 pm (6 pm in summer). Entry to the museum is US$1. The pleasant **Andalusian Gardens** were actually planted by the French. The main entry to the Kasbah is via the enormous Almohad **Bab Oudaia** built in 1195.

Rabat's most famous landmark is the **Tour Hassan**, which overlooks the bridge across the Oued Bou Regreg to Salé. Construction of this enormous minaret – intended to be the largest in the Muslim world – was begun by Almohad sultan Yacoub al-Mansour in 1195, but abandoned on his death four years later. On the same site is the **Mausoleum of Mohammed V**, the present king's father. Entry is free, but you must be respectably dressed.

Beyond the city walls, at the end of Ave Yacoub el-Mansour, are the remains of the ancient Roman city of Sala Colonia, which subsequently became the independent Berber city of **Chellah**. Later still, the Merenids used it as their royal burial ground. It's a pleasant place for a wander. Entry is US$1, and it's open daily from 8.30 am until sunset.

The **Archaeology Museum** is the best of its kind in Morocco. It's on Rue al-Brihi, close to the Hôtel Chellah, and is open daily, except Tuesday, from 8.30 am to noon and 2.30 to 6 pm. Entry is US$1.

Places to Stay

Camping de la Plage (☎ 78 2368) is a clean

MOROCCO

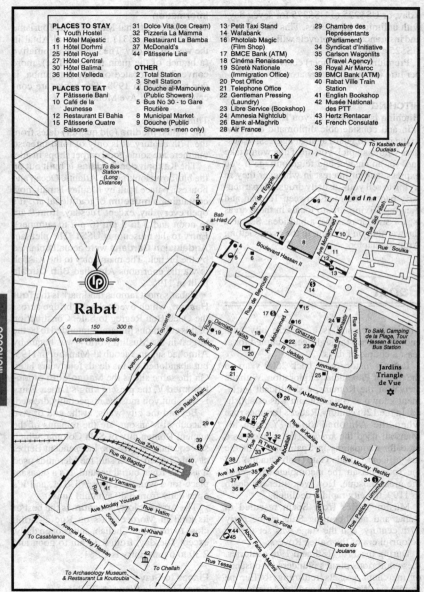

PLACES TO STAY
1 Youth Hostel
6 Hôtel Majestic
11 Hôtel Dorhmi
25 Hôtel Royal
27 Hôtel Central
30 Hôtel Balima
36 Hôtel Velleda

PLACES TO EAT
7 Pâtisserie Bani
10 Café de la Jeunesse
12 Restaurant El Bahia
15 Pâtisserie Quatre Saisons

31 Dolce Vita (Ice Cream)
32 Pizzeria La Mamma
33 Restaurant La Bamba
37 McDonald's
44 Pâtisserie Lina

OTHER
2 Total Station
3 Shell Station
4 Douche al-Mamouniya (Public Showers)
5 Bus No 30 - to Gare Routière
8 Municipal Market
9 Douche (Public Showers - men only)

13 Petit Taxi Stand
14 Wafabank
16 Photolab Magic (Film Shop)
17 BMCE Bank (ATM)
18 Cinéma Renaissance
19 Sûreté Nationale (Immigration Office)
20 Post Office
21 Telephone Office
22 Gentleman Pressing (Laundry)
23 Libre Service (Bookshop)
24 Amnesia Nightclub
26 Bank al-Maghrib
28 Air France

29 Chambre des Représentants (Parliament)
34 Syndicat d'Initiative
35 Carlson Wagonlits (Travel Agency)
38 Royal Air Maroc
39 BMCI Bank (ATM)
40 Rabat Ville Train Station
41 English Bookshop
42 Musée National des PTT
43 Hertz Rentacar
45 French Consulate

Rabat

0   150   300 m
Approximate Scale

place at Salé beach. It costs US$1 per person, US$1 for electricity and US$0.50 for a car. There is no permanent accommodation; you must bring all your own camping gear.

The *youth hostel* (☎ 72 5769) on 34 Rue Marrassa, opposite the walls of the medina, is pleasant enough and costs US$3 per night with communal, cold showers.

Of the basic budget hotels in the medina, the best is the *Hôtel Dorhmi* (☎ 72 3898) at 313 Ave Mohammed V, which has decent singles/doubles for US$8/11. Hot showers are US$1 more.

In the ville nouvelle (new city), one of the best budget deals is the *Hôtel Central* (☎ 70 7356) on the corner of Zankat al-Basra and Rue Dimachk. Spacious rooms without shower cost US$8/11 or with shower US$13/15. A little more expensive for singles but a rival for value in doubles is the *Hôtel Velleda* (☎ 76 9531) at 106 Ave Allal ben Abdallah. Generous rooms with shower cost US$9/12.

The *Hôtel Royal* (☎ 72 1171) on 1 Rue Jeddah Ammane has comfortable rooms with telephone and bathroom. Rooms with shower are US$14/17, and US$17/20 with shower and toilet. Try for a room with views over the park.

If you're having trouble getting a bath or shower at your hotel, head for the Douche al-Mamouniya, just off Blvd Hassan II near the Hôtel Majestic, or the douche (public showers – men only) and hammam (bath-house) inside the medina.

Places to Eat

There is a good selection of cheap restaurants close to the market on Ave Mohammed V. At the *Café de la Jeunesse*, you can get a filling meal of meat and chips with a soft drink for US$2.

Built into the medina walls on Blvd Hassan II is the *Restaurant El Bahia*, a pleasant place for a meal. Main courses with a drink cost around US$3.

The *Restaurant La Koutoubia* at 10 Rue Pierre Parent is a colourful, traditionally decorated place. The house speciality is tajine (stew) which costs US$5.

A block behind the Hôtel Balima is a cluster of places. *La Bamba* offers two set menus of US$6 and US$10. To justify the Spanish name, it promises paella every night. Across the road is one of the best places in Rabat, the pizzeria *La Mamma*, where pizzas cost US$5 and beer is from US$2. Also here is *Dolce Vita* for excellent ice cream.

One of the best places in town for morning coffee and a croissant is the *Pâtisserie Lina* on Ave Allal ben Abdallah, close to the French consulate.

Entertainment

A good place for a drink is the pleasant and very popular terrace outside the *Hôtel Balima* in the ville nouvelle.

For nightlife, you can try one of the rather expensive discos. Currently, the most popular is *Amnesia*, just down from the Hôtel Royal on Rue de Monastir. Entry is US$10, including one free drink.

Getting There & Away

Bus The long-distance bus station is inconveniently located 5km south-west of the city centre on the road to Casablanca. Petits taxis and bus No 30 go into the city centre. Coming from the north, it's easier to get off at Salé and take a local bus or grand taxi from there.

CTM has buses to Casablanca, Er-Rachidia, Fès, Oujda, Tangier, Tetouan and Tiznit (via Agadir).

Train The Rabat Ville train station is in the city centre (don't get off at Rabat Agdal). In addition to the Casablanca shuttles (up to 17 a day), there are departures to Tangier (5½ hours), Meknès and Fès (almost four hours), Oujda (10 hours) and Marrakesh (under six hours).

Taxi Grands taxis to Casablanca (US$3) leave from the long-distance bus station. Other taxis go to Fès (US$6), Meknès (US$5) and Salé (US$0.30) from Blvd Hassan II.

Getting Around

The Airport There are 10 shuttle trains a day to Mohammed V international airport. Some

MOROCCO

involve a change at Casablanca. Tickets cost US$5.

Bus The main local bus station is on Blvd Hassan II. Bus No 16 departs from here to Salé.

Around the Country

AGADIR

Agadir is a modern city which was completely rebuilt after a devastating earthquake in 1960. Most of the activity centres around package tourists from Europe who flock here by the plane-load in search of sun, sand and a sanitised version of the mysteries of the Barbary Coast.

Though one of Morocco's more expensive cities to visit, Agadir is well placed for trips east and further south. To find less crowded beaches and other independent travellers, head out of town. The best beaches are up around **Aghrod**, 27km north of Agadir, and **Cap Rhir**. Closer to Agadir they tend to be crowded.

Information

The ONMT tourist office (☎ 84 6377) is in the market area just off Ave Prince Sidi Mohammed. There's an information desk at the airport, and a syndicat d'initiative (☎ 84 0307) on the corner of Blvd Mohammed V and Ave du Général Kettani.

Amex is represented by the Crédit du Maroc bank (☎ 84 0188) on Ave des Forces Armées Royales (FAR).

Places to Stay

Campervans predominate at Agadir's *camp site* (☎ 84 6683), just off Blvd Mohammed V on the port side of town. There's a general grocery store here.

Most of the budget hotels and a few of the mid-range ones are around the bus station on Rue Yacoub el-Mansour and along Rue Allal ben Abdallah. In the high seasons you must get into Agadir early to be sure of a room.

Dirt cheapies such as the *Hôtel Canaria*

(☎ 84 6727) and the *Hôtel Massa* are pretty grim. Less so is the *Hôtel Select* (public douche next door), which has rooms for US$6/8 for singles/doubles.

Three better places that charge US$7/9 for rooms are the *Hôtel La Tour Eiffel* (☎ 82 3712), the *Hôtel Amenou* (☎ 84 5615) and the *Hôtel Aït Laayoune* (☎ 82 4375).

The two star *Hôtel de Paris* (☎ 82 2694), Ave du Président Kennedy, is comfortable and has steaming hot water. It costs US$9/11 for rooms without bathroom.

The *Hôtel Diaf* (☎ 82 5852) costs US$10/13 for rooms with private bathroom. Hot water is available only in the evening.

More expensive still but very good is the *Hôtel Talborjt* (☎ 84 1832) which is on Rue de l'Entraide. It has pleasant, carpeted singles/doubles, some overlooking lush gardens, for US$25/31.

Places to Eat

There are cheap restaurants and sandwich bars on Rue Yacoub el-Mansour. Just behind here, on Place Lahcen Tamri, the *Restaurant Echabab*, *Restaurant Mille et Une Nuits* and *Café Restaurant Coq d'Or* all offer good three-course menus for around US$2.50.

The *Restaurant Select*, just by the hotel of the same name, does a solid range of old favourites and for about US$2 you can eat well.

If you fancy fresh fish, head to the port entrance west of town where dozens of cheap *seafood stalls* are set up every day for lunch and dinner.

Getting There & Away

The region's main bus station is actually in Inezgane, 13km south of Agadir, and you may arrive here. However, there are plenty of buses leaving from Rue Yacoub el-Mansour in Agadir itself. CTM has daily buses to Casablanca, Dakhla, Essaouira/Safi/El-Jadida, Marrakesh, Laayoune/Smara, Taroudannt and Tiznit.

Most of the grands taxis leave from Inezgane. Destinations include Essaouira, Goulimime, Tan Tan, Taroudannt and Tiznit.

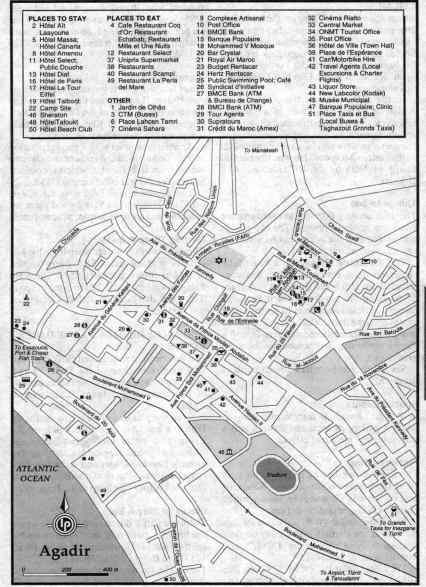

PLACES TO STAY
2 Hôtel Aït Laayoune
5 Hôtel Massa; Hôtel Canaria
8 Hôtel Amenou
11 Hôtel Select; Public Douche
13 Hôtel Diaf
16 Hôtel de Paris
17 Hôtel La Tour Eiffel
19 Hôtel Talborjt
22 Camp Site
46 Sheraton
48 Hôtel Tafoukt
50 Hôtel Beach Club

PLACES TO EAT
4 Cafe Restaurant Coq d'Or; Restaurant Echabab; Restaurant Mille et Une Nuits
12 Restaurant Select
37 Uniprix Supermarket
38 Restaurants
40 Restaurant Scampi
49 Restaurant La Perla del Mare

OTHER
1 Jardin de Olhâo
3 CTM (Buses)
6 Place Lahcen Tamri
7 Cinéma Sahara
9 Complexe Artisanal
10 Post Office
14 BMCE Bank
15 Banque Populaire
18 Mohammed V Mosque
20 Bar Crystal
21 Royal Air Maroc
23 Budget Rentacar
24 Hertz Rentacar
25 Public Swimming Pool; Café
26 Syndicat d'Initiative
27 BMCE Bank (ATM & Bureau de Change)
28 BMCI Bank (ATM)
29 Tour Agents
30 Supratours
31 Crédit du Maroc (Amex)
32 Cinéma Rialto
33 Central Market
34 ONMT Tourist Office
35 Post Office
36 Hôtel de Ville (Town Hall)
39 Place de l'Espérance
41 Car/Motorbike Hire
42 Travel Agents (Local Excursions & Charter Flights)
43 Liquor Store
44 New Labcolor (Kodak)
45 Musée Municipal
47 Banque Populaire; Clinic
51 Place Taxis et Bus (Local Buses & Taghazout Grands Taxis)

MOROCCO

ASILAH

About 46km south of Tangier, the attractive, little port of Asilah has enjoyed a tumultuous history well out of proportion to its size. Settled first by the Carthaginians and then the Romans, it came under Portuguese and Spanish control in the 15th and 16th centuries respectively.

In the early years of the 20th century, Asilah became the residence of a powerful brigand Raissouli, who thwarted all attempts at interference by the sultan and various European powers and became master of all north-eastern Morocco. He was imprisoned finally in 1925 by the Rif chieftain, Abd el-Krim.

Things to See

The 15th century Portuguese **ramparts** are intact, but access is limited. The two prongs that jut out into the ocean can be visited at any time and afford the best views.

The **Palais de Raissouli**, a beautifully preserved three storey building, was constructed in 1909 and includes a terrace overlooking the sea from which Raissouli forced convicted murderers to jump to their deaths onto the rocks 30m below. The palace now houses exhibitions; entry is free. It's closed on Friday and sometimes between exhibitions.

Several decent **beaches** stretch north of the town.

Special Events

In August, Asilah is transformed into an outdoor gallery as local and foreign artists celebrate the Fine Arts Festival.

Places to Stay

There are a number of resorts/camp sites along the beaches north of town. About the best of these is *Camping As-Saada*, which charges US$1 per person and car.

The *Hôtel Asilah* (☎ 91 7286) on 79 Ave Hassan II has small but clean singles/doubles without shower for US$4/7, and with shower for US$10/13.

The *Hôtel Belle Vue* (☎ 91 7747) on Rue al-Khansa offers comfortable doubles (no singles) with shared shower and toilet for US$15, up to US$21 in summer. It also has larger self-contained apartments with lounge, kitchen and refrigerator for US$26 to US$52.

Places to Eat

There is a string of restaurants and cafes on Ave Hassan II and around the corner on Rue Imam al-Assili. One of the best is the *Restaurant Sevilla* at 18 Rue Imam al-Assili, where a main course costs around US$3.

Another restaurant with a good reputation is the Spanish-run *Restaurante Oceano* across from Bab Kasaba, which specialises in fish. A full meal costs around US$8.

The *Boulanagerie Pâtisserie La Plage*, off Place Mohammed V, is a good place for breakfast and tea or to prepare a picnic lunch.

Getting There & Away

The best way to reach Asilah is by bus (US$1) or grand taxi (US$2) from Tangier, or by bus from Larache (US$1). There are trains, but the station is 2.5km north of town. There are also buses to Rabat, Casablanca and Meknès.

BOUMALNE DU DADÈS & THE DADÈS GORGE

The towering ochre-coloured cliffs and fabulous rock formations of the Dadès Gorge, just over 100km east of Ouarzazate, are one of Morocco's most magnificent natural sights.

From the pleasant town of Boumalne du Dadès, a good bitumen road winds up for 27km past *palmeraies* (oasis-like areas where date-palms, vegetables and fruit are grown), Berber villages and some beautiful ruined kasbahs. The road continues as *piste* (dirt track) up into the heart of the High Atlas.

Places to Stay & Eat

There are half a dozen simple hotels where the bitumen road runs out. Recommended are the *Hôtel La Kasbah de la Vallée* (☎ 83 1717) and *Hôtel La Gazelle du Dadès* (☎ 83 1753). The former has comfortable singles/doubles for US$7/9 and better ones with attached shower and toilet for US$13/16. The latter has cheaper rooms still. In both you can pitch a tent by the river or sleep on the roof for about US$1. The new *Hôtel Le Vieux Chateaux du Dadès* has rooms with bathroom for US$12/16. All these places have their own restaurants.

In Boumalne du Dadès itself there are several accommodation options. The *Hôtel Adrar*, across from the bus station, has simple rooms for US$5/7. The new *Kasbah Tizzarouine* (☎ 83 0690) has very comfortable rooms with bathroom for US$27.

Getting There & Away
To get up the gorge, there's an occasional grand taxi from Boumalne du Dadès to the village of Aït Oudinar, 24km up the valley, but you'll probably have to hire one especially – US$6 is the minimum to Aït Oudinar. On market days Berber camionettes travel between villages.

CASABLANCA
With a population of around three million and growing, Casablanca is Morocco's largest city and industrial centre.

Although its history goes back many centuries, including a stint of colonialisation by the Portuguese in the 16th century, it had declined into insignificance by the mid-1880s.

Its renaissance came when the resident-general of the French protectorate, Marshal Lyautey, decided to develop Casablanca as a commercial centre. It was largely his schemes that gave the new city its wide boulevards, public parks and fountains, and imposing Mauresque civic buildings (a blend of French colonial and traditional Moroccan styles).

Keep an eye out for the white, medium high-rise 1930s architecture, the Art Deco detail and the pedestrian precincts thronged with fashion-conscious young people. Casablanca is cosmopolitan Morocco and an excellent barometer of liberal Islam.

Information
The tourist office (☎ 27 1177) is at 55 Rue Omar Slaoui and the syndicat d'initiative is at 98 Blvd Mohammed V.

Amex is represented by Voyages Schwartz (☎ 22 2946) at 112 Rue Prince Moulay Abdallah.

Things to See
The old **medina** is worth a look, and provides a striking contrast with the **ville nouvelle**, centred around Place des Nations Unies. The latter has some of the best examples of Mauresque architecture, including the law courts, préfecture de police, main post office and French consulate.

The **Hassan II Mosque**, completed in 1993, overlooks the ocean just beyond the northern tip of the medina. One of the largest mosques in the world, it took 6000 craftsmen three years to complete. Though expensive, the 45 minute guided tour (US$11/5.50 for adults/students) is well worth it. It's one of the very few mosques in Morocco open to non-Muslims, and is an extraordinary testament to Morocco's continuing tradition of craftsmanship. There are tours every day, except Friday, at 9, 10 and 11 am, and at 2 pm, though times vary in summer.

Casablanca's **beaches** are west of town along Blvd de la Corniche and beyond in the suburb of 'Ain Diab. The beaches are reasonable but get very crowded in summer. Bus No 9 goes to 'Ain Diab from the bus station at Place Oued al-Makhazine, about 500m west of the Place des Nations Unies.

Places to Stay
A long way from the city centre on Ave Mermoz (the main road to El-Jadida), is the *Camping de l'Oasis* (☎ 25 3367). Bus No 31 runs past it.

The *Youth Hostel* (☎ 22 0551) at 6 Place de l'Amiral Philibert, just off Blvd des Almohades in the medina, is a large, comfortable and well-run place, and costs US$4 per person, including breakfast. It's open daily from 8 to 10 am and from noon until curfew time at 11 pm. It has hot showers, kitchen facilities and some 'family rooms' for US$11.

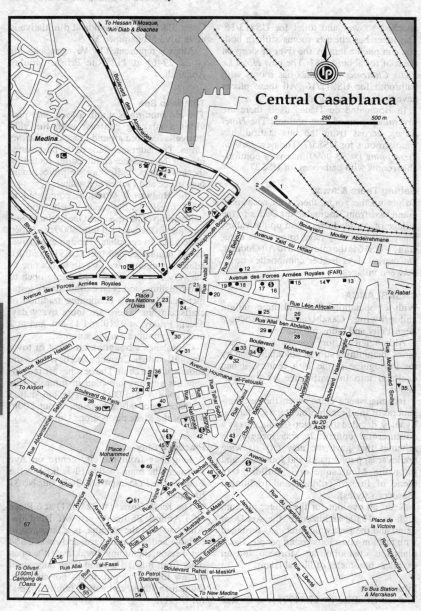

To Hassan II Mosque,
'Ain Diab & Beaches

Boulevard des Almohades

Medina

Central Casablanca

0   250   500 m

Boulevard Moulay Abderrahmane

Avenue Zaid ou Hmad

Blvd Tahar el-Alaoui

Boulevard Houphouet-Boigny

Rue Arabi Jilali

Rue Sidi Belyout

Avenue des Forces Armées Royales (FAR)

Avenue des Forces Armées Royales

Rue Léon Africain

Place
des Nations
Unies

Rue Allal ben Abdallah

Boulevard
Mohammed V

Rue Hassan Seghir

Rue Mohammed Smiha

Avenue Moulay Hassan I

To Airport

Avenue Houmane el-Fetouaki

Rue Tata

Boulevard de Paris

Rue Tahar Sebti

Rue Nationale

Rue Pergola

Rue Chaoui

Rue Ibn Batouta

Rue Abdallah

Rue Ahmed Bouhin

Place
du 20
Août

Rue Abderrahman Sahraoui

Place
Mohammed
V

Rue Prince Moulay Abdallah

Rue Farhat Hachad

Boulevard du 11 Janvier

Avenue
Lalla
Yacout

Boulevard Rachidi

Avenue Hassan II

Avenue Mers Sultan

Rue El Arafir

Rue Brey

Rue Mustapha el-Maani

Rue des Charmes

Rue Essarnbbar

Rue du Capitaine Bèaux

Place de
la Victoire

Rue Strasbourg

Rue Liberté

To Oliveri
(100m) &
Camping de
l'Oasis

Rue Allal
al-Fassi

Rue Omar Sidoui Sultan

To Petrol
Stations

Boulevard Rahal el-Meskini

To New Medina

To Bus Station
& Marrakesh

To Rabat

PLACES TO STAY		41	Swiss Ice Cream		27	Grands Taxis for
5	Youth Hostel		Factory			Rabatè
13	Hôtel Safir	45	Igloo Pâtisserie		28	Central Market
15	Hôtel Sheraton	48	Pâtisserie de l'Opéra		32	Cinéma Rialto
21	Hôtel de Foucauld	53	McDonald's		34	Post Office (PTT);
22	Hyatt Regency Hôtel					Syndicat
25	Hôtel Touring	**OTHER**				d'Initiative
	Restaurant Point	1	Casa-Port Train		38	Parcel Post
	Central		Station		39	Main Post Office
29	Hôtel Colbert	2	Centre 2000; La		40	English Forum
33	Hôtel Rialto		Cage Disco			Bookshop
37	Hôtel de Lausanne	3	Post Office		42	BMCE (ATMs)
49	Hôtel du Palais	4	Hammam		43	Cinéma Lux
		6	Mosque		44	Voyages Schwartz
PLACES TO EAT		7	Pharmacy			(Amex)
9	La Taverne du Dauphin	8	Great Mosque		46	Law Courts
14	Bar Nueva	10	Mosque		47	BMCI (Exchange)
26	Restaurant de	11	Clock Tower		50	Préfécture de
	l'Étoile Marocaine	12	Avis Rentacar			Police
30	McDonald's	16	BMCI (ATMs)		51	French Consulate
31	Pâtisserie Le	17	Budget Rentacar		52	Hammam
	Viennois	18	Royal Air Maroc			Essanoibar
35	Le Marignan	19	Europcar		54	Lynx Cinéma
	Restaurant	20	Hertz Rentacar		55	Tourist Office
36	Restaurant Snack	23	BMCI (ATMs)		56	Petrol Station
	California	24	British Centre		57	Stadium

The hotels in the medina are basic, without hot showers (though there are several hammams around) and cost around US$4 per person. You can do better outside the medina. One of the best cheapies is the *Hôtel du Palais* (☎ 27 6191) at 68 Rue Farhat Hachad near the French consulate, which has clean and spacious singles/doubles for US$7/8. Showers are communal and cold.

At 38 Rue Chaoui is the pleasant and clean *Hôtel Colbert* (☎ 31 4241), where rooms without shower start at US$7/8 or with full bathroom go for US$9/11.

Another popular cheapie is the *Hôtel de Foucauld*, which has rooms without shower for US$8/11 and rooms with shower for US$12/15.

Perhaps the best value of all is the *Hôtel Rialto* (☎ 27 5122) at 9 Rue Salah Ben Bouchaib, which has simple but spotless rooms with cold shower for US$9/12.

Of the two star places, one of the best is the *Hôtel de Lausanne* (☎ 26 8690), 24 Rue Tata. It has 31 immaculate rooms with bathroom for US$19/23.

Places to Eat

The best place for cheap restaurants, particularly rôtisseries (roast chicken joints) is the area opposite the Central Market on Rue Chaoui. Most are open until 2 am. Close by, next door to the Hôtel Touring, is the *Restaurant Point Central*, which is known for its midday tajine (under US$2). It often does couscous on Friday.

For fast food you could try the newly opened *Bar Nueva* on Ave des FAR between the Sheraton and Safir hotels. It serves delicious Lebanese snacks for US$2 and chawarma kebabs for US$5.

Another excellent place is the *Restaurant Snack California* at 19 Rue Tata. It's a bright, clean place, with excellent brochettes/tajine/couscous for US$3. It's also a good choice for vegetarians and women travelling on their own.

The *Restaurant de l'Étoile Marocaine* at 107 Rue Allal ben Abdallah, not far from the Hôtel Touring, is a friendly place where you can eat good Moroccan food in traditional surroundings for very reasonable prices, such as pastilla (pigeon pie) for US$4.

MOROCCO

If you're hankering after South-East Asian food, head for *Le Marignan* on the corner of Blvd Mohammed V and Rue Mohammed Smiha. It specialises in food cooked 'sur plaques' – Japanese style – in front of guests. Main courses cost around US$6. It's also air-conditioned.

For seafood, head straight for the well known *La Taverne du Dauphin* on Blvd Houphouët-Boigny. It's French-run and serves excellent, fresh fare at reasonable prices. A fish fillet costs around US$7 and a small plate of exquisite Dublin prawns US$5.

L'Oliveri at 132 Ave Hassan II is considered the best place in town for ice cream. The *Pâtisserie le Viennois* in the Passage Summica, off Ave Houmane el-Fetouaki, is known for its delicious cakes.

Entertainment
Central Casablanca has plenty of cafes, some of them interesting Art Deco leftovers. For a late night out, you have the choice of fairly sleazy nightclubs (some of them little more than escort bars) or the pricey hotel discos. One of the best of the latter is *Caesar's* at the Sheraton. Entry costs US$12 to US$15. Popular currently with the younger crowd is *La Cage* disco in the Centre 2000, near the port.

Getting There & Away
Bus The CTM bus station is on Rue Léon Africain at the back of the Hôtel Safir. Most of the other companies use the chaotic station off Rue Strasbourg, two blocks south of Place de la Victoire.

There are CTM departures to Agadir (five daily), Essaouira (two daily), Fès and Meknès (nine daily), Marrakesh (five daily) Oujda, Rabat, Safi, Tangier (six daily), Taza and Tetouan.

Train Most trains depart from the Casa-Voyageurs station east of the city centre, but the central Casa-Port station is more convenient. You can get local bus No 30 to Casa-Voyageurs along Ave des FAR and Blvd

Mohammed V. Otherwise it's an hour's walk or a US$2 petit-taxi ride.

Trains to Tangier, Oujda and Fès leave from both Casa-Port and Casa-Voyageurs. From the latter, there are also trains to Marrakesh and El-Jadida. The best bet for Rabat is to catch one of the high-speed shuttles that take 50 minutes and cost US$3 in 2nd class. They leave from both stations.

Taxi Grands taxis to Rabat leave from Blvd Hassan Seghir, near the CTM bus station. The fare is US$3.

Getting Around
The Airport There are 12 daily express trains from Casa-Voyageurs train station (US$2). A grand taxi to the airport, 30km south-east of the city, costs US$16 (US$21 after 8 pm).

Bus Bus No 30 runs along Ave des FAR and Blvd Mohammed V to Casa-Voyageurs station.

CHEFCHAOUEN
Also called Chaouen, Chechaouen and Xauen (pronounced shefsharwen), this delightful town in the Rif Mountains is a favourite with travellers: the air is cool and clear, and the surrounding hills are pleasant for hiking.

The town was founded by Moulay Ali ben Rachid in 1471 as a base from which to attack the Portuguese in Ceuta. With the late 15th century arrival of the Andalucians from Spain (who gave the town its unique Hispanic look of blue-washed houses and tiled roofs), the town prospered and grew.

The old **medina** is small, uncrowded and very easy to find your way around. Keep an eye out for the weavers working in tiny ground-floor rooms on the northern side of the medina. On **Plaza Uta el-Hammam** there is a **kasbah** with a small museum (entry US$1).

Places to Stay
On the side of the hill, behind the Hôtel Asma, are the pleasant *camping ground* and less pleasant *youth hostel* (☎ 98 6031). It's a

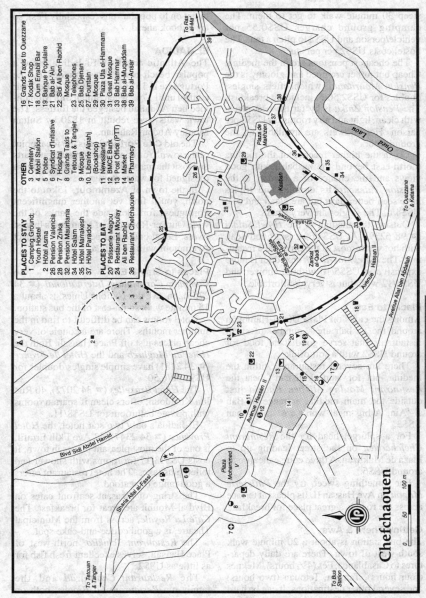

PLACES TO STAY
1 Camping Ground;
  Youth Hostel
2 Hotel Asma
26 Pension Valencia
28 Pension Znika
32 Pension Mauritania
34 Hotel Salam
35 Hotel Marrakesh
37 Hotel Parador

PLACES TO EAT
20 Patisserie Magou
24 Restaurant Moulay
  Ali ben Rachid
36 Restaurant Chefchaouen

OTHER
3 Cemetery
4 Mobil Station
5 Police
6 Syndicat d'Initiative
7 Hospital
8 Grands Taxis to
  Tetouan & Tangier
9 Mosque
10 Librairie Anahj
  (Bookshop)
11 Newsstand
12 BMCE Bank
13 Post Office (PTT)
14 Market
15 Pharmacy

16 Grands Taxis to Ouezzane
17 Kodak Shop
18 Oum Errabii Bar
19 Banque Populaire
21 Bab al-'Ain
22 Sidi Ali ben Rachid
  Mosque
23 Telephones
25 Bab Djenan
27 Fountain
29 Mosque
30 Plaza Uta el-Hammam
31 Great Mosque
33 Bab Hammar
38 Bab al-Muqaddam
39 Bab al-Ansar

Chefchaouen

To Ras al-Ma'

Oued Laou

Plaza de Makhzen

Kasbah

To Ouezzane & Ketama

Shara Assebanine

Plaza Mohammed V

Avenue Hassan II

Avenue Allal ben Abdallah

Blvd Sidi Abdel Hamid

Shara Allal al-Fassi

To Tetouan & Tangier

To Bus Station

Zankat al-Qadi

0   50   100 m

MOROCCO

steep 30 minute walk to get to them. The camping ground charges US$0.55 per vehicle/person and US$2 to pitch a tent. The hostel costs US$2 per person.

The cheapest pensions are in the medina. Cheap but rather cramped and gloomy is the *Pension Mauritania*, which offers singles/doubles for US$2.50/5, including breakfast. The *Pension Znika* is by far the best place, with clean, light and airy rooms for US$3 per person. Hot showers are available on the ground floor.

Up in the higher reaches of the medina (north-east beyond the kasbah), with good views and the chance of a breeze, is the *Pension Valencia*. Its doubles and triples have seen better days but are clean and cost US$4/6. The singles are very small.

Outside the medina is the *Hôtel Salam* (☎ 98 6239). At US$3/6, it is a good deal, with hot water most of the time and a restaurant. The *Hôtel Marrakesh* next door is more expensive at US$5/10 without shower and US$8/12 with, but is very comfortable.

Places to Eat
Among the cafes on Plaza Uta el-Hammam around the kasbah are a number of small restaurants that serve good local food for around US$2 with a soft drink.

There are several restaurants within the medina, but for value you can't beat the *Restaurant Moulay Ali ben Rachid* just outside the main medina entrance of Bab al-'Ain. A big meal won't cost more than US$3.

For a splurge, head for the *Restaurant Chefchaouen* on the street leading up to Plaza de Makhzen. A three course meal costs around US$6.

For something sweet, try the *Pâtisserie Magou* on Ave Hassan II. Its pleasant terrace across the road is a great place for breakfast.

Getting There & Away
The bus station is about a 20 minute walk south-west of town. There are daily departures to Casablanca, Fès (4½ hours), Meknès (four hours), Tangier, Tetouan (two hours) and several other destinations. It can be hard

to get on to popular runs (especially Fès), so try to book ahead.

EL-JADIDA
The Atlantic town of El-Jadida, now a popular beach resort, was founded by the Portuguese in 1513 and remained under their control until 1769 when Sultan Sidi Mohammed ben Abdallah besieged the fortress. The town walls were rebuilt in 1820 by Sultan Moulay Abd ar-Rahman.

The old **Cité Portugaise** is the focal point of the town. You can walk along the ramparts and visit the marvellous **Citerne Portugaise** (designed for water storage).

In the town of **Azemmour**, 15km to the north, you'll find yet another magnificent Portuguese fort alongside the banks of the wide Oum er-Rbia, one of Morocco's largest rivers. Local buses and petits taxis connect Azemmour with El-Jadida.

Places to Stay & Eat
Camping Caravaning International (☎ 34 2755), on Ave des Nations Unies, is about a 15 minute walk south-east of the bus station.

Hotel rooms can be difficult to find in the summer months. There are a couple of very cheap places just off Place Hansali. Both the *Hôtel du Maghreb* and the *Hôtel de France* (☎ 34 2181) have simple singles/doubles for US$4.50/6.50.

The *Hôtel Bruxelles* (☎ 34 2072), 40 Rue Ibn Khaldoun, offers clean if spartan rooms with private bathroom for US$8/11.

El-Jadida's only two star hotel, the *Hôtel Provence* (☎ 34 2347), 42 Ave Fkih Errafil, is one of the most pleasant places in town. It costs US$13/17 for rooms with shower and toilet, plus taxes. The hotel restaurant offers a good range of seafood.

The string of pleasant seafront cafes on Blvd al-Mouhit are great for breakfast. The *Café La Royale*, across from the Municipal Theatre, is a good coffee-and-cake spot.

The *Restaurant Tchikito*, north-west of Place Hansali, serves excellent fresh fish for as little as US$2.

The *Restaurant Chahrazad* and the family-run *Restaurant La Broche*, both on

Place Hansali, serve decent food for US$3 upwards.

Getting There & Away
The bus station is south-east of town on Rue Abdelmoumen el-Mouahidi, close to the junction with Ave Mohammed V, about a 15 minute walk from the town centre. There are several daily runs to Casablanca, Marrakesh, Rabat and Safi.

ER-RACHIDIA & THE ZIZ VALLEY
The pretty drive through the **Gorge du Ziz** north of Er-Rachidia (itself an administrative town) is the main attraction of the area.

Erfoud, the last main town at the southern end of the Ziz Valley, is the take-off point for visits to the **Erg Chebbi**, a fabulous ever-shifting landscape of Saharan sand dunes.

Places to Stay & Eat
Camping Source Bleue de Meski is 23km south of Er-Rachidia along the Erfoud road. It is a pleasant place with a great natural spring and pool.

In Er-Rachidia, the *Hôtel Restaurant Renaissance* (☎ 57 2633) on Rue Moulay Youssef has rooms without/with shower for US$3/8. The new *Hôtel M'Daghra* (☎ 57 4047) on Rue M'daghra Ouad Lahmer, almost opposite the bus station, offers comfortable singles/doubles with bathroom for US$11/17.

The popular *Restaurant Sijilmassa* is on the main street of Er-Rachidia – look for the 'All food is here' sign. The range of dishes (about US$5 for a full meal) is limited, but the food is good. Across the road, the *Restaurant Imilchil* and *Restaurant Lipton* also offer decent cheap meals.

Getting There & Away
All buses from Er-Rachidia operate from the central bus station. CTM has daily departures to Casablanca, Marrakesh, Meknès, Ouarzazate, Rissani (via Erfoud) and Tinerhir. Grands taxis go to Azrou, Erfoud, Fès and Meknès.

ESSAOUIRA
Essaouira, with its colourful fishing port, ramparts, woodcarving workshops and relaxed feel, is the most popular coastal town with independent travellers. It was founded in the 16th century by the Portuguese but the present town dates largely from around 1765, when Sultan Sidi Mohammed bin Abdallah hired a French architect to redesign the town as a centre for trade with Europeans.

Information
The syndicat d'initiative (☎ 47 3630) is on Rue de Caire, just inside Bab-es Sebaa. It's open from 9 am to noon and 3 to 6.30 pm Monday to Friday.

Things to See & Do
You can walk along most of the **ramparts** on the seaward part of town and visit the two main **forts** *(skalas)* during daylight hours.

The small **museum** on Darb Laalouj al-Attarin has displays of jewellery, costumes, weapons, musical instruments and carpets.

The **beach** stretches some 10km down the coast to the sand dunes of Cap Sim. There are a couple of places on the beach where you can hire **windsurfing** gear.

Places to Stay
The best *camp site* is about 3km past the village of Diabat, next to the Auberge Tangaro. Drive about 6km south of Essaouira on the Agadir road and then turn right just after the bridge. *Camping International*, the camp site in town, is pretty basic.

The popular *Hôtel Smara* (☎ 47 2655) on Rue de la Skala has sea views and is quiet and clean. Single/double rooms cost US$6/8, showers are US$0.20 and breakfast costs US$1.

The central *Hôtel Beau Rivage* (☎ /fax 47 2925) overlooks Place Prince Moulay Hassan. Rooms with two beds cost US$8, or US$13 with shower. Hot water is available most of the time.

The *Hôtel du Tourisme* (☎ 47 2075), Rue Mohammed ben Massaoud, has reasonable rooms for US$4/6.

MOROCCO

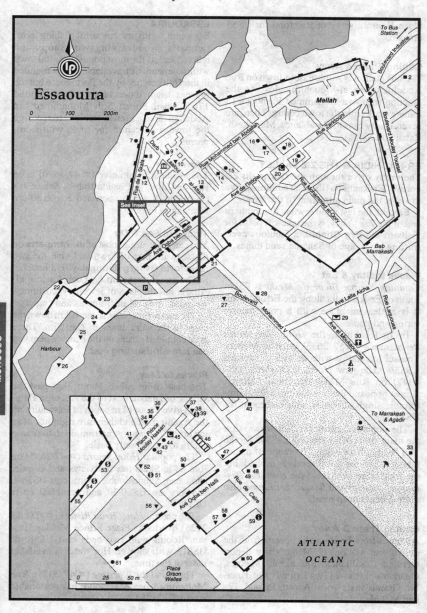

Essaouira

0   100   200m

To Bus Station

Boulevard Industrie

Mellah

Rue Zerktouni

Boulevard Moulay Youssef

Rue Mohammed ben Abdallah

Rue Mohammed el-Qory

Rue de l'Istiqlal

Ave de l'Istiqlal

Darb Laalouj

el-Attarin

Rue de la Skala

Bab Marrakesh

See Inset

Ave Oqba ben Nafii

Harbour

Boulevard Mohammed V

Ave Lalla Aicha

Rue Laaroussa

Ave el Moukaouama

To Marrakesh & Agadir

Place Prince Moulay Hassan

Ave Oqba ben Nafii

Rue de Caire

Place Orson Welles

0   25   50 m

ATLANTIC OCEAN

MOROCCO

PLACES TO STAY			
2	Hôtel Argana		
8	Hôtel Smara		
9	Hôtel Majestic		
12	Hôtel des Remparts		
13	Hôtel Riad Al Madina		
14	Hôtel Chakib		
17	Hôtel des Amis		
28	Hôtel de Iles		
31	Camping International		
33	Hôtel Tafoukt		
35	Hôtel Beau Rivage		
40	Hôtel Tafraout		
48	Hôtel Mechouar		
49	Hôtel Sahara		
50	Hôtel Villa Maroc		
60	Hôtel du Tourisme		

PLACES TO EAT			
1	Cafe		
3	Cheap Eats		
10	Restaurant El Khaima		
24	Restaurant Le Coquillage		
25	Fish Grills		

26	Chez Sam
27	Restaurant Chalet de la Plage
34	Cafe de France
36	Cafe/Pâtisserie l'Opéra
37	Café de la Place
38	Driss Pâtisserie
41	Cafe Marrakech
43	Snack Stand
47	Restaurant l'Horloge
52	Restaurant Essalam
55	Restaurant Bab Laachour
56	Cafe
57	Restaurant El Minzah

OTHER	
4	Bab Doukkala
5	Bab al Bahr
6	Entry to Ramparts
7	Skala de la Ville; Woodworkers' Workshops
11	Museum
15	Women's Hammam

16	Spice, Herbs & Cures Shops
18	Spice Souk
19	Jewellers' Souk
20	Mosque
21	Bab-es Sebaa
22	Skala du Port
23	Customs; Fish Market
29	Post Office
30	Church
32	Windsurfer Hire; Cafés
39	BMCE Bank
42	Afalkai Art
44	Jack's Kiosk
45	Mosque
46	Carpet & Curio Shops
51	Crédit du Maroc
53	Banque Populaire
54	Banque Commerciale du Maroc
58	Galerie d'Art
59	Syndicat d'Initiative
61	Bab al Minzah

The one star *Hotel Tafraout* (☎ 47 2120), 7 Rue de Marrakech, off Rue Mohammed ben Abdallah, is excellent value. Well-maintained rooms cost US$7/9 without bathroom or US$8.50/10 with.

The two star *Hôtel Sahara* (☎ 47 2292), Ave Oqba ben Nafii, has rooms without shower or toilet for US$9/12, and with shower and toilet for US$18/21.

Places to Eat

For breakfast you can't beat the cafes on Place Prince Moulay Hassan. The *Cafe/Pâtisserie l'Opéra* is very good. The *Driss Pâtisserie* sells fine croissants and other pastries.

For snacks there are a few simple little places along Rue Mohammed ben Abdallah, Rue Zerktouni and in the mellah (Jewish quarter of the medina) just inside Bab Doukkala. On Place Prince Moulay Hassan there are two stands selling fresh baguettes (about US$2) stuffed with meat, salad and just about anything else you want.

At the popular *Restaurant Essalam* on Place Prince Moulay Hassan you can enjoy an excellent meal for around US$5. The tajine is exceptionally good.

In the port area are two worthwhile seafood restaurants, *Chez Sam* and *Le Coquillage*, which have set menus starting at US$8. On the eastern side of the port you can take your pick from the catch of the day at the cheap fish grills set up outdoors between 11 am and 7 pm.

Though pricey, the restaurant in the *Villa Maroc*, 10 Rue Abdallah ben Yassin, offers excellent food in exquisite surroundings. Expect to pay around US$17 for a full meal and be prepared to book ahead.

Getting There & Away

The bus station is 1km north-east of the town centre. There are regular departures to Agadir, Casablanca, Marrakesh and Safi. Grands taxis to Agadir (or neighbouring Inezgane) leave from a nearby lot.

JEBEL TOUBKAL

One of the most popular of the endless trekking possibilities in the High Atlas is the ascent of Jebel Toubkal (4167m), North Africa's highest peak. The Toubkal area is just over an hour's drive south of Marrakesh and is easily accessed by local transport.

MOROCCO

You don't need mountaineering skills to climb Toubkal, provided you follow the normal two day route. You will, however, need good boots, plenty of warm clothing, a sleeping bag, plus food and water.

The usual starting point is the pretty village of Imlil, 17km from Asni off the Tizi n'Test road between Marrakesh and Agadir.

Most trekkers stay overnight in Imlil. There are a handful of basic hotels and you can stock up here on food and drink for the trek. In winter it's possible to hire crampons and ice axes.

Trekking in the Toubkal Area
Toubkal Trek The first day's walk takes you up for about five hours to the Toubkal hut (3207m), which sleeps 29 people in two dormitories. It costs US$6 for Club Alpin Français (CAF) nonmembers. In summer you'll need to book ahead through the CAF (☎ 27 0090; fax 29 7292), 1 Rue Henri, BP 6178, Casablanca, or the CAF, BP 888, Marrakesh. There are plans to build a second hut at Toubkal.

The ascent from the hut to the summit should take about four hours and the descent about two. Take water with you as any water from mountain streams is likely to carry giardiasis. It can be bitterly cold at the summit, even in summer.

Other Treks in the Toubkal Area In summer it's possible to do an easy one or two-day walk from the ski resort of Oukaïmeden (the CAF hut here is now open to nonmembers) south-west to Imlil (or vice versa) via the village of Tacheddirt, which also has a CAF refuge. In winter Oukaïmeden offers good skiing (best between February and April). There's regular transport from Marrakesh.

From Tacheddirt there are numerous trekking possibilities, including a pleasant two day walk north-east to the village of Setti Fatma (accessible by public transport from Marrakesh) via the village of Timichi, where there is a welcoming *gîte* (literally 'resting place'; a village house with rooms and basic kitchen facilities). A longer circuit could take you south to Amsouzart and back towards

Imlil via Lac d'Ifni, Toubkal, Tazarhart (there's a refuge here and good rock-climbing) and Tizi Oussem.

Books & Maps Every year the Moroccan Tourist Office publishes the *Great Trek through the Moroccan Atlas* which is full of practical information, including transport details, accommodation options, a list of registered mountain guides and current tariffs.

Volume One of Michael Peyron's book *Great Atlas Traverse*, published in the UK by West Col Productions, covers the Toubkal massif. Another excellent guide (in French) is *Le Haut Atlas Central* by André Fougerolles (Guide Alpin).

Detailed maps are available from Division de la Carte (☎ 70 5311; fax 70 5885), 31 Ave Hassan, Rabat.

Guides & Porters You don't need a guide for the normal two day Toubkal trek, but for longer walks it's advisable to engage a guide, mule-driver and mule (you're looking at around US$30 per day for this). There are plenty of official mountain guides in Imlil; ask at the CAF Refuge or Bureau des Guides.

Places to Stay
Imlil A good place to stay is the *CAF Refuge* on the village square, which offers dormitory-style accommodation for US$2 (CFA members), US$3 (HI members) and US$3.50 (nonmembers). There's a common room with an open fireplace, cooking facilities, cutlery and crockery.

The *Hôtel el Aine* has bright, comfortable rooms for US$3 per person, and the rebuilt *Café Soleil* (☎ 34 9209) has singles/doubles with shower for US$4/8. It also has a good cheap restaurant.

Getting There & Away
There are frequent buses (US$1) and grands taxis (US$1) to Asni from Bab er Rob in Marrakesh. From Asni, camionettes operate fairly frequently to Imlil and will take passengers for around US$2. A grand taxi from Asni costs about US$11.

FÈS

Fès, most ancient of the imperial cities, was founded shortly after the Arabs first swept across North Africa. It has served as Morocco's capital several times and for long periods. It is the most complete medieval city of the Arab world, and Fassis, the people of Fès, justifiably look on their city as the cultural and spiritual capital of Morocco.

The medina of Fès el-Bali (Old Fès) is one of the largest in the world and the most interesting in Morocco. Its narrow winding alleys and covered bazaars are crammed with craft workshops, food markets, mosques, *medersas* (collèges of theology, law, Arabic literature and grammar), and extensive dye-pits and tanneries. The pungent smells, the hammering of the metalworkers, the call of the muezzin, the crowded bazaars and the teams of laden donkeys create a memorable experience. The gates and walls surrounding the medina are magnificent.

Fès was founded by Idriss I on the right bank of Oued Fès in 789 AD, in what is now the Andalus quarter. Idriss II extended the city onto the left bank in 809; these two parts of the city constitute Fès el-Bali.

The city enjoyed its greatest period under the Merenid dynasty, who took it from the Almohads in 1250 and made it their capital. With the rise of the Saadians in the 16th century, Marrakesh once again gained the ascendancy and Fès slipped into relative obscurity. It was briefly revived under the Alawite ruler Moulay Abdallah in the 19th century. In 1916 the French began building the ville nouvelle on the plateau to the southwest of the two ancient cities.

Information

The ONMT office (☎ 62 3460) is on Place de la Résistance in the new city. It offers official guides for tours of the medina at an expensive US$16/13 for a full/half day. Plenty of unofficial guides hang around Bab Bou Jeloud and in the new city and will guide you for a lot less, but you'll have to bargain hard. If you have limited time, or don't like the idea of being lost in a medina, a guide can be useful.

If you don't enlist a guide, you will be hassled to take one, which can be wearing. Once inside the medina, however, you will largely be left alone.

Fès el-Bali

The old walled medina is the area of most interest. The most convenient entry point is **Bab Bou Jeloud**. Unfortunately, many of the religious monuments are closed to non-Muslims.

Just in from Bab Bou Jeloud is the **Medersa Bou Inania**, built by the Merenid sultan Bou Inan between 1350 and 1357. It is one of the few functioning religious buildings that non-Muslims may enter. The carved woodwork is magnificent and there are excellent views over Fès from the roof. The medersa is open daily from 8 am to 5 pm, except at prayer times and Friday mornings. Entry costs US$1.

In the guts of the city is the **Kairaouine Mosque**, one of the largest mosques in Morocco. Founded between 859 and 862 by Fatma bint Mohammed ben Feheri for her fellow refugees from Tunisia, it has one of the finest libraries in the Muslim world. Unfortunately, it's not open to non-Muslims.

Nearby, the **Medersa el-Attarine** was built by Abu Said in 1325 and has some particularly beautiful examples of Merenid craftsmanship. It's open daily from 9 am to noon and 2 to 6 pm, but closed Friday mornings. Entry is US$1.

Near Bab Bou Jeloud, on the boundary between Fès el-Bali and Fès el-Jdid, is the interesting **Dar Batha** (Musée du Batha) on Place de l'Istiqlal. Built as a palace about 100 years ago by Moulays al-Hassan and Abd al-Aziz, it houses historical and artistic artefacts from ruined or decaying medersas, as well as Fassi embroidery, tribal carpets and ceramics. It's open daily, except Tuesday, from 8.30 am to noon and 2.30 to 6.30 pm. Entry costs US$1.

Fès el-Jdid

The other walled city, built next to Fès el-Bali by the Merenids in the 13th century, has the old Jewish quarter (mellah) and a couple

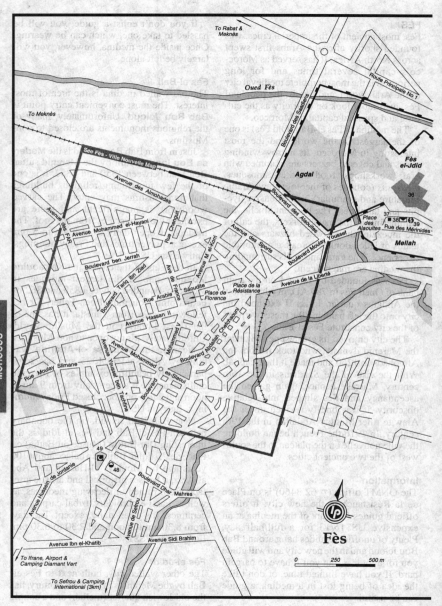

To Rabat &
Meknès

Oued Fès

To Meknès

See Fès - Ville Nouvelle Map

Route Principale No 1

Boulevard des Saadiens

Agdal

Fès el-Jdid

36

Boulevard des Alaouites

Avenue des Almohades

Avenue des FAR

Avenue Mohammed el-Hayani

Rue Chenguit

Avenue des Sports

Boulevard ben Jerrah

Boulevard Tariq Ibn Ziad

Avenue M el-Korri

Ave de France

Séaoûlte

Rue Arabie

Mohammed V

Place de
Florence

Place de la
Résistance

Avenue Hassan II

Avenue Mohammed
es-Slaoui

Boulevard Abdalla Chefchaouni

Boulevard
Youssef ben Tachfine

Rue Moulay Slimane

49

48

Avenue Hussein de Jordanie

Boulevard Dhar
Mahres

Avenue de Sefrou

Avenue Ibn el-Khatib

Avenue Sidi Brahim

To Ifrane, Airport &
Camping Diamant Vert

To Sefrou & Camping
International (3km)

Boulevard Moulay Youssef

Place
des
Alaouites

37

38

39

Rue des Mérinides

Mellah

Avenue de la Liberté

0   250   500 m

Fès

MOROCCO

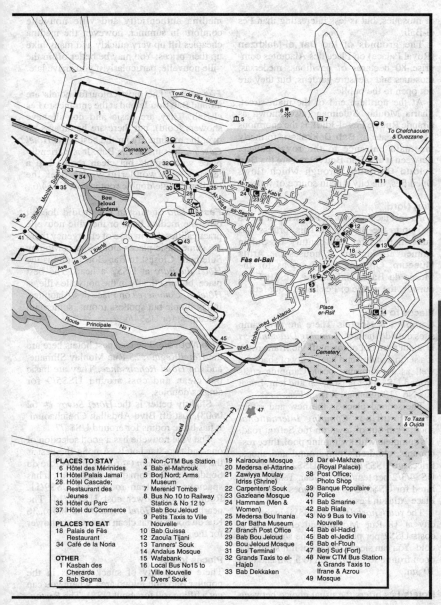

MOROCCO

PLACES TO STAY
1 Hôtel des Mérinides
11 Hôtel Palais Jamaï
28 Hôtel Cascade;
   Restaurant des
   Jeunes
35 Hôtel du Parc
37 Hôtel du Commerce

PLACES TO EAT
18 Palais de Fès
   Restaurant
34 Café de la Noria

OTHER
1 Kasbah des
   Cherarda
2 Bab Segma

3 Non-CTM Bus Station
4 Bab el-Mahrouk
5 Borj Nord; Arms
   Museum
7 Merenid Tombs
8 Bus No 10 to Railway
   Station & No 12 to
   Bab Bou Jeloud
9 Petits Taxis to Ville
   Nouvelle
10 Bab Guissa
12 Zaouïa Tijani
13 Tanners' Souk
14 Andalus Mosque
15 Wafabank
16 Local Bus No15 to
   Ville Nouvelle
17 Dyers' Souk

19 Kairaouine Mosque
20 Medersa el-Attarine
21 Zawiyya Moulay
   Idriss (Shrine)
22 Carpenters' Souk
23 Gazleane Mosque
24 Hammam (Men &
   Women)
25 Medersa Bou Inania
26 Dar Batha Museum
27 Branch Post Office
29 Bab Bou Jeloud
30 Bou Jeloud Mosque
31 Bus Terminal
32 Grands Taxis to el-
   Hajeb
33 Bab Dekkaken

36 Dar el-Makhzen
   (Royal Palace)
38 Post Office;
   Photo Shop
39 Banque Populaire
40 Police
41 Bab Smarine
42 Bab Riafa
43 No 9 Bus to Ville
   Nouvelle
44 Bab el-Hadid
45 Bab el-Jedid
46 Bab el-Ftouh
47 Borj Sud (Fort)
48 New CTM Bus Station
   & Grands Taxis to
   Ifrane & Azrou
49 Mosque

of mosques, but is less interesting than Fès el-Bali.

The grounds of the **Dar el-Makhzen** (Royal Palace) on Place des Alaouites comprise 80 hectares of pavilions, medersas, mosques and pleasure gardens, but they are not open to the public.

At the northern end of the main street, Sharia Moulay Suleiman (also known as Grande Rue de Fès el-Jdid), is the enormous Merenid gate of **Bab Dekkaken**, formerly the main entrance to the royal palace. Between it and Bab Bou Jeloud are the **Bou Jeloud Gardens**, through which flows Oued Fès, the city's main source of water.

Borj Nord

For a spectacular view of Fès, walk or take a taxi up to the Borj Nord. This fortress was built in the late 16th century by Sultan Ahmed al-Mansour. It houses the **Arms Museum**. Opening hours are as for the Musée du Batha and entry is US$1. From outside, the whole of Fès lies at your feet.

Places to Stay

Camping & Hostels There are two camp sites outside the city. *Camping Diamant Vert* is about 6km out of town off the Ifrane road. It's set in a valley and has plenty of shade, as well as a swimming pool. Camping costs around US$3 per person, car and tent. Local bus No 218 runs past it from Fès.

The second place is the new and rather more luxurious *Camping International* about 3km out of town on the Sefrou road. It's complete with swimming pool, three restaurants, children's playground and shops. Prices are US$5 for adults, US$2 for kids and US$4/3/2 per tent/caravan/car. Tents can be hired for US$5. Bus No 38 goes there from Place Atlas in Fès.

The *youth hostel* (☎ 62 4085) is in the new city at 18 Rue Mohammed el-Hansali. It costs US$2 per person and the showers are cold. You can sleep on the roof if it's full. It's open from 8 to 9 am, noon to 3 pm and 6 to 10 pm.

Hotels Fès offers the usual choice between medina authenticity and ville nouvelle comfort. In summer, however, the medina cheapies fill up very quickly and many hike up their prices. You may be better off in the ville nouvelle, particularly if you arrive late.

Fès el-Bali The most colourful hotels are around Bab Bou Jeloud at the entrance to Fès el-Bali. They are basic and not all have showers (cold), but there are hammams all over the medina. By far the best is the *Hôtel Cascade* just inside the Bab. It is a friendly place with simple but clean rooms and a terrace with wonderful views over the medina. Single/double rooms cost US$4/6.

Fès el-Jdid Staying in Fès el-Jdid doesn't offer the medina buzz or the ville nouvelle practicalities, but in case of emergency there are some basic places along Sharia Moulay Suleiman. Closest to Bab Bou Jeloud is the *Hôtel du Parc* at US$2 a head. The best place, but practically in the nouvelle ville, is *Hôtel du Commerce* on Place des Alaouites. It has simple but spotless rooms, some with balconies, for US$4/6.

Ville Nouvelle The cheapest hotels here are the *Hôtel Regina*, 25 Rue Moulay Slimane, and the *Hôtel Renaissance*. They are basic but clean and cost around US$5/9 for singles/doubles.

Slightly better is the *Hôtel Savoy* (☎ 62 0608), just off Blvd Abdallah Chefchaouni. It has basic rooms for around US$4/7.

The ville nouvelle has a good selection of one and two-star hotels. Among the best is the *Hôtel Kairouan* (☎ 62 3590), 84 Rue du Soudan (not far from the train station). It has spacious and clean rooms for US$9/11. Rooms with shower cost US$11/14. The nearby two star *Hôtel Royal* (☎ 62 4656), 36 Rue du Soudan, has clean rooms with shower for the same price.

Places to Eat

There are plenty of snack stands in the popular Bab Bou Jeloud area, where you can get a filling roll for about US$1. The *Restau-*

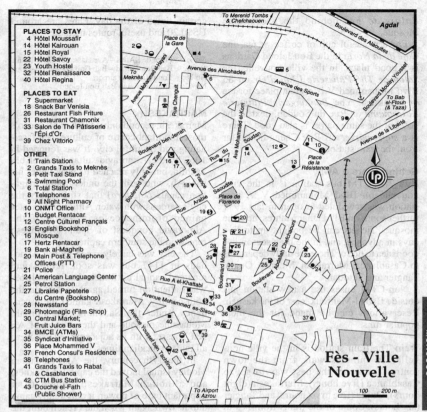

PLACES TO STAY
4   Hôtel Moussafir
14 Hôtel Kairouan
15 Hôtel Royal
22 Hôtel Savoy
23 Youth Hostel
32 Hôtel Renaissance
40 Hôtel Regina

PLACES TO EAT
7   Supermarket
18 Snack Bar Venisia
26 Restaurant Fish Friture
31 Restaurant Chamonix
33 Salon de Thé Pâtisserie
    l'Épi d'Or
39 Chez Vittorio

OTHER
1   Train Station
2   Grands Taxis to Meknès
3   Petit Taxi Stand
5   Swimming Pool
6   Total Station
8   Telephones
9   All Night Pharmacy
10 ONMT Office
11 Budget Rentacar
12 Centre Culturel Français
13 English Bookshop
16 Mosque
17 Hertz Rentacar
19 Bank al-Maghrib
20 Main Post & Telephone
    Offices (PTT)
21 Police
24 American Language Center
25 Petrol Station
27 Librairie Papeterie
    du Centre (Bookshop)
28 Newsstand
29 Photomagic (Film Shop)
30 Central Market;
    Fruit Juice Bars
34 BMCE (ATMs)
35 Syndicat d'Initiative
36 Place Mohammed V
37 French Consul's Residence
38 Telephones
41 Grands Taxis to Rabat
    & Casablanca
42 CTM Bus Station
43 Douche el-Fath
    (Public Shower)

Fès - Ville Nouvelle

0   100   200 m

MOROCCO

rant des Jeunes has simple meals for around US$5.

In the ville nouvelle there are a few cheap eats, along with pâtisseries and cafes, on or just off Blvd Mohammed V, especially around the central market. On Ave de France, the popular *Venisia* is one of the best snack bars in town. Hamburgers/brochettes cost US$2/3.

For something more substantial, the *Restaurant Chamonix*, in a side street a block south of the market, offers a limited range of good food. The set menu costs US$5. Nearby, on Blvd Mohammed V, the pleasant

Restaurant Fish Friture is a new place serving cheap and good fish dishes and pizzas from US$4.

The Tuscan-style pizzeria *Chez Vittorio*, opposite the Hôtel Central on Rue Brahim Roudani, is a pleasant place with reasonable salads/pizzas for US$3/5. It's licensed and is a good choice for vegetarians and women travelling on their own.

For a splurge (minimum of US$21 per head), try the restaurant *Al Fassia* in the Hôtel Palais Jamaï. A little cheaper are the several traditional restaurants set in centuries-old buildings in the medina, such as the

Palais de Fès behind the Kairaouine Mosque.

For a peaceful cup of coffee or tea, the *Café de la Noria* in the Bou Jeloud Gardens is a good place. In the ville nouvelle, the *Salon de Thé Pâtisserie l'Épi d'Or* on 85 Blvd Mohammed V is a great place for tea or breakfast. The *Boulangerie Pâtisserie Kairaouane* on Rue du Soudan, next to the hotel of the same name, is also good. There is a *supermarket* off Rue Chenguit not far from the train station.

Getting There & Away

Bus The CTM bus station is in the ville nouvelle on Blvd Mohammed V. A new station was scheduled to open in late 1997 further south on Blvd Dhar Mahres, near the mosque. Tickets can be bought up to five days in advance, and in the high season is a good idea to do so. There are daily departures to Casablanca, Marrakesh, Meknès, Oujda, Tangier and Tetouan.

Non-CTM buses use a new station just outside Bab el-Mahrouk, east of the kasbah. Reservations can be made for the most popular runs.

Train The train station is in the ville nouvelle, 10 minutes walk from the town centre. Trains are the best way to get to Casablanca (five hours), Marrakesh (eight hours), Oujda (five to six hours) and Tangier (six hours). Some of the trains from Fès to Marrakesh involve changing at Rabat or Casa- Voyageurs (Casablanca). All trains between Fès and Casablanca or Marrakesh stop at Meknès and Rabat.

Taxi Grands taxis for Rabat (US$5) leave from the streets around the CTM bus station on Blvd Mohammed V. Those for Meknès (US$1.50) leave from in front of the train station. Grands taxis for all other destinations leave from the bus station at Bab el-Mahrouk.

Getting Around

Bus Fès has a good local bus service, although the buses are like sardine cans at certain times of the day. Fares are around US$0.20 and useful routes include:

No 9: Place de l'Atlas – Ave Hassan II – Dar Batha
No 12: Bab Bou Jeloud – Bab Guissa – Bab el-Ftouh
No 16: Train station to airport
No 47: Train station to Bab Bou Jeloud

MARRAKESH

Marrakesh, second only to Fès as Morocco's most important centre of culture, is a fascinating and beautiful city. It was founded in 1062 by the Almoravid sultan Youssef bin Tachfin, but only reached its peak under his son, Ali, who built the underground irrigation canals *(khettara)* that still supply the city's gardens with water. Although Fès later gained prominence as a result of the Almoravid conquest of Spain, Marrakesh remained the southern capital.

The city was largely razed by the Almohads in 1147 but was soon rebuilt and renamed capital until their demise in 1269, when attention turned again to Fès. In the 16th century, Marrakesh gained the ascendancy under the Saadians. The mellah, Mouassine mosque and the mosque of Ali ben Youssef with its adjacent medersa were all built in Saadian times.

In the 17th century, the Alawite sultan Moulay Ismail moved the capital to Meknès, and although Marrakesh remained an important base of power, it only really came into its own again when the French built the ville nouvelle and revitalised the old town under the protectorate (1912-56).

Tourism has ensured its relative prosperity since then but it has also been responsible for some less desirable side effects. For a while, Marrakesh had the worst reputation of any place in Morocco for the number and persistence of its *faux guides* (see the boxed item titled Guides). Genuinely concerned about the impact on tourism, the authorities decided to act. Severe penalties for non-official guides have been introduced (up to three years in prison) and a tourist police brigade set up. The problem has improved significantly but will probably never entirely disappear so long as unemployment remains high.

Guides
Soaring unemployment and a very young population (50% under 20 years of age) has given rise to Morocco's most notorious phenomenon: the *faux guide*. The constant attention of these unwanted 'guides' can be the most unpleasant aspect of travelling in Morocco. The secret is not to allow it to be. Politeness and humour go far further than anger and impatience. Whatever you give a Moroccan, he will repay you twofold.

Look on the bright side: for no more than a pittance, you can get almost any service you want, anytime, anywhere. If only that were possible back home. ∎

Information
The tourist office (☎ 44 8889) is on Place Abdel Moumen ben Ali in the ville nouvelle. As in Fès, official guides (US$16/13 for a whole/half day) can be arranged here or in the big hotels.

Amex is represented here by Voyages Schwartz (☎ 43 6600), Immeuble Moutaouakil, 1 Rue Mauritania. The main post office is on Place du 16 Novembre.

The Hôtel Ali (see Places to Stay in this section) is a good place to head if you're interested in organised trips into the High Atlas or south into the desert. Two to 10-day excursions can be arranged with vehicles, camels, cooks and tents all provided.

Things to See
The focal point of Marrakesh is the **Place Djemaa el-Fna**, a huge square in the old city. Although lively at any time of day, it comes into its own in the late afternoon, when the curtain goes up on an extraordinary spectacle of jugglers, storytellers, snake charmers, magicians, acrobats and benign lunatics all competing for attention. In the evening, rows of open-air food stalls are set up and mouth-watering aromas fill the air.

The **souks** of Marrakesh are some of the best in Morocco, producing a wide variety of high-quality crafts, but they are also among the most commercialised. High-pressure sales are the order of the day and you should take any claim of silver, gold or amber with a very large pinch of salt. Even brass plates, leather work, woodwork and carpets vary enormously in quality. Be aware also that guides – official and unofficial – will be very keen to lead you to shops. It's there that they earn their money – on commission from your extortionate sale.

The **Ali ben Youssef Medersa**, adjacent to the mosque of the same name, was built by the Saadians in 1565. It was one of the largest theological colleges in the Maghreb, accommodating an extraordinary 900 students and teachers; entry is US$1. The only annexe to the mosque which survives is the **Koubba Ba'adiyn**, a rare and beautiful example of Almoravid architecture. Entry costs US$1.

The **Koutoubia**, across Place Foucauld from the Place Djemaa el-Fna, is the most famous landmark in Marrakesh. Built by the Almohads in the late 12th century, it is the oldest and best preserved of the three famous minarets (the Tour Hassan in Rabat and the Giralda in Seville, Spain, are the other two).

The most famous of the palaces of Marrakesh was the **Palais el-Badi**, built by Ahmed al-Mansour between 1578 and 1602. Now a ruin, it's open daily, except on certain religious holidays, from 8.30 am to noon and 2.30 to 6 pm. Entry costs US$1.

The **Palais de la Bahia** was built in the 19th century as the residence of the Grand Vizier of Sultan Moulay al-Hassan I, Sidi Ahmed ben Musa. Entry is free, but you must take a guide who will expect a tip. Nearby is the **Palais Dar Si Said**, now serving as the Museum of Moroccan Arts. Well worth a visit, it's open from 9 am to noon and 4 to 7 pm every day, except Tuesday (Friday between 11.30 am and 3 pm); entry is US$1.

Adjacent to the Kasbah Mosque are the **Saadian Tombs**, the necropolis begun by

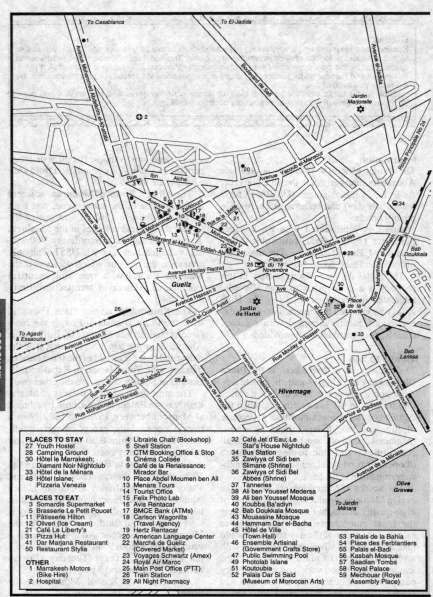

PLACES TO STAY
27 Youth Hostel
28 Camping Ground
30 Hôtel le Marrakesh;
   Diamant Noir Nightclub
33 Hôtel de la Ménara
48 Hôtel Islane;
   Pizzeria Venezia

PLACES TO EAT
3 Somardis Supermarket
5 Brasserie Le Petit Poucet
11 Pâtisserie Hilton
12 Oliveri (Ice Cream)
21 Café Le Liberty's
31 Pizza Hut
41 Dar Marjana Restaurant
50 Restaurant Stylia

OTHER
1 Marrakesh Motors
   (Bike Hire)
2 Hospital

4 Librairie Chatr (Bookshop)
6 Shell Station
7 CTM Booking Office & Stop
8 Cinéma Colisée
9 Café de la Renaissance;
   Mirador Bar
10 Place Abdel Moumen ben Ali
13 Menara Tours
14 Tourist Office
15 Felix Photo Lab
16 Avis Rentacar
17 BMCE Bank (ATMs)
18 Carlson Wagonlits
   (Travel Agency)
19 Hertz Rentacar
20 American Language Center
22 Marché de Geuliz
   (Covered Market)
23 Voyages Schwartz (Amex)
24 Royal Air Maroc
25 Main Post Office (PTT)
26 Train Station
29 All Night Pharmacy

32 Café Jet d'Eau; Le
   Star's House Nightclub
34 Bus Station
35 Zawiyya of Sidi ben
   Slimane (Shrine)
36 Zawiyya of Sidi Bel
   Abbes (Shrine)
37 Tanneries
38 Ali ben Youssef Medersa
39 Ali ben Youssef Mosque
40 Koubba Ba'adiyn
42 Bab Doukkala Mosque
43 Mouassine Mosque
44 Hammam Dar el-Bacha
45 Hôtel de Ville
   (Town Hall)
46 Ensemble Artisinal
   (Government Crafts Store)
47 Public Swimming Pool
49 Photolab Islane
51 Koutoubia
52 Palais Dar Si Said
   (Museum of Moroccan Arts)

53 Palais de la Bahía
54 Place des Ferblantiers
55 Palais el-Badi
56 Kasbah Mosque
57 Saadian Tombs
58 Royal Palace
59 Mechouar (Royal
   Assembly Place)

Marrakesh

0   250   500 m

To Ouarzazate,
Meknès & Fès

Route Principale No 24

Bab
el-Khemis

Bab
Kechich

Rue Assouel

Rue de Bab Taznout

Rue de Bab X-hemis

Route des

Bab
Debbagh

Remparts

Rue el Gza

Rue de Bab Debbagh

Rue de Bab

Doukhala

See Marrakesh
Budget Hotel Area

Rue Dar el-Glaoui

Rue Fatima Zahra

Rue Sidi el-Yamani

Rue Mouassine

Rue Souq ac-Smarine

Rue Azbezt

Rue Isseblyne

Bab
Ailen

Rue de Bab Ailen

Rue el-Kouloubia

Rue Dabach

Medina

Place Djemaa
el-Fna

Sebti

Avenue Mohammed V

Avenue
el-Mouahidine

Rue Graoul

Rue Ba Ahmad

Bab
Ghemat

Rue Riad Zitoun el-Jedid

Rue Riad Zitoun el-Qedim

Rue

Ave Houmane el-Fetouaki

Bab
el-Jedid

Rue de Bab Agnaou

Rue Sidi Mimoun

Ave Houmane
el-Fetouaki

Mellah

Bab
al-Ahmar

Bab
er-Rob

Bab
Agnaou

Rue de la Kasbah

Boulevard el-Yarmouk

To Airport

To Asni &
Taroudannt

Bab
Ksiba

Kasbah

To Ouarzazate

MOROCCO

the Saadian sultan Ahmed al-Mansour. They are open every day, except Friday morning, from 8 am to noon and 2.30 to 7 pm. Entry costs US$1.

Special Events
If you're in Marrakesh in June (the dates vary), don't miss the Festival of Folklore, which attracts some of the best troupes in Morocco. In July, there's the famous Fantasia, featuring charging Berber horsemen outside the ramparts.

Places to Stay
The *camping ground* just off Ave de France is around five minutes south of the train station and costs US$1 per person/per tent.

The *youth hostel* (☎ 44 7713), not far from the train station, costs US$2 a night and US$0.50 for a hot shower. It's a quiet place and a good first stop if you arrive late by train.

Most of the cheap hotels are in the area just south of the Djemaa el-Fna. Among the best are the *Afriquia* (☎ 44 2403) and *Medina* (☎ 44 2997), which charge US$3/6 for singles/doubles.

A little more expensive are the *Hôtel Essaouira* (☎ 44 3805) and *Chellah* (☎ 44 2977), with rooms for US$4/7. A hot shower is US$1. The *Hôtel Souria* has decent rooms for US$6/8.

For a little more money, there are some good one-star alternatives. *Hôtel Ichbilia* (☎ 39 0486) and *Hôtel Ali* (44 4979) are both recommended, with rooms for around US$8/11. On the Djemaa el-Fna itself and with good views is the *Hôtel CTM*. Rooms with shower and toilet are US$8/11.

The pick of the two star places here is the *Hôtel Gallia* (☎ 44 5913), 30 Rue de la Recette. It's spotless and has a quiet courtyard and hot showers. Singles/doubles with shower cost US$16/19, with bidet only US$11/13.

Along Ave Mohammed V heading west towards Bab Larissa is a good two star place, the *Hôtel Islane* (☎ 44 0081), with rooms for US$22/30, including an obligatory breakfast. Some rooms have balconies with views of the Koutoubia. There's also a rooftop restaurant and cafe.

Not far further west is the three star *Hôtel de la Ménara* (☎ 43 6478) on Ave des Remparts. It has a pool, garden and rooms with full bathroom, central heating in winter and air-con in summer for US$27/35, including breakfast.

Places to Eat
In the evening, the Djemaa el-Fna fills with all sorts of specialised food stalls. You can eat snacks for a few dirham, while a full meal won't cost more than US$2. Otherwise there are several small restaurants along Rue Bani Marine and Rue de Bab Agnaou. The *Étoile* offers a filling set menu for around US$4.

Excellent value is the self-service restaurant in the *Hôtel Ali* – all you can eat for US$6 (US$5 for hotel guests). Back on the Djemaa el-Fna itself, and perhaps the best place of all, is the justly popular *Café Restaurant Chez Chegrouni*. The food is cheap and good – couscous costs US$2.50.

The rooftop restaurant *Pizzeria Venezia* at the Hôtel Islane serves pizzas for around US$5 and traditional Moroccan fare for US$6. It also serves beer for US$2 and has good views of the Koutoubia.

If you're desperate to fill up on greens, you could try the decent self-service salad bar for US$3 at *Pizza Hut* on Blvd Mohammed V. Pizzas are not cheap, starting at US$5.

For the full Moroccan feast experience there is no better place than Marrakesh. Though undoubtedly targeting tourists, the food can be superb. If you have just one splurge in Morocco, this is the place to do it, but you'll need to reckon on about US$20 a head. One of the best for sheer atmosphere is the restaurant *Dar Marjana* (☎ 44 5773) near Bab Doukkala.

Just eclipsing it for quality of food is *Stylia* (☎ 44 3587) at 34 Rue Ksour. Here, recipes passed down from generation to generation justify Robert Carrier's description of Moroccan food as 'one of the truly great cuisines of the world'. Both restaurants are lost in the winding alleys of the medina. When you make a reservation (obligatory), a guide will be sent to meet you.

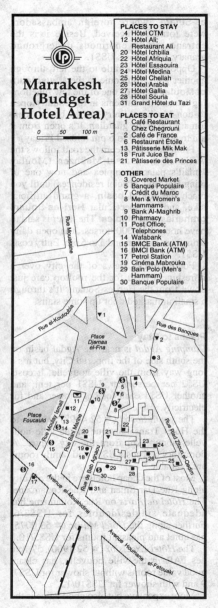

Marrakesh (Budget Hotel Area)

0   50   100 m

PLACES TO STAY
4   Hôtel CTM
12 Hôtel Ali;
    Restaurant Ali
20 Hôtel Ichbilia
22 Hôtel Afriquia
23 Hôtel Essaouira
24 Hôtel Medina
25 Hôtel Chellah
26 Hôtel Arabia
27 Hôtel Gallia
28 Hôtel Souria
31 Grand Hôtel du Tazi

PLACES TO EAT
1   Café Restaurant
    Chez Chegrouni
2   Café de France
6   Restaurant Étoile
13 Pâtisserie Mik Mak
18 Fruit Juice Bar
21 Pâtisserie des Princes

OTHER
3   Covered Market
5   Banque Populaire
7   Crédit du Maroc
8   Men & Women's
    Hammams
9   Bank Al-Maghrib
10 Pharmacy
11 Post Office;
    Telephones
14 Wafabank
15 BMCE Bank (ATM)
16 BMCI Bank (ATM)
17 Petrol Station
19 Cinéma Mabrouka
29 Bain Polo (Men's
    Hammam)
30 Banque Populaire

The ville nouvelle also offers good choices of mostly French and Moroccan cuisine for around US$6.

If you're hankering for something sweet, *L'Oliveri* has the best ice cream in town. It's in the ville nouvelle at 9 Blvd Mansour Eddahbi. For incredibly rich Moroccan cakes and pastries head for the famous *Pâtisserie Hilton* just off Mohammed V, opposite the Café de la Renaissance. A great place to start the day is the *Pâtisserie Mik Mak* next door to the Hôtel Ali, with good coffee and cakes at reasonable prices.

Entertainment

The *Mirador* bar at the top of the Café de la Renaissance is popular for its great views over the city. The best cafe in town is the new *Le Liberty's* at 23 Rue de la Liberté, which has a tearoom and a small garden at the back.

Many ville-nouvelle hotels have night-clubs with entry fees of between US$6 and US$12, including the first drink. Some of the most popular include the *Diamant Noir* in the Hôtel le Marrakesh on Place de la Liberté, and opposite, *Le Star's House*, next door to the Café Jet d'Eau.

Getting There & Away

Bus The bus station is just outside the city walls by Bab Doukkala, a 20 minute walk or a US$1 taxi ride from the Djemaa el-Fna. Popular destinations include Agadir (two buses daily), Casablanca (four daily), Fès (two daily) and Ouarzazate (four daily; four hours).

Train The train station is on Ave Hassan II, a long way from the Djemaa el-Fna. Take a taxi or bus No 8 into the city centre. There are trains regularly to Casablanca (four hours) and Rabat (five hours). From Rabat they continue to either Tangier (10½ hours) or Meknès (seven hours) and Fès (8¼ hours). These trips sometimes involve changing trains.

Getting Around

The Airport A petit taxi from Marrakesh to the airport, 6km south, should cost around

MOROCCO

US$6 but you'll rarely get one for that price. Bus No 11 runs irregularly from the airport to the Djemaa el-Fna. Bus No 8 runs between the train station and the Djemaa el-Fna.

MEKNÈS
Known rather hyperbolically as the Versailles of Morocco, Meknès nevertheless boasts some very impressive buildings. It is an attractive town, much less visited than either of its more famous sisters, Fès or Marrakesh. It also provides a convenient base for exploring the Roman ruins at Volubilis.

Although a town of considerable size even in the days of the 13th century Merenids, it wasn't until the 17th century that Meknès had its heyday when, in 1672, Moulay Ismail made it his capital. Over the next 55 years an enormous palace complex was built, encircled by some 25km of walls.

Information
The tourist office (**☎** 52 4426) and the main post office, on Place de France, are in the ville nouvelle, as are most of the banks.

Things to See
The focus of the old city is the famous **Bab el-Mansour**, one of the most impressive monumental gateways in all Morocco and the main entrance to Moulay Ismail's 17th century **Imperial City**. Opposite the gate on the far north side of the square is the **Dar Jamai**, a late 19th century palace that houses an excellent folk museum. It is open daily, except Tuesday, from 9 am to noon and 3 to 6.30 pm. Entry costs US$1.10.

The **medina** stretches away to the north behind the Dar Jamai; the most convenient access is through the arch to the left of the Dar Jamai. Along the main covered street you'll find the beautiful **Medersa Bou Inania**, built in the mid-14th century. It is open daily from 9 am to noon and 3 to 6 pm. Entry costs US$1, and there's a good view from the roof.

A visit to the Imperial City starts from Bab el-Mansour. Follow the road through the gate around to the small, white **Koubbat**

as-Sufara', where foreign ambassadors were formerly received. Beside it is the entrance to an enormous underground granary. Entry costs US$1.

Opposite and a little to the left, through another gate, you come to the **Mausoleum of Moulay Ismail** – one of the few functioning Islamic monuments in the country open to non-Muslims. Entry is free but it's customary to tip the guardian. It's open from 9 am to noon and 3 to 6 pm (closed Friday).

From the mausoleum the road follows the walls of the Dar el-Makhzen (Moulay Ismail's palace complex and now one of King Hassan's official residences) until you reach the **Agdal basin**, a grand artificial lake, and the spectacular **Heri es-Souani granaries and stables**. The latter is said to have housed 12,000 horses. It is open daily from 9 am to noon and 3 to 6 pm. Entry costs US$1.

For excellent views of the city over a refreshment head for the rooftop cafe just down from the Heri es-Souani. It's through a small unmarked door up some stairs.

Places to Stay
Camping Agdal is near the Agdal basin on the south side of the Imperial City, but it's a long way from the ville nouvelle. It costs US$2 per person/car, US$1 per tent, and another US$1 each for hot shower and for electricity.

The *youth hostel* (**☎** 52 4698) is close to the Hôtel Transatlantique in the ville nouvelle, about 1km from the city centre. A dormitory bed costs US$3 and family rooms are available.

Most of the cheap hotels are in the old city along Rue Dar Smen and Rue Rouamzine. The *Hôtel de Paris* on Rue Rouamzine has adequate singles/doubles for US$3/6. Further along the *Hôtel Maroc* (**☎** 53 0075) has quiet and pleasant rooms for US$5/10.

The *Hôtel Excelsior* (**☎** 52 1900), 57 Ave des FAR in the ville nouvelle, has clean, good value rooms without shower for US$7/9 and with shower for US$10/12.

More expensive but also good value is the

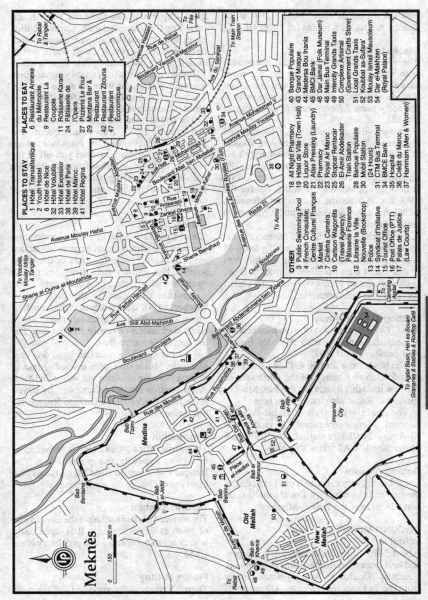

Meknès

0   150   300 m

MOROCCO

PLACES TO STAY
1 Hôtel Transatlantique
2 Youth Hostel
8 Hôtel de Nice
32 Hôtel Volubilis
33 Hôtel Excelsior
38 Hôtel de Paris
39 Hôtel Maroc
41 Hôtel Regina

PLACES TO EAT
6 Restaurant Annexe du Métropole
9 Restaurant La Coupole
11 Rôtisserie Karam
24 Pâtisserie de l'Opera
27 Pizzeria Le Four
29 Montana Bar & Restaurant
42 Restaurant Zhouna
47 Restaurant Économique

OTHER
3 Public Swimming Pool
4 French Consulate; Centre Culturel Français
5 Market
10 Cinéma Caméra
13 Carlson Wagonlits (Travel Agency); Pâtisserie Florence
12 Librairie la Ville Nouvelle (Bookshop)
14 Police
15 Syndicat d'Initiative
15 Tourist Office
16 Post Office (PTT)
17 Palais de Justice (Law Courts)
18 All Night Pharmacy
19 Hôtel de Ville (Town Hall)
20 Liquor Store
21 Atlas Pressing (Laundry)
22 Pharmacy
23 Royal Air Maroc
25 Stopcar Rentacar
26 El-Amir Abdelkader Train Station
30 Banque Populaire
30 Mobil Station (24 Hours)
31 CTM Bus Terminal
34 BMCE Bank
35 Hospital
36 Crédit du Maroc
37 Hammam (Men & Women)
40 Banque Populaire
43 Grand Mosque
44 Medersa Bou Inania
45 BMCI Bank
46 Dar Jamaï (Folk Museum)
48 Main Bus Terminal
49 Intercity Grands Taxis
50 Complexe Artisinal (Government Crafts Store)
51 Local Grands Taxis
52 Koubbat as-Sufara'
53 Moulay Ismail Mausoleum
54 Dar el-Makhzen (Royal Palace)

two star *Hôtel de Nice* (☎ 52 0318) at 10 Zankat Accra, with rooms for US$14/17.

Places to Eat

There are a number of simple restaurants with cheap standard fare in the old town along Rue Dar Smen, between the Hôtel Regina and Place el-Hedim. A good one is the aptly named *Restaurant Économique* at No 123.

In the ville nouvelle, *La Coupole* and *Rôtisserie Karam*, on and near Ave Hassan II, offer good, solid fare at moderate prices.

Pizzeria Le Four is very popular locally and serves delicious pizza for around US$4. It also serves alcohol but watch out for the 19% tax. Across the road is the *Montana*, which has a bar downstairs and a Moroccan restaurant upstairs.

To splash out in traditional Moroccan surroundings, try the *Restaurant Zitouna*, 44 Jamaa Zitouna, in the medina. Slightly less touristy, and with excellent Moroccan food, is the *Annexe du Métropole* on 11 rue Charif Idrissi in the ville nouvelle.

Getting There & Away

The CTM bus station is on Ave Mohammed V near the junction with Ave des Forces Armées Royales (FAR).

The bus station for non-CTM buses is just outside Bab el-Khemis on the north side of the new mellah. Grands taxis to Fès, Moulay Idriss and Rabat also leave from here.

The main train station is on Ave du Sénégal. More conveniently located is the El-Amir Abdelkader station, parallel to Ave Mohammed V. All trains stop here.

Getting Around

Local buses (very crowded) run between the medina and the new city. Local grands taxis leave from near the Bab el-Mansour.

AROUND MEKNÈS
Volubilis

About 33km north of Meknès are the largest and best preserved Roman ruins in Morocco. Volubilis (Oualili in Arabic) dates largely from the 2nd and 3rd centuries AD, when its

most impressive monuments were built, including the triumphal arch, Capitol, baths, basilica and the extraordinary mosaics that have been left *in situ*. It's well worth a visit, even if you're not normally into Roman relics.

If there are several of you, or you can form a group, you might want to share a guide. They do good one-hour tours for US$10. No other information is available on the site.

The site is open daily from dawn to dusk, and entry is US$2. Buses (infrequent) and grands taxis leave from the main bus station in Meknès. Get them to drop you off at the turn-off to Moulay Idriss, from where it's a half-hour walk. Going back you can hitch or walk to Moulay Idriss and wait for a bus or taxi.

OUARZAZATE

Created by the French in 1928 as a strategic garrison and administrative centre, Ouarzazate is a take-off point for tours of the 'deep south'. The journey here from Marrakesh over the Tizi n'Tichka pass is superb.

Another drawcard is the picturesque **Kasbah of Aït Benhaddou**, 32km north of Ouarzazate off the Marrakesh road, where films such as *Lawrence of Arabia* and *The Sheltering Sky* were shot.

From Ouarzazate, you can head due east along the Vallée du Dadès towards Rissani, or travel south-east along the Vallée du Duâa. A third option is to take the new, fully paved route from the Vallée du Duâa to Rissani via Tazzarine.

Information

The tourist office (☎ 88 2485) is in the centre of town, opposite the post office. The Banque Populaire on Blvd Mohammed V is open for exchange on weekends.

Taourirt Kasbah

The restored Glaoui kasbah at the eastern end of town is worth visiting. It is open daily from 9 am to noon and 3 to 6 pm. Entry costs US$1.

Places to Stay

There's a *camp site* (signposted) off the main

road out of town towards Tinerhir, about 3km from the bus station. Charges are US$1 per person and US$1 to pitch a tent.

It can be difficult to find a cheap hotel in Ouarzazate if you arrive late in the day. The *Hôtel Royal* (☎ 88 2258) offers rooms ranging from US$4 for a small single to US$18 for a four person suite. The nearby *Hôtel Atlas* (☎ 88 2307), 13 Rue du Marché, has clean singles/doubles without shower for US$4/7. Doubles and triples with shower are US$8/9.

The extremely pleasant *Hôtel La Vallée* (☎ 88 2668), about 2km out of town on the Zagora road, has comfortable rooms with shared shower for US$13, a decent restaurant and a small swimming pool.

Places to Eat
The *Café de la Renaissance* serves large helpings of brochettes, salad and chips for US$4. The *Restaurant Essalam* offers eight set menus for US$6. The restaurants at the hotels *Royal* and *Atlas* are also good value. You can eat well for about US$2 at the cheerful *Café Mimouza* near the new bus station.

Chez Dimitri, on Blvd Mohammed V, offers good (but not great) French and Moroccan dishes, very pleasant surroundings and an extensive wine list. A full meal costs around US$10.

Getting There & Away
CTM has a bus station on Blvd Mohammed V. SATAS and other lines depart from the new bus station about 2km west of town.

CTM buses go to Agadir (US$10), Casablanca (US$13), Er-Rachidia (US$8 via Boumalne du Dadès), Marrakesh (US$7) and Zagora (US$4). Grands taxis leave from the new bus station to Marrakesh (US$11), Tinerhir (US$7) and Zagora (US$9).

NADOR
This is the first Moroccan town you come to if you are arriving from the Spanish enclave of Melilla. There is little here of interest, but you may have to stay overnight. The *Hotel*

Assalam at the pedestrian mall is clean and quiet, and charges US$3 for a single room.

Bus No 19 goes to the border at Beni Ansar.

OUJDA
This is the last town before the Algerian border (closed at the time of writing). There is little of interest for travellers, but it's a relaxed place with a small but bustling medina. The Algerian Consulate (☎ 68 3740) is at 11 Blvd Bir Anzarane (also called Blvd de Taza). It is open Monday to Thursday from 8 am to 3 pm and Friday until noon.

Places to Stay & Eat
The best area for cheap hotels is in the ville nouvelle in the pedestrian precinct off Blvd Mohammed V. Probably the best value is the *Hotel Al-Hanna* (☎ 68 6003) close to the CTM bus station at 132 Rue de Marrakesh, which has spotless singles/doubles for US$4/6.

In the evenings, cheap food stalls are set up in the medina just inside Bab el-Ouahab. *Sandwich Taroudannt* on Blvd Allal beb Abdallah is quite a good place for traditional Moroccan fare. For breakfast, try the *Café le Tresor* on Blvd Mohammed V.

Getting There & Away
Bus CTM has buses to Rabat and Casablanca from an office behind the town hall. The bus station for all other buses is across Oued Nachef, about 15 minutes walk south from the train station. There are daily departures to Casablanca, Fès, Figuig, Rabat and Taza.

When the Algerian border is open, buses run the 13km every half-hour from near Place du Maroc. There are plenty of taxis at the border.

Train The train station is close to the town centre, at the end of Blvd Zerktouni. There are daily departures for Taza (four hours), Fès (6½ hours) and Meknès (7½ hours). Some trains continue to Tangier, Rabat and Casablanca. There is a morning train to the Algerian border.

Taxi Grands taxis to Taza and Fès leave from near the bus station; those to Nador and the Algerian border leave from Place du Maroc.

TAFRAOUTE

Some 120km south-east of Agadir, in the heart of the Anti-Atlas, is the pretty Berber town of Tafraoute. The nearby **Ameln Valley**, with its stunning rose-pink landscape and mud-brick villages, provides days of hiking possibilities. The journey from Agadir (or Tiznit) is rewarding in itself.

Places to Stay & Eat

Just outside town, off the Tiznit road, is *Camping Les Trois Palmiers*. It costs US$1 per person/per tent.

The *Hôtel Tanger* (☎ 80 0033) offers basic singles/doubles for US$2.50/5. Opposite, the *Hôtel Reddouane* (☎ 80 0066) has rooms for US$4/6.

Much better is the *Hôtel Tafraout* (☎ 80 0060), where you can get clean, modern rooms for US$5/11. There are hot, communal showers.

You can eat fairly well for about US$3 in either of the two cheap hotels. *Restaurant l'Étoile du Sud*, opposite the post office, is a more luxurious splurge – around US$8 for a tasty set menu.

Getting There & Away

CTM has an evening service to Tiznit (just over 100km west of Tafraoute) and another to Marrakesh and Casablanca via Agadir. There are at least two local morning departures to Tiznit.

TANGIER

As a strategic point commanding the Straits of Gibraltar, Tangier had been coveted for millennia. The site has been occupied successively by Romans, Vandals, Byzantines, Arabs, five dynasties of Berbers, the Portuguese, Spanish, British and French.

In the late 19th and early 20th centuries, Tangier became the object of intense rivalry between the European powers. A final solution was only reached in 1923, when Tangier became an 'international zone' controlled by the resident diplomatic agents of seven European countries, plus Sweden and the USA.

The city rapidly became a haven for freebooters, artists, writers, refugees, bankers, exiles and foreign misfits of every variety. It was also renowned for its high-profile gay and paedophile scene. Tangier lost its international status with independence in 1956, but did not lose all its privileges until a few years later.

Not quite as racy and exciting as it once was, the city nevertheless has an atmosphere quite unlike any other town in Morocco. As a major port of entry for tourists, Tangier is also home to the most adept hustlers and pick-pockets in the country. Always keep an eye on your belongings, and before disembarking at the port, know exactly where you're headed. Don't be waylaid by the myriad colourful stories or harmless threats the hustlers may throw at you. Keep your head down, ignore the hassle and get out of the port area; once out, you can ask for directions to your hotel in peace.

Kif

The smoking of Kif (cannabis) is an ancient tradition in northern Morocco. In the Kif mountains around the Ketama region, its cultivation is tolerated until another crop can be found that will grow as successfully.

Discreet possession and use is also, in practice, tolerated. Travellers should never be tempted, however, to buy more than small quantities for personal use. Never travel in possession with it, avoid buying it in Tetouan and Tangier, and mistrust all dealers: many double as police informers.

Never, ever be tempted to smuggle kif. Penalties are severe. About 40 Britons and Americans get arrested every year. ■

Information

The ONMT tourist office (☎ 93 8239) is at 42 Blvd Pasteur. There are plenty of banks along Blvd Pasteur and Blvd Mohammed V.

Things to See

In the heart of the medina the **Petit Socco**, with its cafes and restaurants, is the focus of activity. In the days of the international zone this was the sin-and-sleaze centre and it retains something of its seedy air.

From the Petit Socco, the Rue des Almohades (formerly Rue des Chrétiens) leads up to the **kasbah**, built on the highest point of the city. The entrance is through Bab el-Assa, which opens onto a large courtyard. Just beyond is the 17th century **Dar el-Makhzen**, the former sultan's palace and now an excellent museum. It is open daily, except Tuesday, from 9 am to 3.30 pm in summer and from 9 am to noon and 3 to 6 pm in winter; entry is US$1.

The **American Legation Museum** is in a fine old house in the medina. Opening hours are erratic, but entry is free. Knock to gain entrance.

Places to Stay

The best of the rather poor selection of camp sites is *Camping Miramonte*, about 3km west of the centre of town. Although a bit run-down, it's close to the beach and has a small pool. It charges around US$2 per person/tent/car. To get there, take bus No 12 or 21 from near the Grand Socco.

The clean and welcoming *youth hostel* (☎ 94 6127) is on Rue el-Antaki, just up past the Hôtel El Djenina. Beds cost US$2.50, and US$0.50 gets you a hot shower.

Tangier is full of cheap pensions. If you want to stay in the medina, one of best is the *Pension Mauritania* (☎ 93 4674) in the Petit Socco, which costs US$5/8 for singles/doubles. Showers are communal and cold.

On Ave Mokhtar Ahardan off the Petit Socco, two good bets are the *Hôtel Olid* (☎ 93 1310), which has rooms with cold showers for US$4 per person, and the *Pension Palace* (☎ 93 6128), which charges US$5/10 for spotless rooms without shower. Hot showers cost US$0.70.

There is a string of places along Rue Salah ed-Din el-Ayoubi (Rue de la Plage), running from the waterfront up towards the Grand Socco. The best of them are the *Hôtel Miami*, with rooms for US$5/8, and the *Pension Detroit*, which charges US$4/6. For showers and baths, there are several hammams and public douches in and outside the medina.

On the corner of Rue Ibn Joubair and Rue Targha, and with wonderful harbour views, is the one star *Hôtel Panoramic Massilia* (☎ 37 0703). Rooms with shower, toilet and hot water (in the morning) cost US$9/14.

If you prefer a modicum of luxury but still want to stay in the medina area, try the two star *Hôtel Mamora* (☎ 93 4105), 19 Ave Mokhtar Ahardan, which offers excellent, spotlessly clean rooms with shower for US$12/14 in the low season.

A good choice by any standard is the *Hôtel Continental* (☎ 93 1024), also in the medina. Used for some scenes in the film *The Sheltering Sky*, it is full of character. Rooms, some with views, cost US$16/22 (US$3 more in summer). It is advisable to book ahead.

Places to Eat

There are plenty of cheap eating possibilities in and around the Petit Socco and Grand Socco. Two good snack places, the *Sandwich Cervantes* and *Sandwich Genève*, are close to each other on Rue Salah ed-Din el-Ayoubi. Filled rolls cost under US$1.

For more substantial meals, head for the *Restaurant Populaire* down the steps from Rue de la Liberté. It's a favourite haunt with the locals and has excellent food at reasonable prices. *Restaurant Ahlan* on Ave Mokhtar Ahardan is also popular. A full meal costs around US$3.

The stretch of Rue du Prince Moulay Abdallah around the corner from the tourist office is laden with eating places. *Restaurant Romero* is an upmarket place known for its fish and paella. For food in traditional surroundings at reasonable prices, try *Raïhari*

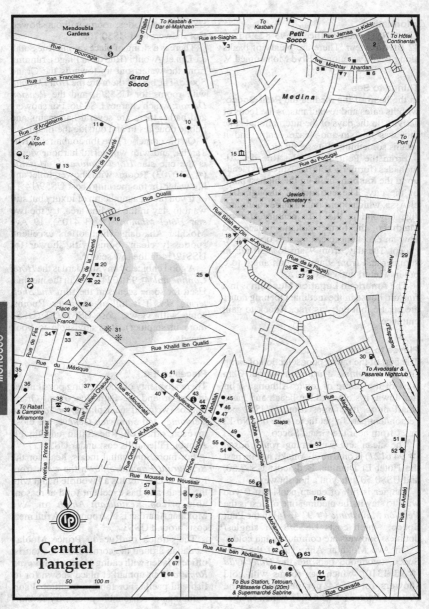

Central Tangier

0   50   100 m

PLACES TO STAY		OTHER		41	BMCE (Late Bank &
1	Pension Mauritania	2	Grand Mosque		ATM)
5	Hôtel Mamora	4	BMCE	42	Cybernet Café
6	Hôtel Olid	9	Hammam	43	Tourist Office
8	Pension Palace	10	Covered Market	44	Telephones & Fax
20	Hôtel El Minzah	11	Cinéma Rif	45	Budget Rentacarè
27	Hôtel Miami	12	Local Bus Terminal	47	Trasmediterranea;
28	Pension Detroit	13	Dean's Bar		Limadet Office
51	Hôtel El Djenina	14	Covered Market	48	Studio Samar (Photo
52	Youth Hostel	15	American Legation		Shop)
53	Hôtel Panoramic		Museum	49	Iberia Airlines
	Massilia	17	Studio Flash (Photo	50	Hôtel El Muniria;
			Shop)		Tanger Inn
PLACES TO EAT		22	Telephones & Fax	54	Avis Rentacar
3	Restaurant Mamounia	23	French Consulate	55	Librairie des Colonnes
7	Restaurant Ahlan	25	Gran Teatro de		(Book Shop)
16	Restaurant Populaire		Cervantes	56	Crédit du Maroc (Amex)
18	Sandwich Genève	26	Telephones	57	Paris Pressing
19	Sandwich Cervantes	29	Tanger Gare Train		(Laundry)
21	Pâtisserie La Española		Station	58	Pub
24	Cafè de Paris	30	Petrol Station	60	Pressing Dallas
34	Cafè de France	31	Terrace & Lookout		(Laundry)
37	Restaurant Raîhari	32	Pharmacy	61	Pharmacy
40	Petit Prince	33	Royal Air Maroc	62	Banque Populaire
46	Restaurant Romero	35	Night Pharmacy	63	Wafabank
59	Pâtisserie Rahmouni	36	Cinéma Le Paris	64	Post Office
		38	Telephones & Fax	65	Hertz Rentacar
		39	Stop Pressing	66	Cady Rentacar
			(Laundry)	67	Cinéma Roxy
				68	London Pub

on 10 Rue Ahmed Chaouki. Set menus are US$8 and main dishes US$5.

For cakes to take away, try the excellent *Pâtisserie Rahmouni* on 35 Rue Moulay Abdallah, or the *Pâtisserie Petit Prince* on 34 Blvd Pasteur. The *Pâtisserie Oslo* on 41 Blvd Mohammed V (with its cafe next door) is a great place for breakfast.

Entertainment
If you're seeking a cold beer, the old-time *Tanger Inn*, below the Hôtel El Muniria, is a good place which opens after 9 pm. The smarter *London Pub* on 15 Rue Mansour Dahabi is more like a jazz bar and is open from 6 pm until 2 am. Beers cost from US$2. The best disco in town is *Pasarela* on Ave des FAR. Entrance plus drink is US$10.

Getting There & Away
Bus Most CTM buses leave from an office near the port entrance. All others leave from the main bus station on Place Jamia el-

Arabia at the end of Ave van Beethoven, a good half-hour walk from the Grand Socco. CTM buses depart regularly for destinations including Casablanca, Rabat, Tetouan and Fès.

Train There are two train stations: Tanger Gare and Tanger Port; the former is more central. Trains run to Casablanca (six hours), Fès (six hours), Marrakesh (10 hours), Meknès (five hours), Oujda (12 hours) and Rabat (five hours).

Taxi Grands taxis leave from the main bus station; there are frequent departures to Tetouan (US$2) and Asilah (US$2).

Ferry If you're heading to Spain or Gibraltar by boat, you can buy tickets from virtually any travel agency or at the port itself. The Trasmediterranea and Limadet office is on Rue du Prince Moulay Abdallah. See the Getting There & Away chapter at the start of

MOROCCO

the book for details of services to/from Tangier.

TAROUDANNT

Taroudannt, with its magnificent, extremely well-preserved, red-mud walls, has played an important part in the history of Morocco. It briefly became the capital in the 16th century under the Saadians, who built the old part of town and the kasbah.

The city narrowly escaped destruction in 1687 at the hands of Moulay Ismail, after it became the centre of a rebellion opposing his rule. Instead, Moulay Ismail contented himself with massacring its inhabitants.

Things to See

You can explore the **ramparts** of Taroudannt on foot, but it is better to hire a bicycle or engage one of the horse-and-cart drivers. It's a long way around the walls.

You can find high-quality items in the small **souks**, especially traditional Berber silver jewellery. Some modest **tanneries** are just beyond Bab Taghount, north-west of Place Assarag.

Places to Stay

There are plenty of cheap hotels in the town centre, around or close to Place Assarag. On the square, it's a toss-up between the *Hôtel de la Place* and the *Hôtel Roudani*. Prices hover around US$4/9 for singles/doubles.

Closer to Place Talmoklate is the *Hôtel des Oliviers* (☎ 85 2021). It has clean beds for US$5/7. The showers are cold. Another reasonable deal is the *Hôtel Mantaga*, which has clean rooms for US$4/5.

The best deal by far is the creaky old *Hôtel Taroudannt* (☎ 85 2416). Its rooms gathered around a tranquil, leafy courtyard are full of character. They cost US$5/7 without bathroom and US$8/10 with shower. The water is boiling hot, the hotel has one of the few bars in town, and the food in the restaurant is good and moderately priced.

Places to Eat

The small cafes that line the street between Place Assarag and Place Talmoklate serve traditional food such as soup, salads and tajine. Several of these places serve seafood at rock-bottom prices.

Also very good are the restaurants on the ground floors of the *Hôtel de la Place* and the slightly more expensive *Hôtel Roudani*, which offers generous serves of brochettes, chips and salad for US$4. The faded but still rather elegant restaurant at the *Hôtel Taroudannt* makes for a good minor splurge, with tasty French and Moroccan food.

Getting There & Away

The main bus companies have stations on Place Assarag. SATAS buses run to Agadir and Marrakesh. CTM has a bus to Casablanca via Agadir and another to Ouarzazate. Local buses leave early in the morning for Marrakesh via the Tizi n'Test pass. Grands taxis and local buses leave from a lot outside Bab Zorgan, the south gate.

TAZA

Highly prized throughout Moroccan history for its strategic position, the town of Taza overlooks the only feasible pass between the Rif Mountains and the Middle Atlas.

Apart from its dramatic setting, the town's old medina is relaxed and worth a wander, particularly around the ramparts to **Bab er-Rih** (Gate of the Wind), from where there are excellent views over the surrounding countryside. The **Grande Mosquée** (Great Mosque), which was begun by the Almohads in 1135, is only open to Muslims.

If you have your own transport Taza makes a good base from which to explore the area around **Mt Tazzeka**, where you'll find the incredible caverns of the **Gouffre du Friouato**. Said to be the deepest in North Africa, the caves have only been partially explored. There are steps down the first 100m and plenty of natural light. After that you'll need a good torch. Pay the guardian to get in (about US$1 should suffice).

Places to Stay & Eat

In Taza's medina, about the only choice is the basic but clean *Hôtel de l'Étoile* inside Bab ek-Guebor. Singles/doubles are around

US$3. The *Hôtel de la Gare* (☎ 67 2443), near the train station, has rooms without shower for US$5/7 and with shower for US$8/9.

In the centre of the new town, the *Hôtel Guillaume Tell* (☎ 67 2347) has spacious rooms with double beds for US$4/6. The communal showers are cold.

The colonial-style *Hôtel du Dauphiné* (☎ 67 3567) is the best place to stay if you can afford it. Rooms without shower cost US$7/9 or with shower US$10/12. There's hot water in the evenings. Downstairs there's a bar and a dining hall.

The best of the few eateries in town is the *Restaurant Majestic* on Ave Mohammed V, where you can eat well for around US$3. The *Pâtisserie Amsterdam* on Avenue Moulay Youssef is an excellent place for tea or breakfast.

Getting There & Away

Buses and grands taxis leave for Fès, Oujda, Al-Hoceima and Nador several times a day from a lot on the Fès-Oujda road. The CTM bus station is more conveniently located on Place de l'Indépendance.

There are daily trains to Oujda, Fès and Meknès. Some continue beyond Meknès to Tangier, others to Casablanca via Rabat.

TETOUAN

With its whitewashed medina, dramatic setting and nearby beaches, Tetouan has an unmistakable Spanish-Moroccan flavour. It was settled by Muslim and Jewish refugees from Andalusia in the 16th century, and was later occupied by the Spanish during the protectorate years (1912-56).

Information

The tourist office (☎ 96 4407) is at 30 Calle Mohammed V, where there are also plenty of banks. The post office is on Place Moulay el-Mehdi.

Things to See

The town's principal square, **Place Hassan II**, links the old and new parts of Tetouan. The main entrance to the bustling **medina** is through Bab er-Rouah. Just inside the gate, the **Musée Marocain** (Museum of Moroccan Art) is built in an old bastion in the town wall and has well-presented exhibits of Moroccan and Andalusian craftsman- ship. It is open daily, except Tuesday, from 8.30 am to noon and 2.30 to 6 pm; entry is US$1.

Just outside Bab el-Okla is the **Artisanat School**, where you can see students learning traditional crafts, such as leather work, woodwork and the making of enamel *zellij* tiles. It's open from 8.30 am to noon and 2.30 to 5.30 pm (closed weekends); entry is US$1.

There is a modest **archaeology museum** opposite, at the end of Rue Prince Sidi Mohammed. It's closed on Tuesday; entry is US$1.

Places to Stay

The nearest *camping ground* is on the beach at Martil, 8km away, but it's not well maintained.

Of the many cheap pensions, one of the best is *Pension Iberia* (☎ 96 3679) on the 3rd floor above the BMCE bank on Place Moulay el-Mehdi. The rooms, some with terrific views over the square, cost US$6/8 for singles/doubles with a shared shower.

The *Hotel Cosmopolita* (☎ 96 4821) on 57 Rue Generalisimo Franco is even better value, with spotless, very adequate rooms for US$4/7.

Hotel Trebol (☎ 96 2018), close to the bus station, has clean rooms without shower for US$5/8 or with shower for US$8/11. There is hot water in the mornings.

More expensive is the *Hôtel Oumaima* (☎ 96 3473) on Rue Achra Mai, which has decent rooms for US$17/21.

Places to Eat

A good place for a cheap meal is *El Yesfi Snack*, which serves good baguettes with various meats, chips and salads for US$1. *Sandwich Ali Baba* on Rue Mourakah Anual serves tajine for under US$2.

The hugely popular *Restaurant Saigon* on Rue Mohammed ben Larbi Torres is a great place, although there's nothing Vietnamese about it. Copious main courses, including couscous, cost US$2.

If you're looking for a splurge in traditional surroundings, try the *Palace Bouhlal* next to the Great Mosque in the medina. It has a set menu for US$8, but is open only for lunch.

For cakes, the two best places in town are the *Pâtisserie Rahmouni* at 10 Youssef Ibn Tachfine and the *Pâtisserie Glacier Smir* at 17 Mohammed V. The latter has ice cream as well.

Getting There & Away

Bus The bus station is at the junction of Rue Sidi Mandri and Rue Moulay Abbas. There are CTM buses to Al-Hoceima, Casablanca, Chefchaouen, Fès, Ouezzane, Rabat and Tangier. Other bus companies go to the same places as well as to other towns.

Taxi Taxis to Chefchaouen (US$2) and Tangier (US$3) leave from a rank on Rue al-Jazeer.

Grands taxis for the Spanish enclave of Ceuta leave from the corner of Rue Mourakah Anual and Rue Sidi Mandri, near the bus station.

TINERHIR & THE TODRA GORGE

The spectacular pink canyons of the Todra Gorge, 15km from Tinerhir, rise up at the end of a lush valley of mud-brick villages and palmeraies. Apart from exploring the gorge itself, you can potter about in the palmeraies to the north and south-east of Tinerhir or, for those with a solid vehicle and a bit of time, head further north into the wilds of the High Atlas. The gorge also offers good climbing.

Places to Stay & Eat

Todra Gorge There are three pleasant camp sites 6km short of the gorge entrance, *Auberge de l'Atlas*, *Camping Auberge* and *Camping le Lac*. They cost around US$1 per person/per tent. There's a small grocery store across the road.

Just before the gorge entrance, the *Hôtel le Mansour* offers ordinary singles/doubles for US$4/7. Next door, the *Hôtel Étoile des Gorges* (☎ 83 5158) has basic rooms for US$6.

Inside the gorge, the *Hôtel Restaurant les Roches* (☎ 83 4814) offers rooms with two beds for US$6 or a place in a big tent for US$2. The *Hôtel Restaurant Yasmina* (☎ 83 4207) has rooms for US$10/12. In summer you can sleep on the roof for about US$2.

Tinerhir The *Hôtel Al Qods*, on Ave Hassan II near the post office, has bright simple rooms for US$3/6. The *Hôtel El Houda* (☎ 83 4613), 11 Rue Moulay Ismail, has clean basic rooms for US$3/7.

Behind Ave Hassan II, near the central market area, is the homey *Hôtel de l'Avenir* (☎/fax 83 4599), which has comfortable rooms for US$7/11. The hotel restaurant serves a good paella.

The market just near the hotel is good for cheap eats. The *Café des Amis* on Ave Hassan serves excellent brochettes.

Getting There & Away

CTM has a couple of buses going east to Er-Rachidia and west to Ouarzazate and on to Marrakesh. Several other bus lines have services east and west, and there are grands taxis too. Some grands taxis head up to the Todra Gorge and, on market days, you can find camionettes heading to more remote High Atlas villages.

ZAGORA & THE DRÂA VALLEY

The 100km journey along the Drâa Valley takes you through a veritable sea of palmeraies and past dozens of imposing, earth-red kasbahs. It's a magical drive, especially in the soft mauve light of the early evening.

Largely a creation of the French, Zagora itself is of little interest, except perhaps for the sign saying 'Tombuktoo 52 jours' (by camel). Market days are Wednesday and Sunday. It's worth considering hiring a car in Ouarzazate to explore this region.

Places to Stay

There are three camp sites. A good one is *Camping d'Amezrou*, about 200m past the Hôtel La Fibule. *Camping Montagne* is signposted about 2km away down a dirt track. Camel treks can be arranged here. *Camping Sindbad* is in the town itself near the Hôtel Tinsouline.

Try to get a front room at the *Hôtel Vallée du Drâa* (☎ 84 7210) on Blvd Mohammed V. Singles/doubles cost US$5/7 with shared bathroom and US$8/10 with full bathroom. Next door is the *Hôtel des Amis*, with basic rooms for US$2/6.

Most rooms at the one star *Hôtel de la Palmeraie*, also on Blvd Mohammed V, have balconies. They cost US$9/13 with bathroom. You can sleep on the roof for US$2.

One of Zagora's most relaxing places is the *Hôtel La Fibule* (☎ 84 7318) on the south side of the Oued Drâa, almost 1km from the town centre. Doubles with shower cost US$16, including breakfast. The hotel has an excellent restaurant, a bar and a swimming pool.

Another attractive option is the nearby two star *Hôtel Kasbah Asmaa* (☎ 84 7599), where palatial rooms with gallons of hot water cost US$26. Both hotels can help organise camel treks.

Places to Eat

All the hotels have their own restaurants, and all produce tasty Moroccan dishes. The *Hôtel Vallée du Drâa* and the *Hôtel de la Palmeraie* offer substantial servings and the latter is licensed. Even if you don't stay at *La Fibule*, try to have a meal there. The locally popular *Restaurant Timbouctou* on Blvd Mohammed V offers delicious meals for around US$4.

Getting There & Away

There's a daily 7 am CTM bus to Ouarzazate (and on to Marrakesh) for US$4, and one at 4 pm to M'Hamid for US$2. Other buses leave from a separate dirt lot on the main road. Grands taxis cost US$5 per person to Ouarzazate. On market days you may be able to get a ride to Rissani. There are no car-rental outlets in Zagora.

South of Zagora

About 18km south of Zagora, **Tamegroute** has a *zawiyya* (religious foundation) containing an old Qur'anic library with texts dating back 700 years.

Five kilometres further on are some minor dunes and two pleasant accommodation options, the *Auberge Repos du Sable* and the three star *Porte au Sahara*. Both places can organise camel treks.

At the end of the road is **M'Hamid**, a small village about 40km north of the Algerian border. M'Hamid is nothing special, but the journey through desert and oasis landscapes is well worthwhile. Watch out for the village of **Oulad Driss**, with its impressive mud-brick mosque and kasbah. There are a handful of basic hotels and camp sites in M'Hamid. The *Hôtel Restaurant Sahara* (☎ 84 8009) can organise camel trips.

Getting There & Away The CTM bus from M'Hamid to Zagora leaves around 5 am. Otherwise you will have to hope for the rare grand taxi or a lift with tourists. You could hire a taxi from Zagora (up to US$45 for the day, but this is negotiable).

Mozambique

For almost three decades war and political unrest were the norm in Mozambique. The country fought a long battle for independence and was later embroiled in a brutal civil war, which ended in 1992. Although the fighting is over, Mozambique is still a desperately poor country, but one where the people are generous and open. The beaches are among the best in Africa, and a few southern resorts are once again filling with fun-and-sun seekers. Further north the roads are bad and other facilities haphazard, so travel here is for the more adventurous. However, Mozambique is fascinating and well worth the time and effort required.

Facts about the Country

HISTORY

The country now called Mozambique was settled by various Bantu tribes who migrated to the area between the 14th and 18th centuries. The early Bantu inhabitants came into contact with Swahili-Arab traders on the east coast of Africa, and became involved in the slave trade (as captives or captors), which reached its height in the mid-19th century. (For more details see the Malawi chapter.)

The first Europeans to reach Mozambique were Portuguese explorers. They competed with the Swahili-Arabs for trade, and by the 16th century had established forts along the coast as collection points for gold, ivory and slaves from the interior. In the late 17th century colonisation began in earnest, with the setting up of privately owned agricultural estates on land granted by the Portuguese Crown or obtained by conquest from African chiefs.

In the 19th century, when the country's borders were defined during the European scramble for colonies, huge land concessions some were granted to foreign charter companies which remained virtually auton-

REPUBLIC OF MOZAMBIQUE
Area: 800,000 sq km
Population: 17 million
Population Growth Rate: 3%
Capital: Maputo
Head of State: President Joaquim Chissano
Official Language: Portuguese
Currency: Metical (Mt)
Exchange Rate: Mt 11,000 = US$1
Per Capita GNP: US$120
Inflation: 60%
Time: GMT/UTC + 2

Highlights
- The beautiful islands and surrounding waters of the Bazaruto Archipelago
- World Heritage Site buildings on Mozambique Island
- Beaches of the southern coast
- The energetic pace of Maputo nightlife

omous until the dictator Salazar came to power in Portugal in the 1920s. A protectionist policy was then introduced in an attempt to seal off the colonies from non-Portuguese investment.

Portuguese colonialism was a particularly backward and unbalanced affair. In the early days it relied heavily on slave labour, and, when that was abolished in the 19th century, forced labour took over. Every man was compelled to work unpaid for six months per year, and in the south most of the workforce was sent to the mines of South Africa.

MOZAMBIQUE

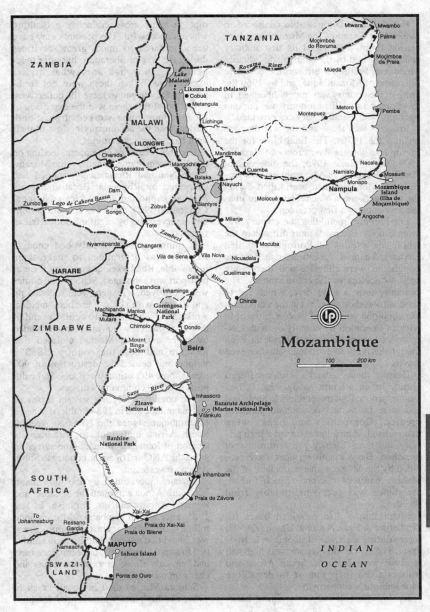

TANZANIA

ZAMBIA

Mtwara Mwambo
Palma
Moçimboa
do Rovuma
Moçimboa
da Praia
Rovuma River
Mueda

Lake
Malawi
Likoma Island (Malawi)
Cobuè
Metangula
Lichinga
Metoro
Pemba
Montepuez

MALAWI

LILONGWE

Chanida
Cassacatiza
Mandimba
Nacala
Mangochi
Cuamba
Namialo
Mossuril
Balaka
Monapo
Nampula
Nayuchi
Mozambique
Island
(Ilha de
Moçambique)
Dam
Zumbo
Lago de Cahora Bassa
Zobuè
Blantyre
Molocuè
Songo
Tete
Milange
Angoche
Nyamapanda
Zambezi
Mocuba
Changara
Vila de Sena Vila Nova
Nicuadala

HARARE
Quelimane
Catandica Caia River
Inhaminga
Chinda
Machipanda Manica
Gorongosa
National
Park
ZIMBABWE
Mutare
Chimoio Dondo
Mount
Binga
2436m
Beira

Mozambique

0   100   200 km

Save River
Inhassoro
Zinave
National Park
Bazaruto Archipelago
(Marine National Park)
Vilankulo
Banhine
National Park

SOUTH
AFRICA
Limpopo River
Maxixe Inhambane

Praia de Závora
To
Johannesburg
Ressano
Garcia
Xai-Xai
Praia do Xai-Xai
Namaacha
Praia do Bilene
MAPUTO
Inhaca Island
INDIAN
SWAZI-
LAND
OCEAN
Ponta do Ouro

MOZAMBIQUE

Resistance to colonial rule coalesced in 1962 when Frelimo – the Mozambique Liberation Front – launched its first military campaigns. Led by the charismatic Eduardo Mondlane, Frelimo's aim was the complete liberation of Mozambique, and by 1966 the north of the country was largely liberated. In these areas a socialist economy was put into operation and essential services provided.

Progress was slow, and the war dragged on into the 1970s. The final blow for the Portuguese was the overthrow of Salazar in 1974. On 25 June 1975, the independent People's Republic of Mozambique was proclaimed. Mondlane had been killed during the war, so Samora Machel was sworn in as the new country's first president.

For Frelimo, rebuilding the country was an enormous task, made more difficult by the wholesale exodus of Portuguese skilled labour and capital. An estimated 90% of the population were illiterate and there were only 40 doctors in the entire country. The economy took a nose dive, which led to serious food shortages. Yet at the same time, Mozambique reaffirmed its commitment to African liberation by complying with UN-sponsored sanctions against Rhodesia, even though this made its economic situation even worse.

Despite these setbacks, Frelimo forged ahead. In an attempt to disperse skilled labour, private land ownership was abolished and state farms and peasant cooperatives created. Companies and banks were nationalised. Education assumed a high priority and mass literacy programmes were launched. Basic health services were provided by the Mozambique equivalent of the Maoist 'barefoot doctors'. Much foreign assistance was received, notably from Sweden.

Mozambique also provided bases for Zimbabwe African National Union (ZANU) forces during their war of liberation in Rhodesia. The cost of this support was high and reprisals were frequent. South Africa and Rhodesia did their utmost to destabilise Mozambique's economy.

By 1983, the country was almost bankrupt. In many areas, collective agriculture was not successful. The peasants may have been prepared to make great sacrifices during the war of liberation, but after independence they had somewhat higher expectations. When these were not forthcoming, they began to leave the collectives.

On top of this there was the expulsion of Mozambique mine workers from South Africa, with the accompanying loss of their vital hard-currency earnings.

Into this picture of gloom, and feeding on the discontent, came Renamo – the Mozambique National Resistance – trained and supported by Rhodesia. Because Samora Machel supported the African National Congress (ANC), there was also direct military intervention by regular South African forces.

If things weren't already bad enough, Renamo was determined to make them impossible. Roads, bridges and any form of transport was sabotaged. Schools and clinics were destroyed. Villagers were rounded up and anyone with skills – teachers, medical workers etc – was shot. Towards the end of this 'civil war' (in which one side was funded by other nations), Machel claimed that Renamo had cost the country US$333 million and caused the destruction of 900 rural shops, 495 primary schools, 86 health posts and 140 communal villages.

The country could not sustain losses of this magnitude and in 1984 South Africa and Mozambique signed the Nkomati Accord. South Africa undertook to withdraw its support of Renamo; Mozambique agreed to expel the ANC and open the country to South African investment.

Mozambique abided by the agreement, but South Africa exploited the situation and Renamo activity did not diminish. In late 1985, after a joint Zimbabwe-Mozambique military offensive against Renamo, proof was found that not only had Pretoria continued to supply the rebels, but senior advisers had regularly flown in to train recruits and check on progress.

Samora Machel died in an air crash in 1986, and his place was taken by Joaquim

Chissano. The war between the Frelimo government and Renamo continued, but by the late 1980s political change was sweeping through the region. The new South African president, F W de Klerk, started to restrict Renamo support, and in 1990 Frelimo switched dramatically from Marxism to a market economy. State enterprises would be privatised, and multiparty elections were to be scheduled. Not everyone, particularly the rural peasants, was happy with these changes, but it pulled the rug from under Renamo.

In 1990 a cease-fire of sorts was arranged, followed by a fully fledged peace agreement in October 1992. Contrary to many expectations, UN-supervised elections held in October 1994 went remarkably smoothly. The outcome of the poll was a comfortable win for Frelimo, with Chissano becoming president. Renamo (transformed from rebel group to political party) agreed to abide by the results.

There's a long way to go before Mozambique's problems are over. The economy is still in a shambles, and political unrest is never far below the surface. However, for the first time in many, many years the outlook is hopeful.

GEOGRAPHY & CLIMATE
Mozambique consists of a wide coastal plain rising to mountains and plateaus on the Zimbabwe and Malawi borders. Two of Africa's major rivers – the Zambezi and the Limpopo – flow through the country. The dry season runs from April to September, during which time the climate is pleasant. In the wet season it's hot and humid, with temperatures ranging from 27 to 29°C on the coast but cooler inland.

ECOLOGY & ENVIRONMENT
Large areas of Mozambique are covered in tropical forest, and the end of the war has allowed the country to exploit this valuable natural resource. Some foreign companies (especially from South Africa) are said to be queuing up to take advantage of lucrative concessions issued by the central government. However, other reports from international observers indicate that trees are being felled at an unsustainable rate, and that local people living in or near forested areas are receiving no benefit from either the logging companies or the government.

Mozambique's population of large mammals was severely depleted during the liberation and civil wars. There are three national parks on the mainland: Gorongosa, Zinave and Bahine, but none can be visited at present due to lack of facilities, lack of animals and the presence of landmines. Gorongosa was actually the base for the Renamo fighters during the civil war, and most animals ended up as soldier rations. However, the park is now being rehabilitated and there are plans to reopen in 1997 or 1998.

POPULATION & PEOPLE
The population is around 17 million. There are 16 main ethnic groups, including: Makua, the country's largest group, inhabiting the north; Makonde, also a northern group, famous for their carvings; Sena, in the central provinces; and Shangaan, dominant in the south.

LANGUAGE
Portuguese is the official language but there are many African languages. English is rarely spoken outside a few tourists areas, so some words of Portuguese are almost essential. See the Language appendix for some useful Portuguese words and phrases.

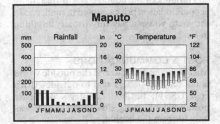

MOZAMBIQUE

Facts for the Visitor

VISAS

Visas are required by all, and generally cost US$10 to US$15 for one month (US$5 for transit, US$30 for three-month multiple-entry).

For visa extensions, each provincial capital has an immigration office. The cost varies (around US$35 for up to 30 days) and the service takes two to three days.

In transit or on a tourist visa, a border tax of US$5 (or 10 rand) is payable on entry. (The value of the rand has fallen over the past few years but the rates have not been adjusted, so if you pay in rand it works out cheaper.) If you overstay your visa, you pay a fine of US$100 cash for each extra day you have stayed.

Other Visas

In Maputo you can get visas for several African countries.

Malawi
  The high commission is open 8 am to noon and visas cost US$23, issued in three days.
Swaziland
  Open 8 am to noon and 2 to 4 pm and visas cost R30 or US$5.
Tanzania
  Open 8 am to noon and visas cost from US$20, up to US$50 for British and some other Commonwealth citizens.
Zambia
  Open 9 am to noon and 2 to 5 pm; visas cost US$20, issued in two days.

EMBASSIES
Mozambican Embassies

In Africa, Mozambique has embassies in Ethiopia, Kenya, Malawi (Lilongwe and Limbe), South Africa, Swaziland, Tanzania, Zambia and Zimbabwe. Elsewhere, it is represented in Belgium, France, Italy, Portugal, Sweden, the UK and the USA.

Foreign Embassies in Mozambique

Foreign embassies and high commissions in Maputo include:

France
  1419 Avenida Julius Nyerere (☎ 491461)
Italy
  130 Rua Pereira Marinho (☎ 491520)
Malawi
  75 Avenida Kenneth Kaunda (☎ 491468)
Portugal
  720 Avenida Julius Nyerere (☎ 490316)
South Africa
  745 Avenida Julius Nyerere (☎ 490059)
Swaziland
  608 Avenida do Zimbabwe (☎ 492451)
Tanzania
  852 Avenida Martires da Machava (☎ 490110)
UK
  310 Avenida Vladimir Lenine (☎ 492151)
USA
  193 Avenida Kenneth Kaunda (☎ 492797)
Zambia
  1266 Avenida Kenneth Kaunda (☎ 492452)
Zimbabwe
  Avenida Martires da Machava (☎ 490404)

MONEY

US$1 = Mt 11,000
Rand 1 = Mt 2500

The unit of currency is the metical (Mt), plural meticais, pronounced 'metacash'. Bank charges are high (especially for travellers' cheques, for which receipts are required – yes, the slips you're supposed to keep separate). There are change bureaus in Maputo and other large towns offering rates about 5% higher than banks, without commission for cash, and with much quicker service. Shops selling imported goods will also change US dollars cash or South African rands, at rates about 5 to 10% higher than the bank. Rip-offs are unlikely. However, changing on the street itself is not safe anywhere.

Throughout the country you'll find many accommodation prices quoted in rand, and in the south you can pay for virtually anything in rand.

POST & COMMUNICATIONS

Mail between Maputo and the outside world is not too bad (letters sent to outside Africa cost US$1), but the country's domestic postal system is very slow. Send your letters only to/from the capital.

Mozambique's telephone service has been completely overhauled, and most towns have efficient public phone offices. Calls cost US$13 for three minutes to Europe, the USA or Australia.

The country code for Mozambique is 258. The area code for Maputo is 01.

PHOTOGRAPHY

The authorities are still very sensitive about photographs of public buildings, bridges or anything connected with the military.

DANGERS

It has been estimated that there are more than one million unexploded antipersonnel mines in Mozambique, which were planted by both sides during the war. While some minefields are marked, most are only discovered when someone gets blown to bits. Do not go into the bush. Stay on roads and well-worn tracks, where other people have obviously gone before. Take special care on rural road verges, for example if you want to head off for a pee. We even heard of men standing *on* the road and pissing into the verge – still setting off mines.

There are also a lot of guns in Mozambique, and a lot of desperately poor people. Armed robberies – aimed mostly at those in smart cars around Maputo – used to be completely unknown, but since 1996 several incidents have been reported. There have also been a few car-jacking incidents on the Tete Corridor route between Malawi and Zimbabwe; preferred targets seem to be fancy 4WD vehicles as these have a high re-sale value.

PUBLIC HOLIDAYS

The following public holidays are observed: 1 January, 3 February (Heroes' Day), 7 April (Women's Day), 1 May, 25 June (Independence Day), 7 September (Victory Day), 25 September and 25 December.

ACCOMMODATION

There are cheap camping grounds and a few backpacker lodges along the coast. Otherwise, cheap hotels *(pensãos)* start at US$5/8 for singles/doubles, and you don't get much for your money. For US$15/20 there are some better options (sometimes called *pousadas)*. Many hotels have a cheaper *casal* rate for married couples.

Getting There & Away

AIR

Mozambique is serviced by several international and regional airlines, plus the national carrier Linhas Aéreas de Moçambique (LAM). A useful flight for travellers is Harare to Beira (US$60 one way, although we heard recently that LAM has cut all regional fares by 30%).

Airport departure tax for international flights is US$10.

Landmine Statistics

It may cost as little as US$3 to produce a landmine.
It costs US$300 to US$1000 to remove one.
In Mozambique, every time a landmine goes off an average of 1.45 people is killed and 1.27 wounded. Households with a landmine victim are 40% more likely to experience difficulty in providing food for the family.

Sources:
Hidden Killers, US State Department, 1993
International Committee of the Red Cross, 1994, quoted in *British Medical Journal*, vol 311, September 1995

MOZAMBIQUE

LAND
Malawi

There are many border crossings. Mozambique is a large country, so where you cross depends on where you are in Mozambique, rather than which part of Malawi you're heading for.

Southern & Central Mozambique From Tete, take a bus to the Mozambique post, Zobué (pronounced 'Zobway'), then walk or hitch 6km to the Malawi border post at Mwanza, from where local buses run to Blantyre (US$3). You'll find there are plenty of moneychangers at both border posts, dealing in kwacha, Zimbabwe dollars, US dollars and meticais, but rates are low.

Northern Mozambique From Nampula there are three passenger trains per week to Cuamba (US$3) and freight trains with a wagon for passengers most other days.

Once in Cuamba, there's usually a daily *chapa* (passenger truck) to the Mozambique border post at Mandimba (US$4). Then it's 6km to the Malawi border post at Chiponde; you can try hitching, or use a bicycle taxi (US$2). From Chiponde minibuses run to Namwera or Mangochi (US$2).

From Cuamba you can also enter Malawi by rail. Take a freight train (twice weekly, but not the same two days each week) to the Mozambique border post; the fare is US$1.50. You then walk about 1km to the Malawi border at Nayuchi (rail crossing only), from where there is a twice-weekly passenger train to Balaka, via Liwonde, which costs US$2.

Three separate train rides, none of which connects, plus a bad line between Cuamba and the border (especially in the rainy season) means this trip can take a day or a week, depending on your luck.

Another road option between northern Mozambique and Malawi involves getting transport from Quelimane or Nampula to Mocuba, from where there's usually a chapa or truck about every other day in the dry season to the Mozambique border post at Milanje (US$4). From Milanje town you walk a few kilometres to the Milanje border post, from where it's about 1km to the Malawi border post at Muloza. Buses go from Muloza to Blantyre via Mulanje (US$3).

South Africa

From Maputo minibuses go to the Ressano Garcia border post (US$3) or Komatipoort (US$5), from where transport runs to Johannesburg. There's also a daily luxury bus called the Panthera Azul from Maputo to Jo'burg (via Mazini). It departs the company's office (☎ 494238) on Avenida Mao Tse Tung (open every day) at 8 am Monday to Friday, later at weekends (US$45). There's also a service to Durban (US$55).

A South African train leaves Maputo at noon on Monday, Wednesday and Friday, arriving Jo'burg the next day at 3.30 pm, for US$23/16/9 in 1st/2nd/3rd class. You leave the train at the border; make sure your gear is safe or take it with you.

Swaziland

Minibuses go from outside Maputo railway station to the Namaacha border (US$3), from where frequent buses go to Mbabane and Manzini.

Tanzania

A few hardy travellers make the journey through northern Mozambique, entering Tanzania at Namiranga on the Rovuma River (the border). From Pemba to Moçimboa da Praia the road is a nightmare but there is regular transport (10 hours) in the dry season. In Moçimboa there is one basic pousada where you can stay overnight. From Moçimboa there is at least one pick-up daily (dry season only) to the border (five hours), leaving at 5 am.

Once through the Mozambique border post, there is a half-hour walk to the Rovuma River, where you cross by canoe (10 minutes) and continue on to Mtwara (irregular transport).

Zimbabwe

The two main crossing points between Mozambique and Zimbabwe are Nyamapanda on the 'Tete Corridor' and Machipanda (just west of Manica) on the Beira to Harare road. Both routes are very busy, with frequent buses plus many trucks and holiday-makers, so hitching is not too difficult.

Buses from Chimoio to Harare (via Mutare) cost US$12.

LAKE & SEA
Malawi
Cuamba is joined to Lichinga by a good road and a terrible railway line. From here infrequent trucks go to Cobué (pronounced 'Kobway') on the shore of Lake Malawi. From here a local boat goes every other day (US$0.60) to Likoma Island. The Malawi ferryboat *Ilala* (see Malawi Getting Around section) connects Likoma with Malawi twice a week.

Tanzania
You might find a dhow heading for Tanzania, although a trip on these boats is not to be taken lightly (see boxed story on Tanzania to Mozambique by dhow): Pemba to Mtwara is about US$20. Other ports include Msimbati (south of Mtwara) and Moçimboa da Praia. All have immigration posts.

There is also a boat called the *Edma*, which makes the trip between Pemba (Mozambique) and Mtwara (Tanzania) via Ibo Island (sometimes) and Moçimboa. It doesn't run to any set schedule so you need to make enquiries to pin it down.

Getting Around

AIR
LAM services internal routes between Maputo and other main centres. Maputo to Beira (daily) is US$120, but recent reports suggest that LAM are cutting prices drastically. Flights are frequently delayed, and baggage often tampered with.

BUS
Where roads are good, buses connect major towns, usually at least once per day. The main operators are: Transportes Olivieras (southern Mozambique); Transportes Virginia (centre); and TransNorte (north). Some sample fares: Maputo to Vilankulo US$7; Maputo to Beira US$18; Beira to Vilankulo US$12; Quelimane to Nampula US$11. Express services are only slightly more expensive but much quicker. You can normally buy tickets a day or two in advance.

Where roads are bad, you'll use converted passenger trucks (*chapas*) or normal trucks (*camions*) to get around.

Large towns have bus stations, but in smaller places transport usually leaves from the start of the road towards the destination. Buses or chapas leave early (between 4 and 6 am), although sometimes chapas simply leave when full – you get there early just in case, then hang around until noon.

Tanzania to Mozambique by Dhow (The Joys of Travel)
We heard from a traveller who had sailed from Msimbati in a Tanzanian dhow. The wind was coming from the south, but the captain promised to take him to Pemba in a day and a night for 10,000 Tanzanian shillings (about US$20). After four days of tacking and being blown backwards they hadn't even reached Moçimboa (less than halfway) and were running out of food. The desperate traveller jumped ship with another local, and somehow managed to get ashore without being eaten by sharks. There followed a three-hour slog though thigh-deep mud and mangrove swamps to reach dry land proper. The main road which he'd been told was 'near' the shore turned out to be several hours away, and he stayed for a night in a remote fishing village. The next day's walk across hot sand and rocks gave him blisters, but he finally reached a road with occasional transport, found a truck to Moçimboa and then another to Pemba, by which time his blisters had gone septic and he could hardly walk.

The moral of the tale is this. The monsoon winds along the East African coast blow north to south from November through February, and south to north from April through September. Never try to go against the wind. ■

MOZAMBIQUE

Maputo

Maputo was once renowned as a beautiful city, rated alongside Cape Town and Rio, but following almost 20 years of deprivation it is very run-down today. Nevertheless, it's still an interesting place, with a very lively atmosphere.

As the country's situation improves, so do the city's facilities – new shops and cafes open, hotels are refurbished, nightclubs reawaken and streets are repaired. Old-timers say Maputo is already regaining some of its old charm.

Information

Time Out is an English-language magazine listing events and places to visit produced by BIP (Public Information Bureau), available from their library on Avenida Eduardo Mondlane, or from large hotels and travel agents.

The main banks are around the junction of Avenida 25 de Setembro and Avenida Samora Machel. Maputo's change bureaus include: AfriCambio, next to Hotel Tivoli on Avenida 24 de Setembro; Expresso Cambio, Avenida de 24 Julho; and one at the Hotel Polana (also open afternoons and Sundays).

The CTT (main post office) is on Avenida 25 de Setembro. The telephone office is on the same street (corner of Avenida Lenine) on the ground floor of a high-rise building; it's open daily from 7.30 am to 9 pm.

Things to See

The oldest historic site is the **Fort** on Praça 25 do Junho. A must-see is the **railway station**, designed and built in the early 1900s by a certain Monsieur Eiffel, who was also responsible for something or other in Paris. Recently renovated, it looks more like a palace, with polished wood and marble decorations, topped by a gigantic copper dome.

The **Museum of the Revolution**, Avenida 24 de Julho (open daily, entrance US$0.05), is worth a visit, but you really need a guide-translator (which can be arranged in advance), unless you read Portuguese. The **National Art Museum** (free) on Avenida Ho

Chi Min has a truly wonderful collection of Mozambique's finest contemporary artists.

On Saturday mornings there's a **craft market** in Praça 25 do Junho. Pottery and basketware are sold on the Marginal roundabout, downhill from the Hotel Polana. Nearby, a shop called Artedif has good craft items (especially leatherwork).

Places to Stay

The *Parque Municipal de Campismo*, on the Marginal, is tatty, with small patches of grass to stick tents on for US$2 per person. Security is questionable unless you're in a vehicle or group.

The best option is *Fatima's* (no phone, but you can book ahead on fax 400425), 1317 Avenida Mao Tse Tung. Rooms are US$7.50 per person, dorm beds US$5 and camping US$3. Meals and drinks are sold. Fatima is a retired backpacker, speaks English, and knows a lot about Maputo and Mozambique. The only problem with this place is its popularity – it's often full.

Otherwise, good cheap accommodation is nonexistent. If you're desperate try the *Hotel Girassol* on Avenida Lumumba which has bare, filthy rooms for US$5 per person. Better is the *Pensão Central* , at 1957 Avenida 24 de Julho, where rooms cost US$7/14. Better again is *Pensão Nini*, Avenida Julius Nyerere, which charges US$15 for a basic double.

Other options include the *Hotel Santa Cruz* (☎ 420147), Avenida 24 de Julio, charging US$16/18; and the *Hotel Universo*, Avenida Karl Marx, charging US$20/22 but worth considering as it's serviced by Transportes Virginia buses (see Getting There & Away, below).

Much better value is the *Residencial Taj Mahal* (☎ 732122), Avenida Ho Chi Min, where clean rooms are US$15/20, or the outwardly tatty *Hotel Central*, near the railway station, where surprisingly smart rooms are US$15 per person.

Places to Eat

At the *market* near the junction of Avenida Lenine and Avenida Mao Tse Tung, there is bread, tinned food, fruit and vegetables. Stalls sell tea and egg or fish sandwiches for around

MOZAMBIQUE

PLACES TO STAY
8 Fatima's
13 Hotel Polana
23 Pensão Nini
25 Hotel Terminus
26 Pensão Martins
28 Hotel Universo
29 Hotel Moçambicano
32 Residencial Taj Mahal
34 Pensão Central
36 Hotel Santa Cruz
48 Hotel Girassol
50 Hotel Cardoso
57 Hotel Tourismo
59 Hotel Tivoli
64 Hotel Central; Pub Mondo

PLACES TO EAT
1 Restaurante Micael
12 Ungumi
17 Restaurant O'Bau
22 Sensações
24 Restaurant Piri-Piri
30 Café Primavera
35 Kitos

42 Taj Mahal Restaurant
43 Impala Steak House
47 Parnaso Restaurant & Pub
54 Café Scala
58 Café Continental

OTHER
2 Zambian High Commission
3 Swazi High Commission
4 US Embassy
5 Malawian High Commission
6 Artedit (Crafts)
7 Market
9 Panthera Azul (bus) Office
10 United States Information
   Service
11 Zimbabwean High Commission
14 Canadian High Commission
15 Oliveiras Bus Depot
16 Praça 16 de Junho
18 Central Hospital
19 Tanzanian High Commission
20 Public Information Bureau (PIB)
21 South African High Commission
27 Interfranca Shopping Centre

31 Museum of the Revolution
33 Express Tours; Exchange
   Bureau
37 British High Commission
38 Cathedral
39 City Hall
40 National Art Museum
41 Minibuses
44 Praça da Independência
45 Centro Cultural
   Franco-Moçambicano
46 Botanic Gardens
49 Natural History Museum
51 Centro do Desportivo
52 Telephone Office
53 Post Office
55 Taxis
56 Municipal Market
60 ENT (National Tourism
   Organisation)
61 Feira Popular
62 Fort
63 Praça 25 do Junho
65 Praço dos Trabalhadores
66 Train Station

Maputo

0   250   500 m

To Camping;
Mini Golf &
Costa do Sol

Avenida Marginal

Avenida Julius Nyerere
Avenida Armando Twane
Avenida Francisco Magumbwe
Avenida Martires da Machava
Avenida Tomas Nduda
Avenida Kim II Sung
Avenida Kwame Nkrumah
Avenida Salvador Allende
Avenida 24 de Julho
Avenida Mao Tse Tung
Avenida Amilcar Cabral
Avenida Agostinho Neto
Avenida Paulo Samuel Kankomba
Avenida Vladimir Lenine
Rua da Base N'Chinga
Avenida do Zimbabwe
Avenida Kenneth Kaunda
Avenida José Mateus
Rua da Argélia
Rua Mahomba
Rua do Machangwea
Avenida Marques de Maeda
Avenida 10 de Novembro
Avenida Patrice Lumumba
Rua da Resistência
Avenida Olof Palme
Avenida Eduardo Mondlane
Avenida Karl Marx
Avenida Filipe Samuel Magaia
Avenida da Guerra Popular
Avenida Albert Luthuli
Avenida Fernandes Farinha
Avenida Mahomed Said Barre
Avenida Lucas Luali
Avenida da Zambia
Avenida do Rio Limpopo
Avenida 25 de Setembro
Avenida Ho Chi Min
Avenida Sekou Touré
Av Samora Machel
Avenida de Maguiguana
Avenida Josina Machel
Avenida Fernão Magalhães
Avenida Zedequias Manganhela
Rua de Timor Leste
Rua de Pedroso
Rua de Bagamoyo

To Eduardo
Mondlane University

To Airport

Rua do Tembe
Rua Paiva Couceiro
Rua do Malanga

Ferries
Port

US$0.50. Near the junction of Avenida Samora Machel and Avenida 25 de Setembro is a *bakery*, with people on the street outside selling jam, fish and other fillings.

For decent coffee and cakes, the *Café Continental* on Avenida 25 de Setembro is popular. Opposite, the friendly *Café Scala* is similar and also does snacks. Other good places are *Kitos* and *Café Primavera*, both on Avenida 24 de Julho, with sandwiches for under US$1 and snacks for US$1.50 to US$2, and *Lanchonete* at the railway station.

For good-value eats the *Feira Popular*, a fun-fair on Avenida 25 de Setembro, has many bars and restaurants. Most do Mozambican standards like steaks and seafood, ranging from US$3 to US$5. The Feira is popular Thursday to Sunday nights (when some of the bars become discos). Stroll around, have a beer, check a few menus, then take your pick.

Entertainment

Maputo has a thriving nightlife. Friday and Saturday nights are very lively after 11 pm, and the partying continues until dawn. The *Feira Popular* has a choice of bars and discos. Taxis wait by the gate to take you home afterwards. Other places which have been recommended include *Eagles Bar* at the Centro Social do Desportivo.

Getting There & Away

The Olivieras Transportes long-distance bus depot is on Avenida 24 de Julho, just beyond Praça 16 de Junho. Some sample fares from Maputo include: Maxixe US$4.50; Vilankulo US$7; Beira US$18.

Transportes Virginia buses go to/from the Hotel Universo, and have a booking office inside the hotel. Sample fares: Vilankulo US$7.50; Biera US$20.

Getting Around

The Airport Buses from Maputo city centre run along Avenida Angola and Avenida Acordos de Lusaka to within about 1km of the airport. Alternatively, taxis to/from downtown cost US$7 to US$10.

Taxi There are ranks near the train station

and central market (daytime) and outside the Feira Popular (evenings). Between the centre and suburbs costs US$5 to US$7.

Around the Country

BEIRA

Beira is a major port and the second-largest city in Mozambique, linked to Mutare in Zimbabwe by road and railway (the 'Beira Corridor'). The central area is compact and the old Mediterranean-style buildings, particularly around the main square *(Praça)*, give this place some faded glamour, well worth visiting for a day or two. Most people head along the *marginal* (sea-front road) to **Macuti**, 9km from the centre, which has a reasonable beach.

Places to Stay

Cheapest is the scruffy *Bem Vindo*, behind the Hotel Estoril (currently disused) in Macuti. It's actually a scrap-metal yard, but the big man who runs it is friendly enough. Camping is US$1, and basic rooms cost US$2 to US$3 per person. Toilets and showers leave a hell of a lot to be desired. To get there catch a 'Macuti' or 'Estoril' bus or minibus and ride to the end. A far better choice is nearby *Biques*, where camping is US$2. It has spotless facilities and a bar with food and English-speaking staff.

In town, cheapest is *Pensão Sofala*, Avenida de Naya, a brothel with filthy toilets and rooms for US$4/6. Better is the nearby *Hotel Savoy*, where clean airy rooms are US$5/9. Also good is the quiet *Pensão Moderna*, with rooms at US$8/15, breakfast US$1.50 and meals around US$4. The *Monaco Hotel*, behind the Hotel Mozambique, charges US$8.50/16.

Up the price band, but still good value, is the *Hotel Miramar* (☎ 322 2830), just off the marginal road, where clean en suite rooms with hot water and air-con cost US$12/17. There's also safe parking.

Places to Eat

A good cheap place is *Tamariz*, on the Praça,

where meals start at less than US$1, up to US$2 for chicken and chips. Nearby are several pavement cafes: *Riviera*, *Capri* and *La Scala* all serve coffee, soft drinks, meals and snacks at reasonable prices.

Near Pensão Sofala, *Takeaway 2 + 1* has outside seats, snacks from US$1 and meals around US$2, and smarter dining upstairs.

INHAMBANE & MAXIXE

About 450km north of Maputo, the town of Maxixe (pronounced 'Masheesh') is where you cross a bay to the sleepy provincial capital of Inhambane. Everybody goes by boat, as the road journey round is over 60km. Dhows charge US$0.15 and take from 20 minutes to two hours, depending on the wind. Motorboats charge US$0.30.

About 20km from Inhambane are two beautiful beaches: **Tofu** is more accessible and more developed; **Barra** is harder to reach and quieter, but has a better setting.

Places to Stay & Eat

Inhambane Your choice is limited to the overpriced *Inhambane Hotel* which charges US$15 per room. About 15km outside Inhambane, where the roads to Tofu and Barra split, is *Bar Babalaza*. Campers are welcome, and simple cabins are planned.

Maxixe *Pousada de Maxixe* has very basic rooms for US$6 and cheap food. The *Campismo de Maxixe* has clean camping pitches with hot showers for US$4.50 (one to four people) and beach huts for US$18 (two people). Best for food is *Restaurant Dom Carlos*, near the bus park, with main meals for US$3 to US$5. *Quiosque o Veleiro* by the jetty is a great place for a cold beer or snack while watching the dhows come and go.

Tofu & Barra Beaches The South African-run *Albatroz Fishing Camp* charges US$25 per person.

Infinitely preferable is the excellent *Barra Beach Backpackers*, run by John Henderson, with camping for US$3.50, simple single/doubles for US$4.50/5.50, plus a kitchen, hot and cold water, and various watersports.

There are regular chapas from Inhambane to Tofu ($0.50), and to Barra village school, from where it's a 4km walk through the palms to Barra Beach Backpackers. Local boys will show you the way.

MOZAMBIQUE ISLAND

Mozambique Island (Ilha de Moçambique) is 2.5km long and about 3km off the mainland (linked by a bridge). There are mosques, churches and various colonial buildings including a fort, a grand palace and a vast hospital, dating from between the 16th and 19th centuries. Most are decayed and decrepit, although a few (including two excellent museums) have been restored in the last few years (see boxed story on Mozambique Island).

A marginal (sea-front road) runs along the east side of the island, with splendid views out across the ocean. Forget about swimming – the beach is the island's toilet – but if you like old relics and a time-warp atmosphere, don't miss 'Ilha'.

Places to Stay & Eat

Until 1996, the only place to stay was the old *Pousada de Moçambique*, almost as tumble-down as the rest of the town, where rooms are US$7/12. A new place to stay is *Casa de Mateus*, opposite the school, charging about US$25 for a good double. The *Piscina*, overlooking the ocean, has food and drinks and there are several other bars and cheap eating places around town, plus a market.

NAMPULA

This major town in northern Mozambique is within easy reach of Ilha de Moçambique and the coast, and linked to Malawi (via Cuamba) by a recently renovated railway. You'll inevitably spend a day or two here, changing transport, money or underwear. The CFVM Piscina (swimming pool) has clean water, shady seating, a bar and restaurant, plus music some evenings (US$2 entrance). Nampula also has an excellent **museum** (with explanations in English).

Mozambique Island

The northern half of Mozambique Island contains so many buildings of historical importance it has been declared a World Heritage Site by the United Nations Education, Scientific and Cultural Organisation (UNESCO). In the southern half of the island most people live in cramped dwellings in poor *bairros* (suburbs) – something perhaps overlooked by UNESCO.

The number one attraction is the **Palace and Chapel of Sao Paulo** – the former governor's residence – dating from the 18th century. Most of it is now a museum, containing original furniture and ornaments – from Portugal, Arabia, Goa, India and even China. It's a fascinating place, but what's even more amazing is that it is still here and in good condition, following almost 20 years of civil strife on the mainland. In the chapel, note the altar and the pulpit, and the upper windows linked to the palace so the governor could receive mass without having to mix with commoners.

Behind the palace is the **Church of the Misercordia**, overshadowed by its large neighbour, but well worth a look. Attached to this is the **Museum of Sacred Art**, containing religious ornaments, paintings and carvings. The museum is housed in the former hospital of the Holy House of Mercy, a religious guild which operated in several Portuguese colonies from the early 16th century onwards, providing charitable assistance to the poor and sick. Both museums are open all day Wednesday to Saturday (closed lunchtime), and also on Sunday morning. They are free, but a small tip for the guide is appreciated.

At the north end of the island the **Fort of Sao Sebastiao** was built by the Portuguese around a spring which was the only reliable source of drinking water on the island. The fort is still in remarkably good condition; it's open all the time and entry is free. Immediately north of the fort, right on the tip of the island is the **Chapel of Nossa Senhora de Balnorte**, reported to be the oldest standing building in the southern hemisphere.

In the main town are several more recent buildings. Look out for the beautifully restored **bank** on Avenida Amilcar Cabral, and the three huge ornate colonial **administration offices** overlooking the gardens south of the hospital. They seem to be disused now, but are still in reasonable condition. Near the municipal market is a **Hindu temple**. There is also a **cemetery** at the southern end of the island with Christian, Muslim and Hindu graves.

Amigos de Ilha (Friends of Ilha) is a cultural and conservation organisation. It has an office near the restored bank and might be able to help with information on places to see around the island. ∎

Places to Stay & Eat

The cheapest places to stay and eat include *Restaurante-Pensão Central* on Avenida Kankomba near the station, and *Pensão Marques* on the same street – both dingy and dirty with singles/doubles for US$3/5.

Much better is *Pensão Parques*, where a bed in the dorm is US$4, a double is US$8, and a triple is US$12. The rooms are clean, the staff friendly, and the food downstairs is good value (meals US$3, snacks US$1.50). You may be allowed to pitch a tent on the flat roof. Other choices include *Pensão Avenida* near the telephone office, with rooms around US$4/8, and the *Hotel Brazilia*, with clean en suite doubles for US$8. Both places do coffee and snacks, plus meals from around US$2.

PEMBA

Pemba is a coastal town in northern Mozambique. Most visitors come for the nearby beach and reef at **Wimbi**. The tourist office is in Wimbi Conches (a shell shop) near the Complexio Nautilus, run by a helpful lady called Fatima (she speaks English).

Places to Stay & Eat

In town, the clean and friendly *Pensão Baia* has rooms (single or double) for US$12. *Pemba Takeaway*, near the top-end Hotel Cabo Delgado, has burgers from US$1, omelettes from US$1.50, and pizzas from US$2.

On Wimbi Beach, your only choice is *Complexio Nautilus*, with en suite bungalows at US$55 (one to three people). Nearby *Celmar Takeaway* offers cheap snacks, and there are some mid-range restaurants nearby.

Be prepared for changes: several hotels and restaurants are planned. There is also talk of a camp site, to be set up by a South African guy who runs a diving outfit called Clube Sportivo Indico.

QUELIMANE

Quelimane (pronounced 'Kelimarny') has a pleasant coastal feel. The **old Portuguese church** near the port and the newer **cathedral** on Avenida 7 de Setembro are both worth a look. The waterfront is a pleasant place to stroll, especially in the evening.

Places to Stay & Eat

There are a few cheap dives near the bus park: *Pensão Moderno* is reported to be OK. Cheapest in the centre is *Pensão Ideal* on Avenida Samuel Magaia, charging US$7 for simple rooms (one or two people).

Next up in price is the *Hotel Zambeze* on Avenida Acordos de Lusaka, charging US$12/18 for simple singles/doubles, plus US$2 for breakfast. Meals are US$3.50 to US$6. A bit smarter is the *Hotel 1 Julio* (☎ 213067) with reasonable rooms for US$15/30.

Café Nicola on Avenida 1 de Julio has snacks for around US$1.50, and meals around US$3. At nearby *Salao Palladium* prices are similar.

The *Salao Aguila* next to Cinema Aguila is also good, especially for coffee, cakes and ice cream. Nearby is the small and friendly *Barette Verde*, where meals start at just over US$1. There are several other bars and cafes in town.

TETE

Tete is a large town on the 'corridor route' through Mozambique between Blantyre (Malawi) and Harare (Zimbabwe). You may find yourself here if you're hitching or breaking away from the beaten track.

Places to Stay & Eat

Cheapest is the basic *Pensão Alves*, in the upper part of town, five blocks from the river, which charges US$2. The nearby *Hotel Kassuende* has en suite singles/doubles at US$8/12. Between these two is *Pastelaria Confianca* and *Snack Bar 2002*, both with good cheap eats. Also good is the *Hotel Zambezi* at US$15 for a big double.

Down on the river bank, almost under the very impressive suspension bridge, is *Restaurant Freita*, a popular expat hangout, with shady outside seating, cold beers, snacks around US$1, and good meals for US$5.

About 20km out of Tete, on the road to the Malawi border at Zobué, is the small town of **Moatize**. On the main street, *Café Agua* has been recommended for safe camping and good cheap food.

VILANKULO & THE BAZARUTO ARCHIPELAGO

The small spread out town of Vilankulo (formerly Vilanculos) is becoming increasingly popular with travellers. It has wonderful beaches and is the main gateway to the beautiful Bazaruto Archipelago. The four main islands of **Magaruque, Benguerra, St Carolina** and **Bazaruto**, plus surrounding islets and reefs, are protected as a national park. It's all here: azure waters, sandy beaches, palm trees, pristine coral, plus tropical fish to goggle at and big game fish to catch.

Places to Stay & Eat

Vilankulo Most travellers head for *The Last Resort*, on the beach, where camping is US$3 and cabins US$3.50. The staff can advise on hikes in the area, snorkelling, diving, boats to the islands, and places to stay once you get there. Nearby is *Simbira Lodge*, with huts for US$2.50 and camping for US$2.

For food, Vilankulo has a market and several shops. Recommended is *Snack Bar Monica* with food for US$2 to US$4 or the smarter *Bar Mozambicano* (US$5 to US$7), where the people who run it are happy to help with local information. On the beach road, *Quiosque Tropical* is a mellow local bar where food must be ordered several hours in advance, but is worth the wait.

Bazaruto Archipelago Most places to stay are in the top-end bracket. The only concession to backpackers is *Gabriel's Lodge* on Benguerra where camping costs US$5 and simple chalets US$6. Bazaruto has the *Zengelemo Campsite*, run by the national park, where prices are reasonable. The people at The Last Resort have the latest details on prices and facilities, and can help you find boats to Benguerra and Bazaruto.

MOZAMBIQUE

Namibia

Wedged between the Kalahari and the chilly South Atlantic, Namibia is a country of vast potential and promise. Rich in natural resources and unquestionably spectacular beauty, it has also inherited a solid modern infrastructure and has a diversity of cultures.

Namibia has fine bushwalking opportunities, rugged seascapes, appealing African and European cities and villages, and nearly unlimited elbow room – features which until recently have been largely ignored, but are well worth exploring.

Facts about the Country

HISTORY

It's generally accepted that southern Africa's earliest inhabitants were San, nomadic people organised in extended family groups who could adapt to even the severest terrain. Population densities were very low and much movement took place. San communities seem to have later come under pressure from Khoi-Khoi (Hottentot) groups, the ancestors of the modern Nama, with whom they share a language group (Khoisan). The Khoi-Khoi were a partially tribal people who raised stock rather than hunted and who were probably responsible for the first pottery-making in the archaeological record. They seem to have come from the south, gradually displacing the San in Namibia, and remained in control of the area until around 1500 AD.

The descendants of the Khoi-Khoi and San people still live in Namibia, but few of them have retained their original lifestyles. The so-called Topnaar Hottentots of the Kuiseb River area are an exception, maintaining ancient ways based on goat-herding.

Between 2300 and 2400 years ago, the first Bantus appeared on the plateaus of south-central Africa. Their arrival marked the appearance of the first tribal structures in southern African societies. Khoisan groups

REPUBLIC OF NAMIBIA
Area: 825,000 sq km
Population: 1.7 million
Population Growth Rate: 2.9%
Capital: Windhoek
Head of State: President Sam Nujoma
Official Languages: English, Afrikaans
Currency: Namibian dollar (N)
Exchange Rate: N\$4.70 = US\$1
Per Capita GNP: US\$2000
Inflation: 10%
Time: GMT/UTC + 2

Highlights
- Etosha National Park and its incredible variety of African wildlife
- Lonely and ethereal Skeleton Coast
- Vast dune-studded Namib Desert
- Spectacular Fish River Canyon

gradually disappeared from the scene – either retreating to the desert or the swamps of the Okavango Delta or being enslaved into Bantu society, a process which has continued right up to today.

Around 1600 AD the Herero people, who were Bantu-speaking cattle herders, arrived in Namibia from the Zambezi area and occupied the north and west of the country, causing conflicts with the Khoi-Khoi with whom they were competing for the best grazing lands and water holes. In what is now called Kaokoland, the more aggressive

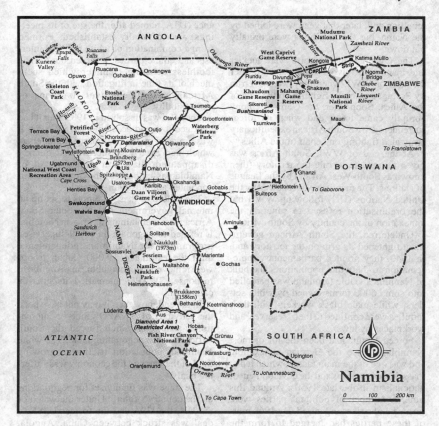

Namibia

Herero displaced not only the Khoi-Khoi but also the remaining San and the Damara people (whose origin is unclear).

It is thought that the Nama people of present-day Namibia are descended from Khoi-Khoi groups who held out against the Herero despite violent clashes in the 1870s and 1880s. In addition, by then a new Bantu group, the Owambo, had settled in the north along the Okavango and Kunene rivers. The Owambo were probably descended from people who migrated from eastern Africa more than 500 years earlier.

Because Namibia has one of the world's most barren and inhospitable coastlines, it was largely ignored by the European maritime nations until relatively recently. The first European visitors were Portuguese mariners seeking a way to the Indies in the late 15th century, but they confined their activities to erecting stone crosses at certain points as navigational aids.

It wasn't until the last minute scramble for colonies towards the end of the 19th century that Namibia was annexed by Germany, except for the enclave of Walvis Bay, which was taken in 1878 by the British for the Cape Colony. In 1904, the Herero launched a rebellion and, later that year, were joined by the Nama, but the rebellions were brutally put down.

The Owambo in the north were luckier and managed to avoid conquest until after the start of WWI, when they were overrun by Portuguese forces fighting on the side of the Allies. Soon after, the German colony abruptly came to an end when its forces surrendered to a South African expeditionary army also fighting on behalf of the Allies.

At the end of WWI, South Africa was given a mandate to rule the territory (then known as South West Africa) by the League of Nations. The mandate was renewed by the United Nations (UN) following WWII but the organisation refused to sanction the annexation of the country by South Africa.

Undeterred, the South African government tightened its grip on the territory and, in 1949, they granted parliamentary representation to the white population. The bulk of Namibia's viable farmland was parcelled into some 6000 farms owned by white settlers, while male black workers with their families were confined to their 'reserves' and workplaces by laws.

Forced labour had been the lot of most Namibians since the German annexation, and was one of the main factors which led to mass demonstrations and the development of nationalism in the late 1950s. Around this time, a number of political parties were formed and strikes organised. By 1960 most of these parties had merged to form the South West Africa People's Organization (SWAPO), which took the issue of South African occupation to the International Court of Justice.

The outcome was inconclusive but in 1966 the UN General Assembly voted to terminate South Africa's mandate and set up a Council for South West Africa (in 1973 renamed the Commission for Namibia) to administer the territory. At the same time, SWAPO launched its campaign of guerilla warfare. The South African government reacted by firing on demonstrators and arresting thousands of activists.

In 1975 the Democratic Turnhalle Alliance (DTA, named after the site of its meetings) was officially established. Formed from a combination of white political interests and ethnic parties, it turned out to be a toothless debating chamber which spent much of its time in litigation with the South African government over its scope of responsibility.

The DTA was dissolved in 1983 after it had indicated it would accommodate SWAPO. It was replaced by the Multiparty Conference, which had even less success and quickly disappeared, at which time control of Namibia passed back to the South African-appointed administrator-general.

The failure of these attempts to set up an internal government did not deter South Africa from maintaining its grip on Namibia. It refused to negotiate on a UN-supervised programme for Namibian independence until the estimated 19,000 Cuban troops were removed from neighbouring Angola. In response, SWAPO intensified its guerilla campaign.

In the end, however, it may not have been the activities of SWAPO alone or international sanctions which forced the South Africans to the negotiating table. The white Namibian population itself was growing tired of the war and the economy was suffering badly.

The stage was finally set for negotiations on the country's future. Under the watch of the UN, the USA and the former USSR, a deal was struck between Cuba, Angola, South Africa and SWAPO, in which Cuban troops would be removed from Angola and South African troops from Namibia. This would be followed by UN-monitored elections held in November 1989 on the basis of universal suffrage. SWAPO collected a clear majority of the votes but insufficient in number to give it the sole mandate to write the new constitution.

Following negotiations between the various parties, a constitution was adopted in February 1990 and independence was granted the following month under the presidency of the SWAPO leader, Sam Nujoma. His policies are based on a national reconciliation programme designed to heal the wounds left by 25 years of armed struggle, and a reconstruction programme based on the retention of a mixed economy and partnership with the private sector.

So far things have gone smoothly and in the elections of December 1994 President Sam Nujoma and SWAPO were re-elected with a 68% landslide victory over rival Mishake Muyongo and the DTA.

GEOGRAPHY & CLIMATE
Namibia may be largely arid, but it encompasses broad geographical variations and can be divided into four regions: the dunes and desert coastal plains of the Namib and the Skeleton Coast, the Central Plateau, the Kalahari, and the bushveld of Kavango and Caprivi.

The whole country enjoys a minimum of 300 days of sunshine a year, but temperatures and rainfall vary considerably both seasonally and geographically. No season is particularly unpleasant, although tourists generally avoid the Namib-Naukluft and Etosha national parks in the extreme heat of summer.

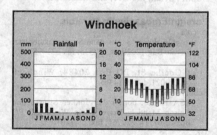

ECOLOGY & ENVIRONMENT
With a small human population spread over a large land area, Namibia is in better environmental shape than most African countries, but challenges remain. Namibia's Ministry of Environment & Tourism (MET) is largely a holdover from pre-independence days, and therefore its environmental policies remain similar to those of its South African counterpart.

Issues such as ranching, agriculture and wildlife-oriented tourism and encroachment on protected areas continue to affect local ecosystems. Many ranchers in the southern part of the country view wildlife as a nuisance, while many people in the more densely populated north see wildlife reserves as potential settlement areas and wildlife itself as a food resource and a threat to crops and human life.

Overfishing and the 1993-94 outbreak of red tide along the Skeleton Coast have decimated sea lion populations, both from starvation and commercially inspired culling. Poaching of desert rhino, elephant and other species in Damaraland, which is not an officially protected area, have caused declines in populations of these unique species.

Namibia was one of the first countries to experiment with the dehorning of rhino, but sadly, dehorned female rhino in Namibia were unable to protect their young from attack by hyenas. During the drought of 1993, when other wildlife was scarce, all calves of dehorned females were lost. The rate of rhino loss to poachers is approximately 5% annually, and growing. By the turn of the century, the desert rhinos of Damaraland may well be wiped out. The non-governmental Save the Rhino Trust (☎ (061) 222281; fax 223077), PO Box 22691, Windhoek, Namibia, has been formed to educate local people about the value of wildlife and to oversee conservation of Namibia's remaining rhino.

Other species, such as the welwitschia plant and the Damara tern, have been compromised by human activities (including tourism and recreation) in formerly remote areas. As yet, efforts to change local attitudes have met with limited success.

POPULATION & PEOPLE
Namibia has an estimated 1.7 million people, an annual growth rate of 2.9%, and one of Africa's lowest population densities, at 1.5 people per sq km.

Of the 11 major ethnic groups, the largest is the Owambo with 641,000 people. Other groups include the Kavango, Damara,

Traditional San Life

Historically, the San lived in nomadic bands of 25 to 35 people. Each group comprised of several families and generally they lived as hunter-gatherers. They had their own land division system; bands had well-defined territories which could measure up to 1000 sq km. During part of the year, the whole band camped together at a water hole; then in the wet season, they'd scatter over the country. They had no political hierarchy or chiefs, and decisions were reached by group consensus; both men and women had a say.

Not all the San lived by hunting and gathering alone. In the early 19th century, the San were responsible for one of the most extensive pre-colonial trade networks which extended across the Kalahari.

Today, the San people are landless and unequivocally impoverished. However, some are finding new lifestyles: learning to farm and keeping small numbers of cattle and goats on what land remains for them, but many still hunt when they have the opportunity. A group of such farmers in Namibia have joined to form the Nyae Nyae Farmers' Cooperative (NNFC), which is supported by the Ju/hoansi Bushmen Development Foundation in Namibia.

In 1991, at the Namibian National Land Conference, the Minister for Land stated that the San system of land-holding would be recognised by the government.

Survival International

Nama, Herero (including Himba), Topnaar, Europeans (mainly German and Afrikaner), Coloured (mixed European and African), Caprivian, Basters, Tswana and San.

LANGUAGE

English and Afrikaans are the official languages, and are used for all official documents, road signs and publications. German is very widely spoken; in some areas, such as Swakopmund, you will hardly hear anything else. In northern Namibia and the Caprivi there's also lots of Portuguese spoken. Other main language groups are Bantu (including Owambo and Herero) and Khoisan (including Nama, Damara and San dialects).

Facts for the Visitor

VISAS

No visas are required by nationals of Australia, Canada, Ireland, New Zealand, South Africa, the UK, the USA, and most other southern African and western European countries.

For visa and length of stay extensions, see the Ministry of Home Affairs (☎ 398 9111),

at the corner of Kasino St and Independence Ave, in Windhoek.

EMBASSIES
Namibian Embassies

There are Namibian embassies in France, South Africa, the UK, and the USA.

Foreign Embassies in Namibia

Angola
  Angola House, 3 Ausspann St, Ausspannplatz, Private Bag 12020 (☎ 227535; fax 221498)
France
  1 Goethe St, PO Box 20484, Windhoek (☎ 229021; fax 231436)
South Africa
  RSA House, corner Jan Jonker Strasse and Nelson Mandela Drive, Klein Windhoek, PO Box 23100 (☎ 229765; fax 224140)
UK
  116A Robert Mugabe Ave, PO Box 22202 (☎ 223022; fax 228895)
USA
  14 Lossen St, Ausspannplatz, Private Bag 12029 (☎ 221601; fax 229792)
Zambia
  22 Sam Nujoma Drive, corner of Republic Rd, PO Box 22882 (☎ 237610; fax 228162)

MONEY
US$1 = N$4.70

The Namibian dollar (N) equals 100 cents

and is on a par with the South African rand (but in South Africa, it fetches only R 0.70). In Namibia, the rand remains legal tender at a rate of 1:1.

You can change major currencies and travellers' cheques to Namibian dollars or South African rand at any bank; opt for rand if there's any chance of having leftover cash to reconvert outside the country. To change travellers' cheques, banks charge up to 7% commission.

Credit cards are widely accepted in most shops, restaurants and hotels, and credit card cash advances are available from BOB, First National Bank's automatic teller.

The American Express representative is Woker Travel (☎ 237946) in Windhoek.

If you're camping or staying in backpackers' hostels, cooking your own meals and hitching or using local minibuses, plan on spending around US$15 to US$20 per day. A general sales tax (GST) of 10% is applied to most purchases, including meals and accommodation, but is factored into advertised rates and prices.

TOURIST OFFICES
Namibia Tourism is at Ground Floor, Continental Building, 272 Independence Ave, Private Bag 13346, Windhoek (☎ 284 2363; fax 284 2364).

Useful publications include the *SWA-Namibia Accommodation Guide for Tourists* and Engen Oil's *Guidebook – Travel in Namibia*. The latter is published annually and available free from government tourist offices or for around US$1.50 at private tourist offices and bookshops.

POST & COMMUNICATIONS
Domestic post is slow, especially as you move away from Windhoek. There are fussy restrictions on parcel wrapping and customs declarations, so check first before you post.

The international telephone rate is US$3.50 per minute to any foreign country.

You can make local and international calls from post office telephone boxes or hotels, but the latter can be very expensive. If you're phoning smaller towns or rural areas, you may have to dial the exchange and ask the operator for the desired number. Some rural areas are connected only by radio telephones or short-wave radio.

The country code for Namibia is 264. The telephone area code for Windhoek is 061, Keetmanshoop 0631, and Swakopmund 064.

DANGERS & ANNOYANCES
Theft isn't particularly rife, but Windhoek does have problems. Don't walk alone at night and either conceal your valuables or leave them somewhere safe. Windhoek townships to avoid, unless you have a local invitation and/or a good reason to visit, include Goreangab, Wanaheda and Hakahana, as well as southern Katutura, where boredom and unemployment are serious problems.

Don't leave anything in sight inside a vehicle, and at caravan parks, particularly in Tsumeb and Grootfontein, guard your valuables at night.

Around Lüderitz, keep clear of the Sperrgebiet, the off-limits diamond area, as the armed patrols can be zealous.

PUBLIC HOLIDAYS
Public holidays in Namibia are: 1 January, 21 March (Independence Day), 1 May (Workers' Day), 4 May (Casinga Day), 25 May (Africa Day), 26 August (Heroes Day), 10 December (Human Rights Day), 25 and 26 December and Easter.

Getting There & Away

AIR
South African Airways (SAA) operates daily flights between Johannesburg, Cape Town and Windhoek's international airport, which is about 42km east of the city. The one-way fare to Johannesburg or Cape Town is around US$175. Air Namibia also flies to Windhoek twice weekly from Harare, Lusaka, Maun and Gaborone.

LAND

Angola

There are three border crossings to Angola – at Ruacana, Oshikango and Rundu – but you need an Angolan visa permitting overland entry. At Ruacana Falls, you can enter the border area temporarily without a visa; just sign in at the border post.

Botswana

A 4WD gravel road from Windhoek through Gobabis to Botswana crosses the border at Buitepos. There's a weekly Trans-Namib bus between Gobabis and Ghanzi (Botswana). Hitching and bus services should improve with the completion of the Trans-Kalahari highway between Gaborone and Windhoek.

You can also drive to Botswana via the Caprivi Strip, crossing at either Ngoma Bridge or Mohembo, but hitching on these routes isn't easy, due to sparse traffic.

The Windhoek to Livingstone bus described under Zambia later in this section passes through Kasane and so offers connections between Namibia and Botswana.

South Africa

A luxury Intercape Mainliner (☎ 227847) coach service from Windhoek to Cape Town (US$90) or Johannesburg (US$92) runs four times weekly. In Windhoek the office is on Gallilei St.

Ekonoliner (☎ (0642) 5935), based in Walvis Bay, leaves Cape Town on Friday and returns on Sunday. One-way tickets cost US$52, with meals. Book through Ritz Reisen (☎ 23 6670) in Windhoek.

You can drive or hitch to Cape Town along good tarred roads, crossing at the Noordoewer border, or to Upington with a border crossing at Nakop. When hitching with trucks, agree on a price before climbing aboard. The standard rate is around US$1.50 per 100km, but drivers may initially ask for more.

Zambia

The only border crossing between Namibia and Zambia is at the village of Katima

Mulilo, on the west bank of the Zambezi River, near Sesheke (Zambia).

From Katima Mulilo it's 5km to the border post at Wenela. There's no bus, but a lift in a pick-up costs US$0.50. It's then less than 1km to the Zambia border post, and a further 500m to the west bank of the Zambezi. Canoes take you across the river, and it's then 5km to Sesheke. Buses from Sesheke to Livingstone, via Kazungula, go twice daily for US$6 to US$8.

The Windhoek-based Zambezi Express (☎ /fax 223478; email bonim@icafe.com.na) has a bus between Windhoek and Livingstone (Zambia), which leaves from Windhoek's Grab-a-Phone bus terminal twice weekly and passes Rundu (US$30), the Zambezi Lodge in Katima Mulilo (US$33), Chobe Safari Lodge in Kasane (Botswana; US$40), Phumula Centre car park in Victoria Falls (Zimbabwe; US$49), and arrives at the New Fairmount Hotel in Livingstone (US$49).

If you are taking your own vehicle into Zambia, you need a Vehicle & Owners Identification Certificate, which must be obtained from the Katima Mulilo police station.

Zimbabwe

Between Windhoek and Victoria Falls, try the weekly Over-Border Minibus (☎ 222873), which uses the Grab-a-Phone terminal in Windhoek. The fare is US$108 for transport only, US$127 including lunch and camping in Rundu, and US$144 with lunch and bed & breakfast in Rundu.

Also see the Zambezi Express bus details in the preceding Zambia section.

Getting Around

AIR

Air Namibia services domestic routes out of Eros airport in Windhoek, including flights to and from Tsumeb; Rundu and Katima Mulilo; Keetmanshoop; Lüderitz and Alexander Bay (South Africa); and Swakopmund and Oshakati.

BUS

Internal bus services aren't extensive. Luxury services are limited to the Intercape Mainliner, which has scheduled runs going from Cape Town to Windhoek and then to Swakopmund, Walvis Bay and Tsumeb.

The Trans-Namib rail service has an expanding system of buses which replace defunct rail services and also tie in places not connected by rail: Lüderitz, Bethanie, Helmeringhausen, Gochas, Buitepos, Ghanzi (Botswana), Outjo, Kamanjab, Opuwo, Khorixas, Henties Bay, Grootfontein, Oshakati and Rundu. There's also a route across the central Namib, between Mariental and Walvis Bay, which sometimes runs via Sesriem.

The main routes are also served by local minibuses, which depart when full. Fares work out to around US$0.03 per kilometre, but there may be a charge of US$2.70 per piece of luggage.

TRAIN

Trans-Namib Railways operates rail services between most major towns but trains are slow – as one reader remarked, moving 'at the pace of an energetic donkey cart' – and services are rarely booked out. Sleepers offer four or six-bed compartments, while economy carriages have only seats. If you want a sleeper, book in advance at railway stations or the Windhoek Booking Office (☎ 298 2032) or they may not attach the 1st class carriage.

Windhoek is Namibia's rail hub, with services south to Keetmanshoop, north to Tsumeb, west to Swakopmund and Walvis Bay and east to Gobabis. On weekends (Friday to Monday inclusive), fares are normally double what they are during the week. Economy/sleeper fares from Windhoek include US$5/16 to Keetmanshoop, US$5/13 to Gobabis, US$3/9 (weekdays) or US$7/20 (weekends) to Swakopmund, US$5/13 (weekdays) or US$10/29 (weekends) to Walvis Bay, and US$13/39 to Tsumeb.

CAR & MOTORCYCLE

Roads are sealed and in excellent repair along the main routes. Even the notorious Golden Highway through the Caprivi is currently being paved, and there are good gravel roads to most of the points of interest off the main routes.

Note that motorbikes aren't permitted in national parks, with the exception of the main routes through Namib-Naukluft Park.

Car hire is expensive, but if you have a group it's the best way of seeing the country. The cheaper companies charge US$50 to US$65 per day with unlimited kilometres (some have a minimum rental period). Most companies require a US$285 deposit and renters must be aged 25 or over.

The best value 4WD hire is with Namib 4WD in Windhoek (☎ 220604; fax 220605) which charges as little as US$90 per day. Enyandi Car Hire in Otjiwarongo (☎ 303898; fax 303892) charges US$110 per day for a 4WD, including insurance, regardless of the rental period; you can contact them through Chameleon Backpackers' Lodge in Windhoek. For Land Rovers, you'll find excellent deals with Swakop-Auto Rent in Swakopmund (☎ /fax 461506). In Windhoek, there's also Asco Car & Motorbike Hire (☎ /fax 233064) and Camping Car Hire (☎ 237756; fax 237757).

HITCHING

Hitching isn't bad, and it isn't unusual to get a 1000km lift, but it's illegal in national parks and there's little traffic on open highways, so expect long waits, especially in the Caprivi.

Lifts wanted and offered are advertised daily on Windhoek radio (☎ 291311), while The Cardboard Box (backpackers' accommodation) and the Ministry of Environment & Tourism (MET), both in Windhoek, have notice boards with share car rental and lifts offered and wanted.

ORGANISED TOURS

Even if you're one who spurns organised trips, there's a good case for joining a camping tour to such hard-to-reach places as Skeleton Coast, Damaraland, Kaokoveld,

NAMIBIA

the Kunene valley, Owamboland, Bushmanland and the wilder sections of the Namib Desert. Some offer nothing but transport and camping options; participants do all the camp work and prepare their own meals. The following operators offer good value:

!Ah N!hore Safaris
    PO Box 5703, Windhoek (☎/fax 220124). Educational cultural tours through remote areas of Bushmanland with skilled San hunters and trackers.
Chameleon Safaris
    PO Box 21903, Windhoek (☎/fax 247668). This backpackers' company runs two classic seven-day safari loops, one each through northern and southern Namibia for US$310.
Charly's Desert Tours
    11 Kaiser Wilhelm Strasse, PO Box 1400, Swakopmund (☎ 4341; fax 4821). Good-value day tours around Swakopmund.
Desert Adventure Safaris
    Namib Centre, Roon St, PO Box 1428, Swakopmund (☎/fax 404459; fax 404664). Inexpensive day tours around Swakopmund, and longer trips to Damaraland and the Kaokoveld.
Footprints
    The Cardboard Box, PO Box 9639, Eros, Windhoek (☎/fax 249190). Recommended hiking and camping safaris, with emphasis on culture, to Kaokoland, Owamboland, Bushmanland and elsewhere. Namibia trips can be combined with options in Botswana, South Africa and Mozambique.
Muramba Bushman Trails
    PO Box 689, Tsumeb (☎ (06738) 6222; fax (0671) 20916). A unique opportunity to meet the Heikum San people and learn from their wealth of bush skills.

Windhoek

Namibia's capital, Windhoek ('windy corner'), at an altitude of 1650m, was once the headquarters of the principal Khoi-Khoi opposition to the German advance, but is now a prosperous and modern city. It has managed to preserve lots of colonial-era buildings.

At its heart is Independence Ave (formerly Kaiser Strasse) which bisects the city and is the major shopping, administrative and tourist centre. Small arcades leading west off

this street are lined with pavement cafes and small shops.

Information
The friendly Windhoek Information & Publicity Office (☎ 391 2050; fax 391 2091), on Post Street Mall, is most helpful. There's also an information desk at the Grab-a-Phone bus terminal.

The Ministry of Environment & Tourism (☎ 233832), or MET, in the Oode Voorpost on the corner of John Meinert Strasse and Moltke Strasse, has detailed information on the national parks. It's open Monday to Friday from 8 am to 1 pm for bookings and payment, and from 2 to 3 pm for bookings only.

You can hire camping equipment from Gav's Camping Hire (☎/fax 251526) at 21 Bevil Rudd St, or Camping Hire Namibia (☎/fax 252995) at 12 Louis Raymond St.

Helpful agents for flights and tours are Trip Travel (☎ 236880; fax 225430) and Woker (Amex) Travel Services (☎ 237946).

For books and maps, there are branches of CNA bookshop in the Kalahari Sands (Frenchbank) Centre and in Wernhill Park Centre. Der Bücherkellar sells novels and literature in English and German. Uncle Spike's Book Exchange, at the corner of Garten Strasse and Tal Strasse, is inexpensive for basic reading material.

Things to See & Do
The whitewashed ramparts of **Alte Feste**, Windhoek's oldest surviving building, date from 1890-92. It houses the historical section of the **State Museum**, which is open weekdays from 9 am to 6 pm and on weekends from 3 to 6 pm.

The other half of the State Museum, the **Owela Museum**, is on Robert Mugabe Ave. Exhibits focus on Namibia's natural and cultural history. It's open the same hours as the historical section.

The throbbing heart of the Windhoek shopping district is the bizarrely colourful **Post Street Mall**, which could have been a set in the film *Dick Tracy*. It's lined with vendors selling curios, art work, clothing and

NAMIBIA

Windhoek

See Central Windhoek Map

1 Club Thriller
2 Minibuses for the North
3 Singles Quarters;
  Minibuses for the North
4 Namibia Star Hotel
5 Backpackers' Lodge
6 Rhino Park Health
  Care Centre
7 Travellers' Lodge
8 June's Place B&B
9 Haus Ol-Ga
10 Yang Tse Restaurant
11 South African Consulate
12 O'Hagan's Irish Pub & Grill
13 Marie's Accommodation
14 Hotel Safari
15 Safari Court Hotel
16 Gav's Camping Hire
17 Camping Hire Namibia
18 Arebbusch Travel Lodge

NAMIBIA

Central Windhoek

[Map of Central Windhoek with street names including: Blenkin, Abt, March, Livingstone, Luther, Street, Schanzen, Promenaden, Road, Independence Avenue, Goethe, Robert Mugabe, Korner, Street, Uhland Street, Osmann Street, Florence Nightingale, Robert Koch, Lister, Johann Albrecht, Pettenkofer, Van Rhijn, Hosea Kutako, Schanzen, Werth Strasse, Hofmeyer, Ross, Pavlov, Schweitzer, Freud, Strasse, Stecler, Walk, Pasteur, Jenner, Pasteur, Adler, Bahnhof, Moltke Strasse, Anderson Strasse, Salk, Strasse, John Meinert, Strasse, Simpson, Curie, Bülow Strasse, Rossini St, Love, Roentgen, Verdi, Roberg St, Kasino, Strasse, John Meinert, Brahms, Bülow, Martin Neumbayo, Post Street Mall, Park, Strauss, Wagner St, Storch, Zoo Park, Brahms, Gluck, Strasse, Peter Müller, Bach, Grieg, Schubert, Mozart, Botha, Independence Avenue, Volans, Louis, Pucini St, Blohm, Bismarck, Neser, Sam Nujoma Drive, Schuster, Strasse, Sam Nujoma Drive, Hügel Strasse, Orban, Sandpiper, Chopin, Hoogenhout, Sam Nujoma Drive, Schwerinsburg Str, Edelvalk, Hosea Kutako, Viljoen, Pursel, Tal Strasse, Garten Strasse, Eulen, Church, Schinz, Church, Papageien, Liszt, Bismarck, Mandy, Trift, Meranten, Avenue, Kalk, Strasse, Egret, Nachtigal, Schinz, Ausspannplatz]

Scale: 0   150   300 m

other tourist items, mostly imported from Zimbabwe.

The walking track known as the **Hofmeyer Walk** through the Klein Windhoek Valley offers a panoramic view of the city and interesting flora and birdlife. It begins at the corner of Orban Strasse and Anderson Strasse and takes about an hour.

In the old **South-West Breweries building**, at 40 Tal Strasse, is the **Namibia Crafts Centre**, open Monday to Friday from 9 am to 5.30 pm and Saturday from 9 am to 1 pm.

True to its partially Teutonic background, Windhoek stages its own **Oktoberfest** towards the end of October, which lovers of the amber nectar should not miss. There's also the German-style **Windhoek Carnival** (or **Wika**), held over a week in late April, which features a series of events and balls.

Places to Stay

A popular camp site is at *Daan Viljoen Game Park*, 18km from town; pre-book at MET (see National Parks & Reserves, later in this chapter).

Closer to town is *Arebbusch Travel Lodge* (☎ 252255; fax 251670) in Olympia, Windhoek, on the road south. Camping costs

PLACES TO STAY		
10	Thüringer Hof Hotel; Jägerstube Restaurant	
15	The Cardboard Box	
16	Chameleon Backpackers' Lodge	
17	Villa Verdi	
18	Hotel-Pension Cela	
19	Hotel-Pension Handke	
25	Continental Hotel	
48	Puccini International Hostel	
49	Kalahari Sands	
58	Hotel Heinitzburg	
59	Hotel-Pension Christophe	

PLACES TO EAT		
9	Espresso Coffee Bar	
11	Nando's	
12	Steenbras Takeaways	
27	Grand Canyon Spur	
29	Central Café; King Pies	
31	King Pies	
32	Gathemann's	
37	Le Bistrot	
38	Mac Pie	
50	Wecke & Voights	
51	KFC	

55	Sardinia's	
56	King Pies	

OTHER		
1	Hospital	
2	Joe's Beer House	
3	Thirty-Something	
4	Train Station	
5	Old Supreme Court (Obergericht)	
6	Kenyan Embassy; Grand China Restaurant	
7	Turnhalle	
8	Ministry of Environment & Tourism (MET)	
13	Paradise Alley	
14	Minibuses to Swakopmund & Walvis Bay	
20	Minibuses for the South	
21	Doctors Rabie & Retief	
22	National Gallery	
23	Owela (State) Museum	
24	Namibia Tourism	
26	Ministry of Home Affairs (Immigration)	
28	Trip Travel	

30	Windhoek Information & Publicity Office	
33	Post Office	
34	South West Africa House (State House)	
35	Old Magistrates' Court	
36	Telecommunications Office	
39	Wernhill Park Centre	
40	Hauptkasse Building	
41	Tintenpalast Building (Parliament House)	
42	Christuskirche (Lutheran Church)	
43	Alte Feste (State Museum)	
44	Kaiserliche Realschule Building	
45	Grab-a-Phone Bus Terminal	
46	Woker Travel Services (Amex)	
47	Der Bücherkeller Bookshop	
52	Officers' House	
53	Namibia Crafts Centre	
54	The Warehouse Theatre	
57	Tucker's Tavern	

US$10 per person and double rooms without/with bath are US$29/35; two/five-bed chalets with bath cost US$52/63. Taxis from the centre cost US$3.50.

A favourite backpackers' hostel is *The Cardboard Box* (☎ 228994; fax 245587; email ahj@windhoek.alt.na), at the corner of Johann Albrecht Strasse and John Meinert Strasse. Dorm beds cost US$6.25, with use of the cooking facilities and swimming pool. Double rooms are US$20, but must be booked in advance. There's a notice board for lifts and it's a convenient place to gather groups for car hire.

The *Chameleon Backpackers' Lodge* (☎ 247668), at 22 Wagner St in Windhoek West, provides a lively alternative. Dormitory beds cost US$8, including a sheet and pillow, and private double rooms are US$25, including linen. Breakfasts, light meals and drinks are available on request, and guests can use the pool, kitchen, video and phone/fax facilities.

Another new possibility is the *Puccini International Hostel* at 4 Puccini St, which charges US$6 for a dorm bed. There's a pool and a sauna and they offer free pick-up from Grab-a-Phone.

The *Travellers' Lodge* (☎ 236547) in Eros Park charges US$8 per person. It's used mainly by local businesspeople. They offer free coffee and tea, kitchen facilities, bedding and a common TV room.

A bit further from the centre but fantastic value is the friendly *Marie's Accommodation* (☎ 251787; fax 252128; email brianhj@mac.alt.na), at 156 Diaz St, with large singles/doubles without bath for US$14/21, including breakfast. Rooms with shared bath and kitchen cost US$16/24.

A pleasant bed and breakfast (B&B) is *June's Place* (☎ 226054), at 91 Nelson Mandela Drive. There are two rooms with private facilities starting at US$19/35 for a single/double. Rates include breakfast

NAMIBIA

served on the patio with a view of the nearby hills.

An inexpensive mid-range hotel is *Hotel-Pension Handke* (☎ 234904; fax 225660) at 3 Rossini St, with singles/doubles for US$38/48, including breakfast.

Places to Eat

One of Windhoek's best takeaways is *Steenbras*, on Bahnhof Strasse near Independence Ave, which serves great fish, chicken burgers and spicy chips. A super-value choice is *King Pies*, with an outlet on Post Street Mall and two on Independence Avenue (at the corner of Garten Strasse and just outside Levinson Arcade). They offer a super lunch deal: a pie and a large soft drink for US$1. A similar place is *MacPie*, on Post Street Mall, which has interesting combinations, including some curry and vegetarian choices.

Among the best chicken options is *Nando's*, which does superb peri-peri chicken, spicy rice, chips and other goodies.

The mid-range *Grand Canyon Spur* has a varied menu and appealing balcony seating. Don't miss the salad bar or the renowned chocolate brownies.

Mike's Kitchen, in Wernhill Park Centre, is a family restaurant serving standard lunches and dinners – salads, steaks, chicken dishes, burgers and chips – seven days a week.

A great splash-out is *Gathemann's*, in a prominent colonial building with a sunny terrace overlooking Independence Ave. In the morning and afternoon they serve rich European-style gateaux and pastries, and downstairs there's a sandwich takeaway.

The *Jägerstube* at the Thüringer Hof Hotel offers Windhoek Lager and German-style cuisine. At lunch, there's an all-you-can-eat buffet of cold cuts, cheese, salad and cooked dishes.

The best Chinese food is at *Yang Tse* on Sam Nujoma Drive, near the petrol stations in Klein Windhoek.

Entertainment

One of Windhoek's best nightspots is *The Warehouse Theatre*, in the old South-West Breweries building on Tal Strasse. This truly integrated club is open almost every night, and emphasises live music and theatre productions – both African and European. It's friendly, secure and lots of fun. The cover charge averages US$3.

In Katutura is the wonderful *Club Thriller* (cover charge US$2.50) – once you're past the weapons search at the door, the atmosphere is upbeat and secure. Foreigners get a minimum of hassle, but don't carry valuables or walk around Katutura at night – always take a taxi (US$0.75 from town).

Less animated pubs include the Irish-style *Tucker's Tavern* and *Joe's Beer House*. Next door to Joe's is the unpredictable *Thirty-Something*, with live music and decent pizza.

Getting There & Away

Most long-distance bus services use the Grab-a-Phone bus terminal on Independence Ave. Services to Swakopmund or Walvis Bay depart from the corner of John Meinert and Mandume Ndomufayo Sts. Southern routes to Mariental and Keetmanshoop leave from the car park north of the Wernhill Park Centre; those going north to Owamboland and Kavango leave from the Singles' Quarters terminal in Katutura township. However, it may be safer to wait on the bridge at the Independence Ave on-ramp to the Western Bypass.

The railway station ticket and booking office is open from 7.30 am to 4 pm, Monday to Friday.

Getting Around

The airport shuttle bus (☎ 263211) between Windhoek international airport (42km from town) and the Grab-a-Phone bus terminal, connects with arriving and departing flights and costs US$7.50. Schedules are posted at Grab-a-Phone.

Taxi fare to anywhere around Windhoek, including Khomasdal and Katutura, is US$0.75, but taxis caught at Grab-a-Phone may well try to overcharge.

Around the Country

CAPRIVI & KAVANGO

The Caprivi Strip, an eccentric extension of Namibia separating Angola and Zambia from Botswana, is the result of a deal in 1890 between Britain and Germany. The two powers agreed on an exchange of territory which left Britain with Zanzibar and Germany with Heligoland (an island in the North Sea) and what would become known as the Caprivi Strip.

The Caprivi and Kavango regions present a very different face of Namibia than places further south; they're largely forested and well watered, and through them flow some of Africa's greatest rivers – the Zambezi, Okavango and Kwando.

Rundu

Rundu occupies a lovely setting on the bluffs above the Okavango River. It's worth checking out the **Mbangura Woodcarvers' Cooperative**; you can buy traditional drums and some lovely handmade furniture. There's also a small **zoo** at Ekongoro, 2km east of town.

The Rundu Tourism Centre (☎ 55910; fax 55909) offers information and local bookings.

Places to Stay & Eat The most central accommodation is the *Rundu Service Centre* (☎ 787), beside Hunter's Tavern at the Shell petrol station. Basic singles/doubles cost US$25/40.

The *Sarasungu River Lodge* (☎ 55161; fax (061) 220694) occupies a shady riverside setting about 4km from the centre. Camping costs US$6.50 per person and single/double bungalows cost US$45/63, with breakfast. With advance notice, Ines or Eduardo will pick you up from the Shell petrol station on the main road.

Kayengona Lodge (radio ☎ (064) 203581, ask for 467), 20km east of town and 4km off the river road, has single/double bungalows with bath for US$30/55. Four/six-bed bun-

galows with shared facilities cost US$18 per person. Campers pay US$5 per person. Transfers from town are free.

The recommended *Nkwasi Lodge* (☎ (061) 250850; fax 250851) offers a friendly retreat with a warm family atmosphere. Meals are superb and guests are treated like family. Single/double bungalows with breakfast cost US$57/87, with high standards and level of service. Camping is US$6.25 per person, including use of the pool and bar.

For super Portuguese-style meals, try *Casa Mourisca* on the river road in the centre.

West Caprivi

The road from Rundu to Katima Mulilo passes through the largely barren West Caprivi Game Reserve. The Mahango Game Reserve near the Botswana border is better for wildlife-viewing, with large numbers of elephants during the dry season. You can drive through Mahango to Shakawe in Botswana but 4WD is required.

At Popa Falls, where the Okavango River plunges down a series of cascades, accommodation is available at *Popa Falls Rest Camp*, with camping for US$7.50 and four-bed chalets for US$25. A small store on site sells tinned food, beer, candles and mosquito coils.

Katima Mulilo

Out on a limb at the end of the Caprivi Strip lies Katima Mulilo, Namibia's most remote outpost. It's as far from Windhoek as you can get in Namibia – over 1200km. It's a pleasant town with lush vegetation and enormous trees, but apart from the hippos and crocodiles in the river, little wildlife remains. The **Caprivi Arts Centre** is a good place to look for handicrafts, such as woodcarvings, baskets, bowls, traditional weapons etc.

Places to Stay & Eat The relaxed *Hippo Lodge* (☎ 3684; fax 3177), 6km downstream from the town centre, offers camping for US$3.75 per person and singles/doubles for

NAMIBIA

US$38/45. Phone and they'll pick you up from town.

The *Zambezi Lodge* (☎ 3203; fax 3631) has single/double self-contained bungalows for US$54/63, with breakfast. You can camp amid flowery garden surroundings for US$2.50 per person plus US$1.25 per vehicle.

The best eatery is the *Lyambai*, in the shopping centre, which is open for lunch. You could also try the *Coimbra Restaurant & Takeaway*, which is just a block away. As the name suggests, it specialises in Portuguese-African items. For a more formal dining experience, the *Zambezi Lodge* serves good lunches and dinners.

Getting There & Away Katima Mulilo is served by the Egoli Liner minibus (☎ 53), which connects it with Rundu and Windhoek several times weekly.

Both the Over-Border Minibus and the Zambezi Express buses from Windhoek pass through Katima Mulilo.

DAMARALAND

Damaraland is characterised by fascinating and unique geological, archaeological and biological features. A convenient base is the *Khorixas Rest Camp* (☎ 196; fax 388), 3km from Khorixas on Torra Bay road. Camping costs US$6 per vehicle plus US$6.25 per person; single/double bungalows are US$43/75. Peripherals include a restaurant, braai (barbecue) area, swimming pool and general shop.

The Petrified Forest

The Petrified Forest, 40km west of Khorixas, takes in open scrubland scattered with petrified tree trunks up to 34m long and 6m around, and estimated to be around 260 million years old.

There's no admission charge (although someone may attempt to collect something anyway), but guides are compulsory and live only from tips; plan on US$1.25 per group for the 500m walking tour. Note that it's strictly forbidden to carry off even the smallest scrap of petrified wood.

Twyfelfontein

The main attraction at Twyfelfontein is the gallery of **rock engravings**, which date back thousands of years. Some are from the early Stone Age and are probably the work of San hunters. Interestingly, many depict animals no longer found this far south, such as elephant, rhino, giraffe and lion.

Admission is US$1.25 per vehicle plus US$1.25 per person. Guides are available, but the route isn't hard to follow and if you want more time than the guide is prepared to spend, you can probably arrange to walk alone. A reasonable tip is around US$1.25 per group for the one-hour tour, but note that guides are salaried, so tipping isn't compulsory.

The nearby *Aba-Huab Camp* (☎/fax (065712) 104), beside the Aba-Huab River, is simple, rustic and natural, and travellers rate it among Namibia's finest camp sites. Camping in tents or small open-sided A-frame shelters costs US$3.75 per person.

Burnt Mountain

Just south-east of Twyfelfontein is the 12km-long ridge of hills known as Burnt Mountain, which appears to have been exposed to fire. Virtually nothing grows in this eerie panorama of desolation, but the vividly coloured rocks light up at sunset. Six kilometres away is an unusual mass of perpendicular basalt columns known as the **Organ Pipes**.

The Brandberg

North of Uis near the upper Ugab River is the massif known as the Brandberg or 'fire mountain', due to the effect of the sun on the red rock. The summit, Königstein, is Namibia's highest peak at 2573m.

The best known Brandberg attraction is the gallery of **rock paintings** in Tsisab ('leopard') Ravine, which was first discovered in 1918 by the German surveyor Dr Reinhard Maack. The site known as Maack's Shelter contains the famous *White Lady of the Brandberg*. It's a 45 minute walk from the car park.

Access to Tsisab ravine is 15km north of Uis, where a gravel track marked 'Witvrou'

NAMIBIA

leads 26km to the parking area. From there, it's at least an hour up a well-defined track to Maack's Shelter, but beyond are other shelters, also containing ancient paintings. Watch for baboon, klipspringer and mountain zebras and carry lots of water.

You can camp at the parking area but no water is available. Alternatively, there's the *Brandberg Rest Camp* in nearby Uis (☎/fax (062262) 235). Single/double units start at US$25/38; bungalows accommodating up to six people cost US$55.

Getting There & Away
There's no public transport anywhere in Damaraland, and hitching can be difficult. The only practical access is with a private or hired vehicle; 2WD is fine for visiting all the sites mentioned in this section.

GROOTFONTEIN
The pleasant town of Grootfontein is characterised by local limestone architecture and avenues of jacaranda trees. The historic **Tree Park**, planted by the South-West Africa Company, features species from around the world. There's also a colonial **cemetery** and a **museum**, which is housed in the old German fort. If it's closed, contact Mr Menge (☎ 2061) to arrange a visit.

For an interesting day, see Thekla and Udo Unkel (☎ (06738) 83130), 8km west of town on the D2859. You'll get the lowdown on one of the world's fastest-growing ventures – ostrich farming – and afterward you can have a meal (guess what's on the menu) or shop for ostrich eggshell jewellery.

Places to Stay & Eat
The *Oleander Municipal Camp & Caravan Park* (☎ 2930) costs US$4.25 for a camp site plus US$1.50 per vehicle and US$1 per person. Simple four-bed chalets cost US$21, and more sophisticated quarters are also available.

The *Meteor Hotel* has singles/doubles starting at US$28/48, with breakfast. The restaurant offers the finest dining in town. Out the Rundu road, opposite the Tsumkwe turn-off, is the recommended *Roy's Rest*

Camp (☎ (06738), ask for 18302; fax (06731) 2139), run by Wimpie and Marietjie Otto. This fabulously rustic place has two-level, four-person bungalows for US$33 for the first person plus US$25 for each additional person. Camp sites are US$2.50 and breakfast and dinner cost US$5 to US$7. There's a nice pool, braai pits and picnic tables, and the owners run tours of their working cattle ranch.

KEETMANSHOOP
Keetmanshoop, with 15,000 people, is the main southern crossroads in Namibia and serves as the centre for a thriving Karakul wool industry. The Southern Tourist Forum (☎ 3316; fax 3813) is in the municipal building.

There's a free **museum** in the 1895 Rhenish mission church.

Namibia's largest stand of the kokerbooms or quivertrees *(Aloe dichotoma)* lies at **Kokerboomwoud**, on the Gariganus Farm, 14km north-east of town. Day admission and access to the picnic facilities is US$3 per vehicle plus US$1.50 per person. This also includes access to the **Giant's Playground**, a natural rock garden 5km away.

Places to Stay & Eat
The large *Municipal Camp & Caravan Park* charges US$1.50 per vehicle and US$1.50 per person. The *Schutzen-Haus*, 200m south, has simple double rooms with shower and toilet for US$30.

There's also the plush new *Lafenis Rest Camp*, 5km south along the road to South Africa. Two/four-bed bungalows cost US$28/43. You can also stay at the *Gariganus Farm* (☎ (0638) 22835); camping costs US$3 per person and simple single/double bungalows cost US$25/42.

The adequate *Travel Inn* (☎ 3344; fax 2138) has budget rooms for US$28. The popular *Canyon Hotel* (☎ 23361; fax 23714) has rooms from US$46/72.

Lara's Restaurant, on the corner of 5th Ave and Schmeide St, is a popular place with strange décor and equally strange music. The

Schutzen-Haus, a German-style pub and restaurant south of the Municipal camp site, dishes up good hardy fare.

Another good choice is the Hungarian-oriented *BalafonTakeaways* (☎ 2539).

Getting There & Away

Intercape Mainliner buses run four times weekly to Cape Town and Windhoek from the Du Toit petrol station. There are also daily Trans-Namib (☎ (0631) 292202) buses to Lüderitz.

Hitching is relatively easy on the B1

between Keetmanshoop and Windhoek or Grünau, but there's less traffic to Lüderitz.

Overnight trains run daily except Saturday between Windhoek and Keetmanshoop.

LÜDERITZ

Lüderitz is a surreal colonial relic – a Bavarian village huddling on the barren, windswept coast of the Namib Desert, seemingly untouched by the 20th century. Here, the South Atlantic is icy but clean, and is home to seal, penguin and other marine life. The desolate beaches also support flamingo and ostrich.

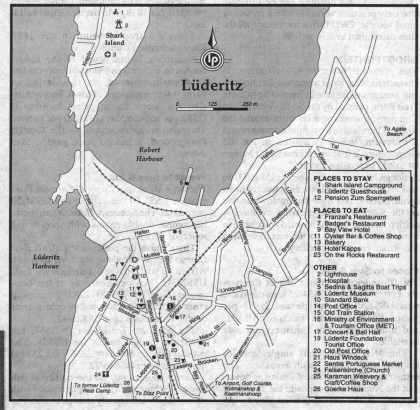

Lüderitz

0   125   250 m

PLACES TO STAY
1 Shark Island Campground
6 Lüderitz Guesthouse
12 Pension Zum Sperrgebiet

PLACES TO EAT
4 Franzel's Restaurant
7 Badger's Restaurant
9 Bay View Hotel
11 Oyster Bar & Coffee Shop
13 Bakery
18 Hotel Kapps
23 On the Rocks Restaurant

OTHER
2 Lighthouse
3 Hospital
5 Sedina & Sagitta Boat Trips
8 Lüderitz Museum
10 Standard Bank
14 Post Office
15 Old Train Station
16 Ministry of Environment
   & Tourism Office (MET)
17 Concert & Ball Hall
19 Lüderitz Foundation
   Tourist Office
20 Old Post Office
21 Haus Windeck
22 Sentra Portuguese Market
24 Felsenkirche (Church)
25 Karaman Weavery &
   Craft/Coffee Shop
26 Goerke Haus

The Lüderitz Foundation tourist office is on Bismarck Strasse. There's also a helpful MET office.

Things to See

Lüderitz has fine examples of German colonial architecture, including the **Goerke Haus (Magistrate's House)**, the **old train station**, and the **Concert & Ball Hall**.

In the evenings at 6 pm (5 pm in summer), you can visit the prominent church, **Felsenkirche**.

The **Lüderitz Museum** on Diaz Strasse is open Monday to Friday from 3.30 to 5 pm, or at other times by phoning (☎ 2562). The **Karaman Weavery** is also worthwhile, and has an attached craft shop and coffee shop.

A popular excursion is to the ghost town of **Kolmanskop**, once a major diamond-mining town which boasted a casino, skittle alley and theatre, but the slump in diamond sales after WWI and the discovery of richer deposits at Orangemund sounded its death knell. Permits to visit cost US$2.50 at the Lüderitz Foundation (☎ 2532) on upper Bismarck Strasse. You must provide your own transport from town.

At **Diaz Point**, 22km south of town, is a lighthouse and a cross commemorating the 1486 landing of Portuguese navigator Bartolomeu Dias. From the point there's a view to the nearby sea lion colony and jackass penguins may sometimes be seen diving and surfing off the rocks.

Organised Tours

Sailing trips to the Cape fur seal sanctuary at Diaz Point leave the harbour jetty daily (US$10). If the seas are calm you can include the penguin sanctuary on Halifax Island for US$5 per person. Book in person through Diaz Souvenirs.

Places to Stay & Eat

The beautifully situated but aggravatingly windy *Shark Island Campground* is connected to the mainland by a causeway 1km north from town. Camping costs US$10 per site. The rustic *Haus Windeck* (☎ 3370; fax 3306) at 6 Mabel St has dorm beds for US$7 and doubles at US$16.

The friendly *Lüderitz Guesthouse* (☎ 3347), which occupies a colonial building near the harbour, has self-contained German-style rooms with shared facilities starting at US$22.

The *Oyster Bar* on Bismarck Strasse serves light meals and snacks, including oysters. For lunch, the recommended *Badger's Restaurant* does great burgers, soup, salad and other light meals.

On the Rocks specialises in seafood and beef dishes; it opens at 7 pm. If there has been a good catch, the affiliated hotels, *Bay View* and *Kapps*, both serve decent seafood. At the stark north end of town is the good-value *Franzel's Restaurant*.

Getting There & Away

Public transport to Lüderitz is limited to flights from Swakopmund to Windhoek and the daily railways' bus from Keetmanshoop.

MARIENTAL

Mariental is a small administrative and commercial centre on the main bus and rail lines between Windhoek and Keetmanshoop.

The main attraction is **Hardap Dam**, 15km north of town. This reservoir on the upper Fish River harbours a variety of birdlife: flamingoes, fish eagles, pelicans, spoonbills and Goliath herons. An attached wildlife reserve shelters hosts of antelope, zebra, birds and other small animals, and offers several loop hiking trails. Maps are available at the office.

Places to Stay & Eat

Camping at Hardap Dam costs US$10 per site, and two/five-bed bungalows cost US$20/40. Other amenities include a shop, restaurant, kiosk, swimming pool and petrol station.

In Mariental, the *Sandberg Hotel* (☎/fax 2291) has singles/doubles for US$29/45. The cheapest place is the *Guglhupf Café* (☎ 718) which charges US$25/35 for singles/doubles.

OKAHANDJA

On the weekend nearest 23 August each year, the Red Flag Herero people come to

Okahandja for their colourful **Maherero Day** procession to honour their fallen chiefs.

The rest of the year, Okahandja's main draws are two immense **craft markets** – one in the centre and the other on the roadside near the southern entrance to town. They operate every day.

Gross Barmen (☎ 502091), 26km south-west of Okahandja, once served as a mission station, but is now Namibia's premier hot-spring resort. Its popularity means that even day visits must be booked through the MET in Windhoek. Admission is US$2.50 per person and US$2 per vehicle.

Places to Stay & Eat

In town the only accommodation is at the *Okahandja Hotel* (☎ 503024), which has a modest restaurant. Basic singles/doubles start at US$15/23.

At Gross Barmen, there are camp sites for US$7.50 for up to eight people; self-contained doubles are US$18 and bungalows range from US$20 to US$40. Picnic sites cost US$16. There's also a shop, restaurant and petrol station.

For meals popular options are the *Ol' Time Pizza Hut*, in the centre, and the *Bürgerstübchen Restaurant* on Post St. Biltong (dried meat) fans may want to check out the *Namibia Biltong Factory* and their delicious peri-peri beef.

Getting There & Away

Okahandja lies on all bus and rail lines between Windhoek, Swakopmund and northern Namibia.

SWAKOPMUND

Although not as ethereal as Lüderitz, Swakopmund is an attractive and interesting town found on the foggy desert coast. It's Namibia's most popular domestic holiday destination and there are plenty of flower gardens and half-timbered houses and lots of German colonial-era structures.

Information

There's a helpful Namib Information Centre (☎ 402224; fax 405101), and the MET office, two blocks away, sells Namib-Naukluft Park permits and also books camp sites. After hours, pick up Namib-Naukluft park entry permits from the Hans Kriess Garage at the corner of Kaiser Wilhelm Strasse and Breite Strasse.

Things to See

Swakopmund's main appeal is its beach frontage and colonial architecture. Sites of interest include the **restored jetty**, the **lighthouse**, the 1901 **railway station** (now a luxury hotel), the old **German barracks** (now the hostel) and the **Hansa brewery**. Especially picturesque is the **Woermannhaus**, formerly a hostel for the crews of a shipping line. Atop the Woermannhaus is the Damara Tower, which once served as a lookout tower.

The **National Marine Aquarium**, on the waterfront, opens up a view of the cold offshore world. Most impressive is the tunnel through the largest tank, which allows close-up views of graceful rays, toothy sharks and other marine beasties. The fish are fed at 3 pm. It's closed Mondays and admission is US$1.50.

If an ill wind blows up, you can take refuge in the **Swakopmund Museum**, at the foot of the lighthouse. It's also worth touring the **Rössing Mine**, the world's largest open-cast (strip) uranium mine. Mine tours leave from Café Anton on Friday at 8 am and cost US$3, including transport. Book at the Swakopmund Museum.

Places to Stay

The bleak *Mile 4 Caravan Park* (☎ 461781; fax 462901), on the beach 6km up the Henties Bay road, has camp sites for US$3 per tent plus US$2 per person and a one-off fee of US$3 for a vehicle. It's exposed to the wind, sand and rain – and security can be a problem.

An atmospheric choice is the delightful *Alternative Space* (☎ 404027) on the desert fringe at 46 Dr Alfons Weber Strasse. Dorm beds cost US$5, including rudimentary cooking facilities and a bizarre turret toilet. Highlights are the castle-like architecture,

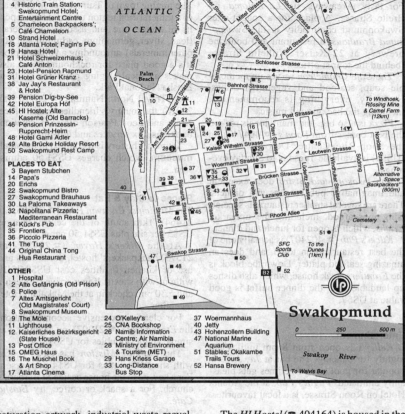

Swakopmund

PLACES TO STAY
4 Historic Train Station;
   Swakopmund Hotel;
   Entertainment Centre
5 Chameleon Backpackers';
   Café Chameleon
10 Strand Hotel
18 Atlanta Hotel; Fagin's Pub
19 Hansa Hotel
21 Hotel Schweizerhaus;
   Café Anton
23 Hotel-Pension Rapmund
31 Hotel Grüner Kranz
38 Jay Jay's Restaurant
   & Hotel
39 Pension Dig-by-See
42 Hotel Europa Hof
45 HI Hostel; Alte
   Kaserne (Old Barracks)
46 Pension Prinzessin-
   Rupprecht-Heim
48 Hotel Garni Adler
49 Alte Brücke Holiday Resort
50 Swakopmund Rest Camp

PLACES TO EAT
3 Bayern Stubchen
14 Papa's
20 Erichs
22 Swakopmund Bistro
27 Swakopmund Brauhaus
30 La Paloma Takeaways
32 Napolitana Pizzeria;
   Mediterranean Restaurant
34 Kücki's Pub
35 Frontiers
36 Piccolo Pizzeria
41 The Tug
44 Original China Tong
   Hua Restaurant

OTHER
1 Hospital
2 Alte Gefängnis (Old Prison)
6 Police
7 Altes Amtsgericht
   (Old Magistrates' Court)
8 Swakopmund Museum
9 The Mole
11 Lighthouse
12 Kaiserliches Bezirksgericht
   (State House)
13 Post Office
15 OMEG Haus
16 The Muschel Book
   & Art Shop
17 Atlanta Cinema
24 O'Kelley's
25 CNA Bookshop
26 Namib Information
   Centre; Air Namibia
28 Ministry of Environment
   & Tourism (MET)
29 Hans Kriess Garage
33 Long-Distance
   Bus Stop
37 Woermannhaus
40 Jetty
43 Hohenzollern Building
47 National Marine
   Aquarium
51 Stables; Okakambe
   Trails Tours
52 Hansa Brewery

saturation artwork, industrial-waste recycling theme and friendly welcome. Transport from the centre is free and they also offer sand-skiing excursions.

Another friendly choice is the *Chameleon Backpackers'* (☎ 402449; fax 404370) opposite the Entertainment Centre. Dorm beds with sheets cost US$5 per person. It has an ideal central location and guests may use the braais in the garden.

The *Swakopmund Rest Camp* (☎ 412807) has two-bed A-frame huts for US$12, four-bed huts for US$19 and six-bed huts for US$34. Guests can use the barbecue facilities.

The *HI Hostel* (☎ 404164) is housed in the Alte Kaserne; mature adults may feel cramped by rules devised for the younger set. Dorm rates are US$5/5.50 for HI members/non-members; private doubles cost US$11.50.

An alternative is *Jay Jay's* (☎ 402909), Brücken Strasse, which has simple singles/doubles for US$8/16 and dorm beds at US$7.

At 81 Seeadler Strasse is a friendly and inexpensive B&B run by *Mrs Viviane Scholz* (☎ 461683). She charges US$11/18 for single/double occupancy in a self-contained flat. It's highly recommended.

NAMIBIA

Places to Eat

For tasty takeaways, try *La Paloma*, on Breite Strasse. A place for a sought-after Swakopmund commodity is the *Swakopmund Brauhaus*, a restaurant and boutique brewery at 22 Kaiser Wilhelm Strasse (behind the tourist office).

The *Café Chameleon* serves up memorable soup, seafood and vegetarian dishes. Basically, everything is recommended, including the background music.

Pizza is also big, and many locals reckon the best comes from *Papa's* (☎ 404747), in the Shop-Rite Centre. Delivery service (US$1) is available Tuesday to Sunday evenings.

The *Swakopmund Bistro* does excellent and imaginative pub lunches and dinners. There are several smaller restaurants specialising in seafood, including the upmarket *Erichs*, which is open for lunch and dinner.

Kücki's Pub (☎ 402407) is actually one of the best restaurants in town, and does an amazing seafood platter. Down the block is the *Frontiers* steak house, which also dishes up laudable fare; the dinner buffet is good value at US$7.

Entertainment

O'Kelley's is open from 8 pm until 4 am nightly for dancing. The bar at *Jay Jay's* is popular for pool and sometimes gets pleasantly animated. *Fagin's Pub*, at the Atlanta Hotel on Roon Strasse, is a local favourite.

Getting There & Away

Between Swakopmund/Walvis Bay and Windhoek, the Dolphin Express (☎ 204118, Walvis Bay) runs five times weekly and the Cheetah Liner (☎ 462454) runs daily (US$15). Between Windhoek and Swakopmund/Walvis Bay, the Intercape Mainliner runs four times weekly (US$25).

Overnight trains from Windhoek depart daily except Saturday.

Hitching is possible, but hitchers risk heat stroke, sandblasting and hypothermia – sometimes all in the same day!

TSUMEB

The mining town of Tsumeb lies in the heart of a mineral-rich region underlaid by deposits of copper ore and associated minerals (lead, silver, germanium, cadmium and 200 other minerals) surrounding a volcanic pipe. It's a good place for rockhounds, and also makes an ideal staging point for visits to Etosha National Park.

At Travel North Namibia (☎ 20728; fax 20916), the country's friendliest tourist office, Anita and Leon Pearson offer information, bookings, fax services and left-luggage.

Tsumeb's history is recounted in the small **museum**, which charges US$1.50 admission.

Places to Stay & Eat

The *Municipal Caravan Park* (☎ 21056; fax 21464), 1km south of the centre, charges US$3 per site plus US$1.50 per adult.

At the *Hiker's Haven* (☎ 20420; fax 21575) backpackers' hostel, dorm beds and use of kitchen facilities cost US$8.75/10 without/with sheets. If you arrive between 2 and 5.30 pm, check in at the Makalani Hotel reception.

For clean, inexpensive accommodation, the *Etosha Café* (☎ 21207), on Main St, has simple singles/doubles for US$18/30.

The *Catholic Mission* has clean rooms with shared facilities for US$4 per person. For a key, go to the house beside St Barbara's church. For a snack or coffee, try *Etosha Cafe*.

A decent snack place is *Burger Shack & Warehouse Disco*. The pizza is recommended, and the disco rages on Friday and Saturday nights.

The *B&B Club* at 3rd and Main serves basic food and alcoholic drinks.

Getting There & Away

Intercape Mainliner runs four buses weekly from Windhoek, and railways' buses run to Oshakati and Grootfontein. Minibuses connect Tsumeb with Windhoek, Oshakati and Rundu, stopping at the Trek petrol station.

WALVIS BAY

Architecturally mundane Walvis Bay, which lies 30km south of Swakopmund on a coastal road bordered by sand dunes, is a busy port with a large fish-processing industry and a saltworks. Because it had the best harbour on the Namib coast, it remained an exclave of South Africa, on the basis of the 1878 British annexation, until 28 February 1994, when it was transferred to Namibian control.

Things to See

Walvis Bay isn't exactly a booming tourist destination, least of all when the wind is blowing the wrong way, but the **bird sanctuary** is worthwhile. The lagoon hosts up to 20,000 flamingoes and other freshwater and coastal birds. For a taste of the wind head out to **Dune 7** on the road east. You can also take a few minutes to visit the **town museum**, which is housed in the library.

Coming from Swakopmund, watch for the offshore platform known as **Bird Island**, 10km north of town, which was built as a roost for coastal birds and a source of guano for fertiliser.

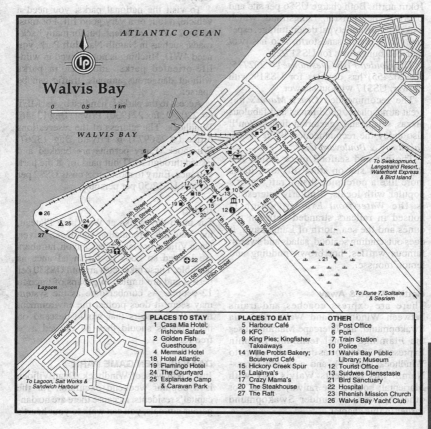

Walvis Bay

ATLANTIC OCEAN

WALVIS BAY

To Swakopmund,
Langstrand Resort,
Waterfront Express
& Bird Island

To Dune 7, Solitaire
& Sesriam

Lagoon

To Lagoon, Salt Works &
Sandwich Harbour

PLACES TO STAY	PLACES TO EAT	OTHER
1 Casa Mia Hotel; Inshore Safaris	5 Harbour Café	3 Post Office
2 Golden Fish Guesthouse	8 KFC	6 Port
4 Mermaid Hotel	9 King Pies; Kingfisher Takeaways	7 Train Station
18 Hotel Atlantic	14 Willie Probst Bakery; Boulevard Café	10 Police
19 Flamingo Hotel	15 Hickory Creek Spur	11 Walvis Bay Public Library; Museum
24 The Courtyard	16 Lalainya's	12 Tourist Office
25 Esplanade Camp & Caravan Park	17 Crazy Mama's	13 Suidwes Diensstasie
	20 The Steakhouse	21 Bird Sanctuary
	27 The Raft	22 Hospital
		23 Rhenish Mission Church
		26 Walvis Bay Yacht Club

NAMIBIA

Fifty kilometres south of town is **Sandwich Harbour**, which was historically a commercial fishing and trading port. It's now a refuge for migratory birds, and over 100 species have been recorded. However, it's only accessible by sturdy 4WD. Half-day trips with Inshore Safaris, at the Casa Mia Hotel, cost US$175 for up to four people.

Places to Stay & Eat
There are two camping grounds: the *Esplanade Camp & Caravan Park* (☎ 206145; fax 204528), in town, and *Langstrand* (☎ 5981), 16km north. Both charge US$6 per site and US$1.50 per person. Langstrand, which looks like an archetypal desert mirage, especially in a fog or sandstorm, also has two/four-bed bungalows for US$17/29.

The *Golden Fish Guesthouse* (☎ 202775; fax 202455) has doubles for US$19 with shower, US$17 without shower.

The recommended *Crazy Mama's* has great atmosphere, good prices and fabulous pizzas, salads and vegetarian dishes. You'll also enjoy the recommended *Willie Probst Takeaway & Boulevard Cafe*.

The bar and seafood place called *The Raft*, which sits on stilts offshore, looks more like a porcupine than a raft, but it's popular with locals. Similarly interesting is the *Water-front Express*, which is housed in railcars stranded between the dunes and the sea, north of Langstrand. It does outstanding seafood, salads and sweets: famous waffles, hot brown pudding and lemon mousse.

Getting There & Away
There are express coaches and trains between Windhoek and Walvis Bay via Swakopmund; the Intercape Mainliner uses the Flamingo Hotel terminal. Dolphin Express (☎ 204118) has daily connections to Windhoek (US$15), and a weekly Trans-Namib bus connects Walvis Bay with Mariental; book at the railway station. For other options, see under Swakopmund earlier in this chapter.

National Parks & Reserves

Despite its harsh climate, Namibia boasts some of Africa's finest national parks, which range from the wildlife-rich bushlands of the centre and north to the inhospitable coastal strip with its huge sand dunes, where sparse wildlife has adapted to the rigours of the desert. In the extreme south is one of Africa's most spectacular sights, in fact one of the natural wonders of the world – Fish River Canyon.

To visit the national parks, you need a vehicle, a tour or a very good lift. For most parks, 2WD is sufficient, but for many back-roads, such as in Namib-Naukluft Park, you need 4WD. Hitching is not allowed in wildlife-oriented parks, and even in parks without dangerous animals, traffic can be sparse.

Access to the parks is handled by the MET (☎ 220241; fax 221930), Private Bag 13346, Windhoek. The address of the reservations office (☎ 236975) is Private Bag 13267, Windhoek. Entry permits are booked and issued through MET but paid for at the park entrance. Entry to most parks costs US$2 per car and US$2.50 per person.

Hiking
For multi-day walks at Waterberg Plateau, the Naukluft Mountains, the Ugab River, Daan Viljoen or Fish River Canyon, numbers are limited so book as far in advance as possible. These hikes cost around US$30 per person and are limited to groups of three to 12 people. As cumbersome as the system may seem, it does protect the environment from the numbers that would descend on these places should they be opened as a free-for-all.

DAAN VILJOEN GAME PARK
Just 25km west of Windhoek, Daan Viljoen is a popular weekend excursion for the capital's residents. Because there are no dangerous animals, you can walk to your heart's

content through lovely desert-like hills and valleys. You'll almost certainly see gemsbok, kudu, mountain zebra, springbok, hartebeest and eland, as well as over 200 bird species. The park is open to day visitors from sunrise to 6 pm; admission is US$1.50.

There are three main walking tracks: the 3km Wag 'n Bietjie; the 9km Rooibos circuit; and the 34km Sweet-thorn Trail. The last takes two days and is open for groups of up to 12 people for US$12.50 per person. Book through MET in Windhoek.

Camping costs US$7 per site, for up to eight people, or you can stay in two-bed rondavels for US$23 per double, with breakfast.

There's no public transport, but hitching from Windhoek is possible, especially at weekends.

ETOSHA NATIONAL PARK

Etosha is certainly one of Africa's most beautiful wildlife parks, and for many well-heeled visitors, it's *the* Namibian destination. The western part of the park is characterised by scrubby savannah but further east, the scrub gives way to mixed woodland.

The heart of Etosha is the 22,270 sq km **Etosha Pan** – a shallow depression which is dry for most of the year. During the winter months, perennial springs around its edges draw large concentrations of birds and other animals. After exceptionally rainy periods, the pan fills with up to a metre of water and enormous numbers of waterfowl arrive to feed and breed.

The best time to visit Etosha is between May and September, when the days are cool and animals gather around the water holes. Park entry is US$5 per adult plus US$5 per vehicle.

Places to Stay

Lodges and camp sites at *Namutoni*, *Halali* and *Okaukuejo* should be booked as early as

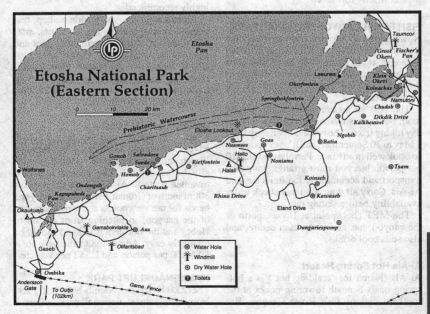

Etosha National Park (Eastern Section)

0   10   20 km

Prehistoric Watercourse

Wolfsnes
Gonob
Salvadora
Sueda
Homob
Ondongah
Kapupuhedis
Pan
Okaukuejo
Gemsbokvlakte
Aus
Gaseb
Olifantsbad
Ombika
Andersson Gate
To Outjo (102km)
Game Fence

Etosha Lookout
Nuamses
Helio
Halali
Rietfontein
Charitsaub
Rhino Drive
Noniams
Koinseb
Kawaseb
Eland Drive
Dungariespomp

Etosha Pan

Leeunes
Okerfontein
Springbokfontein
Goas
Batia
Ngobib
Kalkheuwel
Chudob
Dikdik Drive
Namutoni
Koinachas
Klein Okevi
Groot Okevi
Fischer's Pan
Tsumcor
Tsam

- ⊚ Water Hole
- ✳ Windmill
- ⊙ Dry Water Hole
- ❶ Toilets

possible through MET in Windhoek. Each camp has a shop, restaurant, bar, kiosk, petrol station, swimming pool and floodlit water hole for observing wildlife at night. At Namutoni, take a look at the museum in the whitewashed 19th century German fort.

All camp sites cost US$10 (maximum eight people). At Okaukuejo, two/three/four-bed bungalows start at US$23/33/38. At Halali, double 'bus quarters' (usually reserved for tour groups) cost US$33 and self-contained double bungalows are US$38. At Namutoni, two/three-bed rooms in the fort cost US$18/33 and four-bed flats with a hotplate and fridge cost US$30.

Getting There & Away
The best way to visit Etosha on your own is to muster a group in Windhoek and hire a car. Hitchers have the best luck at petrol stations in Tsumeb. However, park permits must be in order (unless your lift is also willing to share a camp site) and hitching within the park is strictly forbidden.

FISH RIVER CANYON NATIONAL PARK
Nowhere else in Africa is there anything like the immense Fish River Canyon. It's 160km in length, up to 27km wide and 550m at its deepest point, but figures can convey little of the breathtaking vistas afforded by the vantage points.

The best views are easily accessible by road, but there's also a popular four to five-day hiking track. The route is open only from 1 May to 30 September, and it's very popular, so book well in advance. Permits cost US$10 per person but you must arrange your own transport and accommodation in Hobas and Ai-Ais. Carry all your food and check water availability before setting out.

The MET checkpoint at Hobas, north of the canyon, has an information centre, and also sells cool drinks.

Ai-Ais Hot Spring Resort
Ai-Ais (Nama for 'scalding hot') is a hot-spring oasis beneath towering peaks at the southern end of Fish River Canyon. Hot water is piped to a series of baths, Jacuzzis and an outdoor swimming pool.

Admission costs US$1.50 per person and US$1.50 per vehicle. Due to the flood risk, Ai-Ais is closed from 31 October to the second Friday in March.

An excellent excursion is the Fish River Paddle & Saddle, offered by Kobus Jansen (☎ (064) 203581, ask for radio 251). It includes a four day horseback tour from Ai-Ais to the Orange River and two days canoeing for US$167.

Places to Stay
At the pleasant well-shaded Hobas camping ground, 10km from the Main Viewpoint, sites cost US$10. Facilities are clean and there's also a kiosk and swimming pool but no restaurant or petrol station.

Fish River Lodge (☎ /fax (0631) 23762), near the canyon north of Hobas, offers backpackers' specials for US$50/65/80 for one/two/three nights, including transfers from Keetmanshoop and excursions. It's highly recommended.

Amenities at Ai-Ais include a shop, restaurant, petrol station, tennis courts, post office and, of course, a swimming pool and spa and mineral baths. Camp sites cost US$10 for up to eight people. Flats accommodating four people cost US$38 while basic four-bed bungalows are US$25. Pre-book at MET in Windhoek.

Getting There & Away
There's no public transport into the Fish River Canyon and Ai-Ais area, but between March and October hitchers should eventually be successful. The easiest and best travelled route to Ai-Ais is via the turn-off 30km south of Grünau. From there, everyone heads for the viewpoints at the northern end of the canyon, so hitching from Ai-Ais to Hobas and the northern trail head should be relatively easy. Admission to the park costs US$2.50 per person and US$2 per vehicle.

NAMIB-NAUKLUFT PARK
The 23,000 sq km Namib-Naukluft Park, Namibia's largest national park, offers a

range of ecosystems and geological and topographical features: from granite mountains, canyons and estuarine lagoons to some of the world's highest sand dunes.

The central area is a sea of sand consisting of apricot-coloured dunes interspersed with dry pans. The best known of these is **Sossusvlei**, a dusty pan surrounded by 300m-high dunes. The road from Sesriem to Sossusvlei is mostly good, but without 4WD you'll have to walk the last 4km.

Heading north from Sossusvlei, the dunes end abruptly at the Kuiseb River and the Namib assumes a completely different character: a landscape of endless, grey-white gravel plains with isolated kopjes. It supports gemsbok, springbok and mountain zebra as well as the welwitschia plant, which derives its moisture from dew and fog.

The eastern extreme of the park contains the **Naukluft Mountains**, characterised by a high plateau bounded by gorges, caves and springs cutting deeply into the dolomite formations. It's a lovely trekking area, with one-day, four-day and eight-day circuits through the range.

Places to Stay

Camp sites (US$2.50 for the Namib Desert Park camps and US$7.50 for the Sesriem and Naukluft sites) must be pre-booked through the MET offices in Windhoek or Swakopmund. Note that permits for entry and hikes in the Sesriem/Sossusvlei and Naukluft areas may only be booked in Windhoek. *Sesriem*, which is fringed by a luxury hotel, is the most convenient camping ground to Sossusvlei; booked campers must arrive before sunset or they won't get into the main camp, but there is an unappealing emergency overflow area.

A great alternative is the ultra-friendly *Solitaire Guest House* (☎ 3230), at the petrol station in Solitaire, 65km north of Sesriem. This pleasantly anachronistic place could have provided the inspiration for the film *Baghdad Cafe*. Dusty camp sites, or floor space to roll out a sleeping bag, cost US$1.50 and rooms are US$6. At the attached restaurant, you're limited to whatever they're cooking that day, but it's always good.

Getting There & Away

There's no reliable public transport into the park. Your best staging points for lifts will be the backpackers' hostels in Windhoek & Swakopmund.

SKELETON COAST

'Skeleton Coast' refers to the coastline between the Ugab and Kunene rivers, and is derived from the treacherous nature of the coast, which has been a graveyard for ships and their crews.

Between Swakopmund and the Ugab is the bleak 200km coastline of the **National West Coast Recreation Area**. Most visitors head for **Cape Cross Seal Reserve**, 120km north of Swakopmund, which is a breeding reserve for thousands of Cape fur seals. It was here that Portuguese explorer Bartolomeu Dias planted a *padrão* (icon, in this case it's a cross). It's open daily from 10 am to 5 pm. Admission costs US$2.50 per person plus US$2 per vehicle. There's a basic snack bar on the site.

The **Skeleton Coast Park** proper, a wilderness of dunes and gravelly coastal desert, is open to individual travellers only between the Ugab and Hoanib rivers, but everyone requires a permit, which costs US$5 per person plus US$5 per vehicle. To transit the park between Ugabmund and Springbokwater, you can pick up permits at the gates, but you must enter through one gate by 1 pm and exit through the other before 3 pm the same day.

The guided three day, 50km **Ugab River Hiking Trail** starts at Ugabmund for groups of six to eight people. It costs US$30 per person and must be booked through MET in Windhoek.

Places to Stay

In addition to a couple of guesthouses at Henties Bay, there are *camp sites* along the coastal salt road at Mile 14, Jakkalsputz, Henties Bay, Mile 72 and Mile 108, and water is available for a nominal fee. *Torra*

Bay, in the Skeleton Coast Park, has camping only during December and January, and costs US$2.50 per site for up to eight people. *Terrace Bay* has single/double bungalows at US$53/88, including full board, and there's a shop, restaurant and petrol station, but no camping.

Visits to Torra Bay and Terrace Bay must be booked either at MET in Windhoek or Swakopmund; day visitors may not visit either camp.

WATERBERG PLATEAU PARK

The Waterberg Plateau Park takes in a 50km-long and 16km-wide sandstone plateau, which looms 150m above the plain. Around this sheer-sided plateau is an abundance of freshwater springs, which support a lush mosaic of trees and plenty of wildlife. Day admission is US$2 per person and US$2.50 per vehicle. To get up onto the plateau, join a US$15 4WD tour; they depart daily at 8 am and 3 pm.

Each second, third and fourth Thursday of the month, from April to November, visitors can do a four day **Waterberg Wilderness Trail**, beginning at 4 pm at the Onjoka gate. Only one group of eight is permitted at a time, so book early through MET in Windhoek. These walks cost US$30 per person; participants must be reasonably fit and have their own food and sleeping bags.

Places to Stay & Eat

The *Bernabé de la Bat camp site* costs US$10 for up to eight people. For three/four-bed self-contained bungalows with fans, braais and outdoor seating areas, you'll pay US$33/45. The camp also has a restaurant and shop. In Otjiwarongo, the *Municipal Camp site* costs US$6 per site plus US$0.80 per person.

Getting There & Away

There's no public transport to Waterberg but you can take a train, minibus or Cape Mainliner coach to Otjiwarongo and hitch the remaining 53km. Taxis from Otjiwarongo cost around US$25 each way.

Niger

Niger is the second largest country in West Africa, and one of the most fascinating. Much of the country sits on the edge of the Sahara and the towns in the centre and far north (particularly Agadez) exude a unique desert charm. Separated by hundreds of kilometres of barren, windswept land, these towns are the meeting places for the nation's vibrant mix of people – Hausa, Songhai-Zarma, Fulani and Tuareg. Their markets, where cattle, camels and a range of other goods have been traded for centuries, are some of the most exciting in Africa. In the far north the starkly beautiful Aïr Mountains rise as if from nowhere.

Niger (pronounced nee-JAIR in French) lives off its uranium exports, although tourism, mainly in the form of trans-Saharan travellers, has also made inroads. Both industries have been hit heavily in recent years: uranium from depressed world prices and tourism from the closure of Niger's border with Algeria. The tough times have forced many people to migrate to the cities, or, in the case of the nomadic Tuareg, to settle. Although beggars are rife, it is the stoic and resilient nature of the people in this harsh place that creates a lasting impression.

REPUBLIC OF NIGER

Area: 1,267,000 sq km
Population: 9.1 million
Population Growth Rate: 3.2%
Capital: Niamey
Head of State: President Colonel Ibrahim Bare Mainassara
Official Language: French
Currency: West African CFA Franc
Exchange Rate: CFA 575 = US$1
Per Capita GNP: US$200
Inflation: 4%
Time: GMT/UTC + 1

Highlights

- The spectacular Parc National du W
- The Grand Marché in Niamey and market day in Zinder
- An expedition into the remote Aïr Mountains and Ténéré Desert
- Labyrinthine backstreets and Vieux Quartier of Agadez
- The Gerewol ceremony (during the Cure Salée) in the Agadez region

Facts about the Country

HISTORY

Long before the country was colonised by the French (at the end of the 19th century), Niger as it stands today was occupied by the Songhai Empire in the west, the central Hausa kingdoms and the empire of Kanem-Bornu around Lake Chad to the east. The wealth of these states was based on control of the trans-Saharan trade in slaves, gold and salt. Their fortunes diminished during the 18th and 19th centuries as European maritime nations increased trade with West Africa's coastal kingdoms. Even so, trans-Saharan commerce has never actually ceased. Until quite recently, annual caravans of thousands of camels were loaded up with salt at the Bilma oasis before heading for Nigeria and Cameroon.

Islam arrived in the area during the 10th and 11th centuries, but it was the religion of the aristocracy and the urban elite. Rural people continued to follow traditional

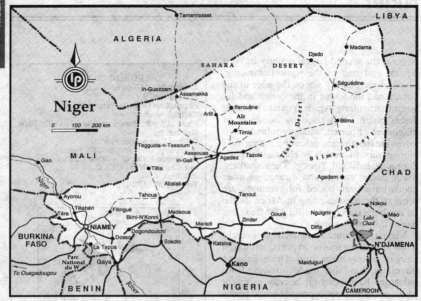

beliefs, even when Islam began to make headway with them in the 19th century.

The British were the first to explore Niger's upper reaches, beginning with the Scottish explorer Mungo Park who disappeared in the area in 1806, but it was the French who colonised it between 1891 and 1911. However, the country was not fully 'pacified' until much later, and resistance movements severely tested the mettle of the colonial authorities. The most serious was the siege of Agadez by Tuareg in 1916-17.

Niger's poor soils and drought hampered the colony's development until groundnuts (peanuts) were introduced in 1930. Along with cattle, this was the country's most important export until uranium took over in the 1970s. After major droughts in the early 1970s, Niger was saved from economic disaster (perhaps at the price of a world ecological disaster) by the uranium mines at Arlit. So valuable were the deposits that Niger's trade balance went into surplus and it was predicted

that uranium would account for 90% of the country's exports by the mid-1980s. These hopes collapsed along with the world market for uranium (although the French continue to buy the bulk of Niger's yellow cake).

Independence was granted in 1960 under the presidency of Hamani Diori. However, economic and social upheaval caused by a drought in 1973 resulted in Diori being overthrown in 1974 in a coup led by Lieutenant General Seyni Kountché, who remained in power until his death in 1987. His chosen successor was Ali Saïbou.

In 1990, students at Niamey University staged a demonstration calling for democratic reform. Several were killed when security forces opened fire and the public outcry which followed forced Saïbou to reluctantly call a national conference. It lasted for three months from July 1991, ending with the installation of an interim government which ruled until multiparty elections were held in early 1993. These ushered in Mahamane Ousmane as the country's first Hausa head of state (the Zarmas previously held power).

His reign was short-lived. A military junta, led by Colonel Ibrahim Bare Mainassara, staged a successful coup in January 1996. A presidential election was held in July and the National Election Commission reported a couple of days later that Mainassara had polled over 50% of the vote (his main opponent, the man he overthrew, polled about 20%).

Elections were held for the 83-seat National Assembly in late November 1996 and mid-January 1997. The authoritarian UNIRD (National Independents' Union for Democratic Renewal) managed to get some 70% of the seats (56 out of 83); the nearest rival got eight seats.

Financially, Niger is still in a precarious state. It has recorded negative GDP growth ever since 1990 and, being heavily reliant on imports, was one of the countries worst hit by the CFA's devaluation in early 1994. Things could improve economically if, as the government hopes, the petroleum giant Elf strikes oil in eastern Niger.

Niger's other major concern is the state of lawlessness in the north and far east of the country which followed the Tuareg rebellion. The rebellion effectively ended in 1995 with the signing of a peace accord between the government and Tuaregs, but many parts of the country are still off-limits. See the Population & People section for more details.

GEOGRAPHY & CLIMATE
A good part of Niger's 1,267,000 sq km is Sahara Desert, with most of the remainder lying in the Sahel. This vast country is mainly flat, only interrupted by the Aïr (pronounced eye-ear) Mountains in the north which rise to 2000m. Beyond these is the Ténéré Desert, a sea of dunes.

Vegetation in the north is sparse or nonexistent, gradually merging into scrub in the Sahel and into lightly wooded grassland in the extreme south. Millet and sorghum are grown in the semi-arid areas, and rice is produced close to the Niger. The Niger, Africa's third-longest river, winds its way through the

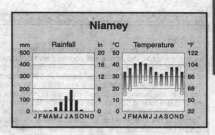

south-west corner and is the country's only permanent body of water as Lake Chad, in the south-east, is now dry on the Niger side.

The climate is hot and dry except for a brief rainy period in July and August. November and January are the coolest months, when the harmattan blows the dust off the desert. Most of the country receives less than 500mm of rain per year.

ECOLOGY & ENVIRONMENT
Desertification is Niger's most serious environmental problem as only 3% of the land is arable. The two main causes of desertification are deforestation, caused by people cutting down wood for cooking and preparation of charcoal, and overgrazing.

There have been concerted attempts at reafforestation, such as the project at Guesselbodi, near Niamey, where villagers have constructed windbreaks and planted nurseries, but these are small attempts in relation to the size of the problem. Well-digging programmes, which one would think would be a salvation for such a dry country, have intensified overgrazing with an increase in the herds contributing to the denuding of the landscape.

POPULATION & PEOPLE
The population of Niger is estimated at 9.1 million. Around 20% of the population remains nomadic.

There are five principal ethnic groups: the southern Hausa (about 50% of the population), the Songhai-Zarma in and around Niamey (22%), the traditionally nomadic Tuareg in the north (10%), the pastoral Peul-Fulani (9%)

Tuareg

The Tuareg are demanding a federal system under which they would have regional autonomy. As an ethnic minority, they have felt scorned and deprived of the rights of normal citizens, and members of their community have been subjected to arbitrary arrest by Niger security forces.

Since their armed struggle began in 1990, more than 100 people – rebels, police and civilians – have been killed. In 1992, as a result of the violent attacks on civilians, the Niger government banned travel in the north and closed its main border with Algeria. It remained closed for more than a year, halting the tourist flow across one of the Sahara's oldest routes and stifling Niger's tourist industry.

In early 1994 the Tuareg Front de Libération de l'Aïr et l'Azaouak (FLAA) and Front de Libération Tamouist (FLT) agreed to an uneasy truce. A peace accord was signed in 1995 after the government and l'Organisation de la Résistance Armée (ORA), representing the Tuareg groups, met in Ouagadougou. Tuareg refugees are now returning to Niger. The aftermath of the rebellion has been outbreaks of sporadic violence and banditry in the north and far east of the country, much of which remains off limits to the traveller. ■

including the well known Wodaabe from west of Agadeaz, and the Kanouri close to Lake Chad. About 85% of the population is Muslim.

SOCIETY & CONDUCT

Foreign women should wear modest clothing; dress is taken very seriously in this Muslim country.

LANGUAGE

French is the official language. Each ethnic group has its own customs and language but the main spoken languages are Hausa, Zarma (written Djerma and pronounced JER-mah in French), Fulani and Tamashek (Tuareg language). See the Language Appendix for French phrases.

Facts for the Visitor

VISAS & DOCUMENTS
Visas

Getting a visa to Niger is one of the greatest hassles of a visit to West Africa. There are few Niger embassies around the world and French embassies are often not empowered to issue Niger visas, so make sure you plan ahead. Australians and New Zealanders have to apply in Paris for a visa. In Africa, visas can be obtained in Algeria (in Algiers and in Tamanrasset), Benin, Côte d'Ivoire, Egypt and Nigeria (Lagos and Kano). You cannot get Niger visas in Mali, Chad, Burkina Faso or Senegal.

Visas are not required for the citizens of Belgium, France, Germany, Italy, Luxembourg, the Netherlands, all the Scandinavian countries, and most of the West and North African countries. Visas are normally issued within 48 hours for a stay of up to one month. Anyone intending to stay for three months needs a visa.

Getting a visa in Europe or North America is fairly straightforward if you are arriving by air. If arriving by land, and you don't have an airline ticket out of the country, you will have to get a letter from your bank showing that you have at least US$500 in your account. In the USA you will need three photos, health card and a copy of your airline ticket; the cost is US$35. Niger embassies outside Africa charge about US$40 for visas; the embassy in France does not ask to see your airline ticket.

Visa Extensions Visa extensions of one month are available from the sûreté (police) in Niamey. You need two photos and US$14; they take 24 hours.

Other Visas
For each visa you need between one and four photos.

Burkina Faso, Central African Republic, Côte d'Ivoire, Gabon & Togo

Visas to these countries are issued in 24 hours by the French consulate in Niamey. For each country, a visa valid for one to five days costs US$12 and a six to 90 day visa costs from US$20 to US$40. The consulate is open until noon.

Benin

The embassy, open weekdays from 8 to 10 am, takes 48 hours to issue visas valid for two weeks (US$20) or for multiple entry (US$30).

Chad

The embassy charges US$12 for a two week visa valid from the date of issue (extendible in N'Djamena) and takes several days to process applications. It opens Monday to Thursday from 8 am to 3 pm, Friday until 12 pm. A Niger exit visa may be required if you're travelling overland to Chad via Nguigmi. You can get one at the Ministry of Interior office in Zinder but you must also get a stamp en route at Diffa.

Mali

The consulate is open weekdays from 9 am to 12 pm and 4 to 6 pm. It requires US$25 and usually gives same day service.

Mauritania

The consulate is open weekdays from 9 am to 12 pm and charges US$12 for visas valid for up to one month.

Nigeria

The embassy is open Monday to Thursday from 10 am to 1 pm but will not issue visas to anyone who is not a resident of Niger. Occasionally travellers get around this, but don't count on it. If you're lucky, the cost varies according to nationality – from US$2 for Americans, US$16 for Canadians and a whopping US$214 for the British.

Senegal

The Senegalese consul lives in a private house out in the suburbs of Niamey. A visa costs US$20/40 for one/two months. Call during normal office hours.

Permits & Other Documents

Yellow fever and cholera vaccination certificates are essential.

In some towns, it is a good idea to report to police if you stay overnight, in particular Arlit and Agadez. They sometimes hold your passport until you leave but more often than not they just look at it and/or stamp it on the spot with what is referred to locally as a *vu au passage*. This stamp saves you getting hassled at the roadblock on the way out of town or by the sûreté at the next town. When leaving Niger across any border, be sure your stamps are in order or you'll be vulnerable to demands for bribes. In Niamey register with the *préfecture* (police headquarters) in the centre, 100m south of the Hôtel Rivoli.

EMBASSIES

Niger Embassies

In Africa there are embassies in Algeria, Benin, Côte d'Ivoire, Egypt and Nigeria. Elsewhere there are Niger embassies in Belgium, Canada, France, Germany, Russia and the USA.

Foreign Embassies in Niger

Foreign embassies in Niamey include:

Algeria

2km north of the centre, just north of Route de Tillabéri, BP 142 (☎ 75 3097)

Benin

Rue des Dallois, 2km north-west of the centre, near Route de Tillabéri, BP 11544 (☎ 72 3919)

Canada

Immeuble Sonara II, Rue du Gaweye (☎ 73 3686)

Chad

off Route de Tillabéri, BP 12820 (☎ 73 4464)

France

corner of Ave Mitterand and Blvd de la République, BP 10660 (☎ 72 2722)

Germany

Ave du Général de Gaulle, BP 629 (☎ 72 2534)

Mali

Blvd de Mali Bero, 4km north-west of the town centre (☎ 73 2342)

Nigeria

Rue Luebke, BP 11130 (☎ 73 2410)

UK (honorary consul)

B Niandou, who speaks little English (and has limited powers), works in the Elf (formerly BP) offices on Route de l'Aéroport, 2km from the centre of town, BP 11168 (☎ 73 2539)

USA

4km north-west of the centre on Blvd de la République, BP 11201 (☎ 72 2661; fax 73 3167)

MONEY

US$1 = CFA 575

The unit of currency is the West African CFA franc. There are no restrictions on imports but export of cash is limited to US$250 (a rule generally not enforced).

NIGER

When entering Niger, it's good to have CFA or French francs on hand especially if you arrive at the weekend when the banks are closed. French francs are interchangeable at a lot of places, including upmarket hotels. The banks outside Niamey charge an exorbitant US$8 to change travellers' cheques – stick to French francs cash.

Whenever you change money, stow it carefully on your person – there are petty thieves lurking outside all the banks ready to snatch and run.

POST & COMMUNICATIONS
Postal services outside Niamey are unreliable. There are two post offices in Niamey – the Grande Poste and Poste de Plateau. Poste restante at the Poste de Plateau is reliable – the charge is US$0.60 per letter collected. It keeps mail for up to four months.

International telephone services are OK and phone calls and faxes can be made from the post offices in Niamey. A three minute (minimum) telephone call to Europe is about US$10. The country code for Niger is 227; there are no area codes. There is also a fax service – the first page costs US$6 and subsequent pages US$3. The 'fax restante' service is particularly handy. You can have faxes sent to you (☎ 73 4470) and collect them free.

DANGERS & ANNOYANCES
Safety
On the whole, Niger is relatively safe although in both Niamey and Agadez theft and armed hold-ups are on the increase. In Niamey, you should steer clear of the area around the Kennedy Bridge after dark and you should also avoid the area around the Hôtel Gaweye and the two corniche roads running parallel to the river on the city side.

Due to the recent Tuareg rebellion, some parts of northern Niger (including the Aïr Mountains in the north-east) may still be off-limits to tourists (even after the signing of the 1995 peace accord). You can check with any US embassy around the world for an update on the situation.

The Algerian side of the border is strictly no-go with the fundamentalist Groupe Islamique Armée (GIA) in full control. Many foreigners and thousands of Algerians have died in the conflict which has been raging since late 1993. Attempts to cross the border would be suicidal.

Harmattan Winds
The harmattan can be particularly strong here and, as a result, some travellers develop respiratory problems, though it's usually nothing worse than a nasty cough. It's a good idea to follow the Tuareg's lead and cover your mouth and nose when travelling.

PUBLIC HOLIDAYS
There are holidays on: 1 January, 1 May, 18 May, 3 August (Independence), 5 September (Settlers' Day), 18 December (Republic Day), 25 December, Easter Monday and variable Islamic holidays (see Public Holidays in the Regional Facts for the Visitor chapter for details).

ACCOMMODATION
Many hotels have reduced their prices to attract the few tourists trickling through. Despite this, accommodation in Niger is still relatively expensive for what you get and rooms in many of the cheaper hotels are extremely ill-kept. Camping (about US$3 per person) is possible in Niamey, Arlit, Agadez, Tahoua, Maradi and Birni-N'Konni.

Getting There & Away

AIR
Air Afrique, Ethiopian Airlines, Air Algérie and Air France fly to Niamey. From Niamey there are flights to/from many West African cities: Ouagadougou (US$75 one way), Abidjan (US$280), Bamako (US$275), Dakar (via Ouaga, US$465 one way), Cotonou (US$195) and N'Djamena (US$365).

Air tickets bought in Niger usually include the US$5 government tax and the US$5 departure tax (for flights within West Africa).

LAND
Algeria
Travel for foreigners in Algeria is seriously risky. You're advised not to enter unless the situation there has eased.

Benin
There are SNTN and private buses from Niamey to the border town of Gaya, but none across the border; you need to take bush taxis to points further south.

A minibus from Niamey to Gaya is US$7 and a Peugeot 504 is US$9 (between Dosso and Gaya it is about US$4). Motorcycle-taxis or pick-ups go from Gaya to the border town of Malanville (in Benin; 8km), cost about US$3 and wait for you at the border points.

Burkina Faso
Three express bus companies run between the SNTN bus station in Niamey and Ouagadougou (500km, 12 to 14 hours). Only one of these is an SNTN bus, but the others (Faso Tours and X9, both Burkina Faso companies) are just as comfortable (US$15 for SNTN and a dollar less for the private companies).

Minibuses from Niamey to the border cost US$4, and from the border to Ouagadougou US$10. Bush taxis often claim that they can cross the border but actually can't – they may collect the whole fare from you and when you realise you have been conned it is too late, so beware! Burkina Faso time is one hour behind Niger, and the border closes at 5.30 pm.

Chad
Niamey to N'Djamena via the top of Lake Chad and Zinder is a hard slog of a week or more. Officials en route, particularly at the Nguigmi border crossing, are brutish and you can't rely on finding food or water between Zinder and Mao. Get your passport stamped in Diffa and Mao and remember that Chad uses Central African CFA francs, so buy some in advance.

Between Zinder and Diffa there are mini-buses (US$10) or Peugeot 504s (US$12).

The minibuses take all day to fill before they leave. From Diffa there are minibuses to Nguigmi (US$3). There's also a weekly bus from Zinder to Nguigmi on Thursdays.

There are infrequent pick-ups from Nguigmi to Nokou in Chad (US$20, 1½ to three days) and from Nokou to Mao (US$6). Equally infrequent pick-ups take the shorter route to Nokou via Rig Rig (US$20 to US$25). Both options are very sandy.

Mao to N'Djamena by bush taxi, probably changing vehicles in Massakori, costs US$10, or by truck it's US$6. Just outside Mao, you can stay at either the *mission catholique* or the *mission protestante* for a reasonable donation. In town, the *Centre de Culture de la Jeunesse* has double rooms at US$15.

Mali
One SNTN bus (actually a truck with a cabin on the back) per week makes the run from Niamey to Gao (450km). The journey is notoriously slow, 30 hours is usual, and costs US$20. Other than these buses, there are also occasional, slow trucks (two to three days) for about US$15.

It is a tough trip, especially from July to September when the route is very muddy. Even in the dry season you should consider breaking the journey for a day or two. The route has been aptly described by a reader as 'a horrific journey of hassles, bureaucracy, time-wasting and general lunacy'. So be prepared and take plenty of drinking water.

Nigeria
There are four main bush taxi routes into Nigeria from Niger. There are SNTN and private buses from Niamey to the border towns of Birni-N'Konni, Maradi and Zinder.

The most popular option is from Zinder direct to Kano (240km, five hours) by taxi (US$8).

The second route is from Birni-N'Konni to Sokoto (95km, US$2 in a share-taxi) but this route is heavily potholed, there are umpteen checkpoints along the way and the Nigerian border officials are known to give travellers with their own vehicle a very hard

NIGER

time. There are motorcycle-taxis from Birni-N'Konni to the border village of Illela (US$1).

Another route is from Maradi to Katsina (92km). From Maradi to Jibiya (Nigerian border) by taxi costs US$4, and from there to Katsina costs US$1.

The fourth route is to Sokoto via Gaya on the Benin border (see Benin above).

Togo & Ghana

There is a weekly service from Niamey to Lomé (Togo) for US$21 and then onto Accra (Ghana) for another US$3.

Getting Around

AIR

Not likely! Perhaps Air Sonita has resumed its service from Niamey and Agadez – ask around. Sometimes Nigeravia (☎ 73 3064), which charters its planes to the mining company in Arlit, sells spare seats to the public (US$380 to Agadez, US$410 to Arlit).

BUS

SNTN, the government bus service (☎ 72 3020 in Niamey), is the most expensive form of transport (about 25% more than the private buses) but its buses are relatively comfortable and generally quicker than bush taxis as they don't stop at all the police checkpoints (there are plenty). You can reserve a seat (you must show your passport) but you often can't actually buy the ticket until the day of travel. The twice weekly service from Niamey to Agadez still travels as part of an armed convoy (beyond Tahoua).

SNTN has a service from Niamey to Birni-N'Konni (440km) for US$16 and to Zinder (950km) for US$30. There are also services from Niamey to Maradi (670km, US$18), Niamey to Arlit (1200km, US$35), Zinder to Nguigmi (600km, US$13) and Agadez to Arlit (245km, US$6). Private buses can be found at autogares.

BUSH TAXI

Bush taxis – either minibuses or Peugeot 504s – cover all the major routes and are cheaper and more frequent than the SNTN buses. Minibuses are generally less expensive than Peugeots. Depending on the destination, however, bush taxis can take a long time to fill up and are generally less comfortable than buses (they also charge about 10% of the passenger fare for baggage). They head in all directions: along the main roads between Niamey, Agadez and Zinder; to the borders of Nigeria, Benin and Burkina Faso; and to smaller places off the main routes.

CAR & TRUCK

There are good sealed roads all the way from Niamey to Agadez and Arlit, and from Niamey to the Burkina border. The Agadez-Zinder road is sealed except for 100km of dirt, due to be sealed soon.

In recent years, the road between Tahoua and Arlit was the target of attacks by militant Tuareg. Following the 1995 peace accord you should be able to go as you please but there are still armed bandits along this route. Convoys may still be operating between Arlit and the border at Assamakka and between Agadez and Zinder. If you are required to go with a convoy, don't expect to have an armed escort protecting your tail the whole way. One group of travellers waited for four days to travel with the escort. Fifty kilometres into the journey they got a flat tyre and never saw the army again.

Private car owners offering lifts charge negotiable rates, but a little more than a Peugeot taxi is usual. Try to arrange lifts in advance and don't hand over any money (even a deposit) until you are on board.

Private cars must pay a *péage* (toll) to use the main routes. You buy a ticket before travelling from a checkpoint on the edge of each town, either for a whole trip (eg Niamey to Agadez, US$2) or in sections. Get the ticket, as you will be fined if you don't.

Petrol costs about US$0.65 a litre, and diesel US$0.55 (significantly cheaper than in Mali or Burkina Faso). In Gaya, Birni-

N'Konni and Maradi you can buy cheap diesel and petrol smuggled from Nigeria. You can't help but notice the sellers waving their red plastic funnels. The petrol should be dyed red; check for added water.

Niamey

Niamey has been the capital of Niger since the administration moved here from Zinder in 1926. It has grown rapidly in recent years and now has a population of about 600,000; in 1940 there were only 2000 people living here. It has most of the amenities of a modern capital city though its character is still distinctly Sahelian. You may see camels kneeling in the sandy streets or plodding across the bridge over the Niger at sundown, though in ever decreasing numbers as the years pass by.

Information

The Office National du Tourisme (ONT; ☎ 73 2447; fax 72 3347) on Ave Luebké has maps of Niamey for US$2 but not much else. It is open on weekdays from 7.30 am to 12.30 pm and 3.30 to 6.30 pm.

For details of banks (there are three banks in Niamey – the BIAO, BCEAO and BDRN) and post and communications services in Niamey, see Facts for the Visitor earlier in this chapter.

The Ascani Bookshop, behind the SCORE supermarket, has a good selection of magazines and newspapers. Also try Indrap on Rue Martin Luther King.

Medical supplies can be bought from Pharmacie Nouvelle near Air Afrique. For medical treatment, the Clinique de Gamkalé (☎ 73 2033), by the river about 2km east of town, has been recommended but it's not cheap – US$40 per consultation. The new Centre Médical Pro Santé (☎ 72 2650) at 10 Rue de la FAO does consultations for US$20; there is also a pharmacy.

Things to See

Musée National du Niger This museum complex in the heart of Niamey has the usual exhibits of local costumes and implements. It also incorporates a very depressing zoo with bored and neurotic birds and animals living in abominable conditions; an area featuring the characteristic dwellings of the country's main ethnic groups, authentically constructed and furnished; and an artisanal section where craftspeople skilled in traditional metalwork, weaving and leather are busy at work.

The museum is open daily except Monday from 8 am to 12 pm and 4 to 6.30 pm. Admission costs US$0.20.

Cultural Centres The **Centre Culturel Franco-Nigérien** (☎ 73 47 68) is opposite the museum. It has a craft workshop, a library and a busy schedule of exhibits, dance and theatre. They show films most nights at 8.30 pm; admission costs US$1.

The **American Cultural Center** is on Ave du Général de Gaulle, west of the Poste Plateau (post office). They have a library, and for those starved of world news they screen CNN every day.

A variety of African cultural activities occur at the **Centre Culturel Oumarou-Ganda** opposite the Grande Mosquée; activities are advertised in Le Sahel newspaper.

Markets The relatively new and impressive **Grand Marché** has managed to maintain a traditional feel despite being spacious and well-maintained. The **Petit Marché** has a good variety of shops and products; bargaining is essential.

Tours Niger-Car Voyages (☎ 72 2331), in the El Nasr building, and the ONT arrange sunset pirogue rides along the river; the cost is US$6 per person for an hour-long trip.

Places to Stay

The only camp site, called both Yantala Camping and Camping Touristique (☎ 73 4206), is 4km out of town on the Tillabéri road and costs US$4 a person, plus the same for a vehicle. It has a pleasant beer garden

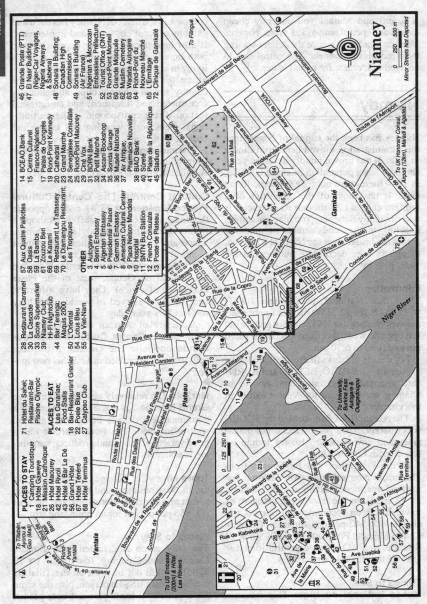

Niamey

0   250   500 m

Minor Streets Not Depicted

PLACES TO STAY
71 Hôtel du Sahel; Restaurant-Bar Pische Olympic
1 Camping Touristique
18 Hôtel Gaweye
21 Mission Catholique
26 Hôtel Maourey
42 Hôtel Rivoli
43 Hôtel & Bar Le Dé
56 Grand Hôtel
67 Hôtel Ténéré
68 Hôtel Terminus

PLACES TO EAT
2 Les Canaries; Food Stalls
16 Bar-Restaurant Grenier
22 Poele Bleue
27 Calypso Club
28 Restaurant Caramel
30 La Cascade
33 Ncore Supermarket
39 Niamey Nyala
44 Hi-Fi Nightclub
50 L'Oriental
54 Lotus Bleu
55 Le Viet-Nam
57 Aux Quatre Paillotes
58 Oasis
59 La Bamba
61 Zouzou Beri
66 Le Karami
69 Restaurant Le Tattassey
70 Le Diamangou Restaurant; Les Tropiques

OTHER
3 Autogave
4 Benin Embassy
5 Presidential Palace
6 Algerian Embassy
7 German Embassy
8 American Cultural Center
9 Place Nelson Mandela
10 Hospital
11 SNTN Bus Station
12 French Consulate
13 Poste de Plateau
14 BCEAO Bank
15 Centre Culturel
17 Palace du Congrès
19 Rond-Point Kennedy
20 Cathedral
24 Grand Marché
25 Senegalese Consulate
29 Ciné Vox
31 BDRN Bank
32 Petit Marché
34 Ascani Bookshop
35 Sonida Garage
36 Musée National
37 Air Afrique; Pharmacie Nouvelle
38 BIAO Bank
40 Sûreté
41 Place de la République
45 Stadium
46 Grande Poste (PTT)
47 El Nasr Building
48 Sonara II Building; Nigeria Airways & Sabena
49 Sonara I Building (Air France)
51 Nigerian & Moroccan Embassies; Préfecture
52 Tourist Office (ONT)
53 Rond-Point Monteil
60 Grande Mosquée
62 Muslim Cemetery
63 Wadata Autogare
64 Rond-Point du Nouveau Marché
65 L'Ermitage
72 Clinique de Gamkalé

To Tillabéri, Ayorou & Gao (Mali)

To US Embassy (200m) & Hôtel Les Rôviers

To Filingué

To UK Honorary Consul, Airport (12km), Maradi & Agadez

To University, Burkina Faso Autogare & Ouagadougou

Niger River

Yantala

Gamkalé

Boulevard de Mali Bero

Route de l'Aéroport

Kennedy Bridge

See Enlargement

Boulevard de la Liberté

and a very slow restaurant (there are plenty of street stalls nearby). A share-taxi into town costs from US$1 to US$4 and there is also a regular bus to the centre.

Highly rated is the *mission catholique* near the cathedral. The clean rooms cost US$6 per person and there is a guests' kitchen. In other parts of West Africa, such missions have stopped taking guests because the hospitality and facilities have been abused – make sure it doesn't happen here.

The *Hôtel & Bar Le Dé* has three-bed rooms with shower for US$6 a person but the rooms and the communal toilets are dirty. There's a popular bar (which can get noisy) and the staff are friendly.

In the middle of town, the noisy *Hôtel Rivoli* (☎ 73 3849) has large singles/doubles with air-con from US$17/21. The *Hôtel Maourey* (☎ 73 2850), between the two markets, looks run-down enough to be a cheapie but it isn't, charging US$24/30 for singles/doubles with air-con.

One of the most popular places these days is the semi-luxurious *Hôtel Terminus* (☎ 73 2692; fax 73 3974) which has single/double bungalows from US$47/56.

Places to Eat

You'll find cheap food around the Petit Marché and in the area around Ciné Vox just off Rue de Kabekoira. There are also good *eating stalls* in the streets near the Grand Marché, at Rond-Point Yantala and at the autogare. Other stalls are set up on Rue du Sahel. Take a torch at night in case of power cuts.

Better than the street stalls for cheap African fare is the popular *Bar Teranga*, a great outdoor garden bar with low tables and a steady flow of cold beers. Meals are US$1. The *Calypso Club* on Rue de la Copro serves up delectable Béninois delights.

For other delicious African food at good prices try *Le Karami*, an open-air, bar/restaurant on Blvd de la Liberté (open for dinner only). Meals, such as tender brochettes, lamb or spicy chicken plus beans or chips, cost about US$3. The *Maquis 2000* is a block south of the Hôtel Le Dé. Good prices com-

bined with the best of Ivoirian cuisine make it a popular place for visitors and locals alike; meals start at US$4.

Near the Hôtel Terminus, the *Oasis* has a wide range of excellent French/European dishes from US$3; don't be put off by the shabby appearance of the place. For Vietnamese food you have the choice of *Le Viet-Nam* on Rue du Terminus (closed on Monday) and the *Lotus Bleu*, a block away (closed Tuesday); dishes are in the US$4.50 to US$6 range. *Le Dragon d'Or*, opposite the Grand Hôtel, open daily for lunch and dinner, is the pick of the Chinese places with dishes from US$5.

There are many expensive restaurants where you might want to splurge, including: *Aux Quatre Paillottes* on Rue du Sahel which has good African meals from US$6 to US$10; *L'Oriental*, near the Rond-Point Kennedy, with Lebanese fare and daily specials (dinners only, closed Wednesday); and *La Cascade*, near the Ciné Vox, for French and Italian cuisine with a menu du jour for US$9 (it is closed on Wednesday).

Entertainment

You will find travellers enjoying the sunset over the Niger and Pont Kennedy from the pool-side bar of the *Grand Hôtel*. Equally good for the view is the *Restaurant-Bar Piscine Olympic* near the swimming pool behind the Hôtel du Sahel; beers are cheap and meals are around US$2.

The open-air *L'Ermitage* on Blvd de la Liberté has live bands nightly (except Sunday) from about 10 pm and admission is US$1. *Le Flamboyant*, across from the Hôtel Ténéré, is similar. Two other lively 'African' bars are *Calypso Club* and *Bar Teranga* (see Places to Eat earlier).

Les Tropiques (☎ 73 3104), on Corniche de Gamkalé, is an open-air disco with a great dance floor. Also good is the fancy *Fofo Club* in the Hôtel du Sahel. The US$4 cover charge (Friday and Saturday only) includes a drink. Similar is the *Hi-Fi Nightclub* near the Hôtel Rivoli and *Le Satellite*, a block away in the El-Nasr building.

Except for the Sahel and Terminus, all the

upmarket hotels have pools which are open to non-guests. The pool at the Grand Hôtel costs US$2 while the best pool, at the Hôtel Gaweye, costs US$4. The public pool (US$1) next to Hôtel du Sahel is quiet on weekdays (and closed Friday) but packed at weekends.

Getting There & Away
The SNTN bus station (☎ 72 3020) is on the Corniche de Yantala river road. The ticket office is open weekdays from 7.30 am to 12.30 pm and 3.30 to 6.30 pm, Saturday from 8 to 9 am and Sunday from 8 am to 12 pm. There is also the Wadata autogare for large private buses, minibuses and bush taxis (note that it is called autogare and not the gare routière).

Getting Around
The Airport Taxis from the airport, 12km from the city centre, charge at least US$6 (and ask triple that at night) – negotiate. Alternatively, walk 150m to the highway and hail a share-taxi which should cost US$1 to the centre.

Taxi There are plenty of share-taxis but they tend to follow set routes which are seldom obvious. This means you may have to change two or three times to get where you want or pay US$3 to hire the cab yourself. Sharing a cab should cost from US$0.50 to US$1.

Car The major car rental agency is Niger-Car (☎ 73 2331) which has offices at the Hôtel Gaweye and at the airport; a small car, which can only be used around town, costs about US$36 per day (insurance and tax included) plus about US$0.30 per kilometre.

Around the Country

AGADEZ
Agadez is a welcome sight after the desert and, with its Sudanese/Sahelian architecture, it is an interesting town to explore. It's quiet and friendly and a high proportion of the bonjours have no ulterior motive. That said, it has been particularly hard hit by the recent drop in tourism (attributable to the sporadic violence and banditry which followed the Tuareg revolt) and, as a result, competition among the street hawkers is fierce. US citizens need ambassadorial permission to visit Agadez.

The old town is a maze of narrow alleyways weaving between single-storey, mud-brick buildings. It's a market town where the nomadic Tuareg and their former slaves, the Bousou, come in from outlying areas to barter their goods for those of the Hausa traders from the south. A popular souvenir is the *croix d'Agadez*, a traditionally silver cross (nickel is now often substituted) which the Tuareg used as currency. You'll also see artisans making *samaras* (leather sandals) and magnificent Tuareg camel saddles.

The Agadez region is renowned for its **festivals**, the most important being the now internationally famous **Cure Salée**. This intriguing festival is held in August or September after the rains, somewhere to the west of Agadez. Bororo males, of the nomadic Fula group, in a ceremony called the Gerewol, adorn and beautify themselves so that only the most obstinate female will refuse their advances. With luck, they find a wife – a woman brave enough to move forward and demand his services, at least for a night. The virility test, the Soro is another story altogether. Read lots before you come and realise that it is very difficult for outsiders to witness these events.

Information
The tourist office (☎ 44 0080) is on the main street, just before the turn-off to Arlit. It is open weekdays from 7.30 am to 12.30 pm and 3 to 6 pm, and also Saturday morning. They may give you a free town map.

You should register with the Commissariat, who will stamp your passport (they may ask for a gift of money always referred to as a *cadeau* but don't pay – think of fellow travellers who will follow you). The PTT, not far from the tourist office, is open Monday to Friday from 8 am to 12 noon and 3 to 5 pm. Most of the banks have closed but there are plenty of moneychangers; however, rates are lower than in Niamey.

Things to See & Do
Camel Market As well as camels this market on the north-western edge of town also has goats and donkeys and is worth a visit. Activity ceases here after 10.30 am.

Grande Mosquée It takes a hefty donation to get in to climb the wooden-studded minaret and more again if you have a camera. However it's worth it for an overview of the

town's narrow alleys and for glimpses of the Aïr Mountains. The three storey building to the north of the mosque is the Palais du Sultan, the residence of the city's traditional ruler (it is not open to tourists).

Vieux Quartier There are some notable traditional facades featuring carved or painted designs; look for houses with horn-like spikes on the roofs or ask people in the street where you can find houses with *les belles façades*. There are many artisan shops here – silversmiths, leather-workers and bronze-smiths are all represented.

PLACES TO STAY
10 Hôtel Agreboun
11 Hôtel Tilden
18 Pension Tellit
19 Hôtel de l'Aïr
23 Hôtel Sahara
24 Bungalows Telwa
26 Hotel Telwa

PLACES TO EAT
12 Street Food
17 Chez Nous
20 Mini Prix Supermarket
29 Supermarket

OTHER
1 Gare Routière
2 SNTN Bus Depot
3 Post Office (PTT)
4 Tourist Office
5 Petrol Station
6 Hospital
7 Pharmacy
8 Commissariat
9 Artisans Ateliers
13 Bar L'Ombre du Plaisir
14 Palais du Sultan
15 Grande Mosquée
16 Artisanal des Handicapés
21 Grand Marché
22 BDRN Bank
25 Centre Artisanal
27 Police Control Post
28 Ternet Voyages
30 Azalait Voyages

To Fort Dufau, Aïr Mountains & Timia
To Algerian Consulate (600m)
To Camping, Camel Market, L'Escale (4km) & Arlit
To Aïr Voyages
To Catholic Church
Vieux Quartier
To Bilma
To Camping L'Escale (4km) & Arlit
To Zinder & Niamey
To Airport (300m)

Agadez

0   100   200 m
Approximate Scale

Art Centres To see silversmiths working on a good selection of jewellery head to the humble **Centre Artisanal** on the southwestern edge of town. Alternatively, tiny private artisans are dotted around the Vieux Quartier to the east. Leather-work and strong sturdy hats are made at the **Artisanal des Handicapés**.

Camel Trek Agadez is the best place to organise a camel trek. In spite of the recent problems, there is still the odd traveller heading east on camel-back. To find someone willing to take you out ask around at the Tuareg Marché, or contact Moussa, a reliable, local guy recommended by many travellers – just ask around for him. If successful, be sure to bring something soft to sit on or your thighs and backside will end up a suppurating mess. Establish the charges early on – even when you think it is all cut and dried, extra costs will probably creep in. Trips start from US$10 per day and include Tuareg guide, accommodation in villages, food and permission from the Commissariat.

Places to Stay & Eat

The *Camping L'Escale* (☎ 44 0522) camp site, about 4km north-west of town on the new Arlit road, charges US$3 a person to camp, US$7 for a filthy mattress in a shocking room, plus US$1 per vehicle; there are cold showers. Watch your gear as security is pretty lax here.

On the western edge of town, the friendly *Hôtel Agreboun* (☎ 44 0307) has pleasant singles/doubles with fans and showers for US$7/9 (more with air-con). The communal toilets are clean and there's secure parking. The shabby *Hôtel Sahara* (☎ 44 0197), opposite the Grande Marché, has basic singles/doubles for US$8/10 with a fan. You can sleep on the terrace for US$3. The restaurant, when it operates, serves large, good value meals.

In the centre, the *Hôtel de l'Aïr* (☎ 44 0147) has rooms with fan/air-con for US$17/27. Even if you don't stay here it's worth visiting for its architecture, a drink on the

rooftop terrace and the excellent view of the Grande Mosquée.

Directly opposite, is the Italian-run *Pension Tellit* (☎ 44 0231) with its four very comfortable rooms complete with air-con, fridge and private baths. Rooms for one to four people range from US$20 to US$40. In the restaurant a good meal will cost about US$8 and on no account miss the real Italian ice cream (a remarkable feat in the Sahara).

You'll get the best *street food* from openair vendors on the main road near the Hôtel Agreboun. Stall owners set up just after sunset and by 7 pm the area is thronging with hungry diners.

As for dining out, the choice is limited to the few hotels with operational restaurants or *Chez Nous*, near the market, run by an amiable Togolese woman. You can eat well here (and drink great coffee) for US$2. *Tafadak*, near the Hôtel de l'Aïr, is the place for Tuareg dishes like hurwa (curdled milk with millet and sugar).

Afterwards (if you think curdled milk sits well in the stomach with beer), go to the lively *Bar l'Ombre du Plaisir* which is popular with local musicians.

Getting There & Away

For information on buses and taxis between Niamey and Agadez, see the main Getting Around section of this chapter.

AROUND AGADEZ
Aïr Mountains & Ténéré Desert

North-east of Agadez are the **Aïr Mountains**, a remote and exotic area which for many travellers is one of the highlights of a visit to Niger. A peace agreement has been signed between the government and the Tuareg, but there is still sporadic armed violence and banditry in the northern and far eastern areas of the country. It is still out of bounds for US citizens unless they have ambassadorial permission, and protected convoys are still necessary. Check with Temet Voyages (☎ 44 0051) in Agadez which, before the troubles, organised all-inclusive tours including food, tent, 4WD and guide for about US$150 a person a day; Niger Ténéré Voyages (☎ 44 0029) is reputedly cheaper.

The **Ténéré Desert**, 500km from Agadez as the crow flies, often receives the label of the Sahara's most beautiful desert. Only the adventurous make it out here (if travel is indeed permitted). The town of **Bilma**, at the end of one of the great desert salt routes, is the end of the line (and as near as you will get to the end of the earth!).

ARLIT

Arlit is the uranium-mining town north of Agadez and was often the first overnight stop in Niger if you were heading south from Algeria (when that was possible and safe). As the Algeria overland route is closed, very few travellers would even contemplate going here. At present, Arlit is off-limits to most travellers as it lies outside the area controlled by government troops. Sporadic violence and banditry are rife in the north and far east of the country.

Whether you enter town from Assamakka or Agadez, police at the checkpoints will take your passport. You must then collect it from the Commissariat de Police before leaving.

There are two banks (BIAO and BDRN) in Arlit but they charge heavy commissions for changing travellers' cheques, so have some French francs handy. There's a tourist office (☎ 45 2249), a good, French-run hospital and a lively market.

Places to Stay & Eat

The two uninspiring *camping grounds* – one to the north, the other to the south – are both 3km from town (a site is about US$3 in either one).

You'd be better off in the centre of town, west of the main street, at the popular *Hôtel l'Auberge la Caravane* (☎ 45 2278). It charges US$3 a person to either camp or sleep on the roof plus US$3 for a vehicle. Clean double rooms with shower, toilet and fan cost US$13; with air-con it costs US$18.

For good food and a lively ambience, head to *Café des Arts*, behind the Hôtel Tamesna, where garlic steak, chips and beans costs US$2.

The *Sahel* on the main street has cheap beer and plenty of drunks. Also popular is the open-air *Cheval Blanc*, where you can get cold beers (US$1.25) and, on weekends, hear a band playing (US$1 cover charge).

BIRNI-N'KONNI

This is very much a border town, with cheap Nigerian petrol, food and sex all for sale along the main drag. Moneychangers, juggling naira (Nigerian currency) and CFA, are everywhere. The main market day is Wednesday.

The *Relais Touristique* (☎ 208), 2km west of town on the Niamey road, is a shady and secure place; it charges US$3 a person and US$2 a vehicle. Double rooms with fans cost from US$7 to US$11, meals are US$4 and the beer price is reasonable.

In town is the depressing *campement* with very run-down rooms from US$7. At the *Hôtel Kado* (☎ 364), two blocks to the north, the rooms aren't as nice as the exterior would suggest. Singles/doubles with bath and fan cost US$11/12; with air-con it is US$15/18.

Along the main street and in the gare routière you'll find plenty of *food stalls* selling rice, meat, sauces and salads. The shady *restaurant* at the Hôtel Kado is expensive but you can get chicken and chips at night.

SNTN has a twice weekly bus to Zinder which passes through Birni-N'Konni (it is usually US$15 to Niamey and US$16 to Zinder).

DOSSO

There are only a few places to stay in Dosso (140km south-east of Niamey). The cheapest is the *Hôtel-Bar Étoile d'Afrique* on the road to Birni-N'Konni and a 20 minute walk from the gare routière; US$2 gets a tiny, airless and dirty cell.

More expensive is the *Hôtel Djerma* (☎ /fax 65 0206), on the main street behind the Mobil station, which offers air-con rooms with shower and toilet for US$16/18 a single/double; the hotel has a half-decent restaurant. The best place is the tidy *L'Auberge du Carrefour* (☎ 65 0017), on the right as you enter town from Niamey; doubles without/with air-con are US$9/12.

The main attraction at *Chez Rita*, near the Grand Marché, is Rita herself (she has immortalised herself on the restaurant walls). The meals are good and cheap.

As Dosso is at the junction of the main road between Zinder and Niamey and the main route to Benin and Nigeria, there are always lots of bush taxis (about US$3.50 to Niamey).

MARADI

Maradi, with 60,000 people, is one of the main commercial and industrial centres of Niger. The present town is only some 40 years old, but the original settlement at Sohongari in the lush Maradi Valley dates back to about 1790 and was founded by the animist Barki. At that time it was part of the territory controlled by the rulers of Katsina, whose regional governor, known as the *maradi* (chief of the fetishers), gave his name to the town.

Market days in Maradi are Monday and Friday. Good buys include Hausa blankets and Fulani cloth. Naira is bought and sold at the gare routière quite openly. The BIAO bank on Rue de la Sûreté and the BDRN on Route de Niamey both charge hefty commissions for changing travellers' cheques.

Places to Stay & Eat

Le Campement Administrative is a crumbling colonial-era building with shady grounds in a wooded valley about 2km from the market. They have single/twin rooms with showers and toilets for US$4/8 or you can camp for US$2 per person. It's easy to get to by taxi (US$1), but returning to town is difficult.

In the centre, the *Hôtel Liberté* has a few decrepit old rooms for US$6/8 a single/double with shower. More modern (and quieter) air-con doubles cost US$14. Better, but a hike from the centre, is the *Hôtel Larewa* which charges US$8/13 for very

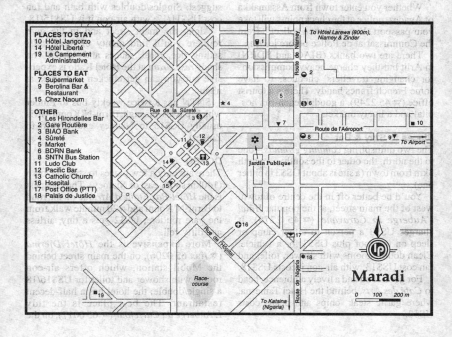

PLACES TO STAY
10 Hôtel Jangorzo
14 Hôtel Liberté
19 Le Campement
     Administrative

PLACES TO EAT
7 Supermarket
9 Berolina Bar &
    Restaurant
15 Chez Naoum

OTHER
1 Les Hirondelles Bar
2 Gare Routière
3 BIAO Bank
4 Sûreté
5 Market
6 BDRN Bank
8 SNTN Bus Station
11 Ludo Club
12 Pacific Bar
13 Catholic Church
16 Hospital
17 Post Office (PTT)
18 Palais de Justice

To Hôtel Larewa (800m),
Niamey & Zinder

Route de Niamey

Rue de la Sûreté

Route de l'Aéroport

To Airport

Jardin Publique

Rue de l'Hôpital

Route de Nigeria

Race-course

To Katsina
(Nigeria)

Maradi

0   100   200 m

clean singles/doubles with fan and shower or US$15 for an air-con double. There's secure parking and a cheap restaurant. The upmarket *Hôtel Jangorzo* (☎ 41 0140; telex 8235) has small rooms for US$12 and standard air-con rooms at US$24/27 for singles/doubles.

Street food is sold at the Jardin Publique (public gardens) facing the south-western corner of the market. The Lebanese-run *Chez Naoum*, about 1km south-west of the centre, several blocks south of the Hôtel Liberté, serves great grilled garlic chicken for US$3. Another cheap place is *Le Cercle de l'Amitié*, on the Route de Niamey, 200m north of the gare routière. Another hot spot, mainly for drinking, is the bar *Les Hirondelles* facing Cinéma Dan Kasswa on the northern side of town; Rolling Stones' fans will appreciate the goat's head soup on offer here.

Berolina is a garden bar-restaurant with African music and meals for US$3. The *Pacific Bar* and the *Ludo Club* are *the* places for dancing and meeting people; street food is sold in front of both of these places.

Getting There & Away

There are SNTN buses, twice weekly in each direction, between Niamey and Zinder, via Maradi; Niamey to Maradi is US$23. Private buses are about US$18 and bush taxis only slightly cheaper.

PARC NATIONAL DU W DU NIGER

This magnificent national park (up there with the Aïr Mountains as a highlight of Niger), on the western bank of the Niger gets its unusual name, W (pronounced 'dou-blay-vay'), from the double bend in the Niger River at the park's northern border. It straddles three countries – Niger, Benin and Burkina Faso. The Niger section of the park is the easiest to reach. You will not see animals in profusion, as you would in East and South Africa, but you will see a large variety of species and many aquatic bird species – perhaps 300 – between February and May.

The park is open from early December to late May, the entrance fee is US$7 and a free map is provided. An obligatory (and undoubtedly useful) guide charges about US$6 to US$10 per day. The park would be a blur without one.

The *camp site*, just before the park entrance and overlooking the Tapoa River, is US$4 per person. The *Hôtel de la Tapoa* has single/double bungalows with half-board for US$35/56 (US$5 more with air-con) and there is a swimming pool. Recently, Niger-Car Voyages set up a safari-style encampment where the tent and extras will cost from US$30.

It is hard to get to the park by public transport. It is about a three hour drive from Niamey to the park entrance at La Tapoa – the road is extremely rough.

TAHOUA

This mainly Hausa town (125km north of Birni-N'Konni) is used as an overnight stop for buses and vehicles travelling between Agadez and Niamey; it is Niger's fourth largest town. On market day, Sunday, you are likely to experience an incredible blend of cultures.

Places to Stay & Eat

Tahoua Camping Touristique is a 30 minute walk north-west from the gare routière; camping costs US$3 a tent and the same for a vehicle. Wrestling rings are nearby; you might be able to lay a wager!

In the town centre, the *Bungalows de la Mairie* (☎ 61 0553) has pleasant bungalows, all with air-con, for about US$17.

One of the most preferred spots for cheap African food is *Chez Fatima*, at the roundabout, one block east of the BIAO Bank.

Getting There & Away

SNTN buses between Agadez and Niamey stop here twice weekly; between Tahoua and Niamey is US$22 (bush taxis are US$16).

ZINDER

Zinder (pronounced zen-DAIR) is a pleasant town and, like Agadez, is one of the country's traditional market towns. It was the capital until 1926 and is now Niger's second largest city with a population of 80,000. But be sure to get your passport stamped at the Commissariat in the heart of town.

On Thursday, the **Grand Marché** is filled with a colourful array of people from outlying villages. The **Zengou Quartier**, the old commercial centre on the north side of town, is a maze of mud-brick houses with castellated walls and patterns in the rendering. The **Birni Quartier** is also an interesting tangle of mud-brick streets with the **Sultan's Palace** (actually inhabited by the Sultan) and the **Grande Mosquée**; for entry to the mosque apply at the Mairie (town hall). The old *banco* houses are everywhere, identified by colourful geometrical designs in relief.

Places to Stay & Eat

The cheapest place in town is the homely *Hôtel Malem Kal Ka Danu* (☎ 51 0568) on Ave de la République (Agadez road) in the Zengou quarter. The friendly owner, Ali, charges US$5/6 for a clean singles/doubles with fans and bucket showers, or US$9 for attached bath.

The *Hôtel Central* (☎ 51 2013) has long been the most popular place to stay for overland trucks. Lately its popularity with prostitutes has lowered its tone somewhat. Large doubles with fans cost US$11, air-con rooms are US$16 and camping is US$3 a person. Its garden is a cool place for a drink and the restaurant is recommended. Nearby,

the *Hôtel Le Damagaram* (☎ 51 0619; telex 8223) is a more expensive version of the same, with singles/doubles from US$18/26. There's a pricey restaurant here and, on weekend nights, a popular nightclub (US$3).

In the mornings and evenings, the best place for good *street food* is the dirt square in front of the Hôtel Central and on the Blvd de l'Indépendance near the gare routière.

For snacks, try *Snack Bar du Damergou* opposite the Hôtel Le Damagaram and for cheap meals *Restaurant Dan Kasina* in the centre, a block or two north of the Hôtel Central.

The best African food – brochettes, chicken in gumbo sauce and pâté – is found at the *Scotch Bar* on Rue de Grand Marché. If you can talk your way inside, you'll be well satisfied at the *Club Privé* – it is open daily until late. Ask locals for directions.

Getting There & Away

SNTN buses run between Niamey and Zinder on Tuesday, Thursday and Sunday; the fare is US$29 and the trip is 14 hours or so. The bus park is just off Blvd de l'Indépéndance, a block north of the Hôtel Central.

A bush taxi between Niamey and Zinder is US$23; these leave from the gare routière near the Petit Marché. From Zinder to Kano in a bush taxi is US$7; the trip takes more than six hours.

Nigeria

Nigeria is Africa's most populous state and, for a while during the 1970s, it was one of the continent's wealthiest. It has a fascinating collection of different peoples, cultures, histories and religions. Always faced with the problem of disunity, today it is trying to find a sense of nationhood out of the rivalries and bloodshed which bedevilled the country for years after independence.

However, there is another, very negative, side to the country. This is the unbridled and often ill-considered 'development' that has taken place, particularly in the cities, fuelled by what appeared to be an endless source of oil money. As a result, many Nigerian cities are sprawling, congested and as ugly as sin. Problems such as overcrowding, pollution, noise, traffic chaos, a soaring crime rate and the inadequacy of public utilities combine to make most urban centres hellholes.

Facts about the Country

HISTORY
The first recorded state to flourish in this part of Africa was Kanem, north-east of Lake Chad. Its wealth was based on control of one of the most important trans-Saharan trade routes from West Africa to the Mediterranean and the Middle East. Islam became the state religion quite early in Kanem's history. A number of Islamic Hausa kingdoms also flourished between the 11th and 14th centuries, based around the cities of Kano, Katsina, Zaria and Nupe.

In the south-west a number of Yoruba empires sprang up between the 14th and 15th centuries, centred in Ife, Oyo and Benin. These three cities became important trading and craft centres. The political systems of these states rested largely on a sacred monarchy with a strong court bureaucracy, each retaining its traditional religion. Islam made very little headway here until the late 18th

FEDERAL REPUBLIC OF NIGERIA
Area: 924,000 sq km
Population: 111 million
Population Growth Rate: 2.9%
Capital: Lagos
Head of State: General Sani Abacha
Official Language: English
Currency: Naira
Exchange Rate: N 80 = US$1
Per Capita GNP: US$230
Inflation: 50%
Time: GMT/UTC + 1

Highlights
- The outstanding museum in green, cool Jos
- The Sacred Groves in rainforest at Oshogbo
- Surviving Lagos

century; the Obas (kings) of these traditional states retain considerable influence today. In the south-east the Ibo and other peoples never developed any centralised empires but instead formed loose confederations.

The first contact between the Yoruba empires and Europeans was made in the 15th century with the Portuguese, who began trading in pepper, though this was later supplanted by the trade in slaves. In contrast, the northern Islamic states continued to trade principally across the Sahara and remained untouched by Europeans until well into the 19th century.

The Portuguese were gradually displaced

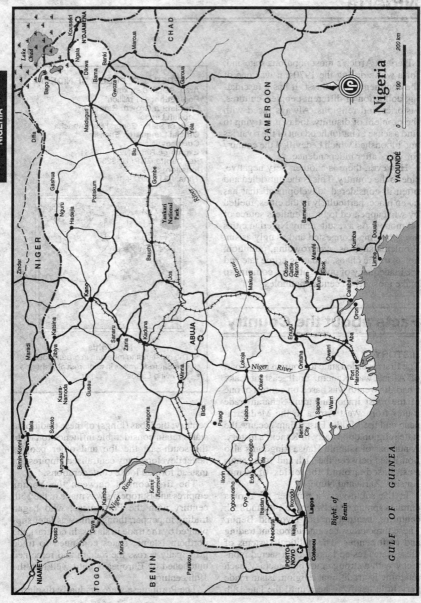

by the northern European maritime nations throughout the 16th and 17th centuries, during which time the slave trade expanded dramatically. It's estimated that 40 million West Africans were dragged off in chains to the Americas, but this human misery wasn't the only result. The political effects of the trade were catastrophic, resulting in continuous wars, instability and the neglect of agriculture and other possible avenues of commerce.

By the time slavery was abolished in the early 19th century, the coastal kingdoms had become dependent on the trade and were unable to adjust to the new circumstances. By that time, however, the British had begun to lay the foundations for direct political control of the hinterland in order to protect their commercial monopoly from a French challenge.

Another important change towards the end of the slave-trade era was a revolutionary upheaval in the Hausa kingdoms of the north. This led to the replacement of Hausa kings with Fulani rulers, and the setting up of the Sokoto caliphate.

Once military conquest was completed, the British ruled indirectly through local kings and chiefs, thereby guaranteeing a stable environment from which economic surplus could be extracted without disruption. The policy worked well in the north but much less so in the south-west, where none of the traditional Yoruba rulers had ever extracted taxes. In the south-east, where there had never been any centralised authority, the policy was even less successful.

As the demand for independence gathered force after WWII, the British attempted to put together a constitution taking into account the interests of the three main areas of the colony – the north, which was mainly Muslim with an ethnic majority of Hausa and Fulani; the east, Catholic and mainly Ibo; and the west, mixed Muslim and Anglican and mainly Yoruba.

It proved to be an extremely difficult task. The northerners feared that the southerners had an educational advantage which would allow them to dominate politics and com-

merce. There was likewise considerable mistrust among the southerners – the result of fierce competition for jobs in the civil service and for business contracts. In the end, each region was given its own civil service, judiciary, and marketing boards (the main earners of foreign exchange). Thus, when independence was granted in October 1960, Nigeria was essentially three nations.

The first six years of independence were disastrous. National politics degenerated into a vicious power game, corruption became rampant and the elite accumulated wealth by any means possible. With their interests ignored, and faced with extortionate rents and rising food prices, the workers organised a general strike in 1963 and another the following year. Their grievances finally exploded in an orgy of looting and violence which swept the country following blatantly rigged elections in the western region in 1965.

In early 1966, a group of young army officers, most of whom were Ibo, staged a coup. The prime minister, the premiers of the west and north, and most of the senior army officers were assassinated. The head of the army, General Ironsi (himself an Ibo), took over as head of state.

Ironsi's accession to power was welcomed by many sections of the Nigerian public, but it didn't last long. A few months later he was killed in a coup staged by a group of northern army officers after anti-Ibo riots had broken out in the north. A new regime was set up under the leadership of Lieutenant Colonel Yakubu Gowon, a Christian from a minority group in the north.

The coup was viewed with horror in the east and the military commander of the area, Lieutenant Colonel Ojukwu, refused to recognise Gowon as the new head of state. His antipathy to the new regime was sealed when large-scale massacres of Ibo again took place in the north, triggering a return to the east by thousands of Ibo from all over the country. In May 1967, Ojukwu announced the secession of the east and the creation of the independent state of Biafra.

Biafra was recognised by only a handful

of African countries, and the civil war dragged on for three years as the Ibo forces fought tooth and claw for every inch of territory which the federal forces took back. By early 1970, as a result of the blockade imposed by the federal government, Biafra faced famine and its forces were compelled to capitulate. Somewhere between 500,000 and two million Biafran civilians had died, mainly from starvation.

Despite the hatreds fanned by civil war, reconciliation was swift and peaceful, and Gowon was careful not to treat the Ibo as a vanquished people. Unfortunately, he was unable to use the same degree of imagination to get the economy moving again, and corruption, once more, got totally out of control. He was overthrown in a bloodless coup by General Murtala Mohammed in 1975.

The new government launched a clean up of the civil service, the judiciary and the universities. Yet, despite his widespread popularity, Mohammed was assassinated in an attempted coup in early 1976. Other members of the regime survived and continued to implement his policies until power was handed back to a civilian government following elections in 1979. The new civilian regime of President Shagari proved to be no better and possibly even worse than previous administrations.

With Nigeria at the height of its political influence, Shagari squandered the country's wealth on grandiose and ill-considered projects until the next crisis loomed in the early 1980s when the price of oil plummeted and the supply of easy money dried up.

Unpaid contractors packed up and left and in an attempt to shore up the crumbling edifice, Shagari turned to bartering oil for essential commodities such as foodstuffs and transport. Next he turned on the millions of other West Africans who had flocked to Nigeria in search of work during the oil boom. Some three million of them were suddenly expelled, causing massive dislocation, unemployment and food shortages in neighbouring countries. Nigeria's action almost destroyed ECOWAS (the Economic Community of West African States). On

New Year's Eve 1983 Shagari was overthrown in a military coup, this time headed by General Mohammed Buhari.

Buhari clamped down heavily and made bold moves to get the country back together. There was a currency changeover to halt the export of naira (to stop black market speculation), land borders were closed to prevent smuggling and many of Shagari's grandiose projects were postponed or cancelled.

Yet during Buhari's rule there were widespread abuses of civil liberties: torture, arbitrary arrests and incarceration without trial became common. In 1985, he was overthrown in another coup headed by General Ibrahim Babangida, the army's chief of staff.

Babangida initially made much headway in restoring some semblance of order to Nigeria without the iron-fisted approach of his predecessor. A year after taking office, he announced he would hand over power to a civilian government in 1990 but this was twice postponed. As each promise was broken, Nigerians began to fear that it was all another case of déjà vu.

In the meantime, Babangida had increased the number of states to 30 in an attempt to ease ethnic tensions prior to the election. He also lifted the ban on political parties but when nominations poured in, he rejected them all and set up two other parties by decree.

The much-delayed presidential election finally went ahead in June 1993 with Moshood Abiola, a Yoruba from the south, claiming victory. Two weeks later, Babangida annulled the results and announced that another election would be held. Seven years of planning that would have given Nigeria some form of democracy went down the drain – but so did Babangida. Pressured by fellow army officers to hand over power, he stepped down in August and appointed Ernest Shonekan as head of an interim, civilian government. A new election date was set for February 1994.

The public's disbelief at Babangida's arrogance and his flagrant contempt for democratic principles resulted in violent riots in Lagos. But there was still no end to military rule. Pre-empting an uprising by junior ranks, General Sani Abacha, the interim government's defence secretary, seized control in a bloodless coup in November and forced Shonekan to announce his government's resignation. Abacha then abolished all 'democratic' institutions including the two political parties, the national and state assemblies and local governments. Steps taken toward free market reform were abandoned in favour of state controls of the sort that allowed corruption to flourish.

General Abacha is still in power and there seems no end in sight to the military regime or Abacha's determination to entrench himself as head of state.

The execution of the playwright Ken Saro-Wiwa, along with eight of his colleagues, in November 1995 for allegedly plotting to overthrow the government stunned the rest of the world and led to Nigeria's expulsion from the Commonwealth.

GEOGRAPHY & CLIMATE

Nigeria's topography is relatively unvaried. The north touches on the Sahel and is mostly savannah with low hills. Mountains are found only along the Cameroon border in the east, although there is also a 1500m-high plateau around Jos in the centre of the country where the climate is pleasantly cool. The coast is an almost unbroken line of sandy beaches and lagoons running back to creeks and mangrove swamps and is very humid most of the year. Rainfall is high in this area.

The climate is hot and dry in the north and hot and wet in the south. The rainy season in

Ken Saro-Wiwa

Ken Saro-Wiwa, the distinguished Nigerian novelist, playwright, and political activist, was hanged in November 1995, along with eight other Ogoni people on the order of the military head of state General Sani Abacha. Saro-Wiwa was found guilty – of complicity in the murder of four pro-government Ogoni chiefs – by a hand-picked military tribunal. The trial was marked by numerous irregularities, the intimidation of witnesses and the refusal of the prosecution to present vital evidence. Its outcome was a foregone conclusion with no possibility of an appeal to an independent court either in Nigeria or elsewhere.

Saro-Wiwa's conflict with the government began in 1993 with the formation of the Movement for the Survival of the Ogoni People (MOSOP), a peaceful resistance organisation which he led. The Ogoni, a minority tribal group of some 500,000 people, inhabit a region of Rivers State which, for decades, has born the brunt of oil drilling operations by Anglo-Dutch Shell which extracts some 300,000 barrels per day from more than 100 wells.

The environmental damage to the Ogoni territory has been severe and rendered much of the land unusable. Between 1976 and 1991, there were almost 3000 oil spills, averaging 700 barrels each. Clean-up operations, where they have taken place at all, have been inordinately slow. In addition, gas flares, burning 24 hours a day (some of them for the past 30 years), are often sited near Ogoni villages and have resulted in acid rain, massive deposits of soot and respiratory diseases in the surrounding community.

Oil revenues account for 80 to 90% of Nigeria's income – around US$8.5 billion each year, some US$3.4 billion of which is consistently unaccounted for. Thirty of the major contracts, covering the export of 800,000 barrels per day, are held by senior officers connected with Nigeria's military regime.

It was against this background that MOSOP was formed. Saro-Wiwa campaigned vigorously. Every protest mounted by the Ogoni (several of which involved hundreds of thousands of people) was met with violence from the armed forces. Hundreds of Ogoni have been killed, many more maimed and tens of thousands have been rendered homeless by vandalism.

Saro-Wiwa's execution caused international outrage, particularly after numerous appeals for clemency had been expressed by many world leaders, including Nelson Mandela. It led to Nigeria's expulsion from the Commonwealth and sanctions being applied by the USA and several European countries. General Sani Abacha dismissed the outcry as attempted interference in Nigeria's internal affairs.

While the focus of world attention has since moved from the Ogoni and their plight, Saro-Wiwa's son, Ken Wiwa, is now one of the leaders in the struggle to save Ogoni land from ruin. ∎

the north is between April and September while in the south it is from March to November. A long dusty dry season stretches from December to March when the cooling harmattan blows off the desert.

POPULATION & PEOPLE

The population is estimated to be around 111 million and rising by around 3% a year.

There are some 250 different ethnic groups, but the largest ones are the mainly Protestant Yoruba in the west, the Catholic Ibo in the east and the predominantly Muslim Hausa-Fulani in the north. About half the people are Muslim, 34% are Christian and the rest follow tribal religions.

LANGUAGE

English is the official language. The main African languages are Hausa, Yoruba and Ibo. There are also large numbers of Edo and Efik speakers.

Facts for the Visitor

VISAS

Visas are required for all except nationals of ECOWAS countries. You cannot get visas at the border or on arrival at an airport.

Most embassies (including the Nigerian high commission in London and the embassies in Benin and Togo, but not the one in the Central African Republic) issue visas only to residents and nationals of the country in which that embassy is located. The high commission in Canberra issues visas only to residents or nationals of Australia, New Zealand, PNG and Fiji. In other words, get a visa before leaving for Africa.

The cost of a visa depends on your nationality. For most, it's about US$27 (or the equivalent) but it's a whopping US$214 for UK citizens (or £138 in London or A$323 in Canberra)! You also need two or three photos, an onward airline ticket (or a photocopy of it) and either a letter of invitation from a person/company in Nigeria or a letter detailing the reason why you want to visit

Nigeria. Processing can take up to two weeks but is usually much shorter. *Never* state your profession as journalist – the visa will be refused.

Visas allow for a stay of up to one month and remain valid for three months from the date of issue, not the date of arrival. Plan accordingly.

Visa Extensions

Extensions are free for most people, but UK nationals must pay a fee and supply one photo and a letter from a citizen or resident vouching for them.

Extensions can be obtained in all the state capitals from the immigration department of the Federal Secretariat. Kano is the easiest place to get them but ask for a letter of introduction first from the manager of the Kano State Tourist Camp.

Other Visas

Benin

> Two-week visas cost US$7.50 and you need one photo. You must apply between 9 and 11 am and collect your passport at 2 pm the same day.

Cameroon

> The Cameroon embassy issues 90 day, multiple-entry visas within 24 hours. The fee is US$60 and you'll need two photos and an onward airline ticket (a ticket ex-Lagos is acceptable). Office hours are weekdays from 8 am to 12.30 pm and from 1.30 to 3 pm.
>
> At the Cameroon consulate in Calabar visa requirements are the same as in Lagos but you may not be asked for an onward ticket. The consulate is open from 9 am to 2.30 pm weekdays.

Chad

> A one-month visa costs US$30, requires two photos and is issued within 24 hours.

Niger

> Visas for Niger are available from either the consulate in Kano or the embassy in Lagos. At both, a one month visa costs US$35, requires three photos and is issued within 24 hours. The embassy is open weekdays from 9 am to 2.30 pm.

EMBASSIES
Nigerian Embassies

In Africa, there are Nigerian embassies or high commissions in all but a very few African countries.

Elsewhere there are embassies or high commissions in most European Union (EU) member states, Australia, Japan, the UK and the USA.

Foreign Embassies in Nigeria

Algeria
26 Maitama Sule St, Ikoyi Island (☎ 68 3155)

Australia
Plot 43, Ozumba Mbadiwe Ave, Victoria Island (☎ 63 6828)

Benin
4 Abudu Smith St, Victoria Island (☎ 61 4411)

Burkina Faso
15 Norman Williams St, Ikoyi Island (☎ 68 1001)

Cameroon
Fermi Pearse St, Victoria Island (☎ 61 2226)
consulate: 21 Ndiden Usang Iso Rd (Marian Rd), Calabar (☎ (087) 22 2782)

Chad
2 Goriola St, Victoria Island (☎ 61 3116)

Congo (Zaïre)
1A Kofo Abayomi Rd, Victoria Island (☎ 61 0377)

Côte d'Ivoire
5 Abudu Smith St, Victoria Island (☎ 61 0963)

France
1 Queen's Drive, Ikoyi Island (☎ 60 3300)

Ghana
21-23 King George V Rd, Lagos Island (☎ 60 1450)

Niger
15 Adeola Odeku St, Victoria Island (☎ 61 2300)
consulate: 12 Aliyu Ave near the Airport Rd roundabout, Kano (☎ 62 5274)

Togo
Plot 976, Oju Olobun Close, Victoria Island (☎ 61 7449)

UK
11 Eleke Crescent, Victoria Island (☎ 61 1551)

USA
2 Eleke Crescent, Victoria Island (☎ 61 0097)

CUSTOMS

Nigerian customs can be a pain in the butt whether you're entering or leaving. Two thorough searches of your baggage on entry and one on exit are normal. They are also very suspicious of individual travellers. This labels you, in their eyes, as a journalist or troublemaker, and they will go through *everything* minutely. If there's evidence that you fit the picture, expect major hassles and delays. You might even be refused entry. If this happens, a *dash* (bribe) will be openly and aggressively demanded. The dash will be substantial – don't offer peanuts.

MONEY

US$1 = N 80

The unit of currency is the naira, which equals 100 kobo (but you'll never see a kobo).

Changing travellers' cheques in Nigeria is complicated. Either banks won't change them at all or they'll have you running around, often for days, until they get the exchange rate from the central bank. They also charge hefty commissions. Bring cash and, if at all possible, avoid banks entirely.

Instead, change at either a bureau de change (foreign exchange bureau) or with a black market (parallel market) dealer. These people are generally quick and reliable but most will only change American Express travellers' cheques at up to 15% less than Thomas Cook cheques. Many will demand to see the proof of purchase slips for the cheques so have them handy. The parallel market rate is substantially higher than the official rate and the bureau de change rates are published daily in the national newspapers.

Another major hassle with changing money is that the largest bill is a mere N 50 (less than US$1). This means that if you're changing US$200 or more, you almost need a laundry bag to carry the bills away because you will rarely get the cash entirely in N 50 bills – N 25 is more common.

Credit cards are all but useless in Nigeria except at five star hotels but you're seriously advised not to use them at all because there are innumerable scams on the go. You cannot get a cash advance against any credit card at any bank in Nigeria.

Currency declaration forms were abolished years ago but corrupt police, especially in the south, will tell you that's not the case. Then they'll proceed to intimidate you with threats of having the lot confiscated unless you pay a substantial dash. They can be very aggressive and persistent. Don't buckle. Instead, go to a bank, see the manager and ask for a letter on headed paper saying you don't need the form. This will cost you much less than paying the dash.

POST & COMMUNICATIONS

Mail sent to/from Nigeria is notoriously slow and the poste restante at Lagos is simply atrocious – avoid having anything sent here if you can. There's no charge for collecting mail from poste restante though you'll most certainly be asked for a dash. Forget about sending parcels – they'll never arrive.

The international telephone service is, thankfully, better than the postal system. You can phone or fax from the NITEL offices in any regional capital (if there's a free line, which is not always the case). The rates are US$2.30 per minute to anywhere in Africa, US$3.40 per minute to anywhere in Europe or America and US$3.85 to Asia or Australasia, all plus 15% VAT.

The country code for Nigeria is 234; area codes include:

Lagos	01
Bauchi	077
Benin City	052
Calabar	087
Jos	073
Kaduna	062
Kano	064
Katsina	065
Maiduguri	076
Onitsha	046
Sokoto	060

DANGERS & ANNOYANCES

Nigerian roads are dangerous, especially in the crowded south where travelling at night is about as sensible as playing Russian roulette. Speeds of 150km/h are not unusual. Entreaties to reduce the speed only elicit laughter despite the hazards of hitting yawning potholes which would total any vehicle and kill its occupants.

Police and army checkpoints are frequent on every single highway throughout the country and it gets tedious. They'll want to see your passport and, half the time, they'll invent a 'problem'. That means a dash. Don't

argue: just give them N 50 and get on your way. The local people get hit up the same as you do. If you're travelling in a bus they don't generally waste too much of your time. These police and army personnel take themselves pretty seriously and it's wise to regard them in the same light if you want to avoid lunatic acts of aggression.

Immigration police can be equally tedious but just as persistent and not shy about knocking on your hotel door at 6 am.

If you fly into Lagos' Murtala Mohammed international airport, you may be in for another treat: the warm greeting you might encounter just outside the airport as you take a taxi into Lagos. It generally takes the form of an army truck which stops the taxi. With a gun against your head, US$1000 will be demanded from you 'for protection'. The intimidation goes on until it's clear you're not impressed with the welcome or until a senior officer intervenes. Welcome to Lagos!

PUBLIC HOLIDAYS

Public holidays observed in Nigeria include: 1 January, 1 May, 1 October (National Day), 25 and 26 December, Good Friday, Easter Monday and variable Islamic holidays (also see Public Holidays in Regional Facts for the Visitor).

ACCOMMODATION

Nigerian hotels, while cheaper than those in neighbouring countries, are generally 'squelched'. What this means is that, regardless of what facilities the hotels advertise, nothing works. Not the air-con or the fan, the water in the bathroom, nor even the lights. The message is this – make do with what you find and hassle the hell out of the management for a discount.

Always check out a room before you pay. There are exceptions but they're few and far between.

Hotels often, but not always, use the term 'single' to refer to a room with one double bed and 'double' for a room with two double beds. Most hotels in the mid-to-high price bracket demand that you pay a refundable deposit upfront.

FOOD

Food in Nigeria is nothing to rave about. The best known dish is pepper soup: a very hot sauce which comes with three pieces of fish, beef or goat meat (though more often than not it's bone or gristle rather than edible meat). It's served with rice or a mound of another grain-based staple such as *gari* or *eba*. A common snack food is *dodo* (pieces of fried plantain), though in the cities you'll find plenty of snack places serving stodgy chicken or fish pies and doughnuts. Meat pies are also popular and cheap but contain little meat.

Getting There & Away

AIR

Carriers flying into Lagos international airport (Murtala Mohammed international airport) include Aeroflot, Air Afrique, Air France, Cameroon Airlines, Ethiopian Airlines, Ghana Airways, KLM, Sabena, and Swissair. British Airways and KLM also fly into Kano.

The national carrier is Nigerian Airways which also flies to many West, Central and East African destinations as well as Europe and America but only a masochist would fly with them. Overbooking is the name of the game and the mad dash across the tarmac for a seat on their planes is plain stupidity. In any case, the airline is uninsurable and has been banned from landing in Britain and Israel. Nigeria has refused British Airways landings in retaliation.

The departure tax for international flights is US$35.

LAND

Benin

The road from Lagos to Cotonou (120km) is in excellent shape. Share-taxis leave from Ebutero motor park near the Udumata bus stop at the end of Carter bridge and cost US$6 (three hours). The time this trip takes depends largely on whether there's a mild or manic traffic jam as you leave Lagos, and on the Nigerian border officials. They can be casual and pleasant if they like you and your dash, or intimidating power freaks. You can also enter Benin via Kamba and Gaya.

Cameroon

The usual road route is from Enugu or Calabar to Mamfé via Ikom. From Calabar take a share-taxi to Ikom (US$3, 2½ hours), and another from there to Mfum (the Nigerian border village) for US$1. Unless you have through transport, it is a 1km walk from Mfum to Ekok (the Cameroon border village). From Ekok there are taxis to most of the towns in western Cameroon via Mamfé. The border closes at 7 pm. You can exchange naira for Central African CFA francs at Ikom at a poor rate.

There's also a crossing in the far north between Maiduguri and Maroua (225km). From Maiduguri to Banki (Nigerian border) a taxi costs US$2 and takes 1½ hours via five police checkpoints. On the Cameroon side there are minibuses to Maroua (US$3, one hour). If Cameroon customs hassle you about having a camera, tell them you're going to the Ministry of Information & Culture in Maroua for a photo permit.

Further north again is the crossing from Ngala to Kousséri, but you would only use this crossing if you were heading straight for N'Djamena (Chad). Another feasible crossing point is from Yola to Garoua.

Chad

Travellers heading from Maiduguri to N'Djamena (247km) must pass through a strip of northern Cameroon to reach Chad, which means you must have a visa for Cameroon. The usual route is via Ngala (on the Nigerian border) to Kousséri (in Cameroon) and then across the bridge to N'Djamena. See the Cameroon chapter for details.

Niger

There are four main routes to Niger but the most popular is from Kano to Zinder (240km, four to five hours). In Kano go to the Kofar Ruwa motor park on the northern edge of the old city, where the Katsina road meets the road to Kofar Ruwa. Direct taxis cost US$8 a person. The best days to hitch a ride are Tuesday and early Wednesday as trucks do the run to pick up produce from the Zinder market which takes place every Thursday. The Nigerian customs are cursory but the Niger customs are extra thorough.

The second route is from Sokoto to Birnin-Konni (95km, US$2 in a share-taxi) but this route is heavily potholed, there are umpteen checkpoints along the way and the Nigerian border officials are known to give travellers with their own vehicle a very hard time. There are motorcycle-taxis from the border village of Illela to Birnin-Konni (US$1).

Another option is to take the road from Katsina to Maradi (92km). From Katsina you'll have to take a taxi (US$1) to Jibiya (Nigerian border) and another one from there to Maradi (US$4).

The fourth route is from Sokoto to Niamey via Gaya on the Niger-Benin border.

SEA
Cameroon
There are boats from Oron, south of Calabar, to Idenao, a small place 50km north-west of Limbe. From Calabar to Oron you can take a speedboat (30 minutes, US$1.50), which will leave when full (12 people), or the ferry (1½ hours, US$0.60) which leaves daily at 11.30 am. Beware of immigration officials at the Calabar dock who will demand to know why you want to go to Oron, take your passport off you and demand a dash of N 1000 (US$12.50). Oron is near the Bakassi peninsula, which is the site of an undeclared war between Nigeria and Cameroon. Basically, travellers won't be made welcome and you can expect hassles there.

If you care to go through this bullshit, there are two types of boats from Oron. The small speedboats are fast and relatively safe (although there are no lifejackets nor any other safety equipment). The average fare is around US$35 and they take around four hours. You can usually find one of these legal boats by asking around.

The other type are long wooden boats fitted with two to three outboard motors and usually loaded with smuggled goods. They generally run about 16km off shore to avoid the Nigerian and Cameroon navies; therefore, if there's a breakdown you could be in trouble. Also keep in mind that you may not arrive where you're supposed to as the captain might decide that the cargo should be unloaded away from prying official eyes. This could mean sloshing through mangroves to a road and a long wait for transport. To find these boats, ask around at Oron port. Expect to pay about US$10.

Getting Around

AIR
Taking a domestic flight in Nigeria is like joining a madhouse. There are schedules – of a sort – but they're vague and constantly subject to delay or cancellation. The only way to get on one is to turn up at the airport a day in advance and make enquiries. The good news is that internal flights are incredibly cheap and you can pay for them in naira.

As with international flights, avoid Nigerian Airways if at all possible. Instead, use one of the private airlines such as KABO Air, Belleview Air and Gas Airlines. They're not quite as chaotic and are more reliable but you can only buy a ticket on the day of departure. As an example of costs, KABO offer Lagos-Kano for US$40 and Kano-Maiduguri for US$30.

BUS & SHARE-TAXI
The best and safest way to travel by road is on a modern luxury express bus – with one reservation: they only leave when full and that can involve a wait of up to three hours, depending on the destination. Alternatively, take a share-taxi. Like the buses, they only go when full but that usually means only six passengers so the waiting time is measured in minutes instead of hours. The drawback with share-taxis is the dangerous speeds at which they travel. If anything unexpected happens, you are history...

Bus and share-taxi fares are about the same over comparable distances and they're both very cheap – petrol is the cheapest in

Africa at around US$0.07 a litre. Fares average around US$1 or less per 100km.

The motor parks for buses and share-taxis are rarely the same, though they may be close to each other. In large cities, there will usually be several motor parks for share-taxis which service specific destinations. Virtually all of them will be on the outskirts of town and you'll have to take a taxi to get there. This can cost you as much as the fare to your intended destination.

TRAIN
The railway system was once a good way to get around Nigeria but it's now at a standstill with most passenger services halted. Its demise is largely due to decades of total neglect in favour of highways. There is still some 3500km of railway line which connects Lagos to Maiduguri via Ibadan, Ilorin, Kaduna and Kano. The other track runs from Port Harcourt to Kaduna via Aba, Enugu and Makurdi with a branch line to Jos. A contract has been signed with China to revitalise the railways but until that happens forget about travelling by rail.

MOTORCYCLE-TAXI ('MACHINE')
In many cities you can get around on the back of a 'machine'. They can manage a backpack on the handlebars and are a great way to cool off. Fares are never more than US$0.15 for a short drop.

HITCHING
Hitching is usually easy but not recommended because of the danger of being mugged. It's also hardly worth the trouble given the cheap fares on buses and share-taxis.

Lagos

Ask any traveller or resident what they think of Lagos and you're more than likely to cop a virulent litany of negatives. They're not wrong – up to a point. It's the largest city in West or Central Africa with wall-to-wall people, bumper-to-bumper cars, noise and pollution beyond belief, a crime rate out of control and public utilities which are simply incapable of coping with the demands of an estimated 10 million people. Elevated motorways ring the city and are jammed with speed freaks and snarl-ups. The dispossessed and the desperate eke out a grim existence in tin and cardboard shacks underneath the same motorways. Power cuts are a daily fact of life.

Yet, while all that's true, particularly of Lagos Island, the city can be a buzz if you've previously lived in large conurbations and have the stamina and street savvy to survive this hot, steamy concrete jungle. The stories you will hear about violent crime and broad-daylight muggings are probably all true so watch what you're doing and where you're going but don't be intimidated. Never walk at night – always take a taxi.

Orientation
For the traveller, there are four main areas of Lagos: Yaba (on the mainland, south of the international and domestic airports); Lagos Island (the heart of the city); Ikoyi Island (a smart suburb with some embassies and top-end hotels), and Victoria Island (an even smarter suburb facing the Atlantic Ocean with the bulk of the embassies and a number of top-end hotels). They're all connected by elevated expressways and bridges. Cheap hotels are to be found only in Yaba and on Lagos Island.

Information
On Lagos Island, the black market dealers hang around the Bristol Hotel. Otherwise, try Majoe Bureau de Change, 5/7 Abibu Oki St. In Yaba, the bureaus de change are on Oja Elegbu Rd between Western Ave and Murtala Mohammed Way. There are many others on Ikoyi Island along Awolowo Rd.

The agent for Thomas Cook is L'Aristocrate Travel & Tours (☎ 266 7322), corner of Davies and Broad Sts, Lagos Island.

Things to See
For street life during the day, take a stroll

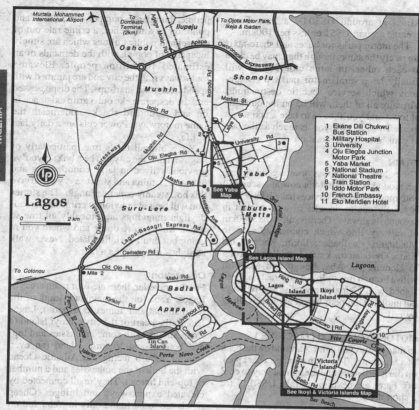

Map Key:
1 Ekene Dili Chukwu Bus Station
2 Military Hospital
3 University
4 Oju Elegba Junction Motor Park
5 Yaba Market
6 National Stadium
7 National Theatre
8 Train Station
9 Iddo Motor Park
10 French Embassy
11 Eko Meridien Hotel

along the length of Broad St on Lagos Island. It teems with human activity and there are all manner of goods and food for sale.

The **National Museum** on Awolowo Rd near Tafawa Balewa Square has some interesting displays and exhibits. It's open daily.

Places to Stay

Lagos Island The women-only *YWCA*, 8 Moloney St at King George V St, has relatively clean, stuffy rooms but it's usually full. Its rates are US$2 a person in a three-bed room and US$3 in a room with two beds. There's an 11 pm curfew.

Close by, the pink *Ritz Hotel* (☎ 52 3148), 41 King George V Rd, charges US$7.50/9 plus 15% VAT for singles/doubles. All the rooms have air-con and a clean bathroom. It's a friendly place and the restaurant/bar is pleasantly dark, sleazy and deliciously cool.

The *Wayfarers Hotel* (☎ 263 0113), 52 Campbell St, has air-con doubles (no singles) with bucket showers for US$13.20 plus VAT. It's fairly clean and secure. There's a popular bar (closed Sunday) and cheap food at the attached Josanna Restaurant. A good meal (eg fish and fried rice) costs just US$2.

Considerably more expensive is the *Bristol Hotel* (☎ 266 1204) at 8 Martins St, right in the centre, which charges US$20/38 for air-con singles/doubles with own bathroom. There's a restaurant and two bars and MasterCard is accepted.

Ikoyi Island The men-only *YMCA* (☎ 68 0516), 77 Awolowo Rd, has dorm beds (four per room) for US$0.50 but it's an absolute flea pit and is for desperadoes only.

Yaba There's a much better choice of cheap hotels in Yaba and it's nowhere near as crowded as Lagos Island. One of the cheapest is the *Hotel Majestic* at 14 Popo St. It's an old place and dilapidated but habitable. Singles with fan are US$4 and doubles with air-con are US$8. All the rooms have their own bathroom but there's no running water. It's handy to the Yaba motor park.

Much better is the nearby *Granada Hotel* (☎ 84 7980) at 29 Jacob St, which is pleasant, quiet and comfortable. Singles/doubles with own bathroom and air-con are US$9/12. It has a bar and food available.

Close to Western Ave is the *Mullard*

Lagos Island

0   250   500 m

Lagos Harbour

PLACES TO STAY
6 Bristol Hotel
17 Wayfarers Hotel;
   Josanna Restaurant
20 YWCA
21 Ritz Hotel

PLACES TO EAT
16 Mr Bigg's

OTHER
1 Udumata Bus Stop
2 Ebutero Motor Park
3 UTB Bank
4 L'Aristocrate Travel
   & Tours (Thomas Cook)
5 UK High Commission
   (Consular Section)
7 UBA Bank
8 KLM
9 Leventis Department
   Store
10 Union Bank of Nigeria
11 Main Post Office
12 NITEL Office
13 Ferry Station
14 Ministry of
   External Affairs
15 NAL Towers
18 Nigerian Airways
19 Aeroflot
22 Police Headquarters
23 Ghanaian High
   Commission
24 National Museum

NIGERIA

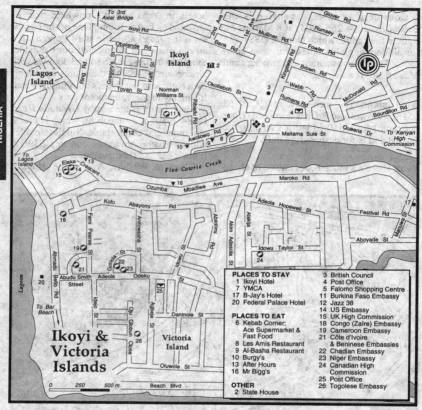

PLACES TO STAY
1 Ikoyi Hotel
7 YMCA
17 B-Jay's Hotel
20 Federal Palace Hotel

PLACES TO EAT
6 Kebab Corner;
  Ace Supermarket &
  Fast Food
8 Les Amis Restaurant
9 Al-Basha Restaurant
10 Burgy's
13 After Hours
16 Mr Bigg's

OTHER
2 State House

3 British Council
4 Post Office
5 Falomo Shopping Centre
11 Burkina Faso Embassy
12 Jazz 38
14 US Embassy
15 UK High Commission
18 Congo (Zaïre) Embassy
19 Cameroon Embassy
21 Côte d'Ivoire
  & Beninese Embassies
22 Chadian Embassy
23 Niger Embassy
24 Canadian High
  Commission
25 Post Office
26 Togolese Embassy

Garden Hotel & Restaurant (☎ 83 7974), 89 Oju Elegba Rd, which is basically a 'short-time' joint but habitable. Singles/doubles with fan and shared bathroom facilities cost US$5.60/6.25; doubles with own bathroom and air-con cost US$7.50. There's a bar and attached restaurant.

Up in price but excellent value and highly recommended is the *Onikirp Hotel* (☎ 86 4767), 328 Borno Way near the junction with Hughes Ave. It's very clean and quiet, all the rooms are air-con with fridge and TV and have their own bathroom with water heater. Singles (two single beds) cost US$13 and

doubles (two double beds) are US$15 including VAT. There's a good bar and restaurant downstairs.

Also good value is the *Niger Palace Hotel* (☎ 80 0010), 1 Thurburn Rd at the junction with Commercial Ave. It's a fairly modern place with doubles (no singles) for US$23 plus VAT. All the rooms are air-con with own bathroom and there's a bar and restaurant.

Places to Eat

Lagos Island Other than hotel restaurants mentioned above, there's an almost total lack of restaurants on Lagos Island but plenty of street stalls along Broad St. For fast food there is *Mr Bigg's*, at the junction of Broad St and Joseph St, which has cheap snacks, meat pies and sandwiches – nothing over US$1. Look for the prominent red and yellow sign.

Ikoyi Island Awolowo Rd is lined with good restaurants and snack places. *Burgy's* at No 72 has excellent burgers and chips for US$5 and sandwiches for less. Beers are US$1.

Ace Supermarket & Fast Food at No 99 has a counter where you can eat meat or fish pies. Across the road, the air-con *Les Amis* has hamburgers (US$3) and felafel (US$2) but drinks here are expensive.

The *Kebab Corner* at No 97 has pricey dine-in or takeaway Chinese and Indian cuisine plus pizzas. *Al-Basha* at No 126 has good pizzas from US$4 and felafel sandwiches for US$2.

Yaba A happy hunting ground for restaurants in Yaba is along Oju Elegba Rd. Apart from a branch of *Mr Bigg's*, others include *Mac Eating Home* on the 1st floor at No 34/36, and *Pico Chicken Restaurant* further west (Nigerian food) – look for the 'Eat as you earn' sign.

Near the Onikirp Hotel is *Tambest bar/restaurant*, Hughes Ave, which is a pleasant little bar with a cool patio where you can get cold beers for US$0.60 plus cheap snacks of dodo, fufu, moi-moi snails, fish, chicken and goat meat. Most of the hotels in Yaba have restaurants with continental and Nigerian food.

Entertainment
There are plenty of bars and music on offer around town; Lagos is full of bars wherever you go. One of the best places is *Afrika Shrine* (also known as Fela's Shrine), on Pepu St, near the Sheraton Hotel in Ikeja. This is the musical home of the renowned Nigerian dissident and musician, Fela Kuti. You're most likely to hear him playing on a Sunday night.

Jazz 38, 38 Awolowo Rd on Ikoyi Island, is also a friendly live-music place but it's best

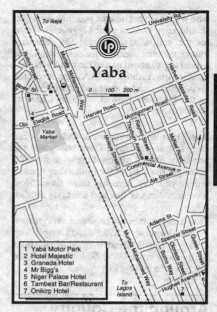

Yaba

0   100   200 m

1 Yaba Motor Park
2 Hotel Majestic
3 Granada Hotel
4 Mr Bigg's
5 Niger Palace Hotel
6 Tambest Bar/Restaurant
7 Onikirp Hotel

on Friday and Saturday nights. There's a US$5 cover charge.

Getting There & Away
Bus & Share-taxi See under Benin in the main Getting There & Away section of this chapter for transport going west to Benin and Togo.

Going north (Ibadan, Oshogbo etc) or east (Benin City etc), you must first take a taxi to the Ojota motor park on the outskirts of the city north of Yaba. The taxi will cost around US$5. The park is well organised and the minibuses and share-taxis display their destinations on the roof.

Getting Around
Airport The Murtala Mohammed airport is approximately a 20 minute taxi ride from the city centre (except during rush hours). A taxi to the airport is much cheaper than one from it.

When emerging from customs you'll be pounced on by taxi drivers and their touts who will try to get hold of your luggage. You should keep hold of your luggage and head for the yellow taxis outside the departure lounge upstairs. Know your destination, and expect to pay about half of the official Nigerian Airports Authority (NAA) fare. Avoid the taxis which can be arranged from this desk as the fares are high (US$15 to Lagos or Ikoyi Islands).

Bus There are normal buses in Lagos – red Lagos State Transport Corp buses and the privately owned yellow buses – but you'll never get the hang of the routes they operate unless you live here for some time. Most travellers don't bother and use taxis instead.

Taxi Yellow taxis can be found everywhere. A short drop costs US$2.50 and a longer drop US$3 (eg Lagos Island to Yaba). Hiring taxis by the hour costs US$3.50 but agree on the price before getting in.

Around the Country

BAUCHI

Bauchi is a nondescript, mainly Muslim town in the midst of some interesting country. Most travellers use it as a take-off point to visit the Yankari National Park.

Places to Stay & Eat

The *De Kerker Lodge*, behind the stadium, is cheap, friendly and has ultra-basic rooms with fan for US$3. The communal toilet is dirty and water comes from the courtyard well.

More impersonal is the *Sogiji Hotel*, on the Maiduguri road, which has rooms with fan/air-con for US$9/11. Much more pleasant is the *Horizontal Bar*, opposite Chicken George on the Jos road, which has comfortable motel-style rooms for US$18.

The town's top lodging is the *Zaranda Hotel* (☎ 43 5902), a multistorey building about 3km west of town on the Jos road, which has rooms from US$23, plus a tax of

about 15% and a US$41 deposit. They organise transport to Yankari for a hefty US$25.

De Sisters Food Centre, on a back street in the town centre, has good cheap food. *Vital Inn*, about two blocks from De Kerker, is one of the very rare watering holes in this almost 'dry' town; various street-food stalls are nearby. *Terry's Place* is a mid-range Chinese restaurant on the Maiduguri bypass road.

BENIN CITY

Benin is one of the old Yoruba capitals. The kingdom which flourished here for centuries before the advent of colonialism gave rise to one of the first African art forms to be accepted internationally – the bronzes of Benin.

The **National Museum** is worth a visit, but although it has a substantial collection of bronze artefacts many of them are on loan elsewhere.

There are plenty of craft shops along Airport Rd close to the Oba's Palace.

Places to Stay

Solo women might like to try the *YWCA* (☎ 25 2186) on Airport Rd. It's big and cheerless but costs just US$1.25 for a dorm bed with shared bathroom facilities. It's often full.

The *Central Hotel* (☎ 20 0780) at 76 Akpakpava Rd has seen better days but is friendly and has singles/doubles with fan at US$5/6.25 and doubles with air-con for US$7. All the rooms have their own bathroom and there's a good bar and restaurant.

Out a further 700m along the same road is the *Edo Delta Hotel*, which is quiet and pleasant and seems well managed. It has singles/doubles with fan and shared bathroom for US$5.60/6.25 and suites with air-con and own bathroom for US$10.

Up in price, the tranquil *Edo Hotel* (☎ 20 0120) on 1st Ave is reasonable but has seen better days. All the rooms are air-con and have their own bathroom and the hotel sits in spacious, manicured gardens. Singles/doubles cost US$8/9.35 with suites at US$14. There's a bar and restaurant.

Much better value than the Edo Hotel is

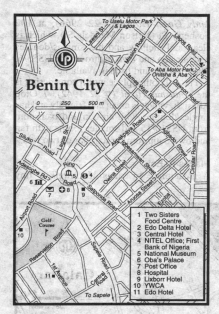

1 Two Sisters
  Food Centre
2 Edo Delta Hotel
3 Central Hotel
4 NITEL Office; First
  Bank of Nigeria
5 National Museum
6 Oba's Palace
7 Post Office
8 Hospital
9 Lixborr Hotel
10 YWCA
11 Edo Hotel

the modern *Lixborr Hotel* (☎ 24 0066), 4 Satponda Rd, just off King's Square (the main roundabout), which is super-clean, imaginatively conceived and friendly. Singles/doubles with air-con and own bathroom cost US$7/11. There's a lively bar and an excellent, if pricey, restaurant.

Places to Eat
In addition to the hotel restaurants listed above, street food is available at a few stalls along Akpakpava Rd. Also on this street, opposite the Edo Delta Hotel, is the popular *Two Sisters Food Centre*. A big bowl of beans, rice and cowtail soup costs US$2 and cold beers are available.

Getting There & Away
There are two motor parks, both of them quite a way from the centre of town. For vehicles going west (eg Lagos, Oshogbo etc) you need the Uselu motor park; for destina-

tions east (eg Onitsha, Aba etc) you need the Aba motor park.

Getting Around
Taxi drivers in Benin City are noted for their rapacious attitude to fares. Always fix the price before getting in. Better still, if you don't have luggage, use a motorcycle-taxi, which costs US$0.20 for a short drop.

CALABAR
Calabar is one of Nigeria's oldest trading cities with European connections going back to 15th century Portuguese mariners.

Much of the old town remains, picturesquely sited on the hill overlooking the river. It was formerly the administrative centre of the British Oil Rivers Protectorate. The town is quite safe to walk around even at night.

Information
Money Forget about banks in Calabar for changing either cash or travellers' cheques. They're useless. Change on the black market (enquire at the Victory Hotel) or at the Standard Bureau de Change on the roundabout at the junction of Goldie and Abu Sts.

Dangers & Annoyances The motor park in Calabar is the hangout of nasty, persistent plainclothes police who will invent 'problems' regarding your documents (especially currency declaration forms, which are no longer required) and then demand a dash and follow you to your hotel room if you refuse. Likewise, immigration police at the dock will demand your passport, grill you about why you are there and demand a substantial dash if you want your passport back.

Things to See
The excellent **museum** is housed in the Old British Residency (brought over in pieces from Glasgow, Scotland in the 1890s) overlooking the Calabar River. It has a large exhibit on the history and effects of the slave trade.

There's also a superb **museum** at Oron, 1½ hours by ferry from Calabar or 30 minutes by speedboat (see under Cameroon in the Getting There & Away by Sea section at the start of this chapter for more information). The museum has carvings, masks, puppets and funerary art.

Places to Stay

The *Stardos Guesthouse*, 7A O'Dwyer St, is the best value in town. It's family-run, spotlessly clean and comfortable and has a range of rooms, some with fan and shared bathroom (US$3.10), others with air-con and private bathroom (US$5.60).

Less convenient but also good value is the

Andy Guest House (☎ 22 2966), at 102 Fosberry St (Nelson Mandela St), which is clean and mellow and has singles/doubles with air-con and own bathroom for US$5/6. There's a bar and food is available.

The only other place worth considering is the *Chalsma Hotel* (☎ 22 1942), 7 Otop Abasi St, which is clean and friendly and has singles/doubles with air-con and bathroom from US$10/15 and smaller rooms with fan and own bathroom for a dollar or two less.

Places to Eat

A great place to eat is *Mr Magik*, a tiny

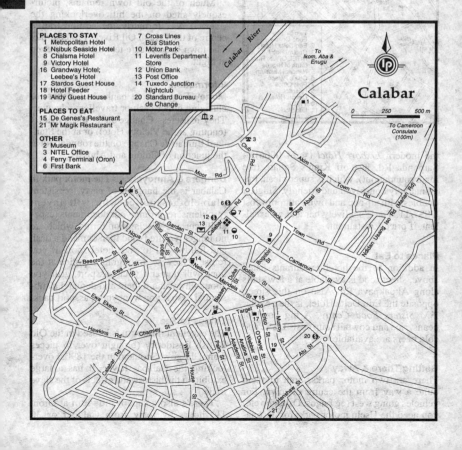

PLACES TO STAY
1 Metropolitan Hotel
5 Nsibuk Seaside Hotel
8 Chalsma Hotel
9 Victory Hotel
16 Grandway Hotel;
   Leebee's Hotel
17 Stardos Guest House
18 Hotel Feeder
19 Andy Guest House

PLACES TO EAT
15 De Genes's Restaurant
21 Mr Magik Restaurant

OTHER
2 Museum
3 NITEL Office
4 Ferry Terminal (Oron)
6 First Bank
7 Cross Lines
  Bus Station
10 Motor Park
11 Leventis Department
   Store
12 Union Bank
13 Post Office
14 Tuxedo Junction
   Nightclub
20 Standard Bureau
   de Change

Calabar River

To Ikom, Aba & Enugu

Calabar

0   250   500 m

To Cameroon Consulate (100m)

bar/restaurant off Henshaw St which has local food and quite a variety of other dishes. Service can take ages but it's a congenial place to have a beer (or three) while you wait.

Alternatively, *De Genes's*, at 36 Nelson Mandela St, is a spotlessly clean restaurant with a casual outside area. It basically only serves meals in the evening (US$1 for goat pepper soup) unless you order in advance. Don't be late in the evening either, otherwise there will be nothing left.

Getting There & Away

The main bus line to/from Calabar and Aba is Cross Lines Buses (the depot is across from the motor park in Calabar and on Factory Rd in Aba). The schedules are erratic but it costs US$2 and takes about 2½ hours. Share-taxis go from the motor park on Ikot Epkene Rd in Calabar, cost US$2.50 and take two hours.

There are minibuses and share-taxis all day from the motor park in Calabar to Ikom (for Cameroon).

IFE

This town is the spiritual centre of the Yoruba people and their highest figure of authority, the Oba of Ife, resides here. The **Oba's Palace** is a treasure chest of antiquities and works of art but it's normally closed to visitors.

What you can visit is the **Antiquities Museum** next door, which is famous for its terracotta and bronze masks. There's also the **Yemoo Pottery Museum**, which has examples of pottery from different areas of the south and a workshop that you can visit.

Places to Stay & Eat

The clean *Green Tops Hotel*, 85 Eleyele Layout, is 2km from the town centre in a quiet residential area. The affable owner charges US$5/7 for a single/double room with fan and communal bath. There's a tiny bar that serves beer, fish pies and rice and sauce.

Also popular is the large *Mayfair Hotel*, conveniently located between the town centre and the university, which has rooms

at US$7 a double. The *Diganga Hotel*, on Ibadan road close to the uni, charges US$10 a double.

The *Conference Centre Guesthouse* (☎ 23 0705), at the Abafemi Awolowo University off the road north-west to Ede, has air-con doubles with attached bathroom and hot water for US$24. It's well maintained plus there's a good restaurant and a popular bar.

JOS

After the steamy mayhem of Lagos, Jos might be the highlight of your visit to Nigeria. The Jos Plateau (1200m above sea level) has a relatively cool climate all year and is green, shrubby and surrounded by small undulating hills.

Things to See

The town's main attraction is the outstanding **Jos Museum** which includes pottery, brassware, ornaments, carved doors and ceremonial headdresses.

Within the same grounds and possibly even more interesting are a number of life-sized reproductions of historic buildings in Nigeria which, in their original setting, are either run-down or have been demolished, or to which entry is prohibited anyway.

The town's big covered **market** and the nearby street scenes are also worth a look.

Places to Stay

The best places for price and facilities are the religious mission guesthouses. The *ECWA Guesthouse* (☎ 54 482) has dorm beds with shared bathroom facilities for just US$1.50, as well as doubles with own bathroom but no fan for US$3 and singles with fan and bath for US$3.75. Cheap, filling meals are available for under US$1.

The two other nearby religious missions, the *COCIN Mission* and the *Tekan Guesthouse/YMCA* (☎ 53 036), both on Noad Ave, are similar, with the COCIN being the better of the two. It takes both sexes and has singles/doubles with own bathroom but no fan for US$2 per bed. It's a friendly place and the restaurant offers cheap Nigerian and continental meals.

NIGERIA

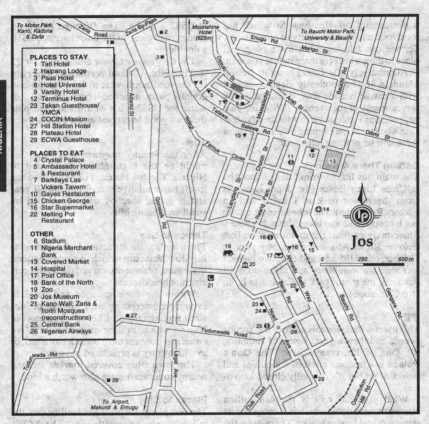

PLACES TO STAY
1 Tati Hotel
2 Haipang Lodge
3 Paas Hotel
8 Hotel Universal
9 Varsity Hotel
12 Terminus Hotel
23 Tekan Guesthouse/
  YMCA
24 COCIN Mission
27 Hill Station Hotel
28 Plateau Hotel
29 ECWA Guesthouse

PLACES TO EAT
4 Crystal Palace
5 Ambassador Hotel
  & Restaurant
7 Barkliays Las
  Vickers Tavern
10 Gayes Restaurant
15 Chicken George
16 Star Supermarket
22 Melting Pot
  Restaurant

OTHER
6 Stadium
11 Nigeria Merchant
  Bank
13 Covered Market
14 Hospital
17 Post Office
18 Bank of the North
19 Zoo
20 Jos Museum
21 Kano Wall; Zaria &
  Ilorin Mosques
  (reconstructions)
25 Central Bank
26 Nigerian Airways

Jos

In town near the market, the *Terminus Hotel* (☎ 54 831), Tafawa Balewa Rd, has doubles (no singles) with no fan and shared bath for US$3.75 and doubles with fan and own bathroom for US$5. The large bar on the 1st floor has a dance floor and a disco at weekends.

Further west off Tafawa Balewa Rd is the large *Hotel Universal*, 11 Pankshin St, which has singles with shared bath for US$2.75 and singles/doubles with own bath for US$3.25/5. There's also a bar and restaurant. Around the block at 1 Azikewe Ave (Zik Ave) is the *Varsity Hotel* which is similar in standard and

has singles/doubles with own bath and fan for US$2.50/3.

Those in search of comfort should try the excellent *Paas Hotel* (☎ 53 851) at 42 Ndagi Farouk Close. All the rooms are air-con with own bath, hot water, TV and fridge. Singles/doubles are US$6/8. There's also a bar and restaurant. Treat yourself!

Places to Eat
The stadium area is a happy hunting ground for cheap restaurants. On Azikewe Ave (Zik Ave) you'll find the *Ambassador Hotel & Restaurant, Senior Cool Restaurant* and

Barkliays Las Vickers Tavern. On Tafawa Balewa Rd there are the *Crystal Palace* (burgers, snacks and coffee) and *Gayes Restaurant* (very good food but more expensive). Down on Ahmadu Bello Way, just beyond the post office, check out the popular *Melting Pot Restaurant*.

Adjacent to the railway station there's fast food at *Chicken George* – chicken and chips for US$1.60. It also has a pool table.

Getting There & Away

Long-distance bus lines (eg Ifeanyi Chukwu, Chukwu Di Transport and Onyennwe) have their offices along Dasuki St on the top side of the stadium. They service destinations south and south-west.

For minibuses and share-taxis going west (Kaduna), north (Zaria, Kano) and north-east (Bauchi and Maiduguri) you need the Jos North motor park (also called Bauchi motor park) which is out on Bauchi Rd near the university. There's also transport from here to Abuja.

KADUNA

Kaduna is a spacious, leafy place developed by the British as an administrative centre. It's a major transport hub, so you may need to pass through or stop here.

Places to Stay & Eat

The *Central Guest Inn*, on Benue Rd, is quiet and the communal shower and toilet passably clean. A double room with fan costs US$2. The *Kaduna Guest Inn* at 15 Ibadan St offers singles for only US$2.

The *Fina White House Hotel* (☎ 21 6597), 23 Constitution Rd, has cramped double rooms with private facilities and noisy aircon for US$5. Despite all this, it's a popular place thanks to its open-air, streetside bar which gets moving each evening.

Those looking for a clean room, good food and tranquil surroundings should head to the *Zodiac Hotel Annexe* (☎ 23 4863) on Yauri St. It costs US$6/8 for a large single/double with an enormous bed and both air-con and

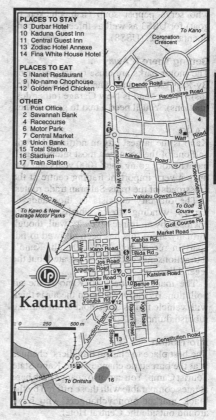

PLACES TO STAY
3 Durbar Hotel
10 Kaduna Guest Inn
11 Central Guest Inn
13 Zodiac Hotel Annexe
14 Fina White House Hotel

PLACES TO EAT
5 Nanet Restaurant
9 No-name Chophouse
12 Golden Fried Chicken

OTHER
1 Post Office
2 Savannah Bank
4 Racecourse
6 Motor Park
7 Central Market
8 Union Bank
15 Total Station
16 Stadium
17 Train Station

Kaduna

0   250   500 m

fan. The restaurant serves reasonably priced salads and chicken and chips.

For cheap African food, the *no-name chophouse* at the intersection of Ahmadu Bello Way and Argungu Rd is unbeatable. The food is cooked in big steaming pots and dished up by huge, sweaty women. Hundreds of people eat here every day (it's open from lunch to 9 pm) and pay no more than US$1 a plate.

Fast food (burgers etc) can be found at the *Golden Fried Chicken* on Yoruba Rd. Up in price, the *Nanet* at 6 Ahmadu Bello Way has air-con, tablecloths and uniformed waiters who serve pepper soup (fish, chicken or goat) for US$3 as well as three-course continental meals (US$8).

Getting There & Away
The motor parks are close to each other on By-Pass Expressway. The first is Kawo (for Jos). The second is New Garage (other destinations). You'll need a taxi to get to either.

KANO
Kano is the largest city in northern Nigeria and one of the country's most interesting. It has a history going back 1000 years and was once a very important trading centre at the crossroads of the trans-Saharan trade routes.

The old city consists of thousands of narrow, winding streets which were once enclosed by an impressive city wall, though virtually all of this has been allowed to fall apart in recent years. As a result, Kano's 'attractions' are definitely overrated, but the legend lives on.

The main drawback to Kano is the air pollution. By early afternoon the air is thick with vehicle fumes and smoke from burning rubbish dumps.

Information
The best place to change travellers' cheques is at the bureau de change at the Kano State Tourist Camp. You can also change cash here at rates comparable with those offered by the black market moneychangers who hang around outside the Central Hotel.

Things to See & Do
Any visit to the old city will probably involve hiring a guide for the day. This isn't a bad idea – they know their way around, charge only a nominal amount (US$4 per person plus the cost of a taxi to the dye pits/museum) and there won't be any pressure to buy crafts or anything else. This is not Morocco. Ask for Hussein, Mohammed or Suleiman at the Kano State Tourist Camp.

You can forget about the **City Walls** but some of the original **gates** on the southern edge of the old city remain. They're of passing interest only.

Inside the old city walls at Kofar Mata (a city gate), the once-famous **dye pits**, said to be the oldest in Africa, are apparently still used though they look somewhat moribund.

The huge old **Kurmi Market** is extensive and definitely worth visiting but the range of craftwork, fabrics and artefacts doesn't match up to the hype. It's a maze of narrow, winding alleys divided by stinking open sewers strewn with garbage but you can find bargains here if you take your time.

The **Emir's Palace** is an outstanding example of Hausa architecture but is essentially not open to tourists. Opposite the Emir's Palace is the **museum**, which is housed in what was formerly a palace. Unfortunately, it's in a sad state of neglect.

For a view over the entire city, climb **Dala Hill** north of Kurmi Market.

The swimming pool at the Central Hotel is open to nonresidents for US$0.60.

Places to Stay
Virtually all travellers stay at the *Kano State Tourist Camp* (☎ 64 6309) at 11A Bompai Rd near the Central Hotel. It's a very friendly, helpful and secure place and Ado Hassan, the enthusiastic manager, is keen to keep it that way. Camping costs US$1.40 per night per person and there are no water problems. There are also dorm beds at US$2 with fans and shared bathroom facilities. Singles/doubles cost US$4.40/7. The place has its own generator, bureau de change, laundry service and the Dewi Restaurant, which serves delicious Indonesian food at reasonable prices.

Similar is the *ECWA Guesthouse*, Tafawa Balewa Rd, which offers dorm beds with shared bathroom facilities for US$1.20 and singles/doubles with attached bathroom and fan for US$4/8. Meals are available on request. The guesthouse is strictly non-smoking.

Die-hards can head for the squelched flea-pits and 'short-time' places scattered throughout the Sabon Gari area. Perhaps the best of the bunch is the *Remco Motel* (☎ 62 8600), 61 New Rd, which has air-con, doubles (no singles) with attached bathroom

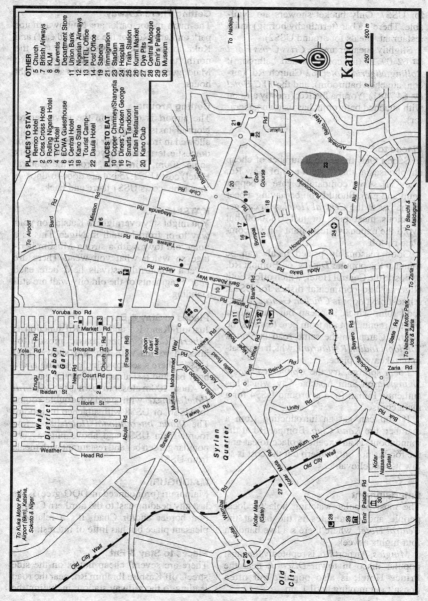

Kano

PLACES TO STAY
1 Remco Hotel
2 Criss Cross Hotel
3 Rolling Nigeria Hotel
4 TYC Hotel
6 ECWA Guesthouse
15 Central Hotel
18 Kano State
    Tourist Camp
22 Daula Hotel

PLACES TO EAT
10 Copper Chimney/Shanghia
16 Diners'; Chicken George
17 Smarts Tandoori
    Indian Restaurant
20 Kano Club

OTHER
5 Church
7 British Airways
8 KLM
9 Leventis
    Department Store
11 Union Bank
12 Nigerian Airways
13 NITEL Office
14 Post Office
19 Sabena
21 Immigration
23 Stadium
24 Hospital
25 Train Station
26 Kurmi Market
27 Dye Pits
28 Central Mosque
29 Emir's Palace
30 Museum

To Hadejia

500 m
250
0

To Kuka Motor Park,
Airport (8km), Katsina,
Sokoto & Niger.

To Airport

To Bauchi &
Maiduguri

To Zaria

To Naibawa Motor Park,
Jos & Zaria

for US$7. Only bucket showers are available. There's a bar (terminally boring) and a restaurant (meals for around US$2).

Slightly cheaper are the *Criss Cross Hotel* (☎ 62 0972) (air-con, attached bathroom); *Rolling Nigeria Hotel*, 82 Church Rd, (air-con, attached bathroom), and the *TYC Hotel* (☎ 64 7491), Yoruba Ibo Rd, (mostly air-con with attached bathroom, has its own generator).

Places to Eat
In Sabon Gari there are a number of cheap chophouses at the western end of New Rd. They all serve comparable fare – pepper soup and gari. Should you be having a beer in the bar at the *Central Hotel*, you can get delicious meat pies for just US$0.60 but avoid the expensive restaurant – it's a complete rip-off.

Good reasonably priced meals can be found at the popular *Diners'* on Bompai Rd, opposite the Central Hotel, which offers both Nigerian and continental dishes for US$2. Almost next door is *Chicken George,* a fast-food joint which is cheap but has only a limited menu. Not far from here towards the Tourist Camp on the same road is *Smarts Tandoori Indian Restaurant*, which is an eat-in or takeaway place.

For a splurge, try the *Copper Chimney/Shangrila* on Sani Abacha Way, which has authentic Indian food at around US$4 for a main course.

If you can get an introduction from a member, the *Kano Club*, Bompai Rd at the roundabout, is an excellent place to eat and the food is not only superb but the cost is so low it's unbelievable.

Entertainment
The most popular watering hole for local people and expatriates is the bar at the *Central Hotel*, where there's a live band on four nights a week.

Mingles, Airport Rd, is reputedly the most popular disco in town. *Disco J*, near the Prince Hotel, is also popular but often doesn't get moving until 1 am.

Getting There & Away
The main motor parks are Naibowa motor park on Zaria Rd (for the south and east) and Kuka motor park on Katsina Rd (for the north, including Niger). A share-taxi to Maiduguri costs US$6 and takes about eight hours.

Getting Around
The airport is 6km from the town centre. Normal taxis charge US$2.50 but are not allowed in front of either the international or domestic terminals so you'll have to walk some 300m. Hire cars (from the Central Hotel) cost US$3.75 but are door-to-door. A 'machine' costs US$1 there and back.

KATSINA
You might stay overnight in Katsina on your way to or from Maradi in Niger. This is a quiet, old town with a strong Muslim heritage so watch what you wear. There are several colourful festivals held here each year. Fragments of the old city wall are still standing.

Places to Stay & Eat
Just off Kano Rd and Ring Rd junction is *Liberty Camp*, where basic mosquito-infested rooms with fan and shower cost US$4. There's secure vehicle parking and a busy bar and restaurant outside the gate.

About 100m closer to town is the *Makurdi Hotel Annexe* with standard double rooms for US$6, or US$8 with attached bathroom. The *Daula International Hotel* has a few rooms from US$6 and above plus a very popular garden bar and restaurant with meals from US$1.

MAIDUGURI
Maiduguri (pronounced m-DOO-gree) is the last city heading east to the northern Cameroon border and/or Chad. It's a relatively pleasant place but has little of interest.

Places to Stay & Eat
There are several cheap hotels on the side streets off Kashim Ibrahim Rd, near the road leading to the railway station, including the

Rainbow Hotel and the *Tourist Hotel* which are habitable but nothing special.

The best place to head for is the *Safari Hotel*, Shehu Laminu Way, which has gloomy décor but is friendly and good value – doubles with own shower, toilet and fan are US$4.60. There's a bar (with no beer) and a cheap restaurant.

Another popular place, set in leafy surroundings, is the *Borno State Hotel* (☎ 23 3191), Italba Rd, off Shehu Laminu Way, which has rooms for US$3.60 with own bathroom and fan and US$7 for private bathroom with air-con. There's also a bar and restaurant.

Just up the road from the Safari Hotel are several local restaurants and street stalls, including the friendly *New Villager Restaurant*, where you can find suya (spiced brochettes) in the evening and a continental breakfast plus spaghetti and beef for lunch.

Getting There & Away

The motor park for Jos and Kano is on the western edge of town on the way to the airport. For destinations to the north, east and south (including the Chad and Cameroon borders) go to the Bama motor park on Bama Rd on the eastern side of town. A taxi to either costs US$1.25.

ONITSHA

Onitsha is a sprawling, polluted holocaust of a city on the Niger River but you may have to stay here overnight.

Places to Stay & Eat

The best choice of a budget hotel here is the *Hotel Eleganza*, 4 O'Connor St, which has doubles with own bath and fan for US$6.25 and doubles with air-con for US$8. It's a friendly place and there's a bar and restaurant.

A good, clean place to eat is the *Apple Rock Restaurant*, also on O'Connor St.

Getting There & Away

The main motor parks are clustered around the flyover at the junction of Lagos-Enugu Expressway and Owerri Rd to the south of the centre. It's absolute chaos here and the traffic congestion is unbelievable. Asking around is the only way to find transport going in the direction you want.

OSHOGBO (OSOGBO)

This is one of Nigeria's most interesting towns, since it's here that the Sacred Groves and Shrine of Oshun, the River Goddess, are to be found. It's also where many of the country's most famous artists have made their homes and the artwork they produce is noteworthy. As a city, Oshogbo is pleasant, relatively quiet and the people are friendly and helpful.

The Sacred Groves

This is Oshogbo's main attraction, covering a large area of rainforest about 2.5km from the town centre. Inside the Groves is the stunning **Shrine of Oshun**. The central point is a rock in the river where annual offerings (around August) are made to the Great Fish – visible only to a lucky few.

In addition to the natural beauty, there are many stunning sculptures, gates and walls put up by Suzanne Wenger, an Austrian painter and sculptor who came here in the 1950s and became, in time, one of the priestesses.

Art Galleries & Craft Shops

Oshogbo is one of the main centres of Nigerian art. Batik, woodwork and painting are the main media. The **Ulli Beier Museum** on Station Rd is worth a visit before you do the rounds of the craft outlets, which are mostly along Iwo Ibadan Rd and the western end of Station Rd.

Places to Stay

On Iwo Ibadan Rd, about 1km before the motor park, the *Pico Allison Hotel* (☎ 23 5046) has rooms with fan and attached bathroom for US$5. Similar, and on the same road but closer to the centre, is the *City Waiters Bar & Restaurant*, which has a few gloomy and none-too-clean rooms with shared bathroom for US$3.75. There's a clean restaurant, bar and pool table.

To the south of town, next to the river, is the *Dreamland Motel Annexe*, Okefia St, which has very basic rooms with shared bathroom for US$3. There's a bar and nightclub in the courtyard but they're not very lively.

Much better value is the *Hotel Terminus International* (☎ 23 0423), Obafemi Awolowo Rd, which has doubles with own bath and air-con for US$6. The beds are lumpy but it's clean and staff are friendly. There's also a bar and restaurant.

Top value is the *Heritage International Hotel* (☎ 23 4285), Okefia St, about 2km from the town centre. It's very pleasant, spotlessly clean and has rooms with huge double beds, own bathroom, air-con and fan for US$7.20. There's no hot water. There's a large bar and delicious suya are available each evening.

Places to Eat
Most of the cheap restaurants are along Iwo Ibadan Rd. They include the *City Waiters Bar & Restaurant, Ultimate Palace Restaurant* (pepper soup etc), the *Side Way Klass Restaurant* (Nigerian dishes), and the *Wakis Restaurant* (Nigerian dishes), opposite the grammar school. All these have a blackboard outside saying 'Food is ready' when they're open.

For a slight splurge, try the *Royal Restaurant*, Okefia St, near the entrance to the Heritage International Hotel.

Getting There & Away
The motor park for Lagos and Ibadan is in the town centre immediately west of the railway tracks. For Benin City, share-taxis congregate at the Total station on the roundabout just east of the railway tracks.

SOKOTO
Sokoto is the last major town before Birnin-Konni in Niger. It became important in the early 19th century as the seat of the caliphate established after Usman dan Fodio's Islamic jihad in 1807, which brought together the various Hausa city-states.

The sultan, Dasuki, effectively remains the spiritual head of Nigeria's Muslims, and his palace and the nearby Shehu Mosque are superb examples of Sudanic architecture. Unfortunately, non-Muslims may not enter either building.

The Argungu Fishing & Cultural Festival, held in early March, is a leading tourist attraction.

Places to Stay & Eat
The *Catering Rest House* near the post office has very run-down rooms for US$8 a double. Nearby on the main road are two mid-range options: the *Sokoto Hotel* (☎ 23 7126), with rooms at US$20, and next door the better *Shukura Hotel* (☎ 20 0019), with air-con doubles from US$30. Both these places have bars and restaurants with meals from US$3.

Going north near the bypass road is the *Ibro International Hotel* (☎ 23 2510) with decent doubles for US$10. Nearby, the relaxed and friendly *Shalom Restaurant* has a wide range of meals from US$1.

Getting There & Away
Taxis to Illela (Nigerian border) usually depart from the new motor park but there are cheaper trucks (and sometimes taxis) at the Illela truck park on the edge of town.

YANKARI NATIONAL PARK
Yankari holds about the only remnant of wildlife left in Nigeria.

Seeing animals here is a hit-and-miss affair; some travellers don't get much more than a glimpse of a monkey but others come across elephant, waterbuck, bushbuck, hippo, crocodile and the occasional lion. The best months to visit are January and February. The other feature of interest in the park is the thermal **Wikki Warm Spring**. Entry to the park costs US$1, plus US$1 if you have a camera.

There's a daily wildlife-viewing truck which starts tours at 7.30 am and 3.30 pm and charges US$1 a person, but it's noisy so the wildlife disappears quickly. Alternatively, arrange with one of the guides to go on a walking tour. For a two hour tour you should pay about US$5 for four people.

Places to Stay & Eat

The park's *Wikki Warm Springs Hotel* (☎ 42 174) is set high above the spring and has a serene view over the lush area. The hotel buildings are fairly decrepit, but prices are cheap, starting at US$6 for a double bungalow. You can also camp for US$2. Make sure your gear (including the window of your bungalow) is secure, as the baboons are master thieves. There's electricity in the evening but the water supply is extremely erratic. The hotel has its own restaurant.

Getting There & Away

From Bauchi, there are minibuses from the motor park at the eastern end of town which will drop you at the park entrance for US$1. From here you have to hitch the 40km to the lodge. This isn't too hard (Friday and Saturday are best) but if a taxi or one of the park's vehicles pick you up, expect to pay US$1.

Réunion

The volcanic island of Réunion is an overseas *département* of France, with an elected local council which sends five deputies to the French National Assembly. The last few decades have seen a push for greater autonomy, but the island remains emphatically French. The baguette is a national institution, instant coffee an abomination, and English-speaking visitors incommunicado without at least a few words of French.

Few people outside *la métropole* (mainland France, that is) know of Réunion, and even fewer know of its natural and scenic wonders. The island's dearth of world-class beaches has prevented an international tourism invasion, but whatever is lacking at sea level is more than made up for in spectacular mountain country.

Facts about the Country

HISTORY

Réunion has a history similar to that of Mauritius, and was visited, though not settled, by Malay, Arab and European mariners. The island was first claimed, in 1664, by the French East India Company, which brought French colonists and Malagasy slaves. Until 1715 the settlers provided for themselves and for passing ships, but the introduction of coffee brought dramatic changes and demanded more slaves – despite the company's prohibition of slave labour. In 1764, the island government passed directly to France, due mainly to poor company management and Anglo-French rivalry. The late 18th century brought numerous slave revolts, and escapees made their way to the interior and organised themselves into villages.

At the time, all the Mascarenes (Réunion, Mauritius and Rodrigues) were French colonies, but Réunion was saddled with the production of food while Mauritius reaped

RÉUNION
Area: 2510 sq km
Population: 675,700
Population Growth Rate: 1.7%
Capital: St-Denis
Head of State: Governed as an overseas department of France
Official Language: French
Currency: French franc
Exchange Rate: FFr 5.68 = US$1
Per Capita GNP: US$8000
Inflation: 2%
Time: GMT/UTC + 4

Highlights
- Spectacular mountain scenery with an exotic tropical twist
- Tremendous trekking possibilities including a live volcano and three rugged cirques
- A rich cultural mix with a distinct French flavour

the profits from sugar exports. When Mauritius was ceded to the British after the Napoleonic Wars, sugar was introduced to Réunion and quickly usurped all agricultural activity. Small subsistence farmers were forced to sell out and migrate to the interior.

Réunion experienced a labour crisis when slavery was abolished in the early 19th century and, as on Mauritius, labour from India was imported to take up the slack.

Unfortunately, competition from Cuba and Europe caused economic stagnation and

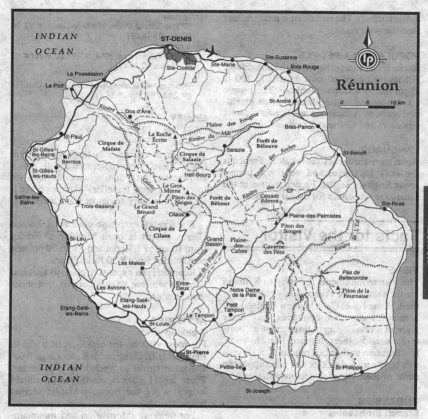

resulted in a concentration of land and capital in the hands of a French elite.

In 1936, the left-wing Comité d'Action Démocratique et Sociale was founded on a platform of integration with France. After WWII, however, when the island became a French département, the party did an about-face. Conservatives, on the other hand, were initially opposed to integration with France, but later feared losing their privileges, realising that independence would unleash resentment which they'd have to face without French assistance.

In the last few decades there has been a push, led mainly by the left, for greater autonomy for Réunion, and for improvements in working conditions and wages.

GEOGRAPHY & CLIMATE

Réunion lies about 800km east of Madagascar and covers an area of 2510 sq km. There are two major mountain zones: the Cirques of Cilaos, Salazie and Mafate, and the active volcanic zone around Piton de la Fournaise. The highest peak is Piton des Neiges (3069m). There are two seasons: the hot, rainy, cyclonic summer (October to March) and the cool, dry winter (from April to September). The east coast is much rainier than the west coast.

POPULATION & PEOPLE

Réunion has a larger land area than Mauritius, but its estimated population of 675,700 is about half that of its neighbour. The people are descended mainly from French plantation owners, African slaves, Indian contract labourers and Chinese merchants.

LANGUAGE

Apart from the local Creole patois, French is the only language, and very few people speak English. See the French section in the Language Appendix for useful phrases.

Facts for the Visitor

VISAS

The visa requirements for entry to Réunion are the same as for France. Only nationals of the EU, the USA, Canada, New Zealand and a handful of other countries may enter without a visa (for up to three months). Australians and others require French visas. Immigration authorities require that all visitors have onward tickets and can supply the name of their intended accommodation.

EMBASSIES
French Embassies

There are French embassies or consulates in many countries, including Australia, Belgium, Canada, Germany, India, Japan, Singapore, South Africa, Switzerland, the UK and the USA.

Foreign Consulates in Réunion

Only a few countries have diplomatic representation in Réunion. They include:

Belgium
    33 Rue Félix-Guyon, BP 785, 97476 St-Denis
    (☎ 90 20 89 or 21 79 72; fax 90 20 88)
Germany
    110 Rue Général de Gaulle, 97400 St-Denis
    (☎/fax 41 84 78)

Madagascar
    77 Rue Juliette Dodu, 97400 St-Denis (☎ 21 66 00; fax 21 10 08)
South Africa
    83 Rue Jules Verne, BP 8, 97821 Le Port (☎ 42 61 18; fax 42 16 12)
UK
    94B Avenue Leconte Delisle, 97490 Ste-Clotilde (☎ 29 14 91; fax 29 39 91)

MONEY

US$1 = FFr 5.68

The unit of currency is the French franc (FF). There's no problem changing major currencies, but punitive commissions on foreign-currency travellers' cheques make it advisable to carry francs or franc travellers' cheques.

The foreign exchange counter at Roland Garros airport is open Monday to Friday from 10 am to 1.30 pm and 3 to 6.30 pm and on Saturday from 8.30 to 11.30 am.

Réunion is an expensive place to visit and bargains are few, so don't arrive on a shoestring budget.

ACTIVITIES
Trekking

For most visitors, the highlight of a trip to Réunion is trekking, which can range from afternoon strolls to week-long expeditions. There are 11 *gîtes de montagne* (mountain lodges) – see the Accommodation section below.

For trekking information and mountain-lodge bookings, visit Maison de la Montagne (also known as Loisirs Accueil Nature et Campagne). The main office (☎ 90 78 78; fax 41 84 29) is at 10 Place Sarda Garriga in St-Denis. Their Cilaos office (☎ 31 71 71; fax 31 80 54) is at 2 Rue Mac Auliffe. The Office National des Forêts (☎ 90 48 00), Colline de la Providence, St-Denis, which looks after most of the tracks, is another good source of information.

ACCOMMODATION

There are official camping grounds in a few places, but security can be a problem. There are three *auberges de jeunesse* (youth hostels) at Bernica, Entre-Deux and Hell-Bourg. The hostels are open to Hostelling International (HI) card holders; membership costs around US$20.

Gîtes de montagne are operated by the government. Accommodation must be booked and paid for in advance through Maison de la Montagne (see the Trekking section above). In addition, there are privately owned *gîtes d'étape* (similar to gîtes de montagne).

Gîtes ruraux are private houses and lodges which can be rented for self-catering holidays. Contact the Relais Départemental des Gîtes de France (☎ 90 78 90; fax 41 84 29), 10 Place Sarda Garriga, St-Denis. Other inexpensive accommodation may be found at *chambres d'hôte* (guesthouses). *Pensions de famille* are essentially budget hotels; fully fledged hotels are very expensive.

For all accommodation, it's wise to make reservations well in advance, especially during the busy months of late July to early September. April, May and around Christmas can also get busy.

FOOD & DRINK
Creole cuisine is a delicious combination of French, Indian and Malagasy cooking, and is beautifully prepared in restaurants.

Regional specialities include the famous lentils and home-made sweet wines of Cilaos. The local beer, Bourbon (affectionately called Dodo), is great.

Getting There & Away

AIR
Airlines which operate flights to Réunion include Air France, Air Madagascar, Air Austral and Air Mauritius.

There is no airport departure tax.

SEA
Mauritius
The MV *Mauritius Pride* operates several times a month between Mauritius and Réunion. The trip takes about 12 hours and costs US$85/100 one way in the low/high season. For further details call ☎ 42 19 45 in Réunion or ☎ 241 2550 in Mauritius.

Getting Around

ROAD
The bus service is very good and covers most parts of the island. For bus information, call ☎ 41 51 10 in St-Denis. Main bus routes include St-Denis to St-Pierre, St-Denis to St-Benoît and St-Pierre to Cilaos.

Mountain bikes may be hired from a number of places, including VTT Evasion (☎ 37 10 43) in St-Philippe, Cilaos Fun (☎ 31 76 99) in Cilaos and VTT Découverte (☎ 24 55 56) in St-Gilles-les-Bains. Most places charge around US$20 per day.

St-Denis

St-Denis is an attractive, clean and expensive capital city, but with all that mountain country out there, it's not a place to linger.

The helpful **tourist office**, Syndicat d'Initiative de St-Denis (☎ 41 83 00), is at 48 Rue Sainte-Marie (however it may be shifting to Maison de la Montagne – see under Trekking in the Facts for the Visitor section above).

Things to See
The interesting **Musée Léon Dierx**, on Rue de Paris, is named after the Réunionnais poet and painter Léon Dierx. The museum has a good collection of French impressionist work, and is open daily except Monday from 9 am to noon and 1 to 5 pm. Admission is free.

The **Jardin de l'Etat & Musée d'Histoire Naturelle** is also worth a look. It's open daily except Sunday from 10 am to 5 pm; entry costs US$1.80.

Places to Stay
The cheap *Pension du Centre* (☎ 41 73 02),

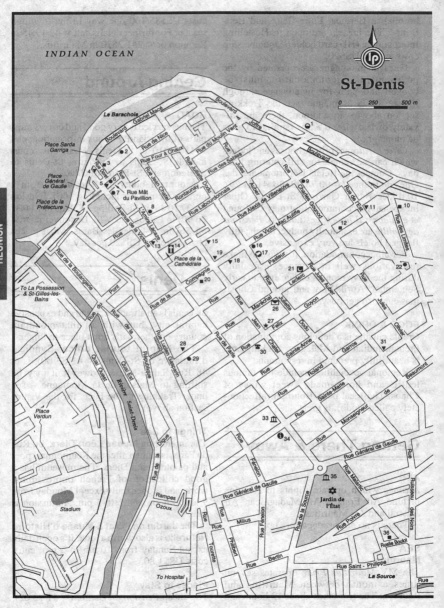

RÉUNION

PLACES TO STAY
3 Hôtel Le Saint-Denis
10 Pension Le Vieux Carthage
12 Hôtel Le Mascareigne
20 Hôtel Central
24 Pension du Centre
25 Pension Touristique Aïcha
32 Pension Amanda
36 La Marianne

PLACES TO EAT
4 Le Roland Garros
5 Le Rallye
11 Le Reflet des Îles
13 Snack Soui-Mine
15 Le Massalé
18 Deutsche Stube
19 L'Igloo Glacerie
28 Kim Son
31 Via Veneto

OTHER
1 Gare Routière
   (Main Bus Terminal)
2 Maison de la Montagne
6 Air Austral
7 Air France
8 Bourbon Voyages
   (Amex)
9 Air Mauritius
14 Cathédrale de St-Denis
16 Air Madagascar
17 Madagascar Consulate
21 Grande Mosquée
22 Prisunic
23 Hindu Temple
26 La Poste (Post Office)
27 Police
29 Grand Marché
30 France Telecom
   (Telephone Office)
33 Musée Léon Dierx
34 Tourist Office
35 Musée d'Histoire
   Naturelle

To Roland Garros Airport
& East Coast

Lancastel

To Roland Garros Airport
& East Coast

23

Rue Maréchal

Leclerc

Boulevard

Rue

Roland Garros

Rue

de

Rue Sainte - Marie

Rue Saint-Jacques

24

25

l'Océan

Place
St-Jacques

Rue Voltaire

Rue de Montreuil

Rue Saint Bernard

Amédée Bédier

Rue Général de Gaulle

32

Rue Jacob

Rue d'Alsace

d'Après

Vauban

Rue de Caen

Rue

Rue Monthyon

Rue

de Nattes

Bois

Mazagran

Rue

To Office
National des
Forêts

des Noirs

Ruisseau

du Pont Neuf

272 Rue Maréchal Leclerc, is more like a hostel, with basic rooms (communal toilet) for US$21 a double. A nicer option is the *Pension Touristique Aïcha* (☎ 20 37 02) at 24 Rue Saint-Jacques, which charges US$26 a double.

The no-frills *Pension Roger* (☎ 41 24 38), 22 Rue Mazagran, has dorm beds for US$10. Moving upmarket, there's the *Pension Amanda* (☎ 21 57 18) at 20 Rue Amédée Bédier, with doubles for US$30.

The popular *Pension Le Vieux Carthage* (☎ 20 24 18), at 13 Rue des Limites, has rooms for US$35 a double. *Pension Le Palmier* (☎ 41 55 55) at 16 Rue Saint-Bernard charges US$26 for double rooms.

For a bit more, you can stay at the one-star *Hôtel Le Mascareigne* (☎ 21 15 28; fax 21 24 19), 3 Rue Lafférière. Double rooms with/without bath cost US$46/37, including breakfast. The friendly two-star *La Marianne* (☎ 21 80 80; fax 21 85 00) at 5 Ruelle Boulot has comfortable doubles for US$53, including breakfast.

Places to Eat
Thanks to the French passion for *la gastronomie*, St-Denis has a restaurant on virtually every corner. At lunch, you'll get a plat du jour from around US$8, but to experience haute cuisine, you'll bid adieu to a pile of francs.

For a quick bite, try the relatively cheap snack bars around Place Sarda Garriga.

The popular *Snack Soui-Mine*, at the corner of Rue Labourdonnais and Ave de la Victoire, does good lunches; the plat du jour is US$6.

The wildly popular *L'Igloo Glacerie*, 67 Rue Jean Chatel, serves magnificent ice cream creations, and also offers reasonably priced light meals. For authentic Indian snacks and sweets, try the little *Le Massalé*, near the corner of Rue Alexis de Villeneuve and Rue Jean Chatel.

If you crave Italian food, there's *Via Veneto* at the corner of Rue Sainte-Marie and Rue Jules Auber. Opposite the Grand Marché is *Kim Son*, which serves good, but expensive, Vietnamese food.

Tasty Creole cuisine is available at *Le Reflet des Îles* at 27 Rue de l'Est; main dishes are around US$14.

For something a little more sophisticated try *Le Roland Garros* on Ave de la Victoire, near Le Barachois; ravioli costs US$12. Nearby is the more down-to-earth *Le Rallye*.

Getting Around
The Airport A taxi between St-Denis and the airport costs about US$18 by day and US$26 after dark. It's cheaper to catch the airport bus, which makes frequent daily trips between the airport and gare routière in St-Denis for US$4.40. To get the regular public bus into St-Denis, cross the airport car park, walk under the motorway flyover and follow the road uphill. The bus stop is about 300m away. The bus to catch is St-Benoît to St-Denis (US$1).

Bus & Taxi St-Denis is relatively small and getting about on foot is a breeze, but there is, nevertheless, a good bus service. Taxis around town are generally expensive and you won't pay less than US$6 for even the shortest distances.

Around the Island

CILAOS
Cilaos is worth visiting for the trip alone: the route turns, switchbacks and zigzags, with cuttings, embankments, tunnels, a flying buttress and even a loop over itself. The mountain scenery is certainly comparable to any in the world.

The village of Cilaos is known for its **sources thermales** (hot springs). A 20 minute sauna costs US$14 at the Établissement Thermal Irénée Accot (☎ 31 72 27). More elaborate options are also available. It's open Monday to Saturday from 8 am to noon and 2 to 5 pm and on Sunday from 8 am to 2 pm.

The **Cirque de Cilaos** offers fine hiking and splendid views. Popular day hikes include **Bras Sec, Roche Merveilleuse** and

La Chapelle. A longer route will take you from Cilaos to the summit of the 3069m **Piton des Neiges**. Most people stay overnight at the gîte at Caverne Dufour on the mountain's flank, and make the summit trip at sunrise, before the view is obscured by cloud. You can either return by the same route or descend to the Cirque de Salazie.

Places to Stay & Eat
The *camp site* owned by the Office National des Forêts (☎ 31 71 40), on Rue du Père Boiteau, is free of charge with authorisation from the office. *Camping de Cilaos*, in Matarum, offers small tent sites for US$7.

The quirky *Le Hameau* (☎ 31 70 94), in the old seminary, has doubles for US$55, including all meals. The basic but cheap convent of the *Soeurs de St-Joseph de Cluny* (☎ 31 71 22), at 80 Rue du Père Boiteau, offers dormitory beds for US$9. Nearby, *Le Sentier* (☎ 31 71 54) has tiny rooms for US$11 per person. In the same area is the more upmarket *Le P'tit Randonneur* (☎ 31 79 55), which has doubles for US$35.

Due to demand, Cilaos has several chambres d'hôte, including *Mme Gardebien* (☎ 31 72 15) at 50 Rue St-Louis, *M Luc Payet* (☎ 31 77 79) at Ruelle des Artisans, *Mme Aurélien Nassibou* (☎ 31 71 77) near the camp site, and *Mme Flavie* (☎ 31 71 23) at Chemin Matarum.

Hôtel Le Marla (☎ 31 72 33; fax 31 72 98), near the lake, is a good budget option with doubles for US$28. The rather dull *Hôtel du Cirque* (☎ 31 70 68; fax 31 80 46), at 27 Rue du Père Boiteau, charges US$56 for a double, including breakfast.

For cheap eats, try the group of mobile snack bars opposite the school; samosas cost US$0.35 and sandwich rolls are around US$3.

Not far from the Hôtel du Cirque, *Le Triton Pizzeria* serves Italian and Creole meals. Nearby is *Chez Noë*, specialising in Creole cuisine.

Near the lake is the pleasant *La Grange*, which offers French and Creole food; main dishes start at around US$9.

CIRQUE DE MAFATE

For an unforgettable wilderness trip, spend a few days trekking through the Cirque de Mafate. This must be one of the world's most dramatic landscapes – and as yet, there's no highway access.

Entry is via several points: from Le Bélier or Hell-Bourg via Bord à Martin or Col de Fourche; from Cilaos via the Col du Taïbit; from Piton Maïdo to Roche Plate; from Sans Souci along the Rivière des Galets; and from La Possession via Dos d'Ane. Inside the cirque are some communities where you can find basic supplies: La Nouvelle, Marla, Aurère, Ilet à Bourse, Ilet à Malheur, Grand Place and Roche Plate.

The routes are well signposted, but you should carry a good map. For further information, see the Trekking section earlier in this chapter. For details about gîtes de montagne, see the Accommodation section earlier in this chapter.

CIRQUE DE SALAZIE

The Cirque de Salazie, the wettest of the three cirques, is busier and more varied than Cilaos. **Salazie** sits at the eastern entrance to the cirque, while **Hell-Bourg** occupies a beautiful setting 9km up the slopes.

A couple of kilometres from Salazie is the **Cascade du Voile de la Mariée**, a towering waterfall spilling from the cloud-obscured heights. A short, pleasant walk west from Hell-Bourg's centre, you'll find the **Anciens Thermes** (old spa) in a ravine. Nearby is the **Élévage de Truites**, or trout farm, operated by Paul Irigoyen. Entry is US$1.50 per person (unless you're fishing, in which case trout cost US$12 per kg).

Many day-hikers ascend the 1352m **Piton d'Enchaing**. For a longer trip, you can walk the 20km to Plaine-des-Palmistes, via Bélouve gîte and the **Forêt de Bébour**.

Places to Stay & Eat

The *Auberge de Jeunesse* (☎ 47 82 65) in Hell-Bourg has dorm beds for US$12.

The rustic chambre d'hôte run by *Mme Madeleine Parisot* (☎ 47 83 48), costs US$20 a double, while *Mme Madeleine Laurent* (☎ 47 80 60) charges US$26 a double.

For inexpensive accommodation, Grand Îlet has some chambres d'hôte, and it's a good jumping-off point for the Cirque de Mafate. *Mme Jeanine Grondin* (☎ 47 70 66) charges US$23 a double; *Mme Jeanne Marie Grondin* (☎ 47 70 51) and *Mme Christine Boyer* (☎ 47 70 87) are similarly priced.

The restaurant *'Ti Chou Chou* offers good Creole meals. Just down the street is *Chez Alice*, which serves hearty plats du jour for around US$12.

PITON DE LA FOURNAISE

This active volcano, which is Réunion's most renowned feature, is relatively safe and straightforward to visit. Although it occupies a single massif, there are two major craters, Dolomieu (the largest) and Bory (inactive since 1791), and a host of smaller, barnacle-like craters strewn across the slopes.

Access is via the 20km road (there's also a walking route) from Le Vingt-Septième to Pas de Bellecombe. The walk to the top takes about five hours return. There's a choice between the steep ascent to Cratère Bory or the easier one to La Soufrière on Cratère Dolomieu. Once at the rim you can circle both craters, or follow the northern rim track, which connects the Bory and La Soufrière routes.

For the best chances of clear weather, start early. Temperatures and climatic conditions swing wildly at times, and warm windproof and waterproof clothing is essential. In the moonlike outer crater, clouds can roll in literally instantaneously, so never wander off the marked route.

ST-GILLES-LES-BAINS

Roches Noires at St-Gilles-les-Bains and nearby Boucan Canot are the best of Réunion's few beaches. On the weekends and during holiday periods, St-Gilles-les-Bains is ridiculously overcrowded.

Up in the hills, don't miss the **Musée de Villèle**, a colonial home dating from 1787, which was owned by the wealthy and powerful Mme Panon-Desbassyns. It's open

RÉUNION

daily except Tuesday from 9.30 am to noon and 2 to 5 pm. Admission costs US$1.80 per person.

Places to Stay & Eat

A small patch costs US$11 at *Camping Municipal* (☎ 24 42 35), Hermitage-les-Bains, south of St-Gilles-les-Bains. Be warned that robbery is rife. At Bernica in the hills behind St-Gilles-les-Bains, is the *Auberge de Jeunesse* (☎ 22 89 75), which charges US$12 per person.

Not far from the beach at Hermitage-les-Bains is a nice pension, *Le Bougainvillier* (☎ /fax 33 82 48), which has doubles for US$41. One of the cheapest budget hotels in St-Gilles-les-Bains is *Le Dor y Flane* (☎ 33 82 41) at 21 Avenue de la Mer, which has doubles for US$32.

There are heaps of inexpensive eating joints around the beach areas. Most restaurants, whatever their appearance or reputation, have set menus from around US$11.

For a quick beach munch, try *La Bobine*, at Hermitage-les-Bains; grilled fish costs US$7. Other swift serves at Hermitage-les-Bains include *Les Trois Roches* (aka *Chez Go)*, with great Creole meals for around US$13. Another good place for Creole food is *Chez Loulou* at Rue Général de Gaulle. On the same road is *Le Bourbon*, which offers French and Creole cuisine from around US$9.

ST-PIERRE

St-Pierre has a pleasantly lively ambience, but there is little to see in or around the town. You could take a look at the **grave** of the African bandit and sorcerer Le Sitarane, marked by a black cross.

If you're here overnight, a good budget choice is the *Pension Touristique Chez Papa Daya* (☎ 25 64 87), at 27 Rue du Four à Chaux, which has doubles from US$26. The pension de famille of *Mme Fontaine Luline* (☎ 25 50 07), 46 Rue Rodier, charges US$18 per person.

For food, a good Chinese and Indian option is *La Jonque*, near the corner of Boulevard Hubert-Delisle and Rue François de Mahy. In the same area is *Pizza Rapido* and *Pizzeria Le Cabanon*. Along Boulevard Hubert-Delisle there is a string of sidewalk cafes with high prices and haughty ambience.

Rwanda

REPUBLIC OF RWANDA
Area: 26,338 sq km
Population: 5 million
Population Growth Rate: 2.7%
Capital: Kigali
Head of State: President Pasteur Bizimungu
Official Languages: Kinyarwanda, French
Currency: Rwandan franc
Exchange Rate: RFr 310 = US$1
Per Capita GNP: US$110
Inflation: 20%
Time: GMT/UTC + 2

Highlights
• View the mountain gorillas in the Parc National des Volcans
• Explore the protected rainforest of Nyungwe Forest

Rwanda has become indelibly etched into the consciousness of the late 20th century as the focus of one of the world's most horrific attempts at genocide. Before the outrages in 1994, many travellers used to come to Rwanda to visit the Parc Nacional des Volcans in the north, where the borders of Rwanda, Uganda and Congo (Zaïre) meet. The thickly forested slopes are one of the last remaining sanctuaries of the mountain gorilla. This endangered species, too, suffered in the civil war, losing quite a few of its dwindling numbers. You can now once again visit two of the family groups, and travellers are starting to trickle back.

Facts about the Country

HISTORY
As in neighbouring Burundi, the original inhabitants of Rwanda, the Twa Pygmies, were gradually displaced from 1000 AD onwards by migrating Hutu tribespeople who, in turn, came to be dominated by the Tutsi from the 16th century onwards.

The similarities with Burundi end there, however. The authority of the Rwandan *mwami* (king) was far greater than his opposite number in Burundi, and the system of feudalism which developed here was unsurpassed in Africa outside Ethiopia.

The Rwandan mwami was an absolute ruler in every sense of the word, with the power to exact forced Hutu labour and to allocate land to peasants or evict them from it. Tutsi overlordship was reinforced by ceremonial and religious observances, and military organisation, likewise, was the sole preserve of the Tutsi.

The Germans took the country in 1890 and

711

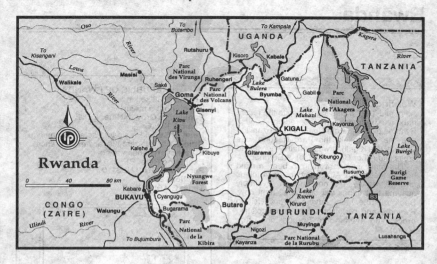

held it until 1916, when their garrisons surrendered to Belgian forces during WWI. At the end of the war, Rwanda was mandated to the Belgians, along with Burundi, by the League of Nations. From then until independence the power and privileges of the Tutsi increased, as the Belgians found it convenient to rule indirectly through the mwami and his princes.

The condition of the Hutu peasantry deteriorated meanwhile, leading to a series of urgent demands for radical reform in 1957. Power is rarely given up voluntarily in Africa, and in 1959, following the death of Mwami Matara III, a ruthless Tutsi clan seized power and set about murdering Hutu leaders.

It was a serious miscalculation and led to a massive Hutu uprising. Some 100,000 Tutsi were butchered in the ensuing bloodletting, and many thousands more fled into neighbouring countries. Faced with carnage on this scale, the Belgian colonial authorities were forced to introduce political reforms, and when independence was granted in 1962 it brought the Hutu majority to power under the prime ministership of Gregoire Kayibanda.

Certain sections of the Tutsi were unwilling to accept the loss of their privileged position. They formed a number of guerrilla groups which mounted raids on Hutu communities, but this only provoked further Hutu reprisals. In the bloodshed which followed, thousands more Tutsi were killed and tens of thousands of their fellow tribespeople fled to Uganda and Burundi.

The massacre of Hutu people in Burundi in 1972 re-ignited the old hatreds in Rwanda and prompted the army commander, Major General Juvenal Habyarimana, to oust Kayibanda. He ruled until he was killed in a plane crash in 1994.

In October 1990, the whole intertribal issue was savagely reopened. On the first day of the month, Rwanda was abruptly invaded by some 5000 well-armed rebels of the Rwanda Patriotic Front (RPF, a Tutsi military front) from their bases in western Uganda. All hell broke loose. Two days later, at Habyarimana's request, France, Belgium and Zaïre (as it was then) flew in troops to assist the Rwandan army to repulse the rebels.

With this support assured, the Rwandan

army went on the rampage against the Tutsi and any Hutu suspected of collaborating with the rebels. The rebels were routed, at tremendous cost in lives and suffering to the Tutsi. President Museveni of Uganda was accused of having encouraged the rebels and supplied them with equipment. The accusations were denied, but the evidence suggests otherwise. It's inconceivable that Museveni was totally unaware of the preparations which were going on, and it was also common knowledge that Uganda was keen to see the repatriation of the 250,000 Tutsi refugees in western Uganda.

The RPF invaded again in 1991, this time better armed and prepared. The government forces were thrown back over a large area of northern Rwanda and by early 1992 the RPF was within 25km of Kigali, at which point a cease-fire was cobbled together and the warring parties brought to the negotiating table. The negotiations stalled several weeks later and hostilities were renewed. A new peace accord between the government and the RPF was signed in August 1993.

In 1994 the whole conflict erupted again on an incomprehensible scale, and the country became the scene for the worst humanitarian crisis the world has seen in the 50 years since WWII. In just three violent months, between 200,000 and 500,000 (some say as many as one million) Rwandans were killed, mostly by *interahamwe* militias – gangs of youths armed with machetes, guns and other weapons supplied by officials loyal to Habyarimana. A further three million people fled the country to refugee camps set up for them in Tanzania, Congo (Zaïre) and Uganda. It has been estimated that seven million of the country's nine million people were displaced.

The spark for the rampage against the Tutsi minority was the death of Habyarimana (and his Burundian counterpart, Cyprien Ntaryamira) when his plane was shot down as it was landing in Kigali. The two leaders were returning from peace talks in Tanzania. It is widely believed that the plane was shot down by Hutu extremists in Habyarimana's own Presidential Guard, who felt he had

become too tolerant of the Tutsi minority. According to some reports, the massacres which followed were not a spontaneous outburst of violence but a calculated plot by the government to rid the country of Tutsi and Hutu reformists.

What the government didn't take into account was the resistance that would be put up by the well-disciplined forces of the Tutsi-dominated RPF. By July 1994 the RPF had overrun the government forces and established a new Government of National Unity in Kigali.

Rwanda seems to be slowly getting back onto its feet. You can walk around in safety again. All the same, not everyone is happy with the RPF government. A number of prominent Hutu have resigned from the government. Other ministers have been sacked for being critical of the army following the RPF's massacre of refugees at the Kibeho refugee camp in 1996. This was certainly a tragic blunder on behalf of the RPF and did nothing to encourage refugees outside the country to feel secure about returning.

It's unlikely, however, that the new opposition party, the Resistance Forces for Democracy, formed by Sendashonga and Twagiramungu, will make much headway.

The RPF may well have a friendly and supportive ally in Uganda but Congo (Zaïre) is still evolving. With the outbreak of hostilities in late 1996, ex-Hutu army soldiers in the Lake Kivu area launched cross-border raids into both Rwanda and Burundi from the refugee camps in the Goma and Uvira regions. Rwanda responded with raids into eastern Congo (Zaïre) and support for Tutsi rebels north of Goma. The Hutu fought alongside the Zaïrese army and the whole situation turned very ugly, with the million or so refugees from 1994 caught in the middle. There were suggestions that the Rwandan plan was to bring about the downfall of President Mobutu in Congo (Zaïre). True or not, Mobutu fell and Congo (Zaïre) now has a government which will no doubt have much improved relations with Rwanda.

RWANDA

Rwanda itself, meanwhile, is still rebuilding following the instability and uncertainty which has devastated the country since 1994.

GEOGRAPHY & CLIMATE

Rwanda's mountainous terrain occupies 26,338 sq km. Like neighbouring Burundi, Rwanda is one of the world's most densely populated countries. To feed the people, almost every available piece of land is under cultivation (except for Parc National de l'Akagera along the border with Tanzania, and the higher slopes of the volcanoes). Since most of the country is mountainous, this involves a good deal of terracing.

The average daytime temperature is 30°C, except in the highlands where the daytime range is between 12 and 15°C. There are four discernible seasons: the long rains from mid-March to mid-May; the long dry from mid-May to mid-October; the short rains from mid-October to mid-December; and the short dry from mid-December to mid-March.

It rains more frequently and heavily in the north-east, where the volcanoes are covered by rainforest. The summit of Karisimbi (4507m), the highest of these volcanoes, is often covered with sleet or snow.

POPULATION & PEOPLE

The population stands at around 8.9 million giving Rwanda one of the highest population densities of any country in Africa. Most of the one million refugees who were living in Congo (Zaïre), Burundi, Tanzania and elsewhere have now returned to Rwanda. Virtually the only ones who haven't are those who had any involvement whatsoever in the genocide of 1994.

About 65% of Rwandans are Christians, 25% follow tribal religions and the remainder are Muslims.

LANGUAGE

The national language is Kinyarwanda. The official languages are Kinyarwanda and French, so if you speak some French you should be able to get by in most areas. English is spoken little, but Swahili is useful in some areas. See the French and Swahili sections in the Language Appendix.

Facts for the Visitor

VISAS

Visas are required by everyone except French and German nationals, and are best applied for in East Africa. They cost about US$30 in most countries, allow a one month stay and generally take 24 hours to issue. Two photos are required.

Most travellers, however, get their visa on arrival at the border. The 15-day transit visa which you get costs US$20 and takes 10 minutes.

Visa Extensions

Both tourist and transit visas can be extended in the capital, Kigali, at MININTER (Ministère de l'Intérieur; ☎ 85856) in the Kacyiru district, about 7km north-east of the city centre. Extensions take one to two days, cost US$13 and you can get up to three months.

Other Visas

Burundi
> Visas are issued only to Rwandan residents, so don't waste your time. Visas are available at the border but you're strongly advised not to travel to Burundi at present.

Congo (Zaïre)
> Visa costs are the same as elsewhere (see the Congo [Zaïre] chapter for details), require three photographs and are issued in 24 hours. Check the security situation in eastern Congo (Zaïre) before applying for a visa.

Kenya
> Visas cost US$30 or the equivalent in local currency, require two photographs and are issued the same day if you apply before 11.30 am. No onward tickets or minimum funds are asked for.

Tanzania
> Visas require two photos and generally take 48 hours to issue. The cost depends on your nationality, but ranges from US$10 to US$55.

Uganda
> Visas cost US$20 or US$25 (depending on your nationality), require two photos and are issued in 24 hours.

EMBASSIES

Rwandan Embassies

In Africa there are Rwandan embassies in Burundi, Congo (Zaïre), Egypt, Ethiopia, Kenya, Tanzania and Uganda. Elsewhere they are found in Belgium, Canada, France, Germany, Japan and the USA.

Foreign Embassies in Rwanda

The following countries have diplomatic representation in Kigali:

Belgium
    Ave de la Paix (☎ 75551)
Burundi
    Rue de Ntaruka, off Ave de Rusumo (☎ 73465)
Congo (Zaïre)
    Rue Député Kamuzinzi, off Ave de Rusumo (☎ 75327)
France
    Rue Député Kayuku (☎ 75225)
Kenya
    Rue Kadyiro, close to the Hôtel Umubano (☎ 82774)
Tanzania
    Ave Paul VI, close to the junction of Ave de Rusumo (☎ 76074)
Uganda
    3rd floor of the building on Ave de la Paix near the corner of Ave des Collines (☎ 76495)
UK
    Ave Paul VI (☎ 84098)
USA
    Ave des Milles Collines (☎ 75327)

MONEY

US$1 =   RFr 310

The unit of currency is the Rwandan franc (RFr).

In Kigali, the moneychangers hang around the main post office. The banking sector is gradually returning to normal after virtually all the banks were shot-up, looted and trashed during the genocide. There are now five banks open in Kigali. There are also banks open again in Butare and Ruhengeri (Banque de Kigali) but one has yet to reopen in Gisenyi.

In addition to the banks, there are several foreign exchange bureaus in Kigali, mainly around the post office.

Costs

Rwanda is a relatively expensive country because of the large number of expatriates and NGOs here. In this landlocked country, a lot of export earnings are spent importing food, drink and transport requirements for the expatriates. As a budget traveller, you will be hard-pressed even if you stay in mission hostels. It's difficult to exist here on a Kenyan, Tanzanian or Ugandan budget, and student cards are only useful to get into the national parks at a discount.

POST & COMMUNICATIONS

Overseas postal rates are relatively high, as is the cost of international phone calls (US$3 per minute). The country code for Rwanda is 250. There are no telephone area codes within Rwanda.

HEALTH

As with most of Africa, you should take precautions against malaria in Rwanda, but mosquitoes generally are not a problem.

Take special care in Rwanda to avoid illness and/or treatment which could require a blood transfusion, as AIDS is rampant.

There are certain parts of Lake Kivu where it is very dangerous to swim, as volcanic gases are released continuously from the lake bed and, in the absence of wind, tend to collect on the surface of the lake. Quite a few people have been asphyxiated as a result. Make enquiries or watch where the local people swim and you'll probably be safe. Bilharzia is also a risk in Lake Kivu.

Cholera vaccination certificates are compulsory for entry or exit by air. If you are entering overland the check is cursory, but officials sometimes ask about it.

It's advisable not to drink tap water. Soft drink, fruit and beer are available even in the smallest places.

DANGERS & ANNOYANCES

Night-time curfews exist in many places around the country and local soldiers have orders to shoot on sight. So far, no tourists have been shot but you're advised not to take

RWANDA

risks. This is especially true in Kigali. Take a taxi after dark.

Out in the countryside, do not walk along anything other than a well-used track; you may step on a landmine.

Never take photographs of anything connected with the government or the military (post offices, banks, bridges, border posts, barracks, prisons, dams etc). Your film and possibly your equipment will be confiscated.

The most common annoyance is the road-blocks on all of the main roads. You must stop at these and your baggage will be searched along with whatever vehicle you are in. The soldiers will also want to check your passport.

PUBLIC HOLIDAYS

Public holidays observed in Rwanda are: 1 January, 28 January (Democracy Day), 1 May, 1 July (National Day), 5 July (Peace & National Unity Day), 1 August (Harvest Festival), 8 September (Culture Day), 25 September (Kamarampaka Day), 26 October (Armed Forces Day), 1 November (All Saints Day) and 25 December.

Getting There & Away

AIR

International airlines flying into Rwanda are Aeroflot, Air Burundi, Air France, Air Tanzania, Air Zaïre, Cameroon Airlines, Ethiopian Airlines, Kenya Airways, Sabena and Uganda Airlines.

Air tickets bought in Rwanda for international flights are very expensive and compare poorly with what is on offer in Nairobi.

LAND

Burundi

Note that at the time of writing it is not safe to enter Burundi overland on either of the routes described below, due to the ongoing civil war there and the unrest in eastern Congo (Zaïre). Your safety is far from guaranteed. The information is given here in the hope that the situation will improve.

The main crossing point between Rwanda and Burundi is near Kayanza on the Butare-Bujumbura road. There are share-taxis which do the trip daily which leave at 8 am, cost US$13 and take five hours.

It's also possible to go from Cyangugu to Bujumbura via the Zaïrese towns of Bukavu and Uvira. Buses from Bukavu go partly via Rwanda (but not via Cyangugu) and partly via Congo (Zaïre) before terminating in Uvira. From there, you'll need to take another minibus or taxi across the Congo (Zaïre)-Burundi border to Bujumbura. You *may* need a Rwandan transit visa or, better still, a re-entry visa, and you will definitely need a dual or multiple-entry Zaïrese visa.

Congo (Zaïre)

As with Burundi, travel into eastern Congo (Zaïre) is not recommended at the moment. Remember that Goma and Bukavu have been right in the centre of the refugee and military crisis which has existed in this area since 1994 and flared in late 1996 so expect a lot of military personnel on either side of the border.

The two main crossing points from Rwanda to Congo (Zaïre) are between Gisenyi and Goma (at the northern end of Lake Kivu) and between Cyangugu and Bukavu (at the southern end of Lake Kivu).

Between Cyangugu and Bukavu, there are minibuses from Kamembe (the border town) to Cyangugu (the border post). It's an easy border crossing and you can walk between the two posts. From the Rusizi (Zaïrese) border post, it's a 3km walk or taxi ride to Bukavu.

Tanzania

Take a share-taxi (daily) from Kigali to Kibungo (US$1), and a minibus from there to the border town of Rusumo (US$2). Once across the border take a pick-up to Ngara, from where there are buses three times a week to Mwanza (12 hours, US$11).

Uganda

There are two main crossing points: Kigali to Kabale via Gatuna/Katuna, and Ruhengeri to Kisoro via Cyanika, but only the former is safe at the moment.

From Kigali to Kabale there are many

minibuses daily (two hours not including immigration formalities and army road-blocks, US$7).

There's also a normal Ugandan bus which does the run between Kigali and Kabale in either direction once daily and leaves Kigali at 6.30 am (US$7).

For those in a hurry to get between Kigali and Kampala, there's a daily bus from Kigali at 6.30 am. The buses are operated by, among others, Jaguar and Happy Trails (in Kampala), cost US$15 and take about 10 hours.

Getting Around

BUS

Rwanda has an excellent road system, mainly due to massive injections of foreign aid.

There are plenty of modern, well-maintained minibuses serving all the main routes. Between dawn and about 3 pm at the bus station in any town you can almost always find one going your way. Minibuses leave when full – this means when all the seats are occupied, unlike in Kenya and Tanzania.

There are also modern government buses (many of them bearing the Japan-Rwanda assistance programme logo) on quite a few routes. These are cheaper than minibuses but take longer and are far less frequent.

Whichever form of transport you take you must be prepared for military checkpoints. These vary in number depending on where you're going but at each you'll be required to get off the vehicle and allow the soldiers to examine your luggage. Other than the time it takes, there's no hassle.

HITCHING

Hitching around Rwanda is relatively easy because of the prodigious number of NGO vehicles on the roads. Most of these people will give you a lift so you may find you hardly need to bother with the minibus system. Drivers will rarely ask you to pay for a lift. They're more interested in talking to you about your experiences in Africa. For more information on hitching, see the main Getting Around chapter at the front of this book.

BOAT

Before the latest civil war, there used to be ferries on Lake Kivu which connected the Rwandan ports of Cyangugu, Kirambo, Kibuye and Gisenyi but these are all suspended at present.

Kigali

Built on a ridge and extending down into the valley floors on either side, Kigali is a small but beautiful city with an incredible variety of flowering trees and shrubs. Unfortunately, there was a tremendous amount of damage done to the city during the latest civil war and many buildings lie in partial or total ruin, though a lot of rehabilitation work has been done and continues to be done.

Law and order has largely been re-established, though there's precious little nightlife because people are afraid of the RPF soldiers patrolling the streets. It's probably best to stay indoors at night if you want to avoid hassles, though this is changing rapidly.

Information

The national tourist office, Office Rwandais du Tourisme et des Parcs Nationaux (☎ 76514), is on Place de l'Indépendance, opposite the post office (PTT). Reservations must be made here to see the mountain gorillas in the Parc National des Volcans. The cost for a gorilla visit is US$126 per person which includes a gorilla permit and the park entry fee, as well as two guides and two armed guards per group.

The post office (and telephone office) is open Monday to Friday from 7.30 am to 6 pm, and on Saturday from 8.30 am to 1 pm. The poste restante is quite well organised.

The immigration office is on Ave du Commerce next to the Air France office in a building set back from the road.

RWANDA

RWANDA

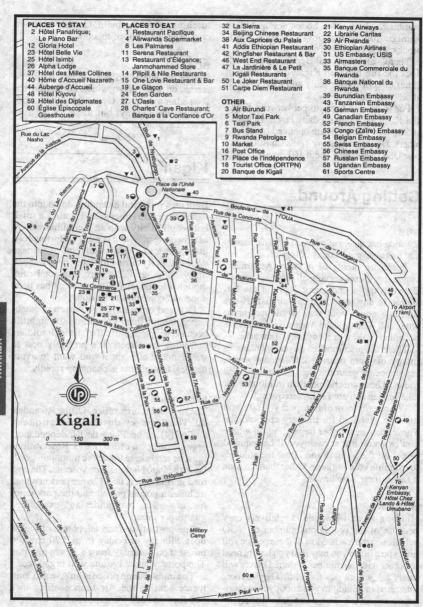

PLACES TO STAY
2 Hôtel Panafrique;
   Le Piano Bar
12 Gloria Hotel
23 Hôtel Belle Vie
25 Hôtel Isimbi
26 Alpha Lodge
37 Hôtel des Milles Collines
40 Hôme d'Accueil Nazareth
44 Auberge d'Accueil
48 Hôtel Kiyovu
59 Hôtel des Diplomates
60 Église Épiscopale
   Guesthouse

PLACES TO EAT
1 Restaurant Pacifique
4 Alirwanda Supermarket
8 Les Palmares
11 Serena Restaurant
13 Restaurant d'Élégance;
   Janmohammed Store
14 Pilipili & Nile Restaurants
15 One Love Restaurant & Bar
24 Eden Garden
27 L'Oasis
28 Charles' Cave Restaurant;
   Banque á la Confiance d'Or

32 La Sierra
34 Beijing Chinese Restaurant
38 Aux Caprices du Palais
41 Addis Ethiopian Restaurant
42 Kingfisher Restaurant & Bar
46 West End Restaurant
47 La Jardinière & Le Petit
   Kigali Restaurants
50 Le Joker Restaurant
51 Carpe Diem Restaurant

OTHER
3 Air Burundi
5 Motor Taxi Park
6 Taxi Park
7 Bus Stand
9 Rwanda Petrolgaz
10 Market
16 Post Office
17 Place de l'Indépendence
18 Tourist Office (ORTPN)
20 Banque de Kigali

21 Kenya Airways
22 Librairie Caritas
29 Air Rwanda
30 Ethiopian Airlines
31 US Embassy; USIS
33 Airmasters
35 Banque Commerciale du
   Rwanda
36 Banque National du
   Rwanda
39 Burundian Embassy
43 Tanzanian Embassy
45 German Embassy
49 Canadian Embassy
52 French Embassy
53 Congo (Zaïre) Embassy
54 Belgian Embassy
55 Swiss Embassy
56 Chinese Embassy
57 Russian Embassy
58 Ugandan Embassy
61 Sports Centre

Kigali

Places to Stay

The one big problem with Kigali is finding accommodation. You'll have to take things as you find them and be very flexible.

The cheapest place is the *Hôme d'Accueil Nazareth*, Blvd de l'OUA, behind Église St-Famille, which has a dormitory with some 15 bunk beds at less than US$1 per bed, but it's really only for those on desperation row.

The *guesthouse* at the Église Épiscopale au Rwanda (☎ 76340), 32 Ave Paul VI, costs US$9 and is much better but not very popular, mainly because it's a long way from the city centre (really only an option if you have transport). If you want to walk, it's 30 minutes from the city centre.

One of the cheapest hotels is the *Hôtel Belle Vie*, Ave du Commerce, which has one single room at US$10 and three doubles at US$13. The toilets (shared) are clean and there's hot water in the shower.

A little higher in price is the *Hôtel Panafrique*, Blvd de Nyabugogo, which has doubles with attached bath (no singles) with cold water only for US$16. It's clean and the rooms are large but it's seen better days.

Also OK is the *Alpha Lodge*, corner of Rue Kalisimbi and Ave des Milles Collines, which has very clean singles/doubles for US$13/23 with shared bathroom and hot water. It's quiet and secure.

Similar is the *Gloria Hôtel*, corner of Rue du Travail and Ave du Commerce, which is pleasant and clean and offers singles/doubles with attached bath at US$13/20. There's only cold water in the showers at present.

Places to Eat

For cheap food try *Les Palmares*, Rue du Travail. Likewise, the *Restaurant Pacifique*, Blvd de Nyabugogo, offers good African fare for US$2. For a good African buffet lunch, the *Pilipili*, Rue de Kalisimbi, is a good bet.

Also good is the *Serena Restaurant*, Ave du Commerce, opposite the market. Further afield is the *Carpe Diem Restaurant*, Ave de Kiyovu, which serves a mixture of African and French dishes.

For snacks, you probably can't beat *L'Oasis*, Ave de la Paix, which has good pies as well as ice cream and fruit juices.

For a very good African buffet as well as some continental dishes at around US$5 try the *West End Restaurant*, Rue de l'Akagera.

The *Eden Garden*, Rue de Kalisimbi, has been a great place to eat for many years with its bamboo décor and informal ambience. It offers very good French steaks, chicken and tilapia with French fries and salad for around US$6.

Entertainment

Perhaps the best disco and one which is very popular as well as being in the city centre is *Le Piano Bar*.

The *Nile Restaurant*, Rue de Kalisimbi, next to the Pilipili Restaurant, has a popular terrace bar.

Getting There & Away

Minibuses run from the gare routière (bus station) to towns all over Rwanda, including Butare (three hours, US$3), Gitarama (about 1½ hours, about US$6), Gatuna (two hours, US$5), Kibuye (US$3), Rusumo (three hours, US$5), Ruhengeri (about two hours, US$2), and Gisenyi (3½ hours, US$3).

Getting Around

The Airport The international airport is at Kanombe, 12km from the city centre. There are taxis (US$10), but it's cheaper to take a direct minibus from the bus station (US$1).

Taxi A taxi within the city centre costs around US$3, more if you're going out to the suburbs.

Around the Country

BUTARE

Butare is the intellectual centre of Rwanda and it's here that you'll find the excellent National Museum, the National University, and the National Institute of Scientific Research.

The huge **National Museum** reopened in 1989 and is probably the best museum in

East Africa. It's certainly the most amazing building in the country. It's well worth a visit for its ethnological and archaeological displays, and is open from 9 am to noon and 2 to 5 pm daily. It's about a 15 minute walk north of the centre, past the minibus station.

Places to Stay

The *Procure de Butare* (signposted *Procure d'Accueil*) is nice and clean and has singles/doubles for US$5/7.

A good and fairly cheap hotel is the clean and friendly *Weekend Hôtel* near the market, with singles/doubles at US$4/7. Better value is the *International Hôtel* across the road. It has double rooms with good beds, a bath and hot water for US$7.

The only mid-range place is the fairly new *Hôtel des Beaux-Arts* (☎ 30584) on Ave du Commerce. It has rooms from US$15.

Getting There & Away

The minibus station is just a patch of dirt about 1km north of the town centre next to the stadium. Taxi-motors abound, so getting there is not a problem.

There are departures to Kigali (three hours, US$3) and Gitarama, and to Kamembe and Cyangugu (US$3) along a spectacular road passing through the Nyungwe Forest, which contains some amazing virgin rainforest between Uwinka and Kiutabe.

CYANGUGU

At the southern end of Lake Kivu and close to Bukavu (Congo [Zaïre]), Cyangugu is an attractively positioned town on the lake shore and the Zaïrese border. A few kilometres south of the border lies **Kamembe**, the region's main town and an important centre for the processing of tea and cotton. Nearby is the **Rugege Forest**, home to elephant, buffalo, leopard, chimpanzee and many other mammals and birds.

The **waterfalls** of the Rusizi River and the **hot springs** of Nyakabuye are here.

The town was the centre of heavy fighting between Tutsi rebels and the Zaïrese army in late 1996 so things have probably changed dramatically.

Places to Stay

A convenient place to stay if you're heading for Congo (Zaïre) (or coming from there) is the *Mission St-François* at the border. Similar is the *Mission Pentecoste* which has great views over the lake. Both cost around US$4 per person.

The only other option is the expensive *Hôtel du Lac* near the border.

Getting There & Away

Minibuses run between Cyangugu and Kamembe and from Kamembe to Butare (four hours total). The road is incredibly spectacular in parts, and it passes through the superb Nyungwe Forest. From Kamembe there are also minibuses to Kigali (via Butare).

GISENYI

Gisenyi was a resort town for rich Rwandans and expatriate workers and residents, but it has suffered severely in recent years.

There are magnificent views over Lake Kivu and, looking north-west, to the volcano of Nyiragongo (3470m).

Information

Moneychangers (doing cash transactions only) hang out around the market and the ERP petrol station outside.

Places to Stay

Most travellers stay at the mission presbytérienne's *centre d'accueil* (☎ 40522), about 100m from the market and bus station. You can get a dorm 'bed' for US$2 or a single room for US$3.

Apart from the mission, there is no decent cheap place to stay in Gisenyi. All the acceptable hotels are near the lake-front. The most reasonably priced of these is the *Hôtel Regina*, with singles from US$20.

KIBUYE

Kibuye is a small town about halfway along Lake Kivu. If coming here by road from Gisenyi, try not to miss the 100m-high waterfall, **Les Chutes de Ndaba**, at Ndaba.

Places to Stay
The only place is the *Guest House Kibuye* (☎ 68191) on the lakeside. It's expensive (US$20/26 for singles/doubles) but you can camp here in the grounds for free.

NYUNGWE FOREST
The Nyungwe Forest ranks as one of Rwanda's foremost attractions. One of the largest protected mountain rainforests in Africa, it covers 970 sq km and offers superb scenery overlooking the forest and Lake Kivu as well as views to the north of the distant volcanoes of the Virunga.

The Nyungwe Forest Conservation Project began in 1988 and is sponsored by the New York Zoological Society, the American Peace Corps and the Rwandan Government. Its current status is unclear.

Its main attraction was guided tours to view large groups of black-and-white colobus monkeys (up to 300 per group). The lush, green valleys also offered outstanding hiking across 20km of well-maintained trails. There are about 270 species of trees, 50 species of mammals, 275 species of birds and an astonishing variety of orchids and butterflies.

Warning
Landmines have been found in Nyungwe Forest so bear this in mind if you intend to go there.

Places to Stay
There are nine camp sites at the Uwinka headquarters, but you must bring everything you need – there is nothing here other than toilets, charcoal and wood. The nearest towns for provisions are Cyangugu and Butare.

Getting There & Away
The Nyungwe Forest lies between Butare and Cyangugu. The Uwinka headquarters is just past the 90km post coming from Butare and is marked by a board on which a black-and-white colobus monkey is painted.

If coming from Cyangugu, take a minibus towards Butare and get off at Uwinka, which is just past the 54km post. The journey takes about one hour.

RUHENGERI
Most travellers come to Ruhengeri on their way to the Parc National des Volcans. It's a small town with two army barracks, a very busy hospital and magnificent views of the volcanoes to the north and west.

Forget any ideas you may have about climbing the hill near the post office, as it's a military area and access is prohibited.

The post office is in the préfecture, opposite the Hotel Muhabura.

Places to Stay
The only place to consider seriously is the *Centre d'Accueil d'Eglise Episcopale*, on the north-west corner of Rue du Pyrethre and Ave du 5 Juillet. It's clean and has dormitory beds for US$3 (six bunk beds in two rooms) and singles/doubles for US$5/8. There's a restaurant with meals for US$2 but you need to order food in advance.

Somewhat cheaper is the *Omukikane Inn*, near the minibus park on Ave du 5 Juillet, which has singles with shared bathroom for US$3 and doubles with attached bath for US$7. It's clean and secure but has only cold water in the showers.

The *Restaurant Renaissance*, on Rue Muhabura, should by now have rooms available, priced at US$5/8 for singles/doubles.

The cheapest mid-range place is the *Auberge Urumuri* (☎ 46229), close to the market, which has no singles but is very clean and pleasant and offers doubles with attached bath and hot water for US$10.

Places to Eat
The *Centre d'Accueil* (see Places to Stay above) offers OK dinners for US$2. Cold beers are available at the usual price.

Cheapest of the African eateries is the *Restaurant La Difference* on Ave de la Nutrition (a suitable location!) which offers cheap kebabs.

The *Hôtel Urumuri*, down a small side street off Rue du Marché, has an outdoor area where you can get good meals of chicken or spaghetti (US$2) from 7 am until evening – if they don't run out. They also have very cold beers.

RWANDA

Getting There & Away

From Kigali, minibuses take about two hours and cost US$2.

PARC NATIONAL DES VOLCANS

This area along the border with Congo (Zaïre) and Uganda has to be one of the most beautiful sights in Africa. There is a chain of volcanoes, one more than 4500m high.

The bamboo and rainforest-covered slopes provide one of the last remaining sanctuaries of the mountain gorilla (*gorilla beringei*). There are four known groups. Dian Fossey's account of her years with the gorillas and her battle with poachers and government officials, *Gorillas in the Mist*, makes fascinating reading.

Visiting the Gorillas

For gorilla visits, advance reservations *must* be made at the tourist office in Kigali, Office Rwandais du Tourisme et des Parcs Nationaux (☎ 76514), Boite Postale 905.

Having booked and paid your fees in Kigali, you must then go to the préfecture (opposite the Hotel Muhabura) in Ruhengeri and arrange to see the gorillas the following morning. Then arrange a vehicle to take you to the point at which you start climbing up to the gorillas. This costs around US$70 shared between however many there are in your group. You must go back to the préfecture before 8 am the next day and you will then be accompanied by the guards and guides to the take-off points. When you've seen the gorillas these people will also accompany you back to the préfecture.

Visits to the gorillas are restricted to one hour and flashes and video cameras are banned unless you are prepared to pay US$6000 for a video permit!

Fees are US$126 per person (US$95 for students) for a gorilla visit (including compulsory guides and guards), payable in hard currency. The guides, guards and any porters will expect a tip at the end.

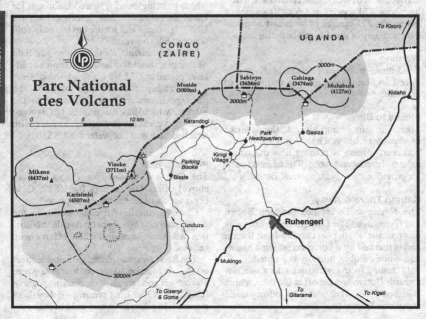

São Tomé & Príncipe

If you get a buzz out of being one of only a few travellers in a friendly country, exploring off-beat places, snorkelling in the clearest waters on the western coast of Africa, or camping on remote beaches still relatively unknown to the outside world, you won't be disappointed with these two remote islands.

Facts about the Country

HISTORY

Despite their relative obscurity, these islands have been of more than passing interest to the outside world. They were first sighted by Portuguese navigators between 1469 and 1472, and the town of São Tomé was founded in 1485. Príncipe was not settled until 1500.

The islands quickly became the largest sugar-producing area in the world, but in 1530 a black revolt frightened the plantation owners off to Brazil. However, slavery, on which the brief sugar boom had been built, remained the basis of the colony's economy. The coffee and cocoa plantations that were set up in the 18th and 19th centuries likewise depended on slave labour. Even when slavery was abolished in 1875, it was replaced by a system of forced labour with minimal wages.

The people of the islands, including those brought in to work the plantations from Angola, Mozambique and Cape Verde, fought the Portuguese on numerous occasions in a bid to win their freedom. Each time, the revolts were put down with much bloodshed by the colonial forces. The worst example was the notorious massacre of 1953 when over 1000 *forros* (the descendants of freed slaves), who refused to work on the plantations, were gunned down by Portuguese troops.

With the fall of the fascist regime in Portugal in 1974, followed shortly afterwards by a mutiny of black troops, the colonial author-

DEMOCRATIC REPUBLIC OF SÃO TOMÉ & PRÍNCIPE
Area: 964 sq km
Population: 130,000
Population Growth Rate: 2.1%
Capital: São Tomé
Head of State: President Miguel Trovoada
Official Language: Portuguese
Currency: Dobra
Exchange Rate: Db 2290 = US$1
Per Capita GNP: US$310
Inflation: 45%
Time: GMT/UTC

Highlights
- Beautiful deserted beaches and crystal clear water
- Old Portuguese colonial architecture

ities were finally forced to come to terms with the liberation movement. A transitional government was set up in December 1974 to guide the country to independence.

When independence was declared in July 1975 almost all of the 4000 or so Portuguese settlers and plantation owners had fled the country, fearful of reprisals.

The European exodus left the country with virtually no skilled labour, a 90% illiteracy rate, only one doctor and many abandoned cocoa plantations. An economic crisis was inevitable. Manual Pinto da Costa, who was the first president and, until then, a moderate, was

São Tomé & Príncipe

ATLANTIC OCEAN

PRÍNCIPE

To Príncipe (150km)

Ilha do Bombom
Sundi
Belo Monte
Praia Grande
Santo António
Praia de Évora
Oeste
Infante Don Henrique

SÃO TOMÉ

Praia dos Tamarindos
Praia dos Governadores
Praia das Conchas
Ilha das Cabras
Praia da Micolo
Lagoa Azul
Guadalupe
Santo Amaro
Airport
Roça Agostinho Neto
SÃO TOMÉ
Neves
Madalena
Trinidade
Cascadas da São Nicolau
Pousada Boa Vista (Casa de Repouso)
Praia das Pombas
Santa Catarina
Pico São Tomé (2024m)
Ilha da Santana
Lemba
Ribeiro Afonso
Praia das Sete Ondas & Agua Izé
Boca de Inferno
São João dos Angolares
Monte Mario
Ribeira Peixe
Praia Grande
Porto Alegre
Ilha das Rolas

0   5   10 km

The invasion never took place but the threat resulted in the dispatch of 1000 Angolan troops to the islands to augment the Cuban soldiers and advisers already there. During the early 1980s the country continued to be economically and militarily dependent on Angola and consequently formed close ties with the communist bloc.

Nevertheless, the islands remained economically aligned with western Europe. Their principal trading partners are still Portugal and the Netherlands (a traditional market for São Tomé's cocoa).

With the collapse of communism in eastern Europe and the demise of the Soviet Union, the country leaned further towards the west. Following mass demonstrations in March 1990, the country's first multiparty elections were held in early 1991 which led to the inauguration of the previously exiled Miguel Trovoada as the new president in April of that year.

Elections held in October 1994 resulted in the ruling Democratic Convergence Party (DCP) being swept from office to be replaced by the Liberation Movement of São Tomé & Príncipe (MLSTP), the party which held power prior to the first multiparty elections in 1991. Trovoada remains president even though his party, the Independent Democratic Action party (ADI), fared badly at the polls in July 1996.

GEOGRAPHY & CLIMATE

Both islands have central volcanic highlands and fast-flowing streams. The highest peak is on São Tomé at 2024m. Partially cleared rainforests are a feature of both islands.

The driest and coolest months are from June to September with temperatures hovering around 28°C. The wettest month is March when temperatures rise to around 30°C.

While this is the general picture, there are many microclimates on São Tomé. The north-east, for instance, has a savannah-like climate while in the south it rains much more, even in the dry season.

POPULATION & PEOPLE

The population of about 130,000 mainly

forced to concede to many of the demands of the more radical members of his government.

The majority of the plantations were nationalised four months after independence, laws were passed prohibiting anyone from owning more than 100 hectares of land, and a people's militia was set up to operate in the workplaces and villages.

Many São Tomé opposition figures were living in exile in Gabon (a staunch pro-western country) and, with unidentified ships and planes sighted frequently in São Tomé's territorial waters and air space during 1978, it appeared an invasion was imminent.

consists of *filhos da terra* (mixed-blood descendants of imported slaves and Europeans who settled the islands in the 16th and 17th centuries).

The rest of the population is made up of *angolares* (legend has it that they are descendants of Angolan slaves who survived a 1540 shipwreck), *forros* (descendants of freed slaves), *serviçais* (migrant labourers) and *tongas* (children of serviçais born on the islands).

Around 90% of the population are Roman Catholic.

LANGUAGE

Portuguese is the official language and *forro*, a Creole language, is widely spoken. See the Language Appendix for useful Portuguese words and phrases.

Facts for the Visitor

VISAS

Visas are required by all. The best place to obtain a visa is in Malabo (Equatorial Guinea). Visas allowing for a stay of 15 days cost US$30 and you need one photo.

Visa Extensions

For visa extensions, see immigration in São Tomé at the Ministério de Negocios Estrangeiros (☎ 22 934) on Avenida Marginal 12 Julho opposite the Portuguese embassy. Even if you overstay your two-week visa, it seems unlikely that you will have any major problems as the government policy is very pro-tourist.

Other Visas

Gabon
    There is no Gabonese embassy in São Tomé but you can get a transit visa on arrival at Libreville airport if you fly directly from São Tomé.

EMBASSIES

São Tomé & Príncipe Embassies

There are embassies, consulates or honorary consuls in Angola, Belgium, Canada, Equatorial Guinea, Gabon, the Netherlands, Portugal, the UK and the USA.

Foreign Embassies in São Tomé

Countries with diplomatic representation in São Tomé include:

Portugal
    Ave Marginal 12 Julho
Spain
    Rua Patrice Lumumba
USA
    c/o UN office, Rua 3 Fevereiro (☎ 21 814)

MONEY

US$1 = Db 2290

The unit of currency is the dobra (Db). Do not exchange much money, at least not at first, because most hotels insist upon payment in US dollars or CFA, and taxi drivers definitely prefer these. Bring plenty of small bills. Restaurants, on the other hand, want dobra.

Many people exchange money on the black market, which is at the Feira do Ponto close to the Conceição Church. The rates can vary but are only marginally better than those at the bank.

Money can also be changed at specially licensed shops such as Tropical, in Rua de Moçambique, and Tyk-Tak in Rua Morta.

The only bank where travellers' cheques can be exchanged is the Banco Internacional de São Tomé e Príncipe (BISTP), on the Praça de Independência (formerly Praça de Portugal).

POST & COMMUNICATIONS

A letter to anywhere in the world costs about US$0.40. There is a poste restante but mail takes a long time to arrive.

There is a card phone outside the telephone office and in the lobby of the Hotel Miramar but cards cost US$40 (hard currency only). Overseas fax services are also available from the telephone office at a cost of US$28 per page. The country code for São Tomé and Príncipe is 23912; there are no area codes.

PUBLIC HOLIDAYS

Public holidays include: 1 January, 1 May, 10 June, 15 August, 5 October, 1 November, 1 December, 25 December, Good Friday and Easter Monday.

Getting There & Away

AIR

For long-haul flights, the only choices are TAP (Air Portugal), which flies from Lisbon to São Tomé via Dakar and Abidjan once a week, and TAAG (Angolan Airlines) which flies from Luanda to Lisbon via São Tomé twice a week.

Air São Tomé e Príncipe (the national carrier) flies to Libreville (Gabon) on a regular basis. The fare is US$160 one way or US$145 with weekend concession. It also flies to Malabo (Equatorial Guinea) for US$148 return, and to Douala (Cameroon) for US$335 return.

The only other international flights are those with Air Affaires Afrique (☎ (012) 21 160) – a Douala outfit – which flies Douala (Cameroon) to São Tomé via Príncipe in either direction on Friday. The fare is US$480 return to São Tomé and US$350 return to Príncipe.

The airport departure tax for international flights is US$20, payable in hard currency.

SEA

Gabon & Cameroon

The *Solmar II* sails between São Tomé and Libreville (Gabon, US$72) and between São Tomé and Douala (Cameroon) on a fairly regular schedule. Make enquiries at the Transcolmar office near the port or enquire at the port itself.

Getting Around

AIR

Air São Tomé e Príncipe has four flights per week between São Tomé and Príncipe (US$130 return).

ROAD

Many roads are sealed but there are a lot of potholes, so the going is slow. On the other hand, there are plenty of taxis and *colectivos* (share-taxis with a boxed 'A' on the front doors) which connect most towns on the island of São Tomé, departing from near the Feira do Ponto market in the capital. Fares are very reasonable: Trinidade US$0.40; São João dos Angolares US$1; and the waterfalls of São Nicolau US$6.50 return, including waiting time. Private rental for the whole day costs US$22. In the town itself, taxi fares are less than US$1, though it's almost as easy to walk.

Príncipe island's only form of public transport is a red minibus. Expect long waits unless you can find a lift in a private vehicle.

BOAT

There are ferries from São Tomé to Príncipe (11 hours, US$10) but the schedule depends on demand and they are not very frequent. Make enquiries at the customs building (Alfandega) at the port in São Tomé.

São Tomé

The capital, São Tomé, is a picturesque little place full of sadly neglected Portuguese colonial buildings but superbly maintained, shady, colourful parks and gardens.

Information

There is a tourist office (Centro de Informação e Turismo) next to the post office on Ave 12 de Julho.

The best travel agent is probably Mistral Voyages (☎/fax (012) 23 344), Praia do Lagarto, opposite the Marlin Beach Hotel. They offer a range of trips, including Príncipe, as well as car rental (from US$70 per day excluding petrol). English is spoken and a free leaflet is available.

Things to See

The **National Museum**, in the old **Fort São Sebastião** at the end of Ave Marginal 12

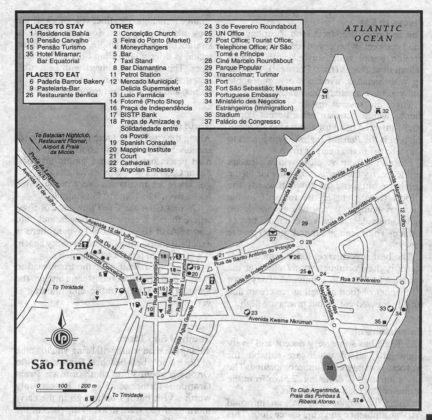

PLACES TO STAY
1 Residencia Bahía
10 Pensão Carvalho
15 Pensão Turismo
35 Hotel Miramar;
   Bar Equatorial

PLACES TO EAT
6 Paderia Barros Bakery
9 Pastelaria-Bar
26 Restaurante Benfica

OTHER
2 Conceição Church
3 Feira do Ponto (Market)
4 Moneychangers
5 Bar
7 Taxi Stand
8 Bar Diamantina
11 Petrol Station
12 Mercado Municipal;
   Delicia Supermarket
13 Luso Farmácia
14 Fotomé (Photo Shop)
16 Praça de Independência
17 BISTP Bank
18 Praça de Amizade e
   Solidariedade entre
   os Povos
19 Spanish Consulate
20 Mapping Institute
21 Court
22 Cathedral
23 Angolan Embassy

24 3 de Fevereiro Roundabout
25 UN Office
27 Post Office; Tourist Office;
   Telephone Office; Air São
   Tomé e Príncipe
28 Ciné Marcelo Roundabout
29 Parque Popular
30 Transcolmar; Turimar
31 Port
32 Fort São Sebastião; Museum
33 Portuguese Embassy
34 Ministério des Negocios
   Estrangeiros (Immigration)
36 Stadium
37 Palácio de Congresso

São Tomé

0   100   200 m

To Trinidade

To Bataclan Nightclub,
Restaurant Filomar,
Airport & Praia
da Micolo

To Trinidade

To Club Argentimõa,
Praia das Pombas &
Ribeira Afonso

Julho, has a good range of displays on agriculture, religion, handcrafts, juju and the slave trade. The latter spares no-one's sensibilities. There's also a section detailing the luxurious lifestyle led by the colonialist plantation owners. It's closed for renovation at present but, otherwise, is open on weekdays from 7 am to 3 pm and on Saturday from 8 am to noon.

Places to Stay

The best and cheapest hotel for independent travellers is the *Residencia Bahía* (near the Conceiçao Church) which charges US$8 for a large, clean room with mosquito nets and shared bath.

Also reasonable is the *Pensão Carvalho*, which is near the town centre on Ave Kwame Nkrumah and charges US$18 for a small room and US$20 for a larger room but the shared toilets are filthy.

Next in line is the nearby, family-run *Pensão Turismo* (☎ 22 340), on Avenida da Independência, which is quite popular and often full. The rooms, which cost US$25, have no fans but the communal baths have reliable running water and the restaurant serves excellent meals for US$3.

Places to Eat

The best place for street food is around the food market where you can find cheap French bread rolls stuffed with canned salami or sausages (from Portugal). Top this up with bananas, avocados or a pineapple and you have a satisfying meal.

There are several restaurants with fixed menus where you can get a decent Portuguese-inspired meal for about US$3. One of the best is the *Pensão Turismo* (see Places to Stay above) in the heart of town.

For an inexpensive place with a pleasant ambience, try the *Restaurant Filomar* on the northern outskirts of town towards the airport (turn right at the turn-off to the Encogas complex). You can eat inside or, better, outside on the refreshingly breezy terrace. The menu is limited but prices are low.

The best supermarket for imported food-stuffs is the Portuguese-run *Delicia* at the entrance to Mercado Municipal. They have all manner of food as well as ice cream and freshly brewed coffee but prices are high.

Entertainment

São Tomé has some very decent and lively nightclubs, all of which are suitable for women, possibly even unaccompanied. The city's top club is *Bataclan*, 2.5km from the centre on the road to the airport.

The *Club Argentimõa* has an informal African ambience and a big dance floor. This partially open-air place becomes lively from around 9.30 pm and it's open every night. The main problem is that it's 4km south of the town centre, so you need transport.

Getting Around

There are plenty of taxis. During the day you can always find taxis at the taxi stand just behind the market on Ave Conceição. A taxi to/from the airport costs US$1.

For car or 4WD rental, enquire at Mistral Voyages (see under Information above).

AROUND SÃO TOMÉ

The island is extremely beautiful. It's full of strange remnants of extinct volcanoes which look like huge pillars, some rising 600m straight up out of the jungle. The north of the island is drier with rolling hills and baobab trees. The coasts are ringed with beautiful, deserted beaches of white sand fringed with palms, and the water is turquoise.

North of São Tomé

Along the road north there is some stunning scenery but not too many good beaches. The road peters out into dense jungle just past Santa Catarina which is as far as taxis will go. There are minibuses every two to three hours from São Tomé to Guadalupe.

Go past Guadalupe to Praia das Conchas, where there's a reasonable beach, and onto **Lagoa Azul** (Blue Lagoon) where there is excellent snorkelling but only a rocky beach. It's possible to pitch a tent there.

From Lagoa Azul, take the truck road to Neves past the wrecked steamship on the rocks. There's little traffic and hitching is very slow.

South of São Tomé

Taking the road south will bring you to some of the island's best beaches. **Praia das Sete Ondas** is about 12km south of town. **Praia Grande** is further south again. It's certainly worth a visit but it's best to go in the early morning if you want to avoid the risks of the sky clouding over. Also worth seeing is the spectacular blowhole, **Boca de Inferno**, near Praia das Sete Ondas.

Minibuses to São João dos Angolares leave daily from near the market in São Tomé. There's also a truck which goes once a week all the way to Porto Alegre, taking all day to get there (the road is diabolical beyond Angolares). It leaves on Fridays from near the secondary school in São Tomé. Otherwise you can walk and hitch but allow two days for the return journey. Traffic is rare, and past Monte Mario the quality of the track limits vehicles to robust trucks and jeeps only. It is also possible to get to Porto Alegre by boat but the schedule is erratic so you should enquire at Transcolmar in São Tomé.

If you get as far as Porto Alegre it's possible to hire a motorised *pirogue* to take you to **Ilha das Rolas**, a small islet off the coast which straddles the equator, though otherwise there's not a great deal to see apart from the non-functioning lighthouse. If the weather is rough, don't go.

Trinidade

Trinidade is a pleasant little town to visit and from there you can continue to the well-known waterfall, **Cascadas da São Nicolau**. There are buses every two to three hours from São Tomé to Trinidade, or you can hitch. If hitching, stop on the edge of Trinidade at the Bar Diamantina. From here, hitch up past Monte Café to Pousada Boa Vista and then follow the painted green stones by the side of the track behind the hotel, La Pousada da Boa Vista, which will eventually lead you (after about 3km) to the Cascadas da São Nicolau. There are steps down to the pool below but the water is chilly.

Cheap lunches of fried fish and bananas can be found at the *Café da Manha* on the main plaza in Trinidade next to the market.

Príncipe

This is a very small island and you can walk anywhere in a day. You'll inevitably attract a lot of attention from the local people, who may follow you and expect a tip for their services, but they're all very friendly. There are only some 12km of road on the whole island.

The island's capital is **Santo António** which is about the size of a large European village. The architecture is similar to that of São Tomé but the whole town is in even greater need of repair.

Places to Stay & Eat

You'll be told that the best place to stay and eat is the *Pensão Residencial Palhota* (☎ 51 060), run by the island's ex-governor, but we have had a few bad reports about this place (theft and intimidation). The rooms have their own bathrooms and are air-con but they're expensive at US$40/60 for singles/ doubles and meals (ordered in advance) are over the top at US$10.

In addition to the Palhota, there are the *Pensão Romar* from US$4, with food available by prior arrangement) and the *Pensão Arca de Noé* which is also reasonably priced.

Senegal

Senegal is the buzz place of West Africa – from its hip music and its sophistication to its fantastic capital, Dakar. Not surprisingly, it gets more visitors than any other country in West Africa. Most are package tourists, confined mainly to the string of top-quality hotels on the Atlantic shore, but Senegal is also popular with independent travellers.

Facts about the Country

HISTORY
Neolithic tools found in Senegal indicate that the country has been occupied for 15,000 years or more. In the 8th century Senegal was part of the empire of Ghana. As this empire waned, the Djolof kingdom arose to flourish during the 13th and 14th centuries, in the area between the Senegal River and modern-day Dakar.

By the early 1500s Portuguese traders had made contact with the coastal kingdoms, which was to last until the mid-16th century. They were displaced by the British, French and Dutch, who hoped to gain control of St-Louis and the Île de Gorée, strategic points where slaves bound for the Americas could be collected. St-Louis was secured by the French in 1659.

By the end of the 19th century, France controlled all of Senegal, and Dakar was built as the administrative centre. As early as 1848 Senegal had sent a deputy to the French parliament, but it wasn't until 1914 that the first African deputy, Blaise Diagne, was elected. He was followed by a new generation of black politicians led by Lamine Guèye and Leopold Senghor.

In the run-up to independence, Senegal joined French Sudan to form the Federation of Mali. The federation gained independence in 1960, but disintegrated two months later. Senegal then became a republic under the presidency of Senghor. At the end of 1980,

REPUBLIC OF SENEGAL
Area: 196,192 sq km
Population: 9.1 million
Population Growth Rate: 2.7%
Capital: Dakar
Head of State: President Abdou Diouf
Official Language: French
Currency: West African CFA franc
Exchange Rate: CFA 575 = US$1
Per Capita GNP: US$450
Inflation: 35%
Time: GMT/UTC

Highlights
- Lazy days and partying nights in the cosmopolitan city of Dakar
- A boat trip to the historic Île de Gorée
- Hiking in the Casamance region and the Basse Casamance National Park
- The beaches of the Petite Côte and the Siné-Saloum Delta

he stepped down and his place was taken by Abdou Diouf (who was soon faced by a string of mounting crises).

In 1989 a minor incident on the Senegal-Mauritania border led to serious riots in both countries, in which many people died. Mauritania deported thousands of Senegalese (killing hundreds in the process), while Senegal retaliated with more of the same. The border was closed, and diplomatic relations were broken off until April 1992.

In the early 1990s there were serious

SENEGAL

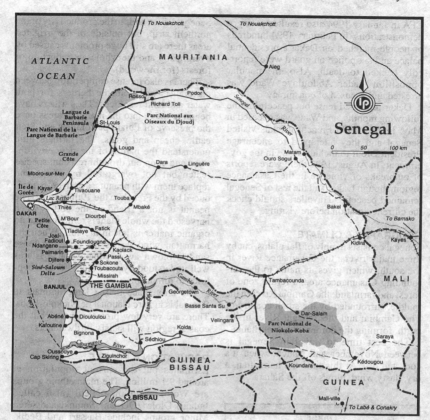

clashes in the Casamance region between the army and separatist rebels. Quite apart from the suffering caused to the local people, the fighting severely affected Senegal's tourist industry. This compounded Senegal's already desperate financial situation.

More violence occurred in Casamance and elsewhere in early 1993 following elections in which Diouf was elected president for a third term. After long negotiations, a cease-fire was declared in July that year, and in the following months peace returned to Casamance. By early 1994 the first tourists had also begun to return.

In April 1996 the Democratic Forces of Casamance (MFDC) boycotted talks to be held in Ziguinchor. The separatist group's secretary general, Augustin Diamacounce, under house arrest, apparently had little influence over the rebels in the bush (who were led by Salif Sadio).

Meanwhile, in other parts of the country, things were still far from peaceful. The government introduced a number of austerity measures, leading to a one day general strike in early September and sporadic outbreaks of unrest in Dakar and other cities during the following months. The devaluation of the

SENEGAL

CFA in January 1994 also resulted in angry demonstrations. In February 1994 hundreds of people marched on Dakar's presidential palace and six police on guard were reportedly hacked to death. Also, the popular opposition leader Abdoulaye Wade was arrested and accused of conspiracy.

Dakar remained tense but peaceful in the following months, and Wade was released in May. In July 1996 French officials visited Senegal and they attempted to encourage President Diouf to include Wade in the government. In August 1997 there were reports of outbreaks of violence in the Casamance region, though Dakar and the rest of Senegal remained peaceful. Travellers should check the current situation before visiting.

GEOGRAPHY & CLIMATE
Senegal consists mainly of flat plains, cut by three major rivers: the Casamance River in the south, which gives its name to the surrounding Casamance area, a fertile zone of forest and farmland; the Gambia River in the middle, surrounded by the small country of The Gambia; and the Senegal River in the north, forming the border with Mauritania.

The best time to travel in Senegal is between November and March, when it's cool and dry. At this time the harmattan, a dry, dusty wind, blows off the Sahara.

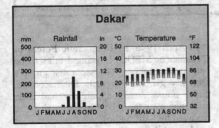

ECOLOGY & ENVIRONMENT
Desertification is the greatest problem facing Senegal, especially in the north of the country. The construction of dams, such as the Manantali and Diama dams on the Senegal River, adds to the productivity of the northern strip, but outside of the irrigated areas there are still huge problems caused by overgrazing and the wholesale reduction of forests (for firewood).

There is also intense competition between pastoralists and nomadic herders for both water and land resources. The farmers have begun to move into the marginal areas once the preserve of Fulani pastoralists and their cattle, sheep and goats. The farmers little understand the nature of the new environment and chop out drought resistant species (eaten but not overgrazed by stock) and replace them with peanuts, a cash crop introduced by the French in the 19th century. The peanut is not a friend of the soil – when harvested the whole plant is removed and no organic matter is left in the soil. When the harmattan wind lashes the soil, the loose sand is blown away. Meanwhile, pastures well understood by the Fulani herders continue to diminish.

The only place to see large animals in Senegal is in Parc National de Niokolo-Koba. There are very few protected areas, but the coastal region will satisfy birdwatchers.

POPULATION & PEOPLE
Estimates put the current population at around 9.1 million. The main ethnic groups are Wolof, Mandinka, Peul (also called Fulani), Diola (JOU-lah), Soninké and Sérèr. Minor groups include Bassari and Bédik. There's also a population of Maurs (from Mauritania), but much smaller than before the crisis of 1989.

RELIGION
Over 80% of the population is Muslim, the remainder being Christians and practitioners of traditional religions. Senegal has its own unique version of Islam that blends magic with a reliance of the priesthood and veneration of saints. Virtually all adherents belong to one of five brotherhoods, the two principal ones being the Mourides, centred in Touba and Diourbel, and the Tidjanes, centred in Kaolack and Tivaouane.

West African Music

Travellers to West Africa cannot help but be overwhelmed by the fantastic variety of music available in nearly all of the countries in this part of the world.

There is a long musical tradition in West Africa that forms an integral part of the cultures of the region and is now being enjoyed throughout the world – thanks to the recognition of a number of West African musicians, such as Salif Keita (and the now legendary Rail Band), Baaba Maal, Anjelique Kidjo, Youssou N'dour, Mory Kanté and Ali Farka Touré (and the western musicians who have entered into a diverse combination of western and African styles and instrumentation with them).

While the world is more familiar with the modern pop compositions emanating from West Africa, the locals are more familiar with the polyrhythmic and polyphonic traditional music created on instruments which are fashioned from materials found close at hand – the *djembe*, *tama* and *sabar* drums, the xylophone-like *balafon*, the reed flute, the sophisticated 21-stringed harp-lute known as the *kora* and the rarer lute-type *kontingo* (thought to be the precursor to the banjo). The creation of much of the music in this part of the world is the domain of a social grouping known as *jalis* (referred to in French as *griots*), almost a wandering minstrel caste who combine the functions of entertainers, historians and genealogists.

Travellers may initially find this traditional music hard to swallow, with melodies and rhythms rising and falling, often simultaneously and in patterns a mite cacaphonic to the western ear. But if they are lucky enough to witness a celebration in an African village – invariably accompanied by music – they will soon be swept away in a wave of appreciation. In short time, pressings of traditional music will sit on their shelves alongside the more easily digestible pop styles.

The pop styles, which mix traditional music with western instruments such as brass and guitar, are probably the best introduction for a westerner. The *mbalax* of Senegal has been popularised overseas and uses the sabar drum in its leading rhythmic role. Afro-Beat fuses African music, soul and jazz, and Juju music, also based on drumming, has its base in Nigerian Yoruba culture. And the enduring *highlife*, originally from Ghana and Sierra Leone, combines traditional African instruments and melodies with just about every western influence imaginable, from gospel to brass. ■

LANGUAGE

French is the official language (see the Language Appendix for useful French phrases). Wolof is the most widely spoken African language.

Facts for the Visitor

VISAS

Visas for stays of up to 90 days are required by all foreigners, except nationals of Denmark, France, Germany, Ireland, Italy, Luxembourg, the Netherlands, the UK and the USA.

It's hard for New Zealanders to get visas; embassies (in Africa and elsewhere) refer requests to Dakar, and the process can take six months.

Other Visas

In Dakar, you can get visas to other African countries (they require one to four photos).

Burkina Faso, Chad & Togo
  The French embassy issues visas for these countries. They cost US$6 and take 24 hours to issue.
Cape Verde
  Visas cost US$10 and take 48 hours to issue.
Côte d'Ivoire
  Visas cost US$10.
The Gambia
  Visas cost US$8. If you come early, you can get the visa by 2.30 pm, otherwise within 24 hours. Seven-day visas to The Gambia are available at the border, but they cost US$36! These are renewable and cost about US$5 (50 dalasi).
Guinea
  Visas cost US$40 and are issued in 24 hours (you need a letter of introduction from your embassy).
Guinea-Bissau
  Visas cost US$20 and are issued in 24 hours. At the consulate in Ziguinchor they are issued on the spot for US$10.
Mali
  Visas cost US$10 and take 48 hours to issue.
Mauritania
  Visas cost US$12 and are issued on the spot (bring a letter of introduction from your embassy).

SENEGAL

Niger
> The embassy has closed but may reopen in the future. Visas used to cost US$15 and were valid for a one month stay.

EMBASSIES
Senegalese Embassies
In West Africa, there are embassies in Cape Verde, Côte d'Ivoire, The Gambia, Guinea-Bissau, Guinea, Mali, Niger, Nigeria and Sierra Leone.

Elsewhere, Senegalese embassies are found in Belgium, Canada, France, Germany, Italy, Switzerland, the UK and the USA. There are also consulates in Australia and Austria.

Foreign Embassies in Senegal
Countries with diplomatic missions in Dakar (and in the Point E and Mermoz areas, 4 to 5km north-west of the city centre via bus No 7 or 12) include:

Canada
> 45 Blvd de la République (☎ 23 9290)

Cape Verde
> 3 Blvd el Haji Djily Mbaye, formerly Ave Pinet Laprade (☎ 21 3936)

Côte d'Ivoire
> 2 Ave Albert Sarraut, one block south of Marché Kermel (☎ 21 3473)

France
> 1 Rue Assane Ndoye, near the Novotel (☎ 23 9181)

The Gambia
> 11 Rue de Thiong, a block north of Ave Pompidou, Ponty (☎ 21 4476)

Germany
> 20 Ave Pasteur (☎ 22 2519)

Guinea
> Rue 7, north of the Nigerian embassy, Point E (☎ 24 8606)

Guinea-Bissau
> Rue 6, near the Guinean embassy, Point E (☎ 24 5922)
>
> consulate: close to the Hôtel du Tourisme, Ziguinchor (☎ 91 1046)

Mali
> 46 Blvd de la République (☎ 23 4893)

Mauritania
> In Mermoz, to the west off Route d'Ouakam, just before the intersection with Corniche-Ouest, at the junction marked by a large Air Afrique sign, then follow signs to the Nigerian Residence. It is an unmarked private house.

Nigeria
> Rue 1, a block north of Route d'Ouakam, Point E (☎ 24 6922)

Sierra Leone
> Clinique Bleu at 13 Rue Castor

UK
> 20 Rue du Dr Guillet, one block north of Hôpital Le Dantec (☎ 23 7392; fax 23 2766)

USA
> Ave Jean XXIII (☎ 23 3424; fax 22 2991)

MONEY
| US$1 | = | CFA 575 |
| FFr1 | = | CFA 100 |

The unit of currency is the West African CFA franc. There is no black market for CFA, and no currency declaration forms.

Most banks are open weekdays, typically from 8.30 to 11.30 am and 2.30 to 4.30 pm (they are closed on Friday afternoon). On Saturday mornings in Dakar, the CBAO is open until 11 am (it accepts MasterCard for cash advances). The bank at the airport is supposedly open until midnight.

Cashing travellers' cheques is easy in Dakar, but difficult elsewhere if they are not denominated in French francs. The golden rule in Senegal, as for most of West Africa, is to carry French francs, especially in cash (as CFA is permanently pegged to the franc).

POST & COMMUNICATIONS
Sending letters from Senegal is expensive. The poste restante in Dakar is slow, unreliable, holds letters for only 30 days and charges US$0.75 per letter.

The telephone service is reasonable, and international connections are good. Dakar has private *télécentres*, usually open until late evening, for phone calls, telexes and faxes. The country code for Senegal is 221; there are no area codes.

DANGERS & ANNOYANCES
Dakar has the worst reputation of any city in West Africa for thieves. The areas around Place de l'Indépendance, the markets and along Ave Pompidou (Ponty) have the most pickpockets. Never let a group of people ('vendors') surround you, as you are being

set up to be robbed – ignore them and keep walking. At night, it's a matter of common sense: stay away from dark alleys and the beaches. Single women should never wear expensive jewellery, watches or 'bum bags'.

Of less concern are the hustlers and 'guides' who pester tourists, usually operating in the same areas as the thieves. A favourite trick is the 'Don't you remember me from ...' line – if you don't remember the person talking to you, tell them to get lost.

Above all, realise that the locals are subjected to these hassles daily but seem to manage. Don't let acute paranoia cloud your opportunity to meet the beautiful Senegalese – among the friendliest people in the world.

Some of the staff at Leopold Senghor (Yoff) international airport have customs identity cards which look authentic – they will produce them and then usher you to customs, where you will be searched. For the privilege of being searched when a 'No' to the question of 'Anything to declare?' usually gets you through without hassles, these 'police' will want a hefty tip. It is hard to ignore them with their IDs – just watch your luggage closely and when the search is over pack up and ignore them.

PUBLIC HOLIDAYS
Public holidays in Senegal are: 1 January, 4 April (Independence Day), Good Friday, Easter Monday, 1 May, 15 August, 1 November, 25 December and variable Islamic holidays. (See the Regional Facts for the Visitor chapter for more information on Islamic holidays.)

ACCOMMODATION
Senegal has a very wide range of places to stay, from the top-class hotels on the coastal resorts to dirty doss-houses in Dakar, plus pleasant guesthouses *(campements)* in the rural areas. All hotels and campements charge US$1 per person tourist tax. This may or may not be included in the price. Some hotels charge by the room, and it makes no difference to the price (apart from the tourist tax) if you're alone or with somebody.

FOOD & DRINKS
Senegal has some of the finest cuisine in West Africa. Common dishes include: *tiéboudienne* (chey-BOU-jen), rice baked in a thick sauce of fish and vegetables with pimiento and tomato sauce; *poulet yassa* or *poisson yassa*, marinated and grilled chicken or fish; *mafé*, peanut-based stew; and *bassi-salété*, millet covered with vegetables and meat.

Senegalese beer is also good. Gazelle comes in half-litre bottles and costs between US$1 and US$2. Flag is a stronger brew: 330 ml bottles cost US$1 in a cheap place, up to US$3 or more in posh bars and hotels (where they wouldn't dream of offering Gazelle). The reddish *bissap*, made from bissap flowers, is a popular non-alcoholic drink.

Getting There & Away

AIR
When flying between Europe and Senegal you have a wide choice of airlines, including Sabena and Alitalia. One-way fares to/from London start at US$480 and returns are from US$690, depending on the season and your length of stay. For a one-way flight back to Europe, Nouvelles Frontières (☎ 23 3434), on Ave Pompidou near the Ali Baba snack bar, sometimes has cheap seats on charter flights for around US$350 (around FFr 2000).

For flights between Dakar and other destinations in West Africa there's a wide choice, including Bamako (US$245 one way), Cape Verde (US$460 return to Santiago), Niamey (via Ouagadougou, US$460 one way), Nouakchott (US$125 one way), Banjul (US$70 one way), Abidjan (US$370 one way) and Bissau (US$125 one way). Most airline offices are on or near the Place de l'Indépendance in Dakar, but it can be easier to use a travel agency; compare prices before buying.

Departure tax is US$15, but most air fares already have that included in the price.

LAND
The Gambia

Senegal surrounds The Gambia, but Senegalese vehicles are not allowed to cross the border, so you have to change. (Only vehicles going through The Gambia on the Trans-Gambia Highway can cross the border, but you can't end your journey in The Gambia.)

Dakar to Banjul From Dakar to the border at Karang costs US$5 by minibus and US$10 by Peugeot 504. Taxis shuttle between the two border posts, or you can walk, and there are pick-ups (US$0.50) to the ferry at Barra which crosses to Banjul (US$0.30, last ferry 7 pm). The journey takes six to eight hours depending on your luck with connections and the ferry.

Ziguinchor to Banjul From Ziguinchor to the southern border with The Gambia costs US$4 by *taxi-brousse* (bush taxi), and from there to Serekunda it's US$3 (in Gambian dalasi or CFA).

Tambacounda to Basse Santa Su Taxi-brousse go to Velingara for US$4. From there pick-ups run to Basse Santa Su (US$1); have your passport stamped by immigration officials at the police station in Basse.

Guinea

Taxi-brousse from Dakar to Labé charge US$55 for the whole trip, although most people do this in stages, breaking at Tambacounda and Koundara. Trucks trundle from Tambacounda to Koundara or Labé, and cost around US$20.

The whole trip between Dakar and Labé takes between 25 and 35 hours. During the wet season the stretch between Koundara and Labé is very slow or impassable as the trucks tear up the road, causing the other vehicles to get stuck.

Guinea-Bissau

Taxi-brousse leave every morning from Ziguinchor to Bissau via São Domingos and Ingore. The road is paved but crosses two rivers, which can cause delays; start early. It costs US$8, plus US$0.20 for each ferry.

The coast route via Canchungo is not viable as there is no longer a ferry between Cacheu and São Domingos (the *Cacheu* is currently beached).

Mali

Train The Dakar to Bamako express train is the best way to travel overland to Mali, as the road is very bad and traffic virtually nonexistent. The train departs from Dakar on Wednesday and Saturday at around 8 am, and takes 30 to 35 hours. Large, comfortable 1st-class seats can be reserved in advance; 2nd class is more crowded with less comfortable seating. From Dakar 1st/2nd-class fares are US$40/30 to Kayes and US$67/50 to Bamako, and *couchettes* (two-person compartments) cost US$114 per person from Dakar to Bamako. There's also an 'omnibus' express on Sunday to Kayes for US$36/19. You can buy tickets the day before the train departs. To be sure of a seat in 2nd class, get to the train about two hours before it leaves. The train has a bar-restaurant car, and you can buy cheap food at stations along the way.

At each border post you have to get your passport stamped. It may be taken by an inspector on the train, but you still have to collect it yourself by going to the office at the border post. Nobody tells you this. So if your passport is taken, ask where and when you have to go to collect it. You may need a stamp at the police station in Kayes too, but this seems fairly arbitrary. Watch out for thieves on the train, especially at night.

Mauritania

Taxi-brousse run regularly from Dakar to Rosso (the border) for US$14. A *pirogue* (dugout canoe) across the river will cost you US$0.50 per person. The trip from Rosso to Nouakchott costs US$10. The whole journey can be done in a day if you leave early.

SEA
The Gambia

Some intrepid travellers get rides on ocean-going pirogues from Dakar and Ziguinchor to Banjul in The Gambia. There are no set schedules or prices, and you should note that these boats are notoriously unsafe.

Getting Around

AIR
Air Senegal has daily flights from Dakar to Ziguinchor (continuing to Cap Skiring four times weekly), and there are weekly flights to Tambacounda and Kédougou. The motto: confirm, and then confirm again.

ROAD
The main routes between Dakar, Kaolack, Ziguinchor and other large towns are covered by buses *(cars)* carrying 30 to 40 people, and good quality minibuses *(petit cars*, between 15 and 30 seats). On many routes you also find more rustic minibuses (sometimes rather misleadingly called *car rapides)*. They are battered, slow, crowded and worth avoiding if possible.

Your other option for long-distance travel is a taxi-brousse. On the main routes these are usually Peugeot 504s with three rows of seats: safe and reliable. On rural routes taxi-brousse are pick-ups (sometimes called *bachés)* seating about 12 people on benches. Fares are reasonable. For example, by taxi-brousse across the country from Dakar to St-Louis is US$7, and to Ziguinchor it's US$12. Buses cost about a third less than taxi-brousse, and minibuses are somewhere in-between. There's normally a small extra charge for luggage (10% of the bill).

TRAIN
For travel around Senegal trains are slower than road transport, but 2nd class is usually cheaper. Trains run daily to St-Louis and Kaolack, and also three times weekly to Tambacounda (and on to Bamako in Mali). For more information, see the Dakar Getting There & Away section later in this chapter.

BOAT
The SENTRAM ferry MV *Joola* plies between Dakar and Ziguinchor (via Carab-

ane Island) twice weekly, leaving Dakar on Tuesday and Friday, and Ziguinchor on Thursday and Sunday. Schedules often change and departure times depend on the tide, so check at the port. The journey takes about 20 hours. Deck class is US$9, while comfortable reclining seats in 1st class are US$18. One and two-person cabins, with bathroom, cost US$45 to US$55 per person.

ORGANISED TOURS
For tours around the country, there's no Kenya or Tanzania-style budget market here. Many companies require a minimum of eight passengers, making it hard for independent travellers, and prices are not cheap, eg around US$55 per person for a one day tour to Joal-Fadiout, US$130 for three days to St-Louis and US$300 for five days to the Casamance or Niokolo-Koba. A good company to get information from is Inter Tourisme (☎ 22 4529), at 3 Allées Delmas in Dakar.

Dakar

Dakar gets mixed reviews from travellers. On the positive side, it's a modern, spacious city, with a temperate climate and many interesting things to see and do (such as good beaches, the Île de Gorée, vibrant nightlife and equally vibrant Dakarois). But other people hate it: the cost of living is very high, and hustlers who won't take no for an answer can ruin a walk around town. If you don't like Dakar, it's easy enough to get away, with daily transport to all parts of the country. But on no account miss it – those that love it end up settling here. Our writer rates it as one of the 20 great cities in the world!

Orientation
The 'Place' (Place de l'Indépendance) is the city's heart. From here, major streets lead in all directions, including Ave Pompidou, the main street, which leads west to Marché Sandaga. From here, Ave Lamine Guèye goes north to Gare Routière Pompiers and the Autoroute, leading inland.

SENEGAL

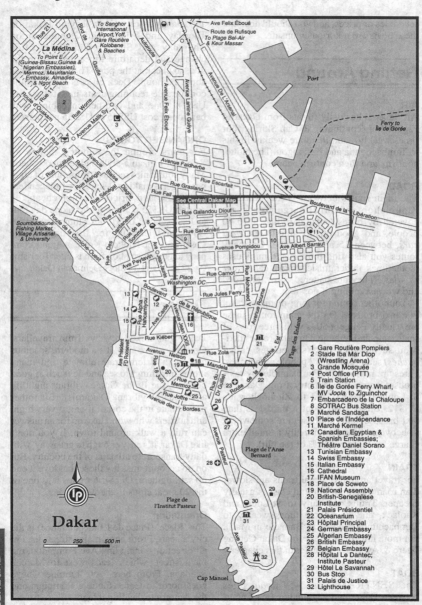

Dakar

0   250   500 m

1 Gare Routière Pompiers
2 Stade Iba Mar Diop
   (Wrestling Arena)
3 Grande Mosquée
4 Post Office (PTT)
5 Train Station
6 Île de Gorée Ferry Wharf,
   MV Joola to Ziguinchor
7 Embarcadero de la Chaloupe
8 SOTRAC Bus Station
9 Marché Sandaga
10 Place de l'Indépendance
11 Marché Kermel
12 Canadian, Egyptian &
   Spanish Embassies;
   Théâtre Daniel Sorano
13 Tunisian Embassy
14 Swiss Embassy
15 Italian Embassy
16 Cathedral
17 IFAN Museum
18 Place de Soweto
19 National Assembly
20 British-Senegalese
   Institute
21 Palais Présidentiel
22 Oceanarium
23 Hôpital Principal
24 German Embassy
25 Algerian Embassy
26 British Embassy
27 Belgian Embassy
28 Hôpital Le Dantec;
   Institute Pasteur
29 Hôtel Le Savannah
30 Bus Stop
31 Palais de Justice
32 Lighthouse

Information

Tourist Office The tourist office has closed; consult the free magazines *Le Dakarois* or *Panda*, available from major hotels. The Librairie aux Quatre Vents on Rue Félix Faure is the best place in West Africa to choose from a vast range of books which will supplement your travel guides.

Money On the western side of the Place are three banks, CBAO, BICIS and Citibank. (For hassle-free MasterCard cash advances go to the CBAO.) Travel agencies may change French francs cash (and only take a small commission) and large hotels will change cash or travellers' cheques. Remember, French francs rule here.

Post & Communications The main post office (PTT) is on Blvd el Haji Djily Mbaye (formerly Ave Pinet Laprade), two blocks north of Marché Kermel; it is open Monday to Saturday from 7 am to 7 pm. There's also a small PTT at the east end of Ave Pompidou.

For phone calls, SONATEL (Senegal's internal phone service) has its city centre offices on Rue Wagane Diouf and Blvd de la République (which is open from 7 am to 11 pm). There are also many private télécentres.

Travel Agencies Senegal Tours (☎ 23 4040) on Place de l'Indépendance is an American Express (Amex) representative and makes flight reservations and sells tours. Also recommended for general booking and tours are SOCOPAO Voyages (☎ 23 1001), 47 Rue Albert Sarraut; Nouvelle Frontières (☎ 23 3434), 1 Blvd de la République; and Sénégambie Voyages (☎ 21 6831) at 42 Rue Victor Hugo.

Cultural Centres The American Cultural Center is south-west of the Place, the French Cultural Centre is on the corner of Rue Carnot and Rue Gomis, and the British-Senegalese Institute is on Rue de 18 Juin, two blocks west of Place de Soweto. They all have libraries and show films.

Things to See & Do

The **Museum of the Institut Fondamental d'Afrique Noir** (IFAN) on Place de Soweto was renovated in 1994, and has a collection of masks, statues, musical instruments and agricultural implements from all over West Africa. It is open daily from 8 am to 2 pm and 3 to 6 pm (closed Monday); entry is US$0.50. A return visit, after witnessing West Africa first hand, is rewarding.

The white **Palais Présidentiel**, five short blocks south of the Place along Ave Roume, dates from 1906 and is surrounded by sumptuous gardens (and the resplendent guards occasionally permit photos).

Dakar has two major markets. **Marché Kermel**, east of the Place towards the port, burnt down in 1993, so now the stalls are out in the surrounding streets, selling mainly fruit, clothing, fabrics and souvenirs. The larger **Marché Sandaga**, on the junction of Ave Pompidou and Ave Lamine Guèye, has more fruit and fewer souvenirs, but for visitors the choice of fabric is a real attraction.

For souvenirs, the **Village Artisanal** on the Corniche-Ouest caters for the tourist trade, but prices are high and the work is nothing special. The plus is that it is next to the fishing village of **Soumbédioune**, where pirogues beach at dusk.

Out of the city centre is the **Grande Mosquée** (built in 1964), with its landmark minaret that is floodlit at night. The mosque is closed to the public, but it's worth coming here anyway because the area around it, called **La Médina**, while not picturesque, is a bustling place contrasting sharply with the sophisticated high-rise city centre.

Plage Bel-Air (Tahiti Plage), a beach 2km north-east of the train station, is fenced and has a bar and sailboards for rent, although the water is not particularly clean. It costs US$1 entry. At the other beaches near central Dakar you run a high risk of being robbed. Better are the beaches at **N'Gor**, 13km north-west of Dakar (and the nearby Pointe des Almadies) and **Yoff**, which has a cheap campement (see Places to Stay).

Central Dakar

0   125   250 m

Places to Stay

When you arrive in Dakar you should have already decided on your first night's accommodation – you can hail a taxi at the airport or train station and go directly there. Dakar is no place to walk around with a backpack.

The cheapest hotel in the city centre is the *Hôtel Mon Logis* (☎ 21 8525) which is on Rue Lamine Guèye, between Rue Bourgi and Rue Galandou Diouf, and charges US$11 for grubby rooms. It's down an alley, upstairs and unmarked.

Next in line is the *Hôtel du Prince* (☎ 21 1855) at 49 Rue Raffenal, where rooms are

US$14, but there are often problems with the water pressure and it's not terribly clean. Both of these hotels are in a part of town which is dark and not safe at night.

Better value is the *Hôtel Provençal* (☎ 22 1069), near the Place at 17 Rue Malenfant, where good singles/doubles with fans cost US$18/20. Upstairs rooms are quiet, airy and have washbasins, and the showers are cleaned daily.

Also good is the *Hôtel du Marché* (☎ 21 5771), 3 Rue Parent near Marché Kermel, which has a lovely back patio. It charges US$14/16 for a room with shared/private bathroom.

PLACES TO STAY
1 Hôtel Le Grasland
2 Hôtel Mon Logis
5 Hôtel du Prince
6 Hôtel Al Baraka
7 Hôtel Continental Annexe
9 Hôtel Continental
10 Hôtel Farid
13 Hôtel Provençal
21 Hôtel du Midi
23 Hôtel Oceanic
31 Hôtel Ganalé; Restaurant '?' 1
48 Hôtel de l'Indépendance
53 Hôtel Nina
55 Hôtel Croix du Sud
60 Hôtel Teranga (Sofitel)
66 Hôtel du Marché
68 Novotel
69 Hôtel du Plateau
73 Hôtel Alafifa
75 Hôtel St-Louis Sun
82 Auberge Rouge
91 Hôtel Miramar
94 Hôtel Lagon II

PLACES TO EAT
3 La Pizzalina
4 La Pizzeria
8 Touba Restaurant (formerly Chez Ousmane)
14 Supermarket
18 Restaurant Darou Salam
19 Tricontin Snacks
20 Restaurant Angkor
24 Le Dagorne
29 Cyber-Café Metissicana
32 La Plaza
33 Mateo Pizza
34 Chawarma La Brioche; Cinéma Plaza

35 Keur N'deye
36 Chez Loutcha
37 Ali Baba Snack Bar
39 Le Sam-Son; Restaurant '?' 2
42 Café de Paris
43 Mic Mac
45 Restaurant Chez Nanette
54 Restaurant La Pergola
62 Score Supermarket
64 Restaurant Le Sarraut; Le Café Théâtre du Kermel
76 Le Hanoi
79 Touba Restaurant
80 Gargotte Diarama
85 Ranch Filfili Supermarket
86 Le Bambou
88 Restaurant Le New Bilboquet
93 Restaurant-Bar Lagon I

OTHER
11 Chez Vous Nightclub
12 Librairie Clairafrique (Bookshop)
15 Inter Tourisme (Tours)
16 Dakar Autotours
17 Austrian & Japanese Embassies
22 Main Post Office (PTT); Poste Restante
25 Marché Kermel
26 Cape Verde Embassy
27 Marché Sandaga
28 Air Guinée
30 Le Pacific Nightclub
38 Orisha; Other Art Shops
40 Chez Claudette Nightclub

41 The Gambia Embassy
44 Bar Ponty
46 Quarante-Deux (Africa Star) Nightclub
47 Small Post Office (PTT)
49 CBAO (for MasterCard)
50 Sabena, M'boup Voyages; CBAO Bank
51 Citibank; Aeroflot; Travel Booking
52 BICIS Bank
56 SOCOPAO-Voyages; Air France
57 Senegal Tours (Amex Agent)
58 Air Afrique
59 Cinéma Le Paris
61 Air Senegal; Air Bissau
63 Safari-Evasion (Tours)
65 Côte d'Ivoire Embassy
67 French Embassy
70 Malian Embassy
71 Cathedral
72 Le Play-Club Nightclub
74 Les Tropiques
77 Black & White Nightclub
78 French Cultural Centre
81 Librairie aux Quatres Vents (Bookshop)
83 King's Club
84 Métropolis Nightclub
87 Keur Samba Jazz Nightclub
89 Nigeria Airways
90 Ethiopian Airlines
92 American Cultural Centre
95 US Embassy
96 Netherlands Embassy
97 IFAN Museum
98 Place de Soweto
99 National Assembly
100 Palais Présidentiel

More expensive but good value is the *Auberge Rouge* (☎ 21 5598), on the corner of Rue Blanchot (ex-Moussé Diop) and Rue Jules Ferry, with clean rooms for US$20, including breakfast. The homely *Hôtel Oceanic* (☎ 22 2044), 9 Rue du Thann, has air-con rooms with attached bathroom for US$20.

Two mid-range places worth a mention are the *Hôtel du Plateau* (☎ 23 4420), at 62 Rue Jules Ferry, where comfortable rooms are US$30, and the more attractive *Hôtel*

St-Louis Sun (☎ 22 2570), at 68 Rue Félix Faure, with rooms for about the same price.

Outside the city centre, near the airport in Yoff village and only 100m from a beach, is the *Campement le Poulagou* (☎ 20 2347), which charges US$18 per person for bed & breakfast or US$28 full board. To get there from the city centre take bus No 7 or 8 to Yoff; it is on the end of a small road off the main road. In the same area is the *Campement Adama Diop* (☎ 20 1367), with rooms for US$7.

SENEGAL

If you'll be in Dakar for a week or more, think about staying on the Île de Gorée, thus avoiding the hassles and high prices of Dakar (see the Around Dakar section).

Places to Eat

On many street corners are stalls selling bread with various fillings – butter, chocolate spread, mayonnaise, sardines. Next to these, particularly along Rue Assane Ndoye, women cook rice and sauce in big pots, and serve meals for around US$1.

One of central Dakar's cheapest restaurants is *Gargotte Diarama* at 56 Rue Félix Faure, with most dishes around US$1. *Touba Restaurant*, just around the corner on Rue Gomis, has mafé, poisson riz or chicken from around US$2.

Lebanese chawarmas are sold throughout the city for about US$2. A good place is *Chawarma La Brioche* on Ave Pompidou, four blocks west of the Place. The chawarmas (and hamburgers) are just as good at the *Ali Baba* and *Mic Mac* snack bars across the street, but you pay a bit extra for the more classy surroundings.

For African food in pleasant surroundings, the best value places in this range are the *Restaurant '?' 1*, on Rue Assane Ndoye, just west of Rue Gomis, and *'?' 2* (ask for 'Point d'Intérogatif'), on the corner of Rue Assane Ndoye and Rue Mohammed V, with good African dishes from US$2.

Dakar also has a wide range of smarter restaurants. A small sample of the more reasonably priced ones follows: *Keur N'deye*, 68 Rue Vincens, with Senegalese specialities (and occasional kora musicians) from US$4 and a set menu for US$8; the popular *Chez Loutcha*, 101 Rue Blanchot (Moussé Diop), with 'Euro-Africaine' dishes from around US$6; *La Pizzeria*, 47 Rue Bourgi, with half/whole pizzas at US$5/8; *Restaurant Le Sarraut*, east of the Place on Ave Albert Sarraut, with a US$9 three-course French menu; and *Le Sam-Son*, 61 Rue Assane Ndoye, and *Le Hanoi*, two blocks further west on the corner of Rue Carnot and Rue Gomis, both with Vietnamese dishes for around US$7.

A favourite, not for its food or ambience but for its friendly staff, is *Café de Paris* on Ave Pompidou. Another great place to eat (especially barbecued meat) is *Cyber-Cafe Metissacana*, an Internet cafe at 30 Rue de Thiong. There is a downstairs restaurant, an upstairs open-air patio and a computer-room bar.

Entertainment

Bars The best known bar in town is the popular but somewhat disreputable *Bar Ponty* on Ave Pompidou, although this is not a place for budget travellers (small Flag beers are US$3) or for the shy (prostitutes cruise for business here).

A better place is the *Bar Gorée*, almost opposite the Gorée ferry wharf, which has cheap beer, snacks and music. It's popular with sailors and anyone who wants a good time without busting the bank. Trouble is rare, but it's not a place for the faint-hearted.

A favourite is the atmospheric *bar* at the rear of the Village Artisanal (see Things to See & Do); the beers aren't cheap but views of Soumbédioune fishing village are priceless.

Nightclubs Dakar is one of the best cities in West Africa for live music, representative of the whole region. (See the West African Music boxed story earlier in this chapter.) In the heart of town is *Keur Samba Jazz* at 13 Rue Jules Ferry, a smart jazz club. Another popular place is the flashy, hot and crowded *Club Kilimandjaro*, on the Corniche-Ouest by the Village Artisanal.

The *Tamango Bar* in the Point E area has good live jazz on Wednesday, Thursday and Friday; it is free to get in but beers are pricey.

Other reputable discos include the *King's Club* at 32 Rue Victor Hugo; the posh *Le Play-Club* near the Hôtel Alafifa at 46 Rue Jules Ferry; the 'flavour-of-the-month' (at the time of writing) *Métropolis* on the corner of Rue Gomis and the Blvd de la République; *Les Tropiques* near the corner of Rue Gomis and Rue Félix Faure; and the expensive but chic *Quarante-deux* (also known as the *Africa Star*) at 42 Rue du Docteur Thèze.

Wrestling Traditional Senegalese wrestling matches *(les luttes)* are held most weekends during the dry season (less often during Ramadan), starting around 4 pm, at the large Stade Iba Mar Diop, on Route d'Ouakam in Le Médina. Matches last only a few minutes, until one contestant forces the other to the ground. Every section of town has its heroes – the event can be very lively.

Getting There & Away
Bus & Taxi-Brousse
Road transport for long-distance destinations leaves from Gare Routière Pompiers off Ave Malik Sy, 3km north of the Place. To Ziguinchor by Peugeot 504 costs US$12, or US$10 by minibus (all vehicles leave before noon). Minibus/taxi-brousse fares are US$5/7 to St-Louis; US$4/5 to Kaolack; US$11/13 to Tambacounda; US$6/7 to the Gambian border at Karang; and about US$2.50 to M'Bour.

Local transport for nearer towns, such as Thiès (US$2) and Rufisque (US$1), leaves from Gare Routière Kolobane, about 2km further away from the city centre on the other side of the Autoroute.

Train Dakar's train station is 500m north of the Place. Trains run daily to St-Louis (US$7/5 in 1st/2nd class) and Kaolack (US$5/4). The Dakar to Tambacounda train (weekly) – the *Bamako Express* – costs US$22/16.

Car Car rental is not cheap. Hertz and Avis, for example, charge US$40 a day plus US$0.40 per kilometre, US$8 a day for insurance and 20% tax for their most compact cars. Some smaller outfits have cheaper deals available.

Boat The MV *Joola* sails between Dakar and Ziguinchor, twice weekly in each direction, via Carabane Island (see the main Getting Around section in this chapter).

Getting Around
The Airport The official taxi rates for trips from Leopold Senghor international airport (formerly Dakar-Yoff) into the city centre are posted in the arrivals hall – US$8.50 during the day and about US$10 from midnight to 5 am – but you'll be doing well if you can negotiate them down to US$15. Going to the airport, you can sometimes get a taxi for less than the official fare.

If you want to avoid taxi rides, SOTRAC city bus Nos 7 and 8, which go to the city centre, stop only a few hundred metres from the airport; these do not run between 9 pm and 6 am.

Bus Bus travel costs from US$0.50 for short rides up to US$1 for long rides; you can get a route map from the information office at the SOTRAC bus station at the northern end of Ave Jean Jaurès. If there is no SOTRAC bus consider a dilapidated blue and yellow car rapide (minibus) – it will cost US$0.20 and drops you at Marché Sandaga. Useful SOTRAC routes include:

No 2 – From Place Leclerc, past the Grande Mosquée to Place de l'ONU
No 4 – From the train station to Marché Tilène in Le Médina
No 6 – From Place Lat Dior past Place de l'Indépendance and the train station, then north to the Gare Routière Pompiers, past the port and Plage Bel-Air, then north-west along the main road between Grand Yoff and Castors
No 7 – From the Palais de Justice, goes past Place de l'Indépendance, along Ave Pompidou to Marché Sandaga and up Ave Blaise Diagne and Route d'Ouakam past Point E to Almadies, N'Gor, the airport and Yoff
No 8 – From the Palais de Justice, goes past Place de l'Indépendance, along Ave Pompidou, out through Le Médina and eventually north up Blvd Bourgiba to Yoff and the airport
No 15 – From Place de l'Indépendance, goes east via the bay to Rufisque
No 21 – From the Palais de Justice, goes north up Ave Lamine Guèye and eventually north-east out of town to Tiaroye-Mer, Malika-sur-Mer and Keur Massar (not to be confused with Keur Moussa)

Train The Monday to Saturday commuter service *(Train Bleu)* runs from the city centre to Tiaroye-Mer and Rufisque; trains leave about every 30 minutes (in both directions) between 6 am and 10 pm.

Taxi Dakar's taxis have meters but they are rarely used, so you must agree on a price before you get in (as the locals do). Short trips (eg from the Place to Gare Routière Pompiers) should be around US$2.

AROUND DAKAR
Île de Gorée

The Île de Gorée, about 3km from Dakar, has been declared a UNESCO World Heritage site. It's a superbly mellow place, with colonial-style houses, a small beach, cheap food and accommodation, no cars and only a few hustlers – the perfect place to wander around alone. You may be plagued by 'guides' at Dakar port; if you hire one, expect to pay US$10 per day for the service.

On a rocky plateau at the far end of the island there is an old fort called **Le Castel** (inhabited by a group of hippyish Baye Fall disciples), with great views of the island and back across to Dakar. You can get drumming lessons here; it costs about US$20 for a four hour lesson. The nearby cliffs featured in the movie *The Guns of Navarone*.

But Gorée's history is a less light-hearted affair: the island was one of the busiest slave centres in West Africa during the 18th and 19th centuries. You should visit the **La Maison des Esclaves** (Slave House; now a museum) and the **IFAN Historical Museum** in the Fort d'Estrées at the north end of the island. Both charge US$0.50 for entry, and are closed on Monday. There's also a small **tourist market**, just behind the row of bars and restaurants, where the bargaining is more relaxed than in Dakar.

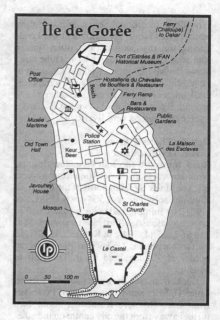

Île de Gorée

Places to Stay & Eat As you come off the ferry you'll see several small bars and restaurants around the small port. They all serve meals for around US$4. Ask at any of these places about renting a room. Local people charge US$10 per night, but with bargaining you can lower the price. For a week US$25 would be a good price.

Accommodation choices include the new *Keur Beer* (☎ 21 3801), 1 Rue du Port, which

---

Gorée's Grim Past

For people of European descent, a visit to Gorée can be very sobering. Reflect as you wander through the Maison des Esclaves that this was the first real point of contact between western civilisations and Africa. Imagine the soon-to-be cargo of 'ebony' – black bodies – cramped in these dank and dark rooms, quivering and frightened, not long dragged from their peaceful village existence, and soon to be thrust into the holds of 'slavers' which would transport them to the New World (to even more misery). The frail and sick were thrust out of a small door of the house onto the rocks below, where they soon died and became fodder for voracious sharks. Feel the moisture on the walls and imagine that it is the tears of the long departed. ■

has comfortable singles/doubles for US$30/36, breakfast included; and the very European *Hostellerie du Chevalier de Boufflers* (☎ 22 5364), where rooms cost about the same and meals are around US$6.

Getting There & Away From Dakar the ferry *(chaloupe)* to Gorée leaves every one to two hours from a wharf in the dock area, a 10 minute walk north of the Place; the trip across takes 30 minutes. A return ticket is US$2 for residents, US$4 for nonresidents.

Lac Retba
Lac Retba, more usually called Lac Rose (by Dakar tour companies) due to its pink colouring, is a popular Dakarois picnic spot attracting tour groups and, inevitably, souvenir sellers. As the terminus of the annual Paris-Dakar motor rally, it has achieved a modern notoriety.

Places to Stay & Eat The campement in Niaga, *Keur Kanni* (☎ 36 5517), offers concrete thatched huts with B&B for about US$20 per person. From here it is a 20 minute walk to the lake.

Getting There & Away From Dakar take a city bus No 15 to Rufisque, then a taxi-brousse to the village of Niaga, from where it's a few more (walkable) kilometres to the lake. Alternatively, take SOTRAC bus No 21 to Malika or Keur Massar and a taxi-brousse or minibus from there to Niaga. The latter is a more interesting route, and if you leave early you can go out one way and back the other, making it a nice day trip. The official round-trip taxi fare is about US$40.

Around the Country

KAOLACK
Kaolack (pronounced KO-lack), between Dakar and Tambacounda, is a busy transport hub, a more active city than sleepy St-Louis or Ziguinchor, and worth visiting for a day or two. The city has a beautiful large

mosque, decorated in the Moroccan style, and the second largest **covered market** in Africa (after Marrakesh), with Sudanese-style arches and arcades. There's no hassle; it's a place to soak up the atmosphere.

Places to Stay & Eat
A cheap hotel is the *Hôtel Napoléon*, two blocks east and one block north of the market, where a dirty room with fan is US$12. Nearby is the *Hôtel Adama Cire*, where clean rooms with attached bathroom are US$17, although they can sometimes be had for US$12. The food is cheap, but the hotel is atop a bar where loud music is *de rigueur*.

The tranquil *mission catholique*, in the south-west part of town, has spotless singles for US$9 (no sharing allowed) or a dormitory for US$4.50 per person. Nearby, Caritas (an aid organisation) has *Chambres de Passage* (☎ 41 2730), where it is US$14 per person or US$21 for a couple sharing.

For cheap eats there are several nameless *gargottes* near the gare routière and street food at the *market*. For snacks and meals try the Lebanese-run *Chez Miriam* and *Chez Marcel*, both in the north-east part of the city centre near Ave Van Vollenhoven.

Getting There & Away
Transport for Dakar (US$4 by taxi-brousse) and northern towns leaves from Gare Dakar, about 2km north-west of the city centre. From Gare Sud, on the south-east side of the city centre, transport goes to Ziguinchor, Tambacounda (US$4 by minibus, US$9 by taxi-brousse) and the Gambian border at Karang (US$7 by minibus, US$8 by Peugeot 504). For details of the daily Kaolack-Dakar train see Getting There & Away in the previous Dakar section.

PETITE CÔTE
The 150km stretch of coast running south from Dakar is called the Petite Côte and is Senegal's best beach area after Cap Skiring.

Joal-Fadiout
The twin villages of Joal and Fadiout (sometimes spelt Fadiouth) are south of M'Bour at

the end of the tarred road. Joal is on the mainland, while Fadiout is on a small island made of oyster and clam shells that have accumulated over the centuries, reached by an old wooden bridge. This place is on the tour circuit, and is plagued by 'guides' and touts. (The villages of Palmarin and Djifere are more pleasant alternatives. For details see the Siné-Saloum Delta section.)

Places to Stay & Eat In Joal, the cheapest place to stay is *Campement Les Cocos* on the road towards Djifere, which charges US$6 for a mattress on the floor of a tatty hut. Much nicer is the nearby *Relais 114* (☎ 57 6114), also called Chez Mamadou Balde, which has basic but clean rooms for US$14, and meals for around US$5. Smarter is the *Hôtel le Finnio* (☎ 57 6112), with expensive air-con bungalows.

M'Bour

This is the main town on the Petite Côte, about 80km south of Dakar. A few kilometres to the north is **Sali-Portudal**, a strip of big ocean-front hotels, packed with European tourists during winter.

Places to Stay & Eat The *Centre d'Accueil et de Séjour* (☎ 57 1002), better known as Chez Marie, in M'Bour near the market, is cheap and popular with singles/doubles at US$13/17, excluding tax and breakfast. Another popular place is the friendly *Chez Zeyna* (☎ 52 1909), where three small rooms, with attached bathroom, cost US$11 per person plus US$2 for breakfast. It's on the southern side of the town, about 1km along the sandy street running nearest the ocean.

One of the nicest places to stay is *La Ferme de Saly*, right on the coast 3km north of M'bour. A bed in a hut costs US$12 per person, and meals are US$6. To get there, if you're heading south from Dakar, then 2km past the turn-off for the big hotels at Sali you'll see a sign on the ocean side for 'La Ferme'. Follow the dirt road for another 3km through grassy sand dunes.

For meals try *Chez Maurice*, near the

market, which has dishes in the US$4 to US$6 range. Just round the corner is a *snack bar* with chawarmas at US$1.50, and near the taxi park are several small *gargottes*.

Getting There & Away A taxi-brousse between M'Bour and Dakar is US$3, and to/from Kaolack it is US$3. If you're going further down the Petite Côte, it is US$1 to Joal-Fadiout and US$2.50 to Djifere.

SINÉ-SALOUM DELTA

This large delta (1,800 sq km), formed where the seasonal Siné and Saloum rivers meet the tidal waters of the Atlantic Ocean, is often overlooked by visitors, but it's a wild, beautiful area of mangrove swamps, lagoons, forests, dunes and sand islands, and worth a visit. About 40% of the area is included in the Parc National du Delta du Saloum (see the Passi, Sokone & Missirah entry later in this section).

Djifere

Djifere is on the western edge of the delta at the tip of a narrow spit of land called the Pointe de Sangomar. You can hire a pirogue here and reach the beautiful islands of **Guior** and **Guissanor**.

You may find a family to put you up here (expect to pay US$6 per person). Alternatively, stay at the excellent *Campement Pointe du Sango-Mar*, which has bungalows (full board) for US$20 per person, or the 'broken-down' *Campement Flamante Rose* (☎ 35 0837), 1km further north, with bungalows for US$16 per person (full board). Both campements can arrange boat trips on the delta (about US$40 for a 20 person boat).

Foundiougne

West of Kaolack, Foundiougne (pronounced FOUN-dune) is easy to reach, and another good place for pirogue trips around the delta.

The *Campement Le Baobab* (also called Chez Anne-Marie; ☎ 45 1108) is a friendly place, with bungalows for US$11/14, including breakfast, and three-course meals for US$4. Ishmael, the resident boatman, offers pirogue trips to the Île aux Oiseaux (great birdwatching) for US$25 per day for the boat (negotiable according to petrol costs and duration of the trip).

Getting There & Away A taxi-brousse from Kaolack to Passi (on the road towards Karang) is US$1.50; Passi to Foundiougne is less than US$1. You can also go to Fatick, on the M'Bour-Kaolack highway, then to Dakhonga and ferry (US$0.40) across to Foundiougne. Returning this way, the first ferry leaves Foundiougne at dawn to meet a minibus which goes all the way to Dakar for US$4.

Ndangane

This is the northernmost village bordering the park and from here you can take a pirogue to any point in the delta.

Apart from the expensive *Pelican* (about US$45 in the low season), there are a number of Senegalese *campements* which have full board for about US$15 per person.

Across from Ndangane are the **Île de Mars**, a perfect getaway and superb birdwatching locale. There are three *campements* lining the shore at Mar Lodj; all charge US$25 for full board (US$18 with breakfast).

Getting There & Away To get to Ndangane from M'Bour take the Kaolack highway to Ndiosomone (3km past Tiadiaye), from where you can take a taxi-brousse to Ndangane. A pirogue across to the Île de Mars is about US$0.60.

Palmarin

In Palmarin (a few kilometres north of Djifere) the superb *Campement Sessene*, with thatched huts on a sandy beach under the coconut palms, offers bed, breakfast and dinner for an unbeatable US$14.

Getting There & Away Palmarin and Djifere are reached from M'Bour, via Joal-Fadiout; Joal to Djifere costs US$2.

Passi, Sokone & Missirah

South of Kaolack on the road to Toubacouta,

Passi is renowned for its huge traditional market.

The *Campement des Tartines* (☎ 48 5413) lives on the reputation of its 'tartes', Marie Chérie and Emma, septuagenarians, who know how to party. A pension with all the extras is about US$20. In Sokone, *Le Caïman* (☎ 48 3140) has huts and a pool, but exists mainly as a base for hunting and fishing excursions; full board is about US$45.

The **Parc National du Delta du Saloum** headquarters is 6km from Missirah; entry to the park is US$6. In Missirah, the friendly *Gîte de Bandiala* has rooms for US$20/30 for half/full board; pirogue trips, fishing and photo safaris are available. To reach Missirah by public transport, you get off at the village of Santhiou el Haji (80km from Kaolack) and walk 6km on a pleasant sandy track through the forest.

ST-LOUIS

The city of St-Louis straddles the mainland, an island and part of the Langue de Barbarie peninsula at the mouth of the Senegal River. You reach the island on the 500m-long Pont Faidherbe, originally built to cross the Danube but shipped here in 1897. Two smaller bridges link the island to the peninsula, a fishing community called Guet N'Dar, and the liveliest section of town.

Things to See & Do

On St-Louis island, local 'guides' will take you up onto the roof of the **post office**, for a small fee, from where you get good views of the bridge and the city. Nearby is the old **governor's palace**, a fort during the 18th century, now a government building and useful landmark. The **museum**, at the southern tip of the island, has some fascinating old photos of St-Louis and wood carvings, including masks.

South of Guet N'Dar is a **Muslim cemetery**, where each grave is draped with a fishing net. Further south down the peninsula are some good **beaches**. Don't go north of Guet N'Dar; the border with Mauritania is 3km away and a restricted area.

Senegal River

Route de la Corniche

N'Dar Tout

Pont Geole

Avenue Dodds

ATLANTIC OCEAN

Rue Adamson

Rue de France

Rue Brue

Rue Brière de L'Isle

Avenue Jean Mermoz

Quai Roume

Rue Khalifa Ababacar Sy

Ave Blaise Diagne

Rue Lt PH Diop

Rue Boufflers

Rue Aynima Fall

Rue P Holle

Rue Seydou Tall

Rue Blanchot

Rue Bisson

Rue du Général de Gaulle

Rue Milles Lacroix

Pont Mustapha Malick Gaye

Pont Faidherbe

Mainland

Rue de L'Eglise

Rue AM Javouye

Boulevard Abdoulaye Mar Diop

Guet N'Dar

Rue Thevenot

Rue Chassagnol

Rue Ibrahim Sarr

Rue Blaise Dumont

Rue Neuville

Rue Ribet

Rue A Fall

Quai Henry Jay

Langue de Barbarie Peninsula

To Campements
(Hydrobase &
Langue de Barbarie)
& Parc National

To Ranch de Bango
& Richard Toll

To Hôtel Coumba Bang,
Gare Routière & Dakar

Sor

St-Louis

0   150   300 m

Approximate Scale

PLACES TO STAY
1 Auberge de Doudou
3 Auberge de
   Jeunesse/L'Atlantide
12 Hôtel Battling Siki
13 Hôtel de la Résidence
15 Hôtel du Palais
20 Hôtel de la Poste
27 Maison des Combattants
35 Hôtel Walo

PLACES TO EAT
7 La Signare
9 Restaurant Galaxie
10 Chawarma Le Folk
11 Restaurant Wuroma
18 Bistro de Phare
19 Chawarma Chez Adja Anta

OTHER
2 Stadium
4 French Consulate
5 Mosquée
6 Mosquée
8 Mosquée
14 Bank
16 Market
17 Lighthouse
21 Post Office
22 Place Faidherbe
23 Governor's Palace
24 Rex Cinéma
25 Cathedral
26 Vox Cinéma
28 Hospital
29 Le Bar Ponty Village
30 Mosquée
31 Museum
32 Muslim Cemetery
33 Train Station
34 Gare Routière

SENEGAL

Places to Stay & Eat

The cheapest place to stay is the basic and grubby *Maison des Combattants*, where rooms cost US$3 per person. Next is the *Hôtel Battling Siki* (☎ 61 1883), north of the Governor's Palace on Rue Brière de l'Isle, where rooms cost US$8/11 for singles/doubles. Couples can share a single. It's a bit grubby but friendly enough, with a lively bar below.

Up a step in quality is the clean and friendly *Auberge de Jeunesse/L'Atlantide*, on Rue Brière de l'Isle opposite the French consulate, where rooms costs US$10 per person with breakfast. A few blocks further north is the *Auberge de Doudou*, slightly more basic at US$9 per person with breakfast.

The mid-range *Hôtel du Palais* (☎ 61 1772), on Rue Brière de l'Isle, has air-con rooms for US$23/30 with breakfast. Meals are in the US$7 to US$9 range.

Some 14km north of town on the Richard Toll road is the *Ranch de Bango* (☎ 61 1981), an old colonial farm which has been restored complete with swimming pool and tennis courts. Rooms with air-con are from US$30/35; breakfast is US$4 extra.

For cheap eats, there are several places in the city centre for chawarma; US$1.50 is the going price. Better and smarter (with tablecloths) is *Chawarma Le Folk*, two blocks north of Hôtel Battling Siki, where the meals are in the US$2 to US$4 range.

For pleasant surroundings and a nice view of the big bridge, try *Le Bar Ponty Village*, where food and drinks are reasonable and there's often live music.

Getting There & Away

The gare routière is on the mainland (Sor), 100m south of Pont Faidherbe. The fare to/from Dakar is US$7 by taxi-brousse (Peugeot 504) and US$5 by minibus. The train station is just north of here (there are daily trains to Dakar; US$7/5 for 1st/2nd class).

TAMBACOUNDA

Tambacounda is a major crossroads on the routes between Senegal, Mali, Guinea and The Gambia. The town, which lies in hot savannah country full of baobab trees, is also a jumping-off point for Niokolo-Koba.

Places to Stay & Eat

A cheap place to stay is *Chez Dessert*, about 1km south of the town centre; rooms are US$5.50 per person. Nearby is the *Hôtel Niji* (☎ 81 1250), with good singles/doubles with attached bathroom for about US$15/17 (an extra US$8 if you want air-con). At the gare routière people will offer to rent you private rooms. For cheap food try one of the small restaurants, such as *Chez Khadim* (meals are US$1.50) and *Chez Francis* (US$3).

Getting There & Away

There are two gares routières: Gare Kidira, on the eastern side of town, for vehicles towards Mali; and the larger Gare Dakar, on the southern outskirts of town, for most other destinations, including Niokolo-Koba. Taxi-brousse charge US$12 to Dakar.

THE CASAMANCE

The Casamance is the region of Senegal south of The Gambia. It differs geographically and culturally from other parts of the country, being a well watered, fertile area and the majority of people are non-Muslim Diola (Jola). The feeling of difference is so strong that a separatist movement has existed here since the 1950s (see the History section earlier in this chapter). There is still a strong military presence, with road blocks and searches common. There were reports of violent unrest in August 1997; check the situation before visiting.

In the Casamance region you can stay at some of the *village-run campements* (officially called *campements touristique rurals integrés* or CTRIs), which provide simple accommodation for visitors and raise money for local projects. Prices at all the CTRIs are standardised: a bed (with net) is US$5; breakfast is US$2.50; and a three-course lunch or dinner US$5. Bucket showers are the norm, and lighting is generally by oil lamp, but the bedrooms and bathrooms are

Casamance

0   5   10 km

Legend:
- Campement/s

THE GAMBIA

To Banjul

ATLANTIC OCEAN

Diouloulou

Abéné

Kafountine

Sitokoto

Marigot de Baïla

Néma

Sindian

Kagnarou

Baïla

Tendième

Bignona

To Sédhiou
& Dakar

Tiobon

Kagnobon

Diégoune

Tionk-Essil

Tendouk

Mangagoulak

Marigot

de

Diouloulou

Casamance River

Pointe
St George

Bandial

Affiniam

Barrage

Djilapao

Tobor

Koubalan

Île aux
Oiseaux

Ziguinchor

To Kolda

Diogué

Karabane

Nikine

Carabane
Island

M'Lomp

Kagnout

Loudia
Ouolof

Etama

Séléki   Essil

Enampor

Kamoubeul

Brin

Toubacouta

Mpak

Diembéring

Elinkine

Ossouye

Oukout

Diohère

Nyassia

Diakène
Ouolof

Niambalang

Diakène Diola

Parc National
de Basse
Casamance

Cap Skiring

Kabrousse

Youtou

Santiaba
Mandjak

Kaguite

To Bissau

GUINEA-BISSAU

always clean. The reservations office for campements is the Centre Artisanal in Ziguinchor but, until tourism in Casamance picks up again, reservations will not normally be required. There are also privately owned campements in the Casamance, offering similar facilities and similar prices.

Affiniam

On the north bank of the Casamance River, opposite Ziguinchor, this village contains a splendid *impluvium* (a large, round mud house), which is also the *campement* where you can stay for standard CTRI prices. (In time of war, the people would shut themselves inside the impluvium for safety. Rain water would be funnelled into a large tank in the centre of the house through a hole in the roof.) To get to Affiniam from Ziguinchor take the public ferry, which runs three times per week. It stops at 'le port d'Affiniam' (about 1km from the campement) for one hour then returns. The fare is less than US$1.

Cap Skiring

The beaches at Cap Skiring are some of the finest in Africa. This is where you'll find most of Senegal's tourist hotels, and several cheap campements too. If you want easy beach-life, this is the place. But if you want to see the 'real' Africa, keep movin' on.

Places to Stay & Eat The cheapest places are in Cap Skiring village itself. The lively *Bar Kassoumaye* has single/doubles for US$6/7 and meals for US$3.

There's a row of *campements* about 1km from the village, near Ziguinchor Junction, all reached by walking south from the junction for 100m, then turning right down a dirt road for 200m towards the ocean.

The friendly and popular *Auberge de la Paix* has rooms for US$4/7; the good-value *Campement Le Paradis* has spotless rooms for US$5 per person; and *Campement Karabane*, a small quiet place, has rooms for US$4.

Up the scale a bit is the *Auberge La Palmier* in Cap Skiring village, where doubles cost US$15. The bar/restaurant is also popular, with French and Senegalese three-course meals from US$8.

There are some cheap *gargottes* in the village, all serving dishes from US$2. Or try *Restaurant Toray Kunda*, off the dirt road towards the top-end Hotel Savana. Run by the affable Ali Baba, this place does huge Senegalese meals for around US$6.

Diembéring

If Cap Skiring is too frantic for you, head for Diembéring (JEM-bay-ring), 9km north and easily reached by bicycle, private taxi (US$11 each way) or the daily minibus from Ziguinchor (it passes through Cap Skiring at 5 pm).

The *Campement Asseb* (☎ 93 3106; ask in town for directions) has bungalows for US$4 per person and meals for US$4. The *Restaurant Le Diola* opposite does similarly priced meals.

On a small hill in the heart of the village is *Campement Aten-Elou* (☎ 93 1705), with rooms for US$5 per person, and at the foot of the hill is the basic impluvium-style *Campement Chez Albert*, where shabby rooms cost about US$4, and meals US$3.

Elinkine & Carabane Island

Elinkine is a busy fishing village at the end of the tar road north-west of Oussouye. From here you can get boats to Carabane Island (sometimes spelt Karabane), which was settled in colonial times. On Carabane, you can still see the Breton-style **church**, with dusty pews and crumbling statues. Along the beach is an old **cemetery** with settlers' graves from the 1840s, now covered in sand.

Places to Stay In Elinkine, the *Campement Villageois* charges standard CTRI prices. It has clean huts (some with showers) in a perfect setting among palm trees on a sandy beach right at the water's edge. (Note: female readers have reported harassment here.)

The private *Campement Le Fromager* is right next to the road where all the taxi-brousse stop. It charges US$6 a person for clean rooms and spotless shared baths; breakfast is US$2.50 and other meals US$6. This place is noisier than the village campement, as it seems to be a hangout for locals, although evenings are lively when the drums resound.

On Carabane, the *Campement Cocotier* has rooms for US$4 a person and meals for US$3.50. More tranquil is *Campement Badji Kunda* (☎ 91 1408), 1km further along the beach, where a solar-powered room is US$9, breakfast US$2, and lunch or dinner US$5. The *Hôtel de Karabane*, on the beach, has rooms from US$6 to US$22, depending on their state of repair.

Getting There & Away Elinkine can be reached by daily minibus from Ziguinchor (US$2). Carabane can be reached by pirogue from Elinkine (US$2.50). You can also get to Carabane on the MV *Joola*, which stops here on its way between Dakar and Ziguinchor twice weekly in each direction (deck class between Ziguinchor and Carabane is US$2).

Enampor

Enampor is 23km west of Ziguinchor. The *campement* is an impluvium, which is worth a visit even if you're not staying here. There are other such houses in the Casamance, but this is a good example. To sleep and eat here you pay standard CTRI prices. The manager will show you around for a small fee.

A traveller suggests the following: walk from Enampor to **Bandial** on the Casamance River. From Bandial, you can get a paddled pirogue to scenic **Pointe St George**, where there is a pleasant *campement*; the great lunches here are US$8. From the point, walk south to picturesque **M'Lomp**.

Kafountine & Abéné

Kafountine is a large village, 15km down the beach from the Gambian border, not far north of the end of the tar road that runs south from Diouloulou. Bikes can be hired in the market; rates start at US$6 per day but are negotiable. Abéné is a smaller place, 6km further up the coast.

Places to Stay & Eat Most places to stay are a few kilometres beyond the village, near the beach. Best is the recommended, quiet and

friendly *Campement Le Filao*, with clean bungalows for US$5 per person. Nearby is *A la Nature Restocases*, where basic bungalows with none-too-clean shared baths cost US$4 per person. On the beach behind the Filao, the small *Soko Bantan Restaurant* serves cheap meals.

In Abéné village is the tidy *Campement La Belle Danielle*, where the friendly Konte brothers charge US$3 for a bed, or US$12 for full board. From the village it's 2km along a sandy track to the beach and the village-run *Campement Samaba*, which charges standard CTRI prices for rooms and meals. Nearby is the upmarket French-run *Campement Le Kossy*, where half board in a bungalow in the beautiful garden costs US$15 per person.

Getting There & Away Ziguinchor to Kafountine is US$4 by taxi-brousse. Abéné can be reached by any transport going to Kafountine, although the village is 2km off the main road, and the beach a further 2km, which you'll have to walk.

Oussouye

Roughly halfway between Ziguinchor and Cap Skiring, Oussouye (OU-sou-yeh) is the main town in the Basse (Lower) Casamance area. Bikes can be hired on the main street.

The well run *village campement* is 1km north of town on the old dirt road leading north-west towards Elinkine. This is a fascinating example of local mud architecture. Rooms and meals are standard CTRI prices. The new *Auberge du Routard*, half a kilometre from town, has nice bungalows for US$4 a person and US$10 for full board.

At **Niambalang**, 12km east of Oussouye, just off the main Ziguinchor road, is a small campement, *Chez Theodor Balouse*, where visitors stay with a friendly family in very simple surroundings for US$3 per night. Meals are cheap (US$1.50), but you have to order a day in advance.

Ziguinchor

Most travellers stay only a few days in Ziguinchor before heading into the Casamance. The **Marché St-Maur** and **Centre**

Artisanal are both well worth a visit. Banks include the SGBS, near the top-end Hôtel Aubert, and the CBAO at the junction of Rue de France and Rue Javelier.

The Guinea-Bissau consulate (☎ 91 1046), near the Hôtel du Tourisme, is open weekday mornings from 8.30 am to noon. Visas cost US$20 and are issued on the spot (bring two photos with you).

Places to Stay Ziguinchor has two cheap campements, both 3km west of the city centre on the road to Cap Skiring: the dull *Centre Touristique de Colobane Fass* (☎ 91 1512), which costs US$4 per person; and the smarter *Campement ZAG* (☎ 91 1557), which costs US$5.50; both do meals.

The friendly *Hôtel Le Bel Kady* (☎ 91 1122), near Marché St Maur, has basic rooms for US$7/9 and a good-value restaurant.

A better deal than these, if you don't mind spending a bit extra, is the *Auberge Chez Clara*, where rooms (one or two people) are US$11, or US$14 with a fan and bathroom, including breakfast. Also highly recommended is the *Relais de Santhiaba* (☎ 91 1199), which has clean 'campement' rooms at US$6 per person with breakfast.

Ziguinchor

0   250   500 m

To Banjul & Dakar

Casamance River

Rue Javelier

Rue du Commerce

Rue du Général de Gaulle

Rue Dialio

Port

Rue de France

Rond-Point

Route de Cap Skiring

Avenue Cherif Bachir Aïdara

To Velingara & Tambacounda

To Campements ZAG, Colobane Fass & Cap Skiring

Boulevard Foch

Rue du Dr Oliver

Ave Lycée Guignabo (Route de l'Aviation)

To São Domingos

PLACES TO STAY
1 Hôtel Le Perroquet; Ferry to Affiniam
2 Hôtel Aubert
3 Hôtel Bambalong
12 Hôtel l'Escale
14 Hôtel du Tourisme; Guinea-Bissau Consulate
20 Auberge Chez Clara
21 Relais de Santhiaba
27 Hôtel Le Bel Kady
29 Le Diamorale
31 Hôtel Le Domaine de Néma Kadior

PLACES TO EAT
4 Chawarma du Port
7 Le Mansah
10 Pâtisserie
13 Le Tam-Tam
17 Restaurant Le Kankuran
23 Hôtel-Restaurant Le Bambadinka
24 Restaurant Busso Niang

OTHER
5 COSENAM (Ferry Office for Dakar)
6 SGBS Bank
8 Post Office (PTT)
9 CBAO Bank
11 Kathmandou Nightclub
15 Shell Station
16 Cathedral
18 Elf Station
19 Gare Routière
22 Total Station
25 L'Arène Folklore (Wrestling)
26 Marché St-Maur
28 Centre Artisanal; CTRI Reservation Office
30 Post Office (PTT)
32 Airport; Air Senegal

SENEGAL

The upmarket *Hôtel du Tourisme* (☎ 91 1227), in the heart of town, is a long-time favourite, charging US$15/18 for rooms with attached bathroom and fans. The food is good too, with most meals for about US$4. Even if you're not staying, it's worth stopping by for a drink. The hotel stores gear if you're touring the Casamance or visiting the beach.

Places to Eat On Ave Lycée Guignabo, in the area of Marché St Maur, are several cheap *cafes*, *bars* and *gargottes*. For fresh bread and cakes, the *patisserie* on the junction of Rue du Général de Gaulle and Rue Lemoine is good value. On the corner of Rue Lemoine and Rue de France is *Le Tam Tam*, serving European and African dishes. For chawarmas at US$1.50, head for *Chawarma du Port* on Rue du Commerce near the port (it also serves pizzas and sandwiches). There are several *coffee stalls* and *shacks* at the gare routière which also serve cheap food.

Slightly more costly, but very good value, is *Le Mansah*, on Rue Javelier, where big meals, including tiéboudienne with chips, are about US$3. The *Relais de Santhiaba* and *Hôtel du Tourisme* both have restaurants serving pizzas, steaks and Senegalese dishes.

Entertainment *The* place to go, especially for good music, is the nightclub at the *Hôtel Bambalong II*. If it is jam-packed go to the *Kathmandou*, just east of the city centre.

Getting There & Away The gare routière is 1km east of the city centre. The fare to Dakar is US$13 by taxi-brousse (Peugeot 504), or US$9 by minibus. Transport to Casamance villages leaves from here also.

There is a ferry between Ziguinchor and Dakar. For more details, see the main Getting Around section in this chapter.

Getting Around For getting around town, or for touring the Casamance in relaxed style, bikes can be hired from the Relais de Santhiaba, Campement ZAG or from outside the Hôtel Aubert. Decent mountain bikes

(vélos tous terrains) cost US$6 per day and old steel bikes US$3.50.

National Parks

PARC NATIONAL AUX OISEAUX DU DJOUDJ

Keen birdwatchers, or anyone else with the slightest interest, should not miss this park on the Senegal River, 60km north of St-Louis. From November to April, some three million birds migrating south from Europe stop here, as it's one of the first places with permanent water south of the Sahara. It is one of the most important bird sanctuaries in the world. Almost 300 species have been recorded. Pink flamingoes, ducks and waders are most plentiful. Others that you might see are white pelicans, spur-winged geese, herons, egrets, spoonbills, black-tailed godwits, bustards and tree-ducks. The park is open daily from 7 am to dusk year-round; entry costs US$6.

The park is 25km off the main road and there's no public transport, so most people take an excursion organised by one of the hotels in St-Louis. Rates vary, ranging from US$20 to US$30 per person (minimum four people) for a day trip. Or you could hire a taxi for the day, paying about US$25 one way or about US$40 for the round trip. As much of the park is inundated with water, you will need to hire a pirogue (US$5) to see it.

The upmarket *Campement du Djoudj* at the park entrance has overpriced bungalows for US$35, or you can camp at the park entrance, with the permission of the warden.

PARC NATIONAL DE BASSE CASAMANCE

This national park is 10km south of Oussouye, south-west of Ziguinchor. It has several vegetation zones, including forest, open grassland, tidal mud flats and mangrove swamps, and animals include red colobus monkey and duiker. The park has a good network of roads, white sandy trails and several hides *(miradors)*. Entrance is US$2 per person per day, plus US$10 per car.

The bungalows at the *campement* were destroyed in the early 1990s – you must camp at the park headquarters or in Oussouye (and visit the park for the day).

Warning

Check the current situation before going to the park; it was recently the scene of fighting between government troops and separatists.

PARC NATIONAL DE NIOKOLO-KOBA

Niokolo-Koba is Senegal's major national park, covering about 9000 sq km, in the south-east of the country. Although neglected in recent years, it's still very beautiful and worth a visit. It has lush and varied vegetation, and is home to 84 species of mammal, including elephant (perhaps the last 20 or so remaining in Senegal), lion, leopard and the giant derby eland, although you shouldn't bet on seeing them. You are likely, however, to see hippo, crocodile, waterbuck, bushbuck, kob, baboon, buffalo, monkey (green and hussar), wart hog, roan antelope and hartebeest. Some 350 species of bird have been recorded in the park.

You must have a vehicle to enter the park and walking is not allowed anywhere, but it is still possible for travellers without a car to visit, using public transport or an organised tour. The best time to come here is between December and May (the dry season), but some park tracks are not cleared until a month after the rains have ended, so don't take anything for granted. For information, visit the park headquarters in Tambacounda, where you might be lucky and find a lift. Entrance is around US$4 per person.

PARC NATIONAL LANGUE DE BARBARIE

This national park, 20km south of St-Louis, covers the southern tip of the Langue de Barbarie peninsula and a section of the main-

land on the other side of the river's mouth. It's easier to reach than Djoudj, and almost as good, but without the volume and variety of birdlife. The park is open daily from 7 am to sunset; entry is US$3.

Camping inside the park is not permitted, so most people reach the park on a trip organised by one of the hotels in St-Louis. It is possible to get a taxi-brousse to Gandiol, from where you can enter the park by pirogue.

Places to Stay

There are several camp sites in the park; try *Camp du Lion*, a beautiful spot 9km from Simenti on the Gambia River. If you camp, bring all the food you need. Water is available, but needs purifying.

A good place for travellers without a vehicle is the *campement* at Dar-Salam park entrance, where the track to Simenti turns off the main road. A basic double bungalow costs US$13, breakfast US$2, other meals US$7 and a half-day safari US$6.

In the centre of the park at Simenti, the *Hôtel de Simenti* overlooks a permanent water hole where animals come to drink. Double air-con rooms are US$36, breakfast US$3 and other meals around US$9. Simpler bungalows are available for about US$14, and the hotel runs half-day safaris for US$15.

Getting There & Away

To reach the park take a taxi-brousse from Tambacounda to Kédougou (US$9) and get off at the Dar-Salam park entrance. Hitch from here, or take a half-day safari from the campement which drops you at Simenti.

Alternatively, hire a taxi in Tambacounda for one or two days. The driver pays his costs, while you pay for your own entry, food and accommodation. Starting prices seem to be around US$130 for a day. Before you do this call at the park headquarters to make sure the track to Simenti is passable for 2WD.

Seychelles

If you're searching for that unspoilt tropical paradise thousands of miles from anywhere, where you can laze on palm-fringed beaches and splash in warm, clear seas, the Seychelles, about 1600km east of the African mainland, fits the bill.

Facts about the Country

HISTORY

The islands were first sighted by Vasco da Gama, the Portuguese navigator, at the beginning of the 16th century, but no settlement was attempted until French planters and their slaves arrived in the 1770s. They introduced cinnamon, cloves, nutmeg and pepper. The British took control of the islands in 1810 and administered them from Mauritius until they became a separate crown colony at the beginning of the 20th century.

Political organisations didn't surface until 1964 when two rival parties were formed: the Seychelles People's United Party (SPUP) led by France Albert René and the Seychelles Democratic Party (SDP) led by James Mancham.

The SPUP advocated complete independence, while the SDP hoped to continue association with Britain. The first democratic elections ended in a stalemate, but in 1970 the SDP won a majority. However, Mancham failed to convince the British authorities to continue association, and independence was granted in 1976.

The first new government was a coalition between the SPUP and the SDP, with Mancham as president and René as prime minister. However, Mancham's plans to quickly modernise the Seychelles and attract outside investment were at odds with René's personal ambitions, and while Mancham was away at the 1977 Commonwealth Con-

REPUBLIC OF SEYCHELLES
Area: 455 sq km
Population: 73,000
Population Growth Rate: 1%
Capital: Victoria
Head of State: President France Albert René
Official Languages: English, French
Currency: Seychelles rupee
Exchange Rate: Rs 5 = US$1
Per Capita GNP: US$5450
Inflation: 4%
Time: GMT/UTC + 4

Highlights
* Stunning beaches, beautiful marine life, and exotic flora and fauna
* Scores of secluded islands offering brilliant snorkelling and diving
* Vallée de Mai on Praslin, with wild and wonderful vegetation, including thousands of coco de mer palms
* The friendly, serene and easy-going little island of La Digue

ference in London, René staged a coup and usurped the presidency.

This didn't deter a group of mercenaries from realising René's greatest fears. A coup attempt took place in late 1981 and nearly succeeded, but its cover was blown by an airport customs officer who found a sub-machine gun in the baggage of what seemed to be a business person on holiday. Gunfire broke out at the airport, and while some of

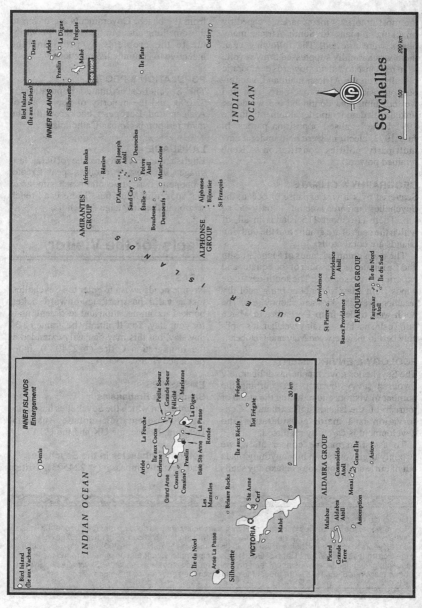

Seychelles

INDIAN OCEAN

INNER ISLANDS

Bird Island
(Île aux Vaches)

Denis
Aride
Praslin
Silhouette
La Digue
Frégate
Mahé

See Inset

Île Plate

Coëtivy

INDIAN OCEAN

AMIRANTES GROUP

African Banks
Rémire
D'Arros
St Joseph Atoll
Sand Cay
Desroches
Étoile
Poivre Atoll
Boudeuse
Desnoeufs
Marie-Louise

ALPHONSE GROUP

Alphonse
Bijoutier
St François

OUTER ISLANDS

Providence
St Pierre
Providence Atoll
Bancs Providence

FARQUHAR GROUP

Farquhar Atoll
Île du Nord
Île du Sud

0   100   200 km

INNER ISLANDS Enlargement

Bird Island
(Île aux Vaches)

INDIAN OCEAN

Denis

Île du Nord

Anse La Passe

Silhouette

Aride
La Fouche
Île aux Cocos
Curieuse
Grand Anse
Cousin
Cousine
Praslin
Baie Ste Anne
La Passe
Félicité
La Digue
Petite Soeur
Grande Soeur
Marianne

Les Mamelles
Brisare Rocks

Île aux Récifs

Ronde

Îlot Frégate
Frégate

VICTORIA
Ste Anne
Cerf
Mahé

ALDABRA GROUP

Picard
Malabar
Grande Terre
Aldabra Atoll
Assomption

Cosmolédo Atoll
Menai
Grand Île
Astove

0   15   30 km

the most notorious mercenaries escaped by hijacking a plane to South Africa, many others were arrested. The following year, there was a rapidly suppressed army revolt.

In response to a swing towards democratic pluralism on the African mainland, vociferous opposition to his one-party rule and western hints that continued aid would be linked with democratic developments, in late 1991 René legalised opposition parties. In July 1993, elections were held under a new multiparty politics constitution – René retained power.

GEOGRAPHY & CLIMATE

Scattered over a vast expanse of ocean, the Seychelles land area amounts to only 455 sq km. There are about 115 islands in all, of which the central are granite and the outlying islands are coral atolls.

The main granitic islands of Mahé, Praslin and La Digue lie just south of the equator and experience two seasons. The south-east trade winds from May to October bring cool dry weather, overcast skies and choppy seas. The north-west trades from December to March bring calm but hot and rainy weather. It's probably best to visit between May and October.

ECOLOGY & ENVIRONMENT

The Seychelles government has deliberately favoured savvy tourism, thus curbing the number of visitors and reducing the strain of tourism on the islands' infrastructure. Conservation is a major consideration and development is carefully regulated.

To assist in marine conservation, we strongly urge you not to buy anything made out of turtle shell nor to buy or take any shells

from the beach. Governments are trying to do something about it; please don't contribute to the problems by providing the incentive to continue the practices.

POPULATION & PEOPLE

The Seychelles estimated population is 73,000, and the majority of people are of African and European background. The main religion is Roman Catholicism.

LANGUAGE

English and French are the official languages, but most Seychellois speak Créole, a phonetic derivative of French similar to that spoken in Mauritius. There is a French section in the Language Appendix.

Facts for the Visitor

VISAS

No-one needs a visa to enter the Seychelles, just a valid passport, an onward ticket, booked accommodation and sufficient funds for your stay. You'll initially be granted a 30 day stay, but this may be easily extended at the Immigration Office (☎ 224030), Independence House, Victoria.

EMBASSIES
Seychelles Embassies

Countries in which the Seychelles has diplomatic representation include Australia, Belgium, France, the UK and the USA.

Foreign Embassies in the Seychelles

The French embassy (☎ 224523), British

Coco de Mer

To the world, the Seychelles is represented by the erotically shaped coco de mer (sea coconut). These extraordinary nuts are the heaviest seeds in the plant kingdom and can weigh over 20kg! They take seven years to mature and some of the 30m-high palms are estimated to be 800 years old. Long before the Portuguese rounded the Cape of Good Hope, empty nuts were found on shores around the Indian Ocean, giving rise to legends about their mystic aphrodisiac powers. Since the Seychelles hadn't yet been discovered, the nuts were thought to come from the sea – hence the name. ■

high commission (☎ 225225) and US consulate (☎ 225256) are all located at Victoria House in Victoria.

Other countries with diplomatic representation include Belgium, China, Denmark, Germany, India, Madagascar, Mauritius, Sweden and Switzerland.

MONEY
US$1 = Rs 5

The unit of currency is the Seychelles rupee (Rs), which equals 100 cents.

You get a better rate for travellers' cheques than for cash. Major credit cards are widely accepted and most banks issue cash advances against the cards.

The Seychelles is an expensive place to visit, so don't arrive on a shoestring budget. Tipping is not obligatory.

POST & COMMUNICATIONS
The Seychelle's mail service is reliable and reasonably fast, and there is a free poste restante service at the central post office in Victoria.

The telephone system is one of the most modern in the world, but, like everything else in the Seychelles, efficiency comes at a price.

The country area code for the Seychelles is 248; there are no area codes.

ACCOMMODATION
The Seychelles tourist industry is heavily controlled by the government. There are no cheap hotels, *pensions de famille*, hostels or doss houses. Furthermore, camping is prohibited and homestays are technically forbidden.

It's wise to make bookings well ahead, as places can fill up in a flash. High-season rates generally apply at Christmas and New Year, Easter and July to August. During these times, most hotels hike their rates by around 15%.

FOOD
Fish and rice are the staple foods; you can indulge in a wide range of seafood, cooked in a variety of ways. Créole cuisine is also prepared in an array of mouth-watering ways.

Avoid anything billed as fruit bat or sea turtle; the former is merely threatened, but sea turtles are highly endangered.

Getting There & Away

AIR
Air France, British Airways, Kenya Airways, Air Seychelles and Aeroflot all have services from the Seychelles.

The departure tax for international flights is US$20, payable in local currency.

Getting Around

AIR
The domestic carrier is Air Seychelles (☎ 381300), which has regular return flights from Mahé to Praslin (US$69), Frégate (US$83), Bird (US$198), Desroches (US$480) and Denis (US$616). The fares to Bird and Desroches include meals and accommodation for one night, while the fare to Denis includes meals and accommodation for two nights.

For information about flights to other outer islands, contact the Islands Development Company (IDC; ☎ 224640) in Victoria.

BUS
Only Mahé and Praslin have sealed roads and bus networks. Mahé has a much more extensive bus service than Praslin. On Mahé, buses run daily from about 6 am to 7 pm. On Praslin, the basic route is from Anse Boudin to Anse Kerlan and buses run each direction every hour from 6 am to 6.30 pm. All bus fares are fixed at US$0.60 on both islands.

BOAT
Schooner ferries run regularly between Mahé, Praslin and La Digue, carrying both

passengers and cargo. There are two schooners, *Cousin* and *La Bellone*, sailing Monday to Friday on the Mahé-Praslin route. The trip takes about three hours, depending on sea conditions, and the one-way fare is US$10. On Praslin, the ferries normally depart from the Baie Ste Anne jetty.

Between Mahé and La Digue, the schooner *La Belle Edma* operates Monday to Friday. The fare is US$10 one way. On the 30 minute run between Praslin and La Digue, *Silhouette* and *Lady Mary II* operate daily. The one-way fare is US$7.

The Marine Charter Association (☎ 322126), beside the Yacht Club in Victoria, has about 30 members who offer boats for hire for around US$78 per person for day excursions.

Occasionally, schooners carry supplies to the Amirantes, Farquhar and Aldabra groups. They don't take passengers, but you may get on as a paying or non-paying crew member. Talk to skippers directly at the ferry piers in Victoria, Praslin and La Digue.

LOCAL TRANSPORT

The taxi fares on Mahé and Praslin are set by the government. On Mahé you'll pay US$3 for the first kilometre and US$1 for each additional kilometre; on Praslin it costs slightly more. Alternatively, you can hire a taxi for a set period and negotiate a fee with the driver.

A great way to zip around Mahé and Praslin is to hire a Mini Moke, which costs around US$70 per day (cheaper for longer rentals). On La Digue and other islands, the best way to get around is on foot or by bicycle. Bikes can be hired on most islands. La Digue also has ox-cart taxis.

Mahé

Mahé is the largest and most heavily populated island of the Seychelles, and is the site of the international airport and the capital, Victoria.

VICTORIA

The **Botanical Gardens** are next to the hospital and are worth visiting to see the island's unique vegetation – including coco de mer palms. The **Natural History Museum**, next to the post office, is open Monday to Friday from 8.30 am to 4.30 pm and on Saturday until 12.30 pm. Admission is free. You may also like to wander in the **Sir Selwyn Clarke Market**.

Places to Stay

All of the following rates include breakfast.

The relatively cheap *Beaufond Lane Guest House* (☎ 322408; fax 224477) on Mont Fleuri Rd has doubles for US$70. A better choice is the nearby *Sunrise Guest House* (☎ 224560; fax 225290), run by the amiable Chung Faye family, where doubles cost US$80.

On the road towards Beau Vallon is the *Hilltop Guest House* (☎ 266555), which charges US$70 for a double.

La Louise Lodge (☎/fax 344349), a good climb up La Misère hill, 3km from town, has nice doubles for US$100. Similarly priced is the homely *Hotel Bel Air* (☎ 224416; fax 224923) on Bel Air Rd.

Places to Eat

The popular *Pirates Arms* on Independence Ave is great for a light meal; a seafood pizza costs US$9. Nearby is the *Tandoor*, which serves Indian cuisine.

In the town centre are several cheap takeaway places, including *Bon Appetit* and *Sandy's*.

The simple *King Wah* on Benezet St has inexpensive Chinese food; main courses cost between US$7 and US$16.

For a minor splurge try *Marie Antoinette*, or the enchanting restaurant at the *Auberge Louis XVII* hotel (☎ 344411), near La Louise Lodge.

For a major splurge, spruce yourself up and head for the very stylish *Bagatelle*, winner of the 1996 Seychelles restaurant of the year award. The food is superb and seafood is a speciality; main courses are around US$20.

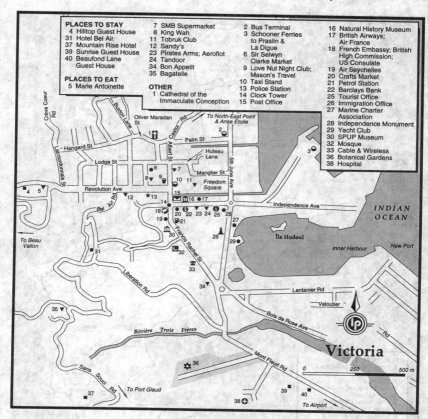

PLACES TO STAY	7	SMB Supermarket	2	Bus Terminal	16	Natural History Museum
4	Hilltop Guest House	8	King Wah	3	Schooner Ferries	17	British Airways;
31	Hotel Bel Air	11	Tobruk Club		to Praslin &		Air France
37	Mountain Rise Hotel	12	Sandy's		La Digue	18	French Embassy; British
39	Sunrise Guest House	23	Pirates Arms; Aeroflot	6	Sir Selwyn		High Commission;
40	Beaufond Lane	24	Tandoor		Clarke Market		US Consulate
	Guest House	34	Bon Appetit	9	Love Nut Night Club;	19	Air Seychelles
		35	Bagatelle		Mason's Travel	20	Crafts Market
PLACES TO EAT			10	Taxi Stand	21	Petrol Station
5	Marie Antoinette	OTHER		13	Police Station	22	Barclays Bank
		1	Cathedral of the	14	Clock Tower	25	Tourist Office
			Immaculate Conception	15	Post Office	26	Immigration Office

(Legend continued:)
- 27 Marine Charter Association
- 28 Independence Monument
- 29 Yacht Club
- 30 SPUP Museum
- 32 Mosque
- 33 Cable & Wireless
- 36 Botanical Gardens
- 38 Hospital

AROUND MAHÉ

Off the east coast opposite Victoria are the six small islands of **St Anne Marine National Park**, offering great snorkelling.

The beach resort on Mahé is **Beau Vallon**, which is popular with both locals and tourists. The sand is good, and inshore it's relatively free of rocks and coral. Buses leave regularly from Victoria. West of Beau Vallon is the **Bel Ombre Treasure Site**, which is hypothesised to be the place where pirate Olivier Levasseur ('La Buse') buried his golden hoard. Even further west, there's a pleasant walk from Danzilles to Anse Major.

Near Port Glaud, opposite the islet of L'Islette, a 10 minute track leads inland to the lovely **Sauzier Waterfall**. For a longer walk, you can climb the 699m **Trois Frères Peak** in Morne Seychellois National Park. Also interesting is the short climb to **Copolia**, where there are large areas of *glacis* (exposed granite) and the Seychelles' most accessible stand of carnivorous pitcher plants. On the Forêt Noir cross-island road, in the shadow of Morne Blanc, is a **tea plantation** and tavern selling locally produced teas.

At the Cable & Wireless station, near the

Mahé

0   2   4 km

PLACES TO STAY
1 North Point Guest House
2 Chez Jean
3 Manresa
4 Calypha Guest House
5 Le Pti Payot
6 Panorama Guest House
7 Beau Vallon Bungalows
9 Le Niol Guest House
10 Mountain Rise Hotel
11 Sunrise Guest House
12 Harbour View Guest House
14 Auberge Louis XVII
15 La Louise Lodge
19 Château d'Eau
21 La Retraite
22 Lalla Panzi
23 La Roussette
27 Auberge Bougainville

PLACES TO EAT
8 Baobab Pizzeria
13 Chez Gaby
18 La Marie Galante Restaurant
20 Katiolo
24 Kaz Kreol
26 Anchor Café & Pizza

OTHER
16 Mission Lodge Ruins;
    Viewpoint
17 Tea Factory
25 Michael Adams' Studio

crest of the Montagne Posée cross-island route, is the start of the rewarding day-walk to **La Brulée**, a granite peak with three spectacular vantage points over the west coast.

If you're interested in Seychelles art, **Michael Adams' studio** at Anse aux Poules Bleues should not be missed.

Near the southern end of the island is **Anse Intendance**, Mahé's wildest beach. Swimming is prohibited, but you can spend hours watching the surf.

For **diving**, the Underwater Centre (☎ 247357) at the Coral Strand Hotel in Beau Vallon and Marine Divers (☎ 247141, ext 8133) at the Berjaya Beau Vallon Bay Beach Resort both offer diving courses. A one hour dive costs around US$50.

Places to Stay

All the following rates include breakfast unless otherwise specified.

North of Victoria at Ma Constance you'll find the homely *Calypha Guest House* (☎/fax 241157), which charges US$55 for a double.

Further north at Pointe Cèdre is the waterfront *Manresa* (☎/fax 241388), with doubles for US$100. At the north end of the island is the *North Point Guest House* (☎ 241339; fax 241850), which offers doubles for US$66, without breakfast and with a minimum of three nights. A bit further around the point is *Chez Jean* (☎ 241445; fax 225430), where doubles go for US$64.

At Mare Anglaise, just north of Beau Vallon, is the deservedly popular *Le Pti Payot* (☎ 261447; fax 261094), with excellent self-catering chalets for US$100 (maximum of four people).

Just off Beau Vallon beach is *Panorama Guest House* (☎ 247300; fax 247947), with good doubles for US$96. Nearby is the similarly priced *Beau Vallon Bungalows* (☎ 247382; fax 247955).

Between Victoria and Beau Vallon is the no-frills *Le Niol Guest House* (☎ 266262), which charges US$50 a double, without breakfast.

At Anse aux Pins is the German/Seychelloise-run *Lalla Panzi* (☎ 376411; fax

375633), which costs US$56 a double. Nearby is the very down-to-earth *La Retraite* (☎ 375816), with doubles for US$52. The southernmost guesthouse on the east coast is the atmospheric *Auberge Bougainville* (☎ 371788; fax 371808), an old plantation house with double rooms for US$84.

Places to Eat

At Beau Vallon, the popular *Baobab Pizzeria*, right on the beach, bakes decent pizzas for US$7.

At Anse à la Mouche you can get cheap snacks at *Anchor Café & Pizza*.

In Anse Royale is *Kaz Kreol*, which serves fabulous Créole meals for around US$14. Similarly priced is *La Marie Galante Restaurant* at Grande Anse, a place which also specialises in Créole food.

For something special, go to *Chez Gaby* on Round Island in St Anne Marine National Park. A meal for two costs about US$40.

Around the Islands

ARIDE ISLAND

Aride Island lies 10km to the north of Praslin. The island was purchased for the Royal Society for Nature Conservation in 1973 by Christopher Cadbury (of chocolate fame). It's now a nature reserve with the islands' greatest concentration of sea birds. From April to October, tours are conducted twice weekly and cost US$79 per person, including lunch. Book through Praslin hotels or tour operators.

BIRD ISLAND

In contrast to the central granite islands of the Seychelles, Bird (also known as Île aux Vaches) is a coral island, ringed by a white coral beach. Its name is derived from the vast colonies of fairy terns, common noddies and millions of sooty terns. Sea turtles also breed on the island. The island is home to the renowned tortoise, Esmeralda, who is believed to be at least 150 years old and weighs around 300kg.

Bungalows cost US$198 per person for the first night on an obligatory full-board basis, including a return flight from Mahé. Subsequent nights are considerably cheaper. For more details, contact the Bird Island office (☎ 224925; fax 225074) in Victoria.

COUSIN ISLAND

This island, about 2km from Praslin, is owned by the International Council for Bird Preservation and serves as a breeding site for sea birds and turtles. It's amazing walking through the thick forest with undaunted birds nesting on almost every branch. There are several endangered species, including the rare brush warbler. Half/full day visits cost US$63/79 and can be arranged through tour operators.

FRÉGATE ISLAND

The privately owned island of Frégate, roughly 20km south of La Digue, is reputed to have been a pirate lair, but today it's a bird stronghold. Attractions include superb beaches, such as **Anse Victorin**, birdwatching and walking.

For details about accommodation, contact the Frégate Island office (☎ 323123; fax 324169) in Victoria.

LA DIGUE

For most visitors, La Digue (population 2000) is the most picturesque and relaxed of the major islands, and its beaches can't be beaten. The ferry terminal and most of the island's activity are in the main settlement of **La Passe**.

Just inland from Anse La Réunion is the **Veuve Reserve**, a swathe of forest which is popular with birdwatchers who come to look for the endangered paradise flycatcher (*Terpsiphone corvina*).

Anse Patates at the north end rates as one of the Seychelles' most scenic beaches, and further down the east coast is the magical stretch of beach at **Anse Gaulettes**.

Just south of the **L'Union Estate & Copra Factory** (the location for the film *Goodbye Emanuelle*) is the oft-photographed beach at **Anse Source d'Argent**. On the east coast

are the incredible beaches of **Grand Anse**, **Petite Anse** and **Anse Cocos**; the strong currents here can make it dangerous for swimming.

Places to Stay & Eat

All of the following rates include breakfast unless otherwise specified.

The old plantation house, *Château St Cloud* (☎/fax 234346), has comfortable doubles for US$80. Almost opposite is the smaller *Sitronnel Guest House* (☎ 234230), which charges US$60 for a double. Nearby, *Bernique Guest House* (☎ 234229; fax 234288) offers pleasant double rooms for US$50 and bungalows for US$84 a double.

Closer to the beach is *Chez Marston* (☎/fax 234023), which has doubles on a half-board basis only for US$80.

For a wonderful homely atmosphere try *Villa Authentique* (☎/fax 234413), inland from La Passe, which charges US$85 for a double.

Moving upmarket, there's the *Paradise Fly Catcher's Lodge* (☎/fax 234015) at Anse Union, which has delightful doubles for US$100. For a real treat stay at *Patatran Village* (☎ 234333; fax 234344), ideally located near the picturesque Anse Patates beach. Doubles, on a half-board basis only, start at US$188. Even if you're not staying here, the restaurant is worth a visit.

For self-catering, you're limited to the shops and a little bakery in and around La Passe. You can get cheap snacks at *Tarosa Cafeteria* near the pier. For reasonably priced Créole cuisine try *Zerof*, opposite the Veuve Reserve.

Getting There & Away

There's no airport on La Digue. The cheapest and easiest access is by ferry from Praslin, which costs US$7 each way. You can hire bikes near the ferry landing for US$5 per day.

PRASLIN

Praslin, the second largest Seychelles island, is 12km long and 5km wide. It is more laid-back than Mahé, and has a distinct tropical flavour.

A major attraction is the lush **Vallée de Mai**, with the Seychelles' greatest concentration of coco de mer palms. There are estimated to be 4000 palms, some of which are around 800 years old. The Vallée de Mai is open daily from 8 am to 5.30 pm. Entry costs US$8.

Praslin's finest beach is **Anse Lazio** on the north-west side of the island, which is accessible by bus.

Places to Stay & Eat

All of the following rates include breakfast unless otherwise specified.

One of the cheapest places is the basic *Orange Tree Guest House* (☎ 233248), above Baie Ste Anne, which charges US$60 for a double. Tucked away on Pointe Cabris is the pleasant *Colibri* (☎/fax 232302), with doubles for US$90.

In Grand Anse, *Cabanes des Pêcheurs* (☎/fax 233320) has clean waterfront bungalows for US$80 a double. Nearby, but not as well located, is *Britannia* (☎ 233215; fax 233944), with nice rooms for US$96 a double. *Villas de Mer* (☎ 233972; fax 233015) has self-catering chalets for US$88 a double.

In the heart of Anse Volbert is *Laurier Guest House* (☎ 232241; fax 232362), with doubles from US$80.

At Anse Kerlan is *Islanders* (☎ 233224; fax 233154), with self-catering chalets for US$100 a double, without breakfast.

For meals, most guesthouses and hotels are open to nonresidents. You can get cheap eats at *Steve's Café* near the Britannia. The beachfront *Berjaya Pizzeria* at Anse Volbert whips up good pizza and pasta. *Bon Bon Plume* on Anse Lazio does terrific lunches in a perfect setting; main courses are upwards of US$20.

SILHOUETTE ISLAND

Located almost 20km from Mahé, the granite island of Silhouette rises steeply from around the shore up to three peaks, of which Mt Dauban is the highest at 750m.

A superb hike is to the summit of 630m **Mont Pot à Eau** to see its namesake phenomenon, the carnivorous pitcher plant, and coco de mer palms. The trip will require the better part of a day and it's a hot climb, so carry lots of water!

For details about accommodation and transfers, contact a tour operator.

Sierra Leone

◆◇◆◇◆◇◆◇◆◇◆◇◆◇◆◇◆◇◆◇◆

Warning
We visited Sierra Leone and updated this chapter before the coup in May 1997. As this book went to press, it was not safe to visit. Check the current political situation before going.

◆◇◆◇◆◇◆◇◆◇◆◇◆◇◆◇◆◇◆◇◆

REPUBLIC OF SIERRA LEONE
Area: 72,325 sq km
Population: 5.5 million
Population Growth Rate: 2.5%
Capital: Freetown
Head of State: Major Johnny Paul Koromah
Official Language: English
Currency: Leone (Le)
Exchange Rate: Le 925 = US$1
Per Capita GNP: US$160
Inflation: 20%
Time: GMT/UTC

Highlights
- The lively city of Freetown, full of African character
- Hiking and climbing on Mt Bintumani
- Tiwai Island Wildlife Sanctuary & Outamba-Kilimi National Park

Before the civil war, Sierra Leone was an excellent place for independent travellers: a bed in an upcountry town was cheap; travel on the main routes fairly easy; the landscape varied and stunningly beautiful; many of the beaches were empty and wildlife reserves could be visited without a vehicle. And the people were eternally friendly; if you bought someone a beer and told a joke or two you'd have a friend for the rest of your visit.

When the military government stood down in 1996, opening the way for free elections, there was real hope of a cease-fire and eventual reconciliation between the new government and the rebel Revolutionary United Front (RUF). In May 1997, full-scale fighting broke out in Freetown when rebel army elements staged a coup, deposing President Ahmad Tejan Kabbah.

Facts about the Country

HISTORY

In precolonial times Sierra Leone was on the edge of the great Mali empire which flourished between the 13th and 15th centuries. The modern state was founded as a homeland for freed slaves. The first settlers landed at Freetown in 1787 and, over the next 60 years, they were joined by about 70,000 ex-slaves from all over West Africa who'd been liberated from ships intercepted by the British navy, and by indigenous people migrating from the interior.

Non-indigenous Africans became known as Krios. They assumed an English style of life and began to regard themselves as superior to the indigenous peoples. The colonial authorities appointed many to senior posts in the civil service. Many others became influential traders but, during the early decades of the 20th century, they were ousted by Lebanese immigrants and later by British entrepreneurs. As the Krios' power continued to be eroded, they clung even more fiercely to their positions in the colonial civil

SIERRA LEONE

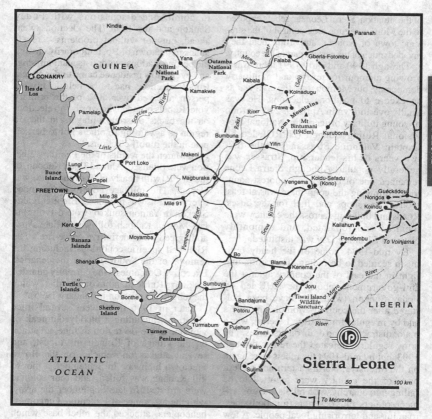

service. In the 1950s, while other African nations were clamouring for independence, the Krios proclaimed loyalty to Britain.

In the last years of the colonial era, Milton Margai, leader of the Sierra Leone People's Party (SLPP), which identified with the Mende people of the south, became prime minister. He died in 1964 and was succeeded by Albert Margai, his brother. In 1967 there were two military coups, and Siaka Stevens, leader of the All People's Congress (APC), was forced into exile in Guinea. In 1968 another coup allowed Stevens to return and become prime minister. The APC went on to

win two further elections, and the country became a republic and a one party state, with Stevens as the first president.

His rule was to last some 18 years but, towards the end of it, his popularity and that of the APC rapidly declined, so Major General Joseph Momoh, commander of the armed forces, was chosen as successor. He inherited huge economic problems and rampant corruption. By 1987, the inflation rate was over 100%.

Things got worse in 1990, when fighting from the civil war in neighbouring Liberia spilled across the border. Taking advantage of the situation, Sierra Leonean rebels opposed to the Momoh regime took control of the strategic town of Koindu, and from there they invaded much of the eastern part of the country.

Through 1990 and early 1991 there was a growing clamour for reform and multiparty democracy, but Momoh used the civil war as an excuse to postpone elections. He was finally overthrown in April 1992 by a group of young military officers, the National Provisional Ruling Council (NPRC), led by Captain Valentine Strasser. For the first two years of his leadership, Strasser was generally popular. Although Sierra Leone remained one of the world's poorest countries, following the coup there was at least food in the shops and fuel for the buses. Roads and buildings across the country were repaired and repainted, and a monthly National Cleaning Day was instituted.

By mid-1994, some of the heady optimism seemed to be fading. The continuing fight in the east of the country against the anti-government rebels, the RUF led by Foday Sankoh (who may have been bolstered after the coup by Momoh supporters and by irregular forces from Liberia), was a major distraction and drain on resources. The army regularly defeated the rebels through 1993, but by mid-1994 the rebels were again on the offensive. North-eastern and eastern parts of the country were reported to be falling into anarchy, with rebels and government soldiers, plus deserters from both sides, roaming and terrorising local people. A few groups turned to banditry, so even some main roads were unsafe.

Early in 1995 the country was engulfed in civil war and thousands of people were displaced. Danger for travellers increased, with a series of kidnappings of foreigners by rebel groups. Much of the area outside the Freetown peninsula remained under control of the RUF. Strasser permitted the formation of opposition parties in 1995 and actively encouraged the holding of free elections.

In late 1995, Strasser was replaced by Brigadier Julius Maada Bio who promised to push forward with elections in February 1996. In early February Bio made overtures to commence discussions with Foday Sankoh and the RUF. The elections went ahead, but not without problems – rebels attacked the town of Bo, temporarily closing the polling stations; voter lists went missing; and even Bio's residence came under attack. Runoff elections had to be held as no one person received over 50% of the primary vote. Rebels branded the words 'no election' on the backs of some villagers in the Bo region as a warning to others not to participate in the runoff elections.

In March the results of the February election were finalised. Ahmad Tejan Kabbah, of the SLPP (with nearly 60% of the vote) was elected. The military government handed over power as was promised. Bio met Foday Sankoh in Yamoussoukro (Côte d'Ivoire) in late March. Kabbah followed in late April and agreed on a 'definitive cease-fire'. The RUF had specific conditions including the removal of the South African mercenaries, Executive Outcomes, who currently guarded the Sierra Rutile titanium oxide mine (which the rebels had overrun in January 1995).

Later in 1996 there were several truce violations, including a bloody outbreak of violence in the Bo region in June, an attack on the village of Koindu in August, and several attacks on vehicles on the Bo to Freetown highway. In September, a plot to kill Kabbah was foiled, and four soldiers were arrested. In late September the army, with the assistance of Executive Outcomes' helicopters, attacked the rebel base which threatened the Bo to Freetown highway. In October it seemed that the cease-fire had ended with many attacks by RUF rebels, especially in the eastern Kenema district and along the Makeni to Kono road. Government troops retaliated by attacking rebel bases, including one near Mile 91.

On November 30 1996 a truce between the government and the RUF was signed, and it was hoped that peace would prevail, although there were reports of another coup attempt within a week of the truce being signed. Sadly, in late May 1997, heavy fighting broke out in Freetown when elements of the army staged a coup, deposing president

Ahmad Tejan Kabbah. Kabbah fled to Guinea, Nigerian troops fought with the rebels, and foreign nationals (and the Sierra Leonean staff) were evacuated by marines and French troops. Ghanaian officials tried desperately to garner a truce. Foreigners were advised not to visit the country.

It is estimated that there are one million people in the Bo, Kenema and Freetown region who have been displaced by the war. Hope springs eternal, but in a country where there are so many refugees, a bloody civil war and the world's worst figure for infant mortality (164 per 1000 live births), widespread child prostitution and sexually transmitted diseases, the outlook for peace and prosperity is grim.

At present the rebels, controlled by Major Johnny Paul Koromah, have control over Freetown and most of the country following a coup in 1997. Members of the Economic Community of West African States (ECOWAS), led by Nigerian forces, have vowed to return the country to democracy and reinstitute the government of Ahmad Tejan Kabbah. How long it will take is anyone's guess. Sadly, it does not seem that the resolution of the conflict will be achieved peacefully. Sierra Leone will probably be off-limits to tourists for some time.

GEOGRAPHY & CLIMATE

Approximately half of the country consists of a flat belt of coastal lowland except on the mountainous Freetown peninsula. The other half rises to mountainous plateaus along the border with Guinea. The climate is hot and humid with heavy rainfall along the coast – up to 3250mm per year. Most of the rain falls between June and September.

POPULATION & PEOPLE

The population of Sierra Leone is around 5.5 million, of which the Temne (mainly in the north) and the Mende (mainly in the south) comprise about 30% each. As well as several smaller indigenous ethnic groups, there are minorities of Europeans and Lebanese. Krios number 2% of the population and mainly live in and around Freetown.

SOCIETY & CONDUCT

Traditional Culture

The Mende and the Temne, and their related groups, have a system of secret societies responsible for maintaining the culture of the tribes, into which boys and girls are initiated at adolescence. Most cultural activities are strictly closed to outsiders. This is particularly the case where 'devils', who dance on special occasions and holidays, are concerned. If you are lucky enough to be allowed to witness the dances, photography is prohibited unless the devils agree to accept money.

LANGUAGE

English is the official language. There are also about 14 tribal languages. The usual spoken language is Krio, which has its roots in English and various African tongues.

Facts for the Visitor

VISAS

Visas (or entry permits which, for Sierra Leone, are almost the same) are required for all. They are normally valid for 30 days, and cost US$30 for Britons, US$15 for Americans and US$10 for most other nationalities.

Extensions are available at immigration (☎ 22 3023) in Freetown at 44 Siaka Stevens St, four blocks east of the Cotton Tree.

Other Visas

In Freetown you can get visas for several African countries. For each visa you need between one and four photos.

Burkina Faso, Chad & Togo
    The French embassy issues visas to these countries, and possibly Mauritania. It's open weekday mornings, and issues visas within 24 hours.
Côte d'Ivoire
    The embassy is open from 9 am to 3 pm. Visas take 24 hours to issue and cost US$25.
The Gambia
    The embassy is open from 8 am to 4 pm Monday to Friday, and issues visas within 24 hours. The cost varies but is about US$15 for Americans.

Ghana

The embassy is open from 9 am to 3 pm. Visas take three days to issue and cost about US$25.

Guinea

The embassy is open from 9 am to 3 pm Monday to Friday. Visas are issued the same day, and cost between US$25 and US$50. A letter of recommendation may be requested. (You can also get a visa to Guinea in Nongoa, just across the border from Koindu in the north-eastern corner of Sierra Leone. However, procedures can change, so double-check this with the embassy in Freetown.)

Liberia

The embassy is currently closed.

Mali

The embassy is open weekday mornings, and issues visas within 24 hours for US$20.

Nigeria

The embassy is open from 10 am to 1 pm Monday to Thursday. Visas take three or four days to process. As at all Nigerian embassies, the cost varies according to nationality, being very cheap for Americans and very expensive for Britons.

Senegal

The consul is usually in attendance from 9 am to 4.30 pm Monday to Friday and from 9 am to 12.30 pm on Saturday. Visas cost US$12 and are issued the same day.

EMBASSIES
Sierra Leonean Embassies
In Africa, there are Sierra Leonean embassies in Côte d'Ivoire, The Gambia, Ghana, Guinea, Liberia, Nigeria and Senegal. If you're in a place with no Sierra Leonean embassy, try the British high commission.

Foreign Embassies in Sierra Leone
Countries with a diplomatic mission in Freetown include:

Côte d'Ivoire

1 Wesley St, east of Pademba Rd (☎ 22 3983)

France

13 Lamina Sankoh St, north of Siaka Stevens St (☎ 22 2477)

The Gambia

6 Wilberforce St, south of Lightfoot Boston St (☎ 22 5191)

Ghana (high commission)

6 Percival St, just north of Siaka Stevens St (☎ 22 3461)

Guinea

eastern end of Wilkinson Rd, next to a Fiat-Lada garage.

Ireland (honorary consulate)

8 Rawdon St (☎ 22 2017)

Mali

40 Wilkinson Rd, 200m beyond Aberdeen Junction (☎ 23 1781)

Nigeria

Nigeria House, Siaka Stevens St, near the Cotton Tree (☎ 22 4202)

Senegal (consulate)

9 Upper East St, a block east of the Leona Hotel

UK (high commission)

Standard Bank Building, on the corner of Lightfoot Boston and Wilberforce Sts (☎ 22 3961)

USA

1 Walpole St, near Siaka Stevens St (☎ 22 6481)

MONEY
US$1   =   Le 925

The unit of currency is the leone (Le). The import or export of more than the equivalent of US$5 in leones is illegal. Currency forms are not used, unless you take more than US$5000 into or out of the country.

At the airport (not at land borders) you have to change US$100, or the equivalent, into leones. Rates are the same as at banks in town. When you leave the country, your money will be counted and you may be searched, although it's all fairly hassle free. At the airport you cannot convert excess leones back into foreign currency.

Banks and foreign exchange (forex) shops offer free exchange rates (ie not artificially fixed), so there is no black market. However, rates and commissions vary considerably between banks and forex shops, according to what you change. You'll get a very bad rate for travellers' cheques at a forex shop, and good rates for most types of cash (especially for large denomination notes). The banks give higher rates for travellers' cheques (but only for US dollars and UK pounds). Travellers' cheques in other currencies (eg French francs) get very bad rates.

POST & COMMUNICATIONS
The postal service in and out of Sierra Leone is unreliable. Aerograms are available and recommended.

The telephone network within Freetown, and to some upcountry towns, is quite good.

For international calls, go to the External Telecommunications office (☎ 22 2801) on Wallace Johnson St, open daily from 8 am to 7 pm.

The country code for Sierra Leone is 232. The telephone area code for Freetown is 022.

DANGERS & ANNOYANCES

Like any city in the world Freetown has its thieves. During the day be on your guard against pick-pockets and bag-snatchers. At night keep to the main streets. The beaches directly in front of the tourist hotels and restaurants outside Freetown are generally safe during the day (although you shouldn't leave things unattended) but risky after dark. Lounging alone further down the beach is asking for trouble, and sleeping there would be suicidal.

Then there's the civil war. If you venture outside the peninsula, make sure you check the current situation – realise that once out there you are pretty much on your own, and in considerable danger from bandits and skirmishers.

PUBLIC HOLIDAYS

Public holidays in Sierra Leone include: 1 January, 27 April (Independence Day), 29 April (Day of Revolution), 25 and 26 December, Good Friday, Easter Monday and variable Islamic holidays (see the Public Holidays section in the Regional Facts for the Visitor chapter).

ACCOMMODATION

In Freetown you can choose between dirty brothels, mid-range guesthouses and international-class hotels. There's less of a choice when you go upcountry, although most large towns have a few cheap hotels and missions which let travellers stay.

FOOD

You buy cheap eats from a chophouse, and most travellers reckon that the chop (food) in this country is some of the best in West Africa. You can nearly always find rice and *plasas*, which is a sauce made from pounded potato or cassava leaves cooked with palm oil and fish or beef.

Other typical Sierra Leonean dishes include okra sauce, groundnut stew and pepper soup. Street food is also good and easy to find in most towns.

Getting There & Away

AIR

European airlines serving Freetown include KLM, Air France, Sabena and Aeroflot. Air Gambia also has a service from London via Banjul, and Ghana Airways flies from London via Accra.

Within Africa, Ghana Airways has many flights between Freetown and other African capitals along the coast, including Conakry (US$65 one way). Other regional airlines include Air Gambia and Gambia Airways (with return flights to Banjul for US$220), Air Guinée, Guinée Air Service, Nigeria Airways and Sierra National Airlines (with return flights to Accra for US$350). All the airlines have offices in central Freetown. Airport departure tax for international flights is US$12.

LAND
Guinea

Peugeot 504 bush taxis and minibuses ply the Freetown to Conakry route, either direct or with a change at the border. The trip costs about US$15 and takes 10 to 12 hours.

It's also possible to enter Guinea from Koindu (in north-eastern Sierra Leone) by taking a canoe across the river to Nongoa, from where you can reach Guéckédou. Or you can go from Kabala (in the north) to Faranah, or from Makeni to Kindia, via Kamakwie (useful if you want to visit Outamba-Kilimi National Park).

Liberia

When the war in Liberia ends, the Freetown to Monrovia route will be via Kenema and the Liberian coast. The whole journey can be done in two days in the dry season, with a change of vehicles and an overnight stop in Kenema.

SEA

Guinea

A fast, luxurious hydrofoil service operated between Freetown and Conakry, Guinea, until the end of 1993. The one-way fare was US$40. It may start again, so enquire at Sierra Link Ltd (☎ 22 2304) at 22 Rawdon St, Freetown, or any travel agency.

Getting Around

AIR

Sierra National Airlines ('Scare-lines'!) has promised a domestic service, perhaps to Kenema and Bo; enquire locally.

ROAD

The once proud fleet of Sierra Leone Road Transport Corporation (SLRTC) buses now lies dormant. Private buses, such as Tilda's Atlantic, cover some routes but

await the end of the war before mounting a fullservice.

Bush taxis (usually Peugeot 504s) and minibuses (called *poda-poda*) generally do relatively short trips between major towns. Bush taxis and poda-poda are often extremely crowded and uncomfortable. The local car rental agencies usually stipulate that their driver accompany the rented vehicle.

Note that many road distances on signposts and maps (including the Michelin) are given in miles.

Freetown

Freetown used to have a dirty and decrepit air and very little worth seeing. But since the coup of 1992, everything has changed and the last few years have seen a sudden surge of activity and optimism. On the main streets are waste bins which people actually use and

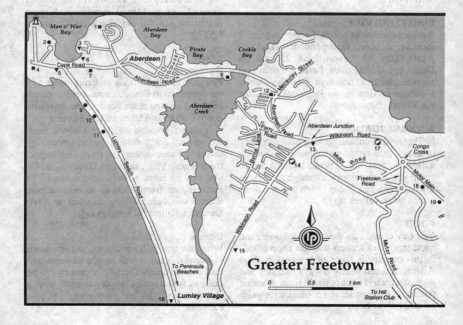

Greater Freetown

which (even more remarkable) are regularly emptied. Things are not perfect yet, but Freetown is not a bad place to visit (and will be even better once the civil war is finally over). As African cities go it's got a good feel and a lot of character.

Information

There is no information office; the Ministry of Tourism & Cultural Affairs (the most underworked of the government departments these days), near the Government Wharf, may distribute out-of-date leaflets.

National Park Information The Sierra Leone Conservation Society (☎ 22 9716) at 4 Sanders St, at the far western end of Siaka Stevens St, has good leaflets and a booklet for sale about the country's protected wildlife areas. The money raised helps to fund the society's various projects. You can also get national park information from the Wildlife Conservation Branch, part of the Forestry

Division, in the government buildings at Tower Hill (☎ 22 5352).

Money Barclays Bank on Siaka Stevens St is the best place to change travellers' cheques, although the service is slow. Nearby are several forex shops including First Foreign Exchange and West Africa Forex Bureau.

Post The post office is on Siaka Stevens St, three blocks east of the Cotton Tree. It's open weekdays and Saturday morning, and the poste restante is free. To send packages, go to the parcel post office on the waterfront at the foot of Lamina Sankoh St.

Cultural Centre The British Council has a library and shows free films most Fridays. To get there, go south on Gloucester St, and turn left just past the Sierra Leone library; it's 200m up the winding road.

Travel Agencies The best travel agencies in

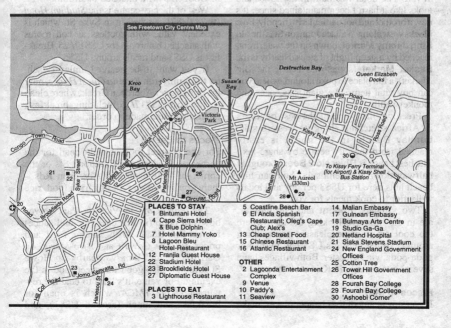

PLACES TO STAY
1 Bintumani Hotel
4 Cape Sierra Hotel & Blue Dolphin
7 Hotel Mammy Yoko
8 Lagoon Bleu Hotel-Restaurant
12 Franjia Guest House
22 Stadium Hotel
23 Brookfields Hotel
27 Diplomatic Guest House

PLACES TO EAT
3 Lighthouse Restaurant

5 Coastline Beach Bar
6 El Ancla Spanish Restaurant; Oleg's Cape Club; Alex's
13 Cheap Street Food
15 Chinese Restaurant
16 Atlantic Restaurant

OTHER
2 Lagoonda Entertainment Complex
9 Venue
10 Paddy's
11 Seaview

14 Malian Embassy
17 Guinean Embassy
18 Bulmaya Arts Centre
19 Studio Ga-Ga
20 Netland Hospital
21 Siaka Stevens Stadium
24 New England Government Offices
25 Cotton Tree
26 Tower Hill Government Offices
28 Fourah Bay College
29 Fourah Bay College
30 'Ashoebi Corner'

town are Yazbeck Tours (☎ 22 2374) and IPC Travel (☎ 22 6860), both in the centre on Siaka Stevens St near the Odeon Cinema. Yazbeck represents American Express. You can also arrange upcountry tours, although the set-up here is geared towards groups – most trips require a minimum of eight passengers.

Things to See & Do

Halfway along Siaka Stevens St is the 500-year-old **Cotton Tree**, which is the city's main landmark. Up the hill from the tree you can see the **State House** (the drive is closed to the public). Just to the east of the tree are the **Law Courts** and, on the opposite side, is the **National Museum**. It has a great collection of masks used by the secret societies. Open weekdays from 10 am to 4 pm (entry by donation), it's well worth a short visit. On Lightfoot Boston St, at the corner of Gloucester St, is the dilapidated **City Hotel**, where Graham Greene wrote *The Heart of the Matter*, while working here for the British Colonial Service during WWII. The hotel was built in the 1920s and looks like it hasn't been maintained since. It's now a brothel and not particularly friendly. Five blocks west along Wallace Johnson St is the old **King Jimmy Market**, down on the waterfront, reached by a steep flight of steps. Nearby is the **Basket Market** (sometimes called the Big Market), a fun place to poke around, where you can buy vital items like giant saucepans and monkey skulls.

Freetown has some of the best **beaches** in Africa stretching along its western side. **Lumley Beach**, in the north, is easily reached from the city centre by share-taxi. The best beach is **River No 2 Beach**, roughly halfway down the peninsula. You can hire beach huts here for US$3 per day and locals will offer to cook meals for you.

Two villages, **Regent** and **Gloucester**, are in the hills overlooking the city, where the cool air is more pleasant for walking around. To get here it's US$0.50 by bus or poda-poda, via Leicester. Both villages have several interesting old Krio-style houses.

Places to Stay

If you stay at any of the cheaper places, make sure you have a good torch (flashlight) or candles as you may spend many nights in the dark.

The best place is the *YMCA* (☎ 22 3608) at 32 Fort St, south-west of the Paramount Hotel. It accepts men and women. Clean single/double rooms with fans cost US$7/10. It's nearly always full, so you may need to wait at the restaurant until someone leaves. Cheaper, but certainly not safer, is the *Tropic of Cancer Hotel* at 4 Gloucester St, where rooms are US$5 per person; a plus is the good value chop served here.

Another possibility is the dingy *Lamar Hotel* (☎ 22 5903), at 21 Howe St, with rooms for US$8/11. Better value is the *Leona Hotel* (☎ 22 3587), on the corner of Regent St and Back St, where clean air-con rooms with attached bathroom cost US$10/12. More expensive but very good value is the *Diplomatic Guest House* (☎ 22 4179) at 152 Circular Rd, near the junction with Fort St, where clean air-con rooms cost US$17/20, or US$20/25 with attached bathroom.

West of the city centre is the *Stadium Hotel* (☎ 24 0387), reached from Syke St, which is excellent value with spotless air-con rooms with attached bathroom for US$17/25. Breakfast is US$3 and meals around US$5.

If you want to be nearer Lumley Beach, try the family-run *Franjia Guest House*, near the bridge over Aberdeen Creek, where clean rooms cost US$17/25 including breakfast; other meals are made to order.

Places to Eat

For cheap street food at night head for the corner of Sanders and Campbell Sts or the corner of Wilkinson and Aberdeen Rds – there you'll find all types of fried food, rice and roast meats.

The *Park Café* in Victoria Park serves bowls of chop (in this case rice and sauce) for around US$1. With similar food and prices are *The Cavern* and *Afro-Merik*, on Garrison St, and *Wendy's* nearby on Howe St, which is also good for street food in the evening. For value, it's hard to beat the restaurant at the *YMCA*, which is open for breakfast and lunch (around US$1), and

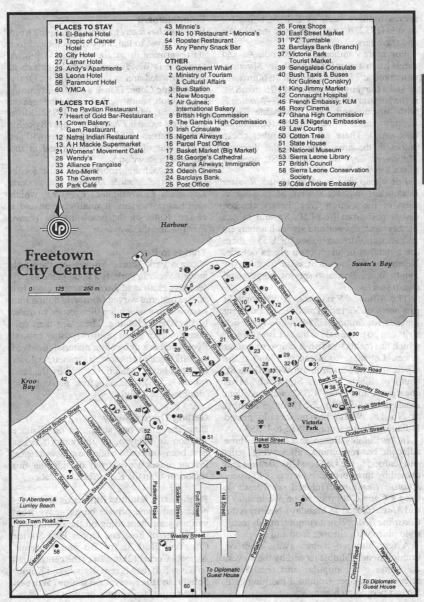

Freetown City Centre

Harbour

Susan's Bay

Kroo Bay

Victoria Park

Kissy Road

To Aberdeen & Lumley Beach

Kroo Town Road

To Diplomatic Guest House

To Diplomatic Guest House

0   125   250 m

PLACES TO STAY
14 El-Basha Hotel
19 Tropic of Cancer Hotel
20 City Hotel
27 Lamar Hotel
29 Andy's Apartments
38 Leona Hotel
56 Paramount Hotel
60 YMCA

PLACES TO EAT
6 The Pavilion Restaurant
7 Heart of Gold Bar-Restaurant
11 Crown Bakery; Gem Restaurant
12 Natraj Indian Restaurant
13 A H Mackie Supermarket
22 Womens' Movement Café
28 Wendy's
33 Alliance Française
34 Afro-Merik
35 The Cavern
36 Park Café

43 Minnie's
44 No 10 Restaurant - Monica's
54 Rooster Restaurant
55 Any Penny Snack Bar

OTHER
1 Government Wharf
2 Ministry of Tourism & Cultural Affairs
3 Bus Station
4 New Mosque
5 Air Guinea; International Bakery
8 British High Commission
9 The Gambia High Commission
10 Irish Consulate
16 Nigeria Airways
16 Parcel Post Office
17 Basket Market (Big Market)
18 St George's Cathedral
22 Ghana Airways; Immigration
23 Odeon Cinema
24 Barclays Bank
25 Post Office

26 Forex Shops
30 East Street Market
31 'PZ' Turntable
32 Barclays Bank (Branch)
37 Victoria Park Tourist Market
39 Senegalese Consulate
40 Bush Taxis & Buses for Guinea (Conakry)
41 King Jimmy Market
42 Connaught Hospital
45 French Embassy; KLM
46 Roxy Cinema
47 Ghana High Commission
48 US & Nigerian Embassies
49 Law Courts
50 Cotton Tree
51 State House
52 National Museum
53 Sierra Leone Library
57 British Council
58 Sierra Leone Conservation Society
59 Côte d'Ivoire Embassy

serves dinners such as fish & chips for around US$2. It's a good place to meet locals and travellers.

For more 'authentic' surroundings, and meals for just over US$1 a dish, try *Minnie's*, unmarked at 7 Lamina Sankoh St, 60m north of Siaka Stevens St. Nearby, at 10 Sankoh St, is the smarter *No 10 Restaurant – Monica's*, with air-con and very reasonable Sierra Leonean meals for about US$3 (open lunch time only). There are several other cheap places in the area, including the *Women's Movement Café* on Charlotte St, north of Siaka Stevens St.

For cheap fast food go to the *Rooster Restaurant* on Siaka Stevens St, two blocks west of the Cotton Tree; hearty chicken dishes cost from US$4.50. Several blocks further west, *Burgerland* serves hamburgers and various African dishes for US$1; there are a number of street chop places outside. Nearby, on Wellington St, is the friendly *Any Penny Snack Bar*, also serving burgers and cheap snacks.

The *Alliance Française*, at 30 Howe St just north of Victoria Park, serves excellent lunches for around US$4, while homesick Brits can go to the cafe at the *British Council*, which has meals like fish & chips for similar prices. Lebanese food can be found at the efficient *Gem Restaurant* on Wilberforce St, south of Siaka Stevens St, which serves chawarma for about US$2 and excellent meals in the US$6 to US$12 range. Nearby, at No 18, *Natraj* has reasonably priced Indian meals for around US$5 to US$8.

In the Lumley Beach area there are three adjacent bar-restaurants, all serving grills and seafood in the US$5 to US$20 range and owned by three brothers: George's *El Ancla Spanish Restaurant* (closed on Tuesday); Oleg's *Cape Club* (closed on Wednesday); and *Alex's* (closed on Monday). Nearby is the *Coastline Beach Bar,* an unpretentious local-style place with cheaper food and beer.

A few hundred metres away, right on Lumley Beach, almost lapped by the waves, are some other popular and reasonably priced places, open from mid-morning until the last people go home.

Entertainment

Freetown has many nightclubs, ranging from the real dives to the fairly respectable. Most start warming up at about 10 or 11 pm. A favourite is *Wendy's* on Howe St, which is very crowded and is free to get in to. Or try the frenetic *Count Down*, a small and smoky reggae club, south-west of the central area on Sanders St, where entrance is US$2. More upmarket again is *Phase 2* on Upper Syke St, which charges US$3 entry. Voyeurs will get a kick out of the show performed at the *Paladio* in Rawdon St.

In the beach area, tourists and richer locals head for the *Attitude Disco* at the modern *Lagoonda Entertainment Complex*, which also has restaurants, a small cinema and a casino. Right on the beach are the *Venue*, *Paddy's* and the *Seaview*.

Things to Buy

Victoria Park Tourist Market, on the north side of Victoria Park, is a good place to buy 'country cloth' and *gara*. Country cloth is a coarse material woven from wild cotton into narrow strips which are then joined to make blankets and clothing. These are then coloured indigo, green or brown using natural dyes. Gara is a thin cotton material, tie-dyed or batik-printed either with synthetic colours or natural dyes. Material is sold by the *lapa* (about 1.5m), and is often pre-cut into 'double-lapa' lengths.

Getting There & Away

Bus The main bus station is on Wallace Johnson St. Many of the upcountry services have been suspended while the civil war rages. Private buses leave from outside the bus station, or from the Kissy Shell bus station.

Bush Taxi & Minibus Bush taxis and poda-poda (and some private buses) leave from various sites, depending on the destination: the corner of Free and Upper East Sts for Conakry; Dan St for Bo and Kenema; Ashoebi Corner (2km east of the central area on Kissy Rd) for Makeni, Kabala and Koidu-Sefadu; and the Kissy Shell station (5km east of the centre) for various destinations.

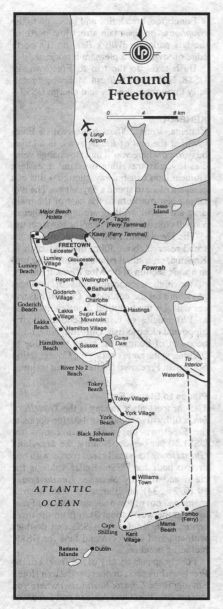

Around Freetown

0   4   8 km

Lungi Airport

Tasso Island

Major Beach Hotels

Ferry Tagrin (Ferry Terminal)

Kissy (Ferry Terminal)

FREETOWN

Leicester

Lumley Village   Gloucester

Lumley Beach

Fowrah

Regent   Wellington

Goderich Village   Bathurst

Goderich Beach   Charlotte

Lakka Village   Hastings

Sugar Loaf Mountain

Lakka Beach

Hamilton Village

Guma Dam

Hamilton Beach   Sussex

River No 2 Beach

To Interior

Tokey Beach

Waterloo

Tokey Village

York Beach

York Village

Black Johnson Beach

ATLANTIC OCEAN

Williams Town

Tombo (Ferry)

Cape Shilling   Mama Beach

Kent Village

Banana Islands   Dublin

Getting Around

The Airport Freetown's Lungi Airport is about 25km from the city on the other side of the bay. A private taxi from the airport should cost around US$5 to Tagrin ferry terminal and US$35 all the way to Freetown (the taxi drives on and off the ferry). Or you can walk 200m out of the airport to the main road and take a share-taxi (on the left as you come out of the gates) for US$0.30 (you pay extra for baggage).

The ferry from Tagrin across to Kissy (US$2/1 in 1st/2nd class) only goes once every two to three hours. From the Kissy ferry terminal share or private taxis go into Freetown (about 4km). Most people walk up the hill to the main road and then take a share-taxi into the city centre (US$0.30).

The express ferry runs between the Tagrin terminal and government wharf in the centre of the city. It costs US$10 one way and normally links with intercontinental flights. If you are staying at one of the large beach hotels you can take the Hotel Ferry from Tagrin to the beach; it costs US$20 one way.

Taxi Taxis do not have meters so for private hire the price must be negotiated. The official fare from the city centre to the beach area is about US$15. There are many private cabs gathered outside the Paramount Hotel on Independence Ave.

Share-taxis run to most destinations. A ride in a share-taxi costs about US$0.30 for a short trip in town. If you get into an empty taxi without discussing the price, you have chartered a private taxi, like it or not.

Around the Country

Since 1990 many parts of Sierra Leone's eastern region have been closed to visitors due to fighting. With the uneasy truce, and a proliferation of armed bandits, this is still very much the case for independent travellers. Make enquiries locally before venturing off the main routes.

BO

Bo is a lively town, and a good place to buy country cloth and gara: ask at Coker's Bar or find Omar & Mohammed, two brothers who prepare fine cloth. Currently, it is near the centre of ongoing rebel activity.

A cheap and pleasant place to stay is the *Catholic Pastoral Centre* on the south-eastern edge of town, about 2km from the centre. Simple rooms with two beds are US$3 to US$5 per night, and meals cost US$3. In the town centre, the *Black & White Hotel* is an old favourite with travellers. Meals start from US$2, and a double with attached bathroom costs US$17.

For cheap food, head for *Coker's Bar* where Pa Coker always has cold beer and his wife, May-Rose, makes good chop. Slightly more upmarket is *The Villa*, a restaurant-bar on the road between the town centre and the Mobil station, but smartest of all is the *ES Minimarket & Snack Bar* which serves good food in the US$4 to US$8 range.

Bush taxis to Kenema (US$2) leave from the bus park on the north side of Fenton Rd.

BUNCE ISLAND

This intriguing destination is in the Sierra Leone River some 20km from Freetown. The British built a fort here in the 17th century from where they traded in camwood (used to make dye), ivory and, sadly, slaves.

Getting there is not easy although Yazbeck Tours (☎ 22 2374) occasionally operates trips in winter. It can also be reached from the north bank village of Pepel. Pepel is 160km by road from Freetown, so only the most determined travellers are likely to make the journey.

KABALA

Kabala is the largest town in the north, at the end of the tar road, about 300km from Free-town. The surrounding hills, with cool streams and waterfalls, are good for gentle hiking.

The central *Gbawuria Guest House* (pronounced BOW-ree-ah) is next to the chief's office on the western side of town. Very clean rooms with one or two beds cost US$3 a night, and the bathroom is spotless.

For coffee, bread, rice and sauce go to the *chophouse* on the main street just north of the bus park. *Pa Willy's Bar*, on the north edge of town, has a pleasant terrace.

Bush taxis do the trip to Freetown for US$8. Bush taxis to/from Makeni go regularly throughout the day and charge US$3.

KENEMA

Kenema, some 300km south-east of Free-town, at the end of the tar road, is a large, busy town where you'll have to change vehicles if you're travelling overland to eastern Guinea. Don't rush away, though – this is a pleasant place to spend a day or two. The two large open **markets** to the east of the main drag are worth strolling around, and there's a small covered market near the town centre.

The **Tiwai Island Wildlife Sanctuary** is a small reserve about 50km directly south of Kenema, on a small island (about 13 sq km) in a wide section of the Moa River. It has one of the highest concentrations of primates anywhere on the continent. Careful observers will see the beautiful diana monkey, up to 120 species of birds, crocodile, pygmy hippo and electric fish. Unfortunately, it has been out of bounds for many years due to fighting in the area; contact the Conservation Society in Freetown for the current status.

Places to Stay & Eat

The cheapest place to stay is the *Travellers' Inn*, a filthy dive at the petrol station opposite the Freetown bus park, with rooms for US$1.50 per person. Nearby, the *Maryland Guest House* has small clean rooms with one or two beds for US$6. Better value is the clean and friendly *Swarray Kunda Lodge* (☎ (022) 534) on Blama Rd (the western main road out of town towards Bo and Free-town in the west) about 3km from the town centre, with singles for US$3 and doubles with attached bathroom and fans for US$8, including breakfast.

For cheap eats try any of the *shacks* in the Freetown bus park, or near the Eastern Hotel. Smarter is the *Capitol Restaurant* where you can get cold beers and African and Lebanese meals. For drinking, try the *Mobil Spot Bar* or the *Super Pub*.

Getting There & Away

Bush taxis to most destinations go from the taxi park in the long dirt street near the clocktower, south of the centre.

MAKENI

Makeni, some 190km from Freetown, is the capital of the northern province and a major transport hub. Here you can buy *shukublais* (Temne baskets) and gara material (see Things to Buy earlier). The vibrant market is a good place to find Bundu masks, but look out for pick-pockets.

Places to Stay & Eat

On the south-western outskirts, close to where the new Freetown to Kono highway bypasses town, is the *Thinka Motel* (pronounced TIN-kah). It is reasonably new and in good condition; rooms with one or two beds cost US$3, or US$4 with attached bathroom. Quieter and more central is the *Caritas Guest House* on Soldier St, about 100m north of Independence Place. Basic, run-down but clean rooms cost US$3 for one or two people; order meals in advance.

For cheap eats, there are several chop-houses in the bus park; *Tamaraneh Brothers* is one of the best, and it also serves coffee and sandwiches. A Makeni institution is *Pa Kargbo's Bar* on Teko Rd next to the Catholic Pastoral Centre, where you can get cold beers and delicious grilled meat sticks prepared by a man named Usman. The motto is 'Usman's Tastes Awesome'.

MT BINTUMANI

Mt Bintumani, also called Loma Mansa (King of the Lomas), lies at the centre of the Loma Mountains Forest Reserve, some 60km south-east of Kenema. At about 1945m, this is the highest point in West Africa (as long as you agree that Mt Cameroun, 2500km to the east, is in Central Africa), and the reserve protects an area of **highland rainforest**, particularly impressive on the western side. There are several species of monkey and you're quite likely to see chimpanzee. Above 1500m the forest gives way to open grassland. After the rains, when the skies are clear, views from the summit (marked by a cairn and a bottle full of messages, from about 30 years ago) are excellent.

The usual approach is from the village of Yifin, to the east of the dirt road that runs between Kabala and Bumbuna, from where it's at least a four day walk to and from the summit. A shorter approach (at least three days) is from Kurubonla, north of Kono. The best time to attempt to climb to the summit is either side of the rainy season (April to May or October to November).

Wherever you start from, you must carry enough food for at least five days, along with camping equipment. There are villages on the lower slopes where you might get a hut to sleep in, but you'll need a tent further up the mountain. A guide is needed for the maze of forest paths. Pay the guide about US$1 per day, and about the same to any person who lets you sleep in their hut, plus a small tip (about US$0.50 or kola nut) to the chiefs in villages where you stay.

OUTAMBA-KILIMI NATIONAL PARK

The Outamba-Kilimi National Park (usually called OKNP) is in the remote north-western part of Sierra Leone. It's easy to reach if you've got your own 4WD.

The park headquarters, visitors' centre and camp are in the Outamba section; an area of rolling hills, grasslands, flood plains and rainforests, dissected by several rivers. The Kilimi section (to the west) is much flatter and not as interesting. The number of species observed is diverse – primates such as the chimpanzee, colobus monkey and the sooty mangabey, pygmy hippo and the rare bongo (as well as many other savannah mammals).

Inside the park there are no roads, so you'll have to walk or hire a canoe (US$2 per day). Guides can also be hired for about US$3. The park entry for overseas visitors is US$8 per day. For more information, contact Wildlife Conservation (see the Information section for Freetown in this chapter).

Somalia

Facts about the Country

HISTORY

The Somali coast once formed part of the extensive Arab-controlled trans-Indian Ocean trading network. Its ports of Mogadishu and Brava were part of the East African chain which stretched through Malindi, Mombasa, Zanzibar and Kilwa as far as Sofala in Mozambique.

The prosperity of these ports was substantially diminished when the trading network was superseded by the Portuguese discovery of a sea route to India and beyond via the Cape of Good Hope early on in the 16th century.

In the 19th century much of the Ogaden Desert – ethnically a part of Somalia – was annexed by the empire of Ethiopia during Ménélik I's reign. This loss has never been accepted by the Somalis. Not only did it poison Somali-Ethiopian relations for more than half a century, but it also led to war on more than one occasion.

At the turn of the century Somalia was divided between the British, who took the northern part opposite Yemen along with Socotra Island, and the Italians, who took the southern part alongside the Indian Ocean. The two parts were reunited when independence was gained in 1960.

SOMALIA
Area: 738,000 sq km
Population: 10 million
Population Growth Rate: 1.6%
Capital: Mogadishu
Head of State: No functioning government
Official Language: Somali
Currency: Somali shilling
Exchange Rate: SSh 2620 = US$1
Per Capita GNP: US$150
Inflation: 25%
Time: GMT/UTC + 3

Nine years later a military coup brought Mohammed Siad Barre to power on a ticket of radical socialism which resulted in enormous changes in Somali society. The government placed great emphasis on self-reliance and on the use of team work. Many roads, houses, hospitals and agricultural projects were created in this manner during this period.

As a result of the coup which brought Barre to power, the USA withdrew the Peace Corps and, in 1970, imposed a trade embargo on the country following news that Somalia was trading with North Vietnam. The USSR immediately stepped into the vacuum with economic and military aid, and several years later Somalia's armed forces became one of the best equipped and best trained on the whole continent.

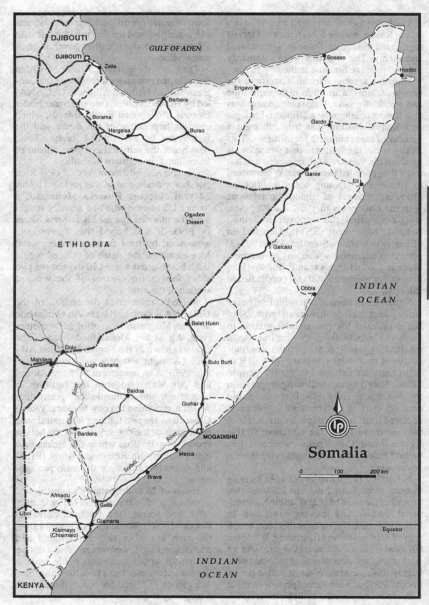

SOMALIA

DJIBOUTI

GULF OF ADEN

DJIBOUTI
Zeila
Bosaso
Hordio

Berbera
Erigavo

Borama
Hargeisa
Burao
Gardo

ETHIOPIA
Garoe
Eil

Ogaden
Desert

Galcaio

Obbia

INDIAN
OCEAN

Belet Huen

Dolo
Mandera
Lugh Ganana
Bulo Burti

Baidoa
Giohar

Bardera
MOGADISHU
Merca

Brava

Afmadu
Gelib

Liboi
Giamana

Kisimayo
(Chisimaio)

KENYA

Somalia

0   100   200 km

Equator

INDIAN
OCEAN

The honeymoon came to an end, however, when Russia rearmed Mengistu's Marxist regime in Ethiopia, Somalia's traditional archenemy. The Russians were summarily ordered to leave Somalia in the late 1970s.

Unusual among African countries, the people of Somalia are all from the same tribe and speak the same language; compatriots also live in neighbouring Djibouti, Ethiopia and Kenya. Within that tribe, though, a number of clans compete for influence. This rivalry is not dissimilar to that which exists between the various Afghan groups and has more than once led to civil war. When forced to vacate their training bases in Ethiopia, following renewal of diplomatic relations with the Ethiopians in 1988, the Isaq clan, who controlled the opposition Somali National Movement (SNM), launched an offensive in northern Somalia. About 50,000 people died, mainly due to government bombing of Hargeisa and Burao (Isaq towns). An estimated 400,000 people fled to Ethiopia.

Somalia has been at war with itself ever since. Just before his overthrow, Siad Barre ordered his presidential guards to flush out rebels from the capital. As a result, they shelled Mogadishu continuously for four weeks, leaving 75% of it in ruins and an estimated 50,000 people killed. Faced with continuing aggression by government forces, the Isaq-dominated northern part of the country (Somaliland) declared itself independent from the rest of the country in 1990. The effects of all this fighting and the distrust which it has fuelled among the various clans have been devastating.

Following fierce battles between warring factions throughout 1992, the USA decided to send in marines to help distribute international food aid to a starving population. In May 1993 the UN took over this role, which proved to be costly and frustrating. While the UN was able to alleviate the problem of starvation, its peacekeeping efforts were largely unsuccessful. When it pulled out its troops, who had been virtual prisoners inside their own compounds, in September 1994,

there were more arms than ever on the streets of Mogadishu, and the country was left with a devastated economy and no government or constitution.

There are more than 25 factions within Somalia, the two major forces being the Congress/Somali National Alliance (USC/SNA) led by Hussein Aideed (son of former leader General Mohammed Farah Aideed), which controls large areas of the south; and the faction led by Mohammed Ibrahim Egal, who heads the self-declared government of Somaliland, in northern Somalia.

General Aideed died in August 1996 from gunshot wounds, and he was replaced by his 34-year-old son, Hussein Mohamed, a former US marine who had actually fought with the marines against his father's forces in 1993. It was hoped that a cease-fire announced by rival factions in the capital Mogadishu on the death of Aideed would hold, but it lasted a scant 10 days as the two sides fought for control of the western section of the city.

Aideed's main rival for control of the USC/SNA is Osman Hassan Ali Otto, while northern Mogadishu is controlled by another rival, Ali Mahdi Mohammed, head of the faction known as the Somali Salvation Alliance. (A bright note here was the signing in late 1996 of an agreement between Aideed and Ali Mahdi to stop the fighting in Mogadishu and dismantle the 'green line' which had divided the city for some years.) Other clans are also fighting for control over other parts of the country, one of the hottest spots being Baidoa, where the Rahanwein clan's Rahanwein Resistance Army (RRA) and Aideed's faction are the main protagonists.

Heads of 26 of the country's clans signed a peace accord in January 1997 after lengthy talks, and formed the National Salvation Council (NSC). While this is a hopeful sign, the two key clan leaders, Aideed and Mohammed Egal, were absent, and a lasting settlement would seem impossible without the participation of these two. So while there is a glimmer of hope for peace, there is still a long way to go.

Refugees

In addition to the destruction of houses, schools and hospitals, Somalia has for years had well over a million refugees, from the war in the Ogaden and its own civil wars. With a population of around 10 million and very limited resources, Somalia is clearly incapable of either feeding or housing more than a fraction of its people. Hundreds of thousands have died of starvation or disease.

Somalia remains a deeply troubled country, and one which will take years to rebuild – should peace ever prevail. ■

GEOGRAPHY & CLIMATE

Severe droughts – and consequent famines – are continuing problems in this part of the world.

The Somali coastline has some of the longest beaches in the world, but they are mostly unsafe for swimming because of the danger of sharks. Visiting them can also be a searing experience because of a lack of shade.

The climate is hot and humid during the rainy seasons (March to June and again between September and December) but otherwise very pleasant. In the mountains and plateaus of the north it is hot and dry with little vegetation and few people. You won't see any evidence of agriculture, only the scattered herds of domestic sheep, goats and camels belonging to the nomads. You can make some beautiful journeys in this part of the country, especially from Hargeisa to Berbera, and along the switchback ascent from the coastal plain to the central plateau on the Berbera-Burao road. South of Mogadishu the land becomes greener, though flat and monotonous.

POPULATION & PEOPLE

Somalia's population is near 10 million and its people are some of the most striking in the world, being tall with aquiline features and ebony skin, and wearing long-flowing robes. They are quiet and dignified and tend to ignore strangers, although Somalis who have learned to speak English are ready to talk, unless you are politically suspicious of you.

LANGUAGE

Somali is the official language. English is widely used in the north but Italian dominates in the south. Written Somali is a very young language and there are many variations in use. Hamar and Xamar, for example, both refer to Mogadishu (which can also be spelled Moqdishu).

Somali script uses the Roman alphabet. Arabic script is only used for religious purposes.

Facts for the Visitor

VISAS

Visas are required by all, but with the current state of affairs it seems that anyone can enter the country without a visa.

EMBASSIES
Somali Embassies

In theory there are Somali embassies in a number of African countries, including neighbouring Djibouti and Kenya, but at the time of writing these were not operating.

Foreign Embassies in Somalia

Countries with diplomatic missions in Somalia are predictably few; one of these is the UK, although foreign staff have been withdrawn. The embassy (☎ 20288) is at Waddada Xasan Geedd Abtoow 7/8 (PO Box 1036), Mogadishu.

MONEY
US$1 = SSh 2620

The unit of currency is the Somali shilling (SSh), which equals 100 centesimi. Trying to change anything other than US dollars cash is probably a waste of time.

ACCOMMODATION

There's likely to be very little in the way of hotels for some time to come. Even before 1992 the choice was very limited.

If you sleep out in the desert (as is often necessary on long truck trips) you need a

SOMALIA

Qat

Another feature of life, in common with Ethiopia and Yemen, is the consumption of *qat*. The leaves of this bush give a kind of mild amphetamine high when chewed and it is one of the few stimulants sanctioned by Islam. Although officially illegal in Somalia, the supply continues to pour in and its sale and distribution are big business. Even at the height of the Ogaden war the daily DC3 Air Somali qat flight from Dire Dawa to Mogadishu was always on time, and shooting at it from either side was strictly out of the question.

More recently, the supply of qat has been driven in at high speed across the scrub from Kenya and Ethiopia in specially modified Toyota Landcruisers. ■

sleeping bag or warm clothes as it gets quite cold at night.

FOOD

The staple diet everywhere is rice, macaroni or spaghetti with a splash of sauce. With luck you may have the choice of mutton or goat. Endless cups of tea are obligatory. The standard breakfast throughout Somalia is fried liver (of sheep, goat or camel) with onions and bread.

Getting There & Away

AIR

There are flights between Nairobi and Mogadishu but they will be cancelled if there is fighting in the capital.

Internal flights are a hit-and-miss affair and are often cancelled altogether. In any case, it might not be wise to take one. Scud and Sam missiles are in use by rebels and government troops and not everyone knows the difference between civil and military aircraft.

LAND

The land border between Somalia and Djibouti is closed.

There's no way you can get overland from Somalia to Kenya at present (unless you're part of a refugee aid convoy). Moreover, the entire border area is infested with well-armed Somali *shifta* (bandits), making any attempt to cross it a dangerous and foolhardy venture.

Getting Around

ROAD

There are sealed roads between Mogadishu and Kisimayo and, except for a few stretches of desert track, between Mogadishu and Hargeisa. Elsewhere the roads are gravel or just tracks through the bush. In the dry season the unsealed roads and tracks are good enough and you'll get from one point to another quickly. In the wet season, however, the stretch between Kisimayo and Garissa (Kenya) alone can take up to two weeks! The road between Hargeisa and Djibouti gets into a similar state, but it isn't quite as bad.

Bus

There is a regular network of buses between the main population centres in the south, but very few run in the north. Most of them travel at night to avoid the heat of the day and air raids.

Since the civil war is still raging, it's impossible to say what transport – if any – is currently running.

Mogadishu

Founded in the 10th century AD by Arab immigrants from the Persian Gulf, Mogadishu had its heyday in the 13th century. It was then that the mosque of Fakr al Din and the minaret of the Great Mosque were built. The city's wealth was based on trade across the Indian Ocean with Persia, India and China, which is what attracted the Portuguese during the 16th century. Unlike the other Arab city-states further south along the coast of East Africa, Mogadishu was never conquered by the Portuguese and continued to be ruled by its sultans until it accepted the overlordship of the Sultan of Oman in the 19th century.

Warning

As a result of the civil war much of the city is in ruins and most of the sights mentioned in this section probably don't exist any more.

Things to See

The **Hammawein**, or **Xamar Weyne**, is the original city of Mogadishu and was once one of the most beautiful sights on the east coast of Africa, rivalling such places as Lamu, Mombasa and Zanzibar.

Other travellers have recommended a visit to the Italian-constructed Roman Catholic **cathedral** and the **museum** next to the Al Aruba Hotel.

The **market** (by the main bus station) is very interesting and worth looking around. You might also like to visit the livestock market, **Suuqa Xoolaha**, early in the morning. It's at the final stop of the Barhadda Taasin-Suuqa Xoolaha bus run.

The most popular beach for both expats and Somalis, especially on Friday, is **Gezira Beach**, but to get there you need to have your own transport. There is a hotel and the beach is supposedly protected from sharks.

Further along the coast are a number of isolated **coves**, though not all are protected from sharks. (One is appropriately called Shark's Bay, though the name is actually derived from a shark-shaped coral reef that juts up out of the water.) Keep an eye out for sharks if you do go swimming.

Getting Around

Buses to other parts of the country leave from

SOMALIA

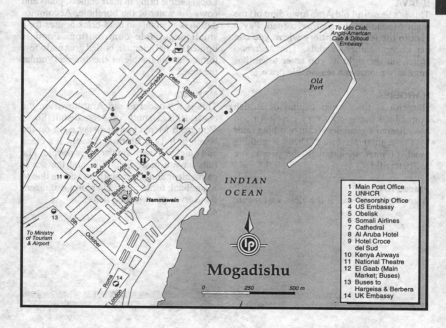

INDIAN
OCEAN

Mogadishu

To Lido Club,
Anglo-American
Club & Djibouti
Embassy

Old
Port

To Ministry
of Tourism
& Airport

Hammawein

0   250   500 m

1 Main Post Office
2 UNHCR
3 Censorship Office
4 US Embassy
5 Obelisk
6 Somali Airlines
7 Cathedral
8 Al Aruba Hotel
9 Hotel Croce
   del Sud
10 Kenya Airways
11 National Theatre
12 El Gaab (Main
   Market; Buses)
13 Buses to
   Hargeisa & Berbera
14 UK Embassy

El Gaab, the big expanse of sand, dust and chaos at the southern end of Lido St, which is also the marketplace.

Around the Country

BERBERA
There is nothing much of interest in Berbera although the people are really friendly and helpful. One traveller reported that it was 'hot, humid and hell – and that's in the cool season'. Be very discreet here about taking photos.

Places to Stay & Eat
Two of the cheapest places are the *Hotel Wabera*, which is clean, and the *Hotel Saaxil*, where you have the choice of a room with fan or air-con. More expensive is the *Hotel Sahel* where all rooms come with air-con.

BRAVA
This is a beautiful old Arab town 5km off the main Mogadishu to Kisimayo road. Pay a visit to the **leather tannery** where you can get cheap leather sandals. The *Kolombo Hotel*, on the right as you enter town, has large airy rooms at a reasonable price.

HARGEISA
Hargeisa is the former capital of British Somaliland but is now very run-down and has suffered a great deal from bombing raids by the regular air force. There is nothing much of interest, although the people are really terrific.

Places to Stay
A good place to stay is the clean and secure

Hotel Daali. The *Hotel Maaweel* is similar. There are also rooms at the *Hargeisa Club*. Also recommended is *State House*, 2km outside town. The staff are friendly and you can camp in the park.

KISIMAYO
Remember to report to the National Security Service on arrival.

Places to Stay
One of the best places to stay is the clean and friendly *Hotel Quilmawaaye*. It's set in a nice garden and the local bigwigs go there. Not as central is the *Hotel Africa* which has good rooms but no electricity. The *Wamo Hotel* is more expensive but it's a good place to meet expatriates and locals, especially if you are looking for a lift to Mogadishu and elsewhere.

LIBOI
This border town is a fascinating little place. Local people bring in their camels, goats and cows for water at the borehole. Accommodation is available in mud-brick houses for a small negotiable contribution. Food is limited to chai, chapati, boiled goat and a few tomatoes, obtainable at the 'market' under the tree.

MERCA
This is a wonderful old Arab town on the coast 100km south of Mogadishu. Some 5km from Merca you can stay right on the beach in huts at **Sinbusi Beach**. It's clean and quiet and there are very few people. The huts have a basic bathroom and the sea is calm, clear and warm with no sharks due to a sandbank further out. There is a *restaurant* that serves good grilled fish.

South Africa

In April 1994, South Africa's first truly democratic elections were held, installing a multiracial government under the presidency of Nelson Mandela. Since then the country has been a popular destination, especially with budget travellers.

Facts about the Country

HISTORY

The earliest recorded inhabitants of this area of Africa were the San (Bushmen) and the closely related Khoi-Khoi (Hottentots). The next arrivals were Bantu-speaking tribes who, by the 11th century, had settled the north-east and the east coast and, by the 15th century, most of the eastern half of southern Africa. These tribes were pastoral, but had trade links throughout the region. They were Iron Age peoples, and the smelting techniques of some tribes were not surpassed in Europe until the Industrial Revolution.

The first European settlement in South Africa was a supply station established in 1652 by the Dutch East India Company at the Cape of Good Hope. This quickly became a colonial settlement (based in Kaapstad, Cape Town) and the Khoi-San people were driven away. The settlers developed a close-knit community with their own dialect (Afrikaans) and Calvinist sect (the Dutch Reformed Church). Slaves were imported from Africa and South-East Asia.

Over the next 150 years the colonists spread east, coming into violent contact with Bantu tribes. In 1779 the eastward expansion of the Boers (Dutch-Afrikaner farmers) was temporarily halted by the Xhosa in the first Bantu War.

Further Boer expansion was hastened after the British annexed the Cape in 1806 and abolished slavery in 1834. The latter was regarded by the Boers as an intolerable interference in their affairs and it led to their migration

REPUBLIC OF SOUTH AFRICA
Area: 1,120,000 sq km
Population: 38 million
Population Growth Rate: 1.7%
Capital: Pretoria (administrative), Cape Town (legislative), Bloemfontein (judicial)
Head of State: President Nelson Mandela
Official Languages: Afrikaans, English, isiZulu, isiNdebele, isiXhosa, siSwati, seSotho, seSotho saLebowa, Setswana, Tshivenda, Xitsonga
Currency: Rand
Exchange Rate: R4.4 = US$1
Per Capita GNP: US$3000
Inflation: 9%
Time: GMT/UTC + 2

Highlights
- Stalking the 'big five' in Kruger National Park
- Tramping around Cape Town
- Surfing Jeffreys Bay
- Sampling some of the thousands of South African wines around Stellenbosch
- Hiking in the dramatic Drakensberg

across the Orange River two years later. This event became known as the Great Trek.

Pressure on the Bantu from both the Boers and the British caused political and social changes among the tribes of the Natal area, resulting in the rise of the Zulu king Shaka. His policy of total war on neighbouring tribes caused immense suffering and mass-migration in a period known as the *difaqane* ('the scattering').

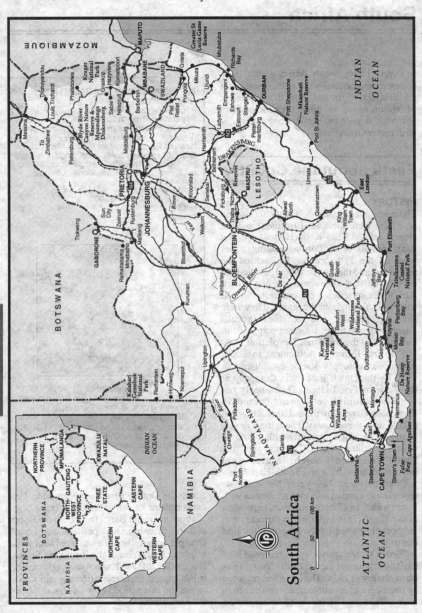

South Africa

Into this scene came the Boers in search of new lands, and not far behind them were the British. The Zulu were eventually defeated, but relations between the Boers and the British remained tense – particularly after the formation of the Boer republics of the Orange Free State and the Transvaal.

When diamonds were discovered in 1867 at Kimberley, then gold in 1886 on the Witwatersrand (Johannesburg), the Boer republics were flooded with British capital and immigrants, creating resentment among the Boer farmers.

The British imperialist Cecil Rhodes encouraged a rebellion among the heavily taxed, but non-voting, English-speaking miners in the Transvaal, with a view to destabilising the Boer republics and inviting British intervention. The resulting tensions led to the 1899-1902 Anglo-Boer War.

The war ended with the defeat of the Boer republics and the imposition of British rule over the whole country. Britain had pursued a scorched-earth policy to combat Boer guerrillas, destroying homes, crops and livestock. Over 26,000 Afrikaner women and children died in the world's first concentration camps.

In 1910 the Union of South Africa was created, giving political control to the whites. This led to black resistance in the form of strikes and the setting up of political organisations. Despite the moderate tone of these early organisations, the government reacted by intensifying repression.

In 1948 came the election victory of the Afrikaner National Party. They went even further in excluding non-whites from political or economic influence, and the security forces brutally enforced the laws. Violence became routine in suppressing any opposition and protest, ranging from the Sharpeville massacre of 1960 and the shooting of school children in Soweto in 1976, to the forcible evacuation and bulldozing of squatter settlements, and the systematic torture and even murder of political activists, such as Steve Biko.

One of the most important organisations to oppose the racist legislation was the African National Congress (ANC). As it

became obvious that the white rulers were unwilling to undertake even the most cosmetic reforms, guerrilla warfare became virtually the only option for the ANC. In the early 1960s, many of its leaders were arrested, charged with treason and imprisoned for long periods – the most famous being Nelson Mandela.

The system of apartheid was entrenched even further in the early 1970s by the creation of the so-called Black Homelands of Transkei, Ciskei, Bophuthatswana and Venda, which were, in theory, 'independent' countries. By creating the Homelands, Pretoria could claim that all blacks within white-designated South Africa belonged to a Homeland and that they were, therefore, foreign guestworkers not entitled to political rights. Any black person without a residence pass could be 'deported' back to a Homeland.

Meanwhile, South Africa was becoming isolated as a result of the success of liberation struggles in Angola, Mozambique and Zimbabwe, which all brought Marxist-leaning governments into power. As a result, a war psychosis came to dominate government thinking and resulted in invasions of southern Angola by South African armed forces, the encouragement of counter-revolutionary guerrilla groups in both Mozambique and Angola, and the refusal to enter into genuine negotiations for the independence of Namibia.

The international community belatedly began to oppose the apartheid regime, and the UN imposed economic and political sanctions. Some concessions were made by the government, including the establishment of a farcical new tricameral parliament of whites, coloureds (mixed race) and Indians – but no blacks.

The 'reforms' did nothing to ease sanctions and after the 1989 elections the new president, FW de Klerk, instituted a programme which was aimed not just at dismantling the apartheid system but introducing democracy. The freeing of political prisoners on 11 February 1990, including Nelson Mandela, the repeal of the Group Areas Act, and the signing of a peace accord with the ANC and other opposition groups, opened the way for hard-fought negotiations on the path to majority rule.

At midnight on 26 April 1994, *Die Stem* (the old national anthem) was sung and the old flag was lowered. Then the new rainbow flag was raised and the new anthem, *Nkosi Sikelele Afrika* (God Bless Africa), was sung.

The new democratic South Africa, with President Mandela at the helm, has some difficult times ahead. The vast majority of the population was economically and politically oppressed for so long that expectations are enormous, and meeting them is impossible, at least in the short term.

GEOGRAPHY

South Africa extends nearly 2000km from the Limpopo River in the north to Cape Agulhas in the south, and nearly 1500km from Port Nolloth in the west to Durban in the east.

There are nine provinces: Gauteng, Northern, Mpumalanga, KwaZulu-Natal, Free State, North-West, Northern Cape, Eastern Cape and Western Cape.

The Homelands no longer exist, but because of their very different histories you still notice a change when you cross one of the old borders. Transkei and Ciskei have been absorbed into Eastern Cape (a small chunk of Transkei has been claimed by KwaZulu-Natal), Venda into Northern Province and Bophuthatswana into the North-West (Thaba 'Nchu, an isolated chunk of Bop, is in Free State). The smaller Homelands (Gazankulu, Lebowa, KaNgwane, KwaNdebele, KwaZulu and QwaQwa) have been more easily absorbed into the surrounding provinces.

CLIMATE

South Africa is mostly dry and sunny, lying just to the south of the Tropic of Capricorn. The major influence on the climate is the topography and the surrounding oceans.

The eastern plateau region (including Johannesburg) has a dry, sunny climate in winter with maximum temperatures around 20°C and crisp nights with temperatures dropping to around 5°C. Between October and April there are late afternoon showers often accompanied by spectacular thunder

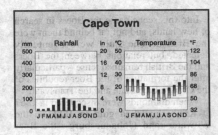

and lightning, but it rarely gets unpleasantly hot. It can, however, get very hot in the Karoo (the interior of the Cape provinces), in Northern Province and the Northern Cape Province.

The south-western cape region has dry sunny summers with maximum temperatures around 26°C. It is often windy, however, and the south-easterly 'Cape Doctor' can reach gale force. Winters can get cold, with occasional snow on the higher peaks.

Along the south coast the weather is temperate, but the east coast becomes increasingly tropical the further north you go. KwaZulu-Natal can be very hot and unpleasantly humid in summer, although the highlands are still pleasant. This is also a summer rainfall area; winter is pleasant.

POPULATION & PEOPLE

South Africa's population is estimated to be about 38 million, of whom about 30 million are black, about five million are white, about three million are coloured and about one million are of Indian descent. Some 60% of whites are of Afrikaner descent, and most of the rest are of British descent. The coloureds live mainly in Western Cape Province, and the Indians (descended from labourers imported by the British in the 19th century) live mainly in KwaZulu-Natal.

Afrikaners

Afrikaner culture doesn't seem to differ much from that in other western countries; however, a violent history, religious fervour and a sense of being isolated in a very dangerous part of the world produce strong undercurrents. The Great Trek has echoes in wagon-wheel fences in suburbia and people are aware of 'old' family names. Folk songs are sung like hymns at political rallies and suspicion of foreign ideas remains. The concepts of culture and race are tightly fused.

Blacks

Just how distinct the various black groups really are is debatable as most classifications date from white scholarship in the 19th century. Also, the difaqane and white invasion meant that the tribes either merged into strong nations or were swept aside. The centralised Zulu, Swazi and Basutho (Lesotho) states are a direct result of this.

Traditionally there have been two major groupings, the Nguni (Zulu, Swazi and Xhosa) and the Sotho (Tswana, Pedi and Basutho). The various groups have much in common. A belief in a distant deity combined with worship of more approachable ancestors forms the basis for religion.

LANGUAGE

There are 11 official languages, but most people speak Afrikaans, English or both, as well as their mother tongue. The most widely spoken African languages are isiXhosa and isiZulu. Both use a variety of 'clicks', very hard to reproduce without practice. It's worth the effort, if only to provide amusement for your listeners.

Afrikaans

Afrikaans developed from the High Dutch of the 17th century. It has abandoned the complicated grammar and adopted vocabulary from French, English, indigenous African and even Asian languages (thanks to Malay slaves).

Greetings & Civilities

Hello.	*Hallo.*
Good morning sir.	*Goeiemôre, meneer.*
Good afternoon madam.	*Goeiemiddag, mevrou.*
Good evening miss.	*Goeienand, juffrou.*
Good night.	*Goeienag.*
Thank you.	*Dankie.*

Useful Words & Phrases

yes	*ya*
no	*nee*
What?	*Wat?*
How many?	*Hoeveel?*
How much?	*Hoeveel?*
When?	*Wanneer?*
Where?	*Waar?*
today	*vandag*
daily	*daagliks*
information	*inligting*
office	*kantoor*

I'm sorry, I don't speak Afrikaans.	*Es es lemmer, ek nie Afrikaans praag.*

Getting Around

left	*links*
right	*regs*
avenue	*laan*
road	*weg*
station	*stasie*
street	*strasse*
town	*stad*

isiXhosa
Greetings & Civilities

Good morning.	*molo*
Goodnight.	*rhonanai*
Do you speak English?	*uyakwazi ukuthetha siNgesi?*
father (term of respect)	*bawo*
Are you well?	*uphilile nanamhlanje?*
Yes, I am well.	*ewe, ndiphilile kanye*
Where do you come from?	*uvela phi na okanye ngaphi na?*
I come from ...	*ndivela ...*

Useful Words & Phrases

How much does it cost?	*idla ntoni na?*
I am lost.	*ndilahlekile*
Is it possible to cross the river?	*kunokwenzeka ukuwela umlambo?*

Is this the road to ...?	*yindlela eya ... yini le?*
When do we arrive?	*siya kufika nini na?*
Would you show me the way to ...	*ungandibonisa na indlela eye ...*
day	*usuku*
month (moon)	*inyanga*
east	*empumalanga*
west	*entshonalanga*

isiZulu

To ask a question, add *na?* to the end of a sentence.

Useful Words & Phrases

please	*jabulisa*
Thank you.	*ngiyabonga*
yes	*yebo*
no	*cha*
Where does this road go?	*iqondaphi lendlela na?*
Which is the road to ...?	*iphi indlela yokuya ku ...?*
Is it far?	*kukude yini?*
north	*inyakatho*
south	*iningizumi*
east	*impumalanga*
west	*intshonalanga*
water	*amanzi*
food	*ukudla*
lion	*ibhubesi*
rhino (black)	*ubhejane*
rhino (white)	*umkhombe*
snake	*inyoka*

Facts for the Visitor

VISAS

Visas are not required by most holiday visitors – you'll be issued with an entry permit on arrival.

If you do need a visa it's worth getting it (free) before you depart for Africa, but allow a couple of weeks for the process. They are not issued at the border.

On arrival you might have to satisfy an immigration officer that you have sufficient funds for your stay. If you arrive by air you'll probably need to show an onward ticket. An air ticket is best, but overland seems to be OK. If you come by land things are more relaxed.

Apply for visa or permit extensions at the Department of Home Affairs, 77 Harrison St, Johannesburg (☎ (011) 836 3228); 56 Barrack St, Cape Town (☎ (021) 462 4970); or at the Sentrakor Building, Pretorius St, Pretoria (☎ (012) 324 1860). This is usually simple, but it's expensive at about US$70.

Other Visas

Botswana
> The visa section of the embassy in Johannesburg (☎ (011) 403 3748; fax 403 1384) is open from 8 am to 1 pm. Most visitors do not require a visa for a stay of up to 90 days. If you do need a visa you'll need to photocopy the first five pages of your passport and supply two passport photos, along with a fee of about US$8.

Mozambique
> The embassy in Johannesburg and the consulate in Cape Town issue one-month visas in six days (US$16, or US$23 for 24-hour service). You'll need two passport photos. The Mozambique tourism authorities in Johannesburg (☎ (011) 339 7275) and Durban (☎ (031) 305 1010) can issue visas faster. However, many travellers get Mozambique visas from the embassy in Swaziland, which charges less.

Namibia
> Most visitors do not require a visa for a stay of up to 90 days. If you need one, get it at the Namibia Tourism office in Cape Town (☎ (021) 419 3190) or Johannesburg (☎ (011) 331 7055). Single/multiple entry visas cost US$5/12. You don't need passport photos but you do need to show an onward ticket or other proof of transport out of the country (such as a hire-car contract).

Zambia
> Most visitors do not need a visa for a stay of up to 90 days. If you need one, get it from the High Commission in Pretoria. You need three passport photos and a fee of US$25 for single entry or US$40 for multiple entry.

Zimbabwe
> Although many visitors don't need a visa there are some significant exceptions. Visas are not issued at the border – go to the consulate in Johannesburg, where there's a wait of up to a week. You don't need passport photos, but there is a fee of US$20 for single entry, US$30 for double entry and US$44 for multiple entry.

EMBASSIES
South African Embassies

There are embassies in Australia, Brazil, Canada, France, Germany, Italy, the Netherlands, Spain, the UK and the USA, among other countries. South Africa has reopened embassies in many African countries.

Foreign Embassies in South Africa

Angola
CPK building, 153 Oliver St, Brooklyn, Pretoria (☎ (012) 46 6104)

Australia
292 Orient St, Arcadia, Pretoria (☎ (012) 342 3740; fax 342 4222)

Botswana
2nd floor, Futura Bank House, 122 De Korte St, Braamfontein, Johannesburg (☎ (011) 403 3748). There is also an office in Cape Town.

Canada
1103 Arcadia St, Hatfield, Pretoria (☎ (012) 342 6923; fax 342 3837)

France
807 George Ave, Arcadia, Pretoria (☎ (012) 43 5564; fax 43 3481)

Germany
180 Blackwood St, Arcadia, Pretoria (☎ (012) 344 3854; fax 343 9401)

Kenya
302 Brooks St, Menlo Park, Pretoria (☎ (012) 342 5066)

Lesotho
6th floor, West Tower, Momentum Centre, 343 Pretorius St, Pretoria (☎ (012) 322 6090)

Malawi
770 Government Ave, Arcadia, Pretoria (☎ (012) 342 0146)

Mozambique
7th floor, Cape York House, 252 Jeppe St, Johannesburg (☎ (011) 336 1819)
7th floor, 45 Castle St, Cape Town (☎ (021) 26 2944)

Namibia
209 Redroute, Carlton Centre, Johannesburg (☎ (011) 331 7055)
Main Tower, Standard Bank Centre, Cape Town (☎ (021) 419 3190)

Netherlands
825 Arcadia St, Arcadia, Pretoria (☎ (012) 344 3910; fax 343 9950)

Swaziland
6th floor, Braamfontein Centre, Braamfontein, Johannesburg (☎ (011) 403 2036)

Sweden
9th floor, Old Mutual Building, 167 Andries St, Pretoria (☎ (012) 21 1050; fax 323 2776)

Switzerland
818 George St, Arcadia, Pretoria (☎ (012) 43 6707; fax 43 6771)

Tanzania
845 Government Ave, Arcadia, Pretoria (☎ (012) 342 4393)

Uganda
Suite 402, Infotech building, 1090 Arcadia St, Arcadia, Pretoria (☎ (012) 342 6031)

UK
Greystoke, 225 Hill St, Arcadia, Pretoria (☎ (012) 43 3121)

USA
7877 Pretorius St, Arcadia, Pretoria (☎ (012) 342 1048; fax 342 2244)

Zambia
353 Sanlam Building, corner of Festival & Arcadia Sts, Hatfield, Pretoria (☎ (012) 342 1541)

Zimbabwe
17th floor, 20 Anderson St, Johannesburg (☎ (011) 838 5620)

MONEY
US$1 = R4.4

The unit of currency is the rand (R), which equals 100 cents. The import and export of local currency is limited to R500. There is no black market.

The Thomas Cook agent is Rennies Travel, a large chain of travel agencies, and there are American Express (Amex) offices in the big cities. Nedbank is associated with Amex. First National Bank is associated with Visa and is supposed to change Visa travellers' cheques free of fees, but many branches don't know this. Most other banks change travellers' cheques in major currencies, with various commissions.

Keep at least some of the receipts you get when changing money as you'll need to show them to reconvert rands when you leave.

Credit cards, especially MasterCard and Visa, are widely accepted. Some ATMs give cash advances on Visa and MasterCard.

Banking hours are usually from 9 am to 3.30 pm.

Taxes & Refunds

There is a Value Added Tax (VAT) of 14%, but foreign visitors can reclaim some of their

VAT expenses on departure. This applies only to goods that you are taking out of the country; you can't claim back the VAT you've paid on food or car rental, for example. Also, the goods have to be bought at a shop participating in the VAT Foreign Tourist Sales scheme.

To make a claim you need the tax invoices (usually the receipt, but make sure that the shop knows that you want a full receipt). They must be originals – no photocopies. When you depart, you have to show the goods to a customs inspector. The total value of the goods must exceed R250. After you've gone through immigration you pick up your refund cheque – at some airports you can then cash it immediately at the bank, in any major currency. If your claim comes to more than R3000 your cheque is mailed to your home address.

You can claim only at the international airports in Johannesburg, Cape Town and Durban, at the Beit Bridge and Komatipoort land borders, and at some harbours.

TOURIST OFFICES
The South African Tourist Corporation (Satour) produces some excellent tourist literature. There are Satour offices in Europe, the USA and some other countries, and embassies can usually supply material. Within South Africa you can usually find Satour material at provincial tourist offices. Satour's web site can be found at: www.africa.com/satour/index.htm

Many towns have tourist offices; if not, information is usually available at the library or the town hall.

POST & COMMUNICATIONS
South Africa has good post and communications services. Most post offices are open weekdays and Saturday morning. Long distance and international telephone calls are expensive – much more so from hotels. If your country has a 'phone home' service (which is billed to your home number or allows you to make reverse-charge calls), take advantage of it.

The telephone system is in a perpetual

upgrade and many numbers and area codes are changing. Following are area codes for the main towns:

Bisho	0401
Bloemfontein	051
Cape Town	021
Durban	031
East London	0431
Jeffreys Bay	0423
Johannesburg	011
Pietermaritzburg	0331
Port Elizabeth	041
Port St Johns	0475
Pretoria	012
Stellenbosch	021
Umtata	0471

Internet cafes are appearing in the big cities and a growing number of hostels offer email.

HEALTH
The main dangers are bilharzia and malaria, mostly confined to the eastern half of the country, especially on the lowveld. Some anti-malarial drugs are sold over-the-counter at chemists.

There are also hot-climate dangers, such as heatstroke and sunburn, plus cold-climate dangers in the Drakensberg.

When hiking, especially in the ex-Homelands where there is little infrastructure, purify water from streams near villages. See the Health Appendix for more information.

DANGERS & ANNOYANCES
Crime rates in many cities are soaring – be very careful at night, and even during the day in parts of Jo'burg, where muggings are common. Until you're certain about what you're doing, don't walk with money or valuables in the cities. Nearly all hostels have safes. If you are mugged, *do not resist*. The mugger will assume that you are carrying a gun, and will be nervous. Don't scare him into shooting you first.

It is unwise for an outsider of any race to venture into a black township without knowing the current situation and without a guide.

Some whites are racist and most are extremely insular. If you aren't of European descent, you're in for a weird time.

PUBLIC HOLIDAYS
Public holidays in South Africa include: 1 January, 21 March (Human Rights Day), 17 April (Family Day), 27 April (Constitution Day), 1 May (Workers' Day), 16 June (Youth Day), 9 August (Women's Day), 24 September (Heritage Day), 16 December (Day of Reconciliation), 25 and 26 December and Good Friday.

ACTIVITIES
Hiking
South Africa has an excellent system of hiking trails, usually with accommodation. They are popular and most must be booked well in advance. Satour's brochure on hiking is useful, and if you plan to do a lot of hiking pick up a copy of Jaynee Levy's *Complete Guide to Walks & Trails in Southern Africa* (hardback, US$25).

There are also many hiking clubs; contact the Hiking Federation of South Africa (☎ 886 6507), 420 Nedbank Centre, Bordeaux, Johannesburg. Several of the adventure travel outfits offer organised hikes.

Most trails are administered by the National Parks Board or the various Forest Regions, although the Natal Parks Board controls most trails in KwaZulu-Natal.

Surfing
South Africa has some of the best, least crowded surfing in the world. Most surfers will have heard of Jeffreys Bay, but there are myriad alternatives, particularly along the east and south coasts. The best time of the year for surfing in KwaZulu-Natal, Transkei and the south-eastern Cape is April to July.

Boards and surfing gear can be bought in most of the big coastal cities. If you plan to surf Jeffreys Bay you'll need a decent-sized board – it's a big, very fast wave.

ACCOMMODATION
Most towns have an inexpensive municipal caravan park or resort close to the centre of town. The National Parks Board and the provincial authorities operate high-quality camping grounds. Camp sites (without power) range from about US$7 to US$10. In summer you might pay US$15 or more for a site at beach resorts, as they are geared to large tents and family holidays. Many backpacker hostels have space for tents.

In some rural backwaters of the ex-Homelands (where there are few official camp sites), you can still camp where you want. *Always* ask permission from the nearest village or home before setting up your tent.

There has been a boom in backpacker accommodation and new places are opening all the time. Dorm beds go for around US$8. There is also good-value accommodation in the national parks and reserves. You'll pay US$15 to US$25 or more for a hut (two or three people).

Many places (other than hostels) have seasonal rates. The highest season is usually the summer school holidays and Easter. The other school holidays are usually classified as mid-season.

FOOD
Despite the fact that South Africa produces some of the best meat, produce and seafood in the world, the food is usually stodgy. The British can take most of the blame. Vegetarians will find the country a nightmare, although things are changing in the big cities and tourist areas.

It is worth sampling some of the traditional Cape cuisine, which is an intriguing mix of Malay and Dutch.

THINGS TO BUY
Crafts, wine and antiques are some of the best things to buy in South Africa. Indigenous crafts are on sale everywhere, from expensive galleries to street corners. The wines of the Western Cape are of an extremely high standard and are also very cheap by international standards. South Africa's long isolation from the outside world means there are troves of old goods for sale at very reasonable prices.

Getting There & Away

AIR

Jo'burg is the most important gateway to the region for both land and air transport, although Cape Town is rapidly catching up as an international air hub. Cheap charter flights from Europe have begun operating.

Most of the major European airlines fly to Jo'burg or Cape Town, some flying via Nairobi (Kenya). South African Airways, Malaysia Airlines and Qantas all offer connections with Australia and Asia. Another alternative is to fly to Singapore and connect with an Air Mauritius flight.

Interesting Asian routes are opening up. For example, Air India flies from Bombay and Malaysian Airlines flies from Kuala Lumpur.

SAA and Varig have flights linking Jo'burg with Rio de Janeiro and Sao Paulo. Malaysia Airlines also flies from Cape Town to Buenos Aires.

South African Students' Travel Service (SASTS) is a national student travel organisation (you don't have to be a student to use its services) and is worth checking out. It has offices in the Student Union building, University of Witwatersrand (☎ 716 3045) in Jo'burg. There are also offices at universities in Cape Town, Durban, Grahamstown, Pietermaritzburg and Port Elizabeth.

There are frequent flights from Jo'burg to regional cities, including Gaborone (Botswana) for US$135, Maseru (Lesotho) for US$72, Windhoek (Namibia) for US$200, Mbabane (Swaziland) for US$93 and Harare (Zimbabwe) for US$260.

LAND
Botswana

The main border posts are at Ramatlhabama, north of Mafikeng (open from 7 am to 8 pm), and Tlokweng Gate, north of Zeerust (7 am to 10 pm).

Greyhound buses run daily between Jo'burg and Gaborone for US$22. Minibus taxis run from Mafikeng (North-West Province) to Lobatese (US$4) and Gaborone (US$6). Mafikeng is accessible from Jo'burg on Transtate buses (US$12).

The weekly Bulawayo (Zimbabwe) train from Jo'burg via Gaborone was cancelled in mid-1997. Check the current situation; the fare previously was US$23/17 (1st/2nd class).

Lesotho

See the Lesotho chapter for information on land routes.

Mozambique

Panthera Azul (☎ 339 7275) runs daily buses from Jo'burg to Maputo (US$45), and also from Durban to Maputo (US$55).

The South African *Komati* train runs three times weekly between Jo'burg and Komatipoort on the Mozambique border (US$28/19/11 in 1st/2nd/3rd class), and continues on to Maputo (US$7/5.20 in 1st/2nd class).

Many travellers cross into Mozambique from Swaziland.

Namibia

The posts at Rietfontein and Vioolsdrif are open 24 hours. Crossing into Namibia from the Kalahari Gemsbok National Park isn't allowed.

Intercape Mainliner has buses departing four times weekly from Cape Town or Jo'burg to Windhoek (US$74), and an indirect service between Windhoek and Pretoria via Upington (US$85).

Ekonoliner has a weekly bus between Cape Town and Windhoek (US$52 with meals).

Swaziland

See the Bus entry in the following Getting Around section for information on the Baz Bus, which includes Swaziland on its interesting itinerary. Otherwise, the best way into Swaziland is the nightly Transtate bus from Jo'burg to Mbabane (US$15). There is a daytime service on Wednesday.

Some minibus taxis run direct between Mbabane and Jo'burg for about US$17.

Zimbabwe

Bus The only road border post between Zimbabwe and South Africa is at Beitbridge (north of Messina) on the Limpopo River, which is open from 6 am to 10 pm. There can be very lengthy waits.

Mini-Zim Luxury Mini-Coaches run twice weekly from Jo'burg to Bulawayo (US$49).

The Jo'burg-Harare bus route is covered by a growing number of operators. The Zimi-Bus runs from Jo'burg to Harare three times weekly; advance bookings are essential. Jacaranda has two weekly minibus services to Harare (US$54) and Silverbird runs twice weekly for US$76.

Train The weekly *Bulawayo Express* between Jo'burg and Bulawayo (via Gaborone) and the weekly *Trans-Limpopo Express* between Jo'burg and Harare were cancelled indefinitely in mid-1997 following an increase in costs imposed by the National Railways of Zimbabwe. Check the current sitation. Previously, fares on the *Bulawayo* cost US$54/37 in 1st/2nd class and the journey was 24 hours; fares on the *Trans-Limpopo* cost US$73/50 and the trip was 26 hours.

Getting Around

South Africa is geared towards travel by private car, with some very good highways but limited and expensive mainstream public transport. If you want to cover a lot of country in a limited time, hiring or buying a car might be necessary. If you don't have much money but have time to spare, you can hitch to most places, and if you don't mind a modicum of discomfort there's the extensive network of minibus taxis, Transtate buses and 3rd-class train seats.

AIR

SAA and SA Airlink are the main domestic airlines, and there are also regional operators. Fares are high, but if you book a week in advance there are some good discounts.

BUS

Translux and Greyhound provide 'luxury' service, good but expensive for getting from A to B. Intercape Mainliner is also good and is slightly cheaper. You'll find booking offices for these services in the big cities, and agents in many towns along their routes.

Transtate buses are slow, but they cover out-of-the-way places with inexpensive services which stop everywhere. Unfortunately, Transtate has disappeared from KwaZulu-Natal, and there are no services in Northern Cape. Getting information about Transtate can be difficult, as it was a 'black only' service in the apartheid days, and most whites have never heard of it. Try asking a black employee at a train station (where Transtate usually stops) or argue *very* hard at a Translux office. There is a Transtate booking counter at the main Jo'burg train station.

The excellent Baz Bus runs a hop-off-hop-on service between Cape Town and Durban, with a feeder service between Jo'burg and Durban. There is also a new and very useful loop between Durban, the north coast of KwaZulu-Natal, Swaziland and Jo'burg. You can either buy section tickets (not much cheaper than the main bus lines) or good-value passes. The Baz Bus runs door-to-door between hostels, which take bookings.

MINIBUS TAXI

Minibus taxis (also known as black taxis) are much more comfortable here than in other African countries, and they run absolutely everywhere. Fares are less than half the equivalent Greyhound bus fare.

Minibus taxis have been attacked in ongoing 'taxi wars' between rival operators. The chances of your taxi being attacked are very low, but it pays to find out what the current situation is in your area. Also, think twice before taking a taxi for an ultra-long trip (say, Jo'burg to Cape Town or Jo'burg to Messina) as tired drivers have accidents.

TRAIN

Spoornet, which runs the railway system, has a number of passenger routes, all on 'name trains'. On overnight trips there are sleepers provided for 1st and 2nd class, but bedding costs an extra US$3.50. Meals are available on the trains. You can't book 3rd class, though 1st and 2nd class must be booked at least 24 hours in advance.

Examples of 1st/2nd/3rd class fares are:

Durban-Bloemfontein	US$54/36/23
Durban-Cape Town	US$127/86/54
Jo'burg-Bloemfontein	US$29/20/12
Jo'burg-Cape Town	US$98/66/42
Jo'burg-Durban	US$50/33/21
Jo'burg-East London	US$65/45/29
Jo'burg-Nelspruit	US$30/21/12
Jo'burg-Port Elizabeth	US$73/49/29
Pretoria-Kimberley	US$39/27/17

CAR

A car can be very useful, despite high petrol prices and high accident rates. Most major roads are excellent, but if you get onto unsealed back roads drive very carefully. In less developed areas, drive slowly to avoid people or animals and be prepared for unannounced dangers, such as giant potholes.

Car theft is rampant in the cities and hijacking is epidemic in Jo'burg. Keep doors locked and windows wound up.

Rental

The major international companies, such as Avis (☎ 0800 021 111 toll-free) and Budget (☎ 0800 016 622 toll-free), are represented. Local companies, which come and go, currently include Imperial (☎ 0800 118 898 toll-free), Tempest (☎ 0800 031 666 toll-free) and Dolphin (☎ 0800 011 344 toll-free).

A step down from these are smaller and cheaper outfits, such as Alisa (☎ 0800 21515 toll-free) and Panther (☎ 397 1469; fax 397 2507 in Jo'burg; ☎ 511 6196; fax 511 7802 in Cape Town). You might get a deal of around US$30 per day with these companies.

Purchase

Jo'burg is the best place to buy a car; prices are generally higher in Cape Town. You will be lucky to find anything reliable for much less than US$2000.

In Jo'burg, Jules St is the main drag for used-car dealers, but you'll pay much less if you buy privately. The *Star* has ads every day and a motoring supplement on Thursday. The Sunday Car Market at the Top Star Drive-in, Simmonds Southway, Park Central, operates every Sunday from 9 am to 1 pm. Hostels are a good place to look for very battered travellers' vehicles.

BICYCLE

South Africa is a good country for cycling. It has a wide variety of terrain and climate, plenty of camping places and many good roads, most of which don't carry a lot of traffic.

Away from the big cities you might have trouble finding specialised parts, although there are basic bike shops in many towns. Mountain bikes are more common than touring bikes.

HITCHING

Hitching is sometimes the only way to get to smaller towns, and even travelling between larger ones the choice is sometimes to wait a day or two for a bus or hitch. The usual common-sense hitching rules, such as not accepting a lift with a drunk, not being dropped off in the middle of nowhere etc apply, and you should enquire about the dangers in a particular area before you stick out your thumb.

ORGANISED TOURS

The boom in backpacker accommodation has brought with it a boom in good-value tours and activities. Most hostels take bookings.

Johannesburg

A mere 100 years old, Jo'burg is by far the largest city in South Africa and is the capital in all but name. It can be an interesting place, with a few good arts venues, and Soweto tours should be a mandatory introduction to the country. However, it is also a very tense city and violent crime is common. If your time is limited, go through it as quickly as possible, or miss it altogether.

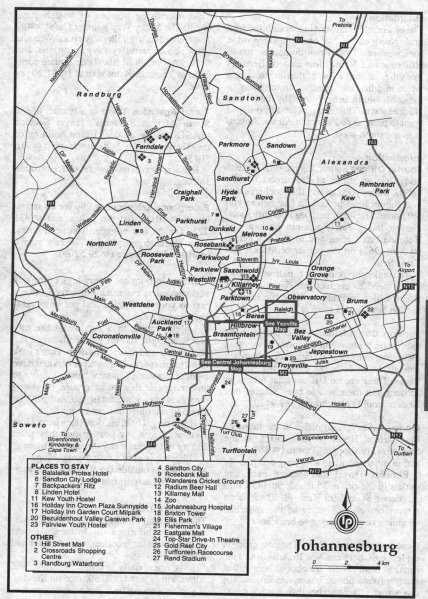

Johannesburg

PLACES TO STAY
5 Balalaika Protea Hotel
6 Sandton City Lodge
7 Backpackers' Ritz
8 Linden Hotel
11 Kew Youth Hostel
16 Holiday Inn Crown Plaza Sunnyside
17 Holiday Inn Garden Court Milpark
20 Bezuidenhout Valley Caravan Park
23 Fairview Youth Hostel

OTHER
1 Hill Street Mall
2 Crossroads Shopping Centre
3 Randburg Waterfront

4 Sandton City
9 Rosebank Mall
10 Wanderers Cricket Ground
12 Radium Beer Hall
13 Killarney Mall
14 Zoo
15 Johannesburg Hospital
18 Brixton Tower
19 Ellis Park
21 Fisherman's Village
22 Eastgate Mall
24 Top-Star Drive-In Theatre
25 Gold Reef City
26 Turffontein Racecourse
27 Rand Stadium

0   2   4 km

Orientation

The city centre is laid out in a straightforward grid. North of the city centre, a steep ridge runs west-east from Braamfontein across to Hillbrow and Berea. Just east of Berea is Yeoville, a centre of nightlife. Jo'burg's white middle-class suburbs stretch away to the north within an arc formed by the N1 and N3 freeways. This is the place to go if you want to pretend you're not in Africa. Soweto is to the south-west.

Information

Tourist Offices Satour, the national tourism body, has an office at the airport (☎ 970 1669), where you can buy the brochures that you should have picked up free before you left home. The Johannesburg Publicity Association has a fairly useless desk at the Rotunda bus station and in the city centre (☎ 336 4961) on the corner of Market and Kruis Sts.

To make bookings for national parks you'll need to contact the National Parks Board office in Pretoria – see the Pretoria section later in this chapter.

Foreign Consulates Most countries have their main embassy in Pretoria; however, a dwindling number of countries also maintain consulates in Jo'burg. Check the Yellow Pages. There are no UK consular offices in Jo'burg, but there is a Jo'burg number that Brits in trouble can ring: ☎ 337 9420.

Money Amex has an office in the lobby of the Carlton Hotel (☎ 331 2301), at the Sandton City shopping centre (☎ 883 2301) and in other suburban shopping centres.

Rennies Travel has foreign exchange outlets in the city at 35 Rissik St, 145 Commissioner St and 95 Kerk St. There is an airport branch and many of the suburban shopping centres also have branches.

Post & Communications The post office is on Jeppe St, between Von Brandis St and the Smal St Mall. There are phones here and at many private phone businesses around the city which charge higher than normal rates.

An increasing number of hostels have email. The Milky Way Internet Cafe (☎ 487 1340; email info@milkyway.co.za; Web site www.pcb.co.za/milkyway) is on the 2nd floor, 38 Raleigh St (the Time Square complex) in Yeoville. Rates start at US$1.20 per hour.

Travel Agencies There is a branch of the South African Students' Travel Service (SASTS) in the Student Union building of the University of Witwatersrand (☎ 716 3045).

Rennies Travel has several offices around Jo'burg.

Emergency Telephone ☎ 999 for an ambulance, ☎ 10111 for the police and ☎ 331 2222 for the fire brigade. You need coins, even for emergency calls. There's also a tourist police service (☎ 29 5209).

Warning Jo'burg has a very high crime rate and caution is essential. On arrival, take a taxi to your destination and put your valuables in the safe.

Unless you're in a car, avoid the city centre at night and on weekends when the shops close and the crowds drop. Don't look like a tourist (or even a backpacker) and have a small amount of money handy to give to any muggers. Beware of groups of young men showing an interest in you, and don't be afraid to ask older passers-by for help.

If you do get held up, don't be a hero. Give your assailants any possessions they want and try not to make any threatening moves.

Hillbrow is now a no-go area. Muggings are common outside the Rotunda, the long-distance and airport bus station.

Museum Africa

This museum, on Jeppe St, has simply outstanding exhibitions on Jo'burg's recent history, and a large collection of rock art and other exhibits.

It is open daily, except Monday, and admission is just US$0.50, free on Sunday. If you're walking here from the city centre, it's reputedly safer to walk along Jeppe St than Bree St.

Market Theatre

This complex on Bree St, at the north-east corner of the city centre, is one of the highlights of Jo'burg. There are theatre venues, an art gallery, some interesting shops, and bars.

Carlton Panorama

The view from the top of the 50-floor Carlton Centre on Commissioner St is spectacular and a good way to orient yourself. It costs US$14 and is open from 9 am to 7 pm Monday to Thursday, and until 9 pm on Friday and Saturday.

Gold Reef City

Gold Reef City is a tourist trap that can't make up its mind whether it's a Disneyland clone or a serious historical reconstruction of old Jo'burg. The admission fee varies from US$1.35 to US$4.40 depending on the time of entrance. The upper terrace, with most of the main tourist attractions, closes at 5 pm, but the pubs and restaurants on the lower terrace stay open. The entire complex is closed on Monday, except public holidays.

Gold Reef City is 6km south of the city, just off the M1 freeway. Catch the No 55 bus from Vanderbijl Square, the main local bus station in the city. Get off at stop No 14, Althan Rd, Robertsham, then walk west along Alamein Rd, go under the freeway and you'll see Gold Reef City on your right.

Yeoville

In the early 1990s Yeoville was in danger of becoming a suburb of junkies and other desperados. This has not happened, thanks to the music venues plus an influx of middle-class blacks. The atmosphere is relaxed and non-racial.

Rockey St, the main street, is practically the only street in Jo'burg where walking around at night is both safe and stimulating.

Bus Nos 19a and 20 run to Rockey St from Vanderbijl Square in the city centre.

Soweto

For the majority of Jo'burg's inhabitants, home is in one of the black townships surrounding the city – probably Soweto. *Don't* attempt to visit unless you have a trustworthy guide or are on a tour. Max Maximum Tours (☎ 938 8703; fax 938 8656) is highly recommended. Max is a long-time resident of Soweto, a nice bloke and a good guide. He charges about US$20. Max also offers tours further afield, such as Sun City and Kruger National Park.

Places to Stay

Camping The *Bezuidenhout Valley Caravan Park* (☎ 648 6302) is at 180 Third Ave, off Observatory Rd, Bezuidenhout Valley, near Bruma Lake, 4km to the east of Hillbrow. If you're a foreigner you can camp, otherwise it's vans only. Sites cost US$5.50.

Hostels Many hostels will pick you up from the airport or the Rotunda (some will try to poach you), and most are excellent sources of travel information. Listed here are a few good choices. If you want to look further afield, there are plenty of brochures at the airport and the Rotunda.

Yeoville is the best area to stay in Jo'burg. *Rockey St Backpackers* (☎ 648 8786; fax 648 8423) isn't on Rockey St, but it is just a short (and safe) walk away at 34-36 Regent St. Dorms go for US$7 and great doubles are from US$20. There are other choices in the area, such as the good *Pink House* (☎ 487 1991); *Explorers Club* (☎ 648 7138), 9 Innes St; and, further from Rockey St, *The Underground* (☎ 648 6132), 20 Harley St.

Further out, but within an easy walk of the Hyde Park (Dunkeld) shopping centre and a longer walk to Rosebank Mall, is the *Backpackers' Ritz* (☎ 325 7125), 1A North Rd, Dunkeld West. If you want to relax in comfort rather than experience the gritty delights of inner Jo'burg, this is the place to come. You can camp here. Prices are similar to the Yeoville places.

Hotels Some of the cheap places to stay in Hillbrow are good value, but that's because

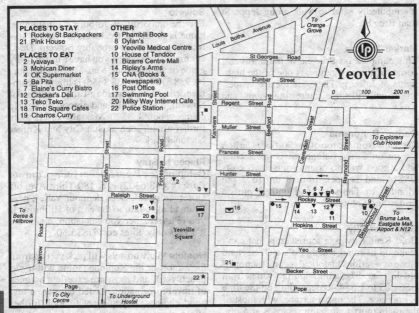

PLACES TO STAY
1 Rockey St Backpackers
21 Pink House

PLACES TO EAT
2 Iyavaya
3 Mohican Diner
4 OK Supermarket
5 Ba Pita
7 Elaine's Curry Bistro
12 Cracker's Deli
13 Teko Teko
18 Time Square Cafes
19 Charros Curry

OTHER
6 Phambili Books
8 Dylan's
9 Yeoville Medical Centre
10 House of Tandoor
11 Bizarre Centre Mall
14 Ripley's Arms
15 CNA (Books & Newspapers)
16 Post Office
17 Swimming Pool
20 Milky Way Internet Cafe
22 Police Station

Yeoville

crime has scared away customers – think twice about staying here. If you're an adrenaline junkie looking for a rock-bottom place to stay, try the run-down but lively *Chelsea Hotel* (☎ 642 4541) on the corner of Catherine and Kotze Sts, Hillbrow. Singles/doubles are around US$12/14.

The *Crest Hotel* (☎ 642 7641), 7 Abel Rd, Berea (right on the edge of Hillbrow), is comfortable and well run. The rooms are well maintained and have phones, and there is security parking. At US$15/22 it's a bargain.

There is a member of the *Formule 1* (☎ 484 5551) chain of spartan, but OK, hotels at 1 Mitchell St, Berea (near the corner of Louis Botha Ave). Rooms sleeping three people cost US$27.

Across the road at 12 Mitchell St, *Vistaero Apartments* (☎ 643 4954; fax 643 3421) are good value and within easy walking distance of Yeoville. Serviced bed-sit apartments with

stove, fridge and phone (TVs can be hired) are US$26/30 or US$164/202 per week. There's a pool and secure parking. Check the bed before you hand over your cash, as they are not very good.

Places to Eat

City Centre For a cheap meal of *pap* (maize porridge) and stew, try the stalls around the long-distance taxi ranks on Wanderers and the nearby streets. Upstairs at 11A Kort St, one of the few remaining Indian streets, *Kapitan's* is a cheerful, old-fashioned restaurant with authentic Indian food. It was a favourite of Nelson Mandela when he was a young Jo'burg lawyer.

Yeoville The Yeoville restaurants are informal places. Wander around and see what takes your fancy.

At 9A Rockey St, *Elaine's Curry Bistro* has an extensive menu and a good reputation.

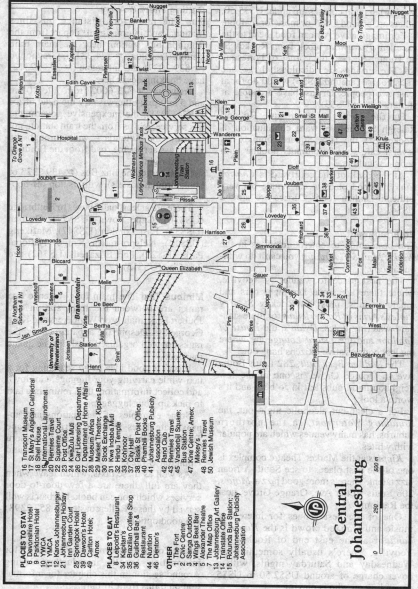

Central Johannesburg

| 0 | 250 | 500 m |

PLACES TO STAY
6 Devonshire Hotel
9 Parktonian Hotel
10 YMCA
11 YWCA
12 Karos Johannesburg Holiday Inn Garden Court
21 Johannesburg Holiday Inn Garden Court
25 Springbok Hotel
39 Dawson's Hotel
49 Carlton Hotel; Amex

PLACES TO EAT
8 Leipoldt's Restaurant
34 Kapitan's
35 Brazilian Coffee Shop
36 Guildhall Bar & Restaurant
44 Nutrition
46 Denton's

16 Transport Museum
17 St Mary's Anglican Cathedral
18 Shell House
19 International Laundromat
20 Rennies Travel
22 Supreme Court
23 Post Office
24 KwaZulu Muti
26 Car Licensing Department
27 Department of Home Affairs
28 Museum Africa
29 Market Theatre; Kipplies Bar
30 Stock Exchange
31 Iswa Indaba Muti
32 Hindu Temple
33 Konnor
37 City Hall
38 Rissik St Post Office
40 Phambili Books
41 Johannesburg Publicity Association

42 Rand Club
43 Rennies Travel
45 Vandenbijl Square; Bus Station
47 Kine Centre; Amex; Mikey's
48 Rennies Travel
50 Jewish Museum

OTHER
1 The Fort
2 Civic Centre
3 Sanga Outdoor
4 Wings Beat Bar
5 Alexander Theatre
7 The Map Office
13 Johannesburg Art Gallery
14 Translate Office
15 Rotunda Bus Station; Johannesburg Publicity Association

Vegetarian main courses are under US$5.50, others are around US$7 or more for seafood.

For imaginative African food, head to the excellent *Iyavaya*, a block from Rockey St on Hunter St, near the corner of Fortesque Rd. The servings are ridiculously large; one main course (around US$6) would do for at least two people. Or just have a couple of starters (about US$3).

On the corner of Fortesque Rd and Raleigh St (the westward continuation of Rockey St), the Time Square complex has several cafe-style restaurants popular with people-watchers.

At the back of the courtyard is *Charros Curry*, a good place to eat simple but very authentic Indian food. Curries are around US$4.

Entertainment

The best guide to entertainment is in the *Weekly Mail & Guardian*; you can't do without a copy.

The best place to wander is Yeoville, where there are some late-night bars and music venues, most on Rockey St. Try *Ripley's Arms* or *Rockerfella's* for more standard watering holes. *Dylan's*, the *House of Tandoor* and the *Lizard Lounge* are where the less conservative citizens hang out.

The *Radium Beer Hall*, 282 Louis Botha Ave in Orange Grove, is one of the few neighbourhood pubs left in Jo'burg and it's worth a look.

For a clean-cut alcoholic night out, the *Randburg Waterfront*, in the northern suburbs, has many venues which are popular with whites.

Kippies at the Market Theatre complex is one of the best places to see South African jazz talent. There's more good jazz at *Mojo's*, 206 Louis Botha Ave, Orange Grove, near the Radium.

One of the best venues for interesting music and a mixed crowd is the *House of Tandoor* at the east end of Rockey St, Yeoville. There's usually something on Wednesday and Saturday nights, with a cover charge of around US$2.50 to US$5 depending on who is playing.

Getting There & Away

Bus The main long-distance bus lines (national and international) depart from the Rotunda bus station, near the main train station. Translux (☎ 774 3313), Greyhound (☎ 839 3037) and Intercape (☎ 333 52312) have booking desks here.

Transtate (☎ 773 6002 from 7 to 10 am and 5 to 9 pm; otherwise try the head office ☎ 774 7741), the inexpensive government bus service, leaves from the train station, not far from the Rotunda – walk through the underpass across the road from the Rotunda and turn right.

Don't forget the Baz Bus (☎ 439 2323 or book through hostels), with its hop-off-hop-on service.

There are at least daily buses to Beitbridge (US$30), Cape Town (US$77), Durban (US$33), East London (US$47), Mafikeng (US$12), Nelspruit (for Kruger National Park, US$25), Port Elizabeth (US$62) and Sun City (US$15).

Minibus Taxi The main long-distance taxi ranks are between the train station and Joubert Park, mainly on Wanderers and King George Sts. Despite the apparent chaos, the ranks are well organised – ask for the queue marshal.

It isn't a good idea to go searching for a taxi while carrying your luggage. Go down and collect information, then return in a taxi to pick up your luggage.

Some examples of destinations and approximate fares from Jo'burg are: Cape Town US$40, Kimberley US$15, Maseru (Lesotho) US$15, Nelspruit US$12 and Upington US$23.

As well as these taxis, which leave when they are full, there are a few door-to-door services which you can book. Durban is well served by these. Rollercoaster (☎ 857 2398) is a good option.

Train Contact Spoornet (☎ 773 5878) for information. See the introductory Getting Around section in this chapter for information on trains from Jo'burg.

Hitching
The organisation Lift Net (☎ (021) 785 3802;) email cch@ilink.nis.za) connects drivers with passengers. A ride will cost about the same as the equivalent minibus taxi fare.

Getting Around
The Airport Between 6 am and 11 pm buses run every half-hour between Johannesburg international airport and the Rotunda. Journey time is about 25 minutes, and the fare is US$8. Private taxis are expensive (around US$25).

Some hostels will collect you from the airport, and some tout there.

Bus Most services stop by 7 pm and most fares are US$0.70.

Routes 19 (Berea), 19A (Yeoville) and 20 (Yeoville) are useful. The buses that run out to Sandton are not part of the municipal fleet; they're operated by Padco (☎ 474 2634). Buses leave the city centre from the corner of Kruis and Commissioner Sts.

Minibus Taxis It's easy to get a minibus taxi into the city centre and, if you're waiting at a bus stop, a taxi will probably arrive before the bus does. Getting a minibus taxi home from the city is more difficult. Try Eloff St if you're heading for Yeoville.

Cape Town

Cape Town, or Kaapstad, is one of the most beautiful cities in the world. It's dominated by a 1000m-high, flat-topped mountain with virtually sheer cliffs, and surrounded by mountain walks, vineyards and beaches. It is the capital of Western Cape Province and the parliamentary capital of South Africa.

Information
At the Tourist Rendezvous, at the main train station, you'll find the Captour desk (☎ 418 5214/5; fax 24 6211) and many other desks of interest.

As well as a desk at the Tourist Rendezvous, the National Parks Board (☎ 22 2810) has offices on the corner of Long and Hout Sts. Cape Nature Conservation (☎ 483 4051), 1 Dorp St, controls several reserves in the province.

Money Amex is at Thibault Square (at the end of St George's Mall; ☎ 21 5586) and at the Victoria & Alfred Waterfront (☎ 21 6021). The Waterfront office is open from 10 am to 5 pm daily.

Rennies Travel is the agent for Thomas Cook and has branches on the corner of St George's and Hout Sts (☎ 26 1789); 2 St George's St; 182 Main Rd, Sea Point (☎ 439 7529); and at the Waterfront (☎ 418 3744).

You can change money at the airport.

Post & Communications The post office is on the corner of Darling and Parliament Sts, and is open weekdays from 8 am to 4.30 pm and Saturday morning.

The public phones in the post office are open 24 hours, but they're often busy. There are plenty of privately run phone businesses where you can make calls without coins. They charge more than public phones.

Several hostels have email facilities and there are at least two cyber cafes: Connection Internet Cafe, Shop 4, Heerengracht Centre, Foreshore; and iCafe on Long St near the Long St Baths.

Atlantic Coast
The spectacular Atlantic coast has the trendiest beaches on the Cape, but the water comes straight from the Antarctic (courtesy of the Benguela current). There are four linked beaches at **Clifton**, accessible by steps from Victoria. There are frequent buses from OK Bazaars on Adderley St, and minibus taxis from the Strand.

Camps Bay is often windy and, although not as trendy as the beaches at Clifton, it is more spectacular.

Cape of Good Hope Nature Reserve
Although the coastline in the reserve is not as dramatic as that between Clifton and

Kommetjie, it is still beautiful. There are walks, beaches, a cross-section of the Cape's unique fynbos ('fine bush'), baboons, buck and birdlife.

The reserve is open daily from 7 am to 5 pm (until 6 pm from October to March).

False Bay

This bay is 25km south-east of the city. Although the east side of the Cape peninsula is not as spectacular, the water is warmer.

Simon's Town was a naval base from 1814 until 1976. **Seaforth** is the nearest beach. South of Simon's Town, turn off St George's Rd onto Seaforth Rd after the navy block. Take the second right onto Kleintuin Rd. Day visitors are charged US$0.55 entry.

Boulders Beach, also near Simon's Town, is home to a colony of penguins.

Kirstenbosch Botanical Gardens

The superb Kirstenbosch gardens on Rhodes Drive, Constantia, are on the eastern side of Table Mountain. The information office has maps and advice on various walks. The gardens are open from 8 am to 7 pm from September to March and until 6 pm from April to August.

Table Mountain & Cableway

The cableway is such a clichéd attraction you might have difficulty convincing yourself that it is worth experiencing. It is. The views from Table Mountain are phenomenal, and there are some excellent walks on the summit.

If you plan to walk, make sure you have warm and waterproof clothing. Table Mountain is over 1000m high and conditions can become treacherous quickly.

The cable cars don't operate when it's dangerously windy. If in doubt, call ☎ 24 5148 or ☎ 24 8409. They normally run from 8 am to 9.30 pm in November and from mid-January to the end of April; 7 am to 10.30 pm from December to mid-January; and from 8.30 am to 5.30 pm from May to the end of October. Once the new, larger cars have been fitted, the prices will jump to around US$12 return.

Catch the Kloof Nek bus from outside OK Bazaars on Adderley St to the Kloof Nek bus station and connect with the cableway bus. You can take a single ticket up the mountain and walk back down, either on the City Bowl side (from Tafelberg Rd past the lower cableway station) or the Kirstenbosch Botanical Gardens side.

Cape Flats

Most of Cape Town's citizens live in townships out on the Cape Flats. Visiting without a black companion who has local knowledge is foolish. One City Tours (☎ 387 5351) has an excellent three-hour township tour for US$17.

Victoria & Alfred Waterfront

This revitalised (but still working) port is packed with restaurants, bars and shops. There are several harbour cruises, starting at US$2. The **aquarium** is well worth a visit, and the kelp forest tank is astounding. Admission is US$5.

A shuttle bus runs regularly from Adderley St in front of the train station to the centre of the waterfront.

Places to Stay

Camping *Sandvlei Caravan Park* (☎ 788 5215), The Row, Muizenberg, is within about 2km of the Muizenberg train station (on the Simon's Town line). Walk east around the civic centre and pavilion, turn right onto Atlantic Beach Rd (which doglegs and crosses the mouth of the Zandvlei lagoon) and take the first left after the bridge down Axminster St, which becomes The Row. The tariff for two people ranges from US$6 to US$12 depending on the season.

Hostels There is a huge and increasing range of hostels. Listed here are a few favourites. On your way to these, stroll up Long St and check out the competition. Prices fluctuate because of the intense competition, but you'll generally pay about US$7 for a dorm and US$20 or so for a double.

The Backpack hostel (☎ 23 4530; email backpack@gem.co.za), 74 New Church St,

Cape Town

PLACES TO STAY
3 St John's Waterfront Lodge
4 Hip Hop Travellers' Stop
5 Diplomat Holiday Flats
26 Tudor Hotel
37 Long St Backpackers
40 Travellers' Inn
47 The Backpack
48 Zebra Crossing
54 Stag's Head Hotel
56 Mount Nelson Hotel
57 Gardens Centre
58 Oak Lodge

PLACES TO EAT
1 Ferryman's Tavern
13 Shebeen on Bree
28 Yellow Pepper
30 Off Moroka Café Africaine
36 Mr Pickwick's Deli
38 Mama Africa
44 Kaapse Tafel Restaurant
46 Rustica
49 Café Bar Deli
50 Mario's Coffee Shop
55 Roxy's Coffee Shop

OTHER
2 Penny Ferry Bertie's Landing
6 Tulbagh Square
7 AA Office
8 Civic Centre
9 Amex
10 Thibault Square
11 Rennies Travel
12 Havana Bar
14 Namibia Trade & Tourism
15 Tourist Rendezvous
16 Train Station
17 Koopmans de Wet House
18 National Parks Board Office
19 Golden Acre Centre
20 Minibus Taxis
21 Castle
22 Grand Parade
23 Bus Information Kiosk; Main Bus Station
24 Post Office
25 Greenmarket Square
27 Bo-Kaap Museum
29 Cape Nature Conservation
31 Manenberg's Jazz Café
32 Cultural History Museum
33 Parliament House
34 District Six Café
35 Department of Home Affairs
39 Lounge
41 Botanical & Company's Gardens
42 Internet Cafe
43 South African Museum
45 Long St Baths
51 National Art Gallery
52 Perseverance Tavern
53 The Shed

Tamboerskloof, is one of the longest running hostels, and it's still very good. It's about a 20 minute walk from the train station, or you can catch the Kloof Nek bus from Adderley St, outside OK Bazaars, to stop No 68. A few doors up at 82 New Church St is friendly *Zebra Crossing* (☎/fax 22 1265), which is smaller, quieter and more personal – and slightly cheaper.

Green Point is a small suburb between the city and Sea Point. *St John's Waterfront Lodge* (☎ 439 1404; fax 439 4875) is a nice place at 6 Braemar Rd in Green Point, not too far from the Waterfront and the city centre. *Hip Hop Travellers' Stop* (☎ 439 2104), 11 Vesperdene Rd, is lively.

Oak Lodge (☎ 45 6182), 21 Breda St, Gardens, is fairly central and has a good atmosphere. It can organise caving trips and other excursions. Take the Vredehoek bus and get off at the Gardens Centre. Buses leave half-hourly from the main bus station.

Guesthouses There are quite a number of guesthouses, especially around Sea Point and the City Bowl (Gardens, Tamboerskloof). Captour is a good place to start looking, although it doesn't have every place on its books – nor will it tell you about the cheapest places unless you insist. Try *Travellers Inn* (☎ 24 9272) at 208 Long St (from US$20/27).

Places to Eat

City *Mr Pickwick's Deli*, 158 Long St, is a licensed, deli-style cafe that stays open very late for good snacks and meals. At *Off Moroka Café Africaine*, 120 Adderley St, near Church St, you can eat inexpensive snacks or light meals in a good atmosphere.

The Tea Garden in the Company's Gardens is licensed and has quite a large menu. There are snacks as well as standards, such as omelettes (US$3.50), salads (from US$2.50) and steaks (from US$6). It's open for breakfast.

Yellow Pepper, 138 Long St (near Dorp St), has a casual atmosphere and interesting food, with main courses under US$3.50. A little further up Long St, *Mama Africa* is a

stylish bar and restaurant. Main courses cost from US$6. There's live African music on Friday and Saturday nights.

Gardens/Tamboerskloof (City Bowl) *Mario's Coffee Shop*, on Rheede St, not far from several hostels, is shabby but has cheap meals. A big breakfast is US$2.75; a ridiculously big breakfast is US$4. Not far away, in a recycled building on Kloof St near the corner of Rheede St, is one of the trendiest places in town, the big *Café Bar Deli*. It's open from breakfast until 1 am (midnight for meals) daily except Sunday and it's usually packed. The food is excellent and not expensive.

The *Perseverance Tavern*, 83 Buitenkant St, is an old pub, built in 1808 and licensed since 1836. In addition to beer (some draught) and an excellent range of wines, it serves decent pub food from US$5.

On the corner of Kloof and Union Sts, *The Happy Wok* is an offshoot of Sukothai, and sells good Chinese and takeaway meals at around US$5 for most main courses.

Victoria & Albert Waterfront As well as the franchised places like *St Elmo's* (pizza) and *Spur* (steak), there are some interesting places to eat, although most are aimed squarely at tourists. There is a group of smaller places in the King's Warehouse, next to the Red Shed Craft Workshop. You can buy from various stalls and eat at common tables. *Ari's*, the Sea Point institution for Middle Eastern dishes, has a branch here.

Musselcracker Restaurant, upstairs in the Victoria Wharf shopping centre, has a seafood buffet for US$15. There's also the relaxed *Musselcracker Oyster Bar*, a good place for a drink and some seafood. Oysters cost US$8 a dozen.

One of the cheap and cheerful options is *Ferryman's Tavern* adjoining Mitchell's Waterfront Brewery. The emphasis is on an interesting variety of freshly brewed beers and good-value pub meals.

Sea Point There are dozens of places to eat along Main (Hoof in Afrikaans) and Regent

Rds, between the suburbs of Three Anchor Bay and Queens. Take a stroll and see what appeals. Perhaps the best restaurant is *San Marco*, 92 Main Rd (on the corner of St James), an excellent formal Italian restaurant, with some of the few professional waiters in town. Prices match the quality, with entrées from US$4.50, pasta from US$8 and main courses between US$10 and US$20. The gelataria in front of the restaurant has delicious takeaway gelati and other ice cream.

Entertainment

The best guide to entertainment is in the *Weekly Mail & Guardian*. *The Argus* newspaper has a comprehensive gig guide on Thursday evening and Sunday. When in doubt, the place to go is the Waterfront.

Hugely popular with young locals is the corner of Bree and Waterkant Sts, where there is a range of pubs and clubs. Most places have a cover charge of about US$3. Not far away are some less suburban places, such as *The Purple Turtle* on Shortmarket St, behind Greenmarket Square, and the laidback *Lounge*, upstairs at 194 Long St.

Away from the city centre, but not too far by Rikki (see the following Getting Around section) or taxi, *The Shed*, De Villiers St, Gardens, is a bar and pool hall attracting an interesting crowd. *The Stag's Head Hotel*, 71 Hope St, Gardens, is a popular grungy pub. It's one of the few English/Australian-style hotels in South Africa.

One of the best places for a drink, a snack and live jazz is *Manenberg's Jazz Café*, upstairs on the corner of Adderley and Church Sts. It's a pleasant place, with tables on the balcony and a relaxed and racially mixed clientele. There's a cover charge of US$2 at night.

One of the best music venues is a long way from the city. The *River Club* (☎ 448 6117), near the corner of Station Rd and Liesbeek Parkway, Observatory, often hosts big-name bands with a cover charge of around US$2.

Getting There & Away

All long-distance buses leave from the main Cape Town train station. Translux (☎ 405 3333) and Intercape Mainliner (☎ 386 4400, 24 hours) have offices there.

All trains leave from this train station.

Most long-distance minibus taxis start picking up passengers in a distant township and only make a trip to the train station's taxi ranks if they need more people, so your choices can be limited. There has been a sporadic 'war' between rival taxi firms, so check the current situation.

Hitching around Cape Town is generally easy. For longer trips, either start in the city centre or catch public transport to one of the outlying towns – the idea is to miss the surrounding suburbs and townships.

Getting Around

The Airport Intercape's Airport Shuttle (☎ 934 5455) links the main train station (outside Platform 24) and the airport for US$7. Taxis cost nearly US$25.

Bus The main bus interchange is on Grand Parade, where there is an information office (☎ 934 0540). If you are travelling short distances, most people wait at the bus stop and take either a bus or a minibus taxi, whichever arrives first.

Train Local trains have 1st and 3rd-class carriages. It's reasonably safe to travel in 3rd class (check the current situation), but don't do it during peak hours (crowds offer scope for pickpockets), on weekends (lack of crowds offer scope for muggers) or when carrying a lot of gear.

Probably the most important railway line for travellers is the Simonstad/Simon's Town line that runs through Observatory and then around the back of the mountain to Muizenberg and along the False Bay coast.

Local trains run some way out of Cape Town into the winelands to Stellenbosch and Paarl.

Rikki These tiny, open vans provide Asian-style transport in the City Bowl and nearby areas for low prices. Telephone Rikki's (☎ 23 4888) or just hail one on the street –

you can pay a shared rate of a few rand or more if you phone for the whole van. They run between 7 am and 6 pm daily, except Sunday, and go as far afield as Sea Point and Camps Bay. From the train station to Camps Bay a single-person trip costs about US$3; to Tamboerskloof costs about US$1.20.

AROUND CAPE TOWN

The winelands region around Stellenbosch, sometimes known as the Boland, is the oldest (dating from the 18th century) and most beautiful wine-growing region in South Africa. Franschhoek, Paarl and Stellenbosch are all historically important towns, and each promotes a wine route around the surrounding wineries.

Stellenbosch

Stellenbosch is the second oldest town in South Africa (established in 1679), and the sense of history is palpable. There are some beautifully restored Cape Dutch buildings and interesting museums, all shaded by magnificent oaks. It is also home to a large university, so there's nightlife.

The publicity association (☎ 883 3584) is at 36 Market St. Pick up *Discover Stellenbosch on Foot* (also available in German) and *Stellenbosch & its Wine Route,* which gives opening times and tasting information about the dozens of nearby wineries.

Places to Stay & Eat *Stumble Inn* (☎ 887 4049; email stumble@iafrica.com), 14 Mark St, is a good hostel offering lots of activities and information. Dorms are US$6 and doubles are US$16.

The publicity association produces a booklet listing many bed & breakfast (B&B) possibilities, from around US$14 per person. *Rustic Café* off Bird St, near Legends, stays open until 4 am. Another late-night student hang-out is the *Gallery Coffee Shop* on Crozier St. There are also various places to eat in the Studentesentrum at the university.

De Volkskombuis (☎ 887 2121), Aan de Wagenweg on the outskirts of town, is one of the best places to sample traditional Cape

cuisine. Try the Cape country sampler (four traditional specialities) for US$10. Booking is advisable.

Boschendal

Boschendal (☎ (02211) 41 252) lies between Franschhoek and Stellenbosch on the Pniel road, and is arguably the most beautiful of all the Cape wineries. Picnic meals are served from 1 November to 30 April – not cheap (US$10), but worth it.

Franschhoek

Franschhoek is a village tucked into the most beautiful valley in the Cape. The information centre (☎ 876 3603) is in a small building on the main street, next to Dominic's Pub. Pick up a map of the area's scenic walks.

There's an interesting **museum** commemorating the French Huguenots who settled in the region, and a number of good nearby wineries and restaurants.

B&Bs in town start at US$30 a double, but there are cheaper farm cottages – ask the information centre.

Le Quartier Francais (☎ (02212) 2248) on the main street is a highly acclaimed restaurant, but it is not ridiculously expensive.

Paarl

Paarl is a large town on the banks of the Berg River; it is surrounded by mountains and vineyards. There are wineries actually within the town limits, and some nice walks nearby. The publicity association (☎ 872 3829) is at 251 Main Rd.

The huge **KWV wine cooperative** both regulates and dominates the South African industry. On Monday, Wednesday and Friday there are English-language tours and tastings, starting at 11 am and 3.45 pm. On Tuesday and Thursday the English-language tours start at 9.30 am and 2.15 pm.

Places to Stay The attractive *Berg River Resort* (☎ 863 1650) is alongside the Berg River at the foot of Paarl Mountain. Sites for two people start at US$7, rising to US$14 in the high season.

The big *Manyano Centre* (☎ 863 2537) on Sanddrift St is used mainly by groups, although there's a fair chance that you'll be the only guest. Beds are US$6 and you'll need a sleeping bag. If you're coming on a weekend, ring in advance. Huguenot train station is closer than the main Paarl station.

Around the Country

BLOEMFONTEIN
Bloemfontein is South Africa's judicial capital. At first sight it's just another sprawling town, but there are some things worth seeing. The tourist office (☎ 405 8489) is in temporary offices in the town hall.

Things to See & Do
The **Military Museum of the Boer Republics** is devoted the Anglo-Boer Wars. Take bus No 14 or 16 from Hoffman Square. There is also the **National Museum** on the corner of Charles and Aliwal Sts.

There are impressive **old buildings**, most along President Brand St, between Charles and St Georges Sts. Get a walking-tour map from the tourist office.

British guns commanded the plains from **Naval Hill** during the Boer War. Marked on the side of the hill is a large white horse – laid out as a landmark for British cavalry coming from the plains. On top of the hill is the small **Franklin Nature Reserve**.

The **zoo** is on Kingsway and includes a large collection of primates.

Places to Stay
Bloemfontein hosts important cricket and rugby games, and accommodation can be scarce on match weekends.

Dagbreek Caravan Park (☎ 33 2490), on Andries Pretorius St, has sites for US$7 and rooms in old railway coaches at US$8/15 for singles/doubles. Two kilometres out on the Petrusburg Rd is *Reyneke Park* (☎ 23 888), with caravan sites for US$12 and chalets. Neither place is close to the centre of town.

Taffy's Backpackers (☎ 31 4533), at 18 Louis Botha St, Waverley, is in a private home and offers dorms for US$7, doubles for US$18 and camping for US$3.50. It's a pleasant place.

Places to Eat
Steak lovers have the usual wide choice for their US$7, including *Camelot Carvery*, 149 Voortrekker St; *Steers*, 200 Zastron Rd; and *Beef Baron*, 2nd Ave, Westdene.

Schillaci's Trattoria on Zastron Rd is a good Italian restaurant. Main courses start at US$5.50 and there are midweek specials.

On the corner of Kellner St and Tweedelaan is *Characters*, a fairly lively but expensive Italian restaurant, with a pleasant bar. Not far away in the Mimosa Mall on Kellner St is *Barba's Café*, recommended by locals.

DRAKENSBERG
The Drakensberg forms the border between Natal and Lesotho, and continues a little way into the Free State. It's the edge of an escarpment rather than a mountain range, but is no less impressive for that. Drakensberg means 'Dragon Mountain'; Zulu call it Quathlamba (Battlement of Spears). Both are accurate descriptions of the awesome formations.

There's a lot of accommodation in this area, with most of the budget options in the parks and reserves.

Access to the Drakensberg is from the N3; Pietermaritzburg, Estcourt and Ladysmith are the main jumping-off points. Towards the southern end of the escarpment, and closer to it, are the small towns of Himeville and Underberg, which can be reached from Pietermaritzburg by minibus taxi, or with a hostel-to-hostel service from Durban.

On the road to **Sani Pass** (a steep route into Lesotho) are two hostels. The good *Sani Lodge* (☎ & fax 702 0330) is on the opposite side of the road from the Sani Pass Hotel, 19km from Underberg. Dorms are US$5.50, doubles are US$13 and camping is US$3.75 per person. Another 5km along the road, *The Wild West Sani Youth Hostel* (☎ 702 0340) has dorms, doubles and rondavels, all for US$6 per person.

Drakensberg Parks & Reserves
All the parks and reserves in the Drakensberg are administered by the Natal Parks Board, except Golden Gate Highlands National Park, which is in the Free State. Accommodation other than camp sites must be booked through the Natal Parks Board in Pietermaritzburg or Durban (see the following Durban section for details).

Golden Gate Highlands National Park
This park is in the Free State, close to the northern border with Lesotho. The main draw is the spectacular scenery, and you can also hire horses. You can book the two day **Rhebuk Trail** with the National Parks Board.

Royal Natal National Park
Royal Natal has some of the Drakensberg's most dramatic and accessible scenery. The southern boundary of the park is formed by the **Amphitheatre**, an 8km stretch of cliff which is spectacular from below and even more so from the top. **Rugged Glen Nature Reserve** adjoins the park on the north-eastern side. Most of the 30-odd walks are day walks.

Giant's Castle Game Reserve
This reserve is in high country – the lowest point is 1300m and the highest tooth in the reserve jags up to 3280m. The reserve is rich in rock paintings, with at least 50 sites. The biggest are **Main Cave** and **Battle Cave**.

No food is available in the reserve. There's a basic shop near the White Mountain resort but the nearest shops for most supplies are in Estcourt, about 50km away.

There are a number of walking trails; most are round trips from either Main Camp or Injasuti, or one-way walks to the various mountain huts. There are also walks between huts, so you can string together overnight hikes.

Hiking in the Drakensberg
The Natal Parks Board is assuming control of the wilderness areas which extend from north of Giant's Castle to south of Underberg, so hikes covering the whole region can be put together. Contact the Natal Parks

Board or the State Forester at Himeville or Cobham.

For the less experienced, there's the five day **Giant's Cup Trail**, running from the Sani Pass Hotel in the north down to Bushman's Nek. While it runs through the same lonely country as the wilderness trails, there are few hard ascents and the daily distances aren't long. Accommodation is in huts.

Most overnight hikes must be booked through the Natal Parks Board.

DURBAN
Durban is a subtropical city on a long surf beach. It's also home to the largest concentration of Indian-descended people in the country. Every summer thousands of inland South Africans arrive for holidays. The steamy nights can get lively.

The busiest area, where you'll find most of the cheaper places to stay and eat (and many of the upmarket ones), is around West St, where it meets Marine Parade and the beachfront.

Information
The main information centre (☎ 304 4934) is in the Old Station on the corner of Pine and Gardiner Sts; the complex is known as Tourist Junction.

There are various booking agencies in the Tourist Junction, including one which takes reservations for both the Natal Parks Board and the National Parks Board (☎ 304 4934).

The foreign exchange counter at the First National Bank on the corner of West and Gillespie Sts is open from 3 to 7 pm on weekdays, 11 am to 6 pm on Saturday and 10 am to 3 pm on Sunday. Note that this branch charges a higher commission than others.

Rennies Travel (the Thomas Cook agent; ☎ 305 3800) is on Smith St, between Gardiner and Field Sts. Amex (☎ 301 5551) is in Denor House on Smith St, next to the AA office.

Things to See & Do
Durban's prime attraction is its long **surf beach** and warm water. The beachfront near the end of West St is a lively place and the

renovated promenade runs north all the way to Carpendale Park.

The **Local History Museum** (free entry) next to the city hall (enter from Aliwal St) has interesting displays of colonial life. On the same block (enter from Smith St) is the **Natural Science Museum** (free), open daily from 8.30 am to 5 pm (Sunday from 11 am). Upstairs is the **Art Gallery**.

The **Indian Market** at the west end of Victoria St is worth wandering around, as are the bustling streets nearby, especially in Grey St. Unfortunately, this area empties at night and the streets become unsafe.

The **African Art Centre**, 8 Guildhall Arcade, 35 Gardiner St, is a non-profit gallery with some exciting work. The excellent **KwaMuhle Museum** is in the former Bantu Administration building on Ordnance Rd. It has a display on the 'Durban System' by which whites subjugated blacks, and temporary exhibitions relating to Zulu culture.

Places to Stay

Durban Beach Youth Hostel (☎ 32 4945; fax 32 4551) is superbly located near the beach at 19 Smith St; however, it's run-down and doesn't have a good atmosphere. Dorm beds are US$6.

Try *Banana Backpackers* (☎ 368 4062), 1st floor, 61 Pine St (corner of Prince Alfred). It's a big, relaxed place that gets good feedback. Its location is excellent for both the beach and the city centre. Dorms are US$7, singles are US$16, twins are US$18 and small doubles are US$25.

Down in The Point area is a new place, *Seafarers Club* (☎ 32 0511) at 154 Point Rd. It's in a big, old building and has the potential for good times, with venues for local bands. The area isn't great, although it's not far from Marine Parade. Dorms are US$6 and there are small singles/doubles for only a little more.

Out in Morningside, popular *Tekweni Backpackers* (☎ 303 1433), 167 9th Ave, is a manageable distance north of the city centre. Dorm beds are US$7 and doubles are US$9 per person. To get there, take a Mitchell Park, Musgrave Rd, Kensington or St

Mathias Rd Mynah bus. Not far away at 743 Currie Rd is another good place, *Travellers Rest* (☎ 303 1064).

In the suburb of Umgeni Park, near Blue Lagoon, *Riverside Lodge* (☎ 83 6570; email riversidelodge@mail.saix.net), 31 Ridgeside Rd, is in a private house and offers camping (US$4.50), dorms (US$6) and doubles (US$21). A taxi from town costs about US$3.50.

On the streets near Marine Parade are some hotels which are cheap, but becoming run-down. Try *Palm Beach* (☎ 37 3451), on the corner of Gillespie and Tyzack Sts, with rooms from US$22/30, including breakfast, and US$38 a double around Christmas; or *Impala Holiday Flats* (☎ 32 3232), 40 Gillespie St, with doubles from US$20 and three or four-bed flats from US$30.

Places to Eat

Many hotels around the beachfront have cheap meals. *Beachhouse*, 237 Marine Pde, has African food. If you head north along North Beach Promenade you get to an enclave of eating places which overlook the sea. *Joe Kool's* is a night spot that serves reasonable food at fair prices. Next door is *Cattleman*, where a steak meal is about US$9. Above this is *The Deck*, a hang-out for surfies and the spot for breakfast after catching those morning waves.

In the city centre in the Old Well Arcade, just off Smith St, is *Africafé*, decked out Ndebele style and *the* place for African food.

The inexpensive outdoor cafe in *Medwood Gardens* on West St, near the post office, is a good place to read your mail. It's open daily, except Sunday, from 8.30 am to 4 pm.

Takeaway places around the city have good Indian snacks. *Victory Lounge*, upstairs on the corner of Grey and Victoria Sts, is an excellent Indian cafe, though only open during the day. Other places on Grey St are the Gujarati-style *Patel's Vegetarian* (closes 3 pm), *Khyber* and *New Delhi*. On Gardiner St across from the town hall, the more expensive *Taj Mahal* is good.

On Florida Rd in Morningside are several

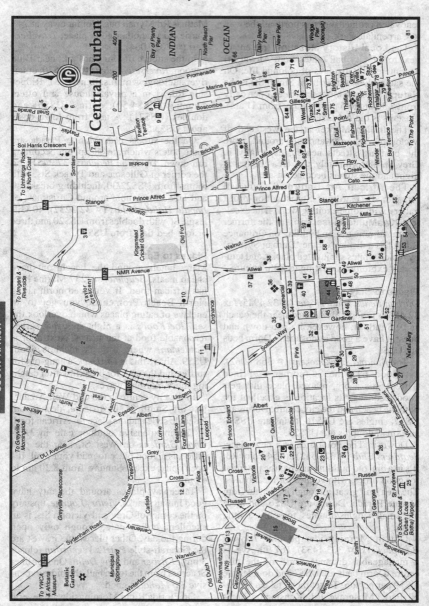

Central Durban

INDIAN OCEAN

SOUTH AFRICA

places to eat and drink. *Christina's Kitchen*, near the corner of 8th St, has pre-prepared gourmet dishes, and next door, *Christina's Restaurant* serves main courses such as roast duck for US$7.50. Nearby is the *Keg & Thistle* pub.

Some way further up Florida Rd is the *Continental Deli*, a must for Aussies hanging out for a decent salad roll. At 16 Stamford Hill Rd, in an historic building, is atmospheric *Queen's Tavern*. The food is ordinary but it's a nice place for a beer.

For some excellent Australian/Californian-style cuisine, go to *Bean Bag Bohemia* on Windemere Rd at the corner of Campbell Ave (near the Florida Rd junction). Cafe meals start at around US$3.50, with larger main courses around US$9.

Entertainment

Many events can be booked with Computicket (☎ 304 2753). The BAT Centre, on the Victoria Embankment and overlooking the Small Craft Harbour, is a new arts centre which is worth checking out for a range of entertainment.

The Wheel on Gillespie St has several bars, and not far away the *Bagdad Café* on Winder St features live bands. The *London Town Pub* is in the Palm Beach hotel. *Magoo's Bar* in the Parade Hotel, Marine Parade, has a band each night.

A block or so back from the beach on Hunter St, *Cool Runnings* is the place for reggae. The *Octagon Jazz Forum* is a popular jazz club on the corner of Field and Queen Sts.

Getting There & Away

Most long-distance buses leave from the rear of the train station. Translux (☎ 361 8333) is located here and Greyhound's office (☎ 309 7830) is nearby. You can also book for Translux and Greyhound at U-Tours (☎ 368 2848; fax 32 8945) on the beachfront.

The Margate Mini Coach (☎ (03931) 21406) runs down the south coast to Margate daily for US$9.

Don't forget the Baz Bus (☎ 439 2323 or book through hostels), with its hop-on hop-off services.

Some long-distance minibus taxis leave from ranks opposite the Umgeni Rd entrance to the train station. Note that a taxi war has been simmering on this rank. Other taxis, running mainly to the south coast and Transkei, are around the Berea train station. From a rank on Theatre Lane, near the cemetery at the west end of West St, several minibuses a day run to Lusikisiki in Transkei.

Getting Around

The Airport A bus (☎ 465 5573, after hours ☎ 21 1434) runs to the airport from the SAA office on the corner of Aliwal and Smith Sts for US$4.50. Some hostels can get discounts and pick-ups for backpackers on the return trip. By taxi, the same trip costs over US$40!

Bus The main bus station and information centre is on Commercial Rd across from The Workshop. The Mynah small buses cover the central and beachfront areas. There are also less frequent full-size buses running more routes and travelling further from the city centre.

Taxi & Tuk-tuk A taxi between the West St beach area and the train station costs about US$4. Tuk-tuks, cheaper than taxis for short trips, congregate on the beachfront near Palmer St.

AROUND DURBAN

There are good beaches on the south coast, which is the strip between Durban and the old Transkei border. There are also shoulder-to-shoulder resorts and in summer there isn't a lot of room to move.

Many of the towns along the coast have caravan parks, though even the cheaper municipal places can be expensive in summer.

Club Tropicana Youth Sanctuary (☎ (039681) 3547) is a hostel overlooking the sea near Anerley, north of Port Shepstone between Melville (Banana Beach) and Bendigo. The Margate Mini Coach stops nearby, as do the main intercity buses running along the N2. It's on an old tropical-fruit farm, and is the headquarters for a non-profit project teaching craft and hospitality skills to people living in traditional villages in the beautiful hinterland. You can treat this place as an ordinary hostel (dorms US$4.50, camping US$2.50, big meals US$2), but it would be much better to stay a while and take advantage of the hikes and activities in participating villages. Better yet, volunteer your time to live in the villages and help with building trail huts, schools, clinics or whatever. This costs US$7 per night, including meals.

The coast north of Durban up to the port city of Richards Bay isn't as developed as the south coast. While the beaches are excellent, most of the towns are quiet retirement villages and time-share resorts.

The **Natal Sharks Board** (☎ 561 1001) in Umhlanga Rocks is a research institute dedicated to studying sharks. You can visit at 9 am Tuesday, Wednesday and Thursday; 11 am and 2 pm on Wednesday; and 2 pm on the first Sunday of the month. Entry costs US$2.50. It's about 2km out of town, up the steep Umhlanga Rocks Dve (the M12 leading to the N3) – a tuk-tuk costs from US$3.50.

EAST LONDON

This port and family resort city is on a bay of surf beaches. The Municipal Tourist Authority (☎ 26 015) is on Argyle St behind the city hall.

Places to Stay

The *municipal caravan park* (☎ 34 9111),

north of the city centre in Nahoon, has sites from US$6 plus US$1 per person, rising by about 50% at peak times.

East London Backpackers' (☎ 23 423), near the beach at 128 Moore St, has dorm beds for US$6. To get there, take the Beach bus from Oxford St. Much better is the new *Sugar Shack* (☎ 21 111), right on the beach near the Holiday Inn. Dorms cost US$7.

GARDEN ROUTE

The Garden Route encompasses a beautiful stretch of coastline between Mossel Bay in the west and the Tsitsikamma Coastal National Park in the east. Inland, its boundary is the Outeniqua and Tsitsikamma mountains, which are between 1000m and 1700m high. The narrow coastal plain is often forested and bordered by lagoons running behind dunes and superb beaches.

The region has some of the most significant tracts of indigenous forest in the country, with giant yellow-wood trees and abundant wildflowers.

The climate is temperate and the area is a favourite for watersports. Although it is beautiful, it is also heavily developed. Prices jump by at least 30% in mid-season (late January to May) and more than double over the high season (December, January and Easter).

There are hostels in **George** (not a very interesting town), **Wilderness** (a beautiful but rapidly developing village), Knysna (see the following entry) and **Plettenberg Bay** (a resort on a spectacular beach).

Knysna

Knysna is a bustling place with a holiday atmosphere. The town is built along the eastern side of a large lagoon, some way from the nearest ocean beaches – **Brenton-on-Sea** (16km west) and **Noetzie** (11km east).

The Tourism Bureau (☎ 82 5510) is on the main street – you can't miss it; there's an elephant skeleton out the front. Rennies Travel is next door.

Gourmets should not miss the tour and tastings at **Mitchell's Brewery** (10.30 am on

weekdays) or a feed of oysters at the **Knysna Oyster Company**.

The famous **Outeniqua Choo-Tjoe**, a steam train running along a spectacular railway line to George, departs twice daily, except Sunday. The trip takes 2½ hours and the fare is US$6 or US$8 return (valid for six months).

Places to Stay & Eat The small and friendly *Knysna Caravan Park* (☎ 22 011) is the closest to town, and has sites from US$3.50 to US$7. *Woodbourne Resort* (☎ 23 223), not far from The Heads on George Rex Dr, is an attractive caravan park which offers chalets and sites.

There are currently five hostels, and with so much competition and such seasonal business, the rates are fairly flexible. Expect to pay a little less than you would in Cape Town.

Highfield Backpackers Guesthouse (☎ 82 6266), 2 Graham St, is just that – a very pleasant little guesthouse for backpackers. *Peregrin* (☎ 23 747), 37 Queen St, is also pleasant, and is well equipped and very clean.

Overlanders Lodge (☎ 62 5920), 11 Nelson St, is behind the Spar supermarket. The owner runs the Knysna Adventure Centre, with good hiking and canoeing trips. *Knysna Backpackers' Hostel* (☎ 22 554), 12 Newton St, is a large Victorian house on the hill a few blocks up from the main street. *Knysna Hikers' Home* (☎ 24 362), 17 Tide St, is a few blocks on the lagoon side of the main street, in a more ordinary house.

JEFFREYS BAY

Surfing is the reason to come to Jeffreys Bay. The town itself is dull and, although it's a nice bit of coast, it is not as scenic as the Garden Route further west.

The publicity association (☎ 93 2588) is in the municipal buildings. A surfie reports that the local library has a copy of *Surfing in South Africa*, a good guide that is no longer on sale.

Jeffreys Bay Hostel rents boards, while the East Coast Surf school rents wetsuits as

SOUTH AFRICA

well – and it gives lessons for about US$2.50 per hour.

Places to Stay

Jeffreys Bay Caravan Park (☎ 93 1111) books out in school holidays. For two people a site costs US$9 (more in summer). There are also cottages from US$6 per person.

The friendly little *Jeffreys Bay Hostel* (☎ 93 1379), 12 Jeffreys St, has dorm beds for US$4.50 and rooms for just US$5.50 per person. Apparently there's now another hostel, *Jeffreys Bay Rest Haven* (☎ 93 1248).

The publicity association can put you in touch with B&Bs and guesthouses. You'll still find places for US$14 a double.

KAROO

For some people the Karoo simply means the boring bit between Jo'burg and Cape Town. For others the Karoo is one of the most exhilarating regions of South Africa, with unlimited space and strange mountain ranges.

The Karoo can get very hot between November and March, and in the mountains (up to 2000m) it can be very cold in winter; snow is not unknown.

Be sure to visit historic **Graaff-Reinet**, with streets of Cape-Dutch architecture, and the very weird **Owl House** in the hamlet of New Bethesda.

Oudtshoorn

Oudtshoorn is the ostrich and tourist capital of the Little Karoo. As well as the **ostrich farms** (entry around US$4), there is **Crocodile & Cheetahland** (entry US$4) and the impressive **Cango Caves** (tours from US$2.50). Oudtshoorn Tourist Bureau (☎ 29 2532) is on Baron van Rheede St near Queens Hotel.

You should explore some of the surrounding countryside; in particular, the **Swartberg Pass** and **Seweweekspoort** are geological, floral and engineering masterpieces – although hitching up here could take a day.

Backpackers Oasis (☎ 29 1163), 3 Church St, is a good hostel charging US$4 for camping, US$7 for dorm beds and US$17 for doubles.

KIMBERLEY

Kimberley is synonymous with diamonds; this was where Cecil Rhodes and the Oppenheimers, among others, made their fortunes, and where De Beers began.

The information office (☎ 82 7298) is beside the city hall.

Things to See

The Big Hole & Kimberley Mine Museum is a reminder of the wild days when thousands of diggers flocked to the town and fortunes were made and lost. The museum incorporates entire streets of Victorian buildings and a diamond museum, all on the edge of the largest hand-made hole in the world. The complex is open daily from 8 am to 6 pm; entry is US$2.50.

De Beers runs tours of the treatment and recovery plants at Bultfontein Mine, departing from the Visitors' Reception Centre at the mine gate. They cost US$2.50, and start at 9 and 11 am on weekdays. Underground tours (☎ 82 9651 for bookings) are run at 8 am on weekdays (9.30 am on Tuesday). They cost US$9.

Places to Stay & Eat

Kimberley Youth Hostel (☎ 82 8577) is about 5km from town, at the intersection of Hull St and Bloemfontein Rd. Dorms cost US$6 and singles/doubles are US$11/16.

The *Big Hole Caravan Park* (☎ 80 6322) is near the Big Hole and has sites for US$4.50 plus US$1.20 per person.

Check out the famous *Star of the West*, near the Big Hole. Said to be the oldest pub in South Africa, it serves good food.

MESSINA

The closest town to the Zimbabwe border, 15km north at Beitbridge, Messina is a dusty little place. You can change money here.

Translux buses stop at the Oasis Bakery; book at the train station. Minibus taxis and local buses stop in the vacant lot behind the main shopping street.

Places to Stay

The *caravan park* (☎ 40 808) is on the southern outskirts of town. Sites cost US$4.50. Next door, the *Impala Lielie Motel* (☎ 40 127) has a pool and restaurant, and single/triple rondavels for US$19/35.

The *Limpopo River Lodge* (☎ 40 205) has singles/doubles from US$20/25.

MPUMALANGA DRAKENSBERG

The highveld comes to a sudden end as the Drakensberg escarpment plunges to the lowveld. There are superb views, especially from **God's Window**. Accommodation abounds in the area, but prices skyrocket during school holidays and sometimes at weekends.

Blyde River Canyon

This immense gorge is one of South Africa's most spectacular sights. Fees on the overnight trails (the only way to get to the canyon floor) are about US$4.50 per person per night. Book well in advance (☎ 768 1216 or ☎ 769 6019).

Places to Stay The only place to stay is the expensive *Blydepoort Resort* (☎ 769 8005), with tent sites and other accommodation. At holiday times the minimum stay is five days.

However, there is an excellent place to stay at the bottom of the escarpment. Rushworth's *Trackers* (☎ 35 033) is a very friendly private reserve on the Blyde River (bilharzia-free here). The reserve caters mainly to educational groups, but individuals are welcome. If there's room you can stay in a dorm for US$7. Otherwise basic camping costs US$3.50 and a cottage is US$12.50 per person. Phone for directions.

Graskop

Graskop calls itself 'the window on the eastern Transvaal', and nearby are some spectacular views of the lowveld, almost 1km below.

The *Municipal Holiday Resort* has tent sites for US$5.50 for two people and rondavels from US$29 for four people. *Panorama Rest Camp* (☎ 767 1091) is about 2km south of town and is stunningly situated on a gorge with views down to the lowveld. Camp sites

are about US$4.50 plus US$2.50 per person. Chalets with cooking facilities start at US$22 for two people.

Pilgrims Rest

This is a well preserved old gold-mining town. There's an information centre on the main street where you can buy tickets (about US$0.40) to visit the town's museums.

The *caravan park* charges US$9 for a site, less out of season. You can stay in restored *miners' cottages* (☎ 768 1211 during business hours) from US$28 for two people.

NAMAQUALAND

Namaqualand is a rugged plateau and coastal plain in the north-west corner of Northern Cape Province, north of Garies and west of Pofadder. The cold Benguela current runs up the west coast and creates a barren desert-like environment. However, after decent winter rains there is an extraordinary explosion of spring flowers. The best time to visit varies from year to year, but from the middle of August to the middle of September is usually best.

It can get very cold in winter and hot in summer. Public transport, except along the N7, is very sparse.

Springbok

Springbok is a copper-mining town. It's considered the capital of Namaqualand, and although there's not much to see or do, the surrounding countryside is magnificent. The nearby **Goegap Nature Reserve** is spectacular in spring.

Springbok Lodge (☎ 21 321) is the best spot in town to get a room (from US$15), a good meal, and maps and information on the surrounding region. The *Namastat* (☎ 22 435) is an interesting place, with accommodation from US$7 in traditional woven Namaqua 'mat' huts. It's about 3km west of the centre of town.

NELSPRUIT

Nelspruit, in the Crocodile River Valley, is the largest town in Mpumalanga's steamy

SOUTH AFRICA

southern lowveld. The publicity association
(☎ 755 1988) is in the Promenade Centre.

Places to Stay
Although there is no hostel (one is planned),
the *Laeveld Verblyfsentrum* (☎ 753 3380) on
Old Pretoria Rd has dorm beds for about
US$9. It's used mainly by youth groups.

The *Municipal Caravan Park* (☎ 759
2113) is some kilometres from the centre of
town. Head west on the N4, go past Eugene
Rd and turn left at the Caltex station. There's
also a member of the good value *Formule 1*
hotel chain (☎ 741 4490).

PIETERMARITZBURG
Pietermaritzburg is an attractive old city,
generally known as PMB. It's worth a day
trip from Durban.

Information
The helpful publicity association office
(☎ 45 1348; fax 94 3535) is at 177 Commercial Rd, on the corner of Longmarket St.

The Natal Parks Board head office (☎ 47
1986) is out in Queen Elizabeth Park. Head
out north on Old Howick Rd (Commercial
Rd) and turn right onto Link Rd about 1km
past the big roundabout. The Natal Parks
Board is about 2km further on. A Wembe bus
from stand No 10 at the city bus station,
behind the publicity association, will get you
to the roundabout.

The KwaZulu Department of Nature Conservation (☎ 94 6696; fax 42 1948) is in the
old YWCA building at 108 Chapel St,
between Pietermaritz and Berg Sts.

Things to See & Do
There are a number of impressive **colonial-
era buildings**. The publicity association,
itself housed in the old borough police and
fire complex (1884), has a walking tour map.

Macrorie House Museum on the corner
of Loop and Pine Sts displays items related
to early British settlement.

For the other side's view, visit the **Voortrekker Museum** on Church St. It's open
weekdays and Saturday morning.

The **Natal Museum** has a range of dis-

plays, including African ethnography. It's on
Loop St, near Commercial Rd, and is open
daily (afternoon only on Sunday).

Places to Stay
The *Municipal Caravan Park* (☎ 65 342) is
on Cleland Rd, around 4km from the train
station. Head south-east on Commercial Rd,
which becomes Durban Rd after you cross
the creek. Veer left onto Blackburrow Rd to
cross the freeway, then take the first right.

There's a reasonable hostel, *Sunduzi
Backpackers* (☎ 94 0072), at 140 Berg St.
The owner is a licensed game hunter, so there
are a lot of animal skins about the place and
photos of hunters gloating over the bodies of
big cats. There are dorms and doubles, and
you can arrange to stay at the owner's game
farm.

The *Crown Hotel* (☎ 94 1601), at 186
Commercial Rd, is handy to the long distance bus station and the town centre. It's a
small place, with singles/doubles from
US$34/43.

Getting There & Away
Greyhound and Translux stop near Publicity
House on a little road between Church and
Longmarket Sts. Book both at the publicity
association.

Cheetah Coaches (☎ 42 0266) runs daily
between Durban and PMB for US$5.50. Its
offices are in the Main City building at 206
Longmarket St.

PORT ELIZABETH
Port Elizabeth (or PE) is not an attractive
city, although it is on a reasonable bit of
coast. On the other hand, PE bills itself as the
Friendly City and quite a few travellers have
had a good time here. It's a big place, with a
population exceeding one million, and
there's nightlife.

Orientation & Information
The train station (for buses and trains) is just
north of the Campanile, the bell tower
(which you can climb for a donation), isolated from the city by the ghastly freeway.
Walk up the steep hill to Donkin Reserve to

orient yourself. The beaches are to the south (or right, looking from Donkin Reserve). The publicity association (☎ 52 1315) is up here in the lighthouse building.

Places to Stay
Sea Acres (☎ 53 2400), Beach Rd, Humewood, opposite the pier, is the caravan park closest to town. Tent sites cost US$6 plus US$2 per person, with a discount if you don't have a vehicle. Basic four-bed huts cost from US$23 a double and there is a variety of fully equipped accommodation.

Port Elizabeth Backpackers' Hostel (☎ 56 0697), 7 Prospect Hill, is within walking distance of both the city centre and the places to eat and drink up on the headland. It offers free trips to the beaches. Dorms are US$6 and double rooms are US$14.

Several other hostels, with prices similar to Port Elizabeth Backpackers' Hostel, have opened recently, including *Port Penguin* (☎ 55 4499), 67B Russel Rd, *Jikeleza Lodge* (☎ 56 3721), 44 Cuyler St, and *Kings Beach* (☎ 55 8113), close to the beach at 41 Windermere Rd.

The publicity association makes B&B bookings and there's also a B&B Association (☎ 33 3716). Most places charge between US$14 and US$20 per person.

Places to Eat
If you haven't yet experienced the full splendour of a South African breakfast, head along to the dining room at the *Edward Hotel* across from Donkin Reserve. A stupendous breakfast is served up in a nice room and, at US$5.50, it's a bargain. Non-guests are welcome.

Roma on Campbell St, near the corner of Russell St, is a pizza and pasta place with an all-you-can-eat deal on Tuesday. If you're paying by the dish, prices aren't bad, with pasta around US$4.

Aviamore, one of the better restaurants in the country, specialises in fresh local produce and game. A three course meal with wine and the odd Scotch costs around US$20.

Entertainment
The *Phoenix Hotel*, 5 Chapel St, is a small, grungy and very friendly pub, with live music some nights. More clean-cut places include: *Rattle 'n' Hum*, Parliament St; *Cagneys*, off Rink St; and *Wings*, on Russel Rd near the corner of Rose St.

Getting There & Away
Buses stop at the train station or the nearby local bus station. The Translux office (☎ 507 3333) is behind the city hall. The Intercape office (☎ 56 005) is nearby on Fleming St.

Getting Around
Some buses leaving from platform No 5 (in the bus station) run south-east along the beachfront to Happy Valley. They are good for getting to the beaches and Sea Acres caravan park.

PRETORIA
Pretoria is South Africa's administrative capital. It's a bland place, only 56km from Jo'burg, though it's a lot more relaxed.

Information
The excellent Tourist Rendezvous is on Prinsloo St between Church and Vermeulen Sts. Here you'll find the Pretoria Information Centre (☎ 323 1222), a National Parks Board desk, a travel agent, and a coffee lounge.

Amex (☎ 322 2620) is in the Tramshed complex, on the corner of Van der Walt and Schoeman Sts. There's also a Nedbank branch here. Rennies Travel (☎ 325 3800) has several branches, including one in the Sanlam Centre, on the corner of Andries and Pretorius Sts.

Things to See
A short walk from Church Square on Church St, the residence of Paul Kruger (president of the Boer republics during the 1899-1902 Anglo-Boer War) has been turned into a museum – **Kruger House**. It's open from 8.30 am to 4 pm Monday to Saturday and from 11 am to 4 pm on Sunday. Admission is US$0.90.

The impressive red stone construction

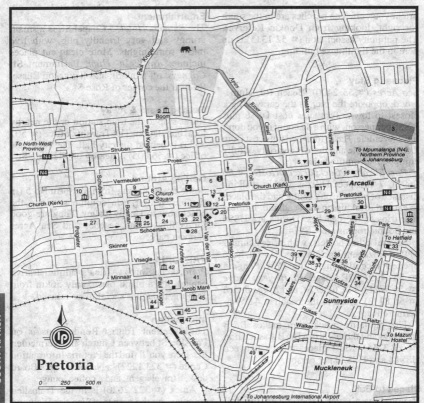

Pretoria

0   250   500 m

Union buildings are government headquarters.

The enormous **Voortrekker Monument**, 12km south of the city, was begun in 1938 to commemorate the extraordinary achievements of the Boers who trekked into the heart of the African veld. Admission is US$1.20. Below the car park there is a small museum (admission US$1.20). The monument and the museum are open from 9 am to 4.45 pm Monday to Saturday and from 11 am to 4.45 pm on Sunday. Catch the Voortrekkerhoogte or Valhalla bus on the south-east corner of Church Square. Ask the driver to let you off at the entrance road to the monument, from where it is a 10 minute walk.

Places to Stay

Pretoria has a growing number of backpacker places, where you'll pay around US$5.50 for a dorm and US$18 for a double. Competition is keen, so see what you can get in the way of (Jo'burg) airport pick-ups, free beers etc.

Mazuri Hostel (☎ 343 7782), 503 Reitz St, Sunnyside, is not bad, and the owner is keen on organising activities and tours. You can send email from here.

PLACES TO STAY		18	Digger's Grill		14	State Theatre
4	Orange Court Lodge	24	Coffee Nest		19	Sterland Cinemas
16	Parkview Hotel	34	Fillings		20	Lesotho Embassy
17	Holiday Inn Crowne	36	Dramant Cafe		21	Tramshed
	Plaza	37	Bimbos			(Amex; Nedbank)
22	Protea Hof Hotel	38	Giovanni's;		23	Sanlam Centre
27	Formule 1 Hotel		London Tavern			(Rennies Travel)
30	Hotel 224	39	Something Fishy		25	Department of Home
31	Malvern House					Affairs
33	Pretoria Backpackers	**OTHER**			26	South Africa Police
40	Burgerspark Hotel	1	Zoo			Museum
43	Park Lodge Hotel	2	Old National Cultural		28	ME Outdoor Shop
44	Victoria Hotel		History Museum		29	19th Hole
46	Karos Manhattan Hotel	3	Union Buildings		32	Pretoria Art Museum
47	Belgrave Hotel	6	Tourist Rendezvous		35	Pharmacy
49	Word of Mouth Hostel	7	Mosque		41	Burgers Park
		8	Local Bus Station		42	Transvaal Museum of
PLACES TO EAT		9	Post Office			Natural History
5	Caponero Restaurant	10	Kruger House		45	Melrose House
13	Buffet de l'Opera	11	Post Office		48	Pretoria Train Station
15	La Gondola	12	Volkskas Bank			

The rapidly expanding *Word of Mouth Hostel* (☎ 341 9661) is at 145 Berea St (corner of Mears St), with another house or two nearby, and a large complex being developed closer to central Sunnyside.

Pretoria Backpackers (☎ 343 9754), 34 Bourke St, Sunnyside, is a short walk from Esselen St.

Orange Court Lodge (☎ 326 6346; fax 326 2492), on the corner of Vermeulen and Hamilton Sts, is an excellent option, with serviced apartments (one, two or three bedrooms) including phone, TV, equipped kitchen and linen. Rates start at US$32/40 for singles/doubles in a one bedroom apartment.

Places to Eat

Roberto's Italian Restaurant is on Schoeman St next to the Tramshed complex. Despite the upmarket décor and service, prices aren't bad and the food is good.

Esselen St in Sunnyside, south-east of the city, has numerous restaurants and takeaway joints. *Fillings* is a trendy cafe and bar selling meals and snacks such as pancakes.

On the corner of Troye St, there's a 24 hour *Bimbos* hamburger joint. *Giovanni's*, upstairs on the corner of Jeppe St, is fairly pricey but the food is good. The large menu

includes pasta from US$4.50 and very good salads from US$3. Downstairs, the *London Tavern* has bar meals.

Entertainment

Upstairs in the Tramshed complex, *Crossroads Blues Bar* stays open late nightly and is usually crowded. There's often live music.

Fillings, on Esselen St, has township jazz on Friday night for free. It's also a cyber cafe. Other popular drinking places on Esselen St include *Casablanca* and *Café Kalua*, and *Café Galleria* sometimes has bands. *Steamers*, near the train station, is a gay-friendly club.

There are more bars and nightspots in the suburb of Hatfield, east of Sunnyside. *Ed's Easy Diner* and *Sports Frog* have been recommended.

Getting There & Away

Pretoria Airport Shuttle (☎ 323 0904 or ☎ 323 1222) operates between Johannesburg international airport (departing outside domestic arrivals) and the Tourist Rendezvous. The journey takes a bit under an hour and costs US$8.50.

A number of international bus services from Jo'burg stop in Pretoria, and most Translux (☎ 315 2111) and Greyhound

SOUTH AFRICA

(☎ 323 1154) services running from Jo'burg to Durban, the south coast and Cape Town originate in Pretoria. Most buses leave from the forecourt of Pretoria train station.

The best method of transport between Pretoria and Jo'burg is the train because almost all buses between the two cities are en route to other destinations and charge high prices for this short sector. The train station (☎ 315 2757) is about a 20 minute walk from the city centre, or catch a bus along Paul Kruger St to Church Square, the main city bus station. A 1st-class train ticket to Jo'burg on the Metro system is US$2.60; there's no 2nd class and you should ask about the danger of mugging before taking 3rd class (US$1).

TRANSKEI

Once a Homeland, Transkei no longer exists as a political entity (it is now in Eastern Cape Province), but it remains a distinct area of South Africa. The main reason to visit is for the spectacular subtropical Wild Coast.

Coffee Bay

Even smaller than Port St Johns, this village has a couple of hostels and opportunities to see traditional Xhosa culture.

To get to Coffee Bay, take the sealed road that leaves the N2 at Viedgesville, 20km south of Umtata. A minibus taxi from Umtata to Coffee Bay costs US$3.40. If you're travelling on the Baz Bus, ask one of the hostels to pick you up in Umtata.

Coffee Bay Trail

This five day trail runs along the spectacular coast between Port St Johns and Coffee Bay. There are huts along the trail where you can get water, but you'll need to treat it (as with water from the streams along the way). You have to make several river crossings and it's essential that you know the tides – 30 minutes after low tide is the safest time.

There's a fee of US$8. Book the trail and buy maps (US$0.40) at the Nature Conservation Division of the Agriculture & Forestry Department (☎ 31 2712) in Umtata. It's on the 3rd floor of the Botha Sigcau building, the office tower on Leeds St.

Port St Johns

This idyllic little town 100km from Umtata has tropical vegetation, dramatic cliffs, great beaches and a relaxed atmosphere. It gets pretty busy around Christmas, when prices rise. A minibus taxi from Umtata costs US$3.75.

Places to Stay *PSJ Backpackers* (☎ (031) 763 4240 in Durban for information) is near the heart of town. From the taxi and bus stop, walk along the main road parallel to the river, take the fourth road on the right past the post office and go up the second driveway on the right. Camp in your own tent for US$3.50 or sleep in the dorm for US$5. Doubles are US$12. Ask here about other budget accommodation in the surrounding area.

A few kilometres out, at the far end of Second Beach, *The Lodge* (☎ 44 1171) is superbly situated on the lagoon with views across to a dramatic surf beach. There can't be many places in the world with a better location. It's a simple old place, but comfortable, with tidy singles/doubles available for US$18/32. Phone from town to be collected.

Umtata

You'll probably pass through Umtata on the way to the coast, as it's on the N2 between Cape Town and Durban and is served by many bus lines. The town was the capital of Transkei.

The tourist office (☎ 31 2885) is upstairs on the corner of Victoria and York Sts. Opposite is a small museum. Wild Coast Central Reservations (☎ 25344), in the Transkei Development Corporation building on the corner of York and Elliot Sts, books various hotels and resorts on the coast. There is a Standard Bank and a First National Bank.

Places to Stay & Eat There are several noisy and decaying hotels in the town centre. The best of them are the *Imperial Hotel* (☎ 31 1675) on Leeds St, which charges from US$18, and the *Grosvenor Hotel* (☎ 31 2118) on the corner of Sutherland and Madeira Sts, which charges US$30 per person for dinner, bed and breakfast.

SUN CITY

Sun City, in North-West Province, is an extraordinary creation, based on gambling and mildly risque shows, plus excellent golf courses, swimming pools, sports facilities, restaurants and high-quality accommodation. Admission is US$9.

The enormous new Lost City complex is worth a look for the scale of the thing. It's a sort of mega-amusement park in high-glitz style, with attractions such as the Bridge of Time, the Valley of Waves (US$9), the Temple of Courage, etc, etc.

Sun City Buses (bookings through Computicket ☎ (011) 331 9991) has several daily buses from Jo'burg and Pretoria. The return fare is US$15.

UPINGTON

Upington is a good starting point for the Kalahari Gemsbok and Augrabies Falls national parks.

The tourist office (☎ 27 064) is at the library. The best place to stay is *Die Eiland Resort* on the banks of the Orange River, 5km south of the town centre. There are tent sites for US$6 and four-bed rondavels at US$26, plus a range of huts and chalets.

VENDA

The Venda region in Northern Province is an ex-Homeland, with some pockets of lush rainforest. There is a sacred lake and forest, but they can only be seen from a vehicle – a spirit lion guards the latter and it's illegal to walk at either place anyway.

The ex-capital, **Thohoyandou**, has a casino, some new government buildings and little else. The tourist office (☎ (015581) 41577) is at the Ditike Craft Centre. *Acacia Park* (☎ (0159) 22506) has chalets for US$28 a double and you can camp for US$4.50.

Near **Vuwani** are remains of furnaces where the Venda people smelted high-grade iron for centuries, and in the north near **Sagole** are ruins of ancient fortifications.

South-east of Louis Trichardt is the fertile **Lebowa** area, home of the Rain Queen, where the main town is **Tzaneen**.

ZULULAND

The Zulu heartland occupies much of central KwaZulu-Natal.

The capital of KwaZulu is **Ulundi**. The town is new, but this area has been the stronghold of many Zulu kings. The **KwaZulu Legislative Assembly** has some interesting artworks and a statue of Shaka, but it isn't always open to visitors. Other than the expensive *Holiday Inn*, there is no accommodation.

The **KwaZulu Cultural Museum** is in town and a few kilometres outside Ulundi is **Ondini**, which was razed by British troops after the Battle of Ulundi, the final engagement of the 1879 Anglo-Zulu War. The Royal Kraal section of the Ondini site is being rebuilt, but you can see where archaeological digs have uncovered the floors of identifiable buildings. You can stay in traditional 'beehive' huts for US$15, including dinner and breakfast. Unless you've made arrangements you must be here by 6 pm. Phone ☎ (0358) 79 1223 for bookings. To get here take the airport turn-off from the highway just south of Ulundi and keep going for about 5km on a dirt road. Infrequent minibus taxis run past Ondini.

Probably the best of the 'Zulu experience' villages, **Dumazulu** (☎ 562 0144 for bookings) is east of the N2, north of Mtubatuba. Four shows are held daily for about US$12. There's accommodation for about US$55 per person, including breakfast. In the Nkwaleni Valley, north of Eshowe, **Shaka Land** (☎ (03546) 655) is an upmarket fake, but the nearby **KwaPhekitungu Kraal**, a co-op craft centre, is real, if not very scenic.

In the small, but lush and beautiful town of **KwaMbonambi** (known as kwumbo), off the N2 about 30km north of Empangeni and the same distance south of Mtubatuba, there are two hostels which are both recommended. *Cuckoos Nest* (☎ 580 1001), 28 Albezia St, is a relaxed place offering lots of activities. *Amazulu Lodge* (☎ 580 1009), 5 Killarney Place, has excellent facilities and runs tours. Both places charge around US$6 for dorms, US$16 for doubles and US$4 for camping.

National Parks & Reserves

National parks and reserves are among South Africa's premier attractions. The scenery is spectacular, the flora and fauna are abundant, and the prices are reasonable. Listed here are just a few of the many parks and reserves. Satour and provincial tourist boards have full details. Also consult the web site at: www.africa.com/venture/saparks/index.htm

In many parks, including most of Kruger, visitors are confined to vehicles. For overnight walks in other parks you need advance permission and you are usually restricted to official camp sites or huts.

The larger parks have rest camps with a variety of accommodation from cottages to camp sites. Although it is not usually necessary to book camp sites, it is necessary to book cottages. The entrances generally close around sunset.

Information can be obtained from the offices listed below. Note that some of the old provincial offices are still operating. You can expect the new provinces to open their own offices, so check with Satour or the National Parks Board for the latest information.

Cape Nature Conservation
    PO Box X9086, Cape Town (☎ (021) 483 4051)
    This organisation controlled all nature reserves in the old Cape Province. It will probably retain control of the Western Cape reserves.
Eastern Cape Tourism Board
    PO Box 186, Bisho 5608, Eastern Cape Province (☎ (0401) 95 2115; fax 92 756)
Free State, Dept of Nature Conservation
    PO Box 517, Bloemfontein 9300 (☎ (051) 70 511)
Natal Parks Board
    PO Box 662, Pietermaritzburg (☎ (0331) 47 1981)
South African National Parks Board
    PO Box 787, Pretoria 0001 (☎ (012) 343 1991; fax 343 0905)
    PO Box 7400, Rogge Bay, Cape Town 8012 (☎ (021) 22 2810; fax 24 6211)

Private Game Reserves
There are many private game reserves. While most cost vastly more than public parks and reserves, you can usually get closer to the animals.

The area just west of Kruger National Park contains a large number of private reserves, usually sharing a border with Kruger and thus including most of the 'big five' animals. Most offer bush camps, walking and open-vehicle game drives. They are often extremely expensive – US$250 a night is only average. Luckily, there are a few cheaper options and occasional specials. Ask a travel agent at Timbavati about these deals.

CEDERBERG WILDERNESS
The Cederberg is a rugged area of valleys and peaks extending roughly north-south for 100km between Citrusdal and Vanrhynsdorp in Western Cape Province. Part of it is protected by the 71,000 hectare Cederberg Wilderness Area.

The Cederberg offers excellent hiking. This is a genuine wilderness area – you are *encouraged* to leave the trails and little information is available on suggested routes. It's up to you to survive on your own.

The main office for the area is at Citrusdal (☎ 921 2288). There's also an office at the Algeria camping ground. Entry costs US$0.70. The Algeria entrance closes at 4.30 pm (9 pm on Friday). You won't be allowed in if you arrive late. Permits have to be collected during office hours, so if you're arriving on Friday evening you'll need to make prior arrangements.

Hiking permits, which cost US$1.20 per day, must be booked through the Chief Nature Conservator (☎ 921 2289 during office hours), Cederberg, Private Bag XI, Citrusdal 7340. The minimum group size is two; three would be safer. Maps (US$1.60) are available at Algeria Camping Ground and the main office in Citrusdal.

Algeria Camping Ground is a beautiful spot alongside the Rondegat River. Camping costs about US$7, more in peak periods. There's another good camping ground in Kliphuis State Forest near Pakhuis Pass on the R364, about 15km north-east of Clanwilliam. Both camp sites must be booked through the Chief Nature Conservator. There are also basic huts for hikers in the wilderness area.

KALAHARI GEMSBOK NATIONAL PARK

The Kalahari Gemsbok National Park is not as well known as many other African parks but it is, nonetheless, one of the greatest. Including the Botswana section (and there are no fences) the park exceeds 36,000 sq km.

Although semidesert, the park supports large populations of birds, reptiles, small mammals and antelope species. These in turn support a large population of predators – lion, leopard, cheetah, hyena, jackal and fox.

The best time to visit is in June and July, when the weather is coolest (below freezing at night) and the animals have drawn in to the bores along the dry river beds. Admission is US$4.50 per vehicle.

There are rest camps at Twee Rivieren, Mata Mata and Nossob, with fully equipped cottages (from US$48 for four people), and huts with shared facilities at Mata Mata and Nossob (US$19.50 for three people). All the rest camps have camp sites (US$7.50 for up to six people). There's a 20% discount on accommodation from November to the end of February – you'll probably spend your savings on cold drinks! All accommodation, including tent sites, must be booked through the National Parks Board.

KAROO NATIONAL PARK

The Karoo National Park near Beaufort West encloses 32,000 hectares of classic Karoo landscape and a representative selection of its flora and fauna. Entry is US$3 per vehicle. There's a three day hiking trail and good accommodation, including camp sites and chalets from US$50 a double.

KRUGER NATIONAL PARK

This huge park, stretching virtually all the way along the Transvaal border with Mozambique, is one of the largest parks in Africa. It's said to have the greatest variety of animals in any game park in Africa, including lion, leopard, cheetah, elephant, giraffe and many varieties of antelope.

The south of the park is the best place to see rhino and hippo. Lions are most commonly seen on the plains north of Skukuza Camp. Olifant's Camp offers dramatic scenery and good game viewing. Elephants are common from here north to the end of the park.

Skukuza Camp is the biggest camp and includes a visitor centre. Pretoriuskop is a little cooler than other camps in summer because of its altitude.

Seven guided 'trails' offer a chance to walk through the park with knowledgeable armed guides. Most trails last two days and three nights, over a weekend. Accommodation is in huts. Trails cost US$215 per person, including meals, and must be booked well in advance.

Entry to the park is US$2.50 per person plus US$4.50 for a car. The number of day visitors admitted to the park is restricted, which can be a problem at weekends and school holidays. It's preferable to avoid the crowds anyway.

The entrance gates open at 5.30 am, except in April (6 am), from May to August (6.30 am) and September (6 am). Gates and camps close at 6.30 pm from November to February, 6 pm in March, September and October, and 5.30 pm from April to August. You can be fined if you arrive late at a camp.

Places to Stay

Accommodation (except tent sites) must be pre-booked through the National Parks Board. The head office (☎ (012) 343 1991; fax 343 0905) is in Pretoria; the postal address is PO Box 787, Pretoria 0001. There is also an office in Cape Town (☎ (021) 22 2810; fax 24 6211) and an agency at the Tourist Junction in Durban (☎ (031) 304 4934).

All rest camps have shops and most sell fuel. Some of the larger camps have restaurants. Huts and cottages are supplied with bedding and towels; most have air-con or fans, and fridges. Most camping sites are not equipped with power points. If you are staying in accommodation with a communal kitchen, you have to supply your own cooking and eating utensils.

The following is a guide to prices: camping costs US$9 for two people; most huts with communal bathrooms and kitchens cost between US$18 and US$25 for two people; huts with bathrooms but no kitchen cost between US$55 and US$65 for two; most self-contained chalets, rondavels or huts cost between US$56 and US$68 for two; and the average price for a self-contained cottage sleeping six is about US$110, more if you want a cottage with two bathrooms(!).

At Hazyview, a small village about 15km north of Numbi Gate and 40km west of Paul Kruger Gate, there's the *Kruger Park Backpackers* (☎ 737 7224), where bunks cost about US$6. You can hire cars here for trips into Kruger. The hostel is about 2km south of Hazyview village, just past the White River turn-off. Transtate buses from Jo'burg come through Hazyview, as do minibus taxis, or you can get here from Nelspruit.

KWAZULU-NATAL RESERVES

As well as the parks in the Drakensberg (see earlier in this chapter), the Natal Parks Board has many other reserves. Entry to most is about US$1.40 plus US$6 per car. Most parks have camp sites (about US$7 per person, less in the low season) and a wide range of other accommodation. All accommodation, except camp sites, must be booked at the Natal Parks Board's head office (☎ (0331) 47 1986) in Pietermaritzburg or at the board's desk in the Tourist Junction in Durban. Its Web site is: www.africa.com/venture/saparks/index.htm

Hluhluwe & Umfolozi Game Reserves

These large, adjoining reserves have lion, elephant, rhino (black and white), giraffe, and many other animals and birds. There is a variety of accommodation in both parks.

Umfolozi's walking trails are open from March to the end of November. Accompanied by an armed ranger and donkeys to carry supplies, hikers spend three days walking in the reserve. You need a party of eight people (no children under 12). Bookings are accepted up to six months in advance. The cost is US$200 per person, including meals and equipment. On weekends there is a two night trail, which costs US$115 per person.

The cheapest accommodation at Hluhluwe is in *rondavels* for US$27/36 a single/double. At Umfolozi it's in four-bed huts for US$18 per person, minimum US$36. Both reserves also have more remote bush camps.

Itala

Itala has all the trappings of a private game reserve at much lower prices. Entry costs US$1.40 per person plus US$6 per vehicle.

Animals include rhino (black and white), elephant, nyala, hyena, buffalo, baboon, leopard, cheetah and crocodile. The diverse habitats support over 320 species of birds.

Ntshondwe is the main centre, with superb views of the reserve below. There's a restaurant and a shop here, as well as a swimming pool. Accommodation starts at US$28 for a unit with communal kitchen. There are a few basic camp sites for US$2.75 per person. Book these on ☎ (0388) 75239. There are also three bush camps.

Itala is entered from Louwsburg, about 65km east of Vryheid on the R69.

St Lucia Area

Several reserves include Lake St Lucia and its surrounds; entry to each of them is US$3.50. This is an interesting coastal lake system with a lot of wildlife. Watch for crocodiles and be careful at night, when hippos roam. Sharks sometimes venture up the estuaries.

One of St Lucia's highlights is the trip on the *Santa Lucia*. It leaves from the wharf on the west side of the bridge on the Mtubatuba road at 8 and 10.30 am and 2.30 pm daily (US$8).

There is Natal Parks Board accommodation at several places, including the holiday village of St Lucia, where there is also lots of privately run accommodation. During slow periods you'll find B&Bs for under US$10 per person.

PILANESBERG NATIONAL PARK

Pilanesberg National Park surrounds Sun City in North-West Province. It covers 500 sq km of extinct volcanic craters, and is well worth visiting. Fauna includes rhino (black and white), giraffe and all sorts of buck. Entry costs US$3. There's a *camping ground* at Manyane Gate, with sites for US$11 (more on weekends and around Christmas). There's also a range of other accommodation, from chalets (from US$40 a double) to a luxury resort. Book all accommodation on ☎ 465 5423.

TSITSIKAMMA COASTAL NATIONAL PARK

Tsitsikamma is a narrow band of spectacular coast between Plettenberg Bay and Jeffreys Bay. It is traversed by one of the most famous walks in the country – the **Otter Trail**, an easy five day, 41km trail along the coast. Unfortunately, it is booked up months in advance. Walking the trail costs US$44 per person. The park headquarters (☎ 54 11607) is at the Storms River mouth, about 5km off the N2. Entry costs US$1.50.

Tsitsikamma is also worth visiting for day walks. There are two good camping grounds. The best is *De Vasselot Restcamp* near the village of Nature's Valley.

Spanish North Africa

All that remains of the Spanish colonies in Africa are the two tiny enclaves of Ceuta and Melilla along with a handful of islets off the northern Moroccan coast.

Like almost all the harbours along the North African shore, Ceuta and Melilla were founded by Phoenician traders, then colonised successively by a host of foreign powers including the Romans, Byzantines and Arabs, and finally the Spanish in the 15th and 16th centuries, following the eviction of the Muslims from Spain. Although currently administered as city provinces of Spain, Melilla and Ceuta are waiting to be granted autonomous status on an equal footing with the mainland provinces.

The Moroccan government occasionally campaigns half-heartedly for the return of the provinces to Morocco, but many of the enclaves' Muslims (mostly Rif Berbers), quite apart from the Spanish who number about 70% of the population, are not overly keen on the idea.

The presence of 10,000 Spanish troops provides a useful boost to the local economy, but it's contraband trade that sustains the towns. Anything up to 80% of the goods entering the enclaves end up not only in Morocco but in countries throughout north-west Africa.

The majority of travellers come here for the ferry services to and from Spain which are cheaper in Ceuta than those to and from Tangier. For those with their own transport, there is also the added attraction of cheap, tax-free petrol.

Facts for the Visitor

VISAS & EMBASSIES
As for Spain, visas are not required by nationals of any European Union country, the USA, Canada, New Zealand, Israel and some countries in Africa.

SPANISH NORTH AFRICA
Population: 150,000
Official Language: Spanish
Currency: Spanish peseta (Ptas)
Exchange Rate: Ptas 140 = US$1
Time: GMT/UTC

Highlights
- Sweeping views over the Mediterranean from the convent of Ermita de San Antonio, Ceuta
- The extravagant new maritime park along Ceuta's waterfront
- The Castilian fortress of Melilla

Nationals of Australia and South Africa are among those who *do* require visas. Visas can be applied for at Spanish embassies. You can ask for a 30 day visa which permits two entries (about US$20) or a 90 day visa which permits three entries (about US$35). Visas are generally issued within 24 hours but to be on the safe side, apply well in advance.

MONEY
US$1 = Ptas 140

The unit of currency is the Spanish peseta (Ptas). Most banks charge around 1% commission on travellers' cheques, with a minimum of US$5 commission for each transaction.

PUBLIC HOLIDAYS
Public holidays include: 1 January, 1 May, 15 August, 12 October, 1 November, 6 December, 25 December and Good Friday.

Getting There & Away

Morocco
Ceuta There are special buses to the border every 15 minutes or so from Plaza de la Constitución in Ceuta. The trip costs US$0.50 and takes about 20 minutes.

If you are arriving by ferry and want to head straight for the border, there is a bus stop just up from the port and off to the right, opposite the ramparts. Look for the sign 'Frontera del Tarajal' on the front of the bus.

The border crossing is straightforward on the Spanish side. Just beyond the banks on the other side of the border there are plenty of *grands taxis* (share-taxis) to Tetouan. A seat costs about US$2.

The whole trip from Ceuta to Tetouan should take no more than two hours; often it takes a good deal less. To keep delays to a minimum, it's worth crossing the border either early in the morning or late at night, particularly if you're going by car.

At the border there are informal money-changers on the Spanish side and national banks on the Moroccan side.

Melilla Local buses go from Plaza de España to the border from about 7.30 am until late in the evening. It's about 150m to Spanish customs from where the buses drop you off, and another 200m to the Moroccan side. There are frequent buses and grands taxis to Nador from the border until about 8 pm.

Mainland Spain
See the introductory Getting There & Away chapter for details of the ferry and jetfoil services to mainland Spain. Daily flights with Iberia link Melilla to Málaga (US$75 one way) and Almería (US$71).

Ceuta (Sebta)

Much maligned by guidebooks, and long used as a gateway to Morocco, Ceuta (Sebta is its Arabic name) is keen to detain many of

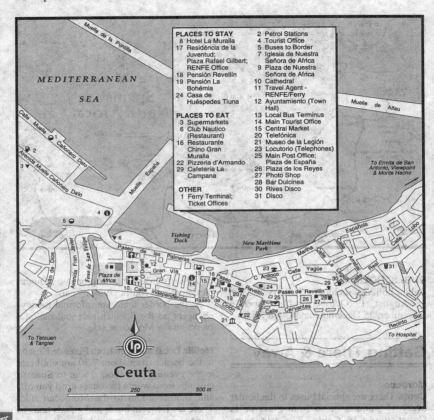

PLACES TO STAY
8 Hotel La Muralla
17 Residéncia de la Juventud; Plaza Rafael Gilbert; RENFE Office
18 Pensión Revellín
19 Pensión La Bohémia
24 Casa de Huéspedes Tiuna

PLACES TO EAT
3 Supermarkets
6 Club Nautico (Restaurant)
16 Restaurante Chino Gran Muralla
22 Pizzeria d'Armando
29 Cafetería La Campana

OTHER
1 Ferry Terminal; Ticket Offices
2 Petrol Stations
4 Tourist Office
5 Buses to Border
7 Iglesia de Nuestra Señora de Africa
9 Plaza de Nuestra Señora de Africa
10 Cathedral
11 Travel Agent - RENFE/Ferry
12 Ayuntamiento (Town Hall)
13 Local Bus Terminus
14 Main Tourist Office
15 Central Market
20 Telefónica
21 Museo de la Legión
23 Locutorio (Telephones)
25 Main Post Office; Plaza de España
26 Plaza de los Reyes
27 Photo Shop
28 Bar Dulcinea
30 Rives Disco
31 Disco

the travellers just passing through. In 1995, an extravagant new park was built on the seafront, designed by the Spanish architect César Manrique.

The town doesn't offer a great deal for the visitor but it's a pleasant enough place to relax for a day or two, particularly if you're feeling travel-fatigued in Africa. It's like stepping momentarily right back into Europe.

Ceuta is not particularly cheap, however, and some travellers may still prefer to catch an early ferry from Algeciras in Spain and head straight for Tetouan or Chefchaouen.

Information

The well-stocked tourist office (☎ 68 4013) is at the junction of Calle de Querol and Avenida General Aizpuru. It's open 8 am to 3 pm from Monday to Friday.

There are plenty of banks along the main street, Paseo de Revellín, and its continuation, Calle Camoens. Banks are open from 8 am to 2 pm, Monday to Friday. Outside business hours, you can change money at the Hotel La Muralla, on Plaza de Africa.

The main post office (Correos y Telégrafos) is at Plaza de España.

Things to See & Do

Just a few minutes from the ferry terminal is the Plaza de Africa, the formal centre of town. Surrounding the square are a couple of Baroque churches, the **Iglesia de Nuestra Señor de Africa** and the **cathedral**, and on the west side, the **Foso de San Felipe**. This fortified trench once formed part of massive ramparts built in 1530, with the help of the Portuguese, and was formerly the object of numerous sieges throughout Ceuta's history.

The **Museo de la Legión** is dedicated to and run by the Spanish Foreign Legion and has an enormous collection of military paraphernalia. It's on Paseo de Colón and is open weekdays (except Wednesday) from 10 am to 2 pm, on Saturday from 4 to 6 pm, and on Sunday from 10 am to 1 pm. Entry is free.

From the convent of **Ermita de San Antonio**, on the hill, there is an excellent view over the Mediterranean to Gibraltar. There are remnants of Spanish and Portuguese **fortifications** atop Monte Hacho and on the south-east end of the peninsula.

If you feel like a swim, visit the new, well designed **maritime park** on the seafront. Entry costs US$4 and the pools are open from May to September.

Places to Stay

Right in the centre, the *Pensión Revellín* (☎ 51 6762) is on the 2nd floor at 2 Paseo de Revellín. Rooms cost US$9/16 for adequate singles/doubles, and hot showers are available in the morning.

The *Residéncia de la Juventud* is not a YHA hostel and, at US$13 a bed, is not cheap. It is nevertheless often full. Tucked away on Plaza Rafael Gilbert, it is open in the early morning and late afternoon (no precise time).

If you can afford a little more, the two best deals in town are the *Casa de Huéspedes Tiuna* (☎ 51 7756), at 3 Plaza Teniente Ruiz, and the slightly better *Pensión La Bohemia* (☎ 51 0615), at 16 Paseo de Revellín. They both charge US$15/25 (add US$7 in summer) for good singles/doubles.

Places to Eat

Food is not as cheap in Ceuta as in neighbouring Morocco but there are plenty of cafes that serve snacks, such as bocadillos and pulgas (rolls with one of several fillings).

For something more substantial, try a local favourite, the *Cafetería La Campana* on 15 Paseo de Revellín. It serves food, including sandwiches, tapas and beer, all day at fairly reasonable prices.

Close to the Museo de la Legión on 25 Paseo de Colon is *Pizzeria d'Armando* (☎ 51 4749). It serves good pizzas from US$5 and is extremely popular with locals so get there before 8.30 pm or you may have to queue.

The *Club Nautico*, Paseo de las Palmeras, is a simple place overlooking the fishing port. It offers generous fish meals for about US$9. A more upmarket place in a side street off Marina Española, on the corner with C Antioco, is the *Restaurant Vicentino* with set menus for around US$11.

Entertainment

Bar Dulcinea on Calle Sargento Coriat is a good place for a couple of beers and tapas. If you're after a late night, the disco *Rives*, off Paseo de Revellín, is currently the town's number one.

Melilla

Melilla is marginally smaller than Ceuta, and somewhat more interesting. Melilla la Vieja, the old town, is a classic fortress stronghold that until the end of the last century contained virtually the entire town within its walls. It still has a distinctly Castilian flavour, with narrow, twisting streets, squares, gates and drawbridges.

The new town was laid out by Don Enrique Nieto, a contemporary of Gaudí, who gave the city centre a Spanish modernist look that is still striking in spite of the many duty-free shopfronts.

The Plaza de España is the heart of the new part of town, and the bulk of the hotels, banks, restaurants and bars are in the grid of streets leading north-west of the plaza.

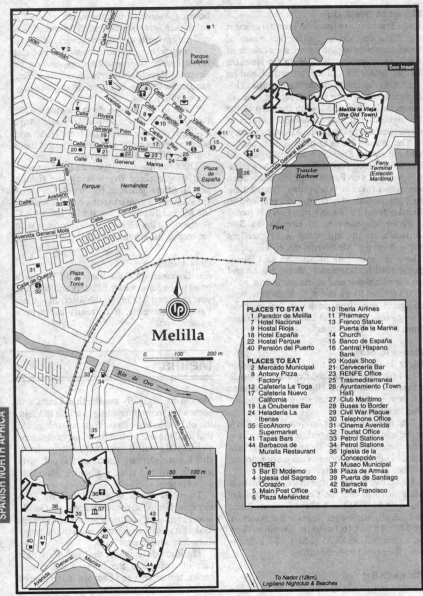

Melilla

0   100   200 m

PLACES TO STAY
1 Parador de Melilla
7 Hotel Nacional
9 Hostal Rioja
18 Hotel España
22 Hostal Parque
40 Pensión del Puerto

PLACES TO EAT
2 Mercado Municipal
8 Antony Pizza
   Factory
12 Cafetería La Toga
17 Cafetería Nuevo
   California
19 La Onubense Bar
24 Heladería La
   Ibense
35 EcoAhorro
   Supermaket
41 Tapas Bars
44 Barbacoa de
   Muralla Restaurant

OTHER
3 Bar El Moderno
4 Iglesia del Sagrado
   Corazón
5 Main Post Office
6 Plaza Menéndez

10 Iberia Airlines
11 Pharmacy
13 Franco Statue;
   Puerta de la Marina
14 Church
15 Banco de España
16 Central Hispano
   Bank
20 Kodak Shop
21 Cervecería Bar
23 RENFE Office
25 Trasmediterranea
26 Ayuntamiento (Town
   Hall)
27 Club Marítimo
28 Buses to Border
29 Civil War Plaque
30 Telephone Office
31 Cinema Avenida
32 Tourist Office
33 Petrol Stations
34 Petrol Stations
36 Iglesia de la
   Concepción
37 Museo Municipal
38 Plaza de Armas
39 Puerta de Santiago
42 Barracks
43 Peña Francisco

0   50   100 m

To Nador (12km),
Logüeno Nightclub & Beaches

SPANISH NORTH AFRICA

Information

The tourist office, on Calle de Querol close to the Plaza de Toros (bullring), is open from 9 am to 2 pm Monday to Friday, and until noon on Saturday.

There are several banks along or near Avenida de Juan Carlos. Their exchange rates are slightly inferior to those you'll find in Morocco, but superior to those offered by the moneychangers who hang around Plaza de España.

The main post office (Correos y Telégrafos) is on Calle Pablo Vallescá. The main telephone office is on Calle Sotomayor, on the west side of the Parque Hernández.

Things to See

The fortress of Melilla la Vieja offers good views over the town and out to sea. Inside the walls, the **Iglesia de la Concepción** is worth a look for its gilded reredos and shrine to Nuestra Señora la Virgen de la Victoria (the patroness of the city). The **Museo Municipal** has a good collection of Phoenician and Roman ceramics, coins and historical documents and is open from 10 am to 1 pm and 5 to 7 pm every day except Sunday. Entry is free.

The **new town**, considered by some to be Spain's second modernist city (after Barcelona), also merits a wander. The **beaches**, south of the so-called Río de Oro, are really only for the desperate.

Places to Stay

The cheapest option is the *Pensión del Puerto*, a basic Moroccan establishment just back from Avenida de General Macías. A bed here costs around US$8 but the place is a bit rough and seems to serve as a brothel too.

Easily the best place for the tight budget is the *Hostal Rioja* (☎ 68 2709), at 6 Calle Ejército Español. It has basic but clean singles/doubles for US$17/24 (more in the high season), with communal hot showers.

Fronting onto the Parque Hernández, another decent alternative is the *Hostal*

Parque (☎ 68 2143), which has singles/doubles with bathroom for US$21/38. A block north-west is the recently redecorated *Hotel Nacional* (☎ 68 4540). It has comfortable double rooms with bathroom and balcony from US$37, depending on the season.

Places to Eat

A good area to search for cheap bocadillos or snacks is along Calle Castelar. A block east on Calle General Pareja is the *La Onubense* bar, which serves excellent tapas in a traditional setting.

A very popular meeting place for young and old alike is the *Cafetería Nuevo California* on Avenida de Juan Carlos. There's a cafe/bar downstairs and a restaurant upstairs which serves traditional Spanish food at reasonable prices. Across the road is the *Antony Pizza Factory* which serves delicious slices of pizza for US$2.

For a splurge, the *Barbacoa de Muralla* is a well-known place in the southern corner of Melilla la Vieja. A three course dinner will set you back around US$28.

If you're hankering for ice cream, the best place in town by far is the *Heladería La Ibense* on Calle de General O'Donnell, just off Plaza de España. It has over 30 different flavours including the delicious *turrón* (nougat) speciality.

For a traditional Spanish breakfast of churros (Spanish doughnuts) and hot chocolate, head for the *Cafetería La Toga* on Plaza de Don Pedro de Estopiñán.

Entertainment

Almost opposite the La Onubense bar is the *Cervecería* which serves at least 20 different types of beer in wonderful Art-Deco surroundings. A popular folk-music club inside the fortress is the *Peña Francisco* (or *Peña Flamenca*). Of the various nightclubs, *Logüeno* on the Carretera Alfonso XIII, outside the town centre, is currently the most popular.

SPANISH NORTH AFRICA

Sudan

Sudan stretches from the deserts of Nubia through the swamps of the Sudd to the equatorial rainforests of the south. Like neighbouring Chad, it straddles the dividing line of two cultures; the Arab, Muslim north and the Black south.

For the moment, large areas of the country are off limits to travellers because of its debilitating civil war. But wherever you manage to go, you'll be struck by the natural charm, dignity and hospitality of the Sudanese, at variance with the fundamentalist excesses of their present government.

Facts about the Country

HISTORY

Egypt's rich past has overshadowed Sudan's own heritage. As early as 2300 BC, the Pharaonic kingdoms had begun to expand south. By 1000 BC, Nubia had become an Egyptian colony and the empire's prime source of gold, producing an estimated peak of 40,000 kg per year.

Further south lay numerous Egyptian towns, the most important being near present-day Merowe, just below the fourth cataract of the Nile. From it, around 1000 BC, grew the independent kingdom of Cush, whose rulers conquered Egypt in the 9th century BC, making Napata their capital.

After the sacking of Thebes by the Assyrians in 666 BC, the Cushite kingdom retreated further south and established a new capital at Meroe, north of modern Shendi. Its wealth was based on the export of ivory, slaves, rare skins and ebony. But after the 1st century AD, it came under pressure from its rival trading state of Christian Axum in Ethiopia, falling to it in the 4th century.

A Christian kingdom then grew up in Nubia, centred around Dongola. Soon after the Arab armies seized Egypt from the Byzantine Empire in 641 AD, Dongola was

REPUBLIC OF SUDAN
Area: 2,505,815 sq km
Population: 28 million
Population Growth Rate: 2.35%
Capital: Khartoum
Head of State: President Lt. General Omar Hassan Ahmad al-Bashir
Official Language: Arabic
Currency: Sudanese pound
Exchange Rate: S£1450= US$1
Per Capita GNP: US$870
Inflation: 83%
Time: GMT/UTC + 2

Highlights
- Dinner at one of the riverside restaurants beside the Blue Nile in Khartoum
- The small but excellent Ethnographic Museum in Khartoum
- The pyramids at Meroe
- The ghost port of Suakin

besieged and the Nubians were forced to sign a treaty with the Arabs. This treaty lasted for five centuries, until Egypt came under the control of the Mamelukes in 1250. Shortly afterwards, Nubia was conquered and Arab migration to Sudan grew from a trickle to a flood.

As Mameluke power in Egypt waned, control of Sudan passed to two sultanates (the Fung and the Fur) whose prosperity was based on taxing the trans-Saharan caravan trade. The Fung were based around Sennar and controlled the Nile Valley between the Egyptian border and Ethiopia, while the Fur's base was in the Jebel Marra mountain range of Darfur. Arabic was gradually adopted as the common language.

The swamps of the Sudd remained an effective barrier against Arab penetration of the south until 1821 when the Turkish viceroy of Egypt, Mohammed Ali, conquered northern Sudan and opened the south to trade. The effect on the south was catastrophic and within a few decades the population had plummeted as a result of pillage, slavery and disease.

After the completion of the Suez Canal in 1869 and Egypt's subsequent indebtedness to foreign creditors, British interference in African affairs increased. Egypt's Khedive Ismail encouraged explorers to enter Sudan, whose governors he appointed. The most famous of these was General Gordon, Governor of Sudan from 1877.

At that time, British colonial policy aimed to control the Nile, contain French expansion from the west and draw the south into a British-East African federation. The European intrusion, and in particular the Christian missionary zeal that accompanied it, was resented by many Muslim Sudanese. In 1881 they rebelled under the leadership of Mohammed Ahmed, known as the Mahdi. Four years later, Gordon and his Egyptian forces were massacred at Khartoum, and for the next 13 years the Mahdi ruled Sudan.

Although nationalist in many respects, the Mahdist uprising was also religious. Traditionally, the Mahdi is a messiah sent by Allah to wage *jihad* (holy war) and the Mahdist movement saw itself as defending Islam. In 1898 the Mahdists were defeated outside Omdurman by Lord Kitchener and his Anglo-Egyptian army.

The British then imposed the Anglo-Egyptian Condominium Agreement which effectively made Sudan a British colony. Over the next 25 years, an export-oriented economy based on cotton and gum arabic was developed, railways and harbours were built and a modern civil service was established.

At the end of WWII, two political parties had emerged in Sudan: the Umma (or Nation) Party formed by the Mahdists and the Ashiqqa (or Blood Brother) Party, formed by the educated supporters of the Khatmiya, forerunners of today's Democratic Unionist Party (DUP). Soon after, they were challenged by the Sudanese Communist Party, which drew its support from factory and rail workers.

Sudan achieved independence in 1956, but the south, disappointed by the rejection of its demands for autonomy, exploded and the country sank into a bitter civil war which lasted 17 years.

The leaders of the Anya-nya (Snake-poison) secessionist movement were largely missionary-educated officers holding strong anti-Communist and anti-Muslim beliefs who had the support of tribal chiefs. Their bid for independence, combined with the falling price of cotton on the world market, led to a short-lived military takeover, followed by elections in 1964. Sadiq al-Mahdi, the great-grandson of the Mahdi, became prime minister. Five years of ineffectual leadership led to another coup, headed by Colonel Jaafar Nimeiri.

Nimeiri ruled for 16 years, surviving several attempted coups during the 1970s and making many twists and turns in policy to outflank opponents and to keep aid donors, particularly Saudi Arabia, happy. However, by signing the 1972 Addis Ababa Agreement granting the southern provinces a measure of autonomy, he quelled the civil war for some years.

In the early 1980s, Nimeiri made a number of ill-considered moves. In 1983 he scrapped the autonomy accord with the south in favour of 'regionalisation' and imposed *shari'a*, or Muslim law, over the whole country. Sudanese courts imposed multiple amputations for such crimes as robbery, and public floggings for possession of alcohol and for real or imagined adultery.

Nimeiri dismissed many experienced advisers, replacing them with a group of mystics and Islamic fundamentalists. This provoked disaffection in the north and, more

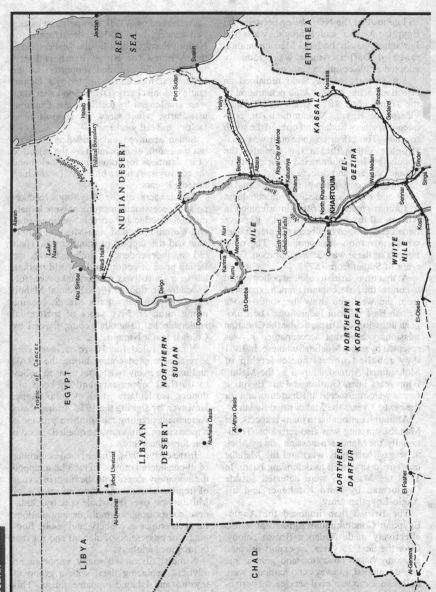

SUDAN

importantly, the southerners reopened hostilities. John Garang went into hiding to form the Sudanese People's Liberation Movement (SPLM) and its armed wing, the Sudanese People's Liberation Army (SPLA), which quickly took control of much of the south.

Nimeiri declared a state of emergency, but was deposed in a coup in 1985. Sadiq al-Mahdi subsequently got a second chance and proved as unequal to the task as the first time around. He was replaced in a bloodless coup in July 1989 by Lieutenant-General Omar Hassan Ahmad al-Bashir, who is the current President. However, Hassan al-Turabi, the fundamentalist leader of the National Islamic Front (NIF), the dominant political organisation, is widely seen as the man holding real power.

The increasing militancy of the government's fundamentalism has cost it all its regional friends, leaving only Iran as a questionable ally. In particular, Sudan has alienated Egypt, its powerful northern neighbour, which holds the junta responsible for a 1995 assassination attempt upon President Hosni Mubarak, and also Eritrea, whose Muslim terrorists Sudan supports.

The civil war, which costs the government over US$1 million a day, has also taken a new turn. The SPLA army is now supplemented by the smaller forces of the National Democratic Alliance, a coalescing of the two major – and primarily Muslim – opposition parties; the Umma and the DUP. For the first time, northern and southern opponents of the regime, although united only in their opposition, are working together. In early 1997, Khartoum was directly threatened for the first time when rebel forces came within striking distance of the Roseires dam (which supplies 85% of the capital's electricity) and of the vital highway between Khartoum and Port Sudan.

GEOGRAPHY & CLIMATE

In the north and west are vast areas of desert that support little life, and in the north-east is the semidesert of Nubia. Rain rarely falls in these areas, and when it does it creates raging torrents in the *wadis* (watercourses)

that can cut communications for days. In summer there are frequent dust storms.

The only areas that support crops of any size are the fertile Gezira, between the Blue and White Niles, south of Khartoum, and a small area south of Suakin on the Red Sea coast.

The desert gradually gives way in the south to savannah and then to rainforest on the borders with Uganda and Congo (Zaïre).

Sudan lies in the northern tropics, with a climate ranging from hot and dry in the north to humid and tropical in the equatorial south. Any rain in the north is normally between July and September and is rarely more than 150mm per annum. In the south, annual rainfall can exceed 1000mm and usually occurs between April and November. Northern temperatures are generally high, climbing to more than 40°C in Khartoum in summer. In the south, the hottest months are February and March.

Water
In the deserts of northern Sudan, water is life. The traditional oxen-driven water wheels and lever-principle *shadoufs* have mostly been replaced by the steady throb-throb of diesel engines, lifting water from the Nile.

Away from the river, when the rare rains fall and rush down the dry riverbeds, villagers construct *hafirs*, small-scale dams at the head of a hollowed-out depression, which will tide their animals over until the next rains. Allah knows when. ■

POPULATION & PEOPLE

Sudan has a population of about 28 million, 75% of whom live in rural areas, including around two million nomads. It is one of Africa's poorest and least developed nations. There are more than 550 ethnic groups and although many Sudanese describe themselves as 'Arabs' this is often little more than a linguistic and religious identification. The number of 'real Arabs' (ie descendants of migrants from the Arabian peninsula) is relatively small.

The Arab-influenced and conservatively Islamic north of the country has a distinctive character. There, most of the men wear flowing white *jalabiyyas* and turbans, while the women enfold themselves in a *tobe*, 9m of fine, colourful fabric. The current regime's dour fundamentalism is not really part of Sudanese Muslims' mind-set and it sits uncomfortably with the strong element of Sufi mysticism that permeates Islam in Sudan. An estimated 70% of the total populace are Muslim.

The further south you go, the more the Arab world gives way to Black Africa. The south is dominated by traditional animists (25% of Sudan's population) and Christians (5%).

LANGUAGE

There are more than 100 languages in Sudan. Arabic, the official language, is the lingua franca almost everywhere and the mother tongue of about half the population, mainly in the north and centre of the country. Nilotic and Nilo-Hamitic languages are spoken in the south, and Darfur is spoken in the western province of the same name. English is widely spoken among government officials.

See the Arabic section within the Language Appendix for a glossary of useful words and phrases.

Facts for the Visitor

VISAS & DOCUMENTS

Visas

Everyone needs a visa. The process is lengthy – up to two months with no guarantee of success – since all applications are normally referred to Khartoum. So, if you're even thinking of visiting Sudan, make sure the visa is in your passport before you leave home. Israeli citizens are barred from entry.

A one month visa costs a fat US$83. Travellers' cheques amounting to US$300 for every two weeks of intended stay are sometimes required and you'll probably be asked to produce an onward air ticket.

Proof of cholera and yellow fever vaccinations is required if you're arriving from an infected area. This is sometimes demanded even if you're arriving from elsewhere (eg Egypt).

Registration

You have to register within three days of arrival in Khartoum or any provincial town. In Khartoum, go to the sinisterly named Aliens Registration Office, (Maktab Tasjil il Ajanib) on Sharia Osman Digna ('we're here for you', proclaims the cheerful notice gummed to the reception window). The cost is US$2.50 and you need one photo.

Visa Extensions

You get visa extensions at the Aliens Office in the Ministry of the Interior, near the post office. You need two photos, varying sums of money and some patience. The amount of time granted seems to be arbitrary.

Other Visas

Chad
    A one month visa costs US$33 and is issued the same day. You need two photos and a letter of recommendation from your embassy. The embassy is open Sunday to Thursday from 8 am to 2 pm.

Congo (Zaïre)
    A one month visa costs US$41 and takes 48 hours to issue. You need three photos and a letter of recommendation from your embassy. Opening hours are Monday, Wednesday and Thursday from 9 am to noon.

Egypt
    The place is a forbidding shambles. If you're travelling to Egypt by air or sea, it will be much better for your pocket and mental wellbeing to pick up a tourist visa (US$19) at Cairo airport or Suez docks. Otherwise, arrive early and pitch into the scrum. Prices vary and you'll need two photos plus a letter of recommendation from your embassy.

Eritrea
    At the time of writing, diplomatic relations were ruptured and the embassy was closed.

Ethiopia
    One month visas cost US$67. Applications are received only on Sunday and Tuesday, and take 48 hours to process. You need two photos, a letter of recommendation from your embassy and, probably, an onward air ticket.

Kenya
> A single entry visa valid for three months costs US$33 and is issued the same day. You need two photos. Consular hours are Monday and Wednesday from 10 to 11 am only.

Uganda
> The embassy closed in 1995 and shows every sign of staying that way until happier times.

Documents
Travel Permits Assume that you need a travel permit for any destination outside Khartoum. Go to the Aliens Registration Office (see Registration earlier in this section), where permits are issued – or denied – on the spot. While you can list on one permit intermediate towns between Khartoum and your destination, you hand over four – yes, four – photos and US$2.25 for *each journey* outside the capital. Functionaries in the provinces often ask to see permits.

EMBASSIES
Sudanese Embassies
Countries in Africa with Sudanese embassies include the Central African Republic, Chad, Congo (Zaïre), Egypt and Ethiopia, and, elsewhere, France, Germany, Japan, the UK and the USA.

Foreign Embassies in Sudan
Countries with diplomatic representation in Khartoum include:

Chad
> Sharia 17, New Extension (☎ 471084)

Congo (Zaïre)
> Sharia 13, New Extension (☎ 471125)

Egypt (consulate)
> Sharia al-Gamhuriyya (☎ 772190)

Ethiopia
> Khartoum 2, at the north-west angle of the cemetery (☎ 471156)

France
> Sharia 13, New Extension (☎ 471082)

Germany
> Sharia al-Baladeya (☎ 777995)

Kenya
> Sharia 3, New Extension (☎ 40386)

UK
> off Sharia al-Baladeya (☎ 770767)

USA (closed at the time of writing)
> Sharia Ali Abdul Latif (☎ 774700)

MONEY
US$1 = S£1450

Sudan is between currencies. Banknotes (there are no coins) are all in the new Sudanese dinar (SD), which is worth 10 Sudanese pounds (S£). However, everyone still expresses prices in S£ unless they're treating you as the simpleton foreigner.

You have to fill in a currency declaration form on arrival.

The black market rate is up to 25% above the bank rate, but you're taking a risk if you play it.

It's difficult to change *any* currency outside the major towns. American cash dollars are the best form of currency to carry in the provinces since travellers' cheques, outside Khartoum, can pose problems.

The big hotels demand hard currency and a few of the smaller ones want to see bank receipts as proof you've exchanged legally. Only major hotels and some airlines accept credit cards.

POST & COMMUNICATIONS
Mail in and out of Sudan is hazardous. Your best bet is to use the main post office in Khartoum or the mailbox in one of the big hotels. There's a poste restante service at the main post office in every city but it's unreliable.

International telephone calls are relatively easy to make in Khartoum. Elsewhere, you may as well forget it. In Khartoum, you can call from the post office or one of the private companies such as Hotline or Key International in the New Extension.

A three minute call to the UK costs US$4.75, to Australia US$8.65 and to the USA US$10.85. Faxes are charged at US$3.45 for the first page and US$1 for subsequent ones.

The country code is 249; the area code for Khartoum is 011 and for Port Sudan 031.

PHOTOGRAPHY
These can be obtained free from the General Administration of Tourism office in Khartoum. The permit is a formality, requiring one photo, but as several travellers have been

picked up by security or accosted by passers-by for taking photos of sensitive sights (such as beggars or run-down areas), it's better to have one. In Khartoum, the locals seem particularly edgy about cameras, but even outside the capital, it's advisable to exercise great caution.

DANGERS & ANNOYANCES
War & Bandits
At the time of writing, travellers' wings are severely clipped. You won't get a travel permit for anywhere south of Kosti: the provinces of Upper Nile, Blue Nile, Bahr al-Ghazal and Equatoria are all war zones. There's also fighting, from sporadic to strong, along swathes of Sudan's frontiers with both Eritrea and Ethiopia. Large areas of the west are also unsafe. Banditry is on the increase in Darfur, particularly near the borders with Chad and Libya, and there have been tribal clashes and government pogroms in southern Kordofan, especially in and around the Nuba mountains.

For the latest information, check with your consulate in Khartoum.

Alcohol Ban
Muslims caught drinking are flogged. You can occasionally find local hooch or booze smuggled in from Eritrea – both at a price – but generally you're in for a dry time.

Power Cuts
In the hottest months, when demand way exceeds supply, power cuts can be long and frequent. So bring a torch (flashlight) and plenty of batteries – and check out the power supply before you invest in a hotel room with air-con.

PUBLIC HOLIDAYS
Public holidays in Sudan include: 1 January (Independence Day), 28 April, 30 June (Revolution Day) and a range of other holidays determined by the Islamic lunar calendar (see Public Holidays in Regional Facts for the Visitor for dates).

ACCOMMODATION
Hospitality from even the poorest Sudanese can be incredible and often you may have no need of a hotel. Rarely will you board a train or lorry and get off at the other end without an invitation to stay with someone. Offers of money for your keep will probably be politely refused, but it's important to offer and better (even expected – though never stated – in the local culture) to leave a small gift.

The most common form of budget accommodation is the *lokanda*, usually a series of basic rooms set around an open courtyard. Beds are normally closely woven rope stretched over a wooden frame. When it's hot – which is often – they're put in the courtyard. A bed can cost as little as US$0.40.

The bigger centres have a range of hotels of varying quality – prices start at US$2 and rise to US$25 for above-average places. There's also a handful of expensive international hotels in the capital.

FOOD
The local staples are mainly *ful mudamis* (stewed brown beans), *fasooliyya* (stewed white beans) – 'beans have satisfied even the Pharaohs', goes an Arab saying – and *dura* (cooked maize or millet). *Ta'amia*, known elsewhere as felafel, is delicious blobs of pounded, fried chickpeas.

Among meat dishes are *kibda* (liver), *sheya* (charcoal barbecued meat), kebabs, *kalawi* (chopped kidney) and *chawarma*, hunks of lamb sliced fresh from a roasting spit. Along the Nile you can find fish dishes of Nile perch.

Mangoes, dates, figs and bananas are plentiful and cheap, as are tomatoes and grapefruit.

DRINKS
Tea is the favourite drink, served as *shai saada* (sweet black tea, sometimes spiced), *shai bi-laban* (sweet tea with milk) or *shai bi-nana* (sweet mint tea). There are also various types of coffees (*gahwa*), the strongest of which are *gahwa turkiya* (Turkish) and *jebbana*, served from a distinctive clay pot and often spiked with cardamom.

Getting There & Away

AIR

At the time of writing, only Lufthansa flew directly (once a week) from Sudan to Europe. Otherwise, you fly to Cairo, Jeddah or Damascus and pick up a long haul flight from there. Flights to neighbouring countries operate only to Cairo and Nairobi.

Olympia Travel Agents (☎ 778580) and Speedbird Travel (☎ 784580) are efficient and reliable, as is Thomson Travel (☎ 452217) in the New Extension.

Tickets must be bought in hard currency. The airport departure tax is a hefty US$20 – to be paid in dollars.

Egypt

Kenya Airways (once a week), EgyptAir and Sudan Airways operate to Cairo. The one-way fare is US$241 and both Arab airlines offer a youth fare of US$145.

Eritrea & Ethiopia

At the time of writing, there were no direct flights to Asmara or Addis Ababa. You have three expensive and irksome alternatives: backtrack to Cairo, transit via Jeddah or double back from Nairobi.

Kenya

A direct flight from Khartoum to Nairobi costs US$403.

LAND

Central African Republic (CAR) & Chad

You have to be hardy to travel the CAR route and decidedly foolhardy to attempt the Chad option. The journey to Bangui, capital of the CAR, can take up to a month and travellers have reported waits of up to two weeks in Birao, over the border.

Travel west of El-Fasher towards Chad is frequently dangerous because of both bandits and tribal skirmishes.

Egypt

At the time of writing, Sudan's land frontier with Egypt was closed. When it reopens, it's physically possible to drive from Wadi Halfa to Aswan, but the Egyptian authorities can be obstructive – to the point of confiscating your vehicle. A much better choice is to put your car on the ferry (see the following Sea section).

Eritrea & Ethiopia

At the time of writing, Sudan's frontiers with both Eritrea and Ethiopia were closed to travellers. When happier times return, buses to Asmara, the Eritrean capital, may again leave regularly from Kassala, and less so from Port Sudan and Khartoum.

SEA & LAKE
Saudi Arabia & Egypt

There are passenger ferries from Suakin, near Port Sudan, to Massawa (very irregularly), Jeddah (1st class US$94, 3rd class $67) and Suez (1st class US$165, 2nd class US$136). Their frequency and timetables often change – particularly for the Suez run – and schedules are abandoned during the Haj, the Muslim pilgrimage. For current sailings, ring the Khartoum offices of the Sudan Shipping Line (☎ 779188) or the Ba'abour Shipping Agency (☎ 770460), or visit their Port Sudan sales offices.

Once the border between Sudan and Egypt reopens, ferries will again run from Wadi Halfa to Aswan. Be prepared for a wait of a few days when you reach Wadi Halfa. You can buy a ticket for the boat in Khartoum, near the train station, or in Wadi Halfa. The trip on Lake Nasser takes anything from 14 hours to two days.

Getting Around

Large areas of Sudan are closed to travellers. For details, see the section on War & Bandits in Dangers & Annoyances in the Facts for the Visitor section. Refer also to the paragraph on Travel Permits in Visas & Documents in Facts for the Visitor.

A sealed road links Khartoum with Port Sudan via Wad Medani, Gedaref and Kassala. The route from Khartoum to Atbara is also sealed, and there are plans to extend this eastwards to Haiya and Port Sudan, thus cutting travel time to the Red Sea significantly. Both the White Nile and Sennar roads to Kosti are tarmac, as is the road between Kosti and El-Obeid.

All other travel is over desert tracks or by snail-rail. It can be slow and unpredictable, but is generally more than compensated for by the hospitality of the people. Off-tarmac travelling times can double during the brief northern rains, which fall between July and September.

AIR

Sudan Airways flies to all of Sudan's major cities, if irregularly since planes are often grounded for repair.

Waiting lists for most flights can be long. Book yourself onto more than one as a precaution against cancellation. Prices are reasonable: the one way flight from Khartoum to Nyala is US$69, and to Port Sudan US$45. And think positive if you're bumped off the flight or the flight doesn't arrive; whenever and wherever you fly, you're saving yourself hours of rigorous overland travel.

There's a domestic airport tax of US$4.

BUS

Buses and other transport leave from a parking lot known as *es-souk esh-sha'bi*, which simply means 'the people's market'. It's usually about 4 or 5km out of town.

There are 'luxury' buses running between Khartoum, Kassala and Port Sudan. The more common varieties are sometimes only one up on cattle lorries and few of them run to anyone's time, but they all travel the dusty tracks that normal buses could never cope with.

When riding the desert trails, take lots of water and a supply of food. And keep your sleeping bag with you – it makes great padding!

LORRY

Where even the toughest buses won't go, souk lorries dare to roll. And when they get bogged in the mud or sand, it's a chance for passengers to flex their muscles and get to know each other!

Beware of sunstroke when travelling up top. Don't expect a free lift. Fares are more or less standardised and you'll usually be charged the same as the locals. A seat inside the cab generally costs double. Unless you're travelling on the tightest of budgets, it's worth the investment.

Fuel shortages are common and can delay or cancel your trip, so take at least a day's extra food and water.

BOX

Relatively new and fast Toyota Hiluxes, 'boxes' (*boksi*, plural *bokasi*) generally serve as local transport between villages. In northern Sudan they also do some routes across the desert between towns, notably from Dongola to Karima and Karima to Atbara.

TRAIN

The state-run rail network, once one of the best in Africa, is now sadly run-down as a result of war and lack of investment and maintenance. All that remains is a line north to Wadi Halfa, with branch lines to Port Sudan and Karima, and a stretch in the west from Er-Rahad to Nyala.

The only remaining passenger services are:

Monday: Khartoum to Wadi Halfa (sleeper US$26, 1st/2nd class US$13/10)
Tuesday: Khartoum to Port Sudan (1st/2nd/3rd class US$12/9/6)
Friday: Khartoum to Karima (sleeper US$23, 1st/2nd/3rd class US$12/9/6)
Saturday: Er-Rahad to Nyala

First class compartments officially carry six passengers but usually more squeeze in. Second and 3rd class compartments have no limit.

Student discounts seem to be according to the whim of the issuing clerk.

BOAT

The Nile steamer between Kosti or Malakal and Juba, once a favourite of overlanders heading for Central Africa, won't sail again until the civil war is over.

Khartoum

Khartoum was founded in 1821 by the Egyptian Khedive Ismail as a military outpost at the confluence of the White and Blue Niles. Its early fortunes were due to the lucrative slave trade when Egypt and Turkey plundered Black Africa. It was captured twice: first by the Mahdi to get rid of Gordon and then by Kitchener to get rid of the Mahdi.

These days, the capital has three parts: Khartoum, North Khartoum (or Bahri) and Omdurman, each separated from the others by an arm of the river. Their combined population is over four million. Omdurman, founded by the Mahdi in the 1880s, was built in the traditional Islamic style and has resisted change. Khartoum owes its present layout to Kitchener, who began rebuilding the city in 1898 after defeating the Mahdi's forces. Its heart retains something of a colonial atmosphere, with its wide tree-lined boulevards and a few leftovers of British imperial architecture.

Information

The post office, telephone and telegraph offices are housed in the same building. For telephone alternatives, see Post & Communications in the earlier Facts for the Visitor section.

The easiest way to change money is at one of the bank implants at the Acropole, Hilton or Meridien hotels.

Shops are usually open from 8.30 am to 1 pm and 5 to 7 pm. Office hours are from 8 am to 2 pm. Breakfast, which most people take between 9 and 10 am, is a Sudanese institution. At this time, don't be surprised if that vital functionary isn't at the desk.

The British Council (☎ 780817) and the French Cultural Centre (☎ 772837) regularly show films.

See also Travel Permits and Photography Permits under Visas & Documents in the Facts for the Visitor section.

Things to See & Do

The **National Museum**, although appallingly badly documented and labelled, has some fine exhibits, particularly the Meroitic jewellery on the ground floor. In the grounds, the temples of Buhen and Semna were saved from the rising waters of Lake Nasser and transported to Khartoum, as were the colourful 1st floor frescoes from early Christian churches in Nubia. It's open Tuesday to Sunday from 8.30 am to 6.30 pm. On Friday it closes from noon to 3 pm.

To appreciate Sudan's ethnic and cultural kaleidoscope, visit the small but excellently documented **Ethnographical Museum** on Sharia al-Gama. It's open Tuesday to Sunday from 8.30 am to 1.30 pm, closing at noon on Friday. Entry at US$0.10 must be the city's best bargain.

Also on Sharia al-Gama'a and observing the same opening hours is the **Natural History Museum** (admission US$0.20). The three slumbering crocodiles in its murky courtyard pool are its only living beings. Inside, beyond the quotation from the Holly Quran (sic), are dioramas with stuffed animals and case upon case of stuffed birds and desiccated insects.

The **Omdurman Souk** is Sudan's largest. It has an amazing variety of wares, though it doesn't compare with Cairo's Khan al-Khalili. Omdurman's most spectacular sight is the **whirling dervishes**, who bob, sway and stir up the dust every Friday afternoon (except during Ramadan) in front of the Hamed an-Nil Mosque. Take a taxi since it's not easy to find.

A quick look (which is all you'll get because foreigners aren't allowed inside) at the **Mahdi's Tomb** in Omdurman is worth the effort, though the original was destroyed by Kitchener and only rebuilt in 1947. Just across the road, the **Khalifa's House** contains a small museum. Look, in

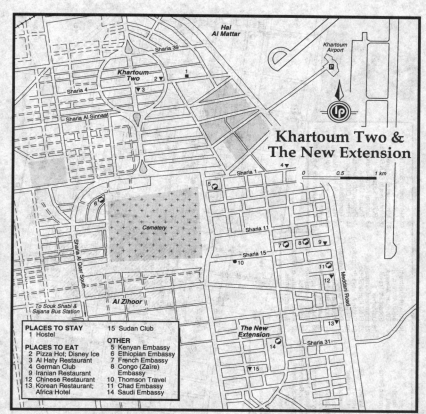

Khartoum Two & The New Extension

Hai Al Mattar

Khartoum Airport

Sharia 39

Khartoum Two

Sharia 4

Sharia Al Sinnaat

Sharia 1

Cemetery

Sharia 11

Sharia 15

Sharia Al Qasr South

Al Zihoor

To Souk Shabi & Sajana Bus Station

Madani Road

The New Extension

Sharia 31

0   0.5   1 km

PLACES TO STAY
1 Hostel

PLACES TO EAT
2 Pizza Hot; Disney Ice
3 Al Haty Restaurant
4 German Club
9 Iranian Restaurant
12 Chinese Restaurant
13 Korean Restaurant;
   Africa Hotel

15 Sudan Club

OTHER
5 Kenyan Embassy
6 Ethiopian Embassy
7 French Embassy
8 Congo (Zaïre)
   Embassy
10 Thomson Travel
11 Chad Embassy
14 Saudi Embassy

particular, for the Mahdist weaponry and period photos.

Upstream, beside the Blue Nile, you can still see **Kitchener's gunboat**, the *Melik*, source of much of the carnage when he decimated the Mahdist forces at the battle of Omdurman.

It's pleasant to stroll the **Blue Nile corniche** beneath the *neem* trees. You can choose any point between the University of Khartoum and the White Nile Bridge except the stretch in front of the People's Palace, where you'll be told politely to make a detour.

The **confluence of the Blue and White Niles** is, for one of the most significant spots on the map of Africa, something of an anticlimax. All the same, it's worth walking over the White Nile Bridge and letting your imagination play over the 6648km route of the world's longest river. For an original perspective, look down upon the confluence from the top of the gondola ferris wheel in adjacent Mogran Family Park.

Abu Roaf, 1.5km north of Shambat Bridge, is a village of boat builders, who saw and nail the small shallow-draft Nile sailing boats, and of blacksmiths, forging ornately

SUDAN

PLACES TO STAY
2 Sudan Hotel;
  Oriental Hotel
20 El-Warithi Hotel
  & Restaurant
25 Acropole Hotel
26 Falcon Hotel
29 Safa Hotel
39 Haramein Hotel
45 Meridien Hotel
46 Sharazad Hotel
47 Bahr al-Ghazal Hotel
48 Salli Hotel
49 Danah Hotel
50 Wadi Halfa Hotel
51 Port Sudan Hotel
52 Medinet-al-Munawwara
  Hotel

PLACES TO EAT
14 Casa Blanka
19 Lebanese Restaurant
22 Sandwich Stand

27 Dac Burger
28 Maxim's Burgers
36 Pizza World
38 Flash Fantastic Foods

OTHER
1 National Museum
3 Coptic Church
4 Ministry of the Interior
  (Visa Extensions)
5 Post Office
6 Catholic Cathedral
7 Melik Gunboat
8 University of Khartoum
9 Natural History Museum
10 UK Embassy; German Embassy
11 Ethnographical Museum
12 Greek Church
13 Sudan Airways
  (International &
  Port Sudan)
15 Olympia Travel Agents;
  EgyptAir

16 Bank of Khartoum
17 British Airways;
  Ethiopian Airways;
  Speedbird Travel
18 Lufthansa
21 Egyptian Consulate
23 El Nil Kodak Studio
24 Sudan Airways (International)
30 US Embassy
31 Sudan Airways (Domestic);
  Industrial Bank of
  Sudan Building
32 Buses to Omdurman
33 Al-Kabir Mosque
34 Minibuses to North Khartoum
35 British Council
37 Aliens Registration Office
  & Travel Permits

40 Minibuses to Souk Two
  & New Extension
41 Minibuses to Saganat
42 Minibuses to Souk Shaabi
  (& Past Saganat)
43 General Administration of
  Tourism Office &
  Photography Permits
44 French Cultural Centre
53 Train Station
54 Wadi Halfa Ferry Booking Office
55 Commonwealth War Cemetery
56 American Club
57 Khartoum Police Administration

Khartoum

To Mogran Family Park;
Hilton Hotel, Riverside
Restaurants, Omdurman
& Abu Road

Blue Nile

Tuti Island

To Blue Nile Bridge

Sharia Osman Digna

Blue Nile

0   100   200 m

May Gardens

Botanical Gardens

Sunt Forest

To Soba (Ring Road)

kitsch iron gates and bedsteads. About 2km north of Omdurman's main souk, there's a colourful daily **camel market**.

Places to Stay

The *hostel* in Khartoum 2, on 47th Ave East, charges US$2 per bed.

The shaded area on the Khartoum map abounds in cheap hotels used by local truckers and travellers. All are basic and in the US$2 to US$4 range for a bed in the courtyard or in a communal room. The *Bahr al-Ghazal Hotel*, the *Salli*, *Port Sudan*, *Wadi Halfa* and *Medinet al-Munawwara* hotels (these last two are signed only in Arabic) are all more than tolerable.

The *Safa* (☎ 779986) is cheap but gloomy. Singles/doubles cost US$3.50/5 without/with bath.

The *El-Sawahli Hotel* (☎ 772544) has clean, simply furnished rooms with desert coolers and fans. Doubles with shared showers and toilets cost US$7.

The *Haramein Hotel* (☎ 780809) is central and popular with travellers. It has rooms with fans for US$2.50/5.

More upmarket but great value for money are the *Danah Hotel* (☎ 783293), where rooms with bathroom, cooler and TV cost US$11/15, and the *Sharazad* (☎ 783577), which has rooms with air-con and satellite TV for US$18/24.

The *Acropole Hotel* (☎ 772860), popular with NGOs, is a home-from-home whose Greek owners, George and Eleonara, are immensely helpful (see the effusive letter of thanks from Bob Geldof on the office noticeboard). More agreeable pension than hotel, its prices (US$70/105 for a room with full board), are altogether less friendly.

Places to Eat

Most Sudanese entertaining takes place within the family, where you find the best cooking. For cheap eats, the choice is fairly limited, apart from the myriad fuul and ta'amiya joints (see Food and Drinks in the Facts for the Visitor section). An exception is the *sandwich stand* at the junction of Sharia al-Khalifa and Sharia al-Gamhuriyya,

where the selection is wide and conditions so clean you could eat off the counter.

Nearby, the unnamed *Lebanese Restaurant*, on the site of the once-raucous and long closed Gordon's Music Hall, offers dishes such as steak with chips and a couple of mezze for US$4.

From the Hilton Hotel to the confluence of the two Niles, there's a series of riverside restaurants. They all offer meat and fish dishes for around US$4, or you can simply enjoy a soft drink and watch the Blue Nile slip by.

At *Casa Blanka*, among other places, you can get a tasty chawarma – but only there can you follow it down with a big ice cream sundae (US$1.40). *Pizza World* does hunky pizzas for US$4 to US$5.50.

In the New Extension, you can eat well for a similar price (including the daily entrance fee) at the *German Club* (☎ 442438). At the nearby *Iranian Restaurant* – which has nothing Iranian but its name and, locals speculate, its owner – you can dine pleasantly enough in the garden and come away with change from US$6.

At the *Korean Restaurant* in the Africa Hotel, you can eat oriental cuisine for US$4.50 to US$6. Try the sizzling barbecues, prepared at your table.

On 47th Avenue, known locally as Chicken Street, there's a range of reasonably priced food. At the eastern end, you can eat international at *Pizza Hot* (no typographical error here), followed by a cooling ice cream in *Disney Ice*. Walking westward, you pass a range of more typical restaurants and cafes, among which *Al Haty*, with its half chicken grilled with herbs (US$2.50), stands out.

For atmosphere, have a drink or a meal (US$4) at the *Liyali Omdurman*, or *Omdurman Nights* – a boat restaurant moored between the Shambat and White Nile bridges.

Getting There & Away

Air British Airways (☎ 774577), EgyptAir (☎ 780064), Kenya Airways (☎ 773429) and Lufthansa (☎ 771322) all have offices in Khartoum.

Sudan Airways has three offices in Khartoum: on Sharia al-Qasr (☎ 780928) for international flights; on Sharia Atbara (☎ 775554) for international and Port Sudan journeys; and in UN Square (☎ 780429) for domestic flights.

Bus & Lorry There are four departure points for all road transport: the souk shabi in south Khartoum (for destinations to the east, north-east and south); Sajana bus station just north of the souk shabi (for Karima, Dongola and Wadi Halfa); Khartoum North (for as far north as Atbara); and Omdurman souk shabi (for westward journeys).

Nyala via Kosti & El-Obeid Check with your consulate that the route west of El-Obeid, where there's occasional strife, is still safe. Note that fares can double during the wet season between July and September.

It's possible to make the trip all the way from Khartoum to Nyala in one extended hit; occasional buses and lorries leave from Omdurman. However, most travellers head first for El-Obeid (see its entry in the following Around the Country section), from where you can organise trips further west on lorries heading to Nyala via El-Fasher.

The whole, exacting trip can take as little as three days, but more likely six – and up to double in the wet season.

Port Sudan via Kassala There are several buses daily to Wad Medani, Gedaref, Kassala and Port Sudan (1270km), leaving between 6 and 7.30 am. Safina, Arrow and Taysir buses are comfortable and some have air-con. For guaranteed air-con, take the Suarty Nasser line or one of the plush new buses of the Dina Magna MC company. For each, book a day in advance to be sure of a seat.

The bus to Port Sudan takes at least 16 hours, may stop overnight and costs US$26. The trip from Khartoum to Kassala, which makes a pleasant overnight stop, is about nine hours.

Wadi Halfa Take one of the daily buses from Khartoum to Dongola via Ed-Debba. At Dongola, you cross the Nile by ferry and, from the east bank, take a direct bus for the long – over 24 hours long – haul to Wadi Halfa, although it's preferable to break the journey into at least a couple of segments.

There's regular bus and lorry traffic along the tarmac road between Khartoum and Atbara, and then intermittent transport going to Dongola via Ed-Debba. Alternatively, between July and February when the Nile's high, there are steamers which run between Karima and Dongola, taking about four days.

Train Rail is the less demanding route to Wadi Halfa. Even so, you're in for a dusty, crowded 50 hour desert journey if there are no breakdowns or derailments. See the Train entry in the main Getting Around section for times and prices.

Getting Around

The short ride from the airport to central Khartoum costs US$3 to US$5, depending on fuel prices and time of day. Buses and minibuses cover most points in Khartoum – see the Khartoum map for bus stations. A ride in a share-taxi travelling a regular route costs US$0.35 or US$0.70, according to distance. A taxi to yourself costs US$1.75 to US$3, also determined by distance.

Around the Country

ATBARA

Atbara, where the railway from Khartoum to Wadi Halfa and to Port Sudan splits, was the scene of the first battle between Kitchener's advancing troops and the Mahdists. Today, , as a graveyard for old steam locomotives, it's fascinating even if you're not a dedicated trainspotter.

You can stay at the roach-infested *River Atbara Lokanda* or, in greater solitude, the *Alneel Lokanda*. Both have beds for US$1. For more comfort, try the *Alneel Hotel* or the *Railway Guest House*.

DONGOLA

Dongola, a pleasant, sleepy town, is famous for its palm groves. The ruins of the **Temple of Kawa**, which you reach by ferry, then box, are on the eastern bank of the Nile.

The best place to stay is the *Al-Manar Hotel*, although, like everywhere in town, it seems a little reluctant to allow women in. Beds in clean rooms with fans cost US$2. The *Ash-Shimal Palace* is also reasonable.

EL-OBEID

El-Obeid, the 'gum-arabic capital of the world', surrounded by inhospitable desert, was once the capital of the Mahdi's Islamic state.

Its **cathedral** is one of the largest in Africa; it's worth going to a service there for the distinctively African music. There is also a small **museum** and two souks.

The best place to stay is the *Kordofan Hotel*, near the airport, with doubles for US$5. Otherwise, try the *Nyala Hotel*. The *International* and *Al-Medina* are both cheap lokandas.

KARIMA

Karima is a base for visiting the nearby archaeological sites. Two kilometres south is **Jebel Barkal**, a sacred site for Egyptians at the time of the 18th dynasty pharaohs. Nearby are some well-preserved **pyramids** and a **temple complex** to Amun.

There are other pyramids in a bad state of repair across the river at **Merowe** and **Nuri**. More equally dilapidated ruins are at **Kurru**, on the Karima bank.

You can stay at the *Al-Nasser Hotel*, the *Lokanda ash-Shimaliyya* or at the *Tirhaga Hotel*, across the river in Merowe.

KASSALA

This area still has a large residual refugee population, caught in a political tug-of-war between Sudan and neighbouring Eritrea.

The town is overlooked by weird mountains like stubby fingers, two of whose digits are called **Taka** and **Toteel**. To get to them, take a local bus to **Khatmiya**. Around town

are extensive fruit orchards. The colourful **souk** is the centre's main attraction.

As the civil war moves closer and since Kassala is so near the Eritrean frontier, the authorities seem particularly jittery about foreigners. You should register at the unmarked security office north-east of the central bus station.

Places to Stay & Eat

Lokandat Mak Nimir, with beds for US$1, is one of several cheap hotels near the minibus station.

The friendly *Toteel Hotel* (☎ 2840) charges US$1.75 per person in a room with a cooler. The *Safa* (☎ 2577) is a particular bargain; a double room with cooler and private bathroom costs US$1 – and for an extra US$0.20 you can have satellite TV. The *Toteel el-Sharq*, where a clean double with bathroom, cooler and TV costs US$7, is also good value. Avoid the surly, joyless *Africa Hotel*.

There are several basic restaurants around the minibus station and behind the Toteel and Hipton hotels. The *Hipton Hotel Cafeteria* does a tasty grill with salad for US$4. For more down-to-earth prices and food, try *Kassala Fantastic Food*, the nearby *Kassala al-A'eli* restaurant or the *Africa Restaurant* near the main mosque.

Getting There & Away

Buses leave from the souk shabi, to which minibuses (US$0.10) from town regularly shuttle. Once the frontier reopens, buses will again run directly to Asmara, the Eritrean capital.

KOSTI

Kosti, named after a Greek shopkeeper and in its time an important riverboat terminal, has little of interest nowadays.

Should you be stuck here at nightfall, the *Om Dom Hotel* has clean rooms and the *Abu Zayd Hotel* on the main street is adequate. Among the lokandas, the *Tabidi* stands out.

MEROE

Over 50 pyramid tombs dominate the site of

the Kingdom of Meroe's capital. The royal city of Meroe thrived from 592 BC until it was overrun by the Abyssinians in 350 AD. There is a *rest house* nearby. To get there, head for Kabushiya, 60km north of Shendi, then on to Bagrawiya by local transport. The pyramids are about 5km from the village.

NYALA

Nyala was the capital of the independent Fur sultanate from the late 16th century until the early 20th century. Nowadays, it's an isolated outpost on the edge of the desert. It's also the departure point for Jebel Marra which, at 3088m, is the second-highest mountain in Sudan, offering rivers, orchards, an extinct volcano and good, hilly walking country, which can, however, be difficult to navigate.

The *El-Ryan Hotel*, once a government rest house and also called the *Ferdous*, is next to the central souk and offers rooms for US$5. Otherwise, try the cheap and basic *Darfur Hotel* or the *Nyala Hotel*.

You can get there either by the long desert drive from El-Obeid, by rail from Er-Rahad or by air from Khartoum.

PORT SUDAN

Port Sudan, now rather run-down, was established in 1905 by the British for exporting cotton and other crops. Along the offshore reef is some of the Red Sea's best snorkelling and diving.

For diving trips, ring Captain Halim (☎ 22649) or contact him through Red Sea Travel & Tourism (☎ 29067). The ebullient captain can organise anything from a day trip to several nights on the reef. Hamido Travel Agency and Ebonus Travel also arrange dives and sea trips.

Places to Stay & Eat

There's a cluster of basic hotels near the minibus lot for Suakin.

The once splendid *Olympic Park Hotel* (☎ 23082) charges US$2 for a room with fan and communal bathroom, and – particularly good value – US$5 for a room with air-con

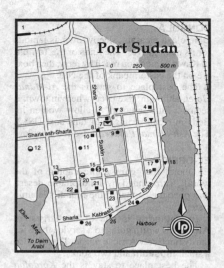

Port Sudan

PLACES TO STAY
4   Samarmaz Hotel
6   Sinkat Hotel
10 Olymoic Park Hotel
13 Omyia Hotel
19 Red Sea Hotel
21 Bohein Hotel; Ebonus Travel
23 Sudan Palace Hotel

PLACES TO EAT
3   Felfela Restaurant
5   Tennis Club Restaurant
18 Marine Gardens Restaurant;
    Quiet Corner Cafe
25 Lu'lu'a Restaurant

OTHER
1   Train Station
2   Aliens Registration Office
7   Post & Telephone Office
8   Osman Digna Roundabout
9   Town Hall
11 Central Market
12 Bus Station (local services)
14 Minibuses & Taxis to Suakin
15 Sudan Shipping Lone Office
    (boats to Jeddah)
16 Bank of Khartoum
17 Red Sea Province Headquarters
20 Sudan Airways Office; Airport Bus
22 Red Sea Travel & Tourism
24 Yacht Jetty
26 Ba'bour Travel (boats to Jeddah)

Osman Digna

If you ask anyone in Port Sudan for directions, you'll be oriented from the statue of Osman Digna, the locally born Mahdist warrior and national hero.

His powerful frame sat squarely on his charger, sword arm outstretched, and people were proud of their statue. However for ultra-orthodox Muslims, representation of the human form is a sin. So one night a mob of fundamentalists tore it from its pedestal and shattered it in the name of Allah.

One small act of desecration which symbolises the schizophrenia and tragedy of Sudan today. ■

and bathroom. The nearby *Sinkat Hotel*, more spartan, has rooms with fan and external bathroom for US$2.

The friendly *Bohein Hotel* has singles/doubles for US$3.50/5.50 with bathroom and fan, and US$5.50/11 with air-con. A spacious room at the *Samarmaz* (☎ 25800) costs US$24 with air-con.

There are several cheap restaurants in and around the market. Beside the creek, the *Lu'lu'a* and *Marine Gardens* restaurants do grills for US$2. You can also eat reasonably under the stars at the *Tennis Club*, open to all. The restaurant at the fancy *Sudan Palace Hotel* has main dishes for US$4.50 to US$6.50.

Getting There & Away

The Sudan Airways bus to the airport, 18km south, costs US$0.70. Buses to Kassala (eight hours) cost US$8/12 with/without air-con, and there are daily air-con buses to Khartoum (US$26, 16 hours). Minibuses and taxis for Suakin leave from near the Omyia Hotel.

For information on passenger ferries, refer to the Sea entry in the main Getting There & Away section earlier in this chapter.

SUAKIN

Before the construction of Port Sudan, Suakin was Sudan's only port, through which, in season, passed thousands of pilgrims bound for Mecca. Abandoned in the 1930s, it became a fascinating ghost town, full of decaying **coral houses**. Today, it fitfully enjoys some of its old bustle whenever a passenger boat for Jeddah, Massawa or Suez puts in.

There are a couple of cheap lokandas, but you're better planning a day trip from Port Sudan.

WADI HALFA

Halfa is the nondescript transit point where the Lake Nasser steamer meets the train, bus and lorries from Khartoum. With their trade decimated now that the ferry from Aswan no longer calls, it's impossible to know which of the hotels will survive until their ship again comes home.

Swaziland

Swaziland, the smallest country in the southern hemisphere, has some good wildlife reserves. It's such a pleasant and easy-going country that it's well worth a visit.

Facts about the Country

HISTORY

The area which is now Swaziland has been inhabited by various groups for a very long time: in eastern Swaziland archaeologists have discovered human remains dating back 110,000 years. However, the Swazi people themselves arrived relatively recently. In the early 19th century when the Zulu nation was violently expanding, King Sobhuza I merged refugees fleeing from the Zulu with his own people to build a nation that could withstand Zulu pressure.

When King Sobhuza I died in 1839, Swaziland was twice its present size. It was whittled down by the Boers between 1840-80. After a period of rivalry between the Boers and the British for control over what remained of the country, Swaziland became a British protectorate.

There was a brief flirtation with a constitutional monarchy after independence from Britain in 1968. But in 1972, when the parties of urban workers and intellectuals began to threaten the Imbokodvo (traditionalist party), the king suspended the constitution, dissolved all political parties and declared a state of emergency.

King Sobhuza II (then the world's longest reigning monarch) died in late 1982 and, in keeping with Swazi tradition, a strictly enforced 75-day period of mourning was announced by Dzeliwe (Great She-Elephant), the most senior of his 100 wives. No soil could be tilled, no harvest reaped and no cattle slaughtered. Only commerce essential to the life of the nation was allowed and sexual intercourse was banned, punishable by flogging.

Highlights
- Good game viewing and safari camps in the splendid Mkhaya Game Reserve
- Enjoyable hiking and white-water rafting

Choosing a successor wasn't easy as Sobhuza had fathered more than 600 children. Prince Makhosetive, born in 1968, was chosen and was crowned King Mswati III in 1986.

Mswati dissolved parliament in 1992 and Swaziland was again governed by a traditional tribal assembly, the Liqoqo. Democratic reform has begun but there is increasingly strident agitation for the pace of change to be increased.

Though Swaziland remains largely traditional, it has been skilfully developed. There are pineapple and citrus orchards, and large areas are irrigated for rice, sugar cane and

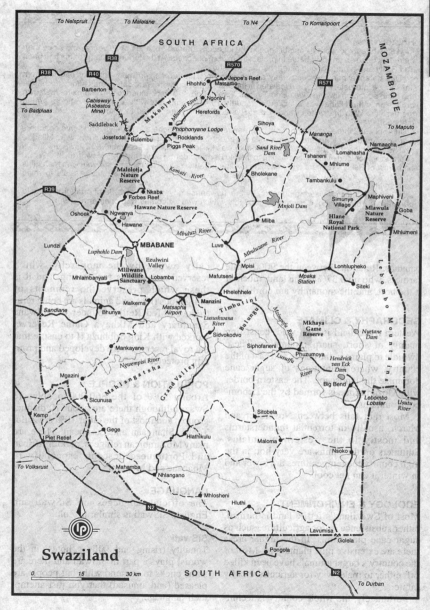

To Nelspruit
To Malelane
To N4
To Komatipoort

SOUTH AFRICA

R38
R570

R38
R40

To Badplaas

Barberton
Cableway
(Asbestos Mine)

Saddleback

Josefsdal
Bulembu

Jeppe's Reef
Matsamo

Hhohho
Ngonini
Herefords

Sihoya

Mlumati River

Makonjwa

Phophonyane Lodge
Rocklands
Piggs Peak

Sand River Dam

Mananga

To Maputo

Namaacha

Lomahasha

R571

MOZAMBIQUE

Tshaneni
Mhlume

Malolotja
Nature
Reserve

Komati River

Bholekane

Tambankulu

R39

Nkaba
Forbes Reef

Hawane Nature Reserve

Oshoek
Ngwenya

Hawane

Mnjoli Dam

Mliba

Simunye
Village

Hlane
Royal
National Park

Maphiveni

Mlawula
Nature
Reserve

Goba

Mhlumeni

Lundzi

Luphohlo Dam

MBABANE

Mbuluzi River

Ezulwini
Valley

Luve

Mbuluzane River

Lebombo Mountains

Mhlambanyati

Milwane
Wildlife
Sanctuary

Lobamba

Mafutseni

Mpisi

Mpaka
Station

Lonhlupheko

Siteki

Sandlane

Malkerns

Bhunya

Matsapha
Airport

Manzini

Hhelehhele

Timbutini

Lusushwana River

Sidvokodvo

Mankayane

Ngwempisi River

Balungu

Mzimpofu River

Mkhaya
Game
Reserve

Nyetane
Dam

Mgazini

Sicunusa

Mahlangatsha

Grand Valley

Siphofaneni

Phuzumoya

Lusutfu River

Hendrick
van Eck
Dam

Big Bend

Lebombo
Lobster

Usutu
River

Kemp

Piet Retief

Gege

Hlathikulu

Sitobela

Maloma

Nsoko

To Volksrust

Mahamba

Nhlangano

Mhlosheni

Hluthi

Lavumisa

Golela

N2

Swaziland

0   15   30 km

SOUTH AFRICA

Pongola

N2

To Durban

SWAZILAND

Rhino Wars

In 1965 white rhino were re-established in the kingdom after an absence of 70 years, and since then there has been an ongoing battle to protect them from poachers. At the forefront of this battle has been Ted Reilly and a band of dedicated, hand-picked rangers.

This defence has not been easy as the poachers have received hefty financial backing from Taiwanese interests. Poaching escalated in the late 1980s and there were determined efforts to change the rhino poaching laws in Swaziland. Rhinos were dehorned and confined to enclosures for their own protection. After Hlane was attacked in January 1992 by poachers with AK47s, the rangers armed themselves. With the rhinos dehorned at Hlane, the poachers shifted to Mkhaya. The battle commenced.

In April 1992 there was a shoot-out between rangers and poachers at Mkhaya, and some poachers were captured. Not long after there was a big shoot-out at Big Bend and two poachers were killed.

The last rhino (the majestic bull Mthondvo) was killed for horn in December 1992 while the Swazi courts still agonised over action relating to the Big Bend incident. The young king, Mswati III, intervened on behalf of Reilly's rangers and poaching declined dramatically. The rangers still wait with their rifles at the ready. You can help – your presence at any one of the big game parks assists in rhino conservation.

A happy postscript was the donation by the Taiwanese government in 1996 of enough money to purchase six black rhino; a gesture of good faith which was welcomed with open arms. ■

---

bananas. Relations between the 9000 white farmers, who own 37% of the land, much of it the best, and the monarchy are cordial.

GEOGRAPHY & CLIMATE

Western Swaziland is high veld, consisting mainly of short, sharp mountains. These dwindle to plains in the centre and east of the country, where plantations of sugar cane dominate the landscape. The eastern border with Mozambique is formed by the Lebombo Mountains.

Most rain falls between November and March, usually in torrential thunderstorms and mostly in the western mountains. Summers on the plains are very hot; in the high country the temperatures are lower and in winter it can get cool.

ECOLOGY & ENVIRONMENT

Most of Swaziland's fertile land is farmed, either subsistence or for agriculture, such as sugar cane plantations. In the higher areas there are extensive pine plantations. Most of the country's larger animals have been killed off, either to make way for agriculture or by hunters.

Fortunately, the whole country is techni-cally owned by the monarchy, which reserved some areas for hunting, and it is these which preserve the remnants of indigenous flora, and animals are being reintroduced. Ted Reilly, founder of Milwane Sanctuary and Mkhaya Game Reserve, worked with King Sobhuza II to ensure that the royal reserves were developed and properly protected.

POPULATION & PEOPLE

Around 90% of the 860,000 people are Swazi (although there are about 70 distinct groups) and most of the other 10% are Zulu, Tonga, Shangaan and European. There are many Mozambican refugees, of both African and Portuguese descent, especially in Mbabane and Manzini.

LANGUAGE

The official languages are SiSwati and English. SiSwati is similar to Zulu.

SiSwati

Tonality (rising and falling 'notes' in the words) plays a part in SiSwati and there are some clicks to contend with, but people are pleased (and amused) that you just attempt their language.

Greetings & Civilities

Hello.

(to one person)	*sawubona* (literally: I see you)
(to more than one person)	*sanibona*

How are you?	*kunjani?*
I'm fine.	*kulungile*

Goodbye.

(if you are leaving)	*sala kahle* (lit: stay well)
(if you are staying)	*hamba kahle* (lit: go well)

please	*tsine*
I thank you.	*ngiyabonga*
We thank you.	*siyabonga*

Useful Words & Phrases

Yes. (all-purpose response)	*yebo*
No.	(click) *ha*
Sorry.	*lucolo*
Do you have ...?	*une ... yini?*
How much?	*malini?*
today	*lamuhla*
tomorrow	*kusasa*
yesterday	*itolo*
Is there a bus to ...?	*kukhona ibhasi yini leya ...?*
When does it leave?	*isuka nini?*
morning	*ekuseni*
afternoon	*entsambaba*
evening	*kusihlwa*
night	*ebusuku*

Yebo is often said as a casual greeting. It is the custom to greet everyone you meet. Often you will be asked *u ya phi?* (Where are you going?).

Facts for the Visitor

VISAS

Most people don't need a visa, but there are some exceptions, including French and German citizens. However, those who need visas will be able to get them free at the border.

Anyone staying for more than 60 days must apply for a temporary residence permit from the Chief Immigration Officer (☎ 42 941), PO Box 372, Mbabane.

Other Visas

Mozambique

The Mozambique Embassy (☎ 43 700) in Mbabane issues visas faster and cheaper (from US$11) than the embassy in South Africa.

EMBASSIES

Swazi Embassies

Countries with Swazi representation include Kenya, South Africa, the UK and the USA. In countries without Swazi representation, try the UK representative.

Foreign Embassies in Swaziland

Countries with diplomatic representation in Mbabane include:

Germany
    3rd Floor, Dhlan'ubeka House (☎ 43 174)
Mozambique (high commission)
    Princess Drive (☎ 43 700)
Netherlands (consulate)
    Business Machine House (☎ 45 178)
UK (high commission)
    Allister Miller St (☎ 42 581/3)
USA
    Central Bank Building, Warner St (☎ 46 441/2)

MONEY

US$1 = E4.40

The unit of currency is the lilangeni; the plural is emalangeni (E). It is tied in value to the South African rand. Rands are accepted everywhere and there's no need to change them. Change your emalangeni before you leave, as they aren't easily changed in other countries.

Several banks change travellers' cheques; Barclays Bank has branches in most major towns.

There is a 10% goods and services tax (GST).

POST & COMMUNICATIONS

You can make international calls (but not reverse-charge calls) at the post office in

Mbabane between 8 am and 4 pm on weekdays and until noon on Saturday. International calls to and from Swaziland are expensive. There are no area codes within Swaziland. The country code is 268; there are no area codes.

HEALTH

Take precautions against malaria. Swimming almost anywhere in the country is risky because of bilharzia and, in some places, crocodiles. Drinking untreated water from streams and wells in rural areas puts you at risk of dysentery and cholera. Also see the Health Appendix for information.

PUBLIC HOLIDAYS & SPECIAL EVENTS

In addition to Christmas, Boxing and New Year's days holidays, Good Friday and Easter Monday, other holidays observed in Swaziland are: 19 April (King Mswati III's Birthday); 25 April (National Flag Day); 22 July (King Sobhuza II's Birthday); variable in August or September (Umhlanga or Reed Dance Day); 6 September (Somhlolo or Independence Day); and variable in December or January (Incwala Day).

The most important events are the Incwala ceremony, held near Lobamba in the Ezulwini Valley, and the Umhlanga, or Reed Dance, held in the same place. Ask at the tourist office in Mbabane for exact dates.

The Incwala ceremony celebrates the new year and the first fruits of the harvest. The king grants his regiments the right to consume his harvest and the rains are expected to follow the ceremony. Photography is not permitted at this deeply religious occasion.

The Reed Dance is performed by unmarried girls who collect reeds for the repair and maintenance of the royal palace, and who symbolically offer themselves as royal brides.

ACCOMMODATION

There are few designated camp sites except in some of the national parks and nature reserves. Away from the population centres it's usually possible (and safe) to pitch a tent, but *always* ask permission.

The only real backpacker accommodation is in Mlilwane Wildlife Sanctuary. There are a couple of church-run hostels in Mbabane. If you're stuck for a room in rural areas you could try the local school.

Many of the hotels are geared towards South African tourists and are expensive.

Getting There & Away

AIR

Matsapha airport, north of Manzini, is the international airport. Royal Swazi Airlines (☎ 86 155) operates from there. Schedules and tickets often refer to the airport as Manzini. Royal Swazi flies to Johannesburg and a number of other Southern African capitals. LAM flies to Maputo.

A departure tax of US$4.50 is levied at Matsapha airport.

LAND
Mozambique

The Lomahasha-Namaacha border post is the entry point to Mozambique (open 7 am to 4.45 pm).

Frequent buses go from Manzini and Mbabane to the border at Namaacha, from where there are minibuses to Maputo (US$3).

South Africa

There are 11 border posts with South Africa, the main ones being Ngwenya-Oshoek, Mahamba, Lavumisa-Golela (each open from 7 am to 10 pm) and Bulembu-Josefsdal (8 am to 4 pm).

Transtate, the South African 'third-class' bus line, runs between Johannesburg and Mbabane for US$15. See the Getting Around section in the South Africa chapter for information on Transtate and the Baz Bus, which includes Swaziland on its circular route.

Some minibus taxis run direct between Jo'burg and Mbabane for about US$17.

Getting Around

BUS & MINIBUS
There's a good system of inexpensive buses, some express, running regular routes but not very frequently. Minibus taxis usually run shorter routes at prices a little higher than the buses. There are also non-share-taxis in some of the larger towns.

CAR & MOTORCYCLE
Most main roads are good but watch out for people and animals on the road. The speed limit is only 80km/h and most people keep to it. Driving down the Ezulwini Valley in heavy traffic can be slow, and the hilly road from Mbabane to Piggs Peak also carries a lot of traffic.

You must wear a seat belt and you must pull over and stop for an official motorcade. There's a US$1.20 road tax if you drive into the country.

HITCHING
Hitching is easier here than in South Africa, as the colour of the driver and the colour of the hitchhiker aren't factors in the decision to offer a lift. However, you have to wait a long time for a car on back roads, and everywhere you'll have lots of competition from locals. For a general warning about hitching, see the Hitching section in the Getting Around chapter.

Mbabane

With about 50,000 people, Mbabane (if you say 'mba-BAA-nay' you'll be close enough) is the largest town in Swaziland. There isn't much to see or do here – the adjacent Ezulwini Valley has the attractions – but it is a relaxing place to hang out. However, it's advisable not to wander alone or even in small groups at night.

Information
The friendly tourist office (☎ 42 531) is in Swazi Plaza, the new shopping complex where you'll find most goods and services, including a Barclays Bank branch (there's also one on Warmer St). Africa South, an excellent bookshop specialising in books on southern Africa, is also in Swazi Plaza.

Places to Stay
The nearest caravan park is about 12km away in the Ezulwini Valley (see the Around the Country section for more details).

There are no youth hostels but accommodation is available in a couple of church missions. The drawback is that they are some way from the centre of town and walking back at night isn't safe. Unless you really want to stay in Mbabane, you're better off heading down the valley to Mlilwane Wildlife Sanctuary, where there is dorm accommodation (see the National Parks & Reserves section for more details).

Thokose Church Centre (☎ 46 682) is on Mhlanhla Rd; rooms are US$8/9 a single/double, but it's often full. Further out, southeast of the centre on Isomi St, the *Youth Centre* (☎ 42 176) charges US$9 per person, including breakfast, in two-bed rooms – you might have to share. The gates are locked at 9.30 pm.

A long-time travellers' favourite is the *City Inn* (☎ 42 406) on Allister Miller St. Singles/doubles cost from US$28/36 or US$18/23 with shared bathroom. It's not great value but it is central. There are more expensive rooms with air-con.

The *Tavern Hotel* (☎ 42 361), off Gilfillan St, charges from US$26/45, with breakfast. Some of the rooms are tiny. The *Swazi Inn* (☎ 42 235), about 3km out on the Ezulwini Valley road, starts at US$43/52, with breakfast.

Places to Eat
Next to the City Inn is *Pablo's*, where the décor and food are Wimpyesque. Further south on Allister Miller St, on the corner of Warmer (Msunduza) St, the *Copacabana* is a friendly Portuguese-run place serving

SWAZILAND

PLACES TO STAY
5 Thokoza Hostel
9 Tavern Hotel
10 Hill St Lodge
16 City Inn
24 Kamtshawe Lodge
26 Youth Centre

PLACES TO EAT
4 Indingiliza Gallery
6 Mediterranean Restaurant
8 LM (Lourenco Marques Restaurant)
12 Ikhwezi Restaurant & Bar
13 Marco's Trattoria
17 Copacabana Restaurant & Bar

OTHER
1 Mbabane Club
2 Pool
3 Swaziland Theatre Club
7 Cinelux Theatre
11 Club 701
14 Police Station
15 Post Office
18 Barclays Bank
19 Bus Station; Taxi Park
20 The Mall
21 Swazi Plaza; Tourist Park
22 Swazi Market
23 Shell Station
25 SAR (Transtate Bus Station)

Mbabane

0   100   200 m

To Manzini & Ezulwini Valley

simple food. Stew with rice costs US$3.50; a big salad is US$2.

Maxim's on Johnstone St is recommended. The restaurant is open daily from 9 am to 1 am, although the bar and disco often stay open later. Best value are the pizzas, which cost under US$5.

The *Mediterranean* on Allister Miller St is in fact Indian, although the menu also has steaks and seafood; curries cost around US$4. It's open for lunch and until 11 pm for dinner. *Marco's Trattoria*, also on Allister Miller St, is upstairs and it has a small balcony.

In Swazi Plaza the popular *Longhorn Steakhouse* (near Barclays Bank) has large steaks from US$7.

Entertainment

The *Cinelux* cinema is at the north end of Allister Miller St and the *Maxi* is in Swazi Plaza. Both show fairly recent mainstream movies for about US$2.50.

At the river side of Swazi Plaza is the *Plaza Bar*, where you will meet locals and travellers. *Maxim's*, the watering-hole for a wide range of people – locals, visitors and expats – is a good meeting place. As well as the bar and pool room there's music most nights and on weekends a basement disco (there's a US$5 cover charge for the disco).

Getting There & Away

Transtate buses leave from the train station on Coventry Crescent. Minibus taxis to South Africa leave from the taxi park near Swazi Plaza, where you'll also find buses and minibus taxis to destinations in Swaziland.

Getting Around

Non-share-taxis congregate near the bus rank by Swazi Plaza, and at night you can usually find one near the City Inn, or try phoning ☎ 42 014 or 42 530. Non-share-taxis to the Ezulwini Valley cost at least US$7, more to the far end of the valley, and still more at night.

Around the Country

BIG BEND

Big Bend is a sugar town on, naturally, a big bend in the Lusutfu River. The *New Bend Inn* (☎ 36 111), on a hill just south of town with good views across the river, is good value at US$24/43 for singles/doubles, without breakfast. There's a restaurant and a pleasant outdoor bar overlooking Big Bend. There's also a friendly workers' bar with a lively disco on Friday and Saturday.

One of Swaziland's best restaurants, the *Lebombo Lobster*, is a few kilometres south of Big Bend. 'Highway hen' (spatchcock cooked with peri peri) is US$6.

Getting There & Away

About four buses a day run south to the South African border at Lavumisa for US$1.50. Coming the other way they continue on to Manzini for US$1.80.

EZULWINI VALLEY

The royal Ezulwini Valley begins just outside Mbabane and extends down past Lobamba village, 18km away. It's a pretty valley but fast turning into a hotel strip. Most of the area's attractions are near Lobamba.

Although you can't enter the **Royal Village**, you can see the monarchy in action at the nearby **Royal Kraal** during the Incwala ceremony and the Umhlanga (Reed Dance). The nearby **Somhlolo National Stadium** hosts events such as coronations.

The **National Museum** has some interesting displays. It's open daily from 8 am to 4 pm and admission is US$2.50 for foreigners. Next to the museum is the **parliament**; sometimes open to visitors. Wear your best clothes.

Mantenga Falls are worth a look, but ask for advice at the nearby Mantenga Hotel before you go. The road is steep and sometimes dangerous, and there have been muggings and worse at the falls.

Places to Stay

There's a hostel and other accommodation at the Mlilwane Wildlife Sanctuary – see the National Parks & Reserves section at the end of this chapter for more details.

Timbali Caravan Park (☎ 61 156), about 12km down the valley road from Mbabane, has sites and accommodation in rondavels and caravans. Camp sites are US$7/10 in the low/high season plus US$2 per person, two-berth, on-site caravans are US$17/20 plus US$3, rondavels are US$17/23 plus US$3/4 and four-bed rooms are US$23/27 plus US$3/4. During the high season (December/January and holidays) you have to pay for a minimum of three nights.

As well as the expensive hotels lining the valley there's *Mantenga Lodge* (☎ 62 168; fax 61 049), which is a pleasant old place where singles/doubles cost US$34/50, with breakfast. To get here, take the turn-off from the highway at Lobamba for Mlilwane Wildlife Sanctuary but turn right rather than left at the T-intersection.

Getting There & Away

Taxis from Mbabane cost at least US$7, and from US$12 if you want to go to the far end of the valley. At night you'll have to negotiate. During the day you could get on a

Manzini-bound bus, but make sure that the driver knows that you want to get off in the valley. Even some non-express buses aren't keen on stopping.

MANZINI

Manzini is the country's industrial centre. Downtown Manzini isn't large but it feels like a different country from easy going rural Swaziland. There are reckless drivers, city slickers and a hint of menace; be careful walking around at night.

The **market** on Thursday and Friday mornings is excellent. Get there at dawn if possible as the rural people bring in their handcrafts to sell to retailers.

Places to Stay & Eat

There's no reason to overnight here, and no cheap accommodation if you want to. The *Prince Velebantfu Hotel* (☎ 52 663), on the Mbabane road near the showgrounds, is the cheapest hotel in town, although it isn't great value at US$20/24 a single/double. This hotel may be closing down.

The cafe at the bus station has cheap local food. In town on Louw St there are three basic places serving local food, mainly during the day. There's a Portuguese restaurant at the *Mozambique Motel*, and a block away on Martins St is another, the *Gil Vincente Restaurant*.

Getting There & Away

A private taxi to Matsapha international airport costs around US$11.50. The main bus and minibus taxi park is at the north end of Louw St. Buses run up the Ezulwini Valley to Mbabane.

PIGGS PEAK

This small town in the hilly north-western corner of the country is the centre of the logging industry. There are huge pine plantations in the area, and some fine views from the ridges.

As well as its scenery, including the **Phophonyane Falls** about 8km north of town, this area is known for its **handcrafts**. At the Highlands Inn in Piggs Peak, Tintsaba Crafts displays a good range; their most expensive items are at the Tekwane shop in the Piggs Peak Casino. There are several other craft centres in this district.

Places to Stay

The *Highlands Inn* (☎ 71 144) is about 1km south of the town centre on the main road. Singles/doubles cost from US$20/38 with breakfast. The rooms are clean and nice enough, but it isn't great value. There's a pleasant garden area with views.

In the area is one of the nicest places to stay in Swaziland. *Phophonyane Lodge* (☎ 71 319; fax 44 246) is in its own nature reserve of lush indigenous forest on the Phophonyane River, where you can swim in rock pools. There is also a network of walking trails. With a maximum of just over 20 guests in three separate locations, this is a quiet and friendly place. This isn't a malarial area but there are plenty of mosquitoes in summer, so bring repellent.

Accommodation is in cottages from US$36 or tents from US$23; both rates are per person. On weekends there's a minimum stay of two nights and prices rise during holidays. There are cooking facilities or you can eat in the tiny restaurant.

To get there, head north-east from Piggs Peak towards the Piggs Peak casino, 10km away, and take the signposted turn-off about 1km before the casino (minibus taxis will drop you off here). Continue down this road until you cross a bridge over a waterfall and the turn-off to the lodge is about 500m further on, to the right. You can usually arrange to be collected from Piggs Peak.

Getting There & Away

The roads across to the north-east of the country are mainly dirt, but they're in reasonable condition.

There are a few non-share-taxis in Piggs Peak. To the casino the fare is about US$4.50; to Mbabane it's US$28. The bus and minibus taxi rank is next to the market at the top end of the main street. There's an express bus to Mbabane for US$1.50.

National Parks & Reserves

Swaziland's two nature reserves, Mlawula and Malolotja, are administered by the National Trust Commission (☎ 61 179) at the National Museum in Lobamba. The other parks and reserves are administered by Royal Swazi Big Game Parks (☎ 44 541; fax 40 957), which has an office in the Mall in Mbabane.

HLANE ROYAL NATIONAL PARK

This park in the north-east is near the royal hunting grounds and is a popular stopover for travellers en route to Mozambique via Lomahasha. There are white rhino and many antelope species. Elephant and lion have been reintroduced but at present they are kept in an enclosure. There are no walking trails.

The entrance at Ndlovu Gate (where there's a shop) is 4km from Simunye. You can walk in. Entry costs US$1.60 on weekdays, US$2.30 on weekends, and US$3 on holiday weekends and all weekends in the high season. Camping costs from US$4.50 per person. Thatched huts with communal facilities and no electricity at *Ndlovu Rest Camp* cost from US$36/40 a single/double (more on weekends). Huts with electricity and attached bathroom at *Bhubesi Rest Camp* cost from US$40/50 (more on weekends).

MALOLOTJA NATURE RESERVE

This reserve, in the hilly north-west, has mainly antelope species. There are walking trails, the longest taking a week. Bring your own food and a camp stove, as fires are not permitted outside the base camp.

Entry is US$2.30 per person and US$1.20 per vehicle. Camping costs US$4 at the established sites and US$2.50 on the trails. There are fully equipped cabins, which sleep six, for US$28, US$38 on weekends.

The entrance is about 35km from Mbabane, on the Piggs Peak road.

MKHAYA GAME RESERVE

Mkhaya is a refuge for endangered species. It has facilities similar to South Africa's exclusive private reserves but at a much cheaper price, and good-value day tours are available. A three hour guided walk costs US$12.50 per person (US$15 on weekends) and a longer Land Rover drive, with lunch, costs US$28 (US$33 on weekends). A white-water rafting tour costs US$55. Minimum numbers for the Land Rover tour are just two, so you don't need to get a huge group together.

Mkhaya is worth staying at for at least a night. Safari tents start at US$105/165 a single/double (more on weekends), including three meals, game-viewing drives and walks. There is also *Nkonjane* (Swallow's Nest), a luxurious stone cottage, at US$165/100 per person single/sharing (more on weekends).

Note that you can't visit without having booked, and even then you can't drive in alone; you'll be met at the nearby hamlet of Phuzumoya at a specified pick-up time.

White-Water Rafting

Mkhaya offers a day-long white-water rafting trip on the Great Usutu River. The river is usually quite tame but near the reserve it passes through the narrow Bulungu Gorge, generating rapids. The second half of the day is a sedate trip through scenic country with glimpses of the 'flat dogs' (crocodiles) sunning on the river bank. The trip costs US$55 per person (minimum of four people or US$220). Phone ☎ 44 541 for bookings.

MLAWULA NATURE RESERVE

In the north-east, taking in both plains and the Lebombo mountains, Mlawula (pronounced something like mull-oo-way) is an 18,000-hectare reserve in harsh but beautiful country. Walking trails are being established. There are antelope species and shy hyenas in remote areas. Aquatic dangers include bilharzia and crocodiles. Watch out for ticks, too. The entrance is about 10km north of Simunye. Entry costs US$2.30. Camping costs US$4, or US$2.50 on the hiking trails.

There is also tent accommodation, from US$10 on weekdays and US$15 on the weekend. These prices haven't risen for a few years, so they may jump soon.

MLILWANE WILDLIFE SANCTUARY

This reserve, near Lobamba in the Ezulwini Valley, has rhino, zebra, giraffe and many antelope species, as well as crocodile and hippo. You can walk or ride a horse through the reserve and night drives are available. Watching the hippos from the restaurant is great entertainment.

Entry costs US$1.60 on weekdays, US$2.50 on weekends and US$3 in peak season (in the most popular South African school holiday periods).

Places to Stay

Camping (no electricity) costs US$4.50 per person. There's a new backpackers' place, *Sondzela House*, with dorm beds for US$7, twin-bedded rooms for US$8.50 per person and double-bedded rooms for US$10 per person. There are also traditional 'beehive' huts for US$17/20, a little less if you provide your own bedding. Rates rise on weekends.

Huts in *Main Camp* sleep six, have bathrooms and a fridge, and cost US$40/50 a single/double (more on weekends). *Shonalanga Cottage* sleeps six and costs US$53/60 a single/double (more on weekends).

All accommodation can be booked through the Royal Swazi Big Game Parks office in the Mall in Mbabane (☎ 44 541; fax 40 957).

Tanzania

Parks and wildlife are not all Tanzania has to offer. In the north near the Kenyan border is snowcapped Mt Kilimanjaro, the highest mountain in Africa. It's the goal of many visitors to scale this 5895m peak. Offshore in the Indian Ocean are several islands including exotic Zanzibar which, like Kathmandu and Timbuktu, has one of those truly evocative names.

Facts about the Country

HISTORY

Not a great deal is known about the early history of the Tanzanian interior except that by 1800 AD the Maasai, who in previous centuries had grazed their cattle in the Lake Turkana region of Kenya, had migrated down the Rift Valley as far as Dodoma.

The coastal area had long been the scene of maritime rivalry, first between the Portuguese and Arab traders and later between the various European powers. The first of these rivals to penetrate the interior were the Arab traders and slavers, who went as far as Lake Tanganyika in the middle of the 18th century.

Zanzibar, which for decades had been ruled from Oman at the mouth of the Persian Gulf, had, by the first half of the 19th century, become so important as a slaving and spice entrepôt that the Omani sultan, Seyyid Said, moved his capital there from Muscat in 1832.

Britain's interest in this area stemmed from the beginning of the 19th century when a treaty was signed with Seyyid Said's predecessor to forestall possible threats from Napoleonic France to British possessions in India. At that time Britain was actively trying to suppress the slave trade and various treaties limiting the trade were signed with the Omani sultans.

European explorers began arriving in the mid-19th century, the most famous being

UNITED REPUBLIC OF TANZANIA
Area: 939,760 sq km
Population: 28.8 million
Population Growth Rate: 3.1%
Capital: Dar es Salaam
Head of State: President Benjamin William Mkapa
Official Languages: Swahili, English
Currency: Tanzanian shilling
Exchange Rate: TSh 530 = US$1
Per Capita GNP: US$160
Inflation: 25%
Time: GMT/UTC + 3

Highlights
- Exploring the winding streets of the old Stone Town in exotic Zanzibar
- Spotting zebra, wildebeest, gazelle and antelope in Serengeti National Park
- Trekking to the snowcapped peak of Mt Kilimanjaro, Africa's highest mountain

Stanley and Livingstone. The famous phrase 'Dr Livingstone, I presume', stems from their meeting at Ujiji on Lake Tanganyika.

A little later the German explorer Carl Peters set about persuading unsuspecting and generally illiterate chiefs to sign so-called treaties of friendship. On the strength of these the German East Africa Company was set up to exploit and colonise what would become Tanganyika.

Like the British in Kenya, the Germans set about building railways to open their colony

TANZANIA

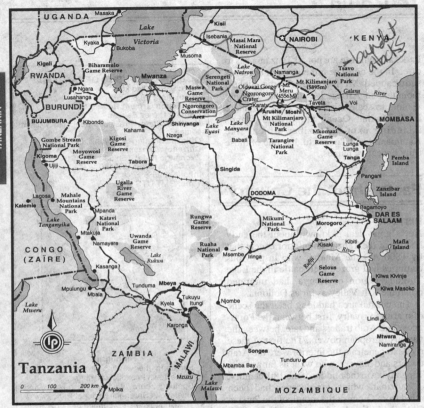

UGANDA   Masaka
Lake Victoria
Kyaka   Kisii
Bukoba   Isebania
Musoma   Masai Mara National Reserve   NAIROBI   'KENYA'   bandit attacks
Kigali   Biharamulo Game Reserve   Mwanza   Lake Natron   Namanga   Tsavo National Park
RWANDA   Ngara   Serengeti National Park   Olduvai Gorge   Mt Meru (4556M)   Mt Kilimanjaro (5895m)   Galana River
Lusahanga   Maswa Game Reserve   Ngorongoro Crater   Arusha/ Moshi   Taveta   Vol
BURUNDI   Kibondo   Ngorongoro Conservation Area   Karatu   Mt Kilimanjaro National Park   MOMBASA
BUJUMBURA   Kahama   Shinyanga   Lake Eyasi   Lake Manyara   Babati   Mkomazi Game Reserve
Gombe Stream National Park   Kigosi Game Reserve   Nzega   Tarangire National Park   Lunga Lunga
Kigoma   Moyowosi Game Reserve   Tabora   Singida   Tanga   Pemba Island
Ujiji   Pangani
Ugalla River Game Reserve   DODOMA   Zanzibar Island
Lagosa   Mahale Mountains National Park   Mpanda   Bagamoyo   DAR ES SALAAM
Kalemie   Katavi National Park   Rungwa Game Reserve   Mikumi National Park   Morogoro   Mafia Island
Lake Tanganyika   Mtakuja   Uwanda Game Reserve   Kibiti   Kisaki
CONGO (ZAÏRE)   Namayere   Lake Rukwa   Ruaha National Park   Msembe   Iringa   Selous Game Reserve   Kilwa Kivinje
Kasanga   Kilwa Masoko
Mpulungu   Tunduma   Mbeya   Rufiji
Lake Mweru   Mbala   Kyela   Tukuyu Itungi   Njombe   Lindi
ZAMBIA   Karonga   Mtwara   Namiranga
Tanzania   MALAWI   Songea   Tunduru
0   100   200 km   Mzuzu   Mbamba Bay   MOZAMBIQUE
Mpika   Lake Malawi

to commerce, although much of Tanganyika was unsuitable for agriculture. Also, in large areas of central and southern Tanganyika, the ravages of the tsetse fly made cattle grazing or dairying impossible.

The German occupation continued until the end of WWI after which the League of Nations mandated the territory to the British. Nationalist organisations developed after WWII, but it wasn't until Julius Nyerere founded the Tanganyika African National Union (TANU) in 1954 that they became effective. Tanganyika gained independence in 1961 with Nyerere as the country's first president.

The island of Zanzibar had been a British protectorate since 1890, and it remained that way until Zanzibar and Kenya gained independence in 1963. Shortly after independence, Nyerere forged a union with Zanzibar (which includes other offshore islands such as Pemba) and mainland Tanganyika to form Tanzania.

No other African country, with the possible exception of Côte d'Ivoire, has been moulded so closely in the image of its first president. Known as *mwalimu* (teacher) in his own country and often referred to as the 'conscience of black Africa' elsewhere,

Julius Nyerere is one of Africa's elder statesmen.

Nyerere inherited a country with few exploitable resources and only one major export crop, sisal. It was an inauspicious beginning and the problems it created eventually led to the Arusha Declaration of 1967. Based on the Chinese Communist model, the cornerstone of this policy was the Ujamaa village – a collective agricultural venture run along traditional African lines.

Nyerere's proposals for education were seen as an essential part of this scheme and were designed to foster constructive attitudes to cooperative endeavour. At the same time, the economy was nationalised, as was a great deal of rental property, and taxes were increased in an attempt to redistribute individual wealth. Nyerere also sought to ensure that those in political power did not develop into an exploitative class by banning government ministers and party officials from holding shares or directorships in companies and from receiving more than one salary. Nevertheless, corruption remained widespread.

In the early 1960s, Kenya, Tanzania and Uganda were linked in an economic union which shared a common airline, telecommunication and postal facilities, transportation and customs. Their currencies were freely convertible and there was freedom of movement. The union fell apart in 1977 due to political differences between socialist Tanzania, capitalist Kenya and the military chaos that stood for government in Uganda.

Tanzania's experiment with radical socialism and self-reliance might have been a courageous path to follow in the heady days following independence, and even during the 1970s when not only Tanzania but many other African countries were feeling the oil-price pinch, but only romantics would argue that it hasn't, ultimately, failed. The transport system is in tatters, agricultural production is stagnant, and the industrial sector limps along at well under 50% capacity. The capital, Dar es Salaam, is dusty and down-at-heel and all economic incentives seem to have been eliminated.

Obviously, many factors have contributed to Tanzania's woes and many of them have been beyond its control, not least the fact that Tanzania is one of the world's poorest countries. This despite the fact that Zanzibar, at the time of independence, was one of the most prosperous countries in Africa.

The winds of democratic change which have swept through Africa in the past few years have not bypassed Tanzania. The country adopted a multiparty system and elections were held in October 1995, but they were described by some as a complete shambles. It was, nevertheless, true that the ruling CCM ('Party of the Revolution') won comparatively easily on the mainland, but the result on Zanzibar was a virtual stalemate where the CCM lost every one of its 21 seats on Pemba island giving the incumbent president, Salmin Amour, only 50.2% of the vote as opposed to the 49.8% of his sole rival, Seif Shariff Hamad, of the Civic United Front (CUF).

Benjamin Mkapa was declared the new president of the union. While the election result reflected the voters' wishes, it also re-activated tribal allegiances particularly amongst the Chagga (Mt Kilimanjaro region), despite all the years of Ujamaa.

It's very unlikely that Tanzania will dissolve into the tribal conflicts which have plagued Kenya in the early 1990s, so there's no cause for alarm, but the near stalemate on the islands is unlikely to go away so easily.

GEOGRAPHY & CLIMATE

A land of plains, lakes and mountains with a narrow, low-lying coastal belt, Tanzania is East Africa's largest country. The bulk of the country is a highland plateau, some of it semidesert and the rest savannah and scattered bush. Much of the plateau is relatively uninhabited because of the tsetse fly which prevents the raising of stock. The highest mountains – Meru (4556m) and Kilimanjaro (Africa's highest at 5895m) – are in the north-east along the border with Kenya.

Tanzania's widely varying geography accounts for its differing climatic conditions. The altitude of the high plateau considerably

TANZANIA

tempers what would otherwise be a tropical climate. In many places it can be quite cool at night.

The coastal strip along the Indian Ocean and the offshore islands of Pemba, Zanzibar and Mafia have a hot, humid, tropical climate alleviated by sea breezes. Only on the mountain slopes of the north-east does the country enjoy an almost temperate climate for most of the year.

The long rainy season is from March to May when it rains almost every day. The short rainy season lasts from November to December, though it frequently rains in January too.

POPULATION & PEOPLE

The population of Tanzania is about 29 million. There are more than 100 tribal groups, the majority of which are of Bantu origin. The Arab influence on the islands of Zanzibar and Pemba is evident in the people, who are a mix of Arabs, Shirazis (from Persia), Comorians (from the Comoros) and Bantus, these days known collectively as the Swahili. People of Asian descent are a significant minority, especially in the towns and cities.

LANGUAGE

Swahili and English are the official languages but there are also many local African languages. Outside the cities and towns fewer people speak English than in comparable areas of Kenya. See the Language appendix for useful words and phrases in Swahili.

Facts for the Visitor

VISAS

Visas are required for all visitors to Tanzania except nationals of most Commonwealth countries (Canada and UK excepted), Scandinavian countries, the Republic of Ireland, Rwanda, Romania and the Sudan. These nationalities require a free visitor's pass, valid for one to three months, obtainable at the border. Visas are also available on arrival at Namanga, Kilimanjaro airport (Arusha), Dar es Salaam airport and at Zanzibar.

If you are travelling from Malawi and need a visa, you must obtain it beforehand in Zimbabwe, Zambia or South Africa as there is no Tanzanian high commission in Malawi – be warned!

The cost of a visa (usually valid for three months) depends on your nationality: US$55 for Britons, US$45 for Americans, US$26 for Japanese, US$16 for Germans and US$10 for others.

Other Visas

The following visas can be picked up in Tanzania:

Burundi
  Visas cost US$20 (or the equivalent in local currency), require two photos and are issued in 24 hours (or while you wait at the consulate in Kigoma).
Congo (Zaïre)
  A single/multiple-entry visa costs US$75/120 for one month, US$135/180 for two months and US$200/225 for three months. Three photos are required, as well as a letter of recommendation from your own embassy. Visas are issued in 24 hours.
Kenya
  Visas cost US$30 (or equivalent in local currency), require two photographs and take 24 hours to be issued.
Rwanda
  Visas cost US$20 (or equivalent in local currency), require two photographs and take 24 hours to be issued. They're valid for a stay of one month.
Uganda
  Visas cost US$20 or US$25, depending on your nationality, require two photographs and are issued in 24 hours.
Other Countries
  Dar es Salaam is a good place to stock up on francophone country visas (the Central African Republic, Chad etc). As there are very few of these embassies in the capital you must get them all from the French embassy.

EMBASSIES
Tanzanian Embassies

In Africa, Tanzania has embassies or high commissions in Burundi, Congo (Zaïre),

Egypt, Ethiopia, Kenya, Mozambique, Nigeria, Rwanda, Uganda, Zambia and Zimbabwe.

Elsewhere they are found in Belgium, Canada, France, Germany, India, Italy, the UK and the USA, among other places.

Foreign Embassies in Tanzania

The following countries have representation in Dar es Salaam:

Burundi
  Plot 1007, Lugalo Rd (☎ 46307)
Canada
  38 Miramba Ave (☎ 46000)
Congo (Zaïre)
  438 Malik Rd (☎ 66010)
France
  corner of Bagomoyo and Kulimani Rds (☎ 66021)
Germany
  10th floor, NIC building, Samora Ave (☎ 46334)
Kenya
  14th floor, NIC building, Samora Ave (☎ 46362)
Madagascar
  143 Malik Rd (☎ 29442)
Malawi
  6th floor, NIC building, Samora Ave (☎ 46673)
Mozambique
  25 Garden Ave (☎ 33062)
Netherlands
  New ATC building, corner of Garden Ave and Ohio St (☎ 46391)
Rwanda
  32 Ali Mwinyi Rd (☎ 46502)
South Africa
  c/o Oysterbay Hotel, Touré Drive, Oyster Bay, 6km north of Dar (☎ 68062)
Sudan
  64 Ali Mwinyi Rd (☎ 46509)
Uganda
  7th floor, Extelecoms House, Samora Ave (☎ 31004)
UK
  Hifiadhi House, Samora Ave (☎ 29601)
USA
  36 Laibon Rd (☎ 66010)
Zambia
  5/9 Sokoine Drive (☎ 46383)
Zimbabwe
  6th floor, NIC building, Samora Ave (☎ 46259)

MONEY

US$1 = TSh 565 (cash)
US$1 = TSh 530 (TC)

The unit of currency is the Tanzanian shilling

(TSh). There is an official exc[...] (around US$1 = TSh 345), but this w[...] affect you if you use international [...] cards, in which case you'll be billed at [...] official rate instead of the foreign exchange [...] (forex) rate. If you have the option, it obviously makes sense not to use credit cards.

There are forex bureaus in most towns and cities where you can change cash and travellers' cheques at the prevailing free-market exchange rate. There is no black market for hard currency so, if anyone offers you substantially more than the forex or bank rates, forget it. You're being set up for a robbery.

There are forex bureaus at Namanga, Arusha, Moshi, Dar es Salaam, Zanzibar, Mwanza and various other places, but none in Morogoro or Bukoba for instance. It's often possible to buy dollars with Tanzanian shillings at a forex bureau.

If you need to change money where there are no forex bureaus, the banks will only exchange currency at the official rate.

Despite the existence of forex bureaus in Tanzania, there are a lot of things which must be paid for in hard currency or travellers' cheques. These include national park entry fees, most mid-range and top-end hotels, airline tickets, and even the hydrofoil between Zanzibar and Dar es Salaam. Most other things (cheap hotels, meals, transport etc) can be paid for with local shillings.

If you pay in travellers' cheques, change is given in local currency at the official bank rate. If you pay in US dollars cash but your banknote doesn't match the charge you have to pay, you have a sporting chance of getting the change in US dollars cash – but don't count on it. Have lots of small US dollar bills handy to counter this. It's not usually a hassle at the national park gates, since they generally have plenty of change in hard currency.

Take note that no bank in Tanzania will issue cash against a Visa or MasterCard.

Kenyan currency is considered to be a more or less 'hard' currency in Tanzania. The current rate is KSh 1 = TSh 10.

IONS

...in Dar es Salaam's ...organised and you ...collecting mail. ...Samora Ave in Dar ...ient international ...y get a connection in just a couple of minutes, but it's expensive. Expect to pay US$10 per minute for a call to Europe, the USA or Australia! Reverse charge (collect) calls cannot be made from here. Calls within Africa (including those to Kenya and Uganda) can be a hassle.

The country code for Tanzania is 255, and local area codes include Dar es Salaam 051; Zanzibar 054; Moshi 055 and Kilimanjaro 0575.

HEALTH

Make sure you have a valid vaccination certificate for yellow fever before arriving in Tanzania. You won't be asked for it at land borders and you probably won't be asked for it if you arrive by air through either Kilimanjaro or Dar es Salaam airports, but it's essential for Zanzibar and Pemba.

HIV/AIDS is a serious risk, though not as prevalent as in Uganda. Make sure you take precautions. Also see the Health Appendix for more information on health issues.

DANGERS & ANNOYANCES

There are very few of these in Tanzania – it's a very law-abiding country. Thieves and muggers hardly exist on the streets, although there are two exceptions – at bus terminals and railway stations. Watch your bags at these places and don't allow your attention to be distracted.

PUBLIC HOLIDAYS

Public holidays in Tanzania include: 1 January, 12 January (Zanzibar Revolution Day), 5 February (CCM Day), 26 April (Union Day), 1 May, 7 July, 9 December (Independence), 25 December, Good Friday, Easter Monday and variable Islamic holidays (see Public Holidays in the Regional Facts for the Visitor chapter for dates).

Getting There & Away

AIR

A number of international airlines serve Tanzania, either through Kilimanjaro or Dar es Salaam airport. There's not a lot of difference between the fares from Europe to Kenya and those to Tanzania. International flight tickets bought in Tanzania have to be paid for in hard currency.

The departure tax for international flights is US$20 or UK£18 and must be paid in hard currency.

Kenya

The cheapest options between Tanzania and Kenya are the flights between Dar es Salaam and Nairobi (US$136) and Zanzibar and Mombasa (US$55), though you must add the US$20 departure tax to these prices. The Zanzibar to Mombasa flight with Kenya Airways is very popular, so book at least two weeks ahead.

LAND
Kenya
Bus There are several land connections by bus between Kenya and Tanzania.

Dar es Salaam to Mombasa Hood Bus/Cat Bus has departures from Dar es Salaam to Mombasa (12½ hours, US$7) via Tanga on Tuesday, Wednesday and Friday at 9 am. The bus office in Dar es Salaam is on Msimbazi St, close to the Kariakoo Market and the Caltex station.

You can also do the trip in stages, but you may have to walk the 6km between the border and Horohoro. *because . . .*

Dar es Salaam to Nairobi Direct buses from Dar to Nairobi operate roughly every second day. Some travel by day, others at night; tickets can be booked with the bus crew who hang out on the bus. The journey takes 10 to 12 hours and costs US$18.

Arusha & Moshi to Nairobi Between Moshi or Arusha and Nairobi there's a choice of normal buses and minibus shuttles.

The minibus shuttles take about four hours and cost US$18. These include Riverside Shuttle in Arusha, which departs daily at 2 pm from its office (☎ 8323 Arusha) next to the Chinese Restaurant on Sokoine Rd, and Davanu Shuttle (☎ 4311 Arusha) which has its office at the Adventure Centre on Goliondoi Rd and departs daily at 8 am and 2 pm.

Much cheaper is Arusha Express, with full-sized buses leaving from Arusha's bus station daily at 2 pm (four hours, US$7).

It's also easy, but less convenient, to do this journey in stages, and since the Kenyan and Tanzanian border posts are next to each other at Namanga, there's no long walk involved.

Moshi to Voi The crossing between Moshi and Voi via Taveta has reliable transport (buses, minibuses and share-taxis), as long as you go on a Wednesday or Saturday, Taveta's market days.

Mwanza/Musoma to Kisii There are no direct buses between Tanzania and Kenya through the Isebania border and doing it in stages is a pain in the arse. There's very little traffic between Musoma and Isebania so give yourself plenty of time.

Train There is a weekly connection between Moshi and Voi on Saturday, leaving Moshi at 2 pm, arriving in Voi at 7.10 pm.

Malawi

The one crossing point here is between Mbeya (Tanzania) and Karonga (Malawi), at the top of Lake Malawi, via Kyela.

Take a bus from Mbeya going to Kyela but get off at the turn-off to the border (US$2). Here you will be besieged by a group of youths with bicycles offering to take you the 5km to the border. For US$1 they'll perch you on the rat-trap luggage rack on the back and pedal away at a suicidal rate. The border closes at 6 pm. Change money with the bicycle boys; their rates are as good as you'll find in Malawi.

The Malawi border post is just across the Songwe River from the Tanzanian post, and the contrast between the two facilities couldn't be greater. Officials on both sides are easy-going and you should encounter no problems as long as your documents are in order.

From the Malawi side there are two daily buses (US$0.50) and occasional minibuses (US$1) for the one-hour trip to Karonga.

Mozambique

A few hardy travellers make the journey into northern Mozambique from Namiranga on the Rovuma River (the border). The only problem is likely to be getting transport from Mtwara to Namiranga, but once here there are boats across the river (10 minutes), from where it's a half-hour walk to the Mozambique border post.

From the Mozambique border there's at least one pick-up daily to Moçimboa, where there's accommodation at a basic *pousada*. From Moçimboa to Pemba the road is a nightmare but there is regular transport (10 hours).

Rwanda

Get one of the daily buses (around 4 am) from Mwanza to Ngara (US$11) from where you take a pick-up to the border at Rusumo (there's cheap accommodation on the Tanzanian side). From the Rwandan side take a bus or share-taxi to Kibungu (US$1) and another from there to Kigali (US$2).

Uganda

The route into Uganda follows the west side of Lake Victoria between Bukoba and Masaka, via Kyaka. It's possible to do the journey from Masaka to Bukoba in one day. The border crossings are hassle-free and there are moneychangers on the Tanzanian side, though they give a lousy rate. The border posts are right next to each other.

There's a daily Land Rover and one bus along the appalling road between Bukoba and the border at Mutukula (about four hours, US$5). Hitching is difficult as there's little traffic.

From the border, pick-ups leave when full for Kyotera (one hour, US$1.50), and there are taxis (minibuses) from there to Masaka (45 minutes, US$1).

Zambia

Bus Most people take the TAZARA railway, but there's also road transport from Mbeya to Tunduma on the Tanzania-Zambia border. From there, you walk to Nakonde on the Zambian side and take a bus from there to Kasama and Lusaka.

Train The TAZARA railway runs between Dar es Salaam and Kapiri Mposhi, in the heartland of the Zambian copper belt, via Mbeya and Tunduma/Nakonde. The line was built by the Chinese in the 1970s and passes through some of the most remote countryside in Africa, including part of the Selous Game Reserve.

There are usually five trains per week in both directions, two express and three ordinary. The express trains depart from Dar es Salaam on Tuesday and Friday at 5.55 pm and the ordinary trains depart on Monday, Thursday and Saturday at 9 am. The journey takes 36 hours by express train to Kapiri Mposhi and fares in 1st/2nd class are US$75/50.

Tickets should be booked at least a couple of days in advance for 1st and 2nd class. Do this in Dar es Salaam at the TAZARA railway station on Pugu Rd, about halfway to the airport. Get there on an airport bus from the junction of Sokoine Drive and Kivukoni Front, opposite the Cenotaph and Lutheran church. A taxi costs about US$6. Third-class tickets are sold only on the day of departure.

Men and women can travel together in 1st and 2nd class only if they occupy an entire compartment (four berths in 1st class, six in 2nd).

Meals are usually available on the train and can be served in your compartment. Bedding is complimentary in 1st and 2nd class.

LAKE & SEA

Burundi & Zambia

Ferry The main ferry on Lake Tanganyika is the historic MV *Liemba* (see boxed story), which operates a weekly service connecting Bujumbura (Burundi), Kigoma (Tanzania) and Mpulungu (Zambia) and is a great way to travel.

The MV *Liemba*

The MV *Liemba* is a legend among travellers and must be one of the oldest steamers in the world still operating on a regular basis. Built by the Germans in 1914 and assembled on the lake shore after being transported in pieces on the railway from Dar es Salaam, it first saw service as the *Graf von Goetzn*. Not long afterwards it was greased and scuttled to prevent the British getting their hands on it. In 1922 the British colonial authorities paid the princely sum of UK£4000 for it. Two years later they raised it from the bottom of the lake, had it reconditioned and put back into service as the MV *Liemba*. The fact that it's still going after all these years is a credit to its maintenance engineers. ∎

Officially, the MV *Liemba* departs from Bujumbura on Monday at about 6 pm and arrives in Kigoma on Tuesday at 8 am. It leaves Kigoma at about 4 pm on Wednesday and arrives in Mpulungu on Friday at 8 am. It calls at many small Tanzanian ports en route between Kigoma and Mpulungu, but rarely for more than half an hour, except at Kasanga where it anchors overnight.

The fares from Kigoma range from US$9/8/6 to Bujumbura to US$25/21/17 to Mpulungu in 1st/2nd/3rd class. Tickets bought at any of the Tanzanian ports can be paid for in Tanzanian shillings.

Third class consists of bench seats either in a covered area towards the back of the boat or in another very poorly ventilated area in the bowels of the vessel. The 2nd-class cabins are incredibly hot, stuffy and claustrophobic. They have four bunks and are very poorly ventilated. If you want a cabin, go the whole hog and take a 1st-class one. These have two bunks, are on a higher deck, have a window and fan, and are clean and reasonably cool. Bedding is available for a small fee.

Third class is not usually crowded between Bujumbura and Kigoma, so this is a possibility if you're on a budget, especially as it's only overnight. It's OK to sleep out on the deck and the best spot is above the 1st-class deck, though you need to be discreet as it's supposedly off-limits to passengers. On the lower decks you need to keep your gear safe, as some petty pilfering does sometimes occur. If you're travelling 3rd class between Bujumbura and Kigoma and want to upgrade to a cabin for the Kigoma to Mpulungu leg, make sure you do this as soon as the boat docks in Kigoma. Third class is not recommended between Kigoma and Mpulungu, as it's usually very crowded.

Meals and drinks are available on board and must be paid for in Tanzanian shillings. Bring enough shillings to cover this. Three-course meals of soup, chicken and rice followed by dessert are not bad value for around US$2, and there's cold beer of course.

A part-lake steamer, part-road route via Kasanga on Lake Tanganyika is also becoming increasingly popular if you're heading from Kigoma to Malawi but don't want to go via Zambia. It will also save you up to US$35. Instead of going all the way to Mpulungu, get off the steamer at Kasanga and, from there, hitch a ride to Sumbawanga (about US$5). From Sumbawanga there are daily 'express' buses to Mbeya via Tunduma (about six hours, US$7).

In addition to the MV *Liemba*, there is another lake steamer, the MV *Mwongoza* which plies between Kigoma and Mpulungu via all the usual Tanzanian lake ports. It departs Kigoma on Monday at 4 pm and arrives in Mpulungu on Wednesday at 8 am. The fares are the same as for the MV *Liemba*.

Lake Taxi & Minibus For getting to Burundi, the alternative to the MV *Liemba* is to travel partly by minibus and partly by lake taxi between Kigoma and Bujumbura, via the Gombe Stream National Park and the Tanzanian border village of Kagunga.

From Kigoma (actually Kalalangabo, about 3km north of Kigoma), there are lake taxis to Kagunga, which cost US$2, leave some time before dawn and take most of the day. The taxis call at Gombe Stream (about halfway), where you can get off if you like. The fare to Gombe Stream is US$1, as is the fare from there to Kagunga. From the Kagunga border post, it's a 2km walk along a narrow track to the Burundi border post, where you take a minibus (US$1) to Nyanza Lac and go through immigration; the office is about 1km from the town centre towards the lake. From Nyanza Lac minibuses go daily to Bujumbura (US$4).

Congo (Zaïre)

SNCZ used to operate boats from both Uvira and Kigoma to Kalemie in Congo (Zaïre) on Lake Tanganyika. With all the disturbances around Uvira in late 1996 it's unlikely these services still operate.

Kenya

Sea It's possible to go by dhow between Pemba or Zanzibar and Mombasa but sailings are very infrequent these days. What is much more reliable is the ferry, MS *Sepideh*, operated by Zanzibar Sea Ferries Ltd (☎ Zanzibar 33725, Dar es Salaam 38025, Pemba 56210), which connects Tanga, Pemba, Zanzibar, and Dar es Salaam with Mombasa. The schedule varies according to the season but it's usually twice a week in either direction. The fares are US$65 Dar es Salaam to Mombasa, US$50 Zanzibar to Mombasa, and US$40 Tanga or Pemba to Mombasa.

Lake Victoria There used to be a ferry service which connected Mwanza (Tanzania) with Kisumu (Kenya) on Lake Victoria once a week but the ship which serviced this route (the MV *Bukoba*) sank in May 1996. It's likely that the schedules of the other two boats – the MV *Victoria* and the MV *Serengeti* – will have been altered so that the two ports are connected again but you'll have to make enquiries. Even when the two ports were connected, cancellations were frequent.

Mozambique

You might find a dhow going to Mozambique although a trip on these boats is not to be taken lightly (see boxed story in the Mozambique chapter): Mtwara to Pemba (Mozambique) is about US$20. Other ports include Msimbati (south of Mtwara) and Moçimboa da Praia. All have immigration posts.

There is also a boat called the *Edma* which makes the trip between Mtwara and Pemba via Ibo Island (sometimes) and Moçimboa. It doesn't run to any set schedule so you need to make enquiries to pin it down.

Uganda

There's a regular Lake Victoria ferry service between Mwanza and Port Bell (Kampala) which leaves Mwanza on Sunday and Wednesday at 3 pm and arrives in Port Bell the following morning at 7 am. From Mwanza the fares are US$14/11/8 plus US$20 port tax.

Getting Around

AIR

Air Tanzania, the national carrier, serves all internal routes. From Dar es Salaam it flies to Kilimanjaro (US$123 one way), Kigoma (US$220), Mwanza (US$187) and Zanzibar (US$43). There are daily departures in either direction on most of these sectors.

A number of private airlines operate light aircraft (six to eight-seaters), mainly to Zanzibar, Pemba and the various national parks.

BUS & MINIBUS

Except for some sections – Namanga to Dar es Salaam via Arusha and Moshi, and Dar es Salaam to Morogoro – Tanzanian roads vary from poor to atrocious. In an effort to cut down on road accidents, public vehicles are

no longer allowed to travel between 10 pm and 5 am.

On the main long-haul routes, there's generally a choice between luxury bus and ordinary minibus (dalla dalla). Advance booking is definitely advisable on a long haul and, if you have the option, it's always better to travel 1st or 2nd class on a train than to go by bus.

Minibuses as found elsewhere in East Africa also travel the roads in Tanzania. They are crowded, but faster than ordinary buses – if you have a choice, take a luxury bus.

TRAIN

Apart from Arusha, Tanzania's major population centres are connected by railway.

As with bus travel, keep an eye on your gear at all times, particularly in 3rd class. Even in 1st and 2nd class, make sure that the window is jammed shut at night. There is usually a piece of wood provided for this, as the window locks don't work.

The difference between 1st and 2nd class is that there are two people to a compartment instead of six. Men and women can only travel together in 1st or 2nd class if they book the whole compartment. Second class on the Dar es Salaam to Moshi and Tanga trains has seats only. You'd have to be desperate to go any distance in 3rd class – it's very uncomfortable.

Some trains (Dar es Salaam to Kigoma, Mwanza, Moshi and Tanga) have restaurant cars which serve good meals (US$1.50), soft drinks and beer. Bed rolls are available in 1st and 2nd class at a cost of US$1, regardless of how long the journey is.

Buying a ticket can be a daylight nightmare, especially in Dar es Salaam and Moshi. It's chaos at the stations and nowhere will you find any schedules. You may well be told that 1st and 2nd class are sold out; if it's a few days in advance this is probably crap, but on the day of departure chances are it's true.

Trains from Dar es Salaam to Kigoma and Mwanza depart at 6 pm on Monday, Wednesday, Friday and Sunday. In the opposite direction, there are departures from both

Kigoma and Mwanza for Dar es Salaam four times a week. The journey normally takes about 36 hours but can take 40 hours. The fare to Mwanza or Kigoma is US$42/30/21/13 in 1st/2nd-class sleeper/2nd/3rd class.

Central Line trains from Dar es Salaam to Moshi and Tanga depart at 4 pm on Sunday and Friday. In the opposite direction, there are departures from both Moshi and Tanga for Dar es Salaam at the same time on the same days. The journey to Moshi takes 15 to 18 hours and to Tanga about 16 hours. The service to Tanga was suspended in early 1996 but should have restarted by now. The fare to Moshi is US$21/15/11/7, and to Tanga US$17/11/7/5.

The TAZARA to Mbeya costs US$34/21 (see the Tanzania Getting There & Away section for details).

BOAT

Lake Tanganyika

The MV *Liemba* which connects Tanzania with Burundi and Zambia also operates between Tanzanian ports on the lake. See the earlier Tanzania Getting There & Away section. The MV *Mwongozo* operates services only in Tanzania, connecting Kigoma with the small Tanzanian ports to the south and the north.

Lake Victoria

There are two Tanzanian ferries, the MV *Victoria* and the MV *Serengeti*, servicing the lake ports of Mwanza and Bukoba on an almost daily basis. The fares are US$13/11/9/7/4.50 in Victoria/1st/2nd class sleeper/2nd/3rd class.

Lake Malawi

Two ferries operate on the Tanzanian part of Lake Malawi, sailing between Itungi and Mbamba Bay via a number of other small ports. There are about three services a week.

Offshore Islands & South Coast

See the Dar es Salaam and Zanzibar sections for details of services to the islands off the Tanzanian coast.

To the mainland ports south of Dar es

Salaam as far as Mtwara, near the Mozambique border, there is the FB *Canadian Spirit*, operated by Adecon Marine Inc (☎ 20856) in Dar es Salaam.

ORGANISED SAFARIS

Most travellers visit Tanzania's national parks on organised safaris. From Arusha, you need a minimum of three days to tour Lake Manyara and Ngorongoro Crater; four days to tour Lake Manyara, Ngorongoro Crater and Serengeti National Park; and six days to tour Lake Manyara, Ngorongoro Crater, and Serengeti and Tarangire national parks.

Safaris from Dar to Mikumi National Park typically last two to three days, to Mikumi and Ruaha national parks five days, and to Selous Game Reserve five days.

Safari Costs

The rock-bottom outfits in Arusha quote US$75 per person per day for a camping safari, but US$85 per person per day is more realistic given the cost of entry fees to the parks. These prices should be all-inclusive in the higher bracket but may not be in the lower bracket. Never assume that they are.

Prices for safaris which involve staying in lodges or tented camps are considerably higher – US$130 to US$160 per person per day, depending on the number of people.

Choosing a Company

Arusha The majority of safari companies here have offices in the Arusha International Conference Centre (AICC). Other companies are located along Boma, Sokoine, Ngoliondoi, Goliondoi and Seth Benjamin Rds. For camping safaris try:

Easy Travel & Tours Ltd
2nd floor, Clock Tower Centre, Joel Haeder Rd, PO Box 1912 (☎/fax (057) 7322)
Equatorial Safaris Ltd
India St and Room 460/1, Serengeti Wing, AICC, PO Box 2156 (☎ (057) 7006)
Hoopoe Adventure Tours
India St, PO Box 2047 (☎ (057) 7011)

Shidolya Tours & Safaris
Room 333/334, Serengeti Wing, AICC, PO Box 1436 (☎ (057) 8506)
Sunny Safaris Ltd
Colonel Middleton Rd, PO Box 7267 (☎ (057) 7145)
Tropical Tours Ltd
Adventure Centre, Goliondoi Rd, PO Box 727 (☎ (057) 8353)

This is by no means a comprehensive list of companies offering camping safaris. There are plenty more on just about every floor of the AICC building. You could easily spend a whole day checking out the various offices.

Mwanza If you enter Tanzania via Isebania and Musoma and wish to tour Serengeti and/or Ngorongoro from the north, you can do this from Mwanza. There's only one safari company in Mwanza and that is Kijereshi Tented Camp Ltd (☎ (068) 4067), Hotel Tilapia, Capri Point Rd, PO Box 190, but they offer only lodge safaris.

Dar es Salaam There are far fewer safari companies in Dar es Salaam, and they cater mainly for safaris to Mikumi, Ruaha and Selous. The following offer lodge-based safaris:

Bushtrekker Safaris
PO Box 5350 (☎ (051) 36811)
Gogo Safaris Ltd
Mkwepu St, PO Box 70647 (☎ (051) 32533; fax 46739)
Savannah Tours Ltd
Kilimanjaro Hotel, PO Box 25017 (☎ (051) 35437)

Balloon Safaris
There are daily flights over the Serengeti which last about two hours and cost US$300 per person, including a champagne breakfast after the flight. Book through Serengeti Balloon Safaris Ltd (☎ (057) 8578; fax 8997), Adventure Centre, Goliondoi Rd, PO Box 12116, Arusha or at either the Seronera Lodge or the Serengeti Sopa Lodge when you're in the park itself.

Walking Safaris
For details of walking safaris offered by

companies in Arusha, check out Tropical Tours Ltd (☎ 8353) PO Box 727, Arusha. This company is fully committed to environmentally responsible tourism and has a wealth of experience in treks north-east and north of Arusha. Prices start at US$220 per person (minimum two people) for three days.

Camel Safaris
As in the Samburu and Pokot lands of northern Kenya, the Maasai lands of north-eastern Tanzania have been hosting camel safaris for several years now. The company running these trips is called Camels Only (☎ (057) 7111; fax 8997), the Adventure Centre, Goliondoi Rd, PO Box 12530, Arusha, and they have their tented headquarters in the northern foothills of Mt Meru, about 85km from Namanga and 56km from Arusha.

Cycling Safaris
About the only outfit which offers a cycling safari is Wild Spirit Safari Ltd (☎/fax (057 4215), India St, PO Box 288, Arusha. On this six-day camping safari you spend 5½ days cycling to the foothills of Mt Kilimanjaro and then round the north-eastern side of Kilimanjaro, ending up in Moshi. The cost is from US$100 per person per day.

Do-It-Yourself Safaris
Tanzania is different to Kenya as far as these go because of the difficulties of hiring self-drive vehicles. Essentially, it's not worth it without your own vehicle, and if you bring a foreign-registered vehicle into Tanzania, the park entry fees for the vehicle alone will be US$30 per 24 hours, as opposed to less than US$2 for a locally registered vehicle.

Dar es Salaam

Dar es Salaam, the 'Haven of Peace', started out as a humble fishing village in the mid-19th century when the Sultan of Zanzibar decided to turn the inland creek, which is now the harbour, into a safe port and trading centre. It became the capital in 1891 when the German colonial authorities transferred their seat of government from Bagamoyo because the port there was unsuitable for steamships.

Since then it has continued to grow and is now a city with about 2.2 million people. Although quite a few high-rise buildings have appeared in the city centre and at various places in the suburbs, it remains mostly a low-rise city of red-tiled roofs, with its colonial character substantially intact. The harbour is still fringed with palms and mangroves, and Arab dhows and dugout canoes mingle with huge ocean-going vessels.

Information

Tourist Office The Tanzania Tourist Corporation (TTC) office (☎ 2485) is on Maktaba St, near the junction with Samora Ave and opposite the New Africa Hotel. The TTC can make reservations at any of the larger hotels in Tanzania and at most of the beach hotels and national park lodges (payment in foreign currency only). It's better though to book national park lodges through a travel agency, as they may offer special deals.

Money Banking hours are Monday to Friday from 8.30 am to 12.30 pm and Saturday from 8.30 to 11.30 am. In addition to the banks, there are many forex bureaus scattered around the centre of Dar. They are generally open between 8 am and 5 pm Monday to Saturday and some are open on Sunday mornings.

American Express is represented by Rickshaw Travels Ltd (☎/fax 29125), Ali Mwinyi Rd, PO Box 1889, Dar es Salaam.

Things to See

The **National Museum** is next to the Botanical Gardens between Samora Ave and Sokoine Drive. It houses important archaeological collections and a section on the Zanzibar slave trade. Entry costs US$2 and it is open daily from 9.30 am to 6 pm.

Another museum which is definitely worth visiting is the **Village Museum**, 10km

from the city centre along the Bagamoyo road. This is an actual village consisting of a collection of authentically constructed dwellings from various parts of Tanzania which display several distinct architectural styles. Traditional dances are performed on Saturday and Sunday between 4 and 8 pm.

Three kilometres further on down the Bagamoyo road at Mpakani Rd is a *makonde* (ebony) carving community known as **Mwenge**. It is an excellent place to pick up superb pieces of this traditional art form at rock-bottom prices.

The **Kariakoo Market** between Mkunguni and Tandamuti Sts has a colourful and exotic atmosphere.

Places to Stay

Finding a place to stay in Dar es Salaam can be difficult. The later you arrive, the harder it gets; so, whatever else you do on arrival, *don't* pass up a vacant room. Take the room and then look for something else if you're not happy with it.

Hostels Three places stand head and shoulders above the rest as being excellent value for money. The first is the very popular *Luther House* (☎ 46687), Sokoine Drive, next to the Lutheran church at the junction of Sokoine Drive and Kivukoni Front. A double with communal bath costs US$15. Advance bookings are required.

Equally popular is the *YWCA* on Maktaba St, next to the main post office, which takes couples as well as women. It's excellent value at US$7/11 a single/double with communal bath and breakfast. Be polite and look clean and tidy when asking about accommodation here, otherwise they'll tell you it's full. Here too, it's advisable to book in advance, but there's more chance of getting a room.

The *YMCA* (☎ 26726), Ali Mwinyi Rd opposite the Mawenzi Hotel, is also excellent value and costs the equivalent of US$10 per person in either a single or a double, including breakfast. The YMCA takes both men and women.

TANZANIA

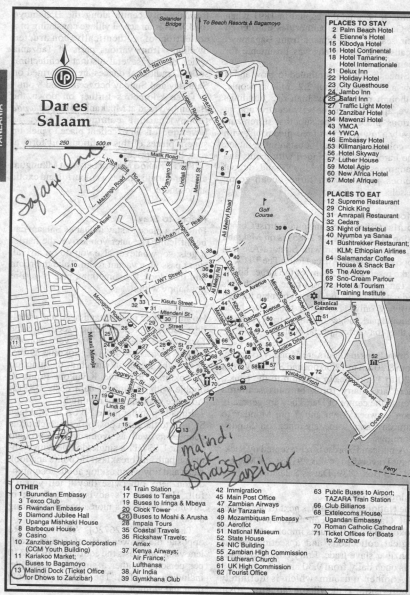

Dar es Salaam

0   250   500 m

(Handwritten annotations on map: "Safari end", "Malindi dock dhaus to Zanzibar")

PLACES TO STAY
2 Palm Beach Hotel
4 Etienne's Hotel
15 Kibodya Hotel
16 Hotel Continental
18 Hotel Tamarine;
    Hotel Internationale
21 Delux Inn
22 Holiday Hotel
23 City Guesthouse
24 Jambo Inn
25 Safari Inn
27 Traffic Light Motel
30 Zanzibar Hotel
34 Mawenzi Hotel
43 YMCA
44 YWCA
46 Embassy Hotel
53 Kilimanjaro Hotel
56 Hotel Skyway
57 Luther House
59 Motel Agip
60 New Africa Hotel
67 Motel Afrique

PLACES TO EAT
12 Supreme Restaurant
29 Chick King
31 Amrapali Restaurant
32 Cedars
33 Night of Istanbul
40 Nyumba ya Sanaa
41 Bushtrekker Restaurant;
    KLM; Ethiopian Airlines
64 Salamandar Coffee
    House & Snack Bar
65 The Alcove
69 Sno-Cream Parlour
72 Hotel & Tourism
    Training Institute

OTHER
1 Burundian Embassy
3 Texco Club
5 Rwandan Embassy
6 Diamond Jubilee Hall
7 Upanga Mishkaki House
8 Barbecue House
9 Casino
10 Zanzibar Shipping Corporation
    (CCM Youth Building)
11 Kariakoo Market;
    Buses to Bagamoyo
13 Malindi Dock (Ticket Office
    for Dhows to Zanzibar)

14 Train Station
17 Buses to Tanga
19 Buses to Iringa & Mbeya
20 Clock Tower
26 Buses to Moshi & Arusha
28 Impala Tours
35 Coastal Travels
36 Rickshaw Travels;
    Amex
37 Kenya Airways;
    Air France;
    Lufthansa
38 Air India
39 Gymkhana Club

42 Immigration
45 Main Post Office
47 Zambian Airways
48 Air Tanzania
49 Mozambiquan Embassy
50 Aeroflot
51 National Museum
52 State House
54 NIC Building
55 Zambian High Commission
58 Lutheran Church
61 UK High Commission
62 Tourist Office

63 Public Buses to Airport;
    TAZARA Train Station
66 Club Billianos
68 Extelecoms House;
    Ugandan Embassy
70 Roman Catholic Cathedral
71 Ticket Offices for Boats
    to Zanzibar

Hotels Two of the cheapest hotels are the *Holiday Hotel*, Jamhuri St, and the *Traffic Light Motel* (☎ 23438), on the corner of Jamhuri St and Morogoro Rd. Both offer singles/doubles with shared bath for US$6/7 and doubles with private bath for US$8.

Going up in price a little, one of the best places to stay is the *Safari Inn* (☎ 38101), on Band St, off Libya St behind the Jambo Inn. It's excellent value at US$9/15 for singles/doubles with attached bath and breakfast. The *Jambo Inn* (☎ 30568) on Libya St is also reasonable value at US$9/15 for singles/doubles with attached bath, fan and continental breakfast.

Similar is the *Kibodya Hotel* (☎ 31312) on Nkrumah St, which has doubles (no singles) with bathroom for US$15. Breakfast is extra. It's a popular place.

For a mid-range place try the *Motel Afrique* (☎ 46557), corner Kaluta and Bridge Sts, which has singles with shared bathroom for US$9 and doubles with attached bath and air-con for US$25. The room rates include breakfast.

The Greek-owned *Palm Beach Hotel* (☎ 22931), Ali Mwinyi Rd near the junction with Ocean Rd, is good but more expensive. There's a variety of rooms, all with air-con and telephone, for US$30/35 a single/double with communal bath. The beer garden's barbecue area is very lively and well patronised.

Places to Eat

Very popular, especially for lunch, is the *Salamander Coffee & Snack Bar*, Samora Ave at Mkwepu St. An average lunch costs about US$3. Right opposite is the *Burger Bite*, a McDonald's clone with prices similar to those at the Salamander.

Other good cheapies include the *Pop-In*, with lunch-time specials such as mutton biryani and pilau or chicken for US$3, and the *Nawaz Restaurant*, Msinhiri St, between Mosque St and Morogoro Rd, which has cheap rice and meat dishes.

Possibly better than all the above for lunch, however, is the *Hotel & Tourism Training Institute* on Kivukoni Front. This is where college students training for the hospitality trade do their practical training. There's a daily set menu served between 12.30 and 2 pm which costs just US$3 and, as you might imagine, the students are doing their best to impress. It's excellent value.

For vegetarian food, *Pandya's Vegetarian Restaurant*, Kaluta and Bridge Sts, is highly rated. Here you can get an all-you-can-eat lunch or dinner for around US$6. Also very good for vegetarian Indian food is the *Supreme Restaurant*, Nkrumah St. This place has been operating for years and has a well-deserved reputation.

Ice-cream freaks should make at least one visit to the *Sno-Cream Parlour*, Mansfield St, near the junction with Bridge St. This place, which is becoming legendary, has the best ice cream in Tanzania.

For a not-too-expensive splurge, the *DSM Chinese Restaurant* in the basement of the NIC building, on Samora Ave at the corner of Mirambo St, is great value and has been a popular place for years.

The *Rendezvous* on Samora Ave is a steakhouse that's popular with local people as well as being good value. Meals cost around US$5.

For a very refreshing change, treat your taste buds to an evening meal at *The Cedars*, on Bibi Titi Mohammed St, which serves excellent Middle Eastern food.

Entertainment

The bar at the *Hotel Embassy* near the main post office is lively and attracts a friendly and garrulous crowd. You need to be fairly well dressed. Another lively bar is the one at the *Palm Beach Hotel*, Ali Mwinyi Rd, though it is further out of town so you'll have to take a taxi (US$1) at night.

Far and away the most popular disco in Dar es Salaam is *Club Bilicanas*, at the back of the former Mbowe Hotel on Mkwepu St. It's open every night until around 4 am and entry costs US$4/5 for a single/couple.

Getting There & Away

Air Air Tanzania (☎ 38300) is at ATC House on Ohio St, and at Tancot House on Sokoine Drive.

Bus There is no central bus station in Dar es Salaam. Instead, buses to various parts of the country leave from a variety of places within the city.

Buses for Bagamoyo, Mwanza, Morogoro and Dodoma leave throughout the day until about 3 pm from outside the Kariakoo Market on Swahili St.

Buses for Moshi and Arusha depart from the bus station on the corner of Morogoro Rd and Libya St. Luxury buses to Arusha (US$12) take about nine hours; ordinary buses are cheaper (US$10) and slower.

Buses to Tanga and Mbeya and other points west and south depart from various offices on the southern side of Mnazi Mmoja park along Bibi Titi Mohammed St between Uhuru and Nkrumah Sts.

Boat Between Dar es Salaam and the islands of Zanzibar and Pemba there's a choice of four different boats: a hydrofoil, a catamaran, and two ordinary ferry boats. It's all very well organised and there are daily departures on most of these boats. They all have booking offices on Sokoine Drive, adjacent to the customs shed.

The one thing you *must* have before you're allowed to board any boat to Zanzibar is a yellow-fever vaccination certificate. This requirement has officially been abolished but this hasn't, apparently, percolated down to the port staff, so make sure you have one in order to avoid unpleasantness.

Whichever form of transport you take, there's a US$5 port charge in addition to the boat fare.

The cheapest ferry boats are the MV *Muungano* (US$10), operated by Azam Marine & Co (☎ 26699 in Dar es Salaam, ☎ 31262 in Zanzibar) and the MV *Noora* (US$10), operated by the Africa Shipping Corporation (☎ 33414 in Dar es Salaam, 33031 in Zanzibar).

Next up is the *Zanzibar Sea Ferries* which plies between Dar and Tanga via Zanzibar and Pemba and costs US$15 (Dar-Zanzibar). It departs Dar four days a week at 10 pm and takes five hours but you stay on the boat until dawn off Zanzibar.

Faster but more expensive is the *Kondor 5*, also operated by Azam Marine, which costs US$20.

The fastest and most expensive boat is the hydrofoil *Sea Express* operated by Sea Express Services Ltd. This departs six times daily and takes just 45 minutes. The fare is US$35/30 in 1st/2nd class. The only difference between 1st and 2nd class is a little extra leg room.

Getting Around
The Airport Dar es Salaam airport is 13km from the city centre. Bus No 67 connects the two but, if you get on at the airport, make sure that it is going right into the city centre as some don't.

A shuttle bus from the centre of town to the airport costs US$1, and a taxi US$9.

Bus The bus to the TAZARA railway station is marked 'Posta Vigunguti'. Fares are fixed and are only a few shillings, but all buses are very crowded. It would be almost impossible to get onto them with a rucksack, let alone to get off at your destination.

Taxi Taxis have no meters and charge a standard US$4 per journey inside the immediate city centre. To the TAZARA railway station, they should cost around US$6.

Around the Country

ARUSHA
Arusha is one of Tanzania's most attractive towns. It sits in lush, green countryside at the foot of Mt Meru (4556m) and enjoys a temperate climate throughout the year. Surrounding the town are many coffee, wheat and maize estates tended by the Waarusha and Wameru tribespeople.

For most travellers, Arusha is the gateway to the Serengeti, Lake Manyara and Tarangire national parks and the Ngorongoro Conservation Area. It's to Arusha that you come to arrange a safari.

Information

The Tanzanian National Parks office (☎ 3471, ext 1104), 6th floor, Kilimanjaro Wing, International Conference Centre, PO Box 3134, usually stocks a few leaflets about the national parks.

There are several forex bureaus in Arusha. The immigration office is on Simeon Rd near the Makongoro Rd junction.

Places to Stay

Campers should think seriously of heading for *Masai Camp*; although it's about 2.5km from the centre of town on the Old Moshi Rd, it's excellent. Camping costs US$3 per person, but there are hot showers, a bar and restaurant (pizzas are a speciality), a volley-ball court, facilities for mechanical repairs and a well-landscaped site.

The area at the back of the Golden Rose Hotel on Colonel Middleton Rd is a warren of budget hotels. Among the most popular are the clean, quiet *Mashele Guest House* (US$5/7 a double with shared/private bath and mosquito nets) and the *Levolosi Guest House* (US$4.50/6 for singles/doubles with shared facilities).

Across the opposite side of Colonel Middleton Rd at the back of Sunny Safaris and along the road running parallel to it is the *Miami Beach Guest House* (☎ 7531) which has doubles (no singles) for US$10 with shared bath, but it can be noisy and dusty because of its proximity to the bus station.

Opposite the main market is the *Robanny-son Hotel* on Somali Rd, which offers singles/doubles with shared bath for US$3/6. Hot showers are available, mosquito nets are provided and the hotel has its own restaurant (no bar), but it's not very clean. In the same area is the better *Amazon Hotel* at US$10/12 for singles/doubles.

More expensive and very popular, though hardly worthy of a mid-range rating, is the *YMCA* on India St. Still, it's an excellent place to meet people, especially if you're trying to get a group together to go on a safari. Bed and breakfast (B&B) costs US$10/13 for singles/doubles with shared bath (cold water only).

One of the cheapest and most popular of the mid-range hotels is the *Arusha Naaz Hotel* on Sokoine Rd. Very clean, pleasant, secure and well maintained, it costs US$20 for a double with private bath.

Somewhat out of town along Serengeti Rd, off the Old Moshi Rd, is *The Outpost* (☎ (057) 8405), a family guesthouse offering B&B for US$16/20. Those who stay here rate the place highly.

Places to Eat

Plenty of simple cafes and cheap restaurants in the lower part of town, along Sokoine Rd, offer standard Afro-Indian fare.

The best place for an excellent and very tasty outdoor barbecue dinner is *Khan's* on Mosque St, off Somali Rd and close to the central market. This place is extremely popular and deservedly so. Expect to pay around US$4. It's only open in the evenings; the rest of the day it's a vehicle spare parts agency!

Also popular but open all day every day is *Roaster's Garden* on the Old Moshi Rd just over the river bridge beyond the New Arusha Hotel. It does a range of dishes but its main function is as a watering hole, especially in the evenings.

For a splurge, most travellers go to one of two restaurants: the *Safari Grill* (part of the New Safari Hotel) or the *Chinese Restaurant*, on Sokoine Rd near the bridge between the two halves of town.

For excellent Indian Mughlai cuisine, go to the *Shamiana Restaurant* at the Hotel Pallson's. Main courses cost around US$5.

Entertainment

Two of the liveliest and cheapest bars are the *Silver City Bar* at the YMCA and the *Naura Yard Bar* next to the Chinese Restaurant. Otherwise, in the afternoons, the beer gardens at the *New Safari Hotel* and the *New Arusha Hotel* are great places to relax and converse.

The indoor bar at the *Hotel Equator* is probably the best and most lively of all the bars any evening of the week. Everyone looking for action comes here.

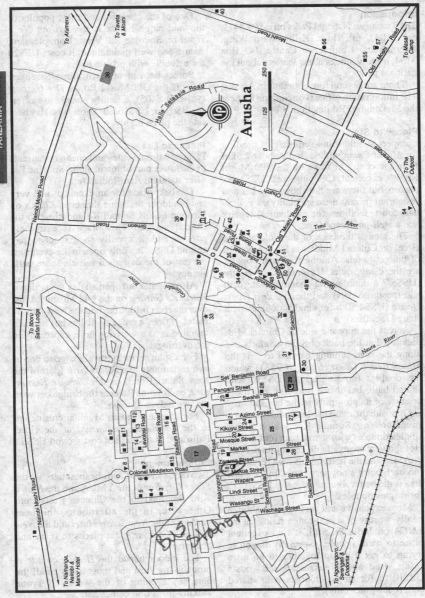

Arusha

To Atumeru

To Taveta & Moshi

Moshi Road

To Masai Camp

Old Moshi Road

Haile Selassie Road

250 m

125

0

Arusha

To The Outpost

Church Road

Serengeti Road

Nairobi Moshi Road

Simeon Road

Temi River

To Tanzania

Old Moshi Road

Sinan Street

Colondai River

To Ilboru Safari Lodge

Nairobi Moshi Road

Ethiopia Road

Stadium Road

Levolosi Road

Naura River

Set Benjamin Road

Pangani Street

Swahili Street

Azimo Street

Kikuyu Street

Mosque Street

Market

Zaramo Street

Makua Street

Wapare

Lindi Street

Wasangu St

Wachaga Street

Colonel Middleton Road

Makongoro Road

Somali Road

Sokoine Road

Bus Station

To Namanga, Nairobi & Manor Hotel

To Ngorongoro, Serengeti & Dodoma

India Street

Boma Road

Goliondoi Road

Sokoine Road

TANZANIA

PLACES TO STAY
1   Eland Hotel
2   Miami Beach Guest
    House
3   Hotel AM 1988
4   Midway Hotel
5   William's Inn
7   Golden Rose Hotel
9   Twins Guest House;
    Annex Mrina Hotel
10 Mashele Guest House
11 Levolosi Guest House
12 Ninja Guest House
13 Monjes Guest House
14 Kitundu Guest House
15 Hotel Arusha by Night
    Annexe
16 Stadium Bar & Guest
    House
19 Amazon Hotel
21 Kilimanjaro Villa
23 Arusha Centre Inn
24 Robannyson Hotel
26 Hotel Pallson's
28 Hotel Arusha by Night

32 Greenland Hotel
35 YMCA; Silver City Bar
39 Novotel Mount Meru
40 Hotel 77
43 New Safari Hotel
44 Hotel Equator
48 Arusha Naaz Hotel
49 Arusha Resort Centre
51 New Arusha Hotel
55 Hotel Impala

PLACES TO EAT
8   Taj Restaurant
20 Khan's
27 Pita Pizzeria
31 Chinese Restaurant
47 Mambo The Caf
53 Roaster's Garden
54 Mandarin Palace
    Restaurant

OTHER
6   Sunny Safaris
17 Stadium
18 Bus Station

22 Uhuru Monument
25 Market
29 Mosque
30 Metropole Cinema
33 Police
34 Adventure Centre
36 Central Bank of
    Tanzania;
    Ngorongoro
    Conservation
    Authority
37 Immigration
38 International
    Conference Centre
41 National Museum
42 Municipal Council
    Offices
45 Air Tanzania
46 Post Office
50 National Bank of
    Commerce
52 Clock Tower
56 Bushbuck Safaris
57 Club 21; Casino

The only nightly disco is at the *Hotel Arusha by Night*. In the basement of the New Safari Hotel is the *Cave Disco*, which is very popular at weekends.

Things to Buy

There are very good craft shops along the short street between the clock tower and Goliondoi Rd. They have superb examples of makonde carving at prices lower than in Dar es Salaam.

Getting There & Away

For details of road transport between Arusha and Nairobi, see the earlier Tanzania Getting There & Away section.

To Dar there are luxury buses (nine hours, US$12) and semi-luxury buses (14 hours, US$11). To Mwanza, there's a choice of buses which go direct through Ngorongoro and the Serengeti National Park, and others which bypass the parks and go via Singida and Shinyanga. The first are much quicker but cost much more because you have to pay two sets of park entry fees (totalling US$40 payable in hard currency) in addition to the fare. There are quite a few bus lines doing both of these routes so there's at least one departure daily. Make enquiries and book a seat the day before. Going via Serengeti/ Ngorongoro the fare is US$34 (plus US$40 park entry fees) and takes 12 to 18 hours. Going via Singida and Shinyanga, the fare is US$18 and takes anything from 36 to 100 hours.

There are buses and minibuses all day, every day (until late) between Arusha and Moshi, which leave when full (1½ hours, US$1.50).

BAGAMOYO

The name of this coastal town, 75km north of Dar es Salaam, is derived from the word *bwagamoyo* meaning 'lay down your heart'. It's a reminder that it was once the terminus of the slave-trade caravan route from Lake Tanganyika.

Bagamoyo later became the headquarters of the German colonial administration and many of the buildings which they constructed still remain.

The only trouble with staying anywhere in Bagamoyo is the very real possibility of being violently mugged.

Things to See

The Catholic mission north of town maintains a **museum**, and the chapel where Livingstone's body was laid before being taken to Zanzibar en route to Westminster Abbey is also here. Don't walk to this museum alone as there's a good chance you'll get mugged.

The 14th-century ruins at **Kaole** involve a one-hour walk south along the beach past Kaole village into the mangrove swamps. When the beach apparently ends, go inland and look for the stone pillars. Don't bring any valuables along this beach and make a decided effort to look poor, otherwise robbery is a near certainty.

Places to Stay & Eat

Most travellers head out to the *Badeco Beach Hotel*. It costs US$9 per person. The *Travellers Lodge* is another beach hotel popular with travellers, and it costs US$5 per person.

Considerably more expensive is the *Gogo Beach Resort*, with doubles with private bath and air-con for US$30/40, but you can also camp here and use the swimming pool.

Getting There & Away

Buses depart from Dar es Salaam throughout the day until about 3 pm from outside the Kariakoo Market (three hours, US$1.50).

BUKOBA

Bukoba is Tanzania's second-largest port on Lake Victoria. It's become quite a popular overnight stop for travellers on their way to Uganda or Rwanda.

The main part of town is some 2.5km from the port so you'll need a taxi if you have heavy bags.

Places to Stay

The cheapest place is the *Nyumba wa Vijana* (youth centre), at the Evangelical Lutheran Church on the road to the hospital. A dormitory bed costs US$1.

You can camp in the grounds of the *Lake Hotel* where it costs US$4 per tent.

Other than the many cheapies around the bus station, a good place to stay is the *Coffee Tree Hotel* (☎ 20412) where singles/doubles with attached bath cost US$5/7 including breakfast. The *Banana Hotel* on Zam Zam St offers singles/doubles with attached bath for US$8/9.

Getting There & Away

For details of the route between Bukoba and Masaka (Uganda) via Kyaka, see the Tanzania Getting There & Away section earlier in this chapter. For ferries to Mwanza, see the Tanzania Getting Around section.

KIGOMA

Kigoma is the most important Tanzanian port on Lake Tanganyika and the terminus of the railway from Dar es Salaam. Travellers used to come through here en route to, or coming from, Bujumbura (Burundi) or Mpulungu (Zambia) on the Lake Tanganyika steamer MV *Liemba*, but with the unrest in Burundi it's very much a backwater these days.

It's a small but pleasant town with one main street which is lined with huge shady mango trees. Life ticks over at a slow pace. If you get stuck waiting for the train (a few days is not uncommon) or the boat (a day or two), you'll have to amuse yourself with walks around town and visits to **Ujiji**, one of Africa's oldest market villages and a good deal more interesting than Kigoma. This is where the famous words 'Dr Livingstone, I presume' were spoken by the explorer and journalist Henry Stanley.

Don't climb any of the hills that flank the town in search of a view, as these are military zones and off-limits to mere mortals.

Kigoma has consulates for Burundi and Congo (Zaïre).

Places to Stay & Eat

The best value for money is the *Kigoma Hotel*, on the main street in the middle of town. Singles/doubles with shared bath cost US$3/4.50.

The *Mapinduzi Hotel* is a basic place charging US$2 for doubles that can accommodate four people without any problem.

Kigoma's only mid-range hotel is the *Lake Tanganyika Hotel*, overlooking the lake, a

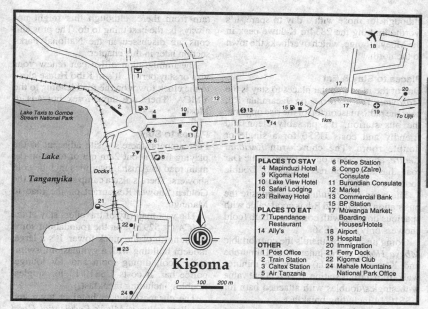

PLACES TO STAY
4 Mapinduzi Hotel
9 Kigoma Hotel
10 Lake View Hotel
16 Safari Lodging
23 Railway Hotel

PLACES TO EAT
7 Tupendance Restaurant
14 Ally's

OTHER
1 Post Office
2 Train Station
3 Caltex Station
5 Air Tanzania
6 Police Station
8 Congo (Zaïre) Consulate
11 Burundian Consulate
12 Market
13 Commercial Bank
15 BP Station
17 Muwanga Market; Boarding Houses/Hotels
18 Airport
19 Hospital
20 Immigration
21 Ferry Dock
22 Kigoma Club
24 Mahale Mountains National Park Office

Kigoma

Lake Taxis to Gombe Stream National Park

Lake Tanganyika

Docks

To Ujiji

0   100   200 m

TANZANIA

few hundred metres south of the town centre. The rates are US$25 for a double with attached bath and breakfast, but beware of the Saturday night disco which usually rocks until 4 am!

The Muslim-owned *Ally's* restaurant has slow service but the best range of food in Kigoma, especially in the evenings.

Getting There & Away
Trains depart at 5 pm on Tuesday, Wednesday, Friday and Sunday for Dar es Salaam and Mwanza. The journey takes from 36 to 40 hours and delays are common. See the Getting Around section earlier in this chapter for fare details.

The buses in this area only serve local towns, but it is possible to find trucks to Mwanza if you are prepared to wait a few days.

For details of the MV *Liemba's* services to Mpulungu and Bujumbura, see the earlier Tanzania Getting There & Away section.

The dock for lake taxis to the Gombe Stream National Park is about an hour's walk up the railway tracks from the station.

KYELA
If it's early in the day and you're on your way to the Malawian border, there's no need to go to Kyela as the turn-off to the border is about 5km back up the road towards Mbeya. From the turn-off, it's 5km to the border which is open until 6 pm.

The *Ram Hotel*, not far from the bus stand, is excellent value with beds for US$1. The *Salaam Hotel* on the main road has beds for US$1 per person, but cold showers only.

MBEYA
Mbeya is on the main road and TAZARA rail line between Tanzania and Zambia. Many travellers stay here overnight en route to Malawi via the Songwe River bridge to Karonga.

There's little of interest for the traveller,

although for those with a day to spare, it's worth climbing the 2834m Kaluwe peak in the Mbeya Range, which overlooks the town to the north.

Places to Stay & Eat

One of the most popular places to stay is the *Moravian Youth Hostel* on Jacaranda Rd, near the radio mast on top of the rise opposite the bus station. It's passably clean and friendly and costs US$6 for a single or double room. The church-run *Karibuni Centre*, about 500m out of town on the Dar road, has also been recommended. Double rooms are US$8.

The basic *Nkwenzulu Hotel*, opposite the bus station on Mbalizi Rd, is good value with spacious doubles with communal bath (cold showers only) for US$6.

Going up in price, there's the comfortable *Mbeya Hotel*, at the junction of Lumumba and Karume (Kaunda) Aves, 15 minutes walk from the bus station. It's excellent value with singles/doubles with attached bath for US$10/14 including breakfast.

The *Mezza Luna Restaurant* near the post office has excellent pizza and pasta.

Getting There & Away

Bus There are express buses between Mbeya and Dar es Salaam (US$5, eight hours).

For details on the trip from Mbeya to Karonga (Malawi), see Malawi in the Tanzania Getting There & Away section.

Train Trains on the TAZARA railway to Dar es Salaam or Kapiri Mposhi (Zambia) are heavily booked, so make a reservation well in advance (see the Tanzania Getting Around section for schedule and fare details). Reservations can be made at the railway station or at the Tanzania Railways Corporation office in town, at the junction of Station Rd and Post St.

MOSHI

Moshi is the gateway to Kilimanjaro but otherwise not very interesting. Rather than stay here, many travellers head straight out to Marangu and arrange a trek up the moun-

tain from there, although this might not always be the best thing to do. The pros and cons are discussed in the National Parks section later in this chapter.

The immigration office can renew your visa or stay permit. It's in Kibo House close to the clock tower on the road leading to the YMCA. There are three forex bureaus in Moshi.

Places to Stay

For campers, there's a site adjacent to the playing field about 2km out of town on the main road to Arusha. Facilities include cold showers. There's also a camp site next to the Golden Shower Restaurant on the road to Marangu.

The vast majority of travellers stay at the *YMCA* (☎ 52923), on the roundabout some 300m north of the clock tower. It's a large, modern building with a gymnasium, swimming pool, dining room and TV lounge/ coffee bar. It costs US$10/13 for singles/ doubles, including breakfast.

The cheapest budget hotel in town and excellent value is *Mlay's Residential Hotel* (☎ 51792) at 72 Market St. It's very clean, always has water and also has a restaurant and bar. Doubles with shared bath are US$4.

Also good is the *Motel Silva* (☎ 53122) where singles/doubles with shared bath cost US$6/7 including breakfast.

Equally good is the four-storey *Kindoroko Hotel* (☎ 52988) on Mawenzi Rd near the junction with Chagga St. Singles/doubles with shared facilities cost US$6/7 including breakfast. The staff are friendly and there are two restaurants and a shady courtyard bar.

The best mid-range choice is the *Hotel New Castle* (☎ 53203), which usually has plenty of rooms available. Doubles with communal bathroom cost US$15, including breakfast.

Places to Eat

Apart from the YMCA and the Swahili menu at the Moshi Hotel, cheap meals are available at *Chrisburger*, a few doors up the road from the clock tower and towards the YMCA on the left-hand side.

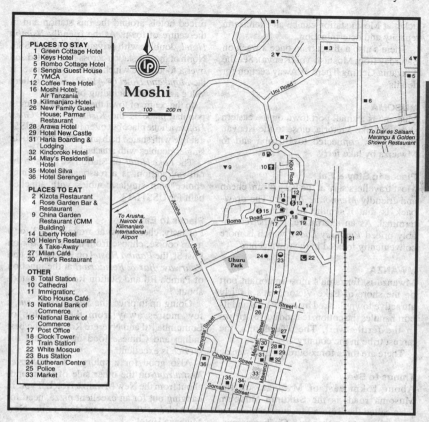

Moshi

0   100   200 m

PLACES TO STAY
1   Green Cottage Hotel
3   Keys Hotel
5   Rombo Cottage Hotel
6   Sengia Guest House
7   YMCA
12 Coffee Tree Hotel
16 Moshi Hotel;
    Air Tanzania
19 Kilimanjaro Hotel
26 New Family Guest
    House; Parmar
    Restaurant
28 Arawa Hotel
29 Hotel New Castle
31 Haria Boarding &
    Lodging
32 Kindoroko Hotel
34 Mlay's Residential
    Hotel
35 Motel Silva
36 Hotel Serengeti

PLACES TO EAT
2   Kizota Restaurant
4   Rose Garden Bar &
    Restaurant
9   China Garden
    Restaurant (CMM
    Building)
14 Liberty Hotel
20 Helen's Restaurant
    & Take-Away
27 Milan Café
30 Amir's Restaurant

OTHER
8   Total Station
10 Cathedral
11 Immigration;
    Kibo House Café
13 National Bank of
    Commerce
15 National Bank of
    Commerce
17 Post Office
18 Clock Tower
21 Train Station
22 White Mosque
23 Bus Station
24 Lutheran Centre
25 Police
33 Market

Uru Road

To Dar es Salaam,
Marangu & Golden
Shower Restaurant

To Arusha,
Nairobi &
Kilimanjaro
International
Airport

Uhuru
Park

Kibo Road

Arusha Road

Boma   Road

Kilima   Street

Kenyatta Street

Chagga   Street

Somali   Street

Market   Street

Mawenzi   Road

TANZANIA

Very popular with local office people, especially at lunch time on weekdays, the *Liberty Hotel* offers cheap traditional African fare, but it hardly functions at the weekend.

For good Chinese food at moderate prices, try the *China Garden Restaurant* at the CCM building on the ring road. It's open daily from noon until midnight.

For a splurge, my favourite is the *Golden Shower Restaurant*, though it's a good 1.5km out of town on the Marangu road. Despite the distance, it is surprisingly popular with travellers, especially those who have climbed Kilimanjaro and feel like celebrating.

Getting There & Away

Bus There are several buses daily in both directions between Moshi and Dar es Salaam. Fares are the same as for Arusha.

There are frequent daily buses and minibuses between Arusha and Moshi which depart when full.

Minibuses to Marangu also leave throughout the day when full and cost US$1.

Train See the Tanzania Getting Around section for details of schedules and fares between Moshi and Dar. Advance booking is essential for 1st and 2nd class. Buying a ticket at Moshi station can be an exercise in tenacity and determination.

There's also a direct train once a week on Saturday from Moshi to Voi (Kenya). See the Tanzania Getting There & Away section for details.

MUSOMA

Musoma is a small port town on the eastern shore of Lake Victoria, close to the Kenyan border. It's connected to Bukoba and to Mwanza by lake ferry.

Places to Stay & Eat

Most travellers stay at the very clean, cheap and friendly *Mennonite Centre*. The drawback is that it's quite far from the ferry terminal. As an alternative, try the reasonably priced *Embassy Lodge* which is more conveniently located in the town centre.

MWANZA

Mwanza is Tanzania's most important port on the shore of Lake Victoria. It's a fairly attractive town flanked by rocky hills and its port handles the cotton, tea and coffee grown in the fertile west. The Wasukuma, the largest tribe in the country, live here.

There are three forex bureaus in Mwanza.

Things to See

About 15km east of Mwanza, on the Musoma road, is the **Sukuma Museum** (also called the Bujora Museum) which was originally put together by a Québecois missionary. Its displays are about the culture and traditions of the Wasukuma tribe. To get there, take a local bus from the dalla dalla bus station in Mwanza to Kisessa from where it's about a 1km walk.

Places to Stay

You can camp at the *Sukuma Museum* (US$5) but if you have no tent there are two-bed *bandas* (huts) for rent. It's a lovely spot and many travellers stay here. Far more convenient for town is the *New Blue Sky Campsite* on Capri Point Rd on the lake shore which costs US$2 per tent.

There's quite a choice of reasonably priced hotels around the bus station and in the centre of town. At the friendly *Nsimbo Hotel*, doubles with private bath cost US$6. North of the bus station across Nyerere Rd and over a footbridge which spans a small river is the *Majukano Hotel* (☎ 41857). It's excellent value at US$6/7 including breakfast.

In the centre of town the cheapest and most popular place is the *Kishamapanda Guest House*, a huge place but often full. It costs US$4 a single with shared bath and US$4.50/5.50 for singles/doubles with attached bath.

The *Lake Hotel*, on Station Rd close to the railway station, is a reasonable mid-range choice with singles/doubles with attached bath for US$11/13.

Places to Eat

For tasty, cheap food at around US$3 for a main course, choose from the *Blue Cafe* on Post St, the *Pamba Hostel* on Pamba Rd, and *Fourways Bar & Restaurant* at the junction of Pamba Rd and Station Rd on the roundabout.

Going up in price, the *Sitar Restaurant*, a few metres away from the junction of Lumumba Rd and Nyerere Rd, does the best Indian and Chinese food in town and the service is excellent.

Also good for a splurge is *The Sizzler Restaurant* on the other side of the roundabout from the New Mwanza Hotel. If you're hanging out for an excellent pizza, head for the *Kuleana Pizzeria* next door to the New Mwanza Hotel.

Getting There & Away

Bus See the Arusha section for details of buses between these two towns. For details of the trip to Rwanda, see Rwanda in the Tanzania Getting There & Away section.

Train There are regular trains between Mwanza and Dar. See the Tanzania Getting Around section for details. Going from Mwanza to Kigoma involves a change at Tabora. There are only 1st and 2nd-class reservations available as far as Tabora.

Boat See the Tanzania Getting Around

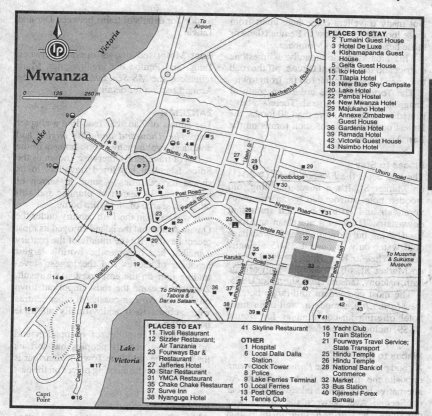

Mwanza

0   125   250 m

Lake Victoria

To Airport

Machemba Road

Customs Road

Bantu Road

Liberty St

Uhuru Road

Footbridge

Post Road

Pamba St

Nyerere Road

Temple Rd

Karuka Road

Lumumba Road

Rwagasore Road

Pamba Road

To Musoma & Sukuma Museum

Station Road

To Shinyanga, Tabora & Dar es Salaam

Lake Victoria

Capri Point Road

Capri Point

PLACES TO STAY
2 Tumaini Guest House
3 Hotel De Luxe
4 Kishamapanda Guest House
5 Geita Guest House
15 Iko Hotel
17 Tilapia Hotel
18 New Blue Sky Campsite
20 Lake Hotel
22 Pamba Hostel
24 New Mwanza Hotel
29 Majukano Hotel
34 Annexe Zimbabwe Guest House
36 Gardenia Hotel
39 Ramada Hotel
42 Victoria Guest House
43 Nsimbo Hotel

PLACES TO EAT
11 Tivoli Restaurant
12 Sizzler Restaurant; Air Tanzania
23 Fourways Bar & Restaurant
27 Jafferies Hotel
30 Sitar Restaurant
31 YMCA Restaurant
35 Chake Chake Restaurant
37 Surve Inn
38 Nyanguge Hotel
41 Skyline Restaurant

OTHER
1 Hospital
6 Local Dalla Dalla Station
7 Clock Tower
8 Police
9 Lake Ferries Terminal
10 Local Ferries
13 Post Office
14 Tennis Club
16 Yacht Club
19 Train Station
21 Fourways Travel Service; State Transport
25 Hindu Temple
26 Hindu Temple
28 National Bank of Commerce
32 Market
33 Bus Station
40 Kijereshi Forex Bureau

section for details of the ferries to Bukoba and the Getting There & Away section for details of the ferries to Port Bell (Uganda) and Kisumu (Kenya).

TABORA

Tabora is a railway junction town where the central railway line branches for Mwanza and Kigoma. You may have to stay the night if you're changing trains and can't get immediate onward reservations.

Places to Stay

The *Moravian Guest House* is probably the best place to stay and is exceptionally cheap. It's pleasant and the staff are friendly. If you'd like more creature comforts try the *Country Roses Hotel*, on West Boma Rd, which charges around US$5 a double.

Getting There & Away

The usual access is by train. See the earlier Tanzania Getting Around section for details.

TANGA

Strolling around Tanga amid its sleepy, semi-colonial atmosphere, you'd hardly be aware that this is Tanzania's second-largest seaport.

Not many travellers come here apart from those looking for a dhow to Pemba Island or those heading north to Mombasa.

This area is predominantly a limestone district and the **Amboni Caves**, off the road to Lunga Lunga, are not too far from town.

The **Tongoni Ruins** are 20km south of Tanga on the Pangani road. There's a large ruined mosque and more than 40 tombs, the largest concentration of such tombs on the East African coast.

Places to Stay
The best bet is the *Planters Hotel* (☎ 2041) on Market St. It's a huge, rambling, old wooden hotel surrounded by an enormous verandah and with a bar and restaurant downstairs. The rooms are clean and have hand basins, but the communal showers have cold water only. It costs US$4/5 a single/double. The *Far Ways Hotel* (☎ 46097), also on Market St, offers doubles with private bath, balcony, fan and clean sheets for US$5.

The most convenient mid-range hotel is the *Marina Inn*, a modern, well-maintained hotel offering air-con doubles for around US$9, including breakfast.

Places to Eat
A good place to eat is the *Patwas Restaurant*, opposite the market in the town centre. An alternative is the *Baht*, a takeaway snack bar on Second Ave, between the two railway crossings. The *Marine Restaurant* on Market St is very popular with the local people at lunch time.

For a minor splurge, you can eat at the *Planters Hotel*. The service is a bit on the slow side but the food is worth the wait.

Getting There & Away
Bus There are usually one or two buses daily from Dar es Salaam to Tanga. The trip takes seven to eight hours and costs US$6.

See the Tanzania Getting There & Away section for details of the Horohoro border crossing.

Train See the Tanzania Getting Around section for details of trains between Dar and Tanga.

Boat Motorised dhows operate between Tanga and Pemba but are irregular. More reliable is the MS *Sepideh*; see the Getting Around section for details.

ZANZIBAR
The annals of Zanzibar read like a chapter from *The Thousand and One Nights* and doubtless evoke many exotic images in the minds of travellers. Otherwise known as the Spice Island, it has lured travellers to its shores for centuries – some in search of trade, some in search of plunder and still others in search of an idyllic home.

It was early in the 19th century under the Omani Arabs that the island enjoyed its most recent heyday. By the middle of the century Zanzibar had become the world's largest producer of cloves and the largest slave-trading port on the east coast. As a result, Zanzibar became the most important town on the East African coast. All other centres were subject to it and virtually all trade passed through it.

The many centuries of occupation and influence by various peoples has left its mark, and the old Stone Town of Zanzibar is one of the most fascinating places on the east coast.

Information
Although Zanzibar is part of the United Republic of Tanzania, it jealously guards its autonomy and requires foreign visitors to go through its own immigration and customs on arrival and departure. Immigration officials also usually want to see your yellow fever certificate.

Lonely Planet's *East Africa* provides more detailed information to Zanzibar, and anyone planning to spend more than a few days on Zanzibar could consider investing in the Bradt *Guide to Zanzibar* by David Else, available in Nairobi and Dar es Salaam, and sometimes on Zanzibar.

Excellent maps of Zanzibar town and of the island are available from the Tanzanian

Tourist Corporation (☎ 32344) which has an office in Livingstone House, on the main road out of town going north. Bookings for government-owned Zanzibar beach chalets must be made here.

There are forex bureaus and a National Bank of Commerce in town.

Warning

Beware of strong currents when swimming off the east coast. Check with your hotel or seek other local advice about safe places for swimming.

Things to See & Do

Stone Town Zanzibar's old Stone Town, much larger than Lámu or the old town of Mombasa, is a fascinating labyrinth of narrow, winding streets lined with quaint little shops, bazaars, mosques, courtyards and squares, former colonial mansions and whitewashed, coral-rag houses, many with overhanging balconies and magnificently carved brass-studded doors. Regrettably, many of these doors have disappeared in recent years.

You'll see a lot of crumbled and crumbling buildings as you walk around the Stone Town, and it's a great pity that so much of the fabric of this historic place has been allowed to fall into disrepair. A determined effort is now being made to restore a lot of the more important buildings. It's a superb place to wander around and get lost in, though you can't really get lost for too long as, sooner or later, you'll end up either on the seafront or on Creek Rd.

One of the most prominent buildings in the old town is the **Beit-el-Ajaib**, or House of Wonders, formerly the sultan's palace and one of the largest structures in Zanzibar. Beside it is a more modest palace to which the sultans moved after vacating the Beit-el-Ajaib in 1911.

On the other side of Beit-el-Ajaib is the **'Arab' Fort**, a typical massive, crenellated and bastioned structure, originally built by the Portuguese in 1700.

The **Old Slave Market**, off Creek Rd, is another landmark but there's very little to see as the first Anglican cathedral in East Africa, the UMCA cathedral (United Mission to Central Africa) stands here.

The old **Hamamni Persian Baths**, east of the cathedral, are perhaps also worth a visit. They're a protected monument and are locked, but if you show a passing interest the guardian (who runs a shop a few metres away) will rush up with the key and show you around, then ask you for a 'donation'.

The **National Museum** on Creek Rd is also worth a visit if you're interested in the history of the island, though it's somewhat run-down.

Scuba Diving In the last few years scuba diving has taken off in a big way on Zanzibar which is not surprising given the numerous beautiful coral reefs off the main island and its many offshore islets.

There are currently three dive operations:

CAT-Diving Ltd
    PO Box 3203 (☎/fax (054) 31040)
Indian Ocean Divers
    PO Box 2370 (☎/fax 33860)
One Ocean – The Zanzibar Dive Centre
    PO Box 608 (☎ 33816; fax 30406)

Sunset Cruises One Ocean – The Zanzibar Dive Centre (see above) offers sunset dhow cruises, given sufficient demand, on Tuesday, Thursday and Saturday. The price is US$20 and includes snacks and soft drinks.

Places to Stay

All accommodation on the island has to be paid for in foreign currency (preferably US dollars) unless you're a Tanzanian resident. There are no exceptions. Make sure you have sufficient small denomination travellers' cheques or bills to pay for this.

One of the cheapest places is the *Flamingo Guest House* (☎ 32850), Mkunazini Rd. It's very friendly but small and lacks character. Rooms with a fan and mosquito net cost US$8/14 including breakfast.

Close by and even cheaper is *The Haven Guest House* (☎ 33454) which offers B&B

TANZANIA

Zanzibar Town (Stone Town)

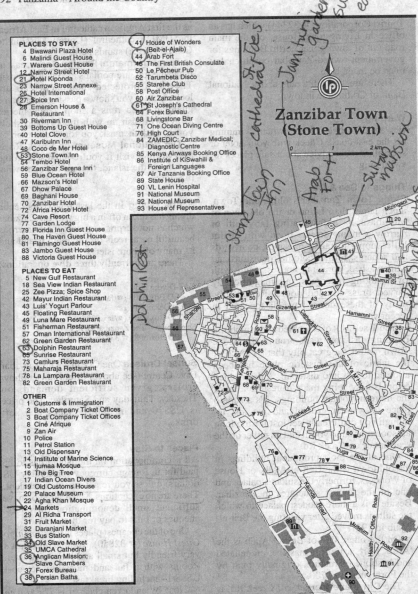

PLACES TO STAY
4 Bwawani Plaza Hotel
6 Malindi Guest House
7 Warere Guest House
12 Narrow Street Hotel
21 Hotel Kiponda
23 Narrow Street Annexe
26 Hotel International
27 Spice Inn
28 Emerson House & Restaurant
30 Riverman Inn
39 Bottoms Up Guest House
40 Hotel Clove
47 Karibulnn Inn
48 Coco de Mer Hotel
53 Stone Town Inn
54 Tembo Hotel
56 Zanzibar Serena Inn
59 Blue Ocean Hotel
66 Mazson's Hotel
67 Dhow Palace
69 Baghani House
70 Zanzibar Hotel
72 Africa House Hotel
74 Cave Resort
77 Garden Lodge
79 Florida Inn Guest House
80 The Haven Guest House
81 Flamingo Guest House
83 Jambo Guest House
88 Victoria Guest House

PLACES TO EAT
5 New Gulf Restaurant
18 Sea View Indian Restaurant
25 Zee Pizza; Spice Shop
42 Mayur Indian Restaurant
43 Luis' Yogurt Parlour
45 Floating Restaurant
49 Luna Mare Restaurant
51 Fisherman Restaurant
62 Oman International Restaurant
62 Green Garden Restaurant
63 Dolphin Restaurant
65 Sunrise Restaurant
73 Camlurs Restaurant
75 Maharaja Restaurant
78 La Lampara Restaurant
82 Green Garden Restaurant

OTHER
1 Customs & Immigration
2 Boat Company Ticket Offices
3 Boat Company Ticket Offices
8 Ciné Afrique
9 Zan Air
10 Police
11 Petrol Station
13 Old Dispensary
14 Institute of Marine Science
15 Ijumaa Mosque
16 The Big Tree
17 Indian Ocean Divers
19 Old Customs House
20 Palace Museum
22 Agha Khan Mosque
24 Markets
29 Al Ridha Transport
31 Fruit Market
32 Daranjani Market
33 Bus Station
34 Old Slave Market
35 UMCA Cathedral
36 Anglican Mission; Slave Chambers
37 Forex Bureau
38 Persian Baths

41 House of Wonders (Beit-el-Ajaib)
44 Arab Fort
46 The First British Consulate
50 Le Pêcheur Pub
52 Tarumbeta Disco
55 Starehe Club
58 Post Office
60 Air Zanzibar
61 St Joseph's Cathedral
64 Forex Bureau
68 Livingstone Bar
71 One Ocean Diving Centre
76 High Court
84 ZAMEDIC: Zanzibar Medical; Diagnostic Centre
85 Kenya Airways Booking Office
86 Institute of KiSwahili & Foreign Languages
87 Air Tanzania Booking Office
89 State House
90 VL Lenin Hospital
91 National Museum
92 National Museum
93 House of Representatives

TANZANIA

with shared bath at US$7 per person. It's very popular with budget travellers.

In the same area and off the main street (signposted) is the *Jambo Guest House* (☎ 33779) where singles/doubles with common bathroom in the low (high) season cost US$8/15 (US$10/20) while those with air-con cost US$10/18 (US$15/25) including breakfast.

Not far from here, just off Vuga Rd, close to the Omani consulate, is the modern and friendly *Victoria Guest House* (☎ 32861). It's quite popular and rooms with private bath cost US$10 per person, including breakfast.

Also in this area and great value is the very pleasant and friendly *Garden Lodge* (☎ 33298) on Kaunda Rd. You can get a bed in a triple room with private bath and fan for US$8 per person, or there are doubles with private bath for US$18.

In the Arab Fort area are two other cheapies. The better in terms of facilities is the *Karibu Inn* (☎ 33058) which has 12 rooms with fan and shared bath for US$15/20, plus doubles with private bath for US$25. All prices include breakfast. Cheaper is the *Bottoms Up Guest House* (☎ 33189), Hurumzi St, where a clean, comfortable room with shared bath, fan, carpet and mosquito net costs from US$6/12 a single/double. All prices include a full breakfast. Quite a lot of travellers stay here.

East of this area close to the UMCA cathedral is another good cheapie, the *Riverman Inn* (☎ 33188), which offers B&B with shared bath for US$10/20 a single/double. It's a quiet place and has a bar.

Possibly the best place to stay is the *Malindi Guest House* (☎ 30165), Funguni Bazaar, also in the Malindi area. This is a beautiful place with bags of atmosphere. The staff are very friendly, and there's a range of rooms, all with shared bath, fan and mosquito net, for US$10 per person including breakfast.

For authentic Zanzibarian character and atmosphere, the best value mid-range place is the *Stone Town Inn* (☎/fax 33658), on Shangani St. It's housed in a beautifully and sensitively refurbished traditional coral-rag house. It offers doubles with private bath for US$25 per person. The place is friendly, secure and the showers have hot water.

Another beautifully restored traditional house which has been opened as a hotel is the *Hotel Kiponda & Restaurant* (☎ 33052; fax 33020), Kiponda St near the UNICEF office. It's spotless and has a superb rooftop restaurant which catches the sea breezes. It offers singles/doubles with shared bathroom for US$18/35 and doubles with private bath for US$45.

In the centre of the Stone Town, the *Spice Inn* (☎ 30728), close to the Agha Khan Mosque, is a popular place to stay. This would have to be the Raffles Hotel of Zanzibar. It's decidedly Somerset Maugham, with its timeless 1st-floor lounge full of easy chairs and local antiques. Prices start at US$20/25 a single/double with fan and shared bath. All prices include breakfast.

Places to Eat
Undoubtedly the cheapest place to eat in the evening is in the *Jamituri Gardens* in front of the fort, where the townspeople gather to socialise and watch the sun go down. Food stalls sell spicy curries, roasted meat and maize, cassava, smoked octopus, sugar-cane juice and ice cream – all at extremely reasonable prices.

Just about as cheap and very popular, especially with local people, is the cafe at the *Ciné Afrique*, where basic African dishes are available. Somewhat more expensive but very popular with travellers is the long-running *Dolphin Restaurant*, close to the GPO on Kenyatta Rd.

Travellers looking for something resembling fast food might like to check out the *Chicken Inn*, next door to the Karibu Inn, or the *Jabco Fast Food International*, on the seafront next door to Africa House Hotel.

One place you *must* visit, especially if you're a fruit juice or ice-cream freak, is the *Baobab Bar* not far from St Joseph's Cathedral which is built, as the name implies, under a baobab tree and designed by someone with imagination. It's excellent.

For a not-too-expensive splurge, there's a choice of very popular restaurants: the *Fisherman Restaurant*, on Shangani St near the Starehe Club; *Camlurs Restaurant*, close to Africa House; the *Maharaja Restaurant*, close to Camlurs; and the *Sea View Indian Restaurant*, on the 1st floor on Mizingani Rd overlooking the harbour.

Also very good, and excellent value, is the *Chit Chat Restaurant* on Cathedral St (near St Joseph's Cathedral), which offers Goan, Indian and Zanzibari food. It's a popular place, so bookings are recommended.

Entertainment
Virtually everyone goes to the *Africa House Hotel* for a cold beer in the late afternoon/early evening. The bar is on the 1st-floor terrace overlooking the ocean and is a favourite spot to watch the sun go down.

Under Africa House Hotel, to the right of the entrance as you face it, is another recently opened bar, the *New Happy Bar & Restaurant*. It's a pleasant place to have a drink and, unlike the bar at Africa House, never runs out of beer. What's more, the beer is consistently cold.

Also very popular, especially after dinner, is *Le Pêcheur*, right next door to the Fisherman Restaurant. It's open all day, every day and basically doesn't close until the last customer leaves.

The bar at the *Bottoms Up Guest House* is another option. It, too, is open all day, every day and has a good selection of music. The beer is always cold, though the lurid décor might make you wonder whether you fell into purgatory en route to pleasure.

The *Cave Resort* opposite Camlurs Restaurant is an intimate little place with no frills where you can mix with local people.

The best disco in town is the *Tarumbeta Club*, part of the Fisherman Restaurant, Stone Town Inn and Le Pêcheur complex. It's open nightly from around 8 pm until early in the morning.

Getting There & Away
There's a range of boats available. See the

Dar es Salaam Getting There & Away section for details.

Getting Around

The Airport There are no buses to/from the airport, only local dalla dalla (pick-ups and minibuses). A taxi costs US$9.

Car & Motorcycle There are a lot of places offering motorcycle and vehicle hire including travel agencies and tour agencies, but some of the cheapest deals can be found by asking around in the bar of the Africa House Hotel any evening. Motorcycles range from around US$30 for one day to US$18 per day for one week or more. Self-drive cars typically cost US$50 for one day to US$35 per day for a week or more.

Bicycle There are many places where you can rent these and most budget and many mid-range hotels can point you in the right direction. Two places which have been operating for years are Al Ridha Transport, close to the Empire Cinema off Creek Rd, and Maharouky's Store, on Creek Rd next to the petrol station in Daranjani.

AROUND ZANZIBAR

There are plenty of **historical sites** around the island worth visiting but seeing them on an individual basis requires a lot of effort and expense. It's far better and cheaper to see a selection of them on one of the 'spice tours'.

Spice Tours

The major components of a spice tour (other than visits to the ruins) are visits to the various spice and fruit plantations around the island. Along the way you'll be invited to taste all the spices, herbs and fruits which the island produces. Spice Tours cost from US$10 to US$50 per person, depending on the quality of the tour, the type of transport, the number of people in the group, the season and if lunch or a picnic is included. Some tours are very good value, others are a rip-off.

Probably the best person to tour with is an elderly Indian man named Mitu, who owns

taxis and has been doing these trips for years. Mitu's office is around the corner from the Ciné Afrique (the street on the right-hand side as you face the Ciné Afrique). Try to book a tour the day before or get there around 8 am.

Also offering excellent value for money are Tembo Tours & Safaris (☎ 30466). A tour lasts from 9 am to 5 pm and includes lunch at a local restaurant. Contact David any night at the bar at Africa House Hotel between 6 and 8 pm.

Also reliable is Kalunga Island Tours (☎/fax 32664), Mkunazini St, which offers both a short spice tour (three hours) and a longer tour (five hours).

Also seek recommendations from other travellers.

Jozani Forest

Some 24km south-east of Zanzibar town, between Chwaka and Uzi bays, is the Jozani Forest, a nature reserve for the rare red colobus monkey, two antelope species and the Zanzibar duiker and sunni. To get there, you need to organise your own transport or get a group together and hire a taxi. A trained guide will show you around the forest. Put aside about half a day for the tour. Entry to the forest costs US$2.

Offshore Islets

Just offshore from Zanzibar town are several islands ringed with coral reefs. Three are simply sandbanks which partially disappear at high tide, but the other four (including Chumbe Island to the south, where there is a lighthouse) are well forested, idyllic tropical islands with small but superb beaches.

The most famous and visited island is **Changuu Island**, also known as Prison Island. In the 19th century it was owned by an Arab who used it, as the sign says, for housing 'recalcitrant slaves'. It was later bought by a Briton who constructed a prison, which was apparently never used, though the ruins remain. Now it's used by day-trippers from Zanzibar for a pleasant day out.

The island is run by the Tanzania Tourist Corporation, which charges an entry fee of US$1, UK£1 or DM 2, payable in *cash*.

It's easy to find transport across from Zanzibar. Enquire at Chemha Brothers Tours (☎ 31751), next to the Fisherman Restaurant; Fisherman Tours (☎ 30468), Creek Rd; Kalungu Island Tours (☎ 32664), Mkunazini St; or the tourist office (all in Zanzibar town).

Beaches

There are some superb beaches, particularly on the east coast of the island, which are as unspoilt as you're likely to find. This is rapidly changing, however, as new guesthouses open their doors each week. All the same, most of the accommodation available is for those who can do without electricity, hot and cold running water, swimming pools and night entertainment. It's totally relaxing and, unlike many of the beaches on the western side of the island close to Zanzibar town, there is no need to worry about being robbed or mugged.

The main beaches on the east coast, in order from the northern tip of the island, are **Nungwi, Matemwe, Pwani Mchangani, Uroa, Chwaka, Bwejuu, Paje, Jambiani** and **Makunduchi**. Everyone has a favourite but they're all pretty similar really.

Places to Stay & Eat There's a choice of government-run bungalows and plenty of privately owned guesthouses.

If you wish to stay at any of the government bungalows, those at Bwejuu, Chwaka and Makunduchi (where there are two) cost US$30 shared between up to five people, and those at Chwaka, Jambiani and Uroa cost US$40 shared between five people.

At Bwejuu the most popular place to stay is the *Bwejuu Dere Beach Resort* (☎ 31017), which consists of three main buildings and associated bungalows. Many of the rooms face the sea, giving you the benefit of sea breezes. The rooms themselves are simple but adequate and provided with a fan, mosquito net, towel and toilet paper. A double with private bath is US$16/20 in low/high season. Rooms with shared bath come a few dollars cheaper.

Close by is the friendly *Palm Beach Inn*, which is good value at US$10/20 for spacious singles/doubles with private bath.

Not directly on the beach but cheaper is the *Kibuda Family Guest House*, which offers accommodation for just US$5 per person including breakfast.

A little further south down the coast, at the entrance to Bwejuu village, the *Seven Seas Guest House* offers B&B for US$8 per person.

In Jambiani the best place in terms of facilities is the *Jambiani Beach Hotel*, which has rooms arranged around a rectangular compound. Bathroom facilities are communal and no mosquito nets are provided but it has a bar and a good restaurant. Rooms here cost US$15 per person including breakfast.

Also popular is the *Shehe Guest House* (☎ 33188), in the centre of Jambiani village, which offers rooms with shared bath, two beds, fan and mosquito net for US$8 per person, including breakfast. Some travellers have recommended the *Lowea Beach Bungalow* which costs US$20 per person including breakfast.

At Nungwi the cheaper places to stay are off to the left of the village as you arrive from the south. The first you come to is *Baraka Bungalows*, with doubles at US$10 per person including breakfast. Camping is permitted on the adjacent beach (US$3 per tent).

Getting There & Away To get to the east coast beaches, you'll have to take a local bus, hire a taxi or rent your own motorcycle or vehicle. The bus station is on Creek Rd opposite the market. Taxis to the east coast tend to be quite expensive. Count on around US$50 to Bwejuu, Paje or Jambiani for a car shared between up to five people.

National Parks & Wildlife Reserves

Like Kenya, Tanzania has a number of world-famous game parks including the Serengeti National Park and the Ngorongoro Crater with the Olduvai Gorge sandwiched between them, plus, of course, Mt Kilimanjaro.

There are other parks in the western and southern parts of the country though access can be either problematical, expensive or both. Accommodation can also be limited if you're not camping. This doesn't mean that the parks aren't worth visiting – they certainly are, especially the Selous Game Reserve which is Tanzania's largest park.

The national parks are open from 6 am to 7 pm. You are not permitted to drive in the parks at any other time.

Park Entry Fees

All foreign visitors must pay the national park fees in hard currency (cash or travellers' cheques). The cost is US$20 per person per day, plus US$30 for a small vehicle (Land Rover size) or US$150 for a large vehicle. Camping costs US$20 per person per night, but some sites are classed as 'special', and so have a special price – US$40!

The only exception to this fee structure is at Gombe Stream National Park on Lake Tanganyika where the entry fee is US$100.

See Organised Safaris in the Getting Around section earlier in this chapter for details of companies offering safaris.

ARUSHA NATIONAL PARK

Although it's one of Tanzania's smallest parks, Arusha is one of its most beautiful and spectacular. It's also one of the few that you're allowed to walk in (accompanied by a ranger), yet few travellers appear to visit it.

The park's main features are **Ngurdoto Crater** (often dubbed Little Ngorongoro), the **Momela Lakes** and rugged **Mt Meru** (4556m), which overlooks the town of Arusha. Because of the differing altitudes within the park (from 1500m to over 4500m) and the geological structure, there are several vegetation zones which support appropriate animal species.

It's possible to see a good deal of the park in just one day – the Ngurdoto Crater, Momela Lakes and the lower slopes of Mt Meru – assuming you're in a vehicle. But this won't give you the chance to walk around, so it's much better to spend two days here, staying overnight at a *camp site*, the *Momela Rest House* or the *Momela Lodge*.

Trekking to the top of Mt Meru at a fairly leisurely pace will take three days. In the dry seasons jogging shoes are sufficient, but if there's a possibility of rain you're advised to wear boots. As for Kilimanjaro, bring along plenty of warm clothing. Temperatures drop to below zero at night up on the saddle and around the peak, and there's often snow there too. You'll need to bring all your own food from Arusha. A guide is compulsory and can be hired from the park headquarters at

Momela. Porters are available and their fees are the same as for porters on Kilimanjaro (see below).

Bookings for the two mountain huts should be made in advance through the park headquarters. It's also a good idea to book a guide in advance here so that you don't waste time waiting around park headquarters.

Companies in Arusha which offer treks on Mt Meru include Hoopoe Adventure Tours (US$390 per person for three days, minimum two people), Tropical Tours (US$480 per person for four days), Euro-Tan (US$280 for three days) and Wild Spirit Safari (US$280 per person for three days).

Getting There & Around

The park is 21km from Arusha and is reached by turning off the main Arusha to Moshi road at the signpost for the national park and Ngare Nanyuki.

There's an excellent series of gravel roads and tracks within the park which will take you to all the main features and viewing points. Most are suitable for saloon cars, though some of the tracks get slippery in the wet seasons (October and November and between March and May). There are also a few tracks which are only suitable for 4WDs.

When driving around the park you don't need a guide, but if you intend to walk, an armed guide or ranger is compulsory because of the danger of buffalo. A guide or ranger is also compulsory if you intend to trek on Mt Meru. Guides and rangers can be hired for US$10 a day from the park headquarters at Momela.

While you can drive or walk around the Ngurdoto Crater rim, you are not allowed to walk down to the crater floor.

GOMBE STREAM NATIONAL PARK

Primarily a chimpanzee sanctuary, this tiny park covers 52 sq km on the shores of Lake Tanganyika between Kigoma and the Burundian border, stretching between the lake shore and the escarpment a little further inland. It used to be popular with travellers going to or from Burundi, but is much less visited these days.

The park is the site of Jane Goodall's research station, which was set up in 1960. It's a beautiful place and the chimps are great fun.

Entry to the park costs US$100 per person for each 24-hour period spent there.

Places to Stay & Eat

Camping is only possible with special permission, which means most travellers stay at the 'hostel'. It consists of huts (which are caged to keep the baboons out), each with six beds and a table and chairs. A bed costs US$10 per night. Bring all your own food, though eggs and fish are sometimes available at the station.

Getting There & Away

There are no roads to Gombe Stream, so the only way in is to take one of the lake taxis. These are small, motorised wooden boats which service the lake-shore villages all the way from Kigoma to the Burundian border.

The lake taxis leave from the small village of Kalalangabo, about 3km north of Kigoma, usually between 9 and 10 am. The trips to Gombe Stream and from there to Kagunga (the last village in Tanzania) take about three hours each and cost US$1 per person for each leg of the journey.

MT KILIMANJARO NATIONAL PARK

An almost perfectly shaped volcano which rises sheer from the plains, Mt Kilimanjaro is one of the continent's most magnificent sights. Snowcapped and not yet extinct, at 5895m it is the highest peak in Africa.

From cultivated farmlands on the lower levels, it rises through lush rainforest onto alpine meadow and finally up a barren lunar landscape to the summit.

It is a traveller's dream to scale the summit, watch the dawn break and gaze out over vast expanses of East African bushland.

Trekking on Kilimanjaro

Who would come to Africa and not climb Kilimanjaro? Certainly not many, but there are a number of things you should know before planning a trek. Firstly, independent trekking is not allowed – all treks must be organised through a tour company. When this rule was introduced budget travellers saw it as a major blow, but it has not changed things very much. Even before the new regulation, it was obligatory to take a guide and porter, and pay park entry fees. Arranging a trek on Kili used to be a real hassle, requiring all sorts of wheeling and dealing between guides, porters and park officials, which often spoilt the trek itself. But now procedures are much simpler, without affecting costs much, as there are a lot of trekking companies competing for business. At the bottom end of the market, some companies arrange treks that are only slightly more expensive than the old DIY price.

Secondly, there's the cost to consider. Most treks are all-inclusive; the cost includes park entry fees, hut fees, rescue fees, meals, guide, porters and usually transport to the park gate, but excludes the hire of camping gear, boots or clothing. Standard five day

(four night) treks up Kili's Marangu Route start at US$350 to US$450 per person. At the absolute bottom end of this price range don't be surprised if your hut is double booked, meals on the small side and porters desperate for tips. Better quality trips on the Marangu Route go from US$500. Some outfits allow you to save more money if you provide your own food, do your own cooking and carry your own bag. You still need a guide though, and he needs a porter even if you don't!

Whatever price you pay, remember that for standard Marangu treks, at least US$300 goes on park fees. With these figures in mind, we honestly can't see how some of the budget outfits make a legal profit.

Unfortunately, because trekking on Kili is seen as expensive, many people try to walk up and down in the shortest time possible. Do not fall into this trap. You should not feel that it is essential to reach Uhuru Peak, or that you have 'failed' if you don't. If time (or money) is limited, you'd be far better off

spending US$350 in another part of East Africa. If you really want to sample Kili, instead of stubbornly pushing for the summit, consider walking up to one of the midway huts and reaching The Saddle, to the appreciate the splendour of the mountain from there before descending. The park has plans to introduce lower routes specifically for people who want to do this.

You can trek on Kilimanjaro at any time of year, but there's usually a lot of rain during April, May and November. It's also best to avoid the Christmas-New Year period, as all huts on the Marangu Route are booked out.

Too many people try to do Mt Kilimanjaro without sufficient acclimatisation and end up with altitude sickness or, at the very least, nausea and headaches. This is obviously going to detract from your enjoyment and prevents quite a few people from reaching the summit. Scaling a 5895m mountain is no joy ride!

To give yourself the best chance of reaching the top, it's a very good idea to stay at the *Horombo Hut* for two nights instead of one, though even this will not guarantee plain sailing.

There's a very funny but accurate description of what it's like trekking on Kilimanjaro in Mark Savage's *Kilimanjaro – Map & Guide*. Make sure you read it! For more detailed information on all aspects of Kilimanjaro, including the standard Marangu Route and the other longer (and more expensive) routes up the mountain, refer to Lonely Planet's *Trekking in East Africa*.

No specialist equipment is required to trek on Kilimanjaro but you do need strong boots and plenty of warm clothing, including gloves, a hat and waterproof overclothes. Even if you stay in the huts on the Marangu Route you also need a sleeping bag and a small mattress or air bed. These can be hired from the two hotels in Marangu village or at the park entrance.

If the huts are fully booked you'll have to camp, and if that's the case, make absolutely sure there are sufficient tents for all of you before setting off.

However you arrange your trek, the guide and porters will expect tips at the end. Be generous about this but don't be profligate. Allow about US$10 per day for the guide and US$5 per day for each porter shared between however many of you there are in your group. Nevertheless, you can expect a hassle and even threats to abandon you on the summit unless you tip them before the descent and by an amount which the guide considers he can squeeze out of you. A lot of people have had nasty altercations about this. You must head this sort of nonsense off before you start. Have it clearly understood that the tips will be given *only on completion of the trek*, and don't compromise on this.

Altitude Sickness
Be aware of the dangers of high altitude sickness. In extreme cases it can be fatal. There are no known indicators as to who might suffer from altitude sickness (fitness, age and previous high altitude experience all seem to be irrelevant), and the only cure is an immediate descent to lower altitudes. See the Health Appendix at the back of the book for more details. ■

Trekking Companies
Competition for business is fierce in both Moshi and Arusha, but it's probably true to say that the cheapest deals are available in Moshi rather than Arusha. This is not always the case, particularly if you want good accommodation the night before and the night after a trek, as some safari companies in Arusha can offer deals on hotel accommodation which you would not be able to match through your own efforts. Treks can also be arranged in Marangu village, a few kilometres before the main entry gate.

If you want a well-organised trek with good food, your heavy gear carried by porters who don't 'disappear' halfway through the trip, and guaranteed transport back to Moshi or Arusha at the end of the climb, think in terms of US$450 per person minimum.

Moshi Check out the following companies:

Keys Hotel
> PO Box 933, Moshi (☎ 52250; fax 50073; email keys@form-net.com)
> This friendly hotel runs good trips: five days on the Marangu Route is US$540 for four people, extra day US$125.

Kilimanjaro Crown Birds Tours & Safaris
> PO Box 9519, Moshi (☎ 51162; fax 52038).
> Its office is in Indoroko Hotel. Five days on the Marangu Route costs US$530 for groups over three, plus US$80 per extra day.

Kilimanjaro Guide Tours & Safaris
> PO Box 210, Moshi (☎ 50120; fax 51220)
> Its office is opposite the Moshi Hotel. It quotes five-day Marangu Route treks at US$550 per person for two or three people, or US$520 for four to six, but we've heard from travellers who have got this trip for US$400. An extra day costs US$100.

Samjoe Tours
> PO Box 1467, Moshi (☎ 52136)
> This company's office is under the Coffee Tree Hotel. A cheap and cheerful outfit, it offers standard five-day Marangu treks for US$420 for two people or US$380 each for six.

Shah Tours & Travel
> PO Box 1821, Moshi (☎ 52370; fax 51449)
> This company's office is on Mawenzi Rd between the clock tower and the bus station. It mainly deals with groups arranged by agents overseas, but will cater for individuals and small parties on the spot. Treks are not the cheapest, but they are well run and good value. For walk-in clients, five-day treks up the Marangu Route cost US$450 starting from Marangu (you can get there by bus, or arrange transport at US$35 for four people).

Trans-Kibo Travels
> PO Box 1320, Moshi (☎/fax 52017)
> This outfit's office is at the YMCA. It's a long-standing and reliable company, offering five-day treks on the Marangu Route from US$500 for groups of four, up to US$570 for two or three people, although prices seem to be negotiable.

Zara Tours
> PO Box 210 (☎/fax 50120)
> This company's office is behind the Moshi Hotel. It's a no-frills outfit, starting at a bargain-basement US$350 for five-day Marangu treks for groups of five or more.

Marangu Village North-east of Moshi, on the road up to the park headquarters and main entrance to Kilimanjaro National Park, are several companies and hotels which operate treks.

Alpine Tours
> PO Box 835 (☎ Marangu 163; fax Moshi (055) 50096)
> This company has its office in the shop at Marangu Gate. You can turn up and arrange budget five-day trips up the Marangu Route on the spot, to leave next day. Groups of three or more pay US$510 per person.

Ashanti Lodge
> PO Box 6004, Arusha
> Budget operator with standard five-day Marangu Route treks from around US$400 to US$450.

Babylon Lodge
> PO Box 227, Marangu (☎ 5 or Arusha 2253; fax 8220)
> Standard five-day treks on the Marangu Route go for US$400 to US$450 per person. Prices are all-inclusive and negotiable.

Marangu Hotel
> PO Box 40, Moshi (☎ 50639; fax 51307; email marangu@users.africaonline.co.ke)
> A good quality and very well-established operation, currently in its sixth *decade* of arranging treks on Kili. Five-day treks on the Marangu Route cost US$350, plus US$70 per extra day, including transport to/from the park gate, food, guides and porters, but excluding park fees. The hotel can also help you do the Marangu Route 'the hard way', by reserving huts and providing the mandatory guide and his porter, while you provide your own food and equipment, do your own cooking and carry your own rucksack. This costs US$170, plus park fees.

Arusha If you do book through an Arusha tour company, make sure they're not going to subcontract it out to a Moshi company – otherwise, you'll have given up your ability to negotiate and will end up paying two lots of commission.

Equatorial Safaris
> 4th floor, Serengeti Wing, Arusha International Conference Centre, PO Box 2156, Arusha (☎ 7006 or ☎ 3302; fax 2617)
> This long-established company does a good value five day Marangu Route trek for US$675, which covers everything, including transport both ways between Arusha and the park gate. This is ideal if you're short of time. A seven day luxury version of the same trip, including two full-board hotel nights, costs US$850.

Hoopoe Adventure Tours

PO Box 2047, Arusha (☎ 7011, 7541; fax 8226)
This company's office is on India St. It's a high-quality outfit, mainly organising wildlife safaris. It also arranges treks on Kilimanjaro; a five day trek on the Marangu Route plus accommodation at the Marangu Hotel before and after the trek is US$790 per person in groups of four.

Roy Safaris

PO Box 50, Arusha (☎ 2115, 8010, 2800; fax 8892)
This company's office is just off Sokoine Rd (Arusha's main street), about 250m down from the clock tower. It's a straightforward, reliable outfit, doing standard wildlife safaris, and five-day Marangu Route treks on Kili from US$520.

LAKE MANYARA NATIONAL PARK

Lake Manyara National Park is generally visited as the first stop on a safari which takes in this park as well as Ngorongoro and Serengeti. It's generally a bit of a letdown, apart from the hippos, since the large herds of elephant which used to inhabit the park have been decimated in recent years.

Even the water birds which come to nest here (greater and lesser flamingos in particular) can usually only be seen from a distance because there are no roads to the lake shore.

Places to Stay

There are two camp sites just outside the park entrance, which is down the road from the village of Mto-wa-Mbu. *Camp Site No 2* is probably the better.

Avoid camping at any sites within the park, as they're all so-called 'special camps', which will cost you US$40 per person per night.

Budget and mid-range accommodation is available in Mto-wa-Mbu village.

MAHALE MOUNTAINS NATIONAL PARK

This national park, like Gombe Stream, is mainly a chimpanzee sanctuary but you won't find it marked on most maps since it was only created in mid-1985. It's on the knuckle-shaped area of land which protrudes into Lake Tanganyika about halfway down the lake, opposite the Zaïrese port of Kalemie.

Unlike virtually all other national parks in

Tanzania, this is one in which you can walk around – there are no roads in any case. Very few tourists come here because of the remoteness of the area, but it's well worth it if you have the time and initiative.

The best time to visit is between May and October.

Places to Stay

Camping is allowed in specific areas if you have equipment (otherwise you may be able to hire some) and camping fees are US$20 per person per day. There's also a *guesthouse* at Kasiha village, though the facilities are still very limited. Bring all your food requirements from Kigoma, since meals are not available. It's a good idea to check with the park headquarters in Kigoma for information on current weather conditions, transport and accommodation before setting off.

Getting There & Away

The only way to get to the park is by lake steamer from Kigoma using either the MV *Liemba* or the MV *Mwongozo*. You have to disembark at Lagosa (otherwise known as Mugambo), usually in the middle of the night, and take a small boat to the shore. From Lagosa, charter a small boat from the local fishers or merchants for the trip to Kasoge (about three hours).

Because you will be reliant on the lake steamers for getting into and out of Mahale, you may have to stay there for a whole week. This is obviously going to be expensive in terms of park entry fees and camping fees. It also means you'll have to bring enough food with you from Kigoma to last a week.

MIKUMI NATIONAL PARK

This 3237-sq-km park sits astride the main Dar es Salaam to Mbeya highway, about 300km from Dar es Salaam. Not many budget travellers visit this park, probably because of the lack of cheap accommodation, but there is a lot of wildlife to be seen.

Mikumi is often visited as a weekend outing from Dar es Salaam and most of the safari companies with branches in Dar es Salaam offer trips here.

Places to Stay

For those on a budget, there are three *camp sites* in the park (US$20 per person per night), and a *hostel* at the park headquarters, which has a room for 50 people. None of the camp sites has water, but they do have toilets and firewood. If you're staying at the hostel, bring your own bedding. There are toilet and cooking facilities. Bookings for the hostel can be made through the Chief Park Warden, Mikumi National Park, PO Box 62, Mikumi, Morogoro.

Considerably higher in price are the luxury *Mikumi Wildlife Tented Camp* (☎ 68631 in Dar es Salaam) and the expensive *Mikumi Wildlife Lodge*, (☎ 27671), owned by the TTC, PO Box 2485, Dar es Salaam.

NGORONGORO CONSERVATION AREA

There can be few people who have not heard, read or seen film or TV footage of this incredible 20km-wide volcanic crater with its 600m walls packed with just about every species of wildlife to be found in East Africa. The views from the crater rim are incredible, and though the wildlife might not look too impressive from up there, when you get to the bottom you'll very quickly change your mind.

Despite the steep walls of the crater, there's considerable movement of animals in and out – mostly to the Serengeti, since the land between the crater and Lake Manyara is intensively farmed. Yet it remains a favoured spot for wildlife because there's permanent water and pasture on the crater floor.

You can visit Ngorongoro at any time of year, but during the months of April and May it can be extremely wet and the roads difficult to negotiate. Access to the crater floor may be restricted at this time.

Olduvai Gorge

The Olduvai Gorge made world headlines in 1959 following the discovery by the Leakeys of fossil fragments of the skull of one of the ancestors of *Homo sapiens*. The fragments were dated back to 1.8 million years.

In 1979 Mary Leakey made another important discovery in the shape of foot-prints at **Laetoli** which she claimed were of a man, woman and child. They were dated back to 3.5 million years, and since they were made by creatures who walked upright, this pushed the origins of the human race much further back than had previously been supposed.

The gorge itself isn't of great interest unless you are archaeologically inclined. However, it has acquired a kind of cult attraction among those who just want to visit the site where the evolution of early humans presumably took place.

Places to Stay & Eat

On the crater rim, there is a choice of five expensive lodges and two camp sites. Most campers stay at the *Simba* site on the crater rim, about 2km beyond Crater Village. The site is guarded, costs US$10 per person and has showers, toilets and firewood. There is also a *camp site* down in the crater, but it has no facilities and you must take a ranger with you. It costs US$40 per person.

The lodges start from US$45/70 for a single/double, the cheapest being the *Rhino Lodge*. Bookings can be made in Arusha at the Ngorongoro Conservation Area Authority (☎ 3339), PO Box 776, Arusha. The other lodges are the *Ngorongoro Wildlife Lodge* (☎ Arusha 2711); the *Ngorongoro Crater Lodge* (☎ Arusha 7803); the stunningly beautiful *Ngorongoro Sopa Lodge* (☎ 6886), PO Box 1823, Arusha; and the *Ngorongoro Serena Lodge* (☎ 8175).

The only option at Olduvai Gorge is the very expensive *Ndutu Safari Lodge* (☎ 6702), PO Box 6084, Arusha, or PO Box 150, Karatu.

For campers' provisions, there's a general store at Crater Village but it only has a limited range of foodstuffs, so bring supplies with you from Arusha or eat at the lodges.

Karatu Karatu (commonly known as 'Safari Junction') is about halfway between Lake Manyara and Ngorongoro. Virtually all camping safaris out of Arusha use this place as an overnight stop in order to economise on park entry fees for Ngorongoro.

TANZANIA

The cheapest place to stay here is *Safari Junction Camp* (☎ Karatu 50), where you can either camp (with your own tent, or hire one for US$2) or rent a log cabin (US$20/30 a single/double). Meals are available.

Getting There & Away
If you are trying to get to the crater independently, there are private buses from Arusha at least as far as Karatu but it may be difficult to find anything going beyond there. There are also plenty of trucks as far as Karatu.

Only 4WD vehicles are allowed down in the crater. Whether you are driving your own vehicle or are on an organised tour, you must take a park ranger with you (US$20 per day).

RUAHA NATIONAL PARK
This 13,000-sq-km park was created in 1964 from half of the Rungwa Game Reserve. Like the Selous, it's a wild, undeveloped area and access is difficult, but there's a lot of wildlife here as a result.

Visiting the park is only feasible in the dry season, from June to December. During the rest of the year the tracks are virtually impassable. The grass is long between February and June, restricting wildlife viewing.

If you're interested in helping this park to expand facilities, control poaching, reduce fire risks and obtain suitable equipment for park maintenance, contact the Friends of Ruaha Society (☎ 20522), PO Box 60 in Mufindi or PO Box 786 in Dar es Salaam.

Places to Stay
Camping is permitted around the park headquarters at Msembe and at various other sites for the usual fee (US$20 per person per night). Also at the park headquarters is a permanent *camp* consisting of bandas equipped with beds. Essential equipment is provided but you must bring your own food and drink. Bookings for the bandas can be made through the Park Warden, Ruaha National Park, PO Box 369, Iringa.

Possibly the most mellow place to stay if you have the money is *Ruaha River Camp*, which is constructed on and around a rocky kopje overlooking the Great Ruaha River. A

double banda with full board costs US$65. It's excellent value and highly recommended. Reservations should be made through Foxtreks Ltd, PO Box 84, Mufindi, or through Coastal Travels Ltd (☎ 37479), Ali Mwinyi Rd, Dar es Salaam.

Getting There & Away
There is a good all-weather road from Iringa to the park headquarters via Mloa (112km). This involves crossing the Great Ruaha River by ferry at Ibuguziwa, which is within the park. The drive should take about four hours. Hitching isn't really feasible, so you'll need your own vehicle or to go on an organised safari.

SELOUS GAME RESERVE
The little-visited, 54,600-sq-km Selous ('sel-oo') is probably the world's largest wildlife reserve. It is quintessential East African wilderness; most of it is trackless and almost impossible to traverse during the rainy season, when floods and swollen rivers block access. The best time to visit is from July to March. In any case, the lodges and camp sites are closed from April to June.

In the northern end of the reserve, where the Great Ruaha River flows into the Rufiji, is **Stiegler's Gorge**, probably the best known feature of the park.

The Selous is one of the few national parks which you are allowed to explore on foot. Walking safaris are conducted from all four camps in the reserve. Boat trips up the Rufiji River are offered by the Rufiji River and Mbuyu safari camps and are a very popular way of exploring the area.

Places to Stay
All park facilities are concentrated in the extreme northern end, and consist of four *lodges* and luxury *tented camps*. There are no budget facilities other than two *camp sites*, one at Mtemere and another close to Matambwe at the Beho Beho bridge.

Getting There & Away
Hitching to Selous Game Reserve is virtually out of the question. To get there, you'll need

to join an organised safari, drive your own vehicle, or go by train and arrange to have someone from a lodge pick you up.

SERENGETI NATIONAL PARK

Serengeti, which covers 14,763 sq km, is Tanzania's most famous wildlife park and is contiguous with the Masai Mara Game Reserve in neighbouring Kenya. Here you can get a glimpse of what much of East Africa must have looked like in the days before the 'great white hunters'. On the seemingly endless and almost treeless plains of the Serengeti are literally millions of hoofed animals.

Nowhere else will you see wildebeest, gazelle, zebra and antelope in such concentrations. The wildebeest, of which there are up to two million, is the chief herbivore of the Serengeti and also the main prey of the large carnivores such as lions and hyenas. The wildebeest is well known for its annual migration.

Places to Stay

Most budget travellers stay at one or other of the *public camp sites* (US$20 per person). There are 12 of these – six at Seronera, two at Kirawira, one at Ndabaka, two at Lobo and one at Bologonja – but facilities are minimal. Some don't even have water, so it's best to bring everything you'll need. In addition, there are six *special camp sites* (US$40 per person) – one at Seronera, two at Kirawira, two at Lobo and one at Bologonja – and 12 *wilderness camp sites* (US$40 per person) – three at Moru, one at Hembe, one at Soit le

Motonyi, two at Naabi Hill and five at Lake Lagarja (Ndutu).

The only other options are the expensive camps and lodges, among them: the *Kijereshi Tented Camp* (Mwanza ☎ 40139), PO Box 190, Mwanza, US$70 a double including taxes and breakfast; the *Ndutu Safari Lodge* (see Olduvai Gorge); the superb *Seronera Wildlife Lodge*, US$110/138 for a single/double; the equally superb *Lobo Wildlife Lodge*, US$110/138 for B&B; the *Serengeti Sopa Lodge* (☎ 6886), PO Box 1823, Arusha; and the *Serengeti Serena Lodge* (☎ 8175), US$116/172.

TARANGIRE NATIONAL PARK

This national park covers quite a large area south-east of Lake Manyara. The park fills with herds of zebra, wildebeest and kongoni, which stay until October when the short rains allow them to move to new pastures. The best season to see birds is from October to May.

Tsetse flies are a pest in this park at certain times of year (February and March), so keep the windows of your vehicle closed when not taking photographs.

Places to Stay & Eat

There are two *public camp sites* where you can pitch a tent for the usual price (US$20). Also, there are six so-called *special camp sites* at US$40 per person per night.

The beautifully sited *Tarangire Safari Lodge* (☎ 7182), PO Box 2703, Arusha, set on a bluff overlooking the Tarangire River, is run by Serengeti Select Safaris. It is expensive at US$52/65 for singles/doubles.

Togo

For many years, Togo was one of West Africa's top spots for travellers. Deserted beaches, hiking and butterfly spotting in the highlands, a fascinating cultural mix and generally enthusiastic and friendly people all made the country an overlander's goal. Then, political turbulence in the early 1990s, together with improving situations in neighbouring Ghana and Benin, reduced the stream of travellers to a trickle.

The tide seemed to be turning in recent years with establishment of a fragile stability and a surge in economic growth. However, an entrenched and oppressive government autocracy has dimmed Togo's outward lustre and left many Togolese frustrated and disillusioned. The next few years will be critical ones. Unfortunately, although many of Togo's charms are as enticing as ever, prospects for a lasting turnaround in the fortunes of this little country remain dubious.

Facts about the Country

HISTORY

Togo's largest ethnic group, the Ewe, migrated between the 14th and 16th centuries from Nigeria to the coast of Togo, where they lived in loose village groupings, relatively isolated from other tribes. In the north, the dominant Kabre were more cohesive, although their influence was limited to the areas surrounding their strongholds near Kara and Sokodé. With the establishment of a European presence in the 16th century, the zone created by this power vacuum was exploited as a conduit for the slave trade centred on the powerful Dahomey kingdom to the east and the Ashanti kingdom to the west.

Togo became a German protectorate in 1894. In 1914 it was split between the British and the French under a UN mandate in which

REPUBLIC OF TOGO
Area: 56,600 sq km
Population: 4.1 million
Population Growth Rate: 3.2%
Capital: Lomé
Head of State: President General Gnassingbé Eyadéma
Official Language: French
Currency: West African CFA Franc
Exchange Rate: CFA 500 = US$1
Per Capita GNP: US$310
Inflation: 6%
Time: GMT/UTC

Highlights
* Hiking in the beautiful hill country surrounding Kpalimé
* Lake Togo, with its watersports and interesting surrounding market towns; also centre of Togo's voodoo cult
* Fascinating village compounds, markets and mountain scenery in the Kandé area

the British acquired the western portion while the French oversaw the larger eastern section. This partition divided the populous Ewe and has been the source of tensions which persist to this day. A 1956 plebiscite in the British part of the colony led to it being incorporated into Ghana, which was about to be granted independence. French Togo gained independence in 1960 under the leadership of Sylvanus Olympio who became the country's first president. Although several

unification movements were spawned during this period, integration was never realised, due in part to diverging decolonisation policies among the British and the French, as well as to interclan rivalries among the Ewe. The opportunity to merge in some form now seems to have passed.

In 1963, Olympio was killed in a military coup and replaced by Nicolas Grunitzky, who in turn was overthrown by General Gnassingbé Eyadéma in another military coup in 1967. Eyadéma, a Kabre from the north, and his party, the Rassemblement du Peuple Togolais (RPT) have ruled since, except for a brief interlude in 1991. For years, this autocratic, military-based regime tolerated no opposition and dissidents were actively sought out. As a result, many Togolese sought political asylum abroad and, until recently, most of the opposition leaders lived in exile in Paris.

Eyadéma resisted local and international demands for democratic change until early 1991 when violent demonstrations in Lomé forced the president to agree to a national conference paving the way for multiparty elections. At the conference, a transitional government was installed with Joseph Koffigoh, a prominent lawyer, at its head. But this situation lasted only briefly, as the new government became the target of a brutal terror campaign carried out by the army which was still loyal to Eyadéma. After a year, Koffigoh dissolved his government and formed a coalition with Eyadéma.

Once back in power, Eyadéma postponed the promised elections, prompting exasperated trade unions to call a general strike in November 1992. The strike continued for months and paralysed Togo's economy. Banks and industries were closed, phosphates and cocoa (the country's main exports) lay stranded in deserted ports, and tourism collapsed. A night curfew was imposed in Lomé and protesters were shot dead by police. Meanwhile, some 250,000 people fled into neighbouring countries.

The election finally went ahead in August 1993 and Eyadéma was re-elected with 96% of the vote in a contest boycotted by the opposition and denounced by international monitoring groups. Parliamentary elections followed in 1994, and a coalition of two opposition parties won a slim majority over pro-Eyadéma forces. However, the polling was boycotted by the Union des Forces du Changement (UFC), the party of Eyadéma's main rival, Gilchrist Olympio, son of the former president, and marred by the killing of three opposition members and a much disputed result. In post-election manoeuvring to maintain his hold on the government, Eyadéma named Edem Kodjo, leader of the smaller of the two prevailing coalition parties, as prime minister. In late 1996, Kodjo resigned following a series of opposition defeats in by-elections, leaving Eyadéma and his RPT once again in total control of the Togolese political scene.

Although Togo's economy has registered several years of positive growth, it is starting to slow, fettered by an uncertain political climate and widespread disillusionment over the pace of political reform. With no credible parliamentary opposition and with frustration increasing among disenfranchised parties, political stability is likely to remain fragile. The next few years will be critical ones for Togo, with attention on Eyadéma to see whether he supports the steps necessary to ensure a revival of the dynamism and charm that once were among the country's hallmarks.

GEOGRAPHY & CLIMATE

Togo's coastline measures only 56km, yet the country stretches inland for 540km. Mountainous, forested areas in the centre yield to savannah in the south and north. The rainy season is from April to July, with shorter rains in October and November. Temperatures in Lomé average 27°C.

ECOLOGY & ENVIRONMENT

With an average of 66 people per square km, Togo is one of the most densely populated countries in West Africa. Land pressures, combined with lack of government commitment, scarce financial resources, and entrenched traditional practices such as slash-and-burn agriculture, have taken a heavy toll on the environment.

The situation in Togo's parks is particularly bad. There is very little wildlife remaining, and poaching and deforestation go on unhindered. In Kéran, Togo's premier national park, it is hard to find any of the antelope, baboon and other animals for which the reserve was once renowned.

Togo's coastline is also in a precarious position. Since construction of a second pier at Lomé's port, several beaches have disappeared and large sections of the original coastal road to Aného are now under the sea. Pollution compounds the situation, as city sewage and runoff from Togo's profitable phosphate parastatal are dumped into the sea.

Although Togo has a surprisingly comprehensive environmental code, environmental policy is not a government priority and there is no enforcement of existing provisions. There are numerous projects at the micro-level being carried out by non-governmental organisations, the Peace Corps and other groups which are having a positive impact.

Ewe & the Afterlife

Togo's diverse cultural composition has given rise to a rich panoply of traditional practices. Many of these, such as Ewe funeral rites and conceptions of life and death, have a strong animist element. According to the Ewe, once a person dies their reincarnated soul or *djoto* will come back in the next child born into the same lineage, while their death soul or *luvo* may linger with those still living, seeking attention and otherwise creating havoc. Funerals are one of the most important events in life and involve several nights of drumming and dancing, followed by a series of rituals to help free the soul of the deceased and influence its reincarnation. ■

However, until government attention and funding are focused on environmental issues, it is likely that Togo's remaining resources will continue to be squandered and irretrievably lost.

POPULATION & PEOPLE

Togo is densely populated with over four million inhabitants. There are some 30 tribal groups, the largest of which are the Ewe in the south and the Kabre in the north. Over half the people are animists, 30% Christian and the remainder Muslim.

LANGUAGE

French is the official language. The main African languages are Ewe and Kabre, while Mina is widely used in commerce. For a listing of useful French phrases, see the Language Appendix.

Facts for the Visitor

VISAS

Visas are required for all except nationals of Economic Community of West African States (ECOWAS) countries. They are rarely issued at the airport. However, 48-hour temporary visas are generally available on land entry through Aflao on the Ghanaian-Togo border near Lomé. Proof of yellow fever vaccination is obligatory for entry at the airport, but is not generally required at land crossings or when seeking a visa extension.

Visa Extensions

Visas can be extended at the *sûreté* (police station) in Lomé upon presentation of three photos and US$20 (US$40 for Canadians). The extension is valid for one month (one year for US citizens) and takes at least three days to issue. The visa section is open Monday to Friday from 7.30 to 11.30 am and 2.30 to 5.30 pm, Saturday from 8 am to noon.

Other Visas

Benin

There is no Benin embassy in Lomé, but you can get a visa at the border on the Lomé-Cotonou road. A 48 hour entry visa (extendible in Cotonou) costs US$8, plus two photos.

Burkina Faso, Côte d'Ivoire & Central African Republic

The French consulate (open weekdays from 8 to 11.30 am) issues three-month visas for these countries. All visas cost US$40, require two photos and take 48 hours to be issued.

Ghana

The embassy is open weekdays from 8 am to 2 pm. Three-month visas cost US$20 for Commonwealth citizens and US$24 for other nationals, require four photos and are generally issued within three days.

Nigeria

Visas are issued for residents of Togo only, although your case may be considered if you have a letter of reference from your own embassy or from the Nigerian embassy in your homeland.

EMBASSIES

Togolese Embassies

In Africa there are Togolese embassies or consulates in Congo (Zaïre), Gabon, Ghana, Libya, Nigeria and Senegal. Elswhere there are in Belgium, Canada, France, Germany, Israel and the USA.

Where there is no Togolese embassy, visas are often issued by the French embassy or consulate.

Foreign Embassies in Togo

Foreign embassies and consulates in Lomé include:

Congo (Zaïre)
    325 Blvd du 13 Janvier (no phone)
France
    Rue Bissagne (☎ 212576)
Germany
    Blvd de la Marina, west of Blvd du 13 Janvier (☎ 212338)
Ghana
    8 Rue Paulin Eklou, just off Route de Kpalimé, Tokoin (☎ 213194)
Netherlands
    Rue du Lac Togo, opposite Chez Marox (☎ 211883)
Nigeria
    311 Blvd du 13 Janvier (☎ 213455)

UK
> c/o The British School of Lomé, Résidence du Bénin (☎ 264606)

USA
> corner of Rue Caventou and Rue Vauban (☎ 212991)

MONEY
US$1 = CFA 500

The unit of currency is the West African CFA franc. There are no limits on its import and export within the West African CFA franc zone. Officially, transfers of sums greater than CFA 50,000 outside of the franc zone require routine approval from the Ministry of Finance.

Banks in Togo will not exchange Central African CFA francs nor Ghanaian cedis. Cedis can be exchanged for West African CFA only with moneychangers, but rates are bad and transactions risky. The main branch of the BTCI gives cash withdrawals against Visa card only. Travellers' cheques in either French franc or US dollar denominations can be exchanged in Lomé and other major cities. Proof of purchase is generally required.

POST & COMMUNICATIONS
Poste restante in Lomé is open weekdays from 7 am to 5.30 pm and Saturday from 8 am to noon. It charges US$0.50 per letter and will hold mail for one month.

International telephone calls can be made Monday to Saturday from 7 am to 6 pm and on Sunday from 8 am to noon at the telecommunications building behind the main post office in Lomé. Rates are US$5 per minute to the USA and US$4 to Australia and the UK. You can also send and receive faxes here (US$1 per received page on fax (228) 215706). Incoming faxes are registered and held indefinitely.

The country code for Togo is 228, and area codes are 021, 022 or 023 for Lomé, 050 for Sokodé and 060 for Kara.

DANGERS & ANNOYANCES
In Lomé, it is not safe to walk on the beach or along Blvd de la Marina at night. Muggings on the beach have been reported even during the day. Hassling is common at the night-time checkpoints on the Blvd de la Marina and elsewhere in central Lomé; a foreigner was killed at one in 1996.

Upcountry, police roadblocks can add hours to journeys, as share-taxis and minibuses are often subject to lengthy searches. Any drivers whizzing through the blockades have certainly paid for the privilege.

BUSINESS HOURS
Businesses are open Monday to Friday from 8 am to noon and 3 to 6 pm, Saturday until 12.30 pm. Government offices generally close at 5.30 pm, while banks are open weekdays from 7.30 to 11 am and 2.30 to 4 pm.

PUBLIC HOLIDAYS
Public holidays in Togo are: 1 January, 13 January (Liberation Day), 27 April (Independence Day), 1 May, 21 June, 15 August, 1 November, 25 December, Easter Monday, Ascension, Whit Monday and variable Islamic holidays (see Public Holidays in the Regional Facts for the Visitor chapter).

ACCOMMODATION
The boom, and subsequent decline, in tourism has left Togo with a relatively extensive but dilapidated tourist infrastructure, although many hotels are making a slow comeback. Basic double rooms start at US$5 (slightly more in Lomé) while a comfortable double with fan/air-con and attached bathroom costs US$12/15. As hotels are generally not full, it's often possible to bargain prices down.

Getting There & Away

AIR
Among the airlines which service Lomé are Air France (☎ 216910), Ghana Airways (☎ 215691), Sabena (☎ 217555), KLM (☎ 220946), Aeroflot (☎ 210480), Ethiopian

Airways (☎ 217074) and Air Afrique (☎ 212042). Both Air Afrique and Ethiopian Airlines offer student discounts on international flights.

Tokoin Airport is 6km north-east of central Lomé. There is no departure tax.

LAND
Benin
Minibuses ply the coastal road between Lomé and Cotonou (155km, US$5, 3 hours) throughout the day, although it is generally faster and cheaper to take a share-taxi from Lomé to the border (US$1), and another one from there to Ouidah (US$2) or Cotonou (US$3).

There are also crossings east of Notsé to Tohoun, north-east of Kara at Kemerida, and at Nadoba, in Vallée de Tamberma, but transport on these routes is infrequent and border officials in Benin will not issue visas.

Burkina Faso
Lomé to Ouagadougou (965km, US$20) takes about 36 hours, with minibuses departing daily at 1 pm from Gare de Agbalepedo (Agbalepedo station), 10km north of central Lomé. The entire route is paved, but frequent police checkpoints on both sides make this trip a nightmare. It is saner and slightly cheaper to travel in stages, breaking at Dapaong and continuing early the next morning, with a second change of vehicles at the border. The Burkina Faso border closes at 6.30 pm.

Ghana
The most popular route to Ghana is via Aflao on the coastal road. From central Lomé it's just 2km to the border (US$0.25 in a share-taxi). There are direct minibuses between Lomé and Accra (200km, US$8, three hours). No departure fees are required, although Togolese border officials may try to convince you otherwise.

Several vehicles a day leave from Kpalimé to the border (15km, US$1), from where you can catch onward transport to Kpandu (25km) and on to Accra (250km,

US$3). From Badou there is an easy, although obscure, crossing to the sparsely travelled Hohoe-Yendi road.

In the north, you can cross from Kara (260km) or Sansanné-Mango (220km) to Tamale via Yendi and from Dapaong via Sinkassé to Bawku (70km), although the routes are rough and transport is fairly infrequent.

Getting Around

TRAIN
Togo has three railway lines but only one – Lomé to Blitta via Atakpamé – is operating. The train to Blitta (US$3, one class only) leaves Lomé on Tuesday, Thursday and Saturday at 6.30 am, arriving in Atakpamé (Agbonou station) around 1 pm and in Blitta by 6 pm. The next morning it returns to Lomé. Food can be bought at stations along the way.

CAR
Most major roads are sealed and in fairly good condition with the exception of a badly potholed stretch between Atakpamé and Kara on the main north-south axis.

Private car rental is prohibitively expensive; you're better off negotiating a fare with a taxi.

BICYCLE
Bicycle is an excellent way to explore Togo, and greatly reduces time spent stalled at police checkpoints. Although most secondary roads are unsealed, they are in generally good condition except during the rainy season.

MINIBUS & TAXI
Togo has an extensive network of minibuses, and most vehicles are in reasonable condition. There is a surcharge for luggage, based on size. Be prepared for hard bargaining; for a standard rucksack, the fee should not

exceed US$0.50 for most journeys (from Kara to Lomé, for example).

Some examples of minibus routes and fares are listed in the following table.

Minibus Routes & Fares			
	Distance	Duration	Fares (US$)
From Lomé			
To Aného	45 km	1 hour	$1
Atakpamé	165 km	3 hours	$3
Dapaong	640 km	14 hours	$11
Kara	420 km	8 hours	$6
Kpalimé	130 km	3 hours	$2
Sokodé	345 km	7 hours	$5
From Kara			
To Dapaong	220 km	5 hours	$3
Kandé	60 km	1 hour	$1
Sokodé	75 km	2 hours	$2
From Atakpamé			
To Kpalimé	100 km	2 hours	$2
Badou	85 km	2 hours	$2

Lomé

Central Lomé, with its high-rises, imposing monuments and busy streets, exudes an urbane although rundown air. Enclosing the central area is the semi-circular Blvd du 13 Janvier (otherwise known as Blvd Circulaire). To the south is a stretch of attractive coastline, although it's not recommended for swimming due to strong currents.

Lomé's most vibrant quarters are around the Grand Marché, where streetside sellers hawk all sorts of wares, and further out in Tokoin, Akodessewa and other outlying areas.

Information

Tourist Information The tourist office (☎ 214313) is on Rue du Lac Togo in an unmarked yellow building near Chez Marox. The friendly staff have free maps plus general information on Togo's major attractions. The office is open weekdays from 7 am to noon and 2.30 to 5.30 pm. More detailed maps are on sale for US$6 in Room 105 of the Direction de la Cartographie Nationale near the French consulate.

Travel Agencies SDV Voyages (☎ 212611) on 2 Rue du Commerce is the American Express representative and will assist in booking flights out of Lomé.

Things to See & Do

The **Grand Marché**, a three storey building in the town centre, is bustling every day of the week. You'll find everything here, from food to modern manufactured goods, spare parts and textiles.

For batiks, wooden sculptures, leather work and other crafts, the best place is the quiet **Village Artisanal**, where you can watch the artists at work. It's on Ave du Nouveau Marché and is open Monday to Saturday from 8 am to 5.30 pm.

There are also **artisan stalls** around the corner from Hôtel du Golfe with a good selection of woodwork and other crafts, but be prepared to fend off the touts.

The **Marché des Féticheurs**, 8km east of the centre in Akodessewa, has a diverse assortment of potions, dried animal organs and other items used in traditional medicine. Although the market has become a tourist trap, it's still worth a visit. To get here, go along Route d'Aného to Hôtel Sarakawa, then continue north for 1.5km.

The **National Museum**, behind the Palais des Congrès, houses a collection of historical artefacts, pottery and woodcarvings. It's open weekdays from 8 am to noon and 3 to 6 pm, weekends from 3 to 6 pm. The entrance fee is US$1.

Hôtel Sarakawa has a superb 50m **swimming pool** which non-guests can use for US$4.

Places to Stay

Near the beach, one of the cheapest places is *Salam Motel* (☎ 222534). Cramped, dirty rooms with fan cost US$6 (US$9 with attached bathroom).

Nearby is the much better *Le Maxime*

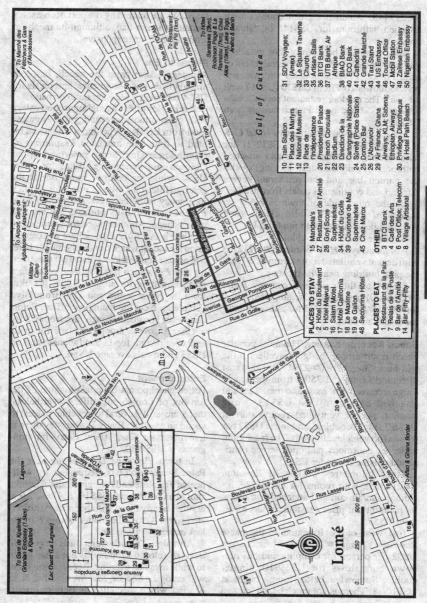

Lomé

PLACES TO STAY
2 Hôtel du Boulevard
4 Hôtel Mawuli
5 Salam Motel
16 Hôtel California
17 Le Maxime
18 Le Gallon
19 Secourina Hôtel
48

PLACES TO EAT
1 Restaurant de la Paix
7 Relais de la Poste
9 Bar de l'Amitié
14 Bar Fifty-Fifty

15 Mandela's
27 Restaurant de l'Amitié
28 Goyi Score
Supermarket
34 Hôtel du Golfe
39 Couronne de Mai
Supermarket
45 Chez Marox

OTHER
3 BTCI Bank
6 Café des Arts
8 Post Office; Telecom
8 Village Artisanal

10 Train Station
11 Place des Martyrs
12 National Museum
13 Place de
l'Indépendance
20 Presidential Palace
21 French Consulate
23 Stadium
23 Direction de la
Cartographie Nationale
24 Sûreté (Police Station)
25 Domino Bar
26 L'Abreuvoir
29 Air France; Ghana
Airways; KLM; Sabena;
Ethiopian Airways
30 Privilege Discotheque
& Hôtel Palm Beach

31 SDV Voyages;
(Amex)
32 Le Square Taverne
33 Church
35 Artisan Stalls
36 BTCI Bank
37 UTB Bank; Air
Afrique
38 BIAO Bank
40 ECO Bank
41 Cathedral
42 Grande Marché
43 Taxi Stand
44 US Embassy
46 Tourist Office
47 Mobil Station
49 Zaïrese Embassy
50 Nigerian Embassy

TOGO

(☎ 217448) which has clean doubles with attached bathroom for US$14/ 24, fan/air-con.

Back from the beachfront, but excellent value, is *Le Galion* (☎ 220030), straight out of rural France. Pleasant doubles with fan and private shower cost from US$10 (US$17 with air-con). The outdoor restaurant serves breakfast for US$2 and good French cuisine from US$6.

In the same area, the attractive *Hôtel California* (☎ 225210) charges US$12/21 for large rooms with fan/air-con and attached bathroom. A paillotte (straw awning) shades the garden bar and the restaurant serves African and continental meals from US$4.

On the other side of town is *Hôtel du Boulevard* (☎ 211591) with clean, good value singles/doubles with fan from US$5/7 (US$11 for an air-con double).

Not far away is *Hôtel Mawuli* (☎ 221275) with decent ventilated rooms from US$7. It's the pink building near the mosque.

Closer to the centre, *Secourina Hôtel* (☎ 216020) has good value singles/doubles for US$15/17 (US$23/25 for attached bathroom and air-con).

Beach Accommodation The most popular beach resort among budget travellers is the laid-back *Chez Alice* (☎ 279172), 12km east of central Lomé and 250m from the beach. Large rooms with mosquito net, fan and attached bathroom cost US$13, while smaller, poorly ventilated rooms start at US$6/7 single/double. Camping is US$2 per person (no vehicles allowed). The restaurant, under an enormous paillotte, serves continental cuisine for under US$5.

Three kilometres west is *Le Ramatou* (☎ 214353), with rooms for US$12/20, including fan/air-con and attached bathroom. Its pleasant but pricey restaurant has meals from US$7.

Just west of Le Ramatou is the passé *Robinson's Plage* (☎ 275814) which charges US$2 per person for camping and has run-down bungalows for US$9/10, single/double. Somewhat better rooms begin at US$10/11. There is not much beach left and

sea views are marred by the port. Robinson's restaurant is not bad, although its meals, at around US$8, are expensive.

Places to Eat
Mandela's, 1km from the beach, has cold draught beer, good brochettes, and meals for US$4 served at a pleasant outdoor patio.

Bar de l'Amitié is a neighbourhood eatery with great atmosphere and good Togolese food from US$1. It's behind a wall and a bit hard to find. The unrelated *Restaurant de l'Amitié* near Goyi Score supermarket, has Guinean and Senegalese dishes for under US$4, while the outdoor *snack bar* at the nearby Hôtel du Golfe is good for a quick meal away from the street. *Restaurant de la Paix* is noisy, but its portions are big and prices cheap. Another place for an inexpensive bite is *Bar Fifty-Fifty*, where you can get good riz sauce; watch out for the salads here.

For excellent African cuisine off the street, try *Pili Pili* which has Togolese meals in a pleasant setting for around US$6. It's 3km from the town centre and 1km from Blvd Circulaire. Near the main post office, *Relais de la Post* has good French fare from US$6.

Chez Marox is a popular place for grills and continental food. Sandwiches start at US$3 and meals average US$6.

Entertainment
Police checkpoints have taken some of the fun out of Lomé's nightlife. Nevertheless, there are still several enjoyable places to spend an evening. Every Wednesday there is live music at *Chez Alice*. Entry for non-guests is US$0.50.

In town, *Privilege Discotheque* near the Palm Beach Hotel is frequented by well-heeled Togolese and foreigners alike. Drinks start at an outrageous US$10. *L'Abreuvoir* is another trendy disco with beers at extortionate prices. Across the road, *Domino Bar* has less expensive *pressions*.

Although it's fairly quiet these days, *Café des Arts* (closed Monday) is not a bad place to while away an evening. Beer connoisseurs will enjoy *Le Square Taverne* on Blvd de la Marina, which specialises in Belgian brews.

Getting There & Away

Taxis and minibuses for Abidjan, Accra, Aného, Togoville, Cotonou, Lagos and the Benin border leave from Gare d'Akodessewa (Akodessewa station), about 1km north of Hôtel Sarakawa. Agbalepedo station, 10km north of the centre, serves all destinations north. Taxis from the Grand Marché to Agbalepedo cost US$0.50. Minibuses to Kpalimé leave from Gare de Kpalimé, 2.5km north of the centre.

Taxis for local destinations leave from the taxi stand south of the market on Rue du Commerce.

Getting Around

Share-taxis around town cost US$0.50 for a short ride. Private taxis charge upwards of US$1; to the airport the fare is US$3 (US$6 from the airport into the city). A share-taxi to the beach resorts east of Lomé costs US$0.50.

Around the Country

ANÉHO

Aného was the colonial capital of Togo until it was moved to Lomé in 1920. There is not much going on these days, but the lagoon setting makes the town a peaceful place to pass an afternoon. Swimming on Aného's beaches is possible but not recommended, as they are not clean and currents can be dangerous.

Places to Stay & Eat

The cheapest place is the friendly *Nous Les Jeunes*, a private home at the north-east end of town. It rents out a few basic rooms with no fans and bucket showers for US$4.

Hôtel Oasis (☎ 310125) is Aného's best. It has rooms for US$14/18 with fan/air-con and attached bathroom, a terrace offering good views of the lagoon and sea, and a pricey but pleasant bar and restaurant. Nearby, the

TOGO

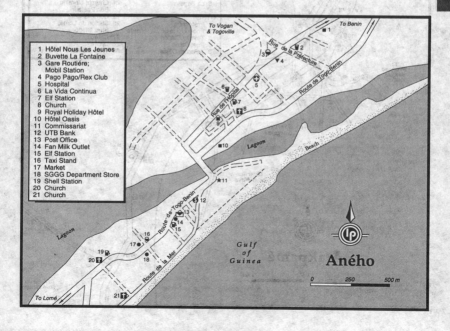

1 Hôtel Nous Les Jeunes
2 Buvette La Fontaine
3 Gare Routiére;
   Mobil Station
4 Pago Pago/Rex Club
5 Hospital
6 La Vida Continua
7 Elf Station
8 Church
9 Royal Holiday Hôtel
10 Hôtel Oasis
11 Commissariat
12 UTB Bank
13 Post Office
14 Fan Milk Outlet
15 Elf Station
16 Taxi Stand
17 Market
18 SGGG Department Store
19 Shell Station
20 Church
21 Church

To Vogan & Togoville

To Benin

Rue de la Préfecture

Route de Togo-Benin

Rue de l'Hopital

Lagoon

Beach

Route de Togo-Benin

Route de la Mer

Gulf of Guinea

Aného

Lagoon

To Lomé

0   250   500 m

rundown *Royal Holiday Hôtel* has dirty rooms with fan for US$7/9 single/double, and no running water.

La Vida Continua is a good place for a drink in the evening with the locals. The women living behind it may offer to make you something to eat. *Pago Pago*, across from the gare routière, has food for US$1, as do numerous street stalls nearby.

Getting There & Away

Aneho's gare routière is at the north-east end of town just beyond the hospital. Some taxis for Lomé also leave from the small taxi stand on the western edge of town near the market.

ATAKPAMÉ

Atakpamé, at 500m altitude, has a pleasant climate and was a favourite hill station for German colonial administrators. It is from here that Togo's famous stilt dancers originate.

Places to Stay & Eat

The cheapest option is the busy *Centre des Affaires Sociales* (☎ 400186) which has beds in crowded four-person rooms with fan for

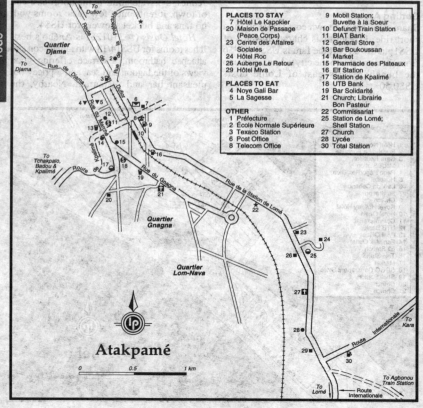

PLACES TO STAY
7 Hôtel Le Kapokier
20 Maison de Passage (Peace Corps)
23 Centre des Affaires Sociales
24 Hôtel Roc
26 Auberge Le Retour
29 Hôtel Miva

PLACES TO EAT
4 Noye Gali Bar
5 La Sagesse

OTHER
1 Préfecture
2 École Normale Supérieure
3 Texaco Station
6 Post Office
8 Telecom Office
9 Mobil Station; Buvette à la Soeur
10 Defunct Train Station
11 BIAT Bank
12 General Store
13 Bar Boukoussan
14 Market
15 Pharmacie des Plateaux
16 Elf Station
17 Station de Kpalimé
18 UTB Bank
19 Bar Solidarité
21 Church; Librairie Bon Pasteur
22 Commissariat
25 Station de Lomé; Shell Station
27 Church
28 Lycée
30 Total Station

Atakpamé

0   0.5   1 km

US$2. More comfortable ventilated doubles cost US$5 (US$6 for attached bathroom and US$8 for air-con).

The Peace Corps' *Maison de Passage* sometimes has spare beds for travellers for US$3. It's on a steep hill overlooking town.

The friendly *Hôtel Miva* (☎ 400437), 2km south of town, has clean ventilated rooms for US$6 (US$5 for smaller rooms in the back annexe).

More central, but not such good value, is *Auberge Le Retour* (☎ 400540), which has basic rooms with bucket shower and fan (if you're lucky) for US$4/8 single/double. Much better is *Hôtel Le Kapokier* (☎ 400284), which has spacious rooms with clean sheets, air-con and shower for US$11, as well as a reasonably priced restaurant.

For dilapidated luxury, climb up to *Hôtel Roc* (☎ 400237) which charges US$19/23 for singles/doubles with air-con and attached bathroom.

La Sagesse has good food at reasonable prices. Across the street, the *Noye Gali Bar* has inexpensive fufu and pâte. *Bar Solidarité* is a popular place for a drink.

Getting There & Away

Minibus & Taxi The main gare routière is at the southern end of town behind the Shell station. Taxis depart in the morning for Lomé (US$3) and Kara (US$4). Taxis to Kpalimé and Badou leave from the Station de Kpalimé south of the market.

Train The closest train station is in Agbonou, 3.5km south-east of Atakpamé centre. Share-taxis from the town centre cost US$0.25. For details of train travel, see the Train section in the Getting Around section of this chapter.

BADOU

Badou, 85km west of Atakpamé, is reached by a sealed but potholed road twisting through beautiful scenery and tropical forest. The best **waterfall** in Togo is near the village of Akloa, 10km south-east of Badou. It's a 35 minute walk from Akloa to the falls on a poorly maintained trail. The negotiable

US$1 entry fee, payable in Akloa, includes a guide if you want one.

Places to Stay & Eat

Bar au Carrefour 2000, opposite the Elf station, has a few stuffy rooms with bucket shower for US$4. *Hôtel Abuta* (☎ 430016) charges US$8/10 for an air-con single/double (US$11/14 with attached bathroom), and allows camping for US$5 per person. Badou's only restaurant is here, with a fixed menu for US$7. Street food is sold on the road leading to the hotel and around Bar 2000.

Getting There & Away

The Atakpamé to Badou road would be a great, although steep, bicycle ride. Bring provisions, as there is little available en route. There is no regular transport on the dirt track linking Badou with Kpalimé; all minibuses and taxis go via Atakpamé.

DAPAONG

Dapaong is a pleasant town near the Burkina Faso border in an important rice and cotton growing area, and is noted for its Saturday **market**. In the corner of the market you'll find tchakpallo, which is made from millet and is the only indigenous beer with a good head.

Dapaong is also the jumping-off point for a visit to the **Réserve de la Fosse aux Lions**, a good example of the sad condition of Togo's parks. Where there once was wild-life, there is now only bushland and the occasional village.

Places to Stay & Eat

The *Centre des Affaires Sociales* (☎ 708029) at the northern end of town is the cheapest option. Basic, grubby doubles are US$4 (US$5/8 with fan/air-con).

Le Sahelien (☎ 708184) on Rue du Marché, south-east of the market, charges US$5 for basic singles, US$7 for ventilated doubles and US$10 for rooms with air-con and attached bathroom.

TOGO

The isolated *Hôtel Lafia*, 800m north of the gare routière, has mediocre doubles for US$7/9 with fan/air-con.

Hôtel Le Campement (☎ 708055), 500m south-west of the market on the Kara road, has comfortable rooms with shower and fan/air-con for US$16/20 and an excellent although expensive restaurant with meals from US$7.

Relais des Savanes, near the market, or the pleasant *Le Fermier* on the northern edge of town both have casual, reasonably priced meals. *Les Retrouvailles*, behind customs, has the same menu as Le Fermier although service can be slow. *Sonu-Bé La Manne Restaurant*, across from the gare routière, has inexpensive meals.

Getting There & Away

Transport to the Ghanaian and Burkina Faso borders (US$1) departs from Station de Korbongou near customs on Route de Nasablé. From the border, you can catch onward transport to Ouagadougou (US$4, 8 to 10 arduous hours) and Koupela (US$3). The main gare routière is 2km south of the town centre.

KARA

Kara is a good base for a trip to the **Vallée de Tamberma** (see later in this chapter) and for excursions to the scenic Mont Kabye region. About 20km north-east of Kara is the village of **Ketao** which on Wednesday holds Togo's second largest market. In Kara you can watch women weavers in the **Groupement de Tissage** making *pagnes* (traditional strips of cloth) at a workshop set up with the help of Peace Corps volunteers.

UTB is the only bank which does foreign exchange.

Places to Stay & Eat

The *Centre des Affaires Sociales* has beds in clean, ventilated two, three or five-bed rooms for US$3 per person. Single rooms with fan are US$5 and air-con doubles US$9.

In the centre, *Hôtel-Restaurant Sapaw* (☎ 601444) has ventilated rooms from

US$3/4, single/double (US$5 for attached bathroom).

Near the gare routière, *Hôtel Tomdé* (☎ 600712) has clean, spacious rooms with fan for US$7, including use of a very large common bath. More expensive, but also good value is *Hôtel de France* (☎ 600342) which has a restaurant and large, attractive rooms with air-con and shower for US$10 (US$11 for attached bathroom).

Le Jardin (☎ 600134) has four small but attractive rooms with air-con and shower for US$16/17 single/double and an excellent, reasonably priced restaurant in a cosy garden setting.

Kara has lots of cheap, good food. *Café-Restaurant Oslo* across from Centre des Affaires Sociales has meals under US$3. Even cheaper are *Bar Columbia* and its nearby sister stall, *Zongo Bar*, which serve fufu and a variety of sauces all day for US$1. *Le Chateau Restaurant* (☎ 606040, closed on Monday) has a wide range of continental and African dishes from US$4.

Getting There & Away

Minibuses leave daily from the Station de Tomdé, east of the market, for Lomé (US$6), Kandé (US$1), Sokodé (US$2), Dapaong (US$3), and the borders of Ghana (US$2) and Benin (US$1). Transport on Wednesday to Ketao is US$0.50.

KPALIMÉ

Kpalimé (pah-lee-may), a resort town near the Ghanaian border, has little to offer in the way of sights, but is a good base for hikes and excursions into the beautiful surrounding hill country. One such trip is to **Pic d'Agou**, Togo's highest mountain at 986m. There are wide views from the top, although visibility is restricted during the harmattan. A share-taxi to the base costs US$0.50.

The other major attractions in this area are the mountains around **Klouto**, 12km north-west of Kpalimé, where the variety of butterflies attracts enthusiasts from all over the world.

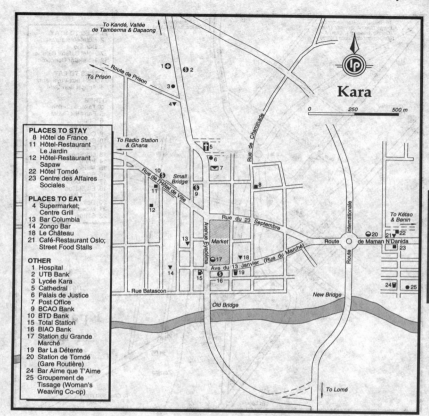

Kara

PLACES TO STAY
8 Hôtel de France
11 Hôtel-Restaurant Le Jardin
12 Hôtel-Restaurant Sapaw
22 Hôtel Tomdé
23 Centre des Affaires Sociales

PLACES TO EAT
4 Supermarket; Centre Grill
13 Bar Columbia
14 Zongo Bar
18 Le Château
21 Café-Restaurant Oslo; Street Food Stalls

OTHER
1 Hospital
2 UTB Bank
3 Lycée Kara
4 Cathedral
5 Palais de Justice
7 Post Office
9 BCAO Bank
10 BTD Bank
15 Total Station
16 BIAO Bank
17 Station du Grande Marché
19 Bar La Détente
20 Station de Tomdé (Gare Routière)
24 Bar Aime que T'Aime
25 Groupement de Tissage (Woman's Weaving Co-op)

In town, the **Centre Artisanal** (closed on Sunday), has local crafts at fixed prices.

Places to Stay & Eat

Chez Solo, 1km south-east of the market, is one of the cheapest places in town. The rooms (US$4) are dirty and the shared bath filthy, but the company is good and Solo is working to improve the place with a new restaurant and paillotte.

Also inexpensive is the noisy but central *Bar Concorde*. Clean rooms with fan and bucket shower start at US$4. The new and quieter *Bafana Bafana* (☎ 410487) has clean

but poorly ventilated rooms for US$7 (US$8 for attached bathroom). *Hotel-Restaurant Domino* (☎ 410187), on a busy intersection, has dark rooms with fan for US$6 (US$12 with air-con).

Further north, near the Centre Artisanal, the new *Auberge Chez Agbeviade* (☎ 410511) has a pleasant, quiet garden and three clean rooms with fan/air-con and attached bathroom for US$8/14.

In Klouto, *Chez Prosper/Auberge des Papillons* has a few simple but OK rooms for US$5. Meals must be ordered in advance. Further up the hill is the cool and peaceful

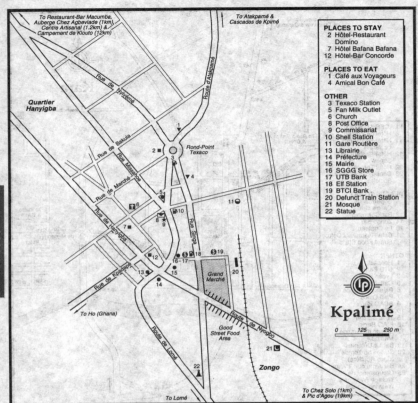

PLACES TO STAY
2 Hôtel-Restaurant
   Domino
7 Hôtel Bafana Bafana
12 Hôtel-Bar Concorde

PLACES TO EAT
1 Café aux Voyageurs
4 Amical Bon Café

OTHER
3 Texaco Station
5 Fan Milk Outlet
6 Church
8 Post Office
9 Commissariat
10 Shell Station
11 Gare Routière
13 Librairie
14 Préfecture
15 Mairie
16 SGGG Store
17 UTB Bank
18 Elf Station
19 BTCI Bank
20 Defunct Train Station
21 Mosque
22 Statue

Kpalimé

0   125   250 m

To Restaurant-Bar Macumba,
Auberge Chez Agbeviade (1km),
Centre Artisanal (1.2km) &
Campement de Klouto (12km)

To Atakpamé &
Cascades de Kpimé

Rue de Nyekonakpoé

Route d'Atakpamé

Quartier
Hanyigba

Rue de Bakula

Rue de Mission

Rond-Point
Texaco

Rue de Marché

Rue de Hanyiga

Rue de Koudani

Rue Sipag

Grand
Marché

Good
Street Food
Area

Route de Nyogbo

Zongo

To Ho (Ghana)

Route de Lomé

To Lomé

To Chez Solo (1km)
& Pic d'Agou (19km)

Le Campement (☎ 485003), which has clean rooms for US$11/16 single/double with attached bathroom and a restaurant with meals for US$8. Camping on the grounds costs US$2 per person. A share-taxi to Klouto costs US$0.50.

In Kpalimé, the attractive open-air *Macumba* (☎ 410086) serves both continental and Togolese food under a paillotte for US$4.

For cheaper fare, try *Amical Bon Café* or *Aux Voyageurs*, both in the centre of town. The *Fan Milk* depot opposite the Shell station sells yoghurt and ice cream.

LAKE TOGO

This relatively shallow lake 30km east of Lomé, believed to be bilharzia free, is a popular weekend getaway for watersports fans.

On the lake's northern shore lies **Togoville**, the centre of Togo's voodoo cult. Wednesday is market day and the best time to visit. The easiest way to get there is by shared canoe (US$0.60) from Agbodrafo on the Lomé-Cotonou road. The departure point is 2km north of the main road, at the end of the signposted dirt track leading to Hôtel Le Lac.

North of Togoville, **Vogan** holds a large and colourful market on Friday, with an impressive selection of fetishes for sale. Transport between Togoville, Aného and Vogan is scarce except on market days.

Places to Stay & Eat
The only accommodation in Togoville is the comfortable *Hôtel Nachtigal* (☎ 216482). Singles/doubles with fan and attached bathroom are US$11/13 (US$15/19 with air-con). Same-sex couples pay a 40% surcharge. The hotel has a pool and a pricey restaurant and bar.

In Vogan, the *Medius Hôtel* (☎ 331000), east of the centre, has ventilated rooms for US$12/25 (US$16/30 with air-con).

In Kpessi, west of Agbodrafo on the lake's southern shore, the beautiful and serenely sited *L'Auberge du Lac* (☎ 270910) has bungalows with fan and attached bathroom for US$14. There is a tourist canoe to Togoville (US$2) and a restaurant with meals for US$7. It's 1km north of the Lomé-Cotonou road and is signposted.

The only other option is the slicker *Hotel Le Lac* (☎ 350005) with air-con rooms for US$25/33 and an expensive restaurant. Both hotels have watersports equipment rental.

Getting There & Away
There are frequent taxis from Lomé's Akodessawa Station which run along the coastal road to Kpessi and Agbodrafo. To get to Togoville by road, continue along the coast to Aného, go past the préfecture and then double back (westward) along the lake for 15km.

Taxis (US$1) between Togoville and Vogan only run on Friday (market day in Vogan) and Wednesday (market day in Togoville).

SANSANNÉ-MANGO
Mango is little more than a convenient overnight stop for those going to or coming from Ghana or Burkina Faso. However, a troop of hippos snort around in a dammed lake on the Oti River, about 7km north-east; you may see them in the early morning or at sunset.

Most people stay at *Hôtel de l'Oti* (☎ 717116), just off the main road at the northern end of town. Basic but relatively clean rooms start at US$4. The friendly, English-speaking owner can help arrange rides; good meals are available for around US$2.

The deserted *Le Campement* has ventilated rooms for US$6/8 single/double. Meals are available upon request, but be prepared for a long wait.

SOKODÉ
Sokodé is a distinctly Muslim town and one of the largest in Togo. It is peopled by the Kotokoli, who migrated in the late 18th century from what is now Mali and brought Islam to the area. However, many animist traditions have survived, one of the most interesting being **Adossa** (Festival of the Knives) which takes place one day after the Prophet's birthday. In this spectacle, men engage in a series of violent dances after drinking a special potion prepared by a marabout (religious saint), which supposedly makes their skin impenetrable.

Places to Stay & Eat
The *Centre des Affaires Sociales*, 1km northwest of the centre on the Bassar road, has basic, dirty rooms for US$3 (US$4 with fan).

A much better option is *Cercle de l'Amitié* next to the BTCI bank, which has simple but clean rooms for US$4 (US$6 with fan and US$7 for attached bathroom). Its new outdoor restaurant should be open by now. Rooms are also available from US$5 at the quiet *Le Campement* (☎ 500786), inconveniently located near customs, south of town. *Buvette Chez-Macau*, down the road, serves Togolese dishes for under US$2.

The popular *Relais de la Cigale* (☎ 500019) on the Lomé road has clean rooms around a nice garden for US$7 and a good restaurant/bar with draught beer and meals for US$5.

Those looking for comfort should head to *La Bonne Auberge* (☎ 500235), 1.5km north of town. Clean rooms with fan/air-con and

TOGO

attached bathroom are US$8/13; the restaurant serves good meals for under US$5.

VALLÉE DE TAMBERMA

The valley of the Tamberma, north-east of Kandé, has a unique collection of fortified villages founded in the 17th century by people fleeing the slaving forays of the kings of Abomey. The family compounds, made of clay, straw and wood, consist of a series of towers connected by thick walls with only one doorway. Inside is an elevated terrace on which the family lives during the day. Animals are kept underneath. The towers, capped with straw, are used for sleeping and grain storage.

As the valley remained isolated until recent times, the culture of the people is relatively intact. It's not easy to get to the villages and even harder to find a family willing to let you look inside their compound. If they do, you can expect to pay. The nearest village is 27km north-east of Kandé on a good dirt track. You are likely to be better received if you go in on bicycle or foot. Otherwise, share taxis (US$0.60) shuttle between Kandé and the fortified village of **Nadoba** on Wednesday (market day in Nadoba) and Friday (market day in Kandé).

There is nowhere to stay in the villages and only a run-down *campement* in Kandé with beds from US$5. A better option is to overnight in **Niamtougou** (26km south of Kandé), where there is accommodation at *Codhani*, a cooperative of handicapped artists with a couple of rooms for US$2. Alternatively, the nearby *Tourist Hôtel* (☎ 650080) has singles/doubles with air-con and attached bathroom for US$12/13. Bicycling is a good option for exploring the valley, and distances are short enough that you could continue over the border into Benin, if you can make it past the guards at the Nadoba checkpoint.

Tunisia

Tunisia, the smallest of the three Maghreb states, has a rich cultural and social heritage stemming from the many empires that have come and gone in this area – from the Phoenicans to the Romans, Byzantines, Arabs, Ottoman Turks and the French.

In the last decade, Tunisia has developed as one of the Mediterranean's major tourist attractions, drawing millions of sun-starved northern Europeans to its shores every year. For the budget traveller, Tunisia used to be a stepping stone into Algeria and on to southern Africa, but with problems in Algeria closing the route south, few travellers visit Tunisia these days.

Facts about the Country

HISTORY

The ancient city-state of Carthage, arch rival of Rome, was only a few kilometres from the centre of the modern capital, Tunis. Carthage began life in 814 BC as one of a series of Phoenician staging posts. It remained relatively unimportant until Phoenicia (situated on what is now coastal Lebanon and Syria) was overrun by the Assyrians in the 7th century BC. As a result, Carthage rapidly grew into the metropolis of the Phoenician world, recording a population of about half a million at its peak.

By the 6th century BC, it had become the main power in the western Mediterranean – bringing it into inevitable conflict with the emerging Roman empire. The two fought each other almost to a standstill in the course of the 128-year Punic Wars, which began in 264 BC. Carthage's legendary general, Hannibal, appeared to have brought the Romans to their knees after his invasion of Italy in 216 BC, but the wars ended in victory for Rome. The Romans showed no mercy after the fall of Carthage in 146 BC. The city was razed and the population sold into slavery.

Highlights
* Exploring the ruins of Roman Carthage, El Jem, Dougga and Bulla Regia
* Strolling in Tozeur's delightful old quarter (the Ouled el Hadef)
* Early morning visits to the ksour, the old Berber granaries, at Tataouine
* Camel trekking in the desert near Douz

Carthage was rebuilt as a Roman city and it became the capital of the province of Africa, an area roughly corresponding to modern Tunisia. Africa's main attraction for the Romans was the grain-growing plains of the Medjerda valley, west of Carthage, which became known as the bread basket of the empire. The remains of the cities they built on these plains, such as Dougga, are among Tunisia's principal attractions.

The Vandals captured Carthage in 439 AD

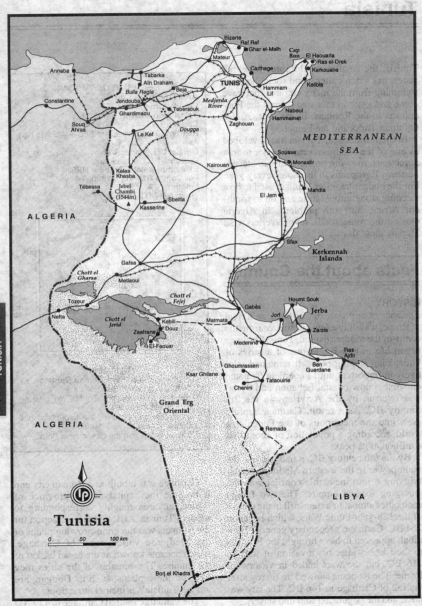

MEDITERRANEAN
SEA

Annaba

Constantine

Soug
Ahras

Tébessa

ALGERIA

ALGERIA

Bizerte
Raf Raf
Ghar el-Melh
Mateur
Cap
Bon
El Haouaria
Ras el-Drak
Kerkouane
Tabarka
Aïn Draham
Beja
TUNIS
Carthage
Kelibia
Bulla Regia
Jendouba
Tebersouk
Medjerda
River
Hammam
Lif
Nabeul
Ghardimaou
Hammamet
Le Kef
Dougga
Zaghouan
Kalaa
Khasba
Kairouan
Sousse
Monastir
Jebel
Chambi
(1544m)
Sbeitla
El Jem
Mahdia
Kasserine
Gafsa
Sfax
Kerkennah
Islands
Chott el
Gharsa
Metlaoui
Chott el
Fejej
Tozeur
Gabès
Houmt Souk
Jerba
Nefta
Chott el
Jerid
Kebili
Matmata
Jorf
Zaafrane
Douz
Zarzis
El-Faouar
Medenine
Ras
Ajdir
Ksar Ghilane
Ghoumrassen
Ben
Guerdane
Chenini
Tataouine
Grand Erg
Oriental
Remada
LIBYA

Tunisia

0   50   100 km

Borj el Khadra

and made it the capital of their North African empire until they were ousted by the Byzantines in 533 AD. The Byzantines never managed more than a shaky foothold, and put up little resistance when the Arabs arrived from the east in 670 AD, ruling from the holy city of Kairouan, 150km south of Carthage. They proved to be the most influential of conquerors, introducing both Islam and the social structure which remains the basis of Tunisian life today.

After the political fragmentation of the Arab empire, Tunisia became the eastern flank of the Moroccan-based Almohad empire. The Almohads appointed the Hafsid family as governors and they ruled, eventually as an independent monarchy, from 1207 until 1574 – a period of stability and prosperity.

The Hafsids were defeated by the Ottoman Turks and Tunisia came to be ruled by a local elite of Turkish janissaries (the professional wing of the Ottoman armies). By the 18th century, this elite had merged with the local populace and produced its own national monarchy, the Huseinid beys. Tunis was notorious as a base for the feared Barbary pirates who terrorised Mediterranean shipping.

After the French arrived in Algeria in the 19th century, the beys took care to avoid giving the French any reason to attack. They managed to delay colonisation for some years by outlawing piracy, westernising the administration and, in 1857, adopting a constitution. However, failure to repay foreign loans finally gave the French an excuse to invade in 1881, and Tunisia became a French protectorate in 1883.

In the 1930s, the Néo-Destour movement for national liberation grew under Habib Bourguiba, who was a Sorbonne-educated lawyer. The French banned the movement and jailed Bourguiba. The movement flourished briefly during the German occupation of Tunis in WWII when Bourguiba was released and the beys appointed ministers from the Néo-Destour movement. This came to an end with the Allied victory in North Africa, and Bourguiba went into exile.

Bourguiba orchestrated two years of guerrilla warfare against the French from Egypt, eventually forcing the French to grant autonomy in 1955. Bourguiba returned to head the new government, and Tunisia was granted independence a year later.

In 1957, the bey was deposed and Bourguiba became the first president of the new republic. In 1975, the National Assembly made him president for life. However, as the 1980s progressed, Bourguiba lost touch with his people and became isolated from the rest of the Arab world. In November 1987, the Interior Minister, Zine el-Abidine ben Ali, orchestrated Bourguiba's downfall and was installed as president. Ben Ali confirmed his hold on power at elections in 1989 and 1994, and Tunisia remains one of the most stable and moderate Arab countries. It has developed close ties with both the USA and Germany, which supply the bulk of its foreign aid.

GEOGRAPHY

Tunisia occupies an area of about 164,150 sq km, bordered by Algeria to the west, Libya to the south-east, and the Mediterranean to the east and north. The mountainous northern third of the country is dominated by the eastern extensions of the Atlas Mountains that run right across North Africa.

The north coast is Tunisia's green belt, with a fertile coastal plain backed by the densely forested Kroumirie Mountains. The forests are home to large numbers of wild boar, as well as jackal, mongoose and genet. The country's main mountain range is the rugged central Dorsale, further south. It runs from Kasserine in the west and peters out into Cap Bon in the east. It includes the country's highest peak, Jebel Chambi (1544m). Between these ranges lies the fertile Medjerda Valley, fed by the country's only permanent river. South of the Dorsale, a high plain falls away to a series of salt lakes (chotts) and then to a sandy desert on the edge of the Sahara known as the Grand Erg Oriental.

The east coast is remarkable for the vast areas under olive cultivation, particularly around Sfax.

CLIMATE
Northern Tunisia has a typical Mediterranean climate, with hot, dry summers and mild, wet winters. The further south you go, the hotter and drier it gets. Some Saharan areas go without rain for years.

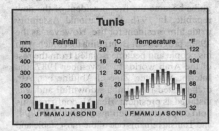

ECOLOGY & ENVIRONMENT
Water is an emerging environmental issue in the oasis towns of the south, where the huge water requirements of the tourist industry has depleted artesian water levels and dried up springs.

POPULATION & PEOPLE
Tunisia has an estimated population of almost nine million, although no census has been taken since 1984. The major cities and their estimated populations are Tunis and suburbs (1.89 million), Sfax (380,000), Bizerte (135,000) and Sousse (110,000).

Most people are of Arab/Berber stock. The original Berbers make up only 1% of the population and are found mainly in the south. Before the creation of Israel, Tunisia had a Jewish population of around 150,000. Only 2000 remain, mainly in Tunis and on Jerba.

SOCIETY & CONDUCT
Culture
Tunisia is easy-going by Muslim standards, especially in Tunis and the major tourist areas. You'll find many western trappings, such as fast food, pop music and women dressed in the latest European fashions. However, traditional life has changed little in rural areas, where the mosque, the *hammam* (bathhouse) and the cafe remain the focal points of life.

Women in Society
Thanks largely to the efforts of their secular, socialist, former president, Habib Bourguiba, conditions for women in Tunisia are better than just about anywhere in the Islamic world – to western eyes, at least. His 1956 Personal Status Code banned polygamy and divorce by renunciation. He called the veil an 'odious rag', and banned it from schools as part of a campaign to phase out a garment he regarded as demeaning. He didn't quite succeed, although it is very unusual to find a women under 30 wearing one.

Avoiding Offence
The residents of Tunis and the resort towns have seen far too many westerners to be offended easily, but the situation is different in rural areas. You can avoid any problems by dressing respectfully, which means long trousers for men and clothes that show off as little flesh as possible for women.

LANGUAGE
Tunisia is virtually bilingual. Arabic is the language of education and government, but almost everyone speaks some French. You are unlikely to come across many English speakers outside the main tourist centres. See the Arabic and French sections in the Language Appendix.

Facts for the Visitor

VISAS
Nationals of most Western European countries can stay up to three months without a visa – you just roll up and collect a stamp in your passport. Americans, Canadians, Germans and Japanese can stay up to four months. The situation is a bit more complicated for other nationalities. Most require no visa if arriving on an organised tour.

Australians and New Zealanders travelling independently can get a two week visa at the airport for US$3, although some have reported being given a month. South Africans can stay a month. Those wanting to stay longer should get a three month visa (about US$6) before they arrive – available wherever Tunisia has diplomatic representation.

Israeli nationals are not allowed into the country.

Visa Extensions

There's little likelihood of needing a visa extension; a month is plenty of time for most people. By all accounts, extending a visa is a process to be avoided. Applications can be made only at the Interior Ministry on Ave Habib Bourguiba in Tunis. They cost US$3 (payable only in revenue stamps) and take up to 10 days to issue. You'll need two photos, bank receipts and a *facture* (receipt) from your hotel, for starters.

Other Visas

People planning on travelling to Algeria (inadvisable at the time of writing) or Libya (very difficult) should apply for visas in their home country.

EMBASSIES
Tunisian Embassies

Tunisian embassies in Africa include Algeria, Libya, Morocco and Senegal. Elsewhere there are in embassies in Germany, Italy, the UK and the USA.

Foreign Embassies in Tunisia

Foreign embassies in Tunis include:

France
     Place de l'Indépendance, Ave Habib Bourguiba
     (☎ 24 5700)
UK
     5 Place de la Victoire (☎ 34 0239)
USA
     144 Ave de la Liberté (☎ 78 2566)

MONEY

US$1 = TD 0.98

The unit of currency is the Tunisian dinar (TD), which is divided into 1000 millimes

(mills). It's illegal to import or export dinar. You can re-exchange no more than 30% of the amount you changed into dinar, up to a limit of TD100. You need bank receipts to prove you changed the money in the first place.

Major credit cards such as Visa, Amex and MasterCard are widely accepted throughout the country at big shops, tourist hotels, car-rental agencies and banks. Cash advances are given in local currency only.

PUBLIC HOLIDAYS

The following public holidays are observed: 1 January, 20 March (Independence Day), 21 March, 9 April, 1 May, 25 July (Republic Day), 13 August, 7 November and variable Islamic holidays (see Public Holidays in the Regional Facts for the Visitor chapter).

POST & COMMUNICATIONS

The Tunisian postal service is slow but reliable.

The phone system works fine. Public telephones are called Taxiphones, easily identified by the yellow signs. They can be used for international direct dialling.

The country code for Tunisia is 216, and area codes are 01 for Tunis, 02 for Bizerte and 03 for Sousse.

ACCOMMODATION

Tunisia has few camp sites with good facilities, but you can pitch a tent anywhere if you have the landowner's permission.

Hostels fall into two categories. There are the Auberges de Jeunesse, affiliated to Hostelling International, and there are the government-run Maisons des Jeunes. They couldn't be more different, although both charge US$4 per night.

The Auberges de Jeunesse are thoroughly recommended. Most have prime locations, such as a converted palace in the Tunis medina and a fascinating old *foundouk* (caravanserai) at Houmt Souk (Jerba). Almost without exception, Maisons des Jeunes are characterless concrete boxes with all the charm of army barracks (and they are run along the same lines). Sometimes they represent the only budget accommodation.

The cheapest hotels offer beds in shared rooms for as little as US$3. These places are not suitable for women.

FOOD

The national dish is *couscous* (semolina). There are apparently more than 300 ways of preparing the stuff, sweet as well as savoury. A bowl of couscous served with some variety of stew costs about US$3 in local restaurants.

A curiosity in Tunisian cuisine is the *briq*, a crisp, very thin pastry envelope that comes with a range of fillings (always including egg).

Getting There & Away

AIR

There are regular flights, both scheduled and charter, from Tunisia to destinations all over Europe, but no direct flights to the Americas, Asia or Oceania.

Cheap tickets are unobtainable in Tunisia. Tickets can be very cheap *from* Europe; last-minute deals in London go as low as UK£69 return. It'll be a two week ticket, but at that price you can afford to throw away the return.

LAND

Algeria

SNTRI runs daily bus services from Tunis to Annaba. There are also *louages* (share-taxis) between the Tunis medina and various towns in eastern Algeria, including Annaba (US$18) and Constantine (US$25).

Libya

The best route is the coast road from Gabès to Tripoli via Ben Guerdane and Ras Ajdir. Shared taxis run from Gabès, Medenine, Sfax and Tunis to Tripoli, and there are daily buses (at 5 pm) from the southern Tunis bus station to Tripoli. The 11½-hour journey costs US$28.

SEA

There are regular ferry services between Tunis and various Italian ports, as well as Marseilles in France. See the Sea section in the Getting There & Away chapter at the beginning of the book for details.

Getting Around

AIR

The domestic airline, Tuninter, operates internal flights from Tunis to Jerba, Sfax and Tozeur.

BUS

Bus is the most popular form of public transport, and can get you just about everywhere you might want to go.

The national bus company, SNTRI, has daily air-con buses between Tunis and every town of any consequence. Advance booking is advisable, especially in summer and around important holidays. Sample one-way fares from Tunis include Sousse for US$6 and Jerba for US$18.

Local transport is handled by regional companies and goes to all but the remotest villages.

TRAIN

The rail network is a long way short of comprehensive. What there is, however, is modern and efficient. The best-serviced route is the line from Tunis to Sousse, Sfax and Gabès.

TAXI

Louages (usually Peugeot 404 share-taxis) seat five passengers and ply the same routes as the buses. They are a bit more expensive, but generally faster and more comfortable. They leave when full.

HITCHING

Hitching is not too bad down the coast to the Libyan border and as far south as Tozeur, although you may be expected to pay (a bit less than the bus fare). It is more difficult, but still possible, for two people. Hitching in the north is easier away from the main tourist areas, and you'll seldom be expected to pay.

BOAT

There are ferries from Sfax to the Kerkennah Islands, but there's little reason to go there. There is also a 24 hour car ferry operating on the short hop between Jorf, on the mainland, and Ajim on the island of Jerba.

Tunis

Tunis, the capital of Tunisia, must be the most laid-back major city in the Islamic world. The main attractions are the ancient medina and the remains of Carthage.

Information

Tourist Office The tourist office (☎ 34 1077) is at the eastern end of Ave Habib Bourguiba, at Place de l'Afrique. Items worth asking for include their map of Tunis and road map of Tunisia and their brochures on Carthage and the medina, all free.

Money The major banks are along Ave Habib Bourguiba. American Express (☎ 25 4304) is represented by Carthage Tours, 59 Ave Habib Bourguiba, and Thomas Cook (☎ 34 2710) by the Compagnie Tunisienne de Tourisme, 45 Ave Habib Bourguiba.

Post & Communications The main post office is on Rue Charles de Gaulle, in the centre of the cheap hotel area, south of Ave Habib Bourguiba. There are convenient Taxiphone offices on Rue Jamel Abdenasser and Ave de Paris.

Things to See

It's worth wandering around the **medina** for half a day or more. Don't miss the **Dar Ben Abdallah Museum**. It's a splendid old Turkish palace that houses a collection of traditional costumes and everyday objects. Two souks to check out are the **Souk el-Attarine** (the perfume souk), and the **Souk**

des Chechias, where the traditional red felt caps are made.

One Tunis attraction not to be missed is the **Bardo Museum**. This magnificent collection of Roman mosaics and marble statuary is housed in an old palace 3km north-west of the city centre. It is open from 8.30 am to 5.30 pm in summer and from 9.30 am to 4.30 pm in winter (closed on Monday). The best way to get there is using Métro Léger (see Getting Around later) line No 4. The Bardo stop is just around the corner from the museum.

The remains of Punic and Roman **Carthage** lie just north of the city centre, and are easily reached by TGM (suburban) train from Tunis Marine station. Get off at Carthage Hannibal station and wander from there. The ruins are scattered over a wide area and include Roman baths, houses, cisterns, basilicas and old streets.

If your time is limited, give top priority to the **Carthage Museum**, next to the bizarre deconsecrated cathedral, and the **Byrsa Quarter**, in the grounds of the museum.

A few stops farther along the TGM line is the beautiful white-washed village of **Sidi Bou Said**, set high on a cliff above the sea.

Places to Stay

Don't bother with the haul out to the nearest camp site, about 15km south of the city near Hammam Lif.

Fortunately, Tunis has an excellent *Auberge de Jeunesse* (☎ 56 7850). It occupies the 18th century Dar Saida Ajoula palace, right in the heart of the medina on Rue Es Saida Ajoula. Rates range from US$4.50 for a dormitory bed and hot shower up to US$10.50 for full board.

There are lots of cheap hotels in the medina charging US$3 for a bed in a shared room. They are not recommended for men, and are totally unsuitable for women.

There are a couple of possibilities around Place de la Victoire. The *Hôtel Medina* (☎ 25 5056) has doubles for US$10, while the *Hôtel Marhaba* (☎ 34 3118), on the opposite side of the square, has doubles for US$7.50.

Most travellers opt to stay outside the medina in the area south of Ave Habib

Bourguiba. A popular choice is the *Hôtel Bristol* (☎ 24 4836) on Rue Lt Mohammed Aziz Taj. It has the best budget rooms in town with singles/doubles for US$5/8.

The *Hôtel Cirta* (☎ 24 1583), at 42 Rue Charles de Gaulle, has long been a favourite with travellers. The place is shabby but clean, and charges US$6/10 for singles/doubles with shared bathroom.

There are plenty of good mid-range hotels to choose from. The *Hôtel Maison Doree* (☎ 24 0632), is a fine old-style French hotel on Rue el Koufa, just north of Place de Barcelone. Singles/doubles with shower cost

US$22/25, including breakfast. Two other good places nearby are the *Hôtel Salammbô* (☎ 33 7498), at 6 Rue de Grèce, and the *Hôtel Transatlantique* (☎ 24 0680), at 106 Rue de Yougoslavie.

The *Hôtel Majestic* (☎ 24 2848), at the northern end of Ave de Paris, is a splendid piece of fading grandeur with one of the finest French colonial facades in town. It has huge singles/doubles with bathroom and TV for US$30/40, including breakfast.

Places to Eat
There's a host of good places to choose from

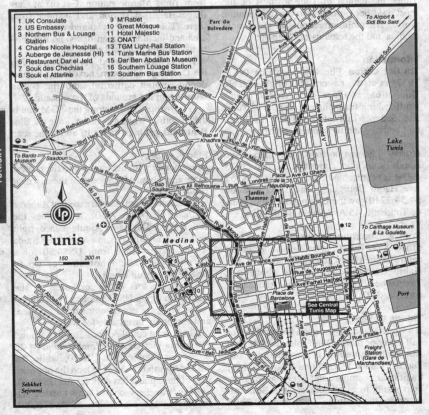

1 UK Consulate
2 US Embassy
3 Northern Bus & Louage Station
4 Charles Nicolle Hospital
5 Auberge de Jeunesse (HI)
6 Restaurant Dar el Jeld
7 Souk des Chechias
8 Souk el Attarine
9 M'Rabet
10 Great Mosque
11 Hotel Majestic
12 ONAT
13 TGM Light-Rail Station
14 Tunis Marine Bus Station
15 Dar Ben Abdallah Museum
16 Southern Louage Station
17 Southern Bus Station

Tunis

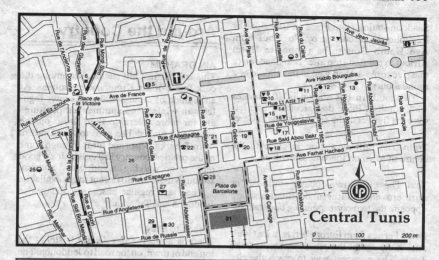

Central Tunis

0   100   200 m

PLACES TO STAY
6   Hôtel Medina
11 Hôtel Africa
14 Hôtel Bristol
19 Hôtel Transatlantique
20 Hôtel Salammbô
21 Hôtel Maison Doree
24 Hôtel Marhaba
29 Hôtel de l'Agriculture
30 Hôtel Cirta

PLACES TO EAT
2   Restaurant Istanbul
9   Café de Paris

15 Restaurants
    Carcassonne &
    Le Palais
16 Restaurant Le Cosmos
17 Restaurant Bolero
18 Restaurant Ezzeitouna
23 Monoprix Supermarket

OTHER
1   Tourist Office
3   Buses to Airport (35);
    Bardo Museum (3)
4   Cathedral
5   American Express

7   UK Embassy
8   French Embassy
10 Taxiphone Office
12 Tunis Air
13 Interior Ministry
22 Taxiphone Office
25 Louages to Algeria
    & Libya
26 Central Market
27 Post Office
28 Place de Barcelone
    Buses & Trams
31 Train Station

TUNISIA

in the streets south of Ave Habib Bourguiba, particularly around Ave de Carthage and Rue Ibn Khaldoun. It's hard to beat the *Restaurant Carcassonne*, 8 Ave de Carthage, for value. It turns out a four-course menu for US$3.50, supplemented by as much bread as you can eat.

The *Restaurant Mahdaoui*, opposite the Great Mosque in the medina, is a good place to stop for lunch. It's the oldest restaurant in Tunis and has a daily blackboard menu of traditional dishes for about US$3.50.

If you want to enjoy a wine with your meal, the *Restaurant Bolero*, on a small side

street off Rue de Yougoslavie, is a good choice. It's always packed with locals at lunchtime and a hearty meal for two with wine will cost about US$20.

Getting There & Away

Bus Tunis has two bus stations, one for departures to the north (Gare Routière Nord de Bab Saadoun) and the other for international buses and buses to the south (Gare Routière Sud de Bab el Alleoua).

The northern bus station is on the north-western side of Bab Saadoun. You can get there on Métro Léger lines Nos 3 or 4 to Bab

Saadoun station from Place de Barcelone or République stations, or by No 3 bus from Ave Habib Bourguiba (opposite Hotel Africa) to the first stop after Bab Saadoun (a massive triple-arched gate in the middle of a roundabout).

The southern bus station is 10 minutes walk south of Place de Barcelone; turn left over the flyover at the end of Ave de la Gare.

Train The railway station is close to the centre of town on Place de Barcelone.

Taxi The city's two louage stations, for northern and southern destinations, are opposite the two corresponding bus stations.

Ferry Ferries from Europe arrive at La Goulette, at the end of the causeway across Lake Tunis. The cheapest way to reach the city from here is by TGM suburban train. A taxi from the port to Ave Habib Bourguiba shouldn't cost more than US$3.

Getting Around

The Airport Tunis-Carthage Airport is 8km north-east of the city. Yellow city buses (Nos 1 and 35) run there from the Tunis Marine terminus every 20 minutes from 6 am to 9 pm for US$0.50. A taxi costs about US$5.

TGM This light-rail system connects central Tunis with the northern beachside suburbs of La Goulette, Carthage, Sidi Bou Said and La Marsa. Trains run from 4 am until midnight.

Tram The modern (Métro Léger) tram system has five routes running to various parts of the city. The useful lines are No 1 for the southern bus and louage stations, No 2 for consulates on Ave de la Liberté and Nos 3 and 4 for the northern bus and louage stations. No 4 also has a stop for the Bardo Museum. The main stations are Barcelone and République.

Taxi Taxis are a fairly cheap way of getting around. They always use the meter.

Around the Country

AIN DRAHAM

This is Tunisia's hill station, set among the cork forest of the Kroumirie mountains. At an altitude of around 900m, it snows regularly in winter, and summer temperatures are far more tolerable than those on the coast and plains. The road to Ain Draham from Tabarka twists and turns through some of the prettiest country in Tunisia. It's a good place to go walking in spring and autumn, although there are no decent maps available.

There are regular buses and louages to Jendouba and Tabarka.

Places to Stay

There is a *Maison des Jeunes* hostel at the top end of town, on the road to Jendouba. The only hotel in town is the pleasant *Hôtel Beauséjour* (☎ (08) 65 5363), where singles/doubles cost US$20/28, including breakfast.

BULLA REGIA

The extensive remains of the Roman city of Bulla Regia lie about 160km west of Tunis near the town of Jendouba. The site is remarkable for its 'underground' villas – the city's bourgeoisie built their houses with one level below ground to escape the summer heat. It is open daily from 7 am to 7 pm in summer and from 8.30 am to 5.30 pm in winter.

Places to Stay

There is nowhere to stay near the site. The closest accommodation is in Jendouba, a dull administrative centre that most people avoid by arriving in time to catch the last train to Tunis at 5 pm.

If you get stuck, there's a choice of the grotty *Pension Saha en Noum*, near the main square on Blvd Khemais el Hajiri (US$4 per person) or the two-star *Hôtel Simitthu* (☎ (08) 63 4043), by the bus station, at US$27/38 for singles/doubles.

Getting There & Away

Jendouba is a regional transport centre. Train

is the best bet for Tunis, and there are regular buses and louages to Le Kef and Tabarka. The simplest way of getting to Bulla Regia is to lash out for a taxi (US$5). Alternatively there are shared taxis that run past the site (US$0.50). If you're making your own way there, the turn-off to Bulla Regia is clearly marked 6km north of Jendouba on the road to Ain Draham. Buses stop at the junction.

DOUGGA

Dougga, 110km south-west of Tunis, is home to the country's most photographed Roman monument, the imposing **Capitol of Dougga**. It looks even better in situ. The site occupies a commanding position on the edge of the Tebersouk Mountains, with sweeping views of the Kalled valley. The well-preserved **theatre** makes a spectacular setting for performances of classical theatre during the Dougga Festival in July and August. The site is open daily from 8 am to 7 pm in summer, and from 8.30 am to 5.30 pm in winter.

Tebersouk is the closest town to the site. The only hotel is the uninspiring two-star *Hôtel Thugga* (☎ (08) 46 5713), which charges US$25/36 for singles/doubles with breakfast. No problem. It's easy to visit the site on a day trip from Tunis or Le Kef – or en route between the two. SNTRI's frequent buses between Tunis and Le Kef all call at Tebersouk. At the bus stop you'll find locals asking about US$5 to take you the remaining 7km to the site and pick you up at a time of your choice.

DOUZ

Promoting itself as the 'gateway to the Sahara', Douz is becoming increasingly popular with travellers, and is packed out during the Sahara Festival in December.

Camel Trekking

Most people come to Douz to organise camel trekking. Trekking touts can be found as far afield as Gabès, and the offers are flying thick and fast by the time you reach Douz. Most of the time they are touting for a couple of big operators at Zaafrane, 10km west of Douz, which is the place to get the best deals. There are regular camionettes and louages (both US$0.50) from opposite the louage station in Douz.

In Zaafrane you will be dropped at a huge vacant lot dotted with hundreds of camels. Among the camels are two small palm-thatch huts, bases for the rival organisations. Both offer trekking for as long as you care to nominate from an hour (US$3.50) upwards. It's a good idea to sit on a camel for an hour before signing up for an adventure such as an eight-day, oasis-hopping trek to Ksar Ghilane. You'll pay about US$30 a day for an experience like this, including all meals. Meals are cooked by campfire, and you'll sleep under basic nomad-style tents.

Places to Stay

Douz has good budget accommodation. There's camping at the *Desert Club* camping ground (☎ (05) 49 5595), in the *palmeraie* (palm grove) at the southern end of Ave 7 Novembre.

The best of the budget hotels is the very friendly *Hôtel 20 Mars* (☎ (05) 49 5495), which charges US$6 per person with free hot showers. If it's full, try the nearby *Hôtel de la Tente* (☎ (05) 49 5468).

EL JEM

The well-preserved **Roman amphitheatre** that dominates the small town of El Jem is rated by many as the most impressive Roman monument in North Africa. It's open daily from 7 am to 7 pm in summer and from 8 am to 5.30 pm in winter. Your US$4 admission also gets you into the **museum**, which is about 500m south of the train station on the road to Sfax. It houses some fine mosaics.

El Jem is easily visited en route between Sousse and Sfax, being a stop on the main train line. All forms of transport leave from around the railway station, so just grab the first service that comes by. If you want to stay, *Hôtel Julius* (☎ (03) 69 0044), right next to the train station, is the only hotel – and only bar – in town. It charges US$8.50/15 for singles/doubles.

GABÈS

There is little reason to linger in this heavily

industrialised port city on the Gulf of Gabès, but it's the transport hub of the south so you'll find probably find yourself passing through at some stage. It does at least have a good budget hotel if you get stuck. The spotless *Hôtel Ben Nejima* (☎ (05) 22 1062) is just 300m from the bus and louage stations at the junction of Blvd Farhat Hached and Rue Haj Djilani Lahbib. It charges US$6 per person, with free hot showers.

JERBA

The island of Jerba is one of Tunisia's most popular tourist spots. Package tourists tend

to stick to the huge 'zone touristique' – 20km of solid hotel development that monopolises the decent beaches to the north-east of the island.

Houmt Souk

Jerba's main town is a tangle of narrow alleys and a few attractive cafe-lined squares. There is a Syndicat d'Initiative (☎ (05) 65 0915) in the middle of town. There are also banks and a post office, as well as countless souvenir shops. The choice is good, but the prices are high – get set for some serious bargaining.

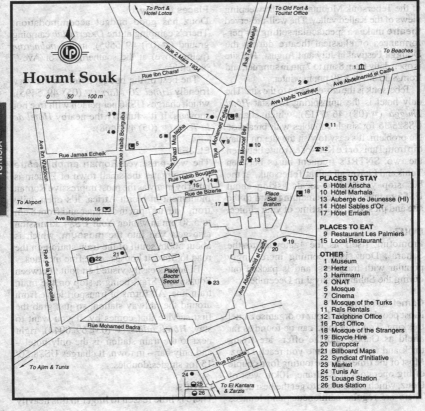

Houmt Souk

To Port & Hotel Lotos
To Old Fort & Tourist Office
To Beaches
To Airport
To Ajim & Tunis
To El Kantara & Zarzis

Rue 2 Mars 1934
Rue ibn Charaf
Rue Taïeb Mehiri
Ave Abdelhamid el Cadhi
Ave Habib Thameur
Rue Ghazi Mustapha
Rue Mohamed Ferjani
Rue Moncef Bey
Avenue Habib Bourguiba
Rue Jamaa Echeik
Ave Ibn Khaldoun
Rue Habib Bougatta
Rue de Bizerte
Ave Boumessouer
Rue de la Municipalité
Place Sidi Brahim
Place Bechir Seoud
Rue Mohamed Badra
Rue Remada

0   50   100 m

PLACES TO STAY
6 Hôtel Arischa
10 Hôtel Marhala
13 Auberge de Jeunesse (HI)
14 Hôtel Sables d'Or
17 Hôtel Erriadh

PLACES TO EAT
9 Restaurant Les Palmiers
15 Local Restaurant

OTHER
1 Museum
2 Hertz
3 Hammam
4 ONAT
5 Mosque
7 Cinema
8 Mosque of the Turks
11 Raïs Rentals
12 Taxiphone Office
16 Post Office
18 Mosque of the Strangers
19 Bicycle Hire
20 Europcar
21 Billboard Maps
22 Syndicat d'Initiative
23 Market
24 Tunis Air
25 Louage Station
26 Bus Station

The Tunis Air office (☎ (05) 65 0159) and the bus and louage stations are at the southern end of the main street, Ave Habib Bourguiba.

The town's main attractions are the old fort, **Borj Ghazi Mustapha** (on the beach, 500m from town) and the **museum** (on the road to the zone touristique). Both are closed on Friday.

Places to Stay & Eat
There is camping on the east coast at the *Auberge Centre Aghir* (☎ (05) 65 7366). To get there, take the bus to Club Med from Houmt Souk.

Houmt Souk has some of most interesting places to stay in the country – old foundouks that have been converted into a range of accommodation to suit every budget. They start with the excellent *Auberge de Jeunesse* (☎ (05) 65 0619) on Rue Moncef Bey. It's great value at US$3.50.

The other foundouk hotels are the *Arischa* (☎ (05) 65 0384), the *Marhala* (☎ (05) 65 0146), and the *Erriadh* (☎ (05) 65 0756). Summer prices for singles/doubles range from US$8/14 at the Arischa to US$18/27 at the Erriadh.

The *Restaurant Les Palmiers* is a great little restaurant on Rue Mohamed Ferjani with most meals under US$2.50.

KAIROUAN
The old walled city of Kairouan is historically the most important town in Tunisia. It was here that the Arabs established their first base when they arrived from the east in 670 AD. The city is also famous for its carpets – and for its carpet sellers.

Information
The tourist office (☎ (07) 22 1664) is inconveniently located right out on the northern edge of town, next to the Aghlabid Basins. Tickets for the main sites are sold here.

The bus and louage stations are north-west of the medina on the road to Sbeitla, signposted off Ave Zama el-Belaoui.

Things to See
In the north-eastern corner of the medina is the city's main monument, the outwardly plain **Great Mosque**. Much of the present structure dates from the 9th century, though the lowest level of the minaret is thought to have been built early in the 8th century, making it the oldest standing minaret in the world.

Other sites include the **Mosque of the Three Doors**, famous for the rare inscriptions carved in its facade; the **Zaouia of Sidi Abid el Ghariani** (a zaouia is a religious fraternity based around a marabout, a Muslim holy man); and the tourist trap known as **Bir Barouta**, which features a camel drawing water from a well whose waters are said to be connected to Mecca.

Places to Stay & Eat
Best value is the *Hôtel Sabra* (☎ (07) 22 0260), just outside Bab ech Chouhada. It charges US$6/10 for clean rooms, breakfast and free hot showers.

Other interesting possibilities are the *Hôtel Marhala* (☎ (07) 22 0736), a converted madrese (Islamic college) in the heart of the medina, and the *Hôtel Les Aghlabites* (☎ (07) 22 0880), which occupies an old foundouk in the market area north of the medina. Both charge US$6 per person.

The *Restaurant de la Jeunesse*, on Ave Ali Belhaouane, does excellent couscous. Stalls everywhere sell the Kairouan speciality, makhroud – honey-soaked pastry stuffed with dates.

LE KEF
Le Kef, 170km south-west of Tunis, has been an important regional centre since Carthaginian times. The setting is spectacular, with the city tumbling down the slopes of Jebel Dyr beneath an impressive Byzantine kasbah. The city centre, around Place de l'Indépendance, is a 10-minute walk uphill from the bus and louage station.

Things to See
The **kasbah** is well worth a look, for the views as much as anything. It's open every

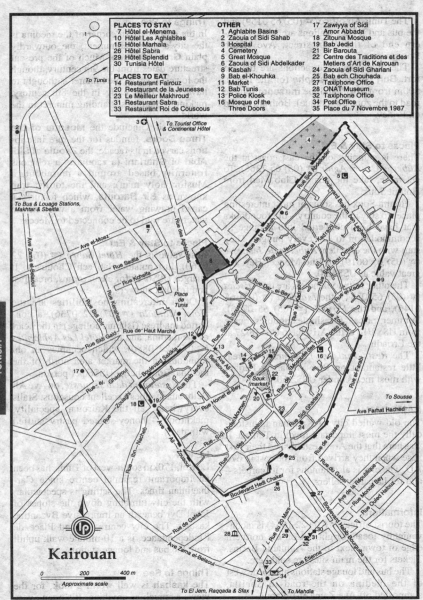

PLACES TO STAY
7 Hôtel el-Menema
10 Hôtel Les Aghlabites
15 Hôtel Marhala
26 Hôtel Sabra
29 Hôtel Splendid
30 Tunisia Hôtel

PLACES TO EAT
14 Restaurant Fairouz
20 Restaurant de la Jeunesse
23 Le Meilleur Makhroud
31 Restaurant Sabra
33 Restaurant Roi de Couscous

OTHER
1 Aghlabite Basins
2 Zaouia of Sidi Sahab
3 Hospital
4 Cemetery
5 Great Mosque
6 Zaouia of Sidi Abdelkader
8 Kasbah
9 Bab el-Khoukha
11 Market
12 Bab Tunis
13 Police Kiosk
16 Mosque of the
   Three Doors

17 Zawiyya of Sidi
   Amor Abbada
18 Zitouna Mosque
19 Bab Jedid
21 Bir Barouta
22 Centre des Traditions et des
   Metiers d'Art de Kairouan
24 Zaouia of Sidi Ghariani
25 Bab ech Chouhada
27 Taxiphone Office
32 Taxiphone Office
34 Post Office
35 Place du 7 Novembre 1987

To Tunis

To Tourist Office
& Continental Hôtel

To Bus & Louage Stations,
Makhtar & Sbeitla

Ave el-Moez

Ave Zama el-Belaoui

Rue Sadia

Rue Kheita

Rue des Aghlabites

Rue Sidi Sfir

Rue Kenahsa

Place de Tunis

Rue de Haut Marché

Boulevard Saidia

Rue Bab Jedid

Rue- el- Ghadroul

Rue Zouaghi

Rue- Ibn–Nachaib

Ave Ali Zouboui

Rue Homer el-Bey

Rue Sidi Abdel Momen

des L'Ancealx

Rue de Gafsa

Ave Zama el-Belaoui

Boulevard Hedi Chaker

Rue de Sousse

Rue du 20 Mars

Ave de la République

Rue Moncef Bey

Rue Ouled Haïouz

Rue Étienne

Boulevard Brahim ben Laghleb

Rue Sidi Abdelkader

Rue de la Kasbah

Rue de Jerba

Rue el-Kadraoul

Rue Sidi Bou Omrani

Rue Dar el-Bey

Rue el-Kadraoul

Rue el-Kedid

Rue Souikat

Rue de la Mosquée des Trois Portes

Rue Sidi Ghariani

Rue el-Farabi

Rue Salah Souali

Rue Ali Belhouane

Souk (market)

Ave Farhat Hached

To Sousse

Rue du Gabsi

Boulevard Habib Bourguiba

Rue Étienne

To El Jem, Raqqada & Sfax

To Mahdia

TUNISIA

Kairouan

0   200   400 m
Approximate scale

Place du 7 Novembre 1987

day from 7 am. To get there, follow the stone steps leading uphill through the old **medina** from Place de l'Indépendance. The road that flanks the kasbah leads to the **Musée des Arts et Traditions Populaires** (closed Monday), which specialises in the culture of the region's Berber nomads.

Places to Stay

All the hotels are on or around Place de l'Indépendance. The *Hôtel Medina* (☎ (08) 22 0214), on Rue Farhat Hached, is a safe pick with clean doubles for US$8 – but no singles.

The *Hôtel de la Source* (☎ (08) 22 4397), on Rue de la Source, is worth a look if you can get past its bizarre custard-coloured lobby. Unfortunately not all the rooms have the style of the family room, with its vaulted stucco ceiling. Regular singles/doubles are US$8/10.

MAHDIA

Mahdia remains a favourite with travellers, in spite of the growing tourist zone on the beaches just north of town. The town dates back to the 10th century, when it was the capital of the Fatimids, a Muslim dynasty that ruled over North Africa from 909 to 1171 AD. Their rulers were called *mahdis*.

There is a small tourist office (☎ (03) 68 1098) just inside the medina. The bus, louage and train stations are about 500m from the town centre, past the fishing port.

Things to See

Anyone with a flickering of interest in architecture will enjoy a stroll in Mahdia's well-maintained medina. Access to the old medina is through the massive **Skifa el Kahla** gate, which is all that remains of the fortifications that protected ancient Mahdia. The unadorned **Great Mosque** is a 20th-century replica of the mosque built by the mahdi in the 10th century.

Places to Stay & Eat

The *Hôtel el Jazira* (☎ (03) 68 1629) is the only hotel in the medina. It's a great spot, with rooms overlooking the sea (US$7/11).

Don't miss having a meal at the *Restaurant el-Moez*, on the edge of the medina near the market. It serves some of the best local food in the country, although the choice is limited to three or four daily specials.

MATMATA

Fascinating though the troglodyte dwellings of Matmata might be, it's hard not to feel sorry for the long-suffering residents of this small village 43km south-west of Gabés. The first tour buses roll up at 9 am every day, and they just keep on coming – day after day. The residents are sick of being stared at like goldfish, and many holes are now surrounded by barbed wire to keep the tourists out. Give it a miss.

SFAX

Tunisia's second-largest city, Sfax is a place with an unglamorous reputation. It has two big things going for it – its unspoilt old medina and the fact that there's hardly a package tourist in sight. The highlight of the medina is the **Dar Jellouli Museum of Popular Traditions**, which is housed in a beautiful 17th-century mansion.

Orientation & Information

The tourist office (☎ (04) 21 1040) is by the port on Ave Mohammed Hedi Khefecha. The SNTRI bus station is by the entrance to the train station, on Rue de Tazarka, and the regional bus station for southern destinations is at the opposite end of Ave Habib Bourguiba. The ferry port for the Kerkennah Islands is 10 minutes walk to the south of the new city. North of the medina is the place for louages to Mahdia and regional buses heading north. The main louage station is on the south-western side of the medina.

Places to Stay

The cheap hotels are in the medina. The *Hôtel Medina* (☎ (04) 22 0354) on Rue Mongi Slim is the best of them with clean rooms for US$4 per person.

The *Hôtel Alexander* (☎ (04) 22 1911), on Rue Alexandre Dumas, has large, comfortable singles/doubles with bath for US$11/16,

TUNISIA

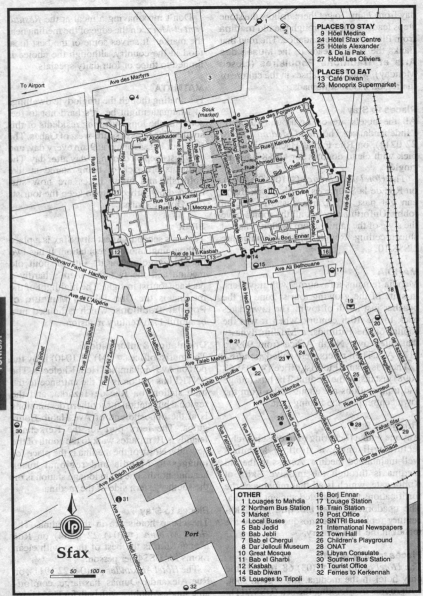

PLACES TO STAY
9 Hôtel Medina
24 Hôtel Sfax Centre
25 Hôtels Alexander
   & De la Paix
27 Hôtel Les Oliviers

PLACES TO EAT
13 Café Diwan
23 Monoprix Supermarket

OTHER
1 Louages to Mahdia
2 Northern Bus Station
3 Market
4 Local Buses
5 Bab Jedid
6 Bab Jebli
7 Bab el Chergui
8 Dar Jellouli Museum
9 Great Mosque
10 Bab el Gharbi
11 Kasbah
14 Bab Diwan
15 Louages to Tripoli
16 Borj Ennar
17 Louage Station
18 Train Station
19 Post Office
20 SNTRI Buses
21 International Newspapers
22 Town Hall
26 Children's Playground
28 ONAT
29 Libyan Consulate
30 Southern Bus Station
31 Tourist Office
32 Ferries to Kerkennah

Sfax

0   50   100 m

Port

including breakfast. Give the place a miss on Saturday night when a folk band plays in the restaurant.

The *Hôtel de la Paix* (☎ (04) 29 6437), a few doors up from the Alexander, has singles/doubles for US10/12.

SOUSSE

Sousse, 142km south of Tunis, is the country's third largest city and a major port. The huge medina and impressive fortifications are the main pointers to the city's long history as a commercial centre. Tourism is big business around here, and the beaches north of town are monopolised by a string of resort hotels.

Orientation & Information

Everything of importance is close to the main square, Place Farhat Hached, on the northern side of the medina. The efficient tourist office (☎ (03) 22 5157) is on the corner of Place Farhat Hached and Ave Habib Bourguiba.

Things to See

The main monuments of the medina are the **ribat**, a sort of fortified monastery, and the **Great Mosque**. Both are in the north-eastern corner, not far from Place Farhat Hached.

The **kasbah** on top of the hill has a **museum** (closed on Monday), featuring some beautiful mosaics. There is no access to the kasbah from inside the medina.

Places to Stay & Eat

The *Hôtel Gabès*, at 12 Rue de Paris, is the most presentable of the medina cheapies. It charges US$6 per person with free hot showers. The best budget place in town is the spotless *Hôtel de Paris* (☎ (03) 22 0564), just inside the medina's north wall at 15 Rue du Rempart Nord. It has (very) small singles for US$6, and good rooms for US$9. There are free hot showers and laundry facilities.

The *Hôtel Medina* (☎ (03) 22 1722), right next to the Great Mosque, has good singles/doubles for US$13/18, including breakfast.

The medina is the place to look for cheap local food. The *Restaurant Populaire*, just

off Place Farhat Hached, is always packed. There's keen competition for the tourist trade from the countless restaurants that line Ave Habib Bourguiba and Place Farhat Hached. You can get a good meal for US$10, plus wine.

Getting There & Away

Train is the way to travel. The station for Sfax and Tunis is just north of Place Farhat Hached, while trains to Monastir and Mahdia leave from Bab Jedid station at the southern end of Ave Mohammed V.

TABARKA

The friendly little town of Tabarka is the last settlement along the north coast before the Algerian border. The setting is beautiful, with the emerald-green backdrop of the Kroumirie Mountains. The small bay and beach to the north of town are watched over by an impressive Genoese fort.

Tabarka is becoming popular and is set to boom following the building of an international airport (charter flights only, to date). Most of the tourist development is 10km to the east of town, leaving Tabarka itself relatively unspoiled.

Places to Stay and Eat

There are a couple of good places, neither of them cheap. Best is the *Pension Mamia* (☎ (08) 64 4058), on Rue de Tunis. Spotless rooms around a courtyard cost US$7 per person in winter (twice that in summer), breakfast included. Next best is the *Hôtel La Plage* (☎ (08) 64 4039), on Rue des Pecheurs, where rooms and breakfast cost US$9/14.

The restaurant at the *Hôtel de France* is good value, offering a three course meal for US$7, while the *Restaurant Khemir* opposite offers good seafood.

TATAOUINE

The modern administrative town of Tataouine lies at the heart of the south's fascinating Ksour district (see boxed story).

Buses and louages leave from the centre of town. There are better transport connections from Medenine, 50km to the north.

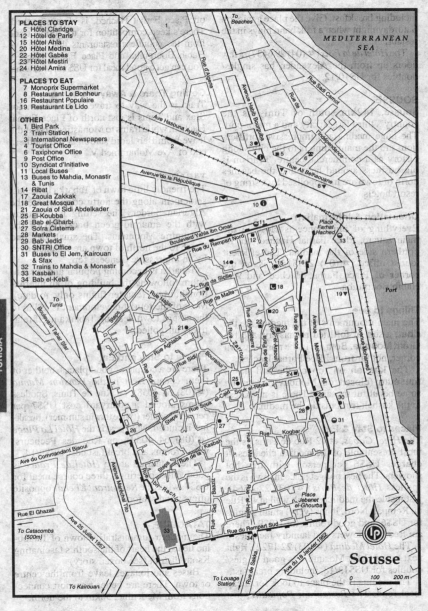

PLACES TO STAY
5 Hôtel Claridge
12 Hôtel de Paris
15 Hôtel Ahla
20 Hôtel Medina
22 Hôtel Gabès
23 Hôtel Mestiri
24 Hôtel Amira

PLACES TO EAT
7 Monoprix Supermarket
8 Restaurant Le Bonheur
16 Restaurant Populaire
19 Restaurant Le Lido

OTHER
1 Bird Park
2 Train Station
3 International Newspapers
4 Tourist Office
6 Taxiphone Office
9 Post Office
10 Syndicat d'Initiative
11 Local Buses
13 Buses to Mahdia, Monastir & Tunis
14 Ribat
17 Zaouia Zakkak
18 Great Mosque
21 Zaouia of Sidi Abdelkader
26 El-Koubba
27 Sofra Cisterns
28 Markets
29 Bab Jedid
30 SNTRI Office
31 Buses to El Jem, Kairouan & Sfax
32 Trains to Mahdia & Monastir
33 Kasbah
34 Bab el-Kebli

MEDITERRANEAN SEA

To Beaches

Rue d'Algérie

Ave Hasouna Ayachi

Avenue Habib Bourguiba

Rue de l'Indépendance

Rue Sidi Camel

Rue Ali Belhaouane

Avenue de la République

Boulevard Yahia Ibn Omar

Rue du Rempart Nord

Rue de Sicilie

Rue de Malte

Rue Najar

Steps

Rue d'Angleterre

Rue de Paris

Rue de France

Rue el-Aarou

Avenue Mohamed Ali

Avenue Mohamed V

Place Farhat Hached

Port

Boulevard Tahar Sfar

To Tunis

Rue Aghlaba

Rue Sidi

Rue Sidi Said

Rue Sidi Bournou?

Rue Zarrouk

Souk el-Ribaa

Rue Souk el-Caid

Steps

Steps

Rue de la Kasbah

Rue el-Maar

Rue Kogbar

Ave du Commandant Bjaoui

Avenue Maréchal Tito

Rue Ibn Rachig

Rue Sidi Bazziz

Rue el-Haïra

Rue du Rempart Sud

Rue de Sakka

Place Jebenet el-Ghourba

Rue El Ghazali

To Catacombs (500m)

Ave 25 Juillet 1957

Ave du 18 Janvier 1952

To Louage Station

To Kairouan

Sousse

0   100   200 m

TUNISIA

Things to See

The closest ksar to the centre of Tataouine is the three-storey **Ksar Megabla**, about an hour's walk from town on the right of the road to Remada. The best sites are the remarkable hilltop villages of **Chenini** and **Douiret**, south-west of Tatouine. Both can be reached by camionette from outside the Banque du Sud on Rue 2 Mars.

The Ksour

Ksour is the plural of *ksar*, the traditional fortified granary built by the region's Berber tribes. A single ksar consists of many *ghorfas*, narrow barrel-vaulted rooms that were used to store grain. They are often stacked three or four levels high and accessed by precarious-looking steps. They were originally built for storage, but when the Arabs invaded they were expanded into formidable defensive positions. They were usually strategically located, and they occupy some spectacular sites. ■

Places to Stay & Eat

The *Hôtel Medina* (☎ (05) 86 0999) is in the middle of town on Rue Habib Mestaoui. It charges US$4 per person and there is no additional charge for hot showers. As an added advantage, this place has the best budget restaurant in town.

TOZEUR

Tozeur is a thriving town on the edge of the Chott el Jerid, the largest of Tunisia's salt lakes. The place has a relaxed atmosphere and is a popular destination for travellers.

The tourist office (☎ (06) 45 0088) is on Ave Abdulkacem Chebbi, and there are several banks on Ave Habib Bourguiba, which is lined with souvenir shops selling the area's colourful rugs.

The bus and louage stations are opposite each other just north of the road to Nefta.

Things to See

The enormous **palmeraie** (palm grove) is

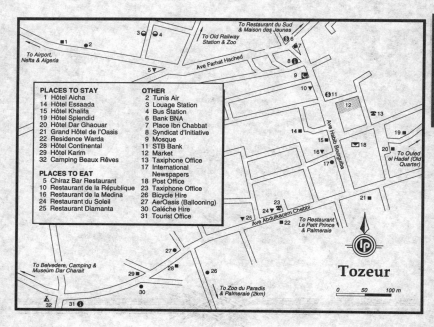

PLACES TO STAY
1 Hôtel Aicha
14 Hôtel Essaada
15 Hôtel Khalifa
19 Hôtel Splendid
20 Hôtel Dar Ghaouar
21 Grand Hôtel de l'Oasis
22 Residence Warda
28 Hôtel Continental
29 Hôtel Karim
32 Camping Beaux Rêves

PLACES TO EAT
5 Chiraz Bar Restaurant
10 Restaurant de la République
16 Restaurant de la Medina
24 Restaurant du Soleil
25 Restaurant Diamanta

OTHER
2 Tunis Air
3 Louage Station
4 Bus Station
6 Bank BNA
7 Place Ibn Chabbat
8 Syndicat d'Initiative
9 Mosque
11 STB Bank
12 Market
13 Taxiphone Office
17 International Newspapers
18 Post Office
23 Taxiphone Office
26 Bicycle Hire
27 AerOasis (Ballooning)
30 Calèche Hire
31 Tourist Office

Tozeur

0   50   100 m

best explored by bicycle, which can be hired on the road signposted to the **Zoo du Paradis** (home to a Coca Cola-drinking camel).

The impressive **Museum Dar Charait** is 1km west of the tourist office at the western end of Ave Abdulkacem Chebbi. It's open every day from 8 am until midnight, admission US$3.50.

The **Ouled el Hadef**, the town's labyrinthine old quarter, is well worth exploring for its striking architecture and brickwork; enter by the road past the Hôtel Splendid.

Places to Stay & Eat
Camping Beaux Rêves (☎ (06) 45 1242), near the tourist office on Ave Abdulkacem Chebbi, is a good, shady site that backs onto the palmeraie. It charges US$3.50 per person, either in your own tent or in one of the communal nomad-style tents. Hot showers are US$1.

The *Residence Warda* (☎ (06) 45 2597) is an excellent place on Ave Abdulkacem Chebbi. It has singles/doubles with shared bathroom for US$11/16, and with bathroom for US$12/18. Prices include breakfast. If it's full, try the *Hôtel Karim* (☎ (06) 45 4574) further along Ave Abdulkacem Chebbi at No 69. It's a modern place offering a similar deal.

The inconspicuous *Restaurant du Sud*, north-east of the city centre on Ave Farhat Hached, has a good choice of meals for under US$3. Another popular place is the *Restaurant du Soleil*, opposite the Residence Warda.

Uganda

For the traveller, Uganda is a safe and friendly country to visit. Certainly the level of comfort is not what you might be used to in Kenya, but the Ugandan people are among the friendliest on the continent and there are some unforgettable sights. Don't be afraid to visit. It's a beautiful country with a great deal to offer.

Facts about the Country

HISTORY

Until the 19th century there was very little penetration of Uganda from outside. Despite the fertility of the land and its capacity to grow surplus crops, there were virtually no trading links with the East African coast.

During the reign of Kabaka Mwanga in the mid-19th century, contacts were finally made with Arab traders from the coast and European explorers.

After the Treaty of Berlin in 1890, which defined the various European countries' spheres of influence in Africa, Uganda, Kenya and the islands of Zanzibar and Pemba were declared British protectorates in 1894. The colonial administrators adopted a policy of indirect rule, giving the traditional kingdoms a considerable degree of autonomy, but favouring the recruitment of Baganda tribespeople for the civil service.

Other tribespeople, unable to gain responsible jobs in the colonial administration or to make inroads in the Baganda-dominated commercial sector, were forced to seek other ways of joining the mainstream. The Acholi and Lango, for example, were dominant in the military. Thus were planted the seeds for the intertribal conflicts which were to tear Uganda apart following independence.

By the mid-1950s a Lango schoolteacher, Dr Milton Obote, managed to put together a loose coalition which led Uganda to inde-

REPUBLIC OF UGANDA
Area: 236,580 sq km
Population: 21.3 million
Population Growth Rate: 3%
Capital: Kampala
Head of State: President Yoweri Museveni
Official Language: English
Currency: Ugandan shilling (USh)
Exchange Rate: USh 1100 = US$1
Per Capita GNP: US$240
Inflation: 6%
Time: GMT/UTC + 3

Highlights
- Taking a boat ride to the base of the spectacular Murchison Falls
- Visiting the mountain gorillas deep in the rainforest of Bwindi National Park
- Superb trekking in the Rwenzori Mountains
- The mellow Ssese Islands, the place to kick back for a few days

pendence in 1962, on the promise that the Baganda would have autonomy.

It wasn't a particularly propitious time for Uganda to come to grips with independence. Civil wars were raging in neighbouring southern Sudan, Zaïre and Rwanda, and refugees poured into the country, adding to its problems. Also, it soon became obvious that Obote had no intention of sharing power with the *kabaka* (the Bagandan king). A confrontation was inevitable.

Obote moved fast, arresting several

943

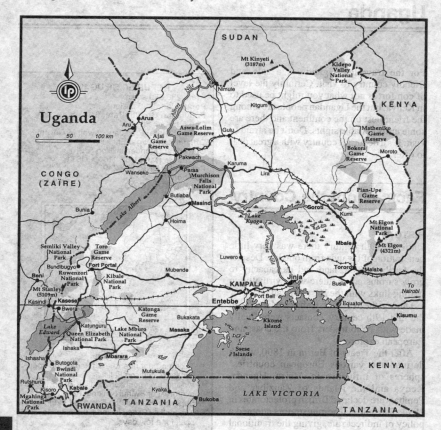

cabinet ministers and ordering his army chief of staff, Idi Amin, to storm the kabaka's palace. Obote became president, the Bagandan monarchy was abolished and Idi Amin's star was on the rise.

Events soon started to go seriously wrong. Obote had his attorney general, Godfrey Binaisa (a Bagandan), rewrite the constitution to consolidate virtually all powers in the presidency. He then began to nationalise foreign assets.

In 1969, a financial scandal put pressure on Amin, and he responded by staging a coup. So began Uganda's first reign of terror.

All political activities were quickly suspended and the army was empowered to shoot on sight anyone suspected of opposition to the regime. Over the next eight years an estimated 300,000 Ugandans lost their lives, often in horrifying ways. Amin's main targets were the Acholi and Lango tribespeople, educated people and the country's 70,000-strong Asian community. In 1972 the Asians were given 90 days to leave the country with virtually nothing more than the clothes they wore.

Meanwhile, the economy collapsed, the infrastructure crumbled, the prolific wildlife was machine-gunned by soldiers for meat, ivory and skins, and the tourism industry evaporated. The stream of refugees across the border became a flood. Inflation hit 1000%, and towards the end, the treasury was so bereft of funds that it was unable to pay the soldiers.

Faced with a restless army in which inter-tribal fighting had broken out, Amin was forced to seek a diversion. He chose a war with Tanzania, ostensibly to teach that country a lesson for supporting anti-Amin dissidents. The Tanzanians rolled the Ugandan army and pushed on into the heart of Uganda, and by the end of April 1979 organised resistance had effectively ceased. Amin fled to Libya where he remained until Gaddafi threw him out following a shoot-out with Libyan soldiers.

However, the rejoicing in Uganda was short-lived. The 12,000 or so Tanzanian soldiers who remained in Uganda, supposedly to assist with the country's reconstruction and to maintain law and order, turned on the Ugandans as soon as their pay wasn't forthcoming.

Yusufu Lule, a modest and unambitious man, had been installed as president with Tanzanian president Nyerere's blessing, but when he began speaking out against Nyerere he was replaced by Godfrey Binaisa, sparking riots in Kampala.

Binaisa quickly came under pressure from other powerful members of the provisional government. Fearing a coup, Binaisa attempted to dismiss army leader David Ojok, who refused to step down and instead placed Binaisa under house arrest. In 1980 the government was taken over by a military commission which set the election date for later that year. Obote returned from exile in Tanzania to an enthusiastic welcome in many parts of the country and swept to victory in an election which was blatantly rigged.

The honeymoon with Obote proved to be relatively short. Like Amin, Obote favoured certain tribes. Large numbers of civil servants and army and police commanders belonging to the tribes of the south were replaced with Obote supporters belonging to the tribes of the north, and the prisons began to fill once more.

Obote was about to complete the destruction that Amin initiated. More and more reports of atrocities leaked out of the country and several mass graves were discovered. In mid-1985 Obote was overthrown in a coup staged by the army under the leadership of Tito Okello.

Shortly after Obote became president for the second time in 1980, a guerilla army opposed to his tribally biased government was formed in western Uganda. It was led by Yoweri Museveni, who had lived in exile in Tanzania during Amin's reign and had served as defence minister during the chaotic administrations of 1979-80.

In the early days, few gave the guerillas, known as the National Resistance Army (NRA), much of a chance, but by the time Obote was ousted and Okello had taken over, the NRA controlled a large slice of western Uganda and was a power to be reckoned with.

Fighting proceeded in earnest between the NRA and Okello government troops, and by late January 1986 it was clear that Okello's days were numbered. The NRA launched an all-out offensive and took the capital.

Despite Museveni's Marxist leanings, he proved to be a pragmatic leader, appointing several arch-conservatives to his cabinet and making an effort to reassure the country's influential Catholic community. Meanwhile, almost 300,000 Ugandan refugees returned home from across the Sudanese border.

The economy took a turn for the better and aid and investment began returning to the country. The mood was buoyant.

After outside pressure for the return of a multiparty system, elections were held in March 1994. However, they were held on a non-party basis and candidates (although members of political parties) had to stand independently. In the end, Museveni and his supporters won more than a two-thirds majority in the Constituent Assembly. Elections in 1996, also held on a non-party basis, returned a similar result, with Museveni gaining 75% of the vote. The only area where

Ssemogerere, the main opposition candidate, had any real support was the anti-NRM north.

The 1996 elections can be seen as Uganda's final step on the road to complete rehabilitation and rebuilding. With the elections out of the way, the country is set to boom. Many potential investors held back, in case the elections didn't go smoothly and the country slid back into chaos. Tourism too is a sector with a bright future. The great pity is that Uganda still has a huge image problem; to most of the world it seems Uganda is still synonymous with two things – Idi Amin and HIV/AIDS. Nevertheless, the future for Uganda and its people is brighter now than it has been for many, many years.

GEOGRAPHY & CLIMATE

Uganda has an area of 236,580 sq km, of which about 25% is fertile arable land capable of providing a surplus of food. Lake Victoria and the Victoria Nile, which flows through much of the country, together create one of the best watered areas of Africa.

The land varies from semidesert in the north-east to the lush and fertile shores of Lake Victoria, the Ruwenzori Mountains in the west, and the beautiful, mountainous south-west.

The tropical heat is tempered by the altitude, which averages over 1000m.

As most of Uganda is fairly flat with mountains only in the extreme east (Mt Elgon), extreme west (Ruwenzori) and close to the Rwandan border, the bulk of the country enjoys the same tropical climate with temperatures averaging about 26°C during the day and 16°C at night. The hottest months are from December to February when the daytime range is 27 to 29°C.

The rainy seasons in the south are from April to May and October to November, the wettest month being April. In the north the wet season is from April to October and the dry season is from November to March.

ECOLOGY & ENVIRONMENT

There is a potential threat is to the ecology of Lake Victoria and the livelihood of the people who live by its shores, with the rapidly growing problem of water hyacinth (*Eichhornia crassipes*). This aquatic weed, originally from South America, floats in large 'islands' on the lake surface. It grows so prolifically that it chokes waterways and is so dense that it stops light penetrating the lake surface, making it impossible for fish to live beneath it. Visitors to the Owen Falls Dam at Jinja can get a graphic idea of how rampant the weed is – the area below the dam is choked almost solid and local people have great difficulty in manoeuvring their canoes through it.

POPULATION & PEOPLE

Uganda's population of about 21 million is increasing at the alarming rate of 3%. It is made up of a complex and diverse range of tribes. The Baganda make up about 20% of Uganda's population. Other tribes are the Lango, Acholi, Teso, Karamojong and Maasai. Pygmies live in the forests of the west.

While about two thirds of the population is Christian, the remaining third still practises animism, while a small percentage is Muslim.

LANGUAGE

The official language is English, which most people can speak. The other major languages are Luganda and Swahili, although the latter isn't spoken much in Kampala. See the Language Appendix for Swahili phrases.

Facts for the Visitor

VISAS

Visas are required for visits to Uganda, although there are many exceptions: nationals of Canada, Denmark, Finland, France, Israel, Germany, Japan, Norway, Sweden, and most Commonwealth countries (but not India, New Zealand and Nigeria).

Visa costs vary depending on nationality: the maximum is US$25 for a three month, single entry visa. Two photos are required and the visas are issued in 24 hours; in Nairobi you can get them the same day.

Visas are available at the border on entry for the usual fee, and you probably won't need a photo. They may give you less than three months but the visa is renewable in the normal way.

Visa Extensions

For visa extensions pay a visit to the immigration department, which is in the lower level of the Crested Crane Towers in Kampala, the ugly landmark building on Nile Ave in the city centre.

Other Visas

Kampala if not a bad place for picking up visas to other countries as there are usually no queues at the various embassies.

Burundi
Don't plan on getting a visa for Burundi in Uganda, as these are only issued to Ugandan residents.

Congo (Zaïre)
A single/multiple entry visa costs US$45/70 for one month, US$80/105 for two months and US$115/135 for three months. Two photos are required, and the visa is issued in 24 hours.

Kenya
If you apply before noon, the visa can usually be issued the same day. The cost is US$30 and two photos are required.

Rwanda
Visas cost US$20 (all nationalities), require two photos and are issued in 24 hours, or the same day if you apply early in the morning. They are also available on the border.

Sudan
Visa applications are only accepted on Monday and Thursday. A one month tourist visa costs US$10 (Ugandan shillings are not accepted) and requires two photos, a letter of introduction from your embassy and an onward ticket. Visas can take anything up to a month to issue, as all applications have to be referred to Khartoum. The border between Uganda and Sudan is effectively closed due to the civil war in southern Sudan.

Tanzania
Visas are valid for three months, take 24 hours to issue and require two photos. Costs vary according to your nationality – French US$25, German US$16, American US$45 and British US$55; others are around US$10 to US$20.

EMBASSIES
Ugandan Embassies

In Africa there are Ugandan embassies in Congo (Zaïre) (Kinshasa and Goma), Egypt, Ethiopia, Kenya, Rwanda, Sudan, Tanzania and Zambia. Elsewhere they are in Canada, France, Germany, Italy, the UK and the USA, among other places.

Foreign Embassies in Uganda

Countries with diplomatic missions in Kampala include:

Burundi
7 Bandali Rise, Bugolobi (☎ 221697)
Congo (Zaïre)
20 Philip Rd, Kololo (☎ 233777)
France
9 Parliament Ave (☎ 242120; fax 241252)
Italy
11 Lourdel Rd, Nakasero (☎ 241786; fax 250448)
Kenya
Nakasero Rd, Kampala (☎ 258235; fax 267369)
Netherlands
Kisozi Complex, Nakasero Lane (☎ 231859)
Rwanda
Plot 2, Nakaima Rd, next door to the Uganda Museum (☎ 244045)
South Africa
Plot 9, Malcolm X Ave, Kololo (☎/fax 259156)
Sudan
Plot 21, Nakasero Rd (☎ 243518)
Tanzania
6 Kagera Rd (☎ 256272)
UK
10 Parliament Ave (☎ 257301)
USA
Rear of British High Commission Building, 10 Parliament Ave (☎ 25791)

MONEY

US$1 = USh 1100

The Ugandan shilling (USh) is a stable currency and floats against the US dollar. It is also fully convertible (ie you can buy Ugandan shillings with US dollars or US dollars with Ugandan shillings) at foreign exchange (forex) bureaus.

It doesn't really matter too much where you change your money, though the forex bureaus generally offer slightly better rates than the banks. You will find forex bureaus at both the Malaba and Busia border posts (Uganda-Kenya border), Jinja, Kabale, Kampala (where there are scores of them), Masaka, Mbarara and Fort Portal. They don't exist in Tororo, Mbale and Kisoro, so if you're going there, plan ahead.

Since the elimination of the black market and the introduction of the forex bureaus, Uganda is one of the more expensive countries in the region.

POST & COMMUNICATIONS

International postal and telephone services are good, at least from Kampala, where you'll even see people with cellular phones!

In towns of any size you'll come across cardphones (yellow phoneboxes) outside the post office. These phones can be used for national and international calls, and cards are available from the post office.

From public phoneboxes international calls are charged at the rate of US$7.50 per minute (!) and the highest denomination phonecard is US$15 – clearly you're not meant to talk for long!

In Kampala there's a much cheaper option: the private operator called Starcom, which has an office and cardphones (green boxes) around town. Their charge is US$2.50 for one minute. See the Kampala section for details.

The country for Uganda is 256. The area code for Kampala is 041.

HEALTH

You must take all the usual precautions, particularly against bilharzia, which is a serious risk in any of Uganda's lakes and rivers.

AIDS continues to be a huge problem in Uganda. The epidemic is worst in the southwest of the country.

When exploring Uganda's higher regions, be aware of the dangers of high-altitude sickness. In extreme cases it can be fatal. There are no known indicators as to who might suffer from altitude sickness (fitness, age and previous high-altitude experience all seem to be irrelevant), and the only cure is an immediate descent to lower altitudes.

See the Health Appendix for further information about health issues.

DANGERS & ANNOYANCES

Even now, more than 10 years after Museveni's rise to power, Uganda still has a lingering image as a dangerous and unstable country to visit. This is a great shame, as it is currently the most stable and least corrupt country in the whole region, and also one of the safest.

Nevertheless, there are still some places where your safety cannot be guaranteed, particularly Karamoja and the area north of Murchison Falls National Park. If you want to visit these parts of the country, make enquiries before setting off.

PUBLIC HOLIDAYS

The following public holidays are observed in Uganda: 1 January, 26 January, 8 March, 1 May, 3 June, 9 October (Independence Day), 25 and 26 December, Good Friday, Easter Monday and variable Islamic holidays. (See Public Holidays in the Regional Facts for the Visitor chapter for dates.)

Getting There & Away

AIR

International airlines which serve Uganda include Aeroflot, Air Tanzania, Ethiopian Airlines, Kenya Airways, Sabena (the Belgian national airline) and Uganda Airlines.

Flying out of Uganda is expensive (there are no discounted fares available in Kampala), and flights to Kenya can be heavily booked.

LAND

Congo (Zaïre)

At the time of writing the situation in Eastern Congo (Zaïre) was uncertain and it was not clear how safe it would be to travel there. Ensure that you make enquiries locally before setting off.

The two main crossing points are south

from Kisoro to Rutshuru via Bunagana, and north-west from Kasese to Beni via Katwe and Kasindi. The Ishasha crossing between Kasese and Rutshuru is also open. There are less used border posts further north, between Pakwach and Mahagi and between Arua and Aru.

Kisoro to Rutshuru Before the recent problems the most reliable crossing was that between Kisoro and Rutshuru, a distance of about 30km. There are daily pick-ups (very crowded) between Kabale and the border via Kisoro.

Crossing into Congo (Zaïre) is straightforward and presents no hassles but check the security situation in Congo (Zaïre) before attempting this crossing. Get to the border early in the day if you want to get to Rutshuru, as there are few pick-ups.

If you intend spending time in Congo (Zaïre), have a visa when you get to the border. Otherwise, you can buy a temporary three day visa to visit the gorillas at Djomba (just over the border) for US$50, but you have to leave your passport at the Congo (Zaïre) border post until you return. You also have to buy a new Ugandan visa to re-enter Uganda (unless you have a multiple entry visa). This arrangement was very well established but things may have changed.

There's reasonable accommodation in Kisoro and basic accommodation on the Congo (Zaïre) side of the border.

Kasese to Rutshuru The Ishasha border post is another possibility. As there's a Friday market at Ishasha, this is probably the best day to go. There's also a Saturday market at Isharo (about halfway between Rutshuru and Ishasha), so there are trucks from Rutshuru early on Saturday mornings.

From Katunguru, the road to Ishasha is pretty good (2WD with care), although in the wet season it can be closed for days.

Kasese to Beni The route from Kasese to Beni via Katwe, Mpondwe and Kasindi involves hitching unless you can find a minibus. Depending on the day you go, this could involve a considerable wait (hours rather than days). Friday is market day so there are a number of trucks in both directions. There's basic accommodation at the border post at Bwera and at Kasindi, 3km from the border in Congo (Zaïre).

Kenya

Bus Akamba operates three direct buses between Kampala and Nairobi daily; the regular services cost US$18, depart at 7 am and 7 pm, and the journey takes around 12 to 14 hours. The Royal service is significantly more expensive (US$42), but very comfortable and includes lunch. The Akamba office in Kampala is on Dewinton St.

Mawingo also operates daily buses at 3 pm. These are marginally cheaper than Akamba (US$16), but are more crowded and take up to 15 hours. The depot in Kampala is right by the old taxi park.

To do the journey in stages, there are frequent minibuses to the Ugandan side of the Malaba border crossing; from Kampala (US$5, three hours), Jinja (US$5, two hours) and Tororo (US$0.30, less than one hour). The road is excellent, though this does mean that drivers can reach terrifying speeds.

The Kenyan and Ugandan border posts are about 1km from each other at Malaba, and you will have to walk between them. On the Ugandan side there's a forex bureau, supposedly open seven days a week, where you can change money at the prevailing rate.

Taking a vehicle through this border crossing is fairly straightforward and doesn't take more than a couple of hours.

From Malaba there are buses and trains to Nairobi.

The other entry point into Kenya from Uganda is via Busia further south. There are frequent minibuses between Jinja and Busia and between Busia and Kisumu in Kenya. Akamba has direct buses on this route which connect Kampala and Kisumu, and cost US$11.

Train The weekly train from Kampala to Nairobi is an excellent way to travel between the two capitals, and the border crossing is a breeze as the immigration officials come through the train and you don't even have to leave your compartment.

Departure from Kampala is at 4 pm on Wednesday, arriving in Nairobi on Thursday at 2 pm. It costs US$58/35 in 1st/2nd class, including meals and bedding.

Rwanda

There are two crossing points: Kabale to Kigali via Gatuna/Katuna, and Kisoro to Ruhengeri via Cyanika. Only the former is considered safe these days.

From Kabale to Kigali there are many minibuses daily which cost US$8 and take about two hours. There are two military checkpoints between the border and Kigali where your baggage will be searched.

Ugandan buses also do the run from Kabale to Kigali, leaving at 7.30 am. The cost is the same as the minibuses.

For those in a hurry to get between Kampala and Kigali, there's a daily bus which leaves Kampala at 6.30 am. These buses are operated by Jaguar or Happy Trails (in Kampala), cost US$15 and take about 10 hours.

Sudan

Overland entry into Sudan is impossible at present, and dangerous even if you managed it.

Tanzania

The route into Tanzania goes through the Kagera province from Masaka to Bukoba via Kyaka. It's possible to do the journey from Masaka to Bukoba in one day. There are minibuses from Masaka to Kyotera (US$1, 45 minutes), and several daily pick-ups go from there to the border at Mutukula (US$1.50, one hour). The border crossings are easy-going and there are moneychangers on the Tanzanian side, though they give a lousy rate.

From the border, there's a daily Land Rover that goes to Bukoba (US$5), which takes about four hours over appalling roads. There's also a bus which departs daily (except Sunday) at 5 pm, costs US$2 and takes about four hours. Hitching is difficult as there's little traffic.

LAKE

There's a regular lake service between Port Bell (Kampala) and Mwanza (Tanzania) which departs from Port Bell on Monday and Thursday at 6 pm and arrives in Mwanza the following day at 10 am. It's a good trip and fares cost US$35/25/20 in 1st/2nd/3rd class. Tickets should be booked by 2 pm on the day of departure at the Port Bell port gate.

This is assuming that ferry services have resumed following the sinking of the MV *Bukoba* in 1996 with the loss of 600-plus lives (the boat had a registered capacity of 430).

Getting Around

BUS & TAXI

Uganda is the land of minibuses (known as taxis), and there's never any shortage of them. Fares are fixed and vehicles leave when full.

Normal buses also connect the major towns. They're cheaper than minibuses but much slower because they stop a great deal to pick up and set down passengers.

Most towns and cities have a bus station/taxi park – simply turn up and tell people where you want to go.

TRAIN

Passenger services in Uganda are 3rd class only, and due to frequent delays and cancellations are generally slow, uncomfortable and not worth the bother. There are services from Kampala to Kasese and to Tororo.

CAR

There's an excellent system of sealed roads between most major centres in the southern part of the country. In the north, minor roads are usually badly potholed, and after heavy rain they become impassable in anything other than a 4WD.

Road signs are almost nonexistent in Uganda, even outside major towns.

Vehicle hire in Uganda is not well developed, but a number of agencies in Kampala offer the service. The cost is around US$40 per day for a small car, US$70 for a 4WD, plus kilometres, insurance and fuel.

Fuel is horrifically expensive. Petrol is US$1.10 per litre; diesel only a few shillings cheaper.

HITCHING

Without your own transport, hitching is virtually obligatory in some situations, such as getting into national parks that are not served by public transport. Free lifts on trucks are the exception rather than the rule, so ask before you get on.

BOAT

There are very limited opportunities for travel by boat on Lake Victoria, the only options being the various methods of getting to the Ssese Islands from Bukakata (east of Masaka) and Kasenyi (a 30 minute taxi ride from Kampala). See the Ssese Islands section for details.

SAFARIS
Organised Safaris

Quite a few reliable companies offer safaris to the national parks and other places of interest, including to the gorillas of Bwindi and Mgahinga in the extreme south-west of the country.

National parks covered by these companies include Murchison Falls, Ruwenzori, Kibale, Semliki Valley, Queen Elizabeth, Bwindi, Mgahinga and Lake Mburo.

Costs Ugandan safari companies rely heavily on lodge and hotel accommodation, so the trips are quite expensive. Even where camping is involved, it's usually the luxury tented camp variety and thus no cheaper.

Since none of the Ugandan companies offer genuine budget camping safaris such as those in Kenya, it's worth considering going with a Kenyan company which covers

Uganda – and usually the gorillas of Congo (Zaïre).

Costs vary a great deal from one company to another but are consistently high. In general, if you assume US$150 to US$250 per day you won't be too far off the mark. This should include all transport, three meals a day, accommodation (including all camping equipment where appropriate) and park entry fees (though some companies exclude these).

Choosing a Company Among the companies which can be recommended are the following in Kampala. These have been listed alphabetically, not in any order of preference or reliability. The area code for Kampala is 041.

African Pearl Safaris
    Lower ground floor, Embassy House (☎ 233566)
Blacklines Tours
    2 Colville St, PO Box 6968 (☎ 255520)
Gametrackers
    Raja Chambers, Parliament Ave, PO Box 7703 (☎ 258993)
Hot Ice Ltd
    Spear House, Dewinton Rise, PO Box 151 (☎ 242733)
Nile Safaris Ltd
    Room 230, Farmers House, Parliament Ave, PO Box 12135 (☎ 244331)

Do-It-Yourself Safaris

Organising your own safari without your own transport is difficult in Uganda, as there's so little traffic into the national parks. That doesn't mean you can't do it – travellers do manage it – but it will certainly involve a fair amount of hitching and waiting around for a ride.

Kampala

The capital, Kampala, suffered a great deal during the years of civil strife that began with Idi Amin's defeat in 1979 at the hands of the Tanzanian army and ended in early 1986 with the victory of Yoweri Museveni's NRA.

In the decade since Museveni's victory,

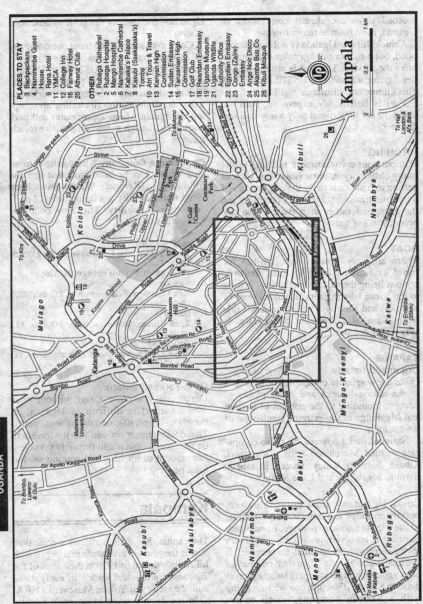

Kampala

PLACES TO STAY
3 Backpackers
4 Namirembe Guest House
9 Rena Hotel
11 YMCA
12 College Inn
16 Fairway Hotel
20 Sheraton Club

OTHER
1 Rubaga Cathedral
2 Rubaga Hospital
5 Mengo Hospital
6 Namirembe Cathedral
7 Kabaka's Palace
8 Kasubi (Ssekabaka's) Tombs
10 Afri Tours & Travel
13 Kenyan High Commission
14 Sudan Embassy
15 Tanzanian High Commission
17 Golf Club
18 Rwandan Embassy
19 Uganda Museum
21 Uganda Wildlife Authority Office
22 Egyptian Embassy
23 Congo (Zaire) Embassy
24 Ange Noir Disco
25 Akamba Bus Co
26 Kibuli Mosque

however, the city has gone from a looted shell to a thriving, modern city befitting the capital of one of the most rapidly developing countries in Africa. These days Kampala even has casinos, nightclubs and decent restaurants. The fact that many Asians have returned has certainly given business and commerce in Kampala a major boost.

The best thing about Kampala, though (and this is in stark contrast to Nairobi), is that it's quite safe to walk around at any time of the day or night in virtually any part of the city. You won't get mugged here, the city is green and attractive, and the people are very friendly – it's a great place.

Information

Tourist Office The tourist office (☎ 242196; fax 242188) is in the IPS Building, near the British high commission on Parliament Ave. The staff here are very well informed and have all sorts of information at their finger tips, although nothing much in the way of printed information.

Uganda Wildlife Authority Office The Uganda Wildlife Authority office (☎ 530574), which is where you make bookings to see the gorillas in Bwindi and Mgahinga, is inconveniently located a few kilometres from the city centre just off Kira Rd at 31 Kanjokya St, Kanjokya. To get there take a Kanjokya (pronounced kamwocha) taxi (US$0.30) from the old taxi park, and get off when you see a row of small market shops below the road on the left; the office is signposted to the right – taxi drivers usually know it.

Post & Communications The post office is on the corner of Kampala and Speke Rds. It also houses the international telephone exchange, which has public international phones and faxes. Phonecards are sold at the post office, and there are many cardphones (yellow phone boxes) around town.

For overseas and STD phone calls it's much cheaper (one-third the price) to use Starcom Communications on Entebbe Rd just down from Kampala Rd. The Starcom

office is open from 7.30 am to 9 pm Monday to Saturday, and from 11 am to 4 pm Sundays.

Things to See

The **Uganda Museum** on Kira Rd is worth a visit. Perhaps its most interesting feature is the collection of traditional musical instruments, which you're allowed to play.

The **Kasubi Tombs** (also known as the Ssekabaka's Tombs) are on Kasubi Hill just off Masiro Rd. Here you will find the huge traditional reed and bark-cloth buildings of the kabakas of the Baganda people.

Also worth a visit are the four main religious buildings in Kampala – the gleaming white **Kibuli Mosque** dominating Kibuli Hill on the other side of the railway station from Nakasero Hill; the huge Roman Catholic **Rubaga Cathedral** on Rubaga Hill; the Anglican **Namirembe Cathedral**, where the congregation is called to worship by the beating of drums; and the enormous **Hindu Temple** in the city centre.

Outside Kampala at Entebbe are the **Botanical Gardens**, which are worth visiting if you have half a day available. Laid out in 1901, they're alongside the lake between the sailing club and the centre of Entebbe.

Places to Stay

Campers and others looking for budget accommodation should head for *Backpackers* (☎ 258469; fax 272012; email ptcu@starcom.co.ug), about a 10-minute taxi ride out of the centre at Kalema Rd, Lunguja, not far from the landmark Namirembe Cathedral. It's a quiet, relaxed place, popular among travellers and overland truckers. Camping costs US$2.30 per person, or there are basic rooms for US$4.60 in a dorm, or US$11.50 for a double. To get there, take a Natete taxi from the new taxi park (US$0.30); there's a sign on a light pole in the middle of the park – just ask for the backpackers.

Closer to the centre of town is the *YMCA* (☎ 230804) on Buganda Rd, about 15 minutes walk from the city centre. You can camp here for US$1.50 but you won't get much privacy, as the site is on a playing field

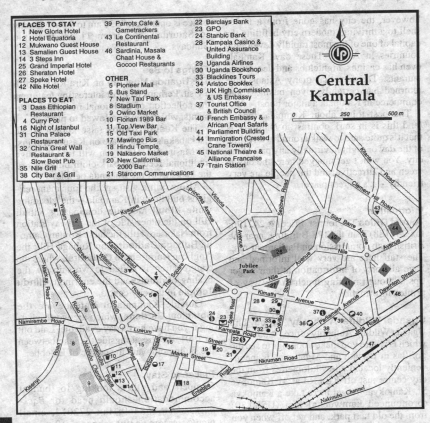

PLACES TO STAY		39 Parrots Cafe &	22 Barclays Bank
1 New Gloria Hotel		Gametrackers	23 GPO
2 Hotel Equatoria		43 Le Continental	24 Stanbic Bank
12 Mukwano Guest House		Restaurant	28 Kampala Casino &
13 Samalien Guest House		46 Sardinia, Masala	United Assurance
14 3 Steps Inn		Chaat House &	Building
25 Grand Imperial Hotel		Gocool Restaurants	29 Uganda Airlines
26 Sheraton Hotel			30 Uganda Bookshop
27 Speke Hotel			33 Blacklines Tours
42 Nile Hotel		OTHER	34 Aristoc Booklex
		5 Pioneer Mall	36 UK High Commission
PLACES TO EAT		6 Bus Stand	& US Embassy
3 Daas Ethiopian		7 New Taxi Park	37 Tourist Office
Restaurant		8 Stadium	& British Council
4 Curry Pot		9 Owino Market	40 French Embassy &
16 Night of Istanbul		10 Florian 1989 Bar	African Pearl Safaris
31 China Palace		11 Top View Bar	41 Parliament Building
Restaurant		15 Old Taxi Park	44 Immigration (Crested
32 China Great Wall		17 Mawingo Bus	Crane Towers)
Restaurant &		18 Hindu Temple	45 National Theatre &
Slow Boat Pub		19 Nakasero Market	Alliance Francaise
35 Nile Grill		20 New California	47 Train Station
38 City Bar & Grill		2000 Bar	
		21 Starcom Communications	

Central Kampala

which fronts on to busy Bombo Rd. In the building itself, you can sleep on a mattress on the floor for US$2. It's a surprisingly popular place to stay, despite the inconvenience of having to pack up and be out by 8 am each day, as it's used as a school on weekdays.

The budget hotels are all in the busy part of town near the taxi parks and bus station. Far and away the best place is the friendly little *Mukwano Guest House* (☎ 232248) on Nakivubo Place right opposite the amazingly busy Owino Market. Dorm beds are US$6, or there's a couple of singles at US$11.50.

Also in this same area is the *Kadepro Tourist Guest House* (☎ 255040), which is OK but as all rooms face the road it is noisy. A bed in the cramped dorm is US$7, or there are singles/doubles with breakfast for US$12/16. All rooms have common bathroom facilities.

Further along towards Entebbe Rd is the *3 Steps Inn* (☎ 24539), another basic but decent guesthouse, with double rooms only for US$16 (common bath).

A reasonably good value mid-range place in the city centre is the *New Gloria Hotel* (☎ 257790) on William St. It's a small, recently renovated place with a cafe. It has singles/doubles with attached bathroom for US$25/45.

A short walk west of the city centre, the *Rena Hotel* (☎ 272336) on Namirembe Rd is good value, at US$18/25 for a single/double with shared facilities or US$25/36 with private bathroom, including breakfast.

Places to Eat

Very close to Nakasero Market in the centre of town is the small *Night of Istanbul*. Main courses here are heavily Indian influenced and cost around US$5. It's a good place which stays open until quite late.

If you're staying in the taxi-park area of town, the choice is limited. Best is the tiny *City Restaurant*, in the small group of shops on the southern side of the new taxi park. Here you can get a good egg and tea breakfast for US$1, and other basic meals for around US$2.

For a cheap Indian meal try the *Masala Chaat House* on Dewinton Rd opposite the national theatre. This is a popular little place which serves vegetarian Indian thali meals for US$3.20.

Surprisingly, one of the best deals in town is at the *Kampala Casino* on Kimathi Ave. On Thursday evenings they put on a Ugandan buffet, and at US$6.50 this is great value. If you haven't tried local food this is a good opportunity, and there's live music while you eat. You do, of course, need to be reasonably smartly dressed to get in.

On the lower part of Kampala Rd, towards the railway station, is the smart *City Bar & Grill*. This very popular lunch time hangout serves excellent tandoori and other Indian dishes, as well as Western meals such as steak. Prices are in the US$5 to US$7.50 range, and there's also a full-sized snooker table and bar.

Further afield, a very popular place with excellent food is the *Half London* on Gaba Rd (sometimes spelt Gqaba). They offer a range of grills and Western-style food and the service is good. You're looking at around US$8 for a meal. For young people, the bar is one of the places to go in the evenings.

Entertainment

One good cheap African bar is the *Florian 1989 Bar* on Nakivubo Place, down near the new taxi park. Another popular local bar here is the open-air *Top View Bar*, which has a live band every night. As the name suggests, it's on a rooftop.

Perhaps the most popular disco is the *Ange Noir* (pronounced locally as Angenoa), which is just off Jinja Rd east of the city centre. Everyone knows it but it's not signposted on the main road.

Getting There & Away

Bus The main bus station is on the corner of Allen Rd and Luwum St, below Kampala Rd. It's a busy place with buses to every main town in the country on a daily basis.

To Butogota (for Bwindi National Park), there is one departure daily at 6 am with Silverline – the trip takes most of the day and costs US$10; there are also daily buses to Kabale (many companies, six hours, US$8) via Mbarara and Masaka; Kasese (Safe Journey, three daily, US$8); Masindi (three hours, US$5); and Fort Portal (two daily, six hours, US$7).

EMS Post minibuses depart at 7 am from the post office on Monday, Wednesday and Friday for Kabale (US$6.50) via Masaka (US$2.50) and Mbarara (US$4); also to Mbale (US$4.50); Masindi (US$4); Hoima (US$5.50) and Fort Portal (US$7) via Mbarara and Kasese (US$6). These are an excellent way to travel, and bookings should be made at the post office a day or so in advance.

Taxi Kampala has two taxi parks. Although on first appearance these places seem utterly chaotic, they are in fact highly organised. Taxis for a particular destination always leave from the same place within each park. The old taxi park, on the triangle formed by Burton, Luwum and South Sts, is the bigger of the two and serves all parts of the city and country to the east; the new taxi park services destinations to the west and north.

As with buses, there are taxis to all major parts of the country on a daily basis.

UGANDA

Getting Around

The Airport The international airport is at Entebbe, 35km south of Kampala. There are public taxis between Kampala and Entebbe town (US$1), from where you can catch another taxi to the airport (3km, US$0.50). A special hire taxi from Kampala to Entebbe airport costs about US$25.

Taxi The ubiquitous white minibus taxis leave from the two taxi parks and fan out all over the city. To find the taxi you want, simply ask around at the taxi parks – people are generally very helpful.

Special Hire In Kampala, there are plenty of 'special hire' taxis, but they're difficult to identify since there's no standardised colour and they have no signs. A standard short-distance fare is around US$2.50.

Around the Country

FORT PORTAL

Fort Portal is a small, pleasant and quiet town at the northern end of the Ruwenzori Mountains. It's also the base from which to explore the Semliki Valley (hot springs and Pygmy villages) and the Kibale Forest National Park.

Kabarole Tours (☎ (0493) 2668l), signposted behind the Esso station, is a good local tour operator.

Places to Stay

One of the cheapest and most popular places is the *Kyaka Lodge* on Kuhadika Rd. You can get a simple room with shared bathroom for US$3/4, but it's pretty awful.

Much better is the *Wooden Hotel* (☎ 22560) on Lugard Rd. Very clean, comfortable rooms with common bath cost US$5/8 for singles/doubles. With private bath it's US$8/10.

The best mid-range option is the very pleasant *Ruwenzori View Guest House*. It's just a small place, signposted off Toro Rd, with a rural aspect and good views of the

mountains. The cost is a very reasonable US$18/30 for singles/doubles with attached bathroom, including breakfast.

Places to Eat

The best food in town is at the *RA Bistro* on Rukidi III St, which serves western-style food. It isn't that cheap, at around US$4 for a main course, but it's excellent, with good service and friendly staff.

Getting There & Away

The taxi park is on Kahinju Rd. There are fairly frequent departures to Hoima, Kasese (US$2.50) and Kampala (US$8).

From the bus station at the other end of Babitha Rd, a daily 6 am bus runs to Kabale (US$8) via Kasese and Mbarara. There are also daily buses to Kampala at 7 and 10 am (US$7, seven hours) via Mubende.

AROUND FORT PORTAL

Kibale Forest National Park

The star attraction at this national park, some 30km south-east of Fort Portal, is the chimpanzees, five groups of which have been partially habituated to human contact.

The park headquarters is at Kanyanchu, signposted on the left about 6km before you reach the village of Bigodi coming from Fort Portal. It's from here that guided walks can be arranged along well-marked tracks (about a 3km round trip) in search of the chimps. There are daily walks from 7 to 11 am (the best time to go) and from 3 to 6 pm, costing US$7 per person, plus the park entry fee of US$15.

You can camp at the headquarters (US$10). Alternatively there's the *Safari Hotel*, which is in Nkingo village, about 45 minutes walk from the park headquarters towards Bigodi village. Here singles/doubles cost US$3/6, or you can camp for US$2.

Right in Bigodi itself is *Mucusu*, a very cosy and friendly place which costs US$3/6 for singles/doubles including breakfast.

Taxis from Fort Portal to Kamwenge pass through Bigodi (US$1.20) and pass the reserve headquarters (US$0.60).

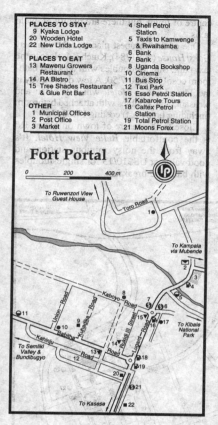

PLACES TO STAY
9 Kyaka Lodge
20 Wooden Hotel
22 New Linda Lodge

PLACES TO EAT
13 Mawenu Growers Restaurant
14 RA Bistro
15 Tree Shades Restaurant & Glue Pot Bar

OTHER
1 Municipal Offices
2 Post Office
3 Market
4 Shell Petrol Station
5 Taxis to Kamwenge & Rwaihamba
6 Bank
7 Bank
8 Uganda Bookshop
10 Cinema
11 Bus Stop
12 Taxi Park
16 Esso Petrol Station
17 Kabarole Tours
18 Caltex Petrol Station
19 Total Petrol Station
21 Moons Forex

Fort Portal

0   200   400 m

To Ruwenzori View Guest House

Toro Road

To Kampala via Mubende

To Kibale National Park

To Semliki Valley & Bundibugyo

To Kasese

Lake Nkuruba

Lake Nkuruba, 25km south of Fort Portal, is a stunning crater lake which is excellent for swimming and believed to be bilharzia free. There are also good walking opportunities from the camp here, including a one hour trek to Lake Nyabikere, from where you can continue to Rweteera and Kibale Forest.

The *community camp site* at the lake is quite basic, but the welcome is warm and the setting ideal for a few days of rest and relaxation. It costs US$2 to pitch a tent. Facilities include a cooking shelter and bush shower.

Taxis from Fort Portal to Kasenda or Rwaihamba pass Lake Nkuruba (US$0.80), which is signposted on the left just before Rwaihamba.

Semliki Valley National Park

Many visitors to Fort Portal make at least a day trip to the Semliki Valley and to **Bundibugyo** on the other side of the Ruwenzoris.

The two main 'attractions' are the **hot springs** near Sempaya and the **Pygmy villages** near the village of Ntandi in the forest of the Semliki Valley, a few kilometres before Bundibugyo. Unfortunately, the Pygmy villagers are horribly commercialised, their culture moribund.

Places to Stay Near the toll station, there's a simple hotel where you can stay the night for US$3 a double. You could also stay at one of the two *bandas* (huts) which are run by Morence Mpora (☎ (0493) 2245) at Kichwamba/Nyankuku, on the way to Bundibugyo.

If you find yourself in Bundibugyo (the local administrative centre) and need to stay the night, there's the *Moonlight Hotel* which costs US$5 per person.

Getting There & Away There are occasional taxis between Fort Portal and Bundibugyo, but as they're obviously not going to hang around while you visit the sights, you'll be left stranded.

The best way to get to the Semliki Valley is to go on one of Kabarole Tours' half-day excursions (US$60 shared between up to four people).

JINJA

Jinja lies on the shores of Lake Victoria and is a major marketing centre for southern Uganda. It's an interesting little place, and one which didn't suffer as badly as many others during the last civil war, so it doesn't wear the same air of dereliction.

Jinja is close to what used to be the Owen Falls, where the Victoria Nile leaves the lake. The **Owen Falls Dam** might be worth a visit, though the actual falls have disappeared under the lake which has been created.

UGANDA

Photography is prohibited. It's several kilometres west of the town towards Kampala on a main road which crosses the top of the dam. The best way to get there is to catch one of the bicycle taxis which hang around outside the market.

Closer to town is the very popular but unspectacular **Source du Nil** (Source of the Nile), formerly Ripon Falls.

Places to Stay

Campers should head for the Timton Hotel, where you can pitch your tent in the garden for US$3 per person. It's about 1km from the

centre of town, but there are plenty of cycle taxis.

One of the cheapest places is the *Fairway Guest House* (☎ 21784), Kutch Rd, close to the taxi park. Singles/doubles with attached bathroom cost US$6.50/7.50. A few doors away is the *Victoria View Hotel*, which is clean and pleasant, with doubles with attached bathroom (including breakfast) costing US$8.

Close to the centre of town on Kutch Rd is the comfortable *Belle View Hotel*. It's away from the noisy minibus station and good value at US$10/13 for singles/doubles with bath and breakfast.

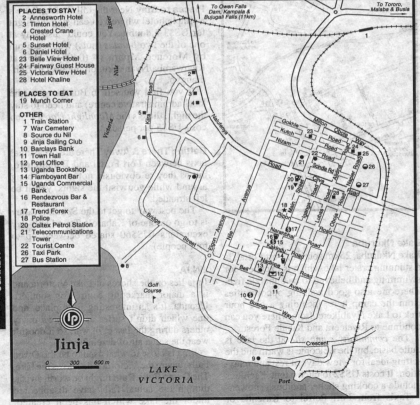

PLACES TO STAY
2 Annesworth Hotel
3 Timton Hotel
4 Crested Crane Hotel
5 Sunset Hotel
6 Daniel Hotel
23 Belle View Hotel
24 Fairway Guest House
25 Victoria View Hotel
28 Hotel Khaline

PLACES TO EAT
19 Munch Corner

OTHER
1 Train Station
7 War Cemetery
8 Source du Nil
9 Jinja Sailing Club
10 Barclays Bank
11 Town Hall
12 Post Office
13 Uganda Bookshop
14 Flamboyant Bar
15 Uganda Commercial Bank
16 Rendezvous Bar & Restaurant
17 Trend Forex
18 Police
20 Caltex Petrol Station
21 Telecommunications Tower
22 Tourist Centre
26 Taxi Park
27 Bus Station

To Owen Falls Dam, Kampala & Bujugali Falls (11km)

To Tororo, Malaba & Busia

Jinja

0   300   600 m

LAKE VICTORIA

Places to Eat

It comes as something of a surprise to find an Indian restaurant, complete with screeching Hindi film-score music, in sleepy Jinja. The *Munch Corner* on Main St does reasonable masala dosas for US$2.50, and also that old Indian favourite – pizza (US$3).

Getting There & Away

There are taxis to Kampala (US$1, one hour), Malaba (US$5) and Mbale (US$5).

KABALE

Kabale is in the Kigezi area, which tourist brochures often and inappropriately refer to as the 'Little Switzerland of Africa'.

This south-western corner of Uganda is certainly very beautiful with its intensively cultivated and terraced hills, forests and lakes. A visit to Lake Bunyonyi is particularly recommended.

Kabale is Uganda's highest town (about 2000m) and it gets cool at night, so have warm clothes handy.

Things to See

Lake Bunyonyi, a famous beauty spot over the ridge to the west of Kabale, is a large and irregularly shaped lake with many islands. The surrounding hillsides, as elsewhere in this region, are intensively cultivated. Many of the villagers have boats and arranging a trip out on the lake shouldn't be a problem.

To get to Lake Bunyonyi, you can either take a minibus (infrequent), hitch or walk (about 6km from Kabale). Ask directions locally.

Places to Stay

If you are camping, there is a free site close to the White Horse Inn but it has no facilities.

The cheapest place to stay is the *St Paul's Training Centre & Hostel*, where double rooms cost US$4.50. It's a clean place, the staff are friendly and simple meals are available.

Two very popular budget hotels here are the *Visitours Hotel*, where singles/doubles will cost you US$3/5, and the *Sky Blue Motel* (☎ 22154), which also has very clean rooms for US$6/8 with shared bathroom facilities.

A good mid-range place is the airy *Victoria Inn* (☎ 22134), with very comfortable rooms with attached bathroom for US$12/20.

Places to Eat

You can find good cheap food at the *Visitours*

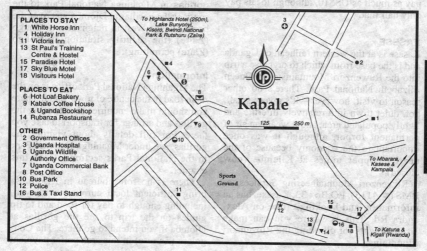

PLACES TO STAY
1 White Horse Inn
4 Holiday Inn
11 Victoria Inn
13 St Paul's Training Centre & Hostel
15 Paradise Hotel
17 Sky Blue Motel
18 Visitours Hotel

PLACES TO EAT
6 Hot Loaf Bakery
9 Kabale Coffee House & Uganda Bookshop
14 Rubanza Restaurant

OTHER
2 Government Offices
3 Uganda Hospital
5 Uganda Wildlife Authority Office
7 Uganda Commercial Bank
8 Post Office
10 Bus Park
12 Police
16 Bus & Taxi Stand

To Highlands Hotel (250m), Lake Bunyonyi, Kisoro, Bwindi National Park & Rutshuru (Zaire)

Kabale

0   125   250 m

Sports Ground

To Mbarara, Kasese & Kampala

To Katuna & Kigali (Rwanda)

UGANDA

Hotel, Sky Blue Motel or the *Rubanza Restaurant*.

The best value, however, is the restaurant at the *Highlands Hotel*. Prices are reasonable and the food good.

Highly recommended is the *Hot Loaf Bakery*, just off the main street and near the post office.

Getting There & Away

Bus There are numerous daily buses to Kampala, which take about six hours and cost US$8. To Fort Portal, there's a daily bus via Mbarara and Kasese at 7 am (US$8, about eight hours).

There are also direct minibuses to Kigali in Rwanda from the bus park near the Visitours Hotel. See the Uganda Getting There & Away section for details.

Taxi The daily taxis between Kabale and Kisoro cost US$4 (US$4.50 to the Congo (Zaïre) border) and take about 2½ hours. They go when full, and 'full' means just that! They depart from the Shell petrol station next to the Visitours Hotel.

For Bwindi National Park there are a couple of vehicles to Butogota daily. You'll pay as much as US$10, although locals pay only half that.

KASESE

Kasese is at the western railhead of Uganda and is the base from which to organise a trip into the Ruwenzori Mountains or to Queen Elizabeth National Park. There's no other reason to visit, however – it's a very small, hot, quiet town in a relatively infertile and lightly populated area, and it wears an air of permanent torpor, although it was once important to the economy because of the nearby copper mines at Kilembe (now closed).

Ruwenzori Mountaineering Services, or RMS (☎ 4115), PO Box 33, Kasese, has an information and booking office on Alexandra Rd. This is where you can make arrangements for climbing the Ruwenzori Mountains.

Places to Stay

The *Rumukiya Inn*, a fairly new place, claims to 'maximumly serve'. As with most hotels in Kasese, the rooms are set around a little courtyard, and cost US$4/6 with common bath. Also good, and very similar, is the *Kogere Modernised Lodge* on Stanley St. Rooms at this little place all have common facilities, and cost US$4/5.

The *Saad Hotel* (☎ 44139) on Ruwenzori Rd has been a very popular travellers' hangout for years. It only has double rooms with attached bathroom (with two single beds), but they allow three people to share a room. It costs US$15/25 for a double/triple.

Getting There & Away

There are daily buses to Kampala (via Mbarara; US$8, about eight hours) and Kabale (US$7.50, 7½ hours). There are frequent taxis to Fort Portal (US$2.50) and Mbarara (US$4).

KISORO

Kisoro is at the extreme south-western tip of the country on the Ugandan side of the Virunga Mountains, across from Ruhengeri in neighbouring Rwanda. Its main draw for travellers is as a base from which to visit the **gorillas** in Mgahinga National Park to the south or the gorillas at Djomba just over the border to the west in neighbouring Congo (Zaïre) (the security situation in Congo (Zaïre) permitting).

Information

The Mgahinga National Park office is on the main road in the centre of town, and it's here you should make enquiries about seeing the gorillas and arrange for transport to take you there. For full details about visiting the gorillas, see under Mgahinga National Park in the National Parks section later in this chapter.

There is no forex bureau in Kisoro, so bring sufficient local currency with you, including enough to pay for food and to tip guides on the trip to see the gorillas at Djomba if you intend to go there. The Congolese (Zaïrese) in this area prefer payment

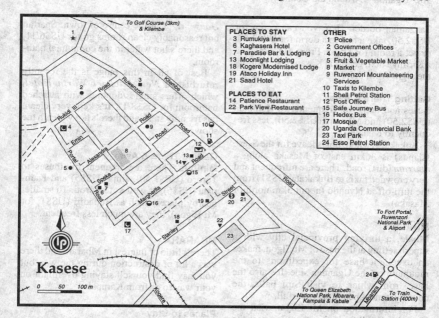

Kasese

PLACES TO STAY
3 Rumukiya Inn
6 Kaghasera Hotel
7 Paradise Bar & Lodging
13 Moonlight Lodging
18 Kogere Modernised Lodge
19 Ataco Holiday Inn
21 Saad Hotel

PLACES TO EAT
14 Patience Restaurant
22 Park View Restaurant

OTHER
1 Police
2 Government Offices
4 Mosque
5 Fruit & Vegetable Market
8 Market
9 Ruwenzori Mountaineering Services
10 Taxis to Kilembe
11 Shell Petrol Station
12 Post Office
15 Safe Journey Bus
16 Hedex Bus
17 Mosque
20 Uganda Commercial Bank
23 Taxi Park
24 Esso Petrol Station

in Ugandan shillings rather than Central African CFA francs.

Places to Stay

About 1.5km from Kisoro on the road to Congo (Zaïre) is the *Rugigana Tourist Valley Campsite*, where you can camp for US$1.50 or take a basic room for US$2 per person.

In Kisoro itself, the best place to stay is the *Mubano Hotel*, which has twin-bed doubles with attached bathroom for US$6. It's reasonably clean, the staff are friendly and there's a bar and restaurant, although no electricity or running water.

A cheaper bet is the *Starlight Guest House*, which charges US$2.50 but is a bit of a dump.

Getting There & Away

There's a direct bus between Kampala and Kisoro daily, leaving Kampala at 7 am and costing US$11. It passes through Kabale

around noon if you want to pick it up there (US$4).

Taxis to the border at Bunagana cost US$0.50. If you intend to head further into Congo (Zaïre) after seeing the gorillas at Djomba, the only public transport to Rutshuru is on Friday. The rest of the time you'll have to hitch, and there's very little traffic.

MASAKA

In 1979 Masaka was virtually destroyed by the Tanzanian army in the closing stages of the war which ousted Idi Amin. A lot of rebuilding has taken place, but a lot more is required.

There's very little to do in Masaka. For most travellers it's just an overnight stop en route to the Ssese Islands in Lake Victoria or south into Tanzania.

Places to Stay

Masaka Backpackers (☎ (0481) 21288) is about 4km from town, just off the road to the

UGANDA

Tanzanian border. Here you can camp for US$2.50, take a bed in a dorm for US$3.50, or get a room for US$5. From Masaka, take a Kirimya taxi, get off at Kasanvu and follow the signs from there.

Getting There & Away
Buses and taxis run frequently to Kampala (US$2.50) and Mbarara (US$2.50), less frequently to Kabale.

Bukakata (where boats leave for the Ssese Islands) is 36km east of Masaka along a *murram* (dirt) road. There are infrequent and very crowded taxis to Bukakata (US$1) from the turn-off at Nyendo (about 3km north of Masaka).

MBALE
Mbale, a thriving provincial city with a superb setting at the base of Mt Elgon, makes an excellent base for expeditions to the mountain on the Ugandan side. It's also the base from which to visit Sipi Falls, the country's most beautiful waterfall.

For information on Mt Elgon, visit the Ugandan Wildlife Authority office near the Mt Elgon Hotel.

Sipi Falls
Sipi Falls is a truly beautiful sight and well worth making the 55km trip north of Mbale to see. The cheapest way of getting to the falls is to take a minibus from Mbale to Kapchorwe and get off close to the falls, but these minibuses are not very frequent, so it may be more convenient to hire a taxi for the day.

If you'd like to stay for the night, there's the *Sipi Falls Rest House* at US$35 per person per night, or you can camp for US$3. Perhaps a better option is the *Elgon Maasai House* in Sipi village, which offers singles for US$5 and also has food available.

Places to Stay
Pick of the very meagre bunch is the *Nile Rest House*, which charges US$3/4 for singles/doubles with attached bathroom, but don't expect too much.

Somewhat more salubrious is the *Upland*

House, right in the centre of town. Spartan but reasonably clean rooms go for US$6/11, and there's hot water in the communal bathroom.

Best of all in this range is the recently refurbished *New Michael Worth Hotel*, which offers singles/doubles with attached bathroom for US$8/11. It's kept very clean, has friendly staff, and there's hot water in the showers.

Getting There & Away
Minibus There are frequent minibuses to Tororo (US$1.50), Jinja (US$5) and Kampala (US$6), as well as to Soroti. To smaller nearby places, such as Budadiri (US$1; for Mt Elgon), they are much less frequent.

MBARARA
There's little of interest in Mbarara and there was a lot of destruction during the war, but you may find yourself staying overnight on your way to or from Kampala.

Places to Stay
A reasonable, cheap place to stay is the *Pearl Lodge* behind the Shell station, which has singles/doubles with shared facilities for US$5/10.

A good mid-range place is the *Mayoba Inn*, on the main road. It has singles/doubles with shared facilities for US$8/10.

If you'd prefer to be off the main road, try the homely *Buhumuriro Guest House* (☎ (0485) 21145), which offers doubles (no singles) for US$11.

Getting There & Away
There are frequent buses and minibuses from Mbarara to Kampala (US$6, four hours), Masaka (US$2.50), Kabale (US$4, two hours) and Kasese (US$4).

SSESE ISLANDS
This group of 84 islands lies off the north-western shores of Lake Victoria, east of Masaka and south of Entebbe.

The main islands of Buggala, Bufumira, Bukasa, Bubeke and Kkome are hilly, and

UGANDA

the noncultivated areas are forested with a wide variety of trees.

Many spots afford beautiful views over the lake and across to the other islands. You'll have no problems persuading the fishers to take you out on their boats. Swimming is also possible off most of the islands, as long as you observe the usual precaution about avoiding reedy areas (where the snails which carry the bilharzia parasite live).

Places to Stay & Eat

The accommodation options are basically limited to Buggala Island. The most popular place is the *Hornbill Camp Site*, about 15 minutes walk from Kalangala. Camping costs US$1.50, and filling meals are US$1.50. The people who run this place are very friendly, and it's a fun place to stay.

Another option is *PTA Andronico's Malanga Safari Lodge* (☎ (0481) 255646) in Kalangala. A bed here in rather scruffy rooms costs US$3. Camping is possible (US$1.50) although there's not much space.

Panorama Camping Safaris, also in Kalangala, has been well set up, with camping in sites among the rainforest for US$2, and a number of bandas for US$15. Excellent meals are available (around US$3), and the service is good and very friendly.

In Liku, about 500m from where the ferry from Bukakata docks, is the *Scorpion Lodge*, a pleasant place with rooms for US$3/7, or you can camp for US$1.50.

Getting There & Away

Boats (fishing boats and outboard canoes) go to the islands from the mainland departure points of Bukakata (east of Masaka) and Kasenyi (a 30 minute taxi ride from Kampala).

In Bukakata there are outboard canoes which ferry people across to Liku, from where pick-ups make the trip to Kalangala.

For fishing boats to Buggala and Bukasa from Kampala, take a taxi to Kasenyi. There is no pier here so you have to pay someone to ferry you out to the boat on their shoulders! The boat for Bukasa leaves around 3 pm daily except Sunday, costs US$3 and

arrives around 6 pm. As these boats travel in the dark and are not well stocked with safety equipment, it may be preferable to take the short ride from Bukakata.

National Parks

BWINDI NATIONAL PARK

Bwindi is one of Uganda's most recently created national parks. In the south-west of the country very close to the Congo (Zaïre) border, the park covers 331 sq km and encompasses one of the last remaining habitats of the mountain gorilla, where half of the surviving mountain gorillas in the world live – an estimated 320 individuals. Because of the unrest in Rwanda and Eastern Congo (Zaïre), Bwindi has become the main place in East Africa for seeing the mountain gorillas.

The park headquarters is at Buhoma, on the northern edge of the park, and it's here that the gorilla visits start from and where you find the only accommodation.

Entry to the park is US$15 per person per day. Be aware that this area is rainforest, and so not surprisingly it rains a hell of a lot – be prepared.

Tracking the Gorillas

Two families here have been habituated to human contact – the Mubare group (12 gorillas) and the Katendegyere group (six gorillas).

Group numbers for gorilla tracking are limited to six people, and unfortunately demand far exceeds supply. One place on each group is set aside as a 'standby' place, so that if you just rock up at the park headquarters and are prepared to wait for a day or so you can usually get on. All bookings must be made through the Uganda Wildlife Authority office in Kampala (PO Box 3530, Kampala; ☎ 530574; fax 530159) and they will often tell you that there are no vacancies for months. Be persistent, and if necessary, turn up at the park and try to get on standby.

Once you do actually get on a tracking group, the chances of finding the gorillas are excellent. The time you actually spend with the gorillas once you find them is limited to one hour.

The cost of gorilla-tracking permits is US$150 per person (in addition to the park entry fee), payable in local currency or US dollars. The trips leave at 8.30 am each day and you have to report to park headquarters 30 minutes prior to that. Note that children under 15 years are not permitted to track the gorillas, and anyone with a cold or other illness is likewise excluded. A full refund is given to anyone who withdraws due to ill health.

Places to Stay & Eat

Buhoma At the *Buhoma Community Campground*, right by the park headquarters, you can camp for US$3. There are also four-bed bandas, which cost US$6 per person. These are very basic, but bed linen (sheets and blankets) is supplied and there's hot water by the bucket.

Right across the track from the camping ground is the *H&P Canteen*, where you can get filling local meals for US$3.50, although they must be ordered in advance.

Also in this area is the *Buhoma Homestead*, a private set-up which is owned and run by African Pearl Safaris (☎ 233566; fax 235770) in Kampala. This is a very pleasant and well-run place. Most of the people who stay here are African Pearl safari clients, but others can also stay for US$65 for full board. Advance bookings are essential.

Butogota There is also accommodation at Butogota, the nearest trading centre to Buhoma and the closest you can get to the park by public transport. Many travellers spend a night here en route from Kabale or Kampala before walking the 17km to Buhoma the next day, and visiting the gorillas the day after that.

The only place in town is the *Butogota Travellers Inn*, a modest place with clean rooms for US$4/6.

Getting There & Away

There is a direct Silverline bus daily in each direction between Kampala and Butogota, which goes via Kisizi. It leaves Kampala at around 6 am, arriving in Butogota around 6 pm (US$10).

The other alternative is the irregular pick-ups and taxis which connect Kabale and Butogota. If you can find one, the fare is US$10.

From Butogota to Buhoma it's 17km and there is no transport, so you'll have to walk although you may get lucky and score a ride. Otherwise you can hire a pick-up (US$20 to US$30 one way) or a motorcycle (US$15) to take you.

MGAHINGA NATIONAL PARK

Mgahinga National Park is tucked away in the far south-western corner of the country. It covers just 34 sq km and its tropical rainforest is another mountain gorilla habitat. The park is contiguous with the Parc National des Volcans in Rwanda and the Parc National des Virungas in Congo (Zaïre). The three together form the Virunga Conservation Area, which covers 420 sq km and is home to an estimated half of the world's mountain gorilla population of around 640 animals (the other half are in Bwindi National Park).

As at Bwindi, it is possible to track gorillas here, but access is less convenient and the gorilla groups have a tendency to duck across the mountains into Rwanda or Congo (Zaïre).

The park headquarters is 12km from Kisoro at Ntebeko Camp, and entry is US$15 per person per day for the first two days; no charge for extra days.

Tracking the Gorillas

A gorilla-tracking group of six people heads out each morning from the park headquarters at 8.30 am. Reservations for the trips are best made at the Uganda Wildlife Authority head office in Kampala (PO Box 3530; ☎ 530574; fax 530159), and the cost is US$120, payable in local currency at the park office in Kisoro. You need to check in at the booking office in Kisoro (by the Mbabano Hotel) by 5 pm on the day before your trip. It's here that you can find out whether the gorillas are actually in the park, and pay your fee.

Places to Stay

There is basic *camping* (US$5) at the park headquarters but you need to be fully equipped as only water and firewood is available. Also at the main gate is the *Arnajambere Iwacu Community Campground* which costs US$3 in your own tent or US$5 in a basic banda.

The only other options are 12km away in Kisoro.

Getting There & Away

There is no transport along the rough 12km track between Kisoro and the park headquarters; without your own vehicle you'll have to walk (a couple of hours) or hope for a lift (very little traffic). Local pick-ups from Kisoro cost US$20.

MT ELGON NATIONAL PARK

This is one of the most recently created of Uganda's national parks and encompasses much of Mt Elgon up to the Kenyan border. Two good trekking routes make this an ideal place to experience African highland wilderness with relatively little hassle and expense.

The mountain (Wagagai is the highest peak at 4321m) is said to have one of the largest surface areas of any extinct volcano in the world. **Sipi Falls**, north of Mbale in the foothills of the mountain, has to be the most beautiful and romantic waterfall in the whole of Uganda.

The best time to trek on the mountain is from December to March and June to September, but the seasons are unpredictable and it can rain at any time.

The Uganda Wildlife Authority office in Mbale (see the preceding Mbale section) can help with any information about trekking on the mountain, as can the park headquarters at Budadiri (where most treks start).

Entry to the park is US$15 for one day, US$30 for two to five days, with additional days at US$5.

MURCHISON FALLS NATIONAL PARK

The largest park in Uganda, at 3900 sq km, is Murchison Falls National Park, through which the Victoria Nile flows on its way to Lake Albert.

Although the wildlife has been virtually wiped out by poachers and retreating troops, it's still worth visiting Murchison, if only for the animals that are left and for the **Murchison Falls** on the Victoria Nile. The three hour launch trip from Paraa up to the base of the falls operates on demand at 9 am and 3 pm daily. It's certainly a highlight of the park. The cost is US$10 per person if there's 10 or more people; if less than 10, then the minimum charge is US$100 for the whole boat. On weekends there's a good chance of finding other people to share the cost with.

Entry to the park is US$15 per person per day; vehicle entry is US$5 for Uganda registered vehicles and US$20 for foreign vehicles; this is per trip not per day.

Places to Stay

Budget options are limited to camping. Paraa, on the southern bank of the river, is the park headquarters. As well as a small African village, there's also the *Paraa Rest Camp*, where you can camp (US$10) on a grassy site with limited views of the river, or in basic but comfortable mud and thatch bandas at US$24 per person.

The *Paraa Lodge* across the river was bombed, burnt and looted years ago, but has recently been completely refurbished by Sarova Hotels (☎ (02) 333233; fax 211472 in Nairobi) and is once again open for business. It has a superb location with views up the river towards the falls. Prices are around US$50/75 for singles/doubles.

The *camp site* at the head of the falls has a very nice position right on the river, although you'll definitely need 4WD to get to the best sites on the river's edge. You'll also need to be self sufficient as there are no supplies of any sort – the only facility is a long-drop toilet. Camping here costs US$10.

Probably the best place to stay actually lies outside of the park's western boundary, between the Bugungu Gate and Lake Albert.

UGANDA

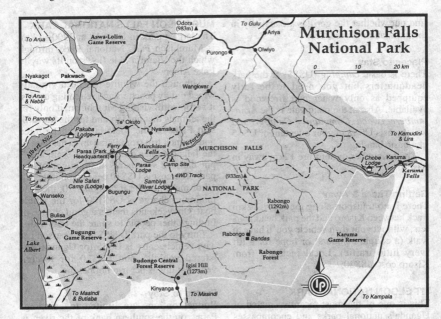

The *Nile Safari Camp* (☎ 258273; fax 231687 in Kampala) has an unrivalled position high up on the south bank of the Victoria Nile with sweeping views over the water. Accommodation is expensive (US$160/240) but there's also a well appointed camp site where you stick up a tent for US$10 per person. One advantage of this place is that as it lies outside the park, you don't have to pay the daily park entry fee of US$15 just to stay here. The turn-off to the camp (well signposted) is 15km from Bulisa town (on Lake Albert) and 4.5km from Bugungu Gate; it's then a further 11.5km along a rough track.

Getting There & Away

The usual access to Murchison Falls is via Masindi, along a good surfaced road from Kampala. From Masindi the only scheduled public transport is irregular daily buses and taxis to Wanseko, on Lake Albert close to where the Victoria Nile joins it and the Albert Nile leaves it.

Without your own vehicle the only other alternative is to hitch. The best chance is with the park vehicles which come in to Masindi a few times a week and may have room to take a passenger back. Enquire at the Game Department office opposite the post office.

QUEEN ELIZABETH NATIONAL PARK

This park covers 2000 sq km and is bordered to the north by the Ruwenzori Mountains and to the west by Lake Edward.

The Queen Elizabeth National Park was once a magnificent place to visit, with its great herds of elephant, buffalo, kob, waterbuck, hippo and topi. But, like Murchison Falls, this park had most of its wildlife wiped out by the retreating troops of Amin and Okello and by the Tanzanian army which occupied the country after Amin's demise. Still, it's worth a visit just to see the hippos and the birds.

Every visitor takes a launch trip up the **Kazinga Channel**, between Lake George and Lake Edward, to see the thousands of hippos and the pelicans. The two hour trip costs US$90 when shared by up to 10 people or US$9 per person if there are more than 10 of you. There are trips at 9 am (the best time) and at 3 and 5 pm.

In the eastern corner of the park is the beautiful **Kyambura** (also **Chambura**) **Gorge**, and a concessionaire operates walking safaris from its Fig Tree Camp at 7.30 am daily. The gorge is home to a variety of primates, including chimpanzee, and these are often seen on the walking safaris, which last from three to five hours and cost US$40 per person.

Entry to the park costs US$15 per day.

Places to Stay & Eat

The places to stay are on the Mweya Peninsula close to the Mweya Safari Lodge. The cheapest option is to camp at the *Students' Camp*, which costs US$1 per person per night. If you don't have a tent, you can get a dormitory bed with shared bathroom facilities for US$1. The *Tembo Canteen* is where the safari drivers hang out. They serve decent meals here for US$3 but you need to order in advance.

A good deal more expensive is the *Ecology Institute*, where you can get a clean and comfortable double room with shared

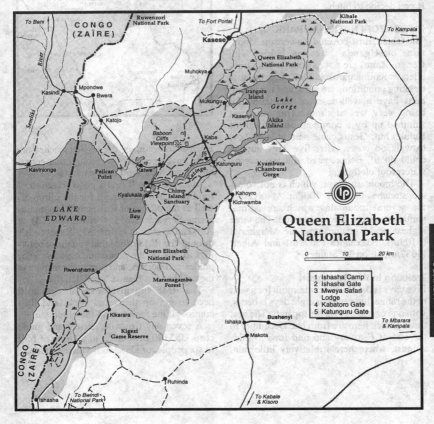

Queen Elizabeth National Park

0   10   20 km

1 Ishasha Camp
2 Ishasha Gate
3 Mweya Safari Lodge
4 Kabatoro Gate
5 Katunguru Gate

UGANDA

bathroom facilities for US$20 per person. The only other option is the expensive *Mweya Safari Lodge.*

Getting There & Away
The main Katunguru Gate is on the Mbarara to Kasese road near the small trading centre of Katunguru. There are regular taxis to Kasese (US$1, one hour) and Mbarara (US$3, two hours).

From the gate it's 7km to the Mweya Safari Lodge, and although the rangers don't seem too keen, they do actually let you walk this stretch. Vehicles are reasonably frequent, so you shouldn't have to wait too long if you decide to hitch.

RUWENZORI NATIONAL PARK
The fabled, mist-covered Ruwenzori Mountains on Uganda's western border with Congo (Zaïre) are not as popular with travellers as Kilimanjaro and Mt Kenya, because trekking conditions are hard, and the mountains have a well-deserved reputation for being very wet at times. This was best summed up by a comment on the wall of Bujuku hut: 'Jesus came here to learn how to walk on water. After five days, anyone could do it'. Be prepared and take warm, waterproof clothing.

The mountain range, which is not volcanic, stretches for about 100km. At its centre are several mountains which are permanently snow and glacier-covered. The three highest peaks in the range are Margherita (5109m), Alexandra (5091m) and Albert (5087m), all on Mt Stanley.

Trekking in the Ruwenzori
Five days is the absolute minimum for a visit to the range, but seven or eight days is better, with one or two days at the top huts. The best times to trek here are from late December to the end of February and mid-June to mid-August, when there's relatively little rain.

Even at these times, the higher reaches are often enveloped in mist, though this generally clears for a short time each day.

In Kasese you'll find a good selection of foodstuffs and equipment for the climb, as well as the offices of Ruwenzori Mountaineering Services (RMS; ☎ (0483) 44115), at Alexandra Rd, PO Box 33, Kasese. It's through the RMS office that you make bookings to trek on the mountain, organise your guides and porters, and arrange transport to the trail head at Ibanda/Nyakalengija.

The RMS organises everything you'll need to get up there and back, and they control all the facilities on the mountain.

A seven day trip with porters and guide costs US$140 per person in a group of four to six people, or US$246 if you are alone.

Zambia

Zambia is a challenge. Distances between major towns are long, getting around by public transport takes persistence (particularly once you get off the main routes), and budget accommodation is limited, especially outside the few tourist centres that do exist. But for many travellers, the challenge of Zambia is the main reason for visiting. This is the 'real' Africa, with genuinely wild national parks, and some of the finest scenery in the region. In the south are the Victoria Falls and the Zambezi River – two of the continent's major highlights.

Despite these attractions, Zambia is often regarded as a place to 'get through' quickly, so not many people sample its rather specialised delights. We heard from a reader proud to have crossed the country in two days, who then went on to say that Zambia had little of interest.

Zambia is not yet an easy destination, but a visit here can be very rewarding. If you like your travel trouble-free and your wilderness neatly bundled then it will not appeal. But if you enjoy a raw edge, Zambia could be just the place you're looking for.

Facts about the Country

HISTORY

The country now called Zambia was known before independence as Northern Rhodesia – created in the 1890s by Cecil Rhodes' British South Africa Company as a place to search for minerals and recruit cheap labour for mines and plantations in Southern Rhodesia (later Zimbabwe) and South Africa.

In the late 1920s, vast deposits of copper ore were discovered in the north of the country. Migrant labour was introduced and became effectively obligatory following the imposition of taxes and commercial farming by European settlers on land appropriated from the local people.

REPUBLIC OF ZAMBIA
Area: 752,615 sq km
Population: 9.5 million
Population Growth Rate: 3.3%
Capital: Lusaka
Head of State: President Frederick Chiluba
Official Language: English
Currency: Zambian kwacha (ZK)
Exchange Rate: ZK 1200 = US$1
Per Capita GNP: US$350
Inflation: 45%
Time: GMT/UTC + 2

Highlights
- White-water rafting and bungy jumping at the spectacular Victoria Falls
- Canoeing on the Zambezi River
- Walking safaris and night drives in South Luangwa National Park

The colony was put under direct British control in 1924. In the following years the settlers pushed for federation with Southern Rhodesia and Nyasaland (present-day Malawi), to make them less dependent on the rule of the colonial authorities in London, but for various reasons (including WWII) this did not come about until 1953.

Meanwhile, African nationalism was becoming a more dominant force in the region. The United National Independence Party (UNIP) was founded by one Kenneth Kaunda; he spoke out against the Federation on the grounds that it promoted the rights of white settlers to the detriment of the local African population.

Through the late 1950s and early 1960s, many African countries gained independence. The Federation was dissolved in 1963 and Northern Rhodesia became independent in 1964 – taking the name Zambia from the Zambezi River which formed its southern border.

As leader of the majority UNIP, Kaunda was made president. He remained in power for the next 27 years, largely because during 1972 he declared UNIP the sole legal party with himself as sole presidential candidate.

Through the rest of the 1970s, Kaunda's rule was based upon 'humanism' – his own mix of Marxist ideals and traditional African values. Nearly all private business was nationalised (including the copper mines), but corruption and mismanagement, exacerbated by a fall in the world copper price, meant that by the end of the 1970s Zambia was one of the poorest countries in the world.

Despite the domestic problems, Kaunda supported several liberation movements in neighbouring countries including those such as the Zimbabwe Patriotic Front (ZAPU and ZANU), the ANC (of South Africa), Frelimo (Mozambique), and SWAPO (Namibia). Naturally, neighbouring governments regarded Kaunda as an enemy, and Zambia's trade was severely restricted as rail routes to the coast were closed.

By the early 1980s Rhodesia had become Zimbabwe, and the TAZARA railway line through Tanzania was complete, giving Zambia access to the sea. Kaunda was able to take his country off a war footing, but things were hardly rosy. The economy was on the brink of collapse, there were serious shortages of food, fuel and other basic commodities, and both the crime and unemployment rates had risen sharply.

In 1986, an attempt was made to diversify the economy and improve balance of payments. Zambia received economic aid from the International Monetary Fund (IMF), but the conditions were severe: basic food subsidies were withdrawn and the currency (the kwacha) was floated. The resultant rise in food prices led to serious countrywide riots in which many people were killed, forcing Kaunda to restore subsidies.

In mid-1990 another round of violent street protests against increased food prices transformed into a general demand for the return of multiparty politics, and Kaunda was forced to accede to public opinion.

He legalised opposition parties, and in full elections in October 1991 Kaunda and UNIP were resoundingly defeated by Frederick Chiluba and the Movement for Multiparty Democracy (MMD). Kaunda bowed out gracefully and Chiluba became president.

Chiluba moved quickly to encourage the return of the IMF and World Bank. Exchange controls were liberalised to attract investors, particularly from South Africa, but tough austerity measures were also introduced – and these were less than appealing to the average Zambian. Food prices soared, the value of the kwacha continued to fall and nationalised industries were privatised or simply closed, leading to many thousands of people losing their jobs. For most Zambians things were even worse than in the 1980s.

By the mid-1990s the lack of visible change in Zambia allowed Kaunda to confidently re-enter the political arena. He attracted strong support but, leading up to November 1996 elections, Chiluba and the MMD were accused of unfair practices, causing Kaunda and UNIP to withdraw in protest. Chiluba took advantage of this situation and won a landslide victory.

Shortly after the election, Chiluba ordered the arrest of two independent monitors who claimed the elections were rigged. Two days later, a group of journalists were suspended from their jobs, apparently because their reports of MMD's role in the election did not contain the required degree of enthusiasm.

However, it was reported by independent sources that a majority of Zambians accepted the result, even if they knew it was rigged, many in the hope that it would at least help Zambia remain peaceful. As leader of the opposition, Kaunda remained active and never far from controversy. In August 1997, a meeting he addressed was broken up by

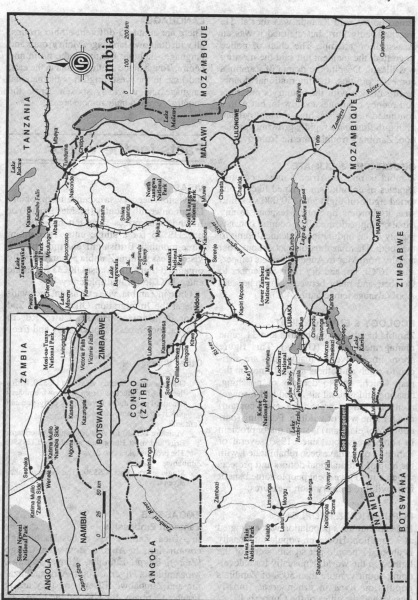

armed police, and Kaunda was shot at. He was not badly hurt, but claimed it was an assassination attempt. The chief of police 'regretted' the incident but said the meeting was illegal. Despite the drama of Zambia's domestic politics, the international donors seem satisfied with the country's progress. Aid money continues to flow in, but with a continued debt crisis, high unemployment, high inflation and a rapidly growing population, Zambia's troubles are far from over.

GEOGRAPHY & CLIMATE

Zambia is one of Africa's most eccentric legacies of colonialism. Shaped like a contorted figure-of-eight and 750,000 sq km in size, its borders do not correspond to any tribal or linguistic area. The country consists mainly of an undulating plateau, sloping to the south. There are three distinct seasons: cool and dry from May to August (average temperature 16°C); hot and dry from September to October; and rainy between November and April (average temperature 24°C).

ECOLOGY & ENVIRONMENT

Zambia has 19 national parks and 31 game management areas (GMAs). This figure seems impressive but many parks are difficult to reach and others are just lines on the map which, due to decades of poaching, clearing and general all-round bad management, no longer protect (or even contain) much in the way of wildlife. Poaching (particularly of elephant) is still a major problem in some areas, but since 1990 several of Zambia's parks have been rehabilitated, with the help of international donors and projects which aim to give local people some benefit from wildlife conservation measures.

POPULATION & PEOPLE

In 1996 Zambia's population was estimated at 9.5 million. However, population density is about 11 people per sq km – one of the lightest in the world. Unusually for a developing country, more than 50% of Zambia's population lives in urban areas (mostly Lusaka and the cities of the Copperbelt).

LANGUAGE

There are about 35 different ethnic groups, all with their own language. Main groups and languages include: Bemba in the north and centre; Tonga in the south; Nyanja in the east; and Lozi in the west. English is the national language and is widely spoken across the country – even in quite remote areas.

Facts for the Visitor

VISAS

All visitors need a visa except citizens of any Commonwealth country (besides Britain) or Ireland. Visa prices vary, but most people pay US$25 for a single entry (maximum three months). British citizens must have a visa (unless visiting Zambia as part of a fully organised tour); these cost UK£33 for single entry, UK£45 for multiple entry.

Once in Zambia, visa extensions are available at the Immigration Office on the 2nd floor of Memaco House, Cairo Rd, in Lusaka; the process is quick, easy and free.

Other Visas

Congo (Zaïre)
> One-month single entry visas cost US$20, with a 'letter of introduction' from your own embassy (standard procedure). If you apply early, you can pick it up the same afternoon.

Tanzania
> Visas are US$20 for Aussies, while Americans, Brits and most Europeans are charged US$50. The process takes two days.

Zimbabwe
> Single entry costs US$30. The process takes seven days.

EMBASSIES
Zambian Embassies

In Africa, Zambia has embassies or high commissions in Angola, Botswana, Congo (Zaïre), Egypt, Ethiopia, Kenya, Malawi, Mozambique, Nigeria, South Africa, Tanzania and Zimbabwe. Elsewhere, they are in France, Germany, the UK and the USA.

Foreign Embassies in Zambia

Unless otherwise stated, the following are in Lusaka:

Botswana
Haile Selassie Ave, near the Tanzanian embassy (☎ 250555)
Canada
United Nations Ave, opposite the Tanzanian embassy (☎ 254176)
Congo (Zaïre)
1124 Parirenyetwa Rd (☎ 229044)
consulate: Mpelembe House, Broadway Rd, Ndola (☎ 614247)
Malawi
Woodgate House, Cairo Rd (☎ 228296)
Mozambique
46 Mulungushi Village, in Kundalile Rd (☎ 290451)
Namibia
6968 Kabanga Rd, Rhodes Park (☎ 252250)
Tanzania
Ujaama House, United Nations Ave (☎ 253320)
UK
Independence Ave (☎ 251133; fax 235798)
USA
Independence Ave (☎ 250955; fax 254861)
Zimbabwe
4th floor, Memaco House, Cairo Rd (☎ 229382)

MONEY

US$1 = ZK 1200

The unit of currency is the kwacha (ZK). You can change money at most banks but most towns have exchange bureaus with slightly higher rates and quicker service. Inflation is high, so only change what you need – the rate will be higher next week. There's no black market worth bothering about; ignore moneychangers on the street as rip-offs are guaranteed. You can get cash with a Visa card at Barclays Bank in Lusaka but it's an all-day process.

PUBLIC HOLIDAYS

Public holidays in Zambia include: 1 January, second Monday in March, 1 May, 25 May, first Monday and Tuesday in July, 1 August, 24 October, 25 and 26 December and Good Friday and Easter Monday.

POST & COMMUNICATIONS

Postal service from Lusaka is quick but from elsewhere in Zambia it's slow and unreliable. Letters to Europe cost US$1; USA and Australia US$1.50. There are public phones in Lusaka and the large towns; calls to Europe or Australia cost about US$25 for three minutes (minimum).

The country code is 260. Area codes in Zambia include: Lusaka 01; Chipata 062; Chirundu 01; Kapiri Mposhi 05; Kasama 04; Kitwe 02, Livingstone 03 and Ndola 02.

DANGERS & ANNOYANCES

The main danger for visitors is the chance of being robbed or mugged in Lusaka. For more details see Dangers in the Lusaka section, later in this chapter. Wherever you go, don't make yourself a target for thieves by behaving imprudently (eg walking the streets late at night) or by showing off your wealth (eg wearing jewellery, carrying cameras).

ACCOMMODATION

Budget choices are limited in Zambia, although a few backpackers' lodges and camp sites exist in tourist areas. Some towns have government rest houses, which are cheap but often in a bad state. Many bottom-end hotels charge by the room so that two, three or even four people can get some real, if crowded, bargains. For information on accommodation in national parks, see the introduction to the National Parks section later in this chapter.

Getting There & Away

AIR

Airlines with long-haul or regional flights to/from Zambia include Air Malawi, Air Zimbabwe, British Airways, KLM and South African Airways. Airport departure tax for international flights is US$20.

LAND

Botswana

The only crossing point between Zambia and

Botswana is the ferry across the Zambezi River at Kazungula, about 60km west of Victoria Falls, which runs between 6 am and 6 pm. It's free for vehicles registered in Botswana, but otherwise it's US$10 for cars and US$20 for pick-ups.

Congo (Zaïre)
The main crossing point is near Chililabombwe, on the main road between Ndola and Lubumbashi. There is a daily direct bus from Lusaka to Chililabombwe, then share-taxis to the border, but from there you must walk to Kasumbalesa before you find pick-ups and taxis on to Lubumbashi.

Malawi
The main border crossing point is about 30km east of Chipata, on the highway between Lusaka and Lilongwe. There's a twice-weekly direct bus service between Lusaka and Lilongwe (for details see the Malawi chapter).

You can also do this journey in stages but it doesn't work out much cheaper. From Lusaka there's a daily bus to the border, or you can take a local bus from Chipata. Local share-taxis and minibuses charge US$1.50 for the 12km trip to the Malawi border post, 2km west of Mchinji, from where there are buses to Lilongwe.

Namibia
The only border crossing point between Zambia and Namibia is at the Zambian village of Katima Mulilo, on the west bank of the Zambezi River, near Sesheke.

The Namibian border post is near the Namibian town of Katima Mulilo. (Locals refer to 'Katima Mulilo Zambia side' and 'Katima Mulilo Namibia side'.) Buses from Livingstone to Sesheke, via Kazungula, run twice daily for US$6 to US$8. The bus may terminate in Sesheke or continue another 5km to the ferry on the east bank of the Zambezi.

Canoes take you across the Zambezi. On the west bank, it's 500m to the Zambia border, and then less than 1km to the Namibia border post (Wenela). From here to Katima Mulilo (Namibia side) is 5km. There's no bus, but a lift in a pick-up costs US$0.50.

A Windhoek-based bus called the Zambezi Express (☎/fax 223478 in Windhoek; email bonim@icafe.com.na) connects Livingstone with Windhoek. See the Namibia Getting There & Away section for more information, or enquire locally at Jolly Boys Backpackers in Livingstone for the latest details on fares and schedules.

Tanzania
The main border crossing point is between Nakonde and Tunduma, on the Great North Road and the TAZARA railway. Most travellers use the train, as bus rides are very long and slow.

Express trains go twice weekly each way between Kapiri Mposhi and Dar es Salaam, leaving Kapiri Mposhi Tuesdays and Fridays at 2 pm (the trip takes 36 hours). Fares are US$60/40/24 in 1st/2nd/3rd class (1st and 2nd are sleeping compartments). Student discount is available.

You need a Tanzania visa before being let on the train. At the border you'll be disturbed by moneychangers. Take care – these guys are sharks. (The train buffet uses the correct currency in each country.)

You can book your ticket in advance (see

Grand Plans
In the next few years, a bridge may be built between Sesheke (Zambia) and Katima Mulilo (Namibia), and the roads from Sesheke to Livingstone and Mongu upgraded. This forms part of a grand long-term transport scheme to link southern Africa's outer reaches to Walvis Bay (Namibia), currently being developed as a major port for the whole region. As part of the same scheme the roads from Katima through the Caprivi Strip and between Livingstone and Lusaka are also due for upgrading. Be prepared for changes, but don't hold your breath. ∎

the Lusaka section), but if they are full here, don't despair: we've heard from travellers who bought tickets on the spot at Kapiri Mposhi without trouble.

There are also slower ordinary trains between Kapiri Mposhi and the border, and on to Dar. For a full rundown of the TAZARA railway, see the Tanzania chapter.

Zimbabwe
Most travellers cross from Livingstone to Victoria Falls. The border is open daily from 6 am to 8 pm. You can take a taxi for a fiercely negotiated US$3, or the twice-daily rail service for US$1.50.

There are also crossings at Kariba and Chirundu. ZUPCO and Giraffe have daily buses to Harare; the first leaves at 6 am, but services get crowded so arrive early. The trip takes nine hours and costs US$7. For more comfort, there's the Power Coach Express with daily service between Lusaka and Harare (US$8).

LAKE
Burundi & Tanzania
A ferryboat called the MV *Liemba* on Lake Tanganyika departs Mpulungu on Friday, arriving at Kigoma on the following Sunday, via other Tanzanian ports. Another boat, the MV *Mwengozo*, leaves every Tuesday and covers the same route.

Fares between Mpulungu and Kigoma are about US$50/40/25 for 1st/2nd/economy class, payable in US dollars. Port tax is US$2. To minimise costs, buy a ticket to Kipili (Tanzania) for US$12, and then buy another ticket for the rest of the journey in Tanzanian shillings on the boat.

Getting Around

AIR
Zambia Airways no longer exists. Internal flights are operated by Aero Zambia and Zambian Express, with one-way fares around US$80 for Lusaka to Kitwe, and US$130 for Lusaka to Livingstone.

BUS
The national bus company, UBZ, has disappeared and all transport is now privately owned, although fares are still standardised. Many routes are served by minibuses and big buses (slower and slightly cheaper). Some sample fares: Lusaka to Livingstone, US$7; Lusaka to Kapiri Mposhi, US$2; Lusaka to Mpulungu, about US$8.

Long-distance buses on main routes tend to leave punctually, although arrival times can be unpredictable. On local services buses leave when full and journey times are even more uncertain. In rural areas the 'bus' is often a truck or pick-up carrying goods as well as people.

TRAIN
Express trains between Lusaka and Livingstone go overnight, thrice-weekly in each direction. Fares are US$7/5/4 in 1st/2nd/3rd class. Ordinary trains between Lusaka and Livingstone run every day; the fare is slightly less but the service is very slow.

Between Lusaka and Kitwe ordinary trains (only) go once per day in each direction. Fares are US$6/5.50/3. This train goes via Kapiri Mposhi (start of the TAZARA line – see Getting There & Away), but there's no connecting service with the TAZARA train.

If you prefer not to stay in Lusaka, the ordinary services to/from Livingstone, Kapiri Mposhi and Kitwe are in fact the same train. This service runs between Livingstone and Kitwe, via Lusaka, stopping here for only a short period.

Lusaka

Central Lusaka is part traditional African and part modern, where dusty markets sit alongside high-rise blocks. From Cairo Rd, the city centre's main drag, wide boulevards lead east to the Government Area (ministries), the 'Diplomatic Triangle' (some embassies) and the smarter residential suburbs.

Although Zambia is a fascinating country, there's very little of interest in Lusaka itself.

The city's main features are a lack of other tourists and (therefore) tourist facilities, and a high crime rate, especially in the centre. Consequently, many people avoid this area, going instead to out-of-town shopping centres. In the last few years, many airline offices and embassies have also relocated to the suburbs.

Information

For changing money, there are banks and exchange bureaus on Cairo Rd; shop around as rates and commissions can vary considerably. However, you're safer at suburban bureaus (eg Kabulonga Supermarket) or a top-end hotel.

The main post and telephone office is on Cairo Rd.

Dangers

Cairo Rd and the streets on its west side are dangerous. Muggings are common, and pickpockets prowl the markets and bus stations. Naturally, rich-looking tourists are a tempting target. While walking on Cairo Rd, don't be distracted by gangs of conmen pretending to sell souvenirs or change money. If you think you've been targeted, go into a shop or bank (many places have their own security guards) and wait until the danger has passed. Even if you're on a tight budget, Lusaka is a place to consider taking taxis.

Places to Stay

City Centre & Suburbs Lusaka has very few budget options. The Salvation Army hostel has closed, partly because travellers abused the hospitality. At the *Sikh Temple*, Mumana Rd off Katima Mulilo Rd, which is off Great East Rd, a bed in the yard is free, but you should leave a donation and obey house rules (no cigarettes, booze, meat or improper behaviour), otherwise this place will close to travellers too.

The *YWCA*, near the hospital, takes men and women for US$10 per person in double rooms. It's basic but very clean and friendly. Your next cheapest option is *Emmasdale Lodge* (☎ 243692), clearly signposted, on the west side of Great North Rd, 2km past North End Roundabout, where single rooms cost US$15. Self-catering flats (one to four

people), with equipped kitchen, cost US$33 – a bargain if you're in a group. Local buses pass along Great North Rd, or a taxi from town costs US$3.

The safe and friendly *Zamcom Hostel* on Church Rd charges from US$20 per person including breakfast, with good evening meals for US$5. The *Hubert Young Hostel*, nearby on the same street, is similar.

Up in price is the *Ndeke Hotel* (☎ 252779), just south of the junction of Haile Selassie Ave and Los Angeles Blvd. En suite doubles cost US$32/56 with breakfast. After 6 pm rooms are half-price.

Outer Lusaka *Pioneer Campsite* is signposted 5km south of the Great East Rd, 18km east of the city centre, 3km east of the airport turn-off. Chalets cost US$10, camping US$5. You can buy food and drinks or self-cater. The friendly owners run a free lift service to/from Lusaka on weekday mornings. From the city to the camp, they pick up at Kachelo Travel (☎ 263973), Kachelo Shopping Centre, between noon and 1 pm. Phone in advance to make arrangements.

If you're coming from the south, *Eureka Camping Park*, about 10km south of the city, is an ideal stop-off. Chalets are US$10, camping US$5. There's a bar, meat and firewood for sale, and some fine showers. Minibuses between Lusaka and Chilanga or Kafue pass the end of the Eureka's drive.

Places to Eat & Drink

There are basic eating houses near the local and intercity bus stations, but the setting is far from pleasant. You're better off at a petrol station snack bar; try the Caltex (open to 5 pm) just beyond North End Roundabout, or the Mobil (to midnight) on the corner of Church and Kabelenga Rds, where burgers, pies and chips start at about US$1. Along Cairo Rd, several snackbars and takeaways offer snacks for around US$1 and meals starting at US$2. These include the long-standing *Rooster King*, opposite Grand Travel at the south end of Cairo Rd, and the nearby *BiteRite*.

Of the smarter restaurants in town, a

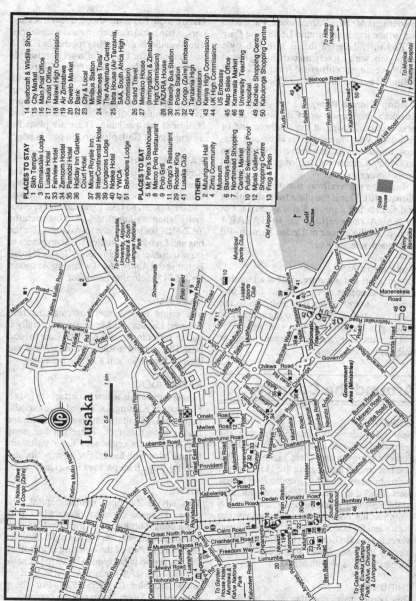

PLACES TO STAY
1 Sikh Temple
3 Emmasdale Lodge
21 Lusaka Hotel
33 Fairview Hotel
34 Zamcom Hostel
35 Pamodzi Hotel
36 Holiday Inn Garden
   Court Hotel
37 Mount Royale Inn
38 InterContinental Hotel
39 Longacres Lodge
40 Ndeke Hotel
47 YWCA
51 Belvedere Lodge

PLACES TO EAT
5 Mr Pete's Steakhouse
8 Marco Polo Restaurant
9 Polo Grill
11 Gringo's Restaurant
29 Rooster King
41 Lusaka Club

OTHER
2 Mulungushi Hall
4 Zintu Community
   Museum
6 Barclays Bank
7 Northmead Shopping
   Centre; Market
10 Public Swimming Pool
12 Mpala Gallery;
   Shopping Centre
13 Frog & Firkin
14 Bushcraft & Wildlife Shop
15 City Market
16 Main Post Office
17 Tourist Office
18 Malawi High Commission
19 Air Zimbabwe
20 Soweto Market
22 Bank
23 City & Local
   Minibus Station
24 Wilderness Trails/
   The Adventure Centre
25 Bata House (Air Tanzania,
   SAA, South Africa High
   Commission)
26 Grand Travel
27 Memaco House
   (Immigration & Zimbabwe
   High Commission)
28 TAZARA House
30 Interchy Bus Station
31 Police Station
32 Congo (Zaire) Embassy
42 Tanzania High
   Commission
43 Kenya High Commission
44 UK High Commission;
   US Embassy
45 Map Samwela Office
46 Kamwala Market
48 University Teaching
   Hospital
49 Kachelo Shopping Centre
50 Kabulonga Shopping Centre

Lusaka

ZAMBIA

favourite is *Mr Pete's Steakhouse*, Panganini Rd, where meals are around US$8. The *Frog & Firkin*, Kabelenga Rd, is a British-style brew-pub, with a lively mixed crowd, music some evenings, 'pub grub' from US$4 and 500ml of perfect draught for US$2.

Getting There & Away

Lusaka's bus depots are City Bus Station, near Kulima Tower, at the southern end of Freedom Way, for local services and surrounding towns and the Intercity Bus Station on Dedan Kimathi Rd, for long distance and cross-border routes.

Lusaka's main railway station is on Dedan Kimathi Rd. This is the place for reservations and tickets for Zambia Railway trains. For TAZARA reservations go to TAZARA House, on the corner of Dedan Kimathi Rd and Independence Ave.

Getting Around

To get a bus to the centre, wait at a bus stop until a bus comes along, with the ticket boy shouting 'town'. From the centre go to the local bus station, or get onto the main road heading in the direction you want to go.

There are taxi ranks at the main hotels or hail a cab in the street.

Around the Country

CHIPATA

Near the border with Malawi, Chipata is the 'gateway' to South Luangwa National Park. For changing money there are two banks. The bus station and market are 1km north of the main street. Nearby, *Kapata Rest House* costs US$5 a double; it's fairly safe but dirty. At the *Zambian Wildlife Conservation Society camp site*, just north of the main street, you can pitch a tent for US$2. About 3km west of town, where the road to Luangwa branches north, the friendly *Chipata Motel* has clean en suite doubles for US$14 with breakfast.

CHIRUNDU

This border town, on the main Lusaka to Harare route has some shops, a few truckers' bars, a bank and a clutch of moneychangers. The *Nyambadwe Motel* has rooms for US$15 and camping for US$5. Infinitely preferable is *Gwabi Lodge*, 11km from Chirundu towards Lower Zambezi National Park, with camping for US$3.50, and rondavels from US$50 per person half board. The view from the swimming pool and bar is stunning and boat rides are available. There are plans for a camp site at Chilapira, on the park's edge.

KAPIRI MPOSHI

Kapiri Mposhi is a busy junction town at the southern end of the TAZARA railway. Thieves and pickpockets love the crowds and confusion, so take great care here, especially when walking the 1.5km between the TAZARA station and the town centre (for the bus and Lusaka line station). Cheap places to stay include the bad-value *Unity Motel*. Better is the *Amity Motel* with double rooms for US$15 including breakfast.

KASAMA

You might find yourself overnighting here between Lusaka and Mpulungu, especially if you're switching from TAZARA train to local bus. The straightforward *Kasama Hotel* has doubles for US$6, and a simple restaurant.

KAZUNGULA

Jungle Junction is a new backpackers lodge, 8km east of Kazungula. Tented accommodation costs US$9 including use of kitchen, and Livingstone transfers. There's a bar, shop and the owners organise village visits and fishing trips with locals. For information ask at Jolly Boys Backpackers in Livingstone.

KITWE

This city is Zambia's mining capital. The centre is more compact than Ndola with more budget options. The friendly *YMCA* on Independence Ave has basic singles/doubles for US$2/3. Part of the building is a brothel, but the action is fairly low-key. Up the scale is the *Hotel Edinburgh* with budget singles/doubles for US$20/30. For cheap eats, try the *Sweet Corner* in the centre.

LIVINGSTONE & THE VICTORIA FALLS

The Zambia side of the Victoria Falls is sometimes forgotten, but here you can sidle right up to the falling water, walk a steep track down to the base of the falls and follow spindly walkways perched over the abyss. The panoramas may not be as picture-post-card-perfect as Zimbabwe's, but they allow closer observation, and the less manicured surroundings create a pristine atmosphere. (Note: a map of Victoria Falls is in the Zimbabwe chapter.)

Livingstone is the nearest large town (11km from the Falls), fast becoming Zambia's 'adventure capital' with good accommodation choices, and plenty of adrenaline pumping activities such as white-water rafting and bungy-jumping.

Warning

Over the last few years, some people have been mugged walking along the main road between Livingstone and the Falls, so hiring a bike has become popular. However, we recently heard reports that even travellers on bikes have been attacked. There's a lot to be said for going in a group and cycling fast. If this sounds too much like the Tour de France, search out one of the infrequent public buses (US$0.25), or get a few people together and go by taxi (US$3 to US$4 each way). Ask at Jolly Boys Backpackers about the latest safety situation and transport options.

Places to Stay & Eat

Near Victoria Falls, between the top-end Hotel Intercontinental and Rainbow Lodge is a rather barren *camp site* charging US$5 per person, which includes the use of Rainbow Lodge facilities. Your belongings should be locked up in the hotel baggage room. For a splurge, the *Hotel Intercontinental* offers all you can eat weekend buffets for around US$16 per person.

In Livingstone town, the simple *Mainstay Campground* charges US$2 per person. At

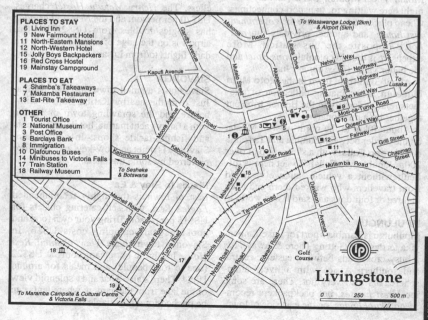

PLACES TO STAY
6 Living Inn
9 New Fairmount Hotel
11 North-Eastern Mansions
12 North-Western Hotel
15 Jolly Boys Backpackers
16 Red Cross Hostel
19 Mainstay Campground

PLACES TO EAT
4 Shamba's Takeaways
7 Makamba Restaurant
13 Eat-Rite Takeaway

OTHER
1 Tourist Office
2 National Museum
3 Post Office
5 Barclays Bank
8 Immigration
10 Djafounou Buses
14 Minibuses to Victoria Falls
17 Train Station
18 Railway Museum

Livingstone

Maramba River Lodge (☎/fax (03) 324189), between Victoria Falls and Livingstone, you can camp on the shady lawn for US$5, and they also have simple chalets. There's good security, a bar and pool, and activities like rafting and safaris can be arranged.

Livingstone's goal to attract tourists from the Zimbabwe side of the Falls will be greatly assisted by the presence of *Jolly Boys Backpackers* (☎ 324278; fax 324229), at 559 Mokambo Way. Dorm beds cost US$6, camping US$2. There's also a pool and kitchen, plus bikes for hire – ideal for trips to the Falls – at US$10 per day.

If you're self-catering the *Shoprite Chequers* supermarket has a good selection. Next door is *Eat-Rite Takeaway* which is OK for lunches, but the best choice is the *Makamba Restaurant*, a block back from the main street. Otherwise, you can resort to the several greasy takeaways along Mosi-oa-Tunya Rd.

MBALA

Mbala is near Mpulungu and you may overnight here waiting for transport connections. Cheap places to stay include the *government rest house*, and another privately run *resthouse* opposite the bus station. More expensive is the old colonial *Arms Hotel* and the better value *Grasshopper Inn*.

About 3km from town is the **Moto Moto Museum**, a fascinating collection of artefacts relating largely to the Bemba tribe put together by a missionary.

About 40km to the north-west of Mbala, on the border between Zambia and Tanzania is **Kalambo Falls**, with a sheer drop of over 200m (double Vic Falls). To get here is difficult without a vehicle, but we've heard from travellers who walked there and back in three or four days and said it was worth it.

MPULUNGU

Mpulungu is Zambia's port for Lake Tanganyika ferries (see Getting There & Away). It's a busy crossroads between eastern, central and southern Africa with a lively atmosphere. It's also very hot. There are some local *rest houses*, but backpackers recommend *Nkupi Lodge*, on the east side of town,

> ### Lake Tanganyika – Some Statistics
> Sitting tightly in the western branch of the Great Rift Valley, Lake Tanganyika is the world's longest lake, stretching almost 700km north to south, and the deepest in Africa (second-deepest in the world) at more than 1.5km. It measures over 33,000 sq km, with a total shoreline of 3000km. Zambian territory covers just 7% of the area, plus about 250km of shoreline. The rest of the lake is shared by Tanzania, Congo (Zaïre) and Burundi. ∎

run by Kathy and Denish Budhia. Camping is US$2 and basic rondavels (not rainproof) US$5. On the lake shore are two other lodges (reached by boat): one is for backpackers, the other more upmarket . Ask at Nkupi Lodge.

NDOLA

Ndola is Zambia's second city, though rarely reached by tourists. Cheap places to stay are limited; most hotels cater for business travellers. The *Henry Makulu Hostel* charges US$20 per person, and the *New Ambassador* has singles/doubles from US$20/40. The airport is on the edge of town, and there are daily flights to/from Lusaka.

SIAVONGA

Siavonga is a small town on Lake Kariba. Just over the nearby Kariba Dam is Zimbabwe and the sprawling town of Kariba with a fancy yacht marina, hotels, restaurants and fishing-tackle shops. In comparison, Siavonga is quiet and low-key, and therefore preferred by some travellers.

Places to Stay & Eat

East of town is the highly recommended *Eagle's Rest*, with self-catering chalets for US$15 per person. Bring your own food and cooking gear; camping costs US$6. In Siavonga town, *Lake View Council Rest House* has basic but clean rooms at US$22 (one to four people) and meals for around US$4. There's also a bar and a splendid view of the lake from the garden, where tents can be pitched for a negotiable fee.

National Parks

Zambia's parks have been called southern Africa's best kept secret, but recently the cover has been blown and wildlife aficionados now come from all over the world to see the impressive populations of birds and animals, or to take part in walking safaris for which Zambia's parks are particularly well known.

After many years of neglect, Zambia's 'high profile' parks (including South Luangwa, Lower Zambezi, Kafue and Mosi-oa-Tunya (Victoria Falls)) have all been improved, with new tracks and the privatisation of (formerly state-run) lodges and camps. This process is on-going, so expect to find more changes by the time you arrive.

For shoestring travellers, many parks are difficult to reach unless you have your own vehicle or the money to pay for exclusive tours (there is no budget safari scene, such as in Kenya or Tanzania). The most accessible park is South Luangwa, and Kafue can also be reached with some persistence.

Entry to South Luangwa costs US$15 per person per day. Kafue is US$10. Entry to other parks is either free or costs anything up to US$15, depending on location or facilities.

Parks usually have four types of accommodation: camping (for about US$5 per person); self-catering, where facilities include basic huts and a staffed kitchen – you just provide your own food, charging between US$10 and US$25; mid-range 'fully-catered' lodges charging between US$50 and US$100; and top-end lodges, charging around US$200 to US$250 all inclusive.

KAFUE NATIONAL PARK

Kafue National Park, about 200km west of Lusaka, covers more than 22,000 sq km; it's the largest park in Zambia, and one of the largest in the world. Vegetation types within the park range from riverine forest through areas of open mixed woodland, to vast grassland plains on its western and northern edges – classic wildlife country. Beyond the northern plains stretch seasonally flooded swamps. Mammals found here include lion, leopard, elephant and buffalo, plus hyena, croc and hippo. Antelope species include impala, roan, kudu, sable and red lechwe, plus sitatunga. Birdlife is also prolific, with over 400 species recorded here.

Places to Stay

The main choice for budget travellers is *Chunga Camp* (also called Chunga Safari Village), at the park headquarters, with basic rondavels overlooking the river for US$12 and camping for US$5. The warden can arrange for a scout if you want to walk in the bush from the camp.

In the north part of the park are three camps run by Busanga Trails (Lusaka ☎ 220897, 221694; fax 274253). These are reasonably priced compared to the other lodges in the park (mostly around US$200 per day): *Lufupa* is US$50 per person full board including park fees; *Kafwala* is US$12 for self-catering huts; and *Shumba*, more remote and overlooking the northern plains, is US$55 for full board. At Lufupa and Shumba wildlife drives (day or night) cost US$15. Access is very hard without your own wheels, but it might be worth calling into the Busanga Trails office on Cairo Rd in Lusaka to see if they have any tours on offer – their prices are cheaper than most other organised safaris in Zambia.

Getting There & Away

From Lusaka, take a bus for Mongu. After about 200km the road crosses a bridge over the Kafue River, where there's a police checkpoint. On the west side of this bridge the main track into the northern sector turns off right. There is a small guard post here where you pay park fees, unless you have a booking with a lodge where this is included. Opposite, the dry-season track leads towards Chunga park headquarters (17km from the main road). About 6km further west is the all-weather road to Chunga (21km from the main road). There's no public transport to Chunga, so you'll have to walk or hitch; ask police or park rangers if vehicles are expected.

History of South Luangwa

The history of South Luangwa National Park is inextricably linked with the story of Norman Carr. He is sometimes known as the 'George Adamson of Zambia', because he raised two lions and returned them to the wild, but his influence and contribution to conservation in Africa goes much deeper.

In 1938, the Luangwa reserves were created to protect and control wildlife populations – notably elephant. A year later Norman Carr became a ranger here. With the area's traditional leader, Carr created Chief Nsefu's Private Game Reserve in 1950, and opened it to the public (until this time reserves had been for the animals only). All visitor fees were paid directly to the chief, thus benefitting both wildlife and local people. Thirty years later 'community involvement' became a buzzword, as conservationists finally realised that the survival of habitats and animals depends on the cooperation of local people.

Norman Carr was years ahead of his time in other fields too. He built Nsefu Camp, the first public camp in the country, and developed walking safaris, a totally new concept then (though commonplace today), to introduce visitors to African bush conditions away from the sometimes more restricting confines of vehicles.

In 1972, Nsefu became part of the South Luangwa National Park. Despite the new title, from the mid-1970s poaching of elephant and rhino became an increasing problem. In 1980, Norman Carr and several other people founded the Save the Rhino Trust; funds raised helped the government parks department combat the poachers.

In 1984, Norman Carr opened Kapani Lodge and operated safaris from this base. He retired from 'active service' in the early 1990s, but still lives in the Luangwa Valley, and meets guests at the lodge on most days.

Just before this book went to print we heard news from Zambia that Norman Carr had died, aged 84, following a serious illness. He will be sorely missed in the Luangwa valley and beyond. ■

SOUTH LUANGWA NATIONAL PARK

For scenery and variety of animals, South Luangwa is one of the best in Africa. Vegetation ranges from dense woodland to open grassy plains, and mammals include lion, buffalo, zebra and Thornicroft's giraffe. The park also contains large numbers of elephant and is noted for leopard. Antelope species include bushbuck, waterbuck, impala and puku. In the Luangwa River you'll see hippo and crocodile. Birdlife is tremendous.

Lodges and camps run tours in open-top vehicles, night drives and walking safaris, either for the day or overnight . Horse riding is also available. One way or another, in South Luangwa you can get pretty close to the 'real Africa'. It's not cheap, but there are more options for the budget-conscious than in any other Zambian park.

Places to Stay

Most campers and overlanders head for *Flatdogs*, just outside the park near the Mfuwe Gate entrance, overlooking the river. Camping costs US$5, and self-catering chalets US$15. There is a small bar and you

can buy snacks and fresh veg. The camp is run by a guy called Jake who is a good source of local information. He also runs Rancho los Pajeros horse riding, and organises game drives (day and night) in the park for US$25. A few kilometres to the west is the well-maintained *Wildlife Camp* (☎ (062) 45026), with camping for US$5, self-catering family chalets (sleeping up to four) for US$15 per person, and pleasant en suite chalets are US$20. There's a bar, which also serves snacks and meals. Game drives are US$20 ($25 at night). This place is popular, so bookings for chalets may be required at busy times. Your other options in South Luangwa are all mid-range and top-end luxury lodges.

Getting There & Away

Local pick-ups run from Chipata to Mfuwe village, near the main gate, at least once daily (US$5), from where you can walk to Flatdogs or hitch to the Wildlife Camp. Some travellers hitch all the way: the junction by the Chipata Motel is the best place to wait. To actually tour the park, the camp sites/ lodges arrange wildlife drives.

Zimbabwe

While it's not without problems, Zimbabwe is a beautiful and relatively safe country. The people are friendly, their music and arts are world famous, the national parks are among Africa's finest, and the bright cities of Harare and Bulawayo boast a variety of attractions.

Facts about the Country

HISTORY

It's generally believed that in the 11th century, the nascent Shona society at Great Zimbabwe encountered the Swahili traders who'd been plying the Mozambique coast for over four centuries. They traded gold and ivory for glass, porcelain and cloth from Asia, and Great Zimbabwe became the capital of Southern Africa's wealthiest and most powerful society. However, by the 15th century, Great Zimbabwe's influence had begun to decline. Although the cause of its fall in the 16th century remains a mystery, possibilities include overpopulation, overgrazing by cattle, popular uprisings and political fragmentation.

During Great Zimbabwe's twilight period, Shona dynasties scattered into autonomous states. In the 1500s, Portuguese traders arrived, bearing tales of wealth which had been passed on to them by Swahili traders, tales of marvellous riches and golden cities across the vast empire of Mwene Mutapa (Monomatapa to the Europeans), whom they thought to be the custodian of King Solomon's mines and the mysterious land of Ophir.

Alliances between Shona states resulted in the creation of the Rozwi state, which encompassed over half of present-day Zimbabwe. Rozwi influence continued until 1834 when Ndebele ('those who carry long shields') raiders under the command of Mzilikazi invaded from the south and assassinated the Rozwi leader. Upon reaching the

REPUBLIC OF ZIMBABWE
Area: 390,310 sq km
Population: 11.3 million
Population Growth Rate: 1.4%
Capital: Harare
Head of State: President Robert Mugabe
Official Language: English, Shona, Sindebele
Currency: Zimbabwe dollar
Exchange Rate: Z$10.65 = US$1
Per Capita GNP: US$580
Inflation: 20%
Time: GMT/UTC + 2

Highlights
- World-famous Victoria Falls and its growing number of adrenaline-junkie activities
- Unexpected lushness of the beautiful Eastern Highlands
- Rich and varied artistic heritage
- Haunting rock formations, ancient San paintings and rare wildlife that characterise Matobo National Park

Matobo hills, Mzilikazi established an Ndebele state. After Mzilikazi's untimely death in 1870, his son Lobengula ascended to the throne and relocated the Ndebele capital to Bulawayo.

Meanwhile, European gold seekers and ivory hunters from the Cape were moving into Shona and Ndebele territory. The best known of the opportunists was Cecil John Rhodes, whose fortune was made in the Kimberley diamond fields. Keen to take

ZIMBABWE

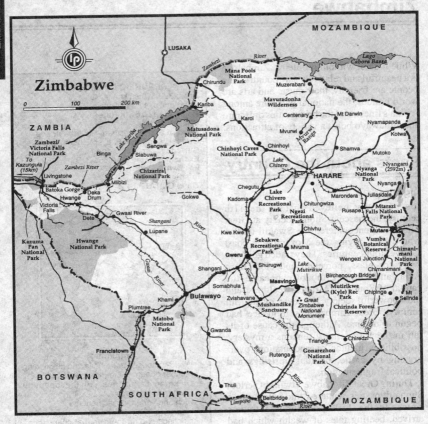

Queen Victoria's interests – and his own enterprise – into the exploitable country north of the Limpopo, he envisioned a corridor of British-style 'civilisation' and a railway stretching from the Cape to Cairo.

In 1889 Rhodes formed the British South Africa Company (BSAC) and received a royal charter awarding him the power to 'make treaties, promulgate laws, maintain a police force ... make land grants and carry on any lawful trade'. The next year, he mustered an army of 500, the 'Pioneer Column', and a contingency of settlers who marched northward into Mashonaland. On 27 June, they

hoisted the Union Jack over Fort Victoria (Masvingo) and on 12 September established Fort Salisbury (Harare).

Finding little gold, the colonists appropriated farmlands on the Mashonaland plateau. By 1895 the new country was being referred to as Rhodesia after its heavy-handed founder, and a white legislature was set up. European immigration began in earnest; by 1904 there were some 12,000 settlers in the country, and double that amount by 1911.

Conflicts between black and white came into sharp focus after the 1922 referendum in which the whites chose to become a self-governing colony rather than part of the Union of South Africa. Although Rhodesia's constitution was in theory nonracial, suffrage was based on British citizenship and annual income, and only a few blacks qualified for it. In 1930 white supremacy was legislated in the form of the Land Apportionment Act, which excluded black Africans from ownership of the best farmland and, in 1934, by a labour law which excluded them from skilled trades and professions. The effect was to force Africans to work on white farms and in mines and factories.

Poor wages and conditions led to rebellion in the black African labour force. By the time Southern Rhodesia, Northern Rhodesia and Nyasaland were federated in 1953, mining and industrial concerns favoured a more racially mixed middle class as a counterweight to the radical elements in the labour force.

Two African parties, the Zimbabwe African People's Union (ZAPU), under the leadership of Joshua Nkomo, and the Zimbabwe African National Union (ZANU), a breakaway group under the leadership of Ndabaningi Sithole, emerged. In the aftermath of the federation's break-up in 1963 – which paved the way for the independence of Northern Rhodesia (Zambia) and Nyasaland (Malawi) – both ZAPU and ZANU were banned and their leaders imprisoned.

In April 1964 Ian Smith took over the Rhodesian presidency and began pressing for independence. British prime minister Harold Wilson countered by outlining conditions to be met before Britain would cut the tether: guarantee of racial equality, a course toward majority rule and majority desire for independence. Smith realised whites would never accept these terms and, in December, he made a Unilateral Declaration of Independence (UDI).

Britain reacted by declaring Smith's action illegal and imposed economic sanctions, which were also adopted by the United Nations (UN) in 1968; however, they were ignored by most western countries and some British companies. As a result, the Rhodesian economy prospered; sanctions provided incentive to increase and diversify domestic production.

At this stage, both ZANU and ZAPU opted for guerrilla warfare. The raids struck deeper and deeper into the country with increasing ferocity, and whites, most of whom had been born in Africa and knew no country but Rhodesia, abandoned their homes and farms, especially in the Eastern Highlands. It finally dawned on Ian Smith that all might not be well in Rhodesia.

On 11 December 1974, the unlikely duo of South Africa's John Vorster and Zambia's Kenneth Kaunda persuaded Smith to call a cease-fire and release high-ranking nationalists – Nkomo, Sithole and Robert Mugabe among them – and begin peace negotiations. The talks, however, broke down in an atmosphere of recrimination between Smith and the nationalists on one hand and among nationalist leaders on the other. ZANU split; Nkomo differed with ANC leader Muzorewa and was expelled from the organisation; and Mugabe, a respected former teacher and 10 year detainee under Smith, went to Mozambique where he replaced Sithole as leader of ZANU. The following year, ZANU chairman Herbert Chitepo was assassinated in Lusaka by Rhodesian intelligence.

Nationalist groups fragmented and re-formed in an alphabet soup of 'Z' acronyms. In January 1976 in Geneva, ZANU and ZAPU were induced to form an alliance known as the Patriotic Front, but the hoped-for spirit of cooperation between them was not realised. Similarly, ZIPRA and ZANLA combined to form the Zimbabwe People's Army (ZIPU) under Rex Nhongo.

At this stage, Smith faced wholesale white emigration and a collapsing economy, and was forced to try a so-called 'internal settlement'. Both Sithole and Muzorewa joined a 'transitional government' in which whites were guaranteed 28 out of the 100 parliamentary seats; a veto over all legislation for 10 years; a guarantee of white property and pension rights; and white control of the armed forces, police, judiciary and civil service. An amnesty was declared for Patriotic Front guerrillas.

The effort was a dismal failure, resulting only in the escalation of the war. To salvage the settlement, Smith entered into secret negotiations with Nkomo, offering to ditch both Sithole and Muzorewa, but Nkomo proved to be intransigent. Finally, Smith was forced to call a general nonracial election and hand over leadership to Muzorewa, but on much the same conditions as the 'internal settlement'. Internationally, he wasn't taken seriously; at best, a few countries regarded Zimbabwe-Rhodesia, as it was known, as simply a passable transitional government.

In 1979, after 14 weeks of deliberation in London, delegations signed the Lancaster House Agreement. It guaranteed whites (3% of the population) 20 of the 100 parliamentary seats and stipulated that private land-holdings could not be nationalised without compensation. At this stage, the various factions began jostling for position in the power queue.

In the carefully monitored election of 4 March 1980, Mugabe prevailed by a wide margin and Zimbabwe and its majority-rule government joined the ranks of Africa's independent nations.

Despite the long struggle, Mugabe kept vengeful tendencies at bay; remaining whites were a nuisance for him, but he didn't want to lose their wealth, technical expertise and access to foreign investment which he, as a committed Marxist, deemed essential for the creation of a one party socialist state.

However, the euphoria, unity and optimism quickly faded with a resurgence of rivalry between ZANU (mostly Shona) and ZAPU (mostly Ndebele), which escalated into armed conflict, and ZAPU leader Nkomo was accused of plotting to overthrow the government. Guerrilla activity resumed in ZAPU areas of Matabeleland, and Mugabe deployed the North Korean-trained Fifth Brigade in early 1983 to quell disturbances. Instead, it launched into an orgy of killing; innocent villagers were gunned down and prominent members of ZAPU were eliminated in order to rout dissidents.

Nkomo, meanwhile, fled to England until Mugabe – who realised his enemies were watching closely as the strife threatened to erupt into civil war – publicly relented and guaranteed his safe return. Talks resulted in a ZAPU-ZANU confederation and amnesty for the dissidents. Thereby, the matter, but not the underlying discontent, was masterfully swept under the rug.

The late 1980s were characterised by scandal and government corruption. While MPs and cabinet ministers loudly professed socialism – some sincerely – many privately amassed personal fortunes. In 1988 student protests against 'dirty government' were put down by cutting university funding and forcing dissidents to admit their 'mistake'.

Despite disastrous experiments with nominal socialism in Zambia, Tanzania and Mozambique, Mugabe guarded his dream of creating a one party state. By mid-1988 the overdue abolition of the law guaranteeing 20 parliamentary seats to whites, the imposition of strangling controls on currency, foreign exchange and trade, and the April 1990 review of white land ownership, indicated steps in this direction.

In the 1990 elections, Edgar Tekere's Zimbabwe Unity Movement (ZUM), which promoted free enterprise and a multiparty democratic state, challenged ZANU in several electorates. However, thanks to ZANU-engineered gerrymanders and an assassination attempt on a candidate who had shown promise in the Gweru North district, ZANU won a landslide victory.

By 1991 Mugabe's dreams of a one party state had faded. Faced with economic crisis, the Zimbabwean government revealed the Economic Structural Adjustment Program (ESAP), which was formulated by the International Monetary Fund (IMF) and the World Bank in an attempt to attract foreign investment. The main goal was the liberalisation of the economy, which required allowing competition from imports and the floating of the Zimbabwe dollar. The immediate result was an increase in most prices – and hardship among the poorer classes.

The hardships of ESAP were magnified by the severe drought of the early 1990s, which caused widespread crop failure and migration to the cities. However, Zimbabwe is gradually recovering from both shocks, and the 1995-6 season brought the best rainfall in decades, and things are now looking up for both people and wildlife.

People scarcely noticed the 1996 elections, which amounted to little more than a rubber stamp for ZANU after the opposition pulled out in protest at government policies denying campaign funding to rival parties.

In August 1996 the social event of the season was President Mugabe's marriage to his 32-year-old former secretary, Grace Marufu. The lavish affair, which accommodated 20,000 guests, seemed a particular affront to disgruntled public workers, who had received a paltry 6% pay rise (in the face of 22% annual inflation) while government ministers saw 130% pay increases, and they walked off the job in protest. In response, the government sacked all striking employees, citing a need to deflate a bloated public sector and improve conditions for the remaining skilled professionals. However, most Zimbabweans are in the unskilled sector, and unless some compromise can be struck, further erosion of confidence in the ZANU government is inevitable.

GEOGRAPHY & CLIMATE

Zimbabwe sits on a high plateau between the Limpopo and Zambezi rivers, with a range of mountains and highlands along the eastern border. It experiences a healthy climate, with temperatures averaging from 22°C on the plateau to 30°C in the Zambezi Valley during summer, and from 13° to 20°C in winter.

ECOLOGY & ENVIRONMENT

Although it may seem inappropriate to mention both hunting and conservation in the same breath, Zimbabwe's official policy is one of 'sustained yield use'; that is, limiting hunting to the level of natural growth in the wildlife population. Safari areas allow game hunting and the government cites their annual net of millions of dollars in foreign exchange as justification for their existence and, therefore, for the conservation of wildlife.

Revenues from hunting on communal lands, where wildlife can become a nuisance to subsistence farmers, is channelled back into the affected communities in the form of schools, hospitals and other infrastructure.

However, the Zimbabwean government seems to realise the value of wild land and preservation of habitat for aesthetic as well as economic values. Since the turn of the century, the human population has grown from 500,000 to 12 million. As pressures to develop and farm wild land increase, so too does the need for retreat from the chaos.

In an effort to foster an appreciation for wildlife and wilderness in school children, several amateur conservation groups have purchased small, protected reserves in urban areas, primarily for the purpose of education. These include Mukuvisi Woodlands near Harare, Cecil Kop near Mutare and Tshabalala near Bulawayo.

POPULATION & PEOPLE

Zimbabwe's population is around 11.3 million. The two main ethnic groups are the Shona (75%), which occupy the north and east, and the Ndebele (18%), who live in the west. Europeans and South Asians comprise about 2%.

LANGUAGE

English is the official language, but most people speak Shona or Sindebele as a first language.

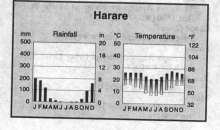

Harare

mm	Rainfall	in	°C	Temperature	°F
500		20	50		122
400		16	40		104
300		12	30		86
200		8	20		68
100		4	10		50
0	J F M A M J J A S O N D	0	0	J F M A M J J A S O N D	32

Facts for the Visitor

VISAS

Visas are not required by nationals of Commonwealth countries, members of the European Union, Japan, Norway, Switzerland or the USA. Citizens of the Republic of South Africa can pick up a visa at the port of entry.

Immigration officials are strict about onward tickets, and Miscellaneous Charges Orders (MCOs) are not acceptable. Anyone without a ticket may buy one on the spot or leave a returnable deposit of US$1000 in cash or travellers' cheques (a credit card with a year until expiry may be acceptable as a substitute).

Visa Extensions

The normal 90 day length of stay may be extended to a maximum of six months at immigration offices, but you may extend for only one month at a time. The Harare office (7th floor, Liquenda House, Baker Ave) has backlogs and therefore the longest waits.

Other Visas

Harare is one of the best places to pick up visas for other African countries. Requirements are constantly changing but nearly all require a fee – some must be paid in US dollars – and multiple passport-sized photos.

Congo (Zaïre)
Visa applications are accepted in the morning and visas are issued at 4 pm that afternoon. Three-month visas cost US$195 for single entry and US$255 for multiple entry (they're considerably cheaper in Nairobi and elsewhere).

Kenya
Single-entry visas cost US$10. They require two photos and are issued in 24 hours. Multiple-entry visas are slower to obtain.

Mozambique
A transit visa, allowing travel through the Tête corridor to Malawi, costs about US$10 (Z$76), requires three photos and is issued in 24 hours. A double-entry transit visa, good for a return trip to Malawi, costs US$24 (Z$190). Tourist visas cost US$18 (Z$135) and also take 24 hours to issue.

Namibia
Visas are free, require two photos and are issued in 24 hours. Few nationalities require them (see the Namibia chapter for details).

Zambia
A double-entry tourist visa for US citizens in Harare costs US$10 and is issued the same day. Seven-day transit visas and 21-day tourist visas are available at the Victoria Falls border (and possibly elsewhere) for US$10. Day trippers to Zambia at Victoria Falls are subject to the same visa requirements, but their visa will be issued only for the day of travel unless otherwise requested, in which case it is valid for 21 days.

Other Countries
The French embassy issues visas for Côte d'Ivoire, Senegal, Burkina Faso, the Central African Republic and Gabon. Check with staff for information on visas for other former French West African countries. Note that the Nigerian high commission won't issue visas if you could have obtained them in your home country, no matter what excuse you have.

EMBASSIES

Zimbabwean Embassies

In Africa, Zimbabwe has embassies in Addis Ababa, Algiers, Dakar, Dar es Salaam, Gaborone, Lagos, Lilongwe, Lusaka, Maputo and Nairobi.

Foreign Embassies in Zimbabwe

The following embassies and high commissions are in Harare:

Angola
Doncaster House, Speke Ave and Angwa St (☎ 790675)

Australia
Karigamombe Centre, 53 Samora Machel Ave (☎ 757774)

Botswana
22 Phillips Ave, Belgravia (☎ 729551)

Canada
45 Baines Ave, on the corner of Moffat St, PO Box 1430 (☎ 733881)

Congo (Zaïre)
Pevensey Rd, Highlands (☎ 498594)

France
Renelagh Rd, near Orange Grove Drive, Highlands (☎ 498096)

Kenya
95 Park Lane (☎ 792901)

Malawi
Malawi House, 42/44 Harare St, PO Box 321 (☎ 705611)

Mozambique
152 Herbert Chitepo Ave (☎ 790837)
Namibia
31A Lincoln Rd, Avondale (☎ 722113/497930)
New Zealand
6th floor, Batanai Gardens, 57 Jason Moyo Ave, PO Box 5448 (☎ 728681)
South Africa
Temple Bar House, corner of Baker Ave and Angwa St (☎ 753147)
Tanzania
23 Baines Ave, PO Box 4841 (☎ 724173)
UK
7th floor, Corner House, corner of Leopold Takawira St and Samora Machel Ave (☎ 793781)
USA
Arax House, 172 Herbert Chitepo Ave, PO Box 3340 (☎ 794521)
Zambia
6th floor, Zambia House, Union Ave, PO Box 4698 (☎ 790851)

MONEY
US$1 = Z$10.65

The unit of currency is the Zimbabwe dollar (Z$), which equals 100 cents. For hotels and organised activities such as rafting or canoeing, non-residents must pay in foreign currency.

Banks are open Monday, Tuesday, Thursday and Friday between 8.30 am and 2 pm. On Wednesday they're open until noon and on Saturday until 11 am. The exchange desk at Harare airport is open for incoming flights, but may limit transactions to US$100. Most hotels exchange currency for a substantial commission.

All brands of US dollars or UK pounds travellers' cheques may be exchanged for Zimbabwe dollars at any bank. Major international currencies are also welcomed, but due to counterfeiting, no-one currently accepts US$100 notes. To exchange travellers' cheques, Zimbank charges 2% commission (minimum Z$10), while Barclays and Standard Chartered banks charge 1% with a Z$20 minimum. To exchange Thomas Cook travellers' cheques, some banks may ask to see your purchase receipts.

Credit cards – American Express (Amex), Diner's Club, MasterCard and Visa – are accepted by tourist-oriented businesses, and at banks you may buy as many Zimbabwe dollars as your limit allows. You can draw instant cash on your Visa card at Barclays Bank ATMs.

There's no black market, but travellers are still caught out by shady exchange artists, mainly in Victoria Falls, who promise unrealistic rates for US dollars cash. What you get is two Z$20 notes around a wad of clipped newspaper.

POST & COMMUNICATIONS
Poste restante is available in major cities and towns but Harare is the most efficient. For shipping handicrafts and artwork, airport freight forwarders are considerably less expensive than the post.

Posting parcels of less than 2kg is inexpensive if they're sent as letters, and it's cheaper to post five 2kg parcels than one 10kg parcel. Posting any item which has a value of more than Z$50 requires you to fill out a bank currency declaration form and a customs form.

The local telephone service is poor, and crowded party lines mean long queues at telephone boxes. Overseas services are better, but there are no card phones and no telephone offices where you can book and pay for calls without plugging coins into the box. Overseas calls are best made from private phones; otherwise, you'll need a whopping big stack of Z$1 coins.

Zimbabwe's country code is 263. Area codes in Zimbabwe include: Bulawayo 019, Chimanimani 0126, Harare 014, Hwange 0181, Kariba 0161, Masvingo 013, Mutare and Vumba 0120 and Victoria Falls 0113.

HEALTH
Malaria is rife in the Zambezi Valley and the Lowveld, particularly between October and April, but elsewhere there's less risk. Bilharzia is present in Lake Kariba, Matobo National Park, and most other lakes and dams. For more information, see the Health Appendix.

DANGERS & ANNOYANCES
Theft and other crime is on the increase,

particularly in Harare and Bulawayo. Don't walk around at night in the cities and, by day, avoid small groups of youths loitering outside hotels; many are pick-pockets and foreigners are prime targets. Always have loose change handy for small purchases, but don't pull out a stash of cash.

Some taxi drivers may drop clients far enough from their door to allow accomplices to rob them with knives; the drivers take a cut. Note taxi number plates before climbing in and insist on being dropped right at your door.

Scams, especially 'sponsorship' scams, are rife and some are expert and inventive. Don't fall for ridiculous stories, don't add your name to the bottom of a list of Z$100 donations and never reach for your money when people are crowding around.

ACCOMMODATION

Zimbabwe is great for camping and has lots of good and mostly secure caravan parks. There is also an increasing number of comfortable and inexpensive backpackers hostels, bed & breakfasts (B&Bs) and guest farms.

At all classified hotels – from seedy dives of ill repute right up to safari lodges and Sheraton-class luxury digs – foreigners must pay in foreign currency. At caravan parks, backpackers hostels and B&B accommodation, foreigners can normally pay in Zimbabwe dollars. Larger hotels and safari lodges – except for the Cresta group – operate on a two tiered system in which foreigners pay up to 200% more than Zimbabwe residents.

Getting There & Away

AIR

Harare is the hub for travel between Zimbabwe and neighbouring countries, and both Air Zimbabwe and Zimbabwe Express Airlines have frequent services between Harare, Johannesburg and other South African cities.

South African Airways and Air Namibia also have connections.

The cheapest flights from Europe are with Balkan Airways, which flies to Harare via Sofia, Bulgaria, for around UK£350. From London, Air Zimbabwe charges around UK£500.

The airport departure tax for international flights is US$20, which must be paid in foreign currency.

LAND

Zimbabwe has border posts with South Africa, Zambia, Botswana and Mozambique. All land border crossings are open between 6 am and 6 pm daily, except Beitbridge (South Africa), which stays open until 10 pm.

Botswana

Bus The main Botswana border crossings are Victoria Falls/Kazungula and Plumtree/Francistown. Twice weekly Chitanda & Sons buses run from Harare to Gaborone, via Bulawayo and Francistown. Book through Manica Travel in Harare (☎ 703421) or Bulawayo (☎ 62521).

A daily (except Sunday) Zimbabwe Omnibus Company service runs from Bulawayo's Lobengula St bus terminal to Francistown. Mach Coach Lines (☎ 60499) has a similar run daily.

The United Touring Company (UTC) bus from Victoria Falls to Kasane crosses at Kazungula and costs US$20 each way.

Train The daily train from Bulawayo to Gaborone costs US$33/27/9 in 1st/2nd/ economy class. See Getting There & Away in the Botswana chapter for more details.

Malawi

The route to Malawi runs from Harare to Blantyre via the Nyamapanda and Mwanza border crossings, transiting Mozambique through the Tête corridor. Note that a Mozambique transit visa is required, and a 'border tax' of US$5 (or Rand 10 or 30 Malawi kwacha) payable (only in hard currency) at the Mozambique border.

It's relatively easy to hitch all the way, but there are also plenty of minibuses between Nyamapanda and Tête and between Tête and Zobué on the Malawi border.

Stagecoach Malawi (three times weekly) or Tauya (daily) buses travel from Nyamapanda to Blantyre in nine to 14 hours and cost around US$13. Stagecoach Malawi also operates from Harare (US$50).

Munorurama (☎ 336593 in Harare) also has daily services from Harare for US$15. If you book a day in advance, you can be picked up anywhere in Harare.

Mozambique
Buses run from Harare to Chimoio (via Mutare) for US$12. Book on ☎ 727231 in Harare. At Nyamapanda there's an informal 'border tax' of US$5 (Rand 10) payable only in hard currency – a nice little money spinner for the border guards.

Namibia
There's no direct route between Namibia and Zimbabwe. The most straightforward route is between Victoria Falls and the Caprivi Strip via Botswana (see Getting There & Away in the Botswana chapter for details).

The comfortable weekly Over-Border Minibus connects Victoria Falls with Rundu (Namibia) and Windhoek. In Victoria Falls, book through Safari Par Excellence in the Phumula Centre. The one-way/return fare is US$123/243; with lunches and camping it's US$143/280.

Another option is the good-value Zambezi Express, which connects Livingstone (Zambia), with Windhoek, via Victoria Falls, for US$49 one way. See Getting There & Away in the Namibia chapter for more details.

South Africa
The only border crossing to South Africa is at Beitbridge; either by road or the Trans-Limpopo rail link.

Bus A growing number of bus companies travel between Zimbabwe and South Africa. Mach Coach Lines runs daily from Mbare to Beitbridge, to connect with the Transtate City-to-City Coach to Johannesburg. Faster are the Mini-Zim Luxury Mini-Coaches (☎ 76644) which run to Johannesburg (US$49) twice weekly from Bulawayo.

The Zimi-Bus (☎ 793081 Harare) runs from Harare to Johannesburg three times weekly; advance bookings are essential. Jac-aranda (☎ 752199 Harare) has two weekly minibus services to Johannesburg for US$54 and Silverbird (☎ 729771, ext 109) in Harare runs twice weekly for US$76.

There are more luxurious (and expensive) options such as Blue Arrow/Greyhound (☎ 69763 Bulawayo; ☎ 791305 Harare) and Translux (☎ 774 3333 Johannesburg).

Daily commuter minibuses depart when full from the Crown Plaza Hotel in Harare (US$30) and the City Hall Car Park in Bulawayo (US$27).

Train The weekly *Trans-Limpopo Express* takes 26 hours from Harare to Johannesburg and costs US$76/55 in 1st/2nd class. The weekly *Bulawayo Express* from Bulawayo to Johannesburg costs US$49/35. Advance bookings are essential; contact Main Line Trains (☎ 773 2944), PO Box 2671, Joubert Park 2044, South Africa.

There's also a daily train from Beitbridge to Johannesburg for US$41/28.

Zambia
Most travellers cross into Zambia at Victoria Falls/Livingstone, which is open daily from 6 am to 8 pm. Between Victoria Falls and Livingstone you can take a taxi for a fiercely negotiated US$3 or the twice daily rail service for US$1.50. If you're crossing for the day, Zambian officials normally aren't fussed about onward tickets or sufficient funds.

There are also crossings at Kariba and Chirundu. From Harare's Mbare musika, ZUPCO and Giraffe have daily buses to Lusaka; the first leaves at 6 am, but services get crowded so arrive early. The trip takes nine hours and costs US$7. For more comfort, there's the Power Coach Express (☎ 60466), 10 Williams Ave, Ardbennie,

Harare, with daily service between Mbare and Lusaka (US$8).

Getting Around

AIR

Air Zimbabwe has domestic routes connecting Harare and Bulawayo with Victoria Falls, Kariba, Masvingo, Gweru and Hwange National Park. Zimbabwe Express Airlines also has domestic flights between Harare, Kariba, Bulawayo, Hwange National Park and Victoria Falls. Sometimes combined flight and accommodation deals are available for the price of the air ticket, so it's worth making enquiries.

BUS

There are two types of buses – express and local (most commonly known as African buses). The relatively efficient express buses operate according to published timetables and make scheduled snack and toilet stops. The best services between major cities and towns are operated by Ajay Motorways and Blue Arrow/United Transport Group.

African buses, on the other hand, go just about anywhere people are living, but they don't run according to schedules. They may depart only in the early morning to smaller villages. They're fairly crowded – particularly after pay days or around school holidays – but they're ultra cheap and you're more likely to meet Zimbabweans on them than on foreigner-oriented express buses. African buses normally depart from township markets outside the main centre.

TRAIN

Zimbabwe's railway network connects Harare, Bulawayo, Mutare and Victoria Falls. All major services travel at night, but sleeping compartments and bedding can be hired for under US$1. Sexes are separated unless you book a family compartment or coupé. Second class compartments hold six adults, but children aren't counted and since most Zimbabwean women travel with at

least one child, women travelling on their own may consider booking a coupé.

Few trains have buffet cars, so bring along snacks and drinks. Tickets for domestic routes go on sale 30 days ahead, and it's wise to book as early as possible.

CAR & MOTORCYCLE

Several relatively inexpensive car-rental companies have emerged in recent years, but vehicles aren't generally well maintained and, in the case of a breakdown, few provide rescue service or replacement vehicles. In fact, many try to charge renters for even routine repairs, so read the fine print carefully. No car-rental company allows renters to take 2WD cars into Mana Pools – or onto any gravel road, for that matter. For that type of travel you need 4WD, which is even more expensive.

You can temporarily import vehicles free of charge, and if you're not covered in Zimbabwe, third party insurance is available at the border. Hired cars from the Southern African Customs Union – Botswana, Namibia, South Africa, Lesotho or Swaziland – may enter Zimbabwe with permission from the rental company, but you need a temporary export permit from the vehicle's home country and a temporary import permit for Zimbabwe. This requires proof of insurance and a 'Blue Book' sheet detailing the vehicle's particulars. Rental companies provide relevant paperwork.

Motorcycles face the same restrictions as cars, with the added stipulation that they are not allowed in national parks.

BICYCLE

Most roads are surfaced and in fair repair, and shoulders are often sealed and marked off from the rest of the road by a yellow line so they can be used as cycle lanes. What's more, the winter climate is predictably good and winds are generally easterly and only rarely strong enough to make cycling difficult. Distances between towns and points of interest are long by European standards, but they're mostly only a day's ride apart and there are plenty of small shops between towns.

Harare's best cycle shops are Zack's on Kenneth Kaunda Ave, opposite the train station, and the nearby Manica Cycles on Second St. Note that spares are hard to come by, even in Harare, so bring as much as possible from home.

HITCHING
Hitching is relatively easy and many travellers prefer it as a way of getting around, although it's not advisable to hitch at night. For the best luck, look for lifts at the last petrol station before the open road. Don't be shy about asking for lifts. Some drivers may expect payment for lifts, so ask before you climb in. Note that hitching is forbidden in national parks. See also the warning on hitching in the main Getting Around chapter.

BOAT
On Lake Kariba, two scheduled ferries connect Kariba with Binga and Mlibizi and are handy for circular tours of Zimbabwe without having to retrace your steps between Victoria Falls and Bulawayo.

The popular Kariba Ferries has two car ferries, the *Seahorse* and *Sea Lion*, which sail twice weekly between Kariba and Mlibizi. The more basic DDF ferry connects National Parks Harbour in Kariba with Binga and Gache Gache. The DDF ferry to Binga departs fortnightly, with overnight stops in Chalala and Sengwa. There are also weekly runs to Tashinga and Gache Gache.

Transport to Binga and Mlibizi to connect with the ferries can be difficult, and those without vehicles must rely on lifts from fellow passengers or taxis from Victoria Falls. Local buses connect Bulawayo and Binga via Dete Crossroads, and they pass within 15km of Mlibizi.

Harare

The capital and heart of the nation in nearly every respect, Harare (population one million), formerly known as Salisbury, was bequeathed a distinctly European flavour by its former colonisers. Its excellent facilities, healthy climate and compact business district make it easy to get around. It's also a good place to splurge on a variety of cuisines and to look for arts and crafts, particularly Shona sculpture.

Warning
Chancellor Ave, an extension of Seventh St, is the site of the Executive President's Residence and the State House. The site is closed between 6 pm and 6 am. Official orders regarding anyone ignoring this curfew are to fire without questioning.

Information
The Harare Publicity Association (☎ 705085) occupies the south-west corner of African Unity Square. It may be Zimbabwe's least helpful tourist office but it's worth picking up its monthly publication, *What's on in Harare*.

For nationwide information, see the Zimbabwe Tourist Board (☎ 793666), 7th floor, Anchor House, on Jason Moyo Ave west of First St.

Buy maps from the Surveyor General, Mapping Section, Electra House, Samora Machel Ave.

National parks information and bookings are made at the National Parks Central Booking Office (☎ 706077) on Sandringham Drive, north of the Botanic Gardens.

Amex is represented by Manica Travel (☎ 703421) at the Travel Centre on Jason Moyo Ave.

The post office is on Inez Terrace. Stamp sales and poste restante are upstairs in the arcade, while the parcel office is in a separate corridor downstairs.

For used books, check out Booklover's Paradise at 48 Angwa St and the Treasure Trove at 26C Second St on the corner of George Silundika Ave. Camping gear, including butane cartridges, is found at Fereday & Sons on Robert Mugabe Rd and Angwa St.

Things to See
The **Queen Victoria Museum**, in the Civic

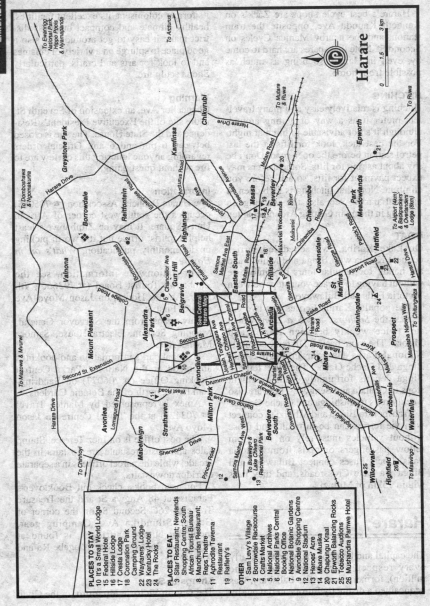

Harare

To Ewanrigg
National Park,
Hippo Pools
& Nyamapanda

To Arcturus

Chikurubi

Harare Drive

Kamfinsa

To Mutare
& Ruwa

Epworth

To Domboshawa
& Ngomakurira

Greystone Park

Harare Drive

Borrowdale

Rehtfontein

Highlands

Arcturus Road

Rhodesville Ave

Mutare Road

Msasa

Beverley

Park

To Mutare
& Ruwa

To Ruwa

Valnona

Gun Hill

Chancellor Ave

Belgravia

Borrowdale Road

College Road

Samora Machel Ave East

Eastlea South

Hillside

Mukuvisi Woodlands

Mukuvisi River

Chadcombe

Meadowlands

Park

To Airport (4km)
& Backpackers
& Bushbackers
Lodge (8km)

Mount Pleasant

Alexandra
Park

Second St

See Central
Harare Map

Arcadia

Harare River

Queensdale

St
Martins

Airport Road

Sunningdale

Prospect

To Chitungwiza

Avonlea

Strathaven

Milton Park

Avondale

West Road

Bishop Gaul Ave

Mbare

Seke Road

Harare
Road

Hatfield

Samora Machel Ave West

To Mazowe & Mvurwi

Maberleign

Sherwood Drive

Princes Road

Belvedere
South

Chiremba Road

George Road

Patrick's Road

Masotsha Ndlovu Way

Harare Drive

Ardbennie

Waterfalls

To Chinhoyi

Lomagundi Road

Harare Drive

Second St Extension

Drummond Chaplin

Kwame Nkrumah Ave

Coventry Road

Simon Mazorodze Road

Highfield Road

Waterfalls Ave

To Bulawayo &
Lake Chivero

Willowvale

Highfield

To Masvingo

0   1.5   3 km

Centre complex near the gold-coloured Sheraton Hotel, contains Mashonaland wildlife and anthropological exhibits. It is open daily from 9 am to 5 pm. Admission is Z$2 for residents and US$2 for foreigners.

More worthwhile is the **National Gallery of Zimbabwe** on Julius Nyerere Crescent near Park Lane. It has excellent displays of African artefacts, with masks and carvings from around the continent. Admission is free on Sunday and US$1 on other days.

Much of Harare's activity focuses on **Mbare musika**, Zimbabwe's largest market and busiest bus terminal. Between 6 am and 6 pm it bustles with shoppers seeking out everything from secondhand clothing and fruit to herbal remedies. On Sunday afternoons, most of Harare shuts down but Mbare keeps buzzing. Take the bus from the Angwa St bus terminal or pay US$1.30 for a taxi.

The **National Botanical Gardens** along Fifth St beyond the golf course are well planned, with extensive lawns and a variety of African plants. They're open daily from sunrise to sunset, and admission is free.

At **Chapungu Kraal**, 8km from the city centre, you can see a typical Shona village and fine stone sculptures. It's open daily from 8 am to 6 pm, and admission is US$0.50 (guided tours pay US$2.50). The sculpture garden and weekend African dance performances (Saturday at 3 pm and Sunday at 11 am and 3 pm) are worth seeing.

Places to Stay

Camping Camp sites at *Coronation Park* off Mutare Rd, 7km east of the city centre, cost US$0.70 for up to four people, but watch your gear. The Menara and Greendale buses from Rezende St bus terminal pass the entrance, and the Msasa bus from Market Square bus terminal stops a few minutes walk away.

Alternatively, try *The Rocks* (☎/fax 734724), an overland truck stop at 18 Seke Rd. Camping costs US$1.50 (tents may be hired), dorm beds are US$4 and doubles are US$8.20. Take a Hatfield emergency taxi from the corner of Robson Manyika Ave and Julius Nyerere Way, or the Zengeza or St Mary's bus from the Angwa St bus terminal. It's a five minute walk from Seke Rd.

Hostels Although it's aimed at business travellers, *Talk of the Town* (☎ 730344) at 92 Central Ave, gets excellent marks for friendliness and cleanliness. Dorm beds cost US$5.50 and single/double rooms are US$9/13. There are cooking facilities available.

A friendly and central place to meet local traders and businesspeople is the *Guest Lodge* (☎ 735450; fax 707900), run by Susan. Dorm beds cost US$6.50 and twin or double rooms cost US$20. Plates of sadza ne nyama (mealies with meat relish) cost just US$0.80.

At 39 Selous Ave is the cosy *Palm Rock Villa* (☎ 724550), where double/triple rooms are US$9/11, including use of kitchen facilities.

Peterborough Lodge (☎ 796735) at 11 Peterborough St, near Water Whirld, is favoured by volunteer organisations; it's great for peace and quiet. Dorm beds cost US$3 and double rooms US$8.

The lively and quirky *Hillside Lodge* (☎ 747961), 71 Hillside Rd, is an old colonial home surrounded by jacaranda trees. Camping in a lovely, tree-studded site costs US$2.10, dorm beds are US$3.50, mattresses are US$3.25, singles/doubles cost US$6.40/7.70 and private double cabins are US$8. It provides free pick-up from town and town/airport transfers for US$1/3.50 per trip. Take the Msasa, Tafara or Mabvuku bus from Speke Ave and Julius Nyerere Way, get off at the Children's Home and walk up Robert Mugabe Rd to Helm Rd, which leads to Hillside Rd.

The bright *It's a Small World Lodge* (☎ 308099) at 72 King George Rd, Avondale, has a pool and comfortable dorm beds for US$5.50 per person, with linen. There's a nominal fee for transfers from town or the airport (initial airport pick-up is free). Great breakfasts are available for US$2. There's also a travellers' communications centre, with fax and email services (fax 33 5341; email backpack@harare.iafrica.com).

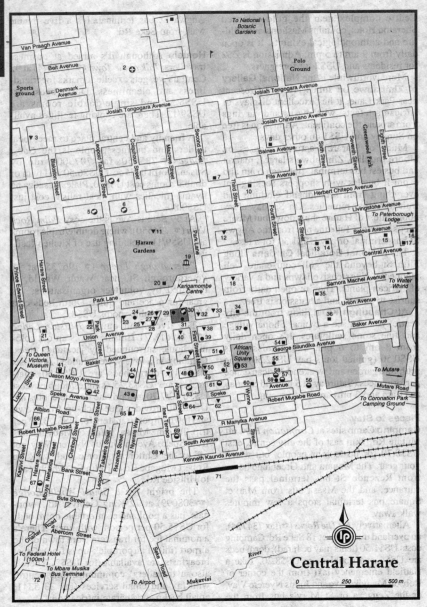

Central Harare

0   250   500 m

To National
Botanic
Gardens

Polo
Ground

Van Praagh Avenue

Beit Avenue

Denmark
Avenue

Sports
ground

Josiah Tongogara Avenue

Josiah Tongogara Avenue

Josiah Chinamano Avenue

Baines Avenue

Fife Avenue

Herbert Chitepo Avenue

Livingstone Avenue

To Peterborough
Lodge

Selous Avenue

Central Avenue

Samora Machel Avenue

To Water
Whirld

Union Avenue

Baker Avenue

George Silundika Avenue

To Mutare

Mutare Road

To Coronation Park
Camping Ground

Robert Mugabe Road

R Manyika Avenue

South Avenue

Kenneth Kaunda Avenue

Greenwood
Park

Harare
Gardens

Karigamombe
Centre

African
Unity
Square

Park Lane

Harare Street

Prince Edward Street

Blakiston Street

Leopold Takawira Street

Colquhoun Street

Mazowe Street

Second Street

Third Street

Fourth Street

Fifth Street

Sixth Street

Seventh Street

Eighth Street

Park Lane

Park
Street

Union   Avenue

Baker   Avenue

Jason Moyo Avenue

Speke   Avenue

Albion
Road

Robert Mugabe Road

Speke

Speke   Avenue

First Street Mall

Angwa   Street

Inez Terrace

J Nyerere Way

Rezende Street

Leopold Takawira Street

Cameron Street

Chinhoyi Street

Mbuya Nehanda Street

Harare Street

Kaguvi Street

Lick   Street

Bank Street

Bute Street

Abercom Street

Charter   Road

To Queen
Victoria
Museum

To Federal Hotel
(100m)

To Mbare Musika
Bus Terminal

To Airport

Seke Road

Mukuvisi

River

Whyne   Avenue

Mutare Road

Kenneth Kaunda Avenue

1 ■
2 ✚
3 ▼
4 ◐
5 ◐
6 ◐
7 ▼
8 ■
9 ◐
10 ■
11 ▼
12 ▼
13 ■ 14 ■
15 ■
16 ■
17 ■
18 ▼
19 ⋔
20 ■
21 ▼
22 ■
23 ◐ 24 ▼ 26 ▼ 29 ● 30 ▼
25 ◐ 27 ● 28 ▼ 31 ■
32 ▼ 33 ▼
34 ■
35 ■
36 ■
37 ●
38 ▼
39 ●
40 ▼
41 ■
42 ●
43 ●
44 ◐ 45 ▼ 46 ▼
47 ▼
48 ● 49 ■
50 ▼ 51 ● 52 ● 53 ℹ
54 ■ 55 ■
56 ◐
57 ● 58 ● 59 ● 60 ● 61 ●
62 ▼
63 ● 64 ▼
65 ■
66 ■
67 ●
68 ★
69 ▼
70 ▼
71 ■
72 ●

PLACES TO STAY
1 Possum Lodge
7 Terreskane Hotel
8 Bronté Hotel
10 Elmfield Lodge
13 Palm Rock Villa
14 Selous Hotel
15 Courteney Hotel
16 Sable Lodge
17 Talk of the Town Lodge
20 Crowne Plaza Hotel
21 Guest Lodge
22 Cresta Jameson Hotel
34 New Ambassador Hotel
35 Holiday Inn
36 Cresta Oasis Hotel
54 Quality International
   Hotel
60 Meikles Hotel
65 Elizabeth Hotel
66 Queen's Hotel

PLACES TO EAT
3 Da Guido Trattoria
9 Clovagalix; Fife Ave
   Laundrette; Spring
   Roll Centre
11 Sherrol's in the Park
12 Alexander's
18 Bombay Duck
23 BB House; Ramambo
   Lodge Restaurant
25 Taco's
26 Café Europa

27 Sandrock Café
32 Sidewalk Café
33 Savoy Sandwich Bar
38 Pino's Restaurant
40 Lido Café
46 Susie's Bistro
47 TM Supermarket
49 Terrace Restaurant
   (Barbour's Dept
   Store)
50 Two Flights Up
62 Shezan
70 Mandarin

OTHER
2 Parirenyatwa Hospital
4 Canadian High
   Commission
5 Mozambican Embassy
6 US Embassy
19 National Gallery
24 Surveyor General
28 Sandro's Nightclub
29 Balkan Bulgarian
   Airlines
30 Australian High
   Commission
31 Aeroflot; Russian
   Cultural Centre
37 Parliament
39 Liquenda House -
   Immigration Office;
   Archipelago's
   Nightclub

41 Solo's Nightclub
42 Chinhoyi Street Bus
   Terminal
43 Town House
44 Rezende Street Bus
   Terminal
45 GPO
48 Zimbabwe Tourist
   Board
51 Treasure Trove
52 Kingston's Bookshop
53 Harare Publicity
   Association
55 Grass Roots Bookshop
56 Fourth Street Bus
   Terminal
57 Blue Arrow Bus Office
58 Manica Travel;
   Ajay's Motorways
59 Air Zimbabwe
61 Trans Lux Bus Office
63 New Zealand High
   Commission
64 Fereday & Sons
   Camping Shop
67 Market Square Bus
   Terminal
68 Police
69 Angwa Street Bus
   Terminal
71 Train Station
72 National Handicraft
   Centre

The popular *Kopje Lodge* (☎ 499097) at 221 Enterprise Rd, Chisipite, has camping for US$2.30, dorms from US$3.30 to US$4.20 and doubles for US$10.30. It offers free pick-up and transfers to/from the Sandrock Cafe, a swimming pool, pizza bakes and Sunday barbecues.

The new *Possum Lodge* (☎ 726851; fax 72 6851) at 7 Deary Ave charges US$5 for well appointed dormitory accommodation. Amenities include meals, a pool, jacuzzi, TV lounge and outdoor bar. From the city centre, it's a 20 minute walk up Second St.

Hotels Most bottom-end hotels double as brothels, and women travelling alone risk being misconstrued. The most popular is the *Elizabeth Hotel* (☎ 753437) on the corner of Julius Nyerere Way and Robert Mugabe Rd.

Singles/doubles with shared facilities cost US$11.50/21, including breakfast.

More respectable is the friendly *Elmfield Lodge* (☎ 728041) at 111 Fife Ave. It's good value at US$9 per person, but the area is risky at night and the facilities marginal; doors don't lock and some rooms lack windows. Backpackers accommodation costs US$5.

For a splash out, make a booking at the delightfully olde worlde *Bronté Hotel* (☎ 796631), 132 Baines Ave, which is set in its own quiet gardens and has a restaurant, bar and pool. In the main building, singles/doubles cost US$45/58, with breakfast. Singles/doubles in the annexe are US$39/51.

Places to Eat
Takeaways in the city centre sell chips, burgers, 'samoosas', soft drinks and other

fast fare. A good choice is the *Spring Roll Centre* in the Fife Avenue Shopping Centre. Institutionalised fast food is available from the several outlets of *Chicken Inn* (chicken and chips), *Baker's Inn* (doughnuts, pastry and sandwiches) and *Creamy Inn* (ice cream). For cheap African fare, the take-aways in the Kopje area offer good value.

Dagwood's in the First St Parkade has inexpensive sandwiches and sadza ne nyama. Nearby *Brazita's* and *Le Paris* both offer real filtered coffee, and the latter also does light meals and sandwiches. The *Lido Café* at 51 Union Ave serves full breakfasts for around US$2, and is recommended for burgers, creative main courses and sweets, which range from US$1.20 to US$4. It's also open for dinner. The *Sidewalk Cafe* on First St serves light inexpensive meals, including vegetarian dishes. The sidewalk seating and simple fare at the *Sandrock Cafe* on Julius Nyerere Way are also popular, particularly with local Rastafarians.

If you're around Coronation Park, don't miss *Rafferty's* on Mutare Rd, 150m from the camping ground turn-off. The delicious, healthy lunches are unbeatable.

For a more elegant meal, there's *Da Guido Trattoria* in the Montagu shopping centre. Pasta specials cost around US$3.50. Don't miss the salads and coffee.

Quality African cuisine is served at *Roots of Africa* on the corner of Seventh St and Livingstone Ave. *Taco's* at 46 Union Ave serves the nearest thing to Mexican food you'll find in Zimbabwe.

For Indian fare, try *Bombay Duck* at 7 Central Ave. The adjoining takeaway serves curry for US$1.50. The best Chinese option is probably the *Mandarin* on Robert Mugabe Rd near First St. For fish and seafood, a good choice is *Pino's* (☎ 792303) at 73 Union Ave; plan on spending around US$10, without drinks.

The *Ramambo Lodge*, on the corner of Samora Machel Ave and Leopold Takawira St, serves wild game dishes, from impala and wart hog to ostrich steak, eland stroganoff and crocodile in cheese sauce. It also does beef, African meals, vegetarian dishes and seafood. The décor and entertainment emulate a 'safari lodge' atmosphere. It's closed on Sunday.

Entertainment

For information on coming events, check the tourist office booklet *What's on in Harare*. To find a *pungwe* (an all-night drinking and dancing musical performance) by a top musician, watch for posters advertised on signs and poles, mainly in the Kopje area of the city centre.

The best places for local bands are the *Federal*, *Queen's* or *Elizabeth* hotels where, on weekends, well known names may occasionally drop by.

Another place which sometimes attracts big names is the New Yorkish *Playboy Night Club* at 40 Union Ave. The garden of the *Nyagonzera Skyline Motel* at Km 19 on the Beatrice-Masvingo Rd also offers superb talent, but at night it's accessible only by taxi.

For a better chance of hearing the greats – the Bhundu Boys, Thomas Mapfumo or Ilanga – try the weekend gigs at *Job's Night Spot* in the Wonder shopping centre on Julius Nyerere Way between Kenneth Kaunda and Robson Manyika Aves.

The most popular places with white Zimbabweans are *The Tube*, with a London tube station theme, at Mbuya Nehanda St 125, and *Archipelago's* in Liquenda House on Baker Ave. *Sandro's* on the corner of Julius Nyerere Way and Union Ave attracts mellower crowds. For a good mixed clientele, try reggae-oriented *Tacos* on Union Ave.

Never walk to or from any late-night spot; take a taxi right to your door.

Getting There & Away

Intercity express buses have their own bus terminals. Local (African) buses leave from Mbare musika, the huge market/bus terminal 5km from the city centre. To get there, take a bus from the Angwa St bus terminal in the city centre, or hire a taxi for US$1.30.

The train station is on the corner of Kenneth Kaunda Ave and Second St.

Getting Around

The Airport The Express Motorways airport bus (☎ 720392) costs US$3. It leaves from the corner of Speke Ave and Second St, near Meikles Hotel.

Taxis to or from the airport cost US$6.50.

Bus The crowded Harare city buses and 15-seat minibuses provide transport for the masses. There are five central bus terminals: Market Square, Fourth St, Angwa St, Rezende St and Chinhoyi St. Buses to Mbare leave from the Angwa St bus terminal. There is also a string of bus stops along Jason Moyo Ave, near Fourth St.

Taxi Official services include Rixi Taxi (☎ 753080), A1 (☎ 706996) and economy-oriented Cream Line (☎ 703333). Using unofficial taxis can be risky. To anywhere in the city centre costs US$0.60 to US$0.90; to the suburbs costs no more than US$2.50.

Emergency taxis – clunky, stripped-down Peugeots with 'emergency taxi' painted on the door – operate within city limits along set routes for less than US$0.20. The main terminals are near the corner of George Silundika Ave and Fourth St, and on Rezende St between Jason Moyo and Baker Aves.

Bicycle Bikes may be hired at Bushtrackers (☎ 303025) at the Brontë Hotel (See Places to Stay earlier in this section for details).

AROUND HARARE
Ewanrigg Botanical Gardens

This leafy national park 40km north-east of Harare contains 40 hectares of botanical gardens and 200 hectares of bushland. Take the Shamva bus from Mbare musika as early in the morning as possible and get off at the Ewanrigg turn-off, which is 3km from the gardens.

Lake Chivero Recreational Park

Lake Chivero, a large reservoir on the Manyame River, is a popular weekend spot with Harare people. Most of the northern shore belongs to clubs and is closed to non-affiliates, but Admiral's Cabin, with picnic sites and boat rental, allows access to the shore for US$1.30.

Much of the southern shore lies within a 1600 hectare **wildlife park**. The **rock paintings** at Bushman's Point are worth a look; other rock paintings, such as those at Crocodile Rock, Pax Park and Ovoid Rock, are accessible only with a park-service guide. For day use, admission is US$1.30. Guided 1½-hour pony safaris cost US$1.30; enquire at the chalet reception office.

Places to Stay There are national park *camp sites* near the Hunyani Hills Hotel on the northern shore. There is also a *rest camp* with chalets and lodges – but no shops or restaurants – on the southern shore. *Admiral's Cabin* (☎ 27144) has camping or caravanning for US$2.50 per person, basic doubles for US$15 and four-bed rooms for US$18.

Getting There & Away From Mbare, there's a daily bus to the northern shore. Otherwise, wait at the bus stop near the Cresta Jameson Hotel on Samora Machel Ave; any Bulawayo road bus will get you to the Manyame bridge, which is within striking distance of the lake.

Domboshawa & Ngomakurira

Domboshawa, a natural site of colourful rock domes, caves and prehistoric paintings, contains a small museum and marked walks. Ngomakurira, further out, is best seen in the afternoon. Its romantic name means 'the mountain of drums', after an effect created by its unique acoustics.

Getting There & Away Take the city bus from the stop in front of Kingston's bookshop, opposite African Unity Square, or from along Seventh St. Alternatively, get the Bindura via Chinamora bus from Mbare, get off at the turn-off 4km north of Domboshawa village and walk the remaining 1km to Domboshawa rock. The Bindura bus continues on to the Sasa road turn-off, which is just 2km west of Ngomakurira.

Hippo Pools

For a friendly wilderness escape, you can't

beat *Hippo Pools* (☎ 708843; fax 750619), a budget resort set idyllically on the banks of the Mazowe River in the Umfurduzi Safari Area. It's ideal for hiking, canoeing and fishing, and the area is rich in wildlife. Camping costs US$3.50 per person and accommodation in rustic open chalets is US$8, but backpackers rates are available. You can self-cater, or order lunch or dinner for US$4. Transfers from Harare (US$8 return) run on Monday and Friday at 2.30 pm from the Brontë Hotel (see the Harare Places to Stay entry for details).

Around the Country

BULAWAYO

Formerly called Gu-Bulawayo or the Killing Place, Bulawayo is Zimbabwe's second city. The name presumably resulted from Mzilikazi's Thabas Indunas (Hill of Chiefs) executions during the early development of the Ndebele state. Safer and more relaxed than Harare (but don't walk around at night), it reminds many travellers of the mid-western USA in the 1950s.

Information

The Bulawayo Publicity Association (☎ 60867), near City Hall, distributes *Bulawayo This Month*, which outlines coming events. Immigration is on the 1st floor of the Central Africa Building Society. Manica Travel (☎ 62521) on Fife St is the Amex representative and books Ajay Motorways buses.

The post office takes up most of the block along Main St between Eighth and Leopold Takawira Aves.

Butane cylinders are available for US$2 at Eezee Kamping on George Silundika St, between Ninth and Tenth Aves. Book exchange is available at Book Mart at 103 George Silundika.

Things to See

The **Natural History Museum**, in Centenary Park on Leopold Takawira Ave, is one of Africa's finest, with extensive cultural, historical, zoological, geological and botanical displays. It's open from 9 am to 5 pm; foreigners pay US$2 admission.

The **Railway Museum** is a must for railway and history buffs. You'll see antique locomotives, rolling stock and even a 'museum on wheels' – a 1904 passenger coach with original fittings.

The **Bulawayo Art Gallery**, in the historical Douslin House on Leopold Takawira Ave and Main St, contains a collection of mainly colonial paintings. Admission is US$0.15 and believe it or not, students get a discount.

To see the creative processes in progress, visit the **Mzilikazi Arts & Crafts Centre** and nearby **Bulawayo Home Industries**, where local people learn artistic skills and produce excellent work. Free guided tours are conducted from 10 am to 12.30 pm and 2 to 5 pm Monday to Friday. Take the Mpilo or Barbour Fields (marked BF) bus from the Lobengula St bus terminal and get off at Bulawayo Home Industries or the Mzilikazi Primary School.

Places to Stay

The *Municipal Caravan Park & Campsite* (☎ 63851), 10 minutes walk from the city centre, has camp sites for US$2.60 per tent plus US$1.20 per person, chalets for US$6 per person and hired caravans for US$9. Don't even consider walking there after dark; taxis cost US$1.30 from the city centre.

A new backpackers place is *Africa Sun Lodge* (☎ 76523) at 398 Thurso Rd, Killarney. It's 7km out, but offers free pick-up from the bus or train and regular shuttles to the city centre. Facilities include a pool, bar, *braai* (barbecue), video lounge and optional meals. Beds cost US$4 per person.

At 11 Inverleith Drive, 4.5km from the city centre, is the quiet *Paradise Lodge* (☎ 46481; fax 64576; email mfsburke @harare.iafrica.com). Dorm beds cost US$4.50, including use of the pool, sun deck, braai, videos, laundry, cooking facilities and transfers to town.

Another cosy place is *20 Devon Lodge*

(☎ 41501), in Hillside, which offers free pick-ups and town transfers, a bar, kitchen, picnic area, TV lounge and volleyball. Camping costs US$3, dorm beds are US$5 and private doubles are US$13. Meals are available on request. Take the Hillside Rd bus from Stand II at City Hall bus terminal and get off on the corner of Weir and Hillside; it's two blocks from there.

The ever-popular *Shaka's Spear* (☎ 69923) on the corner of Second Ave and Jason Moyo St offers a lively atmosphere and pleasant accommodation for US$4.50 per person. Meals are available.

At 7 Hillside Rd is *Hitch Haven*, with camping for US$2.50, dormitory rooms for US$5 and doubles for US$7. Meals and cooking facilities are available. Take the Hillside Rd bus from Town Hall Square.

A good central place is *Berkeley Place* (☎ 67701), where doubles with shower and sink cost US$16.50.

The seedy *New Waverley Hotel* (☎ 60033) on Lobengula St and Twelfth Ave is the cheapest hotel at US$8.20/11.50 for singles/doubles; it's one of Bulawayo's liveliest nightspots.

A touch more plush is the *Plaza Hotel* (☎ 64280) on Fourteenth Ave and Jason Moyo St, with basic rooms for US$14/16.

The quiet *Coach House* (☎ 26009), 27km out along Airport Rd, has camping, braais and kitchen facilities for US$7, or pre-set tents and caravans for US$6 per person. Beds in the lodge cost US$20 and double chalets are US$13.25 per person with breakfast. Horse riding is also available.

For a treat, check out the *Travellers' Guest House* (☎/fax 46059), a B&B/guesthouse/backpackers hybrid run by Alex and Paul. Singles/doubles with bath and use of the braai, pizza oven, TV room, lounge and pool cost US$21/30, including breakfast. Doubles with bath are US$35. Phone for pick-up from town.

Places to Eat

The *Grass Hut* on Fife St has a good value breakfast menu, which includes eggs, omelettes, bacon, sausages and several toast concoctions. If you're famished, visit the buffet at the *Homestead Restaurant* in the Bulawayo Sun Hotel between 7 and 10 am for English/Continental style buffet breakfasts for US$3/5.

At *Oriental Takeaways*, herbivores can chow down on veggie burgers, samosas and vegetarian curry. The *Hot Bread Shop*, near Twelfth Ave and Fife St, also serves good takeaways. You'll find basic Chinese specialities at *Tunku's Chop Suey Centre* on Eighth Ave between Robert Mugabe and George Silundika Sts. For traditional Zimbabwean fare, try *The Pantry*, open from 5 am to 3 pm, on Fifteenth Ave between Main and Fort Sts.

English teas and superb light lunches are served at *Sisters* on the 2nd floor of the Haddon & Sly department store. The popular *Mary's Corner* (☎ 76701), opposite the medical centre on Eighth Ave, serves pizzas, Greek specialities, chicken, beef, sweet snacks and coffee. It's wise to book for lunch.

The clean *YWCA* on Lobengula St is open to nonresidents for lunch between 12.30 and 3 pm; you'll get a filling plate of sadza ne nyama for US$1.

For a pizza, fish & chips, piri-piri chicken or filled jacket potatoes, *Dial-a-Pizza* (☎ 66847) at 101 Lobengula St is open daily from 10 am to 9 pm. It delivers anywhere in Bulawayo.

A good Italian dinner option is the *Capri* (☎ 63639) on the corner of Eleventh Ave and George Silundika St. It's open daily for lunch and dinner, and serves free garlic bread and vegetables. The door is locked for security reasons; just knock through the grating and staff will open up.

The best Chinese food is at *Peking* on Jason Moyo St, with tasty renditions of Sichuan and Cantonese fare. For a dose of Zimbabwean beef, the best choice is *The Cattleman*, near the corner of Twelfth Ave and Josiah Tongogara St.

Entertainment

Most Bulawayo pubs and clubs are more sticky than their Harare counterparts about

ZIMBABWE

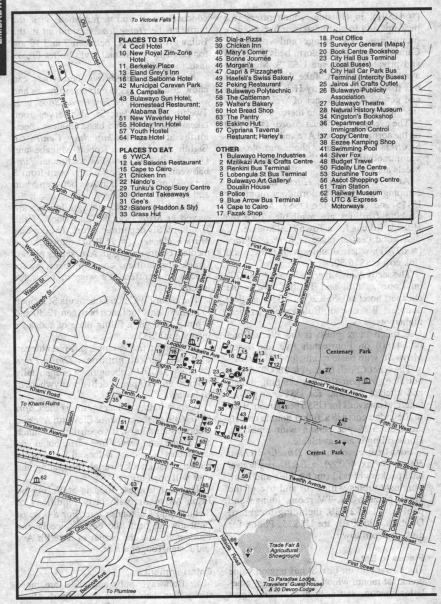

PLACES TO STAY
4   Cecil Hotel
10 New Royal Zim-Zone Hotel
11 Berkeley Place
13 Eland Grey's Inn
16 Eland Selborne Hotel
42 Municipal Caravan Park & Campsite
43 Bulawayo Sun Hotel; Homestead Restaurant; Alabama Bar
51 New Waverley Hotel
55 Holiday Inn Hotel
57 Youth Hostel
64 Plaza Hotel

PLACES TO EAT
6   YWCA
12 Les Saisons Restaurant
15 Cape to Cairo
21 Chicken Inn
22 Nando's
29 Tunku's Chop Suey Centre
30 Oriental Takeaways
31 Gee's
32 Sisters (Haddon & Sly)
33 Grass Hut

35 Dial-a-Pizza
39 Chicken Inn
40 Mary's Corner
45 Bonne Journée
46 Morgan's
47 Capri & Pizzaghetti
49 Haefell's Swiss Bakery
52 Peking Restaurant
54 Bulawayo Polytechnic
58 The Cattleman
59 Walter's Bakery
60 Hot Bread Shop
63 The Pantry
66 Eskimo Hut
67 Cypriana Taverna Resturant; Harley's

OTHER
1   Bulawayo Home Industries
2   Mzilikazi Arts & Crafts Centre
3   Renkini Bus Terminal
5   Lobengula St Bus Terminal
7   Bulawayo Art Gallery/ Douslin House
8   Police
9   Blue Arrow Bus Terminal
14 Cape to Cairo
17 Fazak Shop

18 Post Office
19 Surveyor General (Maps)
20 Book Centre Bookshop
23 City Hall Bus Terminal (Local Buses)
24 City Hall Car Park Bus Terminal (Intercity Buses)
25 Jairos Jiri Crafts Outlet
26 Bulawayo Publicity Association
27 Bulawayo Theatre
28 Natural History Museum
34 Kingston's Bookshop
36 Department of Immigration Control
37 Copy Centre
38 Eezee Kamping Shop
41 Swimming Pool
44 Silver Fox
48 Budget Travel
50 Fidelity Life Centre
53 Sunshine Tours
56 Ascot Shopping Centre
61 Train Station
62 Railway Museum
65 UTC & Express Motorways

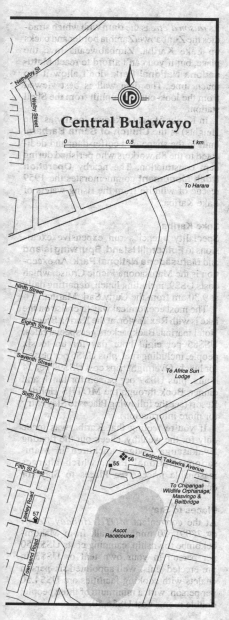

Central Bulawayo

'smart casual dress' requirements, especially after 4.30 pm. The *Alabama* at the Bulawayo Sun Hotel offers live jazz most evenings. The *New Waverley Hotel* stages live African music performances; it's not a great place for unaccompanied women, who often get hassled there.

More down-to-earth is the *Cape to Cairo*, opposite City Hall on Leopold Takawira Ave, with a mellow bar and occasional live music. *Harley's* at the Trade Fair is *the* hangout for young white Zimbabweans.

For Saturday night disco dancing, a respectable option is *Talk of the Town* in the Monte Carlo building on the corner of Fife St and Twelfth Ave; no jeans or trainers are allowed.

On Friday, the public bar at the *Cresta Churchill* has live music and, if featuring a well known name, it can be fabulous. This is one of Zimbabwe's most integrated bars and is popular with locals from all walks of life.

A good bet is the African dance troupe *Sunduza*, which rehearses Monday to Friday from 10 am to noon at the Pumula Hall in Pumula. Access is by minibus from the TM supermarket in town. Admission costs US$6.50.

Getting There & Away

Bus The long-distance African bus terminal is Renkini musika on the Sixth Ave Extension, opposite the Mzilikazi police station.

Express bus companies have their own terminals. Express Motorways is at the Hertz office, but buses leave from the City Hall car park, as do unscheduled Johannesburg minibuses. Ajay's and Trans-Lux use the Bulawayo Sun Hotel. Blue Arrow (☎ 69673) and North Star Coaches leave from Unifreight House at 73a Fife St. Mini-Zim Mini-Coaches (☎ 76644) depart from the Holiday Inn.

Train Daily trains run to/from Harare, Dete (the stop for Hwange National Park) and Victoria Falls. The railway reservations and ticket offices (☎ 322210) are open at various hours for different classes of service, so it's worth phoning first.

Getting Around

The Airport The Air Zimbabwe bus between the Bulawayo Sun Hotel and the airport costs US$3. Airport taxis cost US$5. Reliable taxi companies include Rixi (☎ 60666) and York's (☎ 72454).

Bus For suburban buses, the City Hall bus terminal on Eighth Ave serves the northern, eastern and southern suburbs, while the Lobengula St bus terminal on Lobengula St and Sixth Ave serves the high-density western and south-western suburbs.

Bicycle Miles Ahead Cycle Hire (☎ 41747) rents mountain bikes for US$6.50 per day. Phone and your bike will be delivered. Transit Car & Truck Hire (☎ 76495) on Eighth Ave and Robert Mugabe St hires more marginal bikes for US$6 per day.

AROUND BULAWAYO

Khami

The Rozwi ruins of Khami, 22km west of Bulawayo, are one of Zimbabwe's most important archaeological sites. They date from the 17th century and were occupied until 1820. Foreigners pay US$3 admission. Hitching is difficult and there are no buses, so it's best to rent a bicycle or go by taxi (US$3.20 return). Head out along Khami Rd (Eleventh Ave) and follow the signs.

Tshabalala Wildlife Sanctuary

Tshabalala, 8km from Bulawayo, is open during daylight hours and offers walking, cycling and horse riding. It contains varied wildlife, including giraffe, kudu, zebra, impala, wildebeest and water birds. Foreigners pay US$2.50 admission; horse hire costs US$2.50 per person per hour. No bikes or motorcycles are allowed.

The Kezi bus from Renkini passes Tshabalala, and the Matobo Rd bus from City Hall can drop you at Retreat, 3km from the entrance.

KARIBA

Sticky, sprawling Kariba is a rambling two level jumble with little discernible identity.

Its *raison d'être* is the **dam wall** which straddles the Zimbabwe/Zambia border and backs up Lake Kariba. Zimbabweans love the place, but if you can't afford to reach **Matusadona National Park**, don't allow it too much time. The dam wall is best viewed from the look-out 1km uphill from the Shell station.

In Kariba Heights (known locally as The Heights) is the **Church of Santa Barbara**, built in the shape of a coffer-dam and dedicated to the 86 workers who perished during dam construction. The nearby **Operation Noah Monument** commemorates the 1959 rescue of wildlife from the rising waters of Lake Kariba.

Lake Kariba

Speciality agencies run expensive excursions to **Fothergill Island**, **Spurwing Island** and **Matusadona National Park**. An exception is the Matusadona Picnic Cruise, which costs US$9, including lunch, departing daily at 9.30 am from the Cutty Sark Marina.

The most economical way to cruise on the lake is with Rex Taylor, at the Kariba Breezes Hotel marina. Backpackers get special rates: US$85 per eight hour day for up to six people, including fuel, plus US$5 per person for lunch. Overnight trips cost US$99 per 24 hours, plus US$9 per person for lunch and dinner. Book through the MOTHS Holiday Resort (see the following Places to Stay entry for more information).

If you're feeling that Kariba was made only for the wealthy, check out the floating Nyakasanga Lodge, anchored in Matusadona National Park, which charges reasonable prices (see Places to Stay for details).

Places to Stay

At the convenient *MOTH Holiday Resort* (☎ 2809), 20 minutes walk from Mahombekombe township, camping costs US$1.50 per person in your own tent or US$3 in pre-erected tents. Well appointed six-person chalets with cooking facilities are US$4.50 per person, with a minimum of three people; double rooms cost US$6.50.

Further afield is *Mopani Bay Caravan Park* (☎ 2485) on the shore 2km from the Cutty Sark Hotel. Sites cost US$0.75, plus US$1.30 to US$3 per person. Elephants amble through regularly, and the lawns are trimmed by hippos. There's also the National Parks' *Nyanyana Camp* (☎ 2337) in the Kuburi Wilderness area, 35km from town.

The friendly *Kushinga Lodge* (☎ 2645; fax 2827; email buffalo@kariba.harare.iafrica.com), near the shore at the western end of town, offers double self-catering rondavels with bath for US$25. Camp sites cost US$6 for up to four people.

The *Kariba Breezes Hotel* (☎ 2433; fax 2767) is the best mid-range choice. Single/double rooms cost US$25/42, with breakfast. Because locals and foreigners pay the same rate, standards are far better than the price would imply.

The Christian-oriented *Most High Hotel* (☎ 2965) in The Heights costs US$30 per person for rooms which have hot water, attached bathroom, along with breakfast and an amazing view. Unmarried couples of the opposite sex may not share rooms.

The *Tamarind Lodges* (☎ 2697) charge US$24/36 for lovely four/six-bed lodges; guests may use the Cutty Sark's swimming pool and tennis courts.

Nyakasanga Lodge (☎ 2645), a floating backpackers lodge in Matusadona National Park, charges US$30 per person, including accommodation, meals, use of canoes for exploring the lake and canoe transfers from Kings Camp; otherwise, boat transfers from Kariba cost US$41 per person. Self-caterers get a discounted rate but game walks in the national park and pontoon trips cost extra. Bookings are essential.

Places to Eat

The cheapest meals are found in Mahombekombe township and at the *Country Club* in The Heights, where a hearty spread costs US$1.30 (people have been ignoring the 'members only' sign for years). Another place is *Polly's Takeaways*, where you can munch pasties, burgers or chicken and chips on the lake-view patio.

All hotels have dining rooms; the *Cutty Sark* and the *Lake View Inn* serve a buffet breakfast for US$2.50 and, at the latter, diners have use of the pool. The *Most High Hotel* does snacks, superb breakfasts for US$3.20 and enormous set dinners for US$7.

Getting There & Away

The bus terminal is in Mahombekombe township. MB Luxury Coaches has 12 daily buses from Mbare musika (Harare), and once or twice a week buses connect Kariba with Binga via the Siabuwa road. Blue Arrow runs express buses four times weekly between Harare and Kariba. Between Bulawayo and Kariba, Mini-Zim Mini-Coaches has weekly express runs.

Hitching from Harare is easy on Friday night or Saturday morning but less predictable at other times.

For information on lake ferries to Mlibizi, Binga and other lake ports, see the Zimbabwe Getting Around section.

Getting Around

UTC meets incoming flights and offers transfers between the airport and the Lake View, Caribbea Bay and Cutty Sark hotels in town for US$3 per person. An hourly bus connects the Swift United Freight Depot with Nyamhunga, near the airport, with Mahombekombe and Kariba Heights. Otherwise, hitchhiking around town is easy.

MUTARE

Mutare, Zimbabwe's fourth largest city, is beautifully set in a bowl-like valley surrounded by hills and makes a convenient base for visiting the Vumba region and Nyanga National Park.

The helpful Manicaland Publicity Association (☎ 64711) on Robert Mugabe Rd is open from 8.30 am to 12.45 pm and 2 to 4 pm Monday to Friday. The post office is on the same road, four blocks west.

Things to See

The **Mutare Museum** on Aerodrome Rd has sections on history, people and transport as

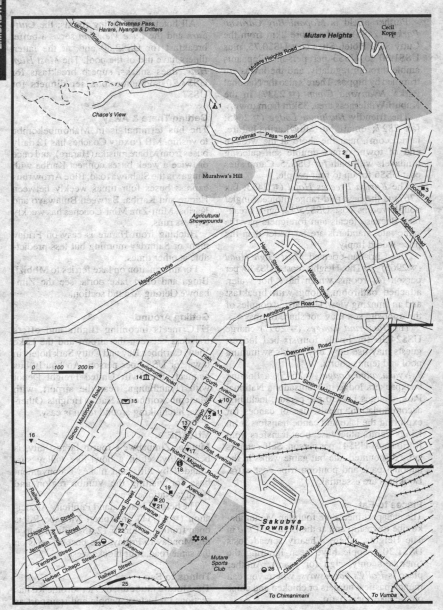

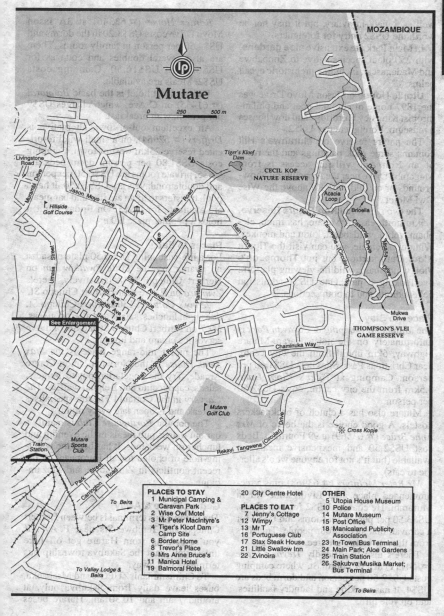

Mutare

MOZAMBIQUE

Livingstone
Road

Jason Moyo Drive

Hillside
Golf Course

Muramvi Drive

Umasa Street

Eleventh Avenue

Tenth Avenue

Ninth Ave

Eighth Ave

Seventh Avenue

See Enlargement

River

Train
Station

Mutare
Sports
Club

Park Street

Carrington Road

To Beira

To Valley Lodge &
Beira

Arcadia Road

Tiger's Kloof
Dam

CECIL KOP
NATURE RESERVE

Acacia
Loop

Broella

Rekayi

Cassonia Drive

Misasa Drive

Tangwena (Circular) Drive

Scenic Drive

Mukwa
Drive

THOMPSON'S VLEI
GAME RESERVE

Bain Drive

Plantation Drive

Chaminuka Way

Sakubvai

Josiah Tongogara Road

Mutare
Golf Club

Rekayi Tangwena (Circular) Drive

Cross Kopje

To Beira

PLACES TO STAY
1 Municipal Camping &
   Caravan Park
2 Wise Owl Motel
3 Mr Peter MacIntyre's
4 Tiger's Kloof Dam
   Camp Site
6 Border Home
8 Trevor's Place
9 Mrs Anne Bruce's
11 Manica Hotel
19 Balmoral Hotel

20 City Centre Hotel

PLACES TO EAT
7 Jenny's Cottage
12 Wimpy
13 Mr T
16 Portuguese Club
17 Stax Steak House
21 Little Swallow Inn
22 Zvinoira

OTHER
5 Utopia House Museum
10 Police
14 Mutare Museum
15 Post Office
18 Manicaland Publicity
   Association
23 In-Town Bus Terminal
24 Main Park; Aloe Gardens
25 Train Station
26 Sakubva Musika Market;
   Bus Terminal

well as a walk-in aviary, but it may not be worth the US$2 entry for foreigners.

In Main Park are extensive **aloe gardens**, with 250 plant species native to Zimbabwe and Madagascar, including prehistoric cycad palms.

Utopia House on Jason Moyo Drive was the 1897 home of colonial poet and philanthropist Kingsley Fairbridge and now houses a museum. Foreigners pay US$2.

The nature reserve on **Murahwa's Hill** contains some rock paintings and the ruins of an Iron Age village; access is from Magamba Drive near the Agricultural Showgrounds or on Old Pass Rd above the Wise Owl Motel.

The two part **Cecil Kop Nature Reserve**, 3.5km north-east of Mutare, has rhino, elephant, zebra, wildebeest, kudu and monkey. Without a vehicle, you can visit the **Tigers Kloof Dam** section, but not **Thompson's Vlei**, which has a wildlife-viewing platform overlooking a pan. One US$1 admission ticket admits you to both sections.

Places to Stay

The *Municipal Camping & Caravan Park* is unfortunately on the noisy Harare-Mutare highway, 6km uphill from the city centre near Christmas Pass. Sites cost US$1.60 per person. Camping at *Tiger's Kloof Dam*, 3.5km from the city centre, costs US$2.50 per person.

Mutare also has a clutch of backpackers hostels. A good choice is the home of *Mrs Anne Bruce* (☎ 63569) at 99 Fourth St. Beds cost US$2.50 and inexpensive meals are available (but it's not for anyone who's allergic to cats).

Mr Peter McIntyre (☎ 63968) runs a recommended place at 5 Livingstone Rd in Murambi. He charges US$2 for dorm beds, US$3.50 per person for rooms and US$7 for a caravan that sleeps four people. Transfers from the city centre are free.

There's also the friendly *Trevor's Place* (☎ 64711) at 119 Fourth St, where camping costs US$2.50 per person and dorm beds are US$4. It has cooking and laundry facilities, and bicycle hire.

Border Home (☎ 63346) at 3A Jason Moyo Drive costs US$3.20 in the dorms and US$4.50 per person in family rooms. There are also several doubles and cottages for US$6.50 to US$16.50. Camping costs US$2. Meals are available.

The cheapest hotel is the basic *Balmoral* (☎ 61435) on C Ave, which charges US$9 per person, with breakfast.

An excellent out-of-town alternative is *Drifters* (☎ 62964), on a small wildlife-oriented reserve 25km west of town. Camping costs US$1.80 per person, dorm beds are US$5, private rooms are US$6.50 per person and double rondavels are US$10.50. It has a pool, transfers to town are free and bar meals are available for US$3. On Friday night it holds a popular pizza bake.

Places to Eat

For a life-sustaining US$0.50 plate of sadza ne nyama, try the *Little Swallow Inn* on Herbert Chitepo St. Alternatively, there's *Zvinoira* on E Ave near Herbert Chitepo St.

Jenny's Cottage, 130 Herbert Chitepo St, does light lunches, salads and afternoon teas. *Mr T* on Herbert Chitepo St and Second Ave serves ice cream and hot snacks.

The nicest mid-range place is the *Stax Steak House* in the Norwich Union Centre Arcade. Try the vegetarian potato burgers, salads, cappuccino and Belgian waffles. *The Carvery* in the Cortauld Theatre specialises in steak and is open late every night.

The popular *Portuguese Club* is mainly a bar but it does pub meals in the evening and lunches on weekends. It has been the watering-hole of choice for all Europeans in the recent conflicts in Zimbabwe and Mozambique.

Getting There & Away

The in-town bus terminal is between Herbert Chitepo and Tembwe Sts near F Ave. If you're coming from Harare get off here unless you want the Sakubva township bus terminal, 5km away.

To Chimanimani, ZUPCO and Msabaeka, buses leave daily from Sakubva only, at around 7 am and 10.30 am. Harare buses leave hourly from the in-town bus terminal, but the nicest way to travel there is by overnight train, which costs US$5/3.50/2.30 in 1st/2nd/economy class.

VICTORIA FALLS

At Victoria Falls, one of the world's most memorable sights, the Zambezi River widens to 1.7km and then plunges 107m into the Zambezi Gorge. The force of the falling water – estimated at around 545 million litres per minute in the rainy season – sends clouds of spray up to 500m into the air and sustains a lush rainforest all around. The falls are best seen during the winter dry season, when you have the advantage of unobscured views, but they're magnificent at any time.

The Victoria Falls Publicity Association (☎ 4202), adjacent to the caravan park, offers limited information. Film is sold at Zambezi Productions in Sopers Arcade.

Things to See

Of course, **Victoria Falls** themselves are the premier attraction. From September to November, you'll get the clearest views with the most rock showing. Between April and June, when the flow is greatest, views are misty and, in windy conditions, the gorge is perpetually spanned by rainbows. In midsummer, the humidity is stifling and the rains hard and frequent. Before visiting the park, wrap your cash and valuables in plastic and be sure your camera equipment is protected from the spray, as it can pour down anywhere from Main Falls to Danger Point and only at times of very low water will you avoid a soaking.

The park, which has a network of surfaced trails along the falls, is open from dawn to dusk, and for foreigners admission is US$20 (US$10 in the low season). Because of the high admission fee many budget travellers are leaving the Zimbabwe side to the tour groups and heading for the Zambian shore, where admission is only US$5 (see the Zambia chapter).

It's worth walking along the Zambezi from the **Livingstone Statue** past the **Big Tree** (a giant baobab) to the Zambezi

National Park entrance, but watch out for wildlife; wart hog, hippopotamus, crocodile, antelope and even elephant, buffalo and lion are present.

The **Zambezi Nature Sanctuary**, which is basically a zoo, offers 5000 assorted crocodiles for the US$2 admission fee, as well as various big cats, birds, insects and domestic animals.

White-Water Rafting

The white-water rafting trips through the Zambezi Gorge are among the world's wildest. High-water runs can be made from either the Zimbabwean or the Zambian side between 1 July and 15 August. Wilder lowwater runs can be made from roughly 15 August to late December.

The main players are Frontiers (☎ 5800), Safari Par Excellence (☎ 4224), Shearwater (☎ 4471) and Supreme Raft (☎ 3300), all in the arcade area. For a half/full day's rafting it's US$80/100 on the Zimbabwean side and US$75/95 on the Zambian side.

Note that we've had numerous reports of belongings – especially cash – going missing from rafting companies 'safe boxes'; take due precautions.

Canoeing & Kayaking

It's fun to paddle around the wide, mostly smooth river above the falls, and several companies offer canoeing and kayaking safaris. Morning or afternoon trips are US$55; all day trips are US$90; and two to four-day trips range from US$135 to US$495.

Other Activities

There is a variety of **river cruises** on the Zambezi above the falls from US$15; boats leave from the jetty near A'Zambezi River Lodge.

Also popular is the **Flight of the Angels**, a 15 minute scenic flight over the falls for US$50, or there's **micro-light flights** from the Zambian side for US$65.

Half/full day **game drives** in Zambezi National Park are available for US$25/50, plus US$2.50 per person park entry. You can also do safaris on horseback; experienced

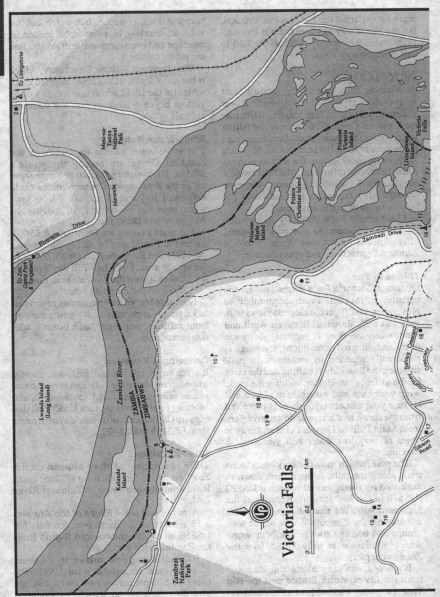

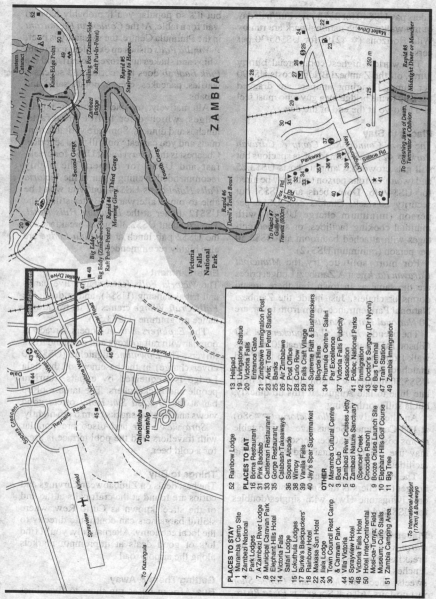

PLACES TO STAY
1 Maramba Camp Site
4 Zambezi National Park Lodges
7 A'Zambezi River Lodge
8 Municipal Caravan Park
12 Elephant Hills Hotel
14 Victoria Falls Safari Lodge
15 Lokuthula Lodges
17 Burke's Backpackers'
18 Rainbow Hotel
22 Makasa Sun Hotel
24 Ilala Lodge
30 Town Council Rest Camp & Caravan Park
44 Villa Victoria
45 Sprayview Hotel
48 Victoria Falls Hotel
50 Hotel InterContinental Mosi-oa-Tunya; Field Museum; Curio Stalls
51 Zambia Camping Area

52 Rainbow Lodge

PLACES TO EAT
16 Boma Restaurant
31 Pink Baobab
33 Cattleman Restaurant
35 Gorge Restaurant
36 Calabash Takeaways
37 Sopers Arcade
38 Wimpy
39 Vanilla Falls
40 Jay's Spar Supermarket

OTHER
2 Maramba Cultural Centre
3 Boat Club
5 Zambezi River Cruises Jetty
6 Zambezi Nature Sanctuary (Spencer Creek Crocodile Ranch)
9 Booze Cruise Launch Site
10 Elephant Hills Golf Course
11 Big Tree

13 Helipad
19 Livingstone Statue
20 Victoria Falls
21 Zimbabwe Immigration Post
23 Avis; Total Petrol Station
25 Banks
26 Air Zimbabwe
27 Post Office
28 Curio Row
29 Falls Craft Village
32 Supreme Raft & Bushtrackers Bicycle Hire
34 Phumula Centre – Safari Par Excellence
37 Victoria Falls Publicity Association
41 Police; National Parks
42 Immigration
43 Doctor's Surgery (Dr Nyoni)
46 Bus Terminal
47 Train Station
49 Zambia Immigration

riders pay US$40 for 2½ hours. Full/half day **game walks** in the national park are run by Wild Horizons (☎ 4219) for US$65/30 per person.

The world's highest commercial **bungy jump**, off the Zambezi Bridge, costs US$90 per jump. Dangling jumpers are dragged back up to the bridge by a guy who must feel like a yo-yo at the end of the day.

Places to Stay

The *Town Council Rest Camp & Caravan Park* (☎ 4210), right in town, is spacious but still gets crowded. Camping costs US$3.25 and two/three/four-person tents may be hired for US$4/5/6. Dorm beds are US$5, but security is slack. Chalets cost US$6 per person (minimum charge US$9), with minimal cooking facilities, or six-bed cottages with attached bathroom are US$6.50 per person (minimum US$12).

For more solitude, try the *Municipal Caravan Park* near A'Zambezi Lodge; prices are the same as in town, but there are no dorms or chalets. Just inside the Zambezi National Park entrance, 6km from town, are 20 *National Parks chalets*.

The friendly *Burke's Backpackers'* at 357 Gibson Rd is a nice, leafy retreat 20 minutes walk from the town centre. Dorm beds and thatched A-frame tents are available for US$5.50 in the low season and US$11 from late June to late August. It fills up quickly, but is still worth trying.

An alternative is *Villa Victoria* (☎ 4386) at 165 Courteney Selous Ave. Comfortable rooms cost US$16.50 per person, and guests may use the pool, braai and self-catering facilities. Ring first.

The only hotel remotely within reach of budget travellers is the *Sprayview* (☎ 4344) on Livingstone Hwy, with singles/doubles for US$38/44.

Places to Eat

Naran's in Soper's Arcade serves a full breakfast for US$2 and good vegetarian lunches, but it's closed in the evenings. For sweets, check out *McDonut's Coffee Shop* just upstairs. Also at Soper's is *Pizza Bistro*,

but it's so popular you'll probably have to wait for a table. At the *Cattleman Restaurant* in the Phumula Centre, the speciality is beef.

Vanilla Falls dishes up excellent ice cream whips and shakes and frozen yogurt, and the *Pink Baobab* does tea, coffee and snacks – waffles, pancakes, crêpes, potato salad and kebabs.

Alternatively, try one of the big hotels/ lodges, which offer buffet breakfasts, lunches and dinners. Some are veritable banquets and you can eat your fill for a set price. Cheapest is the *Sprayview* at US$3 for breakfast and US$6 for dinner. The highly recommended evening braai at the *Victoria Falls Hotel* costs US$14, but you won't be able to move afterwards! Better still is the US$12 dinner at the *Elephant Hills Hotel*. The excellent US$2.30 buffet breakfast and the US$2 pub lunch at the *Ilala Lodge* are also highly recommended.

Entertainment

The *Victoria Falls Hotel* stages live bands and tribal dancing (US$4), and at dusk, the *Falls Craft Village* cranks up its traditional dance programme (US$3.50).

The *Explorers Bar* in Sopers Arcade is popular with raft jockeys and overland truck drivers. The *Downtime* nightclub (US$2.50 cover charge) in the basement of the Ilala Lodge is frequented by expats, tourism people and backpackers. The tame rooftop bar at the *Makasa Sun Hotel* offers good views and free bar snacks from 6 pm nightly.

Sprayview's bar and disco are popular with travellers, and the pool terrace is great for a cold beer.

Things to Buy

The best deals on Zimbabwean carvings and curios are found at the craft halls at the end of the street known as Curio Row, where skilful bargainers can contribute directly to the local economy. Alternatively, you'll find lots of good deals at impromptu markets along the airport road.

Getting There & Away

Bus African buses run three to five times

daily to Bulawayo. The terminal is near the market on Pioneer Rd in Chinotimba township, but they also stop near the Sprayview Hotel. Ajay's Motorways has several daily express services to Bulawayo from the Makasa Sun Hotel.

Train The train station is in front of the Victoria Falls Hotel, and there are daily overnight trains to Bulawayo for US$9/6/4 in 1st/2nd/economy class and twice-daily services to Livingstone (Zambia), over the Zambezi Bridge (30 minutes, US$1.50).

Getting Around
The airport shuttle bus connects with all flights (US$2.50).

Bicycles can be hired from Bush Trackers.

National Parks & Reserves

Bookings are essential for national park accommodation and camp sites, but the reservation system isn't exactly a well-oiled machine; book early and hang on to your receipt. If you're told everything is full, don't despair; the reservation system accepts bookings without payment and there are lots of no-shows. The catch is that you must wait until 5.30 pm on the day you wish to stay to find out if anything is available.

Bookings are most reilably made through the National Parks Central Booking Office (☎ 706077), National Botanical Gardens, corner of Borrowdale Rd and Sandringham Drive, PO Box 8151, Harare, or the Bulawayo Booking Agency (☎ 63646), Lobengula St, PO Box 2283, Bulawayo. You can book up to six months in advance.

Fees for camp sites and cottages are standardised, and foreigners must pay double the advertised rates (all rates given in this section are those for foreigners). Admission to the national parks costs US$5 per day (US$10 to US$20 at Victoria Falls). Tent sites cost US$3 per person and caravan sites are US$4 per person. Basic one/two-bedroom chalets with shared facilities are US$10/21; one/two-bedroom cottages with attached bathroom are US$13/26; and fully equipped one/two-bedroom lodges are US$23/35 (except those at Mana Pools, which are double this rate).

CHIMANIMANI NATIONAL PARK
The name Chimanimani is derived from the Manyika for 'a place that must be passed single file'. The formidable mountain wall that is the heart of the park faces Chimanimani village, a tiny community 19km from the park entrance.

Information
The Chimanimani Publicity Association office (☎ 2294) is in front of the Chimanimani village bus stop. There is a ranger station at Mutekeswane Base Camp, where visitors must sign in and pay park fees. Unless you're staying at the base camp, a tent isn't strictly necessary.

Although fast-flowing surface water in Chimanimani National Park is safe for drinking, water purification is still advisable.

Things to See & Do
In the Park From base camp, **Bailey's Folly** is the shortest and most popular route into the mountains (two to three hours). Alternatively, there's the steeper **Hadange River Track** from the Outward Bound school into the Bundi Valley just below North Cave. The third option, the **Banana Grove Track**, is a gentler ascent than Bailey's Folly, but is mostly used by hikers returning to base camp from Southern Lakes.

From the mountain hut, it's an easy 40 minute walk to **Skeleton Pass**, notorious as a former guerrilla route between Zimbabwe and Mozambique. It's now an active trade route, as you'll probably see. Go in the late afternoon for an unsurpassed view into Mozambique's **Wizard's Valley**. The highest point in the Chimanimani Range, 2437m **Mt Binga** on the Mozambique border, is a stiff three hour climb from the hut. Carry a

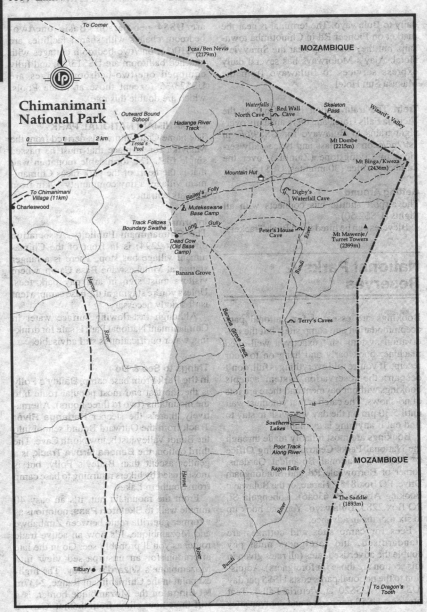

Chimanimani National Park

0   1   2 km

MOZAMBIQUE

To Comer

Peza/Ben Nevis (2179m)

Outward Bound School

Hadange River Track

Waterfalls
North Cave

Red Wall Cave

Skeleton Pass

Wizard's Valley

Mt Dombe (2215m)

Mt Binga/Kweza (2436m)

Tessa's Pool

To Chimanimani Village (11km)

Charleswood

Mountain Hut

Bailey's Folly

Mutekeswane Base Camp

Digby's Waterfall Cave

Track Follows Boundary Swathe

Long Gully

Dead Cow (Old Base Camp)

Peter's House Cave

Mt Mawenje/ Turret Towers (2399m)

Banana Grove

Haroni River

Bundi River

Terry's Caves

Banana Grove Track

Southern Lakes

Poor Track Along River

MOZAMBIQUE

Ragon Falls

Haroni River

Bundi River

The Saddle (1893m)

Tilbury

To Dragon's Tooth

water bottle and fill it up at every opportunity.

Around the Park It's a pleasant day walk to the **eland sanctuary** near the village. However, most of the eland have been poached; only a herd of waterbuck remains. From the village, turn left at the T-junction north of the post office then right at the first turning. Continue north for 5km to the base of **Nyamzure** (Pork Pie Hill), a popular climb. **Bridal Veil Falls**, a 50m drop, is in a lush setting 6km from the village along a scenic winding road.

Tessa's Pool is a classic swimming hole with a rope swing. The area is leased by the nearby Outward Bound school, but travellers can use the swimming hole between 9 am and 4 pm.

Places to Stay & Eat
In the Park There is a camping ground at *Mutekeswane Base Camp*, and the Bundi valley is riddled with caves and overhangs which are ideal for camping (however, they do fill up early). The stone *mountain hut* overlooking the Bundi Valley is an option, but at US$10 per person, it's overpriced.

Chimanimani Village For the best view in town, check out *Heaven Lodge* (☎ 2701), about 1km from the village on the national park road. Camping costs US$2 per tent and US$0.75 per person, dorm beds are US$5.50 and doubles are US$11. Meals are available at the bar. A quieter place is *The Club Rest House* (☎ 2266), with dorm beds for US$4 and singles/doubles for US$8/11.

Moving slightly upmarket, the beautiful *Frog & Fern Guest House* (☎ 2294) has four self-catering cottages scattered around on the hill above town and charges US$22/40 for singles/doubles.

At the expensive *Chimanimani Arms Hotel* (☎ 2511) you can camp on the lawn for US$3.50 per person, but lock up valuables or anything which would tempt baboons (or other thieves) in the hotel storeroom.

The village shops have basic groceries, the market offers fresh produce and the hotel serves meals. *Heaven Lodge* and the *Frog & Fern* sell delicious Chimanimani cheese, which goes well on mountain hikes. The no-frills *Beta Restaurant & Bar* serves tasty, inexpensive meals.

Getting There & Away
There are two daily buses from Sakubva, Mutare. Ajay's Motorways runs two weekly express buses between Chimanimani and Masvingo. FNC Tours (☎ 67890 Mutare) runs twice weekly buses from Mutare for US$5.

Hitching can be difficult, but, generally, the route from Chipinge is easier than from Wengezi Junction.

Nyati Travel (☎ 2513) and three individuals (book through the publicity association) provide transfers to Mutekeswane for US$16.50 per trip for seven to nine people. Otherwise, it's a 19km walk or a doubtful hitch.

GREAT ZIMBABWE NATIONAL MONUMENT
Great Zimbabwe, near Masvingo, is the most significant ruin in sub-Saharan Africa, and provides evidence that medieval Africa reached a level of civilisation not suspected by early scholars. As a religious and temporal capital, this city of perhaps 10,000 governed a realm stretching across eastern Zimbabwe and into Botswana, Mozambique and South Africa.

Probably the first complex to be completed was the **Hill Complex** (once known as the Acropolis), a series of royal and ritual enclosures. The **Valley Enclosures** feature 13th-century walls and *daga* hut platforms, which contain a small conical tower and have yielded such archaeological finds as metal tools and the Great Zimbabwe birds that became the national symbol.

The elliptical **Great Enclosure** is the structure most identified with the site. Nearly 100m across and 255m around, it's the largest ancient structure in sub-Saharan Africa. The mortarless walls are 11m high and, in places, 5m thick. The most accepted theory is that it was used as a royal compound. The greatest source of speculation is the 10m-high **Conical Tower**, a solid and apparently ceremonial structure which probably has phallic significance.

The site **museum** houses most of the Great Zimbabwe archaeological finds. Highlights include the soapstone Great Zimbabwe birds, which were probably Rozwi dynasty totems. Other exhibits of interest include porcelain and glass goods brought by Swahili traders.

Admission to the site is US$5, and foreigners must also pay for photography permits.

Places to Stay
Great Zimbabwe The beautiful and well guarded *camping ground* (☎ 7052) is in a field with a view of the Hill Complex. The *Great Zimbabwe Hotel* (☎ 62449) is expensive, but campers have access to the good value breakfasts and may use the hotel pool for US$2.50.

Masvingo The *Municipal Caravan Park* (☎ 62431) charges US$2.50 per person.

At the recommended *Clovelly Lodge* (☎ 67564), 6km west of town, beds cost US$8.20, including half board, and it offers horse riding and free transfers from town. The *Breezy Brae Bed & Breakfast* (☎ 64650), atop a dwala dome 5km along the Bulawayo road, charges US$14/18 for singles/doubles, including breakfast.

More central is the *Backpackers' Rest* (☎ 65503) in the Dauth building. Double rooms with dinner, bed and breakfast cost US$16. The Masvingo Publicity Association has a list of other B&Bs.

Getting There & Away
Express Motorways has a weekly service from Harare to Masvingo and Great Zimbabwe for US$8.50. DSB Coachlines runs from Harare to Masvingo and Great Zimbabwe twice a week for US$13. Long-distance African buses use the Mucheke musika bus terminal, 2km from Masvingo centre.

To reach Great Zimbabwe from Mas-

vingo, take the three times daily Morgenster Mission bus, which runs from Mucheke musika in Masvingo, and get off at the Great Zimbabwe turn-off, 2km from the ruins. Taxis from Masvingo cost around US$10 for up to five passengers.

HWANGE NATIONAL PARK
Hwange National Park is Zimbabwe's most accessible and most wildlife-packed national park, but unless you hang around Main Camp you won't feel crowded. The best wildlife viewing is in the dry season (which is September and October), when animals congregate near water holes. A popular place with both animals and tourists is **Nyamandhlovu Pan**, 10km from Main Camp.

Organised Tours
From Main Camp, two-hour ranger-guided walks to Sedina Pan depart three times daily and cost US$5 per person; they're limited to seven participants, so book in advance. To get further into the park without your own vehicle, UTC hires vehicles for reasonable rates, and charges US$20/45 per person for two/eight-hour game drives.

A good safari option is with Shamwari Safaris (☎ 248) in Dete, which offers tailored safaris for groups of up to seven people starting at around US$50 per person per day. A two hour game drive costs US$13 and a half-day trip is US$22. Advance booking is advised. The new Singing Bird Safaris (☎ 255), run by O'Brien Masawi in Dete, has also been recommended for economical Hwange game drives and walking safaris.

For walking, camping and backpacking trips through Hwange, you can't beat Khangela Safaris (☎ 49733; fax 68529), PO Box FM 296, Famona, Bulawayo, run by professional guide Mike Scott. These trips are excellent value at US$155 per day, including transport, guide, camping and meals.

Places to Stay & Eat
The big National Parks camps are *Main Camp*, *Sinamatella* and *Robins Camp*. Sinamatella is generally the best; it sits atop a 50m mesa and affords spectacular views.

Robins Camp is known for nocturnal invasion by lions and hyenas. Each camp has a small shop, bar and restaurant.

There are also a number of enclosed picnic sites, each with provision for up to eight campers.

Backpackers accommodation at the *Wildside Hostel* (☎ 395) in Dete costs US$5.50, including pick-up from the train station. Other offerings include private doubles, cooking facilities, transfers to the bus stops and two-hour game drives in Hwange National Park (US$17.50).

The expensive *Hwange Safari Lodge* (☎ 332), 13km from Main Camp, allows nonresidents to use the restaurant/bar for a US$1.30 daily membership fee.

Getting There & Away

Bus African buses stop at Safari Crossroads, 23km from the Main Camp park entrance (6km from Main Camp). The more convenient Ajay's Motorways express buses stop at Hwange Safari Lodge.

Train The Bulawayo-Victoria Falls train passes Dete station in the wee hours of the morning in either direction; as the train station lies 12km north-west of the Main Camp park entrance, you'll probably have to wait there until morning. Dete has a small hotel and a backpackers hostel, but many people just sleep on the floor of the '1st class' lounge at the train station. It's cold so bring a sleeping bag.

Getting Around

Officially, hitchhiking is not permitted inside the park; hitching outside the entrance or discreetly asking for lifts around Main Camp is sometimes tolerated, but don't count on it.

UTC transfers from Hwange Safari Lodge to Main Camp cost US$5.

MANA POOLS NATIONAL PARK

Visiting Mana Pools takes time and effort, but it's magnificent and worth the fuss of getting there. In fact, UNESCO has designated it a World Heritage Site. The park access road is open only from 1 May to 31 October.

Perhaps Mana Pools greatest appeal is its concession to hikers who want to strike out on their own; yes, between 6 am and 6 pm you're free to go wherever you like, even on foot. The best place to view wildlife is **Long Pool**; it's easiest to hitch there just before dusk, when practically the entire park population – both human and wildlife – descends upon it.

Information

It's best to pick up entry and camping permits at the National Parks Central Booking Office in Harare. You can also get them at Marongora, near the park entrance, but your chances of getting a confirmed camp site aren't good. If the camps are fully booked you can get a day permit for US$2.50 per person. Permit applicants must have their own transport into the park; rental vehicles are not permitted. Hitchers can't be added to a driver's permit, so if you're hitching in buy a permit for longer than your intended stay to allow time to find a lift out of the park.

Once you have a permit, turn up at Marongora before 3.30 pm on the day you wish to enter the park, then reach the Nyamepi office before it closes at 6 pm. Hang on to the permit because practically everyone you meet will want to see it.

A popular way to visit Mana Pools is by canoe safari, and several operators organise three to nine-day trips between Kariba and Kanyemba. Trips operate between April and November but six months advance booking is recommended. Reliable operators include Buffalo Safaris (☎ 2645; fax 2827; email buffalo@kariba.harare.iafrica.com), PO Box 113, Kariba, and Chipembere/Wild Frontiers (☎ 2946), PO Box 9, Kariba.

Places to Stay

The main camping ground is *Nyamepi Camp* by the Zambezi. There are also several private concessions, two National Parks lodges and several National Parks exclusive camps, but no shops or restaurants anywhere in the park.

Getting There & Away

There's no public transport into Mana Pools, so you'll need a private vehicle or a tour company transfer from Kariba; Buffalo Safaris has been recommended (see earlier in this section).

MATOBO NATIONAL PARK

You need not be in tune with any alternative wavelength to sense that the Matobo Hills are one of the world's power places. Dotted around the park are a wealth of ancient San paintings and old grain bins, where Lobengula's warriors once stored their provisions. Some hidden niches still shelter clay ovens which were used as iron smelters in making the infamous *assegais*, or spears, to be used against the growing colonial hordes.

Cecil Rhodes also loved Matobo, and less than 2km from the north-west entrance are the remains of his **rail terminus**. When he died on 26 March 1902, his body was taken to **Malindidzimu** (View of the World), the 'place of benevolent spirits', and buried as he'd wanted, amid colourful boulders.

An easy 7km road walk from the Maleme camping ground leads to **Nswatugi Cave** and its well preserved rock paintings. Another easy walk (by road) is to **Pomongwe Cave**, where an early attempt to preserve the paintings resulted in their near obliteration; a site museum offers background information.

Organised Tours

A recommended option for visiting Matabo is with Black Rhino Safaris (☎/fax 41662), PO Box FM 89, Famona, Bulawayo. Day tours run daily (minimum two people) and cost US$33, including lunch. Sandbank Safaris (☎ 41686) at Shaka's Spear and Africa Sun Safaris (☎ 76523) at Africa Sun Backpackers, both in Bulawayo, offer day tours for US$40.

Places to Stay & Eat

Weekends bring the crowds to *Maleme*, but this is the best time for hitching. Sites at any of the park camping grounds cost US$2.50 per person; chalets at Maleme are US$10/21

for one/two bedrooms and lodges are US$16/31. Bilharzia is rife so all water (except the tap water at Maleme) should be boiled or purified. There are a number of other camping grounds.

There's a small kiosk at Maleme and groceries are also sold at Fryer's Store, 10km away. Fryer's also runs the *Inungu Guest House*, which costs US$40 for up to four adults, plus US$10 for each additional person. Book through Sunshine Tours in Bulawayo (☎ 67791).

Another choice is *Matopo Ingwe Motel* (☎ (183) 8217), which charges US$27 per person for bed and breakfast.

Getting There & Away

Hitching can be slow; the easiest access is from Retreat, near Bulawayo. Most tour companies will drop clients at a camp site and pick them up on a prearranged day (see Organised Tours in this section).

NYANGA NATIONAL PARK

Nyanga, which was formerly one of Cecil Rhodes private estates, has long been a summer getaway for heat-weary Harare dwellers. At the park headquarters at Nyanga (Rhodes) Dam you can book park accommodation and guided horse tours around nearby archaeological sites.

Things to See & Do

Near the park headquarters, don't miss the **Nyangwe Fort** ruins, the **Nyangwe Dam Trout Research Centre, Chamowera Fort** ruins, **Rhodes Museum** and the **Pit Structure** ruins. **Nyangombe Falls** lies 5km west of Nyangombe camping ground and 2km from Udu Dam. Wear strong, treaded shoes and avoid the slippery, mossy rocks near the falls.

To climb Zimbabwe's highest peak, misty and myth-ridden **Mt Nyangani**, you'll need 1½ to three hours from the parking lot 14km east of Nyanga Dam. Hikers are meant to register at park headquarters and caution is warranted; mists can roll in suddenly and some locals believe the mountain devours hikers. A three to four day walk continues from Mt Nyangani past Pungwe Drift, Mtarazi Falls and into Honde Valley near the Mozambique border.

Nyanga village, with its manicured English gardens and hedges, village common and stone church, huddles beneath the towering Troutbeck Massif. The **World's View**, 11 winding kilometres above Troutbeck, affords a far-ranging view across northern Zimbabwe, but hitchhiking may be difficult in the low season. The best way is via a steep 4km footpath leading up from the road 6km north of Nyanga village.

For more excitement, contact Far & Wide Zimbabwe (☎ 26329), PO Box 14, Juliasdale, which organises white-water rafting and kayaking trips on the Pungwe River starting at US$55.

Places to Stay

Nyangombe Campground, set amid piney woods, lies between the Nyangombe River and the highway, 7km from Nyanga village.

There are cosy National Parks *lodges* at Udu Dam, Nyanga Dam, Nyangwe Dam and Pungwe Drift.

The basic *Village Inn* (☎ 336; fax 335) in Nyanga village has a nice restaurant, and offers singles/doubles with bath and meals for US$25/41. For budget singles without private facilities, the cost is US$18 and cottages are US$23 per person.

For chilling out in the mellow mountain air, travellers love *Juliasdale Camp & Cabin* (☎ 202) at Juliasdale. Garden camp sites cost US$2.50 per person. Horse riding tours cost US$2.50 per hour and there are also three-day Nyanga tours for US$48.

Inside the park is the *Rhodes Nyanga Hotel* (☎ 377), which starts at US$22/36 for singles/doubles, including dinner and breakfast.

Getting There & Away

DSB Coachlines (☎ 202) runs twice weekly express services between Harare, Rusape, Juliasdale and Nyanga. They leave from the Harare Sheraton.

Masara services from Mbare to Juliasdale and Nyanga (Nyamhuka) run daily, except Saturday. In Harare, catch the Nyanga/Nyamaropa bus from the corner of Glenara Rd and Robert Mugabe St.

From Mutare's in-town bus terminal, ZUPCO, Zvinoira and Masara depart for Juliasdale and Nyanga hourly until midday. Twice a week, FNC Tours (☎ 67890) in Mutare runs buses from Mutare to Rusape, Juliasdale and World's View for US$15 for the return circuit.

VUMBA BOTANICAL RESERVE

The Vumba Mountains, 28km south-east of Mutare, are characterised by cool, forested highlands alternating with deep, almost jungled valleys. In Manyika, the name means simply 'mist'.

The Vumba Botanical Reserve, the private estate of former Mutare mayor Fred Taylor, consists of 30 hectares of manicured gardens and 170 hectares of indigenous forest and bushland. **Leopard Rock** may be climbed via a track from Vumba Rd 2km east of the botanical reserve turn-off. Views from the top are excellent, and just below is the colonial-era Leopard Rock Hotel, which has now been renovated as a golfing and gambling venue.

Organised Tours

For day visits, contact Pickup Tours (☎ 63061), run by Cornelius, who has a pickup truck. For two/four/eight people, an all day Vumba tour, including Burma and Essex Valleys, costs US$16/11/8 per person. UTC (☎ 67484) runs similar tours in more comfortable vehicles for US$26, and FNC Tours (☎ 67890) runs straight transfers from Mutare to the Vumba for US$1.50 each way.

Places to Stay & Eat

In addition to the reserve *camp sites*, there's *Cloud Castle* (☎ 217620), 10 minutes walk away, with super views into Mozambique. Beds cost just US$4.50, and meals and self-catering are available.

More remote is the beautifully situated *Ardroy Guest House* (☎ 217121) on Blue Mountain Rd in Essex Valley, 19km east of the Bvumba and Essex roads junction. Bed and breakfast costs US$7.60, and transfers from Mutare cost US$2 per person (minimum US$4). Otherwise, from the Mutare in-town bus terminal, catch the 8 am Mapofu bus (the quicker option) or the 11 am Burma Valley bus and get off on the corner of Blue Mountain Rd. From there, it's 1km to the guesthouse.

You'll find a growing number of holiday cottages and guesthouses scattered through the region. Pick up the latest listings from the Manicaland Publicity Association in Mutare.

Tony's Coffee House, on Cloud Castle's premises, is a gem which deserves coverage in international gourmet guides – no exaggeration! The chocolate truffle cake has already been dubbed 'Rebirth by Chocolate'! Free transfers from the Manicaland Publicity Association in Mutare run daily at 11 am. There's a small shop at the lodge, or you can buy staples at the *Naro Moru* shop, 500m away.

Getting There & Away

You can reach the Vumba area by bus from Mutare, but once you're there, getting around is difficult without a vehicle. See Organised Tours in this entry for information on day visits and other transport options.

Health Appendix

PREDEPARTURE PLANNING
Immunisations

For some countries no immunisations are necessary, but the further off the beaten track you go the more necessary it is to take precautions. Be aware that there is often a greater risk of disease with children and in pregnancy.

Plan ahead for getting your vaccinations: some of them require more than one injection, while some vaccinations should not be given together. It is recommended you seek medical advice at least six weeks before travel.

Record all vaccinations on an International Health Certificate, available from your doctor or government health department.

Discuss your requirements with your doctor, but vaccinations you should consider for Africa include:

- **Hepatitis A** The most common travel-acquired illness after diarrhoea which can put you out of action for weeks. Havrix 1440 is a vaccination which provides long term immunity (possibly more than 10 years) after an initial injection and a booster at six to 12 months. Gamma globulin is not a vaccination but is a ready-made antibody collected from blood donations. It should be given close to departure because, depending on the dose, it only protects for two to six months.
- **Typhoid** This is an important vaccination to have where hygiene is a problem. Available either as an injection or oral capsules.
- **Diphtheria & Tetanus** Diphtheria can be a fatal throat infection and tetanus can be a fatal wound infection. Everyone should have these vaccinations. After an initial course of three injections, boosters are necessary every 10 years.
- **Meninogococcal Meningitis** Healthy people carry this disease; it is transmitted like a cold and you can die from it within a few hours. There are many carriers and vaccination is recommended for travellers to sub-Saharan Africa. A single injection will give good protection for three years. The vaccine is not recommended for children under two years because they do not develop satisfactory immunity from it.
- **Hepatitis B** This disease is spread by blood or by sexual activity. Travellers who should consider a hepatitis B vaccination include those visiting countries where there are known to be many carriers, where blood transfusions may not be adequately screened or where sexual contact is a possibility. It involves three injections, the quickest course being over three weeks with a booster at 12 months.
- **Polio** Polio is a serious, easily transmitted disease, still prevalent in many sub-Sahara African countries. Everyone should keep up to date with this vaccination. A booster every 10 years maintains immunity.
- **Yellow Fever** Yellow fever is now the only vaccine which is a legal requirement for entry into many countries, usually only enforced when coming from an infected area.
  Protection lasts 10 years and is recommended for travel in Africa. Many African countries are infected areas. You usually have to go to a special yellow fever vaccination centre. Vaccination poses some risk during pregnancy but if you must travel to a high-risk area it is advisable; also people allergic to eggs may not be able to have this vaccine. Discuss with your doctor.
- **Rabies** Vaccination should be considered by those who will spend a month or longer in Africa, especially if they are cycling, handling animals, caving, travelling to remote areas, or for children (who may not report a bite). Pre-travel rabies vaccination involves having three injections over 21 to 28 days. If someone who has been vaccinated is bitten or scratched by an animal they will require two booster injections of vaccine, those not vaccinated require more.
- **Cholera** Despite its poor protection, it may be wise to have the cholera vaccine, especially if you will be visiting many countries in Africa. Very occasionally travellers are asked by immigration officials to present a certificate, even though all countries and the WHO have dropped a cholera immunisation as a health requirement. You might be able to get a certificate without having the injection from a doctor or health centre sympathetic to the vagaries of travel in Africa.
- **Tuberculosis** TB risk to travellers is usually very low. For those who will be living with or closely associated with local people in high-risk areas there may be some risk. As most healthy adults do not develop symptoms, a skin test before and after travel to determine whether exposure has occurred may be considered. A vaccination is recommended for children living in these areas for three months or more.

Malaria Medication

Antimalarial drugs do not prevent you from

being infected but kill the malaria parasites during a stage in their development and significantly reduce the risk of becoming very ill or dying. Expert advice on medication should be sought, as there are many factors to consider including the area to be visited, the risk of exposure to malaria-carrying mosquitoes, the side effects of medication, your medical history and whether you are a child or adult or pregnant. Travellers to isolated areas in high risk countries may like to carry a treatment dose for use if symptoms occur.

Health Insurance

Make sure that you have adequate health insurance. See Travel Insurance under documents in the Regional Facts for the Visitor chapter for details.

Travel Health Guides

If you are planning to be away or travelling in remote areas for a long period of time, you may like to consider taking a more detailed health guide.

Staying Healthy in Asia, Africa & Latin America, Dirk Schroeder, Moon Publications, 1994. Probably the best all-round guide to carry; it's compact, detailed and well organised.

Travellers' Health, Dr Richard Dawood, Oxford University Press, 1995. Comprehensive, easy to read, authoritative and highly recommended, although it's rather large to lug around.

Travel with Children, Maureen Wheeler, Lonely Planet Publications, 1995. Includes advice on travel health for younger children.

There are also a number of excellent travel health sites on the Internet. From the Lonely Planet home page there are links at (http://www.lonelyplanet.com/weblinks/wlprep.htm) to the World Health Organisation, and the US Centers for Disease Control & Prevention.

Other Preparations

Make sure you're healthy before you start travelling. If you are going on a long trip make sure your teeth are OK. If you wear glasses take a spare pair and a prescription.

If you require a particular medication take an adequate supply, as it may not be available locally. Take part of the packaging showing the generic name, rather than the brand, which will make getting replacements easier. It's a good idea to have a legible prescription or letter from your doctor to show that you legally use the medication to avoid any problems.

Medical Kit Check List

Consider taking a basic medical kit including:

- [ ] **Aspirin** or paracetamol (acetaminophen in the US) – for pain or fever.
- [ ] **Antihistamine** (such as Benadryl) – useful as a decongestant for colds and allergies, to ease the itch from insect bites or stings, and to help prevent motion sickness. Antihistamines may cause sedation and interact with alcohol so care should be taken when using them; take one you know and have used before, if possible.
- [ ] **Antibiotics** – useful if you're travelling well off the beaten track, but they must be prescribed; carry the prescription with you.
- [ ] **Loperamide** (eg Imodium) or Lomotil for diarrhoea; prochlorperazine (eg Stemetil) or metaclopramide (eg Maxalon) for nausea and vomiting.
- [ ] **Rehydration** mixture – for treatment of severe diarrhoea; particularly important if travelling with children.
- [ ] **Antiseptic** such as povidone-iodine (eg Betadine) – for cuts and grazes.
- [ ] **Multivitamins** – especially for long trips when dietary vitamin intake may be inadequate.
- [ ] **Calamine lotion** or **aluminium sulphate spray** (eg Stingose) – to ease irritation from bites or stings.
- [ ] **Bandages** and Band-aids
- [ ] **Scissors, tweezers** and a **thermometer** (note that mercury thermometers are prohibited by airlines).
- [ ] **Cold and flu tablets** and throat lozenges. Pseudoephedrine hydrochloride (Sudafed) may be useful if flying with a cold to avoid ear damage.
- [ ] **Insect repellent, sunscreen, chap stick** and **water purification tablets.**
- [ ] **A couple of syringes**, in case you need injections in a country with medical hygiene problems. Ask your doctor for a note explaining why they have been prescribed.

BASIC RULES
Food

There is an old colonial adage which says: 'If you can cook it, boil it or peel it you can eat it...otherwise forget it'. Vegetables and fruit should be washed with purified water or peeled where possible. Beware of ice cream which is sold in the street or anywhere it might have been melted and refrozen; if there's any doubt (eg a protracted power cut in the last day or two) steer well clear. Shellfish such as mussels, oysters and clams should be avoided as well as undercooked meat, particularly in the form of mince. Steaming does not make shellfish safe for eating.

If a place looks clean and well run and the vendor also looks clean and healthy, then the food is probably safe. In general, places that are packed with travellers or locals will be fine, while empty restaurants are questionable. The food in busy restaurants is cooked and eaten quite quickly with little standing around and is probably not reheated.

Water

The number-one rule is *be careful of the water* and especially ice. If you don't know for certain that the water is safe assume the worst. Reputable brands of bottled water or soft drinks are generally fine, although in some places bottles may be refilled with tap water. Only use water from containers with a serrated seal – not tops or corks. Take care with fruit juice, particularly if water may have been added. Milk should be treated with suspicion as it is often unpasteurised, though boiled milk is fine if it is kept hygienically. Tea or coffee should also be OK, since the water should have been boiled.

Water Purification

The simplest way of purifying water is to boil it thoroughly. Vigorously boiling should be satisfactory; however, at high altitude water boils at a lower temperature, so germs are less likely to be killed. Boil it for longer in these environments.

Consider purchasing a water filter for a long trip. There are two main kinds of filter. Total filters take out all parasites, bacteria and viruses, and make water safe to drink. They are often expensive, but they can be more cost effective than buying bottled water. Simple filters (which can even be a nylon mesh bag) take out dirt and larger foreign bodies from the water so that chemical solutions work much more effectively; if water is dirty, chemical solutions may not work at all. It's very important when buying a filter to read the specifications, so that you know exactly what it removes from the water and what it doesn't.

Simple filtering will not remove all the

Nutrition

If your food is poor or limited in availability, if you're travelling hard and fast and therefore missing meals, or if you simply lose your appetite, you can soon start to lose weight and place your health at risk.

Make sure your diet is well balanced. Cooked eggs, tofu, beans, lentils (dhal in India) and nuts are all safe ways to get protein. Fruit you can peel (bananas, oranges or mandarins for example) is usually safe (melons can harbour bacteria in their flesh and are best avoided) and a good source of vitamins. Try to eat plenty of grains (including rice) and bread. Remember that although food is generally safer if it is cooked well, overcooked food loses much of its nutritional value. If your diet isn't well balanced or if your food intake is insufficient, it's a good idea to take vitamin and iron pills.

In hot climates make sure you drink enough – don't rely on feeling thirsty to indicate when you should drink. Not needing to urinate or small amounts of very dark yellow urine is a danger sign. Always carry a water bottle with you on long trips. Excessive sweating can lead to loss of salt and therefore muscle cramping. Salt tablets are not a good idea as a preventative, but in places where salt is not used much adding salt to food can help. ■

HEALTH

dangerous organisms, so if you cannot boil water it should be treated chemically. Chlorine tablets (Puritabs, Steritabs or other brand names) will kill many pathogens, but not some parasites like giardia and amoebic cysts. Iodine is more effective in purifying water and is available in tablet form (such as Potable Aqua). Follow the directions carefully and remember that too much iodine can be harmful.

MEDICAL PROBLEMS & TREATMENT

Self-diagnosis and treatment can be risky, so you should always seek medical help. Although we do give drug dosages in this section, they are for emergency use only. Correct diagnosis is vital.

An embassy, consulate or five-star hotel can usually recommend a good place to go for advice. In some places standards of medical attention are so low that for some ailments the best advice is to get on a plane and go somewhere else.

Antibiotics should ideally be administered only under medical supervision. Take only the recommended dose at the prescribed intervals and use the whole course, even if the illness seems to be cured earlier. Stop immediately if there are any serious reactions and don't use the antibiotic at all if you are unsure that you have the correct one.

Some people are allergic to commonly prescribed antibiotics such as penicillin or sulpha drugs; if this applies to you, carry this information when travelling eg on a bracelet.

ENVIRONMENTAL HAZARDS
Altitude Sickness

Lack of oxygen at high altitudes (more than 2500m) affects most people to some extent. The affect may be mild or severe and occurs because less oxygen reaches the muscles and the brain at high altitude, requiring the heart and lungs to compensate by working harder.

Symptoms of Acute Mountain Sickness (AMS) usually develop during the first 24 hours at altitude but may be delayed up to three weeks. Mild symptoms include headache, lethargy, dizziness, difficulty sleeping and loss of appetite. AMS may become more

severe without warning and can be fatal. Severe symptoms include breathlessness, a dry, irritative cough (which may progress to the production of pink, frothy sputum), severe headache, lack of coordination and balance, confusion, irrational behaviour, vomiting, drowsiness and unconsciousness. There is no hard-and-fast rule as to what is too high: AMS has been fatal at 3000m, although 3500 to 4500m is the usual range.

Treat mild symptoms by resting at the same altitude until recovery, usually a day or two. Paracetamol or aspirin can be taken for headaches. If symptoms persist or become worse, however, *immediate descent is necessary*; even 500m can help. Drug treatments should never be used to avoid descent or to enable further ascent.

The drugs acetazolamide (Diamox) and dexamethasone are recommended by some doctors for the prevention of AMS, however their use is controversial. They can reduce the symptoms, but they may also mask warning signs; severe and fatal AMS has occurred in people taking these drugs. In general we do not recommend them for travellers.

To prevent acute mountain sickness:

- Ascend slowly – have frequent rest days, spending two to three nights at each rise of 1000m. If you reach a high altitude by trekking, acclimatisation takes place gradually and you are less likely to be affected than if you fly directly to high altitude.
- It is always wise to sleep at a lower altitude than the greatest height reached during the day if possible. Also, once above 3000m, care should be taken not to increase the sleeping altitude by more than 300m per day.
- Drink extra fluids. The mountain air is dry and cold and moisture is lost as you breathe. Evaporation of sweat may occur unnoticed and result in dehydration.
- Eat light, high-carbohydrate meals for more energy.
- Avoid alcohol as it may increase the risk of dehydration.
- Avoid sedatives.

Fungal Infections

Fungal infections occur more commonly in hot weather and are usually found on the scalp, between the toes or fingers, in the groin and on the body (ringworm). You get ringworm (which is a fungal infection, not a worm) from infected animals or other people. Moisture encourages these infections.

To prevent fungal infections wear loose, comfortable clothes, avoid artificial fibres, wash frequently and dry carefully. If you do get an infection, wash the infected area at least daily with a disinfectant or medicated soap and water, and rinse and dry well. Apply an antifungal cream or powder like tolnifate (eg Tinaderm). Try to expose the infected area to air or sunlight as much as possible and wash all towels and underwear in hot water, change them often and let them dry in the sun.

Heat Exhaustion

Dehydration and salt deficiency can cause heat exhaustion. Take time to acclimatise to high temperatures, drink sufficient liquids and do not do anything too physically demanding.

Salt deficiency is characterised by fatigue, lethargy, headaches, giddiness and muscle cramps; salt tablets may help, but adding extra salt to your food is better.

Anhydrotic heat exhaustion, caused by an inability to sweat, is quite rare. It is likely to strike people who have been in a hot climate for some time, rather than newcomers.

Heat Stroke

This serious, occasionally fatal, condition can occur if the body's heat-regulating mechanism breaks down and the body temperature rises to dangerous levels. Long, continuous periods of exposure to high temperatures and insufficient fluids can leave you vulnerable to heat stroke.

The symptoms are feeling unwell, not sweating very much (or at all) and a high body temperature (39 to 41°C or 102 to 106°F). Where sweating has ceased the skin becomes flushed and red. Severe, throbbing headaches and lack of coordination will also occur, and the sufferer may be confused or aggressive. Eventually the victim will become delirious or convulse. Hospitalisation is essential, but in the interim get victims

out of the sun, remove their clothing, cover them with a wet sheet or towel and then fan continually. Give fluids if they are conscious.

Hypothermia

Too much cold can be just as dangerous as too much heat. If you are trekking at high altitudes or simply taking a long bus trip over mountains, particularly at night, be prepared. When trekking to high altitudes (eg Mt Kenya, Mt Kilimanjaro, the Ruwenzoris) you should be prepared for cold, wet or windy conditions.

Hypothermia occurs when the body loses heat faster than it can produce it and the core temperature of the body falls. It is surprisingly easy to progress from very cold to dangerously cold due to a combination of wind, wet clothing, fatigue and hunger, even if the air temperature is above freezing. It is best to dress in layers; silk, wool and some of the new artificial fibres are all good insulating materials. A hat is important, as a lot of heat is lost through the head. A strong, waterproof outer layer (and a 'space' blanket for emergencies) are essential. Carry basic supplies, including food containing simple sugars to generate heat quickly and fluid to drink.

Symptoms of hypothermia are exhaustion, numb skin (particularly toes and fingers), shivering, slurred speech, irrational or violent behaviour, lethargy, stumbling, dizzy spells, muscle cramps and violent bursts of energy. Irrationality may take the form of sufferers claiming they are warm and trying to take off their clothes.

To treat mild hypothermia, first get the person out of the wind and/or rain, remove their clothing if it's wet and replace it with dry, warm clothing. Give them hot liquids – not alcohol – and some high-kilojoule, easily digestible food. Do not rub victims, instead allow them to slowly warm themselves. This should be enough to treat the early stages of hypothermia. The early recognition and treatment of mild hypothermia is the only way to prevent severe hypothermia, which is a critical condition.

Motion Sickness

Eating lightly before and during a trip will reduce the chances of motion sickness. If you are prone to motion sickness try to find a place that minimises movement – near the wing on aircraft, close to midships on boats, near the centre on buses. Fresh air usually helps; reading and cigarette smoke don't. Commercial motion-sickness preparations, which can cause drowsiness, have to be taken before the trip commences. Ginger (available in capsule form) and peppermint (including mint-flavoured sweets) are natural preventatives.

Prickly Heat

Prickly heat is an itchy rash caused by excessive perspiration trapped under the skin. It usually strikes people who have just arrived in a hot climate. Keeping cool, bathing often, drying the skin and using a mild talcum or prickly heat powder or resorting to air-conditioning may help.

Sunburn

In the tropics, the desert or at high altitude you can get sunburnt surprisingly quickly, even through cloud. Use a sunscreen, hat, and barrier cream for your nose and lips. Calamine lotion is good for mild sunburn. Protect your eyes with good quality sunglasses, particularly if you will be near water, sand or snow.

INFECTIOUS DISEASES
Diarrhoea

Simple things like a change of water, food or climate can all cause a mild bout of diarrhoea, but a few rushed toilet trips with no other symptoms is not indicative of a major problem.

Dehydration is the main danger with any diarrhoea, particularly in children or the elderly as dehydration can occur quite quickly. Under all circumstances *fluid replacement* (at least equal to the volume being lost) is the most important thing to remember. Weak black tea with a little sugar, soda water, or soft drinks allowed to go flat and diluted 50% with clean water are all good.

With severe diarrhoea a rehydrating solution is preferable to replace minerals and salts lost. Commercially available oral rehydration salts (ORS) are very useful; add them to boiled or bottled water. In an emergency you can make up a solution of six teaspoons of sugar and a half teaspoon of salt to a litre of boiled or bottled water. You need to drink at least the same volume of fluid that you are losing in bowel movements and vomiting. Urine is the best guide to the adequacy of replacement – if you have small amounts of concentrated urine, you need to drink more. Keep drinking small amounts often. Stick to a bland diet as you recover.

Lomotil (diphenoxylate) or Imodium (loperamide) can be used to bring relief from the symptoms, although they do not actually cure the problem. Only use these drugs if you do not have access to toilets eg if you *must* travel. For children under 12 years Lomotil and Imodium are not recommended. Do not use these drugs if the person has a high fever or is severely dehydrated.

In certain situations antibiotics may be required: diarrhoea with blood or mucous

---

Everyday Health

Normal body temperature is up to 37°C or 98.6°F; more than 2°C (4°F) higher indicates a high fever. The normal adult pulse rate is 60 to 100 per minute (children 80 to 100, babies 100 to 140). As a general rule the pulse increases about 20 beats per minute for each °C (2°F) rise in fever.

Respiration (breathing) rate is also an indicator of illness. Count the number of breaths per minute: between 12 and 20 is normal for adults and older children (up to 30 for younger children, 40 for babies). People with a high fever or serious respiratory illness breathe more quickly than normal. More than 40 shallow breaths a minute may indicate pneumonia. ■

(dysentery), any fever, watery diarrhoea with fever and lethargy, persistent diarrhoea not improving after 48 hours and severe diarrhoea. In these situations gut-paralysing drugs like Imodium or Lomotil should be avoided.

Dysentery

As mentioned, diarrhoea with blood and/or mucous is probably dysentery, either amoebic or bacillary. The main difference is that amoebic dysentery has a more gradual onset of symptoms, with cramping, abdominal pain and vomiting less likely; fever may not be present. It will persist until treated and can recur and cause other health problems.

A stool test is necessary to diagnose which kind of dysentery you have, so you should seek medical help urgently. Where this is not possible the recommended drugs for dysentery are norfloxacin (Noroxin) 400mg twice daily for three days or ciprofloxacin (Ciproxin) 500mg twice daily for five days. These are not recommended for children or pregnant women. The drug of choice for children would be co-trimoxazole (Bactrim, Septrin, Resprim) with dosage dependent on weight. A five-day course is given. Ampicillin or amoxycillin may be given in pregnancy, but medical care is necessary.

Giardiasis

This is another type of diarrhoea. The parasite causing this intestinal disorder is present in contaminated water. The symptoms are stomach cramps, nausea, a bloated stomach, watery, foul-smelling diarrhoea and frequent gas. Giardiasis can appear several weeks after you have been exposed to the parasite. The symptoms may disappear for a few days and then return; this can go on for several weeks. Tinidazole (Fasigyn) or metronidazole (Flagyl) are the recommended drugs. Treatment is a 2gm single dose of Fasigyn or 250mg of Flagyl three times daily for five to 10 days.

Hepatitis

Hepatitis is a general term for inflammation of the liver. It is a common disease in Africa.

The symptoms are fever, chills, headache, fatigue, feelings of weakness and aches and pains, followed by loss of appetite, nausea, vomiting, abdominal pain, dark urine, light-coloured faeces, jaundiced (yellow) skin and the whites of the eyes may turn yellow.

Hepatitis A is transmitted by contaminated food and drinking water. The disease poses a real threat to the western traveller. You should seek medical advice, but there is not much you can do apart from resting, drinking lots of fluids, eating lightly and avoiding fatty foods. People who have had hepatitis should avoid alcohol for some time after the illness, as the liver needs time to recover. **Hepatitis E** is transmitted in the same way, it can be very serious in pregnant women.

There are almost 300 million chronic carriers of **Hepatitis B** in the world. It is spread through contact with infected blood, blood products or body fluids, for example through sexual contact, unsterilised needles and blood transfusions, or contact with blood through small breaks in the skin. Other risk situations include having a shave, tattoo, or having your body pierced with contaminated equipment. The symptoms of type B may be more severe than Hepatitis A and may lead to long term problems. **Hepatitis D** is spread in the same way, but the risk is mainly in shared needles.

Hepatitis C can lead to chronic liver disease. The virus is spread by contact with blood usually via contaminated transfusions or shared needles. Avoiding these is the only means of prevention.

HIV & AIDS

HIV, the Human Immunodeficiency Virus, develops into AIDS, Acquired Immune Deficiency Syndrome, which is a fatal disease. HIV is a major problem in many African countries. Any exposure to blood, blood products or body fluids may put the individual at risk. The disease is often transmitted through sexual contact or dirty needles – vaccinations, acupuncture, tattooing and body piercing can be potentially as dangerous as intravenous drug use. HIV/AIDS can also be spread through infected blood transfusions; some African countries cannot afford to screen blood used for transfusions.

If you do need an injection, ask to see the syringe unwrapped in front of you, or take a needle and syringe pack with you.

Fear of HIV infection should never preclude treatment for serious medical conditions.

Meningococcal Meningitis

This very serious disease attacks the brain and can be fatal. There are recurring epidemics in Sub-Saharan Africa.

A fever, severe headache, sensitivity to light and neck stiffness which prevents forward bending of the head are the first symptoms. There may also be purple patches on the skin. Death can occur within a few hours, so urgent medical treatment is required.

Treatment is large doses of penicillin, preferably given intravenously, or chloramphenicol injections.

Sexually Transmitted Diseases

Gonorrhoea, herpes and syphilis are among these diseases; sores, blisters or rashes around the genitals, discharges or pain when urinating are common symptoms. In some STDs, such as wart virus or chlamydia, symptoms may be less marked or not observed at all especially in women. Syphilis symptoms eventually disappear completely but the disease continues and can cause severe problems in later years.

While abstinence from sexual contact is the only 100% effective prevention, using condoms is also effective. The treatment of gonorrhoea and syphilis is with antibiotics. The different sexually transmitted diseases each require specific antibiotics. There is no cure for herpes or AIDS.

Typhoid

Typhoid fever is a dangerous gut infection caused by contaminated water and food. Medical help must be sought.

In its early stages sufferers may feel they have a bad cold or flu on the way, as early symptoms are a headache, body aches and a fever which rises a little each day until it is around 40°C (104°F)or more. The victim's pulse is often slow relative to the degree of fever present – unlike a normal fever where the pulse increases. There may also be vomiting, abdominal pain, diarrhoea or constipation.

In the second week the high fever and slow pulse continue and a few pink spots may appear on the body; trembling, delirium, weakness, weight loss and dehydration may occur. Complications such as pneumonia, perforated bowel or meningitis may occur.

The fever should be treated by keeping the victim cool and giving them fluids as dehydration should also be watched for. Ciprofloxacin (Ciproxin) 750mg twice a day for 10 days is good for adults.

Chloramphenicol (Chloromycetin) is recommended in many countries. The adult dosage is two 250mg capsules, four times a day. Children aged between eight and 12 years should have half the adult dose; and younger children one-third the adult dose.

INSECT-BORNE DISEASES
Dengue Fever

There is no preventative drug available for this mosquito-spread disease which can be fatal in children. A sudden onset of fever, headaches and severe joint and muscle pains are the first signs before a rash develops. Recovery may be prolonged.

Intestinal Worms

These parasites are most common in rural, tropical areas. The different worms have different ways of infecting people. Some may be ingested on food including undercooked meat and some enter through your skin. Infestations may not show up for some time, and although they are generally not serious, if left untreated some can cause severe health problems later. Consider having a stool test when you return home to check for these and determine the appropriate treatment.

Japanese B Encephalitis

This viral infection of the brain is transmitted

by mosquitoes. Most cases occur in rural areas as the virus exists in pigs and wading birds. Symptoms include fever, headache and alteration in consciousness. Hospitalisation is needed for correct diagnosis and treatment. There is a high mortality rate among those who have symptoms; of those that survive many are intellectually disabled.

Malaria

This serious and potentially fatal disease is spread by mosquito bites. If you are travelling in endemic areas it is extremely important to avoid mosquito bites and to take tablets to prevent this disease. Symptoms range from fever, chills and sweating, headache, diarrhoea and abdominal pains to a vague feeling of ill-health. Seek medical help immediately if malaria is suspected. Without treatment malaria can rapidly become more serious and can be fatal.

If medical care is not available, malaria tablets can be used for treatment. You need to use a malaria tablet which is different to the one you were taking (if any) when you contracted malaria. The treatment dosages are mefloquine (three 250mg tablets and a further two six hours later) or fansidar (single dose of three tablets). If you were previously taking mefloquine and cannot obtain fansidar then other alternatives are halofantrine (three doses of two 250mg tablets every six hours) or quinine sulphate (600mg every six hours). There is a greater risk of side effects with these dosages than in normal use if used with mefloquine, so seeking medical advice is preferable.

Travellers are advised to avoid mosquito bites at all times. The main messages are:

- wear light coloured clothing
- wear long pants and long sleeved shirts
- use mosquito repellents containing the compound DEET on exposed areas
  (prolonged overuse of DEET may be harmful, especially to children, but its use is considered preferable to being bitten by disease-transmitting mosquitoes)
- avoid highly scented perfumes or aftershave
- use a mosquito net (best to carry your own)

Schistosomiasis

Also known as bilharzia, this disease is carried in water by minute worms. They infect certain varieties of freshwater snails found in rivers, streams, lakes and particularly behind dams. The worms multiply and are eventually discharged into the water.

The worm enters through the skin and attaches itself to your intestines or bladder. The first symptom may be a tingling and sometimes a light rash around the area where it entered. Weeks later a high fever may develop. A general feeling of being unwell may be the first symptom, or there may be no symptoms. Once the disease is established, abdominal pain and blood in the urine are other signs. The infection often causes no symptoms until the disease is well established (several months to years after exposure) and damage to internal organs irreversible.

Avoiding swimming or bathing in fresh water where bilharzia is present is the main method of preventing the disease. Even deep water can be infected. If you do get wet, dry off quickly and dry your clothes as well.

A blood test is the most reliable test, but the test will not show positive in results until a number of weeks after exposure.

Areas of Malarial Transmission

Limited Risk Malaria Areas

Malarial Risk Area

Yellow Fever
This viral disease is endemic in many African countries and is transmitted by mosquitoes. The initial symptoms are fever, headache, abdominal pain and vomiting. Seek medical care urgently and drink lots of fluids.

Endemic Zones

Yellow Fever Risk Area

CUTS, BITES & STINGS
Bedbugs & Lice
Bedbugs live in various places, but particularly in dirty mattresses and bedding, evidenced by spots of blood on bedclothes or on the wall. Bedbugs leave itchy bites in neat rows. Calamine lotion spray may help.

All lice cause itching and discomfort. They make themselves at home in your hair (head lice), your clothing (body lice) or in your pubic hair (crabs). You catch lice through direct contact with infected people or by sharing combs, clothing and the like. Powder or shampoo treatment will kill the lice and infected clothing should then be washed in very hot, soapy water and left in the sun to dry.

Cuts & Scratches
Wash well and treat any cut with an antisep-tic such as povidone-iodine. Where possible avoid bandages and Band-aids, which can keep wounds wet. Coral cuts are notoriously slow to heal and if they are not adequately cleaned small pieces of coral can become embedded in the wound. Severe pain, throb-bing, redness, fever or generally feeling unwell suggest infection and the need for antibiotics promptly as coral cuts may result in serious infections.

Insect Bites & Stings
Bee and wasp stings are usually painful rather than dangerous. However in people who are allergic to them severe breathing difficulties may occur and require urgent medical care. Calamine lotion will give relief and ice packs will reduce the pain and swell-ing. There are some spiders with dangerous bites but antivenenes are usually available. Scorpion stings are notoriously painful; scorpions themselves often shelter in shoes or clothing.

There are various fish and other sea crea-tures which can sting or bite dangerously or which are dangerous to eat. Again, local advice is the best suggestion.

Jellyfish
Local advice is the best way of avoiding contact with these sea creatures which have stinging tentacles. Calamine lotion, antihis-tamines and analgesics may reduce the reaction and relieve the pain.

Leeches & Ticks
Leeches may be present in damp rainforest conditions; they attach themselves to your skin to suck your blood. Trekkers often get them on their legs or in their boots. Salt or a lighted cigarette end will make them fall off. Do not pull them off, as the bite is then more likely to become infected. Clean and apply pressure if the point of attachment is bleed-ing. An insect repellent may keep them away.

You should always check all over your body if you have been walking through a potentially tick-infested area as ticks can cause skin infections and other more serious diseases. If a tick is found attached, press down around the tick's head with tweezers, grab the head and gently pull upwards. Avoid pulling the rear of the body as this may squeeze the tick's gut contents through the attached mouth parts into the skin, increasing the risk of infection and disease. Smearing chemicals on the tick will not make it let go and is not recommended.

Snakes

To minimise your chances of being bitten always wear boots, socks and long trousers when walking through undergrowth where snakes may be present. Don't put your hands into holes and crevices, and be careful when collecting firewood.

Snake bites do not cause instantaneous death and antivenenes are usually available. Immediately wrap the bitten limb tightly, as you would for a sprained ankle, and then attach a splint to immobilise it. Keep the victim still and seek medical help, if possible with the dead snake for identification. Don't attempt to catch the snake if there is a possibility of being bitten again. Tourniquets and sucking out the poison are now comprehensively discredited.

WOMEN'S HEALTH
Gynaecological Problems

Sexually transmitted diseases are a major cause of vaginal problems. Symptoms include a smelly discharge, painful intercourse and sometimes a burning sensation when urinating. Male sexual partners must also be treated. Medical attention should be sought and remember in addition to these diseases HIV or hepatitis B may also be acquired during exposure. Besides abstinence, the best thing is to practise safe sex using condoms.

Antibiotic use, synthetic underwear, sweating and contraceptive pills can lead to fungal vaginal infections when travelling in hot climates. Maintaining good personal hygiene, and loose-fitting clothes and cotton underwear will help to prevent these infections.

Fungal infections, characterised by a rash, itch and discharge, can be treated with a vinegar or lemon-juice douche, or with yoghurt. Nystatin, miconazole or clotrimazole pessaries or vaginal cream are the usual treatment.

Pregnancy

It is not advisable to travel to some places while pregnant as some vaccinations normally used to prevent serious diseases are not advisable in pregnancy eg yellow fever. In addition, some diseases are much more serious for the mother (and may increase the risk of a stillborn child) in pregnancy eg malaria.

Most miscarriages occur during the first three months of pregnancy. Miscarriage is not uncommon, and can occasionally lead to severe bleeding. The last three months should also be spent within reasonable distance of good medical care. A baby born as early as 24 weeks stands a chance of survival, but only in a good modern hospital. Pregnant women should avoid all unnecessary medication, vaccinations and malarial prophylactics should still be taken where needed. Additional care should be taken to prevent illness and particular attention should be paid to diet and nutrition. Alcohol and nicotine, for example, should be avoided.

LESS COMMON DISEASES

The following diseases pose only a very small risk to travellers, and so are only mentioned in passing. Seek medical advice if you think you may have any of these diseases.

Cholera

This is the worst of the watery diarrhoeas and medical help should be sought. Outbreaks of cholera are generally widely reported, so you can avoid such problem areas. *Fluid replacement is the most vital treatment* – the risk of dehydration is severe as you may lose up to 20 litres a day. If there is a delay in getting to hospital then begin taking tetracycline. The adult dose is 250mg four times daily. It is not recommended for children under nine years nor for pregnant women. Tetracycline may help shorten the illness, but adequate fluids are required to save lives.

HEALTH

Filariasis

This is a mosquito-transmitted parasitic infection found in many parts of Africa. Possible symptoms include fever, pain and swelling of the lymph glands; inflammation of lymph drainage areas; swelling of a limb or the scrotum; skin rashes and blindness. Treatment is available to eliminate the parasites from the body, but some of the damage already caused may not be reversible. Medical advice should be obtained promptly if the infection is suspected.

Leishmaniasis

A group of parasitic diseases transmitted by sandfly bites, found in many parts of Africa. Cutaneous leishmaniasis affects the skin tissue causing ulceration and disfigurement and visceral leishmaniasis affects the internal organs. Seek medical advice as laboratory testing is required for diagnosis and correct treatment. Avoiding sandfly bites is the best precaution. Bites are usually painless, itchy and are yet another reason to cover up and apply repellent.

Rabies

Rabies is a fatal viral infection found in many African countries. Many animals can be infected (such as dogs, cats, bats and monkeys) and it is their saliva which is infectious. Any bite, scratch or even lick from a warm-blooded, furry animal should be cleaned immediately and thoroughly. Scrub with soap and running water, and then apply alcohol or iodine solution. Medical help should be sought promptly to receive a course of injections to prevent the onset of symptoms and death.

Sleeping Sickness

In parts of tropical Africa tsetse flies can carry trypanosomiasis or sleeping sickness. The tsetse fly is about twice the size of a housefly and recognisable by the scissor-like way it folds its wings when at rest. Only a small proportion of tsetse flies carry the disease but it is a serious disease which can be fatal without treatment. No protection is available except avoiding the tsetse fly bites.

The flies are attracted to large moving objects such as safari buses, to perfume and aftershave, and to colours like dark blue. Swelling at the site of the bite, five or more days later, is the first sign of infection; this is followed within two to three weeks by fever.

Tetanus

Tetanus occurs when a wound becomes infected by a germ which lives in soil and in the faeces of horses and other animals. It enters the body via breaks in the skin. All wounds should be cleaned promptly and adequately and an antiseptic cream or solution applied. Use antibiotics if the wound becomes hot, throbs or pus is seen. The first symptom may be discomfort in swallowing, or stiffening of the jaw and neck; this is followed by painful convulsions of the jaw and whole body. The disease can be fatal.

Tuberculosis (TB)

TB is a bacterial infection usually transmitted from person to person by coughing but may be transmitted through consumption of unpasteurised milk. Milk that has been boiled is safe to drink, and the souring of milk to make yoghurt or cheese also kills the bacilli. Travellers are usually not at great risk as close household contact with the infected person is usually required before the disease is passed on.

Typhus

Typhus is spread by ticks, mites or lice. It begins with fever, chills, headache and muscle pains followed a few days later by a body rash. There is often a large painful sore at the site of the bite and nearby lymph nodes are swollen and painful. Typhus can be treated under medical supervision. Seek local advice on areas where ticks pose a danger and always check your skin (including hair) carefully for ticks after walking in a danger area such as a tropical forest. A strong insect repellent can help, and serious walkers in tick areas should consider having their boots and trousers impregnated with benzyl benzoate and dibutylphthalate.

Language Appendix

ARABIC

Even if you don't have the time or inclination to learn Arabic, you need to be familiar with at least some of the numerals. For more detailed help for travellers, see Lonely Planet's *Egyptian Arabic* and *Moroccan Arabic* phrasebooks.

Greetings & Civilities

Greetings.	*salaam al laikoum*
madam (polite)	*lalla*
sir (polite)	*mansour*
sir (very polite)	*sidi*
Thank you.	*shukran*
You're welcome.	*afwan*

Useful Words & Phrases

How much?	*kem?*
yes	*nam*
no	*ley*
camel	*djemal*
market	*souk*
mountain	*jebel*
river bed	*oued/wadi*
sand	*ramia (ramla in Egypt and Sudan)*
fork	*mtaka*
knife	*moos (sekkin in Egypt and Sudan)*
spoon	*tobsi*
bread	*khobz (eesh in Egypt and Sudan)*
coffee	*gahwa*
tea	*atai*
water	*mey/ma*

Numbers

0	*sifr*
1	*wahid*
2	*zouje (itneen in Egypt and Sudan)*
3	*talata*
4	*arba'a*
5	*hamsa*
6	*setta*
7	*seb'a*
8	*thimanya*
9	*tesa'a*
10	*ashara*
11	*hadashara*
12	*etnatashara*
13	*talathashara*
20	*ishrun (ishreen in Egypt and Sudan)*
30	*talat'in*
40	*arba'in*
50	*hamsin*
100	*mia*
200	*miat'in*
1000	*alef*
2000	*alfain*

The pronunciation of Arabic is substantially different in Egypt and Sudan than it is elsewhere. Even between the two countries there are marked differences – for example, camel is *gamal* in Egypt but *jamal* in Sudan.

Somali is the only Arabic-derived language to use Romanised script, though Swahili (also Romanised) contains many Arabic words.

FRENCH

Visitors to West and Central Africa will find that a working knowledge of French is more or less essential. English is not widely spoken and you'll find yourself struggling if you don't have at least the basics in French. There are a number of other countries – such as Rwanda, Burundi, Mauritius, Seychelles, Tunisia and Réunion where French comes in very handy.

African French varies quite widely from 'pure' French, and while you should have no difficulty making yourself understood, you may find it hard to understand other people.

Greetings & Civilities

Excuse me.	*Excusez-moi.*
Good morning.	*Bonjour.*
How are you?	*Comment allez-vous?*
I'm fine, thanks.	*Je suis bien, merci.*
What is your name?	*Quel est ton nom?*

No.	*Non.*	vegetables	*légumes*
Please.	*S'il vous plaît.*	dinner	*le dîner*
Thank you (very much).	*Merci (beaucoup).*	market	*un marché*

Useful Words & Phrases

I don't understand.	*Je ne comprends pas.*
bus	*le bus*
boat/ferry	*le bateau/le bac*
airplane	*l'avion*
I'm looking for ...	*Je cherche ...*
a bank	*une banque*
a hospital	*l'hôpital*
the post office	*le bureau de poste*
a public toilet	*une toilette publique*
youth hostel	*auberge de jeunesse*
hotel	*hôtel*
I'd like to book a ...	*Je voudrais réserver ...*
cheap room	*une chambre bon marchée*
single room	*une chambre simple*
double room	*une chambre double*
room with a bathroom?	*une chambre avec salle de bain*
How much is it ...	*C'est combien ...*
I need a doctor.	*J'ai besoin d'un médecin.*
medicine	*medicine*
Help!	*Au secours!*
Call a doctor/ambulance!	*Appelez un médecin/ l'ambulance-secours!*
Call the police!	*Appelez la police!*
I've been robbed.	*J'étais volé.*
I've been raped.	*J'étais violée.*
I'm lost.	*Je suis perdu.*

Food & Drink

breakfast	*le petit déjeuner*
lunch	*le déjeuner*
banana	*banane*
bread	*pain*
the bill	*l'addition*
beer	*bière*
meat	*viande*
chicken	*poulet*
fish	*poisson*
potato	*pomme de terre*

Numbers

1	*un*
2	*deux*
3	*trois*
4	*quatre*
5	*cinq*
6	*six*
7	*sept*
8	*huit*
9	*neuf*
10	*dix*
11	*onze*
12	*douze*
13	*treize*
14	*quatorze*
15	*quinze*
16	*seize*
17	*dix-sept*
18	*dix-huit*
19	*dix-neuf*
20	*vingt*
30	*trente*
40	*quarante*
50	*cinquante*
60	*soixante*
70	*soixante-dix*
80	*quatre-vingts*
90	*quatre-vingt-dix*
100	*cent*
1000	*mille*
2000	*deux mille*

HAUSA

In Gabon, Niger and Nigeria a knowledge of Hausa, especially numbers, is useful.

Greetings & Civilities

Greetings. (polite)	*ranka ya dade (ranki for women)*
Greetings.	*sannu* (pl *sanunku*)
Welcome. (polite)	*barka da zuwa/ sannu da zuwa*
Welcome.	*lafia/lafia lau*
reply to 'welcome'	*lafia*
Thank you.	*nagode*

Useful Words & Phrases

Yes/OK.	toh
No.	babu
No/I don't want it.	uhuh
good	da kyau
expression of surprise	haba/wallahi!
expression of surprise or disgust	khai!
How much?	nawa?
I don't want it.	shikenah
Are you tired?	ina gajiya?
I am not tired.	ba gajiya
camel	rakumi
cold	sanyi
hot	zafi
house	gida
man	mutum
woman	mache
market	kasuwa
sick	yi shiwo
slowly	sannu sannu
quickly	muza muza

Food & Drink

food	abinchi
chicken	dantsako
cola nut	goro
eggs	kwai
fish	kifi
meat	nama
milk	madara
okra	guro
onions	albasa
rice	shinkafa
salt	gishiri
water	ruwa

Numbers

1	daya
2	biu
3	uku
4	hudu
5	biyar
6	shida
7	bakwai
8	takwas
9	tara
10	goma
11	gomashadaya

12	gomashabiu
20	ashirin
21	ashirindadaya
22	ashirindabiu
23	ashirindaoku
24	ashirindahudu
30	talatin
100	dari

The Hausa greetings don't translate strictly into their English equivalents. *Ranka/ranki ya dade* means 'may your life be long' and is said to seniors or those deserving of respect. *Sannu* is the universal greeting and means 'gently'.

PORTUGUESE

In countries where Portuguese was the colonial language (Angola, Cape Verde, Guinea-Bissau and Mozambique) English is not widely spoken and at least some Portuguese is essential.

Greetings

Excuse me, please.	Faz favor.
Thank you.	Obrigado/a
friend	amigo
Good morning.	Bom dia.
Good afternoon.	Boa tarde.
Good evening.	Bom noite.
How are you?	Como está?
I am fine, thank you.	Muito bem obrigado/a
What's your name?	Cómo se chama?
No problem.	Não faz mal.

Useful Words & Phrases

I don't understand.	Não compreendo.
I don't speak Portuguese.	Não falo Português.
I am lost.	Estou perdido.
Have you got ...? Is there ...?	Tem ...?
cheap	barato
expensive	caro
yes/no	sim/não
no/never/nothing	nada
hotel	hotel/pousada
cheap hotel	pensão

Do you have a room?	*Tem um quarto?*
single/double	*simple/duplo*
room for married couples	*casal*
toilet/bathroom	*casa da banho*
beach	*praia*
train	*comboio*
bus	*ônibus/bus/machimb ombo)*
tomorrow	*amanhã*
When?	*Quando?*
Where?	*Onde?*
How much (does this cost)?	*Quanto custa?*

Food & Drink

market	*mercado*
menu (card)	*cardápio*
menu (a set meal)	*menu*
breakfast	*pequeno almoço*
lunch	*almoço*
dinner	*jantar*
the bill	*quanto*
beer	*cerveja*
tea	*chá*
water	*aqua*
mineral water	*agua mineral*
bread	*pão*
chicken	*frango/galinha*
eggs	*ovos*
fish	*peixe*
fruit	*fruta*
potatoes	*batata*
meat	*carne*
rice	*arroz*
salt	*sal*
steak	*bifel*
steak sandwich	*prego*
sugar	*açucar*
vegetables	*legumes*

SWAHILI

Swahili has become the lingua franca of Tanzania (though educated people still speak English). Much the same thing is happening in Kenya, though the process there will be much slower since English is far more entrenched. Swahili is also useful in parts of Uganda, Eastern Congo (Zaïre), Malawi and Zambia. This is especially so in the rural areas where the local people may only have had a smattering of education or none at all and so are unlikely to be able to speak any English or French. The Comoran language is also derived from Swahili.

Swahili is a composite language and is still evolving. There are still no agreed words for many things, though this is rapidly changing. An extremely useful pocket-sized phrasebook for travellers is Lonely Planet's *Swahili phrasebook*.

Greetings & Civilities

Hello.	*jambo/salamu*
Goodbye.	*kwaheri*
How are you?	*habari?*
I'm fine, thanks.	*mzuri*
Thank you.	*asante*
Thanks very much.	*asante sana*
No worries.	*hakuna matata*
Welcome.	*karibu*
What's your name?	*jina lako nani?*
My name is ...	*ninitwa ...*

There is also a respectful greeting used for elders – *shikamoo*. The reply is *marahaba*.

Useful Words & Phrases

Yes.	*ndiyo*
No.	*hapana*
eat	*kula*
guest house	*nyumba ya wageni*
How much/many?	*Ngapi?*
money	*pesa*
sleep	*lala*
today	*leo*
tomorrow	*kesho*
toilet	*choo*
Where?	*Wapi?*

Food & Drink

bananas	*ndizi*
beef	*ng'ombe*
bread	*mkate*
chicken	*kuku*
egg(s)	*(ma)yai*
fish	*samaki*
food	*chakula*
goat	*mbuzi*

food	*chakula*	10	*kumi*
goat	*mbuzi*	11	*kumi na moja*
meat	*nyama*	20	*ishirini*
milk	*maziwa*	30	*thelathini*
rice	*mchele*	40	*arobaini*
salt	*chumvi*	50	*hamsini*
vegetables	*mboga*	60	*sitini*
water	*maji*	70	*sabini*
		80	*themanini*

Numbers

1	*moja*	90	*tisini*
2	*mbili*	100	*mia*
3	*tatu*		
4	*nne*		
5	*tano*		
6	*sita*		
7	*saba*		
8	*nane*		
9	*tisa*		

OTHER LANGUAGES

The languages included in this appendix are those which are spoken in more than one African country. Also refer to individual country chapters as some chapters also include useful words and phrases for local languages.

Glossary

The following is a list of words that are used in this book and that you are likely to come across in Africa. A country or region in brackets indicates that the word is principally used there. Included is a glossary of food terms, which starts on page 1040.

adobe house – house made of sun-dried bricks
ANC – African National Congress
animism – the base of virtually all traditional religions in Africa; the belief that there is a spirit in all natural things and the worship of those spirits which are thought to continue after death and have the power to bestow protection
asantehene – (Ghana) Ashanti king
askari (Kenya) – guard
auberge – traditionally a simple guesthouse, though some auberges are quite smart hotels

bab (North Africa) – Islamic gate
baché (West Africa) – bush taxi
banda (East Africa) – hut
benzin aadi (Egypt) – normal petrol
BIAO – Banque International pour l'Afrique Occidentale
bijou – service taxi in Egypt
boda-boda (Kenya) – bicycle taxi
boîte – night club
Boîte Postale (BP) – post office box
braai (South Africa) – a barbecue which normally includes lots of meat grilled on a braai stand or pit
buvette (West Africa) – refreshment stall

camion (Mozambique) – truck
campement (West Africa) – guesthouse
caravanserai – courtyard inn
careta (Egypt) – donkey-drawn cart
carnarval – festival
chambre d'hôte – guesthouse
chapa – bush bus
chop bar (West Africa) – streetside restaurant selling inexpensive local food
cirques (Réunion) – crescent-shaped basin

with steep sides formed by the erosive action of ice
colectivo (São Tomé & Príncipe) – share-taxi
commissariat – police station
couchette – two-person train compartment
cundonga – black market

dalla dalla (Tanzania) – pick-up or minibus
dash – bribe
dhow (East Africa) – boat
douche – public shower
duka (Kenya) – shop

ECOMOG – ECOWAS Monitoring Group
ECOWAS – Economic Community of West African States

felucca – Nile River sailing boat
forex – foreign exchange bureau
foro – musical instruments

gare lagunaire – ferry terminal
gare routière – bus or train station
gargotte (West Africa) – cheap restaurant
gité (Morocco) – hiker's accommodation

hammam (Morocco) – Turkish-style bath-house
hantour (Egypt) – horse-drawn carriage
harmattan – dry, dusty Sahara wind which blows towards the West African coast, particularly from November to March
hôtel de ville – town hall

IMF – International Monetary Fund
impluvium – a large, round mud house
ISIC – International Student Identity Card

juju – an object used as a charm or fetish

kasbah (North Africa) – fort or citadel, often outside the administrative centre; also spelt qasba
kente cloth – probably the most expensive material in West Africa, made with finely

woven cotton, and sometimes silk, by Ghana's Ashanti people

kimbanda (Angola) – cult based on Brazilian magic

kinguila (Angola) – woman who changes money on the black market

kizomba (Angola) – African-style nightclub with local music and traditional food

konjo (Mali) – millet beer

kopje – prominent, isolated hill or mountain

koubba (North Africa) – Islamic sanctuary

kraal (Southern Africa) – livestock enclosure or hut village

ksar – (plural ksour) fortified stronghold

louage (Tunisia) – share-taxi

lycée – high school

Maghreb – west (literally 'where the sun sets'); used to describe the area covered by Morocco, Algeria, Tunisia and, sometimes, Libya

mairie (West Africa) – town hall

makonde (Tanzania) – ebony carving

maquis (West Africa) – small open-air restaurant with low, wooden tables, sandy floors and good music

marabout – a religious saint (animist) or holy man (Muslim)

marché (West Africa) – market

marginal – waterfront (Angola); coast road (Mozambique)

matatu (Kenya) – minibus

matola (Malawi) – vehicle, usually a pick-up van, acting as an unofficial public transport service

medersa (Morocco) – college for teaching theology, law, Arabic literature and grammar

medina (North Africa) – old town, usually Arab

mellah (Morocco) – Jewish quarter of a medina

mercado paralelo (Angola) – black market

mestiço (Angola) – people of mixed race

MET (Namibia) – Ministry of Environment & Tourism

mihrab – prayer niche

mobyletter (Burkina Faso) – moped

mokoro (Botswana) – dugout canoe

muezzin – mosque official who does the call to prayer from the minaret

mumtaz (Egypt) – super petrol

musseque (Angola) – shanty

mwalimu (Tanzania) – teacher

NGO – Non-Governmental Organization

OAU – Organisation of African Unity

occasions (Central African Republic) – trucks

ONATRA – riverboat operator in Congo (Zaïre)

pagnes (Togo) – traditional strips of cloth

PAIGC – African Party for the Independence of Guinea-Bissau and Cape Verde

paillotte (West Africa) – straw awning

palmeraie (North Africa) – oasis-like area around a town where date palms, vegetables and fruit are grown

particular (Angola) – truck

pensão – cheap hotel

pinasse (Mali) – motorised boat

pirogue – dugout canoe

plat du jour (West Africa) – dish of the day

pont (West Africa) – bridge

pousada (Mozambique) – better grade cheap hotel

praça – square

prefecture – administrative headquarters

processos (Angola) – share taxis

PTT – post office

qasba – see kasbah

Ramadan – ninth month of the Islamic year, a period of fasting

RMS – Ruwenzori Mountaineering Services

rondavel (Southern Africa) – circular building, often thatched

Sahel – dry savannah area

shari'a – Islamic law

sharia (Arabic) – street

shifta (Kenya & Somalia) – bandit

Socatel – telephone office

souk (North Africa) – outdoor market; also spelt souq

sûreté – police station

SWAPO – South-West African People's Organisation
syndicat d'initiative – government-run tourist office

taxi-brousse – bush taxi
toiles – rough, painted textiles
torgokaha – baskets and hats
tro-tro (Ghana) – small wooden bus

UNITA – National Union for the Total Independence of Angola

vila (Malawi) – town
ville nouvelle – 'new city', towns built by the French alongside existing towns and cities of the Maghreb
voodoo – the worship of spirtis with supernatural powers, widely practised in southern Benin and Togo

waraniéné – woven shirts and trousers

ZANU – Zimbabwe African National Union
ZAPU – Zimbabwe African Peoples' Union
zawiyya (Morocco) – shrine

FOOD GLOSSARY
attiéké – grated manioc, not unlike couscous

bassi-salété – millet covered with vegetables and meat
brochettes – kebabs

capitaine – fish
chai (Kenya & Somalia) – tea
chapati (Kenya & Somalia) – Indian-style bread
chawarma – a popular snack of grilled meat in bread, served with salad and sesame sauce, originally from Lebanon; also spelt shawarma
couscous – semolina

foutou – boiled and pounded yams or plaintains eaten as a staple food with sauce
fuul (Egypt) – fava beans with a variety of ingredients added to spice them up eg oil, lemon, meat, egg

harissa – spicy chilli sauce
hummus – chickpeas paste mixed with sesame puree (tahina), lemon and garlic

karkaday – hibiscus tea
kedjenou – chicken and vegetable stew served with rice or foutou
kushari (Egypt) – popular and cheap dish; oil-based mixture of noodles, rice, black lentils, fried onions, chick peas and spicy tomato sauce

mafé – peanut-based stew
mandazi – semi-sweet African donut

nsima (Malawi) – maize porridge, the regional staple

palava sauce – a sauce made from pounded leaves, palm oil and seasonings, generally eaten with fufu or rice
pâté (Niger) – cornmeal stodge
poisson – fish
poulet braisé – fish or chicken cooked over the embers of a low fire
poulet yassa or poisson yassa – marinated and grilled chicken or fish

riz sauce – very common basic meal (rice with meat sauce)

sahleb – sweet, milky drink made from rice flour, grapes, coconut and nuts
suya (Nigeria) – spiced brochette

ta'amiyya – Egyptian version of felafel (chickpea burgers)
tajine – stew, usually with meat as the main ingredient
tiéboudienne – rice baked in a thick sauce of fish and vegetables with pimiento and tomato sauce
tô (Burkina Faso) – millet or sorghum-based pâté

yaourt (Burkina Faso) – yoghurt

Index

TEXT

Map references are in **bold** type.

NATIONAL PARKS & RESERVES

THANKS

Thanks to the following travellers and others (apologies if we've misspelt your name) who took the time to write to us about their experiences in Africa:

Marjorie Adams, Martin Aigle, Nick Alblas, Lara Allardice, Carl Alviani, Melle Andrea, Nicola Ansell, Oliver Appleyard, Jose Maria Aranaz, Eric Arnett, Kris Attard, Phillipe Aube, Dr J W Bahana, Stephen Baier, Dillon Banerjee, Jan Barrie, Michael Bastow, B Bayman, L Beard, Sarah Beavon, Tamara Bekef, Lars Bernd, Jan Beumeka, Charles Bierley, Mike Bishop, Celine Blazy, Ann Blind, Erik Bouwmeester, Phil Boyd, Gonda Bres, Robert Brierley, Henry Bromelkamp, M & M Buijs, Bruce Burger, Segolene Callard, Julie Calvert, Luis Carlos, Feli Carman, Richard Carr, Mary Cashman, C Caul, R & A Chabanier, Abbie Challenger, Annie Chandler, Andrew Chilton, James Clements, Ilan Cohen, A C Cole, Paolo Cortini, David Cranor, Neville Cregan, Shimon Cregor, Alex Cross, J & J Cutress, Sian L Davie, Rhodri Dean, Miles Denton, Dr Johan Dippenaar, Anno Drameh, Heinz Effertz, John & Sheryl Egli, Jochen Ehmann, Sara Ellison, Terri Emma, Laura Epp, Kay Farmer, Mr & Mrs Farnaby, Jo Faulkner, Neil Feder, Rob Fisher, Annetta Flanigan, Andrew Forbes, Jennifer Ford, Alessandro Fornari, Bob Foster, Jan Willem Francke, Derek Fuller, Clemens Gabler, I & S Giles, Heiko Glander, Helene Goasguen, Shannon Goins, B Goldstein, Bart Goossens, Philip Grayston, David Green, Lynell Greer, Nicole Gregoire, Dr Guido Groenen, Jelger Groenveld, Mike Guadagno, Andre Gupta, A & A Gustafson, Wes Hansen, W A Harrex, Kate Harris, Ruth Harvey, Kevin Harvey, Lynda Hawland, Marcus Hecker, Stefanie Heel, Marko Heusala, Adrienne Hill, Joanne Holmes, Ci Holmgren, Alex Holroyd-Smith, Stephan Holz, Ruth Hunnybun, John & Julie Hurst, Dale Hutchison, Jim Jarrold, Liz Johanson, Adrian Jones, Martin Jones, Denis Kearney, T Kebede, Arthur Kell, Stefan Keller, Andrew Kemball, Christoph Kessel, Helmut Kiathower, Ilze Kinnear, Johannes Kochling, Wilko Krautter, Daniel Kwaku, Wies Lambinon, Suzie La Mont, Dr A Lane, Tara Laundry, Mareike Leist, Ian Leitch, S Lem, Scotty Levings, R & M Lincoln, Kate Longshore, Robert Lowe, Lars Eric Lundgren, H & R MacIntosh, A & M Madeksza, Paolo Maini, David Manchester, Jasper Mann, David Marrill, Seamus Martin, Joanna Martin, Steve McElhinney, William McEwan, Anthony McGovern, Iain McKay, B & C McLaren, Finlay McNicol, Paul Mills, John Mitchell, Shira Mivtach, Paul Moore, Peter Moore, Gareth Morgan, Rosemary Morgan, Natalie Moxhom, Todd Nicholson, Richard Nimmo, Phoenix Ordinatews, Lois Parkin, Inga Parry, Trevor Parry, Astrid Pauwels, Helena Pavan, Jonna Pedersen, Justin & Kath Peer, Mercedes Perez, Paul Piotrowski, Michelle Pirkl, Paul Pometto, J & K Pommerich, Claire Pott, Nick Primavesi, Vanessa Puniak, M & M Rajmajer, Kirsti Raustein, Amanda Raw, Nicholas Redfearn, Simon Reed, Sarah Reilly, Helen Rhodes, J D Rinzema, Lorraine Robinson, P B Rode, Tom Rush, Andrea Russell, Rosel Ruttens, Andrew Salmon, Bruno Sassier, Roger Sathre, Barbara Schade, Sarah Schnepf, Annette Schuster, Tony Seljak, Helen Shields, Robin Short, Richard Shumann, Karen Shupenia, Ezra Simon, Katie Simons, Dani Smith, Graham Snowdon, Robert Snyder, John Soar, Helen Speechley, Nicole Stanners, Craig Stark, Jenny Stary, Bill Staughton, Colin Stevenson, M & M Steyskal, Sean Stitham, Lucy Stone, Steven Suranie, Tony Sweet, K & C Swinburn, Sissel Syvertsen, Grace Tee, Anne Tennent, Amanda Thain, S Theus, Kelsall Thomas, Susanne Thorne, Jon Tillinghurst, Markuu Toivonen, J Tougel, Borice Tuerck, Nathan Turnball, Michael Turner, F & S van Schelven, Andre van den Berg, Janet Vane, Marita Vercammen, C & D Viallet, Michi Vojta, Sarah Walthew, Nicholas Watson, Merrill Watson, Miroslava Weibel, Julian Wheeler, Stephen White, Andreas Wick, Chris Wilcox, Derek Willows, David Wise, R A Yates-Earl, Justin Yoo, Jean Yves and Paul Zdrazil.

LONELY PLANET PHRASEBOOKS

Building bridges,
Breaking barriers,
Beyond babble-on

Nepali phrasebook

Ethiopian Amharic phrasebook

Latin American Spanish phrasebook

Ukrainian phrasebook

Greek phrasebook

Vietnamese phrasebook

Listen for the gems

Speak your own words

Ask your own questions

Master of your own image

- handy pocket-sized books
- easy to understand Pronunciation chapter
- clear and comprehensive Grammar chapter
- romanisation alongside script to allow ease of pronunciation
- script throughout so users can point to phrases
- extensive vocabulary sections, words and phrases for every situation
- full of cultural information and tips for the traveller

'...vital for a real DIY spirit and attitude in language learning' – Backpacker

'the phrasebooks have good cultural backgrounders and offer solid advice for challenging situations in remote locations' – San Francisco Examiner

'...they are unbeatable for their coverage of the world's more obscure languages' – The Geographical Magazine

---

Arabic (Egyptian)
Arabic (Moroccan)
Australia
  Australian English, Aboriginal and Torres Strait languages
Baltic States
  Estonian, Latvian, Lithuanian
Bengali
Brazilian
Burmese
Cantonese
Central Asia
Central Europe
  Czech, French, German, Hungarian, Italian and Slovak
Eastern Europe
  Bulgarian, Czech, Hungarian, Polish, Romanian and Slovak
Ethiopian (Amharic)
Fijian
French
German
Greek

Hindi/Urdu
Indonesian
Italian
Japanese
Korean
Lao
Latin American Spanish
Malay
Mandarin
Mediterranean Europe
  Albanian, Croatian, Greek, Italian, Macedonian, Maltese, Serbian and Slovene
Mongolian
Nepali
Papua New Guinea
Pilipino (Tagalog)
Quechua
Russian
Scandinavian Europe
  Danish, Finnish, Icelandic, Norwegian and Swedish

South-East Asia
  Burmese, Indonesian, Khmer, Lao, Malay, Tagalog (Pilipino), Thai and Vietnamese
Spanish (Castilian)
  Basque, Catalan and Galician
Sri Lanka
Swahili
Thai
Thai Hill Tribes
Tibetan
Turkish
Ukrainian
USA
  US English, Vernacular. Native American languages and Hawaiian
Vietnamese
Western Europe
  Basque, Catalan, Dutch, French, German, Irish, Italian, Portuguese, Scottish Gaelic, Spanish (Castilian) and Welsh

LONELY PLANET JOURNEYS

JOURNEYS is a unique collection of travel writing – published by the company that understands travel better than anyone else. It is a series for anyone who has ever experienced – or dreamed of – the magical moment when they encountered a strange culture or saw a place for the first time. They are tales to read while you're planning a trip, while you're on the road or while you're in an armchair, in front of a fire.

JOURNEYS books catch the spirit of a place, illuminate a culture, recount a crazy adventure, or introduce a fascinating way of life. They always entertain, and always enrich the experience of travel.

THE RAINBIRD
A Central African Journey
Jan Brokken
translated by Sam Garrett

The Rainbird is a classic travel story. Following in the footsteps of famous Europeans such as Albert Schweitzer and H.M. Stanley, Jan Brokken journeyed to Gabon in central Africa. A kaleidoscope of adventures and anecdotes, *The Rainbird* brilliantly chronicles the encounter between Africa and Europe as it was acted out on a side-street of history. It is also the compelling, immensely readable account of the author's own travels in one of the most remote and mysterious regions of Africa.

Jan Brokken is one of Holland's best known writers. In addition to travel narratives and literary journalism, he has published several novels and short stories. Many of his works are set in Africa, where he has travelled widely.

SONGS TO AN AFRICAN SUNSET
A Zimbabwean Story
Sekai Nzenza-Shand

Songs to an African Sunset braids vividly personal stories into an intimate picture of contemporary Zimbabwe. Returning to her family's village after many years in the West, Sekai Nzenza-Shand discovers a world where ancestor worship, polygamy and witchcraft still govern the rhythms of daily life – and where drought, deforestation and AIDS have wrought devastating changes. With insight and affection, she explores a culture torn between respect for the old ways and the irresistible pull of the new.

Sekai Nzenza-Shand was born in Zimbabwe and has lived in England and Australia. Her first novel, *Zimbabwean Woman: My Own Story*, was published in London in 1988 and her fiction has been included in the short story collections *Daughters of Africa* and *Images of the West*. Sekai currently lives in Zimbabwe.

Australia Council for the Arts

This project has been assisted by the Commonwealth Government through the Australia Council, its arts funding and advisory body.

LONELY PLANET TRAVEL ATLASES

Lonely Planet has long been famous for the number and quality of its guidebook maps. Now we've gone one step further and produced a handy companion series: Lonely Planet travel atlases – maps of a country produced in book form.

Unlike other maps, which look good but lead travellers astray, our travel atlases have been researched on the road by Lonely Planet's experienced team of writers. All details are carefully checked to ensure the atlas corresponds with the equivalent Lonely Planet guidebook.

The handy atlas format means no holes, wrinkles, torn sections or constant folding and unfolding. These atlases can survive long periods on the road, unlike cumbersome fold-out maps. The comprehensive index ensures easy reference.

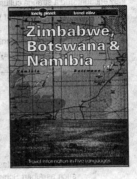

- full-colour throughout
- maps researched and checked by Lonely Planet authors
- place names correspond with Lonely Planet guidebooks
  – no confusing spelling differences
- legend and travelling information in English, French, German, Japanese and Spanish
- size: 230 x 160 mm

Available now:
Chile & Easter Island • Egypt • India & Bangladesh • Israel & the Palestinian Territories •Jordan, Syria & Lebanon • Kenya • Laos • Portugal • South Africa, Lesotho & Swaziland • Thailand • Turkey • Vietnam • Zimbabwe, Botswana & Namibia

---

LONELY PLANET TV SERIES & VIDEOS

Lonely Planet travel guides have been brought to life on television screens around the world. Like our guides, the programmes are based on the joy of independent travel, and look honestly at some of the most exciting, picturesque and frustrating places in the world. Each show is presented by one of three travellers from Australia, England or the USA and combines an innovative mixture of video, Super-8 film, atmospheric soundscapes and original music.

Videos of each episode – containing additional footage not shown on television – are available from good book and video shops, but the availability of individual videos varies with regional screening schedules.

Video destinations include: Alaska • American Rockies • Australia – The South-East • Baja California & the Copper Canyon • Brazil • Central Asia • Chile & Easter Island • Corsica, Sicily & Sardinia – The Mediterranean Islands • East Africa (Tanzania & Zanzibar) • Ecuador & the Galapagos Islands • Greenland & Iceland • Indonesia • Israel & the Sinai Desert • Jamaica • Japan • La Ruta Maya • Morocco • New York • North India • Pacific Islands (Fiji, Solomon Islands & Vanuatu) • South India • South West China • Turkey • Vietnam • West Africa • Zimbabwe, Botswana & Namibia

The Lonely Planet TV series is produced by:
Pilot Productions
The Old Studio
18 Middle Row
London W10 5AT UK

For video availability and ordering information contact your nearest Lonely Planet office.

Music from the TV series is available on CD & cassette.

PLANET TALK

Lonely Planet's FREE quarterly newsletter

We love hearing from you and think you'd like to hear from us.

*When...*is the right time to see reindeer in Finland?
*Where...*can you hear the best palm-wine music in Ghana?
*How...*do you get from Asunción to Areguá by steam train?
*What...*is the best way to see India?

For the answer to these and many other questions read PLANET TALK.

Every issue is packed with up-to-date travel news and advice including:

* a letter from Lonely Planet co-founders Tony and Maureen Wheeler
* go behind the scenes on the road with a Lonely Planet author
* feature article on an important and topical travel issue
* a selection of recent letters from travellers
* details on forthcoming Lonely Planet promotions
* complete list of Lonely Planet products

To join our mailing list contact any Lonely Planet office.

Also available: Lonely Planet T-shirts. 100% heavyweight cotton.

LONELY PLANET ONLINE

Get the latest travel information before you leave or while you're on the road

Whether you've just begun planning your next trip, or you're chasing down specific info on currency regulations or visa requirements, check out Lonely Planet Online for up-to-the minute travel information.

As well as travel profiles of your favourite destinations (including maps and photos), you'll find current reports from our researchers and other travellers, updates on health and visas, travel advisories, and discussion of the ecological and political issues you need to be aware of as you travel.

There's also an online travellers' forum where you can share your experience of life on the road, meet travel companions and ask other travellers for their recommendations and advice. We also have plenty of links to other online sites useful to independent travellers.

And of course we have a complete and up-to-date list of all Lonely Planet travel products including guides, phrasebooks, atlases, Journeys and videos and a simple online ordering facility if you can't find the book you want elsewhere.

www.lonelyplanet.com
or
AOL keyword: lp

LONELY PLANET PRODUCTS

Lonely Planet is known worldwide for publishing practical, reliable and no-nonsense travel information in our guides and on our web site. The Lonely Planet list covers just about every accessible part of the world. Currently there are nine series: *travel guides, shoestring guides, walking guides, city guides, phrasebooks, audio packs, travel atlases, Journeys – a unique collection of travel writing and Pisces Books - diving and snorkeling guides.*

EUROPE

Amsterdam • Austria • Baltic States phrasebook • Britain • Central Europe on a shoestring • Central Europe phrasebook • Czech & Slovak Republics • Denmark • Dublin • Eastern Europe on a shoestring • Eastern Europe phrasebook • Estonia, Latvia & Lithuania • Finland • France • French phrasebook • Germany • German phrasebook • Greece • Greek phrasebook • Hungary • Iceland, Greenland & the Faroe Islands • Ireland • Italian phrasebook • Italy • Lisbon • London • Mediterranean Europe on a shoestring • Mediterranean Europe phrasebook • Paris • Poland • Portugal • Portugal travel atlas • Prague • Romania & Moldova • Russia, Ukraine & Belarus • Russian phrasebook • Scandinavian & Baltic Europe on a shoestring • Scandinavian Europe phrasebook • Slovenia • Spain • Spanish phrasebook • St Petersburg • Switzerland •Trekking in Spain • Ukrainian phrasebook • Vienna • Walking in Britain • Walking in Italy • Walking in Switzerland • Western Europe on a shoestring • Western Europe phrasebook

Travel Literature: The Olive Grove: Travels in Greece

NORTH AMERICA

Alaska • Backpacking in Alaska • Baja California • California & Nevada • Canada • Chicago • Deep South • Florida • Hawaii • Honolulu • Los Angeles • Mexico • Mexico City • Miami • New England • New Orleans • New York City • New York, New Jersey & Pennsylvania • Pacific Northwest USA • Rocky Mountain States • San Francisco • Southwest USA • USA phrasebook • Washington, DC & the Capital Region

Travel Literature: Drive thru America

CENTRAL AMERICA & THE CARIBBEAN

•Bahamas and Turks & Caicos •Bermuda •Central America on a shoestring • Costa Rica • Cuba •Eastern Caribbean •Guatemala, Belize & Yucatán: La Ruta Maya • Jamaica

SOUTH AMERICA

Argentina, Uruguay & Paraguay • Bolivia • Brazil • Brazilian phrasebook • Buenos Aires • Chile & Easter Island • Chile & Easter Island travel atlas • Colombia • Ecuador & the Galápagos Islands • Latin American Spanish phrasebook • Peru • Quechua phrasebook • Rio de Janeiro • South America on a shoestring • Trekking in the Patagonian Andes • Venezuela

Travel Literature: Full Circle: A South American Journey

ISLANDS OF THE INDIAN OCEAN

Madagascar & Comoros • Maldives• Mauritius, Réunion & Seychelles

AFRICA

Africa - the South • Africa on a shoestring • Arabic (Moroccan) phrasebook • Cairo • Cape Town • Central Africa • East Africa • Egypt • Egypt travel atlas• Ethiopian (Amharic) phrasebook • Kenya • Kenya travel atlas • Malawi, Mozambique & Zambia • Morocco • North Africa • South Africa, Lesotho & Swaziland • South Africa, Lesotho & Swaziland travel atlas • Swahili phrasebook • Tunisia • Trekking in East Africa • West Africa • Zimbabwe, Botswana & Namibia • Zimbabwe, Botswana & Namibia travel atlas

Travel Literature: The Rainbird: A Central African Journey• Songs to an African Sunset: A Zimbabwean Story

THE LONELY PLANET STORY

Lonely Planet published its first book in 1973 in response to the numerous 'How did you do it?' questions Maureen and Tony Wheeler were asked after driving, bussing, hitching, sailing and railing their way from England to Australia.

Written at a kitchen table and hand collated, trimmed and stapled, *Across Asia on the Cheap* became an instant local bestseller, inspiring thoughts of another book.

Eighteen months in South-East Asia resulted in their second guide, *South-East Asia on a shoestring*, which they put together in a backstreet Chinese hotel in Singapore in 1975. The 'yellow bible', as it quickly became known to backpackers around the world, soon became *the* guide to the region. It has sold well over half a million copies and is now in its 9th edition, still retaining its familiar yellow cover.

Today there are over 240 titles, including travel guides, walking guides, language kits & phrasebooks, travel atlases and travel literature. The company is the largest independent travel publisher in the world. Although Lonely Planet initially specialised in guides to Asia, today there are few corners of the globe that have not been covered.

The emphasis continues to be on travel for independent travellers. Tony and Maureen still travel for several months of each year and play an active part in the writing, updating and quality control of Lonely Planet's guides.

They have been joined by over 70 authors and 170 staff at our offices in Melbourne (Australia), Oakland (USA), London (UK) and Paris (France). Travellers themselves also make a valuable contribution to the guides through the feedback we receive in thousands of letters each year and on our web site.

The people at Lonely Planet strongly believe that travellers can make a positive contribution to the countries they visit, both through their appreciation of the countries' culture, wildlife and natural features, and through the money they spend. In addition, the company makes a direct contribution to the countries and regions it covers. Since 1986 a percentage of the income from each book has been donated to ventures such as famine relief in Africa; aid projects in India; agricultural projects in Central America; Greenpeace's efforts to halt French nuclear testing in the Pacific; and Amnesty International.

'I hope we send people out with the right attitude about travel. You realise when you travel that there are so many different perspectives about the world, so we hope these books will make people more interested in what they see. Guidebooks can't really guide people. All you can do is point them in the right direction.'

– Tony Wheeler

LONELY PLANET PUBLICATIONS

Australia
PO Box 617, Hawthorn 3122, Victoria
tel: (03) 9819 1877 fax: (03) 9819 6459
e-mail: talk2us@lonelyplanet.com.au

USA
150 Linden St
Oakland, CA 94607
tel: (510) 893 8555 TOLL FREE: 800 275-8555
fax: (510) 893 8563
e-mail: info@lonelyplanet.com

UK
10a Spring Place,
London NW5 3BH
tel: (0171) 428 4800 fax: (0171) 428 4828
e-mail: go@lonelyplanet.co.uk

France:
71 bis rue du Cardinal Lemoine, 75005 Paris
tel: 01 44 32 06 20 fax: 01 46 34 72 55
e-mail: bip@lonelyplanet.fr

World Wide Web: http://www.lonelyplanet.com
or *AOL keyword: lp*

MAIL ORDER

Lonely Planet products are distributed worldwide. They are also available by mail order from Lonely Planet, so if you have difficulty finding a title please write to us. North American and South American residents should write to 150 Linden St, Oakland CA 94607, USA; European and African residents should write to 10a Spring Place, London NW5 3BH; and residents of other countries to PO Box 617, Hawthorn, Victoria 3122, Australia.

NORTH-EAST ASIA

Beijing • Cantonese phrasebook • China • Hong Kong • Hong Kong, Macau & Guangzhou • Japan • Japanese phrasebook • Japanese audio pack • Korea • Korean phrasebook • Mandarin phrasebook • Mongolia • Mongolian phrasebook • North-East Asia on a shoestring • Seoul • Taiwan • Tibet • Tibet phrasebook • Tokyo

Travel Literature: Lost Japan

MIDDLE EAST & CENTRAL ASIA

Arab Gulf States • Arabic (Egyptian) phrasebook • Central Asia • Central Asia phrasebook • Iran • Israel & the Palestinian Territories • Israel & the Palestinian Territories travel atlas • Istanbul • Jerusalem • Jordan & Syria • Jordan, Syria & Lebanon travel atlas • Lebanon • Middle East • Turkey • Turkish phrasebook • Turkey travel atlas • Yemen

Travel Literature: The Gates of Damascus • Kingdom of the Film Stars: Journey into Jordan

ALSO AVAILABLE:

Brief Encounters • Travel with Children • Traveller's Tales

INDIAN SUBCONTINENT

Bangladesh • Bengali phrasebook • Delhi • Goa • Hindi/Urdu phrasebook • India • India & Bangladesh travel atlas • Indian Himalaya • Karakoram Highway • Nepal • Nepali phrasebook • Pakistan • Rajasthan • Sri Lanka • Sri Lanka phrasebook • Trekking in the Indian Himalaya • Trekking in the Karakoram & Hindukush • Trekking in the Nepal Himalaya

Travel Literature: In Rajasthan • Shopping for Buddhas

SOUTH-EAST ASIA

Bali & Lombok • Bangkok • Burmese phrasebook • Cambodia • Ho Chi Minh City • Indonesia • Indonesian phrasebook • Indonesian audio pack • Jakarta • Java • Laos • Lao phrasebook • Laos travel atlas • Malay phrasebook • Malaysia, Singapore & Brunei • Myanmar (Burma) • Philippines • Pilipino phrasebook • Singapore • South-East Asia on a shoestring • South-East Asia phrasebook • Thailand • Thailand's Islands & Beaches • Thailand travel atlas • Thai phrasebook • Thai audio pack • Thai Hill Tribes phrasebook • Vietnam • Vietnamese phrasebook • Vietnam travel atlas

AUSTRALIA & THE PACIFIC

Australia • Australian phrasebook • Bushwalking in Australia • Bushwalking in Papua New Guinea • Fiji • Fijian phrasebook • Islands of Australia's Great Barrier Reef • Melbourne • Micronesia • New Caledonia • New South Wales • New Zealand • Northern Territory • Outback Australia • Papua New Guinea • Papua New Guinea phrasebook • Queensland • Rarotonga & the Cook Islands • Samoa • Solomon Islands • South Australia • Sydney • Tahiti & French Polynesia • Tasmania • Tonga • Tramping in New Zealand • Vanuatu • Victoria • Western Australia

Travel Literature: Islands in the Clouds • Sean & David's Long Drive

ANTARCTICA

Antarctica